PIPE FITTINGS

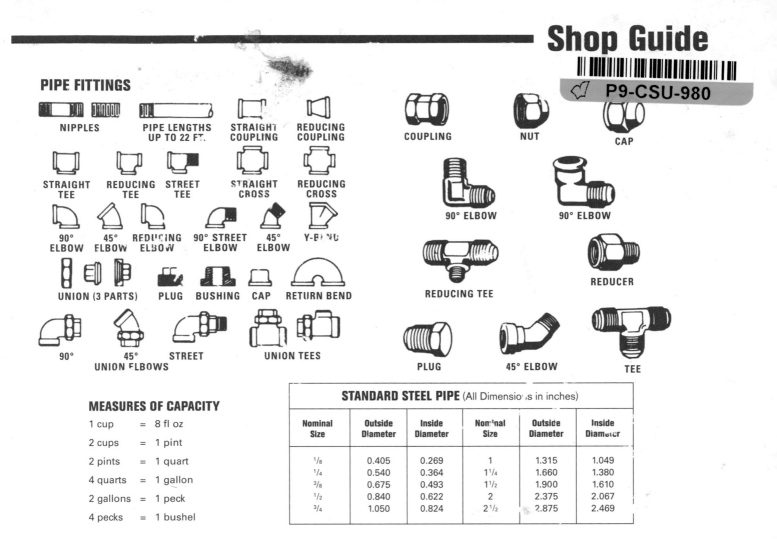

NIPPLES · PIPE LENGTHS UP TO 22 FT. · STRAIGHT COUPLING · REDUCING COUPLING · COUPLING · NUT · CAP

STRAIGHT TEE · REDUCING TEE · STREET TEE · STRAIGHT CROSS · REDUCING CROSS · 90° ELBOW · 90° ELBOW

90° ELBOW · 45° ELBOW · REDUCING ELBOW · 90° STREET ELBOW · 45° ELBOW · Y-BEND · REDUCING TEE · REDUCER

UNION (3 PARTS) · PLUG · BUSHING · CAP · RETURN BEND · PLUG · 45° ELBOW · TEE

90° · 45° UNION ELBOWS · STREET · UNION TEES

MEASURES OF CAPACITY

1 cup	=	8 fl oz
2 cups	=	1 pint
2 pints	=	1 quart
4 quarts	=	1 gallon
2 gallons	=	1 peck
4 pecks	=	1 bushel

STANDARD STEEL PIPE (All Dimensions in inches)

Nominal Size	Outside Diameter	Inside Diameter	Nominal Size	Outside Diameter	Inside Diameter
1/8	0.405	0.269	1	1.315	1.049
1/4	0.540	0.364	1 1/4	1.660	1.380
3/8	0.675	0.493	1 1/2	1.900	1.610
1/2	0.840	0.622	2	2.375	2.067
3/4	1.050	0.824	2 1/2	2.875	2.469

WOOD SCREWS

Length	Gauge Numbers													
1/4 inch	0	1	2	3										
3/8 inch			2	3	4	5	6	7						
1/2 inch			2	3	4	5	6	7	8					
5/8 inch				3	4	5	6	7	8	9	10			
3/4 inch					4	5	6	7	8	9	10	11		
7/8 inch							6	7	8	9	10	11	12	
1 inch							6	7	8	9	10	11	12	14
1 1/4 inch							6	7	8	9	10	11	12	14	16
1 1/2 inch							6	7	8	9	10	11	12	14	16	18
1 3/4 inch									8	9	10	11	12	14	16	18	20
2 inch									8	9	10	11	12	14	16	18	20
2 1/4 inch										9	10	11	12	14	16	18	20
2 1/2 inch														14	16	18	20
2 3/4 inch														14	16	18	20
3 inch															16	18	20
3 1/2 inch																18	20	24
4 inch																18	20	24

WHEN YOU BUY SCREWS, SPECIFY (1) LENGTH, (2) GAUGE NUMBER, (3) TYPE OF HEAD—FLAT, ROUND, OR OVAL
(4) MATERIAL—STEEL, BRASS, BRONZE, ETC., (5) FINISH—BRIGHT, STEEL BLUED, CADMIUM, NICKEL, OR CHROMIUM PLATED.

Popular Mechanics
COMPLETE
HOME
HOW-TO

Popular Mechanics
COMPLETE
HOME
HOW-TO

Albert Jackson and David Day

HEARST BOOKS
A division of Sterling Publishing Co., Inc.

New York / London
www.sterlingpublishing.com

This work was originally published by HarperCollins Publishers under the title: *Collins Complete DIY Manual— 2nd edition,* copyright © 2001 HarperCollins Publishers Ltd.

Every effort has been made to ensure that all the information in this book is accurate. However, in view of the complex and changing nature of building regulations, codes, and by-laws, the authors and publishers advise consultation with specialists in appropriate instances and cannot assume responsibility for any loss or damage resulting from reliance solely upon the information herein.

Popular Mechanics

Steve Willson, U.S. Project Editor
Tom Klenck, U.S. Art Director
Electrical consultant: John Williamson

Created, edited, and designed by Inklink

Concept, editorial, design and art direction:
    Simon Jennings
Text: Albert Jackson and David Day
Design: Alan Marshall
Illustrations: David Day, Robin Harris, Brian Craker,
    Michael Parr, Brian Sayers
Photographs: Paul Chave, Peter Higgins, Ideal Industries, Inc.,
    Intermatic.com, Albert Jackson, Simon Jennings, Leviton
    Mfg. Co., Proliphix, Inc.

Hearst Books

Cover design: Renato Stanisic

The first edition of this book was cataloged by the Library of Congress as follows:

Jackson, Albert, 1943-
    Popular mechanics complete home how-to / Albert Jackson and David Day.
        p. cm.
    Includes index.
    ISBN 1-58816-302-4
Dwellings—Maintenance and repair—Amateurs' manuals. I. Title: Complete home how-to. II. Day, David, 1944- III. Title.

TH4817.3.J32 2004
643'.7—dc22   2003056853

10 9 8 7 6 5 4 3 2 1

First Paperback Edition Published 2009

Published by Hearst Books
A division of Sterling Publishing Co., Inc.
387 Park Avenue South
New York, NY 10016

Popular Mechanics and Hearst Books are trademarks of Hearst Communications, Inc.

www.popularmechanics.com

For information about custom editions, special sales, premium and corporate purchases, please contact Sterling Special Sales Department at 800-805-5489 or specialsales@sterlingpublishing.com.

Distributed in Canada by Sterling Publishing
c/o Canadian Manda Group, 165 Dufferin Street
Toronto, Ontario, Canada M6K 3H6

Printed in China

Sterling ISBN 978-1-58816-803-0

1 PLANNING AHEAD

2 DECORATING

3 REPAIRS & IMPROVEMENTS

CONTINUED

CONTENTS

CONTENTS

4 HOME SECURITY

5 INFESTATION, ROT & DAMP

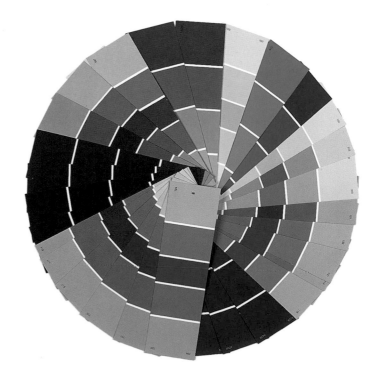

CONTENTS

8 PLUMBING

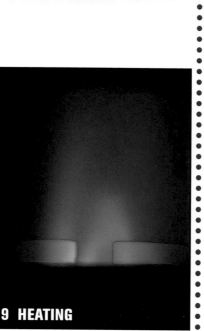

9 HEATING

10 WORKING OUTDOORS

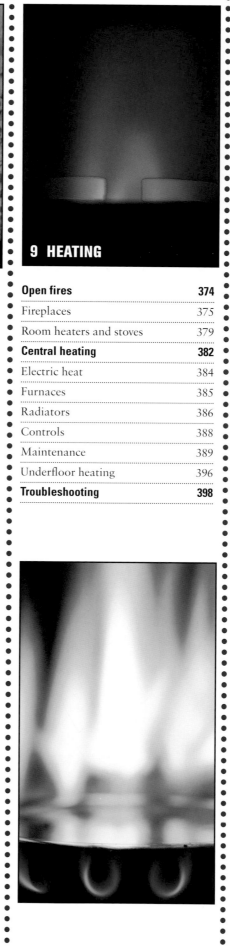

CONTINUED

11 TOOLS AND SKILLS

12 REFERENCE & INDEX

CONTENTS

Popular Mechanics COMPLETE HOME HOW-TO

1 Planning ahead

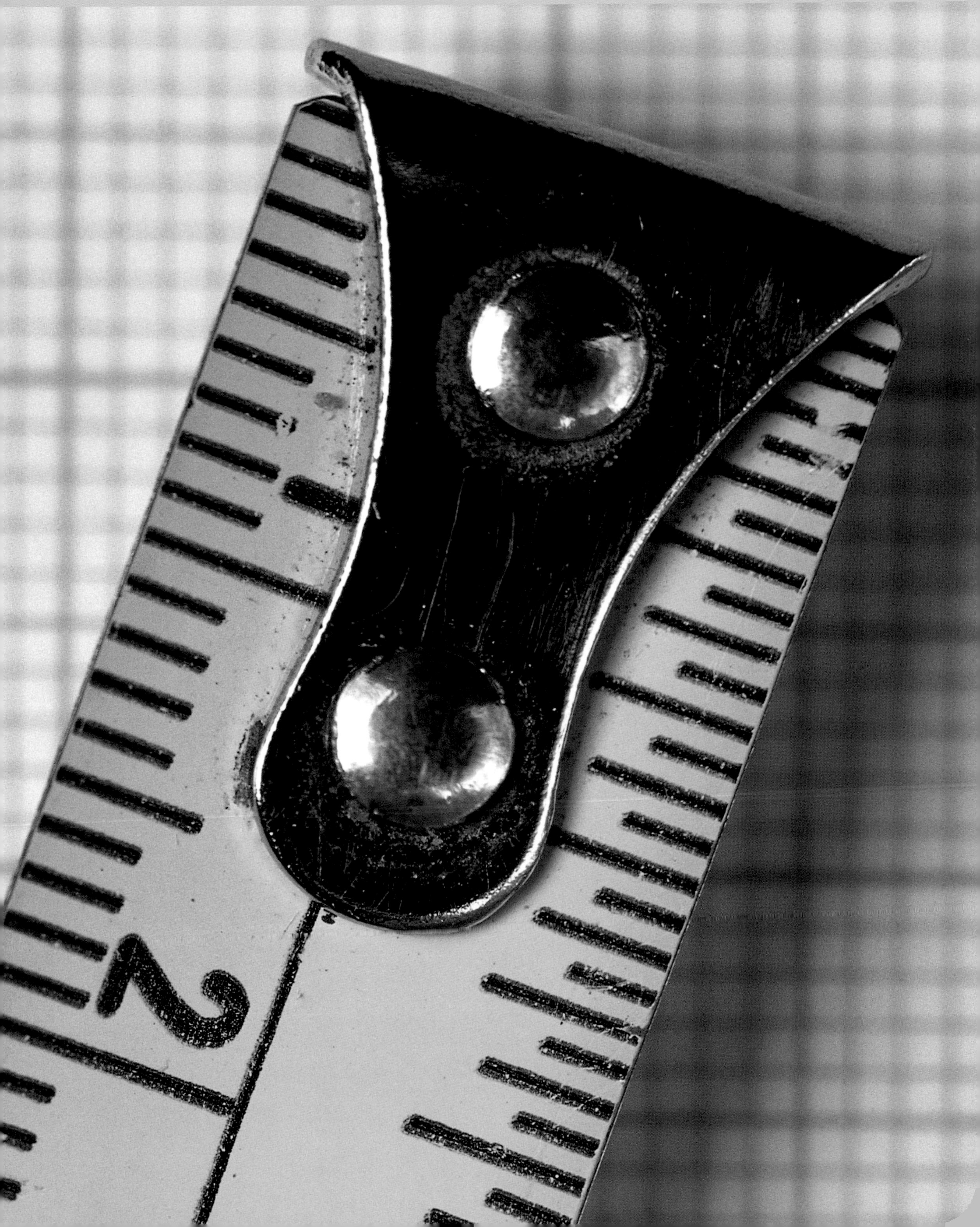

Planning: Assessing property

Carrying out substantial home improvements can be either an enjoyable and stimulating experience or a nightmare. If you plan each step carefully before you begin work, you are more likely to make real improvements, which will benefit your family and add to the value of your property. On the other hand, if you buy a property that is unsuitable for your needs, or launch into an ambitious project without thinking through the consequences, you could waste a lot of time and money.

Checklists

Buying a house is an exciting event—and when you find one that seems to be just what you've been searching for, it can be such a happy moment that it's easy to get carried away and fail to check the essentials. Your first impressions can be so misleading that the shortcomings of what seemed to be your dream home may begin to emerge only after you have moved in. Consequently, it's a good idea to arm yourself with a checklist of vital points when looking at a prospective house, so you are less likely to discover later that it's going to cost a lot to bring the building up to the standards that you want.

In some ways, assessing the potential of the home you live in now can be even harder. You are used to it. Most of it fits like an old glove, and it's hard to be objective about possible improvements. But try to step back and take a fresh look at it by using the same sort of checklist you would use when looking for a new house. No property is ever absolutely ideal, but a little planning can provide you with a framework for making sensible decisions and reducing the number of unhappy surprises in the future.

Before you buy
Buying a home will probably be the largest single investment you ever make, so don't let yourself be misled by first impressions. Check your list of requirements carefully and consider the property fully before spending money on professional consultants.

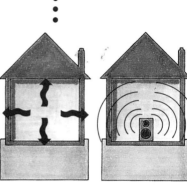

Structural condition

Before you finally decide to buy a house, the building should be inspected by a licensed home inspector or a professional engineer to make sure it is structurally sound. But make some spot checks yourself before calling either in. A pair of binoculars will help you inspect the building from ground level.

Look out for cracks in the walls, both inside and out. Cracked drywall or plaster may simply be the result of shrinkage, but might also indicate foundation problems. Inspect chimneys for faults. Loose bricks can cause considerable damage if they fall; a chimney collapse would be worse. Check the condition of the roof. A few loose shingles can be repaired easily, but a whole section that appears to be misplaced could mean a new roof.

Ask if the house has been inspected or treated for rot or insect infestation. If so, is there a guarantee? If the baseboards look distorted or a floor feels unduly springy, expect trouble. Look for signs of dampness. In hot weather the worst effects may have disappeared, but stained wallpapers or even poor pointing of the brickwork should make you suspicious.

Insulation

Find out how much and what type of insulation is in the house. Once you know what insulation is present, check that its R-value meets your needs. Also, check the past winter's heating fuel bills. If these are more than you want to spend, plan to add some insulation.

HOME SECURITY

Check whether all doors and windows are secured with good-quality locks and catches. You will probably want to change the front-door lock, anyway. A burglar alarm is an advantage only if it is reliable and sensibly installed. Make sure that there are adequate fire-escape routes, especially in apartments with shared access.

Mechanical systems

A real estate agent may know the condition of the various mechanical systems in the house, especially if recent work has been done. And the local building department should have records of building permits and inspections. But to get the complete picture, you should rely on a home inspector: a licensed contractor who can evaluate each system. Simple observation on your part can help establish a starting point.

If you see old-fashioned light sockets, switches, and receptacles, these suggest out-of-date wiring. The age and condition of the cables entering and leaving the main service panel is another good clue. Check that there are enough receptacles in every room and that the lighting seems well planned.

Look at the plumbing too. Are the fixtures old; are the pipes steel instead of copper? Is the water heater new or old, and is it big enough?

Take a look at the heating system. Is it old or new? Is there just a single thermostat for the whole house, or are there several located in different rooms? Does the house have central air conditioning and does this equipment look old?

• Buying an apartment

If you're buying an apartment, make sure to check for acceptable access. Are there stairs, elevators, both? Ask about shared facilities like laundry and trash disposal, and joint responsibilities such as maintenance of public areas. In buildings that have been converted into apartments, check for proper fire-escape routes. Also, visit the municipal building department to see if all the necessary inspections are on record. If possible, talk to some of the other owners in the building.

Appearance

Paint and paper

Is the house decorated the way you like, both inside and out? If it is, are the decorative elements in good shape or do they need work to meet your standards? If the decorative aspects are not what you like, come up with an estimate of how much it would cost to change them. If you don't like something in the beginning, you're not likely to enjoy it later. The future cost of these changes should be factored into the total cost of the house.

Improvements

Decide whether improvements have been carried out tastefully. Ask yourself if you'd be happy living in a house where, for example, the original doors and windows have been replaced with alternatives that don't match the architectural style of the house. This may not be the sort of thing that bothers you. But if it does, over time you'll want to do something to correct the things you don't like. And all these changes will cost money.

Garage and workshop

Is the garage large enough for your car or cars? If there isn't enough space for the garage to double as a work area, is there room in the basement? Is there storage room for all the the stuff we tend to accumulate, like bicycles, lawnmowers, wheelbarrows, snow tires, garbage cans? Keep in mind that when someone is trying to sell a house, the garage and basement are usually cleaned up. Try to imagine them with your possessions in place. Is there room now and room to expand in the future?

Erecting a storage shed or another outbuilding can solve all sorts of storage problems. But if you know that you'll need additional space, you should add the cost of it to the total long-term cost of the house.

Landscaping

Unless you are an avid gardener, you may not want a heavily landscaped lot that requires a lot of attention. If you do enjoy gardening, does the lot provide you with what you need to pursue your interest? For example, is there enough sunlight for the type of plants you want to grow?

Check the type of existing plants and get some sense of their yearly cycle. Are they evergreen or does their foliage drop away in cold months and expose some eyesores that were covered during warm weather? Check the position of trees near the house. If a tree's too close, it could cause foundation problems or damage to the house if it was blown over in a storm. If it's too large, it may block out so much sunlight that other plants have a hard time thriving. Also, make sure that all large trees look healthy. Large, diseased trees cost a lot of money to remove.

Satisfy yourself that any fences or retaining walls are in good shape and performing the way you want. For example, does a backyard fence give you the privacy you prefer or does it have to be replaced? Also, make sure you have access to the opposite side of any fence that runs along your borderline. If it needs paint, can you go onto your neighbor's property to do the work?

Can your children play safely in the yard or does the street have too much traffic? To make sure, visit the house on a weekday and on a weekend day. Traffic patterns can sometimes change drastically depending on the day of the week.

Having checked the condition of the house, refer to other sections of this book to figure out how much work is involved to correct any problems. This will help you to decide whether to do the work yourself, hire professionals, or look for another house.

Structural condition

Insulation

Home security

Mechanicals

Decorating

Improvements

Assessing potential

Assuming the structural condition of the house is okay and that you are willing to take on the the minor repairs and remodeling work that you want to have done, there still may be some things your general survey wasn't designed to highlight.

Is the house in question the right home for you and your family? It takes a good bit of imagination to see how a room will look when it's been divided in two or when a wall has been removed. And it's even more difficult to predict what your lifestyle might be in five or ten years' time. Can the house evolve with you? One way to get a better handle on these issues is simple. Take a tape measure along when you visit a house and get some numbers.

Draw a plan to scale on graph paper.

MEASURING A ROOM

If you think you might want to change the shape of a room, or suspect there may be a problem with fitting certain items of furniture into it, measure the floor area and ceiling height so that you can make a scale drawing later to clarify your thoughts.

Jot down the main dimensions, not forgetting the fireplace hearth, alcoves, and so on. Make a note of which way the doors swing; and of the positions of windows, radiators, electrical receptacles, and other fixtures. Later, transfer the measurements and details to graph paper, drawing them to scale.

When you have drawn your plan of the room, cut out pieces of paper to represent your furniture, using the same scale measurements. Rearrange them until you find a satisfactory solution.

Planning for people

Try to give function, comfort, and appearance equal priority when you are planning your home. The best designers build their concepts around the human frame, using statistics from research into the way people use their domestic and working environments.

Anthropometrics

Although human stature varies a great deal, the study of anthropometrics has determined the optimum dimensions of furniture and of spaces around it that are required to accommodate people of average build. These conclusions have been adopted by both designers and manufacturers so that most fixtures and furniture for kitchens, bathrooms, and living and dining areas are now built to standardized dimensions.

This is especially true of kitchen cabinets, which are designed for compatibility with appliances, like ranges and refrigerators, so the plan fits together as an integrated, functional whole. The standard countertop height, for instance, allows dishwashers to fit underneath while at the same time matching the height of stand-alone ranges. Designers adopt the same type of criteria for furniture, standard-size chairs, tables, and desks, allowing most people to work and eat comfortably.

The intelligent use of anthropometric information helps to reduce accidents. Correctly positioned shelves, for example, make reaching items possible without the need of balancing precariously on a chair. It also helps you choose appropriate furniture. A piece may look appealing and fit your budget, but if it breaks certain design guidelines, it will never be comfortable.

Using available space

As well as the size and function of the furniture itself, its positioning within the room falls within the realm of anthropometrics. An efficient use of floor area is an essential ingredient of good planning, providing people with freedom of action and sufficient room to make use of furniture and appliances with ease.

Whether you are choosing furniture or just planning where to locate the furnishings you already have, take the dimensions shown on the following pages into account. They will help you to buy wisely and make the best use of available space.

The hallway

When you are invited into the house, you will be able to gauge whether the entrance hall is large enough to receive visitors comfortably. Will there be room to store coats, hats, boots, umbrellas, and so on? Is the staircase wide enough to allow you to carry large pieces of furniture to the bedrooms?

If all the family members tend to be out during the day, is there any way to store daytime deliveries safely under cover outside? Is there a way to identify visitors before you open the door to them, especially after dark?

Hallway
5 ft.

Removing a coat
A front hallway should allow 5 ft. from side to side for taking off a coat or jacket.

Headroom
6 ft. 6 in.

Hallway
3 ft.

▲
Staircase headroom
Headroom of 6 ft. 6 in. above a staircase will allow you to carry most large furniture upstairs.

Negotiating a bend
You can turn most large pieces of furniture around a bend in a 3-ft. hallway.

Assessing potential

Living rooms

How many common rooms are there in the house? More than one area will make it possible for members of the family to engage in different pursuits without inconveniencing each other. If there is only one living room, make sure there are facilities elsewhere for private study, music practice, or hobbies that take up a lot of space or make a lot of noise.

Is the living room large enough to do what you want to do? Can it hold the furniture you have, the way you want it arranged? Is there room for expansion into an adjoining room if you need more space?

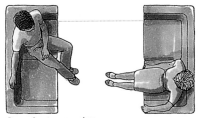

Arranging two couches
Allow a minimum of 3 ft. 8 in. between two couches that are facing each other.

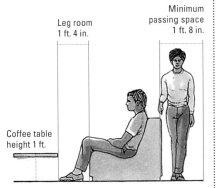

Leg room 1 ft. 4 in.

Minimum passing space 1 ft. 8 in.

Coffee table height 1 ft.

Low seating
The density of upholstery and the dimensions of the seat and back vary so much that it is impossible to suggest a standard, but make certain your back is supported properly and that you can get out of a chair without help. If you place a coffee table in front of a couch, try to position the table so that people can reach it from each end in order to avoid treading on the toes of someone seated.

Allow sufficient passing space around furniture, particularly if a member of the family is a wheelchair user. The chair needs an optimum clearance of 3 ft.

Bedrooms

The number of bedrooms may be adequate for your present needs, but what about the future? There may be additions to the family, and although young children can share a room for a while, eventually a separate bedroom is better for everybody concerned. You may want to put up a guest from time to time or have elderly relatives stay for extended periods. It might be possible to divide a large room with a simple partition, or perhaps a room on the ground floor can double as a bedroom. If an addition or attic conversion will be in your future, now is a good time at least to begin planning for it.

Are all the bedrooms an adequate size? As well as a bed or bunks, the room must accommodate storage for clothes, books, and toys, and room for homework and other pastimes. A guest room may have to function as a private sitting room too, with at least one comfortable chair and possibly a radio and television.

Some older houses have small bedrooms that are accessible only through another bedroom. This arrangement can be a real plus if one of your children is an infant and you want to be close by. But after the child grows out of the room, it's no longer useful as a bedroom, and most people convert it to a dressing room or a large storage closet.

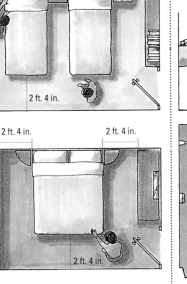

2 ft. 4 in.   1 ft. 8 in.   2 ft. 4 in.

2 ft. 4 in.

2 ft. 4 in.   2 ft. 4 in.

2 ft. 4 in.

Circulating space in bedrooms

Bathrooms

If the bathroom does not provide the amenities you require, estimate whether there is space for extra fixtures, even if this means rearranging the existing layout. Is there room elsewhere in the house for an additional powder room, especially on the first floor for elderly or disabled visitors?

Make a note of the electric fixtures in the room. Are ground fault receptacles present? Is there enough light where you want it? Is there an exhaust fan to remove excess humidity from the room?

Also check for any water damage. Is the paint cracked on windowsills? Do you see any evidence of mildew on the ceiling? Is the flooring stained or loose? Does the room smell musty?

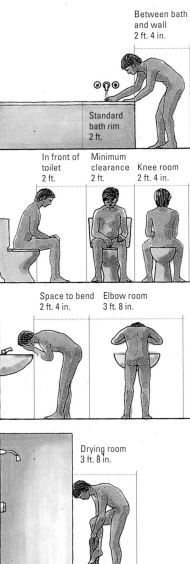

Between bath and wall 2 ft. 4 in.

Standard bath rim 2 ft.

In front of toilet 2 ft.   Minimum clearance 2 ft.   Knee room 2 ft. 4 in.

Space to bend 2 ft. 4 in.   Elbow room 3 ft. 8 in.

Drying room 3 ft. 8 in.

Between bath and wall
Allow sufficient room between the bath and the wall to dry yourself with a towel. The same amount of space will allow you to bend to clean the tub.

Toilet
Allow an adequate space in front and at both sides of a toilet. This will also provide room to maintain and clean the fixture.

Using a lavatory
Allow generous space so you can bend over the lav and also have plenty of elbow room when washing hair. The same space will also give you room to wash a child.

Drying after a shower
This is the minimum space required to dry yourself in front of a shower.

Assessing potential

Kitchen

The quality of kitchen cabinets, fixtures, and appliances varies enormously. But every well-designed kitchen should incorporate the following features.

A labor-saving layout
Preparing meals can be an unpleasant chore unless the areas for food preparation, cooking, and washing up are grouped in a layout that avoids unnecessary movement. The combined lengths of an efficient work triangle should be no more than 20 to 22 feet.

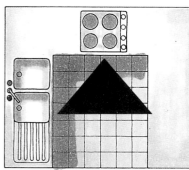

A typical work triangle links preparation, cooking, and washing-up areas.

Storage
Whether you are building storage into a kitchen, workshop, bedroom, or lounge, make sure every item is within easy reach and that there is room to open drawers and doors without hitting a wall or injuring other people.

Storage and appliances
If the work triangle is to be effective, a kitchen must incorporate enough storage space in each area. The refrigerator and food storage should be close to where the meals are prepared, and adequate work surfaces need to be provided. You may be able to find a place for a separate freezer elsewhere, but it should be as close to the kitchen as possible.

If the kitchen has a separate cooktop, it should be located close to the oven with heatproof surfaces nearby to receive hot dishes. Countertop cooking equipment should be within easy reach.

Appliances that require plumbing are best grouped together, with the sink, on an outside wall. In a small house the kitchen area may also contain a clothes washer and dryer, although a separate laundry room is really the ideal solution.

KITCHEN SAFETY

Check the layout of the kitchen with a view to safety. A cramped kitchen can lead to accidents, so make sure that more than one person at a time can circulate in safety.

- If possible, avoid an arrangement that encourages people to use the working part of the kitchen as a passageway to other parts of the house or to the outside.
- Make sure small children cannot reach the range, and construct a barrier that will keep them outside the work triangle.
- Placing a range in a corner or at the end of a run of cabinets isn't a good idea. Plan for a clear countertop on each side. Don't place it under a window, either—a draft could extinguish a gas pilot light, and someone could get burned trying to open the window.

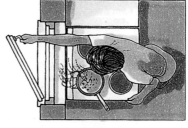

A dangerously placed range
Don't position a range under a window.

Dining room

Is there a separate dining room and, if so, does it have enough room to accommodate the entire family? Does it have extra room for entertaining guests?

Dining rooms are almost always positioned close to kitchens, for obvious reasons of convenience. But sometimes they aren't, and this should be considered a serious design flaw. A dining room too far away will be an ongoing aggravation or simply won't be used much.

If the dining area is part of the kitchen, does it have the room you want? Also, make sure it has efficient ventilation to extract cooking odors.

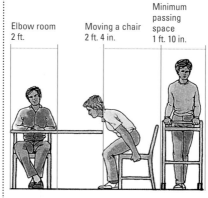

Elbow room 2 ft.

Moving a chair 2 ft. 4 in.

Minimum passing space 1 ft. 10 in.

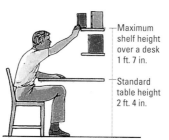

Maximum shelf height over a desk 1 ft. 7 in.

Standard table height 2 ft. 4 in.

Sitting at a table
The same area is needed for sitting at a dining table, writing desk, or dressing table. Arrange dining furniture so people are able to sit down or move a chair out without difficulty.

Breakfast bar
A 3 ft.-high breakfast bar aligns with a countertop.

Minimum knee room 10 in.

Height 3 ft.

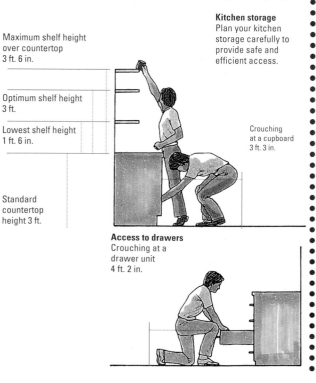

Maximum shelf height over countertop 3 ft. 6 in.

Optimum shelf height 3 ft.

Lowest shelf height 1 ft. 6 in.

Standard countertop height 3 ft.

Kitchen storage
Plan your kitchen storage carefully to provide safe and efficient access.

Crouching at a cupboard 3 ft. 3 in.

Access to drawers
Crouching at a drawer unit 4 ft. 2 in.

Using professionals

Why pay someone to do a job when you can do it perfectly well yourself? There are plenty of skilled amateurs who can tackle just about any job successfully. But getting the job done is only part of the story. How long it takes is another part. And, for most of us, extra time is hard to find.

There are certain jobs that are worth paying a professional to do quickly and efficiently: jobs that are holding up a series of other projects, for example, or that call for techniques that you don't know and don't have time to learn. In many cases, it makes good sense to hire an electrician to do major wiring or a plumber to install new bathroom fixtures while you handle the peripheral jobs and finishing yourself.

Then there are situations that call for certain skills that you haven't developed yet, where you'd like to work along with a professional, or at least observe the work being done so you'll know how to approach it in the future.

Professional advice

In many cases, if you are undertaking a major remodeling project—or if you are building a house from scratch—you will need professional approval (either an engineer's stamp or an architect's stamp) to obtain a building permit. Check with your local building department to see what's required in your area. And if you apply for a mortgage, the bank will insist on a complete title search and a professional property survey. If the surveyor's report discovers any questionable boundary lines, these problems will have to be straightened out before mortgage approval.

If you are buying a house, usually the best protection you can find is the help of a professional home inspector. These people work for you. They check that a building is structurally sound from top to bottom, including all the mechanical systems, and give you a written report on any problems. This document can warn you off a property before you make a serious mistake. But more often it just points out the shortcomings that every house has. You can use the faults identified in the inspection to negotiate a lower purchase price, or demand they be corrected before you buy.

Home inspector

Before you put a bid in on a house you like, you should hire a home inspector to evaluate the property. The inspector's job is to check that the building is structurally sound and to pinpoint anything that needs attention. Unless you are buying a fairly new property, an inspector's report usually makes depressing reading. If the inspector has done a thorough job, the report will list everything that has trouble and could cause trouble, from peeling paint to dry rot in the basement.

Keep in mind that no inspector can guarantee the condition of areas in the house that were inaccessible at the time of inspection. For example, if the house is occupied during the inspection and it has wall-to-wall carpeting installed, the inspector can't fully examine the floors without pulling up the carpeting. The inspection report that you receive should list the areas that weren't accessible and therefore were not inspected.

Study the report for specific references to serious faults that may be expensive to correct, like damage to the foundation, wet or dry rot, termite damage, water seepage, or a badly deteriorating roof. Also take note of things that could lead to trouble in the future, even if there is no evidence of them at the time. For example, if the report points out leaking gutters that are draining onto a wall behind, you should plan to have the gutters fixed before the wall is soaked and rot starts.

To find a good inspector, ask around, look in the Yellow Pages, or contact the American Society of Home Inspectors for a referral in your area. Members of this society have to demonstrate expertise in all areas of residential construction. Membership alone doesn't ensure professionalism, but it's a good place to start. Some construction professionals who have been in the building business for a long time and have a varied background covering all the trades also offer home inspection services. If one of these people is also a professional engineer (P.E.), this person should be qualified to do the work.

Architect

If you are planning ambitious home improvements, especially any involving major structural alterations or additions, consider hiring a qualified architect. These people are trained to design buildings and interiors that are not only structurally sound but aesthetically pleasing. An architect will prepare scaled drawings of the project for submission to the local building department for approval. In most cases, you can also employ the architect to supervise the construction to ensure that it meets all the required specifications.

You and the architect must work as partners. Your part of the bargain, aside from paying the bill, of course, is to explain in the best way you can what it is you want in a house: the way you live, the things that are important to you, how you will use the space, and so forth. The architect should take these concerns to heart, not just give them lip service. But to some extent, the architect should be given some freedom to interpret your desires in ways that might not occur to you. If an architect isn't given some of this freedom, there's no point in hiring him or her in the first place.

Personal recommendations are one of the best ways to find an architect. You can also contact the American Institute of Architects for a list of their members who work in your area. Regardless of how you find an architect, be sure to visit some of his or her recent work before you commit yourself.

Building permits

Before starting just about any building project, you have to get a permit from your local building department. Many homeowners, and some contractors, fail to apply for these permits either because they don't know that they have to or because they want to avoid the bureaucratic process that's involved. This can be an expensive mistake. If you don't have a permit, the local inspector could shut down the job at any time and levy a fine. The inspector could even require that the work be demolished or stipulate alterations that could be very costly.

Building codes, zoning ordinances, and even historic preservation rules that pertain in some areas vary widely. Never be in doubt about what's required. Just make an appointment at the local building department and find out what you need to know. Going through the proper procedures will cause you fewer headaches in the long run and will almost always ensure that a better job is done.

AMERICAN SOCIETY OF HOME INSPECTORS
932 Lee Street Suite 101
Des Plaines, IL 60016
www.ashi.org

AMERICAN INSTITUTE OF ARCHITECTS
1735 New York Ave., N.W.
Washington, DC 20006
www.aia.org

Employing a builder

The search for a builder who is both proficient and reliable can be frustrating. You will hear plenty of stories of clients being overcharged for poor work or being left with a half-completed job for months on end. It's not that good builders don't exist, but there are plenty of careless and inefficient ones who give the entire industry a bad name.

Choosing a builder

A good recommendation is the best way to find a builder. If someone whose opinion you respect has found a builder who is competent, reliable, and easy to communicate with, then the chances are you will enjoy the same experience. Even so, you should inspect the builder's work yourself before you make up your mind. If a recommendation is hard to come by, choose a builder who is a member of a local chapter of the National Association of Home Builders.

A good builder will be booked up for months ahead, so allow plenty of time to find someone who will be free when you need him or her to start work. If a builder is very highly recommended, you may not want to look elsewhere—but unless you get two or three candidates to estimate for the same job, you'll have no way of knowing if the price is fair. A builder who is in demand may quote a high price because he or she doesn't need the work. On the other hand, an inexperienced builder may submit a price that seems tempting but then cut corners or ask for more money later because unanticipated problems come up before the job is completed.

Subcontractors

Unless a builder is a jack-of-all-trades, he employs independent subcontractors (masons, electricians, plumbers, etc.) to do most of the actual work. The builder is responsible for the quality of subcontracted work unless you agree beforehand that you will hire and manage the subcontractors yourself. It's usually better to discuss anything relating to the subcontracted work with the builder, not the subcontractor. The work is the builder's responsibility, and the subcontractors should receive their instructions from one source, otherwise there's bound to be confusion.

● **Estimates and quotations**
A builder's initial estimate is usually an approximate price only. Before you sign a contract, make sure you get a firm written quotation that reflects current prices.

NATIONAL ASSOCIATION OF HOME BUILDERS
1201 15th St., N.W.,
Washington, DC 20005
www.nahb.org

Writing a specification

Many of the disagreements that arise between builder and client are a result of insufficient communication before work begins. Don't give a builder vague instructions. A builder may try hard to provide the kind of work he or she thinks you want, but the guesses might turn out to be wide of the mark. Also, a builder can't possibly quote an accurate price without knowing exactly what you want.

You don't always need a complicated legal document, and you don't have to tell the builder how to do the job. Just write a detailed list of the work you want carried out and, as far as possible, the materials you want used. If you haven't yet made up your mind about the wallcovering you want or the brand of bathroom fixtures, then note the same in the list you give the builder. You can always discuss unresolved details of this kind before the builder submits a quote for the work.

Read the relevant sections in this book to find out what a particular job involves. Or, if the work is complicated, hire an architect or engineer to draw up some specifications for you.

Your agreement with the builder needs to include both a date for starting the work and an estimate of how long it will take to complete. You should insist upon this before signing any agreement. There are often legitimate reasons why a job isn't begun and finished on time. But if you have a signed agreement on dates, the chances of them being met are higher.

Getting an estimate

When you ask several builders to quote a price for a job, what they give you is only an estimate. This will be based on current prices and the amount of information you have supplied at the time. If you take a long time to make up your mind, or alter any specifications, the prices are likely to change.

Before you officially engage the builder you've chosen, always obtain a firm quotation with a detailed breakdown of costs. Part of the quotation may still be estimated, especially if you haven't made up your mind on every detail. For these uncertain things, assign a provisional sum to cover them—but make it clear that you must be consulted before that money is spent. Because a builder has to hire subcontractors to do the work, the builder's estimate is only as good as the subcontractors' estimates. During the course of a project, many things can go wrong and you'll end up paying for at least some of this whether it was your fault or not.

Agree how payment is to be made. Many builders are willing to complete the work before any money changes hands. But most others ask for installment payments to cover the cost of materials. If you agree to installments, make it clear that materials payments will only be made once the materials are on site and that final payment will be made only when all the work meets your approval.

Provided you make it clear to the builder before he accepts the contract, you can retain a figure for an agreed period after the work is completed to cover the cost of faulty workmanship. Between 5 and 10 percent of the overall cost is a reasonable sum to retain.

Neither you nor the builder can anticipate all the problems that might arise. If something unexpected occurs that affects the price for the job, ask the builder for an estimate of costs before you decide what course of action to take.

Working with your builder

Most people find they get a better job from a builder if they create a friendly working atmosphere. You will have to provide access to electricity and water if these are necessary for the job. And the workers will need somewhere to store materials and tools. A certain amount of mess is inevitable, but a builder should make some effort to clean up the site at the end of each working day. And you shouldn't have to put up with mud or other debris in areas of the house that are not part of the building site.

Unless you have an architect to supervise the job, keep your eye on the progress of the work. If you constantly interrupt the builder, that is likely to cause friction. But inspect the job when the workers have left the site at the end of the day to satisfy yourself that the workmanship is acceptable.

Building codes and permits

Building codes

Building codes are comprehensive guidelines intended to set standards for construction practices and material specifications. Their purpose is to ensure the adequate structural and mechanical performance, fire safety, and overall quality of buildings. They are also designed to address various health and environmental concerns related to how buildings are constructed. By setting minimum standards, building codes also limit unfair competitive practices between builders and between contractors.

Building codes address nearly every detail of building construction, from the acceptable recipes for concrete used in the foundation to the permissible fire rating of the roof finish material, and just about everything in between. Partly because codes attempt to be as comprehensive as possible, and also because they must address different concerns in different parts of the country, they are very detailed, complex, and lack uniformity from one region to another. A further complication is that many new building products become available each year that are not dealt with in the existing codes. Model codes, developed by four major organizations, are widely used for reference throughout the United States.

The Uniform Building Code, published by the International Conference of Building Officials, is very widely accepted. ICBO republishes the entire code every three years and comes out with revisions annually. A short form of the Uniform Building Code is available that covers buildings that are less than three stories high and have fewer than 6000 square feet of living space. This publication was designed for the convenience of most builders and remodelers.

The BOCA Basic Building Code, issued by the Building Officials and Code Administrators International is another widely used code. This code also comes in abridged form for residential construction.

A third model code, prepared by the American Insurance Association, and known as the National Building Code, serves as the basis for many codes that are adopted by local communities. It too is available in short form for matters relating only to home construction.

The Standard Building Code is published by the Southern Building Code Congress International. It addresses conditions and problems that are prevalent in the southern United States.

While it's likely that one of these model codes serves as the basis for the building code in your community, municipal and state governments frequently add standards and restrictions that are not in the model codes. It is your local building department that ultimately decides what is acceptable and what is not. Consult your building department for questions about any code issues. And keep in mind that building codes are primarily designed for the safety of the building's occupants and the general welfare of the community at large. It makes sense to follow all the practices outlined by the code in your area.

Anyone can file for a building permit, but if you've hired an architect or builder to handle the construction management for you, they should file for all necessary permits.

Zoning restrictions

Even for projects that do not require a building permit, local zoning regulations may limit the scope and nature of the construction that's permitted. Whereas building codes relate to the building itself, zoning rules address the needs and conditions of the community as a whole by regulating the development and uses of the property. Zoning restrictions may apply to situations such as whether a single-family house can be remodeled into apartments, whether a commercial space can be converted into residential use, or the permissible height of a house or outbuilding.

It's a good idea to check with the local zoning board before you make any plans, especially plans that substantially change the way the property is used. If the planned changes do not conform to existing zoning guidelines, you can apply to the zoning board for a variance. If the board thinks your plans follow the spirit of the regulations, they can approve the changes.

Landmark regulations

Homes in historic districts may be subject to restrictions designed to help the neighborhood retain its architectural character. For the most part, in designated landmark areas, any changes in the exterior of a house are closely regulated. While extensive remodelings that would significantly change the architectural style are almost never permitted, even seemingly small modifications can be rigorously scrutinized. For example, metal or vinyl replacement windows may not be permitted for Victorian homes in designated areas. Or the exterior paint and roof colors may be subject to approval. Even the color of mortar used to repoint brickwork may be specified by the local landmarks commission or similar regulating body. Designs for new construction must conform to the prevalent architectural character. If you live in a historic district, you should apply to the governing body for approval of any plans for exterior changes. If you are interested in buying a house in one of these districts, review the regulations before you make a purchase. The restrictions that apply may be one of the big reasons you wanted to live in the area in the first place.

Building permits

A building permit is generally required for new construction, remodeling projects that require structural changes or additions, and major demolition projects. In some areas, it's necessary to obtain a building permit for constructing an in-ground pool. In others, you even need a permit to erect scaffolding for painting your house.

To get a building permit, you must file an application (provided by your local building department) that answers questions about the proposed site and the project you are planning. You also have to file a complete set of drawings for the entire project along with detailed specifications for all the mechanical systems. A complete set normally includes a site plan, foundation plan, a plan for each floor of the house, section views of the house framing from the ridge to the foundation, elevation drawings of all four sides of the house, and drawings for all the mechanical systems. Permit fees are usually based on some percentage of the construction costs, or the numbers of trips that the inspector is likely to make to the job site, or both.

At the time you apply for a building permit, ask about other permits that may be required. For example, you may need to apply to the local health department for projects that have an impact on sewage facilities or water supply systems. It's important to arrange inspections in a timely fashion, since each ensuing stage cannot proceed until the previous work has been inspected and approved.

Permits and regulations

Although it often seems like it, you don't always need a building permit. Projects that don't significantly alter a home are sometimes excluded from the regulations. The chart on the facing page indicates whether a permit is generally required for the work listed. But remember that local codes are the final authority, and they can be notoriously unpredictable. Use the chart as a reference tool when thinking about a project. But don't proceed without checking with your local code office.

Attic conversion
Permits are not always required for basic attic conversions like adding a single bedroom to the space. But anything more elaborate, particularly if the roofline is changed, would require approval. The same is true of any project that involves substantial electrical and/or plumbing work.

Additions
Unless the local code is atypical, any room addition will require a building permit and a full schedule of inspections along the way.

Painting and minor repairs
You don't need a permit for general maintenance and repair chores such as painting unless you live in a historic district.

Removing trees
Pruning or cutting down trees are two chores that rarely require a permit, except in some historic districts where the landscape around your house may be covered by regulations.

Will you need a permit?

PROFESSIONALS
REGULATIONS

Type of work	Permit required		Zoning approval required	
Interior and exterior painting and minor repairs	NO	Permit may be required to erect scaffolding	NO	Unless in historic district.
Replacing windows and doors	NO		NO	Unless in historic district.
Electrical work	YES	Must be inspected	NO	Some outdoor lighting may be subject to approval.
Plumbing	YES		NO	Work involving water supply or sewage system may require health department approval.
Heating	NO		NO	
Constructing patios and decks, Installing a hot tub	NO		NO	
Structural alterations	YES		NO	Unless house is in an historic district
Attic conversion	NO / YES	No, if work is minor like adding a simple bedroom. / Yes, if major structural work is done and if plumbing and major electrical modifications are called for.	NO	Unless work impacts exterior of house in historic district
Building a fence or garden wall	NO		YES	In cases where a fence or wall is adjacent to public road, there may be height restrictions.
Planting a hedge	NO	Unless it obscures the view of traffic at a junction, or access to a main road.	NO	
Path or sidewalk	NO	Unless it will be used by the public.	NO	Unless in historic district.
Clearing land	NO		YES	
Installing a satellite-TV dish	NO		NO	
Constructing a small outbuilding	YES	Local codes usually have size restrictions. Anything smaller doesn't need a permit.	NO	Unless in historic district.
Porch addition	YES	Local codes sometimes have size limits. Under the limit doesn't require permit.	NO	Unless in historic district.
Greenhouse or sunspace	YES		NO	Unless in historic district.
Building a garage	YES		YES	If used for a commercial vehicle or located close to property line.
Driveway paving	NO		YES	At point where it meets the road.
House addition	YES		NO	Unless house is in historic district or addition will be close to property line.
Demolition	YES	If major work is done that involves any structural elements.	NO	Unless house is in historic district.
Converting single-family house into apartments	YES		YES	
Converting residential building to commercial use	YES		YES	

CHART
Building code requirements and zoning regulations vary from town to town and frequently have county and state restrictions added to them. For this reason, it's impossible to state with certainty which home-improvement projects require official permission and which do not. This chart lists some of the most frequently undertaken projects and is meant to serve as a rough guide only. Taken as a whole, it suggests a certain logic for anticipating what type of approval may be needed. Whether or not official approval is required, all work should be carried out to the standards established in local codes.

11

Do-it-yourself

WORKING SEQUENCE

With most jobs, you can save money by doing the work yourself. You'll probably have to pay more for materials than a contractor, who usually gets a discount, but you will save all the labor costs, which are the lion's share of any professional's bill. By doing things yourself, you can also avoid a whole raft of annoying scheduling problems. And there's a good deal of satisfaction and enjoyment in planning and completing a job that will make your home better.

Planning work priorities
Although planning may not seem so important when you are doing all the work yourself, careful forethought can greatly reduce the strain on you and your family. Work out a schedule, listing the jobs in order of priority. Some may need to be carried out quickly, either to safeguard the structure of the house or because of the damage that could result from bad weather. Others can be tackled at any stage, when you can fit in the time. Try to plan the work in a way that avoids backtracking to earlier stages. Whenever possible, finish one job before moving on to the next.

Planning your time
An important thing to consider in your planning is the amount of time you are able to devote to the work. This may determine how you tackle a long-term project. Unless you can work full time for periods of weeks or even months on end, it will take you several years to completely renovate even a small house. You must decide whether you and your family are prepared to put up with the inconvenience involved. Should you tackle a whole house at once, or would it be better to divide up the work so that part of the house remains relatively comfortable?

Exactly how you plan the work will depend also on the layout of the building. You may be able to seal off one section of the house completely while you work on it. Include in your plans ways to keep from treading dust and dirt from the work area into parts of the house where you are living. And try to clean up as you go. At the end of a long day, it's hard to pick up and sweep up, but it's the best way to keep the mess under control.

No two homes or families are identical. But the chart that follows will help you plan your own sequence of events. You should always give priority to measures that will stop deterioration. Also, it's usually best to repair and decorate the exterior of the house before the interior, so the house will be weatherproof. In practice, you'll almost certainly find it difficult to stick to any schedule. Unexpected problems usually dictate a change of plan, to say nothing of family pressures or budget problems. Try to remember that just about any plan is better than no plan at all.

Priority work ☞

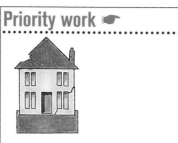

URGENT REPAIRS

Attend to any problems mentioned in the home inspector's report. Repair anything in a dangerous condition or anything that is damaging to the basic structure of the building. These may include:

● Dry rot, rising or penetrating dampness

● Severely cracked or loose masonry

● Termite or other insect infestation

● Faulty plumbing, gutters, and drains

● Faulty electrical wiring

● Unstable retaining walls

● Roof repairs

SECURITY

● Install locks on all vulnerable doors and windows.

● Change the front-door lock on any house you buy. You don't know who has a key.

● Install a smoke and carbon monoxide detector, fire extinguisher, and fire blanket. Consider installing a home security system.

APPROVAL

● Discuss any home-improvement project with your local building department. If necessary, apply for a building permit and zoning board approval.

Roof work ☞

ROOF COVERING

● Repair or replace damaged or missing roofing.

● Repair faulty flashings.

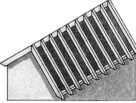

ROOF FRAMING

● Repair or replace any rotten or damaged roof framing members. Consider hiring a professional for this job.

ROOF INSULATION

● Insulate and ventilate the attic space.

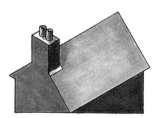

CHIMNEY

● Repoint loose chimney bricks.

● Repair broken or torn flashing.

● Repair broken chimney caps.

Indoor work ☞

REMODELING

Undertake major interior structural changes such as:

● Building or removing dividing walls.

● Lowering ceilings.

● Opening up or closing off doorways.

● Installing or repairing fireplace mantels.

MECHANICALS

PLUMBING
● Undertake new plumbing and heating work.

ELECTRIC
● Wire new electrical fixtures and appliances.

INSULATION

FLOOR INSULATION
● Insulate attic and possibly outside walls.

DOUBLE GLAZING
● Install storm or replacement windows.

VENTILATION

● Provide adequate ventilation.

REPAIRS AND RENOVATIONS

FLOORS
● Repair or replace floors.

WALLS
● Repair or replace drywall or plasterwork.

WOODWORK
● Repair or replace baseboards.

● Repair or replace door and window casings.

BUILT-INS
● Install or repair cabinets and storage shelves.

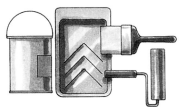

DECORATING

CEILINGS
● Repair and paint ceilings.

WALLS
● Repair and paint walls.

FINISH WOODWORK
● Repair and refinish woodwork.

WALLCOVERINGS
● Repair walls and hang wallcoverings.

FLOORCOVERINGS
● Repair floors and install floorcoverings.

CURTAINS, BLINDS, AND SHUTTERS
● Finish woodwork, then install hardware and hang curtains, blinds, or shutters.

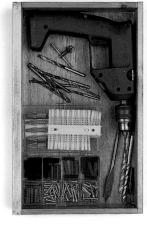

Outdoor work ☞

OUTSIDE WALLS

REPAIRING WALLS

● Repoint brickwork.
● Patch damaged stucco.
● Repair or replace wood siding.

INSULATING WALLS

● Consider installing insulation in exterior walls at this point.

WEATHERPROOFING WALLS

● Waterproof or paint masonry walls.

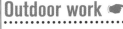

WINDOWS AND DOORS

● Repair or replace doors and windows.
● Repair or replace locks.

WOOD

● Paint or clear-finish all woodwork.

GARDEN WORK

WALLS AND FENCES
● Repair or replace garden walls and fences.

DRIVEWAYS AND SIDEWALKS
● Repair driveways.
● Repair or replace walkways.

LAWNS
● Fertilize and water grass.

TREES AND SHRUBS
● Prune and fertilize on recommended schedule.

GREENHOUSES
● Repair or replace wall and door glass panels.

A basis for selecting color

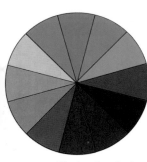

A basic color wheel
A color wheel shows the relationship of primary, secondary, and tertiary colors. Warm and cool colors are grouped on opposite sides of the wheel.

Developing a sense of the "right" color isn't the same as learning how to paint a door or hang a roll of wallpaper. There are no rules as such, but there are guidelines that will help. Often colors are described as tints or shades, and as cool or warm. These terms, though somewhat imprecise, can be helpful when you are developing a color scheme. By considering colors as the spokes of a wheel, you will see how they relate to each other, and how these relationships can create a particular mood.

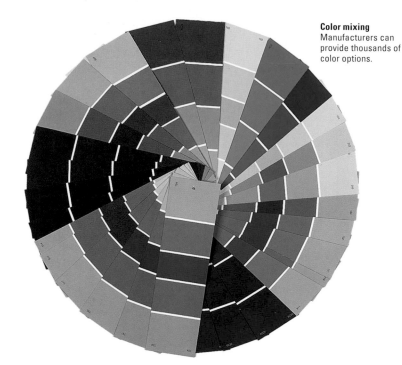

Color mixing
Manufacturers can provide thousands of color options.

Primary colors
All colors are derived from three basic "pure" colors—red, blue, and yellow. They are known as the primary colors.

Secondary colors
When you mix two primary colors in equal proportions, a secondary color is produced. Red plus blue makes violet, blue with yellow makes green, and red plus yellow makes orange. When a secondary color is placed between its constituents on the wheel, it sits opposite its complementary color—the one primary color not used in its makeup. Complementary colors are the most contrasting colors in the spectrum and are used for dramatic effects.

Tertiary colors
When a primary is mixed equally with one of its neighboring secondaries, it produces a tertiary color. The complete wheel illustrates a simplified version of all color groupings. Colors on opposite sides are used in combination in order to produce vibrant contrasting schemes, while those grouped on one side of the wheel form the basis of a harmonious scheme.

Warm and cool colors
The wheel also groups colors with similar characteristics. On one side are the warm red and yellow combinations, colors we associate with fire and sunlight. A room decorated with warm colors feels cozy or exciting, depending on the intensity of the colors used. Cool colors are grouped on the opposite side of the wheel. Blues and greens suggest vegetation, water, and sky, and create a relaxed, airy feeling when used together.

The primary colors from which all other colors are derived.

Secondary colors

Tertiary colors

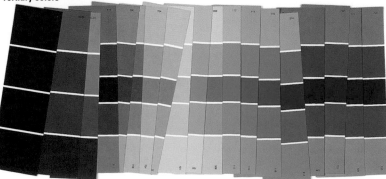

Warm and cool colors

Vibrant primaries
(left)
There's nothing tame or safe about this color scheme—a striking interior created solely by mixing bold areas of primary reds, blues, and yellows.

Cool contrast
(below left)
The contrast between warm wood furniture and cool blue paint creates an understated atmosphere.

Fresh but cozy
(below)
Similar materials look very different when seen in the context of warm pinks. Here, the effect is cozy with a light touch.

Using tone for subtlety

Pure colors can be used to great effect for both exterior and interior color schemes. But a more subtle combination of colors is preferable in most situations. Subtle colors are made by mixing different percentages of pure color or simply by changing the tone of a color by adding a neutral color to it.

Neutrals

The purest forms of neutral are black and white (from which color is entirely absent). The range of neutrals can be extended by mixing the two together to produce varying tones of gray. Neutrals are used extensively by decorators because they do not clash with any other color. But in their simplest forms, they can look either stark or rather bland. Consequently, a touch of color is normally added to a gray to give it a warm or cool feel, so it can pick up the character of another color close by, or to provide an almost imperceptible contrast within a range of similar colors.

Tints

Changing the tone of pure colors by adding white creates pastel colors or tints. Used in combination, tints are safe colors. It's difficult to produce anything but a harmonious scheme. The effect can be very dramatic, however, if a pale tint is contrasted with dark tones.

Shades

The shades of a color are produced by adding black to it. Shades are rich, dramatic colors, used for bold yet sophisticated schemes. It is within this range of colors that browns appear—the interior designer's stock-in-trade. Brown blends so harmoniously into almost any color scheme that it is often considered a neutral.

1 Neutrals

2 Tints

3 Shades

1 Neutrals
A range of neutral tones creates a palette of subtle colors.

2 Tints
A combination of pale tints is usually harmonious and attractive.

3 Shades
Use darker tones, or shades, for rich, dramatic effects.

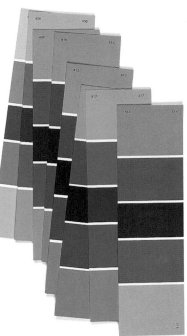

Coordinated harmony
(top left)
Pale colors are often used when a safe, harmonious scheme is required. Darker shades from the same range of colors provide the necessary tonal contrast. With this approach, it is almost impossible to go wrong.

Resolutely neutral
(left)
Some rooms are totally uncompromising in the use of pure neutrals. The starkness is relieved by a single accent of color in the vase of flowers and the dark door trim and picture frames. These accents can be easily varied to shift the balance of the scheme.

17

Taking texture into account

We are far more aware of the color of a surface than of its texture, which we almost take for granted. But texture is a vital ingredient of any decorating scheme and should be considered along with color.

The visual effect of texture is created by the strength and direction of the light that falls on it. A smooth surface reflects more light than a rough one. Coarse textures absorb light, even creating shadows if the light falls at a low angle. Because of this, a color will look different if it's applied to a smooth surface or a textured one.

Even without applied color, texture adds interest to a scheme. You can contrast bare brickwork with smooth paintwork, for instance, or use the reflective qualities of glass, metal, or glazed ceramics to produce some impressive decorative effects.

Like color, texture can be employed to make an impression on our senses. Cork, wood, coarsely woven fabrics, and rugs add warmth, even a sense of luxury, to an interior. Smooth or reflective materials, such as polished stone, stainless steel, ceramic tiles, vinyl, or even black-lacquered furniture, give a clean, almost clinical, feeling to a room.

Bold use of textures
(below)
A wealth of textures, including the color-washed walls, textiles, and wicker pieces, fuse into an interior that is both lively and warm. Clearly, the person who lives here is not afraid of strong colors.

Detailing
(below right)
Carefully chosen and arranged objects can be a source of interest, especially when colors and textures are thoughtfully matched.

Using pattern for effect

Many decorating purists have made us reluctant to use pattern boldly. But our less inhibited forebears felt free to cover their homes with pattern and applied decoration. Often the results were exceptional, creating a sense of excitement that is difficult to create any other way.

An attractive, patterned wallpaper, fabric, or rug can provide the basis for an entire color scheme, if they have been chosen to work well with each other. There is no reason why the dominant colors in a pattern can't be applied to other surfaces in the room. If you are unsure of creating a harmonious scheme with multiple patterns in play, a safe approach is to incorporate a pattern on a single surface or piece of furniture, and then choose plain colors for the other surfaces.

Combining different patterns can be tricky, but a small, regular pattern normally works well with a large, bold pattern. Also, different patterns with a similar dominating color can work well together. Another approach is to use the same pattern in different colors on different surfaces.

Create your own pattern
Stencils give you the opportunity to apply a pattern to furniture, walls, and floors. Below, stenciled grapevines create a personalized backdrop to a kitchen countertop.

Regular patterns
(below left)
Stripes and checked patterns like this red plaid are rarely distracting, even when used in a busy room.

Dominant patterns
(below)
Here, areas of strong color and pattern are the dominant features in a room.

19

Manipulating space

There are almost always areas of a house that feel uncomfortably small or so spacious that you feel like you're in a commercial building instead of your own home. Your first impulse may be to make structural changes, like knocking down a wall or putting one up. In some cases, measures like this will prove to be the best solution. But there is no doubt that they will be more expensive and disruptive than manipulating the space by using color and pattern.

Our eyes perceive colors and tones in such a way that it is possible to create optical illusions that apparently change the dimensions of a room. Warm colors appear to move closer— so a room painted brown, red, or orange, for example, will give the impression of being smaller than the same room decorated in cool colors, such as blues and greens, which have a tendency to recede.

Tone can be used to modify or reinforce the required illusion. Dark tones—even when you are using cool colors—will advance, while pale tones tend to open up a space.

The same qualities of color and tone will change the proportions of a space. Adjusting the height of a ceiling is an obvious example. If you paint a ceiling a darker tone than the walls, it will appear lower. If you treat the floor in a similar way, you can almost make the room seem squeezed between the two. A long, narrow hallway will feel less claustrophobic if you push out the walls by painting them with pale, cool colors, which will reflect more light as well.

Using a linear pattern is yet another way to alter the perception of space. Vertically striped wallpaper or paneling on the walls will counteract the effect of a low ceiling. Blinds make windows seem wider, and wood-strip flooring tends to stretch the room in the direction of the boards. Any large-scale pattern draws attention to itself and, in the same way as warm colors, dark tones will make the room advance toward you. From a distance, small patterns appear to be texture instead of pattern and so tend to make the room recede.

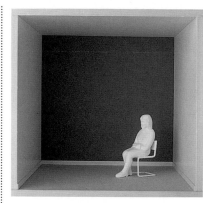

Warm colors appear to move forward

A cool color or pale tone will recede

A dark ceiling will appear lower

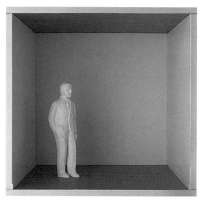

A dark floor and ceiling make a room feel smaller

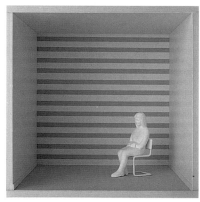

Horizontal stripes make a wall seem wider

Vertical stripes increase the height

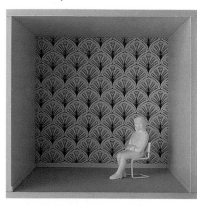

Large-scale patterns make a room feel smaller

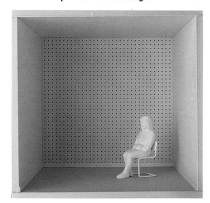

A small, regular pattern recedes

Practical experiments
Apply various decorating treatments to a series of small boxes to see what effect they create.

Before you spend money on paint, carpet, or wallcoverings, collect samples of the materials you want to use and place them next to each other to gauge the effect of the colors and textures on each other.

Collecting samples

Make your first selections from the more limited choice of furniture fabrics and carpets. Collect scraps of the materials that you are considering or borrow sample books from suppliers, so you can compare them carefully at home. Because paint charts are printed, you can never be absolutely sure they will match the actual paint. Some paint stores will give you small samples of the paint you are considering to take home and test on the walls or woodwork.

Making a sample board

Professional designers make sample boards to check the relative proportions of materials as they will appear in a room. Usually a patch of carpet or wallcovering will be the largest dominating area of color. Painted woodwork will be proportionally smaller. And accessories might be represented by nothing more than small spots of color. Make your own board by gluing your materials to stiff cardboard. Butt one piece against another to avoid leaving a white border between the samples, which could change the combined effect.

Incorporating existing features

Most decorating schemes will have to incorporate existing features, such as bathroom fixtures or kitchen cabinets. Use these items as starting points, building the color scheme around them. Cut a hole in your sample board to use as a window for viewing existing materials against those on the card.

Not an inch to spare
(left)
A tiny but well-planned bathroom makes the most of every inch of space. The use of pale neutrals, relieved by simple geometric tiling, keeps the room from feeling claustrophobic.

Optical illusions
(below)
A cramped space can feel like a dungeon, but in this case slightly warm, pale tints are used to push out the walls, and the vertical stripes in the wallpaper help to lift the ceiling. The room is also expanded by floor-to-ceiling mirrors in the alcove and by the natural light from the clerestory windows.

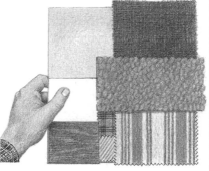

Checking your color selection
View your completed sample board in natural and artificial light to check your color selections.

Schemes for living rooms

In most homes, the living room is the largest area in the house. It's where you spend most of your leisure time and where you entertain friends. Usually, it's also the room where the most money is spent on furnishings, curtains, carpets, and all sorts of electronic entertainment equipment. For all these reasons, you will want to plan your living room decorating to have lasting appeal. After all, you're not very likely to replace costly furniture just to keep a wall color you like.

Unless you are lucky enough to have more than one common room in your house, the living room is the area that must feel comfortable during the day, relaxing in the evening, and be lively enough for occasional entertaining. If the room receives very little sunlight, a warm color scheme is often the best, in order to create a cozy atmosphere. Dark, cool tones will produce a similarly comfortable result under artificial light. But very deep tones can have the opposite effect by creating dark, shadowy areas. Neutral color schemes or a range of browns and beiges will be easy to change in the future simply by swapping the accessories, without having to spend money on replacing essentials. Natural textures are equally versatile.

Patterned carpets or rugs are less likely than plain ones to be ruined by the inevitable spills. But keep in mind that often very dark tones are almost as difficult to keep clean as pale ones.

Curtains and blinds provide the perfect way to easily change the mood of a room. During the day, they are pulled aside or rolled up, and therefore contribute very little to the general appearance of the room. But in the evening, they can become a wall of color or pattern, which can transform the whole environment.

Sheer curtains or blinds are also useful to screen the view through the windows while allowing daylight to fill the room with a soft light that will not damage fabrics and furniture.

Thinking ahead
This fundamental scheme (below) of white-painted walls and woodwork acts as a neutral background for rich colors that can be changed at any time. The mood is one of luxurious comfort, created by heavy drapes, patterned sofa throws, and dark wood tables.

Schemes for bedrooms

A bedroom is first and foremost a personal room. Its decorating should reflect the character of its occupant or occupants, while fulfilling the requirements of a peaceful, relaxing place to sleep. Much depends on the comfort of the furniture and the effects of the lighting. Pattern and color also have big roles to play, especially if the room is small and gets little natural light.

Few people ever think of using pattern on a ceiling, yet a bedroom presents the ideal opportunity. You spend so much time looking up when you're in the room, it just makes sense to have something a little more interesting to look at.

Something less than the best carpeting is often used for bedrooms because it doesn't have to be hard-wearing. The carpet you choose may be inexpensive, but the color doesn't have to be dull. A good color can lift a room more than bland versions of expensive carpeting. If a bedroom faces south, early sunlight will provide the necessary stimulus to wake you up, but a north-facing room will benefit from bright, invigorating colors.

Bedrooms sometimes have to serve a dual function. A teenager's bedroom, for example, usually doubles as a place to study and relax. Because so much time is spent in the room, the decorating should be stimulating rather than reserved. A child's bedroom will almost certainly function as a playroom too. The obvious choice would be for strong, even primary colors. But a neutral background and prominently displayed, brightly colored toys, books, and pictures would work too.

The smallest bedrooms, which are usually reserved for guests, can be made to appear larger and more inviting by selecting the appropriate colors and tones.

Seductive luxury
A combination of pattern and soft textures creates an atmosphere that is both eye-catching and comfortable. The deep rose carpet picks up the background color of the rugs and blankets to unify the whole room.

Kitchen decorating

Kitchens need to be functional areas capable of taking a great deal of wear and tear, so the materials you choose will be determined primarily by practical concerns. However, that doesn't mean you have to restrict your use of color. Kitchen sinks and appliances are made in bright colors as well as the standard stainless steel and white enamel. And tiled countertops, backsplashes, vinyl floorcoverings, and a full range of countertop appliances, offer great opportunities to introduce a many different colors into the room.

Textures are an important consideration, offering a range of possibilities. Natural wood remains a popular material for kitchen cabinets and will provide a warm element that you can either echo in your choice of paint, paper, or floorcovering or contrast with cool-palette colors and textures. Some people prefer to rely entirely on plastic, ceramic, and metal surfaces to create a clean, nearly antiseptic, character.

If the kitchen incorporates a dining area, you may want to decorate the latter in a fashion more conducive to relaxation and conversation. Also, softer textures, such as carpet tiles, cork flooring, and fabric upholstery, will absorb some of the clatter that is generated by kitchen utensils. Another possibility is to decorate the walls in a different way that subtly changes the mood, maybe using darker tones or a patterned wallcovering to define the dining area.

Everything at hand
(above)
Utensils are part and parcel of every kitchen, but they don't have to look utilitarian. Some people prefer to have everything within easy reach, which means that kitchen paraphernalia becomes an integral part of the decor.

Traditional styling with modern amenities
(left)
In this imposing kitchen, flat-painted surfaces are the perfect foil for high-end appliances and countertops of polished stone and natural wood.

Bathrooms

Bathrooms, like kitchens, have to fulfill several functions, which necessitates the use of ceramic and enameled surfaces. Imaginative use of tone, color, and furnishings are especially important if you want to save your bathroom from looking cold or uninviting. Colored fixtures are commonplace. But choose them carefully because they will have a dominating impact on the rest of the room.

Like the bedroom, the bathroom is an area where you can afford to be inventive with your use of color or pattern. A bold treatment that might not be appealing in a large room can be very successful in a smaller room. Also, try to introduce some sound-absorbing materials, like a plush bath mat on the floor and thick towels hanging from the walls to reduce the hard sounds common to fully tiled bathrooms. If you want to use materials that could be affected by steam, make sure the bathroom is properly ventilated.

Bathrooms are usually small rooms with relatively high ceilings. While painting a ceiling a dark color or tone in a large room can improve the proportions, doing so in a small bathroom can make the space feel like a claustrophobic box. A better way to bring down a high ceiling is to divide the walls horizontally, with a chair rail or a wallpaper border, and use a different color or texture above the line and below the line.

Functional simplicity
(left)
White paint, glass, and chrome add up to a refined, no-nonsense bathroom, with its plumbing concealed behind a wall that doubles as a useful shelf behind the lavatories.

Be creative with tiles
(bottom left)
Ceramic tiles are ideally suited to a bathroom. Basic white tile can seem a little clinical, but colorful patterned tiles can add a welcome touch of warmth.

Period-style elegance
(below)
In this bathroom, the fixtures, furnishings, and paneled walls all contribute to a period feel. The deep shade of blue-green makes the room feel warm and intimate.

Small apartments

When you live in one room, or in just a couple of rooms, every square foot of living space has to be as versatile as possible. In large part your plans will be dictated by your lifestyle. If you are out at work during the day, you may want to concentrate on creating a mood for the evening. On the other hand, if you work at home, you'll need to create a daytime environment that is stimulating but not distracting.

Relaxed informality
Whether it's used for preparing a meal, entertaining friends, or working at home, this is a living space to be enjoyed. Although it's an entirely open plan, each area is defined with color and different furniture and light fixtures. It's a mix-and-match scheme that works well because the furnishings complement each other instead of fighting for attention.

Ideally, you would want to design a small interior so it can adapt easily to different activities and different times of day. Some means of screening off a sleeping area is always an advantage. Floor-length curtains hung from a ceiling-mounted track can form a soft wall of color or texture. Or you can use vertical louvered blinds so that with the pull of a cord you can open up or close off the bedroom area. Folding wood screens or louvered shutters give the impression of a permanent screen during the day and are stowed against the wall at night. These dividers also provide the opportunity to introduce naturally finished or stained wood into the room's color scheme.

Dividing the floor area will define areas of activity: soft rugs for seating, polished boards or quarry tile for cooking and eating areas. You can even change the floor level with a simple wooden platform covered in carpet. Wall areas can be sharply defined by using different finishes, textures, and colors.

A small, open-plan apartment suggests other options. Prevailing natural light might persuade you to treat areas differently, either brightening up a dark corner or toning down an area that is constantly sunlit. You can create the impression of greater space by running the same flooring throughout the apartment. White- or pastel-painted walls have a similar effect. Picking out some walls with a strong color or pattern will lead the eye into that area. You could manipulate the ceiling level by using color or tone, visually lowering it over a sitting area or bedroom area, while visually increasing the volume of another space by painting the ceiling with a pale neutral or pastel tint.

In a small apartment lighting is a big issue. If you are fortunate enough to have a lot of natural light, then choose from the wide variety of window treatments available. Curtains provide a soft, diffuse light during the day, but not complete privacy at night. Consider adding blinds or drapes to the curtains for nighttime.

Planning your lighting

To be successful, lighting must allow you to work, read, or study without straining your eyes. It should also brighten areas that are potentially dangerous and provide satisfactory background illumination at all times of the day. With so many needs to fulfill, sometimes the decorative possibilities of lighting are ignored. Good lighting can create an atmosphere of warmth and well-being, highlight objects of interest, transform the character of an interior, and still look good.

Illuminating living rooms

When planning lighting for a living room, the emphasis should be on versatility—creating areas of strong light where it is needed most and areas of subtle light for reading and relaxation. Seating areas are best served by lighting placed at a low level, so that naked bulbs do not shine light directly into your eyes and you're still able to read a book or newspaper in a comfortable chair. Choose lighting that isn't harsh, so it won't cause glare on white paper, and supplement it with low-powered lighting to maintain a suitable level of ambient light in the room.

Working at a desk demands similar conditions, but the light source must be stronger and situated in front of you, to avoid your own shadow being thrown across the work. Choose a properly shaded desk lamp, or conceal lighting under wall storage or bookshelves above the desk.

Similar concealed lighting is ideal for entertainment centers, but you may need extra lighting in the form of ceiling-mounted spotlights to illuminate the shelves themselves. Another good option is track lighting that lets you put any number of light heads on the ceiling so you can shine them wherever you want.

Concealed lighting in other areas of the living room can be very attractive. Strip lights placed on top (and at the back) of high cabinets will bounce light off the ceiling. You can also hide lighting behind window valances to accentuate window treatments, or put it along a wall to illuminate pictures. Individual works of art can be accentuated with a light or two placed above them. Or you can install an adjustable ceiling spotlight that will place a pool of light exactly where you want it. Avoid pointing lamps directly at pictures protected by glass because the reflections will obscure what's behind the glass. Usually, overhead lighting is not used in living rooms because it can be harsh. Wall-mounted sconces work better for general lighting purposes because they reflect softer light off the walls.

Atmospheric lighting
(below left)
A subdued, moody feel is created by a combination of candlelight and electric fixtures controlled by dimmer switches.

Task-lighting
(below)
These days, just about every home office is organized around a computer. Some background lighting is required to reduce the strain of staring into a bright monitor, and you need adjustable task-lighting to illuminate the desktop without reflecting in the screen.

Planning your lighting

Sleeping areas

Bedside lamps or lighting fixtures above a headboard are basic requirements in any bedroom. Most of these are simple incandescent units selected more for how they look than how they work. If you and your partner tend to read in bed, you'll want to equip your lights with dimmer controls operated from the night stand, not the wall. This will allow each of you to adjust the light so it doesn't disturb the other.

A dressing table needs its own light source placed so that it cannot be seen in the mirror but still illuminates the person using it. Wall lights or recessed lights in the ceiling can provide general lighting, but be sure to install them with dimmer switches so you can control the light intensity in the room.

Make sure bedside lamps in a child's room are as tamperproof as possible. A dimmer switch controlling the main room lighting will provide enough light to comfort a child at night but can be turned to full brightness when he or she is playing in the evening.

Dining areas and kitchens

Because its height can be adjusted exactly, a pull-down pendant light (or a chandelier on a dimmer switch) is a good choice for lighting over a dining table. If you eat in the kitchen, have separate controls for the table lighting and work areas so you can create a comfortable dining space without having to illuminate the rest of the room. In addition to a good background light, illuminate kitchen countertops with undercabinet lighting and place track lighting or recessed ceiling spotlights over the sink and kitchen island.

Bathrooms

Safety must be your first priority when choosing light fixtures for a bathroom. They have to be designed to withstand moisture-laden air and still last for a long time. Creating subtle lighting in a bathroom is often challenging, but concealed light directed onto the ceiling from a wall valance is one solution. Be sure to provide strong light above or to the sides of a mirror over a lavatory or vanity.

Staircases

Light staircases from above so that the treads are illuminated clearly, throwing the risers into shadow. This will define the steps for anyone with poor eyesight. Place a light over each landing or at the top, bottom, and middle of circular staircases. Three-way switches at the top and bottom of the stairs are essential to ensure that no one has to use the stairs in darkness.

Workshops

Plan workshop lighting with efficiency and safety in mind. Illuminate a fixed workbench the same way as a desk and provide individual, adjustable light fixtures for machine tools. Most people use inexpensive fluorescent fixtures for general workshop lighting. These provide lots of light, are easy to install, and are economical to run. Daylight bulbs that mimic the look of sunlight are available for these units.

Means of access

Whether you need to reach gutters or require a simple stepladder to paint the living-room ceiling, it is essential to use strong and stable equipment. Working on makeshift structures is inefficient and dangerous. Even for small jobs that don't justify the cost of buying ladders or scaffolding, it's advisable to rent the right equipment rather than make do. For a small outlay, you can buy accessories that make working on a ladder safer and more comfortable.

Before you start any outdoor work, consider the timing, the weather, and the condition of the site. Indoors, you'll have the problem of what to do with a room full of furniture and furnishings while you work.

Outside the house

Plan your work so that you can begin in the spring or late summer when the weather is good but not too hot. The best weather for painting is a warm but overcast day. Avoid painting on rainy days or in direct sunlight, as both rain and hot sun can ruin new paintwork. On a sunny day, follow the sun around the house, so that its warmth will have dried out the night's dew on the woodwork before you apply paint.

It's not a good idea to paint on windy days, because dust is invariably blown onto the wet paint. In order to settle dust that would otherwise be churned up by your feet, vacuum around doors and windows before you start painting.

Walk around the house to check that there are no obstructions that could slow your progress or cause accidents. Clear away any rubbish and cut back overhanging foliage from trees and shrubs. Protect plants, walks, and paved driveways in the work area with drop cloths.

Ladder accessories
There's a range of helpful devices to make working on a ladder easier and safer. This ladder features stabilizers (1) for uneven ground, a footrest for comfort (2), a tool tray (3), a paint-can hook (4), and a stay (5) to hold the top away from gutters or drip edges.

Inside the house

Before painting a room, carry out any necessary repairs and, if you use a fireplace, have the chimney swept—falling soot would ruin your new paint. It pays to clear as much furniture as possible from the room and group what is left under drop cloths. Take up loose carpets and rugs, then lightly spray water on the floor and sweep up the dust. Protect finished wood flooring, tiled floors, and fitted carpets with drop cloths. When painting the baseboard, stick wide low-tack masking tape around the perimeter of the floor.

Remove all furnishings, such as pictures and lamp shades, and unscrew electrical coverplates and door handles.

What to wear

Don't wear wool garments when painting or varnishing, as they tend to shed hairs, which stick to the paint. Overalls that have large pockets for tools and brushes are ideal for DIY work.

Ladder stabilizers
Stabilizers prevent a ladder from rocking on uneven ground.

Ladders and scaffolding

Stepladders are essential when decorating indoors. Traditional wooden stepladders are still available, but they have largely been superseded by lightweight aluminum or fiberglass versions. It's worth having at least one that stands about 6 feet high, so you can reach a ceiling without having to stand on the top step. A shorter second ladder may be more convenient for other jobs, and you can use both, with scaffold boards, to build a platform.

Outdoors, you will need ladders that reach up to the eaves. Wooden extension ladders are very heavy, so consider aluminum ones. Most extension ladders are operated by a rope and pulley, so that they can be extended single-handed.

To estimate the length of ladder you need, add together the ceiling heights of your house, then add at least 3 feet to the length to allow for leaning the ladder at an angle and for safe access to a platform.

There are many versions of dual-purpose or even multipurpose ladders that convert from stepladder to straight ladder. This type of versatile ladder is a good compromise.

Sectional scaffold frames can be built up to form towers at any convenient height for working inside and outside. Broad feet prevent the scaffold from sinking into the ground, and adjustable versions allow you to level it. Some models have locking casters that enable you to move the tower.

Towers are ideal for painting a large expanse of wall outdoors. Indoors, smaller platforms made from the same scaffold components bring high ceilings within easy reach.

Accessories for ladders

Ladder stay
A stay holds the ladder away from the wall. It is an essential piece of equipment when painting overhanging eaves and gutters. You would otherwise be forced to lean back and might lose your balance.

Tool tray and paint-can hook
You should always support yourself with one hand on a ladder, so use a wire hook to hang a paint can or bucket from a rung. A clip-on tray is ideal for holding a small selection of tools.

Clip-on platform
A wide flat board that clamps onto the rungs provides a comfortable platform to stand on while working for long periods.

Stabilizers
These are bolt-on accessories that prevent the ladder from slipping and compensate for uneven ground.

Aluminum stepladder   Dual-purpose ladder   Scaffold tower   Extension ladder

When you buy or rent a ladder, bear in mind that:
- Wooden ladders should be made from knot-free straight-grained lumber.
- Good-quality wooden ladders have hardwood rungs tenoned through the rails (uprights).
- Wooden rungs with reinforcing metal rods stretched under them are safer than rungs without reinforcing.
- End caps or foot pads are an advantage, to prevent the ladder from slipping on hard ground.
- Adjustability is a prime consideration. Choose a ladder that will enable you to gain access to various parts of the building and will convert to a compact unit for storage.
- The rungs of overlapping sections of an extension ladder should align to provide a wide surface for standing.
- Choose an extension ladder with a rope and pulley, plus a latch that locks the extension to its rung.
- Check that you can buy or rent a range of accessories (see opposite) to fit your make of ladder.
- Choose a stepladder with a platform at the top to take paint cans and trays.
- Treads should be comfortable to stand on. Stepladders with wide, flat treads are the best choice.
- Stepladders with extended rails give you a handhold at the top of the steps.
- Wooden stepladders should have a fold-down platform to hold paint cans and roller trays. This platform also helps stabilize the ladder.

Is the ladder safe to use?

Check ladders regularly, and especially before using them after a winter's break. Inspect a rented ladder before using it. Look for splits along the rails, make sure there are no missing or broken rungs, and verify that the joints are tight. Check that the ladder is not twisted, or it could rock when leaned against a wall.

Inspect wooden ladders for rot. Even a small amount of sponginess or a few holes could signify serious damage below the surface. Test that the wood is sound before using the ladder, and treat it with a preservative. If in doubt, scrap the ladder rather than risk an accident.

Check that any hardware on the ladder is secure. Lubricate any moving hardware with a drop of oil. Inspect the pulley rope for fraying and replace it if necessary.

Regularly apply a finishing oil or varnish to wooden ladders so they don't dry out. Apply extra coats to the rungs, which take most wear. Don't paint a ladder. This could hide serious defects.

How to handle a ladder

Ladders are heavy and unwieldy. Handle them properly to avoid damaging property and to make sure you don't injure yourself.

Carry a ladder upright, not slung across your shoulder. Hold the ladder vertically, bend your knees slightly, then rock the ladder back against your shoulder. Grip one rung lower down while you support the ladder at head height with your other hand, and then straighten your knees.

To erect an extension ladder, lay it on the ground with its feet against the wall. Gradually raise it to vertical as you walk toward the wall. Pull the feet out from the wall so that the ladder is resting at an angle of about 70 degrees. If the ladder extends to 26 feet, for example, its feet should be 6½ feet, or a quarter of its height, from the wall.

Hold an extension ladder upright while raising it to the required height. If it is a heavy ladder, get someone to hold it while you operate the pulley.

Handling a ladder
Carry the ladder upright, leaning it back against your shoulder; grip one rung low down, another at head height. When erected, the base of the ladder should be a quarter of its height away from the wall, so that it is correctly balanced.

More accidents are caused by using ladders unwisely than by faulty equipment. Erect the ladder safely before you climb it, and move it when work is out of reach. Never lean to the side; you could lose your balance. Follow these simple, commonsense rules:

Securing the ladder

If the ground is soft, place a wide board under the feet of a ladder; screw a block across the board to hold the ladder in place. On hard ground, make sure the ladder has antislip end caps, and lay a sandbag at the base. Secure the rails with rope tied to stakes driven into the ground at each side and just behind the ladder **(1)**.

When you extend a ladder, the sections should overlap by at least a quarter of their length. Don't lean the top of the ladder against gutters because they are slippery and, if in poor condition, may give way. Never lean a ladder against glass.

If you feel particularly uncomfortable on the ladder, you can often anchor it near the top by tying it to a heavy board held across the inside of the window frame. Make sure that the board extends about one foot on each side of the window, and pad the ends with cloth to protect the wall from damage **(2)**.

Safety aloft

Never climb higher than four rungs from the top of the ladder; you will not be able to balance properly and there will be nothing to hold onto within easy reach. Keep both your feet on a rung, and your hips centered between the uprights. Avoid slippery footholds by placing an old towel at the foot of the ladder to dry your boots before you start climbing.

Unless the manufacturer states otherwise, don't use a ladder to form a horizontal walkway—even with a scaffold board lying on it.

Stepladders are prone to toppling sideways. On uneven surfaces, clamp a brace to one of the stiles **(3)**.

1 Staking a ladder.
Secure the base of the ladder by tying it to stakes in the ground.

2 Securing the top.
Anchor the ladder to a board held inside the window frame.

CLAMPS

BRACE

3 Supporting a stepladder.
Clamp a brace to the rail to stabilize a stepladder.

Erecting work platforms

SCAFFOLD TOWERS

Some workers move a ladder little by little as the work progresses. However, constantly moving ladders becomes tedious and may lead to an accident as you try to reach just a bit further before having to move along. It is more convenient to build a work platform that allows you to tackle a large area without moving the structure. You can rent a pair of trestles and bridge them with a scaffold board, or make a similar structure using two stepladders **(1)**.

Clamp or tie the board to the rungs, and use two boards, one on top of the other, if two people need to use the platform at once.

An even better arrangement is to use scaffold-tower components to make a mobile platform **(2)**. One with locking casters is ideal for painting or papering ceilings.

2 Mobile platform
An efficient structure made from scaffold-tower frames.

It is best to erect scaffolding when working on large areas on the outside of a house. Towers made from slide-together frames are available for rent just about everywhere. Heights up to about 30 feet are common. But taller towers do require diagonal bracing to prevent them from toppling sideways.

Build the lower section of the frame first, and level it with adjustable feet before erecting the tower on top. As you build, climb up and stand on the inside of the tower.

Erect a sturdy platform at the top with perimeter boards around the base to keep tools and materials from being knocked off. Extend the framework and set hand rails all around.

Some towers incorporate a staircase inside the scaffold frame. If you can't rent such a tower, the safest alternative is to use a ladder. But make sure it extends at least 3 feet above the platform, so that you can step on and off safely.

When using a ladder, sometimes it's difficult to reach windows and walls above a shed roof. With a scaffold tower, however, you can construct a cantilevered section that rests on the roof of the addition.

1 Improvised platform
A simple yet safe platform made from stepladders and a scaffold board.

Working in a stairwell

It's not always easy to build a safe platform for painting or papering in a stairwell. The simplest method is to use a dual-purpose ladder, which can be adjusted to stand evenly on a flight of stairs **(1)**. Anchor the steps with rope through a couple of large screw eyes fixed to the stair risers; when the stairs are carpeted, the holes will be concealed. Rest a scaffold board between the ladder and the landing to form a bridge. Screw the board to the landing and tie the other end.

Alternatively, construct a customized platform from ladders and boards to suit your staircase **(2)**. Make sure the boards and ladders are clamped or tied together securely and that the ladders cannot slip on the stair treads. If necessary, screw wooden blocks to the stairs to prevent the foot of the ladder from moving.

Stair scaffold
Erect a platform with scaffold frames to compensate for the slope of a staircase.

1 Dual-purpose ladder
Use this type of ladder to straddle the stairs and support a scaffold board to create a level platform.

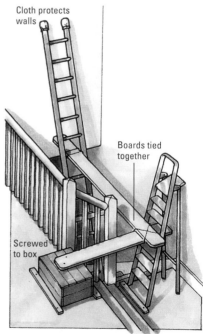

Cloth protects walls

Boards tied together

Screwed to box

2 Customized platform
Build a network of scaffold boards, stepladders, ladders, and boxes to suit your stairwell layout.

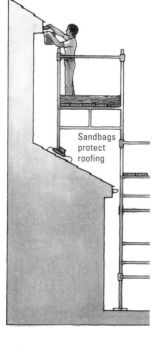

Sandbags protect roofing

Erecting a cantilevered platform
Rest a cantilevered section on a board to spread the load.

Preparation and priming

Thoroughly prepare all surfaces as the vital first step in redecorating. If you neglect this stage, subsequent finishes will be affected. Remove dirt, grease, and loose or flaky previous finishes. Repair serious deterioration such as cracks, holes, corrosion, and decay. It isn't only old surfaces that will need your attention. New masonry, wood, and metals must be sealed, and priming will ensure that a surface is in suitable condition to accept and hold its finish.

Consult the chart below for details on primers and sealers for common materials. Then read the following sections for more information.

The purpose of priming

Deciding whether or not to prime and then selecting the proper priming material depends largely on the condition and special problems of the particular surface.

Generally speaking, the purpose of priming is to seal absorbent surfaces for economical application of the topcoat and to provide a good bonding surface for the finish. In many cases, a diluted solution of the topcoat will be the best primer.

However, this is not always the case, so it's best to read the manufacturer's application instructions before you start the job. Since primers for various materials are formulated using a variety of the common paint resins, you must make sure the paint is formulated for the material and application in which you plan to use it.

In general, all bare woods should be primed before painting for proper adhesion of the finish coats. If the wood was previously painted and the old paint is loose and flaky, the paint first must be scraped away, sanded off, or removed with a chemical stripper. Then the wood must be primed with a product appropriate for the finish coats.

But even wood that isn't painted, when it is used outdoors and is subject to the weather, should be treated with preservative and clear moisture repellent. Even pressure-treated wood needs water-repellent treatment if it is to remain free of cracks and other common defects.

There are various materials formulated to seal against moisture and stain-bleeding and others made to stabilize existing coatings before new paint or adhesives are applied. The chart below suggests a range of choices available for many common finishing projects.

● **Lead in paint**
Lead—which is a poison—was widely used in the past as a dryer in solvent-based paints. Modern solvent-based paints are made without lead.

If you suspect you have lead-based paint in your home, you can have a test done by a laboratory. If you need to remove lead-based paint, hire a lead-abatement specialist for the job.

PRIMERS AND SEALERS: SUITABILITY, DRYING TIME AND COVERAGE

● Black dot denotes that primer and surface are compatible.

	Latex primer	Acrylic primer	Stain-blocking primer	Zinc-rich primer	Oil-cement primer	Aluminum paint	Clear sanding sealer	Clear wood preservative	Clear moisture repellant	Bitumen primer	Masonry sealer	Shellac	Wood-filler paste
SUITABLE FOR													
Wood to be painted	●	●	●			●	●	●	●	●		●	●
Wood to be clear or unfinished							●	●	●			●	
Brick	●				●	●				●	●		
Stone	●				●					●	●		
Concrete	●				●					●	●		
Cinder block	●				●					●	●		
Stucco	●				●	●				●	●		
Gypsum wallboard	●	●										●	
Plaster	●	●									●	●	
Hardboard	●	●				●	●		●			●	
Particleboard	●	●	●			●	●		●			●	●
Iron, steel	●	●		●		●							
Galvanized metals	●	●		●		●							
Aluminum	●	●		●		●							
Copper or bronze		●		●									
Tile, glass													
PROBLEM SURFACES													
Bleed-prone staining			●			●						●	
Pressure-treated wood								●					
Bitumen-primed surfaces	●	●				●							
Resinous woods						●						●	
Open-grained woods		●					●						●
Below-grade, covered masonry					●				●				
Unidentifiable finish		●				●						●	
DRYING TIME: HOURS													
Touch-dry	½	8	8	4	8	8	1	2	2	24	1	½	1
Recoatable	1	24	24	10	24	24	4	24	24	72	4	12	8
COVERAGE (SQ. FT. PER GAL.)													
Smooth surface	450	450	450	450	450	550	600	600	600	300	450	450	—
Rough/absorbent surface	250	250	250	250	250	300	300	300	300	150	250	300	—

Cleaning brick and stone

Before you decorate the outside of your house, check the condition of the brick and stonework and carry out any necessary repairs. There's no reason why you can't paint brick or stonework, but you may want to restore painted masonry to its original condition.

Although most paint strippers cannot cope with deeply textured surfaces, there are thick-paste paint removers that will peel away layers of old paint from masonry.

Treating new masonry

New brickwork or stonework should be left for about three months, until it is completely dry, before any further treatment is considered.

White powdery deposits called efflorescence may come to the surface over this period, but you can simply brush them off with a stiff-bristle brush or a piece of rough cloth. New masonry should be weatherproof and should not require further treatment, unless you want to apply paint.

Cleaning off unsightly mold

Colorful lichens growing on garden walls can be very attractive. Indeed, some people actively encourage their growth. However, since the spread of molds and lichens depends on damp conditions, it is not a good sign when they occur naturally on the walls of your house.

Try to identify the source of the problem before treating the growth. For example, if one side of the house never receives any sun, it will have little chance of drying out. Relieve the situation by cutting back overhanging trees or adjacent shrubs to increase ventilation to the wall.

Cracked or corroded gutters and downspouts leaking onto the wall are another common cause of organic growth. Feel behind the pipe with your fingers, or slip a hand mirror behind it to see if there's a leak.

Removing and neutralizing the growth
Scrape heavy organic growth from the bricks using a plastic putty knife. Then brush the masonry vigorously with a stiff-bristle brush. This can be an unpleasant, dusty job, so wear a face mask and safety glasses or goggles. Brush away from yourself so that debris doesn't land on your clothes.

Starting at the top of the wall, use a nylon brush to paint on a fungicidal solution, diluted according to the manufacturer's instructions. Apply the fungicide liberally and leave the wall to dry for 24 hours, then rinse the masonry thoroughly with clean water.

In extreme cases, give the wall two washes of fungicide, allowing 24 hours between applications and a further 24 hours before washing it down with clean water.

Paint-stained brickwork

Organic growth

Efflorescence

Removing efflorescence from masonry

Soluble salts within building materials such as cement, brick, and stone gradually migrate to the surface, along with the moisture, as a wall dries out. The result is a white crystalline deposit called efflorescence.

The same condition can occur on old masonry if it is subjected to more than average moisture. Efflorescence itself is not harmful, but the source of the damp must be identified and cured.

Brush the deposit from the wall regularly with a dry, stiff-bristle brush or coarse cloth until the crystals cease to form. Don't attempt to wash off the crystals—they will merely dissolve in the water and soak back into the wall. Above all, don't paint a wall that is still efflorescing, as this is a sign that it is still damp.

Masonry paints and clear sealants that let the wall breathe are not affected by the alkali content of the masonry, so they can be used without applying a primer. If you plan to use oil-based paint, coat the wall first with an alkali-resistant primer.

Curing efflorescence
Brush the white deposit from the wall with a stiff-bristle brush or a piece of coarse cloth until the crystals are removed.

Repointing masonry

You can often spruce up old masonry by washing off surface grime with water. Strong solvents will harm certain types of stone, so seek the advice of an experienced local mason before applying anything other than water.

Washing the wall
Starting at the top of the wall, use a hose to spray water gently onto the masonry while you scrub it with a stiff-bristle brush **(1)**. Scrub heavy deposits with half a cup of ammonia added to a bucketful of water, then rinse again. Avoid soaking brick or stone when a frost is forecast.

Removing unsightly stains
Soften tar, grease, and oil stains using a household kitchen cleanser. Check the manufacturer's instructions for proper application and rinsing.

Stripping spilled paint
To remove a patch of spilled paint, use paint stripper. Follow the manufacturer's recommendations and wear old clothes, gloves, and goggles.

Stipple the stripper onto the rough texture **(2)**. Leave it for about 10 minutes, then remove the softened paint with a scraper. Gently scrub the residue out of deeper crevices with a stiff-bristle brush and water. Then rinse the wall with clean water.

If any paint remains in the crevices, dip your brush in stripper and gently scrub it into the problem areas. Use small circular strokes. After the stripper has set, wash it off and repeat if necessary.

1 Remove dirt and dust by washing.

2 Stipple paint stripper onto paint.

A combination of frost action and erosion tends to break down the mortar pointing of brickwork and stonework. The mortar eventually falls out, exposing the open joints to wind and rain, which drive dampness through the wall to the inside of the house.

Cracked joints may also be caused by using a hard, inflexible mortar. Replacing defective mortar is a straightforward but time-consuming task. Tackle a small manageable area at a time, using a ready-mixed mortar made for this job.

Applying the mortar

Scrape out the old pointing with a thin wooden stick to a depth of about ½ inch. Use a cold chisel and a hammer to dislodge sections that are firmly embedded; then brush out the joints with a stiff-bristle brush.

Spray the wall with water to make sure the bricks or stones will not absorb too much moisture from the fresh mortar. Mix up some mortar in a bucket and transfer it to a hawk. If you are mixing your own mortar, use these proportions: 1 part cement, 1 part lime, 6 parts builder's sand.

Pick up a small sausage of mortar on the back of a pointing trowel and push it firmly into the upright joints. This can be difficult to do without the mortar dropping off, so hold the hawk under each joint to catch it.

Try not to smear the face of the bricks with mortar, as it will stain. Use the same method for the horizontal joints. The actual shape of the pointing is not vital at this stage.

Once the mortar is firm enough to retain a thumbprint, it is ready for shaping. Because it is important that you shape the joints at exactly the right moment, you may have to point the work in stages in order to complete the wall. Shape the joints to match existing brickwork, or choose a profile suitable for the prevailing weather conditions in your area.

Once you have shaped the joints, wait until the pointing has almost hardened, then brush the wall to remove traces of surplus mortar from the surface of the masonry.

Shaping the mortar joints

The joints shown here are commonly used for brickwork. Flush or rubbed joints are best for most stonework, though sometimes raised mortar joints are used with stone.

Flush joint
This is the easiest profile to produce. Scrape the mortar flush, using the edge of your trowel, then stipple the joints with a stiff-bristle brush to expose the sand aggregate.

Rubbed (concave) joint
This joint is ideal for an old wall with bricks that are not of sufficiently good quality to take a crisp joint. Bricklayers make a rubbed joint using a jointer, a tool shaped like a sled runner with a handle. Its semicircular blade is run along the joints. Improvise a tool by bending a length of metal tube or rod (use the curved section only, or you will gouge the mortar). Scrape the mortar flush first, then drag the tool along the joints. Finish the vertical joints, then shape the horizontal ones. Having shaped the joints, stipple them with a brush so that they look like weathered pointing.

Raked joint
A raked joint is used to emphasize the bonding pattern of a brick wall. It is not suitable for an exposed site where the wall takes a lot of weathering.

Rake out the new joints to a depth of about ¼ inch, and then compress the mortar by smoothing it lightly with a piece of lath or wood dowel.

Weatherstruck joint
The sloping profile is intended to shed rainwater from the wall. Shape the mortar with the edge of a pointing trowel. Start with the vertical joints, sloping them either to the right or to the left (but be consistent). Then shape the horizontal joints, allowing the mortar to spill out at the base of each joint.

Finish the joint by cutting off the excess mortar with a Frenchman, a tool that has a narrow blade with the tip bent at 90 degrees. Use a board to guide the Frenchman along the joints and nail scraps of wood at each end to hold the board off the wall. Align the board with the bottom of the horizontal joints, then draw the tool along it to trim off the excess mortar.

Mortar dyes
Liquid or powder additives are available for changing the color of mortar to match existing pointing. Color matching can be difficult, and smears can stain the bricks permanently.

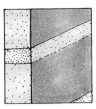
Flush joint

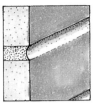
Rubbed joint

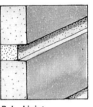
Raked joint

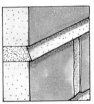
Weatherstruck joint

Use a Frenchman to trim weatherstruck joints.

Repairing masonry

Cracked masonry may simply be the result of cement-rich mortar being unable to absorb slight movements within the building. However, it could also be a sign of a more serious problem—sinking foundations, for example. Don't just ignore the symptoms; investigate immediately and undertake the necessary repairs as soon as possible.

Filling cracked masonry

If a brick or stone wall has substantial cracks, consult a local builder or home inspector to ascertain the cause. If a crack proves to be stable, you can carry out some repairs yourself.

Cracked mortar can be removed and repointed in the normal way, but a crack that splits the bricks cannot be repaired neatly, and the damaged masonry should be replaced by a mason.

Cracks across a painted wall can be filled with mortar that has been mixed with a little bonding agent to help it stick. Before you make the repair, wet the damaged masonry with a hose to encourage the mortar to flow deeply into the crack.

Cracks may follow mortar only.

Cracked bricks could signify serious faults.

Priming brickwork for painting

Brickwork will need to be primed only if it is showing signs of efflorescence or spalling. An alkali-resistant primer will guard against efflorescence. A stabilizing solution will bind crumbling masonry and also help to seal it.

When you are painting a wall for the first time with masonry paint, you may find that the first coat is difficult to apply due to the suction of the dry, porous brick. Thin the first coat slightly with water or solvent.

Waterproofing masonry

Replacing a spalled brick
Having mortared the top and one end, slip the new brick into the hole you have cut.

Colorless water-repellent fluids are intended to make masonry impervious to water without coloring it or stopping it from breathing, which is important because it allows moisture within the walls to dry out.

Prepare the surface before applying the fluid: Repair any cracks in bricks or pointing and remove organic growth; then allow the wall to dry out thoroughly. Cover nearby plants.

The fumes from water-repellents can be dangerous if inhaled, so be sure to wear a proper respirator as recommended by the manufacturer. Also, wear eye protection.

Apply the fluid generously with a large paintbrush, from the bottom up, and stipple it into the joints. Apply a second coat as soon as the first has been absorbed to ensure that there are no bare patches where water could seep in. To be sure that you are covering the wall properly, use a sealant containing a fugitive dye, which disappears after a specified period of time.

Carefully paint up to surrounding woodwork. If you accidentally splash sealant onto it, wash it immediately with a cloth dampened with solvent.

If you need to treat a whole house, it may be worth hiring a company that can spray the sealant. Make sure the workers rig up screens to prevent overspray from drifting across to your neighbors' property.

Moisture that has penetrated soft masonry will expand in icy weather, flaking off the outer face of brickwork and stonework. The result, known as spalling, not only looks unattractive but also allows water to seep into the wall.

If spalling is localized, cut out and replace the bricks or stones. The sequence below describes how to repair spalled brickwork, but the process is similar for a stone wall.

Where spalling is extensive, the only practical solution is to accept its less-than-perfect appearance, repoint the masonry, and apply a clear water-repellent that will protect the wall from further damage while allowing it to breathe.

Spalled bricks caused by frost damage.

Replacing a spalled brick

Use a cold chisel and hammer to remove the pointing surrounding the brick, then chop out the brick itself. If the brick is difficult to remove, drill numerous holes in it with a large-diameter masonry bit; then chop out the brick with a cold chisel and hammer. It should crumble, enabling you to remove the pieces easily.

To fit the replacement brick, first dampen the opening and spread mortar on the base and one side. Then dampen the replacement brick, cover the top and one end with mortar and slot the brick into the hole (see far left). Shape the pointing to match the surrounding brickwork.

If you can't find a replacement brick in the right color, remove the spalled brick carefully, turn it around to the undamaged side, and reinsert it.

Repairing stucco

Brickwork is sometimes clad with a smooth or roughcast cement-based stucco, both for improved weatherproofing and to provide a decorative finish. Stucco is susceptible to the effects of damp and frost, which can cause cracking, bulging, and staining. Before you paint a stuccoed wall, make any necessary repairs and clean off surface dirt, mold growth, and flaky material for a finish that will last.

Cracked stucco allows moisture to penetrate.

Pebbledash can separate and fall off walls.

Leaky gutters can cause rust stains.

Repairing defects

Before you repair cracked stucco, have a home inspector or engineer check the wall for any structural faults that may have contributed to the problem. Apply a stabilizing solution if the wall is dusty.

You can ignore fine hairline cracks if you intend to paint the wall with a reinforced masonry paint, but scrape out larger cracks with a cold chisel. Dampen them with water and fill flush with a cement-based exterior filler. Fill any major cracks with a stucco made of 1 part cement, 2 parts lime, and 9 parts builder's sand, plus a little bonding agent to help it stick to the wall.

Bulges in stucco normally indicate that the stucco has separated from the masonry or sheathing underneath. Tap the wall gently to find the extent of these hollow areas, then remove the material until you reach sound edges. Use a chisel to undercut the perimeter of each hole except for the bottom edge, which should be left square so that it does not collect water.

Brush out the debris, then apply a coat of bonding agent. When it becomes tacky, trowel on a layer of 1 : 1 : 6 stucco, about ½ inch thick. Leave the stucco to set firm, then scratch it to form a key. The next day, fill the hole flush with a weaker mix (1 : 1 : 9) and smooth the surface with a wooden float, using circular strokes.

Reinforcing a crack

To prevent a crack in stucco from opening up again, you can reinforce the repair with a polyester membrane embedded in a primer designed for making stucco patches. When you're done patching, you will need to cover the wall with a textured paint in order to disguise the repair.

To patch cracks, begin by scraping out the crack to remove loose material, then wet it. Fill just over the surface with a mortar mix of 1 part cement and 4 parts builder's sand. When this has stiffened, scrape it flush. When the mortar has hardened, brush on a generous coat of the primer, making sure it extends at least 4 inches on both sides of the crack. Embed strips of polyester membrane (sold for use with the primer) into the coating, using a stippling and brushing action **(1)**. While it is still wet, feather the edges of the primer with a foam roller **(2)**, bedding the membrane into it. After 24 hours, apply a second coat of primer and feather with the roller. When the primer is dry, apply textured coating.

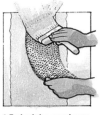
1 Embed the membrane.

2 Feather with roller.

Patching pebbledash

For additional weatherproofing, sometimes small stones are stuck to a thin coat of stucco over a thicker base coat. This process is known as pebbledashing. If water gets behind pebbledashing, one or both layers may separate. Chip off any loose stucco to a sound base, then seal it with stabilizer. If necessary, repair the scratch coat (bottom coat) of stucco.

You can simulate the texture of pebbledash with a thick paste made from bonding agent. Mix 1 part cement-paint powder with 3 parts plasterer's sand. Stir in 1 part of bonding agent diluted with 3 parts water to form a thick, creamy paste. Load a brush and scrub the paste onto the bare surface.

Apply a second generous coat of paste, stippling it to form a coarse texture. Leave it for about 15 minutes to firm up. Then, with a loaded brush, stipple it to match the texture of the pebbles. Let the paste harden fully before painting the repair.

If you want to leave the pebbledash unpainted, make a patch using replacement pebbles. The result may not be a perfect match, but could save you from having to paint the entire wall. Cut back the damaged area and apply a stucco scratch coat followed by a finish coat. While this is still wet, fling pebbles onto the surface from a dustpan. You may have to repeat the process until the coverage is even.

Stipple the texture.

Removing rust stains

Faulty downspouts or gutters can result in rusty streaks on a stuccoed wall. Before painting, prime the areas with a stain-blocking sealer. Rust marks on a pebbledashed wall are sometimes caused by iron pyrites in the aggregate. Chip out the pyrites with a cold chisel, then seal the stain.

Painted masonry

Painted masonry inside the house is usually in fairly good condition, and apart from a good cleaning to remove dust and grease and a light sanding to give a key for the new finish, there is little else you need to do. Outside, however, it's a different matter. Exterior surfaces, subjected to extremes of heat, cold, and rain, are likely to be affected to some degree by stains, flaking, and chalkiness.

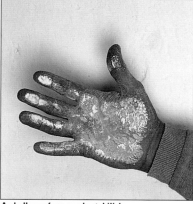

A chalky surface needs stabilizing.

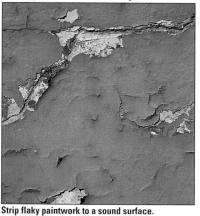

Strip flaky paintwork to a sound surface.

Chimney stained by tar deposits from the flue.

Curing a chalky surface

Rub the palm of your hand lightly over the surface of the wall to see if it is chalky. If the paint rubs off as a powdery deposit, treat the wall before you repaint.

Brush the surface with a stiff-bristle brush, then paint the whole wall liberally with a stabilizing primer, which will bind the chalky surface so that paint will adhere to it. Use a white stabilizing primer, which can also serve as an undercoat. Clean any splashes from surrounding woodwork with solvent.

If the wall is very dusty, apply a second coat of stabilizer after about 16 hours. Wait another 16 hours before applying paint.

Dealing with flaky paint

Poor surface preparation or incompatible paint and preparatory treatments are common causes of flaky paintwork. Damp walls will also cause flaking, so cure the damp and let the wall dry out before further treatment.

A new coat of paint will not bind to a flaky surface, so attend to this before you start painting. Use a paint scraper and a stiff-bristle brush to remove all loose material. Coarse sandpaper should finish the job, or at least feather the edges of any stubborn patches. Stabilize the surface as for chalky walls before repainting.

Treat tar stains with a blocking sealer.

Treating a stained chimney

If the outlines of brick courses show up as brown staining on a painted chimney, you can be sure it is caused by a breakdown of the internal flue liner of the chimney. Defective lining allows tar deposits to migrate through the mortar joints to the outer paintwork. To solve the problem, first repair the old flue liner or install a new one; then treat the brown stains with a stain-blocking primer/sealer before applying a fresh coat of paint.

In the past, even sound brickwork was often painted, simply to brighten up a house. In some areas of the country where painted masonry is traditional, there is every reason to continue with the practice. Indeed, houses with soft, inferior brickwork were frequently painted when they were built in order to protect them from the weather—and to strip them now could have serious consequences. But if the brick on your house is in good condition and doesn't need paint to protect it, then removing the paint is an option—albeit an expensive one.

Restoring painted brickwork to its natural condition is not an easy task. It is generally a messy business involving the use of toxic materials that have to be handled with care and disposed of safely. Extensive scaffolding may be required, and most important, getting the masonry entirely clean demands considerable experience. For all these reasons, it is advisable to hire professionals to do the work for you.

To determine whether the outcome is likely to be successful, ask the company you are thinking of hiring to strip an inconspicuous patch of masonry, using the chemicals they recommend for the job. The results may indicate that it is better to repaint—in which case, choose a good-quality masonry paint that will let moisture within the walls evaporate.

A painted wall in need of restoration.

Repairing concrete

In common with other building materials, concrete suffers from the effects of damp—spalling and efflorescence—and related defects, such as cracking and crumbling. Repairs can usually be made in much the same way as for brickwork and stucco, although there are some special considerations you should be aware of. If the damage is widespread, resurface the concrete before painting.

Sealing concrete

New concrete has a high alkali content. Efflorescence can therefore develop on the surface as it dries out. When treating efflorescence on concrete, follow the procedure recommended for brickwork. A porous concrete wall should be waterproofed with a clear sealant on the exterior. Some reinforced masonry paints will cover tar satisfactorily, but it will bleed through most paints unless you prime first with a bonding agent diluted 50 percent with water. Alternatively, use a stain-blocking primer/sealer.

Cleaning dirty concrete

You can scrub dirty concrete with water (as described for brickwork), but when a concrete driveway or garage floor is stained with patches of oil or grease, you will need to apply an oil-and-grease remover. This is a detergent that is normally diluted with an equal amount of water, but can be used full strength on heavy staining.

Brush on the solution liberally, then scrub the surface with a stiff-bristle brush. Rinse off with clean water. It is advisable to wear eye protection. Keep all windows and doors open when working indoors.

It is worth soaking up fresh oil spillages immediately with dry sand or sawdust to prevent permanent stains.

Binding dusty concrete

Concrete is troweled when it is laid to give it a flat finish. If the troweling is overdone, cement is brought to the surface; and when the concrete dries out, this thin layer begins to break up, producing a loose, dusty surface.

Though not always necessary, it is generally recommended that you paint on a concrete-floor sealer before applying any paint. Treat a dusty concrete wall with stabilizing primer.

Repairing cracks and holes

Rake out and brush away loose debris from cracks and holes in concrete. If the crack is less than ¼ inch wide, open it up a little with a cold chisel so it will accept a filling (see far right). Undercut the edges to form a lip so that the filler will grip. To fill a hole in concrete, add a fine aggregate such as gravel to a sand-and-cement mix. Make sure the fresh concrete sticks in shallow depressions by priming the damaged surface with 3 parts bonding agent and 1 part water. When the primed surface is tacky, trowel in the concrete and smooth it. See also cement-based fillers (far right).

Treating spalled concrete

When concrete breaks up, or spalls, due to the action of frost, the process is accelerated as steel reinforcement is exposed and begins to corrode. Fill the concrete as described above, but paint the metalwork first with a rust-inhibiting primer.

Spalling concrete
Rusting metalwork causes concrete to spall.

An uneven or pitted concrete floor must be made level before you apply any form of floorcovering. You can do this fairly easily yourself using a self-leveling compound, but make sure the surface is dry before proceeding.

Testing for damp

If you suspect a concrete floor is damp, make a simple test by laying a small piece of polyethelene on the concrete and sealing it all around with tape. After one or two days, inspect it for any traces of moisture on the underside.

If the test indicates that treatment is required, apply three coats of heavy-duty, moisture-cured polyurethane sealant. No longer than 4 hours should elapse between coats. The floor should be as dry as possible so that it is porous enough for the first coat to penetrate. If necessary, use a fan heater to help dry the floor.

Before applying a self-leveling compound, lightly scatter dry sand over the last coat of sealant while it is still wet. Allow it to harden for three days, then brush off loose residual sand.

Applying a self-leveling compound

Self-leveling compound is supplied as a powder that you mix with water. Be sure the floor is clean and free from dampness (see previous paragraph), then pour some of the compound in the corner that is farthest away from the door. Spread the compound with a trowel until it is about ⅛ inch thick, then leave it to seek its own level. Continue across the floor, joining the areas of compound until the entire surface is covered. You can walk on the floor after an hour or so without damaging it, but leave the compound to harden for a few days before laying a permanent floorcovering.

● **Leave a new floor to dry out.**
A new floor with a vapor barrier installed should be left to dry out for 6 months before any impermeable covering, such as sheet vinyl or tiles, is laid.

● **Cement-based exterior fillers.**
As an alternative to making up your own sand-and-cement mix, you can buy a cement-based exterior filler for patching holes in concrete and rebuilding broken corners. When mixed with water, the filler remains workable for 10 to 20 minutes. Just before it sets hard, smooth or scrape the filler level.

Filling cracks.
Before you fill a narrow crack, open it up and undercut the edges using a cold chisel.

Applying self-leveling compound.
Pour the compound and spread it with a trowel.

Plasterwork: preparing

Solid masonry walls are usually covered with two coats of plaster: a thicker backing coat and a smooth finish coat. In older houses, ceilings and some internal walls are clad with slim strips of wood known as lath, which serve as a base for the plaster. In modern houses, wire mesh or drywall is generally used instead.

Whatever you intend to use as a decorative finish, the plastered wall or ceiling must be made good by filling cracks and holes.

Preparing new plaster

Smooth the finish. Smooth the surface of small repairs with a wet brush or knife in order to reduce the amount of sanding required later.

Before you paint new plaster, wait to see if any efflorescence forms on the surface. Keep wiping it off with dry cloth until it ceases to appear.

Once fresh plaster is dry, you can stick ceramic tiles on the wall—but always leave it for about six months before decorating with wallpaper or any paint other than new-plaster emulsion. Even then, you should use a masonry sealer followed by a water- or oil-based primer to match your topcoat.

Apply wall sizing to new absorbent plaster before hanging wallpaper or the water will be sucked too quickly from the paste and the paper will simply peel off the wall. If you are hanging a vinyl wallcovering, make sure the sizing contains a fungicide.

Mix the sizing with water according to the manufacturer's instructions; then brush it evenly across the walls and ceiling. If you splash sizing onto painted woodwork, wipe it off with a damp sponge before it dries.

Preparing old plaster

Apart from filling minor defects (see opposite page) and dusting down, old dry plaster in good condition needs no further preparation. If the wall is patchy, apply a primer designed for the topcoat you are using. If the surface is friable, apply a stabilizing solution before painting. Don't try to paint damp plaster. Eliminate the moisture problem, then let the plaster dry out.

Preparing drywall

Finish all the joints between newly installed drywall panels and sand the joints smooth. Make sure to cover all the nail- or screwheads with joint compound too, and when dry, sand smooth.

Before you paint drywall, prime it with a product that matches the topcoat you're planning to use: latex primer for water-based paint, alkyd primer for oil-based paint.

Prior to hanging wallcoverings, seal drywall with a general-purpose primer thinned with mineral spirits. After 48 hours, apply a coat of sizing. Should you want to strip the wallcovering in the future, this treatment will allow you to wet the surface without disturbing the board's paper facing.

Preparing painted plaster

Wash sound paintwork with household detergent. Then use medium-grit wet-and-dry abrasive paper, with water, to scratch the surface of gloss paint, particularly if you are going to paint over it with latex paint.

If the ceiling is stained by smoke or mildew, prime it with a stain-blocking primer/sealer. Stain-blocking sealers are sold in aerosol cans for treating isolated stains. You can then paint over the sealer with either oil-based or latex paint. If you want to hang wallcoverings on oil paint, lightly sand the surface and apply sizing. Cross-line the

wall with lining paper before hanging a heavy, embossed wallpaper.

Remove flaking paint with a scraper or stiff-bristle brush. Feather off the edges of the paintwork with wet-and-dry abrasive paper; then treat the bare plaster patches with a primer. If the edges of the old paintwork continue to show, prime those areas again, sanding lightly once the areas are dry.

You can apply ceramic tiles over sound paintwork. If there is any loose material, remove it first. Then apply the proper mastic and set the tiles.

PLASTER FILLERS

There is an extensive range of materials made specially for filling anything from cracks to deep holes in solid plaster and drywall.

Interior filler
General-purpose cellulose filler comes ready-mixed in tubs or as a powder for mixing to a stiff paste with water.

Deep-repair filler
Ready-mixed lightweight fillers can be used to fill holes and gaps up to ¼ inch deep without slumping. They are ideal for ceiling repairs.

Fast-setting filler
Sold in tube dispensers, fast-setting fillers are perfect for minor repairs. They set firm in 10 to 20 minutes.

Flexible acrylic fillers
Good for filling gaps between plaster and woodwork. When smoothed with a damp cloth, these gun-applied fillers can be painted in 1 hour. No sanding is required.

Expanding foam
Fill large irregular gaps and cavities with expanding polyurethane foam from an aerosol can. Finish the job with cellulose or deep-repair fillers.

Repair plasters
Make more extensive repairs with easy-to-use, slow-drying repair plaster.

Dealing with whitewash.
Whitewash is an old paint made from powdered chalk mixed with glue and water. Most paints and wallcoverings will not adhere to a whitewashed surface, so brush away all loose material and apply a stabilizing primer to bind any traces left on the surface.

You may find that delicate plaster moldings have been obliterated by successive coats of whitewash. Although it's a laborious task, you can remove whitewash with water and a toothbrush, cleaning out clogged detail with a pointed stick. Alternatively, hire a specialist to strip whitewash with steam.

Patching holes in walls

Filling cracks and holes

Special flexible and textured paints are designed to cover hairline cracks, but larger cracks, dents, and holes will reappear in a relatively short time if they are not filled adequately.

Scrape loose material from a crack, using a putty knife or scraper (**1**). Undercut the edges of larger cracks in order to provide a key for the filling.

Use a paintbrush to dampen the crack, then press in joint compound with a knife. Drag the blade across the crack (**2**) to force the compound in; then draw it along the crack to smooth the compound. Leave the compound standing slightly just above the surface, ready for sanding smooth and flush when it's dry.

Fill shallow cracks in one pass. But in deep cracks build up the compound in stages, letting each application dry before adding more. You can fill and sand small holes and dents in the same way.

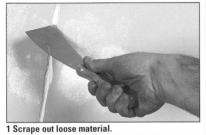

1 Scrape out loose material.

2 Press compound into crack.

Fill gap with expanding polyurethane foam.

Gaps behind baseboards
Large gaps can open up between baseboards and the wall. Most fillers simply fall into the cavity behind, so bridge large gaps with expanding polyurethane foam. When dry, cut the foam flush and sand it smooth. Add caulk and paint.

Patching a lath-and-plaster wall

If the lath strips are intact, just fill any holes in the plaster with repair plaster. If some lath strips are broken, reinforce the repair with a piece of fine metal mesh. Scrape out loose plaster and undercut the edge of the hole with a cold chisel. Use tinsnips to cut the metal mesh to the shape of the hole but a little larger (**1**). The mesh is flexible, so you can easily bend it in order to tuck the edge behind the surface of the plaster (**2**). Flatten the mesh against the lath with light taps from a hammer; if possible, staple the mesh to a wall stud to hold it in place (**3**). For papering and tiling, patch the hole with repair plaster (**4**). If you want a smoother surface for painting, finish the surface with a thin coat of skimming plaster or joint compound.

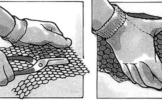
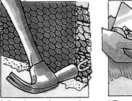

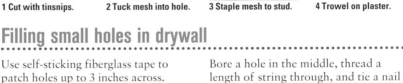

1 Cut with tinsnips. | **2 Tuck mesh into hole.** | **3 Staple mesh to stud.** | **4 Trowel on plaster.**

Filling small holes in drywall

Use self-sticking fiberglass tape to patch holes up to 3 inches across. Apply the strips in a star shape over the hole; then cover the tape with joint compound and feather the edges (**1**).

You can use a scrap of drywall for larger holes. Cut the piece so it's just slightly wider than the hole and narrow enough to slide through it.

Bore a hole in the middle, thread a length of string through, and tie a nail to one end of the string (**2**). Coat the ends of the scrap with compound, then feed it into the hole. Pull on the string (**3**) to force it against the back of the wall panel and let it dry. Cut off the string and fill the hole with compound.

1 Fill and feather the patch.

2 Attach string to patch. | **3 Pull on string.**

Patching larger holes in drywall

A large hole cannot be patched with tape and compound alone or with small scraps. Using a sharp utility knife and a straightedge, cut back the damaged board to the nearest studs or joists at each side of the hole (**1**). Cut a piece of drywall to fit snugly within the hole and attach it to the joists or studs, using drywall nails or screws. Coat the surface with joint compound (**2**), tape the seams, and let the patch dry. Apply a topcoat of compound over the entire area and feather the edges to the wall.

Large holes can't be patched with compound alone.

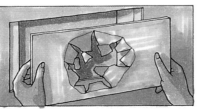

1 Cut back the damaged panel to the nearest supports. | **2 Nail on the new panel and coat with compound.**

Patching damaged corners.
Cracks sometimes appear in the corner between walls or a wall and ceiling. Fill these by running your finger dipped in compound along the crack. When dry, sand the area smooth.

To build up a chipped external corner, dampen the area and then use a knife to apply compound to the damaged edge, working from both sides of the corner (**1**). Let the compound stiffen, then shape it with a wet finger until it closely resembles the original profile (**2**). When the compound is dry, sand it smooth.

1 Apply compound.

2 Shape with finger.

● **Patching lath-and-plaster ceilings.**
If the lath strips are sound, fill the hole flush with repair plaster. If the lath strips are broken, cut them back to the nearest joist. Then install a drywall panel to fit the hole and cover it with a couple of coats of drywall joint compound.

Preparing wallcoverings

It's always preferable to strip a previously papered surface before hanging a new wallcovering. However, if the paper is perfectly sound, you can paint it with latex or oil-based paints (though this will make it more difficult to remove in the future). Use a stain-blocking primer/sealer to prevent strong reds, greens, or blues from showing through the paint. Take similar precautions if there are any metallic inks used in the pattern. Don't attempt to paint vinyl wallcoverings. If you opt for stripping off the old covering, the method you use will depend on the material and its condition.

Steam stripper
Rent or buy a lightweight steam stripper to soften stubborn wall-coverings. Having removed the paper, wash the wall to remove traces of paste.

Stripping conventional wallpaper

To soften the old wallpaper paste, soak the paper with warm water and a little dishwashing liquid or use a commercial stripping liquid. Apply the solution with a sponge or houseplant sprayer. Repeat and leave the water to penetrate for 15 to 20 minutes.

Use a wide metal-bladed scraper to lift the softened paper, starting at the seams. Take care not to dig the points of the blade into the plaster. Resoak stubborn areas of paper and leave them for a few minutes before stripping.

Electricity and water are a lethal combination: Where possible, dry-strip around switches and sockets. If the paper cannot be stripped dry, switch off the power at the service panel before stripping around electrical fittings, and unscrew the coverplates so that you can get at the paper trapped behind. Don't use a sprayer near electrical outlets or fixtures.

Collect the stripped paper in plastic trash bags, then wash the wall with warm water containing a little detergent.

Scoring washable wallpaper

Washable wallpaper has an impervious surface film that you must break through to allow the water to penetrate to the adhesive. Use a wire brush or a wallpaper scorer to puncture the surface, then soak it with warm water and stripper. It may take several applications before the paper begins to lift.

Peeling vinyl wallcoverings

Vinyl wallcovering consists of a thin layer of vinyl fused with a paper backing. To remove the vinyl, lift both bottom corners of the top layer of the wallcovering, then pull firmly and steadily away from the wall.

Either soak and scrape off the backing paper or, if you want to leave it as a lining paper, smooth the seams with medium-grade sandpaper, using very light pressure to avoid gouging the surface.

Stripping painted wallcoverings

Wallcoverings that have been painted can be difficult to remove. If the paper is sound, simply prepare it in the same way as painted plaster or drywall and install the wallpaper over it.

To strip it, use a wire brush or a scoring tool to puncture the surface, then soak the paper with warm water containing paper stripper. Using a steam stripper, you can easily strip painted papers (and washables). Hold the stripper's baseplate against the paper until the steam penetrates, then remove the soaked paper with a wide-bladed scraper.

Scoring wallpaper
Running a wallpaper scoring tool across the wall punches minute holes through impervious wallcoverings.

ELIMINATING MOLD

In damp conditions mold can develop, usually in the form of black specks. It is important to remedy the cause of the mold before you begin to redecorate the walls or ceiling.

If the mold is growing on wallpaper, soak the area in a solution made from 1 part household bleach and 16 parts water, then scrape off the contaminated paper and throw it out. Wash the wall with a fresh bleach solution to remove paste residue.

Apply a liberal wash of the bleach solution to sterilize the wall and leave it for at least three days (but preferably a week) to make sure no further growth develops. If you are planning to repaper the wall, when the wall is completely dry, apply a primer, followed by a coat of sizing containing a fungicide solution. If you want a painted finish, use latex paint that contains a fungicide.

If mold growth is affecting a bare-plaster or painted wall or ceiling, apply a liberal wash of the bleach solution. Wait for at least four hours, and then carefully scrape off the mold, wipe it onto newspaper, and put the paper in the trash. Wash the wall again with the solution, then leave it for three days in order to sterilize the wall completely before redecorating as described above.

Mold growth
Mold, typified by black specks, will grow on damp walls or wallpaper.

Preparing woodwork

Wood is used throughout home interiors for trim, cabinetry, and furniture. Valued for its workability and natural beauty, wood can bring a sense of detail, refinement, and warmth to nearly any room. But it must be treated with special care to retain its special character. A wider variety of wood species is used in interior applications than in exterior ones. Even though interior wood is not subject to damage caused by the weather, other types of abuse like scratching, denting, staining, and splitting, are common.

Preparing new wood for painting

New wood is sometimes primed at the factory, but it is worth checking that the primer is in good condition before you start work. If the primer is satisfactory, sand it lightly with fine-grade abrasive paper, dust it off, then apply a second coat of wood primer to areas that will be inaccessible after installation. Don't leave wood uncovered outside, as primer is not sufficient protection against prolonged exposure to the weather.

Make sure unprimed lumber is dry, then sand the surface in the direction of the grain, using fine-grade abrasive paper. Wrap it around a wood block for flat surfaces, and around a piece of dowel or a pencil for molded sections.

Once you have removed all raised grain and lightly rounded any sharp edges, vacuum the dust from the wood and finish up by wiping the surface with a tack cloth.

Paint bare softwood with an oil-based wood primer or a quick-drying, water-thinned acrylic primer. Apply either primer liberally, taking care to

work it well into the joints and, particularly, into the endgrain—which will require at least two coats for adequate protection.

Wash oily hardwoods with mineral spirits before priming. Use standard wood primers for other hardwoods, thinning them slightly to encourage penetration into the grain.

When the primer is dry, fill open-grained lumber with a fine surface filler. Use a piece of coarse cloth to rub it well into the wood, making circular strokes followed by parallel strokes in the direction of the grain. When the filler is dry, sand it with a fine abrasive paper to a smooth finish.

Fill larger holes, open joints, cracks, and similar imperfections with flexible wood filler. Press the filler into the holes with a putty knife, leaving it slightly over-filled so that it can be sanded flush with fine-grade abrasive paper once it has set. Vacuum the dust before painting.

If, just before starting to apply the undercoat, you find a hole that you've missed, fill it with fast-setting filler.

Sealing knots with shellac

Knots and other resinous areas of the wood must be treated to keep them from staining subsequent layers of paint.

Scrape off any hardened resin, then seal the knots by painting them with two coats of shellac. You can use either clear shellac or pigmented shellac for this job. Shellac usually dries within 30 minutes, so you can apply two coats in less than an hour.

Seal resinous knots with shellac.

Clear finishes

There is usually no need to apply a separate sealer when you intend to finish lumber with a clear varnish or lacquer. However, for very resinous lumber, a shellac sanding sealer is a good idea.

Sand the wood in the direction of the grain using progressively finer grades of abrasive paper, then seal it with a slightly thinned coat of the intended finish.

If the wood is in contact with the ground or in proximity to previous outbreaks of dry rot, treat it first with a liberal coat of clear wood preservative. Check the manufacturer's recommendations to make sure that the liquid is compatible with the finish.

Badly damaged wood can be restored with wood fillers. For interior work, some of these fillers are tinted so they can match the color of a range of wood species. For exterior work, two-part fillers are recommended. They consist of the filler and a separate hardener that is mixed in just before application. These exterior fillers work well but can't be tinted. They're best suited to areas that will be painted.

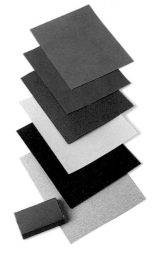

Seal gaps with flexible acrylic caulk. Before painting inside or outside, fill large gaps around trim with acrylic caulk.

Sand along the grain with abrasive paper

Using grain filler

If you plan to finish open-grained wood with clear varnish or French polish, apply a grain filler after sanding. Use a light-colored filler for light-colored wood, a darker filler for dark wood. Rub the filler across the grain with a coarse rag and leave it to harden for several hours. Then rub off the excess along the grain with a clean, coarse rag. Apply successive coats of the clear finish and rub it down with steel wool between coats.

Apply grain filler with a coarse rag

Man-made boards

Versatile and relatively inexpensive, man-made boards are used extensively in the home—for wall, floor, and roof sheathing, and for shelving and cabinets in the kitchen and bathroom.

Preparing man-made boards for finishing

Manufactured panels such as plywood, MDF, particleboard, and hardboard are all made from wood, but they are prepared differently than natural lumber. Their finish varies according to the quality of the board: Some are compact and smooth and may even be presealed and ready for painting; others must be filled and sanded before you can get a really smooth finish.

As a rough guide, no primer will be required when using latex acrylic paints, other than a sealing coat of the paint itself, slightly thinned with water. However, any nail or screwheads must be driven below the surface and covered with wood fillers or wood plugs.

Apply one coat of primer before painting any of these boards with masonry paint. If you are using oil-based paint, prime the boards first with a general-purpose, oil-based primer. Where possible, you should prime both sides and all the edges of the panels. If the boards are preprimed, you need to paint only the surfaces that will be seen.

1 Plywood
2 Lumber-core plywood
3 Particleboard
4 Medium-density fiberboard (MDF)
5 Hardboard (back)
6 Hardboard (face)
7 Fiberboard

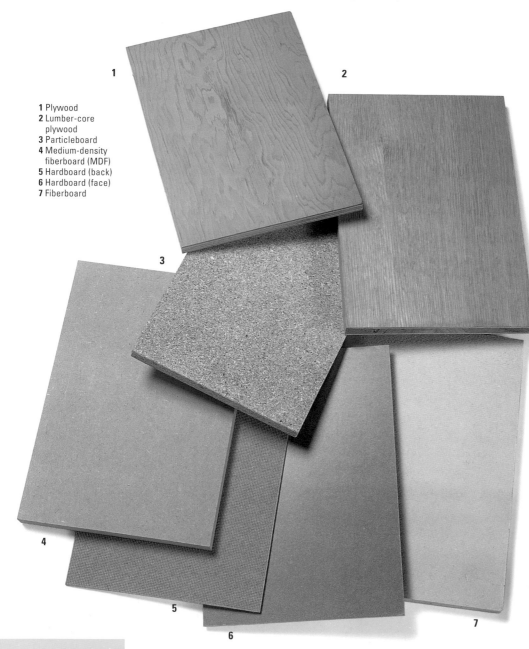

BLEACHING WOOD

Unevenly colored or stained boards can be bleached before applying wood stains and finishes. To avoid a light patch in place of the discoloration, try to bleach the entire area rather than isolated spots.

Using two-part bleach

To use a commercial two-part wood bleach, brush one part onto the wood and apply the second part over the first 5 to 10 minutes later. When the bleach is dry, or as soon as the wood is the required color, neutralize the bleach with a weak acetic-acid solution consisting of a teaspoon of white vinegar in a pint of water.

Put the wood aside for about three days, then sand down the raised grain.

Bleaching wood
Use a paintbrush to apply two-part bleach to stained wood. Leave it until the discoloration has disappeared, then wash off with diluted vinegar.

Safety precautions

Wood bleach is a toxic substance that must be handled with care and stored in the dark, out of the reach of children and pets.

● Wear protective gloves, goggles, and an apron.
● Wear a face mask when sanding bleached wood.
● Ensure that ventilation is adequate, or work outside.
● Have a supply of water handy so you can rinse your skin immediately if you splash yourself with bleach.
● If you get bleach in your eyes, rinse them thoroughly with running water and see a doctor immediately.
● Never mix both parts of the bleach except on the wood, and always apply them with separate nylon brushes.
● Discard unused bleach.

Sanding a wood floor

You can turn an unsightly stained and dirty wood floor into an attractive feature by sanding it smooth and clean with rented equipment. Although straightforward, the job is laborious, noisy, and extremely dusty.

Repairing floorboards prior to sanding

Before you start sanding, examine your floorboards carefully for signs of rot damage. If necessary, replace any weak boards. If the moisture that caused the rot is still present, eliminate the source of the moisture before doing anything else.

Look for boards that have been lifted previously by electricians and plumbers. Replace any that are split, too short, or too weak. Try to find replacement boards to match the rest of the floor. If you have to use new wood, stain or bleach it after the floor has been sanded to match the color of the old boards.

A raised nailhead will rip the paper on the sander's drum, so drive all the nailheads below the surface with a nailset.

Some boards are liable to be cupped, either up or down across the board's width. These can usually be flattened by driving screws through the high areas into the joists or subfloor below.

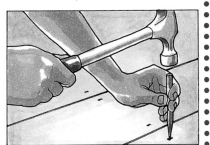

Set nailheads below the surface

Filling gaps between the floorboards

What you do about gaps between boards depends on how much they bother you. Many people simply ignore them; but you will end up with a more attractive floor, and fewer drafts, if you make the effort to fill the gaps or close them up.

Closing up
Over a large area, the quickest and most satisfactory solution is to lift the boards a few at a time and reinstall them butted side by side, filling in the final gap with a new board.

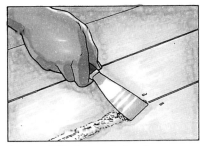

Force wood filler between the boards

Using wood filler
If there are only a few gaps, you can use common wood fillers. Most of these dry to a light color, but some manufacturers offer colored fillers that match different wood species. To use

any filler, just force it into the crack with a putty knife. Then let it dry and sand it flush with the surrounding surface. You can also make a filler paste using sawdust and yellow carpenter's glue. Mix the two into a stiff paste and push into the cracks.

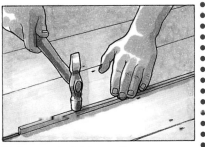

Wedge a wooden lath into a wide gap

Inserting wood strips
Large gaps can be filled with a thin wood strip planed to fit tightly between the boards. Apply a little glue to the gap and tap the strip in place with a hammer until the wood is flush with the surrounding surfaces. If necessary, trim with a hand plane. Don't bother to fill several gaps this way: It is easier to close up the boards and fill one larger gap at the end of the room with a new floorboard.

The area of a floor is far too large to contemplate sanding with anything but industrial sanding machines. You can obtain the equipment from the usual tool rental outlets, which will also supply the abrasive papers. You will need three grades of paper: coarse, to level the boards initially, followed by medium and fine to create a smooth finish.

It is best to rent a large, upright drum sander for the main floor area and a smaller disc sander for tackling the edges. You can sand smaller rooms, such as bathrooms and powder rooms, using the edging sander only. Rent an upright orbital sander for finishing parquet and other delicate flooring that would be ruined by drum sanding.

Some companies also supply a scraper for cleaning out inaccessible corners. If so, make sure it is fitted with a new blade when you rent it.

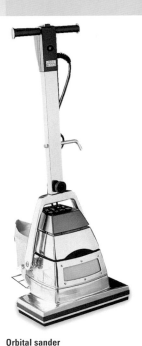

Orbital sander
An orbital sander is comparatively gentle and leaves a smooth finish free from swirls and scratches.

Drum sander
An upright drum sander is used for sanding the main floor area with coarse, medium, then fine-grit abrasive papers to create a smooth finish.

Edging sander
A small disc sander is used for sanding in corners and along edges that the drum sander cannot reach.

Using floor-sanding machines

Fitting abrasive paper to sanders

Precise instructions for fitting abrasive paper to sanding machines should be supplied by the rental store.
If they are not included, ask for a demonstration of what you need to do. Never attempt to change abrasive papers while a machine is plugged into a receptacle.

With most drum sanders, the paper is wrapped around the drum, then secured in place with a screw-down bar **(1)**. Ensure that the paper is wrapped tightly around the drum; if it is slack, it may slip from its clamp and be torn to pieces.

Edging sanders take a disc of abrasive, usually held to the soleplate by a central nut **(2)**.

(1) Drum sander
Tighten the bar clamp to hold the paper securely.

2 Tighten an abrasive disc to an edging sander

Operating a drum sander

At the beginning of a run, stand with the drum sander tilted back so that the drum itself is clear of the floor. Drape the electrical cord over one shoulder to make sure it cannot become caught in the sander.

Switch on the machine, then gently lower the drum onto the floor. There is no need to push a drum sander; it will move forward under its own power. Hold the machine in check so that it proceeds at a slow but steady walking pace along a straight line. Don't hold it still for even a brief period, or it will rapidly sand a deep hollow in the floorboards. Take care you don't let go of it, as it will run across the room on its own, probably damaging the floor or walls in the process.

When you reach the other side of the room, tilt the machine back, switch off, and wait for it to stop before lowering it to the floor.

If the abrasive paper rips, tilt the machine onto its back casters and switch off. Wait for the drum to stop revolving, disconnect the power, then change the paper.

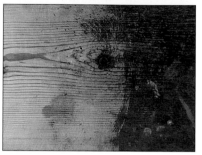

Sanding cleans and rejuvenates wood floors

Using an edging sander

Hand scraper
Use a small hand scraper for removing paint spots from the floor and for reaching into spaces that are inaccessible to the disc sander. The tool cuts on the backward stroke. Various sizes and blade shapes are available to deal with most situations.

Hold the handles on top of the machine and drape the cord over your shoulder. Tilt the sander onto its back casters to lift the disc off the floor. Switch on and lower the machine. As soon as you contact the boards, sweep the machine in any direction, but keep it moving—as soon as it comes to rest, the disc will score deep, scorched swirl marks in the wood, which are difficult to remove. There's no need to press down on the machine. When you have finished, tilt the machine back and switch off, letting the motor run down.

(1) Sand diagonally across the floorboards

Sanding the floor

Health and safety
Wear a dust mask, goggles, and ear protection when working with power sanders.

A great deal of dust is produced by sanding a floor, so before you begin, empty the room of furniture and take down curtains, lamp shades, and pictures. Sweep the floor to remove grit and other debris. Stuff folded newspaper under the door and seal around it with masking tape. Open all the windows. Wear old clothes, a dust mask, goggles, and ear protectors.

Old floorboards will most likely be cupped (curved across their width), so the first task is to level the floor across its entire area. With coarse paper fitted to the drum sander, sand diagonally across the room **(1)**. At the end of the run, tilt the machine, pull it back, and make a second run parallel to the first. Allow each pass to overlap the last slightly. When you have covered the floor once, sweep up the sawdust.

Now sand the floor again in the same way—but this time across the opposite diagonal of the room **(2)**. Switch off and sweep the dust from the floor.

Once the floor is flat and clean all over, change to a medium-grade paper and sand parallel to the boards **(3)**. Overlap each pass as before. Finally, switch to the fine-grade paper in order to remove all obvious scratches, working parallel to the boards and overlapping each pass again. Each time you change the grade of paper on the drum sander, put the same grade on the edging sander and sand the edges of the room so that they are finished to the same standard as the main area **(4)**.

Even the edging sander cannot clean right up to the skirting or into the corners. Finish these small areas with a hand scraper, or use a flexible abrasive disc in a power drill.

Vacuum the floor and wipe it clean with a cloth dampened with mineral spirits. Now you're ready for finishing.

(2) Sand across the opposite diagonal

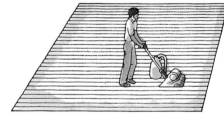

(3) Sand parallel to the floorboards

(4) Finish the edges with a disc sander

Leveling a wood floor

Tiles, sheet vinyl, or carpet should not be laid directly onto an uneven wood floor; the irregularities will cause the tiles or covering to lift or even crack. The solution is to cover the floorboards with ⅛-inch hardboard or, preferably, with more substantial ¼-inch plywood. Both panels are installed the same way.

Conditioning boards

Before you cover the floor with plywood or hardboard, make sure there's no evidence of rot or other moisture problems. If you do detect problems, fix them before installing the new panels.

Also, bear in mind that once the floor is covered with the panels you will not have easy access to underfloor plumbing pipes and electric cables. Make any changes to these components before installing the panels.

It is important to match the moisture content of the panels and the humidity of the room, or the panels could buckle at the joints after they're installed. Stack the sheets on edge in the room for 48 hours so they can adjust to the atmosphere. If you are covering the floor in a large room, stack the panels in several different spots to distribute the weight more evenly over the floor.

Hammer stapler
When leveling a large floor, rent a heavy-duty stapler and mallet for attaching the panels to the floorboards.

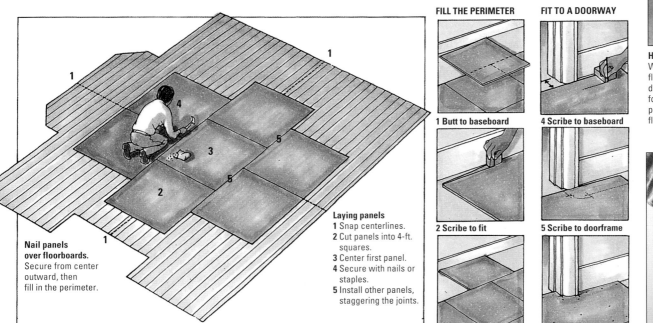

Nail panels over floorboards. Secure from center outward, then fill in the perimeter.

Laying panels
1 Snap centerlines.
2 Cut panels into 4-ft. squares.
3 Center first panel.
4 Secure with nails or staples.
5 Install other panels, staggering the joints.

FILL THE PERIMETER
1 Butt to baseboard
2 Scribe to fit
3 Nail to floor

FIT TO A DOORWAY
4 Scribe to baseboard
5 Scribe to doorframe
6 Cut and nail down

LAYING A BASE FOR CERAMIC TILES

Ceramic floor tiles should be laid in a bed of thin, set mortar. But the water in the mortar can ruin hardboard or standard plywood panels. In this case, use ⅝-inch marine plywood to level the floor. This plywood is highly water resistant and won't be damaged by the mortar. Screw it to the joists every 8 to 12 inches.

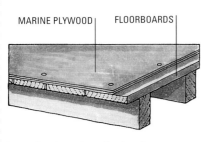

MARINE PLYWOOD   FLOORBOARDS

Lay marine plywood over floorboards

Laying the panels

Cut the panels into 4-foot squares for handling ease. Nail loose floorboards and set the nailheads, then plane high points off the boards.

Use a chalkline to snap two centerlines across the room, crossing at right angles. Lay the first panel in the center, adjusting it so that its edges do not align with the gaps between the floorboards. Unless the panel manufacturer's instructions state otherwise, lay hardboard rough side up, to provide a good gripping surface for the adhesive. Lay the other panels in place to check for any alignment problems.

Nail the first board to the floor with 3/4-inch hardboard nails, or use a rented stapler (see above right). Start near the center of the panel and nail it every 6 inches in the field of the panel. Drive nails every 4 inches around the perimeter. Butt the other panels against

the first panel and nail them in place.

To cut edge panels to fit the margins, lay the panel on the floor touching the baseboard but square to the edges of the nailed panels (**1**). Hold the board firmly and use a pencil and scrap block to scribe a cutline (**2**). Cut the scribed line and butt it up to the baseboard, then mark the position of the nailed panels on both sides of the edge panel. Draw a line between these marks and cut the panel. Nail it in place (**3**).

To scribe around a doorway, butt a panel up to the frame and measure to the doorstop. Cut a scrap block to this size and use it to scribe the panel to the baseboard (**4**). Use the same block to trace the shape of the doorframe (**5**) and cut the shape with a coping saw or jigsaw. Slide the board into the doorway, mark and cut the other edge that butts up against the nailed panels, and nail the panel to the floor (**6**).

Shortening a door
If you install hardboard or plywood over a floor, you may have to plane the bottom of the room doors to provide the necessary clearance. Take the door off its hinges and plane toward the center from each end. When deciding how much stock to remove, be sure to add in the thickness of the new floor-covering that you're installing over the panels.

Painted and varnished woodwork

Most of the woodwork in and around your house will have been painted or varnished at some time, and provided it is in good condition, it will form a sound base for new paintwork. However, when too many coats of paint have been applied, the moldings around door and window frames begin to lose their definition and start to look unattractive. In these cases, it is best to strip off all the old paint, down to bare wood, and start again. Stripping is also essential where the paintwork has deteriorated and is cracked, chipped, or flaking.

Cleaning
Sometimes all that woodwork needs is a good cleaning with household detergent and water.

Acrylic caulk
Acrylic caulk is ideal for filling large cracks or gaps in painted woodwork. Just squeeze into the gap from a caulk gun and smooth it with a wet finger or a damp cloth. No sanding is required. You can paint over it in 1 hour.

Dry, flaky paint

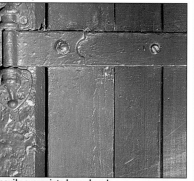

Heavily overpainted woodwork

Badly weathered varnish

Preparing sound paintwork

Wash the painted surfaces, from the bottom upward, with a solution of warm water and household detergent or trisodium phosphate, about 1 teaspoon per gallon of water. Pay particular attention to the areas around the door handles and window locks, where dirt and grease will be heaviest. Rinse with fresh water from bottom to top, to keep runs of dirty liquid from staining the surface.

Rub down high-gloss surfaces with fine-grade, wet-and-dry abrasive paper, dipped in water, in order to provide a key for the new finish coat and to remove any blemishes.

Prime any bare patches of wood, building up these low spots gradually and rubbing down between each application.

Fill open joints or holes with a latex caulk and replace any crumbling wood filler. Once they're dry, cover the new caulk and wood filler with primer.

Preparing badly weathered paintwork or varnish

Unsound paint or varnish, such as the examples pictured on the left, must be stripped to bare wood. There are several methods you can use, but always scrape off loose material first.

In some cases, where the paint is particularly dry and flaky, dry scraping may be all that is required, using a hand scraper followed by coarse, medium, and fine abrasive paper. Where most of the paint is stuck firmly to the woodwork, remove it using heat or chemical strippers.

Stripping paint and varnish with a propane torch

One long-standing method for stripping old paint is to melt it off with a handheld propane torch and canister. You can also rent a propane torch that is connected by a hose to a larger tank that sits on the floor. Both torches have adjustable valves that allow for fine-tuning of the flame intensity, and come with a variety of attachments that create different flame patterns for different working conditions.

It is necessary only to soften the paint with the flame in order to scrape it off. But it is all too easy to heat the paint so that it actually burns. Deposit scrapings in a metal paint can or bucket as you remove them.

Start by stripping moldings from the bottom upward. Never direct the flame at one spot, but keep it moving all the time so that you don't scorch the wood. As soon as the paint has softened, use a molding scraper or putty knife to scrape it off. If it is sticky or hard, heat it a little more and try scraping again.

Having dealt with the moldings, strip flat areas of woodwork using a wide knife. When you have finished stripping, sand the wood with medium-grade abrasive paper to remove hardened specks of paint and any accidental light scorching.

You may find that it is impossible to sand away heavy scorching without removing too much wood. Sand or scrape off loose, blackened wood fibers, then fill any hollows; once the filler is dry, sand it smooth. Apply a coat of good primer that matches the topcoat you are planning to use. Then paint the wood with two topcoats of good paint.

Strip moldings with a molding scraper

Use a scraper to strip flat surfaces

USING CHEMICAL STRIPPERS

You can remove old finish by using a stripper that reacts chemically with paint or varnish. Some general-purpose strippers will soften both oil-based and water-based finishes, others are formulated to react with a specific type of finish, such as varnish or textured paint. Specific strippers are more efficient than general-purpose ones—but come at the cost of having to acquire a whole range of different products.

Traditionally, strippers have been made from highly potent chemicals that have to be handled with care. Working with this type of stripper means having to wear protective gloves and safety glasses, and possibly a respirator, too. The new-generation "green" strippers do not burn your skin, nor do they exude harmful fumes. However, removing paint with these milder strippers is a relatively slow process.

Whichever type of stripper you decide to use, always follow the manufacturer's health and safety recommendations—and if in doubt, err on the side of caution.

Before you opt for a particular chemical stripper, you should also consider the nature of the surface you intend to strip. The thick gel-like paint removers that will cling to vertical surfaces, such as doors and window trim, are perfect for all general household woodwork. Strippers manufactured to a thinner consistency are usually best used on delicately carved work. For good-quality furniture, especially if it is veneered, make sure you use a stripper that can be washed off with mineral spirits, not water, because water can damage the wood.

Working with chemical strippers

Lay polyethelene sheets or plenty of newspaper on the floor, then apply a liberal coat of stripper to the painted surface, dabbing it into any moldings. Leave it for 10 to 15 minutes, then try scraping a patch to see if the paint has softened through to the wood. (You might have to leave one of the milder strippers in contact with the paint for 45 minutes or longer.) Don't waste your time removing only the topcoats of paint; apply more stripper with a brush if necessary, so the stripper will soak through to the wood. Leave it for another 5 to 10 minutes.

Once the chemicals have completed their work, use a scraper or putty knife to remove the softened paint from flat surfaces, and a paint scraper to remove

it from moldings. Wipe the paint from deep carvings with fine steel wool. When stripping oak, use a nylon-fiber pad impregnated with stripper, since oak can be stained by the threads of steel wool.

Having removed the bulk of the paint, clean off residual patches with a pad of steel wool. Rub with the grain, turning the pad inside out to present a clean face as it becomes clogged with paint.

Neutralize the stripper by washing the wood with mineral spirits or water, depending on the manufacturer's recommendations. Let the wood dry out thoroughly, then sand any areas that are rough. Prime, and paint with two topcoats.

Industrial stripping

Any portable woodwork can be taken to a professional stripper, who will immerse the whole thing in a tank of stripping solution that must then be washed out of the wood by hosing down with water. It is an efficient process, but it risks splitting panels, warping the wood, and opening up joints. At best, you can expect a certain amount of raised grain, which you will have to sand before refinishing.

Some stripping companies use a cold chemical dip, which does little harm to solid wood and raises the grain less. However, this treatment is usually more expensive than the water-wash process. Some strippers will dip

pieces for a few minutes only in a warm alkali solution. If carefully controlled, this is safe for manufactured panels, including plywood.

Some stripping companies are willing to pick up and deliver your projects, and others offer finishing services. Never submit veneered items to an industrial stripper unless the company will guarantee that their process won't harm the piece. It's generally a better idea to strip veneered pieces yourself using chemical stripper. Once the finish is removed, be sure to wipe down the whole piece with mineral spirits.

HOT-AIR STRIPPERS

Electrical heat guns do the work almost as quickly as a propane torch, but with less risk of scorching or fire. Even though they don't produce a flame, they operate at an extremely high temperature. Never put your hand near the tip. Some guns come with variable heat settings and a selection of nozzles for various uses.

Using a hot-air stripper

Hold the gun about 2 inches from the surface of the work and move it slowly backward and forward until the paint blisters and bubbles. Remove the paint immediately using a putty knife or paint scraper. Aim to heat the paint just ahead of the scraping tool so you develop a continuous work action. Use a shaped nozzle on the gun when stripping muntins (window center verticals) to deflect the jet of hot air and reduce the risk of cracking the glass.

Old primer is sometimes difficult to remove with a heat gun. This is not a problem if you are repainting the wood: Just sand the surface with abrasive paper. For a clear finish, remove residues of paint from the grain with steel wool dipped in chemical stripper.

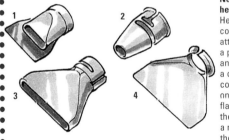

With a heat gun, there is less risk of scorching.

Removing old lead paint.
Wood and metal surfaces in many pre-1960s homes were painted with products that contained lead pigments. Removing these paints can be hazardous. Always use paint remover; never burn off old lead paint, and don't sand it with dry abrasives—power sanding is especially bad. An ordinary domestic vacuum cleaner is not fitted with filters fine enough to capture lead particles, so rent an industrial vacuum cleaner designed for the job.

Nozzles for heat guns
Heat guns usually come with a range of attachments: typically, a push-on nozzle with an integral scraper (1), a conical nozzle to concentrate the heat on a small area (2), a flared nozzle to spread the heat (3), and a nozzle that protects the glass when you strip muntins (4).

Preparing metalwork

Metals are used extensively for window frames, railings, gutters, pipes, radiators, and door hardware in both new and old homes. Metals that are exposed to the elements, or are in close proximity to water, are prone to corrosion. Many paints do not afford sufficient protection against corrosion on their own, so special treatments and coatings are often required to prolong the life of the metal.

Removing rust
Remove heavy rust deposits from pitted metal using a wire brush.

Cast-iron railings deeply pitted with rust

A rusty casement window sheds its paint

Corroded cast-iron downspout

What is rust?

Rust is a form of corrosion that affects ferrous metals—notably iron and steel. Although most paints slow down the rate at which moisture penetrates, they do not keep it out altogether. A good-quality primer is therefore needed to complete the protection. The type you use depends on the condition of the metal and how you plan to finish it. Make your preparation thorough, or the job could be ruined.

Treating bare metal

Remove light deposits of rust by rubbing with steel wool or waterproof abrasive paper dipped in mineral spirits. If the rust is heavy and the surface of the metal pitted, use a wire brush or, for extensive corrosion, a wire wheel chucked in a portable electric drill. Wear goggles while you are wire-brushing to protect your eyes from flying particles.

Use a rust-inhibiting primer to protect metal inside and outside the house. Work the primer thoroughly into any crevices, recesses, or tight corners on railings and other ornamental metalwork. Make sure that sharp edges and corners are coated generously.

Preparing previously painted metal

If the paint is perfectly sound, wash it with water and detergent, then rinse and dry it. Rough up gloss paint with fine waterproof abrasive paper to provide a good bonding surface.

If the paint film is blistered or flaking (where water has penetrated and corrosion has set in), remove all loose paint and rust with a wire brush or a wire wheel in a power drill. Apply rust-inhibiting primer to any bare patches, working it well into joints, bolt heads, and other problem areas. Prime bare metal immediately, as rust can re-form very rapidly.

To repair steel gutters, brush out dead leaves and other debris, then wash clean. Cover the inside with an asphalt coating. Clean the outside and make any repairs. Then prime the outside surface and finish with two topcoats of paint.

Stripping painted metal

Delicately molded sections on fireplace mantels, garden furniture, and other cast or wrought ironwork will benefit from stripping off old paint that can mask fine detail. Ironwork cannot easily be scraped with a wire brush, and a heat gun isn't usually effective because the heat dissipates too quickly for the paint to soften. A propane torch can be used to strip wrought ironwork, but cast iron may crack if it becomes distorted by localized heating.

Chemical stripping is the safest method. Before you begin, check that what appears to be a metal is not some other material covered with many layers of distorting paint. You don't want to vigorously scrape an area that you think is metal and find out after you've seriously gouged it that it's soft wood. Tap the area with a hammer to see if it's metallic, or scrape an inconspicuous section.

Paint the bare metal with a rust-inhibiting primer or with a rust-dissolving gel that will remove and neutralize the rust. Often based on phosphoric acid, these gels combine with the rust to leave it inert, in the form of iron phosphate. Some rust killers will deal with minute particles invisible to the naked eye and are self-priming, so that there is no need to apply an additional primer.

If the metalwork is portable, you may want to take it to a sandblaster or to an industrial stripper. The disadvantages of industrially stripping wood do not apply to metal.

Clean the stripped metal with a wire brush, then wash it with mineral spirits before applying a finish.

Treating other metals

Nonferrous metals such as aluminum, brass, and copper do not corrode to the same extent as steel or iron, but they still require careful preparation before a finish is applied.

Corrosion in aluminum

Aluminum, especially, does not corrode as readily as ferrous metals. Modern aluminum-alloy window frames and doorframes are designed to withstand weathering without a coat of protective paint. In adverse conditions, however, aluminum may corrode to a dull gray and even produce white crystals on the surface.

To remove corrosion of this kind,

sand the aluminum with a fine waterproof abrasive paper, using mineral spirits as a lubricant, until you get back to bright (but not gleaming) metal. Wipe the metal with a cloth dampened with mineral spirits to remove metal particles and traces of grease. When it is dry, prime the surface with a zinc-rich primer. Then follow up with two coats of oil-based paint.

Painting galvanized metal

Galvanized iron and steel have a coating of zinc applied by hot dipping. When new, this provides a poor key for most paints. To remedy this, let the galvanizing weather for six months. However, in many cases the manufacturer of galvanized metalwork will have treated it chemically to permit instant priming. Check when you purchase it.

Priming galvanized metal
If you need to paint galvanized metal before it has had time to weather,

protect it first with two coats of fast-drying acrylic primer formulated for use on nonferrous metals.

Treating chipped galvanizing
Remove any small rust spots resulting from accidental chipping of the zinc coating by gentle abrasion with wire wool, taking care not to damage the surrounding coating. Wash the area with mineral spirits, then allow the surface to dry. Prime with zinc-rich primer, then paint.

Maintaining brass and copper

Ornamental brassware, such as door knobs, escutcheon plates, and hinges, should not be painted, especially as there are clear lacquers available that will protect it from the elements. Strip painted brass with a chemical stripper. Treat corroded brass as described at the right of this page.

Copper, mainly plumbing pipe and fittings, does not require painting for

protection, but visible pipe runs are usually painted so they blend in with the room better. Don't just paint onto the bare pipes—degrease the surface first with fine steel wool lubricated with mineral spirits. Wipe away any metal particles with a cloth dampened with mineral spirits. Then apply two topcoats of paint. No primer is required.

Painting over lead

Before proceeding to paint old lead pipe, scour the surface with steel wool dipped in mineral spirits. No other preparation is required before applying the paint.

Keying lead pipes

Advanced lead corrosion
The cames (grooved retaining strips) of stained-glass windows and leaded door sidelights can become corroded, producing white stains. Unless the glass is etched or sandblasted, clean the lead carefully with detergent and a steel wool pad. Wipe the lead clean, then wash the glass with warm soapy water.

If you want to darken the lead, all you need is a touch of black paint used for coating wood stoves or fireplace grates.

Brass weathers to a dull brown color, but it is usually simple enough to buff up dirty fittings with a metal polish. However, if exterior door fittings have been left unprotected, you may have to use a solution of salt and vinegar to soften heavy corrosion before you can start polishing.

Mix 1 level tablespoonful each of salt and vinegar in ½ pint of hot water. Use a pad of very fine steel wool to apply liberal washes of the solution to the brass. Then wash the metal in hot water containing a little detergent. Rinse and dry the fittings before polishing them with a soft cloth.

Clean brass with salt and vinegar solution.

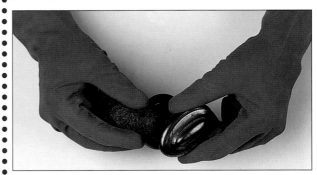

Getting rid of verdigris
Badly weathered brass can develop green deposits called verdigris. This heavy corrosion may leave the metal pitted, so clean it off as soon as possible.

Line a plastic bowl with ordinary aluminum foil. Attach a piece of string to each item of brassware, then place them in the bowl on top of the foil. Dissolve a cup of baking soda in a half-gallon of hot water and pour the solution into the bowl to cover the object.

Let solutions fizz and bubble for a couple of minutes, then use the string to lift out the fittings. Put any that are still corroded back into the solution. If necessary, repeat the process with fresh solution and new foil.

Rinse the brass with hot water, dry it with a soft cloth, and then polish.

Remove verdigris with a baking-soda bath

Preparing tiled surfaces

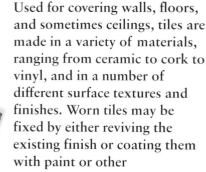

Used for covering walls, floors, and sometimes ceilings, tiles are made in a variety of materials, ranging from ceramic to cork to vinyl, and in a number of different surface textures and finishes. Worn tiles may be fixed by either reviving the existing finish or coating them with paint or other wallcoverings. With some types, it's even possible to install new tiles directly over the old ones.

Washing maintains the color of a tiled floor

CLEANING AN OLD QUARRY-TILE FLOOR

Old quarry tiles are absorbent, so the floor becomes ingrained with dirt and grease. If normal washing with detergent fails to revitalize their color and finish, try one of the industrial preparations that cleaning and maintenance companies use. Suppliers of industrial tile-cleaning materials are often listed in the Yellow Pages. Describe the type and condition of the tiles to the supplier, who will be able to suggest the appropriate cleaner. Loosen stubborn grimy patches by scrubbing with a plastic scouring pad.

Removing ceramic tiles.
To remove old tiles, first chop out at least one of them with a cold chisel, then pry the others off the surface by driving a chisel behind them. Then chop away any remaining tile adhesive or mortar. Wear goggles to protect your eyes.

Removing ingrained dirt.
Scrub stubborn patches of grime with a plastic scouring pad.

Ceramic wall and floor tiles

Ceramic tiles are stuck to the wall or floor with a special adhesive or, in some cases, with mortar. Removing them in their entirety is messy and time consuming, but it is often the most satisfactory solution.

So long as a ceramic tiled wall is sound, you can paint it with a special-purpose primer and compatible gloss paint. Wash the surface thoroughly with a warm water and detergent solution, then apply the primer with a synthetic brush. Let it harden in a dry steam-free environment for a full 16 hours, then use a natural-bristle brush to apply the oil-based gloss paint.

You can lay new tiles directly over old ones, but make sure the surface is perfectly flat—check by holding a long level or straightedge across the surface. Tap the tiles to locate any loose ones and either glue them firmly in place or chop them out with a cold chisel and hammer and then fill the space with mortar. Wash the wall with water and detergent to remove grease and dirt.

It is also possible to tile over old quarry or ceramic floor tiles in the same way. Treat an uneven floor with a self-leveling compound. You can't cover old ceramic wall tiles with wallpaper. The adhesive cannot grip on such a shiny surface.

Ceiling tiles

Ceiling tiles are often stuck directly onto the surface with an adhesive that is difficult to remove. In the past, this adhesive was commonly applied in five small dabs, a method that is no longer approved due to the risk of fire. Now, tile manufacturers normally recommend that a complete bed of nonflammable adhesive be used.

Remove old tiles by prying them off with a wide-blade scraper and then scrape off the dabs of adhesive. Try to soften stubborn patches with warm water or wallpaper stripper, wearing goggles and gloves since it's difficult to avoid splashes.

One way to give old ceiling tiles a face-lift is to paint them—but never with an oil-based paint, which would increase the risk of fire spreading across the tiles. Instead, brush the tiles to remove dust and then apply latex paint.

Vinyl floor tiles

To take up vinyl floor tiles, soften the tiles and their adhesive with a heat gun on a low setting. Use a scraper to pry them up. Remove traces of old adhesive by applying a solution of half a cup of household ammonia and a drop of liquid detergent stirred into a bucket of cold water. When the floor is clean, rinse it with water.

If vinyl tiles are firmly glued to the floor, you can install new vinyl over them. The floor must be cleaned scrupulously, and any silicone-based polish should be removed with a suitable cleaner. You can use either self-sticking tiles or the type that requires a full coat of adhesive over the floor. Check with your tile supplier to see which type is best for your situation.

Cork wall tiles

Dense, prefinished cork wall tiles can be painted directly, provided that they are clean and firmly attached to the wall. Prime very absorbent cork with a general-purpose primer first, then paint over with two topcoats.

Unless the tiles are textured or pierced, you can install wallpaper over them. Just coat the surface with commercial sizing and a heavy-duty wallpaper paste. Then, apply lining paper to prevent the tile seams from showing and install the new wallpaper.

Acoustic ceiling tiles

Acoustic ceiling tiles can be painted with acrylic latex paint. Wash them lightly with water and mild detergent, but don't soak the tiles. Conceal stains with a stain-blocking primer before painting.

Applying finishes

In decorating terms, a finish means a liquid or semiliquid substance that dries or cures to protect, and sometimes color, materials such as wood or masonry. Apart from paint, finishes for wood include stains, varnishes, oil, wax, and French polish, all of which are used to display the natural beauty of wood grain.

The makeup of paint

Paint is made from solid particles of pigment suspended in a liquid binder or medium. The pigment provides the color and body of the paint, while the medium allows the material to be brushed, rolled, or sprayed; once applied, it forms a solid film binding the pigment together. Binder and pigment vary from paint to paint, but the two most common types are oil-based and water-based paint.

Common paint finishes and additives

The type of paint you choose depends on the finish you want and the material you are painting. Various additives modify the qualities of the paint.

Oil-based paints

The medium for oil-based paints is a mixture of oils and resin. A paint made from a natural resin is slow drying, but modern paints contain a synthetic resin, such as alkyd, that makes for a faster-drying finish. Various pigments determine the color of the paint.

Water-based paints

Latex is the most common water-based paint. It is made with synthetic resins similar to those in oil-based paint but dispersed in a solution of water.

Water-based paints are designed for use on the interior and exterior. In high-quality paint, titanium is used for the basic white pigment and other colors are added to this base.

Paint additives

No paint is made simply from binder and pigment. Certain additives are included during manufacture to give the paint qualities such as high gloss, faster drying time, easy flow, and longer pot life, or to make it nondrip.
● **Thixotropic** paints are the typical nondrip types. They are thick, almost jelly-like in the can, enabling you to pick up a brush load without dripping.
● **Extenders** are added as fillers to strengthen the paint film. Cheap paint contains too much filler, reducing its covering power

Paint thinners

If a paint is too thick, it cannot be applied properly and must be thinned before it is used. Some finishes may require special thinners provided by the manufacturer, but most oil-based paints can be thinned with mineral spirits, and latex paints with water. Turpentine will thin oil paint, but it has no advantages over mineral spirits for household paints and is more expensive.

Gloss or matte finish

The proportion of pigment to binder affects the way the paint sets. A gloss (shiny) paint contains approximately equal amounts of pigment and binder, whereas a higher proportion of pigment produces a flat (nonshiny) paint. By adjusting the proportions, it is possible to make satin or eggshell paints. Flat paints tend to cover best, due to their high pigment content, while the greater proportion of binder in gloss paints is responsible for their strength.

Unless you are using one of the specially formulated one-coat finishes, it is necessary to apply successive layers to build up a paint system.

● Painting walls requires a simple system, comprising two or three coats of the same paint.
● Painting woodwork and metalwork usually involves a more complex system, using paints with different qualities. A typical paint system for woodwork is illustrated below.

Bare wood
Sand surface smooth and seal any resinous knots with shellac.

Primer
A primer seals the wood and forms a base for other coats of paint.

Undercoat
This coat is usually the first topcoat. Any color close to the color of the topcoat can be used. The goal is to obliterate the color of the primer and start building a body of paint.

Topcoat
The final finish provides a wipe-clean colored surface.

A paint system for woodwork
Different types of paint are required to build a protective system for woodwork.

SAFETY WHEN PAINTING

Painting exterior masonry

Solvents in oil-based paint, particularly volatile organic compounds (VOCs), contribute to atmospheric pollution and can exacerbate conditions such as asthma. Because of this, it's preferable, when possible, to use paints and varnishes with low VOC emissions. Most manufacturers label their products to indicate the level of VOCs.

Take sensible precautions when using oil-based paints:

● Ensure good ventilation indoors while applying a finish and while it is drying. Wear a respirator if you suffer from breathing disorders.

● Don't smoke while painting or in the vicinity of drying paint.

● Contain paint spillages outside with sand or soil, and don't allow any paint to enter a sewer drain.

●● If you splash paint in your eyes, flush them with copious amounts of water, with your lids held open. See a doctor immediately.

●● Always wear gloves if you have sensitive skin. Use a skin cleanser to remove paint from your skin, or wash it off with warm soapy water. Don't use paint thinners to clean your skin.

● Keep all finishes and thinners out of reach of children. If a child swallows a substance, don't make any attempt to induce vomiting—seek medical treatment instead.

● **Disposing of unwanted paint.**
Before you wash your brushes and rollers, wipe them on newspaper to remove as much paint as possible. Ask your local authority about facilities for disposing of waste paint and cans.

Strain old paint.
If you are using leftover paint, filter it through a piece of muslin or old tights tied over the rim of a paint bucket.

Resealing the lid.
Wipe the rim of the can clean before you replace the lid. Tap a metal lid down all around with a hammer over a wood block.

Preparing paint

Whether you are using paint you've just bought, or some left over from a previous job, there are a few basic rules to observe before you apply it.

● Wipe dust from the paint can, then pry off the lid with a can-opening tool or a flat-blade screwdriver.

● Gently stir the paint with a wooden stick to blend the pigment and the medium. There's no need to stir thixotropic paints, unless the medium has separated; if you have to stir it, let it gel again before using.

● If a skin has formed on paint, cut around the edge with a knife and lift the skin out in one piece with a stick. It's a good idea to store the can upside down so a skin cannot form on top of the paint.

● If the paint is old, it should be strained before use. Just put a scrap piece of muslin over the lip of a paint bucket and tie it under the lip. Pour the old paint into the filter.

The outside walls of houses are painted for two main reasons: to give a bright, clean appearance, and to protect the surface from the weather. What you use as a finish and how you apply it depend on what the walls are made from, their condition, and the degree of protection they need. Bricks are traditionally left bare but may require a coat of paint if they've been painted before. Stuccoed walls are often painted to brighten the naturally dull, gray color of the cement; pebble-dashed surfaces may need a colorful coat to disguise unsightly patches. Or you may, of course, simply want to change the present color of your walls for a fresh appearance.

Working with a plan

Before you start painting outside masonry walls, plan your time carefully. Depending on the amount of preparation that is required, even a small house will take a few weeks to complete.

It is preferable, though, to tackle the whole job at once, since the weather may upset your timetable.

You can split the work into separate stages with days (or even weeks) in between, provided you divide the walls into manageable sections. Use window frames and doorframes, bays, and corners of walls to form break lines that will disguise joints.

Start at the top of the house, working from right to left, if you are right-handed.

● **Black dot denotes compatibility.**
All surfaces must be clean, sound, dry, and free from organic growth.

FINISHES FOR MASONRY

	Cement paint	Exterior latex paint	Reinforced latex paint	Solvent-thinned masonry paint	Textured coating	Floor paint
SUITABLE TO COVER						
Brick	●	●	●	●	●	●
Stone	●	●	●	●	●	●
Concrete	●	●	●	●	●	●
Stucco	●	●	●	●	●	●
Exposed-aggregate concrete	●	●	●	●	●	●
Asbestos cement	●	●	●	●	●	●
Latex paint	●	●	●	●	●	
Oil-based paint		●	●	●	●	●
Cement paint	●	●	●	●	●	●
DRYING TIME: HOURS						
Touch-dry	1–2	1–2	2–3	1–2	6	2–3
Recoatable	24	4	24	24	24–48	12–24
THINNERS: SOLVENTS						
Water-thinned	●	●	●		●	
Solvent-thinned				●		●
NUMBER OF COATS						
Normal conditions	2	2	1–2	2	1	1–2
COVERAGE: DEPENDING ON WALL TEXTURE						
Sq. ft. per quart		150–400	120–250	120–225		180–550
Sq. ft. per pound	30–75				20–40	
METHOD OF APPLICATION						
Brush	●	●	●	●	●	●
Roller	●	●	●	●	●	●
Spray gun	●	●	●	●		●

PAINTS SUITABLE FOR EXTERIOR MASONRY

There are various grades of paint suitable for painting and protecting exterior masonry that take into account economy, standard of finish, durability, and coverage. Use the chart on the facing page for quick reference.

Cement paint

Cement paint is supplied as a dry powder to which water is added. It is based on white cement, but pigments are added to produce a range of colors. Cement paint is one of the cheaper paints suitable for exterior use. Spray new or porous surfaces with water, then apply two coats.

Mixing cement paint

Shake or roll the container to loosen the powder, then add two parts of powder to one part of water in a clean bucket. Stir it to a smooth paste, then add a little more water until you get a full-bodied, creamy consistency. Don't mix more than you can use in an hour, or it will start to dry.

Adding an aggregate

When you're painting a wall that has been treated with a stabilizing solution so its porosity is substantially reduced, it's a good idea to add clean sand to the mix to give it body. This also provides added protection for an exposed wall and helps to cover dark colors. If the sand changes the color of the paint, add it to the first coat only. Use one part sand to four parts of powder, stirring it in when the paint is still in a pastelike consistency.

Masonry paints

When buying weather-resistant exterior-masonry paints, you have a choice between a smooth matte finish or a fine granular texture.

Water-based masonry paint

Most masonry paints are water based, with additives that prevent mold growth. Although they are supplied ready for use, on porous walls it pays to thin the first coat with 20 percent water. Follow up with one or two full-strength coats, depending on the color of the paint.

Water-based masonry paints must be applied during fairly good weather. Damp or humid conditions and low temperatures may prevent the paint from drying properly.

Solvent-based masonry paints

Some masonry paints are thinned with mineral spirits or with a special solvent. But unlike most oil paints they are moisture-vapor permeable, so that the wall is able to breathe. It is often best to thin the first coat with 15 percent mineral spirits, but check the manufacturer's recommendations.

Solvent-based paints can be applied in practically any weather conditions, provided it is not actually raining.

Reinforced masonry paint

Masonry paint that has powdered mica or a similar fine aggregate added to it dries with a textured finish that is extremely weatherproof. Reinforced masonry paints are especially suitable in coastal areas and in industrial areas, where dark colors are an advantage because dirt will not show up as clearly as on a pale background. Although large cracks and holes must be filled prior to painting, reinforced masonry paint will cover hairline cracks and crazing.

Textured coating

A thick textured coating applied to exterior walls forms a thoroughly weatherproof coating that can be painted over to match other colors. The usual preparation is necessary, and brickwork needs to be pointed flush. Large cracks should be filled, although a textured coating will cover fine cracks. The paste is either brushed or rolled onto the wall, then left to harden, forming an even texture. However, if you prefer, you can produce a texture of your choice using a variety of simple tools. It's a relatively easy process, but put in some practice on a small section first.

CONCRETE FLOOR PAINT

Floor paints are formulated to withstand hard wear. They are especially suitable for concrete garage or workshop floors, but they are also used for stone steps and other concrete structures. They can also be used inside for playroom floors.

The floor must be clean, dry, and free from oil or grease. If the concrete is freshly laid, allow it to mature for at least two months before painting. In most cases, it is advisable to prime powdery or porous floors with a concrete sealer, but check the manufacturer's recommendations first.

The best way to paint a large area is to use a paintbrush around the edges, then fit an extension handle to a paint roller for the bulk of the floor.

Apply paint with a roller on an extension handle

Paint in manageable sections.
You can't hope to paint an entire house in one session, so divide each side into manageable sections to disguise the joints. The horizontal molding divides the front of this house neatly into two sections, and the raised door and window trim form convenient break lines.

Techniques for painting masonry

1 Cut in with a gentle scrubbing motion

2 Protect downspouts with newspaper

3 Use a banister brush.
Tackle deeply textured
wall surfaces with a
banister brush.

Using the correct roller
When painting heavy
textures, use a roller
that has a deep pile.
Switch to a medium
pile for light textures
and smooth surfaces.

Spray gun
Rent a high-quality
spray gun and a small
portable compressor.

1 Spray onto the apex of outside corners

2 Spray inside corners as separate surfaces

Using paintbrushes

Choose a brush that is 4 to 6 inches wide for painting walls; larger ones are heavy and tiring to use. A good-quality brush with coarse bristles will last longer on rough walls. For effective coverage, apply the paint with vertical strokes, crisscrossed with horizontal ones. You will find it necessary to stipple paint into textured surfaces.

Cutting in
Painting up to features such as a door, window, and baseboard trim is known as cutting in. On a smooth surface, you should be able to paint a reasonably straight edge following the line of the trim—but it's difficult to apply the paint to a heavily textured wall with a normal brush stroke. Don't just apply more paint in the hope of overcoming the problem; instead, touch only the tip of the brush to the wall, using a

gentle scrubbing action (1), then brush out from the edge to spread excess paint once the texture is filled.

Wipe splashed paint from any trim with a cloth dampened with the appropriate thinner.

Painting behind downspouts
To protect downspouts, tape a piece of newspaper around them. Stipple behind the downspout with a brush (2), then move the newspaper down the pipe to mask the next section.

Painting with a banister brush
Use a banister brush (3) to paint deep textures such as pebble dash. Pour some paint into a roller tray and dip the brush in to load the bristles. Scrub the paint onto the wall, using circular strokes to work it into the uneven surface.

Using a paint roller

A roller will apply paint three times as fast as a brush. Use a deep-pile roller for heavy textures, and one with a medium pile for lightly textured or smooth walls. Rollers wear out very quickly on rough walls, so have a spare sleeve handy. When painting with a

roller, vary the angle of the stroke to ensure even coverage. Use a brush to cut into angles and obstructions.

A paint tray is difficult to use at the top of an extension ladder, unless you install a support bracket.

Using a spray gun

Spraying is the quickest and most efficient way to apply paint to a large expanse of wall. But you will have to mask all the areas you don't want to paint, using newspaper and masking tape, and set drop cloths to prevent overspray.

Thin the paint by about 10 percent, and set the spray gun according to the manufacturer's instructions to suit the particular paint. Make sure to wear a respirator.

Hold the gun about 9 inches away from the wall and keep it moving with even, parallel passes. Slightly overlap each pass and try to keep the gun pointing directly at the surface. Trigger the gun just before each pass, and release it at the end of the stroke.

To cover a large blank wall evenly, spray it with vertical bands of paint, overlapping each band by about 4 inches.

Spray outside corners by aiming the gun directly at the apex so that paint falls evenly on both surfaces (1). When two walls meet at an inside corner, spray each surface separately (2).

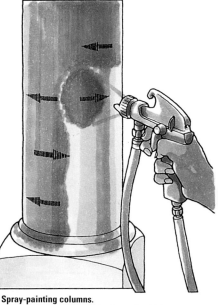

Spray-painting columns.
Columns on porches and porticos should be painted in a series of overlapping vertical bands. Apply the bands by running the spray gun from side to side as you work down the column.

Painting interior walls and ceilings

Unless your house is old, most of the interior walls and ceilings will be drywalled and painted or papered. Preparation varies, but the methods for painting plaster or drywall are identical, and they can be considered smooth surfaces in terms of paint coverage. A flat paint is usually preferred for wall and ceiling surfaces, but there's no reason why you can't use a gloss or satin finish.

Selecting paints for interior surfaces

Latex paint is most people's first choice for interior painting. It is relatively cheap and practically odorless, and there are different qualities of paint to suit different circumstances. However, some situations demand a combination of paints to provide the required degree of protection or simply to achieve a pleasing contrast of surface textures.

Latex paints

Acrylic latex paints are the most popular and practical paints for walls and ceilings. They are available in flat, satin (semigloss), and gloss finishes.

Flat paint doesn't reflect light as much as the others, and so it tends to hide drywall seams better. Satin paint is less likely to show fingerprints or scuffs than flat paint. And gloss paint is the most durable.

One-coat latex
If you want to avoid a patchy, uneven appearance, you need to apply two coats of a standard latex paint, thinning the first coat slightly when painting porous surfaces. A one-coat, high-opacity latex is intended to save you time. But often you'll get poor results, especially when painting over dark colors with a lighter color.

New-plaster latex
These paints are formulated for painting newly plastered interior walls and ceilings. They allow moisture and vapor to pass through. Standard latex paint is not as permeable.

Antimold latex
This low-odor paint contains a fungicide to ward off mold growth.

Latex paint is the obvious choice for walls and ceilings.

Gloss and satin paint

Paints primarily intended for woodwork can also be applied to walls and ceilings that require an extra degree of protection. Gloss paints tend to accentuate uneven wall and ceiling surfaces, so most people prefer a satin finish. But some people want the performance of a harder finish in bathrooms, kitchens, and hallways.

You can use any of the standard oil-based paints on walls and ceilings, and they yield very good results. But if low odor and fast drying are priorities, choose an acrylic latex paint.

Textured paints

Provided the masonry or drywall is basically sound, you can obliterate any unsightly cracks with just one coat of textured paint. A coarse high-build paint will cover cracks up to ⅟₁₆ inch wide. There are also fine-texture paints for areas where people are likely to brush against a wall. Available in either a flat or satin finish, the paint is normally applied with a coarse-foam roller. Use a synthetic-fiber roller if you want to create a finer texture.

Cement paint

This inexpensive exterior finish is also ideal for utilitarian areas indoors such as a cellar, garage, or workshop. Sold in dry-powder form, it has to be mixed with water and dries to a flat finish.

Paints for walls and ceilings
Latex paint is the most practical finish for interior walls and ceilings. But use an acrylic latex or oil-based paint on trim, doors, windows, wainscoting, and cabinetry in the kitchen and bathroom.

Finishes for bare masonry
Interior masonry walls may be left unfinished for the sake of appearance or for convenience in utility rooms such as a basement, workshop, or garage. Sometimes they are deliberately stripped for effect. A brick or stone chimney, for example, can act as an attractive focal point in a room, and an entire wall of bare masonry can make a dramatic impression.

If you want to finish brick, concrete, or stone walls, follow the methods described for exterior walls. However, because they do not have to withstand any weathering, you can use paints designed for interiors. Seal newly stripped masonry with a stabilizing primer, in order to bind the surface.

Using brushes, pads and rollers

Applying paint by brush

Choose a good-quality brush for painting walls and ceilings. Cheap brushes tend to shed bristles—which is annoying and also less economical in the long run. A brush about 8 inches wide will allow you to cover a surface relatively quickly, but if you are not used to handling a large brush your wrist will soon tire. You may find a 4- or 6-inch brush, plus a 2-inch brush for the edges and corners, more comfortable to use. However, the job will take longer.

Loading the brush
Don't overload a brush with paint; it leads to messy work and ruins the bristles if the paint is allowed to dry in the roots. Dip no more than the first third of the brush into the paint, wiping off excess on the inside of the container to prevent drips **(1)**.

Using a brush
You can hold the brush whichever way feels comfortable to you, but the "pen" grip is the most versatile, enabling your wrist to move the brush freely in any direction. Hold the brush handle between your thumb and forefinger, with your fingers on the metal ferrule and your thumb supporting it from the other side **(2)**.

Apply the paint in vertical strokes, then spread it at right angles to even out the coverage. Don't flick the brush, as this will usually cause splatters. Latex paint doesn't tend to show brush marks when it's dry, but oil-based paints do. Because of this, finish oil paints with light upward vertical strokes. This will smooth out the brush strokes and leave a more uniform finish.

1 Dip only the first third of the bristles into the paint.

2 Place fingers on ferrule, and the thumb behind.

Applying paint by roller

A paint roller with an interchangeable sleeve cover is an excellent tool for applying paint to large areas. Choose a roller about 9 inches long for painting walls and ceilings. Larger ones are available, but they can become tiring to use.

There are a number of different sleeves to suit the type of paint and the texture of the surface being painted. Deep-pile sheepskin and synthetic-fiber sleeves are excellent on textured surfaces, especially when applying latex paint. Choose a shorter pile for smooth surfaces, and when using gloss or satin paints. Disposable foam rollers can be used to apply some specialty paints, but tend to skid across the wall.

Special rollers
Rollers with long, detachable extension handles are ideal for painting ceilings

without having to use ladders or scaffolding. Narrow rollers are invaluable for painting behind radiators .

Loading a roller
You will need a paint tray to load a standard roller. Having dipped the sleeve lightly into the paint reservoir, roll it gently onto the ribbed part of the tray to coat the roller evenly **(1)**.

Using a roller
Use zigzag strokes with a roller **(2)**, painting the surface in all directions to achieve even coverage. Keep the roller on the surface at all times—if you let it spin at the end of a stroke, it will splatter paint onto the floor or adjacent surfaces. When applying oil-based paint, finish in one direction, preferably toward prevailing light.

1 Dip roller in paint, then roll it on the ribbed tray.

2 Apply in zigzags, but finish in one direction.

Applying paint by pad

Loading a paint pad. Load the pad evenly by drawing it gently across the tray roller.

Paint pads for large surfaces have flat rectangular faces covered with a short mohair pile. A foam backing gives the pad flexibility so that the pile will always be in contact with the wall, even on a rough surface.

The exact size of the pad will be determined by the brand you choose, but one about 8 inches long is best for applying paint evenly and smoothly to walls and ceilings. You will also need a small pad or paintbrush for cutting in at corners and ceilings.

Loading a pad
Some paint pads come with a special tray. To load the paint, just draw the pad across the captive roller so that you pick up an even amount **(left)**.

Using a paint pad
To apply the paint consistently, keep the pad flat on the wall and sweep it gently and evenly in any direction **(right)**. However, to prevent streaking, finish with vertical strokes when using oil-based paints.

Sweep pad gently in any direction.

Applying paint

Even the most experienced painter can't help dripping a little paint, so always paint the ceiling before the walls. Use a step ladder or erect a work platform, placing it so that you can cover as much of the surface as possible without changing position. Work carefully to achieve a better finish.

● Black dot denotes compatibility.
All surfaces must be clean, sound, dry, and free from organic growth.

FINISHES FOR INTERIOR WALLS & CEILINGS

	Latex paint	Reinforced latex paint	Oil-based paint	Undercoat	Primer/ undercoat	Cement paint	Textured coating
SUITABLE TO COVER							
Plaster	●	●	●	●	●		●
Wallpaper	●		●		●		●
Brick	●	●	●	●	●		●
Stone	●	●	●	●	●		●
Concrete	●	●	●	●	●	●	
Previously painted surface	●	●	●	●	●		●
DRYING TIME: HOURS							
Touch-dry	1–2	2–3	4–5	4	½	1–2	6
Recoatable	4	24	16	16	2	24	24–48
THINNERS: SOLVENTS							
Water	●	●				●	●
Mineral spirits			●	●	●		
NUMBER OF COATS							
Normal conditions	2	1–2	1–2	1–2	1–2	2	1
COVERAGE: APPROXIMATE							
Sq. ft. per gallon	350–400	175–200	400–500	500–600	500		
Sq. ft. per pound						30–75	10–20
METHOD OF APPLICATION							
Brush	●	●	●	●	●	●	●
Roller	●	●	●	●	●	●	●
Paint pad	●		●		●		
Spray	●	●	●	●	●	●	

Painting the walls

Use a small brush to paint the edges, starting at a top corner of the room. If you are right-handed, work from right to left, and vice versa. Paint an area about 2 feet square at a time. When using latex paint, you can work in horizontal bands (1); but apply oil paints in vertical strips (2), because the brush marks are less likely to show this way. Always finish a complete wall before you take a break, otherwise a change of tone may show between separate sections.

1 Paint latex in horizontal bands

2 Apply oil-based paints in vertical strips

ELECTRICAL FITTINGS

Remember to turn off the power before exposing electrical connections.

Painting around electrical outlets

Unscrew a ceiling fixture so you can paint right up to the ceiling opening with a small brush. Remove the coverplates on switches and receptacles so you can paint behind them.

Unscrew ceiling fixture to paint underneath.

Remove coverplates from receptacles and switches.

Painting the ceiling

Starting in a corner, carefully paint along the edges of the ceiling with a small paintbrush.

Paint around the edges first

Starting from the wet edges, paint in bands 2 feet wide, working toward the center of the room. Whether you are using a brush, pad, or roller, apply each fresh load of paint just clear of the previous band, then blend in the two for even coverage.

Blend in the wet edges

Decorative paint effects

In recent years, there has been a resurgence of interest in using paint to create decorative effects. When applied to walls, ceilings, floors, woodwork, and furniture—in fact, any surface to which paint will adhere—these colorful treatments add individuality to any decorating scheme. Some of the more complex effects, which were traditionally the domain of the skilled craftsman, are now easier to achieve using a range of modern tools and materials that are readily available.

Farmhouse kitchen
(below)
Rustic charm is created by colorwashing the walls with two tones of yellow paint, and then superimposing a simple geometric frieze, applied with a homemade stamp.

Practice before you begin

Before embarking on a major project, take the time to select the most appropriate style and colors for your interior. Collect as many color charts as you can and try out any sample colors that your paint store may be willing to supply.

Although many of the techniques are easy to master, it is worth practicing on a piece of board before you tackle an entire room. The texture of the wall itself may influence the finished effect, but at least you will be familiar with the basic techniques. If you don't like the results, paint over the sample and try again.

Although many paint effects can be applied successfully to woodwork, some look better when applied to a flat drywall or plaster surface. Thorough preparation is essential, as with any form of painting. All the following finishes require a flat basecoat, in your choice of color. Apply this initial coat with a brush, pad, or roller. Let it dry completely.

Distressed finish
(above)
It is easy to give newly painted furniture a worn appearance. Let the topcoat dry, then rub through to the underlying color using medium-grit abrasive paper.

Tools and materials for special effects

You can achieve satisfactory results using a selection of ordinary paintbrushes, a sponge or two, and some lint-free rags. But if you plan to move on to the more advanced paint effects, it would be worth investing in the special equipment now available from paint suppliers and some DIY stores. Certain tools and materials are packaged together as kits, but it often pays to buy individual items as you need them.

Paints and glazes

Broken-color decorative effects are based on a two-part paint system. The first layer is a basecoat of opaque paint, usually an eggshell or satin finish, although gloss paint can also be used. Flat paints are not recommended because they are too absorbent. White paint is commonly used as a base for pale shades, or as a background to brightly colored finishes. Colored basecoats are also used to create harmonious or contrasting effects.

When the basecoat is dry, a topcoat of semitransparent colored glaze is applied and then textured using a variety of techniques. Traditional oil-based paints and glazes are available, but water-based acrylic latex materials dry faster and are practically odorless. A clear, flat or satin topcoat is often applied over the paint for protection.

Color choice

You can make your own colors by tinting white latex paint or glaze with pigments, stains, or artist's paints. But it's more convenient to choose colors from one of the standard color charts. You can also have the paint tinted by your paint supplier.

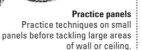

Practice panels
Practice techniques on small panels before tackling large areas of wall or ceiling.

Equipment checklist

Color pigments
Traditionally, powdered pigments were used for coloring all kinds of paints and glazes. Although these are still available from art shops, artist's oil or acrylic paints are easier to use when mixing your own colors, and they are available in a wider range of colors.

Solvents
Solvents are used to dilute or thin paints, to make them easier to work with or to reduce their opacity. They are also used for cleaning paint from brushes and other equipment. Water is used to thin latex paints, and mineral spirits are used for oil-based paints.

Paintbrushes
Paintbrushes ranging from 1 to 6 inches wide will meet most needs. For fine work, supplement these with a selection of artist's paintbrushes. Choose brushes that are compatible with oil paint or latex, and keep them in good condition by rinsing them thoroughly in the appropriate solvent. Finish by washing your brushes in a mild solution of soap and water.

Special-effects brushes
Special brushes are used to manipulate the glaze and create different effects. Long-bristle brushes, known as dragging brushes and floggers, make linear marks and wood-grain effects. Wide colorwash brushes quickly cover an area with paint. Stippling brushes have short hair or plastic bristles for creating textures in glaze. You can use the same brushes for stippling colored paint onto a surface.

Rollers
Rollers are ideal for applying an even coat of paint to large areas. You will need a 9-inch, medium-pile roller for the main areas, and a 4-inch roller for narrow strips.

Special rollers are made for creating effects similar to those produced traditionally with rags and sponges. These rollers are run over a glaze topcoat while it is still workable, producing broken-color effects.

Painting accessories
You will need various containers, such as a paint bucket, screw-top jars, and some old plates to use as palettes for mixing colors. Protect the floor with drop cloths, and use masking tape to create hard-edge effects. When working, wear old clothes, rubber gloves, and a face mask.

Stamps and stencils
Stamps and stencils are used to apply decorative designs or to make a repeat pattern on a painted surface. Stamps are used to imprint designs, and stencils are used to mask off background areas before the color is applied. You can either buy designs or make your own.

Sponges
Use sponges to create random stippled effects. Natural sea sponges, which are available in large and small sizes, produce attractive textures. Synthetic sponges do not perform as well, but you can make interesting marks with plastic sponges torn or cut into different shapes.

Rags and sheet plastic
Lint-free rags and soft sheet plastic are used to create textures, in processes known as rag rolling and bag graining. Similar effects can be produced using a ball of chamois leather.

61

Colorwashing and dragging

Colorwashing

Colorwashing is one of the faster ways of creating a paint effect. It is frequently employed to create Mediterranean-style decor, and provides a useful means of disguising uneven wall surfaces. It can also be applied to gloss-painted woodwork.

Make sure the wall is dry, and prepare the surface thoroughly before painting with a latex paint of your chosen color. Apply the paint with a roller or brush and allow it to dry.

Stir the special-effect paint or glaze as recommended by the manufacturer, and pour a sufficient amount to cover one wall into a paint bucket. Dip the colorwash brush into the glaze and wipe off the excess, then test the paint on a sample board. If it's too thick,

thin it slightly by stirring in a little solvent.

Plan to finish a whole wall in one session. Apply the paint to the wall, covering an area about 3 feet square at a time and working quickly to maintain a wet edge. Use broad brush strokes, varying the angle as you go, to form an irregular crisscross pattern. It doesn't matter if you leave some bare patches showing. But don't allow the paint to dry around the edges, or it will show as a solid band and spoil the free-brush-stroke effect. Finish each brush load before reloading with paint.

When the paint is dry, apply a second coat in a similar way, using the same color or a different one.

Vary the brush strokes when colorwashing

Dragging

Learn to drag the paint if you want a more controlled linear effect. The brush marks are usually applied vertically, but they can be run horizontally; if you are feeling ambitious, use a combination of strokes with one or two colors.

Prepare and paint the walls with latex as described for colorwashing. Then leave them to dry. Apply the special-effect paint or glaze with a roller in even bands about 2 feet wide. Using a dry dragging brush, or a wide paintbrush held at a low

angle to the surface, draw the bristles through the wet paint in one continuous stroke from top to bottom. Wipe off excess paint, then repeat the process alongside the first stripe. Continue along the surface, blending in the edges while they are still wet—it's helpful to have an assistant apply the bands of color with a roller while you follow up with the dragging brush. You can treat the wall in a single color, or use masking tape to create bands of color for a striped effect.

Drag the brush with one continuous stroke

Frescoed walls
A rough, plastered-wall effect can be created by applying a textured coating with a roller or brush and then working it into a troweled effect using a spreader. This coating is designed for use with colorwash.

Mediterranean decor
(below)
A sun-baked wall made by applying a single wash of orange paint over two masked areas of warm color.

Linear texture
(below right)
Dragging a brush through colored glaze leaves a linear texture.

Stippled paint effects

Stippling

Stippling creates an attractive paint effect suitable for walls, woodwork, and furniture. Prepare the surfaces and apply a basecoat, then stipple textures onto the background color with either a natural sponge or a stippling brush. For a two-tone effect, stipple a dark paint over a lighter base color. When selecting the paint, bear in mind that the base color will be the dominant color in the room.

Wear rubber gloves when sponge stippling. Dip a sponge in water until it swells to its full size, then squeeze out the excess water, leaving the sponge moist. Pour a small amount of paint into a paint tray and dip the sponge into it. Touch off excess paint in the tray and blot the sponge on a

piece of scrap paper until it begins to make the required mottled effect. Then apply the sponge lightly to the wall. Don't press too hard, or the sponge will leave a patch of almost solid color.

Cover a manageable area with randomly spaced dabs of color, then fill in the gaps to form an even texture across the wall. Press different parts of the sponge to the wall to avoid a repetitive pattern. If any area appears too dark when dry, stipple the base color over it to tone it down.

When the first stipple coat has dried, sponge another tone or color over it. Step away from the wall occasionally to check that the texture is even. With a stippling brush, paint is applied in a similar way.

Make subtle textures with sponge stippling

Roller sleeves
There are many types of roller sleeves available, including special textured sleeves that allow you to produce large areas of stippling quickly.

Rag stippling

Although the technique is similar, stippling with a cotton rag instead of a sponge produces a bolder effect. Wearing rubber gloves, crumple a piece of rag into a ball and dip it into the paint until the rag is saturated. Squeeze it out and stipple with a creased part of the ball onto scrap paper. When you achieve the required

effect, apply the rag lightly to the wall in a random pattern.

Use different parts of the ball as you work across the wall, refolding it to vary the pattern. Don't let the rag skid on the surface. Once the first stipple coat is dry, you can stipple out mistakes, using a clean rag dipped in the base color.

Rag stippling creates a bold pattern

Sponge stippling
Apply a delicate stipple texture by patting a paint-dampened sponge on the wall.

Stippling off

Just as paint can be applied with a sponge, brush, or rag, so a similar action will remove color and create a reverse-pattern effect. Apply the top coat over the basecoat with a roller, covering an area of about 3 square feet at a time. Dab off the paint to reveal the basecoat color.

Multicolor stippling
This vibrant effect was produced by stippling several colors, one over the other, using a natural sponge.

Rag stippling
Create a stronger textured effect with a crumpled cotton rag.

Stippling-off brush
Use a special brush to create a reverse-pattern effect by removing some of the color.

Bag graining and rag rolling

Bag graining

Stipple off with a rag-filled plastic bag.

Bag graining is similar to rag stippling, but removes paint from the wall instead of applying it. The effect works well if you apply a darker paint over a pale-colored background. It is more efficient if one person applies the paint while another patterns it.

Apply the basecoat and allow it to dry. Pour paint or glaze in a paint-roller tray. You can dilute latex paint with about 50 percent water. Just be sure to mix enough to cover at least one complete wall at a time. If necessary, use newspaper and masking tape to cover areas you don't want to paint.

Use a wide brush to apply the paint over the base color, making sure there are no runs. After you have applied a band of paint about 2 feet wide, take a plastic bag half filled with rags and use it to stipple the wet paint. Overlap each impression to produce an even texture. As paint builds up on the bag, wipe it off onto a rag or paper towel. Your helper should work just ahead of you, applying fresh paint for you to texture before it dries. Bagging rollers are also available to help texture walls quickly.

Two-tone pattern produced by bag graining

Rag rolling

Putting paint on
As an alternative to the usual rag-rolling technique, you can immerse a rag in paint, squeeze it out, and then roll the rag across the wall.

Rag rolling is a popular paint effect, similar in appearance to bag graining and rag stippling. As with other treatments, you will need an assistant to help you paint large areas. You can use latex or oil-based satin paints. Start with a pale-colored basecoat overlaid with a darker color. Or, begin with the darker color and finish with a paler one. Try different combinations on sample boards.

Apply the basecoat and allow it to dry. Continue by applying a band of topcoat, then fold a piece of rag into quarters and twist it into a roll. Starting at the bottom of the wall, roll the rag upward to remove some of the wet paint; by varying the direction, you can produce a texture resembling silk wallcovering.

When you reach the ceiling, if you accidentally blot it, remove the paint immediately with a clean rag dampened with solvent.

Start the next band of texturing at the bottom again, but don't attempt to produce regular strips of color. Change direction constantly to overlap and blend with the previous strip. Re-form the rolled rag each time it becomes saturated with paint.

You can also use a shredded chamois-cloth rag made specifically for rag rolling, or create a similar texture with special-effect rollers.

Rag rolling resembles silk wallcoverings

Bag graining
(far left)
Stippling wet paint with a rag-filled plastic bag tends to move the color around on the surface.

Rag rolling
(left)
Standard rag-rolling removes the wet topcoat to reveal the darker basecoat.

Spattering, speckling and stamping

Spattering and speckling

Spattered paint treatments, which are often used to decorate commercial premises, can be just as effective in your own home. You can achieve an overall speckled texture by spattering two or three contrasting colors onto a latex background. Plan your color scheme using the background as the dominant color.

Cover the floor with large drop cloths and mask off doors, windows, and electrical fittings. Be sure to wear protective clothing and goggles when spattering.

For the spatter colors, use oil-based paints thinned to the required consistency, which is best found through trial and error on a practice board. Don't make the paint too thin, or the intended spatter effect will become a mass of runs. If you have an accident, blot the paint immediately with a paper towel and allow it to dry. Obliterate the mistake by dabbing with a sponge dipped in the base color.

Pour out some paint into a paint tray. Take a stiff-bristle banister brush and dip only the tips of the bristles into the paint. Holding the brush about 4 inches from the wall, drag a ruler toward you, across the bristles. This flicks tiny drops of paint onto the surface. Produce an even or random coverage as you prefer, but avoid concentrating the effect in one place. When the first spatter coat is dry, apply the other colors you want.

Speckled paint sprayed from an aerosol
Furniture, picture frames, and other small objects can be decorated with speckled paint sprayed from an aerosol can. Prepare the surface following the manufacturer's instructions. Holding the can upright, not less than 1 foot from the work, spray on a light coat of paint. Some paints should be protected with a compatible, transparent acrylic topcoat. Check the manufacturer's recommendations.

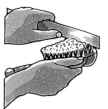

Spattering paint
Produce a spattered effect by drawing a ruler across a stiff-bristle brush.

Spattering creates an even, textured effect

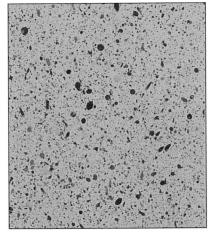

Marking out or eyeballing
It is essential to mark out a wall accurately if you intend to stamp it neatly with a regular pattern *(right)*. When stamping a pattern by eye *(below)*, slight irregularities simply add to the effect.

Stamping

Use stamping to create all-over decorative patterns, borders, or individual effects. If you don't want to use one of the many ready-made stamps, you can cut your own from stiff foam plastic. The simplest way to make a homemade stamp is to photocopy an image and attach it to the foam with low-tack adhesive. Then cut around the image, remove the waste, and peel off the paper pattern.

If you want to decorate your walls with a regular pattern or border, draw guidelines on the surface or use masking tape. Pour a little paint into a tray and dip your stamp into it. Wipe off any excess paint, then test the stamp on clean paper or cardboard. Apply the stamp to the surface, following your guide marks. Dip the stamp in paint as necessary. Don't worry if some of the impressions are less than perfect—a slight difference in surface texture is part of the charm.

Stamping kits contain all you need to get started

Stenciled paint effects

Stenciling

You can paint patterns and designs onto walls and furniture using ready-made paper or plastic stencils. They are available from craft stores and some artist suppliers. If you can't find a stencil that suits your purpose, buy blank sheets of stencil paper from the same outlets, and cut your own design with a sharp mat knife **(1)**. Design your stencil, leaving thin strips between the cutouts to hold the shapes together.

You can buy small jars of acrylic paint for stenciling, but ordinary latex paint works well, too. Unless you intend to spray paint from an aerosol can, you will need a sponge or a special stencil brush that has short, stiff bristles and is used with a stippling action **(2)**.

Lightly mark out the wall to help position the stencil accurately. At the same time, make small marks to indicate the position of repeat patterns. Use small pieces of masking tape to hold the stencil on the wall, or spray the back of the stencil with a low-tack adhesive.

Spoon a little paint onto a flat board, then take a stencil brush and touch the tips of the bristles into the paint. Stipple excess paint onto scrap paper until it deposits paint evenly, then transfer the brush to the wall. Use a sponge in a similar way.

With the stencil held flat against the wall, stipple the edges first, then fill in the center. If necessary, apply a second coat immediately to build up the required depth of color. If you want the design to look three-dimensional, add a shading effect on one side using a darker color. When the design is complete, carefully peel the stencil away from the wall. Wipe traces of paint from the back of the stencil before repositioning it to repeat the pattern.

If paint has crept under the stencil, try dabbing it off with a piece of paper towel rolled into a thin tapered coil. Touch up the background paint if necessary.

Etched-glass effect
Using stencils and a spray can of translucent etching paint, you can create an etched-glass effect on glass or mirrored panels. Mask the area with the stencil and spray the glass with the fast-drying paint. Peel off the stencil to reveal a simulated etched design.

1 Cutting a stencil

2 Stippling with paint

Night sky
(right)
Stipple star and planet designs onto a dark background, using opaque acrylic or metallic paints.

Painting straight edges

Use low-tack masking tape, available in various widths, when you want to paint a band of color or a neat straight edge along a painted panel. This type of masking tape can be peeled off without damaging the painted surface beneath. Never use ordinary transparent adhesive tape.

Marking the lines
Draw straight horizontal lines using a board and a level as a guide. Vertical lines can be marked on a wall by drawing plumb lines with the same board and level.

Painting the edges
Run masking tape along one side of the marked line, taking care not to stretch or twist the tape. Using a small brush, paint away from the tape so that a thick edge of paint does not build up against it. Complete the rest of the area with a roller or larger paintbrush.
Peel off the tape when the paint is dry to the touch. Pull back and away from the edge to leave a clean line. If you happen to pull away specks of paint, touch up the areas with an artist's paintbrush.

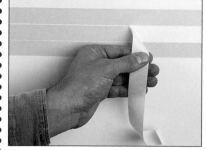

Painting a band of color
To paint a horizontal stripe, complete the background, then mask the top and bottom of the band. Apply the paint, and once it is dry to the touch, remove both tapes.
You can also apply three strips of tape butted side by side. Peel away the central tape, leaving a gap between two masked edges, ready for painting.

Decorating with paint effects

Clouding
(top left)
Similar to colorwashing, this effect is produced by taking a damp rag dipped in colored glaze and rubbing it across the wall, using circular strokes, rather like polishing a window.

Washed over
(top right)
Here the wall was painted with flat color, then stenciled with shell motifs. After the stenciling had dried, the entire wall was colorwashed. The wainscoting was stippled heavily with a sponge.

Combined effect
(left)
A lot of creative energy has been expended on this room. Every surface is either sponged, color-washed, dragged, or stenciled.

67

Creating marbled effects

Marbling

Producing marble effects

Producing a marble-like effect with paint is not an easy technique to master, so be prepared to experiment on a practice board until you achieve a convincing result. It is probably best to confine marbling to small areas such as fireplace mantels or wall panels, but it can be used extensively for a grand decorative treatment. Study some examples of marble, taking note of the basic colors, tones, and markings; then choose a limited color range to produce a variety of similar hues.

Oil paints are traditionally used for marbling because they take a long time to dry. It's necessary to work the whole effect with wet paint, and oil paints blend extremely well. Artist's oil paints are relatively inexpensive for mixing with glazes, but for large areas you should use ordinary satin oil-based paint. However, if you find the smell of oil paint unpleasant, there are slow-drying, decorative-effect acrylic paints, which you can modify using tubes of artist's acrylic paints.

Laying the foundation

Prepare the surface and apply a basecoat to approximate the background color of the marble. While this is drying, make up a colored glaze to be used as a medium for the marbling paints. Apply a coat of the glaze to the background, using a clean, lint-free rag. Rub it evenly over the surface. A light coating will produce the best result.

Applying a mottled pattern

Buy or mix one or two colored glazes. Then, using a 1-inch paintbrush, paint uneven patches onto the surface. Apply the marks randomly, overlapping colors and tones. Take the rag used to apply the glaze and stipple the patches, to blend them in and to lose any distinct edges.

Complete the mottled effect with a wide, soft-bristled paintbrush, sweeping it very gently back and forth across the surface to produce delicately softened areas of shaded color. Adjust areas that appear too dark by wiping off patches of color, then retouch and blend them in again.

Painting veined marble

Use an artist's paintbrush or a large feather to draw the veins, with glazes of contrasting tones or colors. Veins should be painted freely, with varying thicknesses of line. Note carefully the branching fine lines typical of real marble veining.

Blot any thick paint with a paper towel, then blur the veins by brushing back and forth with a soft, dry paintbrush until they appear as subtle, soft-edged lines.

Sealing with varnish

Allow the marbled paintwork to dry thoroughly, then paint on a coat of compatible satin varnish. When the varnish is hard, burnish the surface with a soft cloth to raise a delicate sheen. If necessary, you can modify the finish by applying a little wax polish.

Mottled effects suggest some types of marble

Boldly painted strokes resemble marble veining

Painting a basecoat
Choose a color that approximates the overall background color of the marble you like.

Paints for marbling
Artist's oil paints are the best colors for mixing with glazes, but for marbling large areas you could use ordinary satin-finish latex paint.

Freely applied marbling
(right)
A simple marbled effect enlivens a wood staircase.

Textured coatings

You can apply this coating using a roller or a broad wall brush, but finer textures are possible with the brush. Buy a special roller if recommended by the coating manufacturer.

With a well-loaded roller, apply a generous coat in a band 2 feet wide across the ceiling or down a wall. Don't press too hard, and vary the angle of the stroke.

If you decide to brush the coating on, don't spread it out like paint. Instead, lay it on with one stroke and spread it back again with one or two strokes only.

Texture the first band, then apply a second band and blend them together before texturing the latter. Continue in this way until the wall or ceiling is complete. Keep the room ventilated until the coating has hardened.

Painting around fittings.
Use a small paintbrush to fill in around electrical fixtures and outlets, trying to copy the texture used on the surrounding wall or ceiling. Some people prefer to form a distinct margin around fixtures by drawing a small paintbrush along the perimeter to give a smooth finish.

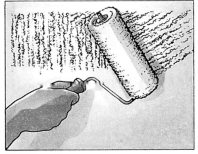

Creating a texture.
You can experiment with a variety of tools to make any number of textures. Try a coarse foam roller or one made with a special surface to produce diagonal or diamond patterns. Alternatively, apply a swirling, ripple, or stipple finish with improvised equipment, as shown on the right.

Textured coatings can be purchased as dry powder for mixing with warm water or in a ready-mixed form for direct application from the container. They are available in a range of standard colors, but if none of them suits your decorative scheme you can use ordinary latex paint as a coloring agent. Textured coatings are suitable for both exterior and interior walls.

Using rollers, scrapers, or improvised tools, you can produce a variety of textures. It's best to restrict distinctly raised textures with sharp edges to areas where you are unlikely to rub against the wall. Create finer textures for children's rooms, small bathrooms, and narrow hallways.

Preparation for textured coatings

New surfaces will need virtually no preparation, but joints between drywall panels must be reinforced with tape first. Strip any wallcoverings, and rough up gloss paint with sandpaper. Old walls and ceilings must be clean, dry, sound, and free from mildew. Treat brittle surfaces with stabilizing primer.

Although large cracks and holes must be filled, a textured coating will conceal minor defects in walls and ceilings by filling small cracks and bridging shallow bumps and hollows.

Masking woodwork and fixtures
Use masking tape 2 inches wide to cover the edges of door and window frames, baseboards, electrical fixtures, and any wainscoting. Lay drop cloths over the floor.

● **Filling a texture.**
If you inherit a textured surface that is not to your liking, you can smooth it with a skim coat of textured paint. Just roll it on and smooth it with a plasterer's trowel.

Creating textures and patterns.
(from left to right)

Geometric patterns
Use a roller with diamond or diagonal grooves. Load the roller and draw lightly across the textured surface.

Stippled finish
Pat the coating with a damp sponge to create a pitted profile. Rinse out frequently. Alter your wrist angle and overlap sections.

Random swirls
Twist a damp sponge on the textured surface, then pull away to make a swirling design. Overlap swirls for a layered effect.

Combed arcs
A toothed spatula sold with the finish is used to create combed patterns, such as arcs, crisscross patterns, or wavy scrolls.

Tree-bark effect
To produce a bark texture, use a special spiral-grooved roller.

Stucco finish
Apply parallel roller strokes, then run the rounded corner of a spatula over the coating in short, straight strokes.

Finishing woodwork

Paint is the most common finish for woodwork in and around the house, offering as it does a protective coating in a choice of colors and surface finishes. However, stains, varnishes, lacquers, and polishes give an attractive, durable finish, enhancing the color of the woodwork without obliterating the beauty of its grain. When choosing a finish, bear in mind the location of the woodwork and the amount of wear it is likely to get.

A natural appearance
A pine staircase in exceptional condition finished with linseed oil.

Top to bottom
1 Oil-based gloss paint
2 Oil-based satin paint
3 Latex gloss paint
4 Unsealed wood stain
5 Protected wood stain
6 Colored preservative
7 Satin polyurethane varnish
8 Lacquer
9 Oil finish
10 Wax polish

Choosing wood finishes

The list below gives a wide range of finishes for protecting and decorating woodwork. Each has qualities to suit a particular purpose, although many can be used simply for their attractive appearance rather than for any practical considerations. This will depend, however, on the location of the woodwork, because some finishes are much more durable than others. Consider wear and tear before making a decision.

Solvent-based paints
Traditional oil-based paints are available in high-gloss, satin, and flat finishes. Indoors, they will last for years, with an occasional cleaning to remove finger marks and other stains. One or two undercoats are essential, especially outside, where durability is considerably reduced by the action of sun and rain. Outdoors, you should plan on repainting every six to seven years.

A one-coat paint, with its creamy consistency and high-pigment content, can protect primed wood or cover existing colors (as long as the new paint is darker than the old) without undercoating. Apply the paint liberally, and allow it to flow freely rather than brushing it out like a conventional oil paint.

Low-odor, solvent-based finishes have largely reduced the smell and fumes associated with drying paint.

Latex paints
These have several advantages over conventional oil paint. Being water-based, they are nonflammable, practically odorless, and constitute less of a risk to your health and to the environment. They also dry very quickly, so that a job can often be completed in a single day. This means, however, that you'll have to work swiftly when painting outside in direct sunlight, to avoid leaving brush marks in the rapidly drying paintwork.

As long as they are applied to adequately prepared surfaces, latex paints form a tough yet flexible coating that resists cracking and peeling. As with other water-based finishes, however, latex paints will not dry satisfactorily if they are applied on a damp or humid day. Even under perfect conditions, don't expect to achieve a high-gloss finish that is as shiny as oil-based enamel.

Wood stains
Unlike paint, which, after the initial priming coat, rests on the surface of wood, a stain penetrates the wood. Its main advantage is to enhance the natural color of the woodwork, or to unify the slight variations in color found even within the same species.

Water-based and oil-based stains are available ready for use. You can also buy powdered pigments for mixing your own. Most common stains don't actually protect the wood. To provide real protection you have to cover the stain with a clear topcoat, usually either varnish or polyurethane.

Protective wood stains
The natural color of wood can be enhanced with protective wood stains. Moisture-vapor permeable stains allow the wood to breathe while providing a weather-resistant finish that resists flaking and peeling.

Protective wood stains should be brushed onto the wood. Some wood-stain manufacturers recommend two to three coats, while others offer a one-coat finish. Exterior stains are usually available in either semi-transparent or opaque versions. The first allows the wood grain to show through. The latter colors the surface of the wood and also penetrates, so you can see the grain texture but not the color. Water-based stains dry faster than oil-based products.

Colored preservatives
Sometimes fencing, siding, and outbuildings tend to look a little too formal when painted, yet they need protection. In these situations, use a wood preservative, which penetrates deeply into the wood to prevent rot and insect attack. Clear preservatives are available in a range of natural wood colors.

Traditional preservatives have a strong, unpleasant smell and are harmful to plants, whereas most modern low-odor products are perfectly safe for all applications.

Varnishes
Varnish is a clear protective coating for wood. Most modern varnishes are made with polyurethane resins to provide a waterproof, scratchproof, and heat-resistant finish. They come in high-gloss, satin, or flat finishes.

Exterior-grade varnishes are more weather-resistant, and some of them, including spar varnish, are tough enough to cope with coastal climates and polluted urban environments.

Some varnishes are designed to provide a clear finish with a hint of color. They are available in the normal wood shades, and some stronger colors. Unlike a wood stain, a colored varnish does not sink into the wood, so there may be loss of color in areas of heavy wear or abrasion unless you apply additional coats of clear varnish to seal the top.

Fast-drying acrylic varnishes have an opaque, milky appearance when applied but are clear and transparent when dry.

Lacquer
This coating is mixed with a hardener just before it is used. It is extremely durable (even on floors) and is resistant to heat and alcohol. The standard type dries to a high gloss, which can be burnished to a satin finish if desired. There is also a flat-finish lacquer, though a smooth, flat surface can be obtained by rubbing down the gloss coating with fine steel wool. Black, white, clear, and pigmented varieties of lacquer are available.

Finishing oil
Oil is a subtle finish that soaks into the wood, leaving a mellow sheen on the surface. Traditional linseed oil remains sticky for hours, whereas a modern oil will dry in a couple of hours and provides a tougher, more durable finish. Oil can be used on softwood as well as on open-grained, oily hardwoods such as teak. It is suitable for interior and exterior woodwork.

Wax polishes
Wax can be employed to preserve and maintain another finish, or as a finish itself. A good wax should be a blend of beeswax and a hard polishing wax such as carnauba. Some contain silicones to make it easier to achieve a high gloss.

Wax polish may be white, or tinted various shades of brown to darken the wood. Although very attractive, it is not a durable finish and should be used indoors only.

French polish
French polish is a specialized wood finish made by dissolving shellac in alcohol. It is easily scratched, and alcohol or water will damage the surface, leaving white stains. Consequently, it can be used only on furniture unlikely to receive regular wear and tear.

There are several varieties. Button polish is the best-quality standard polish. Garnet polish is a good choice for darker woods like mahogany. And white polish works best with light-colored woods.

1 Button polish
2 Garnet polish
3 White polish

Painting woodwork

Wood is a fibrous material with a definite grain pattern and different rates of absorption within a single piece of stock. And some species contain knots that may leak resin. These qualities, and others, have a bearing on the type of paint you use and the techniques and tools you need to apply it.

Basic application

It is essential to prepare and prime all new woodwork thoroughly before applying the finish coats.

If you're going to use conventional oil-based paint, apply one or two undercoats, depending on the covering strength of the paint. After each coat hardens, sand the surface with fine abrasive paper to remove blemishes. Then, wipe the surface with a cloth dampened with mineral spirits.

Apply the paint with vertical brush strokes, and then spread it sideways to even out the coverage. Finish with light strokes in the direction of the grain. Blend the edges of the next band while the paint on the first band is still wet. Don't go back over a painted surface that has started to dry, or you will leave brush marks in the surface.

Use a different technique for spreading latex paints. Simply lay on the paint liberally with almost parallel strokes, then smooth it with gentle brush strokes. Blend wet edges quickly.

High-quality paintbrushes are the best tools for painting woodwork. You will need 1-inch and 2-inch brushes for general work, and a ½-inch brush for painting narrow window muntins.

Using fast-drying latex paints, you may be able to complete a room in one day. But if you are using oil-based paints, plan your work to make sure the paint will be dry enough to close doors and windows by nightfall.

Inside

Paint ceilings first, followed by windows, doors, and walls. Finish with baseboards, so that any dust picked up by the brush from the floor will not be transferred to other areas. If your brush does get dirty, stop and clean it in solvent before starting work again.

Outside

Don't paint in direct sunlight, because it dries paint, especially latex, too quickly. Direct sun also creates annoying glare.

Never paint on wet or windy days. Rain will ruin the finish, and airborne dust can leave specks everywhere.

● **Removing specks and bristles**
Don't attempt to remove brush bristles or specks of fluff from fresh paintwork once a skin has started to form. Instead, let the paint harden, then rub down with sandpaper. Do the same if you discover any runs.

Painting a panel
When painting up to the edge of a door panel, brush from the center out. If you flex the bristles against the edge, the paint will run. Similarly, moldings tend to flex bristles unevenly, so that too much paint flows. Take extra care at corners of molded panels.

Painting a panel

Painting baseboards
Use a simple plastic shield or putty knife to protect the floor when painting baseboards. Cover the edge of carpeting with wide masking tape.

Painting baseboards

Painting a straight edge
To finish an area with a straight edge, use one of the smaller brushes and place it about ⅛ inch from the edge. As you flex the bristles, they will spread out to fill the space.

Making a straight edge

● **Black dot denotes compatibility.**
All surfaces must be clean, sound, dry, and free from organic growth.

FINISHES FOR WOODWORK	Oil paint	Gloss latex	Wood stain	Protective wood stain	Colored preservative	Varnish	Colored varnish	Cold-cure lacquer	Oil	Wax polish	French polish
SUITABLE TO COVER											
Softwoods	●	●	●	●	●	●	●	●	●	●	
Hardwoods	●	●	●	●	●	●	●	●	●	●	●
Oily hardwoods	●	●				●	●	●	●	●	●
Surfaced boards	●	●	●			●	●	●	●	●	●
Rough-sawn boards				●	●						
Interior use	●	●	●	●		●	●	●	●	●	●
Exterior use	●	●	●	●	●	●	●		●		
DRYING TIME: HOURS											
Touch-dry	4	1	½	4	1–2	4	4	1	1		½
Recoatable	14	3	6	6–8	2–4	14	14	2	6	1	24
THINNERS: SOLVENTS											
Water		●	●								
Mineral spirits	●		●	●	●	●	●		●		
Denatured alcohol											●
Special thinner								●			
NUMBER OF COATS											
Interior use	1–2	1–2	2–3	2	N/A	2–3	2–3	2–3	3	2	10–15
Exterior use	2–3	1–2	N/A	2	2	3–4	3–4	N/A	3	N/A	N/A
COVERAGE											
Sq. ft. per gallon	450–600	375–550	600–1000	375–900	150–450	550–600	550–600	600–650	375–550	variable	variable
METHOD OF APPLICATION											
Brush	●	●	●	●	●	●	●	●	●	●	●
Paint pad	●	●	●	●		●	●				
Cloth pad			●			●	●		●	●	●
Spray gun	●	●			●	●	●	●			

Painting doors

Doors have a variety of surfaces and conflicting grain patterns, all of which need to be painted separately. Yet the end result must look even in color, with no heavy brush marks. There are recommended procedures for painting all types of doors.

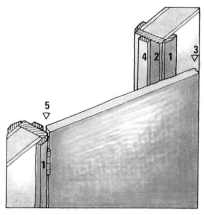

Painting each side with a different color
Make sure all the surfaces that face you when the door is open are painted the same color.

Opening side
Paint the architrave (1) and doorframe (2) up to and including the edge of the doorstop one color. Paint the face of the door and its opening edge (3) the same color.

Opposite side
Paint the architrave and frame up to and over the doorstop (4) the second color. Paint the opposite face of the door and its hinged edge (5) with the second color.

Preparation and technique

Remove the door handles and wedge the door open so that it cannot be closed accidentally before it is dry.

Plan to paint the door and its frame separately so there's less chance of touching wet paint when passing through a freshly painted doorway. Paint the door first, and then when it's dry, finish the door jambs and trim.

If you want to use a different color for each side of the door, paint the hinged edge the color of the closing face (the one that comes to rest against the frame). Paint the outer edge of the door the same color as the opening face, so there won't be any difference in color when the door is viewed from either side.

Each side of the jambs and trim should match the corresponding face of the door. Paint the jambs in the room into which the door swings, including the edge of the stop against which the door closes, to match the opening face. Paint the rest of the doorframe the color of the closing face.

System for a flat door

To paint a flat door, start at the top and work down in sections, blending each one into the other. Lay on the paint, then finish each section with light vertical strokes. Finally, paint the edges, taking extra care to avoid paint runs.

System for a paneled door

The different parts of a paneled door must be painted in a logical sequence. Finish each part with strokes running parallel to the direction of the grain.

Whatever style of paneled door you are painting, start with the moldings (1) followed by the panels (2). Paint the muntins (center verticals) next (3), and then the cross rails (4). Finish the face by painting the stiles—the outer verticals (5). Last of all, paint the edge of the door (6).

To achieve a superior finish, paint the muntins, rails, and stiles together, picking up the wet edges of the paint before they begin to dry.

Glazed doors
To paint a door with glass panels, begin with the muntins, then follow the sequence recommended for paneled doors.

Flat door
Apply paint in sections, working down from the top. Finish up with light vertical brush strokes, picking up the wet edges for a good blend.

Paneled door: basic painting method
Follow the numbered sequence for painting the various parts of the door, finishing each part with strokes along the grain to prevent streaking.

Paneled door: advanced painting method
Working rapidly, follow the alternative sequence—which produces a finish free from lap marks between sections.

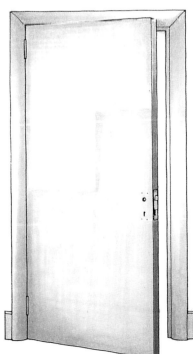

Flat door

Paneled door—basic method

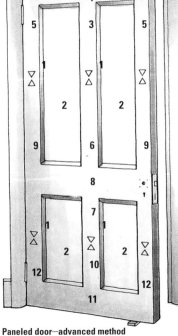

Paneled door—advanced method

Painting window frames

Cutting-in brush
Paint glazing bars with a cutting-in brush. The bristles are cut at an angle to help you work right up to the glass.

Like doors, window frames need to be painted in sequence so that the various components will be coated evenly—and in time to close the windows at night. Be sure to clean the glass thoroughly before painting a window.

Painting a casement window

A casement window hinges like a door, so if you plan to paint each side a different color, follow the procedure recommended for painting doors on the previous page.

It's best to remove the window stay and catch before you paint the window. To operate the window without touching wet paint, you can drive a nail into the underside of the bottom rail and use it as a makeshift handle.

Painting sequence

First paint the muntins (1), cutting into the glass on both sides. Carry on with the top and bottom horizontal rails (2), followed by the vertical stiles (3). Finish the casement by painting the edges (4); then paint the trim (5).

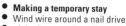

Painting sequence for casement windows

Painting a double-hung window

Follow the sequence below to paint a double-hung window from the inside. To paint the outside face, use a similar procedure, but start with the lower sash. If you are using different colors for each side, the demarcation lines are fairly obvious: when the window is shut, all the visible surfaces from one side should be the same.

Painting sequence

Raise the bottom sash and pull down the top one. Paint the bottom meeting rail of the top sash (1)

and the accessible parts of the vertical members (2). Reverse the position of the sashes, leaving a gap top and bottom, and complete the painting of the top sash (3). Paint the bottom sash (4) and then the trim (5), except for the tracks that the sashes slide in.

Let the paint dry, then paint the inner tracks (6) plus a short section of the outer tracks (7). If there are sash cords, don't paint them. Before the paint has time to dry, check that the sashes slide freely.

Raise bottom sash and lower top one

Reverse position of the sashes

Lower both sashes for access to runners

Keeping the window open

With the catch and stay removed, there's nothing to stop a casement window from closing. Make a stay from a length of stiff wire. Hook one end on the window and the other onto the jamb.

Making a temporary stay
Wind wire around a nail driven into the underside of the frame and use it as a stay.

Protecting the glass

When painting the sides and muntins, overlap the glass by about ¹⁄₁₆ inch to prevent rain or condensation from seeping between the glass and the wood.

If you find it difficult to achieve a satisfactory straight edge, use a plastic or metal paint shield, holding it against the edge of the muntins and the frame, to protect the glass.

You can also run masking tape around the edges of the windowpanes, leaving a slight gap so that the paint will seal the join between glass and frame. When the paint is touch-dry, carefully peel off the tape. Don't wait until the paint is completely dry, or the paint film may peel off with the tape.

Scrape the glass with a razor-blade scraper to remove any dry paint spatters. Many DIY stores sell plastic handles to hold blades for this purpose.

Using a paint shield
A plastic or metal shield enables you to paint a straight edge up to glass.

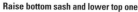

Graining wood

Graining is a technique for simulating the look of natural wood with paint. Once used extensively on inexpensive softwood to imitate expensive hardwoods, it is now used for treating all kinds of woodwork. The basic method is simple to grasp, but practice is essential for convincing results. As a beginner, try to simply suggest wood grain rather than trying to produce a perfect copy.

Mottler

Lining tool

Softener

Flogger

Equipment

Graining tools and brushes
You can use a range of ordinary paintbrushes for wood graining, but subtler results can be achieved if you invest in a few specialized graining tools. Professional graining brushes are not cheap, although if you look after them they should never need to be replaced. A set of metal combs is relatively expensive, but you can get similar effects from cheaper rubber or plastic combs, or cut your own from plastic sheet or cardboard. Graining tools are available from good, general paint stores or craft stores. Some home centers have DIY kits.

Background color
Oil-based or latex satin paint is used to provide the background color for wood-grain effects. Choose a paint that matches the lightest color in the grain pattern of the wood you are copying. This is usually a pale beige that you may want to tint to a warmer or cooler shade. Accurate color matching comes with experience, so try to develop your sense of color by practicing on sheets of paper or cardboard.

Glazes and varnish
You can buy wood-colored glazes, but you will have greater control over the tones and shades if you tint colorless glaze with artist's oil or acrylic paint (see right). To save money, you can use the cheaper, student-quality paints. Earth colors, like raw and burnt umber, raw and burnt sienna, and Vandyke brown, are the most useful for wood graining. You will also need black, to alter the tone of some colors.

Once you are satisfied with your graining results, let the paint dry thoroughly, then protect the surface with two coats of a compatible clear satin varnish.

Preparing surfaces

New wood must be sound, smooth, and dry. After sanding, treat resinous knots with shellac-based primer before you apply a standard primer and undercoat.

Sand previously finished wood to create a good grip for the background color. Scrape and sand peeling paint back to sound, feathered edges. Prime bare patches and then hide the old color with a suitable shade of undercoat paint. When the undercoat is dry, apply two coats of background color, sanding smooth with abrasive paper between coats.

Glazes are practically colorless, ready-made oil or acrylic finishes, similar in consistency to conventional paint. Unlike paint, however, which is designed to form a flat, even covering, glazes are formulated to stay workable and to retain brush strokes and comb marks.

Mixing oil glaze
Professionals frequently carry out wood graining with watercolor glazes, but an oil glaze is easier for amateurs to handle because it dries slowly.

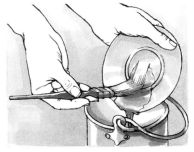

Diluting oil paint
Squeeze a 2-inch length of oil paint onto an old saucer and use a paintbrush to blend in enough mineral spirits to make the paint slightly liquid. Blend in other oil-paint colors until you have mixed the shade you want.

Coloring the glaze
Pour some colorless glaze into a paint bucket. One inch of glaze in a quart pail will be enough for the average room door. Add about 20 percent mineral spirits and mix thoroughly. Gradually add the thinned oil paint until the glaze appears to be the right color and consistency. Test the glaze by brushing it onto a small area of the work surface.

Applying glaze
Whatever your intended final effect, brush a suitable glaze in all directions to cover the work. Finish by brushing parallel to the direction of the grain pattern.

Glazes will remain workable for some time—but when graining a large area, apply the glaze in manageable sections.

Mottler
A soft-bristled mottler is used for simulating bands of highlights.

Lining tool
This special paintbrush with slanted square-trimmed bristles is ideal for removing excess color.

Softener
A 4-inch hog-hair softener is the one special brush you cannot do without. It is used for blending marks left by other brushes and tools.

Flogger
The long stiff bristles are used to simulate large open pores.

COMBS FOR GRAINING

Rubber or plastic combs
You can use a comb to simulate wood grain by dragging its teeth through wet glaze.

Steel combs
Combs are dragged through wet glaze, creating striations that closely resemble real wood grain.

Heart grainers
These are special combing tools that create a highly realistic impression of figured wood grain.

Graining with brushes and combs

Before you even attempt to paint an impression of wood grain, it is worth taking the time to examine the real thing. This will help you to produce convincing effects. No two pieces of wood are exactly the same—so be prepared to accept the irregularities and happy accidents that occur, rather than become frustrated by striving for an exact copy. One of the most useful techniques is simple brush-graining, which re-creates the character of straight-grained wood. Before you create the effect, apply an even coat of glaze to the work.

Flogger
A flogger has extra-long stiff bristles that are used to strike wet glaze, leaving a texture that simulates large open pores. Although you will not use a flogger for every job, it is difficult to achieve the same results with any other paintbrush.

Graining produced with a wet brush

Graining with a wet brush

Produce muted linear effects with a brush still wet from the glaze that you have just applied to the work. Holding the paintbrush between your thumb and fingertips, drag it lightly through the glaze from top to bottom at a shallow angle to the work surface. Apply successive strokes alongside that, until you have covered the workpiece.

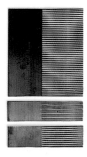

Steel combs
For fine work you can buy sets of precision-made steel combs in three grades—coarse, medium, and fine. Combs 3 to 4 inches wide are the most useful, but you will find 1- and 2-inch combs perfect for graining narrow strips of wood.

Using a wet brush

Open-grain textures

If you want your brush-graining to look like oak, superimpose a coarse open-grain texture, using a flogger.

Using a flogger
Hold the flogger just above and parallel to the surface. Working in bands starting from the base of the panel, strike the wet brush-graining with short overlapping strokes, using the flat of the brush. You can use the side of the brush on narrow work.

Graining produced with a dry brush

Graining with a dry brush

Brush-graining with a dry brush not only displaces the glaze on the surface, but also removes some color at the same time, creating relatively bold stripes. Don't be afraid to wobble the brush slightly as you make the strokes: this will add to the effect. Regularly wipe the tips of the bristles on a rag to remove excess glaze.

Softening the grain
If your brush-graining appears too bold, use a softener brush to blur the lines. Hold the brush at 90 degrees to the surface and gently stroke the painted grain, reducing its intensity without entirely losing the linear effect.

Comb graining

Combing is employed primarily to produce the nearly parallel linear patterns of straight-grained wood, but you can use steel or rubber combs to blur coarse brush-graining. The basic techniques are not difficult to master, and with practice you will discover the degree of variation required to avoid an overrepetitive, mechanical effect.

When combing, add a little more solvent to the glaze to prevent ridges.

Oak-grain pattern created with steel combs

Using a steel comb

Using steel combs
Cover the surface with thinned glaze, then draw a medium steel comb from top to bottom in a series of overlapping vertical strokes. Imitate real grain by occasionally allowing the comb to waver from side to side. Wipe excess glaze from the tips of the teeth between strokes.

Reverse combing
Break up the linear pattern with a fine comb, dragging it upward at an angle of about 10 degrees to the first series of strokes. Blend in excess color at the top and bottom of a panel by stippling with a brush. If you want to create a finer texture, go back over the same area a second time.

Reverse combing

Creating decorative graining

A heart grainer is used to imitate the pattern of heartwood grain that often appears in the center of a door panel. The tool is used much like a comb, in that it is drawn along the work to leave impressions in the wet glaze. But by placing its convex surface against the work at different angles, you can create an almost infinite variety of bold patterns. Grainers are molded with coarse, medium, or fine ribs to suit the character of the wood. You can enhance the character of particular species of wood with mottling effects or knots.

Holding a heart grainer
Hold the grainer between thumb and fingertips, with the concentric curved ribs centered on the bottom edge of the tool.

Heart grainers
These are special combing tools that leave a highly realistic impression of heartwood grain. The convex surface of each heart grainer is molded with concentric ridges, centered on one edge of the tool. Heart grainers are made in coarse, medium, and fine models.

Using a grainer
Position the grainer near one end of the workpiece, with the bottom edge of the tool resting on the glazed surface. Draw the grainer slowly to the end of the panel in one continuous stroke. At the same time, rock the tool over and back to vary the pattern left in the colored glaze.

Creating special effects

Small details applied to basic wood graining add variety and interest, making each panel or frame a unique piece of work. It is essential to be familiar with the effects you are trying to create—so take the time to study examples of real wood.

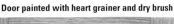

Door painted with heart grainer and dry brush

Ray-flecked oak

Including knots

Softwood is often covered with dark brown knots, which are an essential part of the wood's character. It is well worth including knots to suggest softwood, so make allowance for them while applying the initial graining. As you draw the brush or comb through the wet glaze, swerve the lines where a knot will be placed, to mimic the natural grain.

Imprinting knots in wet glaze
It is surprisingly easy to create a knot by imprinting the wet glaze with the end of a dowel, or even with your fingertip if you are wearing protective gloves. The simple act of touching the glaze disperses the color, leaving a pale patch with a darker rim and sometimes a small dark dot in the center.

If a knot needs still further emphasis, paint in small concentric circles very freely with the point of an artist's brush, stippling afterward to soften the effect. Don't make all your knots the same shape or size.

Creating figured oak

Some hardwoods, especially oak, have a grain pattern crossed with flecks called rays. These pale-colored rays run ribbonlike down a piece of straight-grained wood, or may flank a central band of prominent heart graining. Reproduce rays by wiping off the glaze with different size combs or with a rag-covered stick as shown below.

Wiping out individual rays
Wrap a simple wood dowel or ice-cream stick in absorbent cloth. Draw the tip of the wrapped stick through the glaze, turning the stick to make short, twisting lines that taper sharply toward the ends. No two rays are identical in shape or size, but they tend to follow a similar pattern across a piece of wood.

Stretch the fabric tightly over the rounded tip of the stick, refolding the rag at intervals to maintain a clean working edge. Lightly soften the edges with a brush.

Mottler
Use a soft-bristled mottler to simulate the bands of highlights that are often displayed across wavy-grain woods and veneers, such as fiddleback sycamore or ripple ash. Although a mottler is preferable, you can make do with an ordinary paintbrush.

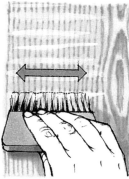

Using a mottler
The easiest way to achieve the wavy bands seen across the surface on some woods is to create the effect when applying the coat of protective varnish. You need to darken the first coat of varnish slightly with artist's paint and create the effect while the varnish is wet.

Holding the mottler at 45 degrees to the surface, wipe away narrow strips of varnish with side-to-side strokes, creating a band of random impressions in the varnish. To soften the mottling, lightly brush along the bands with a softener brush.

Apply a second coat of varnish once the first coat is dry.

Staining with wood dyes

Unless the wood is perfectly clean and free from grease, wood stain will be rejected, producing an uneven, patchy appearance. Strip any previous finish and sand the wood with progressively finer abrasive papers. Always sand in the direction of the grain, as any scratches made across the grain will be emphasized by the stain.

Making a test strip

The final color is affected by the nature of the wood, the number of coats, and the overlying clear finish. You can also mix compatible stains to alter the color, or dilute them with the appropriate thinner.

Make a test strip so that you will have an accurate guide for choosing the depth of color to suit the job at hand. Use a piece of wood from the same batch you are staining, or one that resembles it closely.

Paint the strip with one coat of stain. Allow the stain to be absorbed, then apply a second coat, leaving a strip of the first application showing. It is rarely necessary to apply more than two coats of stain. But, for your test strip, add a third coat and even a fourth, always leaving a strip of the previous coat for comparison.

When the stain has dried completely, apply a band of clear varnish along the strip. Some polyurethane varnishes react unfavorably with oil-based stains, so it's a good idea to use products from the same manufacturer.

Paint pad

Paintbrush

Lint-free cloth

How to apply wood stain

Use a 4-inch paintbrush to apply stains over a wide, flat surface. Don't brush out a stain as you would paint, but apply it liberally and evenly, always in the direction of the grain.

Brushes, pads, and cloths are all useful for applying wood stains.

Working with wood stains

When you wet a piece of wood, water is absorbed and raises a mass of tiny fibers across the surface. Applying a water-based stain does the same—which can spoil the final finish. Avoid the problem by sanding the wood until perfectly smooth, then dampen the whole surface with a wet rag. Leave it to dry out, then sand the raised grain with very fine abrasive paper before you apply the stain. If you are using an oil-based stain, this grain raising process is unnecessary.

If you want to fill the grain, first apply a sealer coat of clear finish over the stain. Choose a grain filler that matches the stain, adjusting the color by adding lighter or darker stains to it. Make sure that the dye and filler are compatible. An oil-based dye will not mix with a water-based filler, and vice versa.

It is essential to blend wet edges of stain, so work fairly quickly and don't take a break until you have completed the job. If you have applied a water-based stain with a brush, it is sometimes necessary to wipe over the wet surface with a soft cloth to remove excess stain.

Using a paint pad is one of the most effective ways to achieve an even coverage over a flat surface. However, you may find that you still need to use a paintbrush for staining moldings and to get the wood stain into awkward corners.

Because stains are so fluid, it's often easier to apply them with a soft, lint-free rag. This will let you control runs on vertical surfaces, and is the best way to stain stair balusters.

Using a lint-free cloth
Wearing gloves to protect your skin, pour some wood stain into a shallow dish and saturate the cloth with stain. Then squeeze some out so that it is not dripping but is still wet enough to apply a liberal coat of stain to the surface.

Staining a flat panel

Whenever possible, set a panel up horizontally for staining, either on sawhorses or a workbench. Shake the container before use, and pour the stain into a flat dish so that you can load your applicator easily.

Apply the stain, working quickly and evenly along the grain. Stain the edges at the same time as the top surface. The first application may have a slightly patchy appearance as it dries, because some parts of the wood will absorb more stain than others. The second coat normally evens out the color without difficulty. If powdery deposits are left on the surface of the dry stain, wipe them off with a coarse, dry cloth before applying the second coat in the same way as the first.

Leave the stain to dry overnight, then proceed with the clear finish of your choice to seal the stain.

Staining floors

Because a wood floor is such a large area, it's more difficult to blend the wet edges of the stain. For the best results, work along two or three boards at a time, using a paintbrush and stopping at the edge of a board each time.

Parquet floors are even trickier, so work with a helper and cover the area quickly, blending and overlapping sections with a soft cloth.

Staining a door

Stain a new or stripped door before it is hung, so that you can lay it horizontally. A flat door is stained like any other panel, but use a lint-free cloth to color the edges so that stain does not run underneath and spoil the other side.

When staining a paneled door, it's a good idea to follow a sequence that will allow you to pick up the wet edges before they dry. Use a combination of brush and cloth to apply the stain, and follow the numbered sequence below.

Unlike the order used when painting a paneled door, it's best to stain the moldings last in order to prevent any overlap from showing on the flat surfaces. Stain the moldings with a narrow brush and blend in the color with a cloth.

Method for staining a paneled door
Follow this sequence, using a combination of paintbrush and lint-free cloth to apply the stain evenly to the various parts of the door. Start with the inset panels (**1**), then continue with half of the vertical muntin (**2**), the bottom cross rail (**3**), and half the stiles (**4**). Pick up the wet edges with the other half of the muntin (**5**) and the stiles (**6**). Stain the central cross rail (**7**), then repeat the procedure for the second half of the door (**8–12**). Finish with the moldings (**13**), using a narrow brush and cloth.

Pads for moldings
It is relatively easy to apply stain to molding using a narrow paintbrush. You can also use a small paint pad intended for painting window muntins.

Interior wood stains are not suitable for exterior use. They don't have protective properties and they have a tendency to fade in direct sunlight. For wood siding and trim, use a stain that has a preservative in its formulation. It should also be moisture-vapor permeable. For rough-sawn lumber, use a colored wood preservative rather than a stain. Both the preservative and the stain are much thinner than paint, so take care to avoid splashing.

Exterior wood stain

Make sure the surface is clean, dry, and sanded. All previous paint or varnish must be stripped off. For extra protection, treat the wood with a clear preservative before staining.

Apply the required number of coats with a paintbrush, making sure that the coverage is even. Stain wall siding one board at a time, coating the lower edge first.

Wood preservative

Before you apply a colored wood preservative, remove surface dirt with a stiff-bristled brush. Existing paint or varnish must be stripped completely, but wood that has been previously coated with preservative can be re-treated. For additional protection against insect and rot attack, treat the wood first with a clear preservative.

Paint a full-strength coat of colored preservative onto the wood and, if necessary, follow up with a second coat as soon as the first has soaked in. Brush out sufficiently to achieve an even color, and cover all edges swiftly before they have time to dry.

Replacing putty

Stains will not color old window putty, so replace it with a colored putty or with new stained beading strips. Begin by applying caulk to the rabbets that hold the glass panes (**1**). Then, set lengths of stained beading into the caulk and secure them with small nails (**2**). You will find it easier to nail the beading if you drive the nails beforehand so that they just protrude through the other side. Use a putty knife to remove excess caulk squeezed from beneath the beading (**3**).

1 Apply caulk

2 Install beading

3 Trim caulk

Varnishing woodwork

Varnish serves two main purposes: to protect the wood from knocks, stains, and other marks, and to give it a sheen that accentuates the grain pattern. Some varnishes can be used to change the color of the wood to resemble another species, or to give it a fresh, new look with a choice of bright colors.

The effect of varnish
The examples above illustrate how different varnishes affect the same species of wood. From top to bottom: untreated softwood, clear flat varnish, clear gloss varnish, wood-color varnish, tinted satin varnish, pure-color varnish.

How to apply varnish

Apply varnish like paint, using a variety of paintbrushes. You will probably find ½-, 1-, and 2-inch widths the most useful. For varnishing a floor, use a 4-inch brush for fast, even coverage.

Keep your brushes clean. Any remaining traces of paint on them can spoil a varnish finish. Load a brush with varnish by dipping the first third of the bristles into the liquid, then dab off the excess on the inside of the container. Don't scrape the brush across the rim of the container, because that creates bubbles in the varnish, which can spoil the finish if they are transferred to the wood.

You can use a soft, lint-free cloth pad to rub a sealer coat of varnish into the grain. You'll find that a cloth is also convenient for varnishing curved or turned pieces of wood.

Applying the varnish

Thin the first sealer coat of varnish by 10 percent and rub it into the wood in the direction of the grain, using a cloth pad. Where a cloth is difficult to use, brush on the sealer coat instead.

Apply a second coat of varnish within the recommended time. If more than 24 hours have elapsed, lightly sand the surface with fine abrasive paper. Wipe the surface with a cloth dampened with mineral spirits in order to remove the sanding dust, then brush on a full coat of varnish. Apply a third coat if the surface is likely to take hard wear.

Using colored varnish

Although wood stains can be used only on bare wood, you can use a colored varnish to darken or alter the color of woodwork that has been previously varnished, without having to strip the existing finish. Clean the surface with fine steel wool dipped in mineral spirits or a furniture cleaner designed to remove old wax and dirt. Dry the surface with a clean cloth, then apply the tinted varnish. It may be worth making a test strip beforehand to see how many coats you will need to achieve the desired depth of color.

Varnishing floors

Varnishing a floor is no different from varnishing any other woodwork. But, due to the size of the area being covered in a confined space, oil-based varnishes can produce an unpleasant concentration of fumes. Open all the windows to provide maximum ventilation, and wear a respirator while you are working. Start in the corner farthest from the door and work back toward it. Brush the varnish out well so that it does not collect in pools.

DEALING WITH DUST PARTICLES

Minor imperfections and particles of dust stuck to the varnished surface can be rubbed down with fine abrasive paper between coats. If you want your topcoat high gloss, take extra care to make sure that your brush is perfectly clean.

If you are not satisfied with your final finish, wait until it is dry, then dip very fine steel wool in wax polish and rub the varnish with parallel strokes in the direction of the grain. Buff the surface with a soft cloth. This treatment removes any high gloss, but it leaves a pleasant sheen on the surface with no obvious imperfections.

Produce a soft sheen with steel wool and wax

French polishing

The art of French polishing has always been considered the province of the expert. It's true that a professional will do a better job of the polishing and will be able to work much faster than an amateur, but there's no reason why anyone cannot produce a satisfactory finish with a little practice.

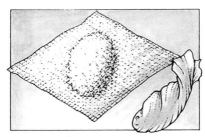

Making an applicator
Traditionally, shellac (French polish) is applied with a soft cloth pad. To make one, take a handful of cotton wool and form it into an egg shape. Then place it in the middle of a 1-foot-square piece of white linen. Fold the fabric over the cotton wool, gathering the loose material in the palm of your hand. Smooth out any wrinkles in the bottom of the pad.

BRUSHING FRENCH POLISH

If you don't have time to practice applying shellac with a cloth pad, use a special French polish that can be brushed onto the surface. It contains an agent that retards the drying process so that brush marks can flow out before the polish begins to set.

The technique for applying this brushing polish is easy to master. Use a soft paintbrush to apply an even coat. After an hour, rub it down lightly with silicon-carbide abrasive paper. Paint on two more coats. Rub down between applications if you notice any blemishes in the surface.

When the shellac has set, dip a ball of 0000-grade steel wool in soft wax polish and rub it gently up and down the panel, using overlapping parallel strokes. Let the wax harden for 15 to 20 minutes, then burnish it vigorously with a soft cloth.

Apply an even coat with a paintbrush.

Preparation for French polishing

Woodwork must be immaculately prepared before French polishing, as every blemish will be mirrored in the finish. The grain should be filled, either with a commercial filler or with layers of polish, which are rubbed down and recoated until the pores of the wood are eventually filled flush.

Work in a warm, dust-free room. A low temperature will make the polish cloudy, known as "blooming," and airborne dust will mar the finish.

Make sure you work in a good light so you can look across the surface in order to gauge the quality of the finish you are applying.

Traditional French polishing

With a cloth pad open in the palm of your hand, pour shellac onto the cotton wool inside until it is fully charged but not absolutely saturated. Fold the fabric over the cotton wool and press the cloth pad against a scrap of wood to squeeze out the polish, distributing it evenly throughout the pad. Dip your fingertip in linseed oil, and spread it on the bottom of the pad to act as a lubricant.

Applying the polish
To apply French polish to a flat panel, first make overlapping circular strokes with the pad, gradually covering the whole surface with shellac. Then go over the surface again, this time using figure-eight strokes, vary the strokes to ensure an even coverage. Finish with straight overlapping strokes parallel with the grain.

Use light pressure with a freshly charged applicator and increase the pressure gradually as the work proceeds. Recharge the cotton wool

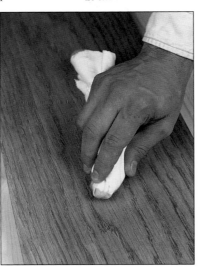

with shellac as necessary, adding another spot of linseed oil to the pad when it stops gliding easily across the surface.

Keep the pad on the move, sweeping it on and off the wood at the beginning and end of each complete pass. If you stop with the pad in contact with the work, the pad will stick to the surface, leaving a scar. If this happens, let the shellac harden thoroughly and rub it down with very fine silicon-carbide abrasive paper.

Assuming the first complete application is free from blemishes, let it dry for 30 minutes, then repeat the process. Build up four to five coats in the same way. Let the polish harden overnight.

Next day, sand out any dust, runs, or pad marks with silicon-carbide paper before applying another four to five coats of polish. In all, 10 to 20 coats will be needed to build a protective coating with the required depth of color.

Removing the oil
The linseed-oil lubricant leaves streaks in the polish that have to be removed with a pad that is practically empty of shellac, but with a few drops of denatured alcohol on the bottom. Apply the pad to the polished surface, using straight parallel strokes only, gliding on and off the panel at the beginning and end of each stroke. Recharge the pad with more denatured alcohol as soon as it begins to drag. Leave the work for a minute or two, and repeat the process if the streaks reappear.

This process not only removes streaking, but eventually burnishes the French polish to a glass-like finish.

Half an hour later, buff the surface with a soft cloth, then leave it to harden for at least a week.

Storing the pad
Keep your pad pliable between applications by storing it in a screw-top jar.

Applying French polish
Make overlapping circular and figure-eight strokes with the pad, gradually covering the whole surface. Then finish with straight parallel strokes.

Lacquer

If you don't prepare the wood properly, lacquer will not cure satisfactorily. You need to strip an old finish, but don't use a caustic stripper, because it will react poorly with the lacquer.

Clean every trace of wax polish from the wood, even from the pores of the grain. Wash it with a ball of fine steel wool dipped in mineral spirits, rubbing in the direction of the grain. When the wood is dry, scrub it with a solution of detergent and water. Then, rinse with clean water, with a little white vinegar added. Sand the wood smooth and remove all the dust.

If you use stain, make sure it is made by the manufacturer of the lacquer, otherwise it may change color. Use the same manufacturer's wood-filler product to fill cracks and holes. Never use general-purpose wood fillers.

Mixing lacquer

For most people, a paintbrush is a good choice for applying lacquer, although professionals generally use a sprayer. If you need to cover a large area, you can also use a foam roller.

When you are ready to apply the lacquer, mix the coating and the hardener in a glass container. Use the proportions recommended by the manufacturer, mixing just enough for your needs. Lacquer will set in an open container in a couple of days. You can extend the pot life to about a week by covering the jar with a lid.

Applying the lacquer

Lacquer must be applied in a warm atmosphere. Use a well-loaded applicator and spread the lacquer onto the wood. There is no need to brush out the liquid; it will flow unaided, and even a thick coat will cure thoroughly and smoothly. The lacquer dries relatively fast, so you need to work quickly in order to pick up the wet edges.

After about an hour, apply a second coat of lacquer. If necessary, rub down the hardened lacquer with fine wet-and-dry paper to remove blemishes. If a third coat is required, apply it the following day.

Self-protection
Wear a suitable respirator when you are applying lacquer to any surface.

Burnishing lacquer
If you want a mirror finish, let the lacquer harden for a few days, then sand it smooth with waterproof abrasive paper and water. Then, use a burnishing cream on a slightly damp cloth to buff the surface to a high gloss. Finish up by rubbing with a clean, soft cloth.

Matting the lacquer
To produce a subtle satin (matte) finish, rub the hardened lacquer along the grain with fine steel wool dipped in wax polish. The grade of the steel wool will affect the amount of matting. Use fine 0000-grade for a satin finish, and a coarse grade for a fully matted surface. Polish with a soft cloth.

SAFETY WHEN USING LACQUER

Although lacquer is generally safe to use, you should always wear a respirator when applying it, especially if you're in a confined area with poor ventilation.

If possible, open all windows and doors for clean air. But remember that you need warm temperatures for lacquer to cure properly. Lacquer hardener is acidic, so wash thoroughly with water if you spill any on your skin.

Applying oil

Clean and prepare the wood and remove previous finishes carefully so the oil can penetrate the grain.

The most efficient way to apply a finishing oil is to rub it into the wood with a soft, lint-free rag. Don't store oily rags; keep them in a sealed tin while the job is in progress, then unfold them and leave them outside to dry before throwing them away. A brush is convenient for spreading oil liberally over large surfaces and into carved areas or deep moldings.

Rub or brush a generous coating of oil into the wood grain. Let it soak in for 10 to 15 minutes, then rub off excess oil with a clean cloth. After about six hours, use an abrasive nylon-fiber pad to rub another coat of oil into the wood. Wipe excess oil off the surface with a rag. The next day, apply a third and then a final coat. When the oil is dry, raise a faint sheen by burnishing with a soft cloth.

Wax-polishing wood

If you want to wax-polish new wood, seal it first with a coat of clear varnish. This will prevent the wax from being absorbed too deeply into the wood. A sealer also provides a slightly more durable finish.

Before waxing an old lacquer finish, clean it with fine steel wool dipped in either mineral spirits or a commercial furniture-cleaning fluid, rubbing in the direction of the grain. Don't rub too hard. You want to remove the old wax and dirt without damaging the finish beneath. Wipe the surface with a rag.

Dip a cloth pad in paste wax and apply the first coat using overlapping circular strokes; then finish in the direction of the grain. After 10 to 15 minutes, use 0000-grade steel wool to rub more wax along the grain, then set the wood aside for 24 hours. When the polish is hard, burnish the surface vigorously with a soft cloth.

When applying liquid wax polish, decant some into a shallow dish and then brush the polish liberally onto the wood, spreading it as evenly as possible. An hour later, apply a second coat of wax, using a soft cloth pad. Use circular strokes at first, then finish by rubbing parallel to the grain. You can apply a third coat after an hour. Leave the polish to harden overnight, then burnish with a soft cloth.

Finishing metalwork

Rusty ferrous metals will shed practically any paint. The most important aspect of finishing metalwork, to prevent corrosion from returning, is thorough preparation and priming. After that, apply the finish in virtually the same way as for woodwork.

When choosing a finish for metalwork in and around the house, make sure it fulfills your requirements. See the chart below for suitable types.

Methods of application

You can use a paintbrush to apply any metal finish. In general, the techniques are identical to those used for painting woodwork—but don't attempt to brush out bitumen-based paints. They should just be laid on with a brush.

Remove metal door and window hardware for painting, suspending it on wire hooks to dry. Make sure that sharp edges are coated properly, because the finish at these points wears quickly.

Some paints can be sprayed, which is useful in the case of intricately molded wrought ironwork on railings, fences, and garden furniture. If you spray-paint indoors, good ventilation is essential. For most other situations, paint-brushes work just as well, without the overspray problems typical of spray paint. A standard roller is suitable for large flat surfaces. Special rollers with V-shaped sleeves work great for painting railings.

● **Black dot denotes** compatibility. All surfaces must be clean, sound, and dry.

FINISHES FOR METALWORK

	Oil paint	Latex paint	Metallic paint	Bituminous paint	Lacquer	Radiator enamel	Zinc-rich finish	Varnish	Epoxy paints	Nonslip paint
DRYING TIME: HOURS										
Touch-dry	4	1–2	4	1–2	½	2–6	½–1	0–3	6–10	4–6
Recoatable	14	4	8	6–24	1	7–14	N/A	1	16–24	12
THINNERS: SOLVENTS										
Water		●		●						
Mineral spirits	●		●	●	●		●	●	●	●
Special						●				
Cellulose thinners								●		
NUMBER OF COATS										
Normal conditions	1–2	2	1–2	1–3	2	2–6	variable	1–2	2	2
COVERAGE										
Sq. ft. per gallon	450–600	325–550	375–500	225–550	400	450	variable	450	450–550	100–180
METHOD OF APPLICATION										
Brush	●	●	●	●	●	●	●	●	●	●
Roller	●	●		●						
Spray gun	●	●		●				●		
Cloth applicator							●			

PAINTING RADIATORS AND PIPES

Let radiators and exposed hot-water pipes cool before you paint them. The biggest problem with painting a radiator is how to reach the back. The best solution is to remove the radiator completely or, if possible, swing it away from the wall. After you have painted the back, reposition the radiator and paint the front.

If this is inconvenient, use a special radiator roller or brush with a long handle (see right). These are ideal for painting between the leaves of a double radiator. It is difficult to achieve a perfect finish, so do your best work on the visible areas.

Don't paint over radiator valves or fittings—otherwise, you won't be able to operate them when the paint dries.

Paint pipes lengthwise rather than across, or drips and runs are likely to form. The first coat on metal pipes will be streaky, so be prepared to apply two or three coats. Allow the paint to dry thoroughly before turning on the heat to radiators and letting hot water into the pipes.

Using a radiator brush
A long, slim-handled radiator brush or roller enables you to paint the back of a radiator without having to remove it from the wall. These same tools can be used for painting between the leaves of a double radiator.

Finishing metalwork

Gutters and downspouts

It is best to coat the inside of gutters with a bitumen-based paint for thorough protection against water, but you can finish the outer surfaces with oil or latex paint.

To protect the wall behind a downspout, slip a scrap of cardboard behind the downspout before painting the back of the pipe.

Protecting the wall
Use cardboard behind a downspout when painting behind it.

Metal casement windows

Paint metal casement windows using the sequence described for wooden casements. This will allow you to close the window at night without spoiling a freshly painted surface.

Lacquering metalwork

Buff the metal hardware to a high gloss, then use a stiff brush to scrub it with warm water and some liquid detergent. Rinse the metal with clean water, then dry it thoroughly with an absorbent cloth.

Apply lacquer with a large, soft artist's paintbrush, working swiftly from the top. Let the lacquer flow naturally, and work all around the object to keep the wet edge moving.

If you do leave a brush mark in partially set lacquer, finish the job and then warm the metal (by resting it on a radiator, if possible). As soon as the blemish disappears, remove the object from the heat and allow it to cool gradually in a dust-free environment.

Applying lacquer
Use a large, soft artist's paintbrush.

Oiling cast iron

Oil dressing produces an attractive finish for cast iron. It is not a permanent or durable finish, and will have to be renewed periodically. It may transfer if rubbed hard.

The material comes in a tube similar to a toothpaste tube. Squeeze some of the oil onto a soft cloth and spread it onto the metal. For the best coverage, use an old toothbrush to scrub it into decorative ironwork.

When you have covered the surface, buff it to a satin sheen with a clean, dry cloth. Build up several applications to give a patina and a moisture-resistant finish.

Applying oil dressing
Use an old toothbrush to scrub the oil into intricate surfaces.

Suitable finishes for metalwork

Oil-based paints

Conventional oil-based paints are suitable for use on metal. Once it has been primed, interior metalwork will need at least one undercoat plus a topcoat. Add an extra undercoat to protect exterior metalwork.

Latex paint

Strictly speaking, latex paint is not suitable for finishing metal. As it is water-based, it will cause corrosion on ferrous metals if applied directly. However, it can be used if the metal surface has already been painted with a suitable metal finish. In this case, the latex is merely a topcoat.

Metallic paints

For a metallic finish, choose a paint containing aluminum, copper, gold, or bronze powder. These paints are water-resistant and are able to withstand very high temperatures—up to about 212°F.

Bituminous paints

Bituminous (often called bitumen-based) paints give good protection for exterior storage tanks and gutters. Standard bituminous paint is black, but there is also a limited range of colors, plus bituminous paint with aluminum.

Security paints

Nonsetting security paint, used primarily for gutter downspouts, remains slippery to prevent intruders from scaling the wall via the downspout.

Radiator enamels

Fast-drying, water-based radiator enamel is supplied in a variety of colors designed to complement existing room colors. A choice of satin and gloss finishes is available.

Radiator enamel can be applied to previously painted radiators, provided the surfaces are thoroughly cleaned and lightly sanded. Bare metal or factory-primed radiators must be coated with a compatible primer.

Turn off the heat and allow the radiators to cool. Then, apply the first coat of enamel, using a synthetic brush. Four hours later, apply a second coat. Wait for at least 8 hours, or as long as the manufacturer recommends, before turning on the heat.

Oil dressing

An oil used for coating cast ironwork, it's reasonably moisture-resistant, but is not suitable for exterior use.

Lacquer

Virtually any clear lacquer can be used on polished metalwork without spoiling its appearance. However, many polyurethane lacquers have a tendency to yellow with age. For long-term protection of chrome plating, brass, and copper, inside or outdoors, use a clear acrylic metal lacquer.

Nonslip paints

Designed to provide secure footing on a wide range of surfaces, including metal, nonslip paints are ideal for metal staircase treads and exterior fire escapes. The surface must be primed before application.

Interior paneling

Walls that are in poor condition—except those that have moisture problems—can be covered with wood paneling to conceal blemishes and to provide a new surface. Installing paneling provides an opportunity for adding insulation. There are two basic types of paneling: solid-wood planking and plywood sheets with veneered wood surfaces.

Tongue-and-groove boards

Solid wood paneling is made from boards with a tongue along one edge and a matching groove on the other. The main function of this joint is to provide room for movement resulting from atmospheric changes, while also allowing for "blind nailing" when attaching the boards to the wall.

The mating edges of tongue-and-groove boards are often machined to produce a decorative V-shaped profile, accentuating the joint between boards. Other types of tongue-and-groove boards have a bead instead of a V-joint. Shiplap versions have matching rabbets along the top and bottom edges. You may find a few hardwoods available as paneling, but most boards are made from softwood, typically knotty pine.

Buy your boards in one batch
Make sure you buy enough paneling boards to complete the job. Boards from another batch may be slightly different, because the machine used to mill their edge joints may have been set to slightly different tolerances.

Plywood panels

Manufactured plywood panels are usually made in 4 x 8-foot sheets in thicknesses ranging from 3/16 to 7/16 inch. Most plywood panels are faced with real wood veneers. But, less expensive panels sometimes feature paper-coated surfaces printed to simulate wood grain. Typical surfaces feature differently colored stains, a satin finish, and V-grooves cut at varying intervals across the surface.

Constructing a framework for paneling

If a wall is flat, you can glue thick plywood panels directly to the surface. But, uneven walls usually call for a frame built from softwood boards, often called furring strips. For solid wood paneling and thin plywood paneling, furring strips are the best solution.

Before you start, carefully pry off the baseboards, door and window casings, and any other trim pieces that are in the way. If you are careful removing these boards, they'll be easier to reinstall later.

Furring strips are usually sold as 1 x 2s, which actually measure 3/4 x 1 1/2 inches. You can also use 2 x 2s (1 1/2 x 1 1/2 inches) if you prefer. Both sizes work well, but if you plan on adding some insulation to the wall, you get twice the R-value with the thicker furring. When insulating, just cut foam insulation boards to fit between the furring strips and attach them to the wall with construction adhesive. You should also add a polyethelene vapor barrier over the insulation before you install the paneling.

The furring strips should be installed on 16-inch centers. If you are installing them vertically, they should fall directly over the wall studs so you have something solid to nail or screw them to. If you are placing them horizontally, make sure to attach the strips to each stud as you move across the wall. Use a level to align the furring strips, whether you're working horizontally or vertically.

Plywood panels are always installed vertically, but tongue-and-groove boards can be installed vertically, horizontally, or diagonally. To install boards vertically or diagonally, attach the furring strips horizontally. If you want to install the paneling horizontally, install the furring strips vertically.

However you decide to run the paneling, remember that all joints must fall on a furring strip, and that the joints should be staggered on furring strips so you don't have joints on adjacent rows lining up.

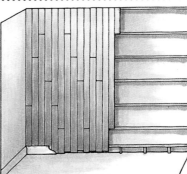

Vertical board paneling—furring strips run horizontally across the wall.

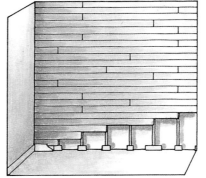

Horizontal board paneling—furring strips run vertically.

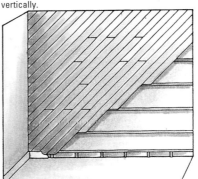

Diagonal board paneling—furring strips are attached horizontally.

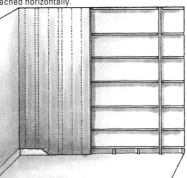

Plywood paneling—horizontal furring strips are installed between the verticals.

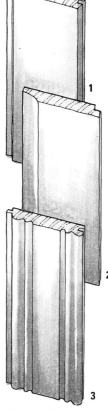

Tongue-and-groove boards
Solid wood paneling boards are often sold by random lengths, from 6 feet up to 16 feet. The most common dimensions are 1/2 x 3 1/2 inches. Prepackaged boards are also available, usually in 6- or 8-foot lengths. Various profiles are made: tongue-and-groove with V-joint (**1**), shiplap (**2**), molded tongue-and-groove (**3**).

Attaching wood paneling

MAKING NEAT CORNERS

Mark out and cut the boards to length, using a circular saw, then sand the outer surfaces smooth before attaching them. Boards purchased in precut packages may be supplied presanded.

Fixing vertical paneling

With the grooved edge butted against the left-hand wall, plumb the first board with a level. Nail it to the strips through the center of its face, using 6d finishing nails.

Slide the next board onto the tongue and, protecting the edge with a strip of wood, tap the second board in place with a hammer. Nail into the furring strips using the blind nailing technique: drive the nail at a 45-degree angle through the inner corner of the tongue (**1**). Sink the head below the surface with a nailset. Slide on the next board to hide the nails, and repeat the same process until all the boards are installed (**2**). Packaged boards sometimes come with metal clips that fit in the groove and nail into the furring. Use up short boards by butting them end to end over a furring strip, but stagger these joints across the wall to avoid a continuous line.

When you reach the other end of the wall, scribe and cut the last board to fit the gap and nail it through the face. If it's a tight fit, carefully remove stock from the edge with a hand plane. Once the last board fits, continue paneling the rest of the walls until the room is done.

Reinstall the baseboards and the window and door casings. The baseboards will have to be cut shorter and the window and door jambs will need to have extensions added to bring them flush with the wall surface. Cut these extension jambs to size and nail them in place. Once you're satisfied with the fit, nail the casings in place. With the room all paneled, apply a finish of your choice.

Paneling a ceiling
It is relatively straight-forward to panel a ceiling with boards, following the methods described for a wall. First locate the joists, then nail or screw the furring strips across them.

1 Blind nailing

HORIZONTAL FURRING
Attach boards with tongue facing out

2 Attaching vertical boards

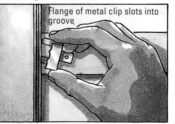

Flange of metal clip slots into groove

Metal clips can be used to fix boards to strips

To panel adjacent walls, shape the paneling boards to make neat internal or external corners.

Internal corners

Where two boards meet in the corner, plane a chamfer along the edge of one board, then nail both boards through their faces to the furring strips.

The detailing is similar for vertical and horizontal boards.

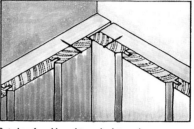

Cut chamfered board to make internal corner

External corners

To join vertical boards, lap one with another and nail them together. Plane a chamfer on the outer corner (**1**). For horizontal boards, nail on a beveled molding to cover the endgrain (**2**).

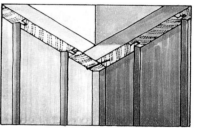

1 Vertical boards

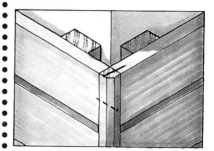

2 Horizontal boards

Fixing horizontal paneling

Follow the procedure described for vertical paneling, but position the first board at the bottom of the wall with its groove pointing down.

Paneling around doors and windows

Remove the casing and sill moldings, and nail the paneling to the furring strips. Add extension jambs to the sill (**1**) and to the window jambs (**2**). Then reinstall the original casings (**3**) and the original sill (**4**).

Adapting the moldings
To adapt moldings around doors and windows, follow the numbered sequence.

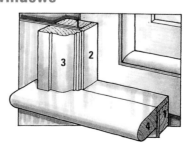

Attaching sheet paneling

ELECTRIC OUTLETS

Existing receptacles and light switches must be adapted to fit the newly installed paneling. The way you deal with these fixtures depends on the thickness of the paneling that's been installed.

Solid wood paneling

Begin by turning off the power to the circuit and the service panel. Then remove the coverplate and pull out the receptacle or switch. Make sure the circuit wires are firmly attached to their connecting terminals and that no bare wire is exposed. Leave the fixture pulled out, with the power off, while you panel around the wall opening.

Your goal is to create a surface for securely mounting the yoke on the receptacle or switch. To do this, carefully fit the paneling over the opening so that the yoke can bear directly on the paneling when it is screwed to the outlet box. If the hole is too wide or high, nothing will back up the yoke and the mounting screws will pull the fixture back to its original position.

On solid panel walls, the standard screws will not be long enough to reach the fixture box behind the paneling. Measure the new length you need and go to a hardware store or electrical supply outlet and get longer screws.

Plywood paneling

Modifying electrical outlets for plywood paneling is usually easier, though the same principles apply. You need to create a bearing surface for the yoke of the receptacle of the switch. Usually, you won't need longer screws. The plywood isn't as thick as the solid wood, and the standard screws will usually reach the fixture box.

Molding option

If you don't want to get involved in electrical work and don't want to hire an electrician to take care of it, you can just run the paneling up to the electrical outlets and add trim around the coverplates. This generally looks odd, especially if you are installing solid boards that are thicker than plywood panels. But, as with many jobs, a little creativity goes a long way. By choosing attractive molding, you can surround the outlets with tasteful treatments. All that's required is to miter the corners of the molding and glue it onto the wall with construction adhesive.

Cut plywood panels to size with a circular saw, making sure the finished side is facing down to avoid splitting the surface grain. Scribe the first board to the adjacent wall and ceiling.

Nailing panels

Nail each panel to the furring strips, using a foot lifter to hold it off the floor (**1**). If possible, hide the nails by driving them through V-grooves running from top to bottom on the surface. Set the nailheads just below the surface with a nailset. Fill the holes with dark-colored wood filler later. Butt subsequent panels to the previous one. Scribe and cut the last panel to fit against the adjacent wall.

Gluing panels

Plywood panels can be nailed to the furring strips as described above, but the nailheads may spoil the appearance. For a better result, use panel adhesive to glue the sheets to the furring. Your furring strips should be spaced to fit the size of the paneling.

When cutting thicker panels, use a circular saw and make sure to keep the finished surface down to avoid splitting the wood veneer. On thin panels, you can use a sharp utility knife to make the cuts. In this case, cut on the finished surface. Fit the first panel to the wall and follow the manufacturer's instructions for applying the glue. Some recommend applying it in patches, others suggest continuous bands. Press the boards firmly against the wall to spread the glue.

You can also use the glue as a contact adhesive. Apply the glue to the furring, press the board in place, then peel it off, leaving glue on both surfaces. When the glue has dried to the touch, press the panel in place again for an immediate bond (**2**).

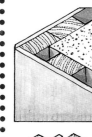

Nailing outside corners
Nail softwood blocks to one furring strip to support the edges of the panel. Add adhesive to the blocks, then nail the panel along the edge. Bevel the edge of one panel and stain the exposed core.

Nailing inside corners
Butt the panels at an inside corner. Conceal the joint by gluing matching strips of paneling into the corner.

Gluing outside corners
Cut a chamfer on the back of both panels, leaving the facing intact, to form a mitored joint. Then glue the panels to the furring strips.

Gluing inside corners
Scribe and cut the panels to fit each other, then glue them to the furring strips.

1 Using a foot lifter

2 Using contact adhesive
Having peeled a panel off the glued strips, wait for the glue to dry slightly and wedge the panel back in place.

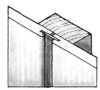

Joining grooved panels
Some boards are grooved along the vertical edges to accept a fillet strip. Nail or staple along the joint, covering the seam with the fillet.

Leaving a gap
Square-edged panels can be butted together or left with a gap between. Stain or paint the furring strip for a finished look.

Fitting a cover strip
The third method of concealing the joints between panels is to leave a slight gap and glue on a cover strip.

Wallcoverings : COVERINGS THAT CAMOUFLAGE

Although wallcoverings are often called wallpaper, only a portion of the wide range available is made solely from wood pulp. There is a huge range of paper-backed fabrics, from exotic silks to woven grass. Plastics have widened the choice of wallcoverings still further: there are paper-backed or cotton-backed vinyls, and plain or patterned foamed plastics. Before wallpaper became popular, fabric wall hangings were used to decorate interiors; this is still done today, using unbacked fabrics glued or stretched across walls.

Ensuring a suitable surface
Although many wallcoverings will cover minor blemishes, walls and ceilings should be clean, sound, and smooth. Eliminate moisture and mildew problems before hanging any wallcovering. Also, consider sizing the walls to reduce paste absorption.

Although a poor surface should be repaired, some coverings hide minor blemishes as well as providing a foundation for other finishes.

Expanded polystyrene sheet
Thin polystyrene sheeting is used for lining a wall before papering. It reduces condensation and also bridges hairline cracks and small holes. Polystyrene dents easily, so don't use it where it will take a lot of punishment. There is a patterned version for ceilings.

Lining paper
This is an inexpensive buff-colored wallpaper for lining uneven walls prior to hanging a heavy or expensive wallcovering. It also provides a good surface for latex paint.

Woodchip paper
Woodchip paper is made by sandwiching particles of wood between two layers of paper. It is inexpensive, easy to hang, and must be painted.

Top right
1 Expanded polystyrene
2 Lining paper
3 Woodchip

Bottom left
4 Hand-printed
5 Machine-printed

Bottom right
6 Lincrusta
7 Embossed-paper wallcovering
8 Blown vinyl

1   2   3

Printed wallpapers
One advantage of ordinary wallpaper is the superb range of printed colors and patterns, which is much wider than for any other wallcovering. Most of the cheaper papers are machine-printed.

The more costly hand-printed papers are prone to tearing when wet, and the inks have a tendency to run if you smear paste on the surface. They are not really suitable for walls exposed to heavy wear. Pattern matching can be awkward, because hand printing isn't as accurate as machine printing.

Relief papers
Wallpapers that have deeply embossed patterns hide minor imperfections. Relief papers are invariably painted, with latex, acrylics, or oil-based paints.

Lincrusta, which was the first embossed wallcovering, consists of a solid film of linseed oil and fillers fused onto a backing paper before the pattern is applied with an engraved steel roller. It is still available, though many people prefer embossed-paper wallcoverings or the superior-quality versions made from cotton fibers. Lightweight vinyl reliefs are also popular. During manufacture they are heated in an oven, which "blows" or expands the vinyl, creating deeply embossed patterns.

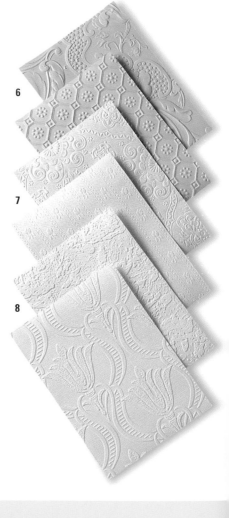

4   5   6   7   8

Wallcoverings

Washable papers
These are printed papers with a thin impervious glaze to make a spongeable surface. Washables are suitable for bathrooms and kitchens. The surface must not be scrubbed, or the plastic coating will be worn away.

Vinyl wallcoverings
A base paper, or sometimes a cotton backing, is coated with a layer of vinyl on which the design is printed. Heat is used to fuse the colors and the vinyl. The result is a durable, washable wallcovering ideally suited to bathrooms and kitchens. Many vinyls are sold prepasted for easy application.

Foamed-plastic covering
This is a lightweight wallcovering made solely of foamed polyethylene, with no backing paper. It is printed in a wide range of patterns, colors, and designs. You paste the wall instead of the covering. It is best used on walls that are not exposed to wear.

Flock wallcoverings
Flock papers have the major pattern elements defined with a fine pile produced by gluing synthetic or natural fibers (such as silk or wool) to the backing paper; the pattern stands out in relief, with a velvety texture.

Standard flock papers are difficult to hang, as contact with paste will ruin the pile. Vinyl flocks are less delicate, can be hung anywhere, and sometimes come prepasted.

You can sponge flock paper to remove stains, but brush to remove dust from the pile. Vinyl flocks can be washed without risk of damage.

Grass cloth
Natural grasses are woven into a mat and glued to a paper backing. While these wallcoverings are very attractive, they are fragile and difficult to hang.

Cork-faced paper
This is surfaced with thin sheets of colored or natural cork. It is not as easily spoiled as other special papers.

Paper-backed fabrics
Finely woven cotton, linen, or silk on a paper backing has to be applied to a flat surface. These coverings are expensive and difficult to hang, so avoid smearing the fabric with adhesive. Most fabrics are delicate, but some are plastic-coated to make them wear-resistant.

Unbacked fabrics
Upholstery-width fabric can be wrapped around panels, which are then glued or nailed to the wall.

Left to right
1 Washable papers
2 Textured and patterned vinyls
3 Foamed polyethylene
4 Flock papers
5 Paper-backed fabric
6 Grass-cloth mats
7 Cork-faced paper

Wallcoverings: estimating quantities

Calculating the number of rolls of wallcovering you need will depend mainly on the size of the roll—both the length and width. However, you also need to take into consideration how the pattern repeats and make allowance for cutting around obstructions such as windows and doors.

The width of a standard roll of wallcovering is 21 inches, the length is 33 feet. Use the two charts on this page to estimate how many rolls you'll need for walls and ceilings.

Nonstandard rolls

If the wallcovering you prefer is not cut to a standard size, calculate the amount you need the following way:

Walls
Measure the height of the walls from baseboard to ceiling. Divide the length of the roll by this figure to find the number of wall lengths you can cut from a roll.

Measure around the room, leaving out windows and doors, to determine how many widths fit into the total length of the walls. To estimate how many rolls you will need, divide this number by the number of wall lengths you can get from one roll. Add in the space around doors and windows.

Ceilings
Measure the length of the room to determine one strip of paper. Work out how many roll widths fit across the room. To estimate how many rolls you need, multiply the two figures and divide the answer by the length of a roll. Check for waste, and allow for it.

Checking for shading

If rolls of wallcovering are printed in one batch, there should be no problem with color-matching one roll to another. When you buy, look for the batch number printed on the wrapping.

Make a visual check before hanging the covering, especially for hand-printed papers or fabrics. Unroll a short length of each roll and lay them side by side. You may get a better color match by changing the rolls around. But if the difference is too obvious, ask for replacement rolls.

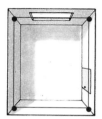

Measuring walls for standard rolls
A standard roll of wallcovering is 21 inches wide and 33 feet long. To be on the safe side, you may want to include windows and doors in your estimate.

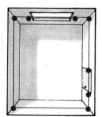

Measuring walls for nonstandard rolls
Do not include doors and windows when estimating for expensive materials. Allow for short lengths above doors and around windows afterwards.

Walls:
Standard rolls
Measure your room, then look down the height column and across the wall column to estimate the number of standard rolls required.

	HEIGHT OF ROOM IN FEET FROM BASEBOARD							
WALLS	7'-0" to 7'-6"	7'-6" to 8'-0"	8'-0" to 8'-6"	8'-6" to 9'-0"	9'-0" to 9'-6"	9'-6" to 10'-0"	10'-0" to 10'-6"	10'-6" to 11'-0"
	NUMBER OF ROLLS REQUIRED FOR WALLS							
30	7	7	8	8	8	9	9	9
32	7	8	8	8	9	9	10	10
34	8	8	9	9	9	10	10	11
36	8	8	9	9	10	10	11	11
38	8	9	9	10	11	11	11	12
40	9	9	10	10	11	12	12	13
42	9	10	10	11	12	12	13	13
44	10	10	11	11	12	13	13	14
46	10	11	11	12	13	13	14	15
48	10	11	12	12	13	14	14	15
50	11	12	12	13	14	14	15	16
52	11	12	13	13	14	15	16	16
54	12	12	13	14	15	15	16	17
56	12	13	14	14	15	16	17	18
58	13	13	14	15	16	17	17	18
60	13	14	15	15	16	17	18	19
62	13	14	15	16	17	18	19	19
64	14	15	16	16	17	18	19	20
66	14	15	16	17	18	19	20	21
68	15	16	17	17	18	19	20	21
70	15	16	17	18	19	20	21	22
72	15	16	17	18	19	20	21	22
74	16	17	18	19	20	21	22	23
76	16	17	18	19	21	22	23	24
78	17	18	19	20	21	22	23	24
80	17	18	19	20	22	23	24	25
82	18	19	20	21	22	23	24	26
84	18	19	20	21	23	24	25	26
86	18	20	21	22	23	24	26	27
88	19	20	21	22	24	25	26	27
90	19	20	22	23	24	25	27	28
92	20	21	22	23	25	26	27	28
94	20	21	23	24	25	27	28	29
96	20	22	23	24	26	27	28	30
98	21	22	24	25	26	28	29	30
100	21	23	24	25	27	28	30	31
102	22	23	25	26	27	29	30	32
104	22	24	25	26	28	29	31	32
106	23	24	26	27	28	30	31	33
108	23	24	26	27	29	30	32	34
110	23	25	26	28	30	31	33	34

(left margin label: MEASUREMENT IN FEET AROUND WALLS, INCLUDING DOORS AND WINDOWS)

Ceilings:
Standard rolls
Measure the perimeter of the ceiling. The number of standard rolls required is shown next to the overall dimensions.

Dimensions
All dimensions are shown in feet.

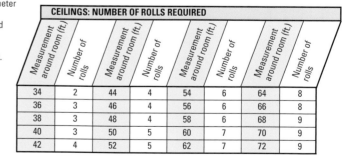

CEILINGS: NUMBER OF ROLLS REQUIRED							
Measurement around room (ft.)	Number of rolls	Measurement around room (ft.)	Number of rolls	Measurement around room (ft.)	Number of rolls	Measurement around room (ft.)	Number of rolls
34	2	44	4	54	6	64	8
36	3	46	4	56	6	66	8
38	3	48	4	58	6	68	9
40	3	50	5	60	7	70	9
42	4	52	5	62	7	72	9

CHOOSING PASTE

Most wallpaper pastes are supplied as powder or flakes for mixing with water. Some come ready-mixed.

All-purpose paste
Standard wallpaper paste is suitable for most lightweight to medium-weight papers. With less water added, it can be used to hang heavyweight papers.

Heavy-duty paste
This is specially prepared for hanging embossed papers, paper-backed fabrics, and other heavyweight wallcoverings.

Fungicidal paste
Pastes often contain a fungicide to prevent the development of mold under impervious wallcoverings, such as vinyls, washable papers, and foamed-plastic coverings.

Ready-mixed paste
Tubs of ready-mixed paste are specially made for heavyweight wallcoverings and fabrics.

Stain-free paste
Use with delicate papers that could be stained by conventional pastes.

Repair adhesive
Sticks down peeling edges and corners. It will glue vinyl to vinyl, so is suitable for applying decorative border rolls.

Trimming and cutting

Most wallcoverings are machine-trimmed to width so that you can join adjacent lengths accurately. Some hand-printed papers are left untrimmed. These are usually expensive coverings, so don't attempt to trim them yourself. Ask the supplier to do this for you.

Cutting plain wallcoverings
Measure the height of the wall at the point where you will hang the first piece. Add an extra 4 inches for trimming top and bottom. Cut several pieces and mark the top of each one.

Allowing for patterned wallcoverings
You may have to allow extra on alternate lengths of patterned wallcoverings to match patterns.

Pasting wallcoverings

You can use any wipe-clean table for pasting, but a narrow, fold-up pasting table is a good investment if you are doing a lot of work. Lay several cut lengths of paper face down on the table to keep them clean. To stop the paper from rolling up while you are pasting, tuck the ends under string tied loosely around the table legs.

Applying the paste

Use a large, soft wall brush or pasting brush to apply the paste. Mix the paste in a plastic bucket and tie string across the rim to support the brush, keeping its handle clean while you hang the paper.

Align the wallcovering with the far edge of the table, to avoid brushing paste on the table, where it could be transferred to the face of the wallcovering. Apply the paste by brushing away from the center. Paste the edges and remove any lumps.

If you prefer, apply the paste with a short-pile paint roller. Pour the paste into a roller tray and roll it onto the wallcovering in one direction only, towards the end of the paper.

Pull the wallcovering to the front edge of the table and paste the other half. Fold the pasted end over—don't press it down—and slide the length along the table to expose an unpasted section.

Paste the other end, then fold it over to almost meet the first cut end. The second fold is invariably deeper than the first—a handy way to tell which is the bottom of patterned wallcoverings.

Hang vinyls and lightweight papers immediately. Drape other wallcoverings over a broom handle spanning two chair backs, or other supports, and leave them to soak. Some heavy or embossed wallcoverings need to soak for 15 minutes.

Pasting the wall
Instead of pasting the back of exotic wallcoverings, paste the wall, to reduce the risk of damaging their delicate faces. Apply a band of paste just wider than the width of the wallcovering, so you won't have to paste right up to its edge for the next piece. Use a brush or roller.

Prepasted wallcoverings
Many wallcoverings come precoated with adhesive, activated by soaking a cut length in a trough of cold water. Plastic troughs are sold for this purpose.

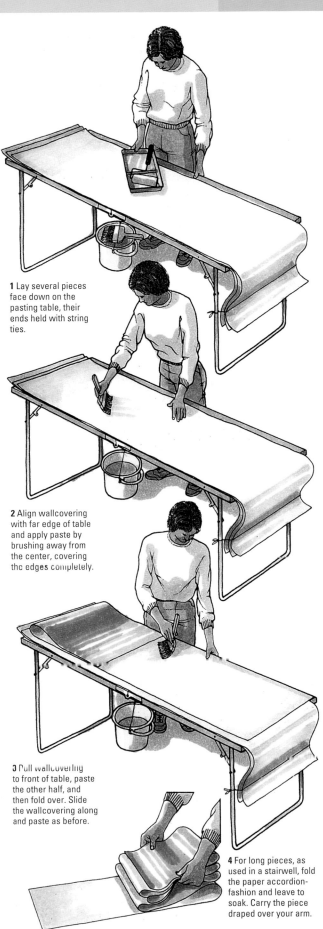

1 Lay several pieces face down on the pasting table, their ends held with string ties.

2 Align wallcovering with far edge of table and apply paste by brushing away from the center, covering the edges completely.

3 Pull wallcovering to front of table, paste the other half, and then fold over. Slide the wallcovering along and paste as before.

4 For long pieces, as used in a stairwell, fold the paper accordion-fashion and leave to soak. Carry the piece draped over your arm.

Papering a wall

Don't apply a wallcovering of any kind until all the woodwork in the room has been painted or varnished and the ceiling painted or papered.

Where to start

The traditional method for papering a room is to hang the first length next to a window close to a corner, then work in both directions away from the light. But, you may find it easier to paper the longest uninterrupted wall first, so you get used to the basic techniques before tackling corners or obstructions.

If your wallcovering has a large, regular pattern, center the first length over the fireplace or between two windows for symmetry—unless that means you will be left with narrow strips at each side. In such cases, it's best to butt two lengths on the centerline.

Center large pattern over a fireplace

Butt two lengths between windows

Hanging paper on a straight wall

The walls of a room are rarely square, so use a plumb line to create a vertical guide for the first length of wallcovering. Start at one end of the wall and mark the vertical line one roll-width away from the corner minus ½ inch, so the first piece will just overlap the adjacent wall (1).

Allowing enough wallcovering for trimming at the ceiling, unfold the top section of the pasted piece and hold it against the plumb line. Brush the paper gently onto the wall, working from the center in all directions in order to squeeze out any trapped air (2).

When you are sure the paper is positioned accurately, lightly draw the point of your scissors along the ceiling line, peel back the top edge, and cut along the crease (3). Smooth the paper back and tap it down with the brush. Unpeel the lower fold of the paper, smooth it onto the wall with the brush, then tap it into the corner. Crease the bottom edge against the baseboard, peel away the paper, then trim and brush it back against the wall (4).

Hang the next length in the same manner. Slide it with your fingertips to align the pattern and produce a perfect butt joint. Wipe any paste from the surface with a damp cloth. Continue to the other side of the wall, allowing the last piece to overlap the adjoining wall by ½ inch.

1 Mark the first piece
Use a roll of paper to mark the wall one width away from the corner, less ½ inch for an overlap onto the adjacent wall. Then mark a line from ceiling to baseboard, using a plumb line.

2 Hang the first piece
Cut the first piece of paper, allowing about 2 inches at each end for trimming. Paste and allow to soak. Hang the top section against the plumb line and brush out from the center.

3 Trim at the ceiling
When the paper is smoothly brushed on, run the tip of your scissors along the ceiling corner, peel away the paper, cut off the excess, then brush back onto the wall.

4 Trim at baseboard
Unfold the lower section of paper. At the baseboard, tap your brush against the top edge, peel away the paper and cut along the folded line. Then brush paper back into place.

● **Hide a join in a corner**
When using a wallcovering with a large pattern, try to finish in a corner, where it will be less noticeable if the pattern doesn't quite match.

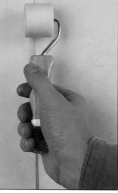

Sticking down the edges
Ensure that the edges of the paper adhere firmly by running a seam roller along the butt joints.

Losing air bubbles
Slight blistering usually flattens out as wet paper dries and shrinks. If a blister remains, you can inject a little paste through it and roll it flat. You can also cut across it in two directions, peel back the flaps, and paste them down.

Lining a wall prior to papering is only necessary if you are hanging embossed or luxury wallcoverings, or if the wall has imperfections that might show through a thin wallpaper. Hang lining paper horizontally, so the joints cannot align with those in the top layer. If you are right-handed, work from right to left and vice versa.

Mark a horizontal line on the wall one roll-width from the ceiling. Holding the folded paper in one hand, start at the top right-hand corner of the wall, aligning the bottom edge with the marked line. Smooth the paper onto the wall with a brush, working from the center towards the edges of the paper.

Work along the wall gradually, unfolding the paper as you go. Take care not to stretch or tear the wet paper. Use the brush to gently tap the paper into the corner at each end.

Use the point of a pair of scissors to lightly mark the corner, peel back the paper, and trim to the crease. Brush the paper back in place. You may have to perform a similar operation along the ceiling if the paper overlaps slightly. Work down the wall, butting each strip against the last, or leaving a minute gap between the lengths.

Trim the bottom length to the baseboard. Let the lining paper dry for 24 hours before covering.

Lining prior to painting
If you line a wall for latex painting, hang the lining paper vertically, as you would with other wallcoverings.

Hanging lining paper horizontally
Hold the folded paper in one hand and smooth it onto the wall, starting at the top right corner. Butt the strips of paper together.

Papering corners

Turn an inside corner by marking another plumb line so that the next length of paper covers the overlap from the first wall. If the piece you trimmed off at the corner is wide enough, use it as your first length on the new wall (**1**).

If there's an alcove on both sides of the fireplace, you will need to wrap the paper around the outside corners. Trim the last length so that it wraps around the corner, lapping the next wall by about one inch. Plumb and hang the remaining strip with its edge about ½ inch from the corner (**2**).

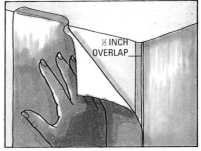

1 Papering into an inside corner

Papering behind radiators

If you can't remove a radiator, turn off the heat and allow it to cool. Use a tape measure to locate the positions of the brackets that hold the radiator to the wall. Transfer these measurements to a piece of wallcovering and slit it

from the bottom to the top of the bracket (**3**). Feed the pasted paper behind the radiator and down both sides of the brackets. Use a radiator roller to press it to the wall. Crease and trim to the baseboard.

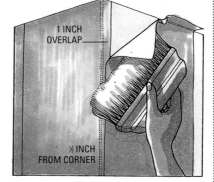

2 Papering around an outside corner

Papering around switches and outlets

Turn off the electricity at the service panel. Hang the wallcovering over the switch or receptacle, then make diagonal cuts from the center of the fixture to each of its corners. Press the excess paper against the edges of the

coverplate with the brush. Trim off the wastepaper, leaving about ¼ inch all around (**4**). Loosen the coverplate, tuck the margin behind, and then retighten the plate. Don't switch the power back on until the paste is dry.

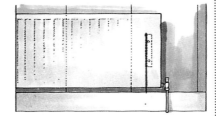

3 Slit paper to fit over radiator brackets

Papering around doors and windows

When you get to the door, hang the length of paper next to a door casing, brushing down the butt joint to align the pattern and allowing the other edge to loosely overlap the trim.

Make a diagonal cut in the excess toward the top corner of the trim (**5**). Crease the waste down the side of the casing with scissors, peel it back and trim off, then brush back. Leave a ½-inch strip for turning over the top of the door.

Fill in with short strips above the door, then butt the next full length of paper over the door and cut the excess diagonally into the trim, pasting the rest of the strip down the other side of the door. Mark and cut off the waste.

Treat window trim in a similar way to door trim. If the window is set into

a reveal, hang the piece of wallcovering next to the window and allow it to overhang the opening. Make a horizontal cut just above the edge of the window reveal. Make a similar cut near the bottom, then fold the paper around to cover the side of the reveal. Crease and trim along the window frame and sill.

To fill in the window reveal, first cut a strip to match the width and pattern of the overhang above the reveal. Paste it, slip it under the overhang, and fold it around the top of the reveal (**6**). Cut through the overlap with a smooth wavy stroke, then remove the excess paper and roll down the joint (**7**).

To continue, hang short lengths on the wall below and above the window, wrapping top lengths into the reveal.

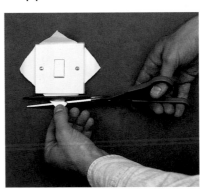

4 Trim off waste, leaving ¼ inch all around

Papering around a fireplace

Papering around a fireplace is similar to fitting wallpaper around a doorframe. Make a diagonal cut in the waste overlapping the fireplace, cutting toward the corner of the mantel. Then tuck the paper in all around, crease it, and cut it.

If the fireplace surround is ornate, first brush the paper onto the wall

above the surround, then trim the paper to fit under the mantelshelf at each side. Brush the paper around the corners to hold it in place. Then, gently press the wallcovering into the shape of the surround, peel it away, and cut the crease with sharp scissors. Smooth the paper back down with the brush.

5 Cut overlap diagonally into corner

Papering archways

Arrange strips to leave even gaps between the sides of the arch and the next full-length strips. Hang strips over the face of the arch, cut around the curve leaving an extra 1 inch margin for folding onto the underside. Snip into this margin to prevent creasing, then brush the piece in place. Fit a strip on the underside to reach from the floor to the top of the arch. Repeat on the opposite side.

Accurate positioning
Brush down the butt joint before you trim.

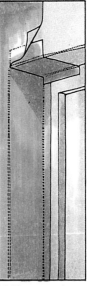

6 Fold onto reveal

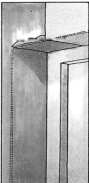

7 Cut with wavy line

Special techniques

No matter what kind of wallcovering you may be using, most of the standard wallpapering techniques previously explained will work. However, there are additional considerations and special techniques involved in applying some types of wallcovering.

The problem when papering a stairwell is having to handle the extra-long pieces on the side walls. For this, you need to build a safe work platform over the stairs. Plumb and hang the longest piece first, lapping the wall above the stairs by ½ inch.

Carrying the large pieces of wall-covering, sometimes up to 15 feet long, is awkward. Paste the covering liberally, so it won't dry out while you hang it, then fold it and drape it over your arm while you climb the platform. You will need a helper to support the weight of the pasted paper while you apply it. Unfold the flaps as you work down the wall.

Crease and cut the bottom of the wallcovering against the angled stair stringer. Don't forget to allow for this angle when cutting each piece to length. Work away from this first length in both directions, then paper the top wall.

To avoid making difficult cuts, it pays to arrange the strips so that the point where the banister rail meets the wall falls between two pieces. Hang the pieces to the rail and cut horizontally into the edge of the last strip at the center of the rail, then make radial cuts so the paper can be pressed in around the rail. Crease the flaps, peel away the wallcovering, and cut them off. Smooth the covering back in place.

Hang the next piece at the other side of the rail, butting it to the previous piece, and make similar radial cuts.

Papering sequence
When papering a stairwell, follow this sequence:
1 Hang the longest piece first.
2 Crease it into the angled stair stringer and trim to fit.
3 Lap the paper onto the top wall.
4 & 5 Work away from the first piece in both directions.
6 Paper the top wall.

Hanging embossed wallcoverings

Line the wall before hanging embossed-paper wallcoverings. Apply a heavy-duty paste liberally and evenly to the wallcovering. Allow each piece to soak for 10 minutes (15 minutes for cotton-fiber wallcoverings) before you hang it.

Tap down butt joints with a paper-hanger's brush to avoid flattening the pattern with a seam roller.

Don't turn an embossed wallcovering around corners. Instead, measure the distance from the last piece to the corner and cut your next length to fit. Trim and hang the offcut to meet at the corner. Once the paper has dried thoroughly, fill outside corners, if necessary, with latex caulk.

Traditional Lincrusta is still available in a limited range of original Victorian patterns for re-creating period interiors. In the long run, it pays to leave hanging this expensive material to an expert, since it requires special techniques that are difficult to master.

Hanging vinyl wallcoverings

Apply paste to paper-backed vinyls in the regular way. Cotton-backed vinyl hangs better if you paste the wall and then let it become tacky before you apply the wallcovering. Use a fungicidal paste.

Hang and butt-join pieces of vinyl, using a sponge instead of a brush to smooth them onto the wall. Crease each length top and bottom, then trim it to size with a sharp utility knife.

Vinyl will not normally stick to itself, so when you turn a corner use a knife to cut through both pieces of paper where they overlap. Peel away the surplus wallcovering and rub down the vinyl to produce a perfect butt joint. You can also glue the overlap, using a repair adhesive.

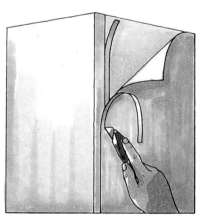

Cut through overlap and remove surplus

Using prepasted wallcoverings

Place the trough of cold water next to the baseboard at the bottom of the first piece. Roll the piece loosely with the paste side facing out and immerse it in the trough for the recommended time indicated in the manufacturer's instructions.

Take hold of the cut end and lift the paper, allowing it to unroll naturally and draining the surface water back into the trough at the same time. Hang and butt-join in the usual way, using a sponge to smooth vinyls and a brush for other prepasted wallcoverings.

Hanging a long wet piece can be difficult if you follow the standard procedure. Instead, roll the length from the top with the pattern on the outside. Place it in the trough and immediately reroll it through the water. Take it from the trough in roll form and drain off excess water, then unroll the strip as you hang it.

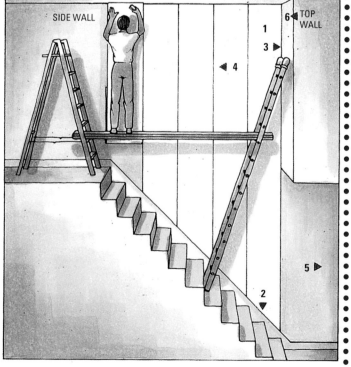

SIDE WALL

TOP WALL

1

6

3

4

5

2

Pull paper from trough and hang it on the wall

Special techniques

Hanging a foamed-plastic wallcovering

A lightweight foamed-plastic wall-covering can be hung straight from the roll onto a pasted wall. Sponge in place, and trim top and bottom with scissors.

Hanging flock paper

Protect the flocking with a piece of lining paper as you smooth out air bubbles with a brush. Cut through both thicknesses of overlapping strips and remove the surplus, then press back the edges to make a neat butt joint.

Fabrics and special coverings

Try to keep paste off the face of paper-backed fabrics and other special wallcoverings. To avoid ruining an expensive paper, ask the supplier which paste to use for the wallcovering you have chosen.

Many special wallcoverings have delicate surfaces, so use a felt or rubber roller to press the covering in place, or tap gently with a brush.

Most fabric wallcoverings will be machine trimmed. But if the edges are frayed, overlap the joints and cut through both thicknesses, then peel off the waste to make a butt joint. Make a similar joint at a corner.

Many fabrics are sold in wide rolls, so even one cut length will be heavy and awkward to handle. Paste the wall, then support the rolled length on a board supported between two stepladders. Work from the bottom up.

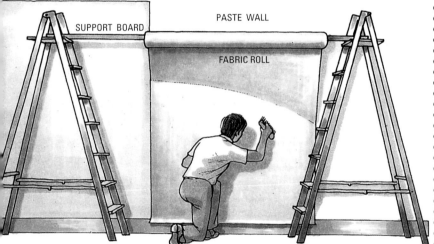

Supporting heavy fabric

Lining with expanded polystyrene

Paint or roll ready-mixed, heavy-duty adhesive onto the wall. Hang the covering straight from the roll, smooth it gently with the flat of your hand, then roll over it lightly with a dry paint roller.

Provided the edges are square, butt adjacent pieces. If they become crushed, overlap each join and cut through both thicknesses with a sharp utility knife. Peel away the cutoffs and rub the edges down.

Trim top and bottom with a knife and straightedge. Allow to dry for 72 hours, then hang the wallcovering over the polystyrene, using a thick fungicidal paste.

Hang polystyrene straight from the roll

There are two ways to apply unbacked fabric to your walls. If you want to hang a plain-colored, medium-weight fabric, you can stick it directly onto the wall.

It can be difficult to align patterns if the fabric stretches. For more control over a patterned fabric, stretch it onto panels of ½-inch-thick insulation board, which gives you the double advantage of insulation and a pin-board, and attach the boards directly to the wall.

Applying fabric with paste

Test a scrap of fabric to make sure the adhesive will not stain it. Use a ready-mixed paste and roll it onto the wall.

Wrap a cut length of the fabric around a cardboard tube and gradually unroll it onto the surface, smoothing it down with a dry paint roller. Take care not to distort the weave. Overlap the joints. If the fabric shrinks, don't cut through the pieces until the paste has dried. Then, reapply paste, cut and close the seams.

Press the fabric into the ceiling line and baseboard, then trim away the excess with a sharp utility knife once the paste has set.

Making wall panels

Cut the insulation board to suit the width of the fabric and the height of the wall. Stretch the fabric across the panel and wrap it around the edges, then use latex adhesive to stick it to the back of the panel. Hold the fabric temporarily with pushpins while the adhesive dries.

Either use a general-purpose adhesive to glue the panels to the wall or nail them, setting the nailheads through the weave of the fabric to conceal them.

Stretch unbacked fabric over insulation board

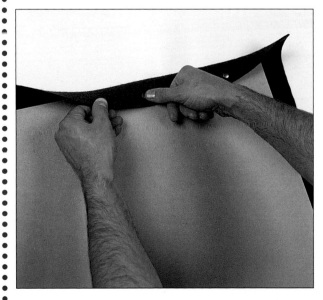

Papering a ceiling

Papering a ceiling isn't as difficult as you may think. The techniques are basically the same as for papering a wall, except that the pieces are usually longer and so more unwieldy to hold while brushing them into place. Set up a sensible work platform—it's virtually impossible to work from a single stepladder—and enlist a helper to support the folded paper while you position one end. Then progress across the room. If you have marked guidelines on the ceiling first, the result should be flawless.

Working from a ladder
If you have to work from a stepladder, get a helper to support the paper while you apply it.

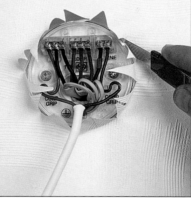

Paper support
A helpful support is made easily by taping a cardboard tube to a broom.

Planning ceiling work

Arrange your work platform after you figure out the papering sequence for the ceiling. The best type of platform to use is one supported by sawhorses, but you can manage with a pair of scaffold boards spanning two stepladders.

Plan to work parallel with the window wall and away from the light, so you can see what you are doing and so that the light will not highlight the seams between strips. If the distance is shorter the other way, then it's easier to hang the strips in that direction.

Mark a guideline along the ceiling one roll-width minus ½ inch from the side wall, so that the first strip of paper will lap onto the wall.

Putting up the paper

Paste the paper as you would for wall-covering and fold it carefully. Drape the folded piece over a spare roll and carry it to the work platform. You will find it easier if a helper supports the folded paper, leaving both your hands free for brushing it into place.

Hold the strip against the guideline, using a brush to stroke it onto the ceiling. Tap it into the corner, then gradually work backward along the scaffold board, brushing the paper on as your helper unfolds it.

If the ceiling has a perimeter molding, crease and trim the paper against it. Otherwise leave ½ inch of paper to lap the walls. This lap will be covered later by the wallcovering. Work across the ceiling in the same way, butting the pieces of paper together. Cut the final strip roughly to width, and trim it to lap onto the wall.

Unlike walls, where you have doors, windows, and radiators to contend with, there are few obstructions on a ceiling to make papering difficult. Problems can occur, however where there is a light fixture or a decorative plaster centerpiece.

Cutting around a light fixture

Where the paper passes over a ceiling fixture, cut several triangular flaps around the baseplate. Press the paper around the fixture with a brush, then continue on to the end of the piece. Return to the fixture and cut off the flaps with a sharp utility knife. Remember to switch off the power if you expose the wiring.

Papering around a centerpiece

If you have a decorative centerpiece, work out the position of the pieces so that a seam will pass through the middle of the centerpiece. Cut long flaps in both papers, then trim to fit.

Cut off triangular flaps when paste is dry

Papering a ceiling
The job is much easier if two people work together.
1 Mark a guideline on the ceiling.
2 Support the folded paper on a tube.
3 Brush the paper on, from the center to the sides.
4 The overlap is eventually covered by wallpaper.
5 Use a pair of boards, to support two people.

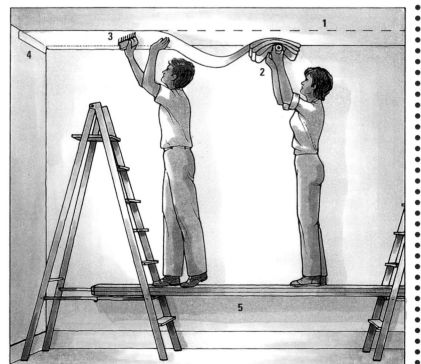

Cut long strips to fit around centerpiece

Choosing tiles

Tiling allows you to cover a surface with relatively small, regular units that can be cut and fitted into awkward shapes far more easily than sheet materials. With an almost inexhaustible range of colors, textures, and patterns to choose from, tiling is one of the most popular methods of decorating walls and floors.

Ceramic wall tiles

The majority of ceramic wall tiles are coated with a thick layer of glaze that makes them durable, waterproof, and relatively easy to cut. Unglazed tiles are generally more subtle in color and may need to be sealed to keep them from absorbing grease and dirt.

Machine-made tiles are perfectly regular in shape and color, and are therefore simple to install. With hand-made tiles, there is much more variation in shape, color, and texture, but many people think this irregularity adds to their appeal.

Although rectangular tiles are available, the majority of wall tiles are 4 or 6 inches square. As well as a wide range of solid colors, you can buy printed and high-relief molded tiles in both modern and traditional styles. Patterned tiles can be used for decorative friezes or individual accents. Some are sold as sets for creating murals, mostly for kitchen countertop backsplashes.

Narrow border tiles are used to create visual breaks that relieve the monotony of large areas of common tiles. You can also buy a wide variety of trim pieces to finish off any tile installation.

Mosaic tiles

These are, in effect, small versions of the standard ceramic tiles. To lay them individually would be time consuming and difficult, so they are usually joined, either by a paper or a mesh backing, into larger panels. Square tiles are common, but rectangular, hexagonal, and round mosaics are also available. Because they are small, mosaics can be used on curved surfaces, and fit irregular shapes better than large ceramic tiles do.

Ceramic floor tiles

Floor tiles are generally larger and thicker than wall tiles so that they can withstand the weight of furniture and foot traffic. As with wall tiles, square and rectangular tiles are the most economical ones to buy and install, but hexagonal and octagonal floor tiles are also available and are often used in combination with accent pieces to create regular patterns. Choose nonslip tiles for bathrooms and other areas where the floor is likely to become wet.

Small, unglazed tiles are laid individually to form intricate patterns that re-create the styles of Victorian and other period tiled floors. They are made in a range of solid colors and patterns.

Quarry tiles

Thick, unglazed quarry tiles have a mellow appearance. The colors are limited to browns, reds, black, and white. Handmade quarries are uneven in color, producing a beautiful mottled effect. Round-edge, bullnose quarry tiles can be used as treads for steps. Trim tiles are commonly available for creating baseboards around a quarry-tile floor. Quarry tiles are more difficult to cut than glazed ceramic tiles, so they aren't often used in areas where complicated fitting is required.

Gap fillers

There are special tiles available to cover the gaps around fixtures like sinks and showers. These tiles have been somewhat replaced by silicone caulks. But, they still add a touch of traditional style to a kitchen or bathroom.

Quadrant
Used to fill the joint between bath and wall.

Mitered tile
Use at the end if you want to turn a corner.

Bullnose tile
Use this tile to finish the end of a straight run.

Field tiles
These are the standard square or rectangular tiles used to create main areas of tiling. Some glazed field tiles are universal tiles, which have two glazed edges so that they can be used for edging on walls and backsplashes. Cross-shape plastic spacers are sometimes used to maintain regular spacing between field tiles.

Tile selection
The examples shown on the left are a typical cross section of commercially available ceramic tiles.
1 Glazed ceramic
2 Shape and size variation
3 Mosaic tiles
4 Quarry tiles

Choosing tiles

Carpet tiles

These have advantages over wall-to-wall carpeting. An error is less crucial when cutting a single tile to fit, and any loose, worn, burned, or stained tiles can be easily replaced. However, you can't always substitute a new tile several years later, because the color won't match. Buy several spares initially and swap them around regularly to even out the wear and color change. Most types of carpet are available as tiles, including cord, loop, and twist piles, both in wool and in a range of manufactured fibers. Carpet tiles come mostly in plain colors or small patterns. Some have an integral rubber backing.

Carpet tiles are hard-wearing and comfortable

Stone and slate flooring

A floor laid with natural stone or slate tiles will be exquisite but expensive. Sizes and thicknesses vary according to the manufacturer—some will even cut to measure. These materials are so costly that you should consider hiring a professional to lay them.

Vinyl tiles

Vinyl can be cut easily and, if carefully installed with good adhesive, will be waterproof. Vinly tiles are also among the least expensive and easiest to install floorcoverings. A standard tile has a printed pattern sandwiched between a vinyl backing and a harder, clear-vinyl surface. Solid-vinyl tiles are made entirely of hard-wearing plastic.

Some vinyl tiles have a high proportion of mineral filler. As a result, they are stiff and must be laid on a perfectly flat base. Unlike standard vinyl tiles, they will block some moisture from rising through a concrete floor.

Most tiles are square or rectangular, but there are interlocking shapes and hexagons. There are many patterns and colors to choose from, including embossed textures that simulate wood, ceramic, brick, or stone.

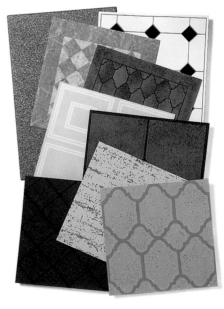

Vinyl tiles can simulate other flooring materials

Choosing tiles

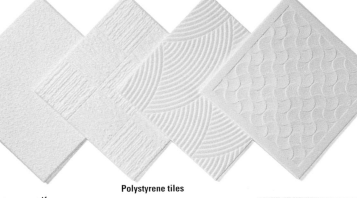

Polystyrene tiles

Polystyrene tiles

Although expanded-polystyrene tiles will not significantly reduce heat loss from a room, they are able to prevent condensation and mask a ceiling that is in poor condition. Polystyrene cuts easily, provided the knife is very sharp. For fire safety, choose a self-extinguishing type and do not coat with an oil paint. Polystyrene wall tiles are made, but they crush easily and are not suitable for use in most homes. Polystyrene tiles may be flat or decoratively embossed.

Mineral fiber tiles

Ceiling tiles made from compressed mineral fiber are dense enough to be sound and heat insulating. They are normally installed in a suspended grid system that may be exposed or concealed, depending on the type of tile. Fiber tiles can also be glued directly to a flat ceiling. A range of textured surfaces is available.

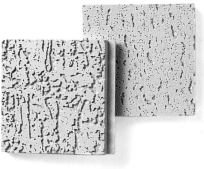

Mineral fiber tiles

Rubber tiles

These were originally made for use in shops and offices, but as they are hard-wearing, soft, and quiet to walk on, they also make ideal residential floor-coverings. Rubber tiles are usually studded or textured to improve the grip.

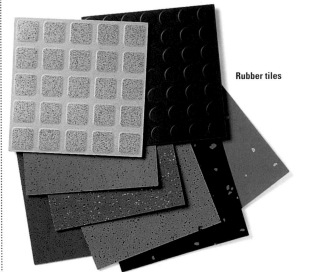

Rubber tiles

Cork tiles

Cork is a popular covering for walls and floors. It is easy to lay with contact adhesive, and can be cut to size and shape with a utility knife. A wide choice of textures and warm colors is available. Presanded but unfinished cork will darken in tone when you varnish it. Or, you can buy prefinished tiles with various plastic and wax coatings.

Mirror tiles

Square and rectangular mirror tiles are attached to walls with a self-sticking pad in each tile corner. Both silver and bronze finishes are available.

Mirror tiles will present a distorted reflection unless they are mounted on a perfectly flat surface.

Plastic tiles

Insulated plastic wall tiles inhibit condensation. Provided you don't use abrasive cleaners on them, they are relatively durable. But, they will melt if subjected to direct heat. A special grout is applied to fill the joints between tiles.

Cork floor tiles

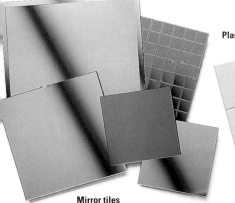

Mirror tiles

Plastic tiles

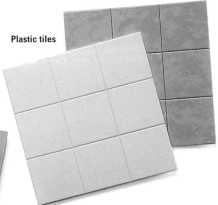

Laying out wall tiles

Once you have prepared the wall surfaces for tiling, measure each wall accurately. Determine where to start tiling and how to avoid having to make too many difficult cuts. The best way to do this is to mark a row of tiles on a straight board, which you can use as a guide for laying out the walls.

Setting out
The setting-out procedure described on this page is applicable to the following tiles: ceramic, cork, mosaics, mirror, and plastic.

Making a guide board
Make a guide board from 1 x 2 lumber to help you plot the position of the tiles on the wall. Lay several tiles along the board, inserting plastic spacers between them if necessary, and mark the position of each tile on the board.

Mark tile increments along a guide board.

Using a guide board
Hold a homemade guide board against the surface and mark the positions of all the tiles.

Laying out a plain wall

On a plain, uninterrupted wall, use the guide board to plan horizontal rows of tiles, starting at the baseboard level. If you are left with a narrow strip at the top, move the rows up half a tile width to create a wider margin. Then, mark the bottom of the lowest row of whole tiles on the wall.

Temporarily nail a thin board to the wall just below this mark (**1**). Make sure the board is level by placing a level on top of it.

Mark the center of the wall (**2**), then use the guide board to set out the vertical rows on each side of the line. If the margin tiles measure less than half a width, reposition the rows sideways by half a tile. Use a level to position a board against the last vertical tile line, and nail it to the wall (**3**).

Laying out a half-tiled wall

If you are tiling only part of a wall, lay out the tiles to leave a row of whole tiles at the top (**4**). If you are incorporating baseboard tiles or border tiles in your design, plan their positions first and use them as starting points.

Arranging tiles around a window

For nicely balanced tiling, you should always use a window as your starting point, so that the tiles surrounding it are equal in size but not too narrow. If possible, begin a row of whole tiles at sill level (**5**) and position cut tiles at the back of a window reveal (**6**).

If necessary, attach a temporary support board over a window to keep the tiles properly aligned (**7**).

Laying out for tiling
Plan different arrangements of wall tiles as shown at right, plotting the symmetry of the tile field to ensure a wide margin all around.

1 Temporarily attach a horizontal board at the base of the field.
2 Mark the center of the wall.
3 Measure from the mark, then attach a vertical board at the side of the field.
4 Start half-walls with whole tiles.
5 Use a row of whole tiles at sill level.
6 Place cut tiles at the back of a window reveal.
7 Support tiles over a window opening until the adhesive sets.

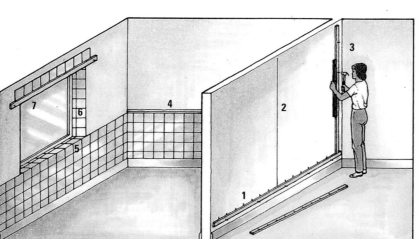

A properly tiled surface should last for many years, but the appearance is often spoiled by one or two cracked or chipped tiles or by discolored grout. There is usually no need to tile the wall again, because both problems can be fixed easily.

Renewing grout

Discolored grout can be cleaned or brightened with one of the many grout maintenance products on the market, but severely cracked or missing grout should be replaced. To remove it, scrape the joints with a grout removal tool available at tile stores. Brush all the dust from the joints, then mix up new grout and spread it over the wall with a rubber-faced grout trowel. Use the trowel to force the grout into the bottom of the joints. When the grout is dry, buff the wall with a clean, soft rag. Then apply a clear liquid sealer.

Brush grout brightener onto grout joints

Replacing a cracked ceramic tile

Scrape the grout from around the damaged tile, then use a small cold chisel to chip out the tile, working from the center out. Wear protective goggles and don't dislodge neighboring tiles. Scrape out the remains of the adhesive, and brush debris from the recess. Coat the back of the replacement tile with adhesive, then press it firmly in place. Wipe excess adhesive from the surface. Once the adhesive has cured, grout the joints.

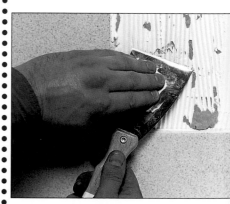

Scrape out remaining tile adhesive

Start by tiling the main areas with whole tiles, leaving the gaps around the edges to be filled with cut tiles later. This allows you to work quickly and accurately, without stopping to make difficult or time-consuming cuts.

Choosing tile adhesive and grout

Ceramic tiles are stuck to the wall with special adhesives that are generally sold ready-mixed, although a few need to be mixed to a paste with water. The product packaging will state the coverage you can expect.

Grout is a similar material that is used to fill the gaps between the tiles. Unless you have specific requirements, it is convenient to use one of the many adhesives that can be used for both jobs.

Most tile adhesives and grouts are water-resistant, but check that any material you use for tiling shower surrounds is completely waterproof and can be subjected to the powerful spray generated by a modern shower. If tiles are to be laid on a drywall, make sure you use a flexible adhesive. Heat-resistant adhesive and grout may be required in the vicinity of a kitchen range and around a fireplace. You should use an epoxy-based grout for kitchen and bathroom countertops.

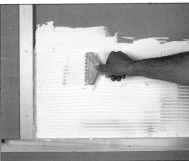

1 Form horizontal ridges with a notched spreader

Applying whole tiles

A serrated plastic spreader is normally supplied with each container of adhesive. But, if you are tiling a large area, it pays to buy a notched metal trowel for applying the adhesive to the wall.

Use the straight edge of the spreader or trowel to spread enough adhesive to cover an area of about 3 square feet. Then, turn the tool around and drag the notched edge through the adhesive so that it forms horizontal ridges **(1)**.

Press the first tile into the corner formed by the layout boards **(2)**. Press the next tile into place with a slight twist, until it is firmly fixed. Many tiles have built-in alignment ears to maintain joint spacing. If your tiles don't, then use plastic spacers. Lay additional tiles to build up three or four rows at a time, then wipe any adhesive from the tiles using a clean, damp sponge.

Spread more adhesive, and continue to install the remaining whole tiles. When you have completed the entire field, scrape the adhesive from the margins and clean any adhesive from the tile surfaces. Once the adhesive has set, carefully remove the alignment boards from the walls.

2 Stick the first tile against layout boards

Cutting and fitting margin tiles

It's necessary to cut tiles one at a time to fit the gaps between the field tiles and the adjacent walls. Because walls are rarely perfectly square and plumb, the margins are bound to be uneven.

Mark each margin tile by placing it face down over its neighbor with one edge against the adjacent wall **(3)**. Make allowance for the normal grout spacing between the tiles. Transfer the marks to the edges of the tile using a felt-tip pen and cut the tile (see next page). Spread adhesive onto the back of each tile **(4)**, and press it into place.

3 Mark back of a margin tile

4 Spread adhesive onto back of a cut tile

Grouting the tiles

Standard grouts are white, grey, or brown, but there is also a range of colored grouts to match or contrast with the tiles. You can also mix color pigments with dry powdered grout, before adding water.

Let the tile adhesive dry for 24 hours, then use a rubber-faced trowel to spread the grout and force it into the joints **(5)**. Spread the grout in all directions to make sure every joint is well filled.

Using a barely damp sponge, wipe grout from the surface before it sets. Sponging alone is sufficient to finish the joints, but compressing each joint helps guarantee a waterproof seal. Do this by running the end of a blunt stick along each joint. When the grout has dried, polish the tiles with a dry cloth.

To make sure the grout hardens thoroughly, don't use a newly tiled shower for about seven days.

5 Press grout into joints with rubber-faced trowel

Cutting ceramic tiles

For any but the simplest projects, you will have to cut tiles to fit around margins, faucets, light fixtures, outlets, and some wall-mounted sinks. Glazed tiles are relatively easy to cut, because they snap readily along a line scored in the glaze. Cutting unglazed tiles is harder, and often requires renting a tile-cutter saw. Whatever method you use, protect your eyes with safety glasses or goggles when cutting ceramic tiles.

Inexpensive cutter
A cutter is drawn down the channel of the guide. Then the tile is snapped with a simple tool.

Cutting thin strips
You can't cut thin strips from a tile with a tile cutter. You have to use tile nibblers to chop off the waste a little at a time. Smooth the cut edge of the tile with coarse sandpaper.

Making straight cuts

It is possible to scribe and snap thin ceramic tiles using little more than a basic tile scorer and a metal ruler, but the job is made easier if you use a tile cutter. Inexpensive plastic versions guide a hand-held scoring tool. Once a tile is scored, it can be snapped in half with a simple tool (above left). But, if you anticipate cutting a lot of tiles, invest in a sturdy lever-action cutter. A good-quality model will be fitted with a tungsten-carbide cutting wheel and angled jaws that will snap most tiles effortlessly.

Mark the cutline on the face of a tile with a felt-tip pen (use a pencil on unglazed tiles). Then, place the tile against the cutter's fence, aligning the marks with the cutting wheel. With one smooth stroke, push the wheel across the surface to score the glaze **(1)**.

Place the tile in the jig's snapping jaws, aligning the scored line with the arrow marked on the tool, then press down on the lever to snap the tile **(2)**.

Cutting a curve
To fit a tile against a curved shape, cut a template from thin card to the exact size of a tile. Cut "fingers" along one edge; press them against the curve to reproduce the shape and trim their ends to fit. Draw around the template to transfer the curve onto the face of the tile and cut away the waste with a rod saw—a thin rod, coated with hard abrasive particles, mounted in a standard hacksaw.

1 Score the marked line with one smooth stroke.

2 Snap the tile by pressing down on the lever.

Using a powered wet saw

Use a wet saw to cut thick unglazed tiles, and to cut the corners out of tiles that have to fit around obstructions. The saw has a diamond-coated blade that runs in a bath of water to keep it cool, and an adjustable fence that helps you make accurate cuts. You can adjust the angle of the blade in order to miter thick tiles that meet in a corner. When using this type of saw, tuck in loose clothing and remove any jewelry that could get caught in the blade.

Adjust the fence to align the marked cutline with the blade, and tighten the fence clamp. Switch on the saw and feed the tile steadily into the blade, keeping your fingers clear of the cutting edge **(1)**. When removing a narrow strip, use a notched stick to push the tile forward.

You have to make two straight cuts to remove a corner from a tile. Make the shortest cut first, then slowly withdraw the tile from the blade. Switch off and readjust the fence, then make the second cut to remove the waste **(2)**.

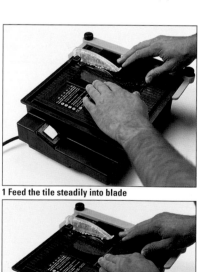

1 Feed the tile steadily into blade

2 Make a second cut to remove corner

Don't use grout to fill the gap between a tiled wall and a shower pan, bathtub, or sink. A rigid seal can crack and allow water to seep in. Instead, use flexible silicone caulk to fill gaps up to ⅛ inch wide. Cartridges of clear silicone in a range of colors are available.

Using silicone caulk

With the cartridge fitted into a caulk gun, trim the tip off the plastic nozzle. The place where you cut the tip dictates the diameter of the bead.

Clean the surfaces with a paper towel wetted with mineral spirits. To apply a bead of silicone, start at one end by pressing the tip into the joint and squeezing the gun handle. Pull backward while continuing to squeeze the handle **(1)**. When the joint is filled, smooth any ripples by dipping your finger into a 50/50 mix of water and dishwashing liquid and running it along the joint **(2)**. You can also use a wetted dowel or teaspoon.

1 Pull back slowly to deposit a full bead of silicone caulk

2 Smooth out any ripples with your fingertip

Removing old caulk

Brush a caulk remover onto a cracked or discolored joint. Wait 15 minutes, then scrape the caulk from the joint.

Installing other wall tiles

Ceramic tiles are ideal in bathrooms and kitchens where at least some of the walls will get splashed with water. But, in other areas of the home, you may decide to use other types of tiles.

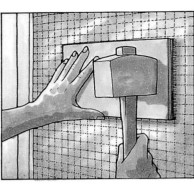

Mosaic tiles

When applying mosaic tiles to a wall, use adhesives and grouts similar to those recommended for standard ceramic tiles. Some mosaics have a mesh backing, which is pressed into the adhesive. Others have a paper facing which is left on the surface until the adhesive sets.

Fill the main area of the wall, spacing the sheets to maintain uniform grout spacing. Place a carpet-covered board over the sheets and tap it with a mallet to set the tiles into the adhesive.

Fill margins by cutting strips from the sheet. Use nibblers to cut individual tiles around obstructions. If necessary, soak off the facing paper with a damp sponge, then grout the tiles.

Bedding mosaics
Tap mosaics to bed them into the adhesive

Mosaics come in sheets

Mirror tiles

It is difficult to cut glass except in straight lines, so avoid using mirror tiles in an area that would require curved cuts.

Mirror tiles are usually attached with self-adhesive pads. No grouting is necessary. Lay out the wall with guide boards like those used for ceramic tiles. Peel the protective paper from the pads and lightly position each tile. Check its alignment, then press it firmly into place, using a soft cloth.

Finally, clean and polish the tiles to remove any dirt or finger marks.

Placing mirror tiles
Carefully align tiles before pressing against wall

Plastic tiles

You can cover a wall relatively quickly with 1-foot-square plastic tiles. Backed with expanded polystyrene, they are extremely lightweight and warm to the touch. Plastic tiles are ideal in bathrooms or kitchens where condensation is a problem. But don't hang them in close proximity to ranges or even radiators, because heat can cause them to soften and distort.

Using guide boards, lay out the area to be tiled. Then spread the adhesive supplied by the manufacturer across the back of each tile. Press the tiles firmly against the wall, butting them together gently. Plastic tiles are flexible and will accommodate imperfect walls.

Grout the joints with the product sold for this type of tile. Use a damp sponge to remove surplus grout before it sets up. If you wait too long, use a solvent recommended by the manufacturer. Straight cuts are easy to make on plastic tiles. Just use scissors or a sharp utility knife. You can also cut curves with scissors.

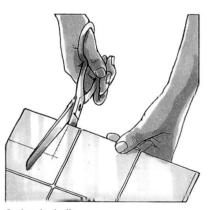

Cutting plastic tiles
Cut plastic tiles with scissors or a utility knife

● **Tiling around curves**
In older houses, some walls may be rounded at the outside corners. Flexible tiles made from vinyl and rubber are easy to bend around tight radii, but cork will snap if bent too far. Cut a series of shallow slits down the back of a cork with a saw, then bend the tile gently to the curve required.

Cork tiles

Set up a horizontal guide board to make sure you lay cork tiles accurately. It isn't necessary, however, to attach a vertical guide, because these large tiles are easy to align without one. Simply mark a vertical line at the center of the wall and install the tiles in both directions from it.

You will need a rubber-based contact adhesive to fix cork tiles. Choose one that allows a degree of movement when positioning the tiles. If any adhesive gets onto the face of a tile, clean it off immediately with the recommended solvent on a cloth.

Spread adhesive thinly and evenly onto the wall and the back of the tiles, and let it dry. As you install each tile, place only one edge against the guide board or the neighboring tile, holding the rest of the tile away from the glue-covered wall. Then, gradually press the tile against the wall and smooth it down with your hands.

Cut cork tiles with a sharp utility knife. Since the edges are butted tightly, you will need to be very accurate when marking margin tiles. Use the same methods shown earlier for laying cork and vinyl floor tiles. Cut and fit curved shapes using a template. Unless the tiles are prefinished, apply two coats of varnish after 24 hours.

Bending a cork tile
To bend cork tile around a tight curve, saw a series of shallow slits across the back of the tile.

Installing ceiling tiles

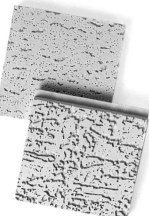

There are basically two types of tiles you can use on a ceiling—expanded polystyrene and mineral fiber. Polystyrene tiles are the most popular, because they are inexpensive and easy to cut. Mineral fiber tiles are usually considered to be an upgrade in appearance and durability. They can be glued directly to the ceiling, but the common tongue-and-groove types are stapled to furring strips that have been nailed or screwed to the ceiling.

Polystyrene tiles can be used in virtually any room in the house, except the kitchen, where they would be directly over a source of heat. Remove any friable material and make sure the ceiling is clean and free from grease.

Installing mineral fiber ceiling tiles

Mineral fiber tiles are stapled to furring strips that are nailed or screwed to the ceiling joists. Determine the direction of the joists with a stud sensor, by looking for drywall nail pops on the surface of the ceiling, or by tapping your knuckles across the ceiling and marking where the sound changes. Poke the ceiling with an awl or drive a couple of test nails to locate the center of a couple of joists. Then measure between these points to determine the spacing between the joists. Except in old houses, joist and stud spacing is almost always 16 inches. Mark the centerlines of all the ceiling joists. Then, mark two bisecting lines across the ceiling, so you can work out the spacing of the tiles to create even margins around the perimeter of the room.

1 Using a tile spacer
Align the furring strips, using a simple jig to gauge tile width.

2 Securing the tiles
Staple through each grooved edge, then slide the tongue of the next tile into the groove.

Nailing up the furring
Nail 1 x 2 furring strips across the ceiling at right angles to the joists, making the distance between centers of the strips equal to the width of one tile.

This job is made easier if you fabricate a simple tile spacer. Just nail together two short boards to use for setting the furring strips the proper distance apart (1). Finish by nailing the last furring strip against the far wall.

Stapling the tiles
When stapling tiles, you must begin with the margins. Measure the margin tiles and cut off their tongued edges. Starting in the corner, attach the two adjacent rows of margin tiles by stapling up through the grooved edges into the furring strips. Attach the other edges by driving small nails through the face of the tiles.

Proceed diagonally across the ceiling by installing whole tiles as you go. Slide the tongues of each tile into the grooves on the mating tiles. Then staple each tile through both grooved edges (2).

Once all the whole tiles are installed, cut and nail the remaining margin tiles to the perimeter furring strips.

Setting out the ceiling
Snap two chalk lines at right angles to each other in the center of the ceiling. Align the first rows of tiles with these chalked lines.

Applying the tiles
You can use a heavy-duty wallpaper paste to glue these tiles to the ceiling. Or, use a nonflammable contact adhesive that is designed for use on expanded polystyrene. Brush the adhesive evenly across the back of the tile and onto the ceiling. When the adhesive is touch-dry, align one edge and corner of the first tile with one of the right angles formed by the marked lines. Then, gently press the tile against the ceiling using the flat of your hand. Don't push hard with your fingertips, because this can crush the tile. Proceed with subsequent tiles to complete one half of the ceiling, then the other.

Cutting the tiles
Mark the margin tiles, then cut through them with a single stroke, using a sharp utility knife. Mark notches or curves on the face of the tile and carefully cut with a utility knife.

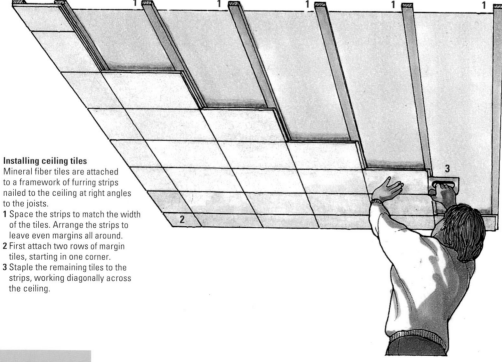

Installing ceiling tiles
Mineral fiber tiles are attached to a framework of furring strips nailed to the ceiling at right angles to the joists.
1 Space the strips to match the width of the tiles. Arrange the strips to leave even margins all around.
2 First attach two rows of margin tiles, starting in one corner.
3 Staple the remaining tiles to the strips, working diagonally across the ceiling.

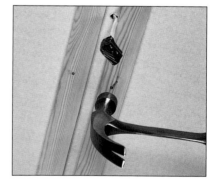

Installing furring strips to support fixtures
Turn off the power at the service panel and remove the light fixture. Nail furring strips to the ceiling joists, positioned so they will support the light fixture after the ceiling tiles are installed. Cut a hole for the circuit cable through the tile that will cover it. Then feed the cable through the hole and staple the tile in place. Reinstall the light fixture and turn the power on.

Setting out soft floor tiles

Arranging tiles diagonally can create an unusual effect, especially if your choice of tiles enables you to mix colors. Laying out the tiles this way is not complicated—it's the same as standard installations, except that you'll be working toward a corner instead of a straight wall.

Mark a centerline and bisect it at right angles, using an improvised compass (see below). Next, draw a line at 45 degrees through the center point. Place a row of tiles along this line to make even margins, and mark another line at right angles to the first diagonal. Check the margins as before. Nail a board along one diagonal as a guide to laying the first row of tiles.

Soft tiles such as vinyl, rubber, cork, and carpet are relatively large, so you can cover the floor quickly. Also, they can be cut easily with a sharp utility knife or even with scissors, so fitting to irregular shapes isn't difficult.

Marking out the floor

It's possible to lay soft tiles onto either a concrete or a wood floor, provided the surface is level, clean and dry. Most soft tiles are installed in a similar way: find the center of two opposite walls, and snap a chalkline between them to mark a line across the floor (**1**). Lay loose tiles at right angles to the line up to one wall (see below left). If there's a gap of less than half a tile width, move the line sideways by half a tile in order to create a wider margin.

To draw a second line at right angles to the first, use string and a pencil as an improvised compass. Scribe arcs on the marked line at equal distances each side of the center line (**2**).

From each of these points, scribe an arc on both sides of the line (**3**). Join the points to form a perpendicular line across the room (**4**). As before, lay tiles at right angles to the new line to make sure margin tiles are at least half-width. Nail a board next to the new line, to help align the first row of tiles.

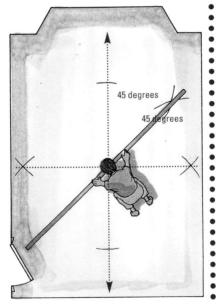

Laying out a floor diagonally
Bisect the room at 45 degrees.

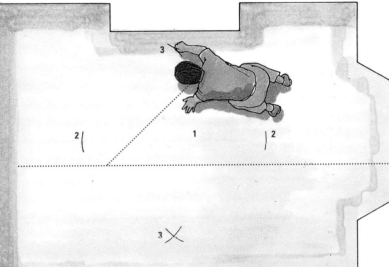

Laying out
Divide the room into quarters to ensure that the tiles are laid symmetrically. This method works for all tiles: vinyl, rubber, cork, and carpet.

4 Right angle complete

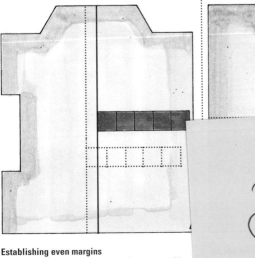

Establishing even margins
Lay loose tiles to make sure there is a reasonable gap at all the margins. If not, move the centerline half the width of a tile.

Laying vinyl floor tiles

Tiles precoated with adhesive can be laid quickly and simply, and there is no risk of squeezing glue onto the surface. If you are not using self-adhesive tiles, follow the tile manufacturer's instructions concerning the type of adhesive to use.

Installing self-adhesive tiles

Stack the tiles in a warm room for 24 hours before you lay them, so they will be as pliable as possible.

If the tiles have a directional pattern, make sure you lay them the correct way; some tiles have arrows printed on the back to guide you.

Remove the protective paper backing from the first tile (**1**), then press its edge against the guide board, aligning one corner with the center line (**2**). Gradually lower the tile onto the floor and press it down.

Lay the next tile on the other side of the line, butting against the first tile (**3**). Form a square with two more tiles. Lay tiles around the square to form a pyramid (**4**). Continue in this way to fill one half of the room, then remove the batten and tile the other half.

Gluing vinyl tiles
Spread adhesive thinly but evenly across the floor, using a notched trowel. Cover an area for about four tiles at a time. Lay the tiles carefully and wipe adhesive from their faces after they are laid.

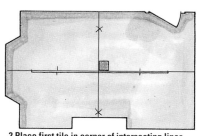
2 Place first tile in corner of intersecting lines

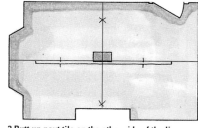
3 Butt up next tile on the other side of the line

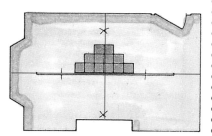

1 Peel paper backing from self-adhesive tiles

4 Lay tiles in a pyramid, then complete half of room

Finishing off the floor

As soon as you have laid all the floor tiles, wipe the surface with a damp cloth to remove any marks. It's not usually necessary to polish vinyl tiles, but you can apply a latex floor polish if you want.

Fit a flat metal threshold bar (available from carpet suppliers) over the edge of the tiles when you finish at a doorway. When the tiles butt up to an area of carpet, fit a single threshold bar under the edge of the carpeting (see left).

Single threshold bar

Lifting an old vinyl tile

Try to remove a damaged tile by chopping it out from the center with a chisel. If the glue is firm, warm the tile with a clothes iron, using a piece of aluminum foil to keep the iron clean. Take care not to damage the surrounding tiles. Scrape the old glue from the floor, and install the new tile. Place a heavy weight on top overnight.

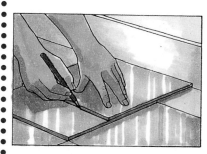

Cutting margin tiles

Floors are usually out of square, so you have to scribe margin tiles to properly fit the gaps next to the baseboard. To scribe a tile, lay a loose tile exactly on top of the last full tile. Then place another tile on top, but with its edge touching the wall. Draw along the edge of this tile with a pencil to mark the tile below. Remove the marked tile and cut along the line, then glue the cut-off portion of the tile into the margin gap.

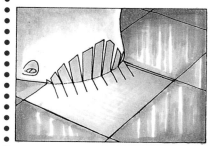

Cutting irregular shapes

To fit around curved shapes, make a template out of thin cardboard. Cut fingers that can be pressed against the object to reproduce its shape, then transfer the template to a tile and cut it to shape.

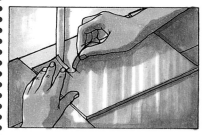

Fitting around pipes

Mark the position of the pipe on the tile using a compass. Starting from the perimeter of the circle, draw two parallel lines to the edge of the tile. Cut the hole for the pipe, using a homemade punch (see opposite page). Then, cut a slit between the marked lines and fold the tile back so you can slide it into place around the pipe.

The procedures for laying floor tiles made from carpet, cork, and rubber are similar in many respects to those described earlier for vinyl tiles. The differences are outlined below.

Carpet tiles

Carpet tiles are laid in the same way as vinyl tiles, except that they are not usually glued down. Lay out centerlines on the floor, but don't nail a guide board in place—just align the row of tiles with the marked lines.

Carpet tiles have a pile that has to be laid in the correct direction. This is sometimes indicated by arrows marked on the back of each tile.

Some tiles have ridges of rubber on the back, so they will slip easily in one direction but not in another. The nonslip direction is also typically indicated by an arrow on the back of the tile. It is best to lay these tiles in pairs, so one prevents the other from moving.

In any case, stick down every third row of tiles using double-sided carpet tape, and tape all squares in areas where there is likely to be heavy traffic. Cut and fit carpet tiles as described for vinyl tiles.

Checking direction of pile
Some carpet tiles have arrows on the back to indicate the direction in which they should be laid.

Using pile for decorative effect
Two typical arrangements of tiles, using the direction of the pile to make different textures.

Cork tiles

Use a contact adhesive when laying cork tiles. Make sure the tiles lay flat by tapping down the edges with a block of wood. Remove any adhesive from the surface of the tiles with solvent.

Unfinished tiles can be sanded very lightly to remove minor irregularities. Vacuum up all the dust, then seal unfinished tiles with two to three coats of clear varnish.

Setting cork tiles
Tap tile seams with a wood block to set the tiles.

Rubber tiles

Lay rubber floor tiles in latex flooring adhesive. Place one edge and corner of each tile against its neighboring tiles before lowering it into place.

Lay rubber tile in latex adhesive

Covering a toeboard with tile

You can make kitchen base cabinets appear to float above the floor by running floor tiles up the face of the toeboard. Hold carpet tiles in a tight bend with a tack strip **(1)**, but glue other types of soft tile in place to create a similar effect.

Glue a plastic molding (normally used to seal around the edge of a bath) behind the tiles to produce a curved detail that will make cleaning the floor a lot easier **(2)**.

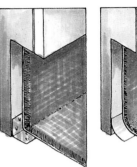

1 Hold in place with tack strip

2 Curved detail for easy cleaning

Cutting holes for pipes

With most soft floor tiles, you can use a homemade punch to cut neat holes for plumbing and heating pipes. Cut a 6-inch length of pipe that is the same diameter as the pipe that's in place. Sharpen the inside rim at one end with a metalworking file. Mark the position for the hole on the tile, then place the punching tool on top. Hit the other end of the punch with a hammer to cut through the tile cleanly, then cut a straight slit up to the edge. With some carpet tiles, you may have to cut the backing to finish the hole.

Punch holes for pipes with a sharpened piece of pipe.

Laying ceramic floor tiles

Ceramic floor tiles make a durable surface that can be extremely decorative. Laying the tiles on a floor is similar to installing them on a wall. But, because they're usually thicker, cutting floor tiles can be more difficult. Therefore, when laying out the tiles, it's a good idea to minimize the cutting, especially around any obstructions that require notched or curved cuts.

Laying out

Mark out the floor as described for soft floor tiles earlier. Work out the spacing to achieve wide, even margins. Nail two guide boards to the floor, perpendicular to each other and aligned with the two adjacent walls farthest from the door. Even a small error will become obvious by the time you reach the other end of the room, so check your layout carefully by laying dry tiles in place in both directions. Check that the margins are satisfactory and the layout lines precisely perpendicular. When satisfied, lift up the dry tiles.

Laying the tiles

Use a floor-tile adhesive that is waterproof and slightly flexible when set. Spread it on, using a notched trowel, according to the directions on the adhesive container. Just like wall tiling, the normal procedure is to apply adhesive to the floor for the whole tiles, and to coat the backs of cut tiles.

Spread enough adhesive on the floor to cover about 3 square feet. Press the tiles into the adhesive, starting in the corner. Work along both guide boards and then fill in between to form the square. Use plastic floor tile spacers (if required for the tile you are using) to create regular joints.

Wipe adhesive off the surface of the tiles with a damp sponge. Then check their alignment with a straightedge, and make sure they are flat on the floor. Work your way along one board, laying one square of tiles at a time. Tile the rest of the floor in the same way, working back towards the far wall. Don't forget to scrape adhesive from the margins as you go.

Allow the adhesive to dry for 24 hours before you walk on the floor to remove the guide boards and to fit the margin tiles. Even then, it's a good idea to spread your weight over a larger area with a wide board or a piece of plywood.

Cutting ceramic floor tiles

Measure the margin tiles as described for wall tiles, then score and snap them with a tile cutter. Because they are thicker, floor tiles will not snap quite so easily, so you may have to resort to using a powered wet saw—even for simple straight cuts. Seal around the edge of the floor with silicone caulk.

Lay out the floor for tiling with mosaics as described for standard ceramic floor tiles. Spread adhesive on the floor, then lay the tiles, using spacers that match the gaps between the individual pieces on the sheets. Paper-faced tiles should be laid paper side up. Press the sheets into the adhesive, using a block of wood to tamp them flat. Twenty-four hours later, remove the spacers and, where necessary, soak off the paper facing with warm water. Grout the tiles.

Cut out enough pieces of mosaic to fit a sheet around an obstruction **(1)**, then replace individual pieces to fit the shapes exactly.

If you are using mosaics in areas of hard wear, protect vulnerable edges, such as steps, with a nosing of ordinary ceramic floor tiles to match or contrast with the main field of mosaics **(2)**.

1 Remove mosaic pieces to fit around obstructions

2 Lay a nosing of ceramic tiles on step treads

Laying out
Mark the floor as described earlier for soft floor tiles. Then:
1 Nail temporary guide boards to the floor along the two adjacent walls farthest from the door.
2 Make sure that the guide boards are exactly perpendicular to each other by measuring out a 3-4-5 right triangle. Mark 6 feet along one wall, 8 feet along the other wall. Then measure the distance between these two marks. It must be exactly 10 feet or the boards aren't perpendicular.
3 Lay a square of 16 dry tiles in the corner as a final check.

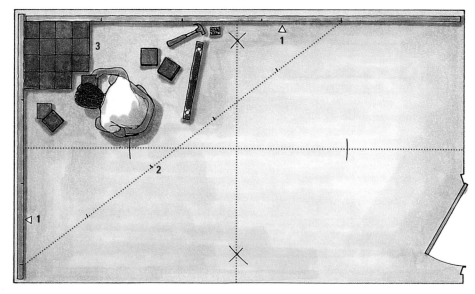

Grouting joints in ceramic floor tiles
Using a rubber-faced float, spread grout over a 3-foot-square area, pressing it firmly into the joints. Clean grout off the surface with a damp sponge, then compress the grout joints with a wood dowel. Polish the tiles with a dry cloth when the grout is dry.

Laying quarry tiles

Tough and hard-wearing, quarry tiles are an ideal choice for floors that receive heavy use. They are relatively thick, however, and making even a straight cut requires a wet saw—so use quarry tiles only in areas that do not require a lot of complex cutting.

Don't lay quarry tiles on an old wood floor. Cover or replace the floorboards with ¾- or ⅞-inch-thick exterior-grade plywood to provide a sufficiently flat and rigid base. A concrete floor presents no problems, as long as it's free from moisture. You can lay quarries using a floor tile adhesive, but the traditional method of laying the tiles on a bed of mortar is the best approach.

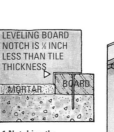

1 Notching the leveling board
Cut matching notches at each end of the board for leveling the mortar.

2 Leveling the mortar
With a notch located over each guide board, drag the leveling board toward you.

Laying out the floor

Set out two guide boards at right angles to each other in a corner of the room, as described for ceramic floor tiles (opposite page). The thickness of the boards should measure about twice the thickness of the tiles, to allow for the mortar bed. If you're working on a concrete floor, attach the boards with masonry nails. The top edge of the guide boards should be level, so check them with a 4-foot level and shim under the guide boards as necessary to keep them level.

Lay a square of 16 dry tiles in the corner, maintaining uniform, recommended grout spacing between the tiles. Then nail a third guide board to the floor, butting against the dry tiles. Level and shim this board if necessary.

Laying out a quarry-tile floor
Laying out a floor for quarry tiles requires three guide boards.
1 Install two guide boards (each about twice the tile thickness) at right angles to each other.
2 Lay 16 dry tiles in the corner to check for proper tile alignment.
3 Install the third guide board parallel with one of the others.

3 Cutting quarry tiles
Mark cutlines as described for wall tiling, and make cuts with a power wet saw.

Period effect
You can re-create Victorian-style floors with modern quarry tiles.

Laying the tiles

Lay quarry tiles on a bed of mortar made from 1 part cement and 3 parts builder's sand. When water is added, the mortar should be stiff enough to hold an impression when squeezed.

Soak quarry tiles in water prior to laying so they won't absorb water from the mortar too rapidly, causing poor adhesion. Cut a sturdy board to span the parallel guide boards: This will be used to level the mortar bed and tiles. Cut a notch in each end to fit between the guide boards **(1)**. Its depth should match the thickness of a tile, less ⅛ inch.

Spread the mortar to a depth of about ½ inch to cover the area of 16 tiles. Level the mortar by dragging the notched side of the board across it **(2)**.

Dust dry cement on the mortar, then lay the tiles along three sides of the square against the battens. Fill in the square, spacing the tiles by adjusting them with a trowel. Tamp down the tiles gently with the unnotched side of the board until they are level with the guide boards. If the mortar is too stiff, brush water into the joints. Wipe mortar from the faces of the tiles before it hardens.

Fill in between the boards, then move the third guide board back to form another bay. Level the board to match the first section, add mortar, and continue tiling in this way until the main floor area is complete. When the floor is dry, remove the guide boards and fill the margins with cut tiles **(3)**.

Leveling mortar for margin tiles
Use a notched piece of plywood to level the mortar, then tamp down the tiles with a block.

Grouting quarry tiles
Push grout into the joints with a pointing trowel or wood dowel. Keep the tiles as clean as possible, wiping excess grout off the surface with a damp sponge. When the grout has set, brush the floor clean.

Parquet flooring

Parquet flooring is a relatively thin covering of decorative wood that is laid in the form of panels or narrow strips. Hardwoods such as oak, birch, and cherry are used for their attractive grain patterns and rich coloring, which can be further highlighted by applying one of the many floor waxes, polishes, and varnishes that are available.

Types of parquet flooring

Laying any type of parquet is as easy as tiling a floor, but you will need to take into consideration the nature of the subfloor.

1 Strip flooring
These short sections of flooring illustrate some of the woods used for this type of parquet. They are available as plywood or solid wood strips, and some are prefinished.

2 Hardwood parquet panels
Small solid-wood strips made up into flat panels for gluing to the subfloor.

3 Wood-faced cork
This type of flooring is easy to lay. Cut to fit with a sharp knife.

Strip flooring
Parquet floors can be constructed from tongue-and-groove or square-edged strips or tiles, either machined from solid wood or made from veneered plywood. They can be nailed to a wooden floor, or left as floating panels by gluing just the edge joints together. Tiles and strips range in thickness from ⅛ to ¾ inch. Install them as parallel strips, or arrange in various combinations to make herringbone or woven patterns.

Hardwood panels
Perhaps the most common form of parquet flooring is 18-inch-square panels made by gluing together ⅜-inch solid wood strips into herringbone or basket-weave patterns. The panels are presanded, and often prefinished as well. Some have a water-resistant backing to protect against moisture damage. Hardwood panels can be glued to wood or concrete floors and their edges butted like floor tiles. Some come with self-adhesive backing.

Wood-faced cork
This is not a conventional parquet flooring, but consists of composite tiles made from a layer of cork backed with vinyl and surfaced with a natural or stained hardwood veneer. The wood is protected by a clear vinyl coating. The tiles are available in 6-inch by 3-foot strips. For laying and cutting wood-faced cork, see the section on installing vinyl and cork tiles.

Whether the subfloor is concrete or wood, it must be clean, dry, and flat before parquet flooring is laid. Use hardboard panels to level a wood floor. Use mortar to level a concrete floor. Some manufacturers recommend that building paper or thin foam underlayment be used under parquet. To reduce the risk of warping, leave parquet panels or strips for several days in the room where they will be laid, so they adjust to the atmosphere.

Preparing solid floors
When laying parquet flooring on a solid concrete base, ensure that the floor is completely dry and make any necessary repairs. For minor depressions, you can screed the surface with a leveling compound (above). For bad floors, you should install a new mortar base.

1

2

3

Cutting curves

Use cardboard templates to mark out curved shapes; transfer them to the strip or panel, then cut along the line with a coping saw or jigsaw.

Fitting into a doorway

If the flooring is to run through two adjoining rooms, take a piece of the flooring and use it to support the blade of a panel saw as you cut off the bottom of the doorjamb. Once the cut piece is removed, the flooring will fit neatly under the jamb.

If the flooring is to change at the door, install a hardwood threshold. This board should be as wide as the doorjambs and as thick as the flooring. Cut the bottom of both doorjambs and nail the threshold in place.

Fitting around a pipe

Measure and mark the position of the pipe on the flooring. Drill a hole slightly larger than the pipe, then cut out a tapered section of the floor tile to accommodate the pipe. Glue the tile to the floor, and put the wedge-shaped cutoff behind the pipe.

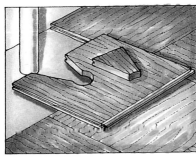

Use a piece of flooring to guide the saw when cutting off the bottoms of door jambs.

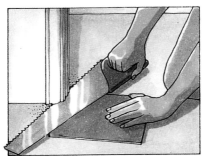

Accommodating a pipe
Cut a hole to match the pipe and a notch behind it to provide clearance. Glue the tile in place and slide the cut-off wedge behind the pipe.

Installing hardwood panels

Lay out the flooring to calculate the position of the panels, as described for vinyl tiles. Instead of fixing a guide board to the floor, just snap a chalkline to mark the edge of the last row of whole panels next to the longest wall.

Using a notched trowel, spread some of the recommended adhesive onto the subfloor alongside the chalkline. Install the first row of panels next to the string, setting them into the adhesive by tapping them with a softwood block and hammer. Check the alignment frequently as you work. Lay subsequent panels, butted against the preceding row, working from the center out in both directions.

Cutting margin panels

Measure and mark margin panels, as described for vinyl tiles, but deduct ½ inch to provide an expansion gap beside the baseboards. Cut the panels with a handsaw or jigsaw.

Glue the margin panels in place, then cover the gap with shoe molding nailed to the baseboard. Don't nail the molding to the flooring.

Finishing the floor

Many panels come prefinished, but if yours are unfinished, begin by sanding smooth any rough areas. Then vacuum the floor, seal the wood, and apply three or four coats of clear finish.

Edge detail
An expansion gap is necessary around a parquet floor. Conceal this gap by nailing a shoe molding next to the baseboard.

Installing the last strip
Pry the last strip in place, using a flat bar with a scrap block to protect the baseboard.

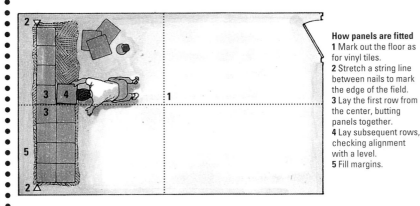

How panels are fitted
1 Mark out the floor as for vinyl tiles.
2 Stretch a string line between nails to mark the edge of the field.
3 Lay the first row from the center, butting panels together.
4 Lay subsequent rows, checking alignment with a level.
5 Fill margins.

● **Floating parquet flooring**
Instead of nailing the pieces to the floor, you can glue them edge to edge by applying a little adhesive to each groove. Place wedges between the parquet flooring and the baseboard to maintain the ½-inch expansion gaps.

Nailing strip flooring

Decide on the direction of the strip flooring, then snap a chalkline parallel to, and about ½ inch away from, the baseboard.

Place the grooved edge of the first strip against the line, and nail it through the face. Tap the next strip into the first strip. The groove on the second strip slides into the tongue on the first strip. Use a scrap piece of flooring to protect the edge you strike.

Nail through the inside corner of the tongue about every 12 inches along the board and within 2 inches of each end. Use a nailset and hammer to drive the nailheads below the surface.

Proceed across the floor, cutting each strip ½ inch short of the baseboard. At the far side of the room, fill the gap with a strip nailed through the face. Install a shoe molding around the perimeter of the room. Finish strip flooring with three or four coats of clear varnish.

How strips are attached
Flooring strips are installed across the floor, working away from the baseboard.
1 Snap a chalkline parallel to the baseboard.
2 Nail a strip through its face, tongue outward, against the chalkline.
3 Drive subsequent strips into place and nail through the tongues.
4 Stagger the end joints.

Carpets

Originally, piled carpets were made by knotting strands of wool or other natural fibers into a woven foundation. But gradually, with the introduction of machine-made carpets and synthetic fibers, a wide variety of different carpet types have been developed. There is a good choice available for virtually any area of the house, whether you want something luxurious or simply practical and hard-wearing.

When selecting carpet, consider your options carefully. The floor area is a very important element in the overall decorating of any room, and the wrong choice can be an expensive mistake.

A properly installed, high-quality carpet will last for many years. So, unless you can afford to change your floorcovering every time you redecorate, take care to choose one that you will be able to live with, even after a change of room colors or furnishings. Neutral or earthy colors are usually thought of as the most versatile. Plain colors and small repeat patterns are suitable for rooms of any size. Large, bold designs are best reserved for grand rooms.

If you are planning to carpet adjoining rooms, consider using the same carpet to link the floor areas. This provides a greater sense of open space and harmony.

You can use patterned borders, in combination with plain carpet, to create a distinctive one-of-a-kind look for any room.

Left to right
1 Cut pile
2 Velvet pile
3 Looped pile
4 Cord pile
5 Twisted pile
6 Woven jute
7 Saxony pile
8 Underlays

Choosing carpet

When shopping for carpeting, there are a number of factors to consider, including fiber content, type of pile, and durability. Although wool carpet is luxurious, synthetic-fiber carpets have a lot to offer in terms of finish, texture, and value.

Fiber content

The best carpets are made from wool, or a mixture of wool and man-made fiber. Wool carpets are expensive, so manufacturers have experimented with a variety of fibers to produce cheaper, but durable and attractive carpets. Materials such as nylon, polypropylene, acrylic, rayon, and polyester are all used for carpet making, either singly or in combination.

Synthetic-fiber carpets were once inferior substitutes, often with an unattractive shiny pile and a reputation for building up a charge of static electricity that produced a mild shock when anyone touched a metal door-knob. Nowadays, manufacturers have largely solved the problem of static, but you should still seek the advice of the supplier before you buy.

As far as appearance is concerned, a modern carpet made from good-quality blended fibers is hard to distinguish from one made from wool. Certain combinations produce carpets that are so stain resistant that they virtually shrug off spilled liquids. To their disadvantage, synthetic fibers tend to react badly to burns, shriveling rapidly from the heat, whereas wool tends only to smolder.

Rush, sisal, coir, and jute are natural vegetable fibers used to make coarsely woven rugs.

Which type of pile?

The nature of the pile is more important to the feel and appearance of a carpet than the fiber content. Piled carpets are either woven or tufted. Axminster and Wilton are names used to describe two traditional methods of weaving the pile simultaneously with the foundation, so that the strands are wrapped around and through the warp and weft threads. With tufted carpets, continuous strands are pushed between the threads of a prewoven foundation. Although secured with an adhesive backing, tufted pile isn't as permanent as a woven pile. The column on the right explains the various ways tufted and woven piles are created. See below for durability.

The importance of underlay

A carpet undoubtedly benefits from a resilient cushion laid between it and the floor—it is more comfortable to walk on and the carpet lasts longer. Without an underlay, dust may emerge from the gaps between the floorboards and begin to show as dirty lines.

An underlay can be either a thick felt or a layer of foam rubber or plastic. When you purchase a foam-backed or rubber-backed carpet, the underlay is an integral part of the floorcovering. In theory, rubber-backed or foam-backed carpets need no additional underlay, but floorboards can still show through cheaper qualities (see margin note).

Choosing a durable carpet

Whether it is woven, tufted, or bonded, a hard-wearing carpet must have a dense pile. When you fold the carpet and part the pile, you should not be able to see the backing to which it is attached.

Carpets are categorized in many ways, but perhaps the most useful is in terms of durability (their ability to withstand wear). Not all rooms in the house receive the same wear, so not every room requires carpet with the highest durability.

DURABILITY RATING	
CLASSIFICATION	APPLICATION
Light domestic	Bedrooms
Medium domestic	Low-traffic rooms
	Dining rooms
	Well-used bedroom
General domestic	Living rooms
Heavy domestic	Hallways/stairs

Tufted and woven carpet pile is treated in a number of ways to give different qualities of finish. With some types, the strands are left long and uncut. With others, the looped pile is twisted together to give a coarser texture. Very hard-wearing carpets have their looped pile pulled tight against the foundation. Cut, velvet, and shag carpets have the tops of their loops cut off, leaving single-fiber strands.

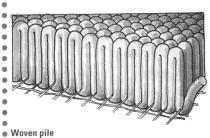

Woven pile
● Continuous strands woven into the warp and weft threads of the foundation.

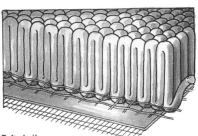

Tufted pile
● Continuous strands pushed through a woven foundation and secured with adhesive backing.

1 Looped pile
Ordinary looped pile gives a smooth feel.

2 Twisted pile
Looped pile twisted for a coarser texture.

3 Cord pile
Loops are pulled tight against the foundation.

4 Cut pile
Loops are cut, giving a soft texture pile.

5 Velvet pile
Loops are cut short for a close stranded pile.

6 Saxony pile
A cut pile up to 1½ inches long.

Fiber-bonded pile
The most modern method of carpet production makes use of synthetic fibers packed tightly together and bonded to an impregnated backing. The texture is like coarse felt.

● **Additional protection**
As well as conventional underlay, it is worth laying rolls of brown paper or synthetic-fiber sheets over the floor to stop dust and dirt from working into the carpet from below.

Fiber-bonded pile
A tough, low-cost carpet, used mostly for commercial interiors.

Laying carpet

Some people install carpet loose, relying on the weight of the furniture to stop it from moving around. However, a properly stretched and attached carpet looks much neater, and, if you are carpeting a fairly simple rectangular room, it isn't very difficult to install.

Installation methods

There are different methods for holding a carpet firmly in place, depending on the type of carpet you have chosen.

Carpet tacks

A 2-inch strip can be folded under along each edge of the carpet, and nailed to the floor with tacks every 8 inches. You can usually cover the tack head by rubbing the pile with your fingertips. With this method, the underlay should be installed 2 inches short of the baseboard, to allow the carpet to lie flat along the wall.

Double-sided tape

Use adhesive tape for rubber-backed carpets only. Stick 2-inch-wide tape around the perimeter of the room. Then, when you are ready to install the carpet, peel off the protective paper layer from the tape and press the carpet into the adhesive.

Tack strips

These wooden or metal strips have fine metal teeth that grip the woven foundation. They are not really suitable for rubber-backed carpets, although they are often used for this job. Nail the strips to the floor, about ¼ inch from the baseboards, with the teeth pointing toward the wall. Cut short strips to fit into doorways and alcoves. Cut underlay up to the edge of each strip.

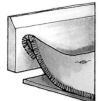

Fixing carpet
Use one of three ways:

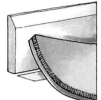

Fold tacked to floor

Double-sided tape

Tack strip

Joining at a doorway
Use one of the bars below:

Double threshold bar

Single threshold bar

Using a knee kicker
The only special tool required for laying carpet is a knee kicker, for stretching it. This has a toothed head, which is pressed into the carpet while you nudge the end with your knee. You can rent a knee kicker from a carpet supplier or tool rental company.

Laying standard-width carpet

If you are installing a separate underlay, join neighboring sections with short strips of carpet tape or secure them with a few tacks to stop them from moving.

Install tack strips around the entire perimeter of the room. Roll out the carpet, butting one machine-cut edge against a wall. Attach this edge to the tack strip. A pattern should run parallel to the main axis of the room.

Stretch the carpet to the wall directly opposite and hook it on the tack strip. Don't cut the carpet yet. Work from the center toward each corner, stretching and attaching the carpet as you go. Do the same at the other sides of the room.

Cut a triangular notch at each corner, so the carpet will lie flat. Adjust the carpet until it is stretched evenly, then attach it to the strips permanently. Press the carpet into the corner, between the baseboard and the floor, with a bolster chisel. Then trim it with a knife held at a 45-degree angle to the baseboard. Hook the cut edge on the tack strip.

Cutting to fit

Cut and fit carpet into doorways and around obstacles, as described for sheet vinyl. Join carpets at a doorway with a single- or double-sided threshold bar.

Joining carpet

Glue straight seams with latex adhesive or, for rubber-backed carpet, adhesive tape. Use as described for sheet vinyl. Expensive woven carpets should be sewn by a professional.

Carpeting a staircase

If possible, use standard-width narrow carpet on a staircase. Order an extra 2 feet, so that the carpet can be moved at a later date to even out the wear. This extra carpet is turned under the bottom step.

You can fit carpeting across the width of the treads, or stop short to reveal a border of polished or painted wood. With the latter method, you can use traditional stair rods to hold the carpet against the risers. Screw brackets on each side of the stairs to hold the rods.

Or you can tack the carpet to the stairs every 3 inches across the treads. Push the carpet firmly into the corner between the riser and the tread with a bolster chisel while you tack the center, then work outward to each side. Unless it's rubber-backed, you can use tack strips to hold the carpet in place.

Installing an underlay

Cut underlay into separate pads for each tread. Attach each pad flush with the riser, and to the front edge under the nosing, with carpet tacks.

Laying a straight run

The pile of the carpet should face down the stairs. Gauge the pile by rubbing your palm along the carpet in both directions. It will feel smoother in the direction of the pile.

Starting at the bottom of the stairs, lay the carpet face down on the first tread. Attach the back edge with tacks, or stretch it over a tack strip. Stretch the carpet over the nosing, and attach it to the bottom of the riser by hooking it onto the tack strip. Run the carpet up the staircase, pushing it firmly into each tack strip with a bolster chisel. Nail the end of the carpet against the riser on the last tread, then bring the landing carpet over the top step to meet it.

Carpeting winding stairs

If using a continuous length of carpet, fold the excess under and secure it to the riser with a stair rod. Or, fold the slack against the riser and tack through the three thicknesses of carpet.

To install fitted carpet, cut a pattern for each step and carpet it individually.

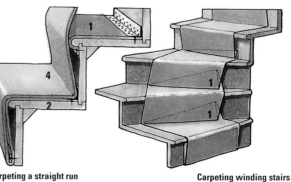

Carpeting a straight run

Carpeting winding stairs

Straight stairs
1 Tack underlay pads.
2 Tack carpet face down on first tread.
3 Pull over nosing and tack to base of riser.
4 Run carpet upstairs, hooking it onto tack strips on each stair.

Winding stairs
Don't cut the carpet, but fold the excess under (**1**) and attach to the risers with stair rods or long carpet tacks.

Sheet-vinyl floorcovering

Measure the floor area and draw a freehand plan, including the position of doors, window bays, alcoves, and so on. Add in the full width of any doorways. Make a note of the dimensions on the plan and take it to your flooring supplier, who will advise you on the most economical way to cover the floor.

The ideal solution is to achieve a seamless wall-to-wall covering. This is often impossible, however, either because a particular width is unobtainable or because the room is such an irregular shape that there would be too much waste if it were cut from one piece. Carpet or sheet-vinyl widths have to be butted together in these circumstances. Try to avoid seams in hallways and heavy traffic areas. You also have to consider matching the pattern and the direction of carpet pile. It must run in the same direction, or each piece of carpet will look different. Remember to order 3 extra inches all around the room for fitting.

Standard widths

Most manufacturers produce carpet or vinyl to standard widths. Some can be cut to fit any shape room, but the average waste factor is reflected in the price. Not all carpets are available in the full range of widths, and you may have difficulty in matching a color exactly from one width to another.

AVAILABLE WIDTHS	
Carpet	**Vinyl**
2 ft. 6 in.*	6 ft.
3 ft.	9 ft.
9 ft.	12 ft.
12 ft.	15 ft.
13 ft.*	
15 ft.*	

*Rare

Carpet widths of 9 feet and over are known as broadlooms. Narrower widths are called strip carpets.

Carpet squares

Carpet squares—not to be confused with tiles—are large, rectangular, loose-laid rugs. Simply order whichever size suits the proportions of your room. Carpet squares should be turned from time to time to even out wear.

Sheet vinyl makes an ideal wall-to-wall floorcovering for kitchens, utility rooms, and bathrooms, where you are bound to spill water from time to time. It is straightforward to install, provided you follow a systematic procedure.

Types of vinyl floorcovering

There are a great many sheet-vinyl floorcoverings to choose from. Make your selection according to durability, color, pattern, and, of course, cost.

Unbacked vinyl

Sheet vinyl is made by sandwiching the printed pattern between a vinyl base and a clear, protective vinyl covering. All vinyls are relatively hard-wearing, but some have a thicker, reinforced protective layer to increase their durability. Ask your flooring supplier which type will best suit your needs.

All varieties of vinyl floorcovering come in a vast range of colors, patterns, and textures.

Backed vinyl

Backed vinyl has similar properties to the unbacked type, with the addition of a resilient underlay to make it warmer and softer to walk on. The backing is usually a cushion of foam vinyl.

Vinyl carpet

Vinyl carpet—a cross between carpet and sheet vinyl—was originally developed for contract use but is now available for the residential market. It has a velvetlike pile of fine nylon fibers embedded in a waterproof vinyl base. It's popular for kitchen use, because it can be cleaned easily with water and a mild detergent. Rolls are usually 5 feet wide.

Vinyl flooring
Hard-wearing and waterproof, sheet vinyl is one of the most popular floorcoverings for bathrooms and kitchens. Vinyl carpet has a pile, but is equally suitable for these areas.

Left to right
1 Unbacked vinyl
2 Backed vinyl
3 Vinyl carpet

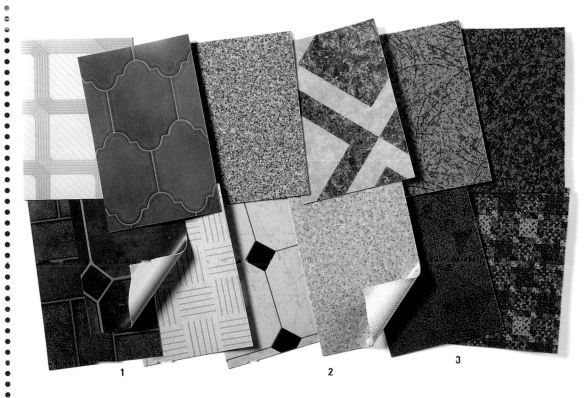

1   2   3

Preparing the floor

Before you lay a sheet of vinyl floorcovering, make sure the floor is flat and dry. Vacuum the surface and nail down any loose floorboards. You can fill shallow depressions on wood floors and concrete floors with fillers made for the job. A concrete floor must have a vapor barrier installed under the new flooring. Never lay vinyl flooring over boards that have recently been treated with preservative.

Laying sheet vinyl

Leave the vinyl sheet in a room (preferably opened flat) for 24 to 48 hours before installing it. If you can't lay it flat, at least stand it on end, loosely rolled. Make a scribing gauge by driving a nail through a piece of furring, about 2 inches from one end. You will use this gauge for fitting the sheet against the baseboards.

Fitting and cutting sheet vinyl

Assuming there are no seams, start by fitting the sheet against the longest wall. Pull the vinyl away from the wall approximately 1½ inches and make sure it is parallel with the wall or the main axis of the room. Use the scribing gauge to score a line that follows the baseboard **(1)**. Cut the vinyl with a utility knife, then slide the sheet up against the wall.

To get the rest of the sheet to lie as flat as possible, cut a triangular notch at each corner. At outside corners, make a straight cut down to the floor. Remove as much waste as possible, leaving 2 to 3 inches turned up all around.

Using a bolster chisel, press the vinyl into the corner, between the baseboard and the floor. Align a metal straightedge with the crease and run a sharp knife along it, held at a slight angle to the baseboard **(2)**. If your trimming is less than perfect, you can nail a shoe molding to the baseboard after the flooring is installed.

Cutting around a toilet or sink

To fit around a toilet bowl or sink pedestal, fold back the sheet and pierce it with a knife just above floor level. Draw the blade up toward the edge of the sheet. Make triangular cuts around the base, gradually working around the curve until the sheet can lie flat on the floor **(3)**. Crease, and cut off the waste.

Trimming to fit a doorway

Fit the vinyl around the doorjambs by creasing it against the floor and trimming off the waste.

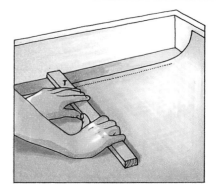

1 Fit to first wall by scribing with a scribing gauge

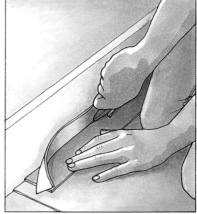

2 Press folded edge to baseboard and cut

Gluing and joining sheet vinyl

Modern sheet-vinyl floorcoverings can be laid loose, but you may prefer to at least glue the edges, especially across a door opening.

Peel back the edge and spread a band of the recommended flooring adhesive, using a grooved trowel. Or, apply 2-inch-wide, double-faced adhesive tape to the floor.

Joining sheets of vinyl

If you have to join sheets of vinyl, lap the top sheet over the sheet underneath and make sure the pattern matches exactly. Cut through both pieces with a sharp knife, then remove the waste strips. Without moving the sheets, fold back both cut edges, apply tape or adhesive, then press the two together.

Secure butting edges with adhesive or tape.

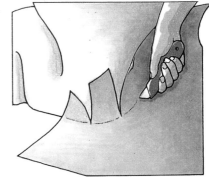

3 Make triangular cuts around a curve

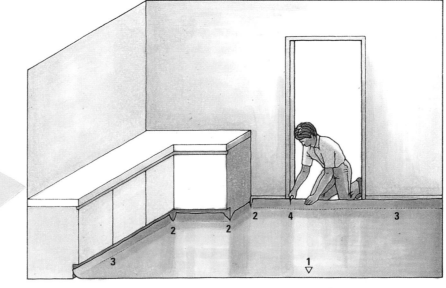

Positioning sheet vinyl
Lay the vinyl on the floor so that it laps the baseboard all around. Then:
1 Start by fitting the sheet to the longest uninterrupted wall.
2 Cut notches at each corner so the sheet will lay flat.
3 Allow folds of about 3 inches all around for scribing to fit.
4 Make a straight cut across the door opening, and install a threshold bar.

Wood-framed house

Wood is the predominant material used in residential construction for both structural and finish applications. While there are several approaches to framing a structure with wood—including traditional post-and-beam framing and balloon framing—the platform framing system shown here is the most common approach.

Foundations

The foundations for frame houses are generally either poured concrete or concrete block. Poured concrete footings should be installed under all foundation walls.

Floor construction

In platform framing, the first-floor structure is fastened to sill plates that rest on top of the foundation walls. The basic floor structure is made with 2-inch-thick joists. The ends of the joists are joined to the rim or band joists, and cross-bracing (often called bridging) is nailed between the joists to prevent them from twisting. When openings occur in the joist layout for stairways, or other passages through the plane of the floor, double headers and double joists are installed around the perimeter of the opening for extra strength. Subflooring and finished flooring are installed over the joists.

Wall construction

The walls of a wood-frame house are ordinarily built by nailing the ends of studs to horizontal members called top and bottom plates. The walls are lifted and nailed to the floor. All the loadbearing walls have a double top plate, and usually the interior partitions do too. Where door and window openings occur, headers are installed in the wall to support the weight above each opening. The outside surface of all exterior walls is covered with sheathing, usually some type of manufactured panel.

Roof structure

A traditional roof calls for rafters that rest on top of the house walls and are joined together with a ridge board at the peak. The roof deck is formed by nailing sheathing (usually manufactured panels) over the top edge of the rafters, and then covering the sheathing with asphalt felt and the roofing material: asphalt or wood shingles, slate, or clay tiles.

Foundations
The foundations carry the whole weight of the house. The type, size, and depth are determined largely by the loadbearing properties of the subsoil and by the frost depth in your area.

Wall foundation
A continuous concrete or block wall resting on top of a concrete footing.

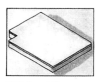

Slab foundation
Houses without basements or crawlspaces may have this type of foundation. In cold climates the footings must be set below the frost line.

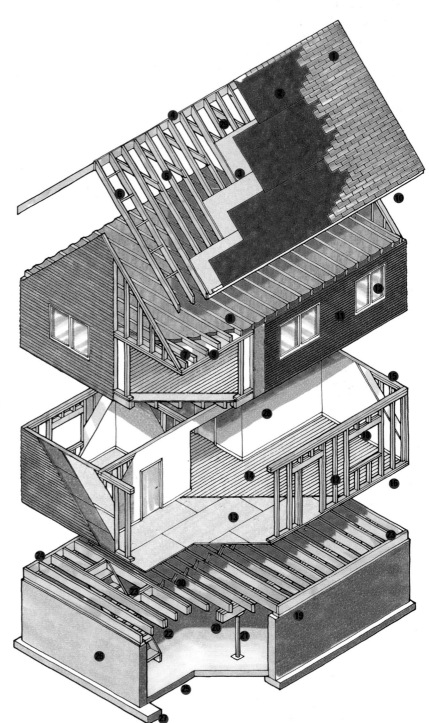

TYPICAL COMPONENTS OF A WOOD-FRAMED HOUSE

1 Asphalt shingles	**9** Vapor barrier	**17** Stud	**25** Concrete slab
2 Asphalt felt	**10** Fascia	**18** Header	**26** Foundation wall
3 Sheathing	**11** Siding	**19** Sill plate	**27** Footing
4 Ridge board	**12** Window unit	**20** Girder or beam	**28** Loadbearing
5 Rafters	**13** Subflooring	**21** Column	partition
6 Lookouts	**14** Finish flooring	**22** Double joist	**29** Collar tie
7 Ceiling joists	**15** Double top plate	**23** Double joist header	**30** Cross-bracing
8 Insulation	**16** Bottom plate	**24** Rim or band joist	

Brick house

Brick houses tend to follow traditional styles and methods of construction. The brickwork gives the building character and is the main structural element. If you have to repair and renovate your home, it is useful to understand the basic principles of its construction.

Foundation
Brick houses generally have a deep foundation made of concrete block or poured concrete. In older houses, stone or brick may have been used for the foundation.

Wall structure
Cavity wall construction is used to build the perimeter walls of most brick houses. Each wall is constructed of an inner and outer leaf separated by an airspace. The two leaves are braced together with metal or brick ties. A flashing just above the finished grade keeps ground moisture from migrating up the walls. Rigid insulation is often placed in the airspace.

For economy, especially in newer brick houses, concrete blocks are frequently used for the inner wall, and the interior surface is generally finished with plaster. Interior partitions are usually framed with wood studs which are covered with wood or wire lath to hold the plaster finish to the walls.

For structural purposes, the tops of door and window openings are covered with lintels made of stone, steel, or cast concrete. Brick arches are a traditional alternative to lintels.

Floor structure
The ends of the floor joists usually rest on recesses in the brick wall. The joists are supported between the perimeter walls with columns or girders. Cross-bracing is nailed between the joists to keep them from twisting. As in wood-framed houses, subflooring is installed over the joists and the finished flooring is applied over the subfloor.

Roof structure
In many brick houses the roof structure is similar to that used in wood-framed houses. But if the roof finish is slate or tile (both of which are extremely heavy), the structure must be reinforced with purlins to support the additional weight.

Foundation problems
Consult an architect or professional engineer when trying to diagnose problems with a foundation.

Settlement
Settlement cracks in walls are not uncommon. If they are not wide and have stabilized, they are not usually a serious problem.

Subsidence
Subsidence is the sinking of a foundation, generally caused by weak or shallow foundations. A wide crack that continues to open is the most common symptom.

Heave
Weak foundations can also be damaged by ground swell or frost heave.

Light foundations
Extensions or bays should never be built on foundations that are lighter or shallower than those supporting the house. If they are, cracks may appear where the two structures meet, as a result of uneven movement between them. This is known as differential movement.

TYPICAL COMPONENTS OF A BRICK HOUSE

1 Tiles or slates	**9** Partition with plaster	**16** Lintel	**24** Concrete slab
2 Ridge board	**10** Internal brick wall	**17** Block partition	**25** Concrete footings
3 Roof battens	**11** Brick cavity wall	**18** Staircase	**26** Ground
4 Roofing felt	**12** Floor joists	**19** Floorboards	
5 Purlin	**13** Cross-bracing	**20** Ground-floor joists	
6 Rafters	**14** Plaster ceiling	**21** Joist plate	
7 Ceiling joists	**15** Brick loadbearing	**22** Interior support wall	
8 Wall plate	wall	**23** Damp-proof course	

Exterior walls

Exterior walls are built to bear the structural loads of the house, to keep out weather and unwanted noises, to trap heat, and to serve as a decorative element in the home's design. There are numerous structural approaches for building exterior walls. The most common ones are illustrated and described below.

Frame wall construction

Wall ties
Wall ties are laid in the mortar joints and bridge the airspace between the inner and outer leaves of a masonry cavity wall. In brick veneer walls, the ties are fastened to the sheathing.

Wire butterfly tie

Sheetmetal tie

In wood-framed houses, exterior walls are usually built with 2 x 4 studs nailed 16 inches on center to top and bottom plates. And since exterior walls carry much of the structural load, wall top plates are doubled.

Sheathing is nailed to the outer surface of the wall frame to add rigidity, and is then covered with a weather-resistant membrane. Wood, plywood, hardboard, vinyl, and aluminum sidings are nailed directly to the membrane-covered sheathing. When the exterior finish is made of brick or stucco veneer, there is generally a 1-inch airspace between the sheeting and the veneer.

Fiberglass batt or mineral fiber insulation is frequently used in the stud cavities. A vapor barrier is applied to the interior edges of the wall frame before attaching the interior wall finish, which may be gypsum drywall, plaster, or paneling.

Masonry construction

Very old stone houses may be built with solid walls, but in most masonry construction, cavity walls, consisting of an inner and outer leaf separated by an airspace, are the norm. The two leaves are braced with wall ties running between them, which are then set in the mortar joints. In modern masonry construction, rigid insulation may be set in the airspace, and cement block instead of brick may be used for the inner leaf for economy.

Exterior wall construction
1 Frame wall with wood siding
2 Concrete-block wall
3 Solid stone wall
4 Frame wall with stucco veneer
5 Brick cavity wall with block inner leaf
6 Frame wall with brick veneer

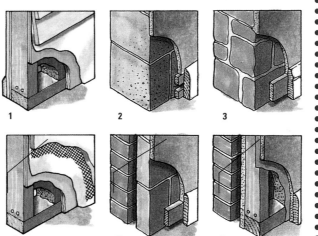

Superinsulated frame walls

Superinsulated frame wall

In recent years, new approaches to wall framing and insulation have been developed in the interest of conserving energy. Typical of various superinsulation approaches has been the use of 2 x 6 studs and plates to create deeper stud cavities that permit thicker insulation. The added insulation significantly improves the R-value of house walls, a standard that measures structural resistance to the passage of thermal energy.

In addition to improving R-values with thicker insulation and insulated sheathing materials, superinsulating techniques also protect insulation from moisture damage and reduce air infiltration through seams and joints by the application of a vapor barrier. The vapor barrier is carefully wrapped around corners and at floor and ceiling joints. The vapor barrier is also carefully sealed around electrical boxes and other mechanical fixtures.

Semipermeable house wraps have been developed for the membrane between the sheathing and the siding. These permit moisture to escape from the wall cavity but screen out drafts.

When appraising the condition of a house or planning a remodeling project, distinguishing between loadbearing and nonloadbearing walls is critical.

In general, the exterior walls of a house are loadbearing, that is, they transmit the weight of the roof and floor loads of upper stories to the foundation. If you took the finish off exterior walls, you would find that they utilize special structural elements: frame walls have double top plates and thick double headers over window and door openings where the normal stud-spacing pattern is interrupted to bear the weight above. If, when you inspect a house, exterior walls appear to buckle, show unusual cracks, or display vertical or horizontal misalignment, this is evidence of a severe structural problem. And if the structural scheme of an exterior wall was altered to build an addition, another means of supporting the loads should have been designed into the job.

Interior walls may be loadbearing or nonloadbearing. If a wall runs parallel to floor joists, chances are it has no structural purpose other than to divide the interior space. But if a wall runs perpendicular to joists and you find a similar wall or columns aligned directly below the wall on a lower story, the wall is loadbearing. A loadbearing wall may also rest on a girder, that is, a heavy horizontal member of steel or wood. Like exterior loadbearing walls, interior bearing walls cannot be removed or structurally altered without providing alternate support. Seek advice from an architect or engineer before proceeding with alterations to loadbearing walls.

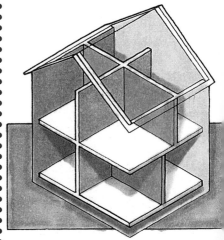

Nonloadbearing walls
The orange walls divide the space into smaller rooms, and could be removed without damaging the structure.

Interior walls

The type of interior wall construction and finish will depend to a certain extent on the age of the building and on the function of the wall within the structure. The most common types are illustrated and discussed on this page.

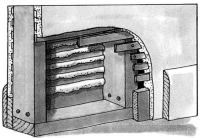

Wood-frame wall with plaster over wood lath

Wood-frame walls

Wood framing is by far the most common structural system used for both interior loadbearing and non-loadbearing partitions. Specific structural differences between the two may consist only of a doubled top plate and more extensive cross-bracing in loadbearing walls. In general, wall studs are spaced 16 inches on center and nailed to top and toe plates. In some nonstructural walls, wall studs are spaced 24 inches on center.

In older houses, thin, closely spaced wood lath strips are nailed to the wall frame to serve as a structural basis for plaster. Plaster is usually applied in two coats—an undercoat of brown plaster followed by a finish coat of white plaster. In newer buildings, metal-wire lath is used as the structural base for plaster instead of wood lath. Metal lath over wood studs is also frequently found where the wall finish is ceramic tile set over a mortar base.

In the vast majority of homes built after World War II, interior walls are wood frame finished with gypsum drywall. The drywall is nailed to the wall frame in sheets, and seams are finished with a drywall joint compound and paper tape. In some cases, a gypsum product similar to drywall is nailed to the wall frame and finished with a skim coat of plaster. Where ceramic tile is applied over a wallboard finish, an adhesive is used as the bonding agent.

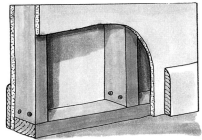

Wood-frame wall with drywall

Metal stud walls

In recent years, metal stud systems have begun to be used to construct interior partitions for economy and because of their fire resistance. It is likely that those living in apartment buildings constructed after 1970 will find partitions framed with metal studs and finished with gypsum drywall, which is fastened to the framing with special screws.

Metal studs and the track that is used for top and bottom plates are normally U-shaped. These materials are easily cut with tinsnips or aviation shears. Studs are crimped into place in the tracks, which are used for plates, and are easy to remove with a firm twist.

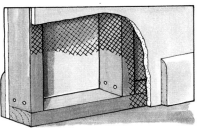

Wood-frame wall with plaster over metal lath

Nonframe walls

In some masonry buildings, especially large apartment buildings constructed between 1890 and 1945, interior partitions may be constructed with lightweight gypsum block or hollow clay block. In most cases with this type of interior wall construction, the wall finish is plaster applied directly to the block. While it is advisable to check with a professional before removing any wall or cutting an opening in it, hollow-block partitions are almost always nonloadbearing. After discovering that such a wall serves no critical structural purpose, you can easily break down or open hollow-block walls with a sledgehammer and cold chisel. The top of openings in block walls will require a lintel for support.

In modern construction, concrete-block walls are frequently used as party walls to separate attached housing units. The wall finish may be plaster or gypsum drywall. Concrete-block walls are designed to contain the spread of fires and also to provide good sound insulation. Generally speaking, party walls are structural and should not be altered without obtaining professional advice and building code permission.

One of the most advanced building technologies—increasingly applied in factory-built, modular homes—is walls made of "stressed-skin panels." While many of the systems are proprietary and the terminology is not entirely uniform, the term usually refers to a wall system that is made with an inner core of rigid foam insulation to which plywood, particleboard, or drywall has been laminated. The panels have interlocking joints. Never alter a stressed-skin panel structure without consulting the manufacturer for the correct procedure and specifications.

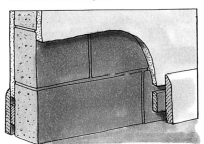

Concrete-block wall finished with plaster

Glass blocks
Hollow glass blocks can be used for nonloadbearing walls. Made in square and rectangular shapes and a range of colors, they are usually laid in mortar.

Converting two rooms to one

Removing a wall may be the best way to improve access between areas frequently used, the dining and living rooms, for instance, and to expand your living space in other areas of the house. Removing a dividing wall, whether it's structural or simply a nonload-bearing partition, is a major undertaking. But it doesn't have to be overwhelming. If you follow some basic safety and structural rules, much of the job is straightforward, albeit very messy and disruptive. Before you start, plan out your requirements and consult the flow chart, right, for a breakdown of just what's involved.

● Hiring professionals
If you're in doubt, hire a professional builder. To save costs, you may be able to work as a laborer or do preparation and clearing work.

Why do you want to remove a wall? Before you go ahead and demolish the wall between two rooms, consider just how the new space might function, its appearance, the time it will take you to carry out the work, and the cost. Ask yourself the following questions:

Will the shape and size of the new room suit your needs? Remember, if you have a young family, your needs are likely to change as they grow up.

Will most of the family activities be carried out in the same room (eating, watching television, playing music, reading, conversation, playing with toys, hobbies, homework)?

Will removing the wall deprive you of privacy within the family, or from passersby in the street?

Will the new room feel like one unit and not a conversion? For example, do the baseboards and moldings match?

Should one of the doorways, if close to another, be blocked off?

Will the loss of a wall make the furniture arrangements difficult, particularly if radiators are in use and take up valuable wall space elsewhere?

Will the heating and lighting need to be modified?

Will the proposed shape of the opening be in character with the room and in the right proportion?

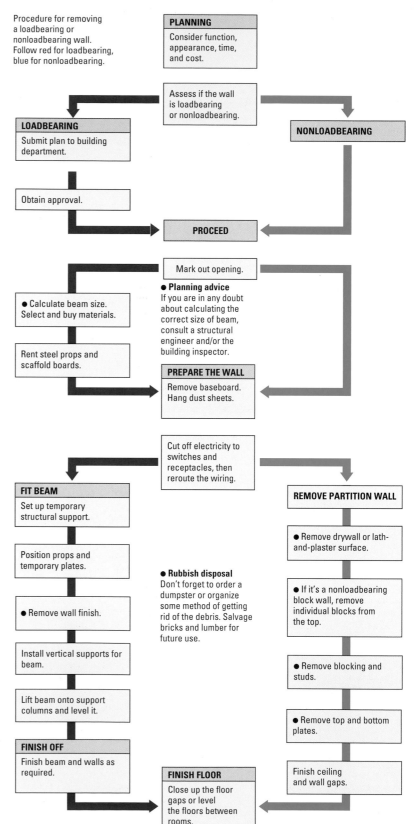

Procedure for removing a loadbearing or nonloadbearing wall. Follow red for loadbearing, blue for nonloadbearing.

PLANNING
Consider function, appearance, time, and cost.

Assess if the wall is loadbearing or nonloadbearing.

LOADBEARING
Submit plan to building department.

NONLOADBEARING

Obtain approval.

PROCEED

Mark out opening.

● Planning advice
If you are in any doubt about calculating the correct size of beam, consult a structural engineer and/or the building inspector.

● Calculate beam size. Select and buy materials.

Rent steel props and scaffold boards.

PREPARE THE WALL
Remove baseboard. Hang dust sheets.

Cut off electricity to switches and receptacles, then reroute the wiring.

FIT BEAM
Set up temporary structural support.

REMOVE PARTITION WALL

Position props and temporary plates.

● Remove drywall or lath-and-plaster surface.

● Rubbish disposal
Don't forget to order a dumpster or organize some method of getting rid of the debris. Salvage bricks and lumber for future use.

● Remove wall finish.

● If it's a nonloadbearing block wall, remove individual blocks from the top.

Install vertical supports for beam.

● Remove blocking and studs.

Lift beam onto support columns and level it.

● Remove top and bottom plates.

FINISH OFF
Finish beam and walls as required.

FINISH FLOOR
Close up the floor gaps or level the floors between rooms.

Finish ceiling and wall gaps.

Removing a loadbearing wall

If a loadbearing wall is to be removed to create a more open plan, a beam must be installed to maintain the home's structural integrity. The basic options for removing a loadbearing wall are discussed below.

Structural concerns

An interior loadbearing wall generally supports the weight of an upper floor and sometimes, depending on the design, part of the weight of the roof. When a loadbearing wall is removed, provisions must be made to support the loads on that wall. Typically, a horizontal beam is installed in the area where joists of the upper floor rested on the top plate of the wall that is being removed. The beam is supported by vertical columns that transmit the load to the foundation and other structural elements of the house frame.

The size of the beam is determined by several factors: the load it must bear, the span between the vertical columns that support it, the distance from the beam to other structural elements that run parallel to it, the material from which the beam is made, and local standards for minimum floor-load capacities. While determining the necessary size required for a beam in any given situation is a matter for a professional engineer, architect, or building official, in general, the greater the load, span between vertical supports, and distance from parallel structural elements, the larger the beam must be. The required thickness and depth of a beam can be changed, based on the number and spacing of support columns and with the introduction of other structural elements running parallel to the beam.

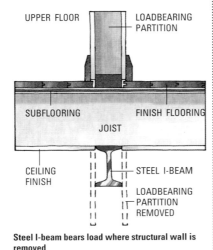

Steel I-beam bears load where structural wall is removed

Choosing a beam

Beams of several different materials can be used to provide structural support where a loadbearing wall is removed. In many cases, rolled steel I-beams are used. Because of steel's great strength, the depth of the beam can be relatively shallow compared with the other options. And this can be an important concern where maximum headroom for an opening is critical. But steel beams can present some difficulties for typical do-it-yourselfers. Most codes require that steel beams be supported by steel columns, and that connections be either welded or bolted—both options that require special equipment and skills. Finishing a steel beam can also be difficult.

Laminated wood beams are a desirable option preferred by do-it-yourselfers and increasingly specified by architects. The beams are made by laminating multiple pieces of lumber. Several appearance grades are available which may either be finished with drywall or left exposed for decorative effect. Laminated beams can be cut and drilled with ordinary tools, and can be joined to columns with structural joints, lagscrews, or approved metal fastening plates

Planning and approval

In most areas, it is necessary to obtain a building permit before removing a loadbearing wall. In order to obtain a permit, you have to provide the inspector with drawings that include key details of the existing structure and specifications for the installation of the new support components. While a knowledgeable do-it-yourselfer may be able to prepare such drawings, others should hire an architect or structural engineer.

Once your plans are approved—and you've paid a fee—work can begin. The inspector will stipulate a schedule for various inspections and it's your responsibility to tell the inspector when the various stages are complete.

How a beam is supported

Beams are supported by vertical columns that transmit the load to other structural elements within the building. The required number and spacing of columns is contingent on the load and the size of the beam.

The drawing below illustrates a typical situation. The structural beam supporting the second-floor joists is supported by a column that transmits the weight to the end of a girder notched into the foundation wall. As you move to the left, you see another column supporting the beam. That column bears directly on the girder and aligns with a column supporting it.

The key point is that columns must align either exactly or very nearly to maintain the structural integrity of the beam. Note that a concrete footing appears below the basement floor slab beneath the columns to bear and spread the weight of the imposed load.

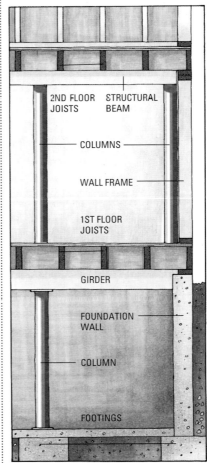

Opening masonry walls

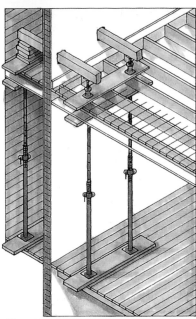

1 Layout for removing wall flush with ceiling

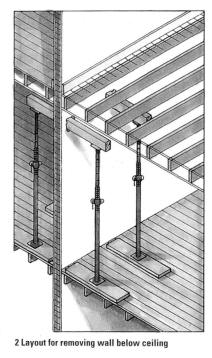

2 Layout for removing wall below ceiling

SAFE PROPPING PROCEDURE

To reduce the risk of structural collapse when opening up walls, it is critical to set up jacks in a safe manner. Use a level to make sure that jacks are plumb and always use heavy boards running perpendicular to the floor joists at the jack bearing points to spread the load. If the floor structure on which jacks are bearing seems springy, set jack posts directly beneath them on the floor below.

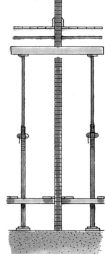

Jacks passing through suspended floor

To remove part of a masonry wall you must temporarily support the wall above the opening. You will need to rent adjustable steel jacks and scaffold boards on which to support them.

Where the beam is to be placed at ceiling level, rent extra boards to support the ceiling **(1)**. Generally you will have to install short beams through the wall to transfer the load to the jacks **(2)**. These beams must measure at least 4 x 6 inches.

Rent sufficient jacks to be spaced not more than 3 feet apart across the width of the opening. If possible, buy the beam after the initial inspection by the building inspector. It can then be cut to your exact requirements.

Preparation

Remove the baseboards from both sides of the wall. Working from one side, mark out the position of the beam on the wall in pencil. Use a steel tape measure, level, and straightedge for accuracy. Hang dust sheets or drop cloths around the work area on the opposite face of the wall to help contain the airborne dust. Seal gaps around all doors with masking tape to prevent the dust from traveling throughout the house. Open windows in the rooms you're working in.

Inserting support beams

Mark the position for the support beams on the wall, then cut away the plaster and chisel a hole through the brickwork at each point. Finish the hole at the bottom of one course of bricks. Make the holes slightly oversize so you can easily pass the beams through. Position a pair of adjustable jacks under each beam not more than 2 feet from each side of the wall. Stand the jacks on scaffold boards to spread the load over the floor.

Adjust the jacks to take the weight of the structure and nail their baseplates to the supporting boards to prevent them from being dislodged.

Supporting the ceiling

If the ceiling needs supporting, stand the jacks on scaffold boards at each side of the wall and adjust them so they're just below ceiling height. (They should be placed 2 feet from the wall.) Place another plank on top of the jacks and adjust the jacks until the ceiling joists are supported.

Removing the wall

Chip off plaster with a sledge-hammer and cold chisel, then cut out the brickwork, working from the top. Once you've removed four or five courses, cut the bricks on the side of the opening. Chisel down pointing to cut the bricks cleanly. Remove all brickwork down to one course below the floorboards. Clear the rubble into garbage bags as you work. If you are removing a lot of debris, it may be worth renting a dumpster. The job is slow and laborious, but a circular saw with a masonry blade can make it easier and quicker.

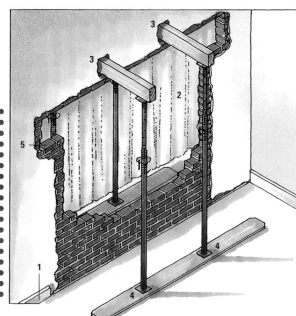

Cutting the opening.
1 Remove or cut back the baseboard and mark the beam's position.
2 Hang dust sheets around the work area.
3 Cut openings and insert support beams.
4 Stand jacks on scaffold boards and adjust them to support the beams.
5 Cut away the plaster, then chisel out the bricks starting from the top of the opening.

Brick-cutting saw

Removing a nonloadbearing wall

Lightweight partition walls that are not loadbearing can be removed safely without consulting the authorities for approval and without the need to add temporary supports. You must, however, be certain that the wall is not structural before doing so because some partitions do offer partial structural support.

Dismantling a stud partition

Remove the baseboards from both sides of the wall and any other moldings. It's a good idea to save these for reuse or repairs in the future. If any electrical switches, receptacles, or light fixtures are attached to the wall, they must be disconnected and rerouted before work begins.

Removing the plasterwork
Use a claw hammer or crowbar to remove the drywall or plaster and lath covering the wall frame. Be sure to wear gloves, goggles, long pants and shirt, and a respirator when doing this work. Remove the debris for disposal.

Removing the framework
First knock away any blocking from between the studs. Then pull out the studs. If they are difficult to remove, saw through them at an angle, to prevent the saw from binding. If you make the cut close to the top or bottom plate, you will be left with useful lumber for future work.

Pry the top and bottom plates from the ceiling joists and floor. If the end studs are nailed to the walls, pry them away with a crowbar.

Finishing off
Fill any gaps in the ceiling and walls by installing narrow strips of drywall. If you have a gap in your flooring, fill it with stock that's the same size and kind of wood.

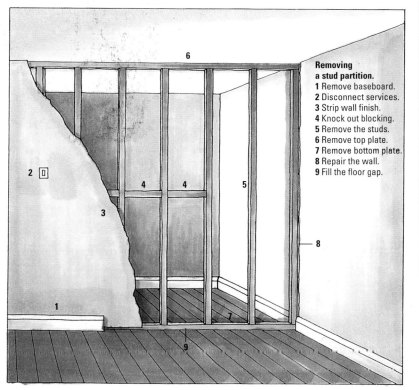

Removing a stud partition.
1 Remove baseboard.
2 Disconnect services.
3 Strip wall finish.
4 Knock out blocking.
5 Remove the studs.
6 Remove top plate.
7 Remove bottom plate.
8 Repair the wall.
9 Fill the floor gap.

Dismantling a block wall

Partition walls are sometimes made using lightweight concrete blocks. To remove the wall, start to cut away the individual units from the top, using a cold chisel and hammer. Work from the center out toward the sides.

Chop off an area of plaster or drywall first, so that you can locate the joints between individual blocks.

Methods of closing a floor gap

When you remove a wall to create one room from two or part of a wall to create a passage, a gap may be left in the finish flooring where the bottom plate of the wall had been fastened to the subflooring.

If a gap runs parallel to the direction of the boards in wood-strip flooring, you can fill it with little disturbance to the pattern. Since floorboards are generally milled with a tongue on one edge and a groove on the other so that they interlock when they are installed, fitting new boards into a confined space can present a problem. If the protruding tongue of an existing floorboard will not allow you to set the filler board in place, chisel away the lower edge of the groove so the filler board can drop over the tongue. If the filler board must be ripped to a narrower width, cut a rabbet to fit over the tongue.

If the gap runs perpendicular to the existing flooring, it will look better to fill it with strips running in the same direction rather than with short strips to match the existing pattern. In this case, match the groove side of a filler board against the ends of existing flooring at one side of the gap and drive finish nails through the tongue. This technique is called blind nailing. Fit the grooves of subsequent rows over the tongues of installed strips and nail in the same way. To fit the final strip in place, remove the tongue with a saw or hand plane, then push the board in place. The last board will need to be face nailed.

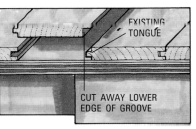

EXISTING TONGUE
CUT AWAY LOWER EDGE OF GROOVE

Gap parallel to floorboards

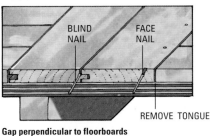

BLIND NAIL   FACE NAIL
REMOVE TONGUE

Gap perpendicular to floorboards

125

Aligning mismatched floors

When a partition wall separating two rooms is removed or when an opening is made to create a passageway, sometimes the levels of the finished flooring on the two sides of the wall are at different heights. This usually happens when the finished flooring of one room is different from the other, or when a floor has been refinished during a previous remodeling project. For the sake of both appearance and safety, you must provide an appropriate transition between the two levels. Several possible solutions to the problem are discussed below.

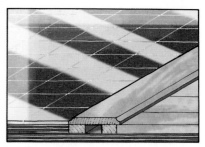

Installing a saddle
Install filler blocks in gap and nail saddle to blocks.

Treating slight mismatches

The slightest mismatch in floor levels can cause people to trip. When a slight mismatch exists, it is desirable to create a distinct visual transition between the two floor surfaces that will catch people's attention. Then they will walk more carefully.

For example, a slight mismatch could exist when one part of a floor surface is finished with ceramic tile and the remainder with wood-strip flooring. Ordinarily, the tile floor could be anywhere from ¼ to ⅞ inch higher than the wood floor, due to the extra subflooring that is usually installed beneath tile. There are three simple ways to correct this problem.

The first is to install a saddle to cover the gap left by the wall that has been removed. The best way to do this is to fill the gap with wood blocks or strips level with the wood floor. The saddle, a stock molding available in several widths at any lumberyard, is then nailed in place over the filler

blocks. The top of the saddle should be level with or slightly higher than the higher of the two surfaces. In most cases saddles are finished with a stain to match the adjacent floors and then covered with at least three coats of polyurethane varnish. They can also be painted, but be sure to use a high-quality enamel paint. Prime the saddle and paint on at least two topcoats.

A second alternative is to nail a small quarter-round molding to the edge of the tile subflooring. This provides the appropriate visual transition and also protects the tile edge from cracking.

A third solution that would unify the room and address a slight mismatch in floor levels would be to fill the gap with a cementitious floor-filling compound finished with a slope to make the transition from one level to the other. The method is used when the entire floor surface is going to be covered with carpeting.

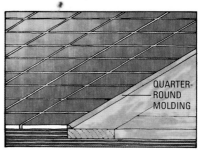

Installing a molding strip
Install quarter-round molding to finish and protect tile edge.

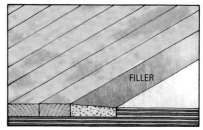

Filling with cementitious filler
Slope the patch from one level to the other. Finish with carpet or vinyl flooring.

Building up floor levels

When you want to create a uniform floor level in two rooms that have been made into one by removing a partition, you can build up the existing floor to create a flat, uniform plane. The methods and materials you choose are based on the amount of differential between the existing floors. This involves installing new subflooring on one or both sides of the gap and, in extreme cases, can also require installing sleepers on the lower floor to support the new subflooring.

Before you make a decision on one of the specific approaches illustrated on this page, it is important to consider what type and thicknesses of materials constitute adequate subflooring for various floor finishes. Plywood, particleboard, tempered hardboard, and fiberboard are generally used for subflooring. Pine, plywood, and hardboard strips can be used for sleepers.

Ceramic and vinyl tile and laminated wood flooring boards require a fairly

rigid subfloor to prevent them from flexing underfoot, which would ultimately loosen the adhesive and might result in cracking. For these applications, a minimum thickness of ½-inch plywood or ⅝-inch particleboard is recommended. If these materials are to be supported by sleepers, the spacing between the sleepers should be no greater than 16 inches. Tempered hardboard can be used as subflooring for tiles only if it is laid directly over an existing floor without sleepers.

Solid wood-strip flooring, which is generally 1 inch thick, can be nailed directly to an existing wood floor, to any existing sturdy subfloor, or perpendicular to sleepers spaced 16 inches apart. Sleepers and subflooring should be fastened either with screws or with ring-shank nails that resist popping. Fasteners should be approximately three times longer than the thickness of the material being fastened. Adhesive can be used along with fasteners.

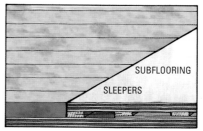

Building up lower floor surface
Match the higher surface with sleepers and subflooring. Treat subflooring or both surfaces.

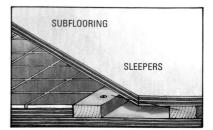

Setting sleepers
Use sleepers to equalize the height on the lower surface, and set subflooring over both surfaces.

Making one room into two

Constructing partitions to divide larger spaces into smaller ones or to alter an existing floor plan is, for the most part, a relatively simple matter. You just construct one or more stud walls and finish the surfaces with drywall or another wall finish. Considerations relating to codes, design goals, and methods of construction are discussed here and on the following pages.

Code considerations

Code regulations concerning the construction of partition walls vary widely from locale to locale. But in general, they govern the amount and type of ventilation that must be provided within an enclosed space, minimum dimensions for hallways, and fire safety provisions. For example, most rooms that can be categorized as living space (living rooms, dining areas, bedrooms, and the like), must have windows of a certain size in relation to the square footage of the room in order to provide adequate light and ventilation. Bathrooms and kitchens, while not necessarily required to have windows, frequently are required to have mechanical ventilation.

With respect to fire regulations, the type and thickness of materials used to construct partitions are frequently specified to ensure that walls can withstand or contain fire for a minimum of 1 hour. For multiple dwellings in some urban areas, metal studs are required and wood studs are not permitted.

Many local codes specify that hallways may be no less than 3 feet wide to provide sufficient room for passage. While it is a good idea to consult with your local building department for code standards relating to your particular project, it's also important to think through the space requirements for activities and room furnishings so that you will arrive at a workable, comfortable design.

Positioning a partition

The frame for a partition wall is generally made from 2 x 4 lumber and consists of a top plate, which is attached to the ceiling, a bottom plate, which is attached to the floor, and studs, which run vertically between the two plates. It is not usually necessary to remove the existing ceiling, floor, or wall finish to fasten a new wall frame to existing structural elements. But you do have to make sure that the fasteners you use are driven into existing structural members. As a rule of thumb, use fasteners that are two to three times as long as the plate is thick.

Determine first whether the new partition will run perpendicular or parallel to existing floor and ceiling joists. If it will run perpendicular, then be sure to establish the exact location of the joists. (Floor joists are usually spaced on 16-inch centers, ceiling joists on 16- or 24-inch centers.) Drive the fasteners through the plates and into the joists.

If the partition is to run parallel with joists, center the plates on a joist or add blocking between existing joists to provide structural anchoring for fasteners. An end stud that abuts an existing wall should be nailed or screwed to a stud in the existing wall. If a stud does not fall where the new wall ends, either open up the wall and add some blocking or use toggle bolts to hold the new wall in place. Use expansion bolts to anchor to masonry walls.

While constructing stud walls finished with gypsum drywall is a simple, convenient way to attain visual privacy, the conventional system of framing and finishing provides low resistance to sound transmission. The typical wall, framed with 2 x 4s and finished with ½-inch drywall, has a sound transmission rating (STC) of only 30 to 34.

Filling stud cavities with batt insulation and using thicker drywall, even doubling the layers of drywall, will improve the resistance to sound transmission. One of the most effective approaches to the problem, however, is to modify the wall framing by using lumber for the top and bottom plates that is wider than that used for the studs. Studs are then fastened in place on 8-inch centers, with edges alternately aligned with opposite edges of the plates.

This reduces the amount of sound-induced vibration that is transmitted from one side of the wall to the other. The STC rating of the model illustrated below, which uses 2 x 4 studs set on 2 x 6 plates and is finished with double layers of ⅜-inch drywall, would have a rating of 50 to 54—nearly equal to that of a 7-inch-thick brick cavity wall.

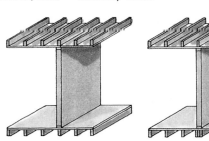

Right-angle alignment
A partition set at right angles to joists is well supported.

Parallel alignment
A partition parallel with the joists must be supported by one of them.

Reinforcement
An extra floor joist may be required to bear the extra weight of the partition.

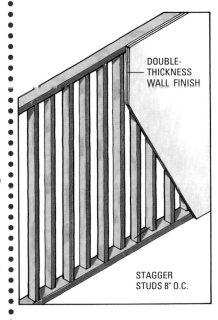

DOUBLE-THICKNESS WALL FINISH

STAGGER STUDS 8" O.C.

Wall framing and finishing designed to reduce sound transmission

Building a stud partition

Making a stud partition wall is the easiest way to divide a room in two. You can construct a plain wall, or add a doorway, pass-through, or glazed area to "borrow" light from an existing window. You can build the partition directly onto the floorboards or the joists below. The ends of the partition can be set against the existing wall finish provided there is a stud or other solid material directly under it, or the existing wall can be opened to add the necessary structural member.

1 Snap chalkline on ceiling

Laying out and spacing the studs

Mark the position of one edge of the bottom plate for the new wall on the floor in chalk. Use a chalkline or a length of 2 x 4 as a guide to draw the line. Continue the guidelines up the walls at each side, using a level and a straight board. Continue the guidelines onto the ceiling, by snapping a chalkline onto the surface **(1)**.

Spacing the studs
Lay the top and bottom plates together with their face sides facing upward. Mark the position of the studs at 16-inch centers working from one edge. Square the lines across both members with a square **(2)**. Center a 2 x 4 scrap over the layout marks and use the edges as a guide for marking the stud

positions. If you are installing ⅝-inch drywall or solid tongue-and-groove paneling, 24-inch spacing can be used.

Laying out a doorway
If you are including a doorway in the wall, make allowance for the width of the opening. The studs that form the sides of the opening must be spaced apart by the width of the door plus the thickness of both doorjambs, plus ½ inch of adjustment space on both sides. Mark the width of the opening on the top plate at the required positions, then transfer these marks to the bottom plate and cut out the opening in the bottom plate **(3)**. The door studs overlap the ends of the bottom plates, which must be cut back to allow for them.

2 Mark top and bottom plate together

3 Mark door opening on top plate first

Attaching the framework

Secure the bottom plate to the floor on each side of the door opening using 16d nails or 4-inch lagscrews. Use the top plate as a guide to keep the two bottom-plate boards in line.

Brace the top plate against the ceiling on its line and check that the stud marks on the top plate line up with those on the bottom plate **(4)**. Use a straight board and a level or a plumb bob to do this. Nail or screw the top plate through the ceiling finish and into the joists above.

Measure the distance between the top and bottom plate at each end and cut the outer wall studs to length. They should fit tightly between the plates.

Fasten the end studs to the walls with nails or screws.

Attaching door studs
Cut the door studs to fit between the plates and wedge them in place but do not fasten them yet. Mark the position of the door header on the studs. Allow for the door height, the jamb thickness, and ⅛ inch of adjustment room.

Attaching the rough header
Nail the door studs to the plates, then nail the header in place through the studs **(5)**. Install short studs, called cripple studs, above the header.

4 Prop top plate against ceiling

Alternative fastening for door studs

Using a chalkline
A retractable self-coating chalkline makes layout easier.

Another method for framing a door opening is to double up the studs on both sides. On the outside are two full studs, but next to them are nailed shorter studs, called jack studs. The jack studs align with the door opening and provide direct support for the header.

Once the header is nailed in place, cut short lengths of 2 x 4 to fit

vertically between the top plate and the header. These cripple studs provide nailing surfaces for the wall finish that's installed later. Make sure when nailing all the parts together that their faces are flush, the studs are plumb, and the header is level. The size of the rough opening must be large enough to accommodate the new door with all the necessary clearances.

Double door studs
1 Jack studs
2 Full studs
3 Header

5 Nail header between studs

Stud partitions

Fastening studs and blocking

Measure and cut each full-length stud and fasten these to the plates (see below). Cut the blocking to fit between the studs and, working from the wall, toenail the first end to the wall stud, then nail through the next stud into the end of the block. One or two rows of blocking may be required. If you are going to install drywall horizontally, place the center of the blocks 4 feet below the ceiling. If you're going to install the drywall vertically, install the blocking in the middle of the wall, staggering it to make blocking easier.

Space studs equally and nail top and bottom

Nail blocking between studs to stiffen them

Use two 10d common nails to toenail each butt joint, one through each side. When driving in the first nail, temporarily nail a block behind the stud to prevent it from moving sideways, or hold your foot against the back side of the stud. Blocks cut to fit between each stud can be permanently nailed in place to provide extra support.

Alternative stud-nailing method

For a very rigid frame, set the studs into ½-inch-deep dadoes notched into the top and bottom plates.

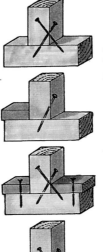

Toenailing
Toenail a butt joint with two nails.

Nailing technique
Support the stud with a block while driving the first nail.

Supporting joint
Blocks nailed to each side brace the joint.

Dado joints
Dado joints make for a very rigid frame.

Fastening to an existing stud wall

Partitions are used for interior walls of rooms. If your new partition meets a wood-frame wall, align it with the framing members in the existing wall.

Fasten the end stud of the new partition to a stud in the existing wall. Locate the stud by drilling closely spaced holes through the wall finish to find the center of the stud.

When the new partition wall falls between the studs of the existing wall, nail the end stud to the blocking and the plates of the existing wall. If you can't get solid nailing, you can use toggle bolts to hold the end stud to the existing wall. Or you can open up the old wall, install a new stud in it, then replace the old wall finish. This is the most difficult option, but it may be the only way to get good support.

Fastening drywall vertically

Start at the doorway with the edge of the first sheet flush with the stud face. Before fastening, cut a 1-inch-wide strip on both sides of the sheet where it falls over the header space.

Fasten the board with 1¼- or 1½-inch nails not more than 12 inches apart. Install the sheets on both sides of the doorway, then cut and install a piece to cover the header space. Allow a ⅛-inch gap at the butt joint. Install the remaining boards.

Fastening drywall horizontally

Drywall can be installed horizontally where it is more economical or convenient to do so. Nail the top row of sheets in place first, followed by the bottom row. If the sheets in the bottom row have to be cut to height, remember to install the cut edge down so it falls behind the baseboard.

Temporarily nail a horizontal support board to the studs ⅛-inch below the centerline of the blocking. Lift a sheet onto the strip, adjust it from side to side until the ends of the sheet fall over the middle of the studs, and nail the sheet in place. Install the remainder of the top sheets in this way. Then install the bottom row. Make sure to stagger the joints between sheets so they don't line up with the joints in the top row.

You'll need help from a second person to carry the sheets and to hold them while you are nailing. Always nail from the center of the sheet to the outside edges. This keeps the sheet flat against the studs.

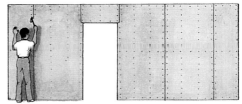

Installing drywall vertically
Work away from doorway or start at one end.

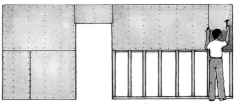

Installing drywall horizontally
Install top row first, then stagger joints on bottom row.

Building a staggered wall

CONSTRUCTING THE CORNERS

A stud wall can be built to divide one room into two and provide closet space at the same time. The construction is the same as described for the straight partition, except for the right-angle junctions.

Constructing a staggered partition with a door at one end and a spacious closet in the middle, as shown below, makes sensible use of available space.

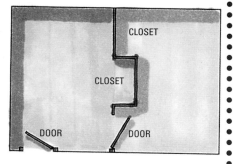

A staggered partition forms storage closets on each side, one for each room.

Positioning the wall

Mark out the bottom-plate position of the main partition across the floor. Mark the position of the recessed partition parallel with it. For clothes storage the recess should be at least 2 feet deep.

Calculate the length of the wall segments by laying them out on the floor. Starting from the wall adjacent to the doorway, measure off the thickness of a stud, the doorjamb, the width of the door, and the finished jamb. Also add ½ inch for clearance around the door. This takes you to the closet opening. Measure from this point to the other existing wall and divide the dimension in two. This gives you the other side of the closet opening. Lay out the remainder of the walls on the floor.

Fastening the top and bottom plates

Mark the position for the top plates on the ceiling. Use a straightedge and a level or a plumb bob to ensure that the stud marks on both plates line up exactly.

Cut and nail the bottom and top plates to the floor and ceiling, as explained earlier for a straight stud partition. Cut and install the studs at the required spacing to suit the thickness of the wall finish. Cut and nail the headers and blocking in place.

Building the wall
1 Mark the bottom-plate stud positions.
2 Transfer the marks to the top plates.
3 Cut and fasten the bottom plates to the floor.
4 Nail the top plates to the ceiling.
5 Make corners from three studs.
6 Nail the other studs at required spacing.
7 Add blocking.
8 Install doorframe.

The right-angled corners and the end of the short partition, which supports the doorframe, need extra studs to stiffen the wall and to provide a nailing surface for the drywall.

Make up a corner from three studs as shown below. Install short 2 x 4 blocks between the studs as spacers **(1)**. For the end of the partition next to the doorway, join two studs with blocks **(2)**. Always nail these blocks flush with the edges of the studs they join.

Once all the wall sections are built and nailed together, check everything for square and plumb. Then hang drywall on both sides of all the walls. Overlap the corners of the drywall sheets **(3)**. At the door opening leave one half of the last stud exposed to provide nailing for the drywall that covers the door framing.

Assemble the doorframe, including both studs, header, cripple studs, and top plate, then lift it into place. Attach one door stud to the partition and cover it with drywall **(4)**. Attach the other door stud to the wall **(5)** and finish trimming out the door.

1 Corner
Use three studs at the partition corners.

2 End post
Use two studs at the end of the partition.

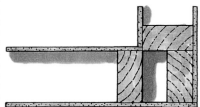

3 Overlap drywall at corners

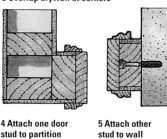

4 Attach one door stud to partition

5 Attach other stud to wall

Hanging fixtures

Unlike solid walls of brick or block, stud walls are mainly hollow, presenting problems when you need to hang wall fixtures. Wherever possible fixtures should be fastened directly to the structural framing members for maximum support. But if the positions of fixtures can't be changed, extra studs, or blocking should be incorporated into the wall before the wall finish is installed.

Mounting a basin

A wall-mounted basin will need sound enough support to carry its own weight and that of someone leaning on it when it's being used.

Buy the basin before building the wall, or work from the manufacturer's literature, which usually specifies the distance between centers for attaching the brackets. Position two studs to take the mounting screws. Mark the center lines of the studs on the floor before applying the drywall or plaster, then draw plumb lines from the marks up onto the wall surface. Measure the height from the floor for the brackets and fasten them securely with screws.

Another approach would be to install a plywood mounting board to fit between the studs to carry both the basin and the faucets, if they are not mounted on the basin. Use exterior-grade plywood at least ¾ inch thick.

Screw 2 x 2 nailing strips to the inside faces of the studs, set back from the front edges by the thickness of the plywood. Cut the panel to size, then nail it to the nailers so it's flush with the edges of the studs.

Install the wall finish to the side of the wall that will carry the basin, leaving the other side open for water supply pipes and drain lines. Drill holes in the plates for pipes. If any pipes need to run sideways, across the wall, notch the studs as shown on the far right. Fasten the basin support brackets through the wall covering and into the plywood block, using lagbolts.

Installing a wall cabinet

It is not always possible to arrange studs as needed for mounting things on the wall because walls tend to be put up well before the exact location of the fixtures is established. If there are no studs where you want them, you will have to use hollow-wall fasteners instead. Choose a type that will adequately support the cabinet.

One good choice is toggle bolts (see far right). These pieces of hardware are pushed through holes drilled in the back of the cabinet and the wall. The spring-loaded wings on the end of the bolt expand when they get through the hole. A washer keeps the screwhead against the cabinet back. By tightening the screw, you pull the bolt wings against the inside surface of the wallcovering. Once the bolt is tight, the back of the cabinet and the wallcovering are sandwiched securely together. For most cabinets, install a toggle bolt at each corner of the back panel.

Hanging shelves

Wall-mounted bookshelves have to carry a considerable weight, so be sure to pick heavy-duty hardware for the job. Use a shelving system that has strong metal uprights that hold and support adjustable brackets. Screw the uprights into studs for the most secure support.

Hanging small fixtures

Load-carrying fixtures with a small contact area can crush the wall finish and strain the fasteners. Mount coat hooks on a board to spread the load, and screw the boards to studs. Hang small pictures on picture hooks secured with steel nails. For heavy frames, try to nail a hook into a stud or use a couple of toggle bolts. Use mirror clips when installing a flush mirror on the wall. And use stranded wire, fastened to a stud, for hanging mirrors. For lightweight items, many different, simple-to-use hollow-wall fasteners are available.

Mounting a basin
Fasten a wall-mounted basin to an exterior-grade plywood board.

It is easy to plan and install pipes and electrical cables in a stud partition wall before finishing it. To guard against future occupants drilling into them, install horizontal runs of pipe and cable no more than 12 inches above the floor.

Plumbing

Plan the runs of supply or waste pipes by marking the faces of the studs, plates, and blocking. Remember that a waste pipe must have a slight fall toward the main waste pipe to drain properly. When you are satisfied with the layout, cut notches in the studs for the pipes (see below).

Transfer the marked lines to the sides of the studs or blocking and drill holes for the pipes in the middle of these framing members. Cut in to the holes to make notches for the pipe.

Also make ¾-inch-deep notches in the outside edge of the studs to receive 1 x 2 fillers that bridge the notch to reinforce the studs.

Install the pipes, followed by the fillers. Make sure the fillers are flush with the edges of the studs. You don't have to add filler strips to any notches that you cut in the blocking.

Running electric cable

Drill ⅝-inch holes at the centers of the studs and blocking for running electrical cable. When the framing members are exposed, you should always mount electrical boxes against the studs or blocking for rigid support. Boxes are available with different types of brackets for this purpose.

But if you need to install a box after the wallcovering is in place, cut-in boxes are available that mount directly into holes cut in the drywall or plaster surface. They have side wings that grip the back of the wall surface.

You can also use a surface-mounted wiring scheme. In this case, the boxes are mounted directly on the wall and the cable is run through rigid conduit to the next outlet in the line.

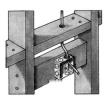

Running plumbing through a stud wall
Reinforce studs with filler pieces

Hollow-wall fasteners
Various fasteners can be used for hanging items from a wall where studs are not available. Some feature screws housed in expanding sheaths. The sheaths expand and press against the sides of the hole when the screw is driven in. Another option is a toggle bolt that has wings that spring out behind the wallcovering as the screw is tightened.

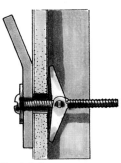

Toggle bolt

Attach electrical boxes to framing member

Suspended ceiling systems

From a practical point of view, a high ceiling can be a liability. It increases heating bills, makes ceiling repairs more difficult, and even makes something as simple as changing a light bulb much more involved than it should be. Lowering the ceiling can help solve these problems and cover up a problem ceiling at the same time. Suspended ceiling systems are made from lightweight metal tracks that hold acoustic or translucent panels. They are easy to install, and don't require specialized tools.

The basic system

The lightweight alloy framework is made from three basic elements: wall angles, which are fastened to walls, main runners, which are similar in function to joists and are usually installed across a room's shorter span, and cross runners, which are set between and perpendicular to main runners.

The loose panels sit on the flanges of the runners. They can be easily lifted out for access to ducts or to service light fixtures, which can be concealed behind them. You need at least 4 inches of space above the framework to install the panels.

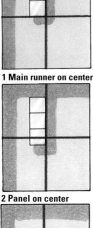
1 Main runner on center

2 Panel on center

3 Center cross runner

4 Panel on center

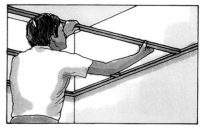
5 Best grid arrangement

Setting out the grid

Normally, 2 x 2-foot or 2 x 4-foot panels are used for suspended ceiling systems. Before installing the framework, draw a plan of the ceiling on graph paper to ensure that the borders are symmetrical. Draw two lines at the halfway point of each wall that bisect in the middle. Lay out the grid on your plan with a main runner centered on the short bisecting line (**1**). Then lay it out again with a line of panels centered on the same line (**2**). Use the grid that provides the widest border panels. Plot the position of the cross runners in the same way, using the other line (**3, 4**). Try to get the border panels even on opposite sides of the room (**5**).

Installing the framework

Before installing a suspended ceiling that has translucent panels under fluorescent light fixtures, remove any flaking material and repair any cracks in the ceiling above. Paint the ceiling with white latex paint to reflect more light from the fixtures.

Install fluorescent light fixtures as needed across the ceiling (16 watts per square yard is recommended as a suitable level of light in most rooms).

Mark the height of the suspended ceiling on the walls with a continuous level line around the whole room. Using a hacksaw or tinsnips, cut lengths of wall angle to fit the longest walls. Mark the stud locations on the wall, then hold up the wall angles and transfer these marks to the angles. Drill screw holes through the angles and attach them to the walls with screws (**1**). Next, cut lengths of wall angle to fit the shorter walls. Their ends should fit on the angles already installed.

Mark the positions of the runners, using your graph-paper plan as a guide. Cut the main runners to span the room. Place their ends on the wall angles (**2**). Use a ceiling panel to check that they are parallel and at right angles to the wall and each other.

Install full-sized cross runners between the main runners according to your plan. Then, cut the border cross runners to fit between the main runners and the wall angles. Align them with the layout marks on the wall. Install the other cross runners in the same way.

Working from the center, drop in the full-sized panels. Measure and cut the border panels to fit the grid and then drop them into place.

Spanning wide rooms

If the size of the room exceeds the maximum length of a standard main runner, join two or more pieces together. A joint-bridging piece is provided if the ends of the runners are not made to lock together.

For spans exceeding 10 feet, support the main runners with wire hangers. Fasten each wire, spaced not more than 5 feet apart, through a hole in the runner and hang it from a screw eye into a ceiling joist above.

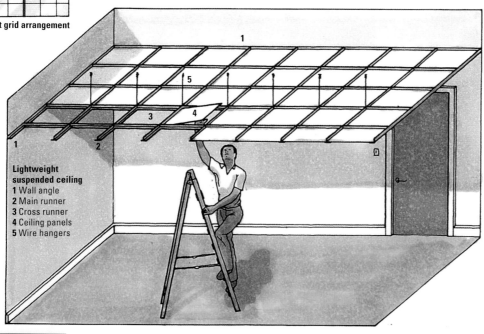

Lightweight suspended ceiling
1 Wall angle
2 Main runner
3 Cross runner
4 Ceiling panels
5 Wire hangers

1 Screw angle to wall

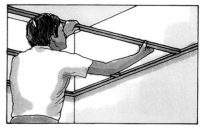
2 Position main runners

Access to the attic space is more convenient and safer if you install a folding ladder. Some are complete with built-in hatch cover, frame, and hardware ready to install in a new opening. Normally, the length of the ladders suits standard ceiling heights, between 7 feet 6 inches and 8 feet. Some can extend up to 10 feet.

Accordion ladder

To install an accordion ladder, securely screw the brackets of the aluminum ladder to the framework of the opening. Install the retaining hooks to the framework to support the ladder in the stowed position. Operate the ladder with a pole, which hooks over the bottom rail. Install the hatch door to the frame with a continuous hinge, followed by the latch that's installed on the other end of the hatch door.

Ready-to-install folding ladder

Cut the opening and trim the joists to the size specified by the manufacturer. Insert the unit in the opening and screw it to the joists.

An accordion ladder is simple to install

Folding ladders are easy to deploy

Many houses are provided with a hatch in the ceiling to give access to the attic space for convenient storage and maintenance of the roof structure. If your house has a large attic space without access from inside the house, installing a hatch could be a valuable addition. Hatch units are available at many home centers. Although the job is straightforward, it does require cutting into the ceiling structure.

When cutting into the structure of a ceiling to create an attic entrance, it's important to consider the effect of the alteration on the ability of the framing to support the existing structure. Some roof frames may incorporate purlins, which are sometimes supported by vertical members that transfer part of the roof load to ceiling joists. If you have any doubts about the effect of cutting joists to install a hatch, consult an architect or engineer.

If you have a choice, site the hatch over a hallway, but not close to the stairs. Access is usually easy from a hallway without having to move furniture, which is more likely if you install it in a bedroom. Make sure your location will provide enough attic headroom so you can climb through the hatch.

Making the opening

If you are planning to install a special folding ladder, the size of the new opening will be specified by the manufacturer. Generally, aim to cut away no more than one of the ceiling joists, which are usually spaced 16 inches apart.

Locate three of the joists by drilling pilot holes in the ceiling. Mark out a square for the opening between the two outer joists. Cut an inspection hole inside the marked area to check that no obstacles are in the way of the cutlines. Saw through the ceiling material and strip it away.

Hold a light into the roof space and climb up between the joists. Lay a board across the joists to support yourself. Saw through the middle joist, cutting it back 3 inches from each edge of the opening. Cut four new pieces of joist lumber to fit between the uncut joists. Use two of these pieces for a header at each end of the cut joist. Nail the headers between the joists using 16d common nails.

Nail the ceiling lath or drywall to the underside of the header joists. Cut jambs from ¾-inch-thick boards to cover the joists and the edges of the ceiling finish. Repair any damage to the ceiling around the opening.

Cut and nail casing boards around the opening to finish it off. If you plan to use a hinged door, install the casing boards flush to the opening. If you want a simple drop-in panel instead, install the casing boards so they overlap the hatch opening by ¾ inch on all sides. Then cut the panel, push it through the opening, and let it rest on the edges of the casing boards.

Attic access traps

Any openings made in the ceiling will encourage the flow of water vapor into the attic space. This can increase the risk of condensation, especially if the attic is not well ventilated. Attic access traps are made with seals to overcome this problem. Each trap has a molded frame that, when installed in a ceiling opening (as described above), forms a seal with the ceiling all around. It also neatly covers the cut edges of the hole. The insulated trapdoor incorporates a flexible vapor seal between it and the hatch frame.

There are hinged trapdoors and lift-out ones. Some of them are fire-resistant. Hinged types can be used in conjunction with an aluminum attic ladder that is available as an accessory.

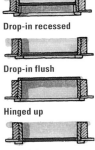

Alternative ways to install hatch covers

Drop-in recessed

Drop-in flush

Hinged up

Hinged down

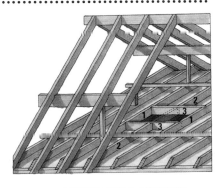

Hatch opening
1 Ceiling joists
2 Cut joist
3 Headers

Frame and insulated trap form an airtight seal

Frame forms seal when attached to joist.

Interior wall finish

As popular interest in authentic restoration of older houses grows, there is a new appreciation for the qualities of a plaster wall finish. While drywall is generally faster, easier, and cheaper to apply, plaster walls have a look and feel that is unmistakable to the discerning eye and sound-reduction properties that are superior to drywall. In the following pages you'll find both traditional and contemporary approaches to the plastering process as well as the methods used for installing and finishing drywall.

Traditional plastering techniques

Traditional plastering uses a mix of plastering material and water, which is spread with a trowel over the rough background in one, two, or sometimes three layers. Each layer is applied with a trowel and leveled accordingly. When set, the plaster forms an integral part of the wall or ceiling. Traditionally, plaster has been applied over masonry walls or wood lath—thin wood strips spaced slightly apart that hold the plaster in place. Over time, metal and gypsum lath have replaced the old wood type. Plastering well requires practice before you can achieve a smooth, flat surface over a large area. With care, a beginner can produce satisfactory results, provided that the right tools and plaster are used and the work is divided into manageable sections. All-purpose, one-coat plasters are now available, which makes traditional plastering easier for do-it-yourselfers.

Gypsum drywall

Manufactured boards of paper-covered gypsum are used to finish walls and ceilings in modern homes. Using drywall eliminates the long drying-out process necessary for wet plasters and requires less skill to apply. The large, flat boards are nailed, screwed, or bonded to walls and ceilings to provide a separate finishing layer. The surface of drywall can be painted, papered, or covered with paneling boards. It can also be covered with a thin coat of finish plaster.

Plaster powder is normally sold in 50- and 100-pound bags. Smaller sizes, including 5-pound bags, are available for repairing damaged plasterwork. It is generally more economical to buy the larger sacks, but this depends on the scale of the work. Try to buy only as much plaster as you need—although it's best to overestimate slightly, to allow for waste and to avoid running out at an inconvenient moment.

Storage

Store plaster in dry conditions. If it is going to be kept in an outbuilding for some time, cover it with plastic sheeting to protect it from moisture. Keep the paper bags off a concrete floor by placing them on boards or plastic sheeting. Once opened, bags are more likely to absorb moisture, which can shorten the setting time and weaken the plaster, so keep an opened bag in a plastic sack sealed with self-adhesive tape. Discard plaster that contains lumps.

Premixed plaster

Ready-to-use plaster is sometimes available in plastic tubs. It's more expensive, but it is easier for most beginners to use and will keep for a long time, provided the airtight lid is sealed well.

Storing plaster
Keep an opened bag of plaster in a plastic sack sealed with adhesive tape.

Traditional plastering
(right)
The construction of a lath-and-plaster ceiling and a plastered masonry wall.
1 Brick background
2 Ceiling joists
3 Lath background
4 First plaster coat
5 Second plaster coat
6 Finish plaster coat
7 Molding

Drywall
(far right)
The construction of a modern drywall and ceiling.
1 Block substrate
2 Furring or stud wall
3 Ceiling joists
4 Blocking
5 Drywall
6 Cove molding
7 Tape
8 Joint compound

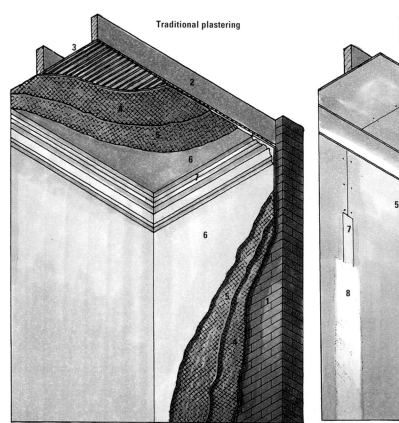

Traditional plastering

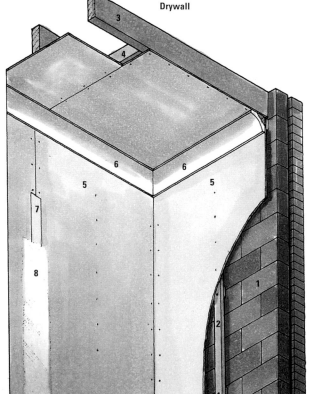

Drywall

Types of plaster

Plastering is carried out with modern gypsum plasters or mixes based on cement, lime, and sand. By varying the process and introducing different additives, manufacturers can produce a range of plasters to suit different substrates and different working conditions.

Plasters are basically produced in two grades: one for base or floating coats, the other for finishing coats. Basecoat gypsum plasters contain cement and lime and must be mixed on site with water and a lightweight aggregate, usually clean, sharp sand. Finish-coat plasters are ready for mixing directly from the bag and require only the addition of water.

The following information on different plaster types deals only with materials designed for residential plastering.

● **Don't buy old plaster**
Plaster can deteriorate if it is stored for more than three months. The paper sacks are usually date-stamped by the manufacturer. If you are buying plaster from a self-service store, choose the sacks with the latest date.

Choosing plaster for domestic work

Gypsum plasters

The majority of plasters are produced from ground gypsum by a process that removes most of the moisture from the rock. This results in a powder that sets when mixed with water. Setting times are controlled by the use of retarding additives, which give each type of plaster a setting time suitable to its purpose.

Gypsum plasters are intended for interior work only. They should not be used on permanently damp walls. Once they have started to set, don't attempt to add more water.

Plaster of paris

This quick-setting nonretarded gypsum plaster gives off heat as it sets. Either a white or pinkish color, it is mixed to a creamy consistency with clean water. It is unsuitable for general plastering, but good for casting, and can be used for repairs on decorative moldings.

Basecoat plasters

In traditional plastering, the finish is built up in two or three successive coats. Basecoat plasters are used for all but the last coat.

Several types of basecoat plasters are available, some needing to be mixed only with water before application, and others that may need to be mixed with sand or other aggregate before they can be used effectively. Which type you choose depends on the substrate, the specific job at hand, the need for economy, and the desired performance and working characteristics. It is crucial to read the package label to determine whether a particular formulation is suitable for the substrate or lath on which the plaster will be applied and to learn the best way to prepare the mixture.

Ordinary gypsum basecoat plaster, which must have sand or other aggregate added, is economical and suitable for most purposes. Wood-fiber basecoat plaster can be used, with the addition of water, only over wood, metal, or gypsum lath. But it must be mixed with sand for application over masonry. Wood- fiber plasters are about 25 percent lighter than sand and gypsum basecoats.

Special lightweight gypsum-based plasters, some premixed with the aggregate, are higher in strength than conventional plasters. These are commonly known by the trade names Structo-base and Structo-lite. Portland cement mixed with lime plaster is suitable for interior applications where a high moisture condition prevails and for exterior stucco work.

Gauging plasters

Gauging plasters are designed to be mixed with lime putty and applied as a finish coat. Some grades are harder and more abrasion resistant than others. The type that is best suited for a particular application can be determined by consulting your supplier. In addition to blending gauging plaster with lime putty to improve workability, users sometimes add aggregate to roughen the finish texture.

Finish-coat plasters

Before the advent of modern gypsums, lime and sand for undercoats and lime for finish coats were employed in traditional wet plastering, often with animal hair added to the undercoat mix to act as a binder. Lime plasters are generally less strong than gypsum and cement-based plasters.

Lime is sometimes still used, but mainly as an additive to improve the workability of a sand-and-cement plaster or stucco. Most finish-coat plasters do not need to be mixed with lime putty. They are mixed with water only and are applied over compatible basecoats, gypsum lath, and moisture-resistant gypsum drywall. Some types are formulated for use over portland cement and lime basecoats in areas with moisture problems.

Molding plaster

With extremely fine grains and controlled set, molding plasters are preferred for casting and running ornamental trim and cornices. Sometimes lime putty is added to improve workability.

Patching plasters

A universal one-coat plaster can, as its name implies, be used in a single application on a variety of backgrounds and then troweled to a normal finish. The plaster is sold in 50-pound bags, ready for mixing with water. It will stay workable for up to an hour, and some types can be built up to a thickness of 2 inches in a single coat.

Ready-mixed, one-coat plaster is also sold in smaller bags or plastic tubs. It is ideal for small repairs. All patching plasters are designed for high bonding strength.

Finish lime

Finish lime is added to plaster to provide bulk and plasticity to make it easier to spread. It also helps to control the setting time. Conventional finish limes must be slaked (saturated with water for 16 to 24 hours) to develop the desired putty consistency. Some specially processed types don't need to be slaked.

Other additives

Plaster retarders can be added to conventional plasters to slow drying to allow adequate working time. Accelerators can be added to speed up hardening when conditions require it.

Types of surface

A well-prepared surface is the first step to successful plastering. New surfaces of block or brick may only need dampening or priming with a bonding agent, depending on their absorbency. Check old plastered surfaces for signs of damage. If the plaster is unsound (separated from the substrate), remove it and leave only stable material. Then treat the surface and replaster the damaged area.

Background absorbency and preparation

Brush down the surface of a masonry substrate in order to remove loose particles, dust, and efflorescent salts. Test the absorption of the background by splashing water on it. If it stays wet, you can consider the surface normal. This means that it will require only light dampening with clean water prior to applying the plaster.

A dry surface that absorbs the water immediately will take too much water from the plaster, so it is difficult to work. It will also prevent the plaster from setting properly and may cause cracking. If the masonry is dry, soak it with clean water, applied with a brush.

Providing a key
Chop out loose mortar joints to help plaster adhere to the surface.

Highly absorbent surfaces

For very absorbent surfaces, such as concrete blocks, prime the surface with 1 part PVA (polyvinyl acetate) bonding agent and 5 parts clean water. When it is dry, apply a bonding coat of 3 parts bonding agent and 1 part water. Apply the plaster when the bonding coat is tacky.

Water-resistant surfaces

Prime smooth brickwork or concrete that is water-resistant with a solution of 1 part bonding agent to 5 parts water. Allow to dry, then apply a coat of 3 to 5 parts bonding agent to 1 part water and trowel on the plaster when the bonding coat is tacky. Alternatively, allow the surface to dry for no more than 24 hours before plastering.

Nonabsorbent surfaces

Glazed tiles and painted walls are classed as nonabsorbent, and so will require a coating of undiluted bonding agent to enable the plaster to stick. The plaster is applied while the agent is tacky. For glazed tiles, an alternative is to apply a slurry of 2 parts sharp sand and 1 part cement, mixed with a solution of 1 part bonding agent and 1 part water. Apply the slurry with a stiff-bristle brush to form a stippled coating. Allow it to dry for 24 hours before plastering.

Remove loose particles with stiff brush

Prime porous surfaces to control too-rapid drying

A bonding agent improves adhesion

You can mix plaster in any convenient container or dish. But it's easier to work with lightweight boards, which will allow you to carry the plaster around the worksite.

Mixing and carrying plaster

You can use ¼-inch exterior-grade plywood to make a useful board for mixing and carrying filler. Cut out a 1-foot square with a projecting handle, or make a thumb hole as in an artist's palette. Seal the surface with varnish, or apply a plastic laminate for a smooth finish.

Mortarboards

Mix plaster in a large plastic tray, or cut a piece of exterior-grade plywood, ¾ inch thick, to make a mortarboard about 3 feet square. Round off the corners and chamfer the edges all around. Screw three lengths of 1 x 2 furring strips (spaced evenly) to the underside of the board.

Using a stand.
You will find it easier to mix plaster at table height.

Using a stand

To help you pick up the mixed plaster easily, use a stand that will support the mortarboard at table height—about 30 inches from the floor.

To construct a folding stand, use 2 x 2 lumber for the legs and 1 x 2 furring for the rails. Make one of the leg frames fit inside the other, and bolt them securely together at the center.

Or you can use a portable folding bench (like a Workmate) to support the board. Just hold the middle support in the table's vise jaws.

Smooth tiles can be keyed with slurry

Mixing plaster

Having prepared the surface, the next step is to mix up the plaster. Mixing plaster can be a messy job, so spread canvas drop cloths, plastic dust sheets, or old newspapers across the floor where you are working, and remember to wipe your feet when leaving the room.

Plaster that is mixed to the correct consistency will be easier to apply. Use a plastic bucket to measure the materials accurately. For large quantities of plaster, simply multiply the number of bucket measures; for small quantities, use half-bucket measures or less.

Old gypsum plaster stuck to your tools or equipment can shorten the setting time and reduce the strength of newly mixed plaster. Discard plaster that has begun to set and make a fresh batch. Don't try to rework it by adding more water. Mix only as much plaster as you will need. For larger areas, mix as much as you can apply in about 20 minutes.

USING BONDING AGENTS

Bonding agents are used to modify the absorption of the surface or improve the adhesion of the plaster. When using a bonding agent, don't apply a basecoat plaster any thicker than ⅛ inch at a time. If you need to build up the thickness, scratch the surface of the plaster to provide an extra key, and allow at least 24 hours between coats.

Bonding agents can be mixed with plaster or with sand and cement to fill cracks. Remove any loose particles and then use a brush to apply a priming coat of 1 part agent to 3 to 5 parts water. Mix the plaster or sand and cement to a stiff consistency, using 1 part bonding agent to 1 part water. Apply the filler with a trowel, pressing it well into the cracks.

Clean up as you go
Wash tools and brushes thoroughly in clean water. On a large job, it may be necessary to rinse out your brushes as the work progresses.

Mixing undercoat plasters

Mix basecoat plasters in a plastic tray or on a mortarboard (see opposite). Measure out each of the materials and thoroughly dry-mix them with a trowel. Make a well in the heaped mix and pour in some clean water. Then turn in the dry material, adding water to produce a thick, creamy consistency.

Just add water to premixed gypsum plasters, which already contain an aggregate. Mix them in a similar way. Always wash down the tray or board after you have finished using it. You can mix small quantities of this type of plaster in a bucket. Pour the plaster into the water and stir to a creamy consistency; 2½ pounds of plaster will need about 1½ pints of water.

Mixing finish plaster

Mix finish plaster in a clean plastic bucket. Pour no more than 4 pints of water into the bucket, then sprinkle the plaster into the water and stir it with a piece of scrap wood or a paint stick until it reaches a thick, creamy consistency. Tip the plaster out onto a clean, damp mortarboard, ready for use. Wash out the bucket.

COVERAGE OF GAUGED-LIME FINISH PLASTERS

Plaster product	Ratio of mix			Average coverage in sq. yds. per 100 lbs. of plaster
	Lime	Gauging	Sand	
Standard gauging plasters	2	1	—	19.5
	2	1	8	14
Structo-gauge	1	1	—	19
	2	1	—	21.5
Keenes cement	2	1	8	13.5
	1	2	—	18.5
	1	2	8	13.5

COVERAGE OF BASECOAT PLASTERS

Plaster product	Mix	Approximate coverage in sq. yds. per 100 lbs. of plaster		
		Gypsum lath	Metal lath	Unit masonry
Standard gypsum basecoat plasters	Sand	10.5	5.75	9.25
	Perlite	9.25	4.5	7.5
	Vermiculite	9	—	8.25
Structo-lite	Regular	7	3.75	6.75
Structo-base	Sand	8.25	5	7.6

Mixing patching plaster

Pour out a small amount of patching plaster onto a flat board. Form a hollow in the center with your filling knife and pour in water. Gradually drag the powder into the center until it absorbs all the water, then stir the mix to a creamy thickness. If it seems too runny, add a little more powder. To fill deep holes and cracks, begin with a stiff mix but finish off with creamy mix.

Plastering techniques

Plastering can seem like an overwhelming task to the beginner, and yet it has only two basic requirements: The plaster should stick well to the surface and be worked to a smooth, flat finish. Thorough preparation and careful choice of plaster and tools should ensure good adhesion. But the ability to achieve a smooth, flat surface will come only after some practice. Most plasterer's tools are somewhat specialized, but their cost will be justified in the long term if you are planning several plastering jobs.

Problems to avoid

Using plasterer's hawk and trowel

Sanding uneven surfaces

Many beginners tackle plastering with the idea of leveling the surface by sanding it down when it has dried. This approach creates a lot of dust, which can permeate other parts of the house, and invariably produces a poor result. It's far better to try for a good surface as you apply the plaster, using wide-bladed tools to spread the material evenly. Ridges left by the corners of a trowel or knife can be carefully shaved down before the plaster sets, using the knife.

When covering a large area with finish plaster, it's not always easy to see if the surface is flat as well as smooth. Look obliquely across the wall or shine a light across it from one side to detect any irregularities.

Crazing

Fine cracks in finished plaster may be due to a basecoat that isn't completely dry before you apply the finish coat. The basecoat shrinks as it continues to dry, which creates cracks in the topcoat. When everything is dry, the fine cracks can be filled with joint compound and painted or covered with wallpaper. Topcoat and under-coat plaster can also crack if made to dry out too fast. Never heat plaster to dry it.

Loss of strength

Gypsum and cement set chemically when mixed with water. If they dry out before setting takes place, they will be friable, having not yet developed their full strength.

● **Using repair plaster**
For small repairs, you can use the ready-mixed plasters that are available in tubs. For shallow repairs, brush on a thick coat of repair plaster and smooth it level with the spreader supplied.

For deeper holes, use a repair plaster designed for treating damaged plasterwork, cement stucco, and masonry. This remains workable for up to 4 hours. Apply it with a plasterer's trowel and work it to a smooth finish. In this instance, you can sand the plaster smooth after it has set.

Picking up plaster

Hold the edge of your hawk below the mortarboard and use your trowel to scrape a manageable amount of plaster onto its surface (**1**). Take no more than a full trowel to start with.

Tip the hawk toward you and, in one movement, cut away about half of the plaster with the trowel, scraping and lifting it off the hawk and onto the face of the trowel (**2**).

1 Load hawk   **2 Lift plaster**

Applying the plaster

Hold the loaded trowel horizontally, tilted at an angle to the face of the wall (**1**). Apply the plaster with a vertical upward stroke, pressing firmly so that plaster is fed onto the wall. Flatten the angle of the trowel as you go (**2**), but never let the whole face of the trowel push against the wall. This induces suction and pulls off the plaster.

1 Tilt trowel   **2 Apply plaster**

Leveling up

To repair a hole in a plaster wall, trowel plaster so it sits just over the surrounding surface. Then use a straight-edged board to level the surface. Hold the board against the original plaster and work it upward while moving it from side to side. Then carefully lift it away, taking the surplus with it. Fill in any hollows with more plaster from the trowel, then level the surface again. Allow one coat of plaster to stiffen before you smooth it with a trowel. For two-coat work, scrape back the edges slightly to provide a key for the finish coat.

Work board up wall to level surface

Finishing the plaster

Apply the finish coat over a gypsum plaster undercoat as soon as it has set. A cement-based plaster must be allowed to dry thoroughly. Dampen its surface in order to reduce absorption before applying the finish plaster. Paper-faced board can be finished immediately, without wetting.

Use a plasterer's trowel to apply the finish plaster, spreading it evenly to a thickness of about 1/16 inch (but not more than 1/8 inch).

As the plaster stiffens, brush it or lightly spray it with water, then trowel the surface to consolidate it and produce a smooth matte finish. Avoid pressing too hard or overworking the surface. Sponge off surplus water.

Spray plaster occasionally as you smooth it

Plastered corners are vulnerable, particularly in hallways, and often need reinforcing.

Using corner beading
If damage to a corner extends along most of the edge, you can reinforce the repair with a metal or plastic corner beading (1). As well as strengthening the new corner, it will speed up the repair work considerably, because it provides a good surface to run your trowel against.

You can obtain beading from a lumberyard or home center. Cut it to length with snips or a hacksaw. Metal beading has a protective galvanized coating, and the cut ends should be sealed with a metal primer before installing them.

Cut back the damaged plaster, wet the substrate, and apply patches of undercoat plaster on each side of the corner. Press the wings of the beading into the plaster patches (2), and use a straightedge to align its outer nose with both of the original plaster surfaces. Also check for plumb with a builder's level. Allow the plaster to set.

Build up the undercoat plaster with your trowel until it is ⅟₁₆ inch below the old finished level (3).

Apply the finish coat, using the beading as a guide to achieve flush surfaces. Take care not to damage the beading's galvanized coating with your trowel, or rust may come through later. To be on the safe side, brush a stain-bloking primer over the new corner after the plaster is dry.

Everybody who works with plaster will at some time have to fill small holes and cracks as part of normal preparation work, and these should present few problems. But once you start tackling more ambitious jobs, like taking down walls or filling in openings where doors or windows have been removed, you will need to develop some of the professional plasterer's skills.

Plastering over openings

Filling in door and window openings might make your room layouts work better. But these tasks require substantial plasterwork for the walls to look right when you're done.

Begin by filling the opening with standard wood framing materials. Measure the opening accurately and build a small replacement wall to fit the space. Add a top and bottom plate to the studs, push the assembly into the opening, and nail it securely to the surrounding framing members. Cover the surface with gypsum lath so you have at least ¼ inch left for plaster across the entire surface. You can either use one-coat plaster or a two-coat system with an undercoat followed by a topcoat.

One-coat plaster
Mix the plaster in a tub according to the manufacturer's instructions. Tip the mixed plaster onto a dampened mortarboard. Then scoop some up onto a hawk and apply the plaster to the surface with a trowel. Work in the sequence shown at right. Start at the bottom of each section and spread the plaster vertically. Work on each area in turn, blending the edge of one into the next. When the sections are done, smooth the whole area with a straight board, fill any hollows, and smooth again.

Let the plaster stiffen for about 45 minutes, until finger pressure leaves no impression, then lightly dampen the surface with a sponge. Wet the trowel and give the plaster a smooth surface.

Two-coat plaster
Apply the undercoat and finish coat of plaster as described above. Just be sure to scrape back the undercoat to a depth of ⅟₁₆ inch to allow for the thickness of the finish topcoat.

Plastering sequence
Divide the area into manageable portions and apply the plaster in the sequence shown.

Repairing a chipped corner

When the plaster covering an external corner breaks away, it usually reveals unsightly patches of lath or masonry. Repair the damage with one-coat or two-coat plaster, using a wide board nailed on one side as a guide to help you achieve a neat corner.

With a cold chisel, cut away the plaster near the damaged edge to create about a 3-inch-wide void on each side of the corner.

If you are using two-coat plaster, nail the guide board on one side of the corner, so that the board's edge is set back about ⅛ inch from the surface of the plaster on the other side of the corner (1).

Mix up the undercoat plaster, wet the substrate and the broken edge of the old plaster, then fill one side of the corner up to the edge of the board but not flush with the wall (2). Scratch the new plaster with your trowel to create a key for the second coat.

When the plaster has become stiff, remove the board, pulling it straight from the wall to keep the plaster from breaking away. The edge thus exposed represents the finished surface. To allow for the topcoat, scrape the plaster back about ⅛ inch, using the trowel and a straightedge as a guide (3).

For the next stage, a professional would simply hold the guide board over the new repair and fill the second side of the corner with plaster. But this leaves only one hand free to lift and apply the plaster, a difficult trick for the beginner. An easier method is to let the new plaster harden, then nail the board in place before applying fresh plaster as before (4). If the new plaster is set hard, you can use the scraped edge as a guide.

Let the undercoat set, then nail the board to the wall as before. But this time align its edge with the original plastered surface, and fill the recess with finish plaster. Dampen the undercoat to reduce the absorption. When both sides are firm, polish the new plaster with a wet trowel, rounding over the sharp edge slightly.

If you use one-coat plaster for the repair, set the guide board flush with the finished surface on each side.

1 Set board back

2 Fill flush with board

3 Scrape back edge

4 Fill second side

OLD PLASTER

NEW UNDERCOAT PLASTER

TOP COAT PLASTER

METAL BEADING

1 Section through a repaired corner

2 Press beading into plaster

3 Apply basecoat

Repairing lath and plaster

A misplaced foot in the attic, a roof leak that has gone unnoticed, a leaking water pipe—any of these can damage a drywall ceiling. Fortunately, serious damage is usually localized and is easily repaired.

Before starting work, turn off the electricity supply at the service panel. Next, check the direction in which the ceiling joists run and whether there is any electrical wiring close to the damaged area. If there's a floor above, you will probably be able to lift a floor-board to inspect the damaged ceiling. Or use a hammer to knock a hole through the center of the damage. You can look through the hole with the help of a flashlight and a mirror **(1)**.

Useful tools for cutting drywall

1 Check for wiring and joists

2 Cut an opening

3 Nail in blocks

4 Nail in furring

Mark out a square or rectangle on the ceiling, enclosing the damaged area. Then cut away an area of the drywall slightly larger than the damage, working up to the sides of the nearest joists **(2)**. Use a drywall saw or a utility knife to make the cut.

Cut and toenail 2 x 4 blocking between the joists at the ends of the cutout. Make sure that half the thickness of the blocking projects beyond the cut ends of the drywall to serve as backing **(3)**. Then nail 1 x 2 furring to the sides of the joists, flush with their bottom edges **(4)**.

Cut a piece of drywall (that is the same thickness as the drywall that's in place) to fit the opening. Leave about a ⅛-inch gap all around. Nail the patch to the blocking and the furring, then fill and tape over the joints to give a flush surface.

Dealing with minor damage
It is not necessary to patch a ceiling that has only minor damage. Eliminate the source of the problem (if the ceiling is damp, let it dry out completely), then use drywall joint compound to make any repairs.

Homemade scratcher

When the plaster of a lath-and-plaster wall deteriorates, it often loses its grip on the lath. The plaster often bulges and may crack in places. It will sound hollow when tapped and tends to flex when you press against it. Loose plaster should be replaced.

Repairing holes in lath-and-plaster walls

Cut out loose plaster with a cold chisel and hammer **(1)**. If the lath strips are sound, you can plaster over them.

After dampening the lath-and-plaster edges around the hole **(2)**, apply a one-coat plaster, using a trowel. Press the plaster firmly between the lath **(3)**, building up the coating until it's flush with the original plaster. Smooth it off with a straight board. Let the plaster stiffen, then smooth it with a damp sponge and a trowel. You can also apply

the plaster in two coats. Scratch the first coat **(4)** and let it set, then apply the second coat and finish as before.

For larger repairs, use two coats of lightweight undercoat plaster, followed by a compatible finish plaster. For a small repair, press drywall joint compound onto and between the lath.

If lath strips are damaged, cut them out and either replace them, using metal mesh, or cover the studs with drywall and finish with plaster.

1 Cut away loose or damaged plaster

2 Dampen edges of old, sound plaster

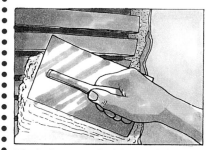
3 Apply plaster, pressing it between lath

4 Scratch undercoat

Repairing a ceiling

A leaking roof or pipe above a lath-and-plaster ceiling can cause localized damage to the plaster. Repair the ceiling with an undercoat plaster, finishing with a topcoat plaster.

Carefully cut back the damaged plaster to sound material. Dampen the

lath and the plaster edges and apply the undercoat **(1)**. Don't build up a full thickness. Scratch the surface and let it set. Give the ceiling a second coat, then scrape it back ⅛ inch below the surface and lightly scratch it. When it has set, apply a finish coat **(2)**.

1 Apply thin first coat with firm pressure

2 Level topcoat over previous undercoat

Decorative moldings

Most distinctive older houses have molded plaster cornices and centerpieces in the main rooms. In comparatively recent times, when they became less fashionable, many of these ceilings were destroyed. Today, thanks to renewed appreciation of period plaster-work, damaged moldings are frequently restored or replaced.

Restoring original centerpieces

A ceiling rose, or centerpiece, is a decorative plaster molding placed at the center of a ceiling, usually with a pendant light fitting hanging from it. Original moldings of this kind are often caked with many layers of old paint that mask the fine detail. Restore them, whenever possible, by cleaning away the layers of old paint and repairing any cracks and chipped details with plaster or joint compound.

Fine detail can be obscured by paint

Installing a reproduction centerpiece

Replace an original ceiling molding that is beyond repair with one of the excellent reproduction moldings made from fibrous plaster. They are available in a range of sizes and period styles.

Reproduction fibrous-plaster centerpiece

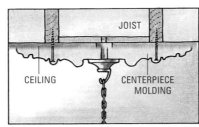

If there's a light fitting attached to the ceiling, turn off the power supply at the service panel, then disconnect and remove the entire fixture.

Use a hammer and cold chisel to carefully chip away the old, damaged molding back to the ceiling plaster. Coat the surface with plaster, then let it dry.

To determine the exact center of the ceiling, stretch lengths of string from corner to corner diagonally. The point where they cross is the center. Mark the center point and drill a hole for the lighting cable. If the new centerpiece lacks a hole for a lighting cable, drill one through its center.

Apply a ceramic tile adhesive to the back of the molding, then pass the cable through the hole in the center and press the molding firmly into place. On a flat ceiling, the adhesive should be sufficient to hold the molding in place, but as a precaution, prop it until the adhesive sets.

Reinforce larger plaster moldings with brass screws driven into the joists above. Cover the screwheads with finish plaster or joint compound, following the contours of the molding. Wipe away surplus adhesive from around the edges of the molding with a damp brush or sponge. When the adhesive has set, attach the light fixture. You may need longer screws to reach through the new molding.

Reinforce larger moldings with screws

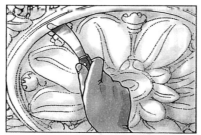

Cover screws, using putty knife

If it is ignored, sagging plaster on a traditional ceiling can develop into an expensive repair job, requiring the services of a professional. But if an area of plaster has broken away from its lath background and is otherwise intact, it can be reattached and prevented from collapsing.

Screw repair

First lift the sagging portion of the ceiling, using wide boards propped in place with lengths of 1 x 4s or 2 x 4s.

Drive countersunk screws, fitted with galvanized or plated washers, through the plaster and into the ceiling joists. The washers should be about 1 inch in diameter, and they should be spaced about 12 inches apart. The screwheads will bed themselves into the plaster and can then be concealed with finish plaster or joint compound.

Plaster repair

A laborious but more substantial repair to a sagging ceiling can be made by using plaster of paris to bond the plaster back to the laths.

After propping up the ceiling as described for the screw repair, lift the floorboards in the room above (usually this is not necessary in an attic), so that you can get at the back of the ceiling. Use a vacuum cleaner to remove dust and loose material. If the lath and the old plaster is not clean, the plaster of paris will not adhere properly.

Wet the back of the ceiling with clean water. Then mix the plaster of paris in a bowl to a creamy consistency and spread it fairly quickly over the whole of the damaged area, covering both the lath and the plaster between the lath **(1)**.

Although plaster of paris sets very quickly, it's best to leave the props in place until it has dried hard.

Use galvanized or plated screws and washers.

Decorative plasterwork
A wide variety of plaster moldings in traditional designs are available.

1 Spread plaster over lath and old plaster

Repairing cornices

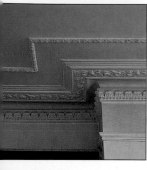

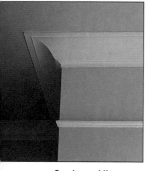

Cornice moldings
Older houses often have highly ornate cornices (top), which call for an experienced specialist. More modern homes usually have simpler moldings (above) which can be repaired using the techniques described on this page.

Cornice moldings are decorative plaster features used to fill the corners between the walls and the ceiling. They are often damaged as a result of a house settling over a long period of time.

Cracks can be repaired with finish plaster or joint compound, but missing sections of molding need to be recreated. Small pieces of straight moldings can be formed in place, but longer sections usually have to be made on a bench and then fixed in place with adhesive. In either case, clean all the old paint off the remaining molding before you start work so you can use the well-defined shape of the existing molding as a guide for a better repair.

Running a cornice

First, temporarily nail a straight guide board to the wall, tucking it up against the lower edge of the molding **(1)**. Make sure it spans the missing section.

Use a contour gauge to make a copy of the molding, including the new guide board, and then transfer it to a piece of stiff aluminum sheet or plastic laminate. Cut along the line with a sabre saw, then finish the edge with various files, regularly checking its fit against a section of molding **(2)**.

Glue and screw the template to a plywood backing board that has been cut to follow the same shape but with its contoured edge cut to an angle of about 45 degrees **(3)**.

Screw a straight board (baseboard) to the template so that it just touches the wall when the template is in position (see template assembly below). Make sure that the template is at 90 degrees to the edge of the baseboard. Screw a triangular brace to the back edge of the template and to the baseboard, to make the whole assembly rigid. Finally, install a fence board to the baseboard on each side of the template, flush with the shaped edge. When the template is in use, the fence runs along the face of the guide board **(4)**.

Clear away any loose material and dampen the area to be restored. Mix plaster of paris to a creamy consistency and spread it over the damage. Build up the thickness gradually, with progressive layers of plaster, running the template along the guide board to form the shape as the plaster stiffens.

You can make long sections of cornice molding on the bench, using a jig made by screwing two lengths of board together to represent the angle between the wall and the ceiling. Glue a triangular board into the angle between the boards. Measure the height of the existing cornice, and at that distance from the ceiling board, attach a guide board to the board representing the wall. Next, paint and wax all the interior surfaces of the jig. Copy the profile of the cornice and make up a template assembly (see bottom left).

Building up the cornice

Mix up the plaster and spread it onto the faces of the jig, then run the template carefully along the guide batten. Build up the cornice gradually, forming the shape as you continue to add layers of plaster. When the molding is hard and dry, remove it from the jig.

Cut back the damaged part of the old cornice to sound material, making square cuts with a fine-toothed saw. Use a hammer and cold chisel to clean out any broken pieces from the corner.

Cut the new section of molding to fit, apply ceramic tile adhesive to its back and top, and then press it into place. A very heavy section should have the additional support of brass screws driven into the ceiling joists. Hide the screwheads with plaster or joint compound.

Scrape away any surplus adhesive and fill the joints where the sections butt together, then wipe down with a damp brush or sponge.

1 Attach board to wall.

2 Make template

45°

3 Bevel backing board.

4 Run fence along guide board

Template assembly
1 Guide board
2 Template
3 Backing board
4 Baseboard
5 Triangular brace
6 Fence board

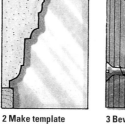

CEILING BOARD

TRIANGULAR FILLER

GUIDE BOARD

WALLBOARD

Cornice molding jig
Run the template assembly along the guide board.

Plastering a wall

The plastering of a complete wall is not usually a job most homeowners will tackle. For new work, it's just easier and cheaper to use drywall. But sometimes there are large areas of damaged plaster, from a substantial roof leak for example, that you want to repair with plaster, not drywall. These jobs can be done by nonprofessionals, though they will likely take you longer. The key to success is to divide the area into manageable sections.

Applying the plaster

Use a plasterer's trowel to scrape some plaster onto a hawk, and start the undercoat plastering at the top of the wall. Holding the trowel at an angle to the face of the wall, apply the plaster with vertical strokes. Work from right to left if you are right-handed; if you're left-handed, work from left to right.

Using firm pressure to ensure good adhesion, apply a thin layer first, then follow it with more plaster, building up to the required thickness. If the final thickness of the plaster needs to be greater than ⅜ inch, key the surface with a scratcher. Let it set, then apply a second or floating coat.

Fill the area between two screed boards (see right), but there's no need to pack the plaster tightly up against them. Smooth the surface with a straight board laid across the screed boards, sliding the board from side to side as you work upward from the bottom of the wall. Fill in any hollows, and then smooth the plaster again. Scratch the surface lightly, to provide a key for the finishing coat, and let the plaster set. Work along the entire wall in this way, and then remove the screed boards. Fill the gaps, smoothing the plaster with the straight board or trowel.

With gypsum plasters, the finish coat can be applied as soon as the undercoat is set. Cement undercoats must be left to dry out for at least 24 hours to allow for shrinkage. Wet them before applying the topcoat.

Because you are bound to drop some plaster, it pays to cover the floor with a drop cloth. Don't try to reuse dropped plaster because it can contaminate fresh plaster.

Setting up

In addition to specialized plasterer's tools, you need a level and some planed softwood boards that are ⅜ inch thick. Known as screed boards, they are nailed to the wall to act as guides when it comes to smoothing the plaster. Professional plasterers form plaster screeds by applying bands of undercoat plaster to the required thickness. These can be laid vertically or horizontally.

After preparing the substrate, attach the screed boards vertically to the wall with drywall screws. The screws make it easy to remove the boards later. Drive the screws just below the surface of the boards so they won't interfere with the trowel. The screeds should be spaced no more than 2 feet apart. Use the level to get them truly plumb, shimming them out if necessary.

Mix the undercoat plaster to a thick, creamy consistency. Use a small batch first. You can increase this to larger amounts when you become more proficient with the process.

Finishing

Cover the undercoat with a thin layer of finish plaster, working from top to bottom using even, vertical strokes. Work from left to right, if you are right-handed (see left); if you are left-handed, work from right to left. Hold the trowel at a slight angle, so that only one edge is touching.

Make sweeping horizontal strokes to level the surface further. You can try using the rule to get the initial surface even, but you may risk dragging the finish coat off. Use the trowel to smooth out any slight ripples.

Wet your trowel and work over the surface with firm pressure to consolidate the plaster. As it sets, trowel it to produce a smooth matte finish, but don't overwork it. Use a damp sponge to wipe away any plaster slurry that appears. The wall should be left to dry out for some weeks before decorating.

Plumb the screeds
Shim out the screed boards, if necessary, until they are plumb.

The order for applying plaster by a right-handed person
Applying the topcoat left to right tends to even out any irregularities in the undercoats.

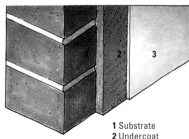

Two-coat plastering
1 Substrate
2 Undercoat
3 Topcoat

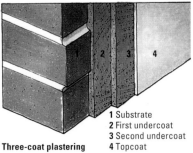

Three-coat plastering
1 Substrate
2 First undercoat
3 Second undercoat
4 Topcoat

Plaster layers
Plaster is applied in layers to build up a smooth, level surface. Three coats may be required on an irregular surface.

Drywall

STORING AND CUTTING DRYWALL

Drywall (gypsum wallboard) provides a quick and simple method of covering walls or ceilings. It offers good sound insulation as well as fire protection. It's easy to cut and to install, either with adhesive, screws, or nails.

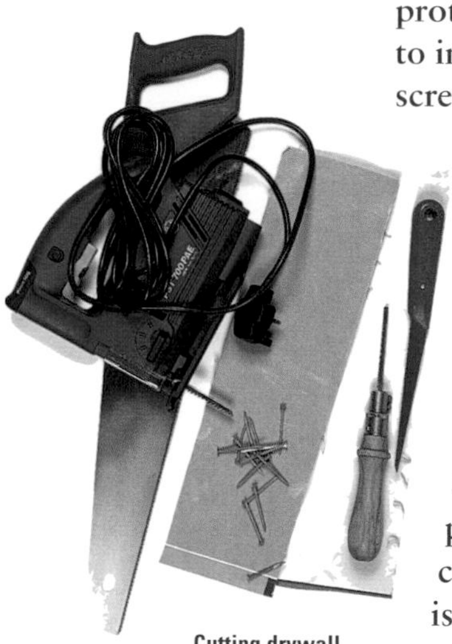

A range of drywall panels is available at home centers and lumberyards. They are made with a core of aerated gypsum plaster, and covered on both sides with a strong paper sheet. Standard panels have a gray paper backing, and an ivory-colored facing paper, which is an ideal surface for paint or wallpaper. If you want to replicate a traditional plastered surface (perhaps to match an adjoining wall) you can also apply a skim coat of wet plaster to the surface of the drywall. The panels are made in a range of thicknesses and sheet sizes, with square-cut ends and tapered edges.

Drywall is fragile, having very little structural strength. But despite its fragility, the sheets are quite heavy, so always get someone to help you carry them. Always carry vertically on edge. There is a good chance of breaking a panel if you carry it face up.

Manufacturers and suppliers store the boards flat in stacks, but this is usually inconvenient at home and isn't necessary for a small number of sheets. Store them on edge instead, leaning them at a slight angle against a wall, with their outside faces together to protect the finished surfaces. Stack the sheets carefully, to avoid damaging their edges.

Cutting drywall

You can cut drywall with a saw or with a utility knife. Support a sheet face-side up on boards laid across sawhorses. Mark the cutting line on it with the aid of a straightedge. When sawing the panel, hold the saw at a shallow angle to the surface. If the cutoff is going to be large, get a helper to support it as you approach the end of the cut, in order to keep the board from breaking.

When slicing plasterboard with a utility knife, cut through the facing paper and slightly into the material, using a straightedge. Then snap the board along the cutting line. Cut through the paper facing on the other side to separate the two pieces. Use a keyhole saw, jigsaw, or drywall saw to cut openings for electrical boxes and other obstructions.

After cutting, remove any ragged paper by smoothing the edges of the board with sandpaper or a coarse file.

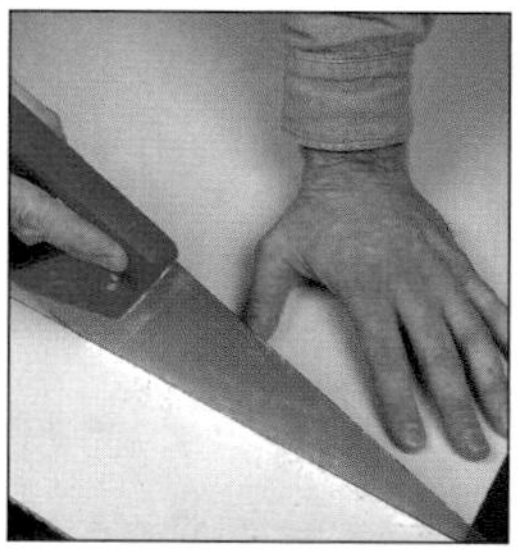

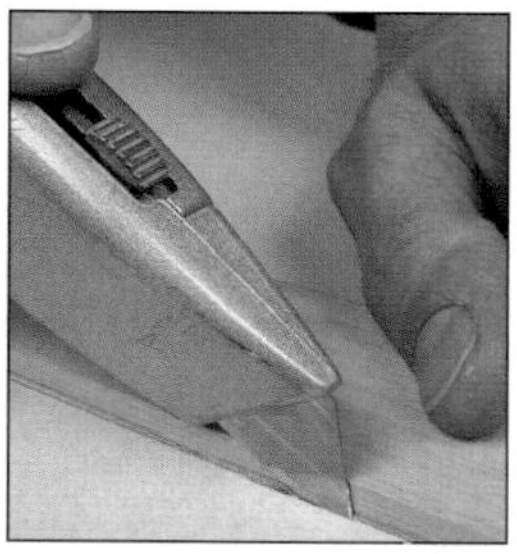

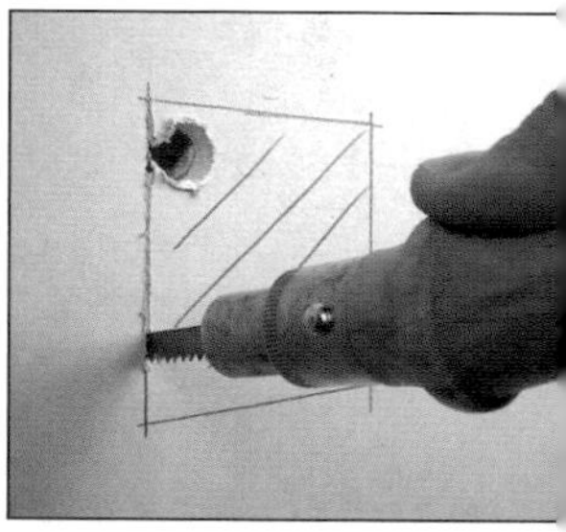

Cutting drywall. *(far right)* Cut the panels to size with a handsaw or a utility knife. Use a keyhole saw, drywall saw, jigsaw, or utility knife to cut any openings.

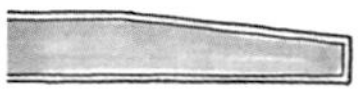

Tapered edge

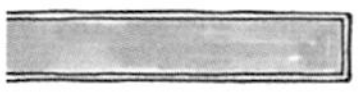

Square end

Types of edge
Tapered edges are filled with joint compound and taped to provide smooth, seamless joints that won't show under a wallcovering or a coat of paint. Square edges need to be filled and taped, too, to ensure sound joints. But these butt joints are invariably more noticeable and so should be kept to a minimum.

GYPSUM PANEL PRODUCTS

GYPSUM PANEL TYPES AND USAGE	THICKNESSES (inches)	WIDTHS (inches)	LENGTHS (feet)	EDGE FINISH
Standard wallboard				
This material is generally used to finish walls and ceilings. The long edges of the panels are tapered to accommodate built-up layers of tape and compound used to finish joints. Available in a variety of thicknesses, ⅝- and ½-inch panels are typically used for single-layer applications direct to studs, while ⅜ inch is normally used over existing wall finishes; ¼-inch wallboard is generally used in multilayer applications for sound control and for curved surfaces with short radii.	¼ ⅜, ½, ⅝	48 48	8 8, 9, 10, 12, 14	Tapered
Water-resistant gypsum panels				
With a specially formulated gypsum-asphalt core and chemically treated face and back papers, this material is recommended for direct application to studs in bathrooms, powder rooms and utility rooms, to combat moisture penetration. Suitable as base for ceramic tile and plastic-faced wall panels.	½, ⅝	48	1, 10, 12	Tapered
Predecorated gypsum panels				
These are standard wallboard panels that have a wide range of factory-applied vinyl and fabric facings. Long edges of panels are beveled to form a shallow V-groove at joints.	½	48	8, 9, 10	Beveled
Gypsum-base panels				
Gypsum bases are used in conjunction with proprietary veneer finishes with less labor, weight, and residual moisture.	½, ⅝	48	8, 10, 12, 14	Square
Gypsum lath				
This product category includes a variety of panel products specially designed as a ground for standard plaster basecoats and finishes.	⅜, ½	16, 24	4, 8	Square

Drywalling a wall

Drywall can be nailed or screwed to wood framing members or to wood furring strips attached to masonry walls. If you're covering old drywall or plaster, the panels can sometimes be glued in place with adhesive. The panels can be installed either vertically or horizontally on the walls. But they should be installed across the joists on ceilings. All edges and ends of each panel must be supported by framing members.

Methods for attaching drywall

Attaching to a stud wall
Partition walls may simply be plain room dividers, or they may include doorways. If you are working on a plain wall, start installing the boards from one corner. If the wall includes a doorway, work away from the doorway toward the corners of the room.

Starting from a corner
Using a foot lifter (see below), hold the first panel in position. If necessary, mark and scribe the edge that meets the adjacent wall. Then fasten the board, securing it to all of the framing members (see fasteners at right).

Install the rest of the boards, working across the wall. Butt the tapered edges together, leaving a gap of about ⅛ inch between panels that will be filled later with joint compound. If necessary, scribe the edge of the last board to fit the end corner before nailing it into place. Cut the baseboard to length, scribe the end where it meets the existing baseboard, and nail the baseboard in place.

Starting from a doorway
Using the foot lifter, hold the first board flush with the door stud and mark the location of the top of the door opening on the front of the panel. From this point, draw a line 1 inch from the edge of the board to the top of the board. Cut out this strip to form a notch for the piece of drywall that will fit over the door. Push the panel back in place and nail or screw it to the wall.

Install the rest of the boards, working toward the corner. Butt the tapered edges and leave a ⅛-inch gap between boards to provide a key for the joint compound used to finish the wall. If necessary, scribe the last board to fit any irregularities in the corner before attaching it.

Cover the rest of the wall on the other side of the doorway in a similar way, starting by cutting a 1-inch-wide strip to create the other side of the notch above the door opening.

Next, cut a piece of drywall to fit above the doorway. Sand off any ragged paper at the edges before pushing the panel in place. Then continue installing the remaining panels on this side of the doorway as you did on the other side.

When all of the drywall is installed, tape and finish the joints, and spread joint compound over the nail- or screwheads. When the finishing is complete, sand the compound with 120-grit paper, install the door and casings, and vacuum up all the dust. Then prime the walls for paint or paper.

FASTENERS

These days drywall screws are the preferred fasteners for professional installers. But unless you've worked with them before, the nails shown below are easier for most people. Space the nails about 12 inches apart and no closer than ⅜ inch to the edges and ends. Drive the nails just below the surface, but don't tear the paper.

Board thickness	Nail length
⅜ inch	1 inch
½ inch	1½ inch
⅝ inch	2⅝ inch

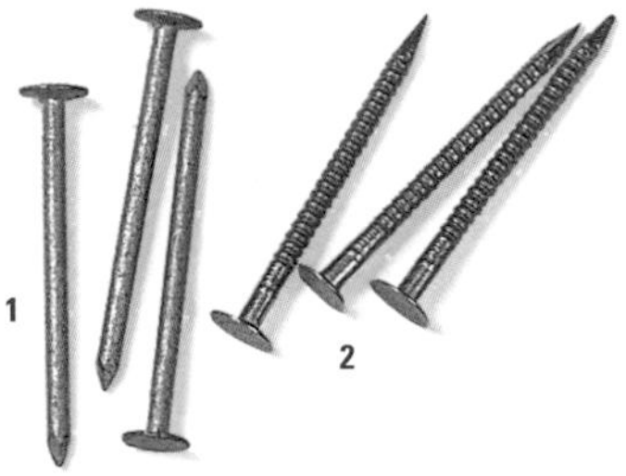

Types of nail used with drywall

Drywall nails
1 Galvanized nails
2 Ring-shank nails

Drywall screws

Drywall screws do a great job of holding drywall panels in place. Screws that are 1¼ or 1½ inches long are used for typical work where a single thickness of drywall is being installed. Longer screws are available for multiple layers of drywall.

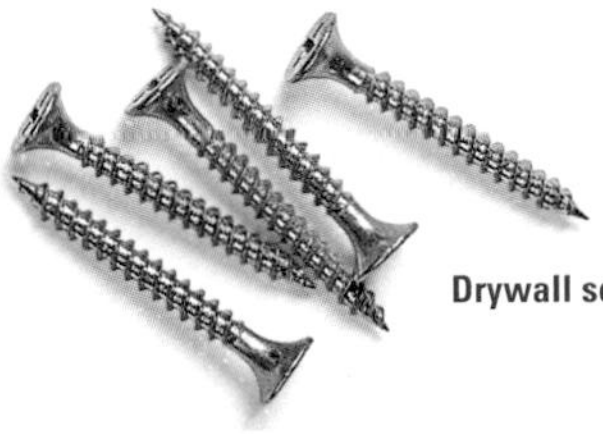

Drywall screws

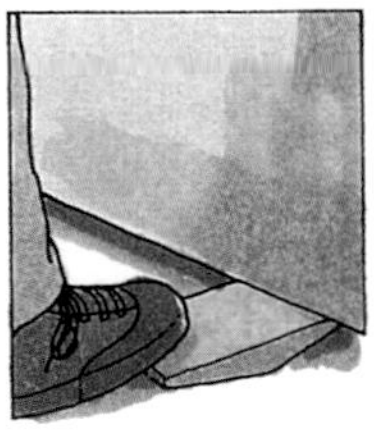

Using a foot lifter
A foot lifter is a simple device that holds the board against the ceiling, leaving both hands free for nailing. You can make one from a 3-inch-wide block of wood. Cut each drywall panel about ⅜ inch shorter than room height, to provide clearance for the foot lifter.

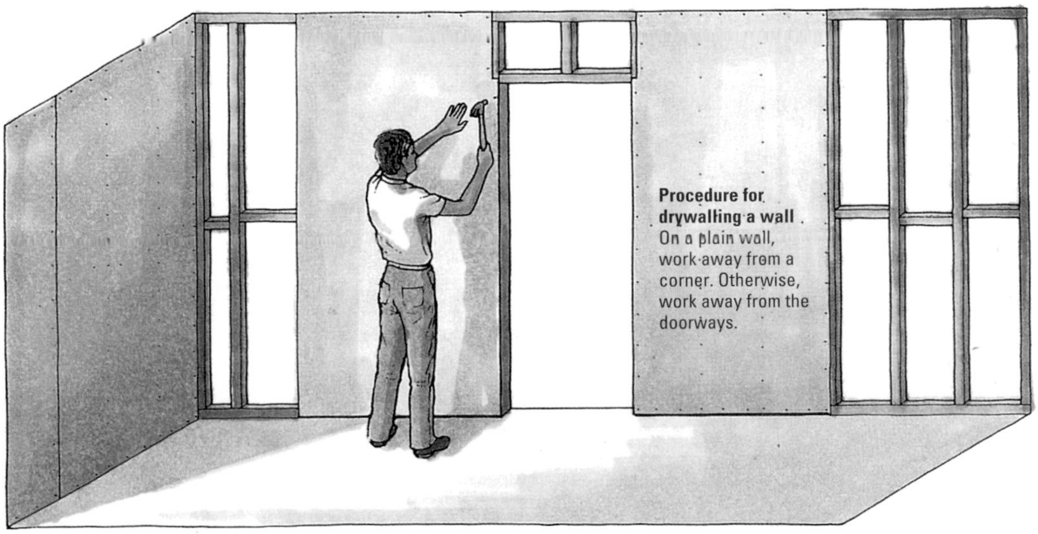

Procedure for drywalling a wall
On a plain wall, work away from a corner. Otherwise, work away from the doorways.

Distances between stud centers
Standard wall construction has studs placed on 16-inch centers. The minimum drywall thickness for these walls is ⅜ inch, but most installers use ½-inch-thick panels. If the studs happen to be on 24-inch centers, you must use either ½-inch panels, or preferably ⅝-inch-thick panels.

Scribing drywall

If the inner edge of the first sheet of drywall butts against an uneven wall, or its other edge does not fall on the center of the stud, the board must be scribed to fit.

Scribing the first board

Begin by placing the first board in position (**1**). The illustration shows an uneven wall pushing the far edge of the sheet beyond the stud. Reposition the panel so that its inner edge lies on the center of this stud. Hold it at the required height, using a foot lifter, and tack-nail it in place.

With a pencil and a board cut to the width of the drywall panel, trace a line that reproduces the contour of the wall on the face of the panel (**2**). Make sure you keep the board level as you scribe down the wall.

Take the board down and use a utility knife or saw to trim the waste away. Cut on the inside of the scribed line, to leave a ⅛-inch gap next to the wall. Place the panel in the corner again, and attach it to the studs with nails or screws (**3**).

Scribing the last board

Temporarily tack-nail the panel to be scribed over the last installed panel (**4**), ensuring that their edges are flush with each other.

Using a guide board and a pencil, as above, scribe a line down the face of the top panel. Remove the marked panel, cut away the waste, then attach it to the studs (**5**). Fill and tape the joints, and cover the nail- or screw-heads with joint compound. When dry, sand all the joints smooth, vacuum up the dust, and prime the walls.

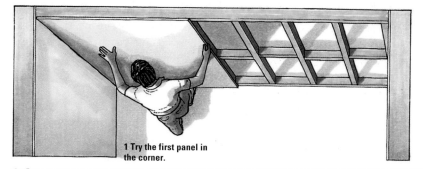

1 Try the first panel in the corner.

2 Reposition the panel and mark the cutting line.

3 Cut the panel to size and nail it in place.

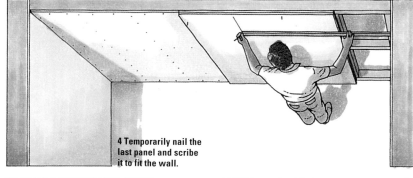

4 Temporarily nail the last panel and scribe it to fit the wall.

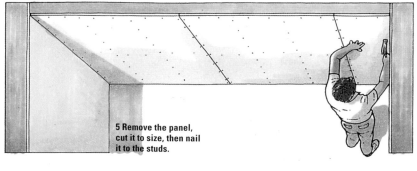

5 Remove the panel, cut it to size, then nail it to the studs.

Drywalling a masonry wall

Drywall can't be nailed directly to masonry walls, so boards known as furring strips are used to provide nailing surfaces and to straighten out any unevenness on the wall surface. If the walls you are covering are in the basement, it's a good idea to use pressure-treated furring strips. You can install the strips directly over old plaster if it is sound. Otherwise, it's best to strip back to the substrate. If the wall is damp, treat the cause and let the wall dry out before starting work. Install any plumbing or electrical components before attaching the furring to the wall.

Layout

Using a straightedge and 4-foot level as a guide, mark the position of the furring strips on the wall. Place the lines 16 inches apart to create 16-inch centers for the drywall panels. The perimeters of windows, doors, and other openings all need to be covered with furring. The wall space above these openings needs furring too. Mark the wall for these pieces, making sure they fall on 16-inch centers, so the layout is consistent from one end of the wall to the other.

Attaching the furring strips

Cut the required number of 1 x 2 furring strips to length. Don't forget that the vertical strips will be about 3 inches shorter than the wall height to allow for the furring strips that fall across the top and bottom of the wall. Be sure to include any shorter strips that fall around and above window and door openings.

Nail the top and bottom strips in place first, using either masonry nails or cut nails. Then fill in between these strips with the vertical strips. Push each vertical strip tightly against the wall to see if it lies flat. You can correct irregularities in the wall by shimming out the furring strips with cedar shimming shingles. If you do install shingles at some point, nail the furring strip through these shingles to hold them in place.

Attaching the drywall

To attach the panels to furring strips, follow the procedure described for nailing to a stud partition. However, there's no need to notch the boards at the sides of windows and doorways, because you can place short furring strips just where you need them above the openings (see below). Follow the usual procedure for finishing the joints between the panels.

Cut the baseboard to length, and nail it through the drywall to the bottom furring strip. If you are using a high baseboard, the top edge should also be nailed to the vertical furring strips.

Masonry walls aren't always flat. Serious irregularities should be corrected so the finished wall surface is as flat and level as practical. You can do this by shimming out the furring before nailing the strips to the wall.

To check that the wall is flat, hold a long straightedge horizontally against it at different levels. If it is uneven, mark the wall at the points where it's most in need of adjustment (**1**).

Hold a straight vertical board against the wall at any problem spot. Make sure this board is plumb and mark the floor behind the back edge of the board (**2**). Draw a line across the floor connecting these marks (**3**). Align all the furring strips with this line.

1 Check wall

2 Mark high point

3 Draw line on floor

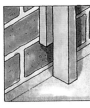
Marking the floor
Use a straightedge to mark the floor.

Attaching furring strips to a wall
1 Mark the positions of furring strips.
2 Attach horizontal strips.
3 Attach vertical strips.
4 Attach short pieces over doors and windows, offsetting them to avoid cutting notches in the panels.
5 Nail panels in place, beginning next to a door or window.

Finishing drywall

All joints between panels and any indentations left by nailing must be filled and sanded before the surface is ready for painting or wallpapering. You will need joint tape, joint compound, and a variety of specialized taping knives to get a high-quality finish.

Tools and materials

To finish drywall joints, you will need joint compound, a premixed plasterlike substance that comes in different size containers. The 5-gallon pails are the most common. The material is also available in dry form that is mixed with water on site. You also need some taping knives that range in width between 3 and 10 inches. To carry workable quantities of the joint compound around you need either a hawk or a drywall pan. To reinforce the joints you need paper or plastic mesh tape to embed in the joint compound. And, once the compound is dry, you need abrasive paper to smooth the joints.

Covering nails or screws

Fill the indentations left by nailing or screwing the panels in place. Use a drywall knife to apply and then smooth the compound. When the compound has set, sand the surface flush with the surrounding panel surface.

Finishing tapered edge joints

Apply a continuous band of compound, about 3 inches wide, down the length of each joint. Press the joint tape into the compound, using a medium-size knife or a plasterer's trowel to smooth the tape in place and remove any air bubbles (1). Apply another layer of compound in a wide band over the tape (2).

When the compound has stiffened slightly, you can smooth its edges with a damp sponge, or allow it to set and sand it smooth with abrasive paper.

When all the filler has set, coat the joint with a thin layer of compound applied in a broad band (3). Once this compound has set hard, lightly sand, then apply another thin but wider band over the first application. Feather the edges with the trowel or knife.

Fiberglass tape can be used instead of traditional paper tape for finishing new drywall or for making small repairs. Because it has adhesive on the back side, this 2-inch-wide tape doesn't need to be embedded in joint compound. Just press it over the joint and then cover it with compound.

Applying the tape

Make sure that the joint surface is dust-free. If the edges of boards have been cut, sand them to remove all the rough paper.

Starting at the top, center the tape over the joint, then unroll it and press it in place as you work down the wall. Cut it to length at the bottom of the joint. If you have to make a seam in the tape, butt the ends, don't overlap them.

Cover the tape with compound, pressing it into the holes in the mesh. Smooth the compound so the mesh of the tape is visible. Allow the compound to set. Then, complete the joint with two more layers of compound, as described for paper tape.

Applying compound
Press compound through fiberglass tape

Finishing butt joints

When a square edge butts against a tapered edge, fill the joint flush before you apply the tape (1).

Where two square edges meet (2), press compound into any gap between the panels and smooth it flush. When the filler has set, apply a thin band of joint cement to it and press the paper tape tight against the board. Cover this with a wide but thin coat of joint cement, then feather the edges.

1 Press tape into compound

2 Apply compound in wide band

3 Apply thin but broad band

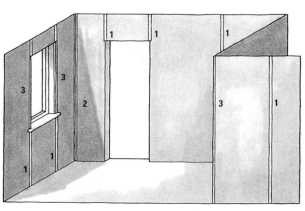

Finishing the joints
1 Use the tape flat for tapered and butt joints.
2 Fold the tape for inside corners.
3 Use metal or plastic corner beads on outside corners.

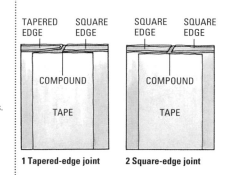

TAPERED EDGE	SQUARE EDGE	SQUARE EDGE	SQUARE EDGE
COMPOUND		COMPOUND	
TAPE		TAPE	

1 Tapered-edge joint   2 Square-edge joint

Finishing corners

Finishing interior corners

Interior drywall corners are finished by a method similar to that used for flat joints. Any gaps are first filled flush with compound. Apply a band of compound about 3 inches wide on both surfaces. Make the surface as smooth as possible.

Cut the paper tape to length and fold it down its center. Then press the tape into the corner. Carefully run a small wood block or a 3-inch knife down each side of the joint to smooth and embed the tape, and to remove any air bubbles (1).

Cover both sides of the joint with a 3-inch-wide band of compound and feather the edges with a damp sponge or a taping knife (2). When the compound has set, apply a second, wider coat and feather the edges again.

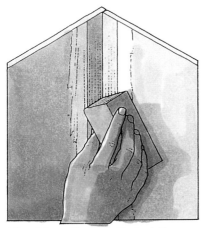

1 Smooth tape with wooden block or knife

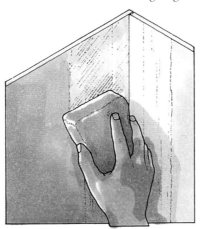

2 Apply compound over tape and feather edges

Finishing outside corners

Outside corners must be finished with a corner bead and compound to reinforce the joint. Plastic or metal beads are available for this job. If the corner is formed with one or two tapered edges, fill the tapers flush before installing the corner bead (1). Apply two coats of joint cement, feathering the edges as described for inside corners.

If both edges are square, then apply a thin coat of compound to both surfaces and install the corner bead (2).

Be careful when you nail or screw the corner bead in place. It's easy to distort its shape by driving nails too deep or overdriving screws. Once the bead is distorted it's very hard to apply the top layers of compound so you get a smooth, straight corner.

Apply a second coat of compound to both sides in a wide band and feather it off with a knife or a damp sponge. When this coat is dry, apply two more coats of joint compound, feathering off as before.

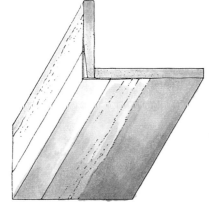

1 Fill tapered edge flush, then bed plastic bead

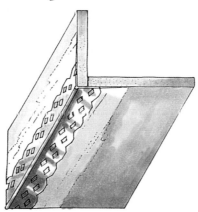

2 Embed metal bead in compound; feather edges

Having attached the drywall securely and finished the joints with tape and compound, now prepare the surfaces for paint or paper. This can be achieved with a thin coat of plaster applied with a trowel or by brushing on a coat of primer.

Finishing with plaster

If you don't want to apply paint or a wallcovering directly to the papered surface of the drywall, you can apply a thin coat of finish plaster instead. This may be necessary if you want to match the characteristics of adjacent plastered surfaces.

Applying a thin finishing coat is not an easy technique to master. Unless you are prepared to put in some practice, it is probably best to hire a professional, especially for ceilings. If you decide to attempt the work yourself, thoroughly study the section on plastering before you begin.

All the gaps and joints between the boards must be filled with compound and reinforced with tape, as described earlier, though in this case there's no need to feather the edges. The entire surface should be dry and the joints sanded smooth before applying the finish plaster.

Priming

Before drywall can be painted or wallpapered, it must be sealed with a primer. One coat of general-purpose primer evens out the absorption of the panels and the joint compound, and provides a sound surface for the wall finish that comes after. It also protects the panels if you steam-strip wallpaper in the future.

For small areas you can apply primer with a brush, but for anything over 10 square feet, a roller makes more sense. Just make sure the wall is dust-free before beginning.

Apply primer to even out absorption

Drywalling a ceiling

1 Support the boards
with simple T-shaped
braces called deadmen.

2 Nail a board to the
wall to give temporary
support to the long
edge of the board.

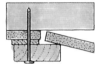

3 Nail a temporary
support board to the
ceiling joists when
butting boards.

Drywall is the finish material of choice for just about all new ceilings, but it can also be used to replace or cover an old lath-and-plaster ceiling that has deteriorated beyond repair.

Any competent person can install the panels and finish them successfully. But the work is hard because the panels are heavy and it's always tiring to work over your head for long periods.

Preparing an old ceiling

Start by stripping away the damaged plaster and lath, and pulling out all the nails. Trim back the top of the wall plaster, so the edge of the ceiling drywall can be tucked in.

This is a messy job, so wear goggles, gloves, a respirator, and protective clothing while working. It is also a good idea to seal the gaps around the door, to prevent dust from escaping into the rest of the house. You will need to dispose of a lot of waste material, so have some strong plastic bags available and rent a dumpster.

Attaching drywall to the ceiling

Measure the ceiling area and select the most convenient size of panels to cover it. The panels should be installed with their long edges running at right angles to the joists. The butt joints between the ends of the boards should be staggered on each row and always supported by a joist.

Some people install ceiling panels working only from a stepladder. But this is difficult and cumbersome, especially if you haven't done it before. A better option for most people is to rent some interior scaffolding.

Nail perimeter blocking between the joists against the walls (if none exists), and for the best-quality job, install intermediate blocking in lines across the ceiling to support the long edges of the panels. If you decide to install intermediate blocking, use 2 x 4s or 2 x 6s and make sure their bottom edges are flush with the bottom edges of the joists.

Start installing the panels, working from one corner of the room. Full drywall panels are heavy material and it normally takes two people to support a large sheet while it is being nailed in place (see below). However, if you have to work on your own, use support boards and T-shaped braces known as deadmen to hold the panels in place while you are attaching them (see far left). Make a pair of braces that are slightly longer than the overall height of the room (**1**), using 2 x 2 lumber. Nail a crosspiece and a pair of diagonal struts to one end of each brace. Temporarily nail a 1 x 2 to the top of the wall to support the long edges of the first row of panels (**2**). Support the next row with boards that overlap the edges of the first panels. Before you nail these support boards to the joists, shim them with a thin board to provide the necessary clearance for the next row of drywall panels (**3**).

Use nails or screws to attach each panel in place, working from the middle of each panel out to the edges. (Space the fasteners about 6 inches apart.) This prevents the panels from sagging in the middle, which is likely to happen if their edges are nailed first.

Cut the last panels in each row with a handsaw or utility knife, and do the same with the last row of panels in the room. Once everything is fastened in place, finish the joints as discussed earlier for walls.

Drywalling a ceiling
1 Cut and install
perimeter blocking
against the wall.
2 Nail intermediate
blocking between the
joists, to suit the width
of the panels.
3 Install the first panel
in one corner. Start
nailing from the center
of the board.
4 Butt the tapered
joints together, leaving
a ⅛-inch gap between.
5 Stagger the end
joints, leaving a ⅛-inch
gap between.

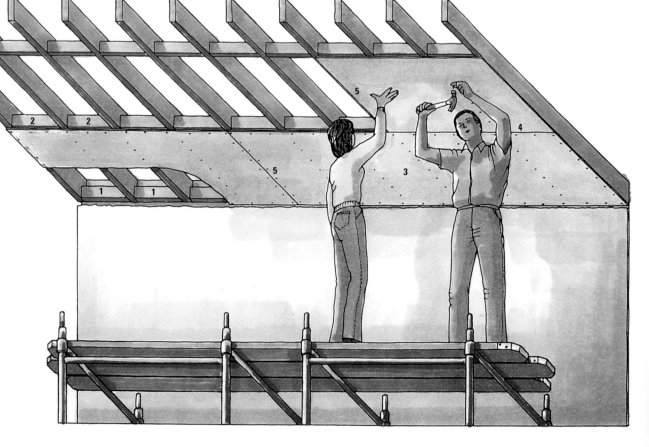

Siding options

Siding is something that you have to live with for a long time—at least you hope you will—because it's so expensive to replace. Unlike floor- and wall-coverings that are easier to change on a whim, siding is usually permanent. You may have to paint it more often than you want, and occasional repairs are sure to come up, but most people dread replacing it.

Just because most people don't want to buy new siding doesn't mean there isn't a lot of it out there. Shown below is just a sampling of the siding options on the marketplace. Certainly the most popular is vinyl because it's a maintenance-free material and it's available everywhere. But other choices can be just as appealing, for different reasons. If you need new siding for your house, do some research at your local lumberyard or home center.

Typical siding materials
1 Vinyl lap clapboard
2 Cedar shake
3 Cement board
4 Vinyl specialty panel
5 Textured Oriented Strand Board (OSB)
6 Stucco
7 Steel
8 Cedar shingle
9 Cedar clapboard
10 Hardboard
11 Texture 1-11 plywood
12 Cultured stone

Horizontal siding

Wood siding

Traditional wood beveled siding, often called clapboards, appears on countless houses across the country. While its popularity has been eclipsed over the last 30 years by aluminum and vinyl versions, it's still used on many new homes. And when it's installed and maintained properly, it can last well over 100 years.

Beveled siding is made from many different wood species including pine, cedar, and redwood. The boards are wedge-shaped; when installed, the thicker edge is on the bottom.

Layout

Plan the siding layout carefully to achieve a uniform exposure around windows, doors, and soffits. For a good appearance and to minimize leaks, try to align the lower edges of the boards with the tops of window and doorframes.

Use a straight length of lumber for a story pole (see left). Mark the heights of all windows and doors. Then, starting at the window and door markings, lay out the story pole with marks for each piece of siding at the recommended exposure (the amount of each siding board that's exposed to the weather). If necessary, expand or decrease the exposure slightly to get the best layout. When satisfied, transfer the story-pole marks to the wall sheathing and the window and door-trim pieces. Also make an exposure guide (see below) from a piece of scrap wood. Use it to align each board as you nail it into place.

Attaching siding

Make sure all the trim boards at the corners and around the windows and doors are installed. Then snap a chalkline for the bottom of the first board. Nail a ½ x 1½-inch primed lumber starter strip along the bottom of the sheathing ½ inch above the chalkline. Beginning at a corner, nail the bottom course of siding flush, by driving siding nails just above the filler strip. Continue all the way around the house, then snap another line to connect the next set of story-pole marks. Attach the second course of siding, checking the alignment of the boards by holding the exposure gauge against the piece of siding below. Continue all the way up the house. Caulk all the siding joints.

Windows and doors

At some window and door openings you may have to notch siding to fit. Carefully measure and mark the siding piece, then cut it with a handsaw or sabre saw. Prime the cut, nail the board in place, and caulk around the opening. Follow the same procedure for notching around all obstructions.

Aluminum is one option for low-maintenance siding. It is available in a number of textures and finishes, and with insulated backing laminated to it. Layout and installation is similar to that for wood. However, framed openings, corners, eaves, and other areas require special trim pieces, which often must be custom-formed using a bending brake. For this reason, most homeowners choose to have aluminum siding installed by professionals.

Vinyl siding is similar to aluminum except that it doesn't bend. Preformed trim, cut to required lengths, is used at edges and openings. Although vinyl siding is usually applied by professionals, there's little reason why a capable do-it-yourselfer shouldn't tackle the job.

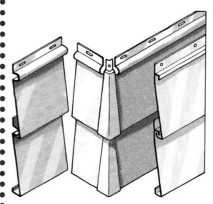

ALUMINUM   CORNER TRIM   VINYL

Wood siding types

BEVEL   RABBETED

STORY POLE   SHEATHING

FRIEZE

TOP OF WINDOW

MARK ON WALL AND FRAME

BOTTOM OF WINDOW

CORRECT EXPOSURE

EXPOSURE GAUGE

Calculating exposure

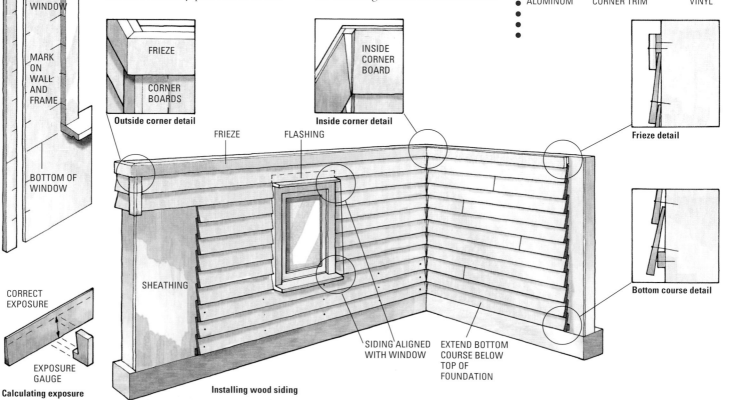

Outside corner detail

FRIEZE
CORNER BOARDS

Inside corner detail

INSIDE CORNER BOARD

Frieze detail

Bottom course detail

FRIEZE   FLASHING

SHEATHING

SIDING ALIGNED WITH WINDOW

EXTEND BOTTOM COURSE BELOW TOP OF FOUNDATION

Installing wood siding

Masonry siding

Mix only as much stucco as you can use in an hour. Keep mixing tools and equipment thoroughly washed so that no mortar sets on them.

Measure level bucketfuls of sand onto a mortarboard or a sheet of exterior-grade plywood placed on the ground. Using a second dry bucket and shovel, measure out the cement, tapping the bucket to settle the loose powder and topping it up as needed. Mix sand and cement together by shoveling them from one heap to another and back again (**1**) until the mix takes on a uniform gray color.

Form a well in the center of the heap and pour in some water (**2**). Shovel the dry mix from the sides of the heap into the water until the water is absorbed (**3**). If you are left with dry material, add more water as you go until you achieve firm, plastic consistency and even color. If after turning the mix it is still relatively dry, sprinkle it with water (**4**). But remember that too much water will weaken the mix.

Draw the back of your shovel across the stucco with a sawing action to test its consistency (**5**). The ribs formed by this action should not slump or crumble, which would indicate that it is either too wet or too dry. The back of the shovel should leave a smooth texture on the surface of the stucco. When you have finished, hose down the work area.

Veneer

Brick and stone veneer, used as siding, do not bear any structure load. They only support their own weight. To apply a masonry veneer, the house foundation must have a ledge in front of the wall framing wide enough to build on. First install metal flashing atop the ledge, extending 6 inches up behind the sheathing. Then attach 15-pound roofing felt to the sheathing. Nail metal masonry ties 2 to 3 feet apart horizontally and 15 inches vertically. Erect the wall, leaving a ¼-inch airspace between it and the sheathing, and anchor the masonry material to the ties as you go.

Stucco

Stucco is a mixture of portland cement and sand. It can be applied directly over brick, stone, or rough-surfaced concrete. Over wood or old siding, first install roofing felt and furring strips, then nail sheets of metal lath onto the furring. Self-furring lath is also available. Check your options at a local masonry supply outlet.

Apply the stucco in three layers. To mix the first, or scratch, coat, add 1 part cement to 3 parts sand. Press generous amounts of this scratch mix into the lath with a trowel. When a layer ⅛ inch thick covers the lath, lightly rake it with a leaf rake to groove the surface. Let the basecoat stand two days, spraying frequently with water to prevent too-rapid drying.

To mix the second, or brown, coat, blend in 1-2 parts additional sand. Apply it as you did the first, in a ⅛-inch-thick layer. Roughen the surface only slightly. Keep moist for two days, then allow to dry for at least five days more. For the final, finish, coat, most DIYers purchase a dry, premixed stucco that contains lime to make the mix smooth and workable. Apply the finish coat in a thin layer, smoothing it with a piece of straight lumber.

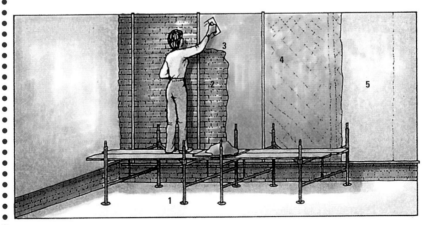

Applying stucco
1 Set up a safe work platform.
2 Attach furring and lath.
3 Apply scratch coat and groove with rake.
4 Apply brown coat and roughen lightly.
5 Apply finish coat.

Patch repairs

Stucco should be applied with a metal plasterer's trowel and the topcoat finished with a wooden float. Start by taking a trowelful of mortar and spread it on the wall with firm pressure, applying it with an upward stroke (**1**).

Build up the undercoat layer so it's no more than two-thirds the thickness of the original stucco or ⅛ inch, whichever is thinner. Level the mortar with a straight strip of wood that fits within the area being patched. Move the strip from side to side. Then scratch grooves in the surface for the topcoat (**2**). Let the undercoat set for a few days.

Finish coat
Before applying, dampen the undercoat. Once you've troweled the stucco onto the wall, level it with a straightedge laid across the surfaces of the surrounding stucco. Work from the bottom to the top of the patch, with a side-to-side motion.

1 Use firm pressure **2 Groove surface**

Wood-framed floors

Floor construction in most houses is based on wood framing members known as joists. These are rectangular in section, placed on edge for maximum strength, usually spaced 16 inches apart, and supported at the ends by the walls. This construction contrasts with the concrete-slab floors that are supported over their whole area by the ground. In older houses, wood-framed floors were usually covered with tongue-and-groove subflooring, with a finish flooring applied over the top. These days, the subflooring is almost always plywood or some type of particleboard.

Floor framing

The joists are usually made from 2 x 8, 2 x 10, or 2 x 12 construction lumber. Their ends are nailed to 2 x 6 sills over foundation walls and to the top plates of wood-framed walls.

The ends of the joists are covered by lumber the same size as the joists, usually called rim joists. Rim joists are nailed to the ends of the other joists and into the sills or plates. Joists are supported on the other end by girders that run down the middle of the floor span. Girders usually consist of three or four 2 x 10s or 2 x 12s nailed together, or a single steel I-beam. They are supported by posts underneath and by the foundation walls at their ends. Bridging is nailed at the midpoint of the joist span to keep the joists from twisting.

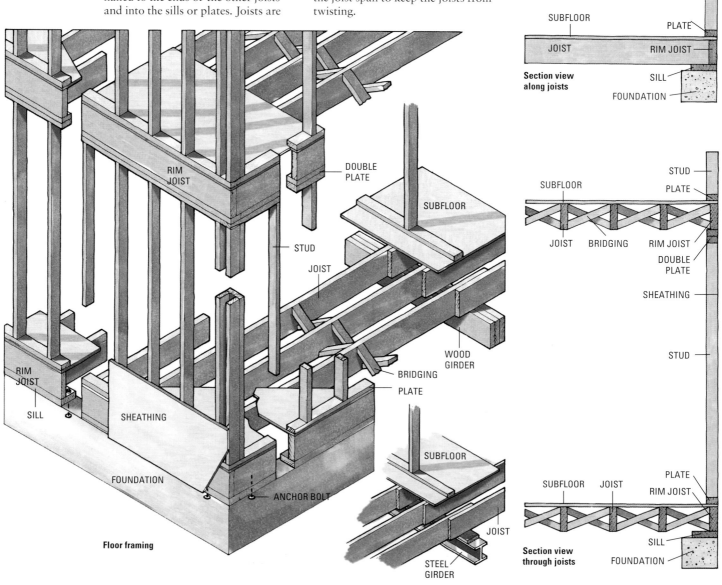

Floor framing

Section view along joists

Section view through joists

Slab floors

For extra stiffness, floor joists are braced either with solid blocking nailed between the joists (**1**), or with bridging boards that are nailed diagonally between the joists (**2**).

Traditional bridging is made from 2 x 2 or 1 x 3 lumber. In modern floor construction, metal bridging (**3**), sized to match the joists, is used. Metal bridging comes in different designs, but always has predrilled flanges to make nailing it easy.

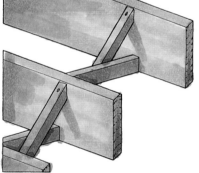
1 Blocking

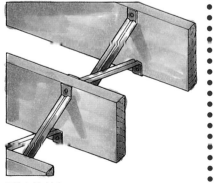
2 Wood bridging

3 Metal bridging

Although concrete slab floors are always used in large industrial and commercial buildings, in houses they are used only for basement and garage floors. A slab floor is a concrete pad poured onto a compacted base of various types of gravel. To prepare for the concrete, the topsoil is removed and gravel is spread to fill the excavation and to level up the site. After being compacted, the gravel is then covered with a layer of rigid foam board insulation and a tough polyethylene plastic sheet that acts as a vapor barrier. This sheet also prevents the moisture in the concrete from draining out into the gravel, which would weaken the finished floor.

The concrete slab is usually about 4 to 6 inches thick and is laid over a layer of wire mesh or rebar reinforcement. The mesh and rebar is supported off the vapor barrier on small stones during the pour so it's embedded in the middle of the concrete. A slab can be poured so it's part of the foundation walls, but it is more often installed between the walls after they have cured.

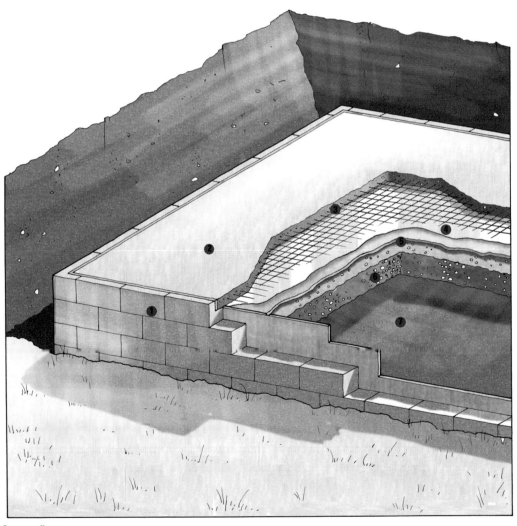

Concrete floors
1 Perimeter foundation
2 Concrete floor
3 Wire mesh
4 Vapor barrier
5 Subslab insulation
6 Compacted gravel
7 Subsoil

155

Flooring

Flooring is the general term used to describe the finished surface that is laid over a floor's structural elements, either floor joists or a concrete slab. The term "wood flooring" pertains to hardwood and softwood boards, or to any number of manufactured panels.

Floorboards

Hardwoods, like oak and maple, are generally used for making floorboards. The standard widths are from 1 to 3½ inches and thicknesses can range from a little as ⁵⁄₁₆ inch to as much as 2 inches. The standard thickness for tongue-and-groove flooring is ¾ inch and the most popular width is 2¼ inches.

Narrow boards produce superior floors, because any movement due to shrinkage is less noticeable. However, installation costs are high, so they tend to be used more in expensive houses. Softwoods, like pine and hemlock, are common in older homes but aren't installed often now.

The best floorboards are quarter-sawn **(1)** from the log, a method that diminishes distortion due to shrinkage. However, since this sawing method is expensive, floorboards are more often cut

tangentially **(2)** to reduce costs. Boards cut in this way, however, tend to cup across their width and should be installed with the convex side facing up. The cut of a board, tangential or quarter-sawn, can be checked by looking at the annual-growth rings on the endgrain (see left).

The joint on tongue-and-groove boards is not at the center of the edges but closer to one face. These boards must all be laid in the same way or the joint won't be flush. Although tongue-and-groove boards are nominally the same sizes as square-edged boards, the edge joint reduces their floor coverage by about ½ inch per board.

In some old buildings you may find floorboards bearing the marks left by an adze on the underside. Such old boards have usually been trimmed to the required thickness only where they sit over the joists.

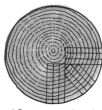

1 Quarter-sawn boards
Shrinkage does not distort these boards.

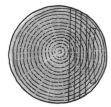

2 Tangentially sawn boards
Shrinkage can cause these boards to cup.

Types of wood flooring
1 Square-edged softwood board
2 Tongue-and-groove softwood board
3 Square-edged particleboard
4 Tongue-and-groove particleboard
5 Square-edged plywood
6 Tongue-and-groove plywood
7 Square-edged medium-density fiberboard (MDF)

Softwood and hardwood boards provide a durable floor that looks great when sealed and polished. Sheet materials such as flooring-grade plywood or particleboard are structural components, and are normally used as a subflooring for other more attractive floorcoverings.

Plywood

Any exterior-grade plywood can be used for subflooring. The panels are available with either square or tongue-and-groove edges. And they come in different grades. Usually one side of the panel is a better grade than the other. This side should be installed facing up.

If it is to be laid directly over the joists, plywood flooring should be ⅝ or ¾ inch thick. When it is laid over an existing floor surface—to level it or to serve as an underlayment for other flooring—it can be ¼ to ½ inch thick. Plywood panels and particleboard panels are laid in the same way.

Particleboard

Particleboard is made from adhesive-bonded chips of wood. Only flooring-grade particleboard—which is compressed to a higher density than the standard material—should be used for subfloors. You can buy either square-edged or tongue-and-groove panels that usually measure 4 x 8 feet and ¾ inch thick. Particleboard is less expensive than plywood and though it can absorb moisture, it doesn't delaminate in wet conditions the way that plywood can.

Medium-density fiberboard

Medium-density fiberboard (MDF) is a dense sheet material made from highly compressed wood fibers and glue. It is produced in different grades, and is suitable for subflooring where a plain, smooth finish is required. MDF is available in 4 x 8 foot square-edged sheets in a wide range of thicknesses. It is usually more expensive than particleboard, but cheaper than plywood.

Lifting floorboards

You can check whether your floorboards have tongues and grooves by pushing a knife into the gap between them.

To lift a tongue-and-groove board, it is necessary first to cut through the tongue on each side of the board. Saw carefully along the line of the joint (**1**), using a dovetail or tenon saw held at a shallow angle. Or you can use a sabre saw or a reciprocating saw with a fine blade. Having cut through the tongue, saw across the board and lift it as you would a plain, square-edged board.

If the original flooring has been blind nailed (**2**), use finishing nails (**3**) to reinstall the boards. Drive the nailheads below the surface with a nailset and fill the hole with a matching-color wood filler.

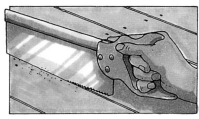
1 Saw along line of joint.

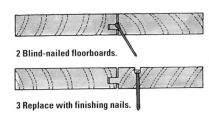
2 Blind-nailed floorboards.

3 Replace with finishing nails.

Refitting a cut board

The butted ends of boards should meet over a joist (**1**). However, a board that has been cut flush with the side of a joist must be supported below when it is replaced. Cut a piece of 2 x 2 lumber and screw or nail it to the side of the joist, flush with the top edge. Screw the end of the floorboard to this support block (**2**).

1 Boards share joist   **2 Support cut board**

Floorboards are rarely long enough to reach the entire length or width of a room, from wall to wall. If you have to remove a floorboard, the end joints between boards are the best place to start. If the board you need to remove has no joints in it, then start with a joint on an adjacent board.

Square-edged boards

Tap the blade of a cold chisel into the gap between the boards, close to the cut end (**1**). Pry up the edge of the board, but try not to crush the one next to it. Push the chisel into the gap at the other side of the board and

1 Pry up board with cold chisel

repeat the procedure. Ease the end of the board up in this way, then work the claw of a hammer under it until there is room to slip the chisel under the other side (**2**). Proceed in the same fashion along the board until it is free.

2 Slide hammer and chisel under board

Lifting a continuous board

Floorboards are nailed in place before the baseboards are installed, so the baseboards will prevent you from lifting out a continuous board. You will have to cut the board in half before you can lift it out. Pry up the center of the floorboard with a wide cold chisel, until you can slip another chisel under it to keep the board bowed up. Remove the nails and, with a tenon saw, cut through the board (**1**) over the center of the joist. You can then lift the two halves of the board off the joists and away from the baseboards.

If a board is too stiff to be bowed upward or is milled with a tongue and groove, it will have to be sawn in place. This means cutting it flush with the

side of the joist, rather then over the center of the joist.

To locate the side of the joist (**2**), push the blade of a drywall saw into the gaps on both sides of the board. (The joints of tongue-and-groove boards will have to be cut beforehand.) Mark both edges of the board where the blade stops, and draw a line representing the side of the joist between these points. Make an access slot for the drywall saw by drilling three or four ⅛-inch holes close together near one end of the line.

Work the tip of the blade into the hole, and start making the cut with short strokes. When the cut is complete, pry up the board with a cold chisel, as described above.

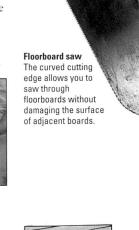
1 Saw across board

2 Find joist's side

Freeing the end of a board

To release the end of a floorboard that is trapped under a baseboard, lift the board until it is almost vertical, then pull it straight out of the gap between the baseboard and the joist (**1**).

A floorboard that runs beneath a partition wall must be cut close to the baseboard before you can raise it (**2**). Drill an access hole so you can insert a keyhole saw blade or a floorboard saw blade (**3**). Then carefully make the cut. Use shallow strokes to reduce the chance of hitting any obstructions underneath the floorboard.

Floorboard saw
The curved cutting edge allows you to saw through floorboards without damaging the surface of adjacent boards.

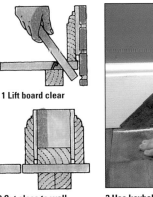
1 Lift board clear

2 Cut close to wall

3 Use keyhole or floorboard saw to make cut

Replacing floorboards

Although floors are subjected to a great deal of wear, it's usually water damage, fire damage, or lumber decay that results in a floor having to be replaced.

Before laying a new floor, measure the room and buy your materials in advance. Leave the floorboards or sheet materials in the room you're working on for at least a week so the material can adjust to the temperature and humidity of the space.

Removing the flooring

To lift all the flooring, you must first remove the baseboards from the walls. If you intend to reinstall the same boards, number them with chalk before removing them. Lift the first few boards as described on the previous page, starting from one side of the room, then pry up the remainder by working a flat bar between the joists and the undersides of the boards. When lifting tongue-and-groove boards, carefully ease them up two or three at a time to avoid breaking the joints, then pull them apart.

Pull all the nails out of the boards and joists, and scrape any accumulated dirt from the boards and the joists. Make sure all the joists are sound and make any necessary repairs.

● **Closing gaps**
It is possible to reinstall floorboards without removing all the boards at once. Lift and renail about six boards at a time as you work across the floor. Finally, cut and fit a new board to fill the last gap.

Laying new floorboards

Although these instructions describe how to install tongue-and-groove boards, the basic method also applies to square-edged floorboards.

First lay a few loose boards together to act as a work platform. Measure the width or the length of the room, whichever is at right angles to the joists, and cut your boards to stop ⅜ inch short of the walls at each end. Lay four to six boards at a time. Where two shorter boards are to be butted end to end, cut them so that the joint will be centered over a joist.

Install the first board with its groove edge no more than ⅜ inch from the wall. Nail it in place with finishing nails that are at least twice as long as the thickness of the board. Use a nailset to drive the heads below the surface of the boards.

Finish the first row of boards, then start the next row by laying the first board so its groove slides over the tongue on the first-row board. For the joint to seat completely, the board being installed usually must be tapped into place. Don't strike the tongue with a hammer to do this. Instead, use a scrap block of flooring to cover the board tongue. Strike the tongue edge of the block to drive the floorboard into place. Continue using the scrap block to strike against as you work down the board. When the joint is tight, toenail the board to the joists by driving the nail into the corner where the top of the tongue meets the board. Set the nailhead. By nailing in this fashion (called blind nailing), the nails won't show when all the boards are in place.

Sometimes boards are too bowed to make a tight joint by driving them with a hammer and block. These boards must be wedged into place. To do this, nail a scrap board a few inches away from the bowed board. Then cut two wedges from scrap flooring and put them between the two boards. Drive the wedges together to force the board into place **(1)**.

When you reach the far side of the room, cut the last boards to width and remove the bottom side of the groove so the board can drop into place **(2)**.

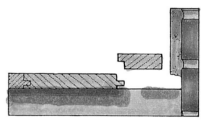

1 Make wedges to drive boards tight **2 Cut away bottom of last board's groove**

Laying floorboards
Work from a platform of loose boards, and proceed in the following order:
1 Fix the first board parallel to the wall.
2 Cut and lay up to six boards, clamp them together, and nail.
3 Lay the next group of boards in the same way, and continue across the floor. Cut the last board to fit.

FLOORBOARD CLAMP

This special tool automatically grips the joist over which it is placed by means of two toothed cams. A screw-operated ram applies pressure to the floorboards when the bar is turned.

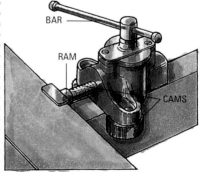

BAR

RAM

CAMS

Hire a special clamp to re-lay floorboards

Laying particleboard sheets

Particleboard is an excellent material for a floor that is going to be hidden under a finish flooring like vinyl or wall-to-wall carpet. It can be laid relatively quickly and is a lot cheaper than the equivalent amount of lumber flooring. It comes with square edges or tongue-and-groove edges.

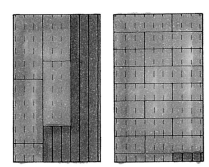

1 Square-edged sheets **2 T&G sheets**

Laying out sheets

When using square-edged sheets, run them in the same direction as the joists to keep the blocking to a minimum. When using tongue-and-groove sheets, there is no need for blocking because the edge joint supports the sheets (see below).

Laying square-edged boards

All the edges of square-edged sheet flooring must be supported. Lay the sheets with their long edges along the joists and nail 2 x 4 blocking between the joists to support the ends of the sheets. Nail blocking against the wall first. The blocking that supports the joints between the sheets can be nailed into place as the sheets are laid.

Start with a full sheet in one corner and lay a row of sheets the length of the room, cutting the last one to fit as required. Leave an expansion gap of about ⅜ inch between the outer edges of the sheets and the walls. The inner edges should fall on the centerline of a joist. If necessary, cut the boards to width, but be sure to remove the waste from the edges closest to the wall, preserving the machine-cut edges to make neat butt joints with the next row. Nail down the boards, using 2-inch ring-shank nails, spaced about 12 inches apart along the joists and blocking. Place the nails about ¼ inch from the sheet edges.

Cut and lay the remainder of the sheets, with the end joints staggered on alternate rows.

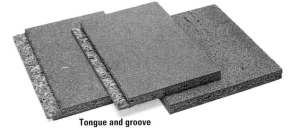

Square edge

Tongue and groove

Laying tongue-and-groove sheets

Tongue-and-groove sheets are laid with their longer edges running across the joists. Blocking is required only to support the outer edges close to the walls. The ends of the sheets should be supported by joists.

Working from one corner, lay the first sheet with its groove edge about ⅜ inch from the walls and nail it in place. Apply construction adhesive to the joint along the end of the first sheet, and then lay the next one in the row. Make sure that the joint between the two sheets is tight. Nail the second sheet as described above, then wipe any surplus adhesive from the surface before it sets, using a damp rag.

Continue in this way across the floor, gluing all of the joints as you go. Cut the last sheet in the row. Then start the second row.

To get the grooves on the sheets in the second row to fit tightly over the tongues in the first row requires driving the two together. Slide the first sheet of the second row against the first-row sheet, place a scrap board along its long edge, and strike along the board until the joint is tight.

Ring-shank nails
Nail down flooring sheets using 2-inch ring-shank nails, spaced about 12 inches apart.

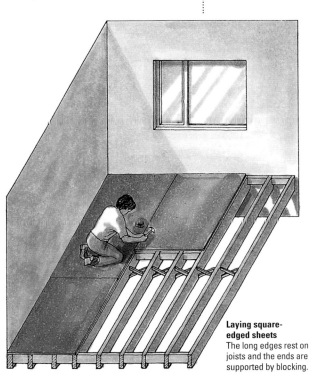

Laying square-edged sheets
The long edges rest on joists and the ends are supported by blocking.

Laying tongue-and-groove sheets
Lay tongue-and-groove sheets across the joists.

Doors: types and construction

At first glance, there appears to be a great variety of doors to choose from—but most of the differences are purely stylistic and they are, in fact, all based on a relatively small number of construction methods.

The wide range of styles can sometimes tempt people into buying doors that are inappropriate for the house they live in. When replacing a front door, it's especially important to choose one in keeping with the architectural style of your house.

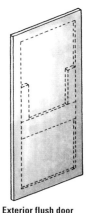

Exterior flush door

Recessed molding

Overlay molding

Buying a door

You can buy interior and exterior doors made from softwood or hardwood, the latter usually being reserved for special rooms or entrances where the natural features of the wood can be appreciated. Softwood doors are for more general use and most are intended to be painted. However, some people prefer to apply a clear finish.

Glazed doors are often used for front and rear entrances. Traditionally these feature wood-frame construction, though modern steel doors can be bought in standard sizes, complete with double glazing and numerous accessories.

Frame-and-panel doors are usually supplied in unfinished wood, so you can stain, paint, or clear finish them to suit your taste.

Door sizes

Doors are made in several standard sizes, which meet most domestic needs. The two most common heights are 6 feet 8 inches and 7 feet. Widths usually start at 2 feet 2 inches and go to about 3 feet in 2-inch increments. Most residential doors are either 1⅜ inches or 1¾ inches thick.

Older houses often have relatively large doors to the main rooms, but modern homes tend to have the same size (6 feet 8 inches by 2 feet 6 inches) throughout the house, except for entrance doors, which most codes require to be 3 feet wide.

When replacing a door in an old house, where the openings may well be of nonstandard sizes, have a door made to fit the opening or buy a larger one and trim it to fit, removing an equal amount from each edge to preserve the door's symmetry.

Panel doors

Panel doors have a hardwood or softwood frame made with mortise-and-tenon or dowel joints. The frame is rabbeted or grooved to house the panels, which can be of solid wood, plywood, or glass. Doors constructed from hardboard, steel, or plastic panels are also available.

1 Muntins
These are the central vertical members of the door. They are jointed into the three cross rails.

2 Panels
These may be of solid wood or of plywood. They are held loosely in grooves in the frame to ensure that they can move without splitting. They stiffen the door.

3 Cross rails
The top, center, and bottom rails are tenoned into the stiles. In some doors, the mortise-and-tenon joints are replaced with dowel joints.

4 Stiles
These are the upright members at the sides of the door. They carry the hinges and the lock.

Panel-door moldings
The frame's inner edges may be plain or molded to form a decorative border. Small moldings are either machined on the frame before assembly or machined separately and nailed to the inside edge of the frame. An ordinary recessed molding (see far left) can shrink away from the frame and crack the paint. An overlay molding, which laps the frame, helps overcome this problem.

Panel door

Flush doors

Most flush doors have a softwood frame faced with sheets of plywood or hardboard on both sides. Mainly used for interior doors, they're simple, lightweight, easy to hang, and inexpensive. Exterior flush doors have internal reinforcement blocks for lock hardware and mail slots.

1 Top and bottom rails
These are tenoned into the stiles.

2 Intermediate rails
These lighter rails, joined to the stiles, are notched to allow the passage of air, in order to prevent mold growth.

3 Lock blocks
A softwood block able to take a lockset is glued to each stile.

4 Panels
The plywood or hardboard panels are left plain for painting or finished with a wood veneer. Metal-skinned doors may be ordered specially.

Core material
Paper or cardboard honeycomb is often sandwiched between the panels in place of intermediate rails.

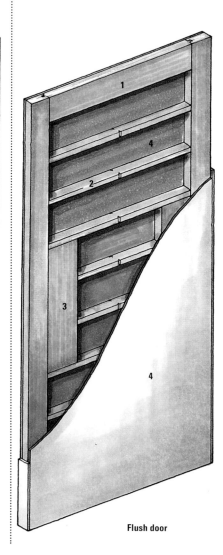

Flush door

Doorframes

Utility doors

These doors have a rustic look and are often found in old houses, outbuildings, attics, and basements. They are strong, easy to build, and when well maintained can last a very long time. These doors are usually hung with strap hinges.

1 Boards
Tongue-and-groove boards are nailed to cross-rail boards.

2 Strap hinges
Long strap hinges are used to carry the weight of a large exterior door.

3 Braces
These diagonal boards, sometimes notched into the cross rails, keep the door from sagging.

4 Cross rails
These are the support boards that the face boards are nailed to.

Framed utility door

Exterior doors

An exterior door is installed in a heavy wood frame consisting of a head jamb at the top, a sill at the bottom that's outfitted with a threshold, and side jambs, which are usually joined to the other pieces with dado joints.

In old houses, a section of the floor framing may need to be notched to accept the sill. But in newer homes, prehung exterior doors are made to rest on top of the subfloor. Thresholds come in different styles and are designed to seal the bottom of the door from the elements while allowing it to swing freely.

Exterior doorframe
1 Head jamb
2 Sill
3 Side jamb
4 Doorjamb rabbet
5 Notched floor
  framing

DOOR
WEATHERSTRIP
THRESHOLD
SILL

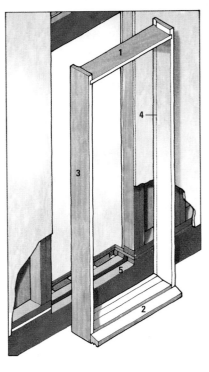

Interior doors

Interior doors are hung in frames that are similar to (but less sturdy than) those used for exterior doors. No sill is present, although in some cases a wood threshold may be added. Usually, interior doors come prehung (the door is already hung on the frame), and are installed with the frame as single units.

The head jamb **(1)** and side jambs **(2)** are fastened to the rough wall opening with shims **(3, 4)** to level and plumb the frame, and to space it evenly from side to side. If the space around the frame is small, wedge-shaped cedar shingles make excellent shims. They are held in place with finishing nails driven through the jambs and shims and into the studs at the sides and the header above.

There are many different styles of interior doors. Generally it's best to choose one that is the same or similar to the other doors in the house. Make sure the jambs on the door you choose are the same width as the thickness of the wall. If you can't find a frame that's a good match, you'll have to cut the jambs narrower or add extension strips to the edges of the jambs.

Interior door frame
1 Head jamb
2 Side jamb
3 Side shims
4 Head shims

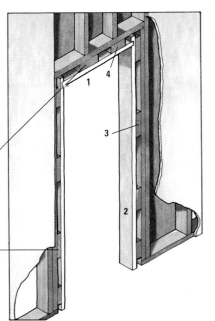

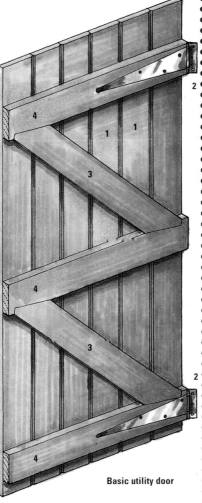

Basic utility door

Fitting and hanging doors

Whatever style of door you want to install, the procedure is similar, with only minor differences. Two good-quality 4-inch butt hinges are enough to support a standard door. But a third, central hinge should be added to an exterior door or a heavy hardwood door.

You will have to try a door in its frame several times to obtain a perfect fit, so it is best to have someone working with you.

Installing a door

Before attaching the hinges to a new door, make sure that it fits well into its frame. It should have a clearance of ⅟₁₆ inch at the top and sides, and should clear the floor by at least ¼ inch; as much as ½ inch may be required for a carpeted floor.

Measure the height and width of the door opening, and the depth from the edge of the jamb to the doorstop molding. Ideally, choose a door that is the right size. But if you can't get one that fits the opening exactly, select one large enough to be trimmed down.

Cutting to size
New doors are often supplied with extensions to their stiles that prevent the corners from being damaged while the doors are in storage. Cut these off with a saw (1) before starting to trim the door to size.

Transfer the measurements from the opening to the door, making allowance for the necessary clearances all around.

To reduce the width of the door, support it on edge and plane the stile down to the marked line. If a lot of wood has to be removed, take some off each stile. This is especially important in the case of panel doors, in order to preserve their symmetry.

If you need to reduce the height of the door by more than ¼ inch, remove the waste with a saw and finish off with a plane. Otherwise, just trim it to size with the plane (2), which must be extremely sharp to deal with the endgrain of the stiles. To avoid chipping out the corners, work from each corner toward the center of the bottom rail.

Supporting the door on thin wedges (3), try it in the frame. If it still does not fit, take it down and remove more wood where appropriate.

1 Saw off extensions

2 Plane to size

3 Wedge door

Installing hinges

The upper hinge is set about 7 inches from the top edge of the door, and the lower one about 10 inches from the bottom. They are cut equally into the stile and the doorframe. Wedge the door in its opening so it is properly aligned, and mark the positions of the hinges on both the door and the frame.

Stand the door on edge, hinge stile up. Open a hinge and, with its knuckle projecting from the edge of the door, align it with the marks and draw around the leaf with a pencil (1). Set a marking gauge to the thickness of the leaf and mark the depth of the recess. With a chisel, make a series of shallow cuts across the grain (2) and remove the waste to the scored line. Repeat the procedure with the second hinge. Then, using the leaves as guides, drill pilot holes for the screws and install both hinges into their recesses.

Wedge the door in its open position, aligning the free hinge leaves with the marks on the doorframe. Make sure the knuckles of the hinges are parallel with the frame, then trace the leaves on the frame (3). Cut out these recesses as you did the others.

Adjusting and aligning
Hang the door with one screw holding each hinge, and see if it closes smoothly. If the lock stile rubs on the frame, you may have to make one or both recesses slightly deeper. If the door appears to strain against the hinges, it is said to be hingebound. In this case, insert thin cardboard pieces beneath the hinge leaves to shim them out. When you're satisfied that the door opens and closes properly, drive in the rest of the screws.

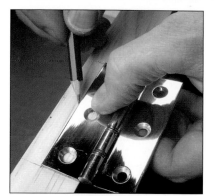
1 Mark around leaf with pencil

2 Cut across grain with chisel

3 Mark size of leaf on frame

MEASUREMENTS

A door that fits well will open and close freely and look symmetrical in the frame. Use the figures given below as a guide for trimming the door and laying out the position of the hinges.

- 1/16 inch clearance at top and sides
- Upper hinge 7 inches from the top
- Lower hinge 10 inches from the bottom
- 1/4 to 1/2 inch gap at the bottom

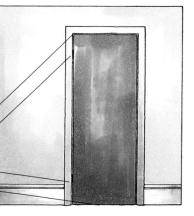

Rising butt hinges

Rising butt hinges, which lift a door as it is opened, prevent it from dragging on a thick carpet. These hinges are made in two parts: a leaf with a fixed pin is screwed to the doorframe, and a leaf with a single knuckle is fixed to the door. The knuckle pivots on the pin.

Rising butt hinges must be installed one way up only, and are therefore made specifically for left-hand or right-hand openings. The countersunk screw holes in the fixed-pin flap indicate which side it is intended for.

Fitting the hinges

Trim the door and mark positions for the hinges (see opposite). But before installing the hinges, plane a shallow bevel at the top outer corner of the hinge stile, so that it will clear the frame as it opens. Because the stile runs through to the top of the door, plane from the outer corner toward the center, to avoid splitting the wood. The top piece of the doorstop will mask the bevel when the door is closed.

Install the hinges to the door and the frame. And then, taking care not to damage the trim above the opening, lower the door onto the hinge pins.

Adjusting butt hinges

If you've got a door that catches on a bump in the floor as it opens, you can fit rising butt hinges to solve the problem.

However, it's sometimes possible to overcome the problem by resetting the existing hinges so that the knuckle of the lower one projects slightly more than the top one. The door will still hang vertically when closed—but as it opens, the out-of-line pins will throw the door upward, enabling it to clear the bump.

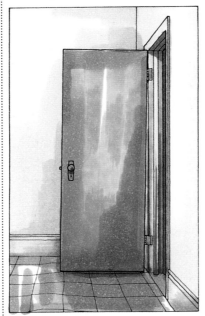

Resetting the hinges
You may have to reset both hinges to the now angle to prevent binding.

Installing a weatherboard

On some older houses, exterior doors don't have weather stripping installed and the sills are not outfitted with a watertight threshold. As a result, driving rain will be forced past the door and into the house. Of course, you can always replace an old door with a new one that comes with proper seals. But if you'd rather keep the door you have, you can create your own weather stripping.

A weatherboard is a molding that goes across the outside bottom edge of the door and sheds water that flows down the door away from the bottom of the door. To install one, measure the width of the opening between the doorstops and cut the molding to fit, shaving one end at a slight angle where it meets the doorframe on the lock side. This will allow it to clear the frame as the door swings open.

Use screws and a waterproof glue to attach the weatherboard to an unpainted door. When attaching one to a door that is already finished, apply a thick coat of primer to the back surface of the weatherboard to make a weatherproof seal. Then screw the weather stripping in place while the primer is still wet.

A door threshold should also have a weather bar installed as shown below. If the door is not typically exposed to driving rain, you can just install a weather bar and cut a rabbet in the bottom edge of the door that will seal against the bar.

Effects of weathering
A sadly neglected panel door that could have been preserved by applying a weather-board before the deterioration had become widespread.

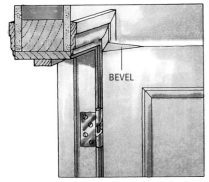

Left-hand opening   **Right-hand opening**

BEVEL

Plane shallow bevel to clear doorframe

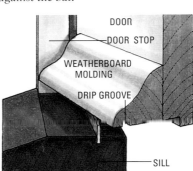

DOOR
DOOR STOP
WEATHERBOARD MOLDING
DRIP GROOVE
SILL

Door with a weatherboard installed

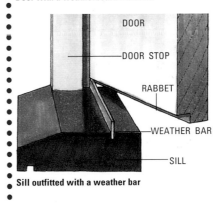

DOOR
DOOR STOP
RABBET
WEATHER BAR
SILL

Sill outfitted with a weather bar

Installing large doors

These days, many houses are built with large, multipurpose rooms. And in houses that don't have these large rooms, there's a design preference for wide archways that create a sense of openness between two smaller rooms. While open floor plans are appealing most of the time, it's a good idea to have some means of occasionally separating the space. Installing large doors is a good option.

Double swinging doors or other door systems allow you to change your living space to meet different needs. Sliding (**1**), bifold (**2**), and accordion (**3**) doors can all divide space efficiently.

Complete door systems, ready for installation, are available. Or you can buy the door system hardware only and install doors of your choice.

Measuring the opening

Before ordering a door system, measure the opening carefully. If you use a steel tape measure, get a helper to keep it taut and avoid a false reading. Measure the width at the top and bottom of the opening and the height at both ends. Also check for square (see below), level, and plumb. If the opening is not square, level, and plumb, it should be fixed before installing the doors.

Sliding doors

Bifold doors

Glazed sliding doors
Glazed room-dividing doors provide an attractive screen when closed.

1 Sliding doors
Sliding doors are hung from a track and are most useful where floor space is limited. They require clear wall space on one or both sides of the opening.

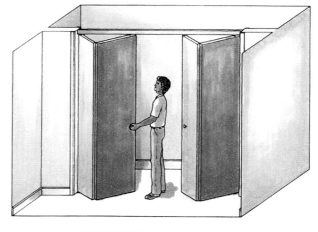

2 Bifold doors
Tracked systems are easy to operate and offer an attractive means of dividing a room, but don't require as much clear floor space as conventional hinged doors.

3 Accordion doors
Like sliding and bifold doors, these operate on a track. They have narrow door panels that fold against each other at the sides of the opening.

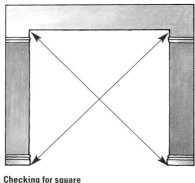

Checking for square
If you are installing large doors, especially in an old house, check that the opening is square. The house may have settled unevenly over time. Measure and compare the diagonal dimensions of the opening. If they are the same, the opening is square. Also, check the jambs for level and plumb.

Sliding doors

A sliding door system is a good spacesaver. Whereas a hinged door needs clear floor space, in an arc at least as wide as the door itself, a sliding door takes up no floor space. But it does require a clear stretch of wall at the side of the opening. In most rooms, this isn't a problem. Furniture can be placed a few inches away from the wall, leaving a gap behind for the door to slide.

A variety of door track sets are available for light, medium, and heavy doors. The doors themselves can range in size from 12 inches up to 6 feet wide, and from ⅜ inch to 2 inches thick. For a double sliding door, two sets of rollers are necessary.

Though designs vary, all track systems for sliding doors have adjustable hanger brackets that are attached to the top edge of the door and to the rollers that make the door slide. A track screwed to the wall above the opening carries and guides the rollers. When the door is closed, it should overlap the opening by about 2 inches at each side.

Installation

Following the manufacturer's instructions, lay out the hanger brackets and screw them to the top edge of the door. The track is usually furred out from the wall with a trim board. This board must be as long as the track and equal in thickness to the baseboards and the casing. Screw the track to the furring board, making sure that it's installed level.

Assemble the hangers and rollers and suspend the door from the track. Adjust the hangers, if necessary, to level and plumb the door. Install the door guide on the floor and the doorstops to the track.

Finish up by installing an attractive valance board over the track. You can trim this with lengths of stock molding to match or contrast with other casing moldings in the house.

Bifold doors

Bifold doors offer a reasonable way of closing off a door opening without intruding too much into the room space when open. The opening should be trimmed in the normal way with smooth jambs and casings to match the others in your house. The head casing can be lowered to cover part or all of the track.

The pivot hinge and track-door rollers are available in standard sets for two or four doors of equal width. Up to six doors can be hung from specialized tracks, but these systems require you to install a bottom guide track, which in most cases is impractical.

The doors range in thickness between ¾ and 1⅜ inches, and in height up to 8 feet. Maximum width for standard bifolds is 2 feet per door.

Installation

Following the manufacturer's instructions, fit the pivot hinges into the top and bottom edges of the end door. Then install the pivoting hangers in the top edges of the other doors.

Hinge the doors together. They will swing to one side of the wall or the other, according to which way the knuckles of the hinges face. Install the track, then hang the doors on the track and install the bottom pivot to the floor so it's exactly plumb with the top one.

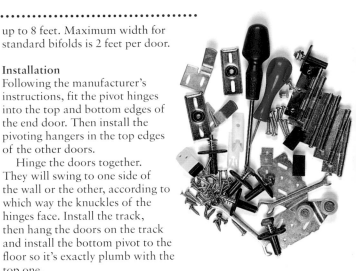

Accordion doors

Accordion-folding doors are designed to fold up and stack at the side of the door opening. They are made up from narrow panels hinged to each other and attached to sliders that hang from a top track. No bottom track is necessary. The panels are thin so that they will stack with a minimum of bulk. Because of this, they don't provide much in the way of sound insulation.

These doors are supplied in kits and are ready for installation. They are available in many different styles, colors, and surface textures. Sizes that fit standard single-door openings are usually stock items; doors to fit larger openings can be ordered.

Installation

Screw the lightweight track to the underside of the wall opening between the rooms. It is possible to recess the track in the head jamb, but it's much easier to face mount it and add a cover molding on each side.

Install the track over the rollers of the stacked panels (**1**), then screw it into place. The track must be installed level. Shim the track if necessary. Then screw cover molding in place to hide the track and any shims you installed (**2**). Screw the end panel of the door to the jamb (**3**) and the latch plate to the opposite side of the opening (**4**) to complete the installation.

TRACK
ROLLER HANGER
DOOR GUIDE

Sliding door system

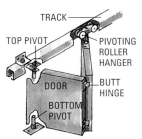
TRACK
TOP PIVOT
PIVOTING ROLLER HANGER
DOOR
BUTT HINGE
BOTTOM PIVOT

Bifold door system

1 Slide panels into track and install track

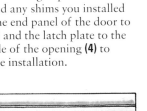
2 Screw on cover moldings

3 Screw door to jamb

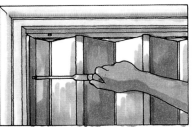
4 Install door latch on opposite jamb

Hardware

Installing hand plates
Designed to protect the paint on interior doors, hand plates are screwed to each side of the lock stile, just above the center rail.

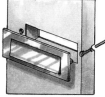

2 Counterbore door for plate and bolts

Installing a door knocker

A traditional set of exterior door hardware includes a mail slot, a doorknob, and a knocker. Of the three, the door knocker is probably considered optional by more people than the other two. From a functional point of view, electric doorbells have made door knockers obsolete. But as decorative hardware, knockers still have their place, especially in renovation work.

On a panel door, install the knocker to the muntin at about shoulder height. Mark a vertical centerline on the muntin at the required height and drill a clearance hole for the mounting screw or screws. Attach the knocker according to the manufacturer's instructions.

Reproduction brass fittings are usually finished at the factory with a clear lacquer to prevent tarnishing. If yours is not, apply a clear acrylic lacquer yourself.

Installing a mail slot

Mail slots are available in a variety of styles and materials—solid brass, stainless steel, plated brass, cast iron, and aluminum. They are designed either for horizontal or for vertical installation. Installing a horizontal mail slot is shown here. But the same methods apply to the vertical type installed in the door stile.

Mark out the rectangular opening

1 Sizing the opening.
Take dimensions from the flap and make the opening slightly larger.

on the center of the cross rail. The slot must be only slightly larger than the hinged flap on the outside (**1**). Drill a ½-inch access hole in each corner of the rectangle for the blade of a keyhole saw or a power jigsaw. After cutting out the slot, trim the corners with a chisel and clean up the edges.

Mark and drill the mounting holes, then attach the mail slot (**2**). You may have to shorten the screws if the door is thin. Plug or fill the counterbored holes that house the screwheads.

Better still, install an internal flap cover. These are held in place with small woodscrews. A flap cover reduces drafts, has a neat, finished appearance, and allows you to remove the mail-slot hardware easily for repairs or replacement.

Installing a doorknob

A period doorknob, whether wrought iron or brass, can be an attractive feature on just about any door. Such knobs are reproduced in many traditional styles and patterns.

A doorknob, often called a pull to differentiate between it and a lockset, is usually installed on the center of the lock stile, at the height of the door's cross rail. But personal preference plays a role here. Some people install them higher on the stile or in the middle of the cross rail.

Drill a counterbored hole from the back side of the door for the head of the screw that holds the knob. The clearance hole for the screw shank passes right through the door.

Hold the backplate and knob on the door, then insert and tighten the screw. For a neat finish, plug the screw hole on the back side of the door to conceal the screwhead.

Counterbore hole for fixing screw

Choose hardware to suit door style

Reproduction door hardware
1 Brass mail-slot plate
2 Brass knocker
3 Brass doorknob
4 Wrought-iron doorknob
5 Wrought-iron knocker
6 Wrought-iron mail-slot plate

Moldings

Interior wood moldings, often called architectural moldings, are in part a legacy of the classic paneled walls found in grand houses of yesteryear. They include molded baseboards, chair rails, picture rails, and decorative cornice moldings. But moldings also have a functional purpose. They often cover up joints in wall finish, hide rough work, and protect the wall from daily abuse. Moldings are usually made from softwoods, and sometimes from hardwoods or even medium-density fiberboard (MDF) if they will be painted after installation.

Baseboards

Architectural moldings are both functional and decorative. A relatively high baseboard lends a period feel to a room and can cover up a lot of rough wall work underneath. By removing them you also have easy access to the wall cavities for such jobs as running new wiring. As a general rule, it's a good idea when choosing new molding to match the style of the other moldings in the house.

Chair rails

The chair rail provides a protective strip to keep the wall finish from being damaged by chairbacks. As such, it's most often used in dining rooms. But it can be used elsewhere too, wherever you want to establish a border between two different wall finishes—wainscoting on the lower part of a wall and paint or wallpaper above, for example.

Picture rails

Like other moldings, the picture rail was originally designed as part of ornate wood-paneled walls. It provided a strong ledge from which to hang heavy, framed pictures. These days picture rails are usually located about 12 inches below the ceiling, and serve a decorative rather than a functional purpose.

Cornice moldings

Cornice, or crown, moldings form a bold decorative feature where the walls of a room meet the ceiling. In old houses they can be made of plaster. But in newer houses, wood is almost always used.

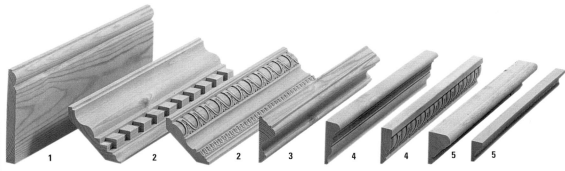

Architectural moldings are decorative and functional

Types of molding
1 Baseboard
2 Crown or cornice
3 Large chair rail
4 Molded and carved chair rails
5 Small chair rails

Making corner joints

Where pieces of molding meet at an outside corner, you have to miter the ends where they join. Cut miters using a handsaw and a miter box, or a power miter saw.

Where pieces meet at an inside corner, the joint has to be coped. To do this, first miter the end of a molding, then cut away the waste with a coping saw following the line formed by the mitered cut **(1)**.

For larger moldings that don't fit in your miter box, mark the profile on the back face, using a cutoff as a template **(2)**. Saw off the waste with the teeth of the coping saw facing backward, to prevent tearing out the wood fibers on the face of the molding.

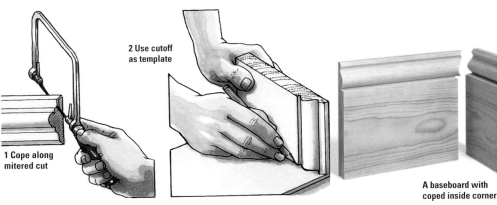

2 Use cutoff as template

1 Cope along mitered cut

A baseboard with coped inside corner

Installing moldings

The best method for installing a molding will depend on the structure of the wall. On wood-framed walls, you can just nail through the molding and wall finish and into the framing members. On a masonry wall, you can use nails, expansion anchors, or plastic anchors. To install the anchors, lay out the wall first where the molding goes and drill clearance holes. Transfer the location of these holes to the molding and drill screw holes at these points. Screw the molding to the wall. In some cases, if the wall is very flat, you can use panel adhesive to glue the pieces of molding in place.

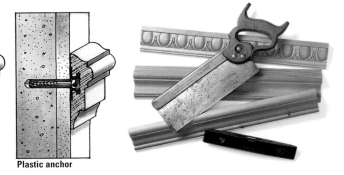

Masonry nail   **Expansion anchor**   **Plastic anchor**

Installing molding

Casing moldings provide a decorative frame to a door, as well as concealing the joint between the doorjambs and the wall. The same moldings are used around windows. Standard casing moldings are stock items at lumberyards and home centers. But a variety of more elaborate casings are sometimes available if you have an architectural molding supplier in your area. If there's a particular profile you want to duplicate, you can have moldings made to order at some cabinet shops.

Installing casing molding

A classical casing treatment includes fluted molding along the sides and top of the door. At the bottom of the side casings, a plinth block is used to make a decorative transition between the casing and the baseboard in the room. At the top corners of the doorjambs, corner blocks are installed, partly for decorative purposes like the plinth blocks. But they also serve a functional purpose. They eliminate the need for miter joints where the side and top casing boards meet. Butt joints are much easier to install.

When casing a door, install the plinth blocks (**1**). Then measure the length from the top of the plinth to ¼ inch above the bottom of the top doorjamb. Cut the casings to this length and nail them into the jambs and the wall. Nail the corner blocks on top of the side casings (**2**), then cut and install the top casing between the corner blocks.

Dealing with out-of-square jambs
If you are restoring an older house, you may find that the doorjambs are out of square and 45-degree miters will not fit tightly together. In this situation, hold each board in place with its inside edge parallel to the jamb and mark along the edges on the wall (**1**). Mark a diagonal line where the lines cross (**2**) to give the angle for the proper miter. Set an adjustable bevel to this angle and mark both casing boards with the bevel. Make the cuts.

1 Mark parallel lines
Hold each component in position parallel with the jambs and mark along the edges.

2 Mark the diagonal
Where the lines cross, mark a diagonal line.

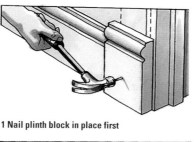

1 Nail plinth block in place first

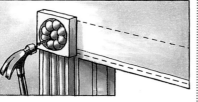

2 Nail corner block on top of side casing

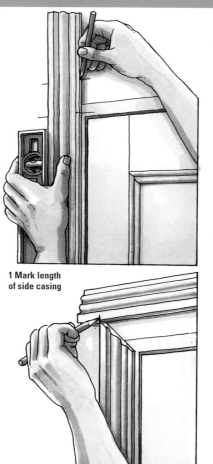

1 Mark length of side casing

2 Mark length of top casing

3 Nail top casing to top doorjamb

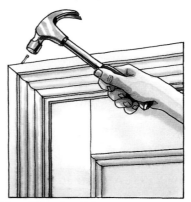

4 Drive nail into mitered joint

Reproduction casing moldings

Installing standard casings

Hold a short length of casing molding about ¼ inch above the door opening, check that it's level, and mark its width on the wall. Next, hold one slightly long side casing board in place about ¼ inch from the edge of the doorjamb. Transfer the marks from the wall onto the casing board (**1**).

Cut a 45-degree miter on the marked end of the casing. Then nail it to the doorjamb, using 2-inch finishing nails driven every 12 inches. Don't drive the nails in fully at this stage, in case you need to move the casing. Cut and install the other side casing, using the same procedure.

Rest the top piece of casing upside down on the ends of the side casings and mark its length (**2**). Cut a miter at each end and nail the molding between the side casings and into the top doorjamb and the wall (**3**). Then line up the miter joints between the two boards, so the surface is flush, and drive a nail through the top casing into the mitered joint at both ends (**4**). Drive all the nailheads below the surface with a hammer and a nailset. Then fill the holes with wood filler, let the filler dry, and sand it smooth. Prime and paint. If you are planning to finish the casings with a clear varnish, fill the nail holes with a colored wood filler that closely matches the color of the wood.

Replacing baseboard

Baseboards are protective "kick boards" that create a decorative border between the floor and walls. Modern baseboards are relatively small and simply formed, with a rounded or beveled top edge. Repairing or replacing baseboards is sometimes necessary just from the wear and tear of normal living. But when you do any extensive remodeling, especially floor work, baseboard damage is inevitable.

In older houses baseboards are usually much bigger and often more ornate. Some lumberyards carry older-style baseboards, but generally they are hard to find. You can either make them yourself or hire a cabinet shop to machine them. Because replacing old baseboards can be time consuming, make an effort to preserve and repair older baseboards rather than discarding them.

Removing the baseboard

Remove a baseboard by prying it away from the wall, using a crowbar or a flat bar. A continuous length of baseboard, with ends that are mitered into inside corners, may have to be cut before it can be removed.

Tap the blade of the crowbar between the baseboard and the wall, and pry the top edge away sufficiently to insert a thin strip of wood behind the crowbar, in order to protect the wall. Then pry out the baseboard again, a little to one side. Work along the baseboard in this way until the board is free. Having removed the board, pull the nails out through the back to avoid splitting the face.

Cutting a long baseboard
A long stretch of baseboard may bend sufficiently for you to cut it in place. Pry it away at its center and insert blocks of wood, one on each side of the proposed cut, to hold the board about 1 inch from the wall (1).

Make a vertical cut with a handsaw held at about 45 degrees to the face of the board (2). Saw with short strokes, using the tip of the blade only.

1 Pry baseboard away from wall and block out

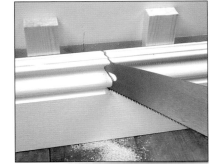

2 Cut through baseboard with tip of saw

Installing new baseboards

Whenever possible, restore a damaged baseboard, particularly if it has an unusual molding for which there is no modern replacement. If that's not possible, you could try to make a replacement from standard molding boards (see below), all of which are readily available.

Measure the length of each wall, bearing in mind that most baseboards are mitered at the corners. Mark the length of the wall on the bottom edge of the new board, mark a 45-degree angle for the miter, and extend the marked line across the face of the board, using a square. Clamp the board on edge in a vise and carefully saw down the line at that angle, using a sharp handsaw.

Sometimes molded baseboards are scribed and butted at inside corners. To achieve the required profile, cut the end off one board at 45 degrees as for a miter joint (1); then, using a coping saw, cut along the contour line on the molded face, so it will fit tightly against its neighbor (2).

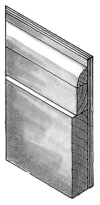

Making a baseboard
If you are unable to find baseboard to match your original, have one machined specially or make one from various pieces of standard moldings.

1 Cut 45-degree miter at end

2 Cut shape following contour line

BASEBOARD MOLDINGS

Most standard baseboards are made of softwood, ready for painting. Hardwoods are not so commonly used; they are usually reserved for special decorative moldings and coated with a clear finish.

Selection of baseboard moldings
Most baseboards sold these days don't have much character. But a well-stocked lumberyard sometimes has a variety of more elaborate options including the types shown at right.

Garage doors

Garage doors, whether sectional or one piece, make a dominant design statement, especially if they are located at the front of your house.

Styles of garage doors

Most garages today are outfitted with sectional overhead garage doors. These are made of horizontal sections that are hinged together and have wheels installed in both ends. These wheels are held captive by, and run in, a continuous steel track that extends from the garage floor to underneath the ceiling joists. When the door is lifted, it moves from a closed vertical position to an open horizontal one.

Overhead doors utilize spring tension to make them easy to lift and pull down. On most units, a large coil spring on the end of the door stretches when the door is dropped. When the door is raised, the accumulated tension of the spring helps pull the door up, making it easier to lift. Large doors that span two-car garages are often equipped with a single horizontal torsion spring instead. This winds up as the door is lowered and unwinds when it is raised. Sectional overhead doors are available in many styles, from basic paint-grade units to high-end, solid hardwood doors.

An older style of spring-assisted door is the one-piece variety that swings out from the bottom and slides overhead, retracting either partially or completely into the garage. These are called "up-and-over doors." Those that retract only partially are called "canopy doors." Some up-and-over doors roll in tracks just like sectional overhead doors. The chief drawback of these one-piece doors is that all of them require at least some clear space in front of the garage to open the door.

Requiring even more space, of course, are the traditional swinging garage doors still found on many older garages. These are wide wood doors (they come in pairs) that are outfitted with heavy-duty strap hinges with long leaves that extend nearly all the way across each door. These doors are constructed with internal bracing to keep them from sagging. Like other garage doors, they can either have glass panes or not. These doors can last a long time, and work well, as long as they are properly maintained. But they do have a tendency to weaken over time because of their weight. As the doors distort from sagging, they start to bind. The most important maintenance requirement is to keep them well painted to prevent swelling caused by water penetration.

Because these doors are under spring tension and have so many mechanical parts, sectional overhead garage doors usually need frequent maintenance. If the door seems hard to lift or drops heavily, the spring tension may need tightening. Overhead doors are connected to their springs (which coil or twist up) by cables that run from the bottom corners of the door, up through a system of pulleys to the ends of the springs.

On doors with coil springs, you tighten the tension by attaching the cable from the bottom of the door to another hole in the cable plate at the end of the spring. On doors with torsion springs, increase the tension by loosening the locknut that holds the spring and twisting the spring a few turns, using a bar supplied with the door or a long screwdriver **(1, facing page)**. WARNING: Never loosen the locknut on a torsion spring without holding the spring with the bar or screwdriver. If overhead doors are hard to lower, or tend to move up too fast when raised, decrease the spring tension on the door.

Binding can be caused by the track being out of alignment. To check, hold a level vertically alongside the track on both sides of the door. Adjust the track by loosening the mounting brackets slightly, tapping the track with a hammer until it is plumb, then retightening the brackets **(2)**. You can also try oiling the rollers **(3)** and applying a thin coat of grease to the tracks.

If the door does not fit the contour of the garage floor when it's closed, you may want to cut the lower panel of the door to fit. Scribe a line that follows the floor onto the face of the bottom panel **(4)**. Set the scribe to the widest gap between the floor and the door, and slowly pull it across the door. Disassemble the door, cut to the line, and reassemble the door.

Lock problems can usually be solved by adjusting the lock-bar guide brackets on both sides of the door, so the bars slide through them easily **(5)**. You should lubricate the lock mechanism also **(6)**. To completely lubricate the lock, you sometimes have to remove the lock and the crank mechanism from the door.

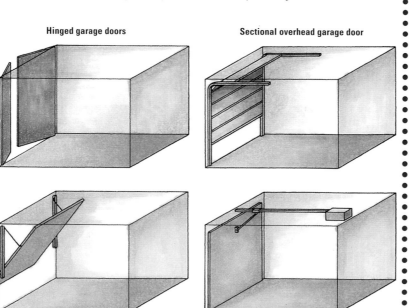

Hinged garage doors

Sectional overhead garage door

Up-and-over garage door

Automatic-opening garage door

Sectional overhead doors

These doors retract within their own space, so they can be used where there's not enough room for doors to swing out, or in. And when properly installed, they are very easy to open because the weight of the door is counterbalanced with heavy-duty steel springs.

There are two common types: one with large coil springs on both sides, the other with a single horizontal torsion spring mounted on the wall above the door.

Installing overhead garage doors is not difficult, but it can take a couple of days if you've never installed one before. Also, when installing a new door, consider adding an automatic garage-door opener to the job. It's a small luxury that makes life easier. Overhead doors should be maintained regularly for good performance.

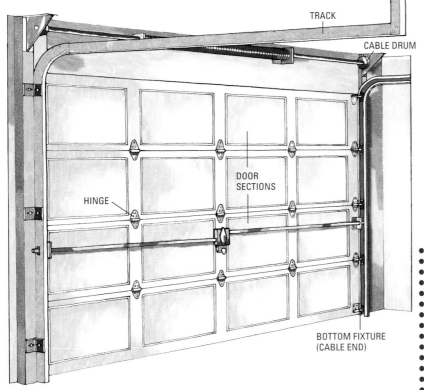

TRACK

CABLE DRUM

DOOR SECTIONS

HINGE

BOTTOM FIXTURE
(CABLE END)

1 Adjust spring tension

2 Tighten track brackets

3 Lubricate track

4 Scribe and cut door

5 Adjust lock-bar guide

6 Lubricate lock mechanism

S-HOOK

PLATE

COIL SPRING

PULLEY

CABLE

Counterbalance system
Sectional garage doors operate with a system of springs, cables, and pulleys that compensate for the weight of the door and make it easy to open and close.

Automatic garage-door openers

Automatic garage-door openers are available for most types of garage doors. These units allow you to open the door by remote control from inside your car and from inside your house. There are many systems designed for do-it-yourself installation, and these come with complete instructions. These openers shouldn't be regarded as simply a luxury. For older or handicapped people, they are practically a necessity.

These systems incorporate an electric motor (mounted on a track) that drives either a chain or a long, threaded rod to lift up the door. Most also come with an integral light fixture that automatically turns on and off at preset intervals.

Systems may operate with either an infrared or radio signal transmitter. The receiver is mounted either outside on a garage wall or inside on the motor housing. Transmitters and receivers have special coded signals for security. The systems also incorporate automatic safety devices that stop the door immediately if it comes in contact with an obstruction.

Windows: types and construction

The purpose of any window is to allow natural light into the house and to provide ventilation. Traditionally, windows were referred to as "lights," and the term "fixed light" is still used to describe a window or part of a window that doesn't open. The part of a window that opens is called a sash. The sash can slide up and down or side to side in tracks or can be hinged on the side or the top. Windows with side-hinged sashes are usually called casement windows. Window sashes can also pivot, and a group of smaller glass panes can be operated together to form a jalousie window.

Most window frames and sashes are made of solid wood. In many cases, the outside surfaces are clad with painted aluminum or colored vinyl.

Casement windows

One of the more common windows is the simple hinged or casement window. Traditional versions are made of wood, and are fabricated much like doors. Vertical side jambs are joined to a head jamb at the top and a sill at the bottom (see below). Depending on the size of the window, the frame is sometimes divided vertically by a mullion with another side-hinged casement on the other side, or horizontally by a transom **(1, left)** and an awning window.

A side-hung casement sash is attached with either a continuous hinge or with butt hinges. A lever handle, sometimes called a "cockspur," is mounted on the sash stile and is used for opening, closing, and locking the sash. A casement stay attached to the bottom rail holds the sash open in various positions. With a top-hung casement (or awning sash), the stay also secures the window in the closed position.

Glazing bars, lightweight, molded strips of wood, steel, or vinyl, are often used to divide the glazed areas of a window into smaller panes **(2)**.

Mild-steel casement windows **(3)** have relatively slim welded frames and sashes. They are strong and durable, but will rust unless protected by galvanized plating or high-quality metal paint. Modern versions are galvanized by a hot-dip process, then finished with a colored polyester coating.

● **Window frames**
Most frames and sashes are made up from molded sections of solid wood. However, mild steel, aluminum, and rigid plastic are also used.

1 Casement window

2 Glazing bars

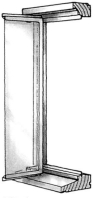

3 Steel casement

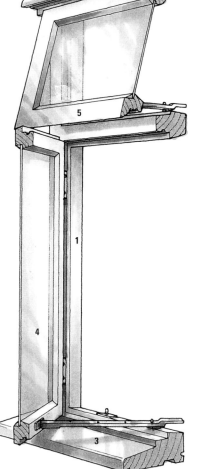

Casement window
1 Jamb
2 Head
3 Sill
4 Casement sash
5 Awning (vent) sash

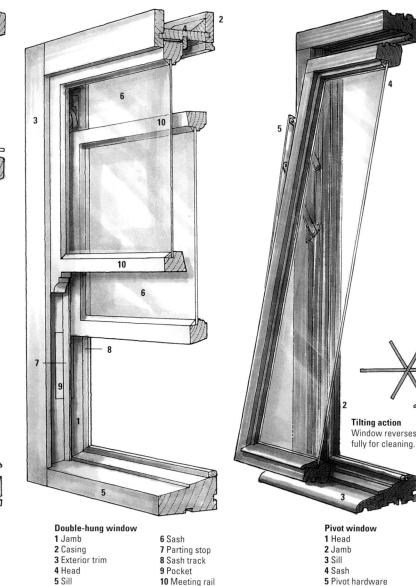

Double-hung window
1 Jamb
2 Casing
3 Exterior trim
4 Head
5 Sill
6 Sash
7 Parting stop
8 Sash track
9 Pocket
10 Meeting rail

Tilting action
Window reverses fully for cleaning.

Pivot window
1 Head
2 Jamb
3 Sill
4 Sash
5 Pivot hardware

Double-hung windows

Vertically sliding windows are usually known as double-hung windows. In this design, both the top and the bottom sash can be opened.

Traditional wooden sash windows (see opposite) are constructed with a box frame in which the jambs are composed of three boards, joined together at the top corners. The side jambs are joined to the sill at the bottom. Windows are sized to fit standard wall thicknesses. When installed, the inside edge of the jambs should be flush with the wall surface and ready for casings to be nailed in place. For thicker walls, extension jambs are nailed to the window jambs to bring them flush with the wall.

If the window has counterweights, they're installed behind the side jambs, with access provided by a small removable piece of the jamb, called a pocket.

The sashes of a double-hung window are held in tracks formed in the side jambs. They are separated by a parting stop. The top sash slides in the outer track and overlaps the bottom sash at horizontal meeting rails. The closing faces of the meeting rails are beveled. This bevel makes the sashes wedge together when closed, which prevents the sashes from rattling. This also allows both rails to separate easily as the window is opened. The sashes are locked by hardware that joins the two when they are in the closed position.

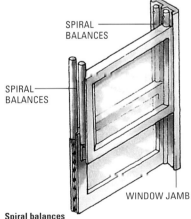

SPIRAL BALANCES

SPIRAL BALANCES

WINDOW JAMB

Spiral balances
The exposed balances are set into grooves in the side jambs of the window.

Spiral balances

Modern wooden, aluminum, and vinyl sashes have spring-assisted spiral balances. The balances are attached to the sides of the jambs.

Pivot windows

Wood-frame pivot windows (see opposite) are constructed in a similar way to casement windows. But their special hinge mechanism allows the sash to be rotated so that both sides of the glass can be cleaned from inside. Using the built-in safety catch, the sash can be locked when open or when fully reversed.

Similar pivoting windows, usually called roof windows, are made for pitched roofs. These windows are usually double-glazed and some come with blinds built into the window. The window is usually protected on the outside by an aluminum cladding, and a flashing kit provides a weatherproof seal between the window and the roof.

Jalousie windows

A jalousie window is a specialized pivot window. The panes are unframed strips of glass, typically ¼ inch thick, that are capped at each end by plastic or aluminum carriers. These carriers pivot on channels screwed to the window frame. The panes are linked by a mechanism that allows them to be opened or closed simultaneously. The exposed edges of the glass are ground and polished.

Jalousie windows provide excellent ventilation and light transmission, but unfortunately offer minimal security unless outfitted with specialized locks.

Use two sets of panes for wide opening.

Aluminum windows

Aluminum window frames are installed in new houses, and often are used as replacement windows for old wood or steel units. The aluminum is extruded into complex sections to hold double-glazed sashes. Finished in several colors—usually white, silver, black, brown, and bronze—aluminum window frames require no maintenance.

They are sold, like wood windows, in many different standard sizes with many different features. They are manufactured in complete units ready for installation. To reduce water damage from condensation, hollow sections of the metal frame incorporate an insulating material to create a thermal break.

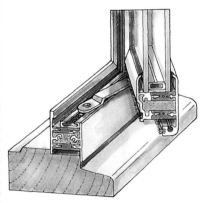

Extruded-aluminum window in a wooden frame

Vinyl windows

Rigid vinyl windows are similar to aluminum ones. They are typically manufactured in white plastic and, once installed, require only minimal maintenance.

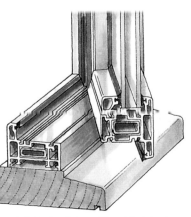

Extruded-plastic window with metal reinforcing

Wood casement—exterior

Wood casement—interior

Metal casements

Vinyl casements

How windows are installed: MASONRY WALLS

Frame walls

Most windows today are prefabricated and set in place as a single unit. Installing them is similar to installing prehung doors. First, measure the rough opening to make sure it is large enough to accept the window. Then cover all four sides of the opening with 15-pound roofing felt to reduce water damage if there is a leak. Set the window in the opening from outside. Center it from side to side.

Check the sill for level and the jambs for plumb. On the outside, drive a 10d finishing nail through the exterior casing and into the wall framing. Start a nail in the opposite top corner, check for level and plumb, and drive the nail into the framing.

Measure between diagonal corners to make sure that the window is square (the measurements should be exactly the same) and insert any necessary shims along the sides of the frame to keep it square. Then nail the lower corners. Operate the sashes to make sure they move smoothly, then finish nailing the window in place.

Push insulation between the window frame and the rough framing from the inside. Then install a drip cap above the window. Set all nailheads and fill the holes. Prime and paint the outside of the window.

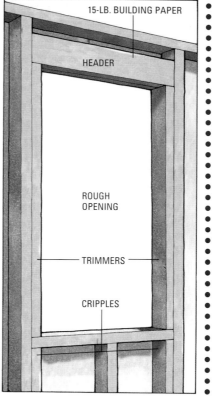

1 Be sure opening matches window
To narrow an opening, install extra trimmers or strips of plywood. To widen an opening, add a new stud next to the framed opening and remove the existing one. Alter the height of an opening by changing the height of the sill, not the header.

In older brick houses, it's common to find the windows set into recesses in the walls, instead of being flush with the outside of the walls. The openings were finished first and the windows were made to fit the openings. The windows were nailed or screwed into wood plugs set into the mortar joints. In a typical 9-inch-thick wall, the window was installed so the inside edge of the jambs was even with the interior wall surface.

In traditional brick construction, the bottom of the opening was defined by a stone sill, and the top of the opening was supported by an arch made of brick or with a stone lintel. Wood lintels were installed behind the arches to help support some of the weight.

Stone lintels were sometimes carved with decorative features and they, too, usually had wood lintels behind them to carry some weight. These traditional window openings—at least in residential construction—were never very wide because of the heavy weight above that had to be supported. When a room called for a wide bank of windows, these usually consisted of multiple smaller openings that were divided by brick or stone columns.

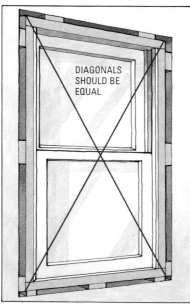

2 Adjust window in opening
Adjust the window with shims until it is level, plumb, and square. Make sure the sashes operate smoothly. If diagonal measurements—from corner to corner—across the window are identical, the window is square.

3 Nail through casing into studs
Nail window at top corners first, then check for square and nail at bottom corners. Nail every 12 inches between corners. Install drip cap, set nailheads, and fill holes. Caulk around the window.

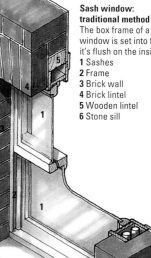

Sash window: traditional method
The box frame of a sash window is set into the w[...] it's flush on the inside.
1 Sashes
2 Frame
3 Brick wall
4 Brick lintel
5 Wooden lintel
6 Stone sill

Types of glass

Glass is made from silica sand and additives like soda and lime. It is heated until it is molten to produce the raw material. The type and quality of the glass produced for windows is determined by how it is processed in the molten stage. Ordinary window glass is known as annealed glass. Special treatments during manufacturing give glass particular properties, like heat resistance or extra strength.

Sheet glass

Clear sheet glass is made for general glazing and was once the most common type used in windows. It is produced by a drawn process which sometimes causes a slight distortion that often can be seen in wide sheets of glass. Though the surfaces are given a smooth "fire finish," they are not always absolutely flat or parallel. Two grades of clear glass are produced, standard grade for general work and a select grade for better work. The thicknesses range from $1/16$ to $5/32$ inch. Horticulture glass is poorer quality, made for use in greenhouses.

Float glass

Float glass is now generally used for glazing windows. It is made by floating the molten glass on a bath of liquid tin to produce flat, parallel, and distortion-free surfaces. It has nearly replaced plate glass, which is a rolled product that is ground and polished on both sides. Clear float glass is made in thicknesses from $1/8$ to 1 inch.

Patterned glass

Patterned glass has one surface embossed with a texture or a decorative design. It is available in clear or tinted sheets, in thicknesses of $1/8$, $5/32$, $3/16$, and $1/4$ inch. The transparency of the glass depends on the density of the patterning. Patterned glass is often used when light and privacy are required, such as for bathroom windows.

Obscure glass, sometimes known as roughcast glass, is another form of patterned glass. It is usually thicker and most often used in commercial buildings.

Tinted glass

Tinted glass is a product designed to cut down the heat from the sun. Because of this, it's often used in roof windows. It can be made of float, sheet, or laminated glass. It reduces glare but does block some of the light. It's available in thicknesses ranging from $1/8$ to $1/2$ inch.

Low-E glass

Low-E (low-emissivity) glass is a clear glass with a special coating on one surface that is selectively permeable. It admits light but reflects heat. It is used primarily for double glazing, and is located on one of the inside glass surfaces. The coating allows a high level of natural illumination. The outer pane of the double-glazed unit can be of any type of glass. Low-E glass is offered as an option by many window manufacturers.

Nonreflective glass

This type of glass is used primarily for glazing picture frames. Its slightly textured surface eliminates the surface reflections associated with ordinary polished glass, yet, when placed within $1/2$ inch of the picture surface, the glass appears completely transparent. Nonreflective glass is $1/16$ inch thick.

Safety glass

Glass that has been strengthened with reinforcement is known as safety glass. It should be used wherever the glazed area is relatively large or where its position makes it especially vulnerable. In domestic situations, safety glass should be used for glazed exterior doors, low-level windows, and shower doors.

Wired glass

Wired glass is a roughcast or clear glass, usually $1/4$ inch thick, that has a fine steel-wire mesh incorporated during manufacture. Though the glass may crack, the mesh serves to hold the pane together, preventing injuries from shattered glass. The glass itself is not any stronger than ordinary glass of the same thickness. Wired glass is considered a fire-resistant material, with a 1-hour fire rating. Though the glass may break, its wire reinforcement helps to maintain the pane's integrity and prevent, or at least inhibit, the spread of smoke and fire.

Tempered glass

Tempered glass is ordinary glass that has been heat-treated to improve its strength. This process renders the glass about four to five times stronger than untreated glass of the same thickness. When it breaks, tempered glass shatters into relatively harmless granules.

Tempered glass cannot be cut. Any holes or other openings must be in place before the glass is treated.

Laminated glass

Laminated glass is made by bonding together two or more layers of glass with a clear, tear-resistant plastic film sandwiched between. The plastic interlayer not only helps to absorb the energy from an impact, it reduces the risk of injury from flying fragments of glass. Clear, tinted, and patterned versions are all available.

Patterned and tinted glass
Embossed and tinted glass is often used for restoring windows in older houses, but it also makes for attractive glazing in new installations.

Cutting glass

You can buy most types of glass from your local hardware store or home center. Often the salespeople can advise you on the type you need and cut the glass to your specifications. If the piece of glass you want is big, or you want to order a lot of glass, look for a glass supply store in the Yellow Pages. Specialty suppliers have a greater selection of different glasses and will usually deliver.

Glass thickness
Once expressed by weight, the thickness of glass is now measured in inches. If you are replacing old glass, measure its thickness to the nearest 32nd of a inch. If you can't find an exact match, buy a slightly thicker glass for safety.

Although there aren't any strict regulations concerning the thickness of glass, it is advisable to comply with the recommendations set out in the Uniform Building Code. The thickness of glass required depends on the area of the pane, its exposure to wind pressure, and the vulnerability of its location, for example, whether it is next to a play area. Tell your supplier what the glass is needed for to ensure that you get the right type.

Measuring
Measure the height and width of the opening to the inside of the frame rabbet. Check each dimension by taking measurements from at least two points. Also check that the diagonals are the same length. If they differ significantly, indicating that the frame is out of square, make a cardboard template of the opening and take it to the glazier. In any case, deduct ⅛ inch from the height and the width to allow room for adjusting the glass when you install it. When ordering an asymmetrical piece of glass, make an exact template of the piece you need and take this to the supplier.

Glass cutters

Glass nibblers
Use nibblers to trim off the edge of a pane.

● **Acrylic glazing**
Use clear acrylic sheet as an alternative to glass when cutting awkward shapes. Use a fret saw and files to shape acrylic.

Always carry panes of glass on edge to prevent them from bending, and wear heavy work gloves to protect your hands. Also wear goggles to protect your eyes when removing broken glass from a frame. Wrap broken glass in thick layers of newspaper before you dispose of it, to reduce the possibility that the people who pick up the trash will be cut. Or check with a local glass shop; it may be willing to add your glass to its scrap pile to be sent back to the manufacturer for recycling.

Basic glass cutting

It is not usually necessary to cut glass at home because most suppliers are willing to do it for you. But sometimes it's more convenient to cut it yourself. A handheld glass cutter with a steel wheel is inexpensive, easy to use, and can handle most common jobs.

Cutting glass successfully is largely a matter of practice and confidence. If you have not done it before, make a few practice cuts on waste pieces of glass and get used to the feel of the tool before cutting the project piece.

Lay the glass on a flat surface covered with a blanket. (Patterned glass should be placed pattern side down and cut on its smooth side.) Clean the cutting surface with mineral spirits.

Place a T-square at the cutline **(1)**, and check your measurement. If you're working on a small piece of glass or don't have a T-square, mark the glass on opposing edges with a felt-tipped pen and use a straightedge to join the marks and guide the cutter.

Lubricate the cutter wheel by dipping it in light machine oil or kerosene. Hold the cutter between your middle finger and forefinger **(2)** and draw it along the guide with a single continuous stroke. Use firm, even pressure throughout the stroke and run the cutter off the end. Slide the glass over the edge of the table **(3)** and tap the underside of the scored line with the back of the cutter. Wearing gloves, grip the glass on each side of the scored line **(4)** and snap it in two. Or you can place a wood dowel under the length of the cutline and push down evenly on both sides of the pane until the glass snaps.

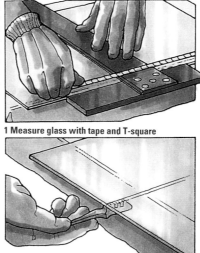

1 Measure glass with tape and T-square

2 Cut glass with one continuous stroke

3 Tap underside to initiate cut

4 Snap glass in two

Cutting off a thin strip of glass

To reduce a slightly oversize pane of glass, remove a thin strip by scoring a line as described above, then gradually remove the waste with nibblers (see far left) or a pair of pliers.

Nibble away thin strip with pliers

Cutting circles and drilling holes

Most glasswork involves cutting straight lines. Occasionally, however, you may need to cut or drill a hole in glass.

Cutting a circle in glass

Stick the suction pad of a compass glass cutter on the glass. Then adjust the cutting head to match the radius of the specified hole. Score the circle around the pivot point, applying firm, even pressure as you go. Now score another, smaller, circle inside the first one (**1**). Remove the cutter and crisscross the inner disc with straight cuts, then make radial cuts about inch apart in the outer rim. Tap the center of the scored area from underneath (**2**), then remove the pieces of glass. Finally, tap the outer rim and nibble away the waste with pliers.

To cut a disc of glass, scribe a circle with the compass cutter, then score tangential lines from the circle to the edges of the glass (**3**).

1 Score circles with even pressure

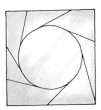

3 Cutting a disc
Scribe the circle, then make tangential cuts from it to the edge of the glass.

Smoothing the edges of cut glass

You can grind down the cut edges of glass to a smooth finish using wet-and-dry abrasive paper wrapped around a wood block. It's fairly slow work, though just how slow depends on how smooth you want the finish. Start with medium-grit paper wrapped tightly around the block. Dip the block, complete with paper, in water and begin by removing the sharp corners along the edge with the block held at 45 degree angle to the edge. Keep the abrasive paper wet. Then sand all the edges flat, using long strokes with the block held flat on the edge.

Repeat the process with progressively finer-grit papers. Finally, polish the edge with a wet wooden block coated with pumice powder.

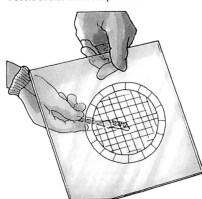

2 Tap center of scored area

Using a glass-cutting template

Semicircular windows and glazed openings above some exterior doors in older homes have segments of glass mounted between radiating bars.

Standard panes may be available for glazing some modern semicircular windows, but if you're doing restoration work on an old house, you may need to cut the glass yourself.

Each piece of glass is a segment of a larger circle. But usually you can't use a compass cutter for the job because the circle is bigger than the capacity of the cutter. You'll need to make cardboard templates to serve as guides for scoring the glass with an ordinary cutter.

Remove the broken glass and clean up the frame. Then tape a sheet of paper over the window and, using a crayon, take a rubbing of the opening (**1**). Remove the paper pattern and tape it to a sheet of thick cardboard. To provide clearance for fitting between glazing bars, and to allow for the thickness of the glass cutter, make the cardboard template about ⅛ inch smaller than the pattern on all sides.

Use double-sided tape to attach the template to the glass. Score around it with the glass cutter (**2**), running all cuts to the edge of the glass, and then snap the glass in the usual way.

1 Take rubbing of shape with crayon

2 Cut around template, using even pressure

Drilling a hole in glass

There are special spear-point drill bits for boring holes in glass. You will need to use a handheld bit brace or a power drill set to run at a low speed.

Mark the position for the hole, no closer than 1 inch to the edge of the glass, using a felt-tipped pen. When drilling mirrored glass, mark the back, coated surface.

Place the tip of the drill bit at the center of the mark and, with light pressure, twist it back and forth until it grinds a small recess and no longer skids over the glass. Use glazing putty to form a small ring around the work area, and fill the inner well with kerosene as a lubricant.

Run the drill at a steady speed and light pressure, since too much pressure may break the glass. When the tip of the bit emerges, turn over the glass and drill from the other side. Drilling straight through from one side risks chipping out the back surface.

Drilling a hole in glass
Use a brace with special glass-cutting bits.

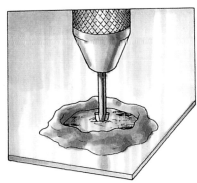

Drilling glass
Always run drill in lubricant to reduce friction

Circle compass cutter

Repairing a broken window

Glazing putty
Traditional linseed-oil putty is made for glazing wood frames. It dries slowly and is hard when set. All-purpose putty for wood and steel frames has similar properties. Both putties tend to crack if they are not protected with paint. Newer acrylic-based glazing putty is an all-purpose type that is easy to use and dries quickly, ready for painting.

Even when no glass is missing, a cracked windowpane is a safety hazard and a security risk, and no longer provides a weatherproof barrier to the elements. It should be replaced promptly.

Temporary repairs
For temporary protection from the weather, tape a sheet of polyethylene over the outside of the window frame until you can replace the glass. If the window is merely cracked, it can be repaired temporarily using a clear self-adhesive waterproof tape. Applied to the outside, this tape gives an almost invisible repair.

Safety with glass
Unless the window is at ground level, it's safer to remove the sash in order to replace broken glass. However, a fixed window has to be repaired on the spot, wherever it is. Large pieces of glass should be handled by two people. Don't work in windy weather, and wear gloves and protective goggles when removing glass.

Repairing glass in wood frames

In wood window frames, the glass is set into a rabbet cut in the frame, and then bedded in putty. Small wedge-shaped fasteners, known as points, are also used to hold the glass in place. Traditionally, linseed-oil putty was used for glazing wood frames. However, acrylic-based glazing putty, which is fast drying and durable, can be used instead. In some cases a wood glass bead is screwed to the rabbet to hold the pane.

Removing the glass
If the glass has shattered, leaving jagged pieces set in the putty, grip each piece separately and try to work it loose **(1)**. It's best to start working from the top of the frame. Old putty that is dry will usually break away easily. But if it won't, cut it out, using a utility knife or a glazier's knife

and a hammer **(2)**. Work along the rabbet to remove the putty and glass. Pull out the points with pliers **(3)**.

If the glass is merely cracked, run a glass cutter around the perimeter of the pane, about 1 inch from the frame, to score the glass **(4)**. Apply strips of tape across the cracks and scored lines, then tap each piece of glass until it breaks free and is held only by the tape **(5)**. Carefully remove individual pieces of glass, working from the center of the pane.

Once all the glass and points are removed, completely clean out the remnants of old putty from the rabbets. Seal the wood with primer. Measure the height and width of the opening to the inside of the rabbets, and have your new glass cut ⅛ inch smaller in height and width to provide some room for adjustment.

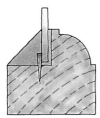
Glass held with putty

Glass held with bead
Some wood frames feature a wood beading, embedded in putty and screwed to the frame. Unscrew the beading and scrape out the putty. Install new glass in fresh putty and replace the beading.

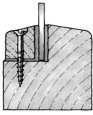
1 Work broken glass loose

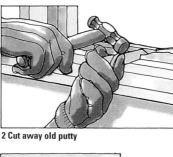
2 Cut away old putty

3 Pull out old points

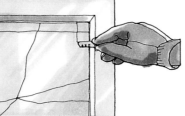
4 Score glass before removing cracked pane

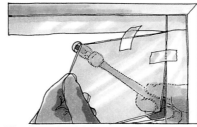
5 Tap glass to break it free

Purchase new glazing points and enough glazing compound for the frame. Your glass supplier should be able to advise you on this. But the rule of thumb is that 1 pound of putty will fill an average-sized rabbet about 13 feet in length.

Working with putty
Knead a palm-size ball of putty (glazing compound) to an even consistency in your hand. Putty is sticky and somewhat annoying to work with, but there's no better approach to making it workable than to knead it with your hands. You can soften putty that is too stiff by adding a little linseed oil.

Press a thin, continuous band of putty into the rabbet all around the frame. Smooth it out with a putty knife. Lower the new pane of glass into the bottom rabbet, then press the rest of the pane into place. Apply pressure close to the edges only, squeezing the putty to leave a continuous seal around the whole pane. Secure the glass by installing glazier's points every 8 inches around the pane. Make sure they lay flat with the surface of the glass **(1)**. Trim the surplus putty from the back of the glass with a putty knife.

Apply more putty to each rabbet on the outside of the glass. Using a putty knife **(2)**, work the putty to a smooth finish at a 45 degree angle. Make neat miters at the corners. Let the putty set for about three weeks, then paint the frame. The paint should lap the glass slightly to form a weather seal.

1 Install new points   **2 Smooth putty**

Acrylic glazing putty
Acrylic glazing putty is packaged in a cartridge and applied with a caulking gun. Run a bead of putty into the rabbet. Bed the glass in place and secure it with glazing points. Then apply a continuous bead of putty all around the frame and smooth it to a 45-degree angle with a putty knife. Allow at least 4 hours for it to cure, then trim off any excess material and clean the glass with water.

Leaded glass windows

Leaded-glass windows are glazed with small pieces of glass joined by strips of lead, known as cames. In many windows, the cames form a lattice that holds rectangular or diamond-shaped panes of clear glass. But in other windows, particularly stained-glass units, the structure is free-form and incorporates colored and textured glass.

Supporting leaded panes

Leaded panes are relatively weak and can sag with age. If you have an old window that is bowing, you can support it with a ¼-inch steel rod.

Drill a ¼-inch hole on each side of the window frame, placing the holes about halfway up the sides, in line with a horizontal piece of came if possible. Drill one hole twice as deep as the other. Flatten the window carefully with the palm of a gloved hand, or use a board to spread the load. Solder a few short lengths of copper wire to the back of the came in line with the planned location of the support rod.

The length of the rod should equal the distance across the inside of the window frame, plus twice the depth of the shallow hole drilled in the frame. Locate the rod in the holes, inserting it in the deeper hole first.

Twist the soldered wires around the rod so that the window is tied to it. Finish the rod with black paint and, if necessary, form a waterproof seal on both sides of the window by pushing glazing compound into the cames.

Twisted-wire tie

Support sagging leaded glass with a metal rod.

Replacing broken glass in leaded windows

It is always easier to replace a piece of glass with the window out of its frame. But because leaded windows are fragile, it's sometimes safer to carry out the repair with the window still in place. If the complete unit does have to be removed, carefully chip out the glazing putty and support the whole panel against a board as it is taken out.

Cut the cames around the broken pane at each joint, using a sharp knife **(1)**. If possible, make the cuts on the inside of the window.

With a putty knife, lift the edges of the cames and pry up the lead until it is at right angles to the surface of the glass **(2)**. Lift or tap out the broken pieces and scrape away any old putty. If you are working with the leaded panel in place, support it from behind with your gloved hand or with a board attached to the back side of the window frame.

Make a paper template of the shape and size of the replacement glass you need. Then lay this template on the new glass and trace around it. Make the cuts with a glass cutter and a straightedge, keeping the cut just to the inside of the line **(3)**. Try the glass for fit and, if necessary, sand down problem spots with wet-and-dry paper.

Mix some black polish (available from glass suppliers) into a ball of ordinary glazing putty and apply a thin bead to the open cames. Then bed the glass into the cames with even pressure. Fold over the edges of the cames to secure the glass. Rub the cames smooth with a piece of wood.

Thoroughly clean the cut joints in the cames with fine steel wool and resolder them **(4)**, using an electric soldering iron and resin-core solder.

Use your thumbs to press colored putty under the edges of the cames on the inside of the window. Run a pointed dowel against the cames to remove excess putty. Remove any smeared putty from the glass with a rag dampened with mineral spirits.

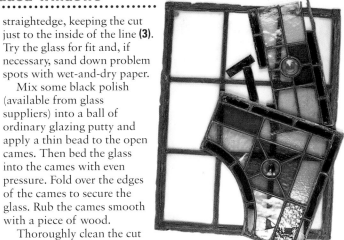

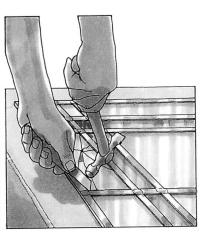

1 Cut cames with sharp knife

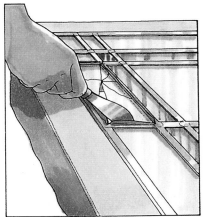

2 Pry lead up with putty knife

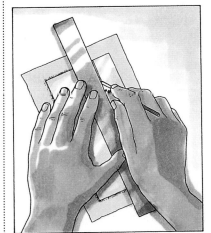

3 Cut glass following paper rubbing

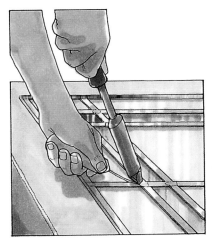

4 Resolder joint after installing glass

Came styles

Round came

Flat came

Beaded came

Double-glazed units

Installing stepped glazing

Some double-glazed window units are designed with a step built into the edge. This provides a positive surface for the unit to bear against. These panes are installed much like regular panels, but a resilient packing piece is added to support the extra weight.

Stepped units
Follow this sequence when installing double-glazed, stepped units.
1 Set the resilient packing in glazing compound.
2 Install the double-glazed unit and secure with glazing points.
3 Fill the rabbet with glazing putty.

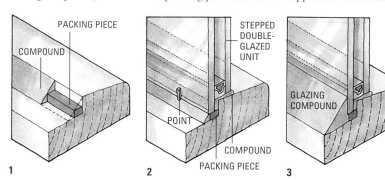

Installing square-edged units

Square-edged units are sealed with butyl glazing compound and held in place with beading. For the conventional method shown here, you will need glazing compound, glazing blocks, and beading nails (see below).

Apply two coats of primer or clear sealer to the rabbets in the frame and let them dry. Lay a bed of the nonsetting butyl glazing compound in the rabbets. To prevent the glass from moving in the compound, place packing blocks on the bottom rabbet and place the spacer blocks against the back of the rabbet. Set the spacers about 2 inches from the corners and about 12 inches apart. Locate the spacers directly behind the points where the beading will be screwed in place.

Set the double-glazed unit into the rabbet and press it firmly in place. Apply an outer layer of compound and place another set of spacers against the glass, positioned to match the spacers installed behind the glass.

Press each bead into the compound and against the spacers. Screw the beading strips in place with brass or galvanized screws. Remove the compound that squeezed out and clean the glass. Prime and paint as needed.

Using beading.
Set square-edged units in butyl compound.
1 Set the packing and spacers in compound.
2 Install the unit, apply more compound, and place spacers behind the beading screw locations.
3 Press the beading against the spacers and attach with screws.

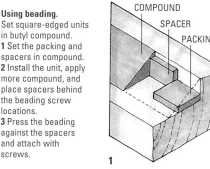

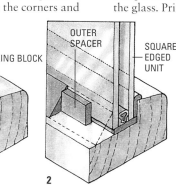

Glazing metal-framed windows

Steel window frames are made with galvanized sections that form a rabbet for the glass. This type of window is glazed in much the same way as a wood-framed window, using general-purpose glazing compound or acrylic glazing putty. The glass is secured in the frame with spring clips (see right), which are set in holes in the frame and covered with putty. To replace the glass in a metal frame, follow the sequence described for wood frames but use clips instead of points. Before installing the glass, remove any rust and apply a high-quality metal primer.

Modern aluminum and plastic double-glazed frames use a dry glazing system that features synthetic rubber gaskets. These are factory installed and should be maintenance free. If you break a pane in a window, consult the manufacturer for the proper way to make the repair.

The sashes of wood casement windows tend to swell in wet weather, causing them to stick in the frame. Once they have a chance to dry out, they should work properly and you should take the time to prime and paint them. This will reduce or totally eliminate the swelling because the water won't reach the wood.

Curing sticking windows

If you have a casement window that sticks persistently in all weather, it may be due to a thick buildup of paint. To repair this condition, strip the old paint from the edges of the sash and the rabbets in the frame. Then prime and paint these surfaces.

If a window has been painted shut, free it by working a utility-knife blade between the sash and the frame. Sand the edges smooth until the sash closes properly, remove any dust, then prime and paint the sanded edges. The same repair advice pertains to all window sashes that have been painted shut.

Curing rattling windows

The rattling of a casement window is usually caused by a poorly installed lever lock. If the lever handle is worn, you can either replace it with a new one or adjust the position of the old one so it works better.

Old double-hung wood windows are notorious for rattling. The most common cause is a sash (usually the bottom one) that fits too loosely in its tracks. To repair it, remove and replace the stop, or glue a thin strip to the side of the stop, to create a narrower track. Rub candle wax on both sliding surfaces if the repair is a little too tight.

If the top sash is rattling, shim it out in a similar way and adjust the position of the lock to pull the sashes together.

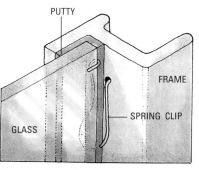

Use spring clips to hold glass

Repairing rotten frames

Old wood windows have always deteriorated to some extent. But regular maintenance and prompt repairs can restore them so they work properly for many years to come. New frames and those that have been stripped of their old finish should be treated with a wood preservative before you paint them.

Regular maintenance

The bottom rail of a wood sash is particularly vulnerable to rot, especially if it is left unpainted. Rainwater seeps in behind old glazing putty, and moisture is gradually absorbed through cracked or flaking paint. Carry out an annual check and deal with any faults. Cut out old putty that has shrunk away from the glass and replace it. Remove flaking paint, repair any cracks in the wood with wood filler, prime, and repaint. Don't forget to paint the bottom edge of the sash.

Replacing a sash rail

Where the rot is so severe that the sash rail is beyond repair, cut it out and replace it. This should be done before the rot spreads to the stiles, otherwise you will eventually have to replace the whole sash frame. Start by removing the sash from the window frame.

It is possible to make the repair without removing the glass, though it is safer to remove it if the window is large. For either approach, you'll need to cut away the putty from the damaged rail.

Usually, the bottom rail is tenoned into the stiles (1). To remove the rail, saw down the joint shoulder lines from both sides of the sash (2).

Make a new sash rail and cut it to length so a full-width tenon is at each end. Position the tenons to line up with the mortises in the stiles. Cut the shoulders of the tenons to match the rabbeted sections of the stiles (3). If there is a decorative molding on the stile, cut it away to leave a flat shoulder (4). Cut slots in the ends of the stiles to receive the new tenons.

Glue the new rail securely into place with a waterproof glue and reinforce the two joints with pairs of ¼-inch hardwood dowels. Drill the stopped holes for the dowels from the inside of the frame so they won't break through the outer surface. Stagger the dowels for a stronger joint.

When the adhesive is dry, plane and sand the surface as needed and remove all the dust. Treat the new wood with a clear preservative. Fill the rail rabbet with glazing compound, then prime and paint as soon as the putty is dry.

The frames of some fixed windows are made like sashes but are screwed permanently to the jamb. After the glass has been removed and the frame unscrewed, this type of fixed window can be repaired in the same way as the casement of sash windows (see below left). If this proves too difficult, you will have to carry out the repair in place.

First remove the putty and the glass, then saw through the rail at each end, close to the stile. Use a chisel to remove what remains of the rail and to carve the tenons out of the stiles. Cut a new length of rail to fit between the stiles, and cut slots at both ends of the rail to receive the loose tenons (1). Cut these slots so that they line up with the stile mortises, and make each slot twice as long as the depth of the mortise. Cut two loose tenons to fit the slots, and two packing blocks to force the loose tenons into place. These blocks should have one sloping edge (2).

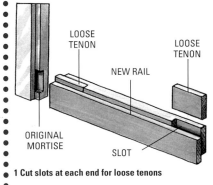

LOOSE TENON

LOOSE TENON

NEW RAIL

ORIGINAL MORTISE

SLOT

1 Cut slots at each end for loose tenons

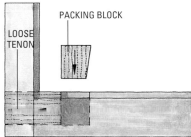

PACKING BLOCK

LOOSE TENON

2 Fitting the tenons
Insert the loose tenons, push them sideways into the mortises, and wedge with packing blocks.

Reassembling the frame

Apply an exterior waterproof glue to all of the joining surfaces. Then place the rail between the stiles, insert the loose tenons, and push them sideways into the mortises. Drive the packing blocks behind the tenons to lock them in place. When the adhesive has set, trim the packing blocks flush with the rabbet in the rail. Then treat the new wood with preservative, replace the glass, and add new glazing compound. Repaint once the putty is dry.

Removing glass.
Removing glass from a window frame in one piece is not easy—so be prepared for it to break. As a precaution, apply adhesive tape across the glass to bind any broken pieces together. Chisel away the putty to leave a clean rabbet, then pull out the points. Steady the glass and lift it out when it's free.

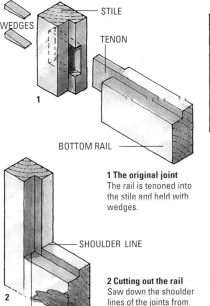

WEDGES

STILE

TENON

1

BOTTOM RAIL

1 The original joint
The rail is tenoned into the stile and held with wedges.

2

SHOULDER LINE

SHOULDER LINE

2 Cutting out the rail
Saw down the shoulder lines of the joints from both sides of the sash.

STILE RABBET

DOWELS

MITER

FLAT SHOULDER

SLOT

SLOT

3

TENON

SHOULDERS

3 Cutting the joint
Cut tenons at each end of the rail, making sure that the shoulders of the joint match the shape of the stile.

MITER

4

4 Molded frames
Cut away the molding on the stile to receive the square shoulder of the rail. Make the cut in the shape of a miter.

Repairing rotten sills

The sill is a fundamental part of a window frame, and because of its size and location, suffers from more exposure to the elements. This exposure can lead to rot. Repairing a sill usually is not a difficult job, but replacing one can be.

A window frame is constructed in much the same way as a doorframe. The head and side jambs are the same width, but the sill is wider and sloped to the outside to shed water. If you just need to repair chips, cracks, and worn depressions, you can work on the sill without removing any window parts. Just choose a day or two when fair weather is forecast. But if you have to replace a wood or stone sill, it's better to remove the window first. If this is impractical, you can replace the sill in place; it's just more difficult.

Replacing a wood sill for a sash window

Ideally, to replace a rotted windowsill you should remove the entire window, carefully disassemble the old sill from the jamb sides, use it as a template, then cut and install a new sill and replace the window. However, sills can be replaced without removing the window, provided you work patiently and have some basic woodworking skills.

Begin by carefully splitting out the old sill. Cut through it crosswise in two places with a saw to remove the middle portion, then gently pry the end

sections away from the jambs. Hacksaw any nails holding the sill to the rest of the frame.

Use a piece of cardboard to make a template for a new sill, shaped to fit between the jambs and beneath the exterior trim. Cut a 10-degree bevel along the upper outside edge of the sill, extending to the inside edge of the sash. Fill the area beneath the sill with insulation, install the sill with 16d finishing nails, then thoroughly fill all the seams with silicone caulk.

Wood sill on sash window in wood-frame wall

Repairing a stone subsill

The traditional stone sills featured in older houses may become eroded by the weather if they are not protected with paint. They may also suffer cracking due to subsidence in some part of the wall.

Repair any cracked and eroded surfaces with a quick-setting waterproof cement. To do this, clean any dust or debris from the cracks. Then dampen the stone with clean water and work the cement well into the cracks. Smooth the surface of the patch flush with the surface of the sill.

Depressions caused by erosion

should be undercut to provide the cement with a good hold. A thin layer of cement simply applied to a shallow depression in the surface will not last. Use a cold chisel to cut away the surface of the sill at least 1 inch below the finished level and remove all traces of dust.

Make a wooden form to the shape of the sill and temporarily nail it to the wall. Dampen the stone, pour in the cement until it's level with the top of the form, then smooth it with a trowel. Allow the patch to cure for a couple of days before removing the form.

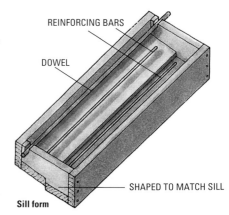

Encase sill in wood form to make repair

Casting a new subsill

Cut out the remains of the old stone sill with a hammer and cold chisel. Make a wood form shaped exactly like the old sill. The form must be made upside down, its open top representing the underside of the sill.

Fill two-thirds of the mold with fine aggregate concrete, tamped down well. Then add two lengths of steel reinforcing bar (rebar), in the middle of the concrete, and fill the remainder of the form. Set a piece of ⅜ inch wood

dowel into notches previously cut in the ends of the mold. This is to form a drip groove in the underside of the sill.

Cover the concrete with polyethylene sheeting or dampen it regularly for two or three days to prevent rapid drying. When the concrete is set (allow about seven days), remove it from the form and clean up any rough edges with a cold chisel or handheld power grinder. Reinstall the sill in a bed of mortar, and caulk all joints with silicone caulk.

Decaying windowsills
Repair deteriorating sills before serious decay sets in.

REINFORCING BARS

DOWEL

SHAPED TO MATCH SILL

Sill form

Replacing broken sash cords

The cords that support sashes in most older windows wear out over time and must be replaced for the window to operate properly. When replacing these cords, always do both sides of the window, even if only one cord is broken. The cords are usually sold by the foot. Each sash requires two lengths about three-quarters the height of the window. Narrow sash chain is also available, and most people consider it more durable than cord.

Removing the sashes

Lower the sashes and cut through the cords with a utility knife to release the weights. Hold on to the cords and lower the weights as far as possible before letting them drop. Using a screwdriver, pry off the side access panels from the sash tracks so the weight pockets will be exposed.

Lean the inner sash forward and mark the ends of the cord grooves on the face of the sash stiles (**1**, see below). Reposition the sash and transfer the marks onto the window jambs. The sash can now be pulled clear of the frame.

Carefully pry out the two parting stops from their grooves in the jambs. You can use a flat-blade screwdriver or a chisel to do this job. Start at one end, prying gradually as you go. If a stop won't budge, grip it with pliers and pull as you pry with the screwdriver.

Once the stops are out, and you've marked the end-cord grooves as before, remove the top sash and place it safely aside. Then remove the window weights from the pockets by pulling them through the access holes. Cut the old cord from the weights and sashes and clean up the weights so they're ready for the new sash cords.

Reinstalling the sashes

The top sash is installed first, but not before all of the sash cords and weights are in place. Clean away any buildup of paint from the pulleys. Tie a length of fine string to one end of the sash cord. Weight the other end of the string with small nuts or a piece of chain. Thread the weight over a pulley (**2**) and pull the string through the pocket opening until the cord is pulled through. Attach the end of the cord to a weight with a special knot (see below left).

Use the sash marks to measure the length of cord required. Pull on the cord to hoist the weight up to the pulley. Then let it drop back about 4 inches. Hold it temporarily in this position with a nail driven into the window jamb just below the pulley.

Cut the cord even with the mark on the pulley jamb (**3**). Repeat this procedure for the cord on the other side of the upper sash and do the same for the bottom sash.

Lift the top sash into its track and remove the nail that holds one of the sash cords. Lean the sash forward, push the cord into its groove in the sash stile, and nail it in place using three or four 1-inch nails. Nail only the bottom 6 inches, not all the way up (**4**).

Do the same thing for the other sash cord, then lift the sash to check that the weights work properly and do not touch the bottom. Replace the pocket-access door and the parting stop. Then install the bottom sash and attach it to the cords the same way.

The components of a double-hung window

1 Pulleys
2 Bottom sash
3 Exterior trim
4 Top sash
5 Parting stop
6 Bottom sash weight
7 Pocket
8 Top sash weight

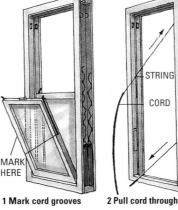

SASH WEIGHT

KNOT

CORD

Sash weight knot

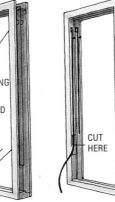

MARK HERE

1 Mark cord grooves

STRING

CORD

2 Pull cord through

CUT HERE

3 Cut cords at mark

NAIL HERE

4 Nail cord to sash

Spiral balances

Instead of cords and counterweights, modern sash windows use spiral balances that are mounted on the inside of the window jambs, eliminating the need for traditional weight boxes. The balances are made to match the size and weight of individual glazed sashes and can be ordered from the window manufacturers at your local lumberyard or home center.

Spiral balance components
Each balance consists of a torsion spring and a spiral rod housed in a tube. The top end is fixed to the jamb and the inner spiral is attached to the bottom of the sash. The complete unit is housed in a sash or jamb groove.

TUBE

SPIRAL

PLATE

Spiral balance unit

Install top limit stop

Install bottom stop

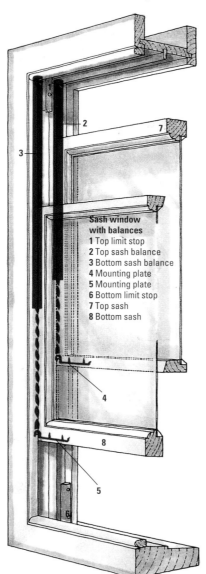

Sash window with balances
1 Top limit stop
2 Top sash balance
3 Bottom sash balance
4 Mounting plate
5 Mounting plate
6 Bottom limit stop
7 Top sash
8 Bottom sash

Installing the balances

One of the great things about spiral balances is that you can use them to replace window weights in older sash windows. To do this, first remove the sashes and weigh them on your bathroom scale. Place your order, giving the weight of each sash, its height and width, and the overall inside height of the window frame. Reinstall the sashes until the balances arrive, then take the sashes out again and remove the pulleys.

Plug the holes in the sashes with wood filler. Cut grooves, as specified by the manufacturer, in the stiles of each sash to take the balances (**1**). Cut a mortise at each end of the bottom edges of the stiles to receive the spiral-rod mounting plates. Install the plates with screws (**2**).

Push the top sash in place, resting it on the sill. Take the top pair of balances, which are shorter than those for the bottom sash, and install each in its groove (**3**). Attach the top ends of the balance tubes to the frame jambs (**4**), pushing the ends tight against the top jamb.

Lift the sash to its full height and prop it with a scrap of wood. Hook the wire "key," provided with the balances, into the hole in the end of each spiral rod. Adjust the tension on the spiral spring according to the manufacturer's instructions (**5**). Attach the end of each rod to its mounting plate and test the balance of the sash. If it drops, add another turn on the springs until it is just held in position. Take care not to overwind the balances.

Install the bottom sash and balances in the same way. Once you're satisfied with the operation of both sashes, install the stops that limit the full travel of the sashes in their respective tracks (see far left).

RENOVATING SPIRAL BALANCES

In time, the springs of spiral balances may weaken. Retension them by unhooking the spiral rods from the mounting plates, then turning the rods counterclockwise once or twice.

The mechanism can be serviced by releasing the tension and unwinding the rods from the tubes. Wipe them clean and apply a coat of light oil, then rewind the rods back into the tubes and tension them as described above.

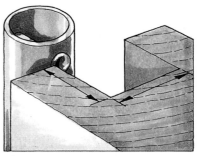

1 Cut groove in sash stiles

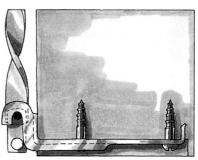

2 Secure mounting plate with screws

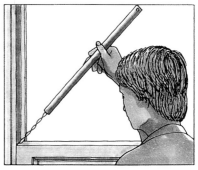

3 Install sash and insert tube in its groove

4 Nail top end of tube to jamb

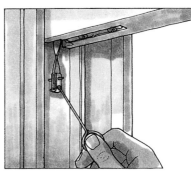

5 Tension springs with the provided key

Replacing windows

Lumberyards and home centers offer a wide range of replacement windows in wood, vinyl, and aluminum. Some typical examples are shown below. Unfortunately, the exact window size you need may not be available. You have two options: Order custom-made windows to fit your openings or modify your rough openings to fit a standard replacement-window size.

Window buying

Most people want to replace their windows either because they aren't working well mechanically, or because they allow too much heat to escape in the winter.

Replacing the windows in your house is an expensive job, so it's tempting to use low-cost units. Unfortunately, these windows don't always solve the problems you're having. It's almost always a better idea to install higher-quality windows. The long-term performance and energy savings are worth the extra cost.

The style of the windows is an important element in the appearance of any house. If you are thinking of replacing the windows in an older house you might find it better, and not necessarily more expensive, to have new windows custom made to fit your openings.

Planning and permits

Window replacement is a job that doesn't usually require a building permit, unless you live in a historic district that regulates what you can do to the exterior of your house. But if you plan to alter your windows significantly—for example, by permanently removing one or by adding a new window in a new place—you should call your local building department to see if you need a permit.

All codes have certain minimum requirements, especially for windows on second and third floors. Code authorities want to make sure that at least some windows are big enough for occupants to get out in case of fire. Some localities are also interested in the R-value of the window glazing, in an effort to improve the energy efficiency of the housing stock.

Buying replacement windows

As mentioned earlier, replacing windows can be a problem if your window openings do not match the standard sizes available from most window manufacturers. You'll either have to alter your openings to fit standard sizes (which can be nearly as expensive as buying the new windows), or you can buy custom-made windows that will fit your openings.

Usually the term custom made is used for one-of-a-kind items that tend to be very expensive. But several large manufacturers will make just about any size window for a relatively small additional charge. Unfortunately, the manufacturers who offer this service are making windows that are expensive in the first place.

Most contractors who install replacement windows supply the new windows and dispose of the old ones after removal. This is the best way to get the job done, but you should carefully compare contractors and window brands before making your choice.

Replacing casements

Measure the width and height of the window opening. Windows in brick walls will need a wood subframe. If the existing one is in good condition, take your measurements from the inside of this frame. Otherwise, take them from the brick and plan on replacing the frame before installing the new window. Order the replacement window accordingly.

1 Pry out pieces of old frame

Remove the old window by first taking out the sashes. Remove any exposed hardware that may be holding the window frame in the opening. Pry out the frame and cut through any fasteners with a hacksaw or a reciprocating saw. Usually the frame can be pried or driven out of the opening in one piece. But if it's wedged tight for some reason, saw through it in several places and pry the pieces out with a crowbar **(1)**. Clean up the opening.

2 Install new window   **3 Drill screw holes**

Remove all the protective packaging from the window and slide it into the opening. Check it for level and plumb **(2)** and shim the jambs to keep the unit from moving. Drill screw holes through the jambs into the jack studs or the subframe behind the window jambs **(3)**. Check for level and plumb again, then drive the screws.

Insulate around the window frame, then install any necessary exterior trim and the interior casings. Set all nailheads and cover them with wood filler or caulk. Prime and paint.

Replacing windows

Bay windows

A bay window is an assembly of smaller windows joined together to yield a big window that projects out from the house wall. The side windows are usually set at one of three angles: 90, 60, or 45 degrees. Curved bays are also available.

The perimeter of a bay window is supported either with brackets of different types or with a shout wall that is part of the wall framing. The bay is protected by a small roof that is attached to the house wall.

Bay windows in brick houses can break away from the main wall because of foundation subsidence. You should hire a contractor for this type of problem. Lesser damage from slight foundation movements can be repaired once the ground has stabilized. Repoint the mortar joints and apply silicone caulk to gaps around the window frame.

Replacement bays

Like other windows, old bay windows can be replaced with new ones. But your chances of finding a new bay in just the right size are slight. Usually the opening has to be adjusted, which for bays is complicated by the presence of the roof. Choosing a custom-made bay is probably your best strategy. It may be more expensive, but using something the right size should keep the installation costs to a minimum.

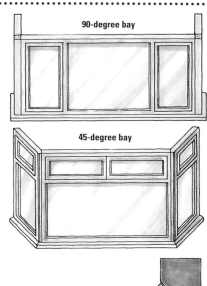

90-degree bay

45-degree bay

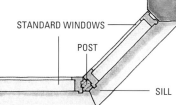

STANDARD WINDOWS

POST

SILL

Standard windows joined to make a bay window

Modern angled bay with decorative lead flashing

Bow windows

These are windows constructed on a shallow curve, and (like bay windows) they normally project from a flat wall. Complete bow windows are available from window manufacturers, ready for installation. You can use a bow window to replace any type of window, as long as the rough opening is big enough to fit the new window.

To install a bow window, modify the rough opening as necessary. Then center the bow in the opening, shim it plumb and level, then nail it into place. Install braces beneath the window to support it. And construct a shallow roof over the top to shed rain and snow. Add flashing and new trim where necessary, then caulk all the joints with silicone caulk. Add insulation between the window and the rough opening, then install the interior trim.

First-floor bow window

Window replacement in a brick wall isn't much more difficult than replacing a window in a wood-frame wall. The job is well within the ability of most do-it-yourselfers.

Remove the sashes, then take out the old window frame from inside the room. Pry off the casing, then the window jamb. Cut away the drywall or plaster if necessary. Remove any obvious fasteners holding the frame to the brick, then strike the outside edge of the sill with a heavy hammer and a wood block. When the window frame is free, lift it out of the opening **(1)** and remove any debris left behind.

Lift the new window into the opening and adjust it from front to back so that both side jambs are the same distance from the outside of the brick wall. Check the window frame for level and plumb and wedge the corners of the frame at the top and the sill. If there's space left at the sides between the window and the brick wall, fill the space with bricks and mortar **(2)**. To solidly anchor the window, you can screw metal brackets to the sides of the window frame and set these brackets in mortar joints in the brick wall.

When the mortar is set, replaster the inner wall and replace the casing. Finish up by applying silicone caulk to the joints between the outside bricks and the window frame to keep the weather out.

1 Lift out old frame   **2 Fill gaps with brick**

Roof windows

Double-glazed roof windows are becoming increasingly popular for replacing old skylights, especially on attic-conversion jobs. The windows usually come with complete flashing kits that are designed to fit a wide range of different roof pitches.

Roof windows that have center-pivoting sashes can be used on just about all roofs. Because the sash in these windows operates, the window can provide ventilation as well as lots of light. They are relatively easy to install using only common remodeling tools. And most of the work is done from inside the house. Once they are installed, the glass can be cleaned comfortably from the inside. Accessories like blinds and remote-opening devices are also available. Most manufacturers also give you glazing options to reduce heat loss and sun glare.

Roof windows used in a traditional building

Internal blinds are available

Choosing the size

The manufacturers of roof windows offer a wide range of standard sizes. Apart from cost considerations, the overall size of the window should be based on the amount of daylight you want in the room.

The installed height of the window is also important. It should be determined by the pitch of the roof and by how the window is going to be used. Manufacturers produce charts that give the recommended dimensions depending on the roof pitch. Ideally, if the window is to provide a good view, the bottom rails should not obstruct that view at normal seating height. And the top of the window shouldn't cut across the line of sight of someone who is standing.

Generally, this means that the shallower the pitch of the roof, the taller the window needs to be. The top of the window should remain within comfortable reach for accessibility.

Smaller window units can be arranged side by side or one above the other to create a larger window. When deciding on a design, bear in mind how it will look on the outside of the house, not just on the inside.

Though you probably won't need permission to install the window if you're replacing an old unit, code restrictions often apply to any job that requires cutting a new hole through the roof. Check with your building department before beginning work.

The manufacturers of roof windows supply instructions for all types of roofs. Below is a summary of how to install a roof window in an ordinary asphalt shingle roof.

Installing a roof window

Start by stripping off the roof-covering materials over the area to be occupied by the window. The final placing of the frame will be determined by the position of the rafters and the roofing. Start by setting the bottom of the window frame at the specified distance above the nearest full course of shingles and try to position it so you'll have half or whole shingles at the sides.

Brace the rafters from inside by installing posts beneath them. Then cut through the roof sheathing and rafters to make the opening, following the dimensions given by the manufacturer. Cut and nail headers and trimmers to the opening (see below) to achieve the correct height and width.

With the glazed sash removed, screw the window frame in place with the brackets provided. Make sure the top of the frame is level, and check that the frame is square by measuring across its diagonals; they should be equal.

Complete the outside work by installing the flashing and new shingles, working up from the bottom of the frame. Replace the sash.

Install insulation between the window frame and the rough opening and replace the insulation in other accessible areas if it was damaged during construction. Install drywall panels to close up the opening around the window and finish all the drywall joints with compound and tape. Add trim to the inside of the window jambs and prime and paint the ceiling.

Window height
The height should enable someone sitting or standing to see out of the window with ease.

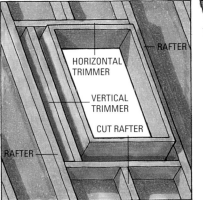

Cut opening and fit trimmers

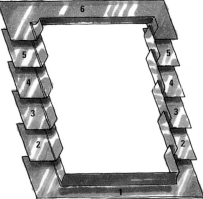

Flashing kit showing order of assembly

Installing curtain rails and rods

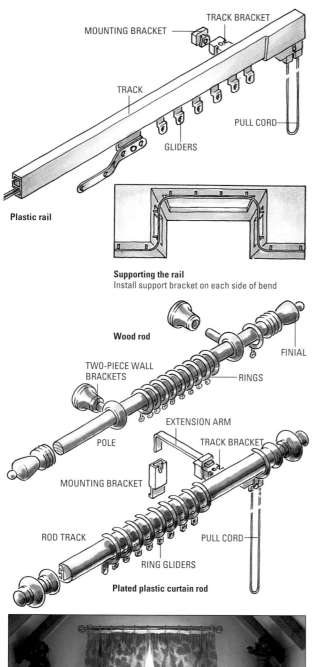

Plastic rail

Supporting the rail
Install support bracket on each side of bend

Wood rod

TWO-PIECE WALL
BRACKETS

Plated plastic curtain rod

Window treatments play an important part in interior design. Although the size and shape of the window itself cannot be altered easily, you can visually modify the proportions of a window with curtains or blinds.

Curtain rails

As well as providing privacy, curtains help insulate the room from the sun, cold, drafts, and noise. They are sold in a variety of fabrics and sizes, or you can make your own. Both the choice of material and the method used for hanging the curtains make an impact.

Modern curtain rods are made from plastic, aluminum, or painted steel. They are available in various styles and lengths and come complete with brackets and rings or hooks. Some are supplied with cords to make drawing the curtains easier and to minimize stains that result from handling.

Although typically used in straight lengths, most rods can be bent to fit a bay window. Rails vary in rigidity, which dictates the minimum radius to which they can be bent.

Curtain rods

Traditional curtain rods are a popular alternative to modern track systems. Made from metal, plastic, or wood, curtain rods come in a range of plated, painted, or polished finishes. Traditional rods are supported on decoratively shaped brackets and are fitted with end-stop finials and large curtain rings. Some modern versions conceal corded tracks, providing the convenience of up-to-date mechanisms while retaining a traditional look.

A pair of wall brackets are all that's normally required to support curtain rods. But a central bracket may be required to support heavy fabrics. Like the rods, the support brackets are available in many different designs and finishes.

Attaching to the ceiling

Joists that run at right angles to the wall allow you to place curtain track rails at any convenient distance from the wall (**1**). Drill pilot holes into the joists and screw the brackets in place.

Joists that run parallel to the wall need blocking nailed between them for the tracks (**2**). Toenail the blocking flush with the ceiling.

If the required track position is close to a joist, nail a 2 x 2 cleat to the face of the joist (**3**).

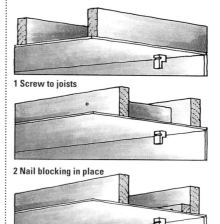

1 Screw to joists

2 Nail blocking in place

3 Nail a cleat in place

Attaching to the wall

Draw a guideline at a suitable height above the window. Mark the positions for the brackets along this line. If you have a wood-frame wall, the brackets must be screwed into framing members behind the wall finish. If you're working on a masonry wall, drill holes for expanding anchors and slide the anchors into place. Then attach the brackets with screws driven into the anchors.

In many cases, you'll be able to mount the brackets on the head casing at the top of the window, especially if you're installing lightweight curtains.

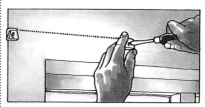

Screw curtain-track brackets to wall

Hanging shades and blinds

Blinds provide a simple, attractive, and sophisticated way to screen windows. Most blinds are sold in standard sizes that you can cut easily to the exact length you need. You can also order blinds made to size in many different materials and colors and with different opening and closing mechanisms.

Roller shades

Low-cost roller shades can be bought in a range of fabric designs and colors in either made-to-order or kit form. A typical kit consists of a roller with two end caps (one of which includes a pull-cord mechanism), two support brackets, a thin piece of wood, and a pull cord. You can buy the fabric separately and cut it to width and length. The rollers come in several lengths. Unless you can find a roller that fits your window exactly, get the next largest size and cut it to fit.

Roller shade and Venetian blinds

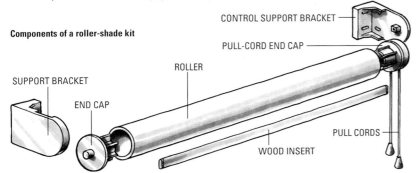

Components of a roller-shade kit

CONTROL SUPPORT BRACKET

PULL-CORD END CAP

ROLLER

SUPPORT BRACKET

END CAP

PULL CORDS

WOOD INSERT

Cutting to size
A shade can be hung within the window recess or across the front of it. When installing the roller inside, place the brackets in the top corners of the frame. Make sure that the pull-cord control bracket is at the end where you want to operate the shade. Measure and cut the roller to fit between the brackets.

If you are installing the roller outside the window recess, you will need to cut the roller about 4 inches longer than the width of the opening. Install the brackets on both sides of the window, using the roller as a guide.

Fitting the fabric
Ideally the fabric should be nonfraying to avoid having to sew side hems. Cut the width ⅛ inch less than the length of the roller. The fabric length should match the height of the window, plus 8 inches. Make a ¼-inch bottom hem,

then turn it up to form a sleeve for the wood insert. Attach the other end of the fabric to the roller with glue or tape. Make sure the fabric is installed squarely on the roller or the shade won't roll up properly.

Installing the shade
With the fabric rolled on the roller, push the square hole of the pull-cord end cap into the control bracket, with the cords hanging down. Clip the other end into the opposite bracket. Identify the cord that lowers the shade, attach a knob on the end of it, then pull down the cord until it's level with the sill.

Remove the shade and unwind the fabric till it reaches the sill. Reinstall the blind and raise it to the open position, using the other cord, then attach its knob. Check that the blind operates smoothly and, if necessary, adjust the length of the cords.

Venetian blinds

Horizontal blinds, or Venetian blinds, as they are often called, are popular and stylish window treatments. They come in a range of standard sizes and can be made to order. They are usually fabricated of metal or plastic and are available in many different colors and finishes. A wide variety of wood-slat blinds is also available.

Installing a Venetian blind
If the blind is to be fitted into a window recess, measure the width at the top and bottom of the opening. If the dimensions differ, use the smaller one. Allow a clearance of about ⅛ inch at both ends. Screw the brackets in place so that the blind, when hanging, will clear any handles or catches. Attach the end brackets about 3 inches in from the ends of the head rail.

Mount the head rail in the brackets. Some are simply clamped, while others are locked in place by a swivel catch (**1**). Raise and lower the blind to check that the mechanism is working freely. To lower the blind, pull the cord across the front of the blind to release the lock mechanism, then let it slide through your hand. Tilt the slats by rotating the control wand.

1 Install head rail on bracket.

Installing at an angle
Venetian blinds can be used on a sloping window. They are supplied with cords that prevent the blind from sagging. When threaded through the slat holes, both cords are attached to the head rail and are held taut by mounting brackets at the bottom (**2**).

2 Attach bottom of blind cords to mounting bracket.

Vertical blinds

Like horizontal blinds, vertical blinds suit simple modern interiors and work well with large glass openings like patio doors. The blinds hang from a track that is mounted to the ceiling or to the wall above the window or door. The vertical "vanes" that clip into hooks on the track are linked together by short chains at the bottom. The vanes are weighted so that they hang straight.

Installing the track
Mark a guideline on the wall or ceiling. Allow sufficient clearance for the rotating vanes to clear obstacles such as door handles. Screw the mounting brackets in place and clip the track into them. Hang the preassembled vanes on the track hooks. Make sure that the hooks are facing the same way and that you are attaching the vanes with their seams all in the same direction.

Interior shutters

Louvered wooden shutters provide an attractive and practical alternative to fabric curtains or blinds, adding a touch of style to just about any interior. Made from a variety of solid woods, they can be varnished to retain their natural appearance or stained or painted to complement any scheme.

Adjustable-louver shutters

Adjustable-louver shutters are usually sold in standard sizes that are cut to fit specific windows. Made-to-order versions are available, though they're usually quite expensive. The adjustable slats are connected by a slim, vertical wood bar that enables the entire bank of louvers to be set at the same angle. This action controls the amount of natural light passing through the window. When shutters are fully closed, they provide complete privacy.

Shutter combinations

The arrangement of shutters is largely determined by the size of the window opening. A single row of shutters (between two and four panels of uniform width) is a common combination. Two pairs of hinged panels, forming bifold shutters, are perhaps the most popular (**1**). Where the shutters exceed about 44 inches in height, they are made with a cross rail in the middle to stiffen the frame.

Two or three shorter rows can be stacked one above the other in order to cover tall windows (**2**). With this arrangement, you can keep one or more rows closed while folding back the remaining row to illuminate the room. When planning for stacked shutters, try to arrange the horizontal divisions between the shutters to align with the cross rails of the window frame. This often looks the best. Or, if you prefer, keep all the panels the same size.

A single row of shutters that cover only half the window are sometimes called café-style shutters (**3**). They provide some privacy but less control over the level of illumination.

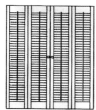

1 Single row shutters

2 Stacked shutters

3 Café-style shutters

Mounting the shutters

Usually, shutters are supplied hinged to a mounting board for screwing to the wall or window frame. You can mount this board on the face of the wall so they span the window opening (**1**). Or, if you have a deep window, you may want to install the board to the inside of the recess (**2**) or to the sides of the window frame (**3**). Large shutters, like those used for French windows, for example, can be hung from the top on a bifold-door track system.

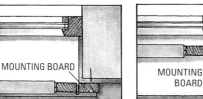

MOUNTING BOARD

1 Wall mounting

MOUNTING BOARD

2 Recess mounting

MOUNTING BOARD

3 Window-frame mounting

Finishing shutters

Shutters are generally sold fine-sanded for finishing but can be supplied ready finished, if required. You can use a brush to apply a clear finish, colored paint, or wood dye—but covering the numerous faces and edges is time consuming, and it's difficult to avoid leaving runs. Consequently, it's preferable to spray a finish onto shutters. You can hire professional spray equipment, though for just one or two shutters, you will probably be able to make do with pressurized spray cans.

Apply a primer to the bare wood, then rub it down and apply one or two coats of finish. For a stained finish—which will allow the grain of the wood to show—apply one or two even coats of wood dye.

Face mounting

For shutters to be attached to the face of a wall (see below left), measure the height (from the sill) and the width of the window opening. Make an allowance for the shutters to overlap the wall at the top and sides of the opening. And check that the mounting screws won't be too close to the edges of the opening.

Recess mounting

For shutters that are to be mounted in a window recess, measure the width of the opening at the top and bottom. Measure the height at both sides. Use the smaller dimension in both cases. Also, be sure to allow for the thickness of the mounting board at both sides. Check this with your supplier for the size of these boards on the shutters you want to buy.

To determine the size of individual shutters, divide the measured area by the number of shutters you want for each window.

Prefinished shutters
Some shutters are available prefinished with paint, stain, or a clear varnish.

Shelving

Shelving can be anything from particleboard planks on simple metal brackets to elegant spans of polished hardwood covering an entire library wall. Shelving is generally the simplest, quickest, and most economical form of storage you can find. And if you opt for one of the many adjustable systems, you can adapt your shelving to suit different needs in the future.

Wall-hung shelves

Shelves can be attached directly to the wall with support boards and end uprights or cantilevered off a wall with any one of a wide range of shelving brackets. These brackets are made of different metals and can support an enormous amount of weight.

Adjustable shelving systems have brackets that clip into upright metal supports screwed to the wall studs. Most uprights have holes or slots at very close intervals so you can make fine adjustments to shelf heights.

One advantage of these systems is that the weight and stress of the loaded shelves are distributed directly to the wall framing, and thus the whole structure of the house. Once the uprights are in place, the shelving arrangements can be changed easily without changing the impact on the support system.

Use inexpensive steel tracks and brackets (with plywood shelves) for utilitarian purposes, such as in your garage or basement. Choose more attractive brackets and shelving for your storage needs around the house.

The simplest way to make built-in, open shelves is to install them in wall recesses, like the alcoves that often flank a fireplace. These areas aren't always plumb and square, so careful fitting of the shelves is usually required to get professional results.

Installing fixed shelves

Mark the position of each shelf, making sure that the spaces between will accommodate all the items you want to store. Using a long level as a guide, draw a level line from each mark across the wall.

Cut wood support cleats for the ends of the shelves. (If the shelves are more than 4 feet long, you should install a cleat across the wall to support the back of the shelf.) For simple shelves, cut the front ends of the cleats to a 45-degree angle (**1**). For a better appearance, apply wood edging to the front edges of the shelves (**2**). These make the shelving look more substantial and hide the cleats. For a sleeker appearance, use painted angle iron for your cleats (**3**).

Stamped steel
shelf brackets

ADJUSTABLE
BRACKET

SLOTTED
UPRIGHT

Adjustable-bracket
systems

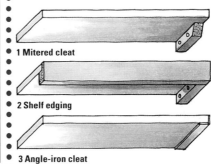

1 Mitered cleat

2 Shelf edging

3 Angle-iron cleat

Choosing the best materials

Precut shelves made from solid wood or manufactured panels are available from lumberyards and home centers in a range of standard sizes. The panels are usually prepainted or covered with wood veneer. Shelves manufactured from glass or painted stamped steel are also widely available. If these kinds of standard shelving don't meet your needs, make your own, using any of the materials shown here.

Materials for shelving

Solid wood

Softwoods, usually pine, hemlock, or fir, are a good choice for shelving, especially if you plan to paint the shelves. Painting covers up the knots that these boards usually have. Softwoods are easy to work with, relatively inexpensive, and available at lumberyards and home centers.

Hardwoods, such as oak, maple, ash, and mahogany are available from hardwood suppliers. These woods are beautiful, but they are harder to work with and almost always more expensive.

Lumber-core plywood

Lumber-core plywood is a relatively expensive manufactured panel made from blocks of softwood glued and sandwiched between two layers of wood veneer. These panels are as strong as solid wood and much more stable. Their exposed edges must be trimmed with veneer or solid wood edging.

Standard plywood

Plywood is built up from veneers, with the grain alternating at right angles in order to provide strength and stability. The exposed edges must be covered with a solid wood edging or veneer.

Particleboard

The least-expensive manufactured panel, particleboard is a popular choice for all types of utility shelving, typically used in basements, garages, and attics.

Medium-density fiberboard

Medium-density fiberboard (MDF) is a dense, stable, man-made panel that is easy to cut and machine. It has a uniform appearance throughout the board, so the edges don't need to be covered with wood or veneer. MDF is ideal for painting.

Glass

Glass is an attractive material for all kinds of shelving. Choose tempered glass and have it cut to size and the edges ground smooth and polished by the supplier.

Stop your shelves from sagging

Solid wood and lumber-core plywood, with its core running lengthways, are the best choices for sturdy shelving. But a shelf made from either material will sag if its supports are too far apart. Particleboard, though popular because of its low cost and availability, will eventually sag under relatively light loads, so it needs supporting at closer intervals than solid wood.

The chart below shows recommended maximum spans for shelves made from different materials. Display shelving for photos and collectibles is generally considered to be under a light load. A shelf full of books is a heavy load. If you want to increase the length of the shelf, then move the supports closer together, add another bracket, or use thicker material for the shelf.

Stiffening your shelves

A wood edging strip or a metal angle attached to or underneath the front edge of a shelf will increase its stiffness. Where needed, a wall-mounted cleat should be used to support the back edge. A front rail can be used to conceal a thin fluorescent light fixture.

Wood stiffeners
1 Wood rail
2 Plywood strip
3 Rabbeted edging
4 Half-round edging

Metal stiffeners
5 Attached angle
6 Grooved T-section
7 Grooved angle
8 Attached T-section

RECOMMENDED SHELF SPANS				
Material	**Thickness**	**Light load**	**Medium load**	**Heavy load**
Solid wood	¾ inch	2 feet 8 inches	2 feet 6 inches	2 feet 4 inches
Lumber-core ply.	¾ inch	2 feet 8 inches	2 feet 6 inches	2 feet 4 inches
Particleboard	⅝ inch	2 feet 6 inches	2 feet	1 feet 6 inches
MDF	¾ inch	2 feet 8 inches	2 feet 6 inches	2 feet 4 inches
Glass	¼ inch	2 feet 4 inches	Not applicable	Not applicable

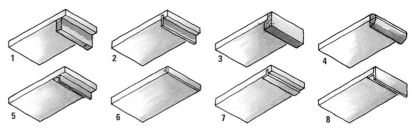

Installing wall-mounted shelving

To a large extent, the nature of your walls will determine the way in which you hang the shelves. On a masonry wall, for example, you can attach the shelf supports almost anywhere, using expansion anchors. On a wood-framed wall, the mounting screws should be driven through the wall finish and into the studs.

Loads cantilevered from wall brackets impose a lot of stress on the installation screws, especially the top ones. If the screws are too small they can be pulled out of the wall by the weight on the shelves.

Shelf supports for wood-frame walls are supplied with the proper screws for the job. If the shelves will be supporting an abnormally heavy load, just use bigger screws.

For ordinary shelving attached to a masonry wall, expansion anchors with 2-inch screws should be adequate. Wide shelves that are to bear a heavy load may well need heavier anchors and screws. Installing extra brackets to prevent the shelf from sagging will help spread the weight. The brackets should be nearly as long as the shelf is wide for the best support.

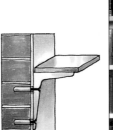

Masonry wall
Use anchors to secure brackets.

Stud wall
Screw brackets into the wall studs.

Installing individual shelf brackets

To install individual shelf brackets on a wood-frame wall, first locate the studs inside the wall. Studs are usually on 16-inch centers, so once you find one you can quickly locate the others. Mark the wall at the stud locations, then draw a level line across the wall at the desired shelf height. Install brackets where the level and stud lines intersect. Drill pilot holes for the screws, then hang the brackets.

On masonry walls, start by drawing a level line across the wall at shelf height. Then establish the bracket locations on the wall. You can install a bracket anywhere along the line because masonry walls are solid.

Mark the bracket-mounting holes on the walls and drill clearance holes into the wall. Slide the anchors in the holes, hold the bracket in place, and drive the mounting screws into the anchors.

Cut the shelving to size and attach each board to the brackets with screws.

Installing a shelving system

The upright supports must be installed plumb. One good way to do this is to loosely attach each upright to the wall with its top screw. Then, hold a level against the upright and adjust it until it's plumb. Mark the position of the bottom screw **(1)** and install it. Next, check that the upright is plumb in the other direction—does it lean into or away from the room? If it's out of plumb, shim behind the upright to correct it **(2)**.

Install a shelf bracket in the first upright and install another bracket in the next upright. Hold the second upright against the wall and get someone to help you lay a shelf across the brackets. Using a level, check to see if the shelf is level from side to side. If it is, mark the top hole of the second upright and attach it to the wall as you did the first.

Continue in this manner until all the uprights, brackets, and shelves have been installed.

1 Plumb the upright support
Use a level to plumb the upright, then mark the bottom screw hole on the wall.

2 Shimming out the upright support
Push wood shims behind the upright until it is plumb.

Glass-block partitions

If you want to screen off an area of a room, but an ordinary partition would cut down the available natural light too much, consider building a wall with glass blocks. A wide variety of individual decorative blocks and a number of modular systems are available from lumberyards, home centers, and glass supply outlets. You can also build a wall using standard, clear glass blocks laid in mortar, as described below.

1 Lay first block in corner

Basic considerations

Glass-block walls are by nature nonloadbearing, so they need to be contained within a rigid frame that's firmly attached to the floor, walls, and ceiling.

Generally speaking, the wall should not be longer than about 18 feet and its surface area should be no more than 200 square feet.

When building a large panel, install an expansion strip between the wood frame and the glass blocks. When all the blocks are installed, grout the expansion joint to hide the strip.

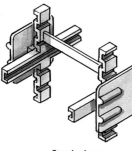

Standard cross-shaped spacer

Making the support frame

To establish the internal dimensions of the support frame, set out a single row of blocks on the floor with standard plastic spacers between them. Measure the total length, then do the same for the vertical dimension. Make a wood frame—using 2-inch-thick lumber that's as wide as the glass blocks are deep—to match these dimensions. Glue and screw the board together. Then install the frame by screwing it to the walls, ceiling, and floor. Make sure the frame is plumb, level, and square.

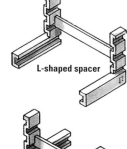

L-shaped spacer

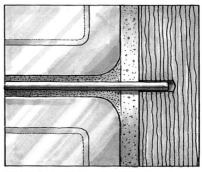

2 Apply mortar to side of each block

Building the glass panel

You will need the appropriate number of glass blocks, sufficient plastic spacers to fit every junction between the blocks and the frame, flexible expansion strips, reinforcing rods, and mortar mix.

Before you start, cut some of the standard cross-shaped spacers into L-shaped and T-shaped ones. These will be used where the blocks meet the frame. Nail the foam expansion strip to the side of the frame using ¾-inch brads.

Mix the mortar to a smooth, buttery consistency and lay a bed of mortar on the bottom of the frame. Starting at one corner, place an L-shaped spacer in the corner and lay the first block. Support its outer end on a T-shaped spacer (**1**). Apply mortar to the side of the next block, making sure there is sufficient to fill the cavity in the block (**2**), and set it in place with another spacer. Continue in this way, laying one course on another. Use a trowel to remove any mortar that squeezes out.

To strengthen the panel, set metal reinforcing rods into each horizontal bed of mortar. For increased strength, drill holes in the frame at the joint level and slide the ends of the rods into them (**3**). You can also set rods in the vertical joints as the blocks are laid up.

T-shaped spacer

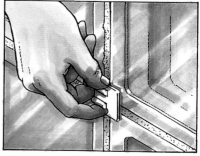

3 Drill holes in side frame for reinforcing rods

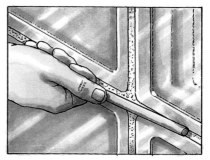

4 Twist and snap off location tabs

Finishing the joints

Twist and snap off the locating tabs from the spacers (**4**), then wipe off the excess mortar from the joints with a damp sponge. Once the mortar is firm, smooth the surface by drawing a ½-inch wood dowel along the joints (**5**). Polish the glass blocks once the mortar has set. Apply a white silicone caulk to all the expansion joints.

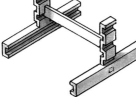

5 Smooth joints with dowel

Stairs

In simple functional terms, stairs are a series of steps that link one floor with another. But a staircase—the stairs and the walls and trim surrounding them—can also be a powerful expression of the style of the house itself. Because of its location, usually in the entrance hall, its large scale, and its interesting shape or decorative features, the staircase is one of the most dominant design elements in the interior of your home.

Steps

Each step of an ordinary straight flight of stairs is made from two boards—the vertical riser that forms the front of the step and the horizontal tread, the board on which you walk. The riser is a stiffening member and is installed between two treads, giving support to the front edge of one and the rear of the other. Treads and risers may be joined together in a number of ways. They can also be joined to the stair stringers on the sides in different ways.

Open-tread stairs have thick treads and no risers. They are often used for utility stairs in basements and attics. For increased strength, metal tie rods are sometimes installed across the stairs where the risers would normally be located.

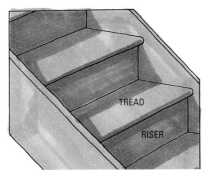

Most staircases have treads and risers

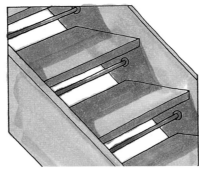

Open-tread stairs sometimes have tie rods

The simplest staircase, and the one that usually takes up the most room, is a straight flight of steps. In houses where space is limited, shorter flights may be used, with an intermediate landing linking one flight with another.

Most staircases have straight treads, but some have tapered treads, often called winders, that are used to make tight turns.

Winders may be used exclusively to form a sweeping, curved staircase. A spiral staircase is constructed around a central column. Unlike the sweeping, curved stair, it can be used in small houses where space is limited.

Staircase with a half-landing

Staircase with two quarter landings

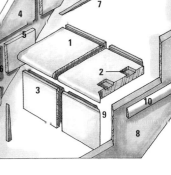

Straight staircase with winders at the top

Stringers

Steps are supported at their ends by wide boards set on edge, known as stringers. These are the main structural members that run from one floor level to another. A wall stringer is the inner one which is fixed to the wall. The stringer on the open side of the stair is called the outer stringer. The appearance of the stairs is affected by the style of the stringers. There are two basic types. A closed stringer covers the ends of the stairs, while an open stringer is cut away for each stair, and the stair tread sits on top of the stringer. The closed version is used for the wall stringer and generally matches the height of the baseboard. The outer stringer can be either the closed or the open type.

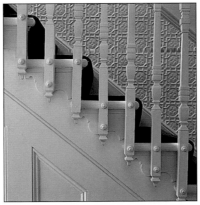

A closed stringer covers stair ends

An open stringer is cut to the shape of stairs

Step to stringer joints

The treads and risers of a typical staircase are set in mortises routed into the face of a closed stringer and secured with glued wedges. The wedges are driven in from underneath to make a tight joint.

In the case of an open stringer, the outer ends of the risers are mitered into the vertical cut edges and the treads are nailed down onto the horizontal edges. The nosing on this type of tread is continued around the end of the tread by adding a short length of molding. This molding hides the endgrain of the nosing and holds the bottom of the balusters captive.

Typical stair joints (above right)
1 Tread
2 Baluster housing
3 Riser
4 Wall stringer
5 Tread groove
6 Riser groove
7 Wedge
8 Open stringer
9 Mitered butt joint
10 Molding

Stair construction

Newel post

In traditional stair building, the wall stringer is screwed to the wall at points underneath the treads and the outer stringer is tenoned into the newels at each end. Newel posts measure at least 4 x 4 inches. They give support to the stair while securing it to the floor and to a structural joist underneath the floor. The newel post at the top of a stairs, or the central newel on stairs with a landing, is usually continued down to the floor. The newels also carry the handrail, which is tenoned into them.

Balustrade

The space between the handrail and the outer stringer may be filled with traditional balusters, modern balustrade rails, or framed paneling. The assembly is known as the balustrade, or banister.

Storage space

In older houses, the space underneath a stair is sometimes enclosed to make a cabinet and provide extra storage room. The triangular space between the floor and the stringer can also be framed in and covered with drywall, plaster, or wood paneling. Because this filler wall is not structural, it can be removed easily in the future.

In most newer houses, the staircases between floors tend to be stacked on top of each other to make the best use of space. So it's impossible to add any storage space under the stairs.

The central stringer

Traditional stairs 3 feet wide or wider should be supported underneath by a central stringer, often called a carriage. This board is usually made of 2-inch-thick lumber that attaches to the floor plate with a birdsmouth joint, and at the top is toenailed to the side of the second-floor landing.

The width of the carriage board is determined by the distance from the corner where a tread and riser meet and the bottom of a side stringer. Short lengths of 1-inch-thick board known as carriage brackets are sometimes nailed to alternate sides of the carriage to make a tight fit under each tread and riser.

This central stringer not only helps to support the staircase, it also provides a nailing surface for any finish material, like drywall or plaster, that you might want to use to cover the underside of the stairs.

STAIRCASE DESIGN

Staircase dimensions and designs are strictly controlled by building codes, which govern such measurements as tread size and shape, rise and run, minimum headroom, handrail position, and spacing of balusters. You must consult your local building department before building or modifying any staircase.

Calculating the rise and run of stairs is probably the most crucial consideration, because this determines the steepness of the staircase. Most codes stipulate 8 inches as the maximum vertical distance (rise) between treads, and 9 inches as the minimum horizontal distance (run) between risers. Minimum headroom between stairs and ceiling is usually 6 feet 8 inches.

When it's properly designed, a finished staircase must fit the exact floor-to-floor height of the opening in equal stair increments. All the treads have to be level, the same size, and the same distance from the last tread. The same requirements pertain to the risers. To check staircase calculations, building inspectors often use one of these three formulas:

1 RISER HEIGHT + TREAD WIDTH = 17" to 18"

2 RISER HEIGHT x 2 + TREAD WIDTH = 24" to 27"

3 RISER HEIGHT x TREAD WIDTH = 70" to 75"

In these calculations, the tread width does not include the nosing (lip) that extends over the riser.

Building your own stairs

Designing and building your own stairs is a lot of work. The process is fairly complicated, requires a lot of tools, demands a high degree of accuracy, and involves some heavy lifting. It's also very challenging and very rewarding if you end up with a good set of stairs. Building stairs for the inside of your house may be more than you want to tackle. But constructing a short run of stairs from a porch or deck to the ground is well within most people's ability.

Manufactured staircases are a standard made-to-order item in lumberyards and even some home centers. Accurate measurement is crucial when ordering stairs, because once they're built you have to buy them.

Stair components
1 Wall stringer
2 Outer stringer
3 Newel post
4 Handrail
5 Balusters
6 Wall panel
7 Carriage
8 Floor plate
9 Birdsmouth joint
10 Carriage brackets
11 Tread
12 Riser

Curing creaking stairs

Creaking in stairs begins when joints become loose and start rubbing. The slight gaps that allow this movement are usually the result of the wood drying out and shrinking, though general wear and tear will also contribute to the problem.

The method you choose for dealing with the problem will depend on whether you have access to the underside of the stairs. A better repair is possible from underneath. But if your stairs are covered, and getting access would mean removing a ceiling, it makes more sense to tackle the repair from above.

Working from underneath

If it's possible to get to the underside of the stairs, have someone walk slowly up the steps, counting them out loud. From your position under the stairs, follow the counting, noting any loose steps and marking them with chalk or a crayon. Have your helper repeatedly step on and off any suspect treads while you look for the source of the creaking.

Loose housing joint
If the tread or the riser is loose in either stringer mortise, it may be because the original wedge has become loose. Remove the wedge (1), clean it up, apply carpenter's glue, and drive the wedge back into the joint (2). If you damaged the wedge when you removed it, make a new one out of hardwood.

Loose blocks
Check the triangular blocks that fit in the corner between the tread and the riser. If the glue has failed on one side of the block, remove it and clean off the old glue. Before replacing the blocks, try to pry slightly open the joint between the tread and riser with a chisel. Squeeze glue into the joint (3), then draw the joint tight by driving 1½-inch screws through the tread and into the riser.

Apply new glue to any blocks you removed and press them into the corner (4). Hold the blocks in place with masking tape until the glue sets. Avoid walking on the stairs for a couple of hours to give the glue a chance to dry.

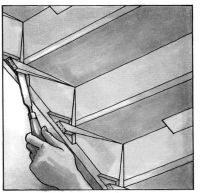

1 Pry out old wedge with chisel

2 Apply glue to joint and drive in wedge

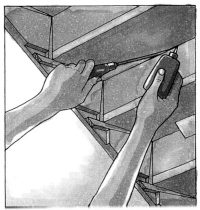

3 Pry open joint and squeeze in glue

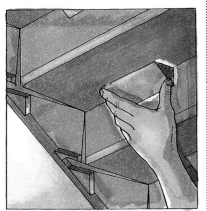

4 Install glued blocks into corner joint

Working from the top

To identify the problem areas, walk slowly up the stairs and stop at each creaking step. Shift your weight back and forth on the problem tread to discover which part is moving. It is best to do this late at night or early in the morning, when the house is quiet and small creaks will not be missed.

Loose front joint
To cure looseness in a joint between the riser and the tread, drill clearance holes for 1½-inch screws in the tread, centered on the thickness of the riser (1). Countersink the hole for the screw-head. Squeeze wood glue into the holes, then drive the screws to pull the joint tight. If the screws won't be concealed by stair carpet you should counterbore the holes and plug them with matching wood.

Loose back joint
A loose joint at the back of the tread cannot be easily repaired from above. You can try working glue into the joint. But because you can't use screws to draw the joint, the glue doesn't usually do much good.

There is a form of reinforcement from above that may help. Glue a piece of ½ x ½-inch triangular wood into the corner between the tread and the riser (2). This technique is appropriate only on wide treads, where the addition of the molding doesn't reduce the tread depth to less than the minimum allowed by code, which is usually 9 inches. Cut the piece of wood slightly shorter than the width of the stair carpet. If you have wall-to-wall carpet on the stairs, this repair doesn't make as much sense. To remove the carpet and install the block is difficult. It's probably easier to live with the creak.

1 Screw joint tight

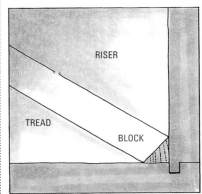

2 Glue triangular block into corner

Repairing worn stairs

Old wood stairs that haven't had the protection of a floorcovering will eventually become very worn. Worn treads can be dangerous and should be repaired promptly. If all the treads are badly worn, consider having the entire staircase replaced.

Treads installed between closed stringers can be replaced only from below. If the stairs are covered underneath with drywall or plaster, you will have to cut an opening to reach the worn tread. If a central stringer has been used in the construction of the stairs the work required to repair the tread can be so extensive that you should consider hiring a contractor for the job.

Renewing a tread

Wear on the nosing of a tread is usually concentrated in the center, and you can repair it without having to replace the whole tread.

Mark three cutting lines just outside the worn area. Draw one line parallel to the edge of the nosing and draw the other two lines at right angles to it (1).

Adjust the blade depth of a portable circular saw to the thickness of the tread. Tack a strip parallel to edge of the tread, to guide the shoe of the saw.

Cutting out

Position the saw, turn it on, then make the cut by lowering the blade into the wood (2). Try not to overrun the short end lines. Once the cut is made, remove the guide strip. Cut the end lines with a handsaw at a 45-degree angle. Make sure you don't cut beyond the saw kerf left by the circular saw. Make these cuts with a tenon saw (3).

You will be left with uncut waste in the corners. Remove most of the cut waste with a chisel, working with the grain and taking care to avoid damaging the riser tongue and triangular reinforcing blocks. Pare away the remaining waste from the uncut corners using a sharp chisel (4).

Replacement

Buy a new stair tread that matches the thickness and species of the existing tread. Then cut a groove for the riser on the underside of the new tread and cut a repair piece to length and width from the new tread. Check its fit in the opening, then apply wood glue to all of the meeting surfaces and press the repair piece in place. Clamp it down with a strip screwed at each end of the tread (5). Place a shim under the strip to hold down the middle of the patch (a piece of polyethylene prevents the shim from sticking to the patch). Drill and insert ¼-inch dowels into the edge of the nosing to reinforce the butt joint and, when the glue is set, plane and sand the repair flush.

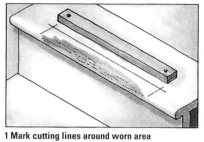

1 Mark cutting lines around worn area

2 Make the cut with saw guided by a strip

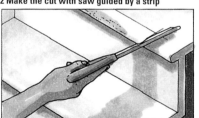

3 Make 45-degree cuts at each end

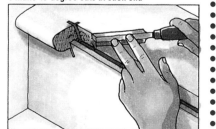

4 Pare away waste from corners

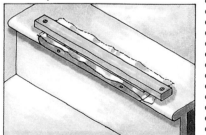

5 Clamp new section of tread with strip

Most stairs have tongue-and-groove joints between the risers and treads. In some others the top of the riser is not machined; it's left square and fits into a matching groove in the tread. In still other stairs, the risers simply butt against the treads and are held in place with nails or screws.

You can determine which type of joint you have by trying to pass a thin knife blade through the joint. Be sure to remove any nails or screws. A butt joint will let the blade pass through, while a tongue-and-groove, or a simple groove joint, will not.

As the joints effectively lock the treads and risers together, those in contact with the damaged tread must be freed before the tread can be removed. A butt joint is relatively easy to take apart; a groove or tongue-and-groove joint will have to be cut.

Dismantling a butt joint

To take a butt joint apart, first take out the nails or screws and, if glue has been used, strike the tread several times with a hammer to break the hardened glue, then pry up the tread with a chisel. Remove the triangular glue blocks in the same way.

Cutting a tongue

Where the tongue of a riser is joined to the underside of a tread, you cut it working from the front of the stair, and where the riser's tongue is joined to the top of the tread, it must be cut from the rear (1). If there is a molding installed under the nosing (the part of the tread that extends beyond the riser), pry it off first with a chisel.

Before cutting a tongue, remove any screws, nails, and glued reinforcement blocks, then drill a row of ⅛-inch holes into the joint to provide access for a hacksaw or keyhole-saw blade (2). You can also use a power reciprocating saw to make this cut, which would speed up the job.

Once the riser-to-tread joints are cut, remove the tread as shown on the facing page.

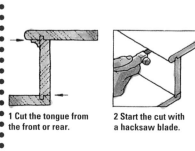

1 Cut the tongue from the front or rear.

2 Start the cut with a hacksaw blade.

Closed stringer stairs

Working from the underside of the stair, chisel out the tread-retaining wedges from the stringer mortises at the ends of the tread **(1)**. Then free the tread by striking its front edge with a hammer and block. Continue to drive the tread backward and out **(2)**.

Make a tread to fit, shaping its front edge to match the nosing on the other steps, and cut a new pair of wedges.

Slide the new tread and wedges into place from underneath. Then measure the gaps left between the risers and the tread and cut wood-shim pieces to match. Test these shims to make sure they fill the joints **(3)**.

Remove the shims, wedges, and tread. Apply wood glue to all parts as you reinstall them. Secure the tread with 1½-inch countersunk woodscrews driven into the risers.

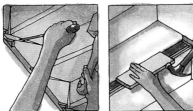

1 Remove wedges   **2 Drive out tread**

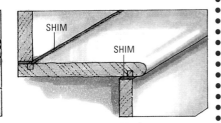

3 Shim saw cuts at front and back

Open stringer stairs

Pry off the molding that covers the endgrain of the tread, taking care not to split it **(1)**. Remove the two balusters from the tread.

Chisel the wedge out of the wall stringer mortise to free the inner end of the tread and drive the tread out from the rear of the stair with a hammer and a block of wood **(2)**.

You will have to cut through or extract any nails that fasten the tread to the outer stringer before the tread can be pulled completely clear.

Use the original tread as a template and mark its shape out on a new board. Then cut the board carefully to

size and shape. Be sure to duplicate the shape of the nosing exactly so the return molding on the end of the tread will match all the others in the staircase.

Lay out and cut the mortises for the balusters **(3)** and make a new wedge for the wall stringer mortise. Apply glue to all the parts, then install the tread from the front, shimming the joints with the riser as described above.

Apply glue to the balusters and replace them. Then glue and nail the return molding to the end of the tread. Also replace the molding piece under the tread nosing if one was used before.

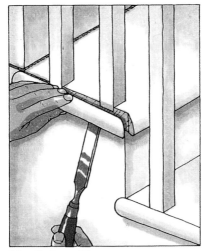

1 Pry off return molding

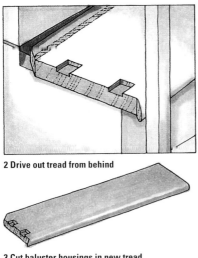

2 Drive out tread from behind

3 Cut baluster housings in new tread

Risers are subjected to much less wear and tear than treads and will not ordinarily have to be replaced. If a riser is split, it can be reinforced from behind by gluing and screwing a new board to the back of the riser. The joining surfaces of both the old and the new wood should be sanded smooth for the glue to hold well. If a riser is broken, you have no alternative; it must be replaced.

Closed stringer stair

In the case of a closed stringer stair, remove the tread below the damaged riser using the method described earlier. Knock the wedges out of the riser mortises, then drive out or pry out the riser **(1)**.

Measure the distance between the stringers and between the bottom of one tread to the top of the other. Cut a new riser to fit. Though you could make tongue-and-groove joints on the new riser, it is easier simply to butt-join its top and bottom edges with the treads **(2)**. Apply glue to all joining surfaces, then wedge the new riser into the mortises **(3)**, and screw it to the tread.

If your stairs are not covered with carpet, counterbore the screw holes and use wood plugs to conceal the screws. You can also secure a riser to a tread by gluing and screwing blocks to both parts from underneath.

Reinstall the tread you removed as described earlier (see left). In this case, you won't have to shim the riser and tread joint because the new riser has been cut to fit.

Open stringer stairs

First remove any molding that's installed under the nosing. Then saw through the joints at the top and bottom of the damaged riser. Remove the wedges from the riser's wall stringer mortise.

Knock apart the mitered joint between the end of the riser and the outer stringer by hammering it from behind. Once the mitered joint is free, carefully pry the inner end of the riser out of its mortise.

Make a new riser to fit between the treads, mitering its outer end to match the joint in the stringer. Cut any necessary shims to size. Then apply glue to all edges of the riser and the shims, and install these parts. Drive the riser wedge into the stringer mortise, screw the treads to the riser, nail the mitered end, and replace the nosing molding.

1 Pry out riser

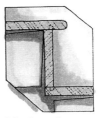

2 Cut riser to fit

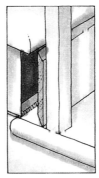

3 Wedge riser

Free the mitered joint
Knock apart the joint on open stringer stairs.

Repairing balusters

A broken baluster is potentially dangerous and should be repaired or replaced promptly. If the baluster is a decorative one, it should be preserved. If the damage is not too extensive, it can be repaired in place. Otherwise, a new baluster should be made to replace it.

Balusters
A range of typical hardwood and softwood balusters.

A period staircase with turned balusters

Buying and installing balusters

Finished balusters of various patterns are available from building suppliers and they can be used for replacing all the old balusters when you are replacing the entire balustrade. They can also be used to replace individual balusters if you can find ones that match your staircase. If you can't find a match, then you'll have to make, or hire someone to make, replacements.

Balusters are mortised into the underside of the handrail and in the edge of a closed stringer or the treads of an open stringer. Sometimes they are simply butted and secured with nails or are set in mortises at the bottom but nailed at the top (see below). You can detect nails by examining or feeling the surface of the baluster at the back. You will find a slight bump or hollow. If the wood is stripped, the nail will be obvious. A light shone across the joint can also reveal a nail.

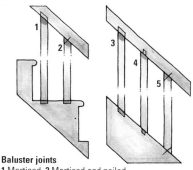

Baluster joints
1 Mortised 2 Mortised and nailed
3 Mortised 4 Tenoned 5 Nailed

Repairing a baluster

A baluster that has split along the grain can be repaired in place. Work wood glue into the split and clamp it with masking tape until it dries. Before clamping the parts with tape, squeeze the joint together and wipe away any surplus glue with a damp rag.

Replacing a baluster

A damaged baluster that is butted and nailed can be knocked out by first removing the nails, then driving its top end backward and its bottom end forward. If it is mortised at the bottom, it can be pulled out of the housing once the top has been freed.

A baluster that's mortised at both ends can be removed by cutting through the joint under the handrail and pulling the baluster from the bottom mortise.

When the baluster is installed in an open stringer, remove the molding that covers the end of the tread and knock the bottom end of the baluster sideways. Then pull it down to remove it

from the handrail mortise.

Installing a baluster
Mark the required length on the new baluster and cut the ends, using the old baluster as a pattern. Install the new baluster in the reverse order of the way you took the old one out.

To replace a baluster which is mortised at both ends in a closed stringer stair first trim off the back corner of the top tenon **(1)**. Then push the bottom of the baluster into the bottom mortise and swing the top end of the baluster into place **(2)**. Secure both ends with nails driven at an angle into the joints.

HANDRAIL REGULATIONS

Building codes require handrails on all staircases. Usually, if the staircase is narrower than 40 inches, you need only one handrail. But if it's wider, most codes demand two handrails.

If the staircase is less than 40 inches wide and has any tapered treads (winders), a handrail must be provided on the side of the stairs where the treads are widest. If this happens to be the wall stringer side, two handrails may be required, one mounted on the wall, the otheras part of the balustrade.

Although these requirements govern new work, there's good reason to retrofit existing stairs to comply with them. Tapered treads, in particular, can be very hazardous, especially for children, who tend to run up and down stairs.

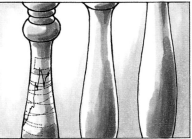

Apply glue and masking tape to split baluster

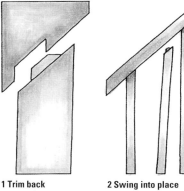

1 Trim back corner of tenon   **2 Swing into place**

Installing a handrail

Measuring and marking

Mark a line on the wall to represent the top of the handrail, setting the height in accordance with building code regulations. Where there are tapered treads, some alterations of the rules may be necessary, but you should check with your local building inspector.

Lay out the line by marking a series of points measured vertically from the nosing of each tread in a straight flight. Where tapered treads occur, take the same measurement from the middle tapered tread and the landing (1).

Marking tips
Marking the points can be simplified by first cutting a straight wood strip to the right height and then using it as a guide. Circle the points with your pencil as you make them so that you can find them easily later.

Marking the handrail
Using a straightedge, join the marks to produce the line of the handrail. Then draw a second line below and parallel to the first, at a distance equal to the thickness of the handrail. Where the rail changes direction, draw lines across the intersections (**A**) to establish the angles at which the components must be cut (2).

Measure the run of the handrail and buy the required lengths, including any special sections required to make turns. Also buy enough handrail brackets for spacing them at 32-inch intervals.

Assembling and installing

Cut the components to the correct lengths and angles, then dowel and glue short sections together or use special handrail bolts. These bolts require clearance holes in the ends of each of the joining parts and mortises cut in the underside of the handrail for the nuts. When using handrail bolts, you must also install dowels (3) to keep the sections from rotating as they are pulled together. Assemble the rail in manageable sections.

Screw the brackets to the rail and have a helper hold it against the wall while you mark the mounting holes. On masonry walls, drill bracket holes in the wall for wall anchors. Insert the anchors and tighten the brackets to the wall with screws (4). On wood-frame walls, locate the brackets so they fall over the studs, then attach the brackets by driving the mounting screws into the studs.

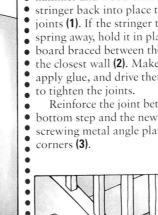

1 Laying out
Mark the wall above each tread and join the marks with a straightedge.

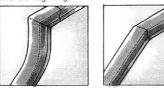

2 Changing angles
The junction of a sloping handrail with a horizontal one can be made with a ramp (left) or a simple angle (right).

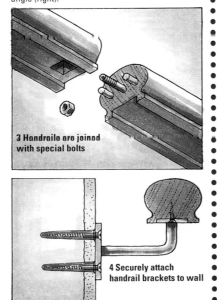

3 Handrails are joined with special bolts

4 Securely attach handrail brackets to wall

When the whole balustrade, including the handrail, balusters, and newel post, feels loose, it indicates a failure of the joints between the steps and the outer stringer. This should be addressed promptly before it get worse. If the stringer breaks, the repair is very involved and can be costly.

You can reattach the steps to a loose stringer and newel post by first removing the wedges from the tread and riser mortises. Then, working along the face of the stringer with a hammer and wood block, knock the stringer back into place to reseat the joints (1). If the stringer tends to spring away, hold it in place with a board braced between the stringer and the closest wall (2). Make new wedges, apply glue, and drive them into place to tighten the joints.

Reinforce the joint between the bottom step and the newel post by screwing metal angle plates into the corners (3).

1 Use a hammer and block to reseat loose joints

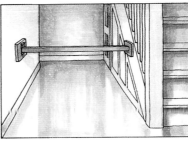

2 Brace stringer against closest wall

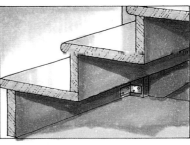

3 Reinforce bottom joint with steel angle plates

Handrail components
In addition to ordinary handrail moldings, you can buy special matched components called turns, ramps, and caps. These are joined to straight sections of handrail with steel bolts.

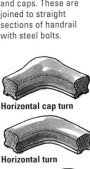
Horizontal cap turn

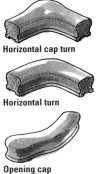
Horizontal turn

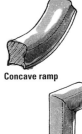
Opening cap

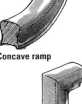
Concave ramp

Gooseneck ramp

Replacing a balustrade

While the staircase in most houses may be a strong design element because of its size and location, the character of the staircase itself is largely defined by the design of its balustrade.

Older houses, and even some houses in newer developments, were often outfitted with ornate balusters, newel posts, and handrails. But over the years, with changes in fashion, many of these old balustrades have been remodeled or replaced. Often these "improvements" have been mistakes. New owners frequently wish that the changes hadn't been made. Although replacing an entire balustrade is not an easy or quick job, the results can be well worth the effort.

Using a kit to replace a balustrade

Kits are available that make it relatively easy to install a traditionally designed balustrade. Usually the kits consist of newel posts made up of three parts, a base section **(1)**, a turned center section **(2)**, and a decorative knob **(3)**, turned balusters in many styles **(4)**, a handrail **(5)**, and a grooved base rail **(6)** that the balusters fit into. Spacer fillets **(7)** are also provided to make installing and finishing the balusters a more straight-forward job. And there are special metal brackets **(8)** for joining the ends of the handrails to the posts. You can use all or any of the parts to meet the demands of most types of staircases. The straight flight staircase (shown below) is a typical example.

Preparation
Remove the existing posts, baluster, and handrail. Clean all the treads and risers and make any necessary repairs. This is also a good time to refinish the stairs if they need it. Complete your preparation by carefully reading and understanding the installation directions for the balustrade kit you purchased.

Installing the newel posts
The simplest way to replace the old newel posts is to start by cutting them off. Leave the joints between their bases and the stringer intact.
Cut off the base of the bottom newel square at the height indicated in the kit instructions.

Mark diagonal lines across the cut ends of the newel posts to establish their centers. Then drill a 2-inch-diameter hole in each to receive the new newel posts. Cut this hole with a drill and an expansion bit or a holesaw. After drilling the holes, shape the cut ends of the posts to a slightly convex contour, to create an attractive transition to the new posts. Set the new posts in the holes, but don't glue them in place.

Installing the rails
Using an adjustable bevel, establish the angle where the stair stringer meets the newel base. Hold the base rail against the stair, following the angle of the stringer exactly, and make a mark at each end where it meets the newels. Then mark the cutting lines at these points, using the bevel and a square. Cut the rail to length.
Mark and cut the handrail in the same way. Screw the base rail to the stringer, then install the handrail brackets in the posts. Loosely tighten them with a wrench. Check that the posts are plumb and that the rails fit properly, then glue the posts into place. Tighten the bolts fully, and when the glue has set, install the cover buttons **(9)** to conceal the nuts.

Installing the balusters
Use one for each tread that's adjacent to a newel post. You'll need fillets for the space between each baluster.
Measure the vertical distance between the grooves in the handrail and the base rail, then transfer this dimension to the balusters. Mark the cut lines, using the adjustable bevel to give the correct angle. Cut the balusters. Glue and nail the balusters and fillets in place, and when the glue is dry, sand all the parts and apply a finish.

Balustrade components
1 Newel base
2 Newel post
3 Decorative knob
4 Turned balusters
5 Handrail
6 Base rail
7 Fillets
8 Metal brackets
9 Cover buttons

Mahogany balustrade constructed from a kit

The roof of a house is an extremely tough environment for any material. Temperatures easily range from 120 degrees in the summer to well below freezing in the winter. Snow, rain, and hail pound away season after season. And sunlight, with its harmful ultraviolet radiation, is a constant throughout the year. If your roof is worn out, everything below it is at risk. Fortunately, you have plenty of roofing options to choose from when you replace it.

Common roofing materials
1 Copper
2 Concrete tile
3 Cedar shingles
4 Slate
5 Stamped steel
6 Steel shakes
7 Asphalt shingles
8 Clay tile
9 Cedar shakes
10 Standing-seam steel
11 Asphalt roll roofing
12 Interlocking asphalt shingle

Roofs

Traditionally most roofs were made with rafters that were cut and installed on site, and this is still the way many roofs are built, especially when usable attic space is required. But most roofs today are built with trusses. These units are fabricated in factories and simply nailed in place on site. Trusses are strong, stable, and usually more economical than rafter roofs. But installing them generally eliminates the attic space.

Basic construction

The framework of an ordinary roof is based on a triangle, the most rigid and economical form for a loadbearing structure. The weight of the roofing and sheathing is carried either by prefabricated trusses, or by framing members called rafters, which are installed in opposing pairs. Rafters are joined at the top to a central ridge board running the length of the roof.

The bottom ends of the rafters are attached to the top plates of the walls.

To stop the roof's weight from pushing the walls out, horizontal members tie the walls together and the rafters together. The bottom ones, installed next to the rafters on the top plates, are the ceiling joists. Members that are nailed to the sides of the rafters, closer to the ridge, are called collar ties.

Roof types

There are many different roof styles, often used in combination. Most of them, however, fall into these basic classifications:

Flat Roof
Flat roofs may be supported on joists to which the ceiling material is also attached, or they may be constructed using trusses which have parallel top and bottom members supported by triangular bracing in between. Most flat roofs actually have a slight slope, formed by the roofing material, to provide drainage.

Shed Roof
This is the simplest type of roof. Sometimes it is called a lean-to roof.

Inside the structure, the ceiling may be attached directly to the rafters to form a sloping surface, or be supported by horizontal joists to form a flat surface.

Gable Roof
Two shed roofs joined together form the classic gable roof, the most commonly used roof in residential construction today. Gable roofs are simple and economical to build and have excellent loadbearing and drainage capabilities. The end walls under the roof are nonloadbearing.

Gambrel Roof
By breaking the slope of a gable roof into two differently pitched sections, more headroom becomes available in

the attic area beneath the rafters. The gambrel design also makes the construction of a wide roof easier because shorter lengths of lumber can be used in combination to span large widths.

Hip Roofs
By sloping the ends of a gable roof toward the center, a hip roof is formed. This roof style provides a protective overhang on all four sides of the building.

Intersecting Roofs
Many houses combine the same or different roof types, built at angles to one another, to form L- or U-shaped floor plans, and other shapes.

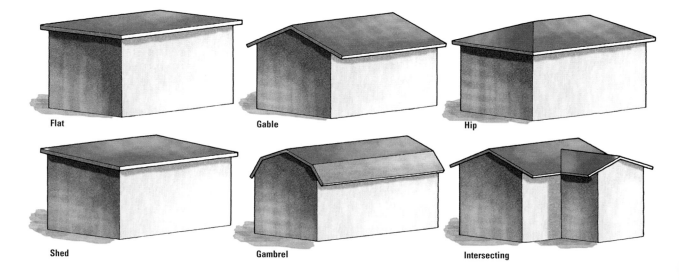

Flat   Gable   Hip

Shed   Gambrel   Intersecting

Roof construction

As mentioned earlier, most roof design is based on a simple geometric form: the triangle. If all the legs of a triangle are firmly attached to adjacent legs, it is very difficult to distort the shape. But holding its shape is not all that a roof system has to do. It must also keep the side walls of the house from spreading apart. To do both, the side walls and the rafters must be joined together with ceiling joists and collar ties to produce a sound structure.

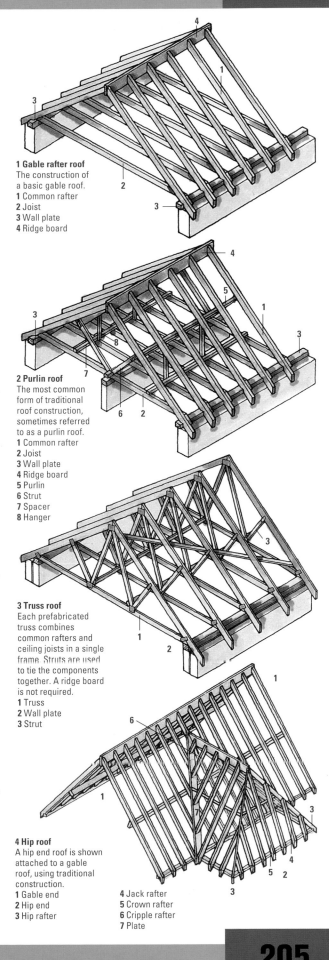

1 Gable rafter roof
The construction of a basic gable roof.
1 Common rafter
2 Joist
3 Wall plate
4 Ridge board

2 Purlin roof
The most common form of traditional roof construction, sometimes referred to as a purlin roof.
1 Common rafter
2 Joist
3 Wall plate
4 Ridge board
5 Purlin
6 Strut
7 Spacer
8 Hanger

3 Truss roof
Each prefabricated truss combines common rafters and ceiling joists in a single frame. Struts are used to tie the components together. A ridge board is not required.
1 Truss
2 Wall plate
3 Strut

4 Hip roof
A hip end roof is shown attached to a gable roof, using traditional construction.
1 Gable end
2 Hip end
3 Hip rafter
4 Jack rafter
5 Crown rafter
6 Cripple rafter
7 Plate

Gable rafter roof

A gable roof **(1)**, is the basic design for residential roof construction. It can be made with trusses (see below) or traditional rafters. Even though building a gable roof is a lot of work, its design is the essence of simplicity: Two flat planes are joined together to form a simple peaked structure.

The top of the framework is called the ridge and it is formed by the junction of the rafters from both sides and a ridge board that runs perpendicular to the rafters. The ridge is supported by the rafters and the rafters are supported by the outside walls. The joint between the rafters and the top wall plate is crucial. If this joint is weak the roof will fail.

To tie the rafters together and form the basic triangle, and to keep the walls from spreading, ceiling joists are nailed to the top plates and the sides of the rafters. These joints are also crucial to the overall strength of the roof.

Purlin roof

In a purlin roof **(2)**, horizontal beams called purlins link the rafters, running midway between the outside wall and the ridge.

The ends of the purlins are supported at the gable wall or, in the case of a hip roof, by hip rafters (see below). The purlins effectively reduce the unsupported span of the rafters, which allows relatively lightweight lumber to be used for the rafters. In order to keep the size of the purlins to a minimum, diagonal struts are installed in opposing pairs to brace them, usually every fourth or fifth rafter. The struts transfer some of the roof weight back to a center loadbearing wall. This type of roof is rarely built anymore; but looking at it suggests the beginning of truss roof construction.

Truss roof

A truss roof **(3)** allows for a relatively wide span and dispenses with the need for a loadbearing partition wall. Like rafters, trusses transfer the entire weight of the roof to the exterior walls.

In the majority of new housing, trusses are computer designed for economy and strength. Each truss combines two roof chords (corresponding to common rafters), a bottom chord (to function like a ceiling joist), and struts that join and brace the chords together. All the joints are butt joints reinforced with heavy-duty plate connectors, often called gang nails. Trusses are usually spaced on 24-inch centers so standard roof sheathing panels will fit the layout without being cut.

Truss roofs are relatively lightweight and can span greater distances than rafter roofs, because trusses don't require a partition wall underneath to support the ceiling joists.

Hip roofs

Hip roofs **(4)** are often used for additions to gable roofs to break up the simplicity of a straight roof. Hips are more complicated to build because their ends are also pitched at an angle. Additional framing members include hip rafters, jack rafters, crown rafters, and cripple rafters. The illustration (right) shows a gable roof and a smaller hip roof added to the side. The points where the two meet are called valleys. The valleys collect and direct rainwater from both roof surfaces down to the gutters.

Checking your roof

The style of a roof is classified not only by the basic shape of the structure but also by the detailing along the eaves. The eaves are where the ends of the rafter meet the exterior walls. The basic eaves variations are shown below.

Flush eaves
When the ends of the rafters are cut flush with the outside wall of the house and covered with a fascia board, the eaves are called flush **(1)**. Gutters are installed directly on the fascia.

Open eaves
If the ends of the rafters extend beyond the outside of the wall, and aren't covered with a fascia board, the eaves are referred to as open **(2)**. This style of eaves is no longer very popular in new construction. But many older houses have them, and frequently the ends have designs cut or carved in them. Gutters are usually in brackets nailed to the top of the rafters before the roofing is installed.

Closed eaves
A closed eave **(3)** is a combination of the flush and the open approaches. The rafters extend past the outside wall, like open eaves. But they are enclosed with a fascia board, like a flush eave. A soffit board is installed under the rafters to close the space.

Eaves vents
Various types of vents are available for installing in fascias and soffits.

A roof structure can fail if its members are exposed to high moisture levels and insect attacks. Failure can also result from overloading due to the use of undersized framing lumber, roofing that's too heavy for the structure, or modifications to the framework to add stairs, dormers, or an attic room without proper reinforcement. A sagging roof, which indicates serious damage, can usually be seen from the ground.

Inspecting your roof

The roof should be inspected from inside. Do this annually to check for any leaks and the presence of destructive insects. For the inspection to be useful, you must have a good source of light. If your attic has no lighting, use an extension cord with a lamp or work light on the end. If the attic has no floor, walk only on the top edges of the joists.

Moisture problems

Rot in roof members is a serious problem which should be corrected by professionals. Rot is caused by damp conditions that encourage the growth of fungi that can destroy the wood.

Inspect the roof sheathing closely for loose or damaged boards or panels in the general area of the rot. Keep in mind that water may be penetrating the roof at a higher level and running down to the rotted area. The source of water damage is not always obvious.

If the rot is close to the intersection of two roofs, you should suspect the flashing. Rot can also be caused by too much condensation in the roof space, a problem that's usually fixed by installing more ventilation.

You should also inspect all the openings in the roof to make sure water isn't leaking around them. This includes the main plumbing vent stack, roof vents, and chimneys. If they're accessible, check the eaves to see if there's evidence that water has backed up due to ice dams or clogged downspouts. Many older homes have windows in the attic that should be checked for leaks and faulty glazing.

Strengthening the roof

A roof that shows signs of sagging may have to be jacked and braced. But some sagging roofs have already been stabilized, so they don't present a structural problem. They may look bad but aren't in any danger of collapsing. In some old buildings a slightly sagging roof line is even considered attractive.

Consult an engineer if you suspect a roof is weak. Apart from a sagging roofline, the walls under the eaves should be inspected for bulging out of plumb. Bulging can occur where improperly framed window openings are close to the eaves, making that section of the wall weak. The walls can also bulge because the roof weight is spreading them apart. This is almost always the result of poor joints between the rafters and the ceiling joists.

A lightly constructed roof can be made stronger by adding extra structural members. This work can often be done from inside the attic. But when the damage is severe, the roofing and sheathing have to be stripped from the outside before the repairs can be made.

This is work for professionals. Make sure they have liability insurance before hiring them.

A well-constructed roof will give many years of service

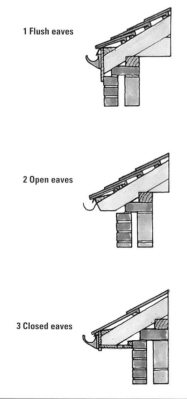

1 Flush eaves

2 Open eaves

3 Closed eaves

Underlayment

New roof sheathing, and sheathing that's been stripped of old roofing, should be covered with 15-pound asphalt felt paper, as underlayment, before new roofing is installed. Felt paper prevents the passage of moisture from outside in but doesn't prevent water vapor from inside getting out. Never use plastic sheeting for underlayment.

Some professional roofers prefer to use 30-pound felt paper as underlayment. Not only is this material heavier and somewhat harder to install, it's also more expensive. But it does provide a thicker base for the roofing and it's not as prone to tearing in the wind.

Most roofers cover the entire roof with underlayment before installing the roofing because of the extra protection it affords a wood roof in case of rain. But because wind easily damages thin felt paper, you may want to apply underlayment in stages.

Before you install the felt paper, you need to install a drip edge along the roof eaves. This material is a stock item at building suppliers. It's easy to cut with tinsnips and is simply nailed to the sheathing with roofing nails. Some roofers also install metal edging, sometimes called rake edge, over the ends of the roof where the sheathing meets the rake trim.

Once all the edging is in place, you can apply the underlayment. First be sure the sheathing surface is dry, smooth, and free of protruding nails and splinters. Apply roofing cement to the upper surface of the drip edge and along the seam where it meets the sheathing. Then set the roll of felt at one end of the roof and unroll it across the roof. Keep it about ¼ inch above the bottom of the drip edge.

Staple or nail the paper to the decking in as few places as possible, just enough to hold it until the new roofing can be applied on top. Lap the next course of paper 2 inches over the first course; overlap 4 inches at vertical seams.

At roof or hip ridges, fold the paper over the peak from both sides to produce a double thickness. Also overlap the paper at the valleys to produce a double thickness there. Install the valley flashing and all other flashings, around chimneys and vents, on top of the felt.

Applying three-tab asphalt shingles

Types of asphalt shingles

The most common type of asphalt shingles are the three-tab variety. These shingles usually measure 3 feet long and 1 foot wide. The length is divided into three sections, called tabs, that are each about 1 foot wide. Other types of asphalt shingles are available. There are strip shingles which have no tabs, interlocking shingles that hook into each other so they're less prone to wind damage, and the newer architectural shingles that have a series of overlapping tabs that are meant to simulate slate and cedar shingle roofing. When properly installed, all these shingles work well.

Installing shingles

To install three-tab shingles, begin shingling at the eaves. First install a single course of full-length shingles, top-edge down, along the length of the roof. Use roofing nails to attach them. Extend the shingles ¼- inch beyond the bottom edge of the drip edge. Then nail a second layer of full-size shingles top-edge up over the first layer to complete the starter course.

So that the cutouts in each shingle will always center over the tabs in the course below, remove half a tab from the first shingle that starts the second course. Attach the shingle so that

5 to 6 inches of the shingle beneath are exposed. This exposure varies depending on the shingles you buy. Follow the manufacturer's directions for the proper exposure.

Lay the rest of the course, nailing about ⅝ inch above each cutout and within 1 inch of both ends. Space subsequent shingles to provide the same exposure as used on the first course. After completing the second course, start the third, removing an entire tab from the first shingle in the course.

Mark where the upper edge of the next course of shingles will fall on both ends of the roof. Snap a chalkline between these two marks. Then lay the shingles in the next course to this line. Snap a line for each ensuing course and continue until you reach the ridge. Install shingles in the same way on the other side of the roof.

Installing the ridge cap

Trim the last row of shingles to lie flat along the ridge. Cover their top edges with a ridge cap made of individual shingle tabs. To do this, first snap a chalkline on each side of the roof, 5½ inches below the ridge. Fold the tabs over the ridge and align them with the chalklines. Nail the caps in place, maintaining the same exposure you used for the rest of the roof.

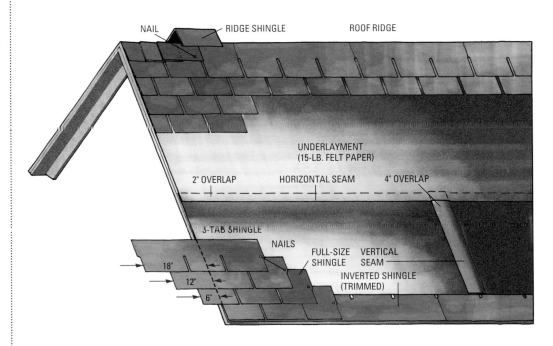

Roof maintenance

Roof coverings have a limited life, the length depending on the quality of materials used, the installation workmanship, and the exposure to severe weather. An average asphalt shingle roof can be expected to last for 20 years. But some materials, like slate and clay tiles, can last for 100 years or more. Of course, proper maintenance will always extend longevity, no matter what type of material is installed on your roof.

1 Pull out nails

2 Nail strip to roof

3 Fold strip over slate

Slate roofs
During the long life of a slate roof, patching can become a regular maintenance chore. But there comes a time when it simply makes more sense to start over. If you have to replace a slate roof, you're in for a big, expensive job, and any way to cut the costs is welcome. One strategy is to remove the old slate carefully so some of it can be reused. For example, you may want new slate installed on the front side of the roof, but be willing to live with the older slate installed on the back side or on a garage roof. If the slate is carefully removed, you may also be able to sell it in bulk to roofing companies that specialize in restoration work. Reinstalling a slate roof is definitely a job for an experienced roofing contractor who has good references.

Inspecting the roof
The roofs of older houses should be checked at least once a year. Start by taking a look at the roof from ground level. Usually, loose or askew slates can be spotted easily against the regular lines of the rest of the roofing. The color of any newly exposed slate will also indicate damage.

Look at the ridge against the sky to check for misalignment and gaps in the joints. Make a closer inspection with binoculars, focusing on all the flashing around chimneys, vents, and roof windows.

From inside an unfinished attic, you will be able to spot daylight through breaks in the slate. Also check the roof framing for water stains, which would indicate failure in the roofing or the flashing.

Individual tiles can be difficult to remove because of the the retaining nibs on their back edges and their interlocking shape.

To remove a plain tile that is broken, lift the nibs clear of the board that it rests on, then pull the tile out. This is easier if the overlapping tiles are first raised on wood wedges inserted at both sides of the tile (1). If the tile is also nailed, try rocking it loose. If this fails, you will have to break it out carefully. You may then have to use a ripper to extract or cut any remaining nails.

Use a similar technique for a single-lap interlocking tile, but in this case you will also have to wedge up the tile to the left of the one being removed (2). If the tile has a deep profile, you will have to ease up a number of surrounding tiles to achieve the required clearance.

If you are removing tiles in order to install something, for example a roof vent, then you can afford to break the one you are replacing. Use a hammer to crack it, taking care not to damage any of the adjacent tiles. The remaining tiles should be easier to remove once the first is taken out.

1 Lift the overlapping tiles with wedges

2 Lift interlocking tiles above and to the left

Removing and replacing a slate

A slate may slip out of place because the nails have corroded or because the slate itself has broken. Whatever the cause, loose or broken slates should be replaced as soon as possible, before a high wind strips them off the roof.

Use a ripper to remove the trapped part of a broken slate. Slip the ripper under the slate and locate its hooked end over one of the nails (1). Then pull down hard on the tool to extract or cut through the nail. Remove the second nail in the same way. Even

where an old slate has already fallen out completely, you still need to remove the nails so you can install the replacement slate.

You will not be able to nail a new slate in place. Instead, use a 1-inch-wide copper strip or a plastic clip designed for holding replacement slates in place. Attach the strip to the roof by driving a nail between the slates of the lower course (2), then slide the new slate into position and turn back the end of the strip to secure it (3).

Cutting slates and tiles

Cut slate with trowel

Or use slate cutter

Cutting slates
You may have to cut a slate to fit the gap in your roof. With a sharp point, scratch a cutline on the back of the slate. Then place the slate beveled side down on a bench or sawhorse. Hold the slate so the cutline is over the edge of the work surface. Then chop the slate with the edge of a mason's trowel. You can also use a slate cutter, if you can find one to rent. It works like a pair of sheetmetal snips. Either drill nail holes or punch them out with a masonry nail. A punched hole leaves a recess for the head of a roofing nail.

Cutting cement slates
Having scribed deep lines, break a cement tile over a straightedge or cut it to size with a circular saw outfitted with a masonry-cutting blade. If you saw cement slates, wear a dust mask and goggles. These slates are relatively brittle, so bore nail holes with a drill.

Cutting tiles
If you need to cut roof tiles, either use an abrasive blade in a circular saw or rent an angle grinder for the purpose. Always wear protective goggles and a dust mask when cutting tile.

Cutting roof tiles with an angle grinder
Follow scored guideline with cutting disc

When the old mortar breaks down, a whole row of ridge tiles can be left with practically nothing but their weight holding them in place.

Lift off the ridge tiles and clear all the crumbling mortar from the roof and from the undersides of the tiles. Be sure to soak the tiles in water before reinstalling them.

Mix 1 part cement and 3 parts sand to make a stiff mortar. Load a bucket about half full and carry it onto the roof. Dampen the top courses of the roof tiles or slates and lay a thick bed of mortar on each side of the ridge, following the line left behind by the old mortar (**1**). Lay mortar for one or two tiles at a time.

Press each ridge tile firmly into the mortar, and use a trowel to slice off mortar that has squeezed out. Try not to smear any on the tile itself.

Build up a bed of mortar to fill the hollow end of each ridge tile, inserting pieces of tile or slate to prevent the mortar from slumping (**2**). Install the rest of the tiles in the same way.

1 Apply bed of mortar on both sides of ridge

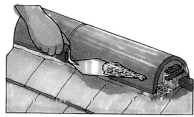

2 Insert pieces of slate to stabilize mortar

Ridge tiles

Thorough ventilation is the key to preserving wood shingles. Unless they can dry out after becoming wet, they will rot. Shingle roofs often have wide spaces between decking boards to allow significant airflow underneath. However, even if a solid sheathing like plywood is used, asphalt felt underlayment should never be installed between the sheathing and the shingles. If the roof has wood shakes instead of shingles, underlayment is recommended.

When you need to repair wood shingles or shakes, your first goal is to avoid causing more damage to the roof while you're working. Old wood shingles can be very brittle. The best time for shingle repair is the day after a soaking rain, when the shingles are still soft and somewhat pliable.

Access
To gain good access to the top of a broken shingle, you must lift the shingles above it with small wood wedges. Carefully drive the wedges under the good shingles until there's a gap of about ¼ inch. Then drive wedges under the bottom edge of the broken shingle to lift it slightly off the roof (**1**).

Removing the shingle
Using a chisel, split the broken shingle in several places, and pull out the waste (**2**). Split the pieces that are still held by the nails until the pieces can be pulled free.

To cut the nails, use a plain hacksaw blade with its end covered in duct tape (**3**). Cut the nails flush with the surface of the shingle below, so the new shingle will lay flat. Remove all the dust and wood chips from the repair area.

Installing the new shingles
Cut a new shingle to width so there's a ¼-inch gap on both sides. Then slide the shingle into the opening so its bottom edge lines up with the ones next to it. Remove the wedges that are holding up the shingles on the next course, and press these shingles down. Drive two nails into the replacement shingle. These should be located 1 inch in from both sides and 1 inch below the shingles above (**4**).

Making ridge repairs
Traditionally the ridge on wood roofs has been covered in two ways. One is with two boards nailed over the last course of shingles and butted together above the ridge. These

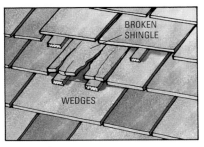

1 Using wedges
Drive wedges beneath damaged shingle and overlapping shingles in upper course.

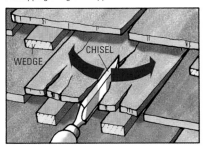

2 Removing damaged shingle
Remove damaged shingle by splitting it apart using a chisel.

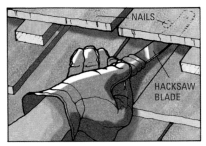

3 Sawing through nails
Saw through nails that held damaged shingle. Use a hacksaw blade wrapped with duct tape.

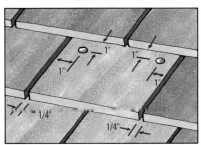

4 Installing new shingle in line with others
Leave ¼-inch gap on each side. Nail in place 1 inch from shingle edges and overlapping shingles.

boards are usually 1 x 4 cedar planks. If these boards are cracked, they should be replaced.

The other ridge-sealing method uses shingles that are nailed together in pairs to form a V-shaped cap. Each cap is nailed in place along the ridge, much like an asphalt shingle ridge cap. All the nails are covered by ensuing caps, and the exposure of the cap shingles matches the exposure on the roof. Broken cap shingles are repaired in the same way as other shingles.

ROOF SAFETY

Roof repairs

Working on a roof can be hazardous, and if you are unsure of yourself when working high off the ground, you should hire a contractor to do the work. If you do decide to do it yourself, it's best not to use ladders alone for roof repairs. Rent sectional scaffolding and scaffolding boards to provide a safe working platform.

All roofing materials are fragile, to a certain extent. Masonry roofing like slate, clay, and concrete tiles can break easily. Wood shingles and shakes get brittle over time. And even common asphalt roofing can be easily damaged, especially if you walk over it on a hot sunny day when the shingles are soft from the heat.

When you combine the possibility of roof damage with the safety concerns related to working off the ground, you may wonder who would ever work on their own roof. The answer is, not many people. But there are ways to work on a roof safely that won't damage the roofing. One of the best is to use a roof ladder (see below).

Roof ladders are common rental items that are made with elevated rails that keep the treads clear of the roof surface and spread the load over a larger area. The top section hooks over the ridge to keep the ladder from sliding. A roof ladder should reach from the scaffold at the eaves to the ridge of the roof. Some models are equipped with wheels, so you can roll the ladder up the slope and then turn it over to engage the hook. Never leave tools on the roof when they are not being used. And keep those that are needed safely inside a tool belt or a drywall bucket hanging from the side of a ladder tread.

A roof ladder allows safe access to roof

Repairing asphalt shingles

Curled shingles, or those that are slightly torn or broken off, can be repaired. Badly damaged shingles should be replaced. It's a good idea to take the weather into account before starting work. Pick a warm (but not hot) day if possible, so that shingles will be pliable but not soft to the touch. Cold stiffens asphalt shingles, causing them to crack easily.

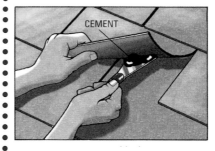

1 Fixing curled shingles
Apply a spot of roofing cement to the underside, then weight down the shingle with a brick. For torn shingles, apply cement liberally, press shingle down, and nail both edges. Apply roofing cement to nail holes before nailing heads down.

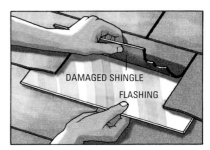

2 Repairing broken shingles
Cut a piece of metal flashing to size of the broken shingle, plus 3 inches on both sides. Apply roofing cement to underside of flashing, slide it in place beneath damaged shingle, then apply cement to top of flashing and press damaged shingle into it.

Replacing a shingle

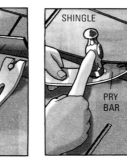

1 Replacing a shingle
Carefully lift the damaged shingle and pry up the nails with a flat bar. Then lift the shingle above the damaged one, pull the nails, and remove the shingle. Stubborn nails that remain should be driven flush with a flat bar and hammer.

2 Sliding the new shingle into place
Align the bottom edge of the new shingle with the edges of the adjacent shingles. Lift up the shingles above so you can nail the new shingle in place. Apply cement to the underside of all lifted shingles, and press them flat.

Ridge shingles

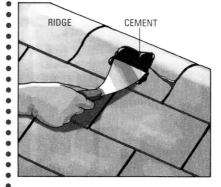

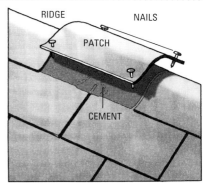

Repairing small flaws
Cover small damaged areas with roofing cement. If the damage is more extensive, repair with flashing as shown above or with a shingle patch (shown here). Apply cement to the damaged shingle, press the patch over it, and nail all four corners. Apply roofing cement to nail holes before driving the heads flush, to reduce the chance of leaks around the nails.

Flashing

Chimney flashing is usually in two parts: the base, or step, flashing that wraps completely around the chimney and under the roofing, and the cap, or counter, flashing that covers the top of the base flashing.

To replace chimney flashing, use a cold chisel to carefully chip out the mortar joints that hold the cap flashing and remove it. Then chisel the joints deeper, to a depth of about 1½ inches. Remove any roof shingles or other covering that overlaps the base flashing, and carefully pry it free. Use the old flashing pieces as patterns to cut new pieces, preferably from copper sheet sold for the purpose. Bend the flashing to shape after cutting, then fasten it in place using roofing cement. Attach the front piece of base flashing first, then the sides. Fasten the back piece last.

Reinstall, or replace, the shingles that cover the base flashing. Then install the cap flashing in the same order as the base flashing: front, sides, back. Fill all the joints with fresh mortar, and when it is fully cured, seal the joints with roofing cement.

Flashing is used to prevent water from getting under the roofing where two or more planes of a roof meet, or where the roof meets a wall. It is also used along edges of roofs, and around windows and doors to direct water away from the inside of the house. Flashing is also required around all vent openings. Roll roofing is commonly used for some flashing, particularly along valleys where two roofs meet. But the most durable flashing materials are aluminum and copper. Both are sold in rolls and rigid pieces.

Inspecting flashing

Inspect flashing at least once a year. Look for cracks or other damage where the flashing meets the chimney **(1)**, vent stack **(2)**, wall **(3)**, and dormer **(4)**, where roof planes meet at valleys **(5)**, along the rakes **(6)** and eaves **(7)**, and over the windows **(8)** and the doors **(9)**.

Very old flashing sometimes develops pinholes which are hard to see. These can be repaired by coating them with plastic roof cement.

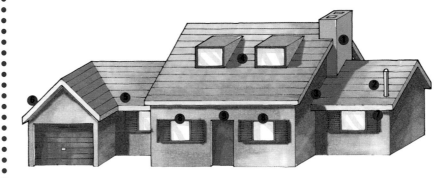

Maintenance and repair

It is not a bad idea to coat all flashing seams periodically with plastic roofing cement, especially at chimneys and around vent stacks. Apply the cement using a small mason's trowel and smooth the surface of the cement so that it does not form hollows and ridges where water may collect. Where you find holes 1-square-inch or bigger, cut a patch from the same material as the flashing. Make it 1 inch larger than the hole all around. Apply cement to the damaged flashing, press the patch into place, then cover the entire area with cement and smooth the surface.

Repointing flashing

Where flashing meets brick, it is usually embedded in mortar. Separations here require immediate repair since the loose flashing actually collects water and funnels it between the bricks where it can spread and do considerable damage. If the flashing itself is sound, just rake out the old mortar from the joint to a depth of about ¾ inch. Press the flashing back into place, wedging it if necessary with small stones. Then, using a trowel, fill the seam with fresh mortar. Smooth the joint carefully. After the mortar has fully cured, seal the flashing with roofing cement.

Rake out joint and repoint with fresh mortar.

Galvanic action

Dissimilar metals touching each other react when wet. As a result, metal flashing must be fastened with nails made of the same metal as the flashing, otherwise one or the other will corrode, often quickly. If it is impossible to match flashing and fasteners, use neoprene washers with the fasteners to prevent direct contact between the two metals. The chart (right) shows common construction metals. When paired, metals farthest apart in the chart corrode soonest and fastest. Metals in contact with acid-containing woods, like redwood and cedar, can also corrode.

Base flashing

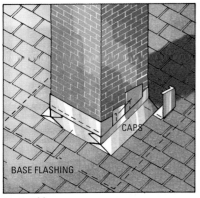

Cap flashing

Corrosion Table
1 Aluminum
2 Zinc
3 Steel
4 Tin
5 Lead
6 Brass
7 Copper
8 Bronze

Flashing repairs

Vertical wall flashing

A row of individual, overlapping flashing shingles are often installed where dormers join roofs and where a roof joins a higher house wall. To locate and repair leaks in these areas, the siding and roofing must be removed.

Look for rotten or discolored sheathing, and evidence that settling has occurred, which may have pulled house sections apart slightly. After repairing any of these problems, fill any gaps between building sections with strips of wood. Apply new felt underlayment over the wood, then reflash the area as you reshingle.

To do this, attach a flashing shingle at the end of each course, fastened to the vertical surface with one nail at the upper corner. Each flashing shingle should overlap the one underneath, and extend at least 4 inches up the adjacent wall and 2 inches under the roofing. After the flashing and the roofing are completely installed, attach new siding to cover the top edge of the flashing.

Wall flashing

Drip flashing

During construction, strips of flashing are installed above doors and windows and along the edges of the roof. These should extend several inches under the siding or roof covering and be nailed well away from the edges. On roofs, the drip edge goes on top of the underlayment along the rake and beneath it at the eaves. If minor repairs do not suffice, remove the siding or roof covering that overlaps the flashing. Determine the cause of the leak, then replace the drip edge, cover any seams with roofing cement, and reinstall the siding or roofing material.

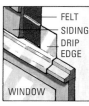

Drip edge

Flat roof flashing

Layers of felt that constitute a built-up roof are generally left long at the edges to create a raised flashing that angles up to adjacent walls. Cracks often develop where the turn begins. To repair, first cement down any loose roofing, then cover the area with a generous layer of roofing cement. Cut additional strips of felt, and build up the flashing by laying down alternate layers of felt and cement to obtain a smooth, even rise with no hollows that can retain water.

Flat roof

Flashing a vent stack

Sometimes you may be able to stop leaks by tightening the lead collar (if one is present) around the neck of a pipe where it passes through the roof.

To do this, tap the collar with a blunt cold chisel and a hammer. Work around the upper rim of the collar, sealing it against the stack.

Also try coating the entire flashing area and lower portion of the vent stack with roofing cement. If a good repair is not possible, then you'll have to install new flashing.

First, carefully remove the shingles that are covering the old flashing. In some cases you can just slip a new piece of flashing over the old one and replace the roofing.

But in most cases, you'll have to pry up the old flashing (**1**), place a new piece of felt on the the roof sheathing, install the new flashing (**2**), and then reinstall the roofing. The flashing should always overlap the bottom shingles and fit under the top shingles (**3**).

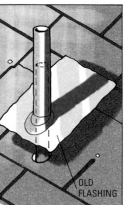 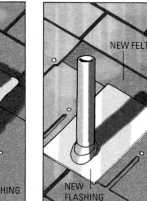

1 Remove shingles and old flashing **2 Install new felt and flashing** **3 Reapply shingles**

Renewing valley flashing

Where shingles are trimmed so that flashing is visible, the construction is called an open valley. When the shingles overlap the flashing, hiding it from view, it's called a closed valley.

Small repairs to open valley flashing can be made with roofing cement. Larger holes can be patched with flashing material coated on the bottom and top with roofing cement. Leaks from no apparent source may sometimes be stopped by applying a bead of cement between the edges of the trimmed shingles and the flashing.

To repair closed valley flashing, first try slipping squares of copper or aluminum flashing material underneath the shingles in the damaged area. Loosen or remove the nails closest to the valley, then bend and install the squares beginning at the bottom of the roof. Overlap them until they extend 2 inches beyond the damaged area. Renail the shingles and cover the nailheads with roofing cement. If leaks persist, remove the valley shingles and install new flashing. Then replace the shingles.

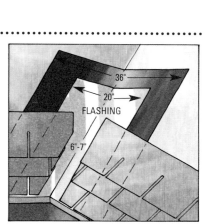

Open valley flashing

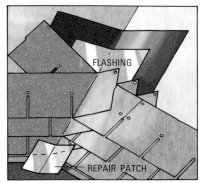

Closed valley flashing

Gutters

A properly sized system of gutters and downspouts, in good working condition, constitutes basic preventive maintenance. Gutters prevent water from running down the sides of the house, causing damage and discoloration. Combined with downspouts, gutters also direct water away from the foundation of the building, lessening the risk of the basement flooding and the foundation settling. Gutters also protect flowerbeds and other landscaping around the perimeter of the house. Inspect gutters frequently.

Gutters and downspouts

Gutters are made of a number of materials. Traditional preferences were for wood or copper. Although both are still used occasionally, most gutters now are made of galvanized steel, aluminum, and vinyl.

The size and layout of a gutter system must allow it to discharge all the water from the roof area it serves. The flow load required depends mainly on the area of the roof.

For roofs with areas less than 750 square feet, 4-inch-wide gutters usually suffice. Choose 5-inch gutters for roofs with areas between 750 and 1400 square feet. Six-inch gutters are available for even larger roofs.

Downspouts also should be properly sized to carry away runoff. For roof areas up to 1000 square feet, 3-inch downspouts are usually sufficient. Larger roofs require 4-inch downspouts.

The location of downspouts can affect the system's performance. A central downspout can serve double the roof area of one with an end outlet. A right-angled bend in guttering will reduce the flow capacity by about 20 percent, if it is placed near the outlet downspout.

GUTTER HANGERS

There are three basic types of hanging hardware for gutters (see below). Although 30-inch spacing is standard, 24-inch spacing provides better support to withstand snow and ice loads.

Gutter spike is driven through gutter into fascia board. Sleeve fits in trough.

Strap hanger fastens under shingle

Bracket fastens to fascia board

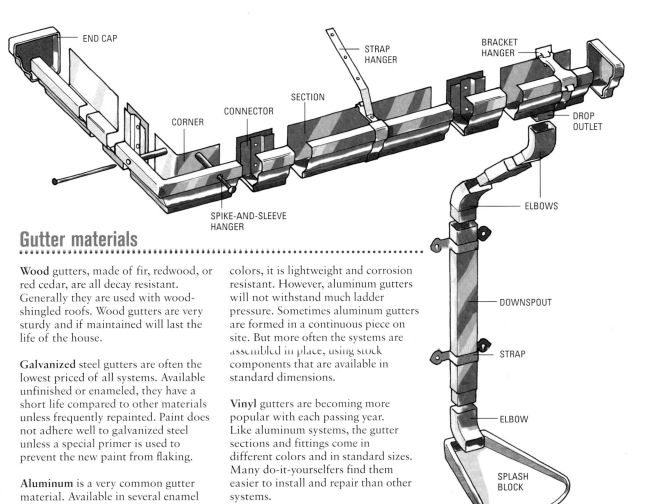

Gutter materials

Wood gutters, made of fir, redwood, or red cedar, are all decay resistant. Generally they are used with wood-shingled roofs. Wood gutters are very sturdy and if maintained will last the life of the house.

Galvanized steel gutters are often the lowest priced of all systems. Available unfinished or enameled, they have a short life compared to other materials unless frequently repainted. Paint does not adhere well to galvanized steel unless a special primer is used to prevent the new paint from flaking.

Aluminum is a very common gutter material. Available in several enamel colors, it is lightweight and corrosion resistant. However, aluminum gutters will not withstand much ladder pressure. Sometimes aluminum gutters are formed in a continuous piece on site. But more often the systems are assembled in place, using stock components that are available in standard dimensions.

Vinyl gutters are becoming more popular with each passing year. Like aluminum systems, the gutter sections and fittings come in different colors and in standard sizes. Many do-it-yourselfers find them easier to install and repair than other systems.

Gutter maintenance

Repairing small holes

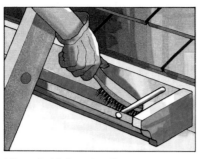

1 To repair pinholes and small rust spots
First clean the gutter and scrub the damaged area using wire brush or coarse abrasive paper. Wipe away residue using a rag dipped in paint thinner.

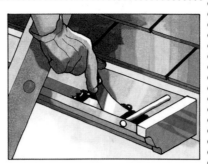

2 Apply coat of roofing cement
On holes larger than ¼ inch, sandwich layers of heavy aluminum foil between coats of roofing cement. Smooth topcoat so water won't collect.

Patching large areas

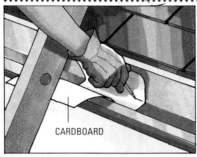

CARDBOARD

1 To repair a large hole
First use thin cardboard to make a pattern, then cut a patch of the same material as the gutter to fit over the area, overlapping the hole at least 1 inch.

2 Coat with roofing cement
Press the patch into a bed of roofing cement, then crimp it over the edge of the gutter. Apply another layer of cement, smoothing it so water won't collect.

Maintaining wood gutters

Repaint wood gutters at least once every three years. Be sure to work during a period of warm, fair weather.

First clear the gutter and allow a few days for the wood to dry thoroughly. Next, sand the interior of the gutter smooth and remove the residue with a whisk broom and handheld vacuum. Wipe the sanded trough with paint thinner, then apply a thin coat of roofing cement mixed with paint thinner to brushing consistency. This helps the cement enter the pores of the wood.

After the first coat of cement has dried, wait two days, then apply a second thin coat. Sand and repaint the gutter exterior with two coats of high-quality house paint.

Snow and ice

Gutters can be badly distorted and even broken when large amounts of snow and ice accumulate inside. Dislodge the buildup with a broom from an upstairs window—if you can reach it safely. Otherwise, climb a ladder to clean the gutter.

If snow and ice become a regular seasonal problem, you should screw a snow board to the roof. Make it out of 1 x 3 lumber treated with a wood preservative. Install it about 1 inch above the eaves, using steel straps as shown on the right.

Inspect and clean out the interiors of gutters at least twice a year, in autumn after the leaves have fallen and again in early spring. Check more often if you live in a heavily wooded area. Use a ladder to reach the gutter. At least 12 inches of the ladder should extend above the gutter to provide safe working conditions.

First block the gutter outlet with a rag. Then, wearing heavy work gloves to avoid cuts, remove debris from the gutters. Scrape accumulated silt into a heap using a shaped piece of plastic or light sheetmetal. Then scoop it out with a garden trowel and deposit it in a bucket hung from the ladder.

Sweep the gutter clean with a whisk broom, then remove the rag and flush the gutter using a garden hose. Check whether the water drains completely or remains in standing pools, indicating a sagging gutter section.

Leaking seams where gutter sections are joined can be sealed using silicone caulk. For the best seal, disassemble the sections, apply caulk inside the seam, then reassemble the joint. Otherwise, spread caulk over the seam on the inside of the gutter and smooth the surface to avoid producing ridges that might trap water.

If downspouts are clogged, free them using a plumber's snake or drain auger. Work from the bottom if possible, to avoid compacting debris further. If necessary, disassemble the downspout sections to get at the blockage.

If downspout blockages are frequent, install leaf strainers in the gutter outlets. Or in severe situations, attach wire-mesh leaf guards over the entire length of the gutters to slow the accumulation of debris.

Leaf strainer

Wire-mesh leaf guard

A snow board protects gutters from snow and ice

Home security

It is, without a doubt, well worth taking reasonable precautions to protect yourself, your family and your property against the risks of fire and burglary. The cost and effort involved is small compared with the expense of replacement or even rebuilding—not to mention the hardship caused by personal injury or the loss of items of sentimental value.

How a burglar gains entry

Vulnerable areas of a house

1 The front door
Inadequate locks invite forced entry.

2 Darkened porch
Makes identification of callers difficult.

3 Back and side doors
Often fitted with inadequate locks.

4 French windows
Can be sprung with one well-placed blow.

5 Downstairs windows
A common means of entry if unlocked.

6 Upstairs windows
Vulnerable if they can be reached and opened easily.

Statistics prove that most intruders are opportunists in search of one or two costly items, such as electronic hardware (typically video cameras, television sets and computers), jewelry, or cash.

The average burglar takes only a few minutes to break into a house—often in broad daylight. Although it's virtually impossible to prevent a determined burglar from breaking in, you can do a great deal to make it difficult for the inexperienced criminal.

The illustration below indicates the vulnerable areas of an average house, and some methods for safeguarding them. Check each point and compare them with your home, to make sure that your security is adequate.

7 Attic trap door
The only way to enter a house from the attic.

8 Skylight
Quiet access to attic from back of house.

9 Ladder
Available ladder gives easy access to second floor windows.

10 Unlocked gate
Provides a convenient exit for a burglar removing bulky items.

11 Garage or shed
A potential source of housebreaking tools.

12 Downspout
As good as a ladder for an agile burglar.

13 Glass
Weak putty allows a thief to remove glass silently.

14 Burglar alarm
Valuable deterrent.

If you require more detailed information about home security, you can obtain free advice tailored to your needs.

Crime Prevention Officer
Local police usually have special officers responsible for advising both commercial establishments and private individuals on ways to improve the security of their premises. Telephone your nearest police station to arrange for a confidential visit to discuss any aspect of home security that may concern you.

Fire Prevention Officer
Contact your local fire department for advice on how to balance your concerns about home security against the need to provide adequate escape routes in case of fire. The fire department can also explain the merits of various types of simple firefighting equipment that are available to home owners.

Insurance companies
Check with your insurance company to see if your home and its contents are adequately covered against fire and theft. Most policies pay out only according to the value of objects at the time of their loss, which is usually not enough to replace covered items with new ones. You can opt for a higher-priced replacement-value policy that will guarantee the full replacement cost of lost or destroyed property.

In many cases you can reduce your premiums for both types of policies by installing a variety of security equipment such as motion detecting alarms or a whole house alarm system monitored by police.

Guarding against intruders

You can reduce the likelihood of burglary by adopting security-conscious habits. Discourage opportunist burglars by closing and locking all windows and doors, even when you're only going to be out for a short time. Break-ins have been known to occur while the whole family is watching television—so lock up before sitting down for the evening. When you leave the house at night, close the curtains and leave a light on that's attached to an automatic timer.

Don't open your front door to callers unless you know them or they've made a prior appointment. Even then, don't be afraid to ask for identification. Bona fide gas or electricity officials will expect to be challenged, so keep your door locked until you're satisfied that their identification is genuine.

When you go on vacation, cancel milk and newspaper deliveries. Install a timer switch that turns lights on and off to give the impression that the house is occupied. Also notify the Post Office to hold your mail until you return. And, it's a good idea to tell the police you're away and that a neighbor has a key. Deposit your valuables in a bank.

Marking your possessions with an invisible marker or engraving tool will help police identify your possessions if they are recovered after a theft.

Photograph jewelry, paintings, and other valuables that are difficult to mark, and keep a record of them at the bank in case of fire. You can also install a strong but compact floor or wall safe for storing valuables and important documents.

A checklist for guarding your home

1 Front door

If there's no answer when an intruder rings the doorbell, he may be tempted to force an entry. Install a high quality entry lockset and a strong deadbolt lock to your front door.

It's also a good idea to install a heavy duty security chain to the door and the jamb to prevent an intruder from bursting in as you open the door to see who's there. Also consider installing a peephole door viewer so you can identify callers without unlocking the door.

If you live in an apartment and the entrance door is the only vulnerable point of entry, consider having a multi-point lock fitted: it throws bolts into all four sides simultaneously. Make sure your door security will not prevent you from escaping in the event of a fire.

2 Darkened porch

Install a porch light so that you can identify callers after dark. Bright lighting on any porch may also make an intruder think twice before attempting to break in.

3 Back and side doors

A burglar can often work unobserved at the rear or side of a house. Consider motion-activated security lighting for these areas and install good entry locksets and deadbolt locks.

4 French windows

Insecure French windows can be opened easily with a heavy push or a kick. It is therefore essential to install bolt locks on the top and bottom of each sash. Also install locks on any sliding doors or windows.

5 Downstairs windows

These are always vulnerable—especially at the back and at the side of the house. Install locks that suit the material and style of the windows.

6 Upstairs windows

Even if these can be reached only with a ladder, to be on the safe side fit key-operated locks. Windows accessible by scaling a downspout, flat roof, or wall should be secured in the same way.

7 Attic trap door

Install a bolt on the trap door leading to your attic. Some attached houses have common attics, and burglars can break through dividing walls between houses.

8 Skylights

Windows at roof level are at risk if they can be reached easily by means of downspouts or from an adjacent building. Install a lock or a bolt to deter thieves.

9 Ladders

Some homeowners store ladders on the outside of their house or garage. These can provide easy access to the second floor or roof of any home.

10 Side gate

If your house has a side gate, lock it to prevent burglars from carrying away bulky items. Installing a trellis above the gate may stop them from vaulting over it.

11 Garages and sheds

Keep outbuildings locked to protect the contents and to prevent burglars from using your own tools to break into your house. Install either standard door locks or a heavy duty padlocks that can't be easily cut. Install the padlock plates with bolts instead of screws to prevent the lock from being pried off.

12 Downspouts

Paint downspouts with high-gloss enamel paint to keep burglars from climbing them. This paint makes it difficult to get a good grip.

13 Glass

Most people accept the risk that glass can be broken or cut. However, for greater security you can install plexiglass (which is much harder to cut and break) in the most vulnerable places. Other alternatives are to cover ordinary glass with a metal grille or to install exterior security shutters operated from inside.

14 Burglar alarm

Although an alarm is a useful deterrent, it should not be regarded as a sufficient safeguard on its own.

Outbuildings
Use a strong padlock and steel hasps to secure a garage or shed door.

● **Leaded windows**
Lead strips holding stained glass can be peeled silently and the glass removed. The only way to prevent this is to install a metal grille or a plexiglass storm window.

Securing doors

Doors are vulnerable to being forced, and are often used by burglars for a quick exit. For both reasons, it's worth installing strong locks and bolts. Don't just rely on the old lock that's currently installed in your door. It's very likely worn and nowhere near as secure as newer high-quality units. Some locks and bolts are designed specifically for use on front doors, while others are made for securing back or side doors.

Choosing the right lock

The door by which you leave the house —normally the front door—needs a particularly strong lock because it can't be bolted from inside except when you are at home. Back and side doors need extra protection against them being

forced open from outside. It's a good idea to add an extra keyed lock on the inside to prevent thieves from making an easy getaway with their spoils. Your basic choice of locks is between mortise and rim types.

Deadlocking cylinder rim locks

A deadlocking cylinder rim lock can be attached to an exit door as an alternative to a mortise lock—it locks automatically as the door is closed, so that the bolt cannot be forced back without a key except by turning the knob on the inside. On some models, one complete turn of the key prevents the lock from

being operated even from inside, so an intruder can't walk out of the front door with your property. The staple should be fixed into the edge of the door frame with screws so a well-placed kick won't easily rip the lock from the door.

Door latch
This type of lock does not provide adequate security on its own.

Mortise sashlock
Suitable for back and side doors.

Deadlocking cylinder rim lock
1 Cylinder
2 Lock body
3 Staple

Mortise locks

A mortise lock is installed in a deep slot cut in the edge of the door, so it cannot easily be tampered with. There are various models to suit the width of the door stile and the location and style of the door.

A mortise sashlock is suitable for back and side doors. It has a handle on each side to operate a springbolt, and a key-operated deadbolt that can't be pushed back once the door is closed.

Purely key-operated mortise locks or deadbolt locks are separate units usually installed on main exit doors because they are very difficult to force once they're locked. When used with high-quality keyed lockset you get the convenience of a knob on both sides of the door and the security offered by two keyed locks.

● **Changing locks**
There's no need to buy a new lock just because your key is lost or stolen. Simply take the old one to a locksmith, who will swap the internal mechanism for one that comes complete with a different set of keys.

Mortise lock
1 Striking plate
2 Faceplate
3 Lock body

Automatic timer switches
You can give the impression that someone is at home by using an automatic timer switch, plugged into an ordinary electrical wall socket, to control a table lamp or radio. Set the program to switch the light or radio on and off several times over a period of 24 hours. Alternatively, buy a more sophisticated switch that will turn the lighting on and off at different times every day of the week. Some models also provide for random program switching.

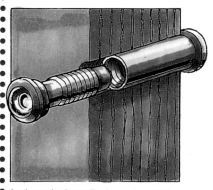

24-hour time switch

Installing a door viewer
A peephole door viewer enables you to identify callers before opening the door. Select a viewer with as wide an angle of vision as possible: you should be able to see someone standing to the side of the door or even crouching below the viewer. Choose one that is adjustable to fit any thickness of door.

Drill a hole of the recommended size—usually ½ inch—right through the center of the door at a comfortable eye level. Insert the barrel of the viewer into the hole from the outside. Then screw on the eyepiece from inside.

A telescopic viewer fits doors of any thickness

Installing door locks

Installing a mortise lock

Scribe a vertical center line on the edge of the door with a marking gauge and use the lock body as a template to mark the top and bottom of the mortise (**1**). Choose a drill bit that matches the thickness of the lock body and drill out the majority of the waste wood for the mortise between the marked lines.

Square up the edges of the mortise with a chisel (**2**) until the lock fits snugly in the slot. Mark around the edge of the faceplate with a knife or pencil (**3**), then chop a series of shallow cuts across the waste with a chisel. Clean out the recess until the faceplate is flush with the edge of the door.

Hold the lock against the face of the door and mark the center of the keyhole with an awl (**4**). Clamp a block of scrap wood to the other side of the door, over the keyhole position, and drill right through on the center mark —the block prevents the drill bit from splintering the face of the door as it breaks through on the other side. Cut out the keyhole slot on both sides with a keyhole saw or a sabre saw.

   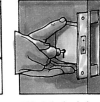

1 Mark the mortise   **2 Chop out the waste**   **3 Mark the faceplate**   **4 Mark the keyhole**

Screw the lock into its recess and check its operation; screw on the coverplate and then the escutcheons over the holes on each side of the door (**5**). With the door closed, operate the bolt to mark the position of the striking plate on the door frame. If the bolt has no built-in marking device, turn the bolt fully out, then push the door closed so you can draw round the bolt on the face of the frame (**6**).

Mark and cut the bolt mortise and shallow recess for the striking plate (**7**), as described for the lock itself.

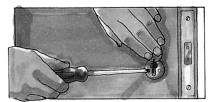 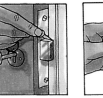

5 Screw the escutcheons on to cover the keyhole   **6 Mark bolt on frame**   **7 Fit striking plate**

Installing a cylinder rim lock

Although instructions vary from model to model, the following method shows how easy it is to install a cylinder rim lock. Using the templates provided with the lock, mark then drill the holes for the cylinder (**1**). Hold the lock body against the door, so that you can mark and cut a recess for its flange (**2**).

Pass the cylinder into the hole from the outside and check the required length of the flat connecting bar. If necessary cut it to size with a hacksaw (**3**). Bolt the cylinder to the door.

Screw the mounting plate for the lock on the inside of the door (**4**) and attach the lock body to it. Screw the lock's flange into the recess in the edge of the door, making sure it lies flush.

Use the lock as a guide for positioning the staple on the door frame. Chisel out a shallow recess for the staple, then screw it to the frame.

1 Mark cylinder center   **2 Scribe around flange**   **3 Cut connecting bar**   **4 Attach mount plate**

There are many types of bolts for securing a door from the inside. Rack bolts can be fitted into the edge of the door and have the advantage of being unobtrusive as well as secure.

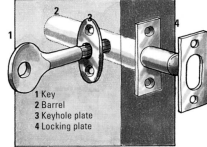

The components of a standard rack bolt

1 Key
2 Barrel
3 Keyhole plate
4 Locking plate

First mark the locations of the two door holes. Then drill a hole—usually ⅝ inch in diameter—in the edge of the door for the barrel of the bolt. Use a square to transfer the center of the hole to the inside face of the door. Mark the keyhole, then drill it with a ⅜-inch bit and insert the bolt (**1**).

With the key holding the bolt in place, mark the recess for the face plate (**2**); then pare out the recess with a chisel. Screw the bolt and keyhole plate to the door. Operate the bolt to mark the frame, then drill a ⅝-inch hole to a depth that matches the length of the bolt. Install the locking plate.

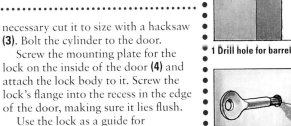

1 Drill hole for barrel and key, install bolt

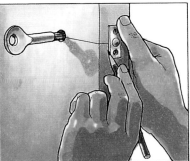 

2 With key in place, draw around face plate

Attaching a security chain
No special skills are needed to install a security chain. Simply screw the mounting plates to the door and frame; the security chain should be positioned just below the main door lock.

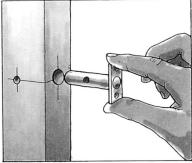

Securing windows

Since windows are particularly vulnerable, it's worth making sure they're adequately secured. There are all sorts of locks for wooden and metal windows, including some that lock automatically when you close the window. Locks for metal frames are more difficult to install because you may have to cut threads for the screw hardware.

How windows are locked

The type of lock suitable for a window depends on how the window opens. Sliding sashes are normally secured by locking the sashes together, whereas casements—which open like doors—should be fastened to the outer frame or locked by rendering the catches and stays immovable.

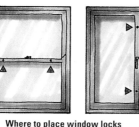

Where to place window locks
The black dots indicate the best positions for bolts or locks.

Window locks must be strong enough to resist forcing and have to be situated correctly for optimum security. On a small window, for example, fit a single lock as close as possible to the center of the meeting rail or vertical stile; on larger windows, you will need two locks, spaced apart.

Locks that can be operated only by a removable key are the most secure. Some keys will open any lock of the same design—an advantage in that you need fewer keys for your windows, though some burglars carry a range of standard keys. With other locks, there are several key variations.

Wooden windows need to be fairly substantial to accommodate mortise locks, so surface-mounted locks are frequently used instead. These are perfectly adequate and, being visible, act as a deterrent.

If the mounting screws are not concealed when the lock is in place, drill out the center of the screws after installation so they cannot be withdrawn.

Sash windows

Installing dual screws

Cheap but effective, a dual screw consists of a bolt that passes through both meeting rails so that the two sashes are immobilized. The screw is operated by a special key, and there is little to see when the window is closed.

With the window shut and the catch engaged, fit a dual screw by drilling through the inner meeting rail into the outer one; wrap tape around the drill bit to gauge the depth. Slide the sashes apart and tap the two bolt-receiving devices into their respective holes. Then close the window again and use the key to insert the threaded bolt until it is flush with the window frame. If necessary, saw the bolt to length.

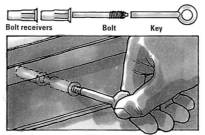

Bolt receivers   Bolt   Key

Turn a dual screw until it is flush with the frame

Fitting a key-operated lock

These are simple locks that screw to the top surface of the two meeting rails, effectively clamping the rails together.

Installing sash stops

When the bolt is withdrawn with a key, a sash stop mounted on each side of a window allows it to be opened slightly for ventilation. As well as deterring burglars, sash stops prevent small children from opening the window any further.

To install a stop, drill a hole in the upper sash for the bolt, then screw the faceplate over it (on close-fitting sashes, you may have to recess the faceplate). Screw the protective plate to the top edge of the lower sash.

Extract sash stop with a key to secure window

Casement windows

Installing rack bolts

On large casement windows, install rack bolts – as described for doors.

Installing a casement lock

A locking bolt can easily be mounted on a wooden window frame: the bolt is engaged by turning a simple catch, but can only be released with a removable key. With the lock body screwed to the part of the window that opens, mark and cut a small mortise in the fixed frame for the bolt. Then screw on the coverplate.

A similar device for metal windows, is a clamp which, when fixed to the opening part of the casement, shoots a bolt that hooks over the fixed frame.

A good casement lock has a removable key

Locking a cockspur handle

A cockspur handle, which secures the opening edge of the casement to the fixed frame, can be locked by means of an extending bolt that you screw to the frame below the handle. However, make sure that the handle is not worn or loose – otherwise the lock may be ineffective.

Lockable handles that allow you to secure a window that's left ajar for ventilation can be substituted in place of a standard cockspur handle.

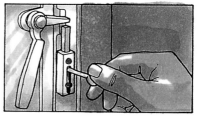

An extending bolt stops the handle from turning

Pivot windows

If a pivot window is not supplied with an integral lock, use rack bolts or locks recommended for casement windows.

Burglar alarms

Fanlight windows

You can buy a variety of casement locks, as well as devices that secure the stay to the window frame. The simplest kind is screwed below the stay arm to receive a key-operated bolt passed through one of the holes in the stay arm. Manufactured lockable stays are also available.

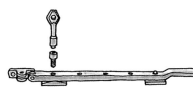

The device bolts the stay to the window frame

A better alternative is a device that clamps the window to the surrounding frame. Attach the lock first, then use it to position the staple.

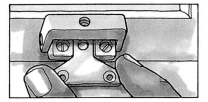

Attach the lock first in order to locate the staple

French windows

French windows and other glazed doors are vulnerable to forcing—a burglar only has to break a pane to reach the handle inside. Key-operated locks are essential to prevent a break-in.

Each door of a French window needs a rack bolt both at the top and bottom, positioned so that one bolt shoots into the upper frame and the other into the sill below. It's necessary to take each door off its hinges in order to install the lower bolt; if that's difficult, install a lockable surface-mounted bolt instead.

Locking sliding doors

If you have aluminum sliding patio doors, install additional locks at the top and bottom to prevent the sliding frame from being lifted off its track. These locks are sometimes expensive, but they are easy to install and provide good security.

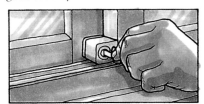

Install top and bottom lock on sliding door

Although it is no substitute for good locks and catches, an alarm system provides extra security and may deter intruders if there are less well-protected premises nearby. The system itself must be reliable, and you and your family need to be disciplined in its use. If your neighbors are constantly subjected to false alarms, they are less likely to call the police in a genuine emergency. In most areas, the police will not respond unless they are alerted by a member of the public or the system is professionally monitored. However, it pays to give the police a record of two alarm-key holders they can contact if your alarm does goes off.

Typical alarm systems

Alarm systems differ greatly, but there are two basic categories: passive systems that detect the presence of an intruder inside the house, and perimeter systems that guard all likely means of entry. The best systems incorporate a combination of features.

Control unit

Where one is installed, the control unit is the heart of the system, all the detectors being connected to it. From it, the signal is passed to a bell or siren. The control unit has to be set to allow sufficient time for legitimate entry and exit. If it has a zone-monitoring option, you can activate door contacts or sensors in selected parts of the house—to permit freedom of movement upstairs at night, for example, while entry doors and downstairs areas remain fully guarded.

The control unit must be tamper-proof, so that it will trigger the alarm if disarming is attempted by any means other than a key or the correct digital code. It is usually wired directly to the house electrical service panel, but it should also have a rechargeable battery, in case of power failure.

Detectors

Entrances can be outfitted with magnetic contacts that trigger the alarm when broken by someone opening a door or window. Other types of detectors sense vibrations caused by

an attempted entry, including breaking glass. They must be accurately placed and set to distinguish between an intrusion and vibration from external sources.

Scanning devices

Infra-red sensors can be strategically positioned to scan a wide area. The height of the beam can be adjusted to ignore pets. Detectors of this type are usually connected to a central control unit, but there are independent battery-operated sensors for single room.

The alarm

Most burglar alarms have a bell or siren mounted on an outside wall. These should switch off automatically after a set period, but some alarms are designed to continue signaling with a flashing light and some will automatically rearm themselves. Many systems transmit a warning directly to a monitoring center for quick response. Whichever type you choose, it is important that the alarm is triggered by any attempt to tamper with it, either by dismantling or by cutting wires.

Personal-attack button

With most systems you can have a "panic button" installed beside entry doors or elsewhere in the house to press in the event of an attack. Pressing a personal-attack button trips the alarm even when the system is switched off.

DIY systems

If you want to avoid the expense of professional installation, there are several DIY alarm systems that are quick and easy to install. However, you may need advice from the supplier of the equipment on the choice and siting of sensors and detectors. Consult your insurance company to check whether your choice of alarm affects your policy in any way.

Make sure the system will enable you to select the type and number of detectors you require, and that it incorporates a reliable tamper-proof control unit.

Wireless systems, which use secure coded radio signals to trigger the alarm, avoid the need for extensive wiring and can be extended to monitor sheds and garages.

● **Infrasonic alarms**
Some alarm systems can detect the ultra-low noise levels created by the displacement of air caused by opening or closing doors and windows. Even when the alarm is set, neither you nor your pets will trigger it unless you open a door or window. Infrasonic alarms are particularly easy to install.

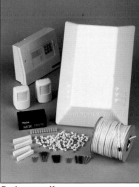

Do-it-yourself burglar alarm system

Protecting against fire

No one needs to be reminded about the potential risk of fire, yet nearly all domestic fires are caused by carelessness. Many fires could be prevented by taking sensible precautions.

Avoiding the risks

Make sure your electrical installations and equipment are safe and in good order. Don't overload receptacles with adaptors and extension cords. Install more receptacles instead. Don't trail long extension cords under carpets or rugs If the wiring becomes damaged it could overheat and start a serious fire.

Never leave fires or space heaters unguarded, especially when there are children in the house. And don't dry clothes in front of a fire—they could easily fall into the flames.

Take particular care with smoking materials. Empty ashtrays at night, but dampen the contents before discarding them. Don't rest ashtrays on chair arms: a burning cigarette's center of gravity shifts as it burns, which may cause it to topple off and ignite the upholstery. Never smoke in bed. Fires are frequently caused by smokers falling asleep and setting fire to the bedding.

Keep your workshop or garage clear of shavings and trash, especially oily rags, which can ignite spontaneously. If possible, store flammable chemicals and paints in an outbuilding away from the house.

As a means of fighting a fire, install an all-purpose fire extinguisher in a prominent position, preferably on an escape route. Mount a fire blanket close to—but not directly above—the range or cooktop. Members of your local fire department will be able to recommend equipment for domestic use. Don't buy inferior items: they may not work in an emergency.

Fire blankets and extinguishers
Portable extinguishers should located in, at least, the kitchen, basement and garage. Extinguishers must be serviced regularly.

Smoke detectors
A detector provides an early warning of fire.

Providing escape routes

Your first responsibility is to ensure that your family can escape safely if your house should catch fire. Before you go to bed, close internal doors—which will help to contain a fire—but don't lock them. Locked internal doors rarely deter burglars anyway.

Although you shouldn't leave a key in an external lock, keep it close by but out of reach of the door or window. Make sure everyone in the house knows where the key is kept, and always return it to the same place after use. Ensure some accessible part of double-glazed windows can be opened to afford an emergency escape route.

Keep stairs and hallways free from obstructions as they may be difficult to see in dense smoke. Avoid using space heaters to warm these areas in case they get knocked over during an escape and spread the fire further. Communal stairs to apartments are especially important, so try to persuade neighbors to keep them clear.

In the event of a fire, get everyone out of the building quickly, alert neighbors and call the fire department. If it is safe to do so, close doors and windows as you leave, but never open a door that feels warm—it could be protecting you from a fire on the other side.

Fighting a fire

Don't attempt to tackle a fire yourself unless you discover it early. Make sure that everyone in your family knows what to do in the event of a fire.

Fat fire
Cooking oil ignites when it reaches a certain temperature, and unattended frying pans are one of the most common causes of domestic fires. Don't attempt to move a burning pan. Instead:
● Turn off the source of heat.
● Smother the fire with a close-fitting lid or a fire blanket. Alternatively, quickly soak a towel in water, wring it out, and drape it over the burning pan.

● Let the pan cool for half an hour.
● If you aren't able to extinguish the fire immediately, call the fire department.

Chimney fire
If there is a blaze in a chimney, call the fire department and cover the fireplace opening with a screen. Remove rugs, in case burning material drops onto them.

Clothes on fire
If someone's clothes catch fire, throw the person onto the ground and roll him or her in a blanket or rug. Seek medical attention in the event of burns.

A smoke detector will identify the presence of smoke, even before flames start, and sound a shrill warning. Although detectors can be incorporated into an alarm system, self-contained battery-operated units are easier to install yourself. Make sure you change the battery at least once a year, and remember to check that the detector is working by pressing its test button every month.

There are two basic types of smoke detector. Photoelectric devices detect smoke from smoldering or slow-burning fires which give off large quantities of smoke. Ionization detectors are marginally less sensitive to smoldering fires but are more attuned to small particles of smoke produced by hot, blazing fires such as a burning frying pan. There are also detectors that combine both systems to give good all-round performance.

Siting a smoke detector
The best place for a smoke detector is on the ceiling, at least one foot away from any wall or light fixture. If it has to be wall mounted, make sure it is six inches to one foot below the ceiling. Don't install a smoke detector in a kitchen or bathroom, as steam can trigger the alarm; and don't fix one directly above a heater or an air-conditioning vent.

If you live in a one-story house, install a smoke detector in the hallway between the bedrooms and living area(s). For a two-story home, place at least one detector in the hallway, directly above the bottom of the stairs. If possible, install a second alarm on the landing. Some alarms can be linked with bell wire—if one detects smoke, they are all triggered at once.

Gas detectors
There are devices that warn you before escaping gas reaches a dangerous concentration. They are normally designed to detect natural gas, so are usually screwed to a wall no more than one foot below the ceiling of the kitchen or the room where the main gas appliance is installed.

If the alarm sounds, extinguish any open flames, including cigarettes, and don't operate electrical switches. Turn off the gas supply at the meter and open all the doors and windows. Then, call the gas company's Emergency Service number.

Infestation: insects

Your homes and surroundings are often invaded by insect pests. Some of them are quite harmless, although they can be very annoying. But others can cause real problems by seriously weakening your home's basic structure. Unfortunately, these pests can often go unnoticed until the damage is done. At the first sign of infestation, try to identify the cause and then eradicate it as quickly as possible, before it gets out of control.

Termites

Termites are wood-eating insects, prevalent in nearly all parts of the country. Although if neglected they can cause severe damage, infestation is easily eradicable by professional pest-control experts. And in many cases, it can be prevented by incorporating special, relatively inexpensive building techniques during construction.

Of the three significant species of termites in the U.S., subterranean, damp-wood, and dry-wood, the subterranean variety does the most damage. These ¼-inch-long pests live underground, often at depths of up to 25 feet, and travel to the surface for food. They eat only cellulose, the material of wood fiber, and must avoid both light and the drying effects of open air. If they are shut off from moisture, which they receive by living in the ground, they die in only a few days.

Termites colonize as ants do, and their societies are composed of groups of specialized members. Within a colony there are winged termites,

Damp-wood termite

whose job it is to reproduce, and wingless termites, some of which act as soldiers to defend the colony, and others that are workers, whose job it is to construct tunnels and forage for food. It is the workers that do the most damage.

Because termites avoid light, they feed entirely within the wood they find, so their presence is often hard to detect. As they travel upward from their nests, they feed on any wood in contact with the ground and will sometimes build earth-covered tunnels up the sides of impervious materials, such as masonry foundation walls or pipes, to reach still higher. They can also burrow through weak mortar joints and poorly laid concrete.

Once a year, in the spring or early summer, the winged, reproductive termites swarm, leaving their nest to fly to a new location to found another colony. Often the migration takes place only for a few hours. At the new site, the termites drop their wings and tunnel underground.

Damp-wood and dry-wood termites

Damp-wood termites do not require soil moisture. They may reach 1 inch in length and have a 2-inch wingspan. They inhabit only moisture-soaked wood and presently are a problem mostly along the Pacific coast.

Dry-wood termites resemble subterraneans but require very little moisture to survive. Instead of dwelling underground, they bore

directly into above-ground wood (even furniture) then plug their holes behind them as they begin to colonize. Currently, dry-wood termites are not a widespread problem in the U.S. They threaten only a narrow zone along the Atlantic and Gulf coasts south from Virginia, the lower portions of Texas, and the Pacific coast up to northern California.

Identifying termites

Winged subterranean termites are sometimes mistaken for flying ants, and vice versa. But the two can be distinguished by inspecting their wings and bodies. Termites have 4 equal-size wings. Flying ants also have 4 wings, but one pair is smaller than the other. Characteristic of flying ants is their distinctive pinched-in waist, separating their bodies into distinct sections: thorax and abdomen. Termites have thick waists and, compared to ants,

their body sections are harder to distinguish.

Winged termites, like ants, are dark-colored (sometimes even black) and have completely formed, hard-walled bodies. Soldier termites are also dark. They have large, hard heads, strong jaws and strong legs, but their bodies are soft. They are blind. Workers are also blind, but their bodies are pale yellow, gray or white, and almost completely soft.

Termites
1 Winged adult
2 Soldier
3 Worker
4 Queen
5 King

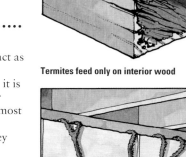

Termites feed only on interior wood

Termite tunnels along foundation wall

Freestanding termite tunnels

Probe suspect wood with penknife

Insect infestation

Locating termites

Termite inspections are required as part of most house sales, particularly when a mortgage is involved. In areas where infestation is common, once- or twice-yearly inspections should be made as well, although termites progress slowly and severe damage may take 2 or more years to develop. Here is where and how to look for termites:

Search for tunnels leading from moist earth towards a wood supply. Termite tunnels are half-round, approximately ¼ to ½ inch in diameter, and appear to be made of cement. Normally tunnels are attached to some other surface, but in some instances they may be free-standing. Inspect foundation walls (inside and out), pipes rising from damp earth, and foundation piers. Also check for evidence around foundation cracks,

pipe openings, and especially sill joints, where the wood walls of a house rest on top of the foundation. Inspect the seams where concrete patio, garage, or basement slabs meet the house. Also check around basement windowsills and crawlspace ventilators.

Examine any wood that is in contact with the ground for direct entry of termites. Such sites include the bottoms of wooden stairs and railings, fence posts, trellises, firewood, and lumber piles, even dead tree stumps.

In spring and early summer, watch for swarms of flying insects which may be termites. They normally enter wood at points near ground level, such as around house foundations, and leave piles of discarded wings at the entrance to the new colony.

Installing metal termite shields between foundation walls and wood sills and around pipes entering the soil from the house structure above is an effective way to prevent termite infestation. In addition, foundation walls should extend at least 6 inches above ground level, and the distance between joists and soil in crawlspaces should be a minimum of 18 inches.

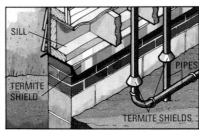

Protecting possible entry points

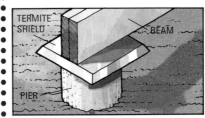

Protecting structural wood members

Testing for damage

Because termite damage is seldom visible, probe suspect wood with a penknife, screwdriver, or ice pick. If the tool penetrates the wood easily to a depth of ½ inch or more, damage is present. Pry away a portion of the soft

wood. If this procedure uncovers chambers or cavities, suspect termites or other wood-boring insects. If the wood seems intact but is uniformly spongy, most likely the problem is not termites, but rot.

Sources of termite infestation
1 Foundation too low
2 Sill and joists contact soil
3 Soil heaped against pier
4 Wood framing contacts soil
5 Porch and steps contact soil
6 Construction scraps, or firewood, left on dirt basement floor
7 Post extends through concrete
8 Exterior wood siding too near grade
9 Wood framing around vent contacts soil
10 Softened, cracked lime mortar in old brick wall
11 Improper roof drainage (runoff collects around foundation)
12 Loose stucco
13 Cracks in concrete slab floor
14 Unshielded beam end
15 Wood framing beneath chimney (heat attracts termites)
16 Insufficient crawlspace height
17 Rotting stumps in yard
18 Untreated fence posts contact soil

Control measures

Once termites are present, the only effective method of extermination is to treat the soil with chemicals to create a toxic envelope surrounding the house. Chlordane is the chemical used most often. Using chlordane and other termite-controlling chemicals is permitted, but in some regions of the

country may be restricted to application by licensed professionals only. Pest-control poisons are hazardous and difficult to handle safely and apply effectively. If you suspect or locate termite damage, contact a reputable extermination company for help.

Eradicating insect pests

Insecticides are dangerous and should be used with caution. They can contaminate soil for long periods of time. They can work their way into our food supply from both plants and animals. And some are deadly to beneficial insects as well as the pests we don't want.

Ants

The common black ant will enter a house foraging for food. Once established, the workers follow well-defined trails. In summer, great numbers of winged ants emerge from the nest to mate but the swarming is over in a matter of hours, and the ants themselves are harmless. If winged ants stray into the house, they can be overcome with an aerosol insecticidal spray.

To locate the nest, follow the trail of ants. It will be situated under a path, at the base of a wall, in the lawn or under a flat stone, perhaps 20 feet from the house. Destroy the nest by pouring boiling water into the entrances. If this will damage plants, use an insecticidal dust or spray.

Common black ant

Wasps

Wasps are beneficial in spring and early summer, as they feed on garden pests, but later in the year they destroy soft fruit. They will also kill bees and raid the hive for honey. Wasps sting when aroused or frightened.

Trap foraging wasps in open jam jars containing a mixture of jam, water and detergent. Flying wasps can be killed in the air with an aerosol fly spray. You can destroy wasps at the nest by depositing insecticidal powder near the entrances and the areas where they alight. Approaching a nest can be hazardous, so tie a spoon to a long stick to extend your reach. You can also use a smoke generator where there is no risk of fire. Light a pellet, place it in the entrance and seal the opening.

Treat a wasp sting with a cold compress soaked in witch hazel or use an antihistamine cream or spray.

Wasp

Flies

Depending on the species, flies breed in rotting vegetables, manure, decaying meat, and offal. They can carry the eggs of parasitic worms and spread disease by leaving small black spots of vomit and excreta on foodstuffs. Make sure to cover exposed food and keep refuse sealed in plastic bin liners.

Tight-fitting window screens and screen doors will prevent flies from entering the house. An aerosol fly spray will deal with small numbers, but for swarming flies in a roof space, for instance, use an insecticidal smoke generator. These are available at hardware stores and agricultural supply outlets. Large numbers inside the house often can be sucked into a vacuum cleaner. After they're in the bag, vacuum up some insecticidal powder and wait a few hours before emptying the bag.

Housefly

Cockroaches

Cockroaches can appear anywhere there's a supply of food and water in warm conditions. Cockroaches are unhygienic and have an unpleasant smell. Being nocturnal feeders, cockroaches hide during the day in crevices and walls, behind cupboards, and especially under ranges, refrigerators, and near central heating pipes. A serious outbreak should be dealt with by a professional, but you can lay a finely dusted barrier of insecticidal powder between suspected daytime haunts and supplies of food. Don't sprinkle insecticides near food itself. Use a paintbrush to stipple powder into crevices and under baseboards. When you have eliminated the pests, fill all cracks and gaps to prevent their return.

Cockroach

Silverfish

Silverfish are tapered wingless insects about ½ inch long. They like moist conditions found in kitchens, bathrooms and basements. You may find them behind wallpaper, where they feed on the paste. Use an insecticidal spray or powder in these locations.

Silverfish

Carpenter ants

Damage from carpenter ants is often mistaken for termite infestation. However, ants tunnel only to construct nesting places; they remove excavated wood to the outside of their nests and keep the passageways clear. Termite galleries, on the other hand, are packed with sawdustlike material which is actually woody feces. This difference is a clear means of identifying which pest is at work.

Carpenter ants can be seen entering and leaving wood. They vary in size but a common variety is about ½ inch long, and either all black or black mixed with brown. All members of a colony are fully formed except the larvae. Small, isolated colonies can be eliminated by injecting pesticide dust into the galleries or into holes drilled at intervals along infested wood. For best results, hire a professional exterminator.

Winged adult   **Worker**

Carpenter bees

Carpenter bees most often resemble large bumblebees. They have black bodies with patches of yellow, and may be 1 inch long. Bees bore an individual tunnel approximately ¼ inch in diameter directly into wood, then turn at right angles and excavate extensive galleries running in the same direction as the wood grain in which they lay eggs. Control is the same as for carpenter ants.

Carpenter bee

Other insect pests

Beetle damage occurs chiefly in dry wood, including furniture. Adult beetles enter the wood through small natural openings, then lay eggs. The larvae then feed on the wood as they develop, causing damage that looks a great deal like termite damage. Beetles breed in the same wood generation upon generation, often for hundreds of years. Eventually the wood becomes so honeycombed with burrows that, as with termite damage, the structure collapses of its own weight. Evidence of beetle infestation is only slightly more noticeable from the outside than infestation by termites. You can sometimes see tiny "shot holes:" in the wood where adult beetles have chewed their way to the outside, particularly during spring or early summer.

In the U.S., three types of wood-boring beetles are collectively termed powder-post beetles. The two most common are the death watch beetle and the true powder-post beetle. Both are tiny—approximately ⅛ inch long. Death watches in America attack primarily Douglas fir (European species are known for destroying hardwoods), whereas powder-posts are attracted especially to hickory, ash, and oak. The third type, commonly called the lead cable borer, reaches 1 inch in length. Presently it thrives only in the semiarid southwest and California. Named for its habit of chewing into lead-lined electrical cables and similar materials during hot weather, this beetle is also prevalent in furniture and paneling made of oak and California laurel wood.

As with termites, extermination by professionals is the only reliable control. Infested furniture can be removed from the home and fumigated in a special chamber. On-site extermination in woodwork, paneling, and floors requires residents to vacate the building for several days.

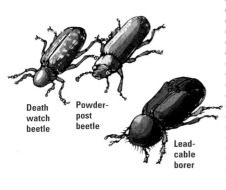

Death watch beetle

Powder-post beetle

Lead-cable borer

Centipedes and millipedes

These multilegged pests inhabit damp, dark areas and decaying vegetable matter. Usually they remain out of doors. However, they may frequent unused basements and wander into the house from below or from outside. Some centipedes may bite if they are injured. If that happens, apply antiseptic to the swelling and call your physician if symptoms persist. To control centipedes and millipedes, apply insecticide on doorsills, windowsills, and other places where pests are entering the house. Pay particular attention to baseboard areas where pests may migrate from the basement.

Earwigs

Easily recognized by their large rear pincers, these pests have become epidemic in many parts of the U.S. Earwigs inhabit moist, sheltered areas such as lawns and leafy garden vegetables, and damp stored fabric and carpeting. They are also frequently found in the hollow tubing of lawn furniture, in foundation cracks, and behind baseboards. Control these pests with insecticide sprayed or applied to these areas. Major infestations are not a do-it-yourself proposition. Call a professional exterminator.

Crickets

Crickets normally reside outdoors but may enter houses as autumn approaches or when populations increase during periodic cricket plagues. One or two of these insects are merely annoying because of their nocturnal chirping. An infestation can endanger many household items, including woolens, silks and paper, not to mention foodstuffs. To control crickets, spray insecticide around building entrances, baseboards and the edges of carpets. Also spray beneath furniture, in closets, and on floors behind drapes. Tight-fitting window screens and screen doors are effective, along with other preventive measures to physically bar crickets from the house.

Spiders

Any area of undisturbed space within a house may be home to spiders; however, most prefer dark places. Though all spiders inject venom when they bite, only two species, the black widow and the brown recluse, are considered dangerous to humans. To be on the safe side, treat all spider bites with antiseptic and report them immediately to a physician. Regular and frequent sweeping and dusting can help keep spider populations down, but spraying insecticide is the best cure for infestations. To be sure of eradicating spiders, spray the webs with insecticide, then remove them after the spiders within them are dead. Black widows are especially fond of dry piles of lumber and firewood. Use caution in these areas and spray often.

Ticks

Most ticks found in homes have been transported indoors by family pets, usually dogs. Filled with blood, the ticks drop off the animal and become lodged in bedding, upholstery, carpets and behind baseboards. Although many varieties of ticks carry diseases that affect humans, the common brown dog tick is considered harmless. To remove an individual tick, hold a lit match close to its body, then pluck it away after it retracts its head from within the skin. You can also touch the tick with a red-hot needle, or swab it with kerosene or alcohol to remove it. Take an infested animal to a veterinarian for treatment. To effectively control ticks indoors, spray insecticide wherever an animal sleeps, and destroy old bedding by burning.

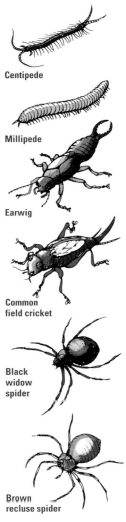

Centipede

Millipede

Earwig

Common field cricket

Black widow spider

Brown recluse spider

Tick (normal and engorged)

Mice, rats and bats

HANDLING POISONS

Insects are not the only pests that invade buildings. Mice and rats can be a menace, particularly in large older houses where there are plenty of places to hide. These enable them to live and prosper uninterrupted, and to benefit from a plentiful supply of food by invading your living quarters. Mice are just a nuisance, but rats present a health hazard and should be eliminated.

Bats sometimes shelter inside houses, too, usually in the attic. Although they can be beneficial, consuming large quantities of insects, they can also carry rabies, which can be a fatal disease.

Mice

Domestic mouse
Not a serious threat to health, though mice are unhygienic rodents.

Mice are attracted by fallen scraps of food, so the easiest remedy is to keep floors clean. However, mice can move easily from house to house, through roof spaces or wall cavities and under floors, and so may be difficult to eliminate entirely without professional help.

You can buy poisoned bait, which should be sprinkled onto a piece of paper or a paper plate so you can remove uneaten bait easily and safely. Be sure to keep pets and children away from the bait. If signs of mice still persist after three weeks, resort to traps. Humane traps capture mice alive in a cage or box, enabling you to deposit them elsewhere. Or you can use spring-loaded traps. Keep in mind that most people don't set enough traps. If possible, position them every 6 feet along mouse runs. The best place is against the baseboard.

Bait mouse traps with oatmeal or chocolate. Dispose of the dead bodies by burying, burning, or putting in the garbage to be picked up.

Rats

Common rat
A serious health risk. Seek expert advice.

Rodent damage
As well as posing a health risk, rodents can cause material damage, too.
(left to right)

Gnawed electrical-plug casing

Electrical cable chewed by rats

Rat damage to old pipework

Serious rat infestation occurs rarely in the average domestic situation, but rats can be a problem in rural and inner-city areas or near rivers, canals and docks. They can be killed with anti-coagulant poisons, large traps, or by professional exterminators. Contact your local Health Department for expert advice.

Poisons designed to kill rodents are deadly to humans, too—so it is vital to follow carefully the manufacturer's handling and storage instructions. Store poisons where pets and other animals cannot get at them, and make sure they always remain out of the reach of children. Never store poisons under the kitchen sink—where they could easily be mistaken for household products—or anywhere where they might contaminate food. If poison is accidentally consumed by humans or animals, keep the container so that the poison can be identified by a doctor or vet. Some containers are color-coded specifically for this purpose. Wear gloves when you are handling poisons.

Handling poisons safely
Wear protective gloves when preparing poisoned bait.

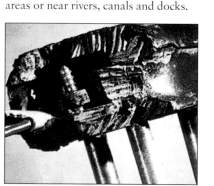

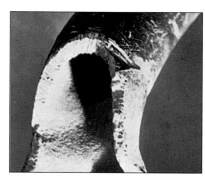

Bats

Bats prefer to roost in uninhabited structures such as barns, caves, mines and tunnels. But occasionally they take up residence in houses. If possible, bats should be left undisturbed because they eat large numbers of insects, particularly flies and mosquitoes. Only a few species of tropical bats drink blood. However, bats are known to harbor diseases, particularly rabies, and as such constitute a health hazard.

To rid an attic of a bat colony, seal all the openings except one and install a bright light to shine directly on the roosting area. Wait a week. Then about ½ hour after dark, when any remaining bats are out feeding, seal the last hole.

If an individual bat strays into a room, try to keep calm. It will avoid you if possible. And it won't become tangled in your hair as the old wives' tale suggests. Open all the windows and doors, turn off the lights and in time the bat will find a way out.

Bat
Bats may carry rabies and should be considered a health risk.

Wet rot and dry rot

Rot can occur in unprotected lumber inside your house, and in buildings and fences outside that are subject to moisture or high levels of water vapor. Damp conditions allow fungal spores to develop and multiply, until eventually the piece of lumber is destroyed. Severe fungal attack can cause serious damage throughout a structure and requires immediate attention. The two most common types are wet rot and dry rot.

Recognizing rot

Signs of fungal attack are easy enough to detect—but certain strains are much more damaging than others, and so it is important to be able to identify them.

White furry deposits or black spots on lumber, drywall or wallpaper are mold growths. Usually, these are the result of condensation. When they are wiped or scraped off, the structure shows no sign of physical deterioration except some staining. Repair the source of the condensation. Then, treat the moldy area by washing it with a fungicide solution or a mixture of 16 parts warm water and one part household bleach.

Wet rot

Wet rot only occurs in lumber that has a high moisture content. Once the cause of the moisture is eliminated, further deterioration is stopped. Wet rot often attacks the framework of doors and windows that have been neglected, allowing rainwater to penetrate the joints and adjacent lumber. The first sign is often peeling paint. Removing the paint will reveal wood that is spongy when wet, but dark brown and crumbly when dry. In advanced stages the grain splits, and thin dark-brown fungal strands will be evident. Always treat wet rot as soon as you find it.

Dry rot

Once it's established, dry rot can be an extremely serious form of decay. It attacks wood that has a much lower moisture content than wood that's attacked with wet rot. Dry rot occurs in badly ventilated and confined indoor spaces, unlike wet rot, which usually thrives outdoors.

Dry rot exhibits different characteristics depending on the extent of its development. It spreads by sending out fine pale-gray strands in all directions (even through masonry) to infect drier lumber. It will even pull water from damp wood. Dry rot can progress at an alarming rate. In damp conditions these strands are accompanied by white growths resembling cotton wool, known as mycelium.

Over time, dry rot develops wrinkled pancake-shaped bodies. These produce rust-colored spores, and when expelled, the spores cover surrounding lumber and masonry. Infested wood becomes brown and brittle, with cracks across and along the grain, causing it to break up into cube-like pieces. You may detect a strong, musty, mushroom-like smell, produced by the fungus.

Wet rot

Dry rot spores

Dealing with wet rot

Once you have eliminated the cause of the moisture, cut away and replace any damaged wood. Then paint the repaired areas and the surrounding woodwork with three heavy coats of fungicidal wood preservative. Brush the liquid into all the joints and end grain.

Then apply a wood hardener to reinforce the damaged wood and fill any voids with epoxy wood filler. Finish up by priming and painting.

Coat damaged wood with hardener

Dealing with dry rot

Unless the outbreak is minor and self-contained, dry rot should be treated by a professional who specializes in this work. Because this fungus is able to penetrate masonry as well as wood, figuring out just how far it has spread can be very difficult.

If you do decide to treat small areas yourself, begin by eliminating any sources of dampness. And make sure there is adequate ventilation to prevent the rot from returning. Cut out all infected lumber to at least 18 inches beyond the last visible sign of rot. Wire brush any infected masonry. Then, collect all the debris in plastic bags and burn it.

Use a liquid fungicidal preservative to kill any remaining spores. Apply three generous coats to all woodwork, masonry, and plaster or drywall within five feet of the infected area. You can also spray on three coats of the preservative. Just be sure to wear any and all protective clothing recommended by the manufacturer.

If you have a wall that has been penetrated by strands of dry rot, drill regularly spaced staggered holes into it from both sides. Angle the holes downwards, so the fluid will collect in them and saturate the wall internally. Repair the holes after you've completed the treatment.

Coat all replacement wood with preservative, and if possible, immerse the end grain in a bucket of preservative for five to ten minutes. Once the preservative is dry, prime and paint the affected areas.

Preventive treatment

Because fungal attack can be so damaging, it is well worth taking precautions to prevent it. Regularly paint and maintain door and window frames, where water is able to penetrate easily. Seal around them, and fill any cracks in the siding with caulk. Provide adequate ventilation in all areas, especially the attic and basement. Eliminate any sources of moisture, such as leaks from plumbing pipes, the roof, and foundation walls.

Looking after lumber

Any lumber that's used outside or in high moisture areas inside the house, should be treated with wood preservative. Brush or spray at least two coats on all boards, paying particular attention to joints and end grain.

Immersing lumber

Any lumber that will be in contact with the ground, especially fence posts, needs to be treated with preservative. Either buy treated lumber for the job, or do the treating yourself. Fence posts can be coated on the outside by simply brushing on preservative. But the end of the post that will go in the ground should be immersed in a bucket of perservative to protect the end grain of the wood. Keep each post in the bucket for at least 10 minutes.

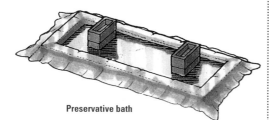

Preservative bath

You'll get the best results, however, if you totally immerse the posts in a preservative bath. To do this, fabricate a tub by stacking up loose bricks for the walls and lining the depression with a thick sheet of polyethylene. Fill the trough with preservative and immerse the posts, holding them down with bricks to prevent them from floating. Leave them in the preservative overnight.

Wood preservatives

There are many different chemical preservatives on the market, designed for specific uses outside and inside the house. Be sure you choose the correct one for the job at hand.

Liquid preservatives

For treatment of existing indoor and outdoor wood, choose a liquid preservative that you can apply with a brush. Although all wood preservatives are toxic, if you follow the manufacturer's instructions for proper use, they can be used safely.

Common preservatives are zinc and copper napthenate, and trubutylin oxide (TBTO). Traditional creosote and pentachlorophenol (penta) are no longer sold for consumer use. These chemicals are carcinogens and are highly toxic.

Liquid preservatives are sold in hardware stores, lumber yards and home centers. Some are also sold in paint stores. When buying preservatives make sure you get a preservative, not a water repellent. Preservatives carry antifungal chemicals that penetrate the wood. Repellents are exterior coatings that simply protect the outside of the wood against water damage. Some preservatives are paintable, others are not. And some come with stains incorporated into their formulation to color the wood.

Clear   Wood Colored   Green

Pressure-treated lumber

Pressure-treated lumber is the best choice for any new outdoor construction where the wood will come in contact with the ground or concrete. Decks and fences are the two most common examples.

Usually this lumber is rated for two different applications: ground contact and above-ground use. Inhaling the treatment chemicals can be harmful. So wear a dust mask when sawing and don't burn scraps.

SAFETY WITH PRESERVERS

All preservatives are flammable—so don't smoke while you are using them, and extinguish any open flames. Wear protective gloves and goggles when applying preservatives. And wear a face mask respirator when using them indoors. Provide good ventilation while working, and don't sleep in a freshly treated room for 48 hours to allow time for the fumes to dissipate completely. Immediately wash off any preservative from your skin. If some splashes in your eyes, flush them with water immediately and get medical help right away.

Moisture problems

Moisture problems and the dampness they cause can be detrimental to your health and to the condition of your home. So try to locate and eliminate any sources of moisture as quickly as possible, before wet or dry rot develops. There are three major types of moisture problems: penetrating moisture from external leaks, rising moisture from osmosis through basement floors, and condensation moisture that's generated inside the house.

Principal causes of penetrating moisture
1 Broken gutter
2 Leaking downspout
3 Missing shingles
4 Damaged flashing
5 Faulty pointing
6 Porous bricks
7 Cracked masonry
8 Cracked stucco
9 Loose shingles
10 Defective seals
   around frames
11 Missing
   weatherstripping

Penetrating moisture

Penetrating moisture is the result of water entering the structure from outside. This is usually considered the most damaging type of moisture problem and therefore the one that worries homeowners the most. The obvious symptoms, like water dripping from a ceiling, collecting below the front door, or running down the inside of windows, occur only during wet weather. And they dry out after a couple of dry days, sometimes leaving only subtle stains behind.

Isolated damage suggests that water has entered only at a single point. With a little methodical investigation, you should be able to locate the source accurately. But general dampness and humidity indicate a larger overall problem, one that may be hard for a non-professional to diagnose. Roof leaks are notorious for being difficult to trace.

Obvious problems like worn out weatherstripping, defective caulk, and a few missing roof shingles aren't hard to fix. To diagnose and solve more complicated problems, it's a good idea to call in a contractor.

Rising moisture

Rising moisture is caused by water from the ground soaking through basement walls and floors. Most newer houses have concrete foundations and floors with impervious vapor barriers installed when they were being built. These barriers are designed to eliminate, or at least greatly reduce, the amount of moisture passing through. But they are only as good as the product used and the installation methods employed. Too often these barriers are treated almost as an afterthought.

In many older homes, especially those with stone foundations and dirt or gravel floors, there are no barriers to water penetration, to say nothing of any vapor barriers in place. The amount of rising moisture entering these structures can be very high. During wet weather it's not uncommon to have water pouring through the walls and floor. This is why so many old houses have big sump pumps. With no barriers in place, moisture is a constant problem, even during dry spells. The weather may be dry outside, but the soil around the house is always damp.

231

Dampness: causes and cures

PENETRATING Moisture: PRINCIPAL CAUSES

CAUSE	SYMPTOMS	REMEDY
Broken or blocked gutter Rainwater overflows, typically at the joints of old gutters, and saturates the wall directly below, preventing it from drying out normally.	Damp patches appearing near the ceiling in upstairs rooms, and mold growth immediately behind the leak.	Clear leaves and silt from the gutters. Repair the damaged gutters or replace with new gutters.
Broken or blocked downspouts A downspout that has cracked or rusted through soaks the wall behind the leak. Leaves get lodged at the break and plug the entire spout.	An isolated patch of wet, often appearing halfway up the wall. Mold growth behind the downspout.	Clear the blockage and repair or replace the cracked or corroded downspout. Paint wall with stain blocker primer and repaint.
Loose or broken roof shingles Defective shingles allow rainwater to penetrate the roof.	Damp patches appearing on upstairs ceilings, during a heavy downpour.	Replace the faulty shingles and repair any damage underneath.
Damaged flashing The joint between any section of the roof and a side wall of the house, and the roof areas around chimneys, plumbing stacks and roof vents are sealed with flashing. Flashing is usually made of aluminum or occasionally copper. If the flashing breaks or is torn, water draining off the roof will enter the building behind or below it.	Wet patches on the ceiling extending from the wall toward the roof ridge, or around a chimney or a roof vent. Damp patch on the side wall near the walls junction with an adjoining roof. Water dripping from an exhaust fan in the bathroom.	If the existing flashing appears to be intact, cover the leaking area with plastic roof cement. If it is damaged, replace it, using similar material.
Faulty pointing Aging mortar between bricks in an exterior wall or chimney is likely to crack or fall out; water is then able to penetrate to the inside of the wall.	Isolated damp patches or sometimes widespread patches on walls and near chimneys, depending on the extent of the deterioration.	Repoint the joints between bricks, then treat the entire wall with a water-repellent coating.
Porous bricks Bricks in good condition are weatherproof, but old soft bricks become porous. As a result, the wall behind the problem bricks becomes saturated, particularly on the side of the house or chimney that faces prevailing winds and therefore most of the driving rain.	Widespread dampness on the inside of exterior walls. A noticeable increase in dampness during a downpour. Mold growth appearing on walls and ceilings.	Repair or replace faulty bricks and coat the area with a clear water-repellent sealer.
Cracked brickwork Cracks in a brick wall allow rainwater (or water from a leak) to seep through to the inside wall.	An isolated damp patch on the inside wall of the house directly behind the crack.	Replace any damaged bricks and mortar, and cover with a clear water-repellent sealer.
Defective stucco Cracked or damaged stucco encourages rainwater to seep between the stucco and the wall sheathing underneath. The water can't evaporate before it's absorbed by the wall.	An isolated damp patch, which may become widespread. The trouble can persist for a day or two after rain stops.	Fill small cracks with stucco repair and reinforce the crack. Remove and replace extensively damaged sections. Then paint the whole area with exterior paint.
Damaged coping If the coping stones (on some brick houses) are missing or the joints are open, water can penetrate the wall.	Damp patches on ceiling below or near where the coping stones are located.	Install new stones in fresh mortar or replace the mortar between sound stones.

Dampness: causes and cures

PENETRATING Moisture: PRINCIPAL CAUSES

CAUSE	SYMPTOMS	REMEDY
Blocked drip groove Exterior window sills should have a groove running along the underside of the sill from one end to the other. When rain runs under the sill, the water falls off at the groove. If the groove is full of paint, water will go over it and into the wall.	Damp patches along the underside of a window frame. Rotting wood sills on the inside and outside. Mold growth appearing on the inside face of the wall below the window.	Clean out the drip groove. Then coat the sill with wood preservative and repaint.
Failed caulk around windows and doorframes Wood trim around windows and doors often shrinks, causing the caulk to crack and let in rain water.	Rotting woodwork and patches of damp around windows and doors.	Repair the trim and seal the gap between the trim and siding with silicone caulk.
No weatherstripping Weatherstripping around and under doors should keep out rain water. When it's worn or missing, water can easily enter.	Damp floorboards just inside the door. Rotting along or next to the door threshold.	Replace old weatherstripping around door. Repair threshold with epoxy filler, coat with preservative, and paint.
Bridged wall cavity Mortar inadvertently dropped onto a wall tie connecting the inner and outer leaves of a cavity wall allows water to bridge the gap.	An isolated patch of damp appearing anywhere on the wall, particularly after a heavy downpour.	Open up the wall and remove the mortar bridge, then waterproof the wall externally with paint or clear repellent.

RISING Moisture: PRINCIPAL CAUSES

CAUSE	SYMPTOMS	REMEDY
Stone foundation walls If a house has a stone foundation, water and moisture can enter through any spaces between the stones or cracks in the mortar.	Standing water or very high humidity in the basement. Mildew or rot on the floor framing members above.	Excavate the perimeter of foundation wall and parge with a heavy layer of mortar. Install a sump pump and dehumidifier.
Dirt or gravel floor Water and water vapor evaporates into basement air from the soil.	Wet or damp floor. Mildew or rot on the floor framing members above.	Pour reinforced concrete floor or install a sump pump and dehumidifier.
No sump pump A sump pump removes standing water from basement floors after floods or long periods of rain have saturated soil surrounding the foundation.	Standing water in your basement.	Install a sump pump and dehumidifier.
Severely cracked concrete floor Superficial cracks are of no concern, but deep cracks that go though the floor into the soil below let ground water into the basement.	Standing water on the floor or damp areas next to the crack. Worse during very wet weather.	Fill the cracks with hydraulic cement
Severely cracked concrete wall Cracks in solid concrete or concrete block walls that go through the wall allow water from the surrounding soil to enter.	Water stains on the wall and standing water on the floor below the crack.	Make sure the gutters and foundation perimeter drain system are working properly. Then fill cracks with hydraulic cement.

Curing moisture problems | Condensation

Remedies for curing different moisture problems are suggested in the charts on the previous pages. And you will find detailed instructions for carrying out many of them in other sections of this book, especially where they contribute to other problems like heat loss, poor ventilation, and paint failure. Below are a few repair techniques not shown elsewhere.

Waterproofing walls

Waterproofing foundations walls is the sort of thing that is best done when a house is being built, not years later.

Foundation walls work best when they are made of solid concrete or concrete block and mortar. Both types need extensive waterproofing added to the outside of the wall and a complete perimeter drainage system installed before the foundation is backfilled with soil. If the water-proofing or drainage fail, the only certain way to make the repairs is to excavate around the walls and replace the waterproofing

and drainage.

Exterior walls are easier to treat, because in most cases this just means repainting them and caulking all the gaps between the siding boards and the siding and trim. In the worst cases, where the siding has remained unpainted for so long that the wood is split, cracked and coming loose from its fasteners, the siding has to be replaced. If you replace it with wood siding, make sure that all boards are back primed before they're installed. Then apply two top coats of high quality paint.

1 Water drips to ground

2 A bridged groove

3 Drip molding

Providing a drip molding

Because water cannot flow uphill, a drip groove on the underside of an external window sill forces rainwater to drip to the ground before it reaches the wall behind **(1)**. When painting the house, scrape out all the old paint from drip grooves so a bridge can not form

(2). If an external window sill does not have a precut drip groove, it's worth adding a drip molding underneath. Just glue and nail a ¼-inch square strip about 1 ½ inches from the front edge of the sill **(3)**. Paint or stain the drip molding to match the sill.

Sealing around window frames

Scrape out the old or loose caulk from around window and door trim and fill the cracks with silicone caulk. Run the tip of the caulk tube along the edge of the trim to get a smooth even bead. If the gap is too wide to be filled with one bead,

fill it with a second after the first has dried.

To fill especially deep gaps, first spray a layer of expanding foam filler into the crack. Let it dry according to the manufacturer's instructions. Then finish filling the gap with caulk.

Fill gaps around window and door trim with silicone caulk.

Bridged cavity

A bridged cavity is sometimes a problem in brick veneer houses. When bricks are being laid, mortar occasionally drops behind the bricks into the cavity between the house wall and the brick veneer wall. When this dropped mortar hits and sticks to wall ties, it can collect moisture that is between the walls and sometimes transfer it through the inner wall and stain the room wall.

The easiest way to deal with the problem is to coat the outside of the brick with a water repellent sealer. This should reduce the amount of moisture between the walls and thus the amount of moisture leaking into the house.

Bridged cavity results from mortar being dropped on wall ties

Condensation

Air carries moisture in the form of water vapor. Its capacity to carry depends on its temperature. As air becomes warmer, it absorbs more water, something like a sponge. When water-laden air comes into contact with a surface that is colder, the air cools until it can no longer hold the water it has absorbed. The water condenses and is deposited, in liquid form, on the cold surface.

Conditions for condensation

A great deal of moisture vapor is produced by cooking and by using baths and showers, and even by breathing. The air in a house is normally warm enough to hold the moisture without reaching its saturation point—but in cold weather the low temperature outside cools the external walls and windows below the temperature of the heated air inside. When this happens, the moisture in the air condenses and runs down windowpanes and soaks into the window trim and wall surface below. Matters are made worse in the winter when windows and doors are kept closed, so that fresh air is unable to replace humid air before it condenses.

The root cause of condensation is rarely simple because it is usually the result of a combination of air temperature, thermal insulation, humidity and poor ventilation. Tackling just one of these problems in isolation may exaggerate the symptoms or transfer the condensation elsewhere. The chart on the facing page lists major factors and some common remedies.

Condensation usually appears first on cold glass

Condensation: Causes and cures

CONDENSATION: PRINCIPAL CAUSES

CAUSE	SYMPTOMS	REMEDY
Insufficient heat In cold weather the air in an unheated room may become saturated with moisture.	General condensation.	Heat the room to increase the ability of the air to absorb moisture without condensing.
Kerosene heaters This type of heater produces as much water vapor as the fuel it burns, causing condensation to form on cold windows, exterior walls and ceilings.	General condensation in rooms where the heater is used.	Substitute another form of heating.
Uninsulated ceilings Moist air readily condenses on cold ceilings.	Widespread damp and mold. Lines of ceiling joists are clear because mold doesn't grow as well along the joists, which are relatively warm.	Install attic insulation.
Uninsulated walls Moist air condenses on cold walls.	Damp patches or mold, particularly around the window casings.	Install wall insulation and/or storm windows.
Uninsulated pipes Cold-water pipes attract condensation. The problem is often wrongly identified as a leak in the pipe.	A line of dampness on a ceiling following the path of a pipe. An isolated wet spot on a ceiling where water drops from a pipe. Beads of moisture on the underside of a pipe.	Insulate your cold-water pipes with plastic foam tubes.
Cold windows When exterior temperatures are low, windows usually show condensation before other features do. The glass is thin, so it cools quickly and stays cold until it warms up outside.	Foggy windowpanes and water collecting in pools at the bottom of the glass.	Reduce moisture in the room and/or install storm windows.
Sealed fireplace If a fireplace opening is blocked up, the air trapped inside the flue cannot circulate and therefore condenses on the inside and eventually leaks.	Damp patches appearing anywhere on the chimney, the firebox or the hearth.	Ventilate the chimney by inserting a grille through the area that's blocked.
Attic insulation blocking vents If attic insulation blocks soffit or roof vents, air cannot circulate properly and condensation appears on rafters and roof sheathing.	Widespread mold or rafters, attic floor joists and the underside of roof sheathing.	Unblock the vents and install a roof fan if necessary.
Condensation after remodeling If you've done work that involved new mortar or plaster, condensation may be the result of these materials expelling a lot of moisture as they dry out.	General condensation affecting walls, ceilings, windows and floors.	Wait for the new work to dry out, then review the situation.

Damp basement

Being below ground level, the walls and floors of a basement invariably suffer from dampness to some extent. The best way to solve serious moisture problems is from outside by installing new waterproofing on the walls and a new perimeter drainage system. But this can be very expensive. For this reason, minor moisture problems usually are solved from the inside as described below. To improve the chances that interior treatment will work, check the following: all gutters and downspouts should be working properly, the soil around the foundation should be graded away from the house, the basement should be sufficiently ventilated and well heated, and a room dehumidifier should be installed.

Treating the floor

New concrete floors should always have a vapor barrier installed. But many old ones don't have one, or it isn't working properly. To create a surface barrier, you can seal the floor with a heavy-duty, moisture curing polyurethane.

To prepare the floor, make sure it's clean and grease free. It might take several washings to get it clean, but good preparation is time well spent. The bond between the polyurethane and the floor will be much stronger as a result.

Then fill any cracks and small holes by first priming these areas with one coat of polyurethane. One hour later fill the crack and holes with a mortar made from six parts sand, one part cement, and enough polyurethane to produce a

stiff paste. Fill deep cracks carefully, making sure to push the mortar all the way into the cracks with the edge of your trowel. Smooth the surface of the mortar so it's flush with the surrounding area.

Let the mortar cure and do your best to dry out the entire floor. The polyurethane can work in damp conditions but it will penetrate a dry floor better. Use a wide floor brush to apply the first coat. Do not exceed the coverage recommendations printed on the container. After two or three hours, apply a second coat, wait for it to dry, then follow up with a third and a fourth coat, with proper drying in between. After three days curing time, the floor should be ready for use.

Moisture-curing polyurethane can be used to seal the walls of a basement as well as the floor. If want to paint the walls, do so within 24 hours after treatment to achieve maximum adhesion. After the first coat of paint is dry, you can add another coat of paint at any time.

Bitumen-latex emulsion

If you plan to plaster the basement walls, you can seal out modest moisture by using a relatively cheap bitumen-latex emulsion. This is sometimes used in a concrete floor as a waterproofing agent and as a water-proof adhesive for some tiles and parquet flooring. But it isn't suitable as an unprotected covering, for either walls or floors.

If old plaster is in place, remove it and repair the wall underneath with a skim coat of mortar to create a smooth surface. Once the mortar is cured, paint the wall with two coats of the bitumen emulsion. Before the second coat dries, embed some clean, dry sand into the emulsion to provide a key for the plaster.

Polyethylene barriers

If you want to use drywall to finish the basement walls instead of plaster, you should still prepare the walls as described above. But once the bitumen emulsion has cured, install furring strips, to receive the drywall, on the foundation walls. These can be nailed in place with masonry nails or attached with self-tapping concrete screws. In most cases, attaching the furring on 24-inch centers is the accepted approach.

This is a good time to consider adding rigid polystyrene foam insulation to the walls. It's easy to work with (just press it between the furring strips), impervious to moisture, and affordable. The improved R-value of your basement walls will make the living space much more comfortable and it will cost less to heat. Different thicknesses are available. Choose the best one for you and match the thickness of the furring strips to the thickness of the insulation.

After the furring strips (and insulation) are in place, install a continuous polyethylene sheet vapor barrier against the furring. Staple it in place and make sure to tape all the seams. Then install the drywall panels and finish the joints with tape and joint compound. Prime the surface and paint it.

Treating a wall with bitumen-latex emulsion
1 Skim coat of mortar
2 Bitumen latex coating
3 Dry sand layer
4 Plaster

Treating a floor with moisture-curing polyurethane
Cover the floor with three or four coats of polyurethane.

Patching active leaks

You can patch any cracks that are actively leaking water, using quick-drying hydraulic cement. Sold in powder form, you just mix it with water and it expands as it hardens, sealing out the moisture. To apply it,

first undercut the crack using a cold chisel and hammer. Mix some cement and hold it in a gloved hand until it's warm, then push it into the crack. Hold it in place with your hand for a couple of minutes, until it is hard.

Insulating your home

No matter what fuel you use, the cost of heating a home continues to rise, and shows no signs of stopping. So it makes good sense to do what you can to reduce your heating bills. Turning down the thermostat is one strategy, albeit a chilly one. But this doesn't attack the problem at its source, which is usually poor (or no) insulation.

Specifications

Homes in nearly all parts of the United States benefit from some amount of insulation. Even in the warmest parts of the country, insulation is valuable in keeping excessive heat from infiltrating living spaces. It can also improve the efficiency of air conditioners by preventing cooled air from rapidly escaping. Reputable insulation contractors or your local building inspector can tell you the amount of insulation recommended for your region. When comparing thermal insulating materials, you'll be faced with these technical specifications:

U-values

The building materials that are already present in your house have been rated by the construction industry and government housing authorities according to the way the materials conduct heat. For individual materials, these ratings are called K-values and represent the total heat transmitted (per square foot, per hour) between the surfaces of two materials when there is a temperature difference between the two of 1°F. When the passage of heat is measured through an entire structure (such as a wall, ceiling, or floor), which is made up of several different materials plus air spaces, the rating is called the U-value. The higher the U-value, the more rapidly heat passes from one surface of the structure to another.

R-values

Adding insulation reduces U-values (but not K-values) by resisting the passage of heat through a structure. The degree of resistance is termed the R-value. Insulation is compared and sold by this rating. Materials with superior insulating qualities have the highest R-values.

Deciding on your priorities

For many people, the initial expense of total house insulation is prohibitive, even though they may concede that it is cost-effective in the long term. Nevertheless, it's important to begin insulating as soon as you can, because every measure you take contributes some savings.

Many authorities suggest that in an average house, 35 percent of lost heat escapes through the walls, 25 percent through the roof, 25 percent through drafty doors and windows, and 15 percent through the floor. At best, this is no more than a rough guide, as it is difficult to define an "average" home in order to estimate the rate of heat loss.

A town house, for example, will lose less than a detached house of identical size, even though their roofs have the same area and are in similar condition. And other factors are relevant, too—for instance, large, ill-fitting, double-hung windows permit far greater heat loss than small, tightly fitting casements.

Although these statistics identify the major routes for heat loss, they don't necessarily indicate where you should begin your insulation program in order to achieve the quickest return on your investment or, for that matter, the most immediate improvement in terms of comfort. In fact, it is best to start with relatively inexpensive measures.

1 Water heater and pipes

Begin by insulating your water-heater tank and any exposed pipes running through unheated areas of your house. This improvement will result in noticeable savings in just a few months.

2 Radiators

Attach aluminum foil to the walls behind your radiators. The foil will reflect heat into the room before the wall absorbs it.

3 Weather stripping

Seal off air leaks around windows and doors with weather-stripping materials. For a modest expense, weather stripping provides a substantial return economically and in terms of your comfort. It's also easy to install.

4 Roof

Tackle the insulation of your roof next, because it's usually considered the most cost-effective major insulating job. It not only reduces fuel bills, but can make you eligible for utility company rebates or credits.

5 Walls

Depending on the construction of your house, insulating the walls may be a sound investment. However, it's likely to be expensive and it will be several years (if not more) before you recoup your initial investment.

6 Floors

Most floors are insulated to a certain degree by carpet and rugs. But, adding insulation between the floor joists is not usually cost-effective. Let your comfort be the deciding factor. If a floor is too cold with carpet and rugs in place, then consider adding some insulation.

7 Storm windows

Contrary to typical advertisements, storm windows produce a slow return on your investment. However, they do help increase the value of your home, make your rooms less drafty, and cut down on some of the noise coming from outside. Installing new windows instead of new storms is a better idea when it comes to energy conservation, but it can be very expensive.

Pipes, water heaters, and radiators

Insulating a water heater

One of the least expensive and most effective energy-saving projects is to insulate your water heater. Even so-called insulated heaters rarely have more than 1 inch of insulation surrounding the tank. Many hardware stores, home centers, and heating supply outlets sell commercial kits containing precut fiberglass insulation for wrapping around the outside of many different size tanks. These kits are normally inexpensive and perform so well that it's worth taking some time to find one.

If you can't find one for your heater, make one. Just cut some strips of paper-faced fiberglass insulation (the thicker the better) with a sharp utility knife. Then wrap the strips horizontally around the tank, beginning at the bottom. Joint the strips at the seams with duct tape.

Be sure to leave the thermostat, temperature-and-pressure (T&P) relief valve, and any control knobs exposed so you'll have easy access later for servicing the tank. And when working on gas- or oil-fired heaters, cut the insulation to stop within 2 inches of the vent stack at the top of the tank and 2 inches from the air-intake holes at the bottom of the tank. These should be exposed to prevent fire and to make sure the tank performs properly.

Insulating a hot-water cylinder
Fit insulation snugly around the cylinder and wrap pipe insulation around the pipework.

Insulating pipes

You should insulate hot-water pipes in those parts of the house where their radiant heat is not contributing to the warmth of the rooms, and cold-water pipes in unheated areas of the building, where they could freeze. The best way to insulate these pipes is with foam pipe insulation, designed just for this job.

This insulation comes in tube form, and is produced to fit pipes of different diameters. Usually it's available in ½-inch and ¾-inch diameter, and sometimes you'll have the option of ½- or ¾-inch-thick tube walls. The thicker tubes, of course, provide more insulation. Some tubes incorporate a metallic foil backing that reflects some of the heat back into hot-water pipes.

Most tubes are preslit along their length so that they can be stretched over the pipe (1). Butt each successive length against the one before, end to end, and seal the joints with tape.

At a bend, cut small segments out of the split edge so that it bends without crimping. Fit it around the pipe (2) and seal the closed joints with tape. Cover a 90-degree elbow with two mitered pipes. Just cut the ends with a utility knife, slide the pieces together (3), and seal with tape. Cut lengths of tube to fit snugly around a T-joint, using a wedge-shaped butt joint (4), and seal with tape as before.

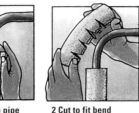

1 Stretch onto pipe   **2 Cut to fit bend**   **3 Miter over elbows**   **4 Butt at T-joints**

Foam pipe insulation
This type of insulation is lightweight and easy to work with. You can cut it with a utility knife or scissors and join it with tape.

Reflecting heat from a radiator

As much as 25 percent of the radiant heat from a radiator can be lost to the wall behind it. You can reclaim as much as half of this wasted heat by applying aluminum foil or a foil-faced polystyrene panel to the wall behind the radiator. Both will reflect the heat back into the room, but the panel is the more durable option. The material is usually available in sheets and is easiest to apply when the radiator has been moved for other remodeling work. But, you can do it with the radiator in place.

Turn off the radiator and measure it and the location of any wall-mounted brackets. Use a sharp utility knife or scissors to cut the sheet to to size. For the best appearance, make it slightly smaller than the radiator all around. Cut narrow slots to fit over any brackets (1).

Apply wallpaper paste to the back of the material, then slide it behind the radiator (2). Smooth it onto the wall and allow the paste to dry before turning on the radiator. You can also used double-sided tape to hold it in place.

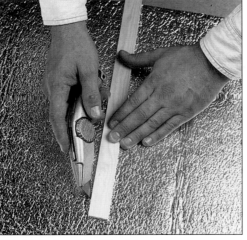

1 Cut slots to align with wall brackets

2 Slide lining behind radiator and press to wall

Draftproofing doors

A certain amount of ventilation is desirable to maintain good indoor air quality and to keep condensation at bay. However, allowing uncontrolled drafts is hardly an efficient way to ventilate a house. Drafts account for a large amount of heat loss in any house, and are also responsible for a good deal of discomfort. Adding threshold seals is the best way to combat substantial door drafts. These devices are easy to install, require no special tools or knowledge, and are available in many different shapes and sizes.

Flexible strip

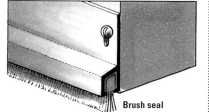

Brush seal

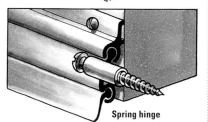

Spring hinge

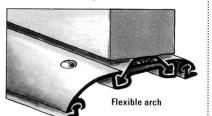

Flexible arch

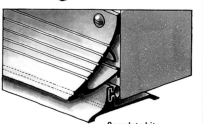

Complete kit

Locating and curing drafts

Tackle the exterior doors first. Then turn your attention to interior doors and seal only those that border unheated rooms—for example, a door from the kitchen to a mudroom, or one from a hallway to an unused bedroom or to the attic stairs.

Locate drafts by running the flat of your hand along the bottom of the door. If you dampen your skin, it will enhance its sensitivity to cold. Otherwise, wait for a very windy day in order to conduct your search.

Threshold sealing devices are made by many different manufacturers, and there are so many variations that it's impossible to describe every type here. But the following examples illustrate the principles that are commonly used to seal out drafts.

Threshold seals

The gap between the bottom of an exterior door and the floor can be very large and, if not properly sealed, can admit fierce drafts, especially on the coldest days. To close this opening, install a threshold seal. Buy one that fits the opening exactly if possible. Otherwise, buy the next bigger size and cut it to fit your door.

Flexible-strip seals

The simplest form of threshold seal is a flexible strip of plastic or rubber that sweeps against the floorcovering to close the gap. The most basic versions are simply self-adhesive strips. Other types have a rigid plastic or aluminum extrusion that is screwed to the face of the door. This securely holds the sealing strip in contact with the floor.

Flexible-strip seals are inexpensive and easy to install. But they tend to wear out quickly. They work best over smooth flooring.

Brush seals

A long nylon-bristle brush, set into a metal or plastic extrusion, can be used to exclude draft under doors. This kind of threshold seal is suitable for slightly uneven floors and textured floorcoverings. It is the only type that can be fitted to sliding doors as well as hinged ones.

Spring-hinge seals

This seal has a plastic strip and extruded clip that are spring-loaded, so they lift from the floor as the door is opened. When you close the door, the seal is pressed against the floor by a stop screwed to the doorframe. Suitable for both interior and exterior doors, these seals operate silently and inflict little wear on floorcoverings. They are also ideal for uneven floors.

Flexible-arch seals

This type of seal consists of an arched vinyl insert, fitted to a shallow aluminum extrusion, that presses against the bottom edge of the door. Because it has to be nailed or screwed to the floor, a flexible-arch excluder is difficult to use on a solid concrete floor. For an external door, choose a version that has additional underseal to prevent rain from seeping beneath it. To install it, you may have to plane the bottom edge of the door.

Door kits

The best solution for an exterior door is to buy a kit combining an aluminum weather trim, which is designed to shed rainwater, and a weather bar fitted with a tubular seal that's made of rubber or plastic. The trim is screwed to the face of the door, and the weather bar is screwed to the threshold.

Weather-stripping doors

Sealing gaps around the door

Any well-fitting door needs a ¹⁄₁₆-inch gap at the top and sides so that it can operate smoothly. However, a gap this large can let a great deal of heat escape. There are several ways to seal these gaps, some of which are described here. The cheaper versions have to be replaced regularly.

Foam weather stripping

The most straightforward seal is a self-adhesive foam strip, which you stick around the doorjamb next to the stop. The strip is compressed when the door is closed, forming a seal. The cheapest polyurethane foam will be good for one or two seasons (although it's useless if painted) and is suitable for interior doors only. The better-quality vinyl-coated polyurethane, rubber, or PVC foams are more durable. When applying foam strips, avoid stretching them, because this reduces their effectiveness. The door may be difficult to close at first, but the strip will compress slightly over time and the door will work better.

Flexible-tube weather stripping

A small vinyl tube, held in a plastic or metal extrusion, is compressed to fill the gap around the door. The cheapest versions have a flange that can be nailed or stapled to the doorstop.

Spring strips

These thin metal or plastic strips have a sprung leaf that is either nailed or glued to the doorjamb. The top and closing edges of the door brush past the sprung leaf, sealing the gap. The hinged edge simply compresses the leaf on that side of the door. This type of strip does not work well on uneven surfaces unless the leaf comes with a foam strip glued in place.

V-strips

This design is a variation on the spring strip: The leaf is bent back to form a V-shape. The strip is mounted on the jamb to fill the gap around the door. These products are inexpensive and easy to install.

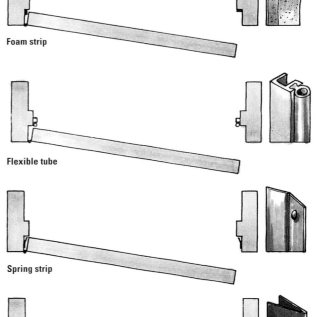

Foam strip

Flexible tube

Spring strip

V-strip

Weather stripping
Flexible foam and vinyl strips are easy to cut and apply

Sealing keyholes and mail slots

An external keyhole should be fitted with a coverplate to keep out drafts during the winter. You can buy a hinged flap that screws onto the inside of the door to cover a mail slot. The best ones have a brush seal behind the flap.

Keyhole coverplate
The coverplate is part of the escutcheon

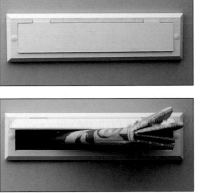

Brush seal
An integral brush seal prevents drafts from entering when the flap is open.

Window weather stripping

Sealing hinged casement windows is straightforward. You can use most of the options suggested for doors (see previous page). But weather-stripping a double-hung window is a bit more complicated, because there are more mating surfaces.

Double-hung windows

The top and bottom rails of a double-hung window can be sealed with any type of compressible weather stripping. The sliding edges admit fewer drafts, but they can be sealed with a brush seal fixed to the frame. Mount it on the inside for the lower sash, on the outside for the top one. To seal the gap between the central meeting rails, use a V-strip or a compressible strip. For square faces, use a blade-seal strip.

1 Brush seal

2 V-strip

3 Compressible strip

4 Blade seal

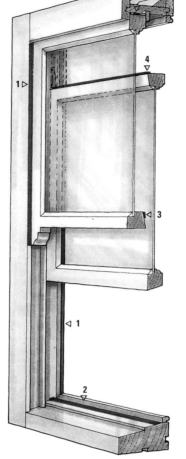

Sealing a pivoting window

When you close a pivoting window, the movable frame comes to rest against fixed stops. Adding weather stripping to these stops will seal off the worst drafts. You can use compressible strips, V-strips, or high-quality flexible tubes for this job. Just make sure you pick products that are weatherproof.

Flexible-tube seal for a pivot window

Filling large gaps

Large gaps left around newly installed windows (or doors) are often a source of big drafts. The same is true of holes drilled through the walls for vents and electrical services. Use an expanding-foam filler to seal these gaps. Once the filler has set, trim it flush with the surrounding surfaces.

Seal large gaps with expanding foam

Floors and baseboards

A ventilated crawlspace below a first-floor room can be the source of significant drafts, through gaps either in the floorboards or underneath the baseboard. The best way to seal the floorboards is to install fiberglass insulation between the joists. To seal the gap between the baseboard and the floor, fill it with caulk and then cover the caulked area with shoe molding for a clean appearance.

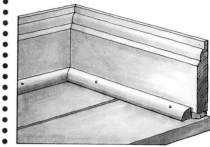

Seal gap with mastic and wooden quadrant

Drafts from attic access panels

Newer houses don't always have big attics that are accessible from stairs. Too often the roof is made with trusses instead of rafters, so there isn't much usable space to justify easy access. Instead, attic access is provided by a simple panel that covers an opening in the ceiling, usually in a closet or hallway. You lift up the panel and crawl into the attic from a ladder.

Some attics have fold-down staircases that are nothing more than ladders. In this case the ceiling panel is hinged, and when you pull it down, the ladder unfolds and rests on the floor.

To reduce drafts from an attic stairway door, just weather-strip the door as explained earlier. Sealing access panels or fold-down stairs requires adding weather stripping to the framing that the panels rest against. Usually, foam strips or V-strips are the best choices.

Drafty fireplaces

A chimney can be an annoying source of drafts. If you want to retain the look of an open fireplace, cut a sheet of thick polystyrene to seal the flue of the chimney, but leave a hole about 2 inches across to provide some ventilation. When you want to use the fireplace again, don't forget to remove the polystyrene—it's flammable.

Insulating roofs

Approximately a quarter of the heat lost from an average house goes through the roof, so minimizing this should be one of your top priorities. Usually, insulating your roof means insulating the ceiling just below the roof. To do this, you just add insulation between the ceiling joists. But if you want to convert your attic into living space, now or in the future, it makes sense to insulate between the rafters. This is harder to do, but it stops heat loss and it gives extra living space.

Preparing the attic

On inspection, you may find that the ceiling under your roof already has insulation, just not enough of it. At one time even an inch of insulation was considered to be acceptable. It's worth installing extra insulation to bring it up to the recommended minimum R-value rating for your region. Also, check the roof framing for signs of rot or roof leaks so they can be treated before you begin.

Remember that the plaster or drywall ceiling below will not support your weight. When working in the attic, lay several planks across the joists so you can move about safely.

If you don't have a light fixture in the attic, now is a good time to install one. But if you don't want to go through the trouble, just run an extension cord with a work light on the end into the attic and hang it high up to provide overall light.

Most attics are very dusty, so wear old clothes (long sleeves and long pants) and a dust mask. Also, wear gloves and safety glasses, especially if you're handling fiberglass insulation, which irritates the skin.

Types of roof insulation

There's a wide range of insulating materials available, so it is important to check the recommended types for your area with the local building code authorities.

Blanket insulation

Fiberglass and mineral- or rock-wool blanket insulation is commonly sold as rolls, sized in widths to fit snuggly between joists and rafters. The most common width is 16 inches, because this is the normal joist spacing. The label on the roll tells how many square feet it covers. The same material, usually cut into 4-foot lengths, is sold as "batts." A minimum thickness of 10 inches (for cold climates) and 8 inches (for warm climates) is recommended for attic insulation.

Blanket insulation is sold in three ways: unfaced, paper-faced, and foil-faced. The unfaced type is usually used for laying on attic floors where existing insulation with a vapor barrier is already in place, so a second vapor barrier should not be used.

The paper-faced product has a vapor barrier built into the facing. It is used when there is no other insulation present and a vapor barrier is required. The vapor barrier should always be installed against the warm surface; in the case of an attic, this means at the bottom of the joist space next to the plaster or drywall on the ceiling below.

The foil-faced product is used in the same way as the paper-faced product. In addition to acting as a vapor barrier, its facing is covered with foil that reflects some of the radiant heat back into the room.

Loose-fill insulation

Loose-fill insulation, in pellet or granular form, is poured between the joists, up to the recommended depth. Exfoliated vermiculite, made from a mineral called mica, is the most common form. But others, like mineral-wool and polystyrene granules, are also available. Loose fill is sold in bags that generally cover 25 square feet to a depth of 4 inches. This product works best on jobs where the joist spacing is irregular. It should not be used in very drafty attics where the material can blow about easily.

Blown insulation

This insulation is installed by contractors who blow fiberglass, mineral wool, or cellulose fibers into the attic. It's very effective in old houses where joist spacing is not consistent.

Rigid insulation

Boards made of dense foam, either polystyrene or polyurethane, are very efficient insulators. Most lumber yards stock them in 4 x 8 sheets, in thicknesses that range from ¾ inch to 2 inches. The boards are simply nailed to framing members and are usually used in new construction.

Vapor barriers

Installing insulation makes the attic colder than before, which increases the risk of condensation either on the framing members or within the insulation itself. In time, this could cause serious rot problems and significantly reduce the effectiveness of the insulation. When insulation is wet, it functions more like a conductor than an insulator.

One way to reduce this condensation is to provide adequate attic ventilation. Another solution is to install a vapor barrier on the warm side of the insulation. This prevents moisture-laden house air from passing through the ceiling and into the attic. A vapor barrier is often bonded directly to the insulation. In new construction, it tends to be a separate polyethylene sheet. This type is stapled to the framing members underneath the insulation before the drywall is installed. All vapor barriers should be continuous and undamaged.

● **Ventilating the attic**
Laying insulation between the joists increases the risk of condensation in an unheated roof space. To keep the attic dry, make sure there are adequate roof, soffit, gable, or ridge vents to keep the air circulating properly.

243

Insulating an attic

Blanket insulation

Before starting to lay blanket insulation, use flexible caulk to seal gaps around pipes, vents, or wiring entering the attic.

Remove the blanket's wrapping in the attic (since the insulation is compressed for transportation and storage, but swells to its true thickness on being released) and begin by placing one end of a roll into the eaves, vapor-barrier side down. Make sure you don't cover any soffit vents in the eaves. On a shallow-pitch roof, it's a good idea to trim the end of each blanket to a wedge shape so that it doesn't obstruct the airflow.

Unroll the blanket between the joists, pressing it down to form a snug fit—but don't compress it. Continue filling between the joists until the first layer is complete. Just butt the leading end of

the new roll tightly against the last blanket. Cut any blankets that are too wide for the space with a utility knife.

Most attics are not easy to work in. The headroom is often too low, the air too hot, and any number of obstructions will make a neat installation practically impossible. Do the best you can, and remember that the tighter the insulation blankets fit against the framing and each other, the more money you'll save on fuel costs in the future.

Don't cover with insulation any exhaust-fan housings or lighting fixtures that may protrude into the attic. Leave at least 3 inches of clearance around them to keep the insulation from overheating. Or, replace the fixtures with ones designed for direct contact with insulation.

Loose-fill insulation

When installing loose-fill insulation, keep in mind that it doesn't come with a vapor barrier. If there is already insulation with a vapor barrier in place, you can just spread the loose fill over it. But if there is no barrier, one must be installed before adding any loose-fill insulation. Take special care not to cover the soffit vents. To avoid blockages, wedge strips of plywood or thick cardboard between the joists so an open air passage to the soffit vents is maintained.

Pour the insulation between the joists and distribute it roughly with a broom.

Level it with a spreader cut from a piece of hardboard about 2 feet wide.

If you want to achieve a higher R-value than you'd get with the insulation level with the top of the joists, just add more. Start at the perimeter of the room, or at the point farthest from the access hole or stairway, and pour more insulation above the joists. Work backward toward the attic access so you'll be able to get out without crawling through the insulation. Once the extra insulation is added, you won't be able to use the attic floor for storage.

Double layers of insulation
If you want to install more than a single layer of insulation—to achieve a much higher R-value—lay the second layer at right angles to the first one.

Insulating around chimneys
To avoid a fire hazard, the wood framing around a chimney should be installed so it is at least 2 inches from the chimney on all sides. To insulate this area, it's best to use fiberglass batts. Just remove the facing from the insulation and loosely stuff the insulation into the spaces around the chimney. Don't pack it too tightly. If the fibers don't have some loft, their effectiveness is significantly reduced.

Insulating pipes
If you live in a cold climate and there are water pipes running between the joists, prevent them from freezing by laying blanket insulation over them. In areas where this isn't practical, insulate each pipe separately with pipe-insulating tubes.

You can also use loose-fill insulation to protect pipes. Before pouring the loose fill over them, lay a bridge made from cardboard over the pipes. This will tend to trap some of the heat coming up from the room below and prevent the pipes from freezing.

Insulating pipes between joists.

Laying blanket insulation *(right).* Seal all gaps around pipes, vents, and wiring (**1**). Place end of roll against eaves, and trim ends (**2**) or add soffit vent protectors (**3**). Press rolls between joists (**4**).

Spreading loose-fill insulation *(far right).* Seal gaps to prevent condensation (**1**). Use strips of plywood to prevent insulation from blocking ventilation (**2**) or add soffit vent protectors (**3**). Cover any water pipes with cardboard (**4**), then use a board to level the insulation (**5**). Insulate and weather-strip the access panel (**6**).

Laying blanket insulation

Spreading loose-fill insulation

Insulating between the rafters

If you plan to use your attic for living space, you will need to insulate between the roof rafters instead of the floor joists. Before starting, check for any roof leaks and make sure any necessary repairs are done.

Condensation is another source of trouble that must be considered before starting work. Because the roof surface will be colder after installing insulation, the likelihood of condensation increases. To eliminate condensation, you have to provide two things.

The first is proper ventilation. You should maintain a gap of at least 1½ inches between the top of the insulation and the bottom of the roof sheathing. (Because this gap is necessary, the depth between the rafters that's available for

insulation is reduced. To add more insulation and still maintain the proper minimum ventilation gap, you'll have to add strips to the bottom of the rafters to create extra depth.) You also need continuous soffit vents on all eaves, and a continuous ridge vent along the top of the roof.

Second is a vapor barrier on the warm side of the insulation. You can use blankets with an integral vapor barrier, or install unfaced blankets between the rafters and staple a polyethylene sheet to the lower edges of the rafters to act as a vapor barrier. After installing the insulation, you can cover the rafters with sheets of drywall, tongue-and-groove boards, or sheets of 4 x 8 plywood paneling.

Installing blanket insulation

Cut a faced blanket to length, then lift it up and push it between the rafters. Unfold the side flanges on the facing

and staple them to the undersides of the rafters. Be sure to overlap the edges on successive blankets.

Installing insulation boards

You can also use rigid polystyrene boards to insulate between rafters. To keep the boards properly aligned, and to maintain the ventilation gap above them, nail furring to the sides of

the rafters. Then cut the boards for a tight fit and push them up against the furring. Cover the insulation with a polyethylene-sheet vapor barrier.

Generally, when you make an attic space into living space, you end up adding short walls under the rafters. The space where the rafters meet the floor is considered unusable, and these walls help define the space better.

Blankets or batts are usually the best choice. They're economical and easy to install. And, because there is plenty of ventilation behind the wall, you can fill the stud spaces completely with insulation. Faced insulation has an integral vapor barrier. Unfaced insulation doesn't; it needs a polyethylene vapor barrier over it.

Insulating a room in the attic.
Surround the room itself with insulation, but leave the floor uninsulated so the attic will benefit from heat rising from the rooms directly below.

● **Where space is tight**
It is usually difficult to install enough insulation to achieve high R-values between standard-size rafters. Once you allow for a 1½-inch ventilation gap above the insulation, there's not much room left. Your options are to increase the depth of the rafters by nailing boards to the bottom edges, or to install polystyrene insulation between rafters, because it has a higher R-value per inch.

Insulating an attic from the inside.
Fit either blanket or board insulation between the rafters.
1 Minimum gap of 1½ inches between insulation and roof sheathing for ventilation.
2 Blanket or batt.
3 Vapor barrier stapled to rafters.
4 Board insulation wedged between rafters.
5 Drywall nailed over vapor barrier.
6 Roofing felt.
7 Roofing.

Other insulating methods

Flat roofs

Flat roofs don't have the virtue of shedding water quickly, as pitched roofs do. Because of this, they need an elaborate roofing system that is almost always contractor-installed. If you're having a flat roof redone and you have no insulation between the rafters below, it's a good time to add insulation to the roof. Discuss this with the contractor and sort out the options you have.

There are several different approaches to waterproofing a flat roof. One of the most common is to apply multiple layers of waterproof roofing materials. To do this, contractors usually start by stripping off all the old roofing down to the roof deck. This is a messy job, and almost always requires a dumpster on the premises. Then they apply a waterproof covering or membrane to the top of the roof deck. This is followed by a heavy-duty vapor barrier and some rigid insulation boards. The system is completed by covering the insulation with a topcoat of hot tar. Sometimes aggregate of some type (often small stones) is spread over the topcoat to protect the roofing from high winds and high temperatures.

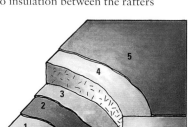

Insulating a flat roof. Expert contractors can insulate the roof from above.

1 Roof deck
2 Waterproof covering
3 New vapor barrier
4 Insulation
5 New waterproof covering

Hot roof system

Insulating from below the ceiling

If you live in an old house that has no insulation and you have a room below a flat roof or a cathedral ceiling, the prospect of tearing off the ceiling plaster or the roofing to get at the rafter cavities may be daunting. And it should be. Both jobs are difficult, expensive, and create a terrible mess. In some situations, it's better to pay high heating bills than to do what needs to be done to add some insulation.

There is another option: installing rigid insulation below the ceiling joists. To do this job, start by nailing or screwing 2 x 2 boards to the under-side of the ceiling. Run these boards perpendicular to the direction of the joists. Make sure the fasteners you use are long enough to extend through the 2 x 2s and plaster (or drywall), and into at least 2 inches of the joists.

Then, cut rigid insulation boards to fit between the 2 x 2s and glue them to the ceiling with construction adhesive. Once all the insulation is installed, cover the boards and the 2 x 2s with a polyethylene-sheet vapor barrier. Then screw or nail new drywall in place and finish the seams with tape and joint compound. Paint the ceiling with primer and then two coats of acrylic latex paint.

Insulating the ceiling

1 Existing drywall or plaster ceiling
2 Softwood 2 x 2s screwed to the joists
3 Insulation glued to existing ceiling
4 Polyethylene vapor barrier stapled to the 2 x 2s
5 Drywall nailed to the 2 x 2s

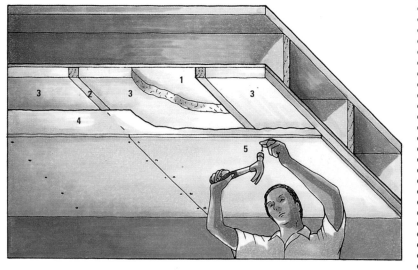

Although a great amount of heat escapes through the walls of a house, installing insulation in finished walls can be more expensive than the savings you get in reduced fuel bills. If you have no insulation in your walls, plan on a payback period of 5 to 10 years. (The shorter time applies to cold climates, the longer one to mild climates.) If the walls already contain some insulation, it could take as long as 25 years for energy savings to match the cost of adding more insulation.

Fiberglass

In new construction, or on major remodeling jobs, installing fiberglass batts or blankets between the studs is the most common and practical method for insulating walls. The thickness of the insulation you install depends on the width of the lumber used for the wall studs.

A typical wall, built with 2 x 4 lumber and finished on the inside with drywall and on the outside with wood siding, has an R-value of about 5 without any insulation in place. Installing 3½ inches of fiberglass raises the R-value to at least 16.

Loose fill

With finished walls, the most common practice is to have a contractor drill holes through the exterior of the house and blow loose-fill insulation into the cavities between the studs. This usually delivers about R-12 rating.

Rigid foam

If you are planning—or are willing—to re-side your house, adding rigid insulation over the sheathing before re-siding is a good idea. The insulation is nailed in place, the seams covered with duct tape, and the joints next to trim boards and other fixtures are filled with exterior-grade caulk. The new siding is installed over the insulation.

This system works well. It provides some insulating value and greatly reduces cold-air infiltration. But it is expensive and worth it only if you need new siding. Some vinyl siding products come with rigid-foam inserts that fit behind the siding panels. This raises the R-value of the wall even more.

Insulating walls

Installing fiberglass blankets

Choose insulation wide enough to fit tightly between wall studs. To cut, unroll the insulation facing-side down, then use a framing square or straight board to compress the insulation and act as a cutting guide. Cut the insulation 2 inches longer than the bay, using a utility knife. Afterward, pull the facing away from the fiberglass at each end to create 1-inch stapling tabs.

Press the insulation into each bay, with the facing toward the room. With foil-faced material, staple the tabs to the inside faces of the studs so the insulation is recessed at least ¾ inch. With paper-faced material, staple the tabs flat along the outer edges of the studs, leaving no recess. Fit insulation behind obstructions, such as pipes and electrical boxes, so it lies against the exterior sheathing. Pack unfaced insulation into gaps between window and doorframes.

After installation is complete, staple a polyethylene vapor barrier across the entire wall, allowing the plastic to extend a few inches all around—to be covered later by finished ceiling, floor, and adjacent wallcovering. Carefully cut out around windows, doors, electrical boxes, and other openings before attaching interior wallcovering.

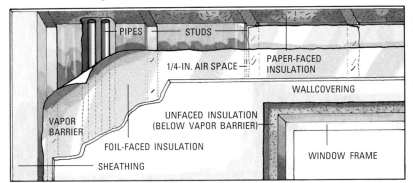

Details for installing batt insulation

Insulating masonry walls

Above ground, masonry walls can be insulated with either blanket or rigid insulation. Below ground, because blanket insulation is susceptible to moisture damage, only rigid foam is recommended. (If you live in an extremely cold climate, insulating basement walls can cause foundation damage. Be sure to check with a local building inspector before proceeding.)

To apply blanket insulation, first cover the masonry surface with a polyethylene vapor barrier, attaching it with dabs of construction adhesive. Then, construct an ordinary stud wall against the masonry, nailing it to the floor and ceiling. Pack the bays with insulation, as described on this page.

Cover the insulation with a second vapor barrier before finishing with drywall, paneling, or plaster.

To install rigid insulation, first attach a vapor barrier to the masonry, then nail vertical 1 x 2 furring strips to the wall, spaced 16 inches apart on center. Use masonry nails or cut nails for this job. You can also use concrete screws, which take longer to install and cost more than nails, but do a much better job of holding furring in place. Press insulation panels into the bays between strips. Make sure you have a snug fit. Then, cover the wall with a vapor barrier and the finished wallcovering, fastened to the furring strips.

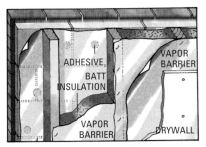

Details for installing batt insulation

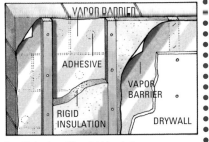

Details for installing rigid insulation

BLOWING IN INSULATION

For most homeowners, this is a job best left to professional insulation contractors. However, equipment is available at rental centers if you want to blow in loose-fill insulation yourself.

To perform the task, begin by locating all the wall studs, usually by noting the pattern of siding nails. Then shut off all power to the house. Remove a strip of siding 3 to 4 feet from the bottom of the walls and drill a pair of holes (the diameter recommended by the insulation or equipment supplier) side by side in each bay between studs. Check, using electrician's fish tape, for obstructions such as fire blocks (horizontal boards fastened between studs) below the holes. If you find any, drill holes below them to gain access to the area beneath.

Insert the blower nozzle and blow insulation into each bay through one of the holes in each pair. Be sure the bays fill completely, then plug the holes with corks. Drill another series of holes 4 feet above the first and repeat the procedure. Continue until you reach the top of the walls. When finished, reinstall the siding.

Blowing in loose-fill insulation

Safety

Fiberglass and mineral wool can severely irritate skin, lungs, eyes, and mucous membranes. When handling, always wear long sleeves and pants, gloves, goggles, and a respirator.

Insulating floors

Even with carpet or other covering above, heat can readily escape through the ground floor into an unheated basement or crawlspace below.

Floors are best insulated from underneath by pressing fiberglass or mineral-wool insulation between the floor joists, much the same way as in insulating a stud-frame wall. Foil-faced insulation is the best choice, since it reflects escaping heat back in the direction it came from. Because joists are normally wider than wall studs, greater thicknesses of insulation may be used. Insulation may be pressed snugly against the subfloor (allow a ¼-inch gap if using foil-faced insulation), or fastened level with the bottom edges of the joists. Be sure the insulation extends over the foundation sills at the ends of the joists. This is a primary heat-loss area.

Whether you use foil- or paper-faced insulation, the facing, which acts as a vapor barrier, must face the warm living space above. This makes fastening the insulation in place difficult, because the tabs on each side are no longer accessible. One solution is to staple wire mesh, such as chicken wire, across the joist edges as you install the insulation. Another solution—recommended especially if a basement ceiling will be installed—is to cut lengths of stiff wire, each slightly longer than the distances between joists, and press these wires, at 18- to 20-inch intervals, up into each bay to hold the insulation in place.

Hot-air ducts running through unheated basements or crawlspaces should be insulated to prevent heat loss, unless such loss is desirable to warm the space. Also, ducts carrying air from central air-conditioning systems should be insulated to retain cool air if they pass through areas that are not air-conditioned. Fiberglass and mineral-wool blanket insulation, with and without a reflective vapor barrier, are sold for this purpose at heating and air-conditioning supply stores. Choose reflective-barrier insulation for air-conditioning ducts. Ordinarily, no barrier is needed for hot-air ducts.

To install the insulation, cut it into sections where necessary, wrap it around the duct, then secure the seams with duct tape.

Exposed steam and hot-water pipes should also be insulated. For these, purchase foam insulation sleeves sold especially for the purpose at plumbing and hardware stores. The sleeves are slit along one side. To install, slip the sleeve over the pipe, then seal the seam with duct tape. Insulated, adhesive pipe-wrapping is also available. To attach this, merely remove the backing paper, then wrap the tape in a spiral, overlapping it slightly, around the pipe along its entire exposed length.

Insulating from below. To secure insulation between floor joists, either staple wire mesh to the lower edges of the joists (right) or press lengths of heavy wire between the joists (far right).

Crawlspaces

It is seldom necessary to fully insulate crawlspaces, provided insulation is installed beneath the house floor above. A polyethylene vapor barrier should be spread over the crawlspace floor and extended at least partway up the walls to prevent moisture buildup. The space itself should be adequately vented to the outside. The vapor barrier may be left exposed if the space is unused.

If insulation is required, proceed as described earlier for insulating a masonry wall. Or, you can merely drape fiberglass batts down from the top of the foundation. Anchor the insulation with bricks along the top and with bricks or a length of 2 x 4 lumber at the bottom.

Batt insulation for crawlspace

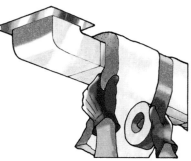

Blanket insulation for ducts

Foam insulation for pipes

Insulation tape for pipes

Double glazing

A double-glazed window consists of two sheets of glass separated by an air gap. The air gap provides an insulating layer that reduces heat loss and sound transmission. Condensation is also reduced, because the inner layer of glass remains warmer than the glass on the outside.

Both factory-sealed units and secondary glazing are used for domestic double glazing. Sealed units are unobtrusive, while secondary glazing is cheaper and helps to reduce the noise from outside. Both provide good thermal insulation.

What size air gap?

For heat insulation, a ¼-inch gap will give the optimum level of efficiency. If the gap is less than ½ inch, the air can conduct a proportion of the heat across the gap. If it's greater than ¾ inch, there is no appreciable gain in thermal insulation, and air currents can transmit heat to the outside layer of glass.

For noise insulation, an air gap of 4 to 8 inches is more effective. Triple glazing—a combination of sealed units with secondary glazing—may be the best solution.

The amount of heat lost from your house through windows is significant; a rule of thumb is about 10 to 12 percent. The installation of double glazing can cut this loss in half.

Another benefit is the elimination of drafts. Cold spots, experienced when sitting close to large windows, will be reduced too.

Installing double glazing with good window locks will also improve security against forced entry, particularly when sealed units or tempered glass are used. However, make sure that some accessible part of appropriate windows can be opened in order to provide an escape route in case of fire.

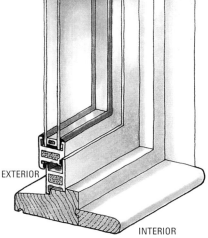

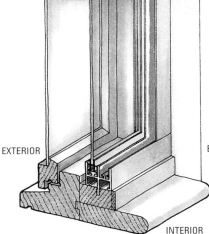

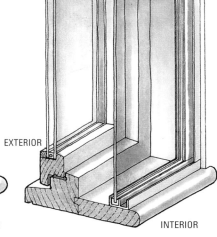

Factory-sealed unit
A complete frame system installed by a contractor.

Secondary double glazing
Installed in addition to a single-glazed window.

Triple glazing
A combination of secondary and sealed units.

Double-glazed sealed unit

Heat-retentive sealed unit

Double-glazed sealed units

Double-glazed sealed units consist of two panes of glass that are separated by a spacer and hermetically sealed all around. The gap may contain dehydrated air, which eliminates condensation between the two panes of glass, or inert gases, which also improve thermal and acoustic insulation.

The thickness and type of glass used are determined by the size of the unit. Clear float glass or tempered glass is commonly employed. When obscured glazing is required to provide privacy, patterned glass is used. Heat-retentive sealed units, incorporating special low-emissivity glass, are offered by many window manufacturers.

Generally, factory-sealed units are installed by contractors or builders. But you can also buy sealed units that you can install yourself, particularly in the replacement-window marketplace. And, of course, you can have windows custom-made at some cabinetmaking shops. This option gives you just what you want, but for most people is prohibitively expensive.

Double-glazed sealed units with vinyl or aluminum frames are popular because they require almost no exterior maintenance. But these windows are not always appealing on older houses. A secondary system—similar to traditional storm windows—that leaves the original window intact is a better option for most restoration work.

Secondary double glazing

Secondary double glazing consists of a separate pane of glass or sheet of plastic fitted over an ordinary single-glazed window. It is normally installed on the inside of the existing windows, and is one of the more popular methods of double glazing, because it's easy to install yourself and much less expensive than new, sealed units.

How the glazing is mounted

Secondary glazing can be fastened to the sash frame (1) or window frame (2), or across the window reveal (3). The method depends on the ease of installation, the type of glazing chosen, and the amount of ventilation needed.

Glazing mounted to the sash will reduce heat loss through the glass and provide accessible ventilation, but it won't stop drafts. Glazing attached to the window frame has the advantage of cutting down heat loss and eliminating drafts at the same time. Glazing installed across the reveal offers improved noise insulation too, since the air gap can be wider. Any system should be easy to remove, or preferably to open, to provide a change of air, especially if the room doesn't have any other form of ventilation.

A rigid plastic or glass pane can be mounted to the exterior of the window. Windows set in a deep reveal are generally the most suitable ones for external secondary glazing (4).

● **Providing a fire escape.**
If you fit secondary glazing, make sure there is at least one window in every occupied room that can be opened easily.

Glazing with plastic film

Quite effective double glazing can be achieved using double-sided adhesive tape to stretch a thin flexible sheet of plastic across a window frame. The taped sheet can be removed at the end of the winter.

Clean the window frame (1) and cut the plastic roughly to size, allowing an overlap all around. Apply double-sided tape to the edges of the frame (2), then peel off the backing paper.

Attach the plastic film to the top rail (3), then pull it tightly onto the tape on the sides and bottom of the window frame (4). Apply only light pressure until you have positioned the film, then rub it down onto all the tape.

Remove all creases and wrinkles in the film using a hair dryer set at high temperature (5). Starting at an upper corner, move the dryer slowly across the film, holding it about ¼ inch from the surface. When the film is taut, cut off the excess plastic with a knife (6).

Secondary double glazing, in one form or another, is particularly suitable for DIY installation. It's possible to fit a secondary system to almost any style or shape of window, from a traditional double-hung window to a modern casement.

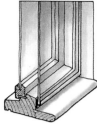

1 Sash
Glazing attached to sash of window.

2 Frame
Glazing attached to structural frame.

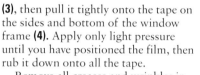

3 Reveal
Glazing mounted to reveal and interior windowsill.

4 Exterior
Glazing attached to reveal and exterior windowsill.

1 Clean woodwork to remove dust and grease

2 Apply double-sided tape to window frame.

3 Stretch film across the top of frame

4 Pull film taut and press to sides and bottom

5 Use a hair dryer to shrink film

6 Trim waste with a sharp knife

Removable systems

A simple method of interior secondary glazing uses clear plastic film or sheeting. These lightweight materials are held in place by self-adhesive strips or rigid molded strips, which form a seal. Most strip fastenings use magnetism, which allows the secondary glazing to be removed for cleaning or ventilation. The strips and tapes usually have a flexible foam backing, which takes up slight irregularities in the woodwork. This type of glazing can be left in place throughout the winter and removed for storage during the summer months.

Installing a removable system
Clean the windows and the surfaces of the window frame. Cut the plastic sheet to size, then hold it against the window frame and draw around it (1). Lay the sheet on a flat table. Peel back the protective paper from one end of the self-adhesive strip and stick it to the plastic sheet, flush with one edge. Cut the strip to length and repeat on the other edges. Cut the mating parts of the strips and stick them onto the window frame, following the guidelines marked earlier. Press the glazing into place (2).

When using rigid molded sections, cut the sections to length with mitered corners. To attach an extruded molding (3), stick the base section to the frame, then insert the outer section to hold the glazing in place.

1 Mark around glazing

2 Position glazed unit

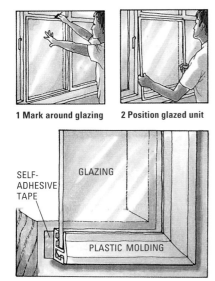

SELF-ADHESIVE TAPE

GLAZING

PLASTIC MOLDING

3 Rigid plastic moldings support glazing

Plastic materials for double glazing

Plastic materials can be used in place of glass to provide lightweight double glazing. They are available as clear, thin flexible film and as clear textured or colored rigid sheets.

Unlike glass windows, plastic glazing has a high impact resistance and does not splinter when broken. Depending on its thickness, plastic can be cut with scissors, drilled, sawn, planed, or filed.

The clarity of the newer types of plastics is as good as that of glass. Although they have the disadvantage of being easily scratched, slight abrasions can be rubbed out with metal polish. Plastics are also liable to degrade with age, and are prone to static. It's best to wash plastic sheeting with a liquid soap solution.

Film and semirigid plastics are sold by the square foot or in rolls. Rigid sheets are available in a range of standard sizes, or can be cut to order.

Rigid plastic sheets are generally supplied with a protective covering of paper or thin plastic on both faces. In order to avoid scratching the surface of the sheets, don't peel off the covering until after cutting and shaping.

Polyester film

Polyester film is a form of plastic often used for inexpensive secondary double glazing. It can be trimmed with scissors or a knife and attached with self-adhesive tape or strip fasteners. The fact that polyester is tough, virtually tearproof, and very clear makes it an ideal plastic for glazing windows.

Polystyrene

Polystyrene is an inexpensive plastic that is available in both clear and textured sheet form. Clear polystyrene doesn't have the clarity of glass, and degrades in strong sunlight, so it shouldn't be used for south-facing windows or for situations where a distortion-free view is desirable. Depending on the climate, the life of polystyrene is estimated to be between three and five years. Its working life can be extended if the glazing is removed for storage in the summer.

Acrylic

Acrylic is a good-quality rigid plastic. It is up to ten times as strong as glass, without any loss in clarity. Although it costs approximately twice as much as polystyrene, the working life of acrylic is estimated to be at least 15 years. It is manufactured in a useful range of translucent and opaque colors.

Polycarbonate

A light weight, vandalproof glazing with a high level of clarity, this plastic is most commonly available in $\frac{1}{16}$-, $\frac{1}{8}$-, and $\frac{3}{32}$-inch-thick sheets. It costs about twice what acrylic costs. Polycarbonate sheeting has a hollow ribbed section that gives it exceptional rigidity, while at the same time keeping both heat loss and weight to a minimum.

PVC glazing

PVC is available as a flexible film or rigid sheet that is ultraviolet stabilized and therefore unaffected by sunlight. PVC film provides inexpensive glazing where a high degree of clarity is not essential, such as in the basement or attic.

Storm window systems

Secondary glazing applied to the exterior of windows usually takes the form of storm sashes, either one-piece, single-pane windows that are installed in the fall and taken down in spring, or permanently mounted, sliding-sash panes that remain in place all year. Single-pane storm windows can be homemade, often at considerable savings over purchased windows. However, installing sliding windows is best left to professional storm-window installers.

Storm window mounting details

Single-pane storm window

FRAME
GLASS
CORNER CLIP
GASKET
CHANNEL

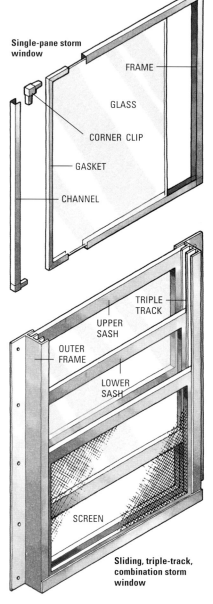

TRIPLE TRACK
UPPER SASH
OUTER FRAME
LOWER SASH
SCREEN

Sliding, triple-track, combination storm window

Combination storm/screen door
To fit, measure height (H) and width (W) of door opening in at least two places.

How to make a single-pane storm window

Measure the length and width of the window opening by holding the tape against the outside edges of the blind stop against which the storm window will sit. Single-pane storm-window kits are often available at hardware stores and home centers. If you can't find a kit in the size you need, purchase lengths of aluminum storm-window channel (prefitted with a U-shaped rubber glazing gasket), and friction-fit corner clips (usually sold with the channel) to make the frame. Don't attempt to make windows taller than 5 feet, because such large areas of glass are hard to handle.

Remove the gasket, then cut four pieces of channel so that when assembled, the outside dimension of the frame measures ⅛ inch less in both height and width than the window opening. Assemble three sides of the frame using the corner clips to hold the pieces together. Drive the clips into the channel ends using a small ball-peen hammer.

Purchase double-strength glass for the pane, cut so it will fit between the channels of the frame with the gasket installed. Fit the gasket around the edge of the pane, mitering the gasket sides at each corner with a utility knife (discard the triangular scraps of waste gasket), then slide the pane into the frame and install the final length of channel.

Attach two-piece, storm-window hanging brackets from the top edge of the storm window, then mount the window to the outside of the opening. The storm window should sit firmly. However, you may wish to fasten it at the bottom and apply removable weather stripping around the inside.

Sliding storm windows

Sliding storm windows, usually called combination windows (because they incorporate a screen for use during summer), are available from home and building supply centers. Most often, they are designed to fit the outside of double-hung window frames, and can be operated merely by raising the interior window to gain access to the latches controlling each sash. In triple-track units, the upper storm-window sash is mounted—sometimes permanently—on the outermost track of the storm-window frame. The lower sash slides up and down in the middle track, and a screen slides up and down in the innermost track. In double-track units, the lower sash and screen are interchangeable, to be switched according to season.

It's important that sliding storm windows are well made and tight fitting. When purchasing, look for quality corner construction, gasketing on both sides of the glass, and deep tracks in the channel. Metal latches are more durable than plastic ones. At the bottom of each frame should be small (¼-inch-diameter) holes to prevent condensation.

When having storms installed, be sure caulk is applied to the existing frame before the storm frame is mounted. And, always make sure the windows operate smoothly before accepting the job.

Combination storm and screen doors

Combination storm doors are usually made of aluminum. However, wood doors offer greater energy savings. Both are usually sold mounted in a frame, ready for installation. To measure the door opening, measure both the height and the width in at least two places. Use the smallest measurement in each case. For the height, measure between the doorsill and the inside face of the head jamb. For the width, measure between the two door rabbets in the side jambs. On most entry doors, there will be a flat surface already milled into the doorjambs to accept a screen, storm, or combination door.

Ventilation

Ventilation is essential for a fresh, comfortable atmosphere, but it has a more important function with regard to the structure of our homes. Ventilation wasn't a problem when houses were heated with open fires, drawing fresh air through all the natural openings in the structure. With the introduction of central heating, insulation, and draftproofing, well-designed ventilation is vital. Without a constant change of air, centrally heated rooms quickly become stuffy. Before long, the moisture content of the air becomes so high that water easily condenses, often with serious consequences.

There are various ways to provide ventilation. Some are simple; others are much more sophisticated.

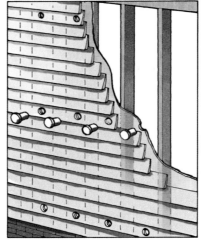

Ventilator plugs for drying out damp wall cavities

Initial consideration

Whenever you undertake an improvement that involves insulation in one form or another, take into account how it is likely to affect the existing ventilation. It may change conditions sufficiently to create trouble in areas outside the habitable rooms, where the symptoms can't be seen, such as under floorboards or in the attic. If there is a chance that damp conditions might result from a project, provide additional ventilation.

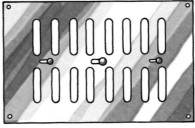

Operable ventilator

Ventilating wall cavities

Faulty vapor protection can lead to moisture accumulating within walls. The problem is common in renovated houses where insulation has been added to older buildings. Suspect the need for ventilation especially if you notice blistering paint on the exterior of the house.

To ventilate wall cavities, install vent plugs, small cylindrical louvers available in several diameters from hardware and building supply stores. Drill holes from the exterior of the house into each cavity where moisture is suspected, at the bottom, top, and at 4-foot intervals in between, and insert the plugs.

Ventilating a fireplace

An open fire needs oxygen to burn brightly. If the supply is reduced by thorough draftproofing or double glazing, the fire smolders and the slightest downdraft blows smoke into the room. There may be other reasons why a fire burns poorly—a blocked chimney for example. But if the fire picks up within minutes of partially opening the door to the room, you can be sure that inadequate ventilation is the problem.

One efficient and attractive solution is to cut holes in the floorboards on each side of the fireplace and cover them with a ventilator. Cheap plastic grilles work just as well, but you may prefer brass or aluminum for a living room. Choose an operable ventilator, which you can open and close to seal off unwelcome drafts when the fire is not in use. If the room has carpeting, cut a hole in it and screw the ventilator into the floor.

Another solution is to install a sealed fireplace-door unit, which comes with inlet pipes and a small blower. Cut holes in the exterior wall at each side of the fireplace, insert the pipes, and attach vents on the outside.

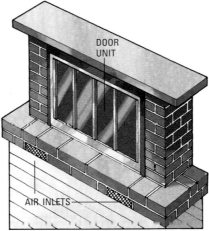

Sealed fireplace doors vent directly outdoors

Ventilating an unused fireplace
An unused fireplace that has been blocked by bricks, blocks, or drywall should be ventilated to allow air to flow up the chimney and dry out any moisture. Some people believe a vent from a warm interior aggravates the problem by introducing moist air to condense on the cold surface of the brick flue. However, as long as the chimney is uncapped, the updraft should draw moisture-laden air to the outside. A brick vent installed in the flue from outside is a safer solution, but it is more difficult to accomplish and, of course, impossible if the chimney is located within the house. Furthermore, the vent will have to be blocked if you want to reopen the fireplace later.

To ventilate from inside the room, leave out a single brick or block, or cut a hole in the drywall. Then, cover the hole with a ventilator that's at least ½ inch wider and higher than the hole.

Face-mounted ventilator for a fireplace

Ventilating below floors

Perforated openings known as air bricks are built into the external walls of a brick house to ventilate the space below the wood floors. If they become clogged with earth or leaves, there's a strong possibility of dry rot developing in the wood framing members. So, if you have a brick house, check the condition of air bricks regularly.

Checking out the air bricks

Ideally, there ought to be an air brick every 6 feet along an external wall, but in many brick buildings the air bricks are spaced farther apart without any harm being done. Sufficient airflow is more important than the actual number of openings in the wall.

In some older brick homes, the floor joists that span a wide room are supported at intervals by low sleeper walls made of brick. Sometimes these are perforated to facilitate an even airflow throughout the space. In other cases, there are merely gaps left by the builder between sections of solid wall. This method of constructing sleeper walls can lead to pockets of still air in corners that drafts never reach. Even

when all the air bricks are clear, dry rot can break out in areas that don't receive an adequate change of air. If you suspect there are dead areas under your floor (particularly if there are signs of damp or mold growth), install an additional air brick in a wall nearby.

Old ceramic air bricks sometimes get broken, and are often ignored because there is no detrimental effect on the ventilation. However, even a small hole can provide access for vermin. Don't be tempted to block the opening, even temporarily. Instead, replace the broken air brick with a similar one of the same size. You can choose from single or double air bricks, made from ceramic or plastic.

To build an air brick into a cavity wall, bridge the gap with a plastic telescoping unit, which is mortared into the hole from both sides. The telescoping function allows the unit to fit a range of different wall thicknesses. If need be, a ventilator grille can be screwed to the inner end of the unit.

Single ceramic brick

Double plastic air brick

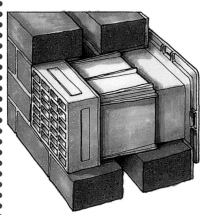

Air brick with telescoping sleeve
Bridge a cavity wall with this type of unit.

Installing or replacing an air brick

Use a masonry drill to remove the mortar surrounding the brick you are removing, and a cold chisel to chop out the brick itself. Spread mortar on the base of the hole and along the top and

both sides of the new air brick. Push it into the opening, keeping it flush with the face of the exterior brick. Repoint the mortar to match the profile used on the surrounding wall.

Cavity tray
A cavity tray sheds any moisture that penetrates the cavity wall above the unit. It is necessary only when the air brick is fitted above the damp-proof course on the house wall.

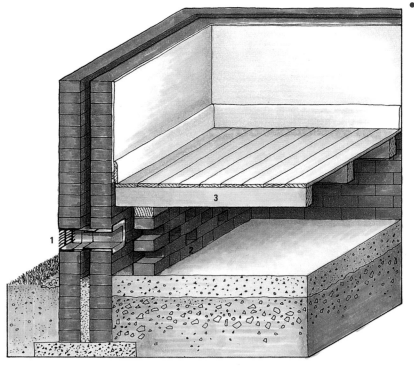

Ventilating the space below a wood floor.
The illustration (left) shows a cross section through a typical, brick cavity-wall structure, with a wood floor suspended over a concrete slab. A house with solid-brick walls is ventilated in a similar way.
1 Air brick fitted with sleeve.
2 Sleeper wall built with staggered bricks to allow air to circulate.
3 Floorboards and joists are susceptible to dry rot caused by poor ventilation.

When attic insulation first became popular as an energy-saving measure, many people were told to tuck insulation right into the eaves to keep out drafts. What this advice failed to recognize was that a free flow of air is necessary in the roof space to prevent moisture-laden air from condensing on the structure.

Inadequate ventilation can lead to serious deterioration. Wet rot can develop in the roof framing, and water can drip onto the insulation, eventually rendering it ineffective. If water builds up into pools, the ceiling below becomes stained and there is a risk of short-circuiting the electrical wiring throughout the attic. For these reasons, efficient ventilation of the roof space is essential.

Ventilating the eaves

Building codes specify ventilation requirements, so check with your local building department before installing vents yourself. One common rule of thumb for estimating ventilation is 1 square foot of ventilation opening for every 300 square feet of roof.

The best configuration of ventilators for your house depends on how much air needs to circulate and the way your roof has been framed. Most standard gable roofs include either vent plugs or continuous vent strips in the soffit under the eaves. Both types of vents have screened backs to allow air in and to keep insects out. These soffit vents are usually combined with louvered vents at the top of both gable ends. In houses that don't have gable roofs, gable vents are replaced by roof vents that are cut into the back side of the roof near the ridge.

Both systems work well, until any of the components are blocked and the air can't get through. This can happen, particularly with soffit vents, when extra insulation is added to the attic and is pushed down over the top of the vents. Always allow uninterrupted air flow over any new insulation.

Slate and tile vents

In houses where soffit vents are not installed, adding the plug-type vents is easier than the continuous-strip vents. Just drill holes in the soffit between all the rafters and push the vents into these holes. If necessary, install baffles between the rafters to keep the insulation from blocking the airflow.

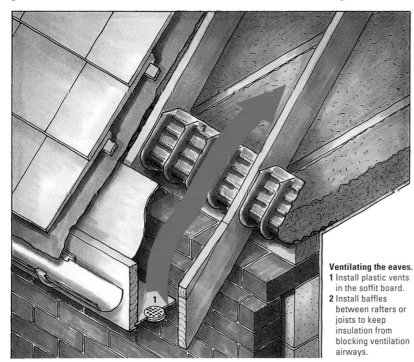

Ventilating the eaves.
1 Install plastic vents in the soffit board.
2 Install baffles between rafters or joists to keep insulation from blocking ventilation airways.

Because warm air rises, air entering through the eaves is most effectively vented at or near the ridge. Below are some common venting arrangements.

Soffit vent

An attic space
If insulating between rafters, provide a minimum 2-inch airway between the insulation and the roof sheathing. Install soffit vents and roof vents.

An attic room
Install a ridge vent and roof vents (as close to the eaves as possible) to draw air around an insulated attic room.

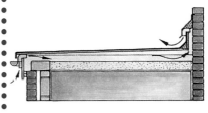

Roof vent

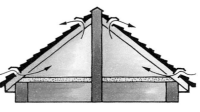

A fire wall
A solid wall built across an attic space prevents eaves-to-eaves ventilation. Install roof vents near the eaves and near the ridge on both sides of the roof.

A flat roof
An insulated flat roof can be ventilated by installing continuous soffit vents along the eaves and above the fascia board where the roof meets the house.

Fitting roof vents

Installing a ridge vent

A continuous ventilating strip running the length of the roof provides very effective outflow ventilation. Ridge venting may be installed on any pitched roof, during new construction or reroofing, or as a task by itself.

If a ridge vent is to be included in the new construction of a roof, the roof decking is laid to leave a gap on either side of the ridge board, creating an open slot along the roof peak approximately 2 inches wide.

Determine the actual width from the size of the ridge vent. The gap allows exiting air to pass through. If felt roofing paper is laid, trim it even with the top edge of the sheathing. Fasten the ridge vent over the gap, nailing it into the decking and rafters on both

sides. Lay the final course of shingles on each side of the roof so that they cover the base of the vent.

To install a ridge vent to a finished roof, you will have to cut a gap along the roof peak to create a passage for exiting air. Use a chalkline to mark the cutting line on each side of the peak, then cut through the shingles and felt paper first, using a utility knife, to expose the sheathing. Set the blade of a circular saw slightly deeper than the thickness of the sheathing, then cut along each chalked line to open the roof. Be careful to avoid nails.

Caulk the underside of the ridge-vent sides, then fasten it over the slot using roofing nails long enough to penetrate at least 1½ inches into the rafters.

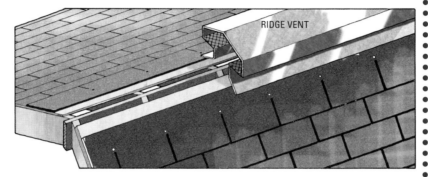

RIDGE VENT

Installing roof ventilators

Installing ventilators on the sloping portions of a roof requires careful cutting and sealing to prevent leaks. You may want to hire a professional roofer to do the job.

First, determine the location of the vent. It must lie between rafters. Use the vent itself or a template made of cardboard (sometimes supplied with the vent) to mark the area of the roof to be cut out. It should be smaller than the overall dimensions of the vent base so that the vent can be pushed beneath adjacent shingles. Cut out the area by

first removing the roofing (use a utility knife to cut through asphalt shingles), then sawing through the wood sheathing using a sabre saw. Apply plastic roof cement to the underside of the vent. Then slide it into place and fasten it with galvanized roofing nails. As you slide the vent in, you'll have to hold up the neighboring shingles so the top of the vent rests flat against the sheathing. Cover the nailheads with cement, and smooth down the shingles around the vent so they lay flat. Glue them in place with roof cement.

ROOF VENT

As mentioned earlier, the proper amount of roof ventilation is an issue controlled by local building codes. So make sure to ask for these guidelines from the building inspector. A good rule of thumb is 1 square foot of open ventilation for every 300 square feet of attic area. For a house with 1200 square feet of attic, the total vent area would have to be at least 4 square feet. This rule assumes a vapor barrier is in place below the attic floor.

If no vapor barrier is in place to restrict some of the moisture flow into the attic, then the ventilation requirements increase. The rule of thumb for this situation is 1 square foot of open ventilation for every 150 square feet of attic area. Using the 1200-square-foot attic example from above, the house without a vapor barrier would require 8 square feet of venting.

Unless the local code has other recommendations, your goal is to split the ventilation square footage as evenly as possible between the eaves and the ridge. So on a typical gable roof with a vapor barrier in place, you'd want about 1 square foot of ventilation incorporated into each of the eaves, and 1 square foot on both sides of the ridge.

Thirty years ago, the standard approach would have been to install a rectangular vent every 6 to 10 feet along the soffits and a triangular gable vent on both ends of the house, or a couple of roof vents near the ridge on the back side of the house.

But now that we know how important proper ventilation is to the long-term health of a house, the tendency has been to increase this ventilation substantially. These days, it's common to have a 1½-inch continuous vent built into each soffit and a continuous ridge vent installed along the full length of the roof ridge. This arrangement provides more, and better, airflow because there are no pockets of dead air in the attic that aren't moved out. Each rafter or truss bay is continually bathed in fresh air from the bottom to the top.

Extractor fans

Since kitchens and bathrooms are particularly prone to condensation, it's important to have some means of expelling moisture-laden air and unpleasant odors. An electrical extractor fan can freshen a room quickly without creating drafts.

Locating the fan

The best place to site a fan is either in a window or on an outside wall, but its exact location depends on where the room door is. Stale air extracted from the room must be replaced by fresh air, which normally happens through the door leading to other areas of the house. But if the fan is too close to the source of replacement air, it will draw air directly from the doorway and have little effect on the rest of the room. The ideal position for the fan is directly opposite the source of replacement air, as high as possible, to extract the hot air (1). In a kitchen, try to locate the fan above or adjacent to the range, so that cooking smells and steam will not be drawn across the room before being expelled (2).

If the room contains a fuel-burning appliance with a flue, you must make sure that there is enough replacement air to prevent fumes from the appliance from being drawn down the flue when the extractor fan is switched on.

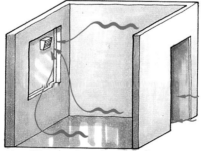

1 Install fan opposite replacement-air source

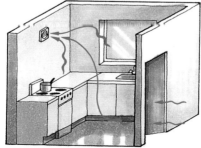

2 In a kitchen, place extractor near range

Types of extractor fans

Many fans have an integral switch. If not, a switched connection unit can be wired into the circuit when you install the fan. Some types incorporate a built-in controller to regulate the speed of extraction, and a timer that switches off the fan after a certain interval. Some fans will switch on automatically when the humidity in the room reaches a predetermined level. Axial fans can be installed in a window, and with the addition of a duct, some models will extract air through a wall. To overcome the pressure resistance in a long run of ducting, a centrifugal fan may be required. To prevent backdrafts, choose a fan with external shutters that close when the fan is not in use.

Window-mounted axial fan
1 Inner casing
2 Motor assembly
3 Interior clamping plate
4 Glass
5 Grille-clamping plate
6 Exterior grille

Wall-mounted axial fan
1 Motor assembly
2 Interior backplate
3 Duct
4 Exterior grille

Choosing the size of a fan

The size of a fan, or to be accurate, its capacity, should be determined by the type of room in which it is installed and the volume of air it has to move.

A fan installed in a kitchen must be capable of changing the air completely 10 to 15 times per hour. A bathroom requires 6 to 8 air changes per hour, or 15 to 20 changes if a shower is installed. A living room normally requires about 4 to 6 changes per hour, but it's best to install a fan with a slightly larger capacity if the room will be smoky.

In order to determine the minimum capacity required, calculate the volume of the room (length x width x height) and then multiply the volume by the recommended number of air changes per hour (see example below).

● **Low-voltage fans**
A low-voltage fan, which comes with its own transformer, can be mounted directly above a shower.

DUCTING TO EXTERIOR

FAN

Centrifugal fan

CALCULATING THE CAPACITY OF A FAN FOR A KITCHEN

Size of kitchen			
Length	Width	Height	Volume
11 ft.	10 ft.	8 ft.	880 cu.ft.

Air changes	Volume	Fan capacity	
15 per hour x	880 cu.ft.	13,200 cu.ft.	

Make sure there are no plumbing pipes, electrical wiring, or other obstructions buried in the wall before you begin work.

Cutting the hole
Wall-mounted fans are supplied with a length of plastic ducting for inserting in a hole cut through the wall. Mark the center of the hole and draw its diameter on the inside of the wall. Use a long masonry drill to bore a hole through the wall.

If you have masonry walls on the outside of your house, use this fit hole as a reference point for the center of the vent duct. Hold the duct up to the wall and trace around it. Then, bore a series of holes through the masonry with a masonry bit. The more holes you drill, the easier it will be to remove the bricks, stones, or stucco. Use a cold chisel and a hammer to cut the masonry between the holes. Work carefully to create a hole as close to the duct size as possible. If you make a sloppy hole, the exterior grille may not be able to cover it. Once the masonry is removed, cut away the wood sheathing with a reciprocating saw or a keyhole saw. Cut out the drywall or plaster on the inside of the house according to the fan manufacturer's directions.

Installing the fan
Separate the components of the fan, then attach a self-adhesive sealing strip to the backplate to receive the duct **(1)**.

Insert the duct in the hole so that the backplate fits against the wall **(2)**. Mark the length of the duct on the outside, remembering to allow for sliding the duct onto the outer grille. Cut the duct to length with a hacksaw. Reposition the backplate and duct in order to mark the installation holes on the wall. Drill the holes into the wall and install toggle bolts or wall anchors. Then, feed the electrical supply cable into the backplate before screwing the plate to the wall. Apply the sealing strip to the exterior grille and push it onto the duct. Mark and drill the mounting holes for the exterior grille, then screw it in place **(3)**. If the grille doesn't fit flush with the wall, seal the gap with caulk. Wire the fan according to the manufacturer's instructions, then attach the motor assembly to the mounting plate.

Metal detector
Detect buried pipes or wiring with an electronic sensor placed against the wall.

1 Seal plate spigot

2 Insert duct in hole

3 Screw-fix grille

Installing a fan in a window

An extractor fan can be installed only in a fixed window. If you want to fit one in a sliding sash window, you will need to secure the top sash, in which the fan is installed, then fit a sash stop on each side of the window in order to prevent the lower sash from damaging the casing of the fan.

Cutting the glass
Every window-mounted fan requires a round hole to be cut in the glass. The size is specified by the manufacturer. It is possible to cut a hole in an existing window, but stresses in the glass will sometimes cause it to crack. All things considered, it is generally better to install a new pane of glass that has been cut exactly to fit the requirements of the fan you bought.

Cutting a hole in glass is not easy for most people, so it's usually a better idea to have it cut by a local glass shop. You will need to provide exact dimensions, including the size and position of the hole. Order glass that matches the existing pane.

Installing the fan
The exact assembly may vary, but the following sequence is a typical example of how a fan is installed in a window:

Take out the existing window pane

and clean up the frame, removing retaining points and traces of old putty. Then install the new pane with the precut hole.

To get a good seal, brush all the dust away from the window-frame rabbet and coat the rabbet with mineral spirits. Roll a golf-ball-size piece of glazing compound into a ¼-inch-thick rope and press it into the rabbet. Continue until you've worked your way around the entire window. Then, smooth the compound and remove the excess with a putty knife. Install the pane and glazier's points to keep it in place, then fill the rabbet with compound.

From outside, install the exterior grille by locating its circular flange in the hole **(1)**. Attach the plate on the inside to clamp the grille to the glass **(2)**. Tighten the installation screws carefully in rotation to achieve a good seal and an even clamping force on the glass. Screw the motor assembly to the clamping plate **(3)**. Wire the fan in accordance with the manufacturer's instructions. Then, install the inner housing over the motor assembly **(4)**.

Finally, switch on the fan to check that the mechanism runs smoothly and that the backdraft shutter opens and closes automatically when the unit is switched on and off.

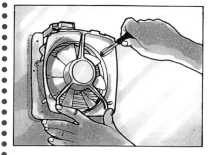
1 Place grille in hole from outside

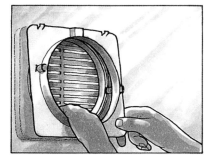
2 Screw inner and outer plates together

3 Screw motor assembly to plate

4 Attach housing to cover assembly

WARNING
Never attempt to make electrical connections before you have switched off the power at the service panel.

Installing a range hood

Window-mounted and wall-mounted fans are primarily intended for overall room-air extraction. But the most effective way to rid your kitchen of water vapor and cooking smells is to mount a ventilator hood directly over your range or cooktop.

Where to mount the range hood

Unless the manufacturer's recommendations indicate otherwise, a range hood is typically positioned between 2 and 3 feet above a range or cooktop.

Depending on the model, a range hood may be either cantilevered from the wall or screwed between or beneath kitchen wall cabinets. Some cabinet manufacturers produce special range-hood housing units that match the style of their cabinets. If you're installing all new cabinets, you should consider ordering one of these.

Most range hoods have either two or three speed settings and built-in light fixtures to illuminate the cooking surface below.

Installing ducting

When a range hood is mounted on an external wall, air is pulled through the back of the unit into a straight duct passing through the wall.

But, if the range is situated against an interior wall, you'll need to connect the hood to the outside with ductwork. The straight and curved components of the standard duct simply plug into one another to form a continuous shaft running between the hood and the outside wall.

Placement of this duct is often a complicated job. You have to determine where there is space available. Sometimes the duct can run over the top of wall cabinets until it reaches an outside wall. This is the easiest solution, and requires only the addition of a valance or soffit on top of the cabinets to hide the duct from view. If this option isn't available to you, it makes sense to hire a contractor to install the duct elsewhere.

To install the duct, begin by attaching the female end of the first component to the top or back of the hood. Then continue piecing together sections of straight duct with elbows until you reach the outside wall. Cut a hole through the wall and install straight duct to the exterior grille.

Installing the hood

Range hoods are hung from brackets that are sold with them. These brackets are screwed either between wall cabinets or directly to the wall. Cut a hole through the wall (or the cabinets above) for the duct, and run new electrical cable to the hood for driving the fan.

Some range hoods filter out odors and grease and then return the air to the room. Others direct stale air outside through a duct in the wall. The extraction design is generally considered the better option, though sometimes installing the duct can be so difficult and expensive that using the recirculating method makes more sense.

In order to install an extracting hood, it is necessary to cut a hole through the wall and install ducting. Although hoods that recycle the air are much simpler to install, they do not remove moisture from the room and do not filter out all of the grease and cooking odors. To keep any range hood working at peak efficiency, change or clean the filters regularly.

Recirculation hoods return air to room

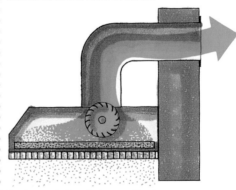

Ducting can be installed at top of hood...

Or ducting can be installed at back of hood

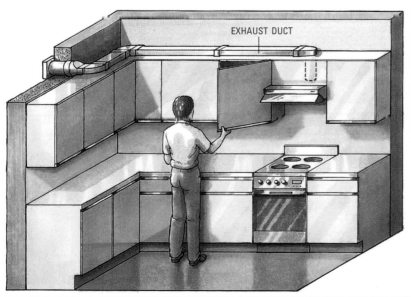

Installing exhaust ducts.
When a range is located against an interior wall, run the duct from the hood along the top of the wall cupboards.

EXHAUST DUCT

Heat-recovery ventilation

It has been estimated that more than half the energy produced by burning fossil fuels is used to keep our homes warm. Although the installation of efficient insulation significantly reduces heat loss, a great deal of heat is still wasted as a result of ventilation.

Heat-recovery ventilators are designed to balance the requirements of conserving energy and the need for a constant supply of clean fresh air by capturing some of the heat from the air that's leaving the house and transferring it to the clean air coming in.

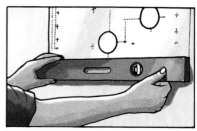
1 Position template to mark ducts and fasteners

2 Bore holes for ducting with holesaw

How a heat-recovery ventilator works

Heat-recovery ventilation unit
The diagram shows the layout of a typical wall-mounted heat-recovery ventilator.
1 Stale air from room
2 Stale air exhaust
3 Fresh air supply
4 Warmed fresh air
5 Heat exchanger
6 Induction fan
7 Exhaust fan

Heat-recovery ventilation can range in scale from compact units for continuous low-volume ventilation of individual rooms to whole-house ducted systems.

The simple ventilator shown here contains two low-noise electric fans. Stale air from the interior is extracted by one fan through a highly efficient heat exchanger. This absorbs up to 70 percent of the heat that would otherwise be wasted and transfers it to a flow of fresh air drawn into the room by the second fan. Because the two airflows are not allowed to mingle, odors and water vapor are not transferred along with the heat.

Self-contained heat-recovery ventilators can be installed in exterior walls or windows. The extraction unit of larger ducted systems is usually mounted in the basement, or sometimes in the attic.

3 Pass ducts through wall

4 Plug gaps around ducts with insulation

5 Seal edge of duct covers with caulk

Installing a heat-recovery ventilator

With the aid of a level, use the manufacturer's template to mark the position of the ventilator on the wall, including the centers of both ducts **(1)**. Locate the unit high on the the wall, but with at least a 2-inch clearance above and to the sides.

The ducting is likely to be narrower than that used for standard exhaust fans, so it may be possible to use a holesaw **(2)**. Drill a pilot hole through both the interior wallcovering and the exterior sheathing and siding first. After cutting the hole in the interior wall, cut the hole in the exterior wall slightly lower so that the ducting will slope to drain condensation to the outside. If the

ducting is too large to use a holesaw, use a keyhole or sabre saw instead, and trim the holes using a rasp. Use a hacksaw to cut the ducting to a length that equals the depth of the wall plus ⅜ inch. Use aluminum flashing tape to hold both ducts to the back of the wall-mounting plate. Insert the ducting into the wall holes **(3)**, push the panel against the wall, and mount it with screws.

Outside, plug the gaps around the ducting with fiberglass insulation **(4)** and screw the covers over the ends of the ducts. Seal around the edges with caulk **(5)**. Fit the main unit to the mounting plate on the inside wall **(6)** and wire it to a nearby outlet box.

6 Install ventilator unit on mounting plate

Ventilators

Mounting a flush ventilator

Most flush-mounted ventilators require a wooden frame to line a hole cut through the wall. Make it to the dimensions supplied by the man-ufacturer of the ventilator. Construct the frame with glued and screwed butt joints. Decide on the approximate position of the unit, then locate the wall studs to align one with the side of the unit. Mark the rectangle for the wooden lining onto the wall, then drill through the drywall or plaster at the corners of the outline. Cut out the rectangle with a keyhole saw or sabre saw and remove the wall insulation. Working from outside, cut away the siding and sheathing along the same lines. Saw off any studs obstructing the hole flush with its edges. (Do not remove studs from a bearing wall without consulting a building inspector.)

Insert the lining. The ventilator must be angled downward a few degrees toward the outside to drain away condensation. If this angle is built into the ventilator unit, the wood-frame lining can be set flush with the wall. Otherwise, tilt the frame a fraction by shimming it underneath before nailing. Compare diagonal measurements to make sure the lining is square in the hole.

Slide the ventilator unit into the liner, screw it in place, and install the front panel. Outside, seal the joints between the sheathing, the lining, and the ventilator unit with caulk.

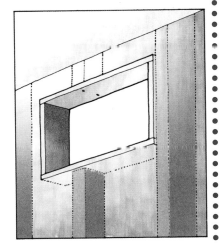

Mounting a flush ventilator
Install a wood-frame liner in the wall close to the ceiling where it will be in the best position to extract hot rising air. Attach the ventilator to the liner with screws.

Installing through a masonry wall

Decide on the approximate position of the unit, then mark its position on the wall by scribing around it with a pencil or awl. Use a masonry drill to bore a hole through the wall at each corner. Then cut through the drywall with a utility knife or through plaster with a cold chisel. Continue to drill holes around the perimeter of the hole and chop out the masonry with a cold chisel. After cutting halfway into the wall, drill a hole that goes the rest of the way through, using a long masonry bit. Use this hole as a reference point for drawing the cutout on the outside of the wall. Finish cutting the hole from the outside.

Mounting a ventilator liner

Clean up the rectangular hole you cut through the masonry. Then construct a wood liner using butt joints at the corners. Insert the liner, tilting it slightly toward the outside if necessary.

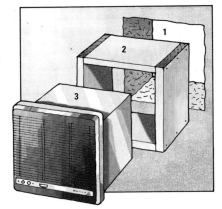

Mounting liner
1 Cut rectangular hole through masonry with cold chisel.
2 Build wood liner to fit size of ventilator and install in hole.
3 Slide ventilator into liner and attach.

Dehumidifiers control condensation

To combat condensation, you can either remove the moisture-laden air by ventilation, or warm it so that it is able to carry more water vapor before it becomes saturated. A third possibility is to extract the water itself from the air using a dehumidifier.

A dehumidifier works by drawing air from the room into the unit and passing it over a set of cold coils, so that the water vapor condenses on them and drips into a reservoir. The cold (but now dry) air is then drawn by a fan over heated coils before being returned to the room as additional heat.

The process is based on the simple refrigeration principle that gas under pressure heats up—and when the pressure drops, the temperature of the gas drops too. In a dehumidifier, a compressor delivers pressurized gas to the hot coils, in turn leading to the larger cold coils, which allow the gas to expand. The cooled gas then returns to the compressor for recycling.

A dehumidifier for domestic use is usually built into a floor-standing cabinet. It contains a humidistat that automatically switches on the unit when the moisture content of the air reaches a predetermined level. When the reservoir is full, the unit shuts down in order to prevent overflowing, and an indicator lights up to remind you to empty the water in the container.

When a dehumidifier is installed in a damp room, it should extract the excess moisture from the furnishings and fabric within a week or two. After that, it will monitor the moisture content of the air to maintain a stabilized atmosphere.

A portable version can be wheeled from room to room, where it is plugged into a standard wall outlet.

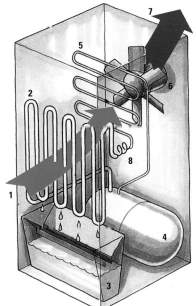

Working components of a dehumidifier
The diagram illustrates the layout of a typical domestic dehumidifier.
1 Incoming damp air
2 Cold coils
3 Water reservoir
4 Compressor
5 Hot coils
6 Fan
7 Dry warm air
8 Capillary tube where gas expands

Air conditioners

Central air-conditioning systems should be checked once a year in early spring by a professional service technician. During the air-conditioning season, the homeowner should check and replace the filters once a month, or more frequently in dusty areas.

Even small window- or wall-mounted air conditioners are usually factory-sealed and lubricated. However, it is important to keep the indoor and outdoor grilles dust-free to maintain high cooling efficiency and to avoid overstraining various components. Vacuum the front of the unit frequently. Once a year, remove the cover and vacuum behind it.

How air conditioning works

An air conditioner works on the same refrigeration principle described for a dehumidifier, and incorporates similar gas-filled coils and a compressor. However, airflow within the unit is different. Individual units are divided into separate compartments within one cabinet. Room air is drawn into the cooling compartment and passed over the evaporation coils, which absorb heat before a fan returns the air to the room at a lower temperature. As moisture vapor condenses on the coils, the unit also acts as a dehumidifier, a welcome bonus in hot, humid weather. Condensed water is normally drained to the outside of the house.

Gas in the evaporation coils moves on, carrying absorbed heat to the compartment facing the outside, where it is radiated from the condenser coils and blown outside by a fan.

A thermostat operates a valve, which reverses the flow of refrigerant when the temperature in the room drops below the setting. The system is automatic so that the unit can heat the room if it is cold in the early morning. As the sun rises and boosts the temperature, the air conditioner switches over to maintain a constant temperature indoors.

Choose a unit with variable fan speed and a method for directing the chilled air where it will be most effective in cooling the whole room. Usually this is at ceiling level, where the cold air falls slowly over the whole room area.

To reduce the running costs of an air conditioner, try to match its capacity—the amount of heat it can absorb—to the size of the room it will be cooling. A unit that is too small will be running most of the time without complete success, while one that is much too large will chill the air so quickly that it won't be able to remove much moisture vapor, and the atmosphere may still feel uncomfortable because it is humid. Ideally, the unit should only be working all the time on the hottest days.

The capacity of an air conditioner is measured in British Thermal Units (BTU). A unit with a capacity of 9000 BTU will remove that amount of heat every hour. As a rough guide to capacity, find the volume of the area you wish to cool (length x width x height), then allow 5 BTU per cubic foot. Ask the supplier to provide a more accurate calculation, which includes the size and number of windows, insulation, and heat-generating equipment in the room.

Mounting the unit

Cut a hole through the wall and fit a wood lining as described earlier for a heat-recovery ventilator. Being a larger and heavier unit, an air conditioner needs some sort of supporting cage or metal brackets.

Units designed for installing in windows are supplied with adjustable frames and weather stripping. After attaching the frame to the window opening, lift the air conditioner into the window, then slide it into place.

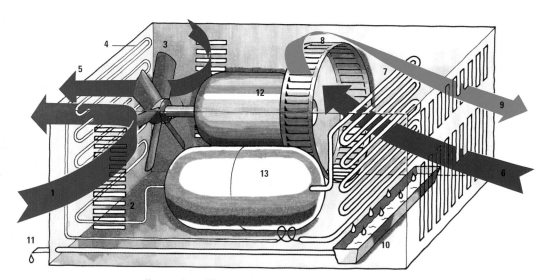

How an air conditioner works
The diagram shows the mechanism of a small wall-mounted or window-mounted air conditioner, but it illustrates the principle employed by all air conditioners.
Outside air (1) is drawn through the side vents (2) by a fan (3) which blows it over the hot coils (4). The air extracts heat from the coils and takes it outside (5). Warm, humid air from the interior (6) is drawn over the cold coils (7) by a centrifugal fan (8) and returned to the room cooled and dry (9). The condensed water drips into a reservoir (10) and drains to the outside (11). The motor (12) powers the fans and the compressor (13), which pumps gas around the system.

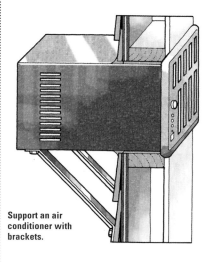

Support an air conditioner with brackets.

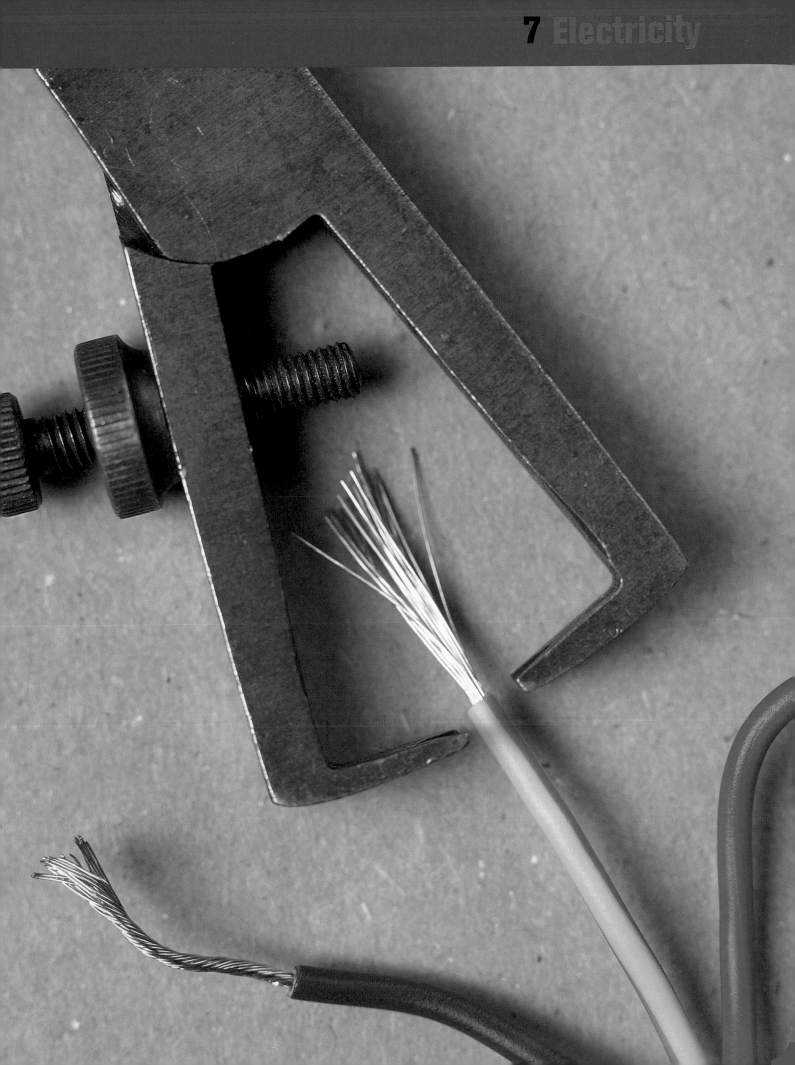

Electricity in our homes

Electricity has been so much a part of our lives for so many years that now it's hard to imagine living without it. We instinctively reach for a switch in the dark and a light comes on. We give little thought to circuitry, to switches, to the flow of current. We expect it to be there, and most of the time it is. Only when our electrical systems fail do we give them much thought. And then we are likely to be more confused than curious. For many of us, it all seems an unapproachable mystery. Electricity sounds dangerous, and any discussion of it seems hopelessly and deliberately obscured by difficult technical jargon.

The truth of the matter is that electricity is complicated when used to do complicated things, as in advanced electronics. But you don't have to start at that level. You can start with the simplest repair and work up.

Electricity is learnable because it is logical and sequential, and therefore predictable. Electrical current runs along wires as simply as water passes through plumbing pipes. Switches interrupt current just as valves and faucets interrupt water. If this analogy seems too simple, it probably is, but learning to think in simple progressions

is the key to understanding your home's electrical system.

Like so many other areas of home improvement, electrical projects are now made easier with improved materials. Manufacturers are designing more and more items with the inexperienced do-it-yourselfer in mind. In many ways, electrical work has never been easier. Start by doing the little things. Small projects will give you the confidence to approach larger projects. Eventually, doing your own electrical work will offer real savings and the satisfaction of greater self-sufficiency.

Think safe to be safe

One of the most intimidating aspects of electricity is its ability to injure or even kill. With a few precautions, however, you can eliminate the danger factor and work without fear of being hurt. In fact, you are probably more likely to electrocute yourself through

Don't overload circuits

Use screw for adapter

Test for voltage

careless living habits than when attempting a do-it-yourself wiring project. The following list of dos and don'ts will protect you from electrical hazards, both in your daily living and when working on your home's electrical system.

- Always wear safety glasses when working with electricity and remove all jewelry and wrist watches.
- Always shut the power off at the main service panel to any circuit you intend to work on.
- Do not overload a receptacle with adapters and extension cords.
- Do not run extension cords under carpets or throw rugs. Constant traffic can fray a cord's insulation, creating a fire hazard.
- When bathing, keep radios, hair dryers, and other small appliances a safe distance from the tub.
- When adapting a three-prong plug to a two-prong receptacle, make sure the adapter is grounded to the screw on the receptacle's coverplate and that the box is grounded.
- When a fuse blows, never install a substitute fuse with an amperage rating greater than the one you are replacing.
- Do not pull a plug from a receptacle by its cord. The cord will soon tear loose inside the plug, overheat, and become a fire hazard.

- Always unplug an appliance or lamp before attempting a repair.
- Before starting any work, use a voltage tester to make sure the power is off. A lamp or small appliance will also work in testing outlets for power.
- Do not use aluminum ladders when working near overhead service lines or when testing live circuits.
- If you must work on wet floors, wear rubber boots and stand on planks to provide a buffer between you and the moisture.
- Electrical systems are mechanically and electrically bonded to metallic plumbing and gas piping systems. When working on electrical wiring avoid coming in contact with grounded metal pipes, ductwork or other grounded objects.
- When making plumbing repairs, make sure that you do not splice a length of plastic pipe into a metal plumbing pipe unless you install a copper wire bonding jumper the length of the plastic pipe that maintains the continuity of the metal piping system.

Even if you understand nothing about the wiring in your home, you can still save on energy consumption by following these basic conservation measures.

Kitchen

- Use flat-bottom pans roughly the same size as the burner when cooking on electric range tops.
- Cover foods when boiling to speed the heating process and reduce energy consumption.
- Use microwaves when possible, as they cook faster and use less wattage.
- When hand-washing dishes, use a sink stopper to hold water. A continually running hot rinse uses much more water.
- Clean dust and grease from refrigerator condensers at least three times a year. Dirty condensers are very inefficient to operate.

Heating and cooling

- Set thermostats at 68° F in winter and 78° F in summer. Each degree under 68° F and over 78° F will save approximately 3 percent of your total heating or cooling costs.
- Open drapes facing the sun during the day in winter and close them during the day in summer. In wintertime, close all drapes at night to reduce heat loss.
- Apply caulk and weather stripping to leaky windows and doors to further reduce heat loss.

Laundry and bath

- Wash only full loads of clothing. When possible, wash with warm water and rinse with cold water.
- Because clogged filters interrupt efficient airflow, clean dryer lint filters after every load.
- Showers generally require less hot water than baths. To reduce further the amount of hot water needed, install a simple volume-reduction washer in the showerhead.
- Repair all leaky faucets, as they can cost you hundreds of gallons of hot and cold water each year.

Lighting

- Make your home more energy efficient and save money by updating your lighting with compact fluorescent lamps (CFL) and other new lighting technologies.

Until you understand the basics of electricity, your electrical skills will be limited to simple repair projects. Luckily, once you get past the usual apprehensions, electricity is quite easily understood. Electricity is logical and so can be learned in small steps. The basics are explained on this page.

Volts x Amps = Watts

The electrons flowing through a circuit cause a current measured in amperes. The rate of flow can vary greatly, according to demand and power source. Current flows only when called for by an appliance. Amperes are moved along the circuit by pressure, called voltage. In simplified terms, when we multiply voltage (pressure) times amperes (current) we get wattage, which is a measure of how much electricity is being used. If the current passes through a 75-watt bulb, for example, the electricity consumed will be 75 watts. Similarly, a 1500-watt electric space heater consumes 1500 watts of power.

Amperes

Amperes, often shortened to amps, are precise units of measurement. Approximately 6.25 quintillion (18 zeros) electrons moving at 186,000 miles per second past a point in a circuit each second equals 1 amp. Among many other things, amps are used to rate appliances, power tools, and your home's electrical circuits. A typical service panel will carry a variety of circuits with different amp ratings, usually between 15 and 50 amps.

Volts

Just as water pressure is measured in pounds per square inch, electrical pressure is measured in volts. The greater the voltage, the greater the pressure behind the amperes. Some voltage is lost when forced through a long conductor due to the resistance of the conductor material. Although a short and a long conductor might have the same voltage input, the long

conductor will deliver a lower output. The difference in output is called voltage drop. When voltage arrives at your service panel, it may fluctuate. This voltage could vary as much as plus or minus 5%. You should generally be receiving from 115 to 125 volts at any given time. To establish some workable standard, the National Electrical Code and electrical utilities have established 120/240 volts as the assigned nominal voltage. Today, all electrical materials are designed to these standards and rated accordingly.

Watts

Watts measure how much power is being used at a given time. To size a circuit and breaker, you must first determine the maximum wattage needed for a given room or group of rooms. We do this by adding up the watts as listed on light bulbs and appliances. (Sometimes you will see watts expressed as volt-amps, or VA.) A normal kitchen circuit might be quickly overloaded by a refrigerator, microwave, and a few small appliances.

We also need to know how many watts a 15- or 20-amp breaker will deliver, so we multiply 15 amps times 120 volts, to get 1800 watts of potential power. If your maximum anticipated wattage is more than 1800, extra circuits will be necessary.

Watt-hours are also the measure used by power companies to keep track of the electricity we use. To make the billing more manageable, watt-hours are calculated in units of one thousand, known as kilowatt-hours. Each Kwh equals 1000 watt-hours, as measured by your service meter.

Low-voltage circuits

Low-voltage wiring has long been used for doorbells and thermostats because they require so little energy. Low-voltage systems are used for indoor lighting, landscape lighting, security systems, central vacuum systems, garage door openers and

many others as well. Low-voltage systems are often rated from 12 to 30 volts. Transformers or electronic power supplies are used to reduce voltages. These transformers or power supplies are usually supplied with low-voltage systems and kits.

For electricity to work, you must establish a circuit. A circuit is simply a wire loop that travels from an electrical source to an electrical load and back. Billions of electrons flow down one side of the loop, through the load and back along the other side. Only when a loop remains closed can electricity flow through it. If the loop is interrupted, as with a switch, the flow stops. The electrons must travel full circle to create a current. When a circuit is incomplete, it is said that an "open circuit" exists. This can be the result of a broken wire or an improper connection.

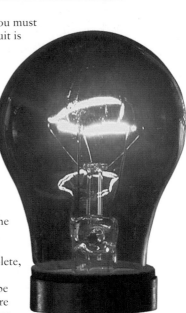

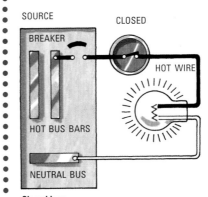

Closed loop
When switch is closed, current flows

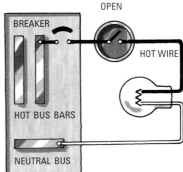

Open loop
When switch is open, current cannot flow

240-volt circuits
Many major appliances such as clothes dryers, water heaters, and air conditioners require more voltage than can be handled by a 120-volt circuit. To accommodate these greater voltage needs, 240-volt circuits are used. A 240-volt circuit will have two hot wires and a grounding wire, and may include a neutral wire if needed by the appliance.

Basic electrical toolbox

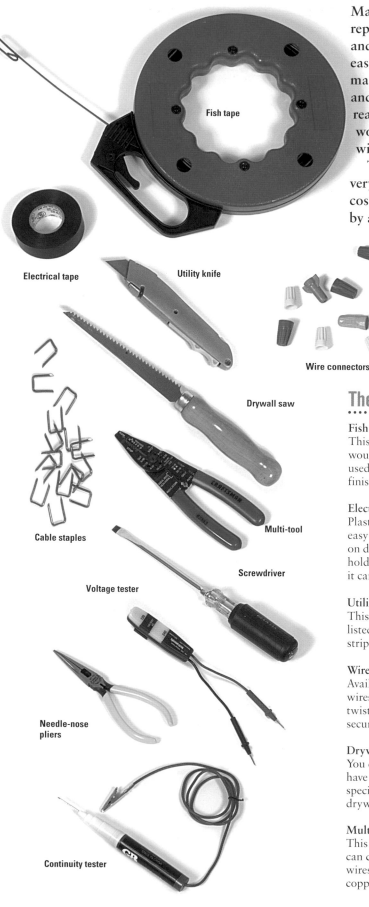

Fish tape

Electrical tape

Utility knife

Drywall saw

Multi-tool

Cable staples

Screwdriver

Voltage tester

Needle-nose pliers

Continuity tester

Wire connectors

Many homeowners are intimidated by the prospect of electrical repairs, though they really shouldn't be. When approached safely, and with the proper tools, basic repairs and installations are quite easy and involve little risk. Bookstores, home centers, and magazines abound with information on basic electrical projects, and with some study, even complicated upgrades are within the reach of most do-it-yourselfers. There isn't much about electrical work that is physically demanding, but the right selection of tools will make any job easier.

The good news is that assembling a basic electrical toolkit isn't very hard because it includes relatively few tools. And the total cost of these tools is often less than the cost of a single service call by an electrician. Your tool kit may vary slightly, depending on your specific needs. But the tools and accessories shown here make a good starting point for most people. When supplemented by other, more common household tools, you'll be able to tackle most jobs successfully. Of course, any major project will require a permit beforehand and an electrical inspection afterward to conform to local codes.

The tools you'll need

Fish tape
This tool has a rigid coil of metal tape wound around a retractable wheel. It's used for pulling new cable within finished floors, walls, and ceilings.

Electrical tape
Plastic tape is flexible, durable, and easy to use. For making minor repairs on damaged cable sheathing, and for holding cable to the end of a fish tape, it can't be beat.

Utility knife
This tool has more uses than can be listed. It's the best tool for cutting and stripping cable sheathing.

Wire connectors
Available in different sizes to match the wires being joined, these small devices twist wires together and hold them securely.

Drywall saw
You don't need this if you already have a keyhole saw. But it's made specifically for cutting holes in drywall.

Multi-tool
This tool is the heart of the toolkit. It can cut cable and wires and can strip wires cleanly without damaging the copper under the insulation.

Cable staples
Staples are required to fasten new cable to studs and joists.

Screwdriver
Only one flat-blade screwdriver is shown here. But you'll need an assortment of sizes in both flat blade and Phillips heads.

Voltage tester
This tool has two wire probes joined by a small neon light. It's used to determine if power is present in a receptacle, switch, or any wire in any circuit. When current passes through the probes, it lights the bulb.

Needle-nose pliers
These pliers are used for any number of small tasks, but are particularly useful for bending the ends of wire to fit around a terminal screw.

Continuity tester
This tester differs from a voltage tester because it has its own battery power source. It's used to determine if there is continuity in a device or circuit. For instance, when the clip touches one switch terminal and the probe touches the other terminal, a glowing bulb indicates a completed circuit through the switch. Never use a continuity tester on energized equipment or circuits!

If you own a single-family home, state or local laws may allow you to do electrical work on your side of the meter. This does not mean that you can invent your own standards, however. The next person to live in your house has a right to be protected against dangerous or substandard workmanship and materials. Permits and on-site inspections are required by code officials. Check your local building department's Web site for permit and inspection information and forms.

When do you need a permit?

You need a permit anytime you alter or add to existing wiring. You will also need a permit when wiring major home appliances or when installing any outdoor or accessory building wiring. When wiring will be concealed by finished walls or ceilings, a "rough-in" inspection is required, in addition to a "final" inspection upon completion. Minor repairs, such as replacing defective switches and receptacles, generally do not require permits. When in doubt, call your local building department.

Your local code authority will be happy to supply the forms you will need to apply for a permit. You will be charged a fee to defray the costs of inspection, and in some cases you may be required to take a simple competency test to demonstrate your understanding of basic electrical principles.

You may also be required to supply a rough drawing of the work you have in mind. Don't panic; this drawing need not be complicated, and besides, it offers the perfect opportunity for you to clarify any technical questions you might have.

Try not to be intimidated by inspectors; they have an obligation to inform you as to what the code requires, but they also have an obligation to identify code deficiencies, hopefully with a professional, courteous and helpful demeanor.

UL listings

Just as you should maintain the highest standards of workmanship, you should always use equipment and materials that are third party certified. All electrical equipment and materials must be labeled by Underwriters Laboratories (UL), Canadian Standards Association (CSA), or another government-accredited testing laboratory. Electricity is only as safe as the materials used to bring it to you. A small savings on unapproved materials could cost you plenty in property damage or personal injury.

Property insurance and your wiring

Home insurance policies are not likely to include exclusionary clauses concerning your electrical work. Even so, if a fire starts in your home and can be directly tied to your faulty electrical work, your insurance company may consider you a permanent bad risk and decide not to renew your policy.

Similar complications can result from work performed in your home by someone other than a licensed electrical contractor, such as an unlicensed handyman. Furthermore, you may be liable to a future owner of your home under the latent-defect laws of your state. If you knowingly hide an electrical defect when the contract is signed, the future owner can sue you for damages after the sale, or at least require you to correct the problem.

Obtaining a permit, paying a nominal inspection fee, and setting up the proper inspections is the best insurance policy you can have. Once your code authority approves your work, you are in the clear. Any questions of liability will be directed elsewhere.

In short, acquire permits and follow code regulations. Codes protect you and the person who buys your home when you move on. In most cases, wiring to code does not make your work any more difficult or expensive, just safer. It only makes good sense to wire your home in the safest way.

Codes and the grandfather clause

What if you are adding wiring to a home that does not meet current code requirements? When the inspector sees the existing wiring, will he make you upgrade it as well? The answer is almost always no. As codes change, you are not expected to change your home's wiring too. If your home was wired to code when it was built or remodeled, it falls under the grandfather clause. Only those sections you alter (and those sections affected by the alteration) must meet current code specifications.

Of course, there are exceptions. If existing wiring poses a serious threat to property and lives, you can be required to correct the problem.

About the NEC®

The first electrical code in this country was proposed in 1881 by the National Association of Fire Engineers. It was written in response to the many fires started by electricity then. It had only three rules. The National Electrical Code® was first published in 1897. It is revised every three years and now contains over 900 pages. The NEC® is not intended as an instruction manual for untrained persons. For the pertinent information it contains, buy, instead, one of the simplified guidebooks available at bookstores.

Applying for an electrical permit

As mentioned earlier, you may be required to take a simple competency test to demonstrate your electrical know-how.

You may also be required to sign an affidavit stating that you are the owner and occupant of the home listed in the permit application. Generally, homeowners are only allowed to do electrical work in the single-family detached home that they own and occupy; never in apartments, condominiums, attached townhouses, and other multifamily housing where innocent people could be put at risk.

When a permit is issued to you, you may have to post it on the job site. Like a fishing license, most permits expire after 12 months, at which time you will need to get a new one if you have not completed your project.

Typical building permit

From the source to you

Electricity is created by generators that may be powered by water, oil, gas, coal, nuclear reactor, wind, solar or other renewable sources. From these generators electricity is transmitted to distribution stations at very high pressure, or voltage. From the distribution stations, the voltage is reduced and distributed to major cities and rural areas.

From a local substation, electricity is distributed down your street, either through overhead lines or underground cables. Each home is then connected by an overhead service drop or underground service lateral. An older home might have a two-wire service capable of carrying only 30 amps of power at 120 volts of pressure. Homes built in the last 60 years are likely to have three-wire services capable of carrying from 60 to 200 amps at 120/240 volts.

With today's increased electrical needs, 60-amp services are seldom adequate. Lending institutions and insurance companies often require 100-amp services as a minimum these days, even for smaller homes. Installing a new meter socket, conduit, service conductors and a new service panel should always be left to a licensed electrical contractor. Consult with your electrical contractor, your power company, and your local code authority to coordinate any major service upgrades. In all cases, strict adherence to the electrical code is a must.

One of the advantages of installing a new service is that you can usually convert from overhead to underground wiring. Overhead services, called "service drops," detract from the appearance of a home and are subject to storm damage. Overhead services can also kill you if you touch them with aluminum ladders or tree-pruning equipment. Even if you have an overhead service, you can have your power company and your electrical contractor convert it to an underground service, called a "service lateral." Of course, your yard must be large enough to allow a trencher to maneuver. Directional boring equipment and underground piercing equipment can bypass patios and other large expanses of concrete that used to be obstacles for converting to an underground service.

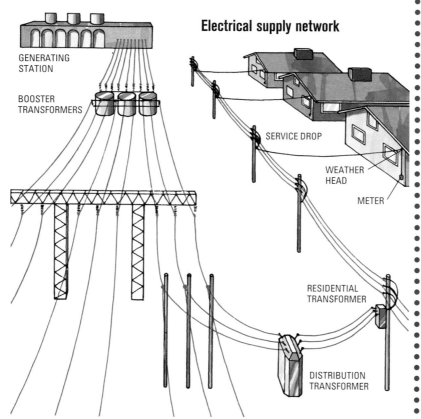

Electrical supply network

GENERATING STATION

BOOSTER TRANSFORMERS

SERVICE DROP

WEATHER HEAD

METER

RESIDENTIAL TRANSFORMER

DISTRIBUTION TRANSFORMER

Service lateral
1 Service entrance meter
2 Meter grounding conductors
3 Grounding electrode
4 Water pipe
5 Underground conduit riser

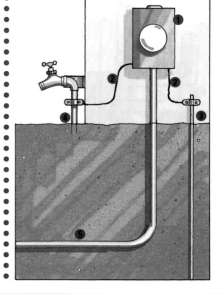

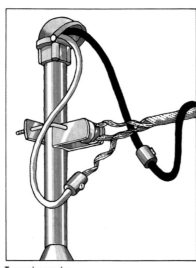

Two-wire service

Three-wire service

How we use the electricity we buy

The rates listed below are for a specific area. Yours will be higher or lower. Information supplied by the Lincoln Electric System, Lincoln, Nebraska.

CONSUMPTION AND COSTS FOR COMMON ELECTRICAL APPLIANCES

Appliance	Average Wattage	Avg. Hrs. Per Mo.	Avg. Kwh Per Mo.	Avg. Cost Per Mo.	Avg. Cost Per Hour
Food preparation					
Blender	386	3.2	1.24	$ .07	2.3¢
Broiler	830	6.0	5.00	$ .30	5.0¢
Coffee Maker (drip)					
Brew	1440	3.0	4.32	$ .26	8.7¢
Warm	85	240.0	20.40	$ 1.23	.5¢
Deep Fryer	1448	4.7	6.80	$ .41	8.8¢
Electric Frying Pan	1196	13.0	15.50	$ .94	7.2¢
Electric Knife	92	1.0	.09	$ .01	.6¢
Garbage Disposer	445	6.0	2.70	$ .16	2.7¢
Microwave	1500	11.0	16.50	$ 1.00	9.1¢
Mixer (hand)	127	1.0	.13	¢ .01	.8¢
Oven	1500	11.0	16.50	$ 1.00	9.1¢
Range					
Bake	2833	8.0	22.70	$ 1.37	17.1¢
Broil	2900	6.0	14.70	$ 1.05	17.5¢
Surface Units					
6"-unit, high setting	1400	—	—	—	8.5¢
8"-unit, high setting	2600	—	—	—	15.7¢
Sandwich Grill	1161	2.3	2.67	$ .16	7.0¢
Slow Cooker	200	57.0	11.40	$ .69	1.2¢
Toaster	1146	3.0	3.40	$ .21	6.9¢
Toaster Oven	1500	2.0	3.00	$ .18	9.1¢
Waffle Iron	1161	1.6	1.90	$ 11	7.0¢
Food preservation					
Freezer					
15 cu. ft. upright	341	262.0	99.60	$ 6.02	2.1¢
15 cu. ft. upright frostless	440	334.0	147.00	$8.89	2.7¢
Refrigerator/Freezer					
15 cu. ft.	326	291.0	94.90	$5.74	2.0¢
15 cu. ft. frostless	616	248.0	152.50	$9.20	3.7¢
Utility					
Central Vacuum System	4300	8.0	34.40	$ 2.08	26.0¢
Clock	2	730.0	1.46	$ .09	—
Dishwasher	1200	25.0	30.00	$ 1.82	7.3¢
Dryer	4856	17.0	83.00	$ 4.99	29.4¢
Fluorescent Light (40w)	40	92.0	3.68	$ .22	.2¢
Fluorescent Light (20w)	20	92.0	1.84	$ .11	.1¢
Incandescent Light (100w)	100	92.0	9.20	$ .56	.6¢
Iron	1100	12.0	13.00	$ .80	6.7¢
Sewing Machine	75	12.0	.90	$ .05	.5¢
Vacuum Cleaner	630	6.0	3.80	$ .23	3.8¢
Washing Machine (automatic)	512	17.0	8.70	$ .53	3.1¢
Water Bed (king size, operating 50% of the time)	375	321.0	120.00	$7.28	2.3¢
Water Heater	4500	111.0	500.00	$ 30.22	27.0¢

Summer rate=7.15¢/Kwh   Winter rate=4.9¢/Kwh   Average=5.7¢/Kwh

Meters and service entrances

All the electricity you use is recorded in Kwh by your meter. In older meters, you can actually watch them count. A numbered disc spins when electricity is used and these revolutions are recorded by four or five small dials. Newer models have a digital readout. In both types, the counter on the meter works much like the odometer in your car. Every watt that is consumed is recorded.

Your meter is banded in place and the band is sealed by your power company. It is actually part of the service entrance circuit. When a meter is removed, the circuit is interrupted. Only when it is plugged back in can you draw electricity from the power source.

If you wish to monitor your energy consumption, you can note the reading at the beginning of the month and again at the end of the month and subtract the former from the latter. Your meter will also give you an exact measure of energy saved when you experiment with energy-saving devices and practices. And of course, if you pay an estimated monthly bill, you can check for accuracy by comparing your actual use with the estimated billing.

Breaker panel

The service entrance panel

From the meter, your service wires enter your home, either through the roof or through a wall. (Thirty-amp services usually have one black and one white wire, while 60- to 100-amp or greater services usually have two black wires and one white wire.) Service wires are usually encased in metal or plastic conduit from the weather head to the service panel. Once inside the panel, the two hot (black) wires attach to a main switch, or disconnect. The neutral (white) wire is attached to the neutral bus bar. At this point, a ground wire, usually bare No. 6 copper, is connected to the bus bar as well and then fastened to a copper grounding rod or metal plumbing pipes or both. (Some panels have separate neutral and ground bus bars, which are bonded together in the panels.)

How your home's wiring connects to the service panel depends upon the age of the system and whether or not subpanels are used. An older home may have a main panel with a disconnect switch, a bus bar, and a ground conductor. In this case, the panel serves only as a distribution box and a main disconnect. From the main panel, one black hot and one red hot wire (the NEC no longer requires one hot conductor to be coded red), together with a white neutral wire and a green ground, travel to one or more

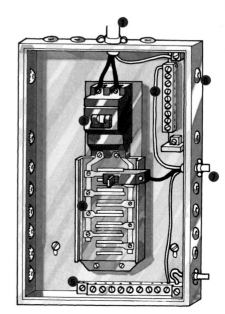

subpanels where the hot wires are connected to hot bus bars and neutral wires are connected to neutral bus bars. Older homes may also be wired directly to a main panel, without subpanels. In this case, each circuit would have its own fuse in the main panel.

A new home is likely to have a panel with circuit breakers. In this case, subpanels are not generally used. All the circuits are connected to hot bus bars through snap-in, or slide-in circuit breakers. In this configuration, the hot wire of every 120-volt circuit will be attached to a single-pole circuit breaker and the neutral and ground wires will be connected to the neutral bus bar. 240-volt circuits will be similarly wired, except that the two hot wires will be attached to a double-pole circuit breaker. Once the panel is wired, connecting breakers and new circuits is relatively simple.

Main components of a typical service panel
1 Power supply from meter
2 Neutral bus
3 Main disconnect
4 Hot bus
5 Ground bus
6 Knockout
7 Cable to house circuit

Fuse panel

How to read a meter

If your meter is an older model, it will likely have four or five dials. Each dial will be numbered from 0 to 9. As you look at these dials, you will see that they move in opposite directions.

To record your meter reading, write down the numbers from each dial starring at the left. This will give you the approximate number of kilowatt-hours consumed. To determine how much electricity you use in a month, read the meter at the beginning of the month and again at the end of the month. Automated Meter Reading (AMR) is being deployed in many areas as a

means to automatically and accurately capture electricity usage (water and gas consumption can also be automatically collected). Data from smart electric meters is sent via radio signals to handheld or mobile receivers or to fixed network receiving equipment that is installed throughout the neighborhood. Other types of technologies are also in use. These new technologies eliminate estimated bills, they ensure accurate billing for exact usage, and the meter reader no longer needs access to the home; the utility reduces costs and the homeowner is not inconvenienced.

Subpanel

Reading a meter
The reading indicated here would be 76579.

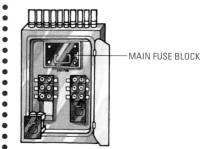

MAIN FUSE BLOCK

Older service panel
These have pull-out fuse blocks

Breakers and fuses

Fuses and breakers are safety buffers that keep an electrical malfunction from starting a fire. A fuse can blow or a breaker trips when one of three things happens. The most frequent cause is an overloaded circuit. When too many lights or appliances are plugged into a circuit, they call for more amperage than the circuit can deliver. This amperage overload causes the thermal elements in fuses and breakers to heat up, which causes the fuses or breakers to blow. A short circuit will also cause a fuse to blow because of the greatly increased amperage in the circuit. And finally, a fuse will blow if a hot wire touches a grounded object; this is called a ground fault. It is crucial to determine what may be causing a fuse to blow or a breaker to trip repeatedly.

Types of fuses

Edison-base fuses

A traditional Edison-base fuse contains a thin metal strip or wire that melts when a circuit heats up excessively. When the strip melts, it separates and interrupts the flow of electrons. The glass and ceramic housing, encasing the strip, keeps the molten metal from escaping and becoming a fire hazard.

The glass window on the front of an Edison-base fuse allows you to see if the strip is intact. When the fuse blows, the window also offers some clues in tracking down the source of the problem. If the window is blackened by carbon, the cause of the overload is probably a short circuit. A short circuit creates heat very quickly and burns the fuse at high temperature, which smokes the glass. If the glass is clear and you can see the melted strip, then the circuit probably heated up more slowly, as it would with an amperage overload.

If after replacing an Edison-base fuse, the new fuse blows as well, take notice of how long it took to blow. If it blew immediately, assume a short circuit. Often you will find the short in an appliance, most likely in its cord or plug. Your only recourse is to repair the appliance and install a new fuse.

If a single circuit blows frequently but with no apparent pattern, assume an overloaded circuit. You will have to unplug one or more lamps or appliances until a new circuit can be added.

Time-delay fuses

Some heavy tools and electric motors require three times as much amperage for startup as they need for running, once started. If a fuse blows only when you start an electric shop tool or a window air conditioner, you can circumvent the startup overload by installing a time-delay Edison-base fuse. If the time-delay fuse blows,

however, unplug a few lamps or appliances or quit using the power tool until a new circuit can be installed.

Type-S fuses

Through the years, many frustrated homeowners have installed 20-amp fuses in 15-amp sockets. This method does put an end to blown fuses, but it also cancels the only safety feature an electrical system has. Don't be tempted to up-size a fuse. If an overloaded fuse in your panel can't overheat, the wiring in your home will. Overheated wires cause fires.

If you move into an older home, check to see that the previous owner has not made a dangerous substitution. To further protect yourself and all future owners, install nontamperable Type-S fuses. These fuses come with variously sized threaded adapters that screw into Edison-base fuseholders. Once installed, they cannot be removed. From then on, only 15-amp Type-S fuses can be used for this circuit. Twenty-amp Type-S fuses won't fit.

Cartridge-type fuses

Cartridge fuses can be found in many older homes and are often used as main panel fuses. They may also be used to protect subpanels, but the most common installation has two cartridge fuses at the main disconnect.

There are two types of cartridge fuse. The differences are in the end connections and in amp ratings. Ferrule-type cartridges can be rated between 10 and 60 amps and are frequently used in subpanels and on branch circuits or appliance circuits. Knife-blade cartridges are the other type. The blade ends of these fuses snap into service panel clips. Because they are rated higher than 60 amps, they are often used as main panel protectors.

BREAKERS

Breakers have replaced fuses almost entirely in the last 40 years. Unlike a blown fuse, a tripped breaker does not have to be replaced. When a short or overload trips a breaker, all you need to do is turn it back on. In addition to being a perpetually renewable circuit protector, a breaker can withstand the temporary amperage surges often created when electric motors first start up. So, in a sense, a breaker has a built-in time-delay feature. You can also buy Edison-base replacement breakers that screw directly into older service panels. To reactivate these breakers, you simply push a small button in the center of the breaker.

Breakers differ slightly in appearance and operation from one manufacturer to another. The main difference is that some breaker switches do not return to the off position when tripped. You will have to shut them off all the way before flipping them on again. Breakers are also not universal in terms of how they snap into panels. You will have to buy breakers to match the brand name on your service panel.

20-amp Edison-base fuse

20-amp time-delay fuse

15-amp Type-S fuse

Type-S fuse adapter

Edison-base replacement breakers
By pushing button, power is restored

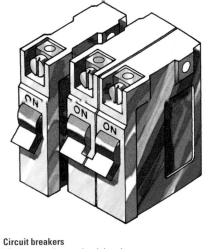

Circuit breakers
Modern panels use circuit breakers

100-amp knife end cartridge fuse

50-amp ferrule end cartridge fuse

Assessing your system's potential

Two things determine the expansion capabilities of your home's electrical system. Most important is the maximum amp rating of your service entrance. The other is the amount of circuit space left—if any—in your service panel.

Mapping your home's wiring

Before you can know how much expansion your electrical system will safely handle, you will need to determine how much amperage is now being used by each circuit. The best way to do this is to make a map of your home's circuitry. While tracing circuits sounds complicated, it need not be. All you will need is a floor-plan drawing of your home, a voltage tester, circuit tracer tester, lamp or portable radio, and a little deductive reasoning.

Making the map

Start by drawing the perimeter of your home on graph paper. Use a simple ⅛-inch-to-1-foot scale. In other words, each little square on the graph paper equals 1 square foot of living space. Then draw in the approximate location of all interior walls. If you have a two- or three-story house, make an additional drawing for each floor. If you have a basement, lighted patio, or deck and a wired garage or other outbuilding, draw them too. Then indicate the location of each outlet box and each permanent light fixture in your home.

Start by removing the fuse or tripping the breaker on the first circuit in the panel. Mark that breaker or fuse No. 1. Then take your voltage tester or small lamp and plug it into all outlets near the circuit you've just interrupted. Next to each outlet on the map that doesn't work, place the number 1. Then go back to the service panel, restore power to the circuit you've just checked, and shut off the power to the next circuit in the panel. Be sure to number each fuse or breaker in the panel as you go.

With power to the second circuit shut off, locate and number all fixtures and outlets on the map that do not work. Do this with each circuit until you have isolated each circuit and determined how many outlets and fixtures are served by each. Also check and mark down your major electrical appliances, such as a range, water heater, or clothes dryer that have dedicated 240-volt circuits. When you are finished, every outlet and fixture should have a number. Tape the map to the inside of the panel cover for future reference.

Rating your panel

To determine what rating your service panel has, open the panel cover and look for the amperage designation near the main disconnect. If your service and panel are rated at 100 amps or more, you are in luck. If it is rated at 60 amps or less, expansion will be limited. If your needs require a substantial upgrade, consider having a larger service panel installed by a licensed electrical contractor.

Your ability to install new circuits will depend on the number of breaker or fuse spaces left in the panel. A home's wiring doesn't always need all the breaker slots provided in a 100-amp, or greater, panel. If you see vacant breaker slots, an expansion will be easy. Each slot will hold one new 15- or 20-amp single-pole circuit breaker. If you have two adjacent vacant slots, your panel will accommodate a new 240-volt double-pole circuit breaker.

If yours is one of the many older 60-amp panels, however, all available fuse spaces will likely be taken. A 60-amp service panel will also limit the number of 240-volt appliance outlets you can have. One 240-volt and four 120-volt circuits is the limit in 60-amp panels. If your 60-amp panel has the room and the available amperage, wiring a new circuit will be as easy as wiring from a new breaker. If the panel is full, but you have two underutilized circuits, you can sometimes combine the two and free one circuit for expansion.

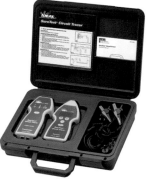

Circuit tracer tester

Determining total amperage

As a rule of thumb and to keep things simple, general purpose lighting outlets and receptacle outlets should each be calculated at 1.5 amps. This means that a 15-amp fuse or breaker (on No. 14 wire) will support 10 outlets. A 20-amp fuse or breaker (on No. 12 wire) will support 13 outlets. If your mapping identifies a circuit that can support additional outlets, you can tap into that circuit to add new outlets.

If your map identifies two circuits with so few outlets that both circuits could be protected by a single fuse, you may be able to combine those two circuits in the panel, thus freeing one whole circuit for expansion.

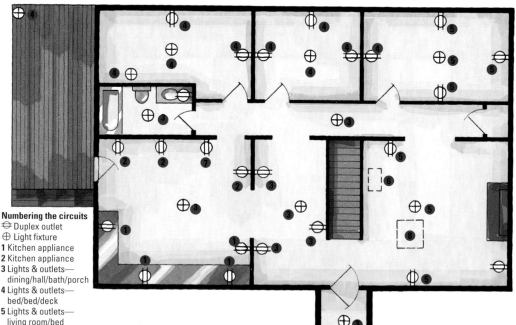

Numbering the circuits
⊖ Duplex outlet
⊕ Light fixture
1 Kitchen appliance
2 Kitchen appliance
3 Lights & outlets—
   dining/hall/bath/porch
4 Lights & outlets—
   bed/bed/deck
5 Lights & outlets—
   living room/bed
6 Basement—
   furnace/basement
   light
7 120/240 range
8 240 dryer (basement)

Weatherproof box

Cut-in box

Handy box

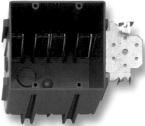

2-gang box

Switch box

15-amp duplex receptacle

20-amp duplex receptacle

GFCI receptacle

Single-pole switch

Three-way switch

Keyed light fixture

Coverplates

• Once you decide to tackle a project, you'll have to shop for materials, and here's where things can get confusing. There's a wide variety of electrical hardware out there and it's not always easy to know what goes where. Here are some of the most common items with a brief description of what each one is commonly used for and why.

All electrical connections must be housed in closed electrical boxes. Boxes also hold switches, lights, and receptacles securely in place. You'll find several different shapes in plastic and metal and each type has a specific use.

Weatherproof box is designed for outdoor use and, when fitted with the correct coverplate, is watertight.

Cut-in box is used for retrofit work. You just cut a hole in the wall and slide the box in. The side flanges hold it in place.

Handy box is made for surface mounting and is used with armored cable or conduit.

Two-gang box has space for two receptacles, two switches, or one of each.

Switch box is designed for one switch, but the sides can be removed so it can be ganged with other switch boxes. Switch boxes are used in flush installations.

The most common receptacles are the duplex variety for 15- and 20-amp circuits. Most come with screw terminals and push-in slots for attaching wires. A more specialized model is the GFCI (ground fault circuit interrupter) receptacle. GCFIs are required in bathrooms; garages; outdoors; in crawl spaces and basements; kitchen countertops; and at all laundry, utility and wet bar sinks. GFCIs help protect people from fatal electrical shocks.

Switches are usually single pole, for turning power off to a fixture from a single location, and three-way for switching power from two different locations. But not all lights are switched remotely. Some have a pull-chain switch built in, like the keyed light fixture shown.

Various coverplates round out this selection of basic hardware. They're available in different sizes, configurations, and colors.

Electrical tape

Grounding pigtail
This allows you to join ground wires together with a wire connector on the bare end, and then to attach them to the back of a metal box with the grounding screw on the other end.

Cable connectors
Conduit connector (top) attaches conduit to box. Cable connector (above) joins cable to box.

Continuity testers

Continuity testers allow you to test conductors without having the power on, which makes them ideal for testing appliance switches and connections. Unlike voltage testers, continuity testers have their own battery-supplied power. The light in a continuity tester comes on when its circuit is completed by a switch, conductor, or appliance. It is important to turn off power to any circuit or part before testing it with a continuity tester. Never use a continuity tester on energized equipment or circuits!

Testing fuses

To see if a fuse is still working, touch the probe of the tester to the metal threads of the fuse and the alligator clip to the contact at the base of the fuse. If the fuse is good, the light in the tester's handle will glow.

To test a cartridge fuse, simply touch the probe to one end and the clip to the other. If the fuse completes the circuit and lights the bulb, it's good.

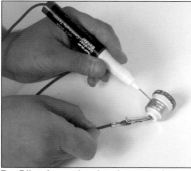

Test Edison fuse on threads and contact point

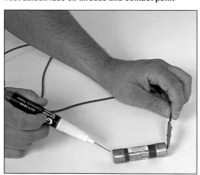

Test cartridge fuse at both ends

Testing lamp switches

To test a lamp switch, unplug the lamp and fasten the alligator clip to the brass-colored terminal screw and touch the probe to the contact tab inside the socket. When you turn the switch on, the light in the tester should glow. If it does not, replace the switch.

Testing three-way lamp switches

A three-way lamp switch has three opportunities to malfunction because it has three separate circuits inside the device. If you have a lamp with a three-way switch that is giving you trouble, unplug the cord and remove the switch. Then attach the alligator clip to the brass screw terminal. (The other terminal will be bright silver colored.)

Turn the switch to the first "on" position. When you touch the probe to the small vertical tab in the base, the tester light should come on. Then turn to the second on position. Touch the probe to the round center tab and the tester light should come on.

Finally, turn the lamp to the third on position. If the tester light comes on when you touch both tabs simultaneously, the switch is not defective. You will probably find the problem in the cord or the plug. (If you can't get the probe to touch both tabs at the same time, use the clip end of the tester to touch the tabs and use the probe end of the tester to touch the terminal screw.) If the tester fails to light in any one of the three on positions, replace the switch.

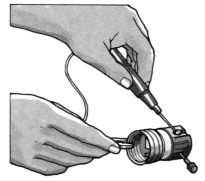

Testing a lamp switch
With the alligator clip clamped to the socket threads, touch the probe to the silver screw.

Testing a three-way lamp switch
Touch the probe to the vertical tab, the rounded tab, and finally, both tabs at once.

Testing toggle switches

When testing any switch with a continuity tester, shut off the power and remove the switch completely. To test a single-pole switch, place the alligator clip on one terminal and touch the probe to the other. When the switch is in the on position, the tester should light up.

To test three-way switches, determine which of the three terminal screws is the "common" terminal. The traveler screws will be brass in color and the common screw will be a darker color. Place the alligator clip on the common screw and touch the probe to one of the other terminals. Flip the switch one way and the tester light should go on. Then touch the probe to the other terminal; the tester light should go on this time when the switch is in the opposite position.

Testing a switch
In the case of this three-way switch, both toggle positions should be tested.

Voltage testers

A voltage tester is a simple, inexpensive device that tells you if there is electricity in a cable, outlet, or switch. The illuminated neon bulb signals the presence of voltage. Because a voltage tester can keep you from inadvertently touching a hot wire, you should buy one before you begin any wiring project. Voltage testers are also useful in testing your work for proper grounding and for determining which wire in a cable is hot. New "non-contact" voltage testers add another level of safety to avoid touching energized wires. Receptacle testers also check for voltage, GFCI functionality, reversed polarity and many other problems.

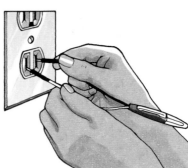

Testing receptacle
Slide one tester probe into each slot.

Testing a receptacle

To see if a receptacle is working, insert one wire of the tester into each plug slot. If the tester light comes on, the receptacle is energized. If not, the receptacle is defective or a fuse has blown. To determine if the problem is in one receptacle only, test the other receptacles on the circuit. If none works, the problem is in the circuit. If only one receptacle is defective, shut off the power to the entire circuit at the panel and test again to make sure the circuit is off, then replace the defective receptacle.

Locating the hot wire in a cable

When working in a switch, receptacle, or light fixture box that contains two or more black wires, you will need to determine which black wire is hot. It is always possible that someone before you wired the white wire hot instead of the black wire, which can be confusing.

To find which wire is hot, separate the wires at the box so that they cannot make contact with each other. Then touch one tester probe to the metal box and the other to each of the black wires. The one that lights the tester bulb is the incoming hot wire. For future reference, you may wish to mark that wire with a piece of tape. If you are working inside a plastic outlet box, you will not be able to test the ground against the box. Instead, touch one probe to the bare ground wire in the box and the other to one of the black wires.

Testing for hot wire
Place one probe on black wire, the other on metal box.

Non-contact voltage tester

Checking for proper grounding

Properly grounded receptacles are very important to the safety of your electrical system. Use your voltage tester to make sure every receptacle is grounded well. Insert one tester probe into the hot slot of the receptacle and touch that other probe to the coverplate screw. (The hot slot on newer receptacles is the smaller of the two. If the coverplate screw is painted, chip some paint from its head or turn the screw out far enough to reach the unpainted threads.) If the receptacle is a three-prong model, insert the ground probe into the U-shaped ground slot. The tester light should burn brightly. If the light seems weak, check for a poor ground wire connection.

Checking grounding
If the box or receptacle is grounded, the light will come on brightly. A dim light suggests a poor ground wire connection.

Voltage tester
This simple tool lights up when current flows through it.

Testing a switch

To determine whether a switch is hot, remove the coverplate and touch one probe of your tester to the metal box or bare wire ground. Then touch the other probe to each of the wired terminals. If the light burns from each of these terminals, the switch is hot. If the switch is hot, shut the power off in the panel before working on the switch or the circuit.

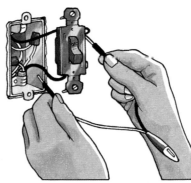

Testing switch
To check if switch is hot, place one probe on the metal box, the other on a screw terminal.

Dealing with electric shock

Severe electric shock can arrest the heart and interrupt the victim's breathing. Immediately call 911 or the local emergency number. Often, when someone is exposed to a source of electrical energy, they will not be able to let go. Don't put yourself at risk of an electrical shock by touching the victim. Try to turn off the source of electricity. If that is not possible, try to move the source of electricity away from the victim with a dry, non-conducting object made of wood, plastic or similar. The longer a person is in contact with the source of electricity, the more damage is done.

First-aid kit
Always have a well-stocked first-aid kit around the house to help with any injuries.

Isolate the victim from the electrical source

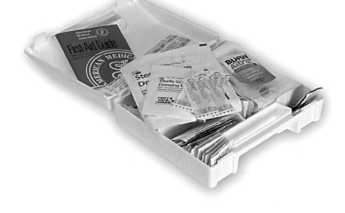

Clear away obstructions

Tilt head back to open airway

Check for breathing

Breathe into the victim's airway

Open the airway

Unless the victim's airway is opened, air cannot enter the lungs. If the victim is not breathing, the airway may be blocked. Clear the mouth of obstructions (food, gum, objects). Lay the victim on his or her back and tilt the head back by placing your hand on the forehead and lifting the chin up with your other hand. This keeps the tongue from blocking the airway.

Check for breathing

Once the airway is open, check for signs of breathing. Look to see if the victim's chest is rising and falling, listen for air being exhaled, and feel with your cheek and ear for air escaping through the victim's nose and mouth. If the victim is not breathing, you should begin rescue breathing.

Mouth-to-mouth

Keeping his head tilted back with one hand on the forehead, pinch the victim's nostrils shut with your thumb and forefinger. Take a deep breath and cover the victim's mouth with your own, making a seal. Blow deeply and slowly into the mouth, watching to see if the chest is rising and falling. Ventilate the victim's lungs two times with slow, full breaths. After the first two full breaths, continue giving one breath every five seconds for as long as you can. Check the victim often to see if breathing has begun.

Mouth-to-nose

If the victim's mouth is burned for any reason, you might breathe through the nose. Keeping the head tilted back, push the victim's mouth closed with your free hand. Place your mouth over the nose while sealing the mouth with your cheek. Proceed as you would for mouth-to-mouth.

Reviving a child

If the victim is a baby or small child, cover both the nose and the mouth with your mouth, then proceed as above, but use gentle puffs of air.

Recovery

Once the victim starts breathing, place him or her in a semi-prone position. Observe carefully to see if the breathing continues regularly. Keep the victim warm with blankets until medical help arrives.

Breathe into a child's mouth and nose

Repairing cords and plugs

A variety of cord types are used to supply lamps, power tools, portable heaters, and small appliances. These cords usually consist of No. 16 or No. 18 stranded wire covered with thermoplastic plastic. The wire strands and the minimal insulation allow cords to be flexible. But over time, the insulation breaks down and the protective covering wears thin. When bare wires are exposed, short circuits and ground faults can occur.

Years of use can threaten plugs as well. Plugs frequently tear loose, and rough handling can also break a plug's housing, which can cause a short circuit or ground fault to occur between the prongs.

Replacing plugs

To replace a defective plug, cut the cord several inches away from the plug. Then separate the two wires for about 3 inches and strip ⅜ inch of insulation from each wire. Disassemble the new attachment plug. Then feed the separated and stripped cord into the plug housing. Connect the white wire or identified cord wire to the silver screw and the black wire or unidentified cord wire to the brass screw. Then reassemble the plug.

Polarized plugs
Older two-prong non-polarized plugs should be replaced with polarized two-prong plugs that have one prong that is wider. The wider prong matches with the wider neutral slot on receptacle outlets. Proper polarization is required for safety and helps reduce the chance of an electrical shock.

Replacing cords

You can buy replacement cord by the foot or in precut lengths that have attachment plugs already on them.

Regardless of which cord you buy, the appliance end is a pretty simple hookup. In many cases, you will have to take the appliance apart, usually by loosening several screws in the housing. Some appliances have access panels that make connecting the cord easier. Many lamps have felt or cardboard base covers that can be pried loose. In any case, let the old cord be your guide to installing a new one. You can even tie the new cord to the old one and pull it through.

Once you've brought the cord into the lamp or appliance, you will find two or three wire terminals, or in some cases, color-coded factory leads. If you find terminals, strip approximately ⅜ inch of insulation from the end of the wires. Twist the stranded wire and bend it into a clockwise hook. Lay the hook under the terminals and tighten them down.

Caution: All jacketed cords contain wires that are color-coded white (neutral), black (hot), and green (grounding). The neutral wire in a non-jacketed two-wire cord will be identified with raised, ribbed lines that run the length of the wire. The other wire in the same two-wire cord will have a smooth surface. In cords that have transparent insulation the neutral wire will be silver colored and the hot wire will be copper colored. The black wire or unidentified (non ribbed) cord wire is always connected to the brass (hot) terminal, the white wire or the identified (ribbed) cord wire is always connected to the silver (neutral) terminal, and the green or bare grounding wire always connects to the green (grounding) terminal.

Replacing a lamp socket

Because lamp sockets get a lot of use, they wear out sooner than other components. Luckily, they are inexpensive and easy to replace. Start by unplugging the cord and removing the lamp shade and bulb. Then find the place on the socket marked "press." Press firmly against the socket and the components will separate. Once apart, remove all components and thread the new socket base onto the threaded nipple with the wires pulled through the new base. Then tie the two wires together and connect them to their respective terminals. Finally, replace the brass shell, bulb, and shade.

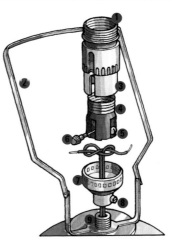

Lamp cord

Heater cord

Vacuum cleaner cord

Power cord

The components of a typical lamp
1 Socket shell
2 Harp
3 Insulating sleeve
4 Socket
5 Terminal screw
6 Switch
7 Socket cap
8 Set screw
9 Threaded nipple

Incandescent fixtures

Ceiling or wall-mounted light fixtures can be expected to last a long time. Even when they appear to be defective, often the problem can be traced to wall switches or the wiring between the switch and fixture. Light fixtures, therefore, are usually replaced for reasons of style or because they don't have the bulb capacity to provide adequate light. When shopping for a new fixture, make sure it can deliver the amount of light you need and try to find one that has a cover, or canopy, as large as the one on your existing fixture. A smaller canopy may require some touch-up painting or even some drywall or plaster repair.

Whatever the reason for replacing a light fixture, you'll be glad to know that the project is a simple one because all fixtures, regardless of outward appearance, have similar internal parts. And because the switch for the fixture is already in place, you don't have a lot of retrofit wiring to do. Also, nearly all fixtures (whether mounted on the wall or the ceiling) are fastened to ceiling outlet boxes, which makes the fixture-to-box connection nearly universal.

Removing a light fixture

To remove an old ceiling or wall fixture, start by shutting the power off at the panel. Then loosen the set screws or center nut that holds the glass diffuser to the fixture body. With the diffuser off, undo the center nut or canopy screws from the decorative cover or canopy. Pull the canopy down to expose the wires and the mounting strap. Then remove the strap from the box and pull the wires out. Separate the wire connections or remove the wire connectors and the fixture will come free.

Installing a new fixture

Caution: Before installing new fixtures, verify the temperature rating of your existing wiring. Newer light fixtures are often marked "MINIMUM 90 DEGREE CELSIUS SUPPLY WIRING" or similar. The thermoplastic insulation on house wiring installed before 1985 often does not meet this higher temperature rating. Consult with a licensed electrical contractor to replace the branch circuit supply wiring if necessary. Also be sure that the existing box is securely mounted to framing members and will support the new fixture.

To install a new fixture, start by fastening the strap to the box. If your fixture requires a threaded nipple, turn it into the strap. Then, hold the fixture up to the box so that the fixture wires can be attached to the wires in the box. Hold each color-matched set of wires together and secure the connections with twist-on wire connectors. Fasten the canopy either to the strap with the mounting screws or to the threaded nipple with a nut. Install the globe or diffuser onto the fixture.

Caution: Never install a bulb with a higher wattage rating than the fixture is designed to hold. Bulbs of higher wattage can overheat the fixture wiring and start a fire. Check the manufacturer's warning label on the fixture for the allowable types of bulbs.

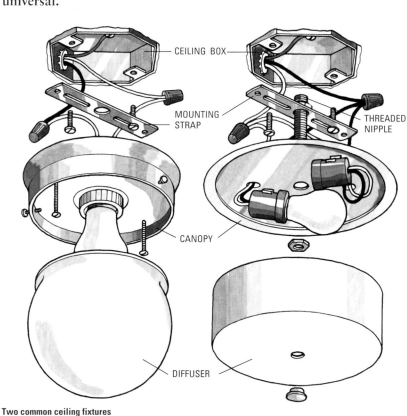

CEILING BOX

MOUNTING STRAP

THREADED NIPPLE

CANOPY

DIFFUSER

Two common ceiling fixtures

Chandelier-type fixture construction

SWITCH LOOP

Wall-mounted light with receptacle

CAUTION: TO REDUCE THE RISK OF FIRE, USE TYPE A 60-WATT LAMP MAX.

Bulb wattage rating printed on light fixture

REPLACING A BALLAST

Fluorescent lights offer the best energy buy around when it comes to lighting your home. You can receive five to six times as much light from a fluorescent bulb as from an incandescent bulb of the same wattage. Fluorescent fixtures operate under a completely different principle from incandescent fixtures. When electricity is routed to a fluorescent fixture, a booster station, called a ballast, sends a surge of electricity into the fluorescent tube. Older models also include a starter to help the ballast reach maximum power in less time. This increased surge of electricity then charges gases in the bulb which in turn create a faint light. The light is then picked up and intensified by a chemical coating on the inner wall of the bulb. This three-step activation explains the familiar hesitation found in older models when first turned on. Newer models come on much faster, some almost instantly.

Installing fluorescent fixtures

Installing fluorescent fixtures is no different than installing incandescent fixtures. In both cases, the body of the fixture is held to the ceiling by a threaded nipple or screws that go into a ceiling box. Both have lead wires that are joined inside the ceiling box with wire connectors. The rest is a matter of design variation.

When replacing an incandescent fixture, shut off the electricity, undo the center nut or screws that hold the canopy in place, and remove the wire connectors from the fixture leads. Then install the new threaded nipple (if required) and strap. Hold the lamp near the box and connect the fixture leads to the switch wires. With the wires connected, slide the fixture body, called the channel, over the threaded nipple or against the strap and tighten the center nut or strap screws. Larger channels may also need to be fastened to ceiling joists with wood screws for extra support. If you have trouble finding joists, use toggle bolts or another type of hollow-cavity fastener.

Diagnosing and repairing fluorescent fixtures

The most frequent problem you are likely to encounter with fluorescent lights is worn-out bulbs. Unlike incandescent bulbs, fluorescent tubes do not burn out abruptly. They flutter and flash on and off and act up in ways that lead homeowners to believe more serious problems exist. Don't assume the worst. Always start with the tube. If a tube will not come on at all, wiggle and twist it slightly in its sockets. Often the end pins are not seated properly.

To determine whether a troublesome tube needs to be replaced, look to the discoloration on each end. It is normal for a tube to show gray rings through the glass on each end, but when these rings turn black, the bulb needs to be replaced. Make sure that you replace it with a tube of the same wattage.

Defective starters

When older fluorescent fixtures flutter but do not come on, the problem is likely to be the starter. A starter is a small cylinder located under one of the tubes near a socket. Twist the tube out so that you can reach the starter. Then, check to see if the starter is seated properly. Push it in and try to turn it to the right. If it moves or turns to the right, replace the bulb to see if reseating the starter helped. If the light does not come on, you can assume a defective starter.

Remove the old starter by pushing in slightly and turning it a quarter-turn counterclockwise. Be sure to buy another starter with the same amp rating. Then push it into its socket and turn it to the right until it seats. Finally, replace the tube and turn the power back on. The new starter should eliminate the flickering problem immediately.

Nonstarter fixtures

Newer fluorescent fixtures come on instantly. Because of a few internal changes, starters are no longer needed. If you have trouble with one of these newer fixtures, first look to the tubes, then to the ballast, for the problem.

The ballast is the heart of a fluorescent fixture and is therefore the most costly component to replace. In fact, if you watch the specials, you can often buy a completely new fixture for the same price as a new ballast.

A faulty ballast is characterized by a continuous buzzing sound, often accompanied by a sharp odor. To replace a ballast, shut the electricity off at the panel and remove the tubes and channel lid. Inside, you will find the ballast screwed to the channel. Clip the wires near the ballast and loosen the retaining screws that hold the ballast in place inside the fixture.

Replacement ballasts come with lead wires. Simply fasten the new ballast to the channel and join the fixture wires to the ballast leads with wire connectors. Follow the manufacturer's wiring diagram carefully to avoid joining the wrong wires together.

Unscrew the old ballast and pull it down from the channel.

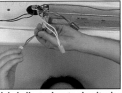

Push the new ballast into place and attach it with screws.

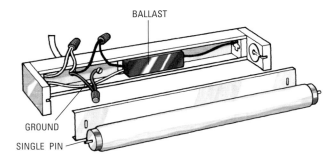

Join ballast wires to circuit wire with wire connectors.

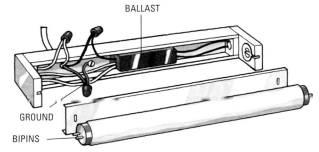

BALLAST
GROUND
SINGLE PIN

Instant-start fluorescent fixture

BALLAST
GROUND
BIPINS

Rapid-start fixture

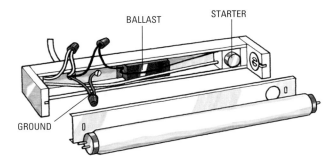

BALLAST   STARTER
GROUND

Starter-type fixture

Doorbells and thermostats

Repairing a broken doorbell may require a little detective work, but it's normally a simple task. Low-voltage doorbell and thermostat wiring is essentially free from fire or shock hazard. Just be sure to turn off the 120-volt power if you need to replace the transformer. Wireless chimes are great for updating or expanding old doorbell systems.

Testing the button

Start with the most likely culprit, the button. It gets the most use and abuse over the years. Undo the screws that hold the button to the house trim and locate the wires. Remove one of the two thin wires from its terminal and touch it to the other wire or terminal. If the bell rings, you probably need a new button. Simply attach the two existing wires to the terminals of the new button and fasten the new button to the door trim or house siding. Some buttons fasten directly, others have baseplates. Low voltage requires no ground wire.

Repairing broken wires

As you work your way through the system, carefully check for loose connections, broken wires, or frayed insulation. If you find broken wires, splice them with small wire connectors and tape. If you find frayed insulation, tape each wire individually near the problem area. And of course, restore any loose connections you find.

Cleaning clapper and bell

If, when someone rings your doorbell, you hear a muffled buzz instead of the bell, suspect a dirty or gummed up clapper contact. Remove the cover and clean the clapper contact thoroughly. If it does not respond at all to an electrical charge, you probably need a new one. First, remove the old cover, bell, and wall bracket. To keep the wires from falling into the wall space, pull them out as far as you can and guide them through the opening of a new wall bracket. Then screw the new bracket to the wall so that it is level. Connect the existing wires to the new terminals and snap the cover over the bell or chime mechanism.

Checking the transformer

If the bell does not ring when you test the button, look to the transformer. The transformer will be attached to the side of a 120-volt junction box, usually in the basement. Check for voltage at the transformer terminals with a low-voltage tester (see page 275) or a digital multimeter. It should match the low-voltage rating marked on the transformer.

If no voltage is indicated, assume a faulty transformer. Shut the power off that serves the transformer. Then remove the screws that hold the old transformer to the box. Attach the leads from the new transformer to the 120-volt conductors inside the box and mount the new transformer on the outlet cover. Install the outlet cover, attach the low-voltage wires to the transformer terminals, and restore power to the circuit.

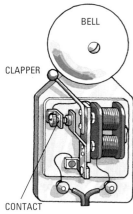

A typical clapper-type doorbell

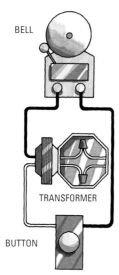

A typical doorbell loop

Replacing a thermostat is an easy job when you buy the right replacement. Before shopping for a new one, pry the cover off of your current thermostat and check to see how many wires come through the wall. Furnaces without air conditioning will require only two wires, while furnaces with air conditioning require four or more wires. Make sure that the thermostat you choose is compatible with your existing system. Look for a brand name and model number and try for an exact replacement, or consider upgrading to a digital programmable thermostat that can actually help reduce your heating and cooling costs. The energy savings can be substantial and new innovations including internet managed energy conservation add greater efficiency, access and flexibility to your thermostats.

Start by removing the cover from the old thermostat. Disconnect the color-coded wires, but make sure you note how they were hooked up. Then remove the screws holding the baseplate to the wall. Be careful not to let the wires fall behind the wall finish into the stud space.

Then slide the wires through the new baseplate and fasten it to the wall. Make sure that the baseplate is perfectly level. With the base installed, connect the wires to the terminal according to the manufacturer's instructions.

To replace an old thermostat, begin by removing the thermostat cover.

Digital multimeter

Unscrew the doorbell button from the side of the house.

Tape the wires to the house so they won't fall into the hole.

Connect wires to back of new button and screw to the house.

Find the screws that attach the thermostat to its baseplate and remove them.

Working with wire

Most electrical wiring today is made of copper. Copper is a good conductor and is flexible enough to handle the twists and turns of a typical installation without breaking. Because the wires of a circuit, generally called conductors, will create a fire hazard if they touch each other, they are covered with plastic insulation. The familiar Type NM (nonmetallic) cable found at your favorite home center is a factory assembly of two or more insulated conductors that are enclosed within an overall nonmetallic jacket or sheath. Individual conductors that travel from one location to another without being part of a cable must be installed in conduit.

Electrical wire is sized by the American Wire Gauge (AWG) number in sizes ranging from No. 18 to No. 3/0 or larger. Wire size is a critical factor in a home's wiring system. Just as a small pipe size can carry only so many gallons of water, small conductors can carry only so many amperes. When a wire is forced to carry more amperes than its size can handle, resistance increases and the wire heats up. As a wire heats up, the wire's insulation will

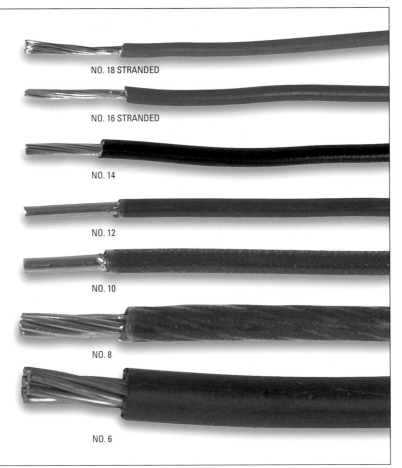

NO. 18 STRANDED

NO. 16 STRANDED

NO. 14

NO. 12

NO. 10

NO. 8

NO. 6

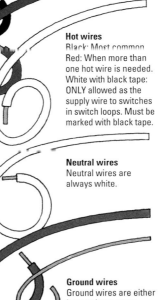

Wire types and uses
The wire sizes used in a typical home range from No. 18 wire for doorbells to No. 3/0 wire for service conductors.

fail, which results in a fire hazard. When you do any wiring project, make sure to follow the NEC specifications.

The following general sizing guide will help you choose the right wire size for each project.

RESIDENTIAL WIRE SIZING GUIDE

Wire size	Common use	Amps
No. 18	Low voltage doorbells, thermostats, garage door openers	6
No. 16	Low voltage doorbells, thermostats, garage door openers	8
No. 14	General lighting and receptacle circuits	15
No. 12	Appliance, bathroom, laundry, equipment circuits	20
No. 10	Dryers, A/C, wall-type and countertop-type cooking units	30
No. 8	Feeders and large appliances, etc.	40
No. 6	Feeders and large appliances, etc.	55
No. 3	Service conductors and feeders	100
No. 1/0	Service conductors and feeders	150
No. 3/0	Service conductors and feeders	200

Identify wires by color

To give electrical wiring an instantly recognizable standard in the field, the NEC has designated an insulation color for each conductor function. A black wire, for example, is always the "hot" side of a circuit. Red wires are also "hot" wires. If you see a black wire and a red wire in the same cable, you know the circuit has two hot wires and therefore usually means a 240-volt circuit. A white wire is always neutral, unless used the supply wire for single-pole, three-way, and four-way switch loops. In that case, the white insulation is required to be marked with black paint or black tape to distinguish it from the white neutral in the same box. Blue wires can also be hot when substituted for black in conduit. Grounding wires are either green or bare.

While these designators are excellent indicators, don't trust your life to them. The homeowner before you may have invented his own coding system. Protect yourself from nonconformists by testing each circuit you work on with a voltage tester before starting the job.

Hot wires
Black: Most common
Red: When more than one hot wire is needed.
White with black tape: ONLY allowed as the supply wire to switches in switch loops. Must be marked with black tape.

Neutral wires
Neutral wires are always white.

Ground wires
Ground wires are either bare or have green insulation.

Cable types and uses

In the field, the terms wire and cable are often used interchangeably. To be exact, however, the term "wire" refers to an individual conductor, insulated or uninsulated. The term "cable" is used to describe two or more wires encased in a single jacket or sheath. Type NM 12/2 cable with ground, for example, contains two insulated No. 12 wires and one No. 12 paper-wrapped ground wire. This same arrangement of wires might also be run as individual wires inside of conduit, but in this case would not be called cable. Although ground wires are generally permitted to be bare, it's more practical to use green insulated wire for conduit installations.

Types of wire

Type THHN wire is most commonly used in residential installations where conduit is used. It has a tough insulation, called thermoplastic, that will accommodate both hot and cold weather extremes. Type THWN is a designation for all-weather installations and can be used in aboveground outdoor installations. It has a slightly heavier plastic coating that provides more protection from temperature extremes and moisture.

Types of cable

Because residential wiring is simpler than commercial wiring and requires fewer provisions for change, cable is used instead of conduit and wire. A variety of cable types have been developed to meet a variety of special needs. In most cases, the job will dictate the cable type you use.

Type NM cable is the most commonly used in residential systems. It is made of two or more Type THHN wires and a bare ground wire, all enclosed in a nonmetallic jacket. The ground wire is wrapped in paper and is positioned between the two insulated wires. The paper wrap restricts this cable to normally dry locations only.

Type NMC is no longer manufactured because Type UF has the same corrosive-resistant properties and can be used in its place.

Type UF cable is designed to be used in underground installations of outdoor lighting and as a lateral cable to outbuildings. Type UF cable is permitted to be used in wet, dry, or corrosive locations.

Type AC armored cable and Type MC metal-clad cable are found in both old and new installations. Type AC cable has been around since the early 1900s and is often called by its early trade name BX. It was designed to be used where ordinary cable might be punctured by nails. The flexible metallic enclosure of Type AC cable is approved for grounding, whereas Type MC cable is not but it includes a green insulated wire. Armored cable is harder to work with than Type NM or Type UF.

In the early fifties, manufacturers looking for a less expensive conductor introduced aluminum wire to the market. The industry soon learned, however, that aluminum wire came with some very serious problems.

It is not as efficient a conductor as copper and therefore offers more resistance to current. Terminations are the main problem. As the aluminum wire heats up, it expands, and repeated expansion and contraction eventually cause the wires to loosen under terminal screws. Loose connections create heat, melt wire insulation, and start fires.

Replacement switches and receptacles rated 15- or 20-amps must be marked CO/ALR, which indicate their terminals are approved for aluminum, copper-clad aluminum, and copper wire. Special twist-on connectors are now available for adding new copper "pigtails" to existing aluminum wiring, which allows for copper connections to regular switches and receptacles.

It's best to hire an electrical contractor who has experience with aluminum wire. The U.S. Consumer Product Safety Commission has more information at www.cpsc.gov.

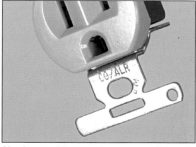

Aluminum wiring requires receptacles and switches designated CO/ALR.

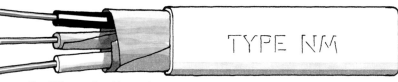

Type NM, two-wire with ground

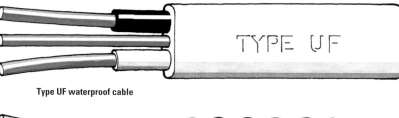

Type UF waterproof cable

Armored cable

Cutting, stripping, and splicing wire

Working with wire does not require a large investment in tools. In fact, you can do a lot with needle-nose pliers and a sharp pocket knife. If you do more than replace an occasional receptacle, however, you should consider investing in a few wireworking tools. Your first purchase should be a multipurpose tool, pliers that cut and strip many different sizes of wire. A sharp utility knife is also a big help. Needle-nose pliers are a must, as are sturdy side cutter pliers. Add a Phillips and flat-blade screwdriver and you should have all you need for just about every job.

Stripping wire

You can buy a sheathing stripper, but a sharp knife works just as well if you are careful **(1)**. Because the uninsulated ground wire runs through the center of the sheathing, make your cut in the middle of one side. Make the cut shallow to avoid nicking the insulated wires. Then pull the split sheathing back from the wires and cut it off **(2)**.

With the sheathing gone, strip approximately ½ inch of insulation from each insulated wire **(4)**. You can use a knife, but a multipurpose tool works better. In any case, avoid cutting into the copper. Slide the end of the wire into the correct numbered slot in the handle of the tool **(3)**, then squeeze, twist, and pull. If you have the wire in the right hole, the insulation will strip right off the wire and won't nick the copper in the process.

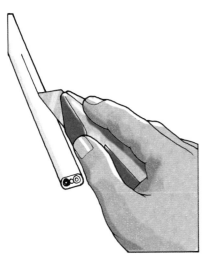

1 When cutting sheathing, cut in center only

2 Cut the excess sheathing from the cable

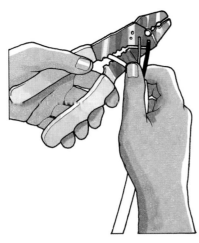

3 Select the correct wire-size opening

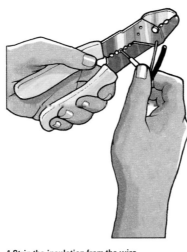

4 Strip the insulation from the wire

Making connections

Wire connections, no matter where they are made, must be very tight. Loose connections will only get looser over time and in the process will create resistance, which in turn creates heat. Hot connections cause wire insulation to breakdown, and if they are allowed to spark, can cause fires.

To join two solid wires, strip ½ inch of insulation from each wire and twist the stripped wires together with pliers in a clockwise direction. Then select a wire connector large enough to slide over the twisted wires about half way. Insert the wires into the connector and turn it until the wire is drawn in and the connector no longer turns. The more wires you join, the larger the connector you will need. Make sure that no copper shows outside the connector. If it does, take off the connector, trim the wires to length with side cutter pliers, and reinstall the connector.

Stranded wire connections

When connecting stranded wire, strip about ½ inch of insulation from each wire and twist the strands together in a clockwise direction until no loose ends can be seen. Then turn the connector on until it is tight.

When connecting stranded wire to solid wire, strip ½ inch of insulation from the solid wire and about ¼ inch from the stranded wire. Wrap the stranded wire tightly around the solid wire in a clockwise direction and leave about ⅛ inch of stranded wire extended past the solid wire. Then tighten a connector over them.

When connecting wires to switch or receptacle terminals, strip about ⅝ inch of insulation from each wire, then use needle-nose pliers to form a small loop or hook. Hook the wire clockwise under the terminal screw and tighten. Screw terminals are not approved for multiple wires so it's best to use pigtails to connect the circuit wires to the receptacle or switch.

When connecting to a switch or receptacle that has push-in terminals with self-locking slots, strip only ½ inch of insulation from the wires and push each wire into the back of the device until no copper can be seen. Push-in terminals are restricted to No. 14 solid copper wire only and they are not approved for stranded wire.

Join solid wires with wire connector.

Wrap stranded wire around solid wire.

Install pigtails on receptacle terminals.

Strip wire and slide into push-in terminals.

Grounding the system

You can always expect electricity to find the path of least resistance back to the utility transformer. Proper grounding of electrical systems and equipment helps to ensure that people do not become a path for electricity.

The electrical current in your home's system starts its circular flow at the electric utility transformer, through the service panel and the main breaker, and then through the hot wire. After it passes through a light fixture, it travels back to the service panel and the utility transformer through the neutral wire. Downstream from the service, the hot and neutral circuit wires are accompanied by an equipment grounding wire. Equipment is grounded to limit the voltage to ground on conductive surfaces and to facilitate the operation of circuit breakers under ground-fault conditions. From the service panel, a grounding electrode conductor runs outside and is attached to a copper rod driven into the ground. This connection to earth helps stabilize the voltage to ground on the household wiring system during normal operation, and it helps to prevent excessively high voltages caused by lightning or accidental contact with high voltage power lines.

Short circuits

Sometimes when lamp cords wear thin, a hot wire may come into contact with a neutral wire. When this happens, the current takes a shortcut. The term short circuit is often used incorrectly to describe any kind of electrical fault. A "short circuit" and a "ground fault" are actually different. A short circuit occurs when a hot wire touches the neutral wire or another hot wire. Good short circuits cause the breaker to trip immediately because the wires are in direct contact with each other and lots of current is flowing. Bad short circuits may create an arcing condition through an air gap. This type of short circuit may not trip the breaker and can often lead to an electrical fire.

Grounding a system

How your electrical system is grounded will depend upon the age of your home. Many homes are grounded through their water pipes to the city water main. In this case, the grounding electrode conductor travels from the service panel to the house side of the water meter. It is then clamped to both sides of the water meter.

Other homes may be grounded directly through copper ground rods. In this case, the ground rod is driven into the earth at least 8 feet deep, usually near an outside basement wall. An approved ground rod clamp connects the grounding electrode conductor to the ground rod.

If present at the house, the NEC now requires that an underground metal water pipe and the steel reinforcing bars in the concrete footing shall both serve as the grounding electrodes. If the only electrode present is an underground metal water pipe, it must be supplemented with a ground rod in case the metal pipe is replaced in the future with plastic pipe. All interior metal water piping systems are also required to be bonded to the electrical system.

A ground fault often happens when a hot wire comes loose and touches a metal outlet box or the metal housing of an electrical tool or appliance. Because an equipment grounding conductor is attached to the metal surface, the ground fault current abandons the neutral wire and travels back to the panel through the equipment grounding conductor. The equipment grounding conductor provides an effective low-resistance path back to the panel for fault current. This intentional path allows for the maximum amount of fault current to flow. Lots of fault current will trip the circuit breaker as quickly as possible. The equipment grounding conductors also help to keep all of the metal surfaces as near as possible to zero-volts-to-ground, thereby minimizing any shock hazard for persons.

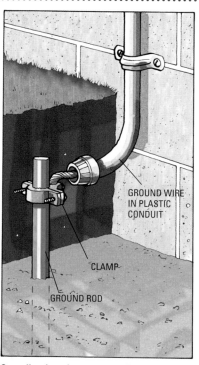

Grounding through copper grounding rods
When possible, the connection should be made below grade.

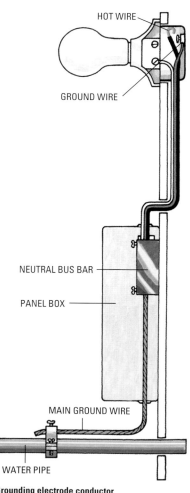

Grounding electrode conductor
Underground metal water pipes are used as grounding electrodes for grounding the electrical system.

Grounding individual circuits

In addition to grounding the electrical "system," electrical "equipment," receptacles, and light fixtures must be grounded. Many older homes only have two-wire circuits and two-slot outlets, with no grounding wire. If your home has three-wire circuits or metallic cables or conduits, you may be able to upgrade to three-slot receptacles.

Equipment grounding

Turn off the power and pull the receptacle out of the box. If you see a bare or green wire fastened to the metal box, or you have determined the box grounded with a voltage tester, feel free to install three-slot receptacles. Another option is to replace old two-slot receptacles with GFCI receptacles. They work even when not grounded. Be sure to install the "No Equipment Ground" labels that come with GFCI receptacle. Note—You may need to install a new box to accommodate the larger GFCI receptacle.

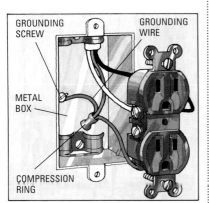

Copper compression ring
All ground wires can be crimped together.

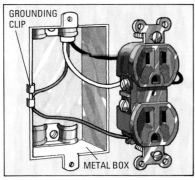

Gounding clip
If no grounding screw is present, use a grounding clip.

Ground fault circuit interrupters

As already mentioned, a ground fault can be dangerous. If you touch an appliance or tool that has a loose hot wire and the metallic surfaces become energized, you may become the path of least resistance for electrical current back to the source. When you are on wet ground or in a damp location, your body improves as a conductor. Ground faults can be fatal.

To protect yourself from a deadly ground fault shock, all receptacles in your bathrooms, kitchen countertop areas, garages, outdoor locations, basements or crawl spaces, and laundry, utility, or wet bar sink areas should be equipped with ground fault circuit interrupters, called GFCIs. They are required by the NEC for all new installations.

GFCIs work by monitoring the current in the hot and neutral wires. As long as current is equal in both wires, the circuit remains energized. As soon as a GFCI senses an imbalance in current, as typifies leakage current in a ground fault, it shuts off the power to that circuit or receptacle within a fraction of a second.

You can acquire GFCI protection with one of three devices. The most expensive and most versatile GFCI is contained in a breaker **(1)**. When you install a GFCI breaker, everything on that circuit is protected. The second device is a GFCI receptacle that is quite easy to install **(2)**. When you install this receptacle, all receptacles on the circuit after the GFCI are also protected. The last alternative is the simplest. It is a GFCI receptacle adapter **(3)**. You simply plug this adapter into a standard receptacle and then plug your appliances into the adapter. An adapter works well but protects only the receptacle it is plugged into. Adapters are a good choice in older bathrooms. GFCIs have saved countless lives.

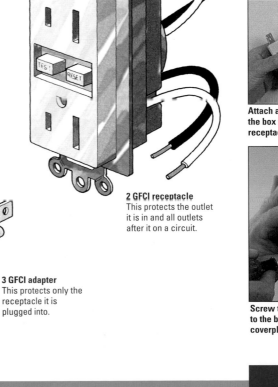

1 GFCI breaker
This protects an entire circuit from inside the panel.

3 GFCI adapter
This protects only the receptacle it is plugged into.

2 GFCI receptacle
This protects the outlet it is in and all outlets after it on a circuit.

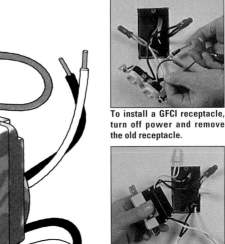

To install a GFCI receptacle, turn off power and remove the old receptacle.

Attach all the wires in the box to the new GFCI receptacle.

Screw the new receptacle to the box and add the coverplate.

Electrical circuits

As mentioned earlier, a circuit is a flow of electricity that starts at the utility power source, through the service panel, continues through the fixtures, and comes back to the source in a continuous pattern. On a practical level, it helps to think of a circuit not as some kind of mysterious flow of electrons but rather as simply a system of wires that carry that flow. It's just easier to visualize wires threaded through our homes, like plumbing pipes carrying water, bringing electricity to our lights and appliances.

Branch circuits

The circuits that serve the rooms of your home are called branch circuits. Indeed, if you could see through your home, these wires would look like tree branches, all reaching out from your service panel. There are three basic kinds of circuits: general lighting circuits, small-appliance circuits, and individual circuits.

General lighting circuits serve the general purpose lights and receptacle outlets found in living rooms, bedrooms, and bathrooms. General purpose lighting circuits are rated 120-volts at 15-amps, although bathroom and laundry circuits are required to be rated at 20-amps.

Small-appliance circuits are rated 120-volts at 20-amps and are required in kitchens and dining areas. They run the usual gamut of small kitchen appliances, such as toasters, food processors, and even refrigerators. The NEC now requires at least two

small appliance circuits for kitchens, though many older homes get by with only one.

Individual circuits are rated either 120- or 240-volt and are dedicated to only one utilization equipment. These circuits serve clothes dryers and water heaters but can include refrigerators, air conditioners, microwave ovens, furnaces, and dishwashers. Cord-and-plug connected utilization equipment rated at more than 80% of the circuit rating should have its own circuit and breaker, likewise any fastened-in-place equipment rated more than 50% of the circuit rating. Many individual circuits carry 30-, 40-, or 50-amps at 240 volts to meet the greater demands of the appliances involved. Others, like computer circuits, might be dedicated for other reasons. Computers are very sensitive to voltage dips and spikes and so are sometimes given a circuit of their own.

As previously mentioned, the NEC is not intended to be an instruction manual for untrained persons; calculations can get very complicated. Let's keep it simple and conservative. As you already know, conductors are rated by their ampacity. The ampacity of a conductor is the current that a conductor can carry continuously, within its limitations, without exceeding its temperature rating and degrading the thermoplastic insulation. In theory, a No. 12 wire can carry 20 amperes on a continuous basis without failing. However, it's best to adopt a conservative rule for conductors and circuit breakers. Unless marked otherwise, circuit breakers should not be loaded to more than 80 percent of their current rating where the load will be operated continuously for three or more hours. You might think a 20-amp breaker can handle 2400 watts (120-volts x 20-amps), but it's best to keep the load at 80 percent, or 1920 watts. A 15-amp circuit should be loaded to no more 1440 watts (120-volts x 15-amps = 1800 watts x .8 = 1440 watts). Another example is a continuous electric heat load of 1500 watts x 1.25 = 1875 watts; no problem for a 20-amp circuit that has a safe capacity of 1920 watts.

Arc fault circuit interrupters

Arcing faults are a leading cause of fires and deaths. They are caused by damaged or deteriorated wiring and cords, faulty connections at devices, and many other electrical hazards. Arcs, sparks, and the resulting heating effect can cause wood, carpet, paper, and other combustible materials to catch on fire.

Arc fault circuit interrupter (AFCI) protection is now required by the NEC. The 2002 NEC required all circuits supplying lighting and receptacle outlets in dwelling unit bedrooms to be protected by AFCIs. For the 2008 NEC, the requirement for AFCI protection was expanded to circuits supplying lighting and receptacle outlets in all areas of the home, other than outlets in kitchens, bathrooms, garages, unfinished basements and outdoors (these outlets already are provided with GFCI protection). Like GFCI protection that has gradually expanded over time, look for AFCI protection to also be expanded in the future.

While standard circuit breakers trip due to short circuits, overloads, and ground-faults at relatively high current flow, and GFCIs protect people from fatal electrical shock and trip in the milliamp range, AFCIs are intended to detect unwanted arcing characteristics and de-energize the entire circuit before a fire can occur.

The modern kitchen
A modern kitchen has at least two small-appliance circuits in addition to individual circuits for major appliances. Overhead lights can be part of a general lighting circuit.
1 120-volt, 20-amp circuit for refrigerator/small appliance
2 120-volt, 20-amp circuit for dishwasher
3 120/240-volt circuit to range
4 120-volt, 20-amp circuit for small appliances
5 Dishwasher
6 Range
7 Light switch
8 Overhead lights

The number of circuits your home should have depends mostly on its size and also on your own special needs. The NEC essentially requires one general lighting and receptacle circuit for every 600 square feet of floor space, but many electricians prefer a 1/500 ratio to cover future needs. In the final analysis, your lifestyle, personal needs, and your plans for the future have the most to do with how many circuits you install. For example, if you are converting a den into an entertainment center, your electrical needs in that room will be greater than before.

Adding outlets to a circuit

If you don't need a new circuit but would appreciate a few more outlets, you may be able to add outlets to existing circuits. If you determine that a 15-amp circuit has less than 10 outlets or a 20-amp circuit has less than 13, you can cut new boxes where you need them and run wire from one of the existing boxes to the first new box. From there on, you simply run wire from one box to another in sequence and install new receptacles.

Making room in a full panel

In many cases, expansion will seem impossible because no fuse or breaker slots are left in the panel. Expansion may still be possible by adding a new subpanel, by combining circuits in the existing service panel, or by installing "tandem" breakers.

The first step is to determine which two circuits serve so few outlets that together they could be combined and protected by a single fuse or breaker. For example, each outlet is given a rating of 1.5 amps, so a 15-amp breaker can protect 10 outlets. If you find one circuit that serves four outlets and another circuit that serves six, those two circuits can be combined. Kitchen circuits and multi-wire circuits that share a common neutral cannot be combined.

To combine circuits, remove each terminal from its breaker slot or fuse terminal and tie both wires and a short pigtail (a 4- to 6-inch piece of wire) together with a wire connector. Then tie the pigtail wire to the fuse terminal or breaker. This will leave one circuit vacant for expansion.

Previously, when 60-amp service panels were filled to capacity with fuses and wires, you could tie onto the tap screws between the four fuses and create a new subpanel. Taps such as this do not have overcurrent protection where they receive their supply. They are required to terminate in a breaker that provides only "overload" protection for the conductors. The larger fuses or breakers upstream only provide catastrophic short circuit protection. Taps are not recommended and must comply with special rules in the NEC. Un-fused taps should be left up to a licensed electrical contractor.

If you do have room in the panel, a subpanel is still a good way to supply several circuits from a remote location. If you need more circuits in a workshop or an outbuilding, you can run a 60- or 100-amp feeder circuit to a subpanel and then let the subpanel serve several additional circuits.

Start by running the feeder cable between panel locations. Make the connections at the subpanel first, and then the service panel. The NEC now requires that all feeders to subpanels include an equipment grounding conductor, whether the subpanel is in your workshop in your home or an outbuilding. In other words, the feeder circuit will include two hot wires, a neutral wire, and an equipment grounding wire. Subpanels must have separate neutral bars and equipment grounding bars. At a remote outbuilding, a grounding electrode conductor will need to be installed from the subpanel's equipment grounding bar to a ground rod.

To combine circuits, remove black wire from one breaker.

Remove black wire from breaker for second circuit.

Join black wires to pigtail wire with wire connector.

Attach pigtail to one breaker and circuits are combined.

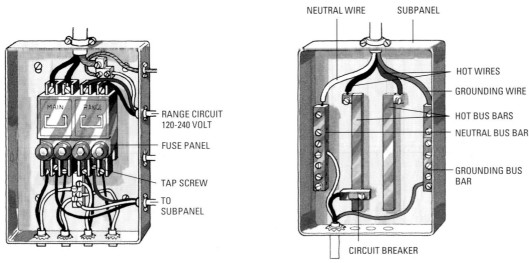

RANGE CIRCUIT
120-240 VOLT

FUSE PANEL

TAP SCREW

TO
SUBPANEL

This method is no longer allowed

NEUTRAL WIRE   SUBPANEL

HOT WIRES

GROUNDING WIRE

HOT BUS BARS

NEUTRAL BUS BAR

GROUNDING BUS BAR

CIRCUIT BREAKER

Subpanel with neutral and ground buses

Extending circuits

Drilling
When drilling holes through studs and joists, drill only within the middle third of the board. Never, under any circumstances, notch the bottom of a joist. A notch on the bottom side of a joist seriously threatens its load-carrying capacity. And when you drill near the edge of a stud, you are running the cable within reach of drywall fasteners. If you must drill near the edge of a stud or joist (less than 1¼ inches) cover that section of the framing member with a ⅟₁₆-inch-thick protection plate.

There are several possible methods for extending circuits. The approach that will be best for you depends on available space in the service panel and your existing wiring. Several options are discussed below.

Extending a knob-and-tube circuit

If you own one of the many thousands of homes with old knob-and-tube wiring, expansion is difficult but not impossible. Knob-and-tube is a two-wire system with each individual wire encased in treated fabric. The wires run side by side through ceramic insulators, called knobs, that are nailed to joists or rafters, and through ceramic tubes that are inserted in holes drilled in studs.

Knob-and-tube wiring is no longer installed, but existing installations can be extended, providing you follow a fairly strict procedure. Start by shutting the power off to the circuit to be extended. Then install a square junction box (preferably plastic) between or near the two knob-and-tube wires.

Next, run Type NM 14/2 with ground cable from the new outlets to this junction box and clamp the cable in the box. Strip the sheathing from the cable so that you have three 6-inch leads (one black, one white, one ground) in the box. Then strip about 2 inches of insulation from both knob-and-tube wires near the junction box. Cut one black and one white THHN wire long enough to reach the knob-and-tube wires. Slide these wires into a sheath made for this type of work called a loom. Then clamp the loom-covered THHN wires to the box with

approved clamps.

To tie the THHN wires to the knob-and-tube wires, first wrap each THHN wire tightly around its knob-and-tube wire so that the wrap is at least ¾ inch long within the stripped area of the old wire. Then solder the connections with rosin-core solder. Hold a soldering iron to the wires until the solder melts and adheres to the wires. When the solder has cooled, wrap the exposed portions of the wire with electrical tape. For added protection, continue the tape at least 2 inches past the joint on each side.

With the soldered connections made, move back down to the junction box and join the cable leads to the THHN wires with wire connectors. To ground the extension circuit, first mount a grounding pigtail to the back of the box. Then run a separate ground wire to the service panel. Screw this wire to the equipment grounding bar in the panel Then return to the box and join the cable ground wire, the separate ground wire and the pigtail with a wire connector. Note—The NEC no longer allows the equipment grounding conductor in this type of circuit extension to be connected to the nearest cold water pipe. This fact alone makes these circuit extensions very impractical.

A typical knob-and-tube extension
1 New circuit
2 Existing knob-and-tube wiring
3 Cable clamp
4 Grounding wire to neutral bus or to cold-water pipe
5 Soldered splice
6 Loom clamp
7 Junction box
8 Tube
9 Knob

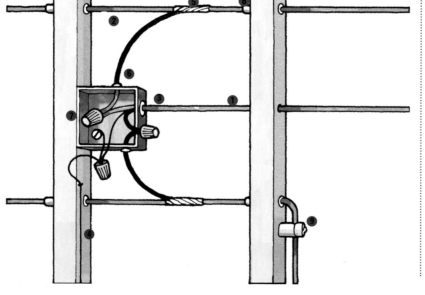

Using tandem breakers

If your service panel contains circuit breakers, but all the breaker slots are filled, you may be able to get one more circuit by substituting a standard-sized single-pole breaker with a tandem breaker; be sure to check the label inside your panel. Tandem breakers contain two single-pole breakers and can supply two separate circuits. A tandem breaker is inserted in the space formerly occupied by the standard-size breaker. A tandem breaker is not the same as a two-pole breakers.

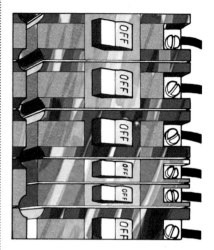

Common circuit routes

How you get from here to there with a circuit is largely a matter of choice. However, it can be greatly influenced by the layout of the house and by whether you are wiring a new house or expanding the wiring in an older one. Circuits in new homes generally take a direct route, while new circuits in existing homes find the path of least resistance, both physically and financially.

As you plan your circuits, think first about how you will get from the service panel to the outlet area. Plan for the most economical use of cable. The cost of cable or conduit and wires makes long circuits more costly, of course, and long circuits also offer more resistance to the flow of current and, therefore, greater chance for overheating.

When possible, run several cables through the same holes until each must branch off to its own service area. This will result in fewer holes in load-bearing joists and less time spent drilling them. Usually you'll have a lot of holes to drill so it makes sense to reduce that number when you can.

Outlet and fixture boxes

Boxes are made of metal or nonmetallic material (fiberglass or plastic). Nonmetallic boxes cost substantially less than metal boxes and often work just as well. All equipment grounding wires get spliced together in every box. In addition, when wiring into metal boxes, you must attach one equipment grounding pigtail to the box so the box is grounded, and a separate pigtail to the receptacle. In nonmetallic boxes you only need a ground wire pigtail to the receptacle. Cable is always clamped to metal boxes, whereas in nonmetallic boxes, cable is held in place by internal clamps or with self-gripping tabs. For single-gang nonmetallic boxes that do not have clamps, cables can be secured within 8 inches of the box by staples driven into framing members.

How to calculate minimum box sizes

Every electrical box is required to have sufficient volume for the number of wires, switches, receptacles and cable clamps contained within the box to avoid overcrowding and damage to wires.

Nonmetallic boxes are marked with their volume in cubic inches inside the box. The official volume for metal boxes is only found in the NEC (if you measure the inside of a metal box to calculate the approximate volume it should be acceptable to most inspectors).

The "Volume Allowance" (for brevity let's just call it "unit") required for each conductor, device, and clamp, to ensure enough free space within the box, is as follows:
- No. 14 wire (2 cu. in.)
- No. 12 wire (2.25 cu. in.)
- No. 10 wire (2.5 cu. in.)

Following are the simplified rules:
- Each insulated hot and neutral wire will count as one unit each.
- All ground wires combined count as one unit.
- All cable clamps combined count as one unit.
- All devices that mount in the box count as two units each.

Multiply the number of "units" by the volume allowance required for the largest conductor in the box. Sound confusing? The following typical example (at right, "How to calculate minimum box sizes") will help to make it perfectly clear.

MAXIMUM NUMBER OF WIRES PER METAL BOX

Size of box	No. 14	No. 12	No. 10
Round or octagonal			
4 X 1½"	7	6	6
4 X 2⅛"	10	9	8
Square			
4 X 1½"	10	9	8
4 X 2⅛"	15	13	12
Switch Boxes			
3 X 2 X 2¼"	5	4	4
3 X 2 X 2½"	6	5	5
3 X 2 X 2¾"	7	6	5
3 X 2 X 3½"	9	8	7
Junction Boxes			
4 X 2⅛ X 1⅞"	6	5	5
4 X 2⅛ X 2⅛"	7	6	5
All ground wires in a box can be counted as one wire.			

How to calculate minimum box sizes

The "Volume Allowance" required per conductor for free space within each box is as follows: No. 14 wire (2 cu. in.); No. 12 wire (2.25 cu. in.); No. 10 wire (2.5 cu. in.).

Example: How do you calculate the proper size box that will contain one duplex receptacle outlet, one light switch and 4 Type NM 14-2 with ground cables:

Volume Allowances (Units)	Cubic Inches
8 insulated wires @ 2 cu. in.	16 cubic inches
All ground wires combined @ 2 cu. in.	2 cubic inches
One switch @ 4 cu. in.	4 cubic inches
One receptacle @ 4 cu. in.	4 cubic inches
All cable clamps combined @ 2 cu. in.	2 cubic inches
Total	*28 cubic inches*

Metal box cover
If you have a lot of different boxes to install, one way to simplify the job is to install the same metal double box for each location. Then just add a metal cover designed for the specific box use: double or single switch or receptacle or ceiling fixture.

Which box should you use?
The shape of a box is your best clue to its intended use. Round boxes are most frequently used with ceiling fixtures, while square or rectangular boxes most often contain switches or receptacles mounted in the walls. While wall fixtures and special adapter plates allow some crossover, shape is still a good indicator.

New-work boxes are designed to be attached directly to studs or rafters. A variety of fastening devices, including screws, nails, brackets, and bars hold these boxes in place. Cut-in (sometimes called old-work) boxes, on the other hand, attach directly to the surface materials between studs or joists. Take the time to familiarize yourself with the many kinds of boxes and their varied applications. When the time comes to start a project, you will know just which boxes to buy.

Wall and ceiling boxes

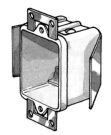  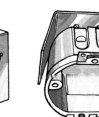  

Plastic cut-in wall box   **Nonmetallic wall box**    **Metal wall box**   **Plastic cut-in ceiling box**   **Metal ceiling box**

Methods of mounting

GAUGING NOTCH

CONNECTOR
CONDUIT

JOIST

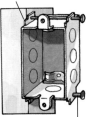 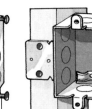   

DRIVE NAILS

SCREW BOX TO WALL
WITH ANCHORS

JOISTS

Nail-in box   **L-bracket wall box**    **Utility (handy) box** 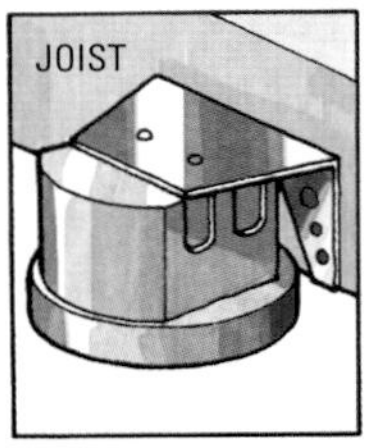   **Hanger bracket box**    **Bar hanger box**   **L-bracket ceiling box**

Switches

Switches are used to open and close circuits. When in the closed position, the circuit is completed and current flows according to demand. When in the open position, the circuit is interrupted and current cannot complete the circuit.

Basic switches

There are four basic types of switches. The one most frequently used is the single-pole switch. Single-pole switches are used to open or close simple lighting circuits. The next most frequently used is a three-way switch. Three-way switches are most often used to provide two switching locations for light fixtures. The third most common is the four-way switch, which when used in conjunction with at least two three-way switches allows you to control light fixtures from three or more locations. The fourth type is the double-pole switch. This device can handle two hot wires and is commonly used to switch 240-volt outlets and appliances.

Toggle switches

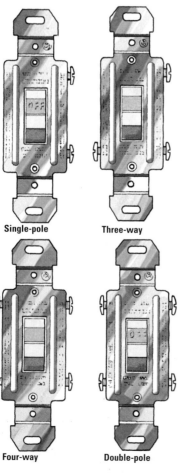

Single-pole   Three-way

Four-way   Double-pole

In addition to the four basic types, switches are also made for special needs and with special features. Some of these switches are just slightly more convenient than the basic models. But others offer real advantages, like dimmer switches, locking switches, lighted toggle switches, and others shown below. Consider installing one of these special switches to make a part of your life a little easier. Almost all are simple to install; it's usually just a matter of pulling out your current switch and replacing it with the new one, using the same box and wire.

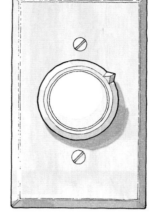

Dimmer switches
Dimmer switches, or rheostats, are popular because they allow you to adjust standard lighting fixtures to create different lighting effects. Low light makes a room seem warmer and more inviting, while brighter light offers a better work environment.

Dimmer switches give you both options and everything in between. If used properly, dimmer switches can also save energy by using less wattage.

Locking switches
Locking switches do not have "on/off" toggles, but require a key to operate. These switches are ideal for protecting electrical tools, computers, or stereo equipment from children. Simply switch an entire tool circuit off with a locking switch.

Lighted toggle switches
These switches are ideal for basement or garage use. The toggle lever contains a tiny light that remains on when the light is shut off. The light uses very little energy and will save you from having to feel your way to the switch in the dark.

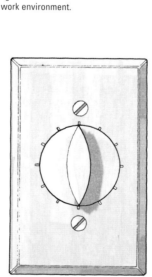
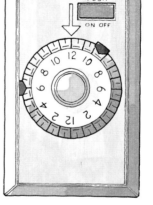

Time-delay switches
Time-delay switches are perfect for those situations where you need to get from here to there before the light goes out. The most frequent use of a time-delay switch is on a flood light between a garage and house. You

can turn the time-delay switch off in the garage and still have time to unlock the back door before the light goes out.

Time-clock switches
Time-clock switches can be set to come on or go off at programmed intervals. They are commonly used to discourage burglars. They allow you to simulate your regular lighting habits when away.

Pilot-light switches
Pilot-light switches tell you when they are on. If you have trouble remembering to shut the backyard light off, the glowing light will help you remember.

Replacing a switch

If you have never looked closely at a switch, now is a good time. A great deal of information is stamped into the metal yoke and the plastic body of a switch. You will see the amp rating, the volt rating, the approved wire type, the testing lab's approval, and the type of current it can carry. Newer models will also give you a gauge to show you how much wire to strip from the conductors. And if you make a mistake pushing the wires into the push-in terminals, the release slots are even marked so you can pull the wires back out without damaging the switch. Probably the most important designations on a switch are the UL approval stamp and the CO/ALR rating. The UL listing is your assurance of quality and the CO/ALR rating tells you that that particular switch can be safely used with aluminum, aluminum-clad, or copper wires.

Replacing a single-pole switch

Switches do eventually wear out. They may quit with one flick of the toggle, or they may work once in a while if you push on the toggle just right. In either case, there is no need to put up with a faulty switch. Single-pole switches are not expensive and are easy to replace.

Start by shutting the power off to the circuit serving the bad switch. Then remove the coverplate and loosen the screws on the mounting yoke. Pull the switch out of the box so that you can work on it. You will notice that both wires fastened to the switch terminals are either black or marked with black tape. Because a switch needs only to control the hot side of the circuit, this makes perfect sense. You will also notice that the white neutral wires are simply spliced together and are not involved with the switch at all. Never install a switch in the white neutral wires of any circuit.

Check to make sure that your replacement looks like the faulty switch. It may have newer push-in terminals in addition to the screw terminals, but it should have only two terminals.

Because the existing conductors will be shaped to fit the screw terminals, skip the push-in option and just use the terminals. Remove the old switch and attach the black wires to the new switch terminals. It will not matter which black wire you connect to which terminal. Slip the hook-shaped wires under the new screws so the open side of the hook is facing right, or clockwise. Then tighten the screws.

The NEC now requires switches to be connected to an equipment grounding wire. To maintain proper circuit grounding join the cable ground wires and two pigtail wires together with a wire connector. Attach one grounding pigtail to the grounding screw at the back of the box and the other grounding pigtail to the grounding terminal on the switch. Push the switch into the box, attach the yoke to the box, and replace the coverplate.

Several contributing factors related to the installation of aluminum wire have been known to cause loose connections at terminals. Loose connections cause resistance and may cause sparks and a fire. Electrolysis also sets in to corrode, or oxidize, the connection. For this reason, CO/ALR-rated switches must be used when connecting aluminum wire directly to switches. Standard switches can be used with aluminum wire if an indirect connection is made. In this case, a copper pigtail attaches to the switch and is then joined to the aluminum wire with special UL listed wire connectors. Remember, aluminum wires must never be used in push-in terminals.

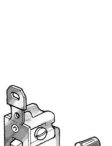

Connecting to terminals

Many switches come with push-in terminals and binding screw terminals. You can use either one, but the push-in terminals are easier. However, electricians prefer using the screw terminals. The gauge on the back of a switch shows you exactly how much insulation to strip from each conductor. If you strip too much or too little insulation, you should redo the connection. To release the locking clip inside the switch, insert a piece of wire into the release slot next to the terminal and press in. At the same time, push the conductor in slightly and then pull it out.

Typical pigtail connection
The term "pigtail" is the accepted vernacular for a short piece of wire. It is used as a lead to a receptacle, switch or fixture. A typical pigtail wire is about 6 inches long and is stripped on both ends. One end attaches to a terminal and the other is joined to the circuit wires in a wire connector. Because pigtails are so often used for joining ground wires to the grounding screw in a metal box, pigtails with a grounding screw attached are commonly available.

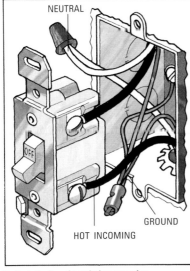

NEUTRAL

OFF

HOT INCOMING

GROUND

Typical single-pole switch connection

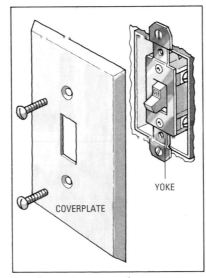

YOKE

COVERPLATE

Coverplate screws mount to yoke

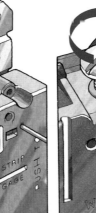

CLOCKWISE

STRIP GAGE · PUSH

TO WIRE

Push-in terminal connection

Screw-type terminal connection

Three-way and four-way switches

Three- and four-way switches allow you to control a single overhead light from two or three locations. This is especially handy when that light is at the top of stairs or in the middle of a large room. Instead of making your way across a darkened room or up dark stairs, you can shut the light off when you leave the area, no matter which end you are on.

Installing three-way and four-way switches where only one switch has been before can be time consuming. You have to cut in new boxes and run new cable through finished walls, ceilings, or floors.

To install new switches, first cut a box hole, then fish cable.

Replacing a four-way switch

Four-way switches allow control of light fixtures from three locations. Four-way switches have four terminals and are used in conjunction with two three-way switches. If a continuity test shows a bad four-way switch, replace it.

A four-way switch receives two traveler wires, one from each three-way cable attached to the two three-way switches. To replace a four-way switch, shut off the power and pull the switch from the box. Then disconnect the top two travelers and connect them to the top two terminals of the new switch. Do the same with the bottom two travelers. By transferring only two wires at a time, you will avoid making a wiring mistake.

Pull cable up through wall cavity and over to ceiling box.

Pull cable through box holes and push box into ceiling.

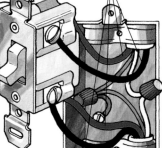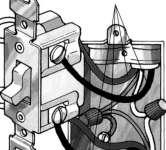
Install light fixture and hang globe in place.

Replacing a three-way switch

If you have one three-way switch, you must have another. If one of them fails, you will have to check both (with a continuity tester) in order to isolate the defective switch. When you've determined which switch no longer works, shut off the power to that circuit. Then remove the coverplate and mounting yoke screws and pull the switch out of the box. To protect yourself further, test the circuit conductors with a voltage tester.

With 2 three-way switches, three options are required: on/off, off/on, and off/off. When you pull a three-way switch out of its box, you will see that it has three terminals and a grounding screw. Like single-pole switches, three-ways control only hot wires. You may see a red wire, a black wire, and a white wire attached to the three terminals, but all are considered hot. Two of these hot wires are "travelers" and one is a common wire. The common wire will be attached to the third terminal, which will be marked either "COM" or will have a darker colored screw. The two travelers will be attached to matching screws of a lighter color.

When replacing a defective three-way switch, start by marking the common wire with a piece of tape. Then remove each wire from its terminal. Attach the two travelers to the two like-colored terminals of the new switch. It doesn't matter which terminal gets which traveler. Then fasten the common wire to the darker, or marked, screw. If the ground wire was connected to the defective switch only, use a pigtail to attach it to the new switch and to the metal box. If the box is plastic, attach a pigtail from the switch to the other ground wires.

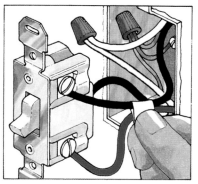
TRAVELER TERMINAL   MASKING TAPE

A typical three-way hookup
Tape the common hot wire.

Creating a three-way circuit loop

If one of your ceiling lights is still an old-fashioned pull-chain model, you may want to install a new fixture that can be controlled from either side of the room.

Start by shutting off the power to the circuit. Undo the old ceiling fixture so that you have access to the wiring in the box. Then check to see how best to run the new switch loop. When you have determined which is the easiest route to the new switch locations, install cut-in boxes at the appropriate locations. Then fish a Type NM 14/2 with ground cable from the ceiling box, across the ceiling, and down one wall to the first switch box.

From the first box, run a Type NM 14/3 with ground cable to the second switch box. Fasten the new cables to the new boxes and to the ceiling box. Allow about eight inches of cable to extend past the opening of each box to make working easier.

Strip seven inches of sheathing off each cable, and ⅝ inch of insulation off each wire. Then connect the new fixture leads to the ceiling cable with wire connectors. And attach the switch wires to the switches. Ground all boxes properly and restore power to the circuit.

TRAVELER WIRES

A four-way switch

A three-way circuit loop
1 Light fixture
2 Two-wire w/ground cable
3 First switch
4 Three-wire w/ground cable
5 Second switch

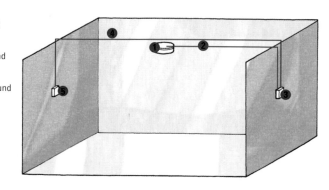

Special-use switches

Special-use switches can make your existing lighting more effective and more useful. They can also make your switches easier to see and easier to use. Dimmer switches, whether used on fluorescent or incandescent lights, can create softer moods and save money, too. The special switches shown earlier in this chapter are not expensive and are easy to install. Each should come with wiring diagrams to suit a variety of situations.

Installing time-clock switches

Like pilot-light switches, time-clock switches can be installed only in middle-of-the-run outlets. You will also need to use a voltage tester to locate the incoming black conductor. Time-clock switches sometimes come with wire leads instead of terminals.

Start by shutting the power off and removing the old switch. Then fasten the special mounting bracket to the box. Tie the black lead to the incoming black wire and the red wire to the outgoing black wire. Connect the white neutral wire to the circuit neutral wires and the ground wire to the box. Screw the switch to the mounting bracket and restore power.

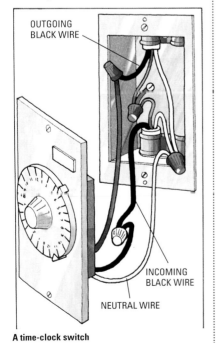

OUTGOING BLACK WIRE

INCOMING BLACK WIRE

NEUTRAL WIRE

A time-clock switch

Installing dimmer switches

To install a simple three-position dimmer switch on a two-wire circuit, shut off the power to the circuit and remove the single-pole switch. Shutting off the power here is doubly important because of the electronic circuits in the switch. A spark could easily ruin its diode rectifier. Then connect the black wire to the positive terminal and the white wire to the neutral terminal, just as you would a single-pole switch. Attach the ground to the box or switch; replace the switch and coverplate. These three-position switches can carry a maximum of 300 watts, so don't use them on circuits that require more wattage.

For circuits that serve up to 600 watts, use a dimmer switch with a knob-controlled rheostat. These too are wired just like a standard single-pole switch, unless you need a three-way version or a special fluorescent dimmer.

Three-way dimmer switches are wired the same as standard three-way switches but will often come with wire leads instead of terminals. In this case, you will make all connections inside the box with wire connectors.

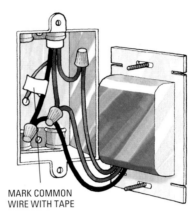

MARK COMMON WIRE WITH TAPE

Three-way dimmer switch

Installing a pilot-light switch

Pilot-light switches come in two varieties, but both must be installed in middle-of-the-run boxes. One has the light inside the toggle switch and the other has a larger light below a horizontal toggle. The lighted toggle version takes a switch coverplate and the separate light version requires a receptacle coverplate. They are wired a little differently, but perform the same task. Before starting any switch replacement, be sure to shut the power off to that circuit.

If you choose the toggle-light version, you will find two brass terminals at the top of the switch and one silver-colored terminal at the bottom of the switch. Remove the single-pole switch and attach the incoming and outgoing black wires to the brass terminals on the new switch. Then join the incoming and outgoing white neutral wires to a pigtail inside the box and run the other end of the pigtail to the silver terminal on the new switch. Finish by attaching the ground wires to the metal box or to the ground screw on the switch. If after restoring power to the circuit, the pilot light stays on in the off position, reverse the black wires on the switch.

If you choose the separate light version, you will find three brass terminals and a silver terminal. Attach the outgoing black wire to the side with two brass terminals; either terminal will do. Then connect the incoming black wire to the brass screw on the other side of the switch. Finally, tie the white neutral to the silver screw terminal with a pigtail and connect the ground to the back of the metal box.

Push the switch back into the box, taking care not to push any wires away from the terminal screws. Then fasten the yoke screws to the box and install the coverplate. Test your work. The light should come on when the switch is turned on.

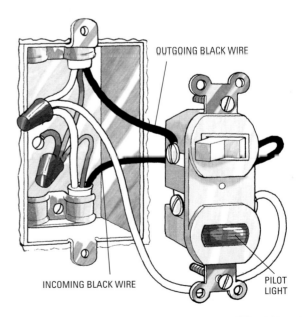

OUTGOING BLACK WIRE

INCOMING BLACK WIRE

PILOT LIGHT

Receptacles

**Standard tamper-
resistant receptacle**

There are several reasons why you might want to replace a receptacle. You may need to upgrade from two-slot to three-slot outlets to match your three-prong plugs. Of course, the circuit must include an equipment grounding wire if you intend to make this upgrade. But in most cases, you install a new receptacle because the old one no longer works or the receptacle face is cracked or broken.

In general, there are three basic types of receptacles. One is the standard duplex receptacle with both push-in and wire-binding screw terminals. Secondly, GFCI receptacles are now required in many locations. And the new third type is the tamper-resistant receptacle. For new installations, the NEC now requires all 15- and 20-amp receptacles throughout the home to be tamper-resistant, indoors and outdoors. Tamper-resistant receptacles are required due to a proliferation of electrical burn accidents involving young children. They are designed to prevent the insertion of foreign objects into the receptacle slots. All of the receptacles come in a variety of styles and colors to match any décor.

Receptacle switches

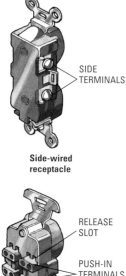

SIDE
TERMINALS

**Side-wired
receptacle**

RELEASE
SLOT

PUSH-IN
TERMINALS

**Back-wired, push-in
terminals**

**Switch/receptacle
combination**

A receptacle/switch combination offers greater versatility in a single box. These models are popular in simple remodeling projects where additional boxes are not feasible or practical. There are a multitude of different configurations available.

This combination can be wired together or separately. For example, the switch might control a bathroom exhaust fan and light, while the receptacle half could be wired directly, so that it is always hot. In another situation, where an appliance needs to be controlled by a switch, the switch half of the combination would control the receptacle half. This combination

is one way to add a receptacle to an older bathroom without a major rewiring project.

Of course, every bathroom and appliance circuit must be protected by a ground fault circuit interrupter to meet code. In this case, a GFCI circuit breaker would probably be installed in the panel.

As previously mentioned, GFCI receptacles are also acceptable as a replacement for old two-slot receptacles that do not have an equipment grounding wire. Check with your local home center or hardware store for all of the different styles, figurations, and colors.

Reading receptacles

Like switches, receptacles are marked with a variety of symbols that you should check before you buy. The amp and voltage ratings will be stamped on the body, as will the testing lab's name and approval symbol. The mounting yoke may also tell you what type of wire is permitted to be connected to the terminals. Receptacles that include push-in terminals are restricted to 15-amp circuits and are for connection with No. 14 solid copper wire only. Receptacles approved for the connection of aluminum wire are marked CO/ALR. If you connect aluminum wiring directly to a standard receptacle, you are risking a fire (see the previous discussion on aluminum wiring).

The NEC does allow standard receptacles to be used with aluminum wire if the receptacle connection is made with a copper pigtail. Special

UL-listed connectors are now available for adding new copper "pigtails" to existing aluminum wiring, which allows for copper connections to regular switches and receptacles.

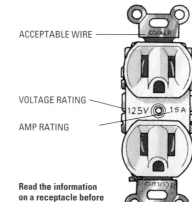

ACCEPTABLE WIRE

VOLTAGE RATING

AMP RATING

125V 15A

**Read the information
on a receptacle before
you buy it.**

The familiar plastic twist-on wire connector, often called by the trade name Wire-Nut®, is used for joining wires in fixtures, appliances, and boxes. Any joint made with a wire connector must remain accessible and contained within a proper electrical enclosure. Even though electricians often use other methods to join wires, plastic wire connectors are the best choice for homeowners. They're easy to use (you just twist them onto the ends of the wires being joined), inexpensive, and available in any hardware store or home center. Be sure to pick the one that's designed for the wires you are splicing and always check the manufacturer's listing of acceptable wire sizes and combinations. The most common ones are shown below.

Gray connector
The smallest commonly available wire connector, it can hold a minimum of one No. 20 with one No. 22 wire, and a maximum of two No. 16 wires.

Blue connector
It can hold a minimum of three No. 22 wires and a maximum of three No. 16 wires.

Orange connector
It can hold a minimum of three No. 22 and a maximum of two No. 14 with one No. 18.

Yellow connector
This can hold a minimum of one No. 14 with one No. 18 and a maximum of one No. 10 with one No. 14.

Red connector
This can hold a minimum of two No. 14 and a maximum of four No. 12.

Installing receptacles

There are two basic wiring methods for standard receptacles. The method you use will depend upon where the receptacle is located in the circuit. If the receptacle you are about to install is in the middle of the circuit, you will follow the middle-of-the-run wiring method. If it is the last receptacle on a circuit, you will follow the end-of-run method.

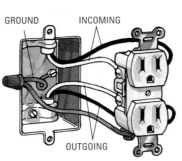
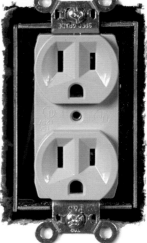

A typical middle-of-the-run receptacle

Installing middle-of-the-run receptacles

Because a middle-of-the-run receptacle must pass electricity along to other receptacles on a circuit, it must be wired accordingly. A middle-of-the-run outlet box will contain two cables carrying six wires: two black, two white, and two bare ground wires.

To wire a middle-of-the-run receptacle, attach the two black wires to the two brass-colored terminals. Then attach the two white wires to the two silver-colored terminals. To ground a receptacle in a metal box, make a pigtail connection between the two bare ground wires and the ground screw on the receptacle. Then attach another pigtail to the box with a machine screw or grounding clip. If installing a receptacle in a nonmetallic box, simply make a pigtail connection from the ground wires to the receptacle.

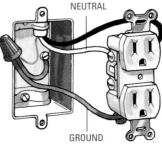

A typical end-of-the-run receptacle

Installing end-of-the-run receptacles

An end-of-the-run receptacle only needs to be wired so that the circuit is completed across its own terminals. To wire an end-of-the-run receptacle, attach the single black wire to one of the brass terminals and the single white wire to one of the silver terminals. Then pigtail from the incoming ground wire to the ground screw on the receptacle and to the metal box. For a nonmetallic box, simply attach the ground wire to the receptacle ground screw.

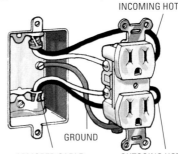

Armored cable uses its armor as a ground

Armored cable and receptacles

Some older homes have armored cable instead of nonmetallic sheathed cable. Some armored cable uses the metal armor as a grounding conductor and has no separate ground wire. To ground a receptacle with armored cable that doesn't have a ground wire, use a pigtail between the box and the receptacle ground screw. Because the metal box is fastened to the metal cable, a permanent ground connection is made.

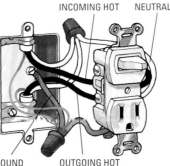

The switch controls a remote light

Installing switch/receptacle combinations

If you have a switch where you also need a receptacle, you can often have both in one unit. A switch/receptacle combination gives you both, while allowing you to use the wiring already in the switch box. But before buying a switch/receptacle unit, make sure you know which wiring method you will be able to use. The location of the unit on a circuit will dictate how the switch/receptacle will work.

The most popular use of a switch/receptacle combination has the receptacle wired hot and the switch controlling a remote light or small appliance. Because the receptacle must have both a hot and a neutral wire to complete the circuit, this switch/receptacle combination must be installed in a middle-of-the-run location. If you want the switch to control the outlet and the light, you will have to pull another cable to get a neutral for the receptacle.

To wire a switch/receptacle to a middle-of-the-run outlet, join the white neutral wires with a wire connector and pigtail to the silver-colored terminal screw. Attach the incoming black wire to one of the brass screws and the black outgoing switch wire to the copper screw. Then ground the receptacle and box with a pigtail to the receptacle ground screw.

To have the switch control the receptacle and the light at the same time, reverse the black wires. The incoming black wire should be connected to the copper screw and the outgoing black switch wire should be connected to the brass-colored screw.

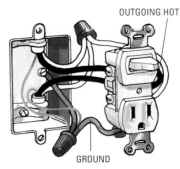

The switch controls the receptacle

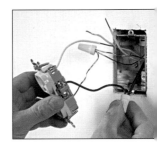

Pigtail connections
Some municipal codes require that all standard receptacle connections be made with pigtail leads. In this case, the black pigtail is tied to one brass terminal and the white pigtail is tied to a silver terminal on the opposite side of the receptacle. In this way, one faulty terminal connection cannot disable an entire circuit. While this practice is not part of the NEC, local authorities may enforce its use. In any case, a pigtail should be used whenever more than one wire must be tied to a single terminal.

Installing receptacles

Switching half of a receptacle

If most of the lights you use in your living room and bedrooms are lamps instead of permanent light fixtures, you may wish to wire half of some receptacles to switches. In this case, the bottom half of each outlet is wired directly and is always hot. TVs and other small appliances can be plugged into those. All lamps, on the other hand, could then be plugged into the switched half of the receptacles.

The obvious advantage of this arrangement is that you can turn on lamps as you come through the door.

To split a receptacle so that half of it is hot full time and the other half is switch-controlled, start with the receptacle. As you hold a receptacle with the sockets facing you, you will see that the terminals on both sides are tied together with metal strips. You will also see that the strips have metal tabs that are scored part way through. These metal strips join both halves of the receptacle, which is what allows you to wire to only one terminal on each side and still have power to both sockets.

In the case of a split receptacle, you will no longer want the top and bottom sockets tied together on the hot side. To separate the top and bottom sockets, use pliers and break the tab off the metal strip on the hot side only. Do not break the tab on the neutral side.

Wiring split receptacles

To wire a split receptacle to a switch, use 14/2 with ground Type NM cable. Bring this cable from the power source to the receptacle box and then continue it to the switch box.

Fishing this cable through finished walls and ceilings can be difficult and time consuming. If you have access to the room from a basement directly below or an attic directly above, the job is easier. Take accurate measurements in the room to be sure that you drill in the right places.

At the receptacle box, the white wire in the cable that goes to the switch box will be the hot supply for the switch. Re-identify this white wire with black tape at both ends. The black wire in the switch loop cable will be the switched hot wire and it will connect to the brass terminal on the switched half of the receptacle.

At the receptacle box, splice the incoming black hot wire and the re-identified white hot wire together

with a black pigtail over to the remaining brass terminal on the un-switched half of the receptacle. Splice the ground wires together with a double pigtail. Attach one pigtail to the box and the other to the ground terminal on the receptacle.

To connect the switch, all you will have to do is attach the black wire to one terminal and the re-identified white to the other. Then double-pigtail the incoming ground wire, with one pigtail to the ground terminal on the switch and one pigtail to the back of the box.

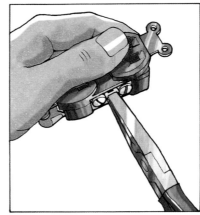

Split receptacles
To separate the top half of a receptacle from the bottom half, break the connecting tab.

Like a receptacle/switch combination, a receptacle/light combination is a good way to gain a receptacle without the work and expense of installing new boxes. Receptacle/light combination units are most commonly used over bathroom lavatories, but can be installed elsewhere. They are usually rated at 15 amps, so only low-wattage appliances should be plugged into them. Electric razors and hair dryers will not overload receptacle/light combinations. Because the NEC requires every bathroom outlet to be protected from ground fault, a receptacle/light should always be protected by a GFCI.

Receptacle/light combinations can also be wired in two ways. A switch can control both the light and the receptacle, or the receptacle half of the fixture can be wired hot, leaving the switch to control only the light. How you wire your own depends on whether your existing light is in an end-of-the-run or middle-of-the-run outlet box.

If only two wires enter your existing fixture box, you are dealing with an end-of-the-run connection, in which case both the receptacle and the light must be operated by the switch.

If you find four wires (plus a ground) in your existing box, you will be able to wire the receptacle hot and switch the light independently.

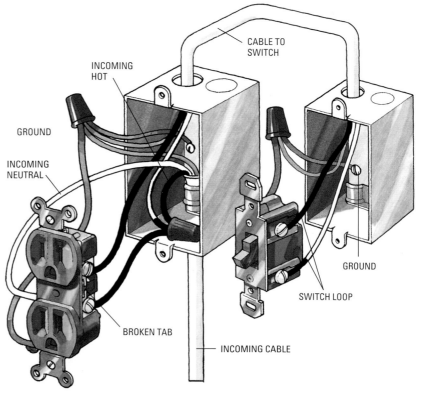

New wiring for new rooms

If you will be wiring a new home, new addition, or gutted older home, getting wiring from here to there seems an easy task. It is, in fact, much easier than fighting the structural barriers in remodeling work. Even so, there will be plenty of practical decisions to make, including the most efficient use of costly materials.

This is where thinking things through is important. To do a professional job, you must start with a well-considered plan. Do it on paper. Work it out so you know where your receptacles, lights, and switches will be. Decide in advance how many circuits you will need. And give some thought to your future needs while you are at it. Figure it out the best you can and then determine the most economical way to get it all done.

How many outlets

Ultimately, the number of receptacles, switches, and fixtures you install should be determined by your needs. It's far easier to install extra boxes now than it will be later.

The NEC has its own minimum standard. In simple terms, you need at least one receptacle for every 12 feet of wall space (in other words, no point in the wall space can be more than 6 feet from a receptacle). Any wall 2 feet or more in width must have one. And you must put one within 6 feet of both the latch and hinge sides of every entry door. Fixed glazing, railings, room dividers, and bar-type counters are considered wall space and are included in your measurements. Doors, fireplaces and similar wall opening are not counted.

Even with these rules, the layout of a home may be confusing. To check your preliminary receptacle layout, take a table lamp that has a six-foot long cord and move it around the room where the wall meets the floor; you should be able to reach six feet in either direction and hit a receptacle. It may seem like a lot of receptacles when you're installing them. But after you start using them, you'll probably wish you had more.

Planning light locations

NEC lighting regulations generally involve safety, not issues of practicality. The two areas of concern are fire protection and the prevention of personal injury due to insufficient lighting.

Closet lighting
Lights in closets are not mandatory. If installed, however, there are some very stringent NEC codes concerning closet lighting.

The chief concern of code and fire officials is that blankets, clothing and boxes would come in contact with broken or hot lamps, thereby creating a fire hazard. Many fires do start in closets every year.

The list of allowable fixtures for closets includes surface-mounted or recessed incandescent with completely enclosed lamps, surface-mounted or recessed fluorescent fixtures, or new LED fixtures that are identified for use in storage areas. Incandescent and LED fixtures with open or partially enclosed lamps and cord pendant lampholders are not allowed. Falling hot filaments from broken incandescent lamps are a fire hazard.

The NEC has a complex definition for "closet storage space" that can leave experienced electricians scratching their heads. Illustrations are rare in the NEC, but there is one for closets. The required clearances are between the fixture installed in the clothes closet and the nearest point of the defined closet storage space.

Recessed lighting
Recessed light fixtures are very popular for providing general lighting, specific task lighting, or for accenting rooms. These "can" lights are available for flat or sloping ceilings, for new construction with open framing or the remodel-type for existing ceilings, with incandescent, fluorescent, or low-voltage lamps, and with a wide variety of trims. Energy codes often require cans to be air-tight to prevent air leakage, infiltration, and condensation problems.

To avoid any fire hazards, you need to precisely follow the manufacturer's installation instructions with respect to clearances, trim styles, and lamp sizing. Recessed cans incorporate thermal protection sensors that will cause the lamp to blink on and off to warn of overheating. Type IC (insulation contact) cans are permitted to be in contact with thermal insulation. Non-Type IC cans must maintain ½ inch of clearance from combustible materials and 3 inches from thermal insulation.

Front- and back-door lighting
The NEC requires that each entrance to a house, attached garage, or a detached garage that has electric power, must be illuminated by a wall-switched exterior fixture. The fixture does not have to be mounted near the door but must illuminate the entrance. An exception in the code allows remote, central, or automatic control of lighting at entrances in lieu of a wall switch.

Other lighting considerations
In general, the NEC requires at least one wall switch-controlled lighting fixture in every habitable room and bathroom. In other than bathrooms and kitchens, it's allowable to switch one or more receptacle outlets in lieu of light fixtures. The code allows occupancy sensors in addition to wall switches, or occupancy sensors at the customary switch locations with built-in manual override.

Wall switch-controlled fixtures are also required in hallways, stairways, and attached garages. At interior stairways with six or more risers, switches are required at each floor, and each landing that has an entryway. Similar to outdoor entrances, remote, central, or automatic control is allowed for hallways and stairways.

Lighting is also required for attics, crawl spaces, utility rooms and basements where these areas are used for storage or contain equipment that requires servicing, such as furnaces and water pumps.

Installing a recessed light fixture in the ceiling

Cut hole, feed switch cable to light box, and join wires.

Angle mounting bracket on light into hole and attach to joists.

Slide trim ring onto light, snap in place, and install bulb.

TABLE OF FIXTURE CLEARANCES IN CLOSETS

Type of fixture	Clearance
Surface-mounted incandescent or LED fixtures with a completely enclosed light source installed on the wall above the door or on the ceiling	12 inches
Surface-mounted fluorescent fixtures installed on the wall above the door or on the ceiling	6 inches
Recessed incandescent or LED fixtures with a completely enclosed light source on the wall above the door or on the ceiling	6 inches
Recessed fluorescent fixtures installed in the wall or ceiling	6 inches
Surface-mounted fluorescent or LED fixtures shall be permitted within the defined storage space where the fixture is specifically approved and identified for this use	

Consult the NEC or a qualified electrician for detailed information related to the definition of closet storage space.

Running new cables

When you know how you will run each circuit, start by installing boxes and drilling holes for the cables. With the boxes mounted and the holes drilled, start pulling cable through the holes, one cable at a time.

Because you will have many cables hanging near your panel when it comes time to install the breakers, you should design some method of keeping them straight as you go. The best way is to write directly on the sheathing of each cable with a permanent marker. Each cable hanging near the panel will represent a circuit, serving a given area of the house. Write "#1 kitchen" on the first of two kitchen appliance circuits, for example. A professional electrician can walk up to a tangle of cables and somehow make sense of them. To the rest of us, however, a dozen unmarked cables looks much more like a can of worms.

Where to run circuit cables

As mentioned earlier, often the most efficient route for you to run cable is right down the center of the house. This will not be true of circuits near the panel, of course, but for those circuits serving the far end of the house, a trunk-line approach is often the easiest. Start by drilling a slightly larger hole than usual, say ⅞ inch in diameter, in each joist near the center beam in the basement. If your home is built on a concrete slab, go through the attic. Then pull three cables through that single row of holes.

As you near each circuit's location, route a cable to the first outlet box on that circuit. From there, thread a cable through drilled holes in the framed walls or ceiling until all outlets are connected. This trunk-line (with branch runs) approach will help you keep the layout clear in your mind and will also save a lot of unnecessary drilling and pulling.

Mounting the boxes

Receptacle boxes should all be at a uniform height, usually 12 to 14 inches from the floor. Switch boxes should be mounted 44 to 48 inches from the floor and are usually on the latch side of the door. Thermostats and similar controls are often installed at 60 inches. Adjust all boxes up or down for persons with special needs. Ceiling boxes should be installed with brackets or fastened to framing members to support heavier fixtures or ceiling fans.

Where to drill

When threading cables through your home, you should always drill through the framed walls, ceiling joists, and floor joists. In unfinished basements and crawl spaces, smaller cables must be run through bored holes in the joists or installed on running boards. Larger cables can be installed on the lower

edges of joists. Cables installed on unfinished basement walls are required to be installed in conduit for physical protection. Cables installed within the webbing of floor and roof trusses shall be properly secured and routed away from metal truss connection plates.

When drilling holes in joists and studs, do everything you can to protect the wire and the structure. Always drill through the center of a 2 x 4 stud. If a bored hole and cable is less than 1¼ inches from the face of the framing member, a ¹⁄₁₆-inch steel plate is required for protection. When drilling floor or ceiling joists, drill only in the center one-third of the board. If you drill near the bottom of a joist, you will weaken it. If your new home has engineered floor trusses instead of joists, drill through the plywood center of the trusses and never through the bottom or top rails.

Take the most direct route possible. Drill through bottom wall plates and floor decking and pull the cable into the framed walls. From there, drill through each stud on your way to the outlet boxes. Drill holes 12 inches or so above the boxes to allow for securing the cable at the box locations. If you come to a door frame, drill above it, either through the short studs above the header or through the ceiling joists. Then travel back down and through the studs again. When you come to a framed corner with several thicknesses of 2 x 4s, drill into the studs from two directions and fish the cable around the corner. Type NM cable shall be secured within 12 inches of boxes and every 4½ feet thereafter.

Wiring into boxes
Before bringing cable into metal boxes, you will have to pry one or more knockouts from each box. These knockouts have slots that allow you to twist them out with a screwdriver. Nonmetallic boxes have molded knockout areas that are very thin. To create an opening for a cable, force a screwdriver through the knockout area.

Stapling cables to studs and joists
Anytime you run cable along the side of a stud or joist, you must staple it, at least once every 4 feet. The NEC also requires that any cable that enters a box must be stapled within 8 inches of the box. The exception to this rule is when fishing cable into cut-in boxes on remodeling projects, where studs and joists cannot be reached. In these cases, boxes with cable connection clamps must be used.

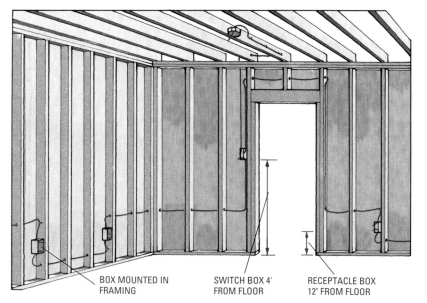

BOX MOUNTED IN FRAMING

SWITCH BOX 4' FROM FLOOR

RECEPTACLE BOX 12" FROM FLOOR

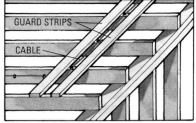

GUARD STRIPS

CABLE

Guard strips
When you must run cable across ceiling joists, protect it with guard strips.

1/16" PLATE

Metal protection plates
Use when wire is within 1¼ inch of the face of a stud.

The service panel

Whether you are wiring a new home or a new addition, you are likely to start in the panel. For the purpose of completeness, we will assume a new panel that is empty and de-energized. How you lay out your new panel, that is, in what order you install the new breakers, is really up to you. Electricians usually install the heavy-duty circuits at the top of the hot bus, just below the main disconnect. An average home might have three 240-volt breakers at the top, followed by ten or more 120-volt breakers below them for the appliance, laundry, bathroom, and lighting circuits.

Connecting circuit breakers

Two-hundred-forty-volt breakers
Practically speaking, a 240-volt circuit is two adjacent 120-volt circuits tied together in a panel and at a receptacle. But technically, there is much more to it. Utility transformers supply 120/240-volt, 3-wire, single-phase power for dwelling services. A single-phase, 3-wire supply consists of the "A" leg, the "B" leg, and "N," the neutral. You'll have 120-volts each from A-N and B-N, and 240-volts from A-B. Three-phase power is used in commercial occupancies. Appliances requiring 240-volts are wired to draw current from two hot wires, A and B.

Your 240-volt cables will each contain one red hot wire, one hot black wire, one white neutral wire, and usually one green or bare equipment grounding wire.

Start by making sure that the main service disconnect is shut off. Then insert the cable through one of the panel knockouts and fasten it with a cable connector. Strip off all but ½ inch of the cable's sheathing inside the panel. Then fasten the white wire and the ground wire to the neutral bus bar. Fasten the black hot wire to one of the two terminals on the two-pole circuit breaker. Follow by fastening the red hot wire to the other breaker terminal.

With the hot wires connected, move the breaker into position on the hot bus. Tip one edge of the breaker under the small retainer on the bus and press the other end onto the two copper tabs projecting from the bus. The breaker should snap firmly in place. Different manufacturers will have slightly different breaker/bus connections.

One-hundred-twenty-volt breakers
Ordinary 120-volt breakers snap into place just like 240-volt breakers. The main difference is that a single-pole 120-volt breaker will take up only one slot and cover only one copper tab. Remember that each wire size must be matched to a compatible breaker ampere rating.

Bring a 120-volt cable into another of the panel knockouts. If you have many circuits, you may wish to bring several cables into the panel through the same knockout opening. In that case, wait to tighten the cable connector until all wires are installed. Strip the sheathing from the cable and connect the white neutral and bare equipment grounding wires to the neutral bus bar. (Use the separate grounding bus for grounding wires if it's available.) Then fasten the black wire to the breaker terminal.

Grounding the panel

At the service panel, the equipment grounding conductors, the neutral conductors, and their respective terminal bars, are bonded together with a main bonding jumper that may be a green screw, a bonding strap, or similar. This critical connection provides a path for ground-fault currents to make a complete circuit and return to the source transformer, thereby tripping circuit breakers as quickly as possible.

From the neutral bar, a grounding electrode conductor is run to one or more grounding electrodes. The most common connection is to a metal underground water pipe within five feet of where it enters the house. The code also requires a connection to a concrete-

encased electrode, which consists of a least 20 feet of ½ inch steel reinforcing steel bars in the concrete footing. If the underground metal water pipe is the only electrode present, it must be supplemented with a ground rod in the event the underground metal pipe is repaired with plastic pipe in the future.

Be sure to use grounding clamps that are specifically approved for water pipe connections. Likewise for ground rod clamps that must be suitable for direct burial.

An equipment bonding jumper connection is also required to the interior metal water piping system. This can be accomplished by simply installing a bonding jumper around the water meter, which is required anyway.

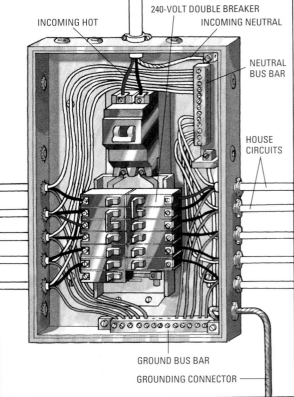

Circuit cables exiting the sides of the panel
They could also exit the few knockouts at the top.

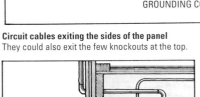

Grounding the panel
A service panel must be grounded or its circuit grounding conductors will not be effective.

New wiring in older homes

The trick to electrical remodeling is to work past structural barriers in an inconspicuous way. A few specialized tools will be useful—fish tapes, sabre saws, and extension bits make reaching into blind spaces and blocked passages a lot easier. But a good understanding of how your home was built is your best help. Take some time to consider how your wall studs and floor and ceiling joists are laid out. Look for nail patterns that suggest the location of a framing member. Check out your basement and attic to determine which way joists run and how far apart they are. As a general rule, walls, floors, and ceilings are laid out on 16-inch centers, that is, framing members are 16 inches apart. Ceiling joists may also be laid out on 24-inch centers. These measurements are standard references, but every home will have its exceptions. Joists, for example, will frequently be doubled up for support under walls, while corners, doors, windows, and intersecting walls all require extra studs.

Drilling top and bottom plates

The best places to run wiring are unfinished basement ceilings or unfinished attics. If you have either, make all of your long runs there and wire into the wall only to connect switches or receptacles. In many cases, you will have to go from the basement to the attic at least once. If you have a two-story home, you may have to cut into walls at several levels.

If you have a single-story home, however, getting from the basement to the attic can be as simple as drilling through the top and bottom plates of a center wall and fishing wire from one level to another. The secret to this and all remodeling work is accurate measuring. You will be able to see the top plate in the attic because the ceiling joists will be resting on it. In the basement, however, all you may see are the tips of nails showing through from the bottom plate. You may not see even

that much. If not, you will have to measure for the exact location from an outside wall. Take the measurement from the upstairs center wall to an outside wall and transfer that measurement to the basement.

If measuring is too difficult because of structural barriers, try driving a long nail straight down, right next to the wall from upstairs. Then go in the basement and try to locate where the nail broke through the decking. Measure over 3 inches from the nail and drill straight up into the wall.

When both top and bottom plates are drilled, slide two fish tapes into the wall cavity, one from each direction and hook one with the other. Then pull the bottom fish tape down until the end of the fish tape from the attic is exposed. Attach a cable to the attic fish tape and pull the fish tape and cable up through the wall and into the attic.

Attach cable to end of fish tape that comes from attic and pull up.

Staple cable to joist, mount box and install cable.

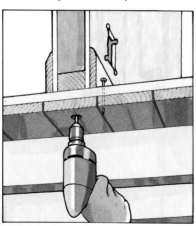

Drill hole into bottom plate using nail as guide.

Hook fish tape onto cable and pull up into box.

The easiest and most certain way to locate obstructions behind plaster or drywall is to buy an electronic density sensor. These "stud finders" are not the usual magnetic sensors that react when near nails, but actually sense the extra density of a stud, joist, or fire block. Furthermore, a density sensor will pinpoint the exact edges of a framing member. It also works well through metal lath walls, where magnetic sensors are helpless. You can find a density sensor at most local hardware stores and home centers.

Density sensors are handy but certainly not necessary. You can locate most studs and fire blocks by visual inspection or by tapping on the wall with your knuckles and listening to its resonance. A hollow sound suggests a hollow space between studs. A dull sound suggests the presence of a stud. To check for fire blocks (short 2 x 4 blocks nailed between studs to stop the spread of fire through the wall cavities), rap every few inches between studs in a line between the floor and ceiling. A sudden dull sound between studs will indicate a blockage.

Another easy way to locate studs is by looking for nail holes in baseboards. Baseboard nail holes are usually covered with filler that is noticeable at close range. Always look to the nails at the top of the board for clues. The nails at the bottom may be driven into the bottom plate of the wall, which is continuous and therefore deceiving. With a little close inspection, you will be able to predict where most studs and joists are likely to be.

If an area doesn't yield much in terms of clues, as a last resort you can always drive a small nail every inch across the wall until it hits something solid. If you keep the holes small, the repair shouldn't be too difficult.

Cut-in boxes are used to upgrade older electrical systems. Unlike standard boxes used in new construction, where walls are unfinished, cut-in boxes are not fastened to studs or joists. They are mounted directly to plaster or drywall. They come in several styles with different clamping methods. Some have sheet metal spring clamps on the sides, while others have wing nuts or expansion clamps.

The kind you choose is less critical than how you mount it. In each case, you will have to custom fit the opening to the physical dimensions and characteristics of the box. And of course, what the wall is made of will have a lot to do with how you proceed.

Cutting wood lath

Cutting into plaster and wood lath is really not much different from cutting into metal lath. The main difference is that wood is usually easier to cut than metal. You will find the cuts on one side of the opening relatively easy. This is because the lath is still supported from both directions. Once you cut through one side, however, the lath may vibrate too much when you cut it again. If it vibrates too much or tends to spring back when you cut, try a slightly different angle, speed, or pressure. You can usually find a way by making minor adjustments in your approach.

Cutting into drywall

Drywall is the easiest of the common wall finishes to cut. Again, the objective is to stay away from studs, joists, or fire blocks. Drywall is thin and resonant, which makes finding studs easy. It will also reveal slight nail depressions, which are usually visible with bright sidelight from a bare bulb. Use a drywall saw, keyhole saw, or utility knife to make the cut.

When using a utility knife, always use sharp blades. Cut the paper all the way around first to establish the perimeter, then work the blade deeper with each cut thereafter. Cut in downward strokes with steady, even pressure.

Cutting into metal lath and plaster

Plaster-covered metal lath can be the most difficult kind of wall finish to cut. The problem is that the expanded metal base that holds the plaster will flex if you attempt to chisel or saw through it. Too much flexing will cause the wall to crack and can cause the plaster to release from the lath.

Installing cut-in boxes into metal lath requires care, but it can be done with very few special tools. Patience is the key here. Start by locating the studs in the area where you would like your new box. If you do not own a stud finder, rap on the wall to see if you can hear any variation in tone. Where the tone sounds most resonant, pick the spot for your new box.

Before making a cut, drill a very small hole through the plaster and metal lath. Spend a little time reaming the back side of the plaster out with the drill bit. Then bend about 2 inches of a thin wire at a 90-degree angle. Slide the bent part of the wire into the drilled hole and spin it **(1)**. If the wire hits a stud, move to the right or left accordingly. When the bent part of the wire spins all the way around without hitting anything, make your cut.

Before cutting into the plaster, cover the box area with masking tape. This will reinforce the plaster and keep it from chipping during the cut. Then hold the cut-in box, or its paper template, up to the tape and trace around it **(2)**. With the shape of the box

established, drill four holes in the wall, one at each corner of the box. Then use a sharp utility knife to cut into the plaster **(3)**. Do not try to cut all the way through in one slice. Cut a little at a time until you reach the metal lath. Then make several smaller cuts across the section to be removed so that it will come out easier.

With the plaster cut, use a sharp chisel that you don't mind getting dull to cut and pry the plaster square from the metal. Remember, you must not vibrate the lath too much. Just chip a little at a time, in a downward motion. Never tap the chisel straight back toward the lath.

With the plaster out, you will be ready to cut the lath. You can use a hacksaw or a sabre saw **(4)**. The hacksaw works well enough if you take your time. Be careful not to push too hard in case the blade binds against the wire. A quicker and safer way is to use a sabre saw. Make sure that you use a new blade and that you hold the base of the saw firmly against the wall. To reduce vibration further, you might hook a wire through the metal lath and pull toward you with roughly the same pressure you use against the sabre saw. This will steady the saw and the lath. Cut all sides slowly and consistently until the lath drops out.

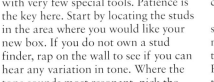

Utility knife

Keyhole saw

Drywall saw

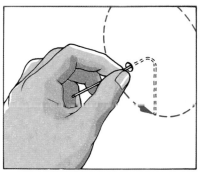
1 Check for blockage by inserting a bent wire.

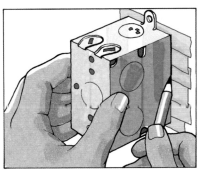
2 Trace around an old-work box.

3 Use a sharp utility knife to cut the plaster.

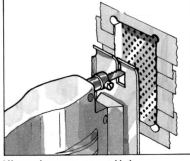
4 Use a sabre saw to cut metal lath.

Pulling cable with fish tapes

Fish tapes are the workhorse tools of retrofit wiring. With them, you can reach into closed areas behind walls, ceilings, and floors and pull new wire into otherwise inaccessible places. They are simple to use. You just drill into a wall or joist space and slide the tape along until you can reach it at another location. You can then tie cable to the end of the tape and pull it back through.

In blind spots, you can slide two fish tapes into a space, one from each end. With a little maneuvering, you will be able to hook one tape with the other, giving you the choice of pulling wire from either direction. When working from above, where gravity is a factor in your favor, a small chain offers another option. Your home will dictate the method of use.

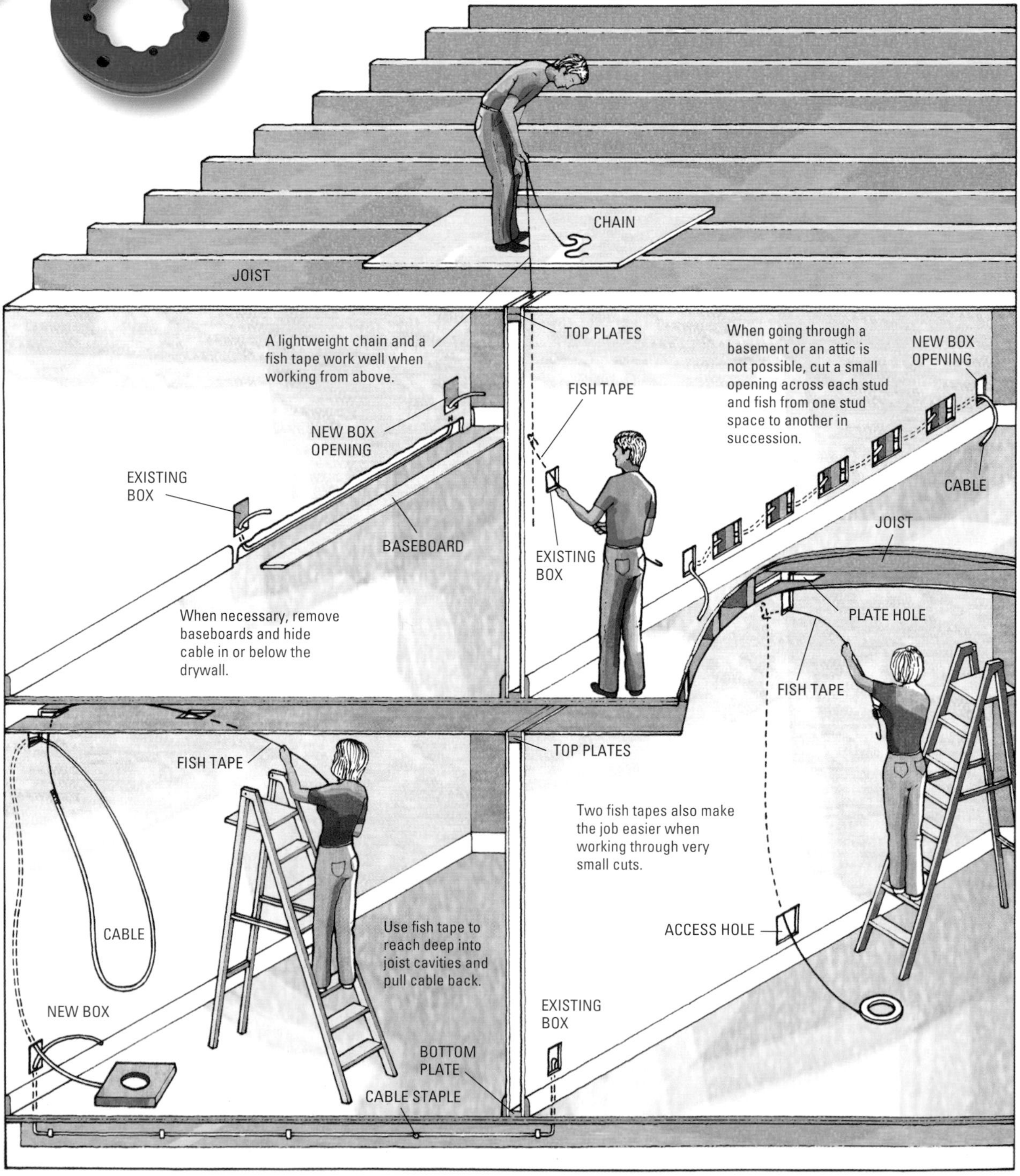

CHAIN

JOIST

A lightweight chain and a fish tape work well when working from above.

TOP PLATES

When going through a basement or an attic is not possible, cut a small opening across each stud and fish from one stud space to another in succession.

NEW BOX OPENING

FISH TAPE

NEW BOX OPENING

EXISTING BOX

CABLE

BASEBOARD

JOIST

EXISTING BOX

PLATE HOLE

When necessary, remove baseboards and hide cable in or below the drywall.

FISH TAPE

FISH TAPE

TOP PLATES

Two fish tapes also make the job easier when working through very small cuts.

ACCESS HOLE

CABLE

Use fish tape to reach deep into joist cavities and pull cable back.

EXISTING BOX

NEW BOX

BOTTOM PLATE

CABLE STAPLE

As you survey your home for possible electrical upgrades, you will see that many changes could be made if you could only get cable from one wall to another. Fortunately, the problem is old enough to have a solution. All it will take is two fish tapes, common household tools, a little planning, and a lot of patience.

Begin with the basics. Make sure that the circuit you want to expand can handle more outlets. Decide which existing outlet offers the easiest tie-in location. Then consider the best route to the new outlet location.

Start by shutting off the power to the circuit you will be tapping. Then remove the coverplate and receptacle from the tie-in box to make sure the circuit is grounded and the wiring is what you expected. For example, is it a middle-of-the-run or an end-of-the-run receptacle? While you are at it, remove a knockout from the bottom of the box for the new cable to come through.

When the existing box is ready, cut the box opening in the new location across the room. Then go into the basement and drill up into both walls below each box location. Use a ⅝-inch bit and stay near the center of the wall to avoid drilling into drywall or baseboard nails.

Slide one fish tape through the knockout in the existing box and another fish tape through the hole drilled from the basement **(1)**. You will need help at this point, but the object is to hook one fish tape with the other. When you hook them together inside the wall, pull the lower fish tape up and into the box. Fasten cable to the lower fish tape **(2)** and pull cable back into the basement and across the floor **(3)**. Then cut the cable so that it will reach well into the new box and push it up into the wall. Have someone reach into the new box opening and pull the cable into the room. Then staple the cable to the floor joists. Slide the cable into the new box and mount the box in the wall. Finally, wire the receptacles and install the coverplates.

If you need to run cable down a wall or to the other side of a door but can't get there from an unfinished attic or basement, consider removing a little woodwork and hiding the cable there. The trick is to remove baseboards or trim without damaging them. Use a flat pry bar and a small block of wood to pry against. Push the pry bar behind the trim and gently pry against the block at various locations until the trim comes loose. Then carefully pull out the nails from the back side of the board using a locking pliers to prevent the face of the trim from being damaged.

If the drywall is held up from the floor ½ inch, tuck the cable under the drywall. If you do not find a gap, use a chisel to cut a small groove for the cable. When you re-nail the trim, be sure to keep the nails above the cable location.

When hiding cable behind door trim, tuck it between the frame and the jamb. If the cable will not fit, you may have to chisel into the drywall or plaster. In either case, staple the cable in place as often as the situation allows. When you reach the box location, drill into the wall behind the trim and run the cable to the opening from inside the wall.

Cables must always be protected from physical damage. Cables in notches and shallow grooves must be protected by 1/16-inch thick steel nail plates.

To gain access from above on a finished floor, pry up floorboard.

Use a hammer and chisel to carefully pull floorboard up.

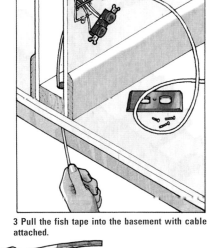

1 Use two fish tapes to pull new wire into existing boxes.

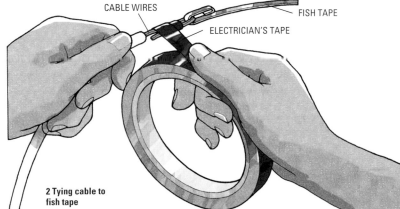

CABLE WIRES
FISH TAPE
ELECTRICIAN'S TAPE

2 Tying cable to fish tape

3 Pull the fish tape into the basement with cable attached.

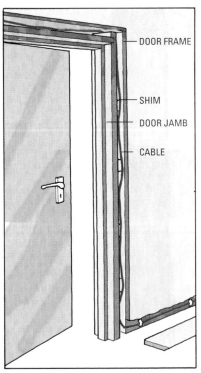

DOOR FRAME
SHIM
DOOR JAMB
CABLE

Running wire around a door

Extending existing circuits

A junction box is simply a box that is covered with a blank plate. Junction boxes are used to house and protect wire connections made between outlet boxes and must remain accessible at all times. As discussed before, a wire connection must never be made outside a box, even if hidden in an attic or crawl space.

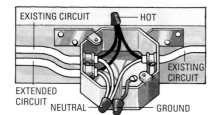

1 Running a new circuit from existing ceiling box

EXISTING CIRCUIT — HOT
EXISTING CIRCUIT
EXTENDED CIRCUIT
NEUTRAL — GROUND

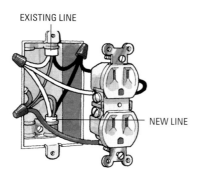

EXISTING LINE
NEW LINE

2 Running a new circuit from existing receptacle

NEW CABLE
EXISTING CABLE

3 Adding an extension to an existing box

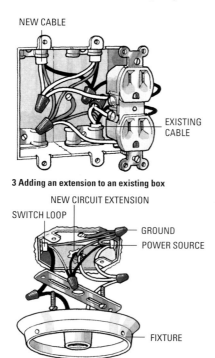

NEW CIRCUIT EXTENSION
SWITCH LOOP
GROUND
POWER SOURCE
FIXTURE

4 Extending circuit from an overhead fixture

Installing a new junction box

You will sometimes have the amp capacity to add fixtures or outlets, but doing so will require cutting into the middle of a circuit. A case in point would be when the easiest and most economical tie-in location is in the attic and not near receptacle or light fixture boxes.

Start by shutting off power to the circuit. Then mount a round or octagonal box on an attic ceiling joist right next to the circuit cable (1). Cut the cable and pull as much slack out of it from each direction as you can. This will give you longer leads to work with in the box. Then bring both ends of the existing circuit and the new branch cable into the box. Secure each cable with a cable connector or staple them within 8 inches of the box.

Assuming you already have the add-on boxes wired, you will now be ready to tie the new branch line into the existing circuit. To make this connection, simply join each color-coded set of wires in the box with a wire connector. To ground a metal junction box, you should also run a pigtail from the ground wires to the box screw. In plastic boxes, just join all the ground wires together in a wire connector.

Finally, cover the box with a blank plate and restore power. Remember, the plate of the box must remain accessible, so don't cover it up.

Converting an existing box

Often a receptacle box can serve as a junction box while continuing to serve its original purpose. (Ceiling boxes can also serve as junction boxes if they are not end-of-run outlets.) In the strictest terms, these boxes are not junction boxes because they still hold receptacles or fixtures, but whenever possible, use them as junction boxes. Junction boxes are always in danger of being covered up by someone in the future. Ceiling and receptacle boxes generally are not.

End-of-the-run junctions
If you wish to add a circuit branch from a receptacle used as a junction box, try to find the last receptacle on the existing circuit. Because it will have only two existing wires, you will not be exceeding the NEC's allowable number of wires per box. You will also not have to worry about interrupting other receptacles down the line.

Just shut off the power and bring the new cable into the end-of-the-run box. Then remove the wires from the receptacle and tie each set of corresponding wires together with pigtails. Connect the loose ends of the pigtails to opposing receptacle terminals (2). Replace the coverplate.

Middle-of-the-run junctions
Middle-of-the-run receptacles are more trouble, because by adding two more wires and a ground, you exceed the number of wires allowed by the NEC for such a small box. You will either have to install a larger cut-in box or add a box extension (3). (Adding an extension is possible only if the original box is the expandable type.)

Choose the method that makes the job easiest. Once the box size has been fixed, start by bringing the new branch cable into the box. Then join all corresponding wires with wire connectors and pigtail the joined black and white wires to the original receptacle terminals. Join all the ground wires and a grounding pigtail with a wire connector. Attach the other end of the pigtail to the grounding screw in the back of the box. Finally, cover the receptacle and restore power to the circuit.

Ceiling box junctions
If a ceiling box is served by a cable that's hot all the time instead of just a switch leg, then it can be used easily as a junction box. Sometimes ceiling fixtures wired in this manner are switched by a pull chain, and at other times they are connected to a switch loop. When tapping into a fixture operated by a pull chain, just tie all corresponding wires together in the box with wire connectors and pigtail from the wires to the original fixture terminals (4).

When tapping into a box with a hot cable and a switch loop, start by cutting the white wire from the incoming power cable that leads to the fixture. Then use a wire connector to join the white wire from the extension to the two wires produced by the cut. Next, join the black wires from the power source and the extension circuit, and the re-identified white wire in the switch loop cable. Then join the black wire from the switch loop cable to the black fixture lead. Connect all the ground wires and attach them to the box with a pigtail.

Installing a ceiling box

If you would like a ceiling light fixture or a ceiling fan added to a room but are put off by the prospect of cutting a hole for a new box into your finished ceiling, don't worry. While ceiling installations can sometimes result in a lot of repair work, in most cases the damage will be minimal and easy to repair. The most difficult part of the job is usually installing the box. As always, the design of your home will determine just how much trouble installing a ceiling fixture will be.

Working from above

If you live in a single-story home with an accessible attic, installing a ceiling box and running wire to it will be easy. Start by deciding exactly where you would like the fixture located. Then drill a small pilot hole in the ceiling from below. Insert a wire about a foot long through the pilot hole so you can see it sticking above the insulation in the attic.

When you find the wire in the attic, make sure there's room for a box and its bracket between joists. If there is, then hold the box up to the ceiling, centered over the pilot hole, and trace around it with a pencil. Cut the hole.

Working through floors

In some cases, working through a second-story floor is easier than cutting into a first-floor ceiling. Floors can be easier to repair, especially when they are covered with rugs. Of course, accurate measurements are a must.

Most homes have two layers of flooring: subflooring and finished flooring. To cut through both layers, make two neat crosscuts, preferably over the top of two joists. Then make two more cuts perpendicular to the first cuts. Remove any visible nails keeping the cut boards in place. Then, use a chisel or a flat pry bar to pry the flooring away from the joists and lift the boards up.

Working from below

If fine hardwood floors or a flat roof prevent you from working from above, you may be constrained to cut into the ceiling from below. While this will require some plaster or drywall repair, you should not let it get in the way of your lighting needs. Plaster and drywall repairs are straightforward and can be learned in short order.

If you need to cut into the ceiling from below, make a big enough access hole to fit a standard bracket box (or an NEC-approved fan box) and a 2 x 4 nailer. A large hole will make fishing cable to a power source or switch a lot easier. And when it comes time to repair the ceiling, a large hole is no harder to repair than a small one.

The wiring method you use to bring power into the ceiling box will depend on the location of your most convenient power source, and whether you want to control the fixture from one or two locations.

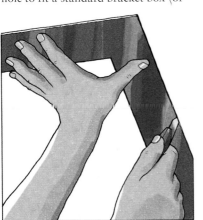

Making a square opening
Use a framing square to draw a square opening. The opening will be easier to repair if it is uniform.

Replacing the drywall piece
You can often use the same square of drywall you cut out to cover the hole.

CHOOSING A CEILING BOX

The kind of ceiling box you buy will depend upon the access you have to the ceiling joists and the kind of fixture you wish to install. If you have access to joists from above or if you have no access and must cut an access hole in the drywall or plaster, then a bracket box is your best choice. Bracket boxes give the best support. If you are installing a lightweight ceiling fixture, a cut-in box or a pancake box will do the job. A pancake box should be used only in an end-of-the-run installation because the box area is too small to contain more wires.

The NEC specifies that paddle-type ceiling fans must be installed in specially approved ceiling boxes. If a box conforms to this NEC standard it will be stamped accordingly. To give yourself even more protection, you should bolt these boxes to 2 x 4 blocks nailed between joists.

SPRING EAR

METAL EXTENSION

Cut-in box
For lightweight ceiling fixtures only, never for ceiling fans.

Pancake box
For end of circuit use where only one cable will be in the box.

TWO-PIECE BAR   CLAMP FITTING

Clamp fittings on bracket boxes

Surface wiring

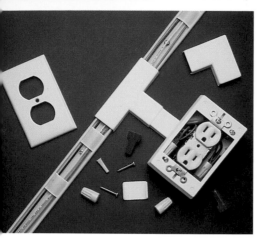

If cutting into finished walls, ceilings, and floors is more than you feel like taking on, consider making your electrical improvements with surface raceways. Metal surface raceways have been popular for years, and now plastic versions with snap-on covers are available. Because surface wiring adds to the cost of the job, plan carefully to avoid buying unnecessary parts or making any wrong cuts. While wiring an entire house with surface-mounted circuits would be quite expensive, simpler projects are much more affordable and convenient, especially when compared to cutting and repairing holes in walls or ceilings.

Raceways come in pieces that you assemble to fit your needs. A raceway consists of a base channel and a trim channel that together form a small rectangular tube that carries the circuit wires. The base channel screws directly to walls or ceiling. Once the wires are in place, the trim snaps over the base channel. To cover in-line joints, small cover clips are provided. And a variety of elbow and tee clips are used when turning corners and changing directions.

When installing raceways, first screw all the base channels and electrical-box baseplates to the walls and ceiling. Then lay the wires into the base channels and hold the wires in place with wire clips. Carefully measure the lengths of the trim channel pieces. Cut them and snap them in place. Then add any connecting pieces that are necessary, mount the boxes, and install the receptacles, switches, and light fixtures the job requires.

Tapping into existing receptacles

The advantage of surface wiring is that you can tap into an existing receptacle without cutting into the wall. This is accomplished by an extension adapter. The adapter fits over an existing box, and the wires from the raceway are joined to the receptacle wires with pigtails to continue the circuit.

To install this adapter, shut off the power to the circuit and remove the coverplate from the box. Pull out the receptacle and screw the adapter plate to the box. Break out the slot you need in the raceway-extension frame box to accommodate the raceway channel. Then place the extension frame over the channel and snap it onto the adapter plate.

To connect the wires, start by making four 5-inch pigtail wires, one

black, one white, and two green. Join the incoming-power black wire to the black raceway wire and the black pigtail inside a wire connector. Then tie the other end of the black pigtail to the hot side of the receptacle. In like manner, join all white wires and pigtail them to the neutral side of the receptacle.

To properly ground the system, attach one pigtail to the grounding screw on the receptacle and the other pigtail to the grounding screw at the back of the box. Then join both pigtails and the grounding wire from the power line and from the raceway with a wire connector.

Fasten the receptacle to the extension frame with screws and replace the coverplate.

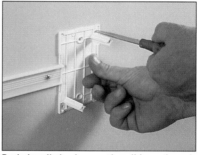

Begin installation by mounting all base channels and box base plates on wall and ceiling.

Place all wires in base channel, then carefully snap trim channel over all base channels.

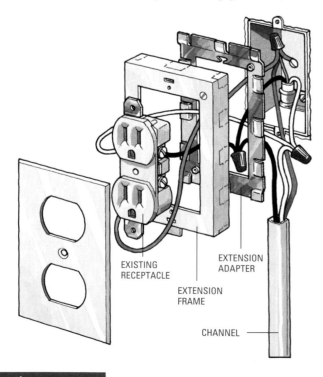

EXISTING RECEPTACLE

EXTENSION ADAPTER

EXTENSION FRAME

CHANNEL

Attach an extension frame to ceiling-fixture base plate with screws.

Join fixture leads to raceway wire with wire connectors, then screw fixture to extension frame.

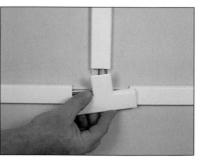

Finish all trim channel joints with variety of trim connecting pieces.

The major appliances that use 240-volt circuits make our lives a lot easier. Clothes dryers, water heaters, ranges, wall-mounted ovens, counter-mounted cooking units, and air conditioners have become indispensable components of our comfortable lives. If you need another 240-volt appliance and your service panel has the space and the amperage to handle it, don't let working with 240 volts scare you.

If you can wire a 120-volt circuit, you already have the skills to wire a 240-volt circuit. A 3-wire 240-volt circuit will have 120-volts each from the "A" and "B" legs to "N", and 240-volts between "A" leg and "B" leg. A 2-wire 240-volt circuit for an appliance that does not need the neutral wire will have 240-volts between "A" leg and "B" leg. When you run wires and hook up breakers and receptacles, the techniques are very similar.

Three-wire and four-wire receptacles

It won't take you long to discover that the receptacle for your electric range does not look the same as the one for your electric clothes dryer. For one thing, the socket holes are different. You can't plug a 50-amp range into a 30-amp dryer receptacle, or vice versa.

Some 240-volt appliances such as air conditioners and water heaters need 240 volts only. Other appliances, like electric ranges and dryers, need both 240-volt and 120-volt power in a single receptacle. A range, for example, requires 240 volts for high heat but might require only 120 volts for lower settings. And any built-in timers or lights would use only 120 volts. As you can see, the needs of the appliance involved affect how many wires a circuit should have and therefore which receptacle you must use.

A water heater on the other hand only needs straight 240-volt power. Typically a two-wire with ground cable

will be used. In this case, the white wire is allowed to be used as a hot wire as long as it is re-identified with black tape. The black wire and the re-identified white wires are connected to the water heater's hot terminals, and the ground wire is connected to the water heater's grounding terminal.

A 120/240-volt dryer or range receptacle needs three wires and a ground wire to complete its circuit. In this case, four wires, black, red, white and a ground wire, are brought into a four-terminal receptacle. The two hot wires are connected to the two hot terminals. The white wire is connected to the neutral terminal. The ground wire from the service panel is attached to a pigtail from the receptacle and a pigtail to the grounding screw at the back of the box. This is all there is to wiring a four-wire, 120/240-volt dryer or range receptacle.

Wiring at subpanel

The feeder from a service panel to a subpanel will always be a four-wire circuit. Two insulated hot wires, an insulated neutral wire, and an insulated or bare equipment grounding wire depending on if you use plastic-sheathed cable, plastic conduit, or metal conduit.

Unlike the service panel where the neutral bar is bonded to the panel enclosure and the equipment grounding bar, the neutral bar must never be bonded in a subpanel. The neutral bar is installed on plastic spacers to insulate it from the grounded metal enclosure. If the neutral was bonded at the subpanel, then normal operating current that should only travel through the insulated neutral wire back to the service would also travel on the bare equipment grounding wires and other grounded metallic surfaces, thereby creating a shock hazard.

Installing a 240-volt breaker

To install a 240-volt breaker, shut off the main disconnect breaker and bring the circuit cable into the panel. Fasten it with a cable connector. Then strip the sheathing from all but about ½ inch of the cable, and connect the ground and neutral wires to their respective bars. Snap the circuit breaker into place. Connect the black wire and the red wire to the breaker terminals. Replace the panel cover.

A 240-volt breaker has two terminal screws; attach red hot wire to one and black hot wire to other.

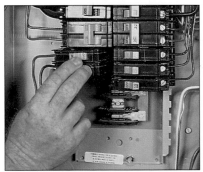

Once circuit wires are attached to the breaker, push breaker into hot bus bar.

Running 240-volt cables
Heavy-duty circuits require larger wire, such as No. 8 or No. 6. When several of these larger wires are contained in a single cable, that cable is very stiff. In some situations, it is too stiff to be pulled through drilled joists. To accommodate this problem, the NEC allows No. 8 and larger cable to be secured directly to the lower edges of joists or on running boards nailed to the open joists. Smaller cables are required to be installed through bored holes, and larger cables are permitted to be secured as stated. In either situation, the NEC wants to ensure that the cables are protected from physical damage.

A 240-volt window air conditioner receptacle

A 120/240-volt dryer receptacle

A 120/240-volt range receptacle

Wiring to 120-volt appliances

While fixed appliances like dishwashers, trash compactors, and garbage disposers are sometimes found on kitchen-appliance circuits, they should have their own circuits. And so should refrigerators. The same is true of microwave ovens, sump pumps, and garage door openers.

So much for the ideal. The truth is, many older homes simply do not have enough room in their service panels for so many circuits.

The NEC allows waste disposers, built-in dishwashers, and trash compactors to be connected with flexible cords. Also, in some situations, a dishwasher and a disposer can share a circuit, but dedicated circuits are preferable. Basically, the rating of any one cord-and-plug-connected appliance should not exceed 80 percent of the circuit rating. The rating of an appliance that is fastened in place should not exceed 50 percent of the circuit rating where other loads are also supplied by the same circuit.

Wiring a disposer

If you are installing a garbage disposer in a sink that has not previously had one, you will have to bring power to a new disconnect switch and then into the sink cabinet. A 14/2 with ground cable will give you the number of wires and the amperage you need.

Start in the panel to make sure you have the expansion room to support another appliance. The first step is to bring cable from the panel to the wall behind the sink. If the basement is open, simply run from the panel directly to the sink wall and drill up through the bottom wall plate. If your house doesn't have a basement, you'll have to approach the job from the attic. Once in the attic, the cable can travel directly to the sink area and fish down into the wall cavity through the wall's top plate.

Next, cut a hole for a cut-in switch box in the sink wall and pull the cable through this hole. Then fish a second cable from the sink cabinet to the switch box opening. With both cables through the hole, slide them into the box and mount the box in the wall. Splice the neutral wires together and fasten the

black wires to the single-pole switch terminals. Then join the ground wires and two grounding pigtails together with a wire connector, with one pigtail to the grounding screw at the back of the box and one to the ground screw on the switch. Attach the switch to the box and install a coverplate.

With the switch installed, go into the sink cabinet and slide flexible metal conduit over the cable from the disposer to the wall. The conduit should stick through the wall a little and be fastened to the disposer with a conduit connector. Inside the disposer housing, you will find a black stranded wire, a white stranded wire, and a ground screw. Attach the ground wire from the cable to the ground screw in the disposer. Next, use wire connectors to join the black cable wire and the black disposer lead. Then join the white wires the same way. Finally, fold the wires and connectors into the disposer housing and fasten the coverplate over the opening. Then hang the disposer from the bottom of the sink, install a 15-amp breaker in the service panel, and test the disposer.

Wiring a dishwasher

The method used to wire a dishwasher is similar to that used for a disposer, including a disconnecting means within sight of the appliance. Start by bringing 14/2 with ground cable through the wall or floor of the dishwasher cabinet. Because the cable will be hidden under the dishwasher and out of reach, you will not need to encase it in flexible conduit. Simply bring it into the cabinet space so that it is long enough to reach the front of the dishwasher. Slide the dishwasher into place, level the legs, and secure its brackets to the countertop. Then remove the access panel and complete the plumbing connections.

With everything else connected, remove the plate from the electrical box containing the lead wires. Bring the stripped cable into the box and fasten it with a cable connector. Then join the dishwasher leads to the like-colored cable wires with wire connectors. Attach the cable ground wire to the grounding screw in the box. Replace the box cover and the front access panel of the dishwasher. Then install a 15-amp breaker in the service panel.

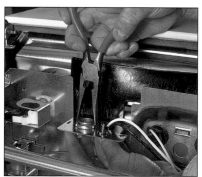

Install a cable connector in dishwasher electrical box and slide cable through connector.

Install a conduit connector on the bottom of the disposer, then attach flexible conduit.

Join like-colored wires with wire connectors and attach ground wire to disposer grounding screw.

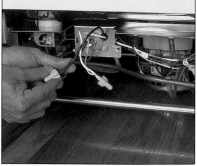

Join cable wires to dishwasher leads with wire connectors; attach ground wire to ground screw.

Installing an attic fan

Attics hold an incredible amount of heat in the summer. Temperatures that can easily exceed 150°F are not much affected by simple louvers and vents. Very high attic temperatures put an extra load on your home's cooling system and, in extreme cases, can damage roofing and plywood sheathing.

The solution is as simple as installing a power-exhaust attic fan. A thermostatically controlled model will make your home more comfortable in summer while protecting your roof and saving you a lot on your cooling bill.

Selecting a fan

An attic fan simply pulls cooler air through soffit and gable vents into the attic and exhausts the hot air to the outside. When shopping for an attic fan, make sure you buy one with a high enough CFM (cubic feet per minute) rating. Your dealer should be able to help you select a size to fit your needs. If you prefer making your own estimates, multiply your attic's square footage by 0.7. The total will give you the CFM rating you need. If your roof shingles are black or very dark, add 10 to 15 percent to the CFM total.

Mounting a fan

Start by going into your attic and locating the best spot to install the fan. Choose a rafter or truss space near the center of your home and about 3 feet down from the peak of the roof, usually on the side opposite the street. Then measure for the center of the space and drill a small pilot hole through the sheathing and shingles from the inside **(1)**.

With the pilot hole made, take a sabre saw, a utility knife, and the fan up on the roof. Center the fan housing over the pilot hole and slide it to a position that requires cutting the fewest number of shingles. The top two-thirds of the flashing on the fan is designed to slide under the shingles and the bottom one-third will fit on top of the shingles. To do this, you may need to slide a hacksaw blade under some of the shingles and cut a few nails.

Mark the top and bottom positions of the flashing lightly with the knife and then set the fan aside. The directions that come with the fan will indicate the size and position of the hole that must be cut in the roof. If your fan comes with a template, use it.

Once the correct hole location is established, use a sharp knife to cut the shingles away. With the shingles and roofing felt removed, use a sabre saw to cut through the sheathing **(2)**.

Slide the upper part of the flashing under the shingles. Then carefully lift the shingles and nail the flashing at each side so that the nails are under the shingles. While the bottom of the flashing is still loose, coat the underside with plastic roofing compound. Also coat the underside of any shingles that lie on the flashing. Then nail the bottom of the flashing over the shingles **(3)**.

To get power to the fan, start by screwing the thermostat to a rafter or truss near the peak. Then run flexible conduit over to the fan motor.

The easiest way to get power to the thermostat is to tap into an existing circuit in the attic either inside a pull-chain light-fixture box or by installing a junction box next to a cable. (A cable that serves an attached garage is often a good candidate.) Simply shut off the power to the circuit you've chosen and bring a 14/2 with ground cable from the thermostat to the light fixture or junction box. Once inside the box, tie the like-colored wires together with wire connectors.

Return to the thermostat and join the white cable and white fan lead together with a wire connector. Do the same with all the ground wires. Then join one lead from the thermostat to the black lead coming from the power source with a wire connector. Join the other thermostat lead to the black wire going to the fan with a wire connector. Put the coverplate on the thermostat box and the junction box, if you installed one. Or reinstall the light fixture if one was used. Turn on the power and check your work.

1 Drill up through roof at center of rafter space

2 Cut through roof sheathing with sabre saw

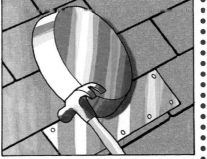

3 Slide fan into place and nail flashing

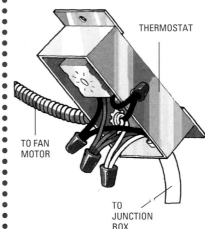

THERMOSTAT

TO FAN MOTOR

TO JUNCTION BOX

Temperature adjustments
Inside the thermostat box, you will see a set screw pointer on a dial. By turning this screw, you set the temperature at which the fan will come on. Try 90°F as a starting temperature. The fan will automatically shut off when the attic temperature drops 10°. If you find that the fan runs continuously, adjust the setting for a little higher startup temperature.

Installing a bathroom fan

Building codes typically require that your bathroom must have either a window that opens or an exhaust fan. Even if you have two windows offering cross-ventilation, a fan is a good idea. The reason is that building materials and high concentrations of moisture do not get along. Excess moisture causes paint to peel and can cause wood to rot. Moisture tends to warp cabinet doors. It can also fill a bathroom with mold spores, which are a common cause of serious health problems.

Exhaust fans come in a variety of styles with a choice of features. A simple exhaust fan is easiest to install and supply with power, but a fan/light combinations and fan/heater combinations offer greater utility in a single unit. In many cases, you will be able to install fan/light combination in place of an existing overhead light fixture, thereby saving a light and adding a fan. If your bathroom feels cold when you step out of the tub, a fan/heater combination can help take the chill out of the air.

The kind of fan you choose depends first on your needs, of course. But structural constraints will play a role, too. If you cannot run a three-wire cable from an existing switch to the fan location without going through a lot of trouble, it might be better to settle for a simple fan or fan/light combination. Plan out your wiring before you buy any unit.

Installing a fan switch box

Determine best spot for switch, then trace box onto wall.

Cut box hole and fish cable from fan and power source.

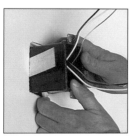

Slide cables into cut-in box and push box into hole.

Fan/light/heater installations

A combination fan/light/heater unit will require five wires (one neutral wire, three switched hot wires, and a grounding wire). One 14/3 and one 14/2 cable (or three 14/2 cables) will be needed between the switch unit and the combination fan/light/heater unit. You could also install flexible metal conduit with individual insulated wires (one white neutral wire, one green grounding wire, and three black switched hot wires. Fortunately, combination fan/light/heater units usually come with special switches that control all three operations in one switch unit.

Venting the fan

The way you vent your bathroom fan is important. When improperly vented, condensation will form and run back into the ceiling, causing stains and ruining drywall. The best way to vent a fan is to connect listed flexible insulated duct between the fan and the soffit vent. Flexible insulated duct is easy to cut and bend and slips easily into tight spaces. When in a horizontal position, condensation is not likely to run back into the ceiling.

Another method is to cut a vent into the roof and vent the fan through an insulated vertical exhaust duct. This method is acceptable but includes several pitfalls. One potential trouble spot is the flashing. Cutting into an existing roof is always a risk; anything less than a perfect seal will leak, maybe not always, but whenever there is a driving rain. Secondly, with the vent duct in a vertical position, condensation can run straight back into the fan and ceiling. When you have a choice, vent horizontally to a soffit by using either flexible insulated duct or insulated sheet metal duct and fittings.

Fan or fan/light installation

If you use the switch loop from an existing light to control a new fan/light unit, both the fan and the light will go on when you flip the switch. Start by shutting off the power to the circuit and removing the old fixture and ceiling box. Then measure carefully and cut the ceiling to accept the fan housing. Fasten the housing to the ceiling joists and bring the existing wiring into the housing. If the fan and light are not factory installed in the housing, install these components and plug each into its receptacle.

Then connect the switch wires to the fan/light unit leads with wire connectors and attach the ground wire to the grounding screw in the box. Finally, install the light diffuser and decorative cover and restore power to the circuit.

If separate switches for the fan and light are important to you, then you will have to run a three-wire with ground cable between the switch box and the new fan/light unit and install a double switch in the switch box. The wiring between the switch box and the fan/light unit will include a white neutral wire, a grounding wire, and two switched hot wires, one for the fan and one for the light.

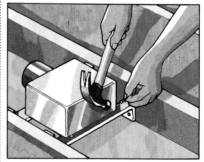

Anchor fan housing into ceiling from above

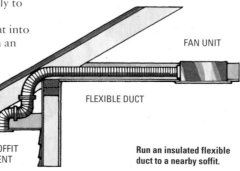

FAN UNIT

FLEXIBLE DUCT

SOFFIT VENT

Run an insulated flexible duct to a nearby soffit.

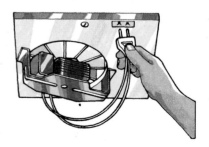

Mount fan and plug it in

Indirect lighting can be installed anywhere you feel like putting it, provided NEC minimum clearances are observed. The four most common ways to hide indirect lights are behind a cornice board, valance, soffit, or cove. In each case, you will build a trough to hide the fixture. You can be as creative as you wish, but remember to leave enough clearance so that the enclosure is not trapping too much heat and is accessible for maintenance.

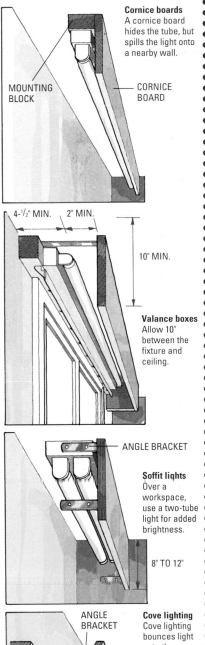

Cornice boards
A cornice board hides the tube, but spills the light onto a nearby wall.

MOUNTING BLOCK

CORNICE BOARD

4-1/2" MIN.   2" MIN.

10" MIN.

Valance boxes
Allow 10" between the fixture and ceiling.

ANGLE BRACKET

Soffit lights
Over a workspace, use a two-tube light for added brightness.

8" TO 12"

ANGLE BRACKET

Cove lighting
Cove lighting bounces light onto the ceiling, into the room.

10" MIN.

Architects are taught to think of lighting not only as a tool of daily living but as a part of a home's design. Today, lighting manu-facturers are directing more and more of their energies to fixtures that can create dramatic effects.

Even with all the technical advancements available to you, some of the most creative lighting techniques can still be created with inexpensive fixtures, common materials, and a little imagination. You can change the entire mood of a room by hiding a few lights behind coves and valances and letting them spill soft lighting onto ceilings or down from cabinets. The idea of indirect lighting is not to flood a room with light, but to direct attention toward or away from some feature of a room. If you would like your lighting to do more, consider the indirect approach.

Choosing the right fixtures

Fluorescent fixtures are the most commonly used in indirect lighting. They produce soft white light without glare or hot spots. They also produce very little heat and so can be installed in tight spaces. Fluorescent lights come in a variety of sizes that can be easily adapted to any length of cove, soffit, valance, or ceiling recess.

Wiring indirect lighting

Another advantage of fluorescent fixtures is that they can easily be ganged together and wired in sequence. Just mount the fixtures end-to-end or spaced apart as desired, and connect them together with chase nipples, close nipples, Type NM cable, or flexible metal conduit as needed. Connect the white neutral wires and black hot wires to the factory fixture wiring as per the installation instructions. Be sure to ground each fixture with a bare or green equipment grounding wire run with the white and black wires. With the fixtures wired together, switch the entire series with a single-pole switch located in a convenient spot.

Installing an undercabinet light

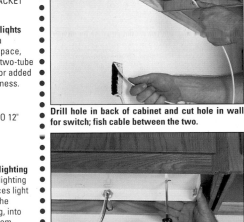

Drill hole in back of cabinet and cut hole in wall for switch; fish cable between the two.

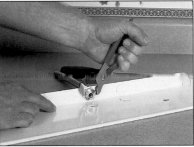

To protect cable until it goes into wall, attach short length of flexible conduit to back of fixture.

Attach fixture channel to underside of cabinet with one screw at each end.

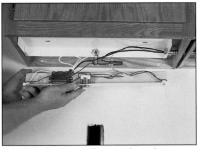

Join switch wires to fixture wires, then mount fixture in channel.

Installing a ceiling fan

If you're tired of looking at that old, outdated ceiling fixture and you'd prefer a ceiling fan/light combination, don't be intimidated by the prospect of installing one yourself. There are a lot of models to choose from in a wide price range. But all are installed in a similar way.

Many people use these fans to keep a room cool in the summer. But they can be almost as effective for keeping a room warm in the winter by circulating the warm air that tends to hover near the ceiling.

You need to beef up the support for the ceiling box so it can safely handle the weight of the fan. Code requires either a 2 x 4 brace nailed between joists to support the box, or an approved box with a bracket designed to carry the weight.

Access to the box from above makes a 2 x 4 block the simpler option. Just pull the insulation away from the box, cut a 2 x 4 to fit tightly between the joists, and nail it in place. Then go below and screw the box securely to the block.

If you don't have access from above and must come through the box hole in the room's ceiling, then use the bracket box. These units are designed to fit through a ceiling-box opening. To install one, you first remove the existing box, then insert the circuit wires into the box and push the box with the bracket into the joist cavity. Once in the cavity, you turn the mounting bar from below and sharp prongs are driven into the joist. Installed properly, the bracket can support the fan.

Hanging the fan

Begin by installing the fan mounting plate that comes with the fan. Use 4-inch-long wood screws, and drive them through the mounting plate and the ceiling box into the support block nailed between the joists. Pull the switch wires through the hole in the mounting plate. If the fan mounting plate does not already have a factory installed support hook, then fabricate a temporary hook from coat hanger wire and hang it from the plate, making sure it is strong enough to temporarily support the fan.

Lift the fan assembly onto the hook and join the black wire to the black fixture lead with a wire connector. Do the same with both white wires. Join the two ground wires to a grounding pigtail and attach the pigtail to the grounding screw in the ceiling box.

Remove the temporary support hook and push the fan canopy over the mounting plate. Then screw the canopy to the plate. Because these screws are what hold the fan in place, make sure they are tight. With the fan assembly in place, mount each fan blade on its metal bracket and then mount the brackets on the fan.

If your fan came with a light kit, remove the cap on the bottom of the fan housing to access the light wires. Pull down the white neutral wire and the black hot wire. Next attach the light-kit adapter ring , supplied with the fan, to the fan housing. Lift the light fixture close to the fan and make the wire connections. Join white to white, and black to black, with wire connectors.

Fasten the light fixture to the fan with the screws provided and install the bulbs in the fixture. To avoid a fire hazard, always use the bulbs recommended by the fixture manufacturer.

Remove mounting screws to existing light fixture and pull down fixture; remove wires.

Remove insulation from around box and cut 2 x 4 block to fit between joists; nail it into joists.

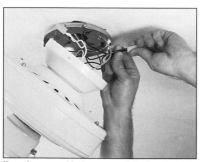

Hang fan assembly from mounting plate and join fan leads to power cable leads.

Drive screws through mounting plate and ceiling box into support block until plate is tight to ceiling.

Attach fan securely to mounting plate, then install fan blades on mounting brackets.

Drive 1½-inch-long wood screws through fixture box and into support block.

Installing outdoor lighting

If you can do your own wiring inside your house, you can certainly do it outside too. The principles are the same. Because outdoor wiring is exposed to all kinds of weather, it must be impervious to water. It must also be resistant to the effects of extreme hot and cold temperatures. Knowing how to work with these materials is most of what you need to know to run electricity outdoors.

Connecting to the house circuits

You can bring indoor electricity outside with one of two exterior fittings:

90° fittings

If you are starting with a new circuit in the breaker panel or tapping into an existing circuit with a junction box, the fitting you will use to get through the house wall will be an LB conduit fitting. An LB allows you to come through an exterior wall and make a 90-degree turn along the wall. It is threaded on each end to accept conduit adapters or pipe nipples. Because it creates a 90-degree turn, its front can be removed so that you can help the wires make the turn. The coverplate for this opening fits over a rubber gasket, which makes the conduit fitting watertight.

An LB is always installed between two pieces of conduit. In some cases, an LB might fit back-to-back with a junction box just inside the wall.

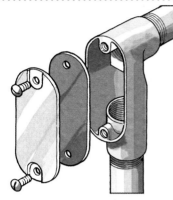

An LB allows you to wire at a 90° angle.

Generally, splices are not permitted inside conduit bodies, so the conversion between cabled wire and individual wire should be made inside the junction box. If you want to exit a basement wall below ground level, use a junction box mounted to the inside wall, then run conduit through the wall. Conduit bodies must always remain accessible.

Extension boxes

If you are tapping into an outside outlet or light fixture, you will not need an LB. Instead you can sandwich a weatherproof extension box between the receptacle or fixture and its outlet box.

To install an extension box, shut the power off, remove the coverplate and receptacle or fixture, and pull the wires out of the box. Then screw the extension box to the outlet box mounted in the wall. Bring the conduit into the extension box and pull the conduit wires through the opening so that you can work on them comfortably. Connect all the same-colored wires to pigtails with plastic connectors. Attach the pigtails to the receptacle or fixture.

An LB and a junction box, back-to-back

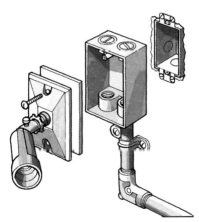

Tapping an existing light or receptacle

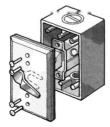

Features of a switch with an external lever

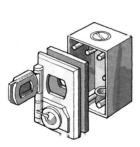

Features of an outdoor receptacle box

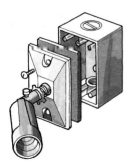

Features of an outdoor floodlight box

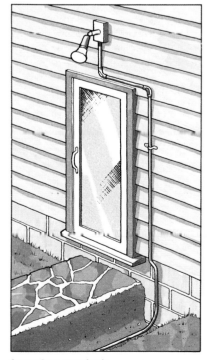

Connecting a new circuit
A box extender and metal conduit

Working beyond the house

All outdoor wiring must be protected from physical damage. All fixtures and boxes, including switch and receptacle boxes, must be weatherproof and rated for exterior use. And all floodlights and their sockets must be rated for exterior use. As long as you satisfy these requirements, the improvements you make can be as varied as your outdoor needs. In general, burial depths for different wiring methods are as follows: 1) Type UF cable or other suitable direct buried cables (24 in.), 2) PVC conduit (10 in.), 3) rigid metal conduit (6 in.), and 4) approved low-voltage landscape lighting cables (6 in.). Electrical metallic tubing (thin-wall conduit) is not permitted to be used for direct burial installations without corrosion protection.

Outdoor receptacles

A weatherproof receptacle cover

Installing outdoor receptacles

If you cut your grass with an electric mower, or if you need an electric trimmer to reach under a backyard fence, you should consider installing receptacles nearer your work. All you need is a few weatherproof receptacle boxes, both Schedule 40 and Schedule 80 plastic, conduit, type UF cable, and the willingness to dig a trench between your house and the new receptacle locations.

Once you know where you plan to access the power from inside the house, mark this location on the outside of the foundation wall. Then drive a stake in the ground at this point and another where you want your first outdoor receptacle and stretch a string between the two. If you want more receptacles, run a string between each location.

Begin digging the trench by using a spade to cut the sod about 4 inches deep and 12 inches across. (If you do a neat job of cutting the sod, when you replace it, your lawn will look much better.) Once cut, dig up the sod and pile it on one side of the trench. Continue digging until the trench is 18 inches deep along its entire length. To protect your lawn, pile the loose dirt on a tarp placed on the opposite side of the trench from where you piled the sod.

With the ditch ready, run Schedule 40 plastic conduit between the house and the receptacle locations. Cut the conduit with a hacksaw. At every receptacle location, sweep the conduit up out of the ground with pre-molded bends called "factory elbows." Then use another elbow to re-enter the ditch

in the direction of the next receptacle. Factory elbows are connected with glue. Plastic conduit that transitions from below ground to above ground will need to be Schedule 80, which is heavy duty conduit.

With the conduit in place, install a weatherproof junction box on each set of two risers. Use plastic fittings that glue or screw into the box and glue the fittings to the conduit risers. The plastic conduit cannot be used as the sole support for the box—a wood or metal post will need to be installed to support the box.

To secure the conduit risers, or elbows, slide a concrete block over each set of risers and pour concrete into the block cavities. You don't need to wait for the concrete to set. Go ahead and fill in the trench with the loose soil. Tamp the soil with your feet until it is firm, then replace the sod and give it a good watering.

All that remains is to pull the cable through the conduit, install the receptacles and weatherproof in-use type receptacle covers and connect the underground wiring to the circuit in the house.

Other outdoor options

Other electrical options might include a string of landscape lights or a front-yard pole light. The installation of these fixtures does not differ substantially from that of the receptacles described here. The same basic techniques are used to carry power to outbuildings or storage sheds.

Installing a GFCI

Every outdoor receptacle must be protected from ground fault. When installing a new circuit, you might install a GFCI breaker, but when wiring only one box, use a GFCI receptacle. A GFCI receptacle senses any imbalance between the hot and neutral sides of the circuit. When an imbalance occurs, as it does with leakage current to ground through a faulty power tool, the sensing mechanism immediately interrupts the flow of electricity.

If installing an outside receptacle mounted to your house would make your outdoor cooking or lawn and garden work easier, you will be happy to know that the job is not that difficult. In most cases, tapping an existing circuit will work. Before you cut into any wall, however, shut the power off.

Start by finding a receptacle on the inside near where you would like one on the outside. Then take careful measurements and mark the box location on the outside of your home. Hold a cut-in box against the siding and trace around it to mark the cut. To keep the corners neat, drill each with a ¼-inch bit. Drill completely through the siding and the sheathing. Then use a sabre saw to cut the box opening.

With the opening made, probe through it to find the existing box. If insulation is in the way, push it up and away from your work area. Then go back inside and remove the receptacle from the existing box and open a new knockout hole at the bottom of it. Push a short length of cable through the knockout opening until you think you've pushed enough to reach the new box. Then go back outside and pull the cable out through the opening.

With the cable in place and the new box ready to install, pull the insulation back down. Insert the cable through a knockout opening and mount the box in the wall. Install a GFCI receptacle in the box and add an in-use weatherproof cover to keep the rain out.

Supporting the conduit
Fill block cavity with concrete.

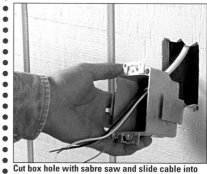

Cut box hole with sabre saw and slide cable into box; push box into hole.

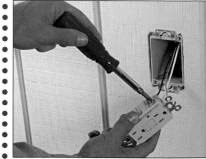

Attach wires to GFCI receptacle, then attach receptacle to box and add watertight coverplate.

Working with conduit

Not many residential electrical improvements will require the use of conduit, but some will, and you should know what is available and how to use it. Conduit is required any time individual wires are run in place of cabled wire. It is also required when a cable or wire is in danger of being cut, torn loose, or stepped on, that is, when it is in harm's way. There are several different types of conduit.

Types of conduit

There are two basic types of conduit or tubing: metal and nonmetallic.

Metal conduit and tubing comes in 10-foot lengths and three wall thicknesses. Rigid metal conduit (RMC) is a heavy-wall conduit. It's difficult to bend without special benders—factory elbows are available to make installation a little easier. It can be cut and threaded, or you can use threadless fittings in some situations. It offers the greatest physical protection for wiring. Intermediate metal conduit (IMC) is very similar to RMC, but it has a thinner wall thickness. Electrical metallic tubing (EMT) is often called thin-wall conduit. There are a multitude of factory elbows and lots of different fittings, but EMT is easily bent with an inexpensive EMT bender—an installation with fewer factory fittings always looks nicer too. RMC and IMC are widely acceptable for direct burial and only need to be buried 6 inches deep. However, EMT is generally not acceptable by many inspectors as being suitable for direct burial without additional corrosion protection.

Flexible metal conduit (FMC) and liquidtight flexible metal conduit (LFMC) are useful for making convenient final connections to appliances or where equipment may vibrate or require re-positioning. FMC

is no longer permitted in wet (outdoor) locations. LFMC is approved for use outdoors and is often used for the connection of air conditioners and other outdoor equipment.

Nonmetallic (plastic) conduit and tubing is very popular and easy to work with. Rigid polyvinyl chloride conduit (PVC) comes in 10-foot lengths and in two varieties: Schedule 40 and heavy-wall Schedule 80. Schedule 40 can be used in trenches and aboveground, but Schedule 80 is required where wiring transitions from underground to above ground to guard against damage from lawn mowers and similar hazards. PCV conduit can be readily bent with a heat gun or similar heat source. Of course, similar to metal conduit, factory elbows and a host of other fittings are available. PVC conduit is glued together with PVC cement. PVC conduit needs to be buried at least 18 inches for underground installations. Other plastic raceways include liquidtight flexible nonmetallic conduit (LFNC) and electrical nonmetallic tubing (ENT).

All raceways have to be installed, supported and secured in accordance with their respective allowances or restrictions in the NEC. To avoid damaging conductors that are installed in raceways be sure to trim or ream all cut ends to remove all rough edges.

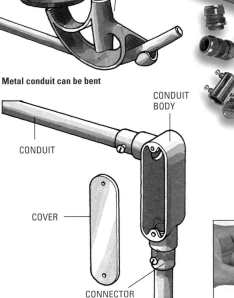

Metal conduit can be bent

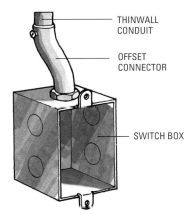

CONDUIT BODY
CONDUIT
COVER
CONNECTOR

Conduit bodies make wiring at right angles easy

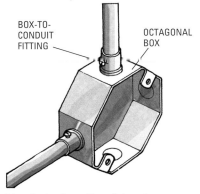

THINWALL CONDUIT
OFFSET CONNECTOR
SWITCH BOX

Offsets keep conduit tight against walls

Attach conduit to box with connector

Pulling elbows with removable covers simplify wiring

Connector joins conduit to panel

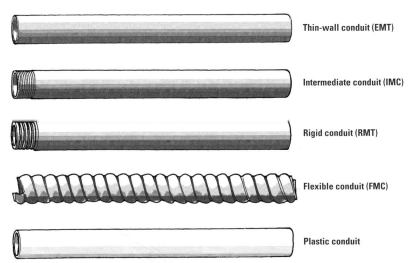

Thin-wall conduit (EMT)

Intermediate conduit (IMC)

Rigid conduit (RMT)

Flexible conduit (FMC)

Plastic conduit

BOX-TO-CONDUIT FITTING
OCTAGONAL BOX

A junction box is used for splicing wires

Installing a floodlight

There's no better way to extend the day than with a house- or garage-mounted floodlight. Aside from offering a measure of security and safety, a floodlight can also improve a wide range of outdoor activities, from backyard barbecues to nighttime dips in the pool, to after-dark driveway basketball games, and even to cooler-temperature, late-night gardening. If none of these ideas appeal to you, rest assured that most of them will appeal to the kids around the house. And to top it all off, floodlights are usually easy to install just about anywhere.

1 Find power source and knock hole in box.

2 Run cable through framing members to switch.

Access to power

In many cases the easiest access to power is through the garage. Unfinished garages make the wiring a breeze, especially if you don't mind having the switch in the garage. If this doesn't work for you, your next best choice is a ceiling fixture on a circuit that has room for another light.

Once you pick your circuit, shut off the power to it and remove the light fixture. Remove one of the knockouts on the side of the box and install 14/2 with ground cable into the box (1). Attach it with a cable connector. Strip the sheathing off the cable and strip

about ⅜ inch of insulation off each wire. Join the black cable wire to the black hot wire in the box with a wire connector. Do the same thing with the neutral cable wire and the neutral box wire. Join the cable ground wire to the other ground wires in the box. Replace the light fixture.

Run the cable to the switch box location and run the same-size cable from the switch location to the floodlight box location. Bore holes through framing members as needed (2), and staple the cable in place at least every 4 feet.

3 Thread plastic nipple to back of floodlight box.

Installing the fixture

Floodlight options
Floodlights take a variety of forms and are installed in a variety of ways. A quick trip to your local home center will reveal several design options. There are traditional fixtures, like the one shown above, and rectangular quartz fixtures. Some mount on the wall, others in the roof soffit, and still others have motion-activated switches. All do have one thing in common, however: they're designed for outdoor installations and so their components are weathertight.

The typical floodlight fixture consists of a metallic weathertight box, two adjustable lamp holders, a rubber weather gasket, and a coverplate. To keep water from entering the box through the cable opening, it's a good idea to install a plastic conduit nipple into the back opening on the box (3).

Drill a hole through the side of the house and pull the switch cable through this hole. Then slide the floodlight box over the cable and push the nipple on the back of the box into the hole. Screw the box to the side

of the house.

To wire the fixture, first join the cable ground wire to the grounding lead on the fixture and to a grounding pigtail with a wire connector. Then attach the pigtail to the grounding screw at the back of the box.

Join the white neutral wire from the cable to one of the fixture leads with a wire connector. Then join the black cable wire to the other fixture lead with a wire connector. Attach the fixture securely to the box (4) and screw in the bulbs.

4 Attach fixture securely to the box.

5 Push cut-in switch box into wall opening.

Connecting the switch

If you are working in an open garage you can use a standard switch box for this job. Just nail it to a stud about 48 inches from the floor. If the switch location is in a closed wall, cut a box hole where you want it and install a cut-in box (5). A closed location will require fishing cable through the wall. Pick the most efficient route that does the least damage.

Feed the cable from the floodlight and from the power source into the box and strip the sheathing from both cables and about ½ inch of insulation

from each wire. Join the ground wires from both cables to a grounding pigtail using a wire connector. Then attach the pigtail to the grounding screw at the back of the box.

Join both white wires in a wire connector. Then hook the black wire from the power source to one switch terminal and the other black wire going to the floodlight to the other switch terminal (6). Screw the switch yoke to the box and install a coverplate. Turn the circuit power on and test the installation.

6 Attach hot leads to switch.

Low-voltage alternatives

Low-voltage wiring was once limited to doorbells and thermostats. Today, however, low-voltage lighting is available in a wide variety of fixtures and systems for general purpose lighting, task lighting, and accent lighting. The reason, of course, is that low-voltage systems give you more light for less money, and rising electric rates have made efficiency an issue. Low-voltage wiring is also safe; the low-voltage circuits are inherently power-limited and do not produce enough energy to be a fire or shock hazard. Also, power supplies often contain integral protection that will de-energize circuits due to overloading or short circuits.

Low-voltage kits

The only way to buy low-voltage components is in kit form. The NEC requires that low-voltage lighting systems shall be listed as a complete system, or assembled from matching, listed parts. When you buy a kit, for example, the transformer size, the length and size of the wire and the number of allowable fixtures are all figured for you.

Contrary to popular opinion, low-voltage systems can start fires when overloaded. Too many fixtures or too long a run can cause low-voltage wires to overheat. When shopping for a system, make sure you buy a transformer with a built-in breaker.

If you don't find exactly what you want in one brand, try another brand or another style: track lighting offers a good illustration of this point. Here's just one example. You can get a fixture that fastens to the ceiling and has a surface cord that runs to a receptacle-mounted transformer. Or you can get a system, the same size and similar style, that has a surface-mounted transformer that ties directly into the ceiling box, so it's not visible from anywhere.

Mushroom light

Installing a transformer

In order to reduce your house current from 120 volts to 12 volts, a transformer is needed. There are several sizes of transformers to meet a variety of needs. Most transformers used in residential wiring are rated at 100 to 300 watts. The greater the rating, the more 100-foot branch circuits can be served. If a transformer is underrated, the lights it serves will not go on or the wire that serves them will overheat.

Transformers for indoor fixtures can be located in a number of places on or near their fixtures. In some fixtures, they can be part of an electronic circuit, similar to that of a stereo. But in many cases, you will fasten the transformer directly to a 120-volt metal outlet box. Just remove a knockout plug and attach the transformer to the box with a clamp. Then fasten the leads from the transformer to pigtail connections inside the box. The low-voltage UF wires can then be tied to the terminals of the transformer.

A transformer designed to be used outdoors, however, must be sealed in its own weathertight box. You can buy transformers with on/off switches built in, or you can use a conventional switch between the outlet and the transformer. The transformer box must be connected to the outlet box with weathertight conduit. Then, from the transformer, low-voltage UF cable should be laid underground to each fixture. Low-voltage fixtures do not need to be grounded, and because they pose no physical threat, do not have to be buried deep or encased in conduit when installed outdoors. But it makes good sense to keep them out of harm's way, if for no other reason than you don't want to have to repair them after they're installed.

Low-voltage fixture connection

Low-voltage connections are made inside protective boxes on indoor lighting fixtures. In some cases, the low-voltage side of the fixture is wired and sealed at the factory. When you install these fixtures, you will only have to wire the 120-volt connection. The

Well light

terminals on the low-voltage side of a transformer can remain exposed provided the transformer is not covered by drywall or otherwise concealed.

All outdoor connections must be made in weathertight boxes. This can be done the conventional way with binding screws or with special low-voltage connectors. These connectors use screw-and-clamp devices. The cable is placed in a slot and the clamp is screwed down over it. As the clamp tightens, it pierces the cable, making contact with the wires inside. In this case, you do not even have to cut the wire at the fixture. Both connections are code approved.

Deck light

Spot light

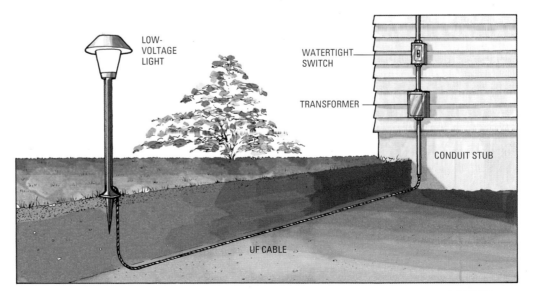

LOW-VOLTAGE LIGHT

WATERTIGHT SWITCH

TRANSFORMER

CONDUIT STUB

UF CABLE

Installing low-voltage outdoor lights

When it comes to electrical projects, installing low-voltage outdoor lighting is as easy as it gets. These kits are much less expensive to buy and operate than their 120-volt counterparts. For example, a six-head system uses about the same energy as a single 100-watt lightbulb. And the complicated weather protection and shock prevention measures required for outdoor 120-volt systems are almost entirely absent. Low-voltage wires don't even need to be buried deeply; a few inches is all that's necessary.

Installing cable and fixtures

First determine the layout you want and mark the cable route. Do this from the transformer location to the last light. Then use a spade or flat-blade shovel to cut a slice into the ground about 5 inches deep. Push the shovel back and forth to create a V-shaped trench. Lay the cable into the trench, and wherever it sticks up, push it down with a wooden stick. There's really no depth requirement for 12-volt cable. But a couple of inches deep offers the cable some protection and keeps it from being a tripping hazard.

The light fixtures come in different styles. The ones shown here are very common. Each consists of a stake, a riser pipe, and a lamp head. Each lamp head has a lead cable that passes through the riser and is fitted with a cable-piercing connector.

To install the fixture, first drive the stake into the ground a couple of inches away from the cable. Make sure the stake is plumb, otherwise the lights, especially if they're lined up in a row, will look sloppy. Then slide the lamp head onto the riser tube and join the two with the set screw on the riser. Take this assembly and attach it to the stake, again by tightening a set screw.

Drive stake into ground

Connect lamp head to riser

Wiring the transformer

The transformer needs to be installed next to an outdoor receptacle. In most cases, all you have to do is screw the transformer box to the house wall and plug it into the receptacle. But systems do vary, so follow the instructions that came with your unit.

Next, bring the low-voltage cable up to the bottom of the transformer box and cut it to length. Split the last 2 inches of cable in two and strip about ½ inch of insulation off each wire. Crimp a ring connector (usually provided with the kit) onto the end of each wire. Then hook these connectors onto the transformer terminals. Install the transformer cover.

Attach ring connectors to ends of cable wires

Attach cable-wire connectors to transformer

Shopping for lights

You'll find a lot of different low-voltage lighting products at your local home center and quite a range of prices too. But after you work through all the noise and clutter, you'll probably find just two basic product categories wherever you shop. At the low end are the familiar packaged kits, consisting of a transformer, cable, and six to eight plastic light heads. The head designs may vary and some kits come with light sensors that can automatically turn on your lights, but most of the difference is only cosmetic. These kits are a snap to install and are very durable.

Your other option is an a la carte mix of listed fixtures and components from the same manufacturer. When you buy individual components you may pay more for a customized system, but the fixtures usually look great, the lights are generally brighter, and you often have a bigger selection of styles.

Wiring fixtures

To make the fixture and cable connections, begin by checking that the cable lead from the fixture rests in its slot at the base of the riser. Then expose several inches of buried cable and lay it across the connector fitting on the end of the cable lead. Thread the fitting cap onto the fitting. As the cap is turned down, it pushes the cable into two sharp prongs that pierce the cable and the contact wires.

Make sure lead cable fits in riser slot

Lay cable in connector and tighten cap

Installing track lighting

How you chose to light each room in your house can go a long way toward creating enjoyable and functional living spaces. While there are many lighting options out there, one of the most versatile is track lighting. In this system individual lamps, or heads as they're often called, are attached to tracks mounted on the ceiling. Because the tracks can be installed practically anywhere, you can place them where they'll do the most good. And because the lamps are designed to move along the tracks, you can easily vary the light intensity in different parts of the room. You can also change the lighting arrangement at the drop of a hat, to accommodate new requirements or just to try something new.

Installing the tracks

First, study the layout of your room and decide on the best placement for your track sections. Plan on the first track to start at an existing light fixture. This will be the power source for the tracks. Keep in mind that all the lamps can be adjusted in any direction to provide general room illumination and specific task lighting.

Start by shutting off the power to the ceiling fixture and removing the fixture from the ceiling box. Remove the existing fixture mounting strap from the box and replace it with the one that came with your system. Then slide a feed connector into the first piece of track.

The track is held to the ceiling with toggle bolts. The toggle bolts require holes in the ceiling that are big enough for the expanding spring clamps to fit through. To locate these holes, hold the track in place and mark the bolt holes on the ceiling. Then remove the track and drill the holes.

Install the toggles in the track holes, hold the track up near the ceiling, and squeeze the spring clips so they can fit through the holes. Tighten the bolts most of the way but leave some room for adjustment. Repeat this process for the other tracks. When all are joined, finish tightening all the toggle bolts.

Install connectors in ends of track.

Hang tracks from ceiling with toggle bolts.

Once all tracks are assembled, draw bolts tight.

Choosing your lights
The clearest choices in track lighting systems focus on the head design. Some have small, unobtrusive can-shaped heads. Others have large, high-tech lamps that lend drama to a room, even when they're turned off. A quick trip to a lighting showroom will provide you with options that can fit any room and any budget.

Wiring and light heads

With all the tracks assembled and secured to the ceiling, attach the wires that power the system. Connect the black and white wires from the ceiling box to the feed connector on the first piece of track. The black wire goes to the brass screw and the white wire goes to the silver screw. Attach the ground wire to the grounding screw on the connector. Push the feed connector cover over the end of the track and the bottom of the ceiling box and attach it.

To install the first lamp, push the top of the fixture into the track with the lamp contacts parallel to the length of the track. Rotate the fixture a quarter of a turn, so its polarity arrow points to the polarity line on the track. You should hear the lamp click into place. Each lamp has a switch. Turn it on before installing the next lamp.

When all the lamps are installed, turn on the circuit power at the service panel and turn on the wall switch. If any of the lamps don't light, first check if the switch on the lamp is turned on. Also check that the lamp is properly seated in the track. When everything is working, adjust the lamps to provide illumination exactly where you want it. And don't be afraid to experiment with new arrangements. That's the beauty of this system.

Screw feed connector to track light strap.

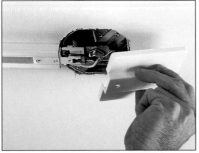
Install cover over feed connector and box.

Insert lamp in track and rotate to lock in place.

Installing a garage-door opener

Overhead garage doors can be dangerous things. Just ask emergency room attendants about crushed fingers. These injuries occur when people try closing sectional garage doors by sticking their fingers into the gap between panels and pulling down. Naturally, the gap closes. Electric garage-door openers solved this problem, but created another: serious injuries to children who have been trapped under doors when the openers bring them down.

Because of these injuries, door-opener manufacturers have made real strides in safety. Auto-reversing mechanisms are now standard. As soon as the door hits anything above floor level it automatically reverses. And openers now come with infrared sensor units that are installed just above the floor. When the infrared beam between the units is interrupted by an object or a person, the door stops automatically and then reverses.

Controls

When shopping for a garage-door opener, you'll find many control options. In addition to operating the power unit and the light fixture (both manually and remotely), some systems allow you to hard-wire a passage door so the light comes on for 5 minutes after the passage door is opened. The options you choose will dictate how the unit is wired. Follow the manufacturer's instructions carefully.

Even though specifics change, the general approach is fairly consistent. Current to the power unit comes via a power cord that's plugged into a ceiling-mounted receptacle. The infrared sensors are mounted just above the floor, where the door comes down, and are joined to the power unit with a low-voltage cable. The power unit is controlled by remote units and by a fixed, keypad control unit that's usually mounted on a wall in the garage.

Hanging the opener

Preliminary considerations
With redundant safety mechanisms built in, there is little chance that a door opener will cause serious injury or damage. That's the good news. The bad news is that equipment that's designed to be sensitive requires careful adjustment and a good door that works properly. If your garage door could use some adjustment, consider calling a professional door-repair technician before installing a new opener. Door adjustments are not as easy as they look and they can be dangerous if not done properly.

The first step in the installation process is to assemble the opener components according to the manufacturer's instructions. Then you must establish the center of the door opening and hang the support bracket on the door header at this center point. Once the bracket is in place, lift the idler-arm assembly into the bracket and secure it with a locking pin.

Lift up the power unit and idler-arm assembly and rest it on top of a step-ladder. Then fabricate a support bracket for the power unit using perforated angle iron. There are a number of reasonable support hanger designs. One good one is to attach a 3-foot-long 2 x 4 block to the ceiling using 4-inch-long wood screws driven into the joists above. Then attach two angle-iron support legs to the block using ¼-inch lagbolts.

Lift the power unit up and attach it to these hangers using the hardware supplied with the opener. To keep the power unit from twisting during operation, install a diagonal brace made of angle-iron between the two support legs.

Attach the door to the traveler arm that's connected to the opener. Then check that all the bolts joining the door panels are tight. Do the same with all the hardware that's supporting the door tracks. Once the power is hooked up, test the door operation to make sure it's working properly.

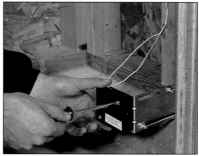
Attach infrared sensors to brackets mounted on wall studs next to garage door.

Slide the traveler assembly onto the end of the track tube about 40 inches from the power unit.

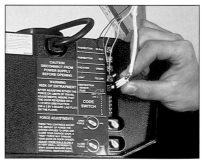
Attach the low-voltage cables from both infrared sensors to the back of the power unit.

Carefully slide the capped end of the track tube into the bracket on top of the power unit.

Bring the chain around the drive sprocket on the power unit, making sure all links are engaged.

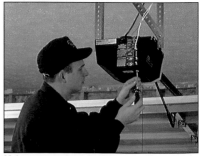
Make any necessary performance adjustments by turning screws at the back of the power unit.

Home office planning

Working from home has become a practical option for a great many people. And even those who commute to the office usually need someplace at home where they can catch up on extra work and sort through personal papers. Homework and hobbies can put the younger members of the family in a similar position.

Increasingly, these activities are centered on a computer and a network of other electronic equipment. Whether you make do with a corner of the dining room table or have the luxury of a dedicated workspace, some planning—and maybe new wiring—will avoid a tangle of wires and some severely overloaded receptacles.

To assess the number and the locations of the receptacles, first plan your office layout to make the best use of the space available. Think about where your desk or worktable should be. You will probably want to take advantage of natural light—but before you make any permanent alterations, try out the position of your computer monitor to avoid reflections from windows and fixed lighting.

Even the most sophisticated computer is of limited use without some accessory equipment.

You'll need a printer for any number of things, from old-fashioned correspondence that you still send by snail mail, to recording and filing information of interest that you downloaded from the Internet. And you may want a scanner for putting your own photos and graphics onto the computer so you can send them to friends and family by e-mail.

But a printer and scanner only scratch the surface of the world of computer peripherals. CD burners, DVD burners, video game hardware for the kids, external hard drives, and more are all waiting to clog your workspace. The list goes on and on.

The cable jungle

Each new piece of equipment needs a power supply and a connection to the computer—which is why so many home offices end up with a tangle of wires and overloaded receptacles.

To reduce the number of cables, you could get a new computer with more of this extra stuff already installed. But if you're not in the market for one right now, consider adding some more receptacles to the room. If your home office is directly above a basement, adding the new outlets and the wiring that connects them isn't very hard, expensive, or time consuming. And if your office is on the second floor, under an attic, the job isn't much more difficult. Just run a cable from the service panel directly to the attic. Then fish the cable down to the receptacles.

Also consider installing surge protectors on any receptacle that serves a computer. Fluctuations in voltage are not uncommon, and some of these can damage your equipment.

Workstation
Specially made units can greatly improve efficiency.

Lighting your office
Use dedicated task-lighting to illuminate the work area without creating distracting reflections. A portable desk lamp is one option, or you could install a small spotlight above the desk. A dimmer switch that controls the room lighting will allow you to set the best level of light for the time of day or the task at hand.

A place for your computer

Most people can work comfortably on a desk or table that is 28 to 30 inches high. Ideally a computer keyboard should be slightly lower. This is why manufactured computer workstations are usually made with a slide-out keyboard shelf that can be stowed beneath when not in use. Make sure to get a comfortable chair. And if your children are likely to use the same workspace, chose a chair that is adjustable in height.

A work surface needs to be at least 24 inches deep to provide enough room for the average computer and related add-ons. You'll also need extra space for papers and reference books, plus shelves and drawers to store items like stationery, computer disks, and typical office supplies.

USB hub
This small hub allows you to connect several pieces of equipment to a single port on the back of your computer.

Installing telephones

Telephone lines used to be just for voice communication. But now they're used for transmitting documents, images, e-mail, data, video and so much more from the Internet. In fact, for some people their place of work can be just about anywhere as long as a phone is close at hand. If you want to improve the phone system in your home, today's home centers have the latest equipment, cables, components, and tools to allow you to install a modern communication system in your home.

Most homes already have two phone lines installed, even if only one is being used currently. So if you just want to add a second line you're set. But if you want two or more additional lines, the phone company will have to run new cable to your house.

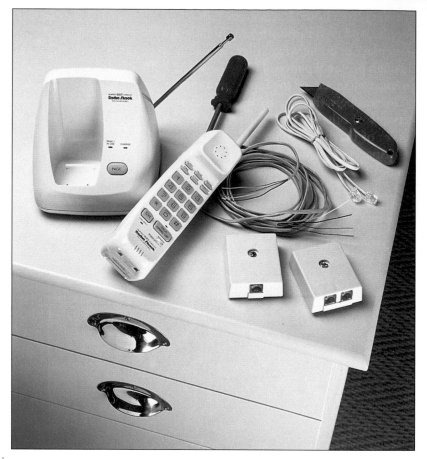

Slide new cable through rubber gasket on end of Network Interface Device.

Strip sheathing from new cable and insulation from wires.

Run new cable to jack location and staple it to joists.

Running new line

For most houses, there's a phone company Network Interface Device (NID) installed in the basement or on the exterior of the house. The NID carries two lines from the telephone pole or pedestal. So if you want a second line, you just run a new cable to the NID.

To install the cable, first feed it into the end of the NID through the rubber gasket that's mounted there. Then strip about 3 inches of sheathing from the cable, and about ¾ inch of insulation from each wire. This wire is very fine, so be careful when you strip it. Once the stripping is done, loop the wire ends around the matching color terminals in the NID and tighten the terminals.

Then run the new phone line to the jack location. Staple the cable every 8 to 12 inches along the floor joists. And drill holes through the joists, as required, to reach the jack location. Once you're there, drill a ³⁄₁₆-inch hole through the floor and into the room. Feed enough cable through this hole to reach the jack. Then staple the cable to the joist as close to the floor hole as possible.

Installing jacks

There are many different kinds of phone jacks available, and even more accessories for the jacks. But for basic two-line service, a duplex jack is a good choice. This unit has two separate jacks, so you can make individual connections to two separate phone lines.

To install one, mount the jack on the baseboard molding with the screws provided with the jack. Then feed the phone cable into the bottom of the jack and strip the sheathing off the cable. Also strip about ¾ inch of insulation off the wires. Attach the wires to the matching-color terminals and tighten the terminal screws in place.

Use pliers to remove the knockout on the bottom of the jack cover. Then screw the cover onto the jack and test the jack. If a line is not working, check for loose terminal screws.

Mount jack on baseboard.

Strip wires and hook on terminals.

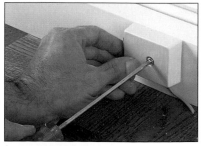

Screw cover onto jack.

There's nothing like a power outage to make us realize how much we rely on electricity. It powers the furnace, the refrigerator, the TV, the computers, the lighting circuits, and in many homes the water well that supplies the showers and toilets. A prolonged power outage can leave us cold, hungry, bored, unwashed, uncomfortable, and largely in the dark.

While an inexpensive portable generator will power the TV and a lamp or two, what's really needed is a unit that's large enough to keep some of the most important circuits running. A good-size generator that can handle these circuits is not cheap, but neither is a long outage in bad weather, when the family has to stay at a motel and eat every meal in a restaurant. In order to protect the lives of electric utility workers, back-feeding your home's electrical system with a generator requires special equipment and safety considerations.

Attach pipe nipple to hole in side of main panel.

Transfer switch

Generators must be connected to a home's wiring system in a way that's electrically safe You must use an approved transfer switch that routes electricity from either the electric utility or the generator to important house circuits. Also be careful about where the generator will be located and the risk of carbon monoxide poisoning from exhaust emissions.

Both manual and automatic transfer switches are available. A basic manual transfer switch is actually two breakers positioned side by side in an auxiliary panel. One breaker is powered by the main service panel and the other by the generator. A mechanical interlocking mechanism only allows one breaker at a time to be in the "on" position. This design protects the generator if it's still connected when the utility power comes back on. But more importantly, it protects utility workers from being electrocuted by the generator when they are working on the utility system.

A manual transfer switch does not automatically route the important circuits to the generator when the utility power fails. You have to manually flip the switch to the generator mode. Then you plug in the generator and start the engine. When utility power returns, you have to stop the generator and flip the transfer switch. Permanently installed generators use automatic transfer switches and provide backup power even if no one is home.

Slide switch panel over other end of nipple; screw to wall.

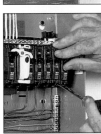

Pull 10/3 with ground NM cable from one box to the other through nipple.

Wiring the transfer switch panel

Mount the transfer switch panel next to the main service panel. Then shut off the power at the main panel and remove a knockout plug from the facing sides of both panels. Install a short threaded nipple with locknuts between the panels. Run a piece of 10/3 with ground NM cable through the nipple and strip the sheathing from both ends. Connect the neutral and ground wires to the main panel's neutral bus bar. Then attach the red and black wires to a 30-amp, 240-volt breaker in the main panel. Connect the other end of the wires to the "utility supply" breaker in the transfer switch panel.

Identify the "generator" circuits you want to move and remove the wires from the main panel breakers and the neutral bus bar. To bring these circuits into the transfer switch panel, they may need to be extended. If there is adequate space available, the NEC allows circuit extensions to be spliced in the main panel. Otherwise, you may need to install junction boxes in order to properly extend the generator circuits. Once the circuit extensions are complete, connect these wires to branch circuit breakers in the transfer switch panel.

Attach circuit wire to new breakers in switch panel.

Connecting the generator

Consult with local code officials before you proceed with connecting portable or permanent stand-by generators. Some areas allow portable stand-by generators to be connected to a weatherproof flanged male inlet connector by means of a heavy-duty extension cord. Other areas require a generator cord be hard-wired directly into the house electrical system. In addition to electrical safety, there may be zoning and noise ordinances related to larger, permanently installed stand-by generators.

If local codes permit, make extension cord for generator hookup. Warning: Extension cords must not have two male ends. The male plug on one end connects to the generator receptacle, and the female connector on the other end connects to a matching flanged male inlet at the house.

Estimating needs
The output of a generator is rated in watts. This figure indicates the maximum power that the unit can deliver. To determine the wattage of the generator you need, total the wattage of the fixtures and appliances you'd like to power. Then add about 20 percent as a reserve to handle increased startup demand of most electrical motors. Here's an example of how this works: let's say you wanted to power at least two lighting circuits (240 watts), a sump pump (1500 watts), a refrigerator (600 watts), and a blower on a gas furnace (1200 watts). This gives a total of 3540 watts without reserve power. With about 700 watts of reserve added in, the total comes to about 4260 watts. This is the minimum-size generator this example requires.

Lightning protection

Lightning storms are more prevalent in some areas of the country than others. When lightning strikes, the results are not predictable. It can melt electrical wiring, destroy electrical appliances and equipment, injure or kill inhabitants, and, of course, burn a house to the ground. The basic components of a lightning protection system include air terminals, interconnecting copper conductors and down leads, grounding electrodes, and bonding and mounting hardware. And those with surge arresters installed in their service panels or at their meters are safest. Lightning protection systems are best left to qualified professionals who can design and install a certified lightning protection system that is unique to your home.

Grounding antennas

TV and radio antennas and satellite dishes are prone to lightning strikes. Lightning surges can easily destroy any entertainment equipment that is connected to an ungrounded antenna or dish.

Grounding an antenna is easy. From an approved clamp on the frame of the antenna, run a No. 6 ground wire to a second clamp on a copper-clad ground rod.

Because some satellite dishes do not have grounding terminals, you may have to improvise a connection. The best method is to drill and tap a ¼-inch hole in the support post and fasten the ground wire to the frame with a brass bolt. Then run the No. 6 bare wire to an approved clamp and ground rod. To prevent an electrical shock hazard, ground rods for antennas and satellite dishes must be bonded with a solid No. 6 copper inter-system bonding jumper to the main electrical system ground rod.

Antennas can be grounded with approved clamps, No. 6 wire, and ground rods
1 Steel antenna
2 Approved clamp
3 No. 6 conductor
4 Finished grade
5 ½" x 8' grounding rod
6 Undisturbed soil
7 Concrete pad

Surge protection

Surge-protective power strip

Surge protective device incorporated into a duplex receptacle

Type 3 surge-protective devices (often called transient voltage surge suppression devices) are connected anywhere on the load side of the branch circuit breaker. These devices are available as panel modules, receptacles or the ever popular multi-outlet power strips. These types of surge-protective devices are intended to protect sensitive electronic equipment such as computers and entertainment equipment from spikes and surges that occur on electrical wiring, communication wiring and coaxial cabling.

Surges can be caused by electrical utility lines or natural phenomena such as lightning. Surges can also originate in the home from motors and other types of electrical equipment. Regardless of the source of the surge, these devices provide inexpensive protection for your expensive entertainment and computer equipment.

They need to be installed, tested, and maintained in accordance with the manufacturer's instructions in order to maintain the warranty coverage often provided by the manufacturer of the surge-protective device.

Surge-protective devices are rated in joules, a unit of electrical energy. The higher the joule rating, the more protection that is provided by the device.

Installing a lightning arrester

A lightning arrester (surge-protective device) is a device that routes a high-voltage lightning charge away from an electrical system and into the earth. Lightning arresters are inexpensive and are not that difficult to install. Type 1 surge-protective devices are permitted to be connected to the supply side (hot side) or the load side of a home's main disconnect switch. For supply side connections you will need to have the power to your home shut off by your local utility or a licensed electrician. Never attempt to install a surge-protective device with the power on.

With the power off, locate a knockout plug on the top of your service panel the size of the threaded nipple on your arrester. Remove this plug and insert the nipple through the opening. Then tighten the arrester in place with the provided fastening nut.

Next, slide the white wire from the arrester under an unused terminal on the neutral bus bar and tighten the terminal screw. Then loosen one of the terminal screws on the incoming side of the main disconnect switch. Slide one of the black wires from the arrester under that terminal, next to the incoming service wire already in place, and retighten the screw. Finally, fasten the other black arrester wire under the remaining disconnect terminal.

Be sure to only purchase a quality UL listed and labeled surge-protective device and carefully follow the manufacturer's installation instructions that are provided with the device.

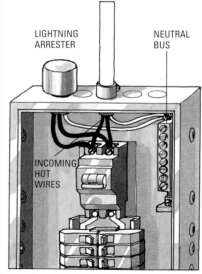

LIGHTNING ARRESTER   NEUTRAL BUS

INCOMING HOT WIRES

Lightning arrester installed in a typical panel.

8 Plumbing

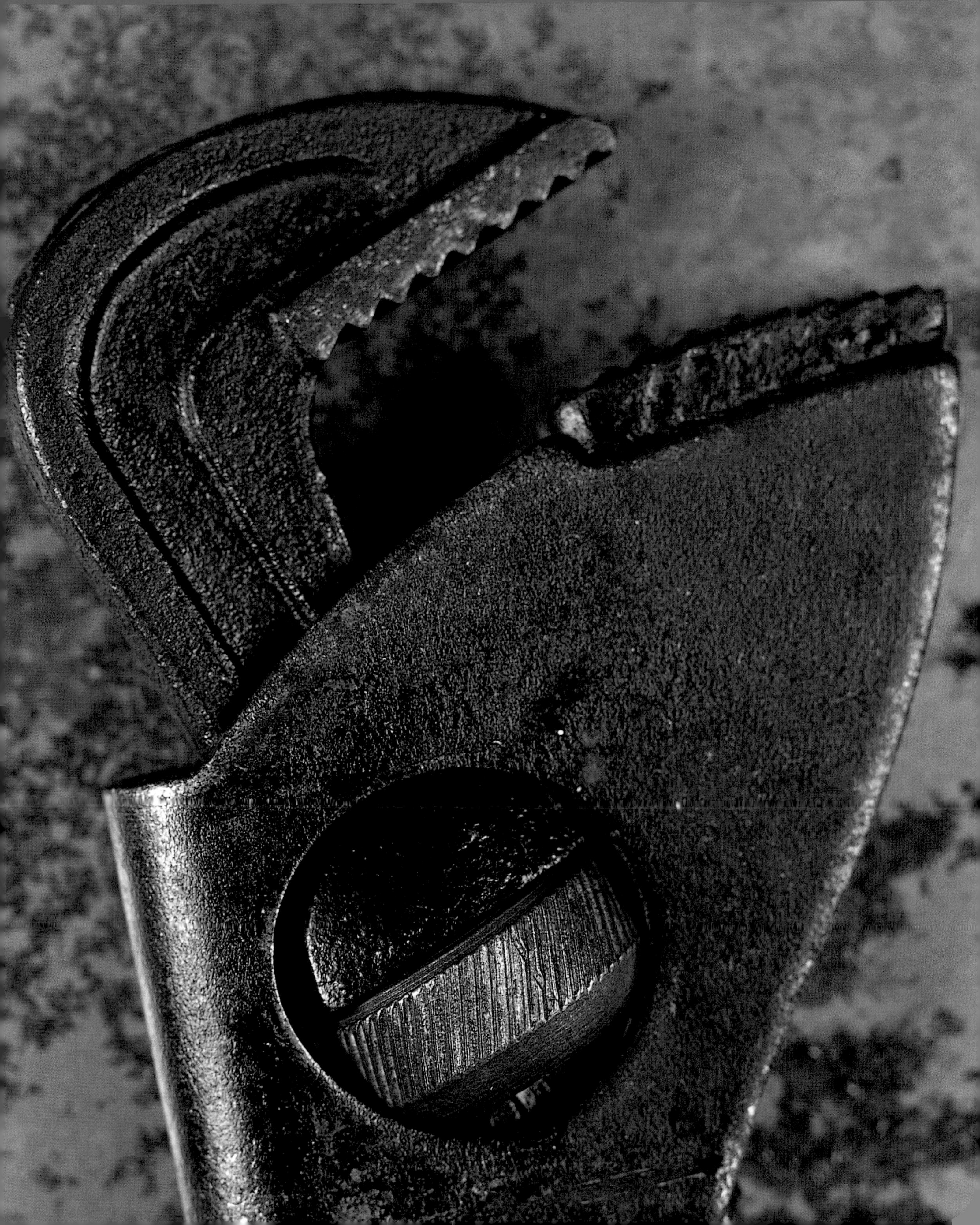

Understanding the system

Today, more and more homeowners are willing to tackle their own plumbing repair and remodeling projects. As with most do-it-yourself endeavors, cost is a motivating factor. The lion's share of most plumbing bills is the cost of professional labor, so doing your own repairs and installations makes good economic sense, and offers as a bonus the satisfaction of greater self-sufficiency.

Fortunately for the do-it-yourselfer, the plumbing supply industry has wasted no time in recognizing the opportunities provided by the growing consumer market. Instead of selling plumbing supplies in bulk quantities to wholesale houses and plumbers, manufacturers are now marketing for the consumer as well. They are also making their products easier to use. Repair and replacement parts are now likely to be attractively packaged with instructions and a "you can do it" pep talk on the back of each blister pack.

To the further benefit of the homeowner, design and manufacturing trends have also steered the industry in the direction of lighter, less expensive, and easier-to-install materials.

If you own your home, you can work on any of its plumbing. Your work will have to meet accepted plumbing standards as defined by local code regulations. Plumbing codes are written and enforced locally in the United States, but are based on specifications of the national *Uniform Building Code*. Before starting any major plumbing project, check with your local code office to see if the work you have planned meets specific code requirements.

A typical plumbing system

A residential piping system can be divided according to function into five basic categories. These categories are: pressurized water and fuel pipes, gravity-flow soil pipes, vent pipes, fixtures, and appliances. All pipes in a system serve specific fixtures (sinks, lavatories, and tubs) and appliances (water heaters, disposers, dishwashers, and clothes washers).

Take time to familiarize yourself with this network of pipes in your home before beginning any repair or remodeling project. An understanding of how each component in your system works with other components will help you feel more confident about the project at hand. Think about each pipe, valve, and fixture in your home as it fits within one of the five basic categories of function. Consider each item within the system separately. Until each element is examined according to its use, the system as a whole will likely remain a mystery. Plumbing is best learned one step at a time.

PLUMBING SYSTEM

1 **Water service**
Water supply from water company.

2 **Water meter**
Records water usage.

3 **Cold water supply**
Carries cold water to fixtures and appliances.

4 **Sillcock**
Cold water access from outside house.

5 **Gas line**
Gas supply from gas company.

6 **Water heater**
Heats water for fixtures and appliances.

7 **Hot water supply**
Carries hot water to fixtures and appliances.

8 **Supply riser**
Water connection just below fixture.

9 **Drain and trap**
Carries waste from fixture or appliance.

10 **Main drain**
Carries waste from all fixtures and appliances.

11 **3-in. stack**
Main vent for entire waste system.

12 **Vent**
Individual vent for fixture or appliance.

13 **Cleanout**
Access to waste system to remove blockages.

14 **Floor drain**
Carries water from basement floor.

15 **4-in. soil pipe**
Carries house waste to public sewer system.

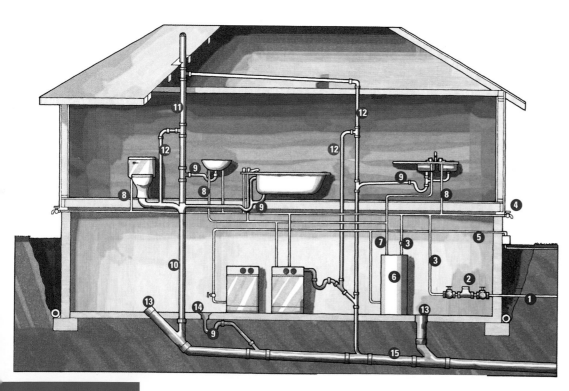

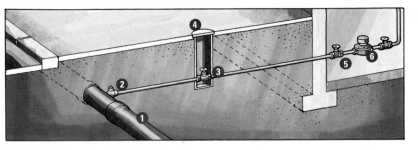

Supply lines

The water that flows from your tap enters your home through a single water-service pipe. This pipe is buried below frost level in your yard and extends from the city water main to a meter valve just inside your home. If water is supplied from a well, it flows to a pressure tank where it is stored until needed. In some cases, the water meter will be located in a meter pit just outside the home.

The water service is then connected to a meter, which measures the amount of water you use. From the meter, a single trunk line, carrying cold water, usually travels up and along the center girder of a home. At convenient intervals along the way, smaller branch lines extend from the trunk line to service various fixtures throughout the house. One goes to the water heater which supplies hot water to another trunk. This hot trunk line usually travels side by side with the cold line and branches off to wherever hot water is needed.

SUPPLY COMPONENTS

1 Water main
The water company uses this pipe to carry water to all the homes in the neighborhood.

2 Corporation stop
This valve is used to shut off water supply at the water main.

3 Curb stop
This valve shuts off water supply just before it enters the house.

4 Iron cover
This cover gives access to the curb stop at grade level.

5 Meter stop
This valve shuts off water before it reaches the meter. This makes replacing the meter much easier.

6 Meter
The meter records water consumption for water-company billing.

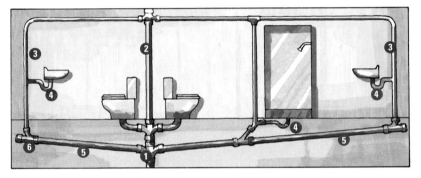

Drainage and venting

Drainage lines are the pipes that carry soiled water from your fixtures to the public sewer system. They generally consist of one or more vertical stacks with horizontal drains attached. It is important that drainage lines are installed at just the right pitch. Too little fall will cause water and solids to drain sluggishly and may cause the line to clog. Too much fall, particularly on long runs, will cause the water to outrun the solids, which may also cause the line to clog. A fall of ¼ inch per foot is ideal.

As a public sewer system is vented through the roofs (via plumbing stacks) of the homes connected to it, sewer gas is always present in large quantities in drainage systems. Each fixture must therefore have a seal to keep noxious sewer gases from entering the home through fixture drains. This seal is created by a U-shaped pipe, called a trap, beneath each fixture. Traps allow water to pass through them when a fixture is drained. After a fixture is drained, however, the trap holds a measured amount of water in its bend so that sewer gas cannot pass through the pipe and into your home. Every fixture in your home must have a trap, and every trap must be vented.

Venting is one of the most critical aspects of a drainage system. Without correctly vented drain lines, toilets won't flush properly, sink and lavatory drains choke, and high-volume appliance drains may overflow. But most important, unvented drain lines siphon water from fixture traps. Once a trap seal is broken, sewer gas quickly enters your living quarters. Even in quantities too small to detect by smell, sewer gases can cause respiratory problems and headaches.

The type of vent used depends upon the number of fixtures and floor levels involved and the structural constraints peculiar to each home.

DRAINS AND VENTS

1 Soil stack
This is the main waste line in the house. It directs all the waste from fixtures and appliances to the sewer line, or septic-system line, outside the house.

2 Main vent stack
This pipe carries sewer gases from the system into the air above the house. It also serves to equalize the air pressure in the system.

3 Vent line
The vents carry sewer gases from the fixtures and appliances and equalize the air pressure in the waste system.

4 Trap
This fitting contains water to keep sewer gases from entering the house.

5 Drain line
These pipes capture waste from the fixtures and appliances and carry it to the soil stack.

6 Cleanout
This fitting provides access to the waste system for removing blockages with a plumber's snake or drain auger.

Draining a water system

Being able to locate and shut off your meter valve, or if you live in the country, your pump switch is an important homeowner responsibility. You must be able to act quickly in an emergency.

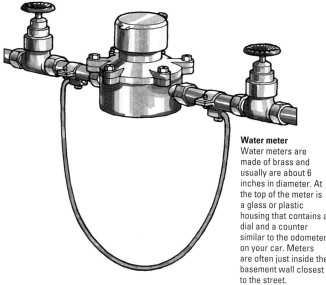

Water meter
Water meters are made of brass and usually are about 6 inches in diameter. At the top of the meter is a glass or plastic housing that contains a dial and a counter similar to the odometer on your car. Meters are often just inside the basement wall closest to the street.

Draining the system

To drain your water system, first shut off the valve on the street side of the meter. Then shut off the valve on the house side of the meter. With both valves closed, place a bucket under the meter and loosen the meter union next to the house side-valve. The small amount of water trapped in the meter will trickle through the opened union. Then go through your house and open all faucets to prevent air lock. When these are open, return to the basement and open the house-side valve and slowly drain the water into a bucket.

Open the house-side union with pipe wrenches

Draining your water heater

There can be several reasons why you might want to drain your water heater. The most likely occasion will be when removing an old heater. Sediment, faulty electrical elements, and stuck relief valves are three other common problems that require draining.

Start by shutting off the water supply to the heater. If your heater has a cold-water inlet valve, use it and leave the cold-water side of the system on. If no inlet valve is present, you will have to shut down the water supply to the entire house at the meter.

Once water to the heater is shut off, open all hot-water faucets in the house to prevent air lock. Then, attach a garden hose to the drain valve and empty the tank. If yours is an electric heater, an added precaution: Energized electrical elements burn out in a matter of seconds when not immersed in water, so you must shut off the power to the heater before draining it.

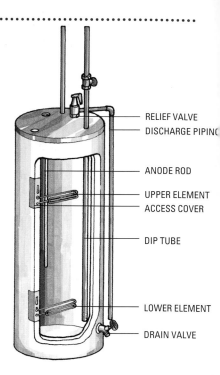

RELIEF VALVE
DISCHARGE PIPING
ANODE ROD
UPPER ELEMENT
ACCESS COVER
DIP TUBE
LOWER ELEMENT
DRAIN VALVE

Partial drain-downs

In many instances, such as toilet repairs, there will be no need to drain the entire system. A toilet usually has a shutoff valve between the riser and the supply line under the tank. Some homes have shutoff valves under sinks and lavatories as well. When these valves are present, use them. It is almost always easier to isolate a single fixture than to put the entire system out of order.

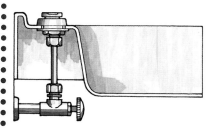

Shutoff valve under sink

Shutoff valve under toilet

Recharging the system

Just as you opened all faucets to prevent an air lock when draining the system, you will need to open them to bleed air from the lines when recharging the system with water. Open the meter valves only partway. Then bleed the air from the newly charged lines. After all the air in the system has escaped through the faucets, turn the faucets off and turn the meter valves all the way open. Small bursts of air may still escape through your faucets when you first use them, but all the air should be dissipated after the first full pressure draw. If you do not bleed trapped air from supply lines, the shock of air released under full pressure could damage faucet and supply-pipe seals.

Open faucets to bleed air when recharging system

Emergency repairs

It seems that plumbing leaks occur when we are least prepared to deal with them, at night, during the winter, when we're away from home, or just about always on a weekend. In such cases, a plumber may not be readily available, and you may not have the time and materials on hand, or the expertise for that matter, to make a permanent repair. There are, however, a number of stopgap measures that you can use to repair leaks temporarily. And most of them make good use of commom materials that just about all of us have on hand around the house.

Frozen and split pipes

In colder climates, pipes located in exterior walls, crawl spaces, and attics are often subject to freezing. The best preventive measure is to insulate these pipes. Even insulated pipes, however, can freeze when exposed to drafts of extremely cold air. When pipe freezes, a plug of ice forms in a small

Frozen water can easily split even the best copper pipe

section of the pipe and expands against the pipe walls. The expansion swells the pipe and, in most cases, ruptures the pipe wall.

Even a well-protected pipe may crack after years of use. Factory defects and corrosion are often responsible for these leaks. Regardless of how a pipe cracks or splits, emergency repair methods are usually the same.

A sure sign that a pipe has frozen is that no water passes through the pipe to the faucets nearest the freeze. You will often be able to feel along the pipe and locate the frozen area. If the pipe has not yet ruptured, use a portable hair dryer to warm the frozen area until water again flows to the nearest faucet. Once the pipe has thawed, you should wrap it with

Repair coupling
This kit uses a rubber sleeve and a hinged metal clamp.

Thawing a frozen pipe
Move a hair dryer back and forth across the frozen pipe until the water starts to flow again.

insulation. If no insulation is available, use old rags and fasten them to the pipe with tape, string, or wire.

If you can see that the pipe has already split, you will need to drain the system before thawing the frozen area. Once the area has thawed, you will need to make some sort of emergency repair. If you are able to find a plumbing supply outlet, the best solution is to buy a sleeve-type repair coupling. These couplings can be purchased in a number of standard sizes. They consist of two metal halves that are hinged on one side and bolted together on the other. A rubber sleeve fits inside and wraps completely around the pipe.

To install a sleeve repair coupling, first clean the pipe with a wire brush or sandpaper. Then fit the rubber sleeve around the pipe so that the seam is opposite the leak. Fit the metal halves of the collar over the sleeve and tighten the two halves together. While this method is usually thought of as an emergency repair, if the area has been properly prepared, it can be permanent.

If conventional repair materials are not available, you can sometimes make do with materials found around the house or at your local all-night service station.

To create a makeshift sleeve coupling, use a piece of tire inner tube, or a section of old garden hose, and a few radiator hose clamps. Wrap the inner tube around the split pipe several times and clamp it in place with hose clamps. This is at best a stopgap measure, but it will slow the leak until you can make a more permanent repair.

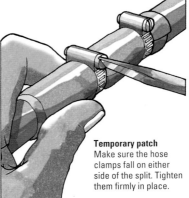

Temporary patch
Make sure the hose clamps fall on either side of the split. Tighten them firmly in place.

Epoxy patch repair

If you do not have access to plumbing materials, you may still be able to buy a general-purpose epoxy kit. These kits consist of two sticks of putty that you knead together. Once the parts are completely mixed, you will have about fifteen minutes to work before the mixture begins to set. Start by cleaning and drying the area around the split with sandpaper and alcohol. Knead the two components until they are a single consistent color and begin to give off heat. Then press the epoxy putty around the pipe. Smooth the ends with a damp cloth until the epoxy forms a seamless bond around the pipe extending several inches on either side of the split.

Epoxy takes a full 24 hours to cure, but, after a few hours, you should be able to turn the water on slightly. Do not put full pressure in the pipes for at least 24 hours after applying an epoxy patch.

Epoxy patch
Must cure properly before turning on water.

Plastic waste pipe and fittings

3-in. PVC pipe

3-in. sanitary tee with 1-1/2-in. side inlet

11/2-in. PVC pipe

11/2-in. wye

11/2-in. banded coupling

11/2-in. standard sanitary tee

11/2-in. 45° street ell

11/2-in. 90° ell

Male adapter

Adjustable plastic toilet flange

Female insert adapter

Standard glue-joint coupling

Working with plumbing pipe is better today than it was thirty years ago, largely because of plastic and copper. Both are much easier to work with than their predecessors, cast iron and steel. And both are highly resistant to corrosion.

Waste pipe and fittings

Shown here are common residential drainage and vent pipes and fittings. Others are available to solve specific problems. And most come in diameters from 1½ in. to 4 in.

3-in. and 1½-in. PVC pipe
Used for drain and vent lines.

3-in. sanitary tee with 1½-in. side inlet
Feeds 3-in. toilet waste line and 1½-in. shower drain into main stack.

1½-in. wye
Has less severe 45-degree inlet angle than a standard 1½-in. tee.

1½-in. standard sanitary tee
Most often used as a dry-vent fitting above the highest wet-drainage fitting.

1½-in. 45-degree street ell
Used in close quarters, the fitting has one male end and one hub end.

1½-in. 90-degree ell
Standard elbows have female hub on both ends.

Male adapter
For joining plastic pipe to female pipe threads, usually on iron, brass, or copper pipe.

Female insert adapter
For joining plastic pipe to male pipe threads, usually on iron, brass, or copper pipe.

Standard glue-joint coupling
For joining two pipes with solvent cement.

1½-in. banded coupling
Can join plastic pipe to cast-iron, copper, brass, and chrome pipe. Consists of a rubber sleeve, stainless steel band, and two hose clamps.

Adjustable toilet flange
For joining a toilet bowl to the waste piping and the bathroom floor.

Supply pipe and fittings

Supply pipes and fittings carry potable water throughout the house. Rigid copper pipe and copper and brass fittings have long been the standards for residential water systems, and will likely remain so because of their durability. The pipe and fittings shown here are the most common components used for residential water supply systems.

Copper pipe, ¾- and ½-in.
Standard water supply pipes. The ¾-in. pipe is used for main trunk lines. The ½-in. pipe is used for branching off to individual fixtures.

Soft copper tubing, ⅜-in.
Most often used for riser pipes between supply lines and fixtures. Available in other sizes for other jobs.

Prefitted stainless-steel risers
Flexible pipes that join shutoff valves under sinks and toilets to the fixtures.

Tees, ells, street ells, and couplings
Standard fittings for copper pipe. Available in ½- and ¾-in. diameters, they are joined to pipe with solder. Other specialized fittings are available for unusual situations.

Male adapter
Most often used to join copper pipe to threaded fittings on water meters, heaters, and softeners.

Dielectric union
For joining copper pipe to steel pipe. Prevents electrolytic corrosion between dissimilar metals.

Brass union
Provides a mechanical, instead of soldered, joint between pipes so they can be quickly disassembled.

Ball valve
In-line valve that allows full flow—no water restriction—when open.

Boiler drain
A compression valve, often used to connect supply lines with washing-machine supply hoses.

Chrome compression valve
Standard shutoff valve for under sinks and toilets.

3/4-in. tee   **45° standard ell**   **90° street ell**   **Slip coupling**

3/4-in.copper pipe

1/2-in. copper pipe

3/4-in. male adapter   **Dielectric union**   **Brass union**

3/8-in. soft copper tubing

Ball valve   **Boiler drain**   **Chrome compression valve**

Prefitted stainless-steel risers

Hanging accessories

Code requirements stipulate that horizontal pipes must be supported every 4 to 6 feet, depending on pipe size. There are a variety of hangers for getting this job done. Two of the most common are shown on the right.

Plumber's strap
This perforated strapping is very flexible and comes in rolls, so you just cut what you need for the job at hand. The holes make it easier to nail or screw the strap to floor joists. It is particularly useful for large drain and vent pipes.

Copper two-hole strap
These straps are sized for the pipe being supported, usually ½- or ¾-in. diameters. They are nailed or screwed to wood framing members.

Plumber's strap

Copper two-hole strap

Working with pipe

Lead-and-oakum joint
Before plastic pipe, joints were made by driving oakum into the hub and sealing it with molten lead.

Until you learn to work with pipe, your plumbing capabilities will be limited to simple maintenance. While neoprene gaskets, no-hub couplings, and plastic pipe and fittings have greatly reduced the need for special knowledge and specialized tools, most remodeling still requires that you understand how traditional plumbing materials are put together. In most cases, these newer, easier-to-use materials will have to be tied into existing pipes. You may also need to dismantle some existing piping in order to repair or extend your plumbing system. In short, knowing how to use plastic pipe is of little use if you do not also know how to tie it to other kinds of pipe in your existing system.

The good news is that the skill needed to work with cast-iron, steel, and copper pipe has been seriously overrated. You can do it. You may need a few specialized tools, but you can rent those. What is necessary is a basic understanding of how these materials are put together and which fittings and tools make the job easier. The rest is a matter of practice.

Making the connection

With the acceptance of plastic as a plumbing material, several new methods of joining plastic to conventional soil pipe have been developed. These connectors have virtually eliminated the skill once needed to form mechanical joints. Where once molten lead and oakum (an oily, ropelike material) were packed into bell-and-spigot joints, now neoprene gaskets make the seal. Instead of dismantling a run of pipe all the way back to its nearest hub, you can join two hubless pipes in minutes with no-hub couplings.

Bell-and-spigot gaskets
Neoprene gaskets are made for every standard-size, cast-iron soil pipe. They are fitted rubber collars that snap into the bell of a cast-iron pipe. The inside of the gasket is then lubricated with

detergent (dish soap works well), and the male end of the adjoining pipe is forced into the gasket until it seats.

No-hub couplings
No-hub couplings are rot-resistant rubber sleeves with stainless-steel bands around them. They are designed for use on drainage pipes and are approved by most code authorities. To install no-hub couplings, you simply slide one end of each pipe into the sleeve and tighten the bands. No-hubs come in many sizes, including increasing and decreasing couplings that allow you to join different pipe sizes to one another. They are particularly handy in joining dissimilar pipe materials.

Drain and vent sizing

FIXTURE	DRAIN SIZE	VENT SIZE	MAX. LENGTH TO STACK
Toilet	4"	2"	10'
Toilet	3"	2"	6'
Sink	1½"	1½"	3'6"
Lavatory	1½"	1½"	3'6"
Tub	1½"	1½"	3'6"
Shower	2"	1½"	5'
Laundry	2"	1½"	5'
Floor drain	2"	1½"	5'

No-hub coupling

When installing drainage pipe, there are a few rules you will need to follow in order to ensure mechanically sound joints and even flow patterns. They are as follows:

1. The grade or elevation of a drainage pipe should not be less than ¼₆ inch per running foot of pipe. In total, the fall of a given pipe run should not be greater than the diameter of the pipe involved. For example, a 2-inch pipe should not drop more than 2 inches along its entire length. If structural constraints require that a pipe drop more than its diameter, fittings should be used to "step" the pipe down to a lower plane. In this case, a vent will be required before stepping down.

2. When drainage pipes are wet, or carry water, fittings with gradual flow patterns should be used. For example, tees should be used only when they are the highest fittings on a vertical pipe. They should never be used in horizontal positions or when other fixtures are served above them. Because wyes offer much more gradual flow patterns, they should always be used instead of tees, except as the highest branch fitting on a vertical stack.

3. When drainage pipes are suspended from floor or ceiling joists, they should be supported by pipe hangers at a rate of at least one every 6 feet, or one for every pipe less than 6 feet long.

4. Every vertical stack must have a cleanout fitting at its base before entering a concrete floor.

5. All pipes installed underground or under concrete must be laid on even, solid soil. No voids or low spots are permissible under a pipe. If voids exist, or if the grade has been over-excavated, the ditch should be lined with fill sand. You should never fill voids or raise a pipe with soil. Soil is sure to settle with time, causing the pipe to sag and clog, or to shear off entirely.

When excavating a ditch for soil pipe, dig a small impression in the soil for each pipe hub. This will keep the entire length of the pipe from resting only on the hubs. Because soil pipe is buried permanently, either underground or under concrete, always work for a permanent installation.

Plastic pipe is the easiest pipe to handle because it is lightweight, can be cut with a hacksaw, and is joined to its fittings with glue. Plastic drainage pipe comes in two forms. ABS pipe is black and PVC is white. Both are schedule #40 weight, which is the wall thickness required by code for drainage pipe. There is no appreciable difference between the two, except that ABS has become more expensive in recent years, and the plumbing industry in general seems to be moving away from it. For consistency, you should match the type already in your home.

Joining plastic to iron

Plastic drainage pipe can be joined to cast-iron pipe in two ways. One is to cut the cast iron with a rented snap cutter and then join the pipes with a no-hub, or a banded, coupling. The other is to use a neoprene gasket.

To do this, buy a gasket that matches the size of the pipe being joined. Then push it into the cast hub and lubricate it with some dishwashing liquid to make joining the pipes easier. File over the sharp edge on the end of the plastic pipe and firmly push the pipe into the gasket.

Cut cast iron pipe with rented snap cutter

Push neoprene gasket into hub, followed by pipe

Cutting and assembling

To cut and fit plastic pipe, measure for the desired length and mark the pipe with a pencil. Then, using a hacksaw, cut carefully across the pipe (1). Take particular care in making straight cuts. A crooked cut will keep the end of the pipe from fitting properly into the hub of the fitting. Smooth the cut edge with a file (2).

It is always a good idea to assemble pipe and fittings before gluing to make sure that all measurements are accurate and all fitting angles correspond. Then, before dismantling, mark the fitting and pipe (3) at each joint so that you will have an easy reference point when gluing them together permanently. You can also scratch a mark with a utility knife (4). This won't smear as pencil marks often do.

Gluing pipe and hubs is easy but requires accuracy and speed. Apply glue to the inside of the hub of the fitting. Then glue the outside of the pipe, covering to a depth consistent with the depth of the hub (5). Press the fitting onto the pipe with the pencil marks about an inch apart. When the pipe is in all the way, turn the fitting so that the pencil marks line up. By turning the fitting on the pipe, the glue is spread out evenly around the entire joint.

Glued joints (technically, cemented joints) set in about 30 seconds, so if you make a mistake, you have to pull the joint apart very quickly. Plastic pipe cement does not really glue one surface to another; rather, it melts the two surfaces, causing them to fuse. Once a joint has set, it is permanent.

When buying materials, be sure to choose a cement made for the type of pipe you buy. ABS glue will not cement PVC pipe and fittings. PVC glue does work with ABS pipe, so you have to use compatible materials.

Drainage pipe must often be installed in interior walls. Because plastic pipe expands and contracts with hot and cold water, make sure that holes drilled in the wall studs are large enough to allow for this expansion. Stud and joist holes should be at least ⅛ inch larger than the exterior diameter of the pipe. Plastic pipe should never be shimmed tightly against wood. Without room for expansion, plastic pipe will produce an annoying ticking sound in the wall after hot water has been drained through.

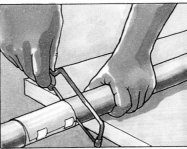

1 Use paper as a guide to keep the cut square

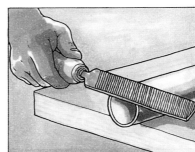

2 Smooth the end with a file

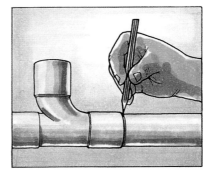

3 Preassemble the joint and mark pipe and fitting

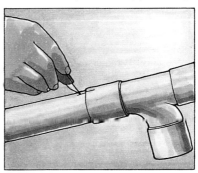

4 Or, scratch the pipe and fitting with a knife

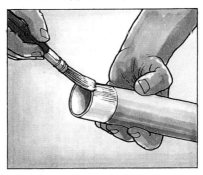

5 Brush cement on pipe end and fitting hub

Plastic water pipe

CPVC (chlorinated polyvinyl chloride) plastic water pipe has been used for water supply lines in some parts of the country for many years. If installed properly, it's got a good track record. And there is no question that it's easier to work with than rigid copper pipe and fittings. No soldering is required, and people who don't have any experience with the materials can get good results on the first job. Unfortunately, the building codes in some areas don't allow it for potable water piping. So be sure to check with your local code authorities before putting it in your house.

Joining CPVC plastic pipe

With one exception, CPVC plastic water pipe is put together the same way as plastic drainage pipe. Plastic pipe has a shiny residue on its surface that should be either lightly sanded or treated with a solvent primer before the cement is applied. A fine-grit sandpaper works well for the ends of the pipe but is a little harder to use for the inside of the fittings. Most people opt for a solvent primer instead because it's faster to use and more thorough. Simply brush the surfaces to be joined with the primer, wait a few seconds, and wipe them clean with a soft cloth. Then apply the glue to the pipe and fitting and push them together with a slight twist.

Make cuts with plastic pipe cutting shears

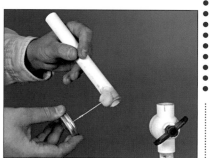
Apply primer to fitting and pipe end

Test-fit joint and mark final alignment

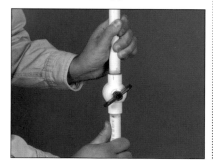
Apply cement and push pipe into fitting

Joining PEX to fittings

PEX pipe is the new kid on the block. It's made of polyethylene plastic and is becoming more popular, particularly with DIYers. It usually comes in red, white, or blue colors and is sold in easy-to-handle rolls. It has little coil memory and is not affected by corrosive soil or water. And it's much more forgiving than copper or CPVC in freezing temperatures. It's usually joined to rigid brass or plastic fittings with simple-to-install clamps. It doesn't have the track record of copper or even CPVC at this point, but it's gaining code acceptance all the time.

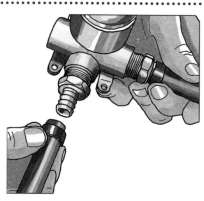
PEX pipe attaches to fitting with simple clamps

Plastic water pipe can also be joined to steel and copper pipe by means of plastic threaded adapters.

Both male and female plastic adapters are available. One end of the plastic adapter is glued to the plastic pipe and the other is threaded into a fitting or onto a pipe. When joining plastic water pipe to existing metal piping, wrap the male threads with plastic pipe-joint sealant tape. Because plastic female adapters can expand when threaded onto male threads, a better choice is to use a plastic male adapter threaded into a copper or steel female adapter or other fitting.

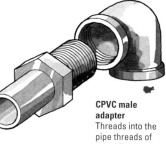
CPVC male adapter
Threads into the pipe threads of metal fittings.

Plastic supply-pipe types

Chlorinated polyvinyl chloride (CPVC)
A versatile plastic pipe suitable for both hot and cold supply lines, local codes permitting.

Polybutylene (PB)
An easy-to-install pipe that was popular in the seventies and eighties but is no longer on the market. To make repairs to a PB piping system, install CPVC or copper transition fittings.

Cross-linked polyethylene (PEX)
This pipe is most often used for in-floor radiant heating systems. And it's been used for some time in mobile and modular houses. But it's gaining in popularity for hot and cold water supply lines in site-built houses. Generally, it's available only at professional plumbing supply outlets.

CPVC
PB
PEX

Working with steel pipe

Steel pipe is available in galvanized and black versions. Galvanized pipe is used for water supply lines and drainage and vent lines, while black steel (often called black iron) is used primarily for gas piping. Though they are put together in exactly the same way, you should avoid mixing the two. When galvanized iron is used on gas installations, the gas in the line can attack the zinc plating and may cause it to flake off. These zinc flakes can be carried through the system and may clog the orifice and control valve of a water heater or furnace. On the other hand, if black pipe is used in water supply lines, it will rust shut in a matter of months.

Cutting and threading steel pipe

Steel pipe can be cut with a hacksaw. In fact, when cutting out a section of existing pipe, a hacksaw is your best choice. When you intend to thread the cut end, however, a wheel cutter will give you a much more uniform cut. Wheel cutters can be found at most tool rental stores along with the threading dies you'll need.

To determine the exact length of pipe, measure between the two fittings and add the depth of the threads inside each fitting for your total length. Then mark the pipe with a crayon. Place the pipe in a pipe vise and tighten the cutter on the pipe so that the wheel is directly on your mark. Then tighten the wheel one-half turn and rotate the cutter around the pipe. When the cutting wheel turns in its groove easily, tighten it another turn and rotate the cutter again. Repeat the process until the pipe is cut completely through.

Once the cut is made, leave the pipe in the vise and get ready to cut new threads. Cover the first inch of the pipe with cutting oil and slide the cylinder of the die onto the pipe. Set the lock on the die to the "cut" position. Then, while pressing the die onto the pipe with the palm of your hand, crank the die handle. When the die teeth begin to cut into the metal, you will feel some resistance. You will then be ready to crank the handle steadily around the pipe to cut the threads.

About every two rounds, stop and pour oil through the die head and onto the new threads. This is very important. Without oil, the pipe will heat up and swell until you can no longer turn the handle. Dry pipe threads will also ruin the die cutters in short order.

Continue cranking and oiling until the first of the new threads shows through the front of the die. Then reverse the direction lock on the handle and spin the die off the pipe. Thread the other end and you're done. All threaded steel joints should be put together with Teflon pipe-joint tape or pipe-joint compound, on the male side only.

Cutting threads
To cut threads on a steel pipe you need a pipe vise to hold the workpiece and a cutting die mounted in a long cranking handle.

Teflon tape
Use this sealing tape on the threads of all steel pipe joints.

Steel pipe fittings

Steel pipe is put together with threaded joints. Because steel was the predominant residential piping material for most of the twentieth century, you will find it in many older homes. You may never need to install steel piping, but chances are you will confront it when making changes and repairs.

Steel pipe comes in 21-foot lengths and is threaded on each end at the factory. It also comes in short precut, prethreaded lengths called nipples that graduate in ½-inch increments from 1 inch to approximately 1 foot. When you need custom lengths, you have to cut and thread them yourself, using a die cutter. Some well-equipped, and usually older, hardware stores will do the job for you.

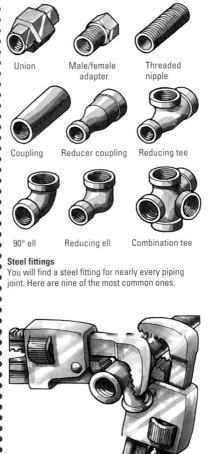

Union

Male/female adapter

Threaded nipple

Coupling

Reducer coupling

Reducing tee

90° ell

Reducing ell

Combination tee

Steel fittings
You will find a steel fitting for nearly every piping joint. Here are nine of the most common ones.

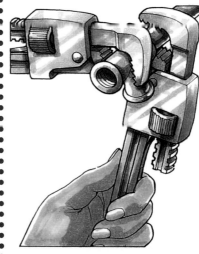

Joining steel pipe and fittings
You need two pipe wrenches to tighten threaded steel joints. One holds pipe, one holds fitting.

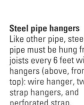

Steel pipe hangers
Like other pipe, steel pipe must be hung from joists every 6 feet with hangers (above, from top): wire hanger, two strap hangers, and perforated strap.

Joining copper pipe

Soldered joints are found in runs of copper pipe. To install them, all you'll need is an inexpensive torch, the correct solder and flux, some abrasive, and a willingness to try.

Applying solder

Because comfort is important when soldering at odd angles, it's a good idea to precut some solder and hold this shorter piece in your hand instead of trying to handle the whole spool. Wind about 2 feet around your hand and leave about 10 inches free. Then pull the loop from your hand and squeeze it into a handle.

If you are right-handed, place the solder in your right hand and the torch in your left. Light the torch and open the valve all the way. Place the torch tip so that the flame hits the hub of the fitting straight on. The tip should be about ¾ inch away from the fitting. If yours is not a turbo tip, heat one side for a few seconds until the flux begins to liquefy, and then move around the fitting and heat the far side while touching the solder to the fitting.

Keep the solder opposite the torch flame and continue to touch the fitting until the solder liquefies and wraps around the fitting quickly. As soon as the fitting is hot enough to pull solder around it, take the heat away and push solder into the fitting.

If the fitting will not take solder easily, pull the solder

away and heat the fitting for a few more seconds. Then push the solder in. A ¾-inch fitting should take about ¼ inch of solder. When the hub has taken enough solder, move on to the next hub on that fitting. Always start with the bottom joint on a fitting and work up. When all joints on that fitting are soldered, watch the rim of the last joint carefully. When the fitting starts to cool, it will draw solder into the joint. This cooling draw is your assurance that the joint is a good one. If the solder around the rim of a joint stays puddled and does not draw in when it cools, heat until the solder liquefies, and then wait again for it to draw in slightly. When you are satisfied that the last joint is a good one, wipe the fitting of excess solder and move on to the next fitting. When all fittings have cooled, turn the water on and check each joint periodically for leaks.

Of course, working with a torch requires a few precautionary measures. When soldering a fitting that is next to a floor joist or any combustible surface, you will have to protect that surface. The simplest protection method is to fold a piece of sheet metal over so that it has a double thickness. Then slide this double wall of metal between the fitting and the combustible surface. If you cannot sufficiently protect the area around the fitting, you may wish to solder that section elsewhere and install it already soldered.

To avoid scorching the rubber washers and diaphragms inside valves, always solder them with the handles turned open. This will diffuse enough heat to keep the seals from being ruined. Remember, use only as much heat as is needed to draw the solder evenly around the joint. The most common beginner's mistake is too much heat, not too little.

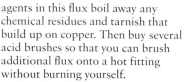

Torches

Most hardware stores offer small, inexpensive torch kits (about $20) that include a replaceable propane, or MAPP gas, bottle, a regulator valve and a flame tip. The best of these kits offer a turbo tip that spins the flame as it exits the tip. Turbo tips are useful because they wrap flames around a pipe so that you do not have to heat both sides of a fitting. You can also rent larger propane tanks with hose-mounted tips that hold much more gas.

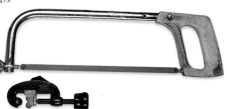

Flux and solder

The next ingredient you will need is a good self-cleaning flux. The right flux is critical to achieving a leak-proof soldering job. Because you will sometimes need to reflux heated fittings, you will want to avoid soldering paste. Choose, instead, a can or jar of self-cleaning flux that has the consistency of butter. The cleaning

agents in this flux boil away any chemical residues and tarnish that build up on copper. Then buy several acid brushes so that you can brush additional flux onto a hot fitting without burning yourself.

Choosing the right solder is also important. Until the late eighties, lead in varying amounts was always present

in solder used for plumbing systems. It was easy to use and was very durable. But it was banned by the EPA because of the health risks of lead leaching into drinking water. The only solder you should use on plumbing joints is lead-free solder. And resist all urging by salespeople to use acid-core solder for plumbing work.

Clean fitting with small wire brush

Clean pipe with steel wool or sandpaper

Apply flux to the fitting and the pipe

Heat joint with torch and apply solder

Fittings for remodeling and repair

Repair and remodeling work often require that you cut a section of pipe from between two fittings. This is easily done with a hacksaw. Once the cut is made, you will need to back each section of remaining pipe out of its fitting. Use two pipe wrenches, one to unthread the pipe and one to hold the fitting so that joints farther down the line won't be disturbed. If other joints are inadvertently turned, you might cause leaks.

Steel replacement pipes need a union fitting

Reconnecting with copper or plastic pipe

Splicing in new pipe between two existing steel fittings is easier to do with copper or plastic. In both cases, threaded adapters can be screwed into the steel fittings. In the case of copper, the remaining joints between the replacement pipe and the adapters will have to be soldered. In the case of plastic pipes, all the joints will be glued. Because plastic water pipe is not universally accepted for water supply lines, you should check with your local code authorities before installing it for that purpose. Plastic drain and vent lines are accepted everywhere.

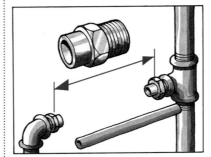

Copper pipe is joined to steel pipe with adapters

Working with copper pipe

Copper pipe is available in four wall-thicknesses. Type K is the thickest and is used primarily for underground water services and under concrete for supply lines. It comes in soft coils.

Type L offers the next thickest pipe wall. It is available in soft coils or rigid sticks. The soft version is typically used in gas pipe installations and is connected with flare fittings.

The thinnest allowable supply-line pipe is type M. It is made only in 20-foot rigid lengths and is the most widely used in residential water systems.

The thinnest-walled copper pipe is

DWV. As its initials imply, it is used as drain, waste, and vent piping. Although seldom used now for drainage and vent piping, it was widely used in the fifites.

All copper pipe can be cut with a hacksaw, but if you intend to use flare fittings on soft copper, a wheel cutter will give a more uniform edge. All copper can be soldered, and all soft copper can be flared for use with flare fittings. Copper drainage pipe can be joined to steel, plastic, or cast-iron pipe with no-hub couplings. Hard-copper supply connections can also be joined with compression fittings.

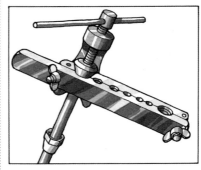

Flaring tool forms flare on end of soft pipe

Flare and compression fittings

As its name implies, a flare fitting requires that you flare the pipe to fit the fitting. Slide the flare nut onto soft copper pipe and clamp the flaring die within ⅛ inch of the end of the pipe. Thread the flaring tool into the pipe end until the end of the pipe expands evenly against the tapered die seat. Remove the tool and draw the fitting together with two wrenches.

A compression fitting operates in reverse fashion and so it does not require a special tool. Simply slide the fitting nut and brass compression ring onto hard or soft copper pipe and thread the nut onto its fitting. Hand-tighten the nut, one to one and a half turns. Use pipe-joint compound on all flare and compression fittings.

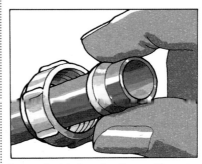

Compression joint is made with nut and brass ring

Working with cast-iron pipe

You can cut cast-iron pipe with a chisel by tapping lightly in a line around the pipe until it breaks. But the best way is to use a snap cutter. This is a ratchet-like tool with a chain that wraps around pipe and cutting wheels that clamp onto the pipe. As the tool turns, the wheels cut the pipe. Snap cutters

are available at most tool rental outlets.

Traditional hub and spigot joints are now made with neoprene gaskets. Where hubs are not available or where hubless cast iron is joined to plastic, steel, or copper pipe, no-hub couplings make the easiest connection.

Rented snap cutter cuts cast iron

Drain-cleaning techniques

CLEARING TOILET BLOCKAGES

Soap, hair, food particles, and cooking grease all help to clog drainage lines. Occasionally a fixture trap will accumulate a blockage that can be forced clear with a plunger or compressed air. Most blockages build up inside pipes over an extended period of time, however, and must be cabled, or "snaked," to be opened. The method you choose will depend upon the fixture involved and the size of the drainage line.

Forcing fixture traps

Plungers and cans of compressed air can both be used to free simple trap clogs. When forcing a clog from a trap with either of these, be sure to plug any connecting airways. When plunging a lavatory, for example, use a wet rag to plug the overflow hole in the basin. When forcing the trap of a two-compartment sink, plug the opposite drain. After the debris has been forced through the trap and into the drain line, run very hot water through the line to move the clog into the main stack or soil pipe.

Snaking fixture drains

When you wish to clean the drain line of any fixture with a snake, you will first have to remove the trap. Use a pipe wrench or adjustable pliers to loosen the nuts at the top of the trap and at the drain connection near the wall. With S-traps, loosen the nuts near the floor and at the trap. To avoid cracking or breaking a chrome P-trap, hold it firmly and turn the nut with steady, even pressure.

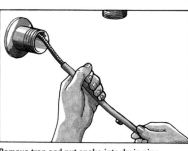

Remove trap and put snake into drain pipe

Snaking a shower

If drain water backs up into a tub or shower from another fixture, it probably means that the main sewer line is clogged. If a tub or shower drains slowly, or not at all, then you should snake the tub or shower trap and drain line. To snake a tub, remove the coverplate from the overflow valve and push the cable into the overflow pipe. This is easier than working through the drain opening. Stand-alone showers don't have overflow openings, so they have to be snaked through the drain.

Snaking a sewer line

You can rent a sewer-cleaning machine, but before doing so, get several bids from professional drain-cleaning companies. Often they can do the job for just a little more than the cost of the machine rental. And you can avoid all the aggravation that's involved. Most sewer clogs are either from tree roots or collapsed pipes and both repair jobs are better left to a professional.

Occasionally a toilet will clog and overflow. Most toilets clog at the top of the trap because that is where the trap is the smallest. Toothpaste caps, hairpins, and combs are regular culprits.

Start by trying to plunge the toilet trap. A plunger with a collapsible funnel works best. If plunging doesn't do the trick, remove the water from the bowl and use a small mirror and a flashlight to look up into the trap. If you can see the obstruction, chances are you can reach it with a wire hook.

If all else fails, rent a closet auger and crank the auger through the trap several times. The auger's cable is just long enough to reach the toilet flange. As you pull the cable out of the trap, keep cranking the handle.

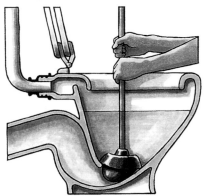

To free clog, first try plunger

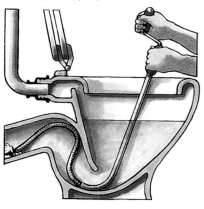

If plunger doesn't work, use auger

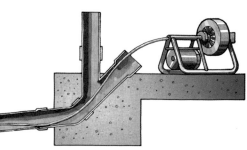

Sewer-cleaning machines
These tools are aggressive pieces of equipment that can clear out serious blockages.

Faucet replacement

Faucet installation has not changed much over the years. While plastic fasteners and flexible supply risers have made the job easier, the process remains much the same. Often the most complicated part of the job is selecting the faucet itself. One faucet-buying trip to a plumbing supply showroom, to say nothing of visiting the average home center megastore, can set your head spinning. The number of different models and the jargon (single-handle, double-handle, compression, cartridge, ceramic cartridge, retro, modern) can be overwhelming. Start by matching your existing faucet design. By doing this you'll know at least one model that will work for you.

Removing a faucet

The most troublesome part of replacing a faucet is getting the old faucet off. Start by shutting off the faucet's water supply, either at the meter or at a shutoff valve located under the sink. Turn the faucet on to relieve the pressure. Then loosen the nuts that connect the riser pipes to the supply lines and the faucet. A basin wrench will help you reach the coupling nuts high up under the sink. When these nuts are loose, bend the risers slightly so that they can be pulled out of the faucet and supply fittings.

Next, use a basin wrench to undo the nuts that hold the faucet to the sink. If the faucet is old and the nuts corroded, first spray penetrating oil on the threads. If this does not help loosen the nuts, use a small cold chisel and hammer and gently tap the nuts in a counterclockwise direction to break them loose. Once they are broken loose, back off the nuts with a basin wrench.

In a few cases, even these methods

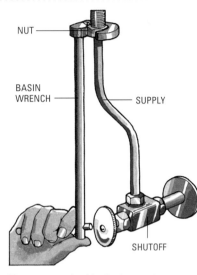

NUT
BASIN WRENCH
SUPPLY
SHUTOFF

Disconnect supply with a basin wrench

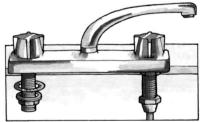

Top-mount faucet
This is installed from above and is held in place with a locknut and washer from below.

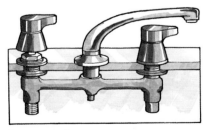

Bottom-mount faucet
This is installed from below and is held in place with a locknut and washer from above.

will not free the fastening nuts. If this happens to you, your only recourse is to saw through the nut with a hacksaw blade.

Some faucet styles mount from the bottom and are held to the sink or countertop by a locknut under the handle escutcheon. To remove a bottom-mounted faucet, first remove the handles, then the escutcheons. Escutcheons are usually screwed on and can be removed by threading them counterclockwise. Under the escutcheon, you will find the locknuts. Undo these nuts and the faucet should fall out.

Because years of soap and mineral buildup can leave a ridge around the edge of the faucet plate, you may have to clean the faucet area of the sink before installing a new faucet. A fifty-fifty mixture of white vinegar and warm water used in conjunction with a single-edged razor blade will help you remove this ridge. Just soak the buildup and scrape it away.

Installing a new faucet

After you've cleaned the sink, set the new faucet in place with the rubber or plastic spacer between the faucet and sink. Then reach under the sink and thread the new washers and nuts onto the faucet until the nuts are fingertight. Before tightening the faucet nuts, however, go back and straighten the faucet so that the back of the coverplate is parallel with the back edge of the sink. When the faucet is straight, tighten the nuts.

When the faucet is fastened in place, you will be ready to reconnect the supply risers. It is usually a good idea to start with new risers. Different types are available. Soft copper risers are okay if they aren't visible, in places like under a kitchen sink or bathroom vanity. But where the risers do show, chrome-plated copper is a better choice, as are stainless-steel flexible risers. Both include a bulb-shaped head that fits into the ground joint surface of the faucet's hot- and cold-water inlets. The riser nuts slide onto the pipe from the other end. When you tighten these nuts to the faucets, the bulb-shaped head is pressed into the ground joints and makes a watertight seal. The supply-line ends of the risers are connected to shutoff valves with compression fittings.

Remove old faucet and lower new one in place

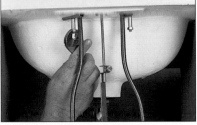

Tighten nuts from below to hold faucet

Attach supply risers to shutoff valves

WASHER
PERFORATED DISC
SCREEN
BODY

Cleaning aerators
Most kitchen faucets have aerators that can clog. To clean them, unthread the body and wash the screen, disk, and washer.

Faucet repairs

Faucet repair is as simple or as complex as the design of the faucet involved. In general terms, there are four basic faucet mechanisms in use today. The oldest type, still found in many faucets and in most valves, uses the stem-and-seat principle. More recent designs feature replaceable cores, rotating balls, and ceramic disks. With each of these types, the internal mechanism turns or rotates until holes in the mechanism align with holes in the faucet, allowing water to pass through. The degree of alignment determines the mixture of hot and cold water. In each case, repair is relatively simple and inexpensive. Only when a faucet body itself is defective is faucet replacement absolutely necessary.

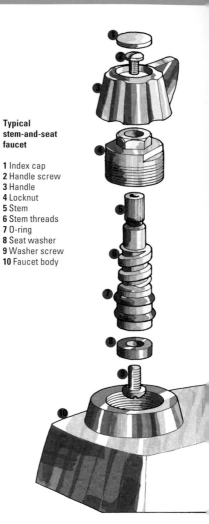

Typical stem-and-seat faucet

1 Index cap
2 Handle screw
3 Handle
4 Locknut
5 Stem
6 Stem threads
7 O-ring
8 Seat washer
9 Washer screw
10 Faucet body

Heat-proof grease
Before reassembling any faucet, cover all moving parts with heat-proof grease. As the name implies, heat-proof grease will not dissolve in hot water. It greatly increases the life of replacement parts and makes the faucet much easier to take apart the next time service is needed. Remember to grease the handle sockets as well. Heat-proof grease will separate dissimilar metals enough to prevent corrosion.

Repairing stem-and-seat faucets

To repair stem-and-seat faucets, start by removing the handles. Most handles have decorative coverplates (also called index caps) under which are handle screws. Pry off the caps and remove the screws. If a handle has not been removed recently, it may be stuck to the stem. Gently pry up under both sides of the handle with two screwdrivers to free the handle. If the handle will still not loosen, you may need to buy an inexpensive handle puller from your local hardware dealer.

On better faucets, all external parts are made of chrome-plated brass and these faucets usually come apart easily. Cheaper models feature chrome-plated pot metal corrodes easily, making the handles hard to remove. If you damage a pot-metal handle, your best bet is to replace it with a universal-fit replacement handle.

When you have the handle off, undo the escutcheon (if necessary) to get to the locknut. Loosen the locknut with an adjustable wrench. If the locknut backs out several rounds and then stops, turn the stem in or out, depending on the brand, to free the locknut. When the locknut is loose, back the stem out of the faucet. To remove most stems, turn the nut counterclockwise.

On the end of the stem you will find a rubber washer secured by a brass screw or nut. Undo this screw or nut and find a replacement washer that fits the rim of the stem. A tight fit is important here. The washer should not be too big or too small. Press the washer into the seat and install the screw or nut. Because brass screws can become brittle with age, it's a good idea to replace the screw when you replace a washer. If you are uncertain about which washer to use, take the stem to a well-stocked hardware store and ask the clerk to pick out the right one for you.

Pry washer off stem

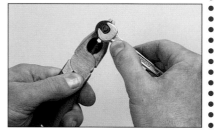

Remove nut or screw

Blade removes coverplate

Remove handle to reach stem

Dealing with seat damage

When a defective washer is allowed to leak for an extended period of time, the pressure of the water will cut a channel in the faucet seat. For this reason, always repair a leaking faucet immediately. A defective seat will chew up new washers in short order, so always check the seat when you replace a washer.

If you find a channel in the seat, replace the seat. A seat wrench will allow you to unscrew a removable seat from a faucet body. Some seats are machined into the brass body of a faucet and therefore cannot be removed. If your faucet seats are pitted and cannot be replaced, your only alternative is to grind the entire seat rim to a level below the surface of the pit. While this may sound difficult, it is not. You can buy an inexpensive seat grinder from your local hardware store and once the faucet is apart, you can do the job in a matter of minutes.

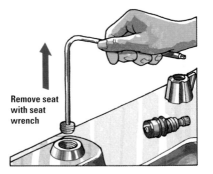

Remove seat with seat wrench

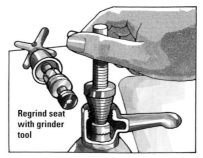

Regrind seat with grinder tool

Faucet repairs

Seat-and-spring faucet repairs

Seat-and-spring type faucets, one of a variety that are known as washerless faucets, have become quite popular in recent years, both because of their durability and because they are easy to repair. The operating mechanism of a seat-and-spring faucet consists of a stainless-steel or plastic ball that is turned and aligned with water openings in the faucet body as the single handle is manipulated. The openings in the faucet body contain spring-loaded rubber caps, or seats, which press against the ball and prevent leaking when in the off position. When this type of faucet drips, it is because these rubber caps and springs are worn.

Repair kits for seat-and-spring faucets are inexpensive and come with everything needed to completely rebuild a faucet. It is important to identify the faucet by brand name when asking for a repair kit in order to get the correct parts. The common brand names are Delta and Peerless. Kits come with complete instructions. The repairs you make will depend upon the location and nature of the leak.

Typical seat-and-spring faucet

1 Handle
2 Set screw
3 Cap
4 Spout
5 Spout collar
6 Cam collar
7 Cam seal
8 Ball
9 Spring cap
10 Spring
11 O-ring
12 Faucet body

Repairing handle leaks

If your seat-and-spring faucet leaks around the handle but does not drip from the spout, all you have to do is tighten the faucet cap. The cap is the threaded dome that holds the mechanism in place. The repair kit comes with a small cap wrench, or if you prefer you can use slip-joint pliers to tighten a cap. You simply remove the handle with an Allen wrench, then turn the cap clockwise until the leak stops. Do not overtighten. Pliers can sometimes scratch the chrome. For added protection, wrap the jaws with a soft cloth.

Allen wrench removes handle

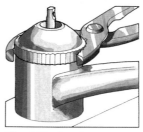

Pliers tighten faucet cap

Replacing seats and springs

If the faucet drips, you must take the faucet apart. This is easily done by using the proprietary cap wrench. Use the Allen wrench side of the tool to loosen the handle set screw. Pull the handle off. Then use the cap wrench to loosen and remove the cap. Under the cap you will find a nylon and rubber cam covering a stainless-steel ball. Remove the cam assembly and pull the ball up and out of the faucet body. Inside the faucet you will see two or three hollow rubber caps, or seats, mounted on two small springs.

Insert a needle-nose pliers into the faucet body and pull the seats and springs out. Throw the worn seats and springs away. It is too easy to get the old confused with the new. Then slide the new springs and seats into the faucet holes. When the spring-loaded seats are in place, you will be ready to reinstall the ball-and-cam assembly.

The kit will come with a new cam seal that should be installed before putting the cam in place. The cam assembly will have a tab on one side that corresponds with a slot in the faucet. Match the tab with the slot and press the cam assembly in place over the ball. You can then tighten the cap and replace the handle.

If your seat-and-spring faucet also leaks around the spout collar, you should replace the collar O-rings before putting the cap and handle back on. To replace collar O-rings, pull up evenly and firmly on the spout until it comes free. Use a knife to cut the old O-rings from the slots and slide the new rings over the body until they fit into the O-ring slots. Then grease the rings with heat-proof grease and press the spout collar back on, rotating it gently as you go. Complete the job by reinstalling the cap and handle.

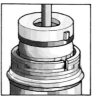

To remove the cam and ball, simply pull them out of the faucet body.

Remove the springs and cap seals with a pair of needle-nose pliers.

To replace ball, line up the tab in the ball with the slot in the faucet.

Faucet repairs

Repairing cartridge-type single-handle faucets

Cartridge-type washerless faucets have enjoyed wide popular use because of their simplicity and durability. They are available in single-handle and two-handle versions. Unlike the single-handle seat-and-spring mechanism, the cartridge type has a core instead of a ball. This type of faucet is marketed widely under the Moen trade name.

All single-handle Moen faucets use the same core mechanism, but other aspects vary with price. In terms of repair, the only notable difference is in the way the handle covers come off.

If your Moen single-handle faucet has a flat chrome coverplate with the trade name pressed into it, you must first pry the coverplate up with a knife to get to the handle screw. Other models have a plastic hood that covers the handle screw and top of the faucet. These hoods simply pull up and off.

Below the handle you will find the cartridge stem. If yours is a chrome coverplate model, you will also need to remove a retainer nut. Just below the stem, or pivot nut, you will see a brass clip inserted into the side of the cartridge stem. This clip locks the cartridge in place. After you have turned off the water, pull the clip out with pliers. When the clip is removed, you will be able to pull the cartridge out of the faucet body.

Press the new cartridge in place, making sure that it's aligned the same way as the one you took out. Seat the cartridge by pressing it down until the cartridge is in far enough to accept the clip and you can slide the clip into place. Then replace the retainer nut, spout, and handle. Make sure that the handle slips into the groove in the retainer nut before replacing the screw. The handle works properly when it lifts and lowers the stem smoothly.

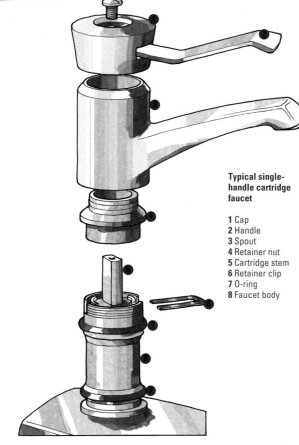

Typical single-handle cartridge faucet

1 Cap
2 Handle
3 Spout
4 Retainer nut
5 Cartridge stem
6 Retainer clip
7 O-ring
8 Faucet body

Repairing washerless two-handle faucets

Washerless faucets are also available in two-handle designs. The repair kit includes a cartridge and a seat assembly.

To make the repair, start by prying off the index cap and removing the handle screw. When the handle is off, remove the locknut that holds the cartridge in place. Then pull the old cartridge up and out of the faucet. Replace the seat and spring as you would with a single-handle faucet.

The new cartridge must be properly aligned before it can be installed. On the side of each cartridge you will see a tab, called a key. And on the faucet body side you will see a slot, called a keyway. Also note a stop at the top of the cartridge (see above). Align the key so that it is directly over the keyway. Then insert the cartridge so the stop is facing the spout. Replace and tighten the locknut until it is snug. Press the handle onto the new stem and replace the handle screw and index cap.

Remove handle screw and handle

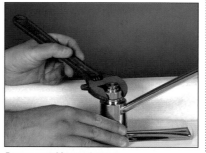

Remove cartridge retainer nut

Remove locknut and cartridge

Remove retainer clip with needlenose pliers

Pull old cartridge straight up and out

Replace seat assemblies

Faucet repairs

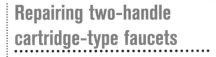

Repairing ceramic-disk faucets

When a ceramic-disk faucet leaks, the leakage is likely to show up around the base of the faucet. Getting to the operational part of these faucets is different than in other models. Instead of prying off the index cap to remove the handle, you must tip the handle back to reveal a set screw under the front of the handle. Use an Allen wrench to loosen the screw. But having the handle removed still does not give you access to the internal mechanism. You must also remove the chrome faucet cover. With older models, you will need to loosen the pop-up drain lever and undo two brass screws from the underside of the faucet. Newer models have a slot screw in the handle

and a brass keeper ring that allows you to remove the cover from above.

When the faucet cover is off, you will find a ceramic disk secured by two brass bolts to the base of the faucet. Undo these bolts and the disk should lift off. Take this disk with you to your plumbing supply store and buy an identical replacement disk.

To install the new disk, align the ports of the disk with those of the faucet base. Make sure that the flange under the cartridge bolt holes fits into the rim around the bolt holes in the body plate. When all is perfectly aligned, replace the disk bolts and refasten the faucet cover and handle. Turn on the water and test for leaks.

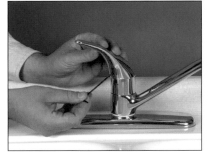
Remove handle set screw with Allen wrench

Remove faucet cover to reach ceramic disk

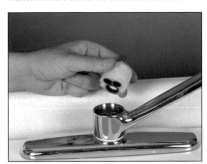
Unscrew bolts and remove ceramic disk

Slide new disk into faucet and screw in place

Repairing two-handle cartridge-type faucets

Some two-handle faucets also use cartridges for their internal mechanisms. To remove a defective two-handle cartridge, start by removing the index cap with a knife. Then remove the handle screw and handle. Under the handle is a large nut that holds the cartridge in place. Undo this nut with pliers. Then lift the cartridge out by the stem.

To install a new cartridge, turn the cartridge stem in a counterclockwise direction so that the holes of the cartridge are aligned. Then push the cartridge straight down into the faucet, making sure that the key at the top of the cartridge fits into the slot in the faucet. When you've seated the cartridge, screw the cartridge nut back on and tighten with pliers until snug. Then replace the handle, handle screw, and index cap.

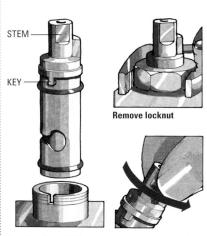

STEM

KEY

Remove locknut

Two-handle cartridge

Turn to align cartridge

Sillcock repair

A sillcock is simply a stem-and-seat faucet with a long stem. To repair one, start by shutting off the water at the meter or shut off valve. Then loosen the locknut that holds the stem and pull the stem out. If the stem is particularly stubborn, twist and pull it out with locking pliers. Replace the washer, apply heat-proof grease, and replace the stem.

Sillcocks often wear out faster than ordinary faucets due to a common mistake: Because water continues to drain from the spout for a few seconds after the valve is shut, many people think that the valve is starting to leak, so continue to turn the handle. This extra, unnecessary pressure ruins stem washers in a hurry.

Replacing freezeless sillcocks

Freezeless sillcocks differ from ordinary outside faucets in that they can be left on during freezing weather. Instead of stopping the water outside the home, they stop water inside by means of a long faucet stem. The only way a freezeless sillcock can freeze is if a hose is left connected in cold weather or if it has been installed without

sufficient pitch to drain. When either situation occurs, sillcocks will freeze and split just inside the home near the valve seat.

To replace a sillcock, turn off the water and unthread the sillcock from the pipe in the basement. Buy a new one the same length and thread it back into the supply line.

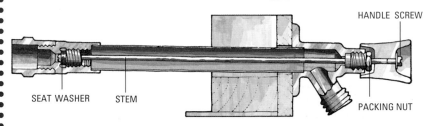

HANDLE SCREW

SEAT WASHER   STEM

PACKING NUT

Replacing lavatories

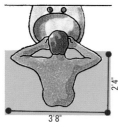

Replacing a wall-hung lavatory with a pedestal sink or a vanity cabinet and countertop basin can have a big design impact on a small room. Add some fresh paint, new light fixtures, maybe some new flooring, and a new mirror or medicine cabinet and you'll completely change the room. This approach to remodeling not only makes for a better place to live but also can add real value to your home while taking only a couple of weekends to do yourself.

Replacing a wall-hung lavatory with a vanity and basin

The first step is to measure the space around the existing lavatory to determine what size cabinet your bathroom will allow. Because storage space is always at a premium, it's a good idea to try for the biggest vanity that will fit in your space. Factory-made cabinets come in standard dimensions to fit many opening widths and depths, and most cabinet stores have a staggering variety of material and finish choices available. You'll also be able to choose what combination of doors and drawers the cabinet will have. Buying one of these vanities is generally less expensive than having your vanity custom built.

Countertops and lavatory basins are other major considerations. For standard-size cabinets, cultured-marble tops with basins molded into them are economical choices. Other options are plastic laminate countertops with china, cast-iron, or enameled-steel basins. Solid surface tops with integral basins and natural stone tops with undermount sinks occupy the high end.

If you're replacing your lavatory, you might consider new faucets. Plumbing supply stores, kitchen-and-bath cabinet shops, and your local home center store have a wide selection, with something for every budget.

Removing a wall-hung lavatory

First remove plumbing pipes and then take out anchor screws

To remove a wall-hung lav, start by disconnecting the trap and water supply risers. If your lav does not have shutoff valves between the risers and supply lines, now might be a good time to install them. With valves on both supply lines, you will not have to shut down the entire water system when working on just one fixture.

Once the piping is disconnected, check to see if the back of the lavatory is secured to the wall by anchor screws. These screws will be located at the back of the lav just under the apron. If anchor screws are present, remove them. Then grab the lav by its sides and pull up. It should lift right off the mounting bracket. Remove the mounting bracket by undoing the screws that fasten it to the wall. Before installing the new vanity, check to see if the wall above the vanity needs to be

repaired or painted. Sometimes the screw holes from the mounting bracket will show above the new vanity. Filling these holes and other cosmetic repairs may be necessary before the vanity can be set in place.

With the opening ready, slide the new vanity in place and secure it to the wall with long screws driven through the back of the cabinet and into the studs inside the wall. In some cases you may have to cut openings in the vanity for the drainpipe and supply lines. Once the cabinet is in place, you are ready to install the countertop. In the case of a cultured-marble top, simply set it on the vanity and glue it to the cabinet top with construction adhesive. In the case of a factory- or custom-made countertop, screw the top to the corner brackets of the vanity from inside the cabinet.

Carefully lift lavatory off mounting-bracket and set aside

Cutting a basin opening

Repair any damage to the wall before installing vanity

Some lav basins come with a paper template for marking the correct cutline on the countertop. But if yours didn't, you can simply turn over the sink on the countertop and trace around its perimeter. Then measure the width of the basin lip and draw a second line inside the first to allow for the lip. Bore an access hole on the waste side of the cut line for the blade

of a sabre saw. Cut the opening. To avoid chipping the countertop, use a fine-tooth blade and advance the saw with steady, even pressure.

Because it is much easier to install a faucet and pop-up assembly from above, attach the faucet and the pop-up now. Then turn over the basin, put it in the opening, and attach it to the countertop. Caulk around the rim.

To install a lavatory faucet, insert the faucet supply shanks through the basin faucet holes. Then slide the large spacing washer onto the shanks from below and tighten the locknut on each shank. Make sure that the faucet is centered before tightening the locknuts.

To install a pop-up drain assembly, pack putty around the drain flange and thread the pop-up waste pipe into the basin gasket until the flange is seated in the drain opening. Follow by threading the tailpiece into the pop-up waste pipe.

To connect the pop-up mechanism, insert the lift rod into the opening at the back of the faucet. Then slide one end of the adjustment strip onto the lift rod and the other onto the pop-up lever. Finally, pull the pop-up lever all they way down and tighten the adjustment screw.

When the basin is in place and hooked up to its trap and water supplies, use water-soluble latex caulk to seal the basin to the counter. Wet the areas to be caulked first. Then apply a bead of caulk around the faucet base. Push caulk into the cracks. Then wipe all excess caulk away with a damp cloth.

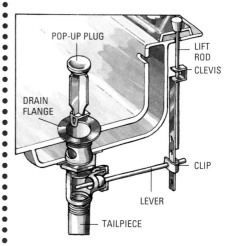

Typical pop-up drain assembly

Invert basin on countertop and trace perimeter

Replacing a kitchen sink

There are a bewildering number of design choices when it comes to residential kitchen sinks, faucets, and accessories. And the material and finish options are equally daunting. Here's a sampling of the kind of options you'll see when you go shopping at your local home center or kitchen-and-bath supply outlets.

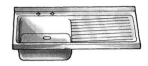

Double sink with left-hand drainboard

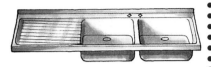

Single sink with right-hand drainboard

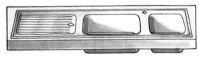

Double sink with cutting-board insert

Sink with disposer bowl and cutting-board insert

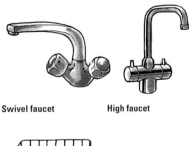

Swivel faucet   **High faucet**

Wire basket   **Spray hose**

Cutting boards

Replacing a kitchen sink is not a difficult task. But how you proceed depends on the sink you choose and whether you'll be replacing the countertop or keeping the old one.

Typical sink installation details

1 Shutoff valve
2 Supply tube
3 Pipe threads
4 Lock nut
5 Aerator
6 Strainer
7 Putty
8 Rubber washer
9 Paper washer
10 Spud nut
11 Slip nut
12 Rubber washer
13 P-trap
14 Cleanout plug

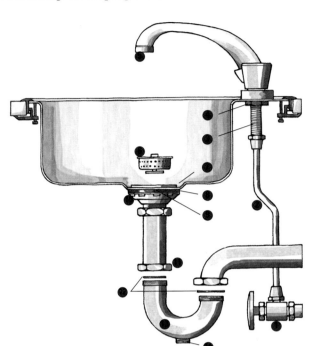

The components of a kitchen sink are fairly standard, no matter what model you choose. The sink has to do three things without leaking: receive water, drain waste and stay attached to the countertop.

Removing the old sink

If you plan to replace your old countertop, there is probably no need to pull the sink from it. Simply disconnect the trap, disposer, and water supplies, remove the screws from the underside of the countertop, and pull the sink and countertop up together. If you wish to save the basket strainers, disposer flange, or faucet, these are much easier to remove when the countertop is off the cabinets.

If you plan to save the countertop and replace only the sink, start by disconnecting the water supplies, trap, and disposer. Then loosen the clips around the underside of the sink rim,

using a screwdriver or socket wrench. Carefully slide a putty knife under the sink rim to break the seal of any caulk that's present.

Lift the sink straight up by placing one hand around the faucet base and the other through the disposer opening. With the sink out, you will likely need to clean mineral, putty, and soap buildup from the countertop where the old sink rim rested. A putty knife and household cleanser work well for this job. Just be careful. Both the cleanser and the putty knife can easily scratch the surface of the countertop.

Replacement sinks

The replacement sink you choose will have one of three possible rims. If you select an enameled cast-iron sink, for example, you will be able to pick between a "self-rimming" model and one that requires a sink rim to fasten it to the countertop.

The self-rimming type has a rolled edge that rests on top of the counter and is caulked in place. The edge of this sink is raised above the counter. The disadvantage of a self-rimming sink is that when wiping the counter,

you cannot simply push spills and food particles into the sink.

As a result, some people prefer a sink that fits flush with the countertop. For a flush fit, choose a sink that uses a rim to suspend it in the counter opening. Sink rims are common on porcelain-steel sinks.

A third rim type is found on stainless-steel sinks. No separate rim is needed but rim clamps are required to fasten the sink to the countertop.

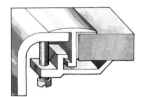

Sink with sink rim

Self-rimming sink edge

Mounting a stainless-steel sink.
Stainless-steel sinks are available in a wide range of prices. The more shiny the surface, the more expensive the sink. Stainless-steel sinks do not require sink rims to hold them in place. Instead, the rim of the sink rests on the top of the counter and is held against the countertop by fastening clips from the underside of the counter. Stainless-steel sinks will usually fit the same opening as a sink-rim type and therefore make good replacements. Measure before you buy.

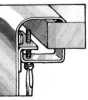

Self-rimming stainless-steel sink attachment

Strainers and disposers

The chrome trim parts you see in the drains of your sink are not part of the sink basin. They are merely the most visible parts of your disposer and basket strainer. As such, they can be replaced when cosmetic or mechanical problems arise. The job is involved but not difficult and requires only a few tools.

Replacing a basket strainer

To remove a basket strainer, disconnect the drainpipe from the basket drain threads. Then use a spud wrench or large adjustable pliers to loosen the locknut. To keep the strainer body from turning when you loosen this nut, insert the handles of small pliers into the drain crosspiece from the top. While you turn the nut from below, have someone hold the pliers from above.

If the nut is corroded on the strainer body, you may need to use a small chisel and a hammer to break it loose. If the hammer and chisel do not loosen it, use a hacksaw blade to cut the locknut. Cover one end of the blade with tape to create a handle. Cut across the nut in an upward diagonal motion.

When the locknut is loose, push the strainer body up through the drain opening. Clean the brittle old putty from the flange recess on the sink opening. Then roll new putty out between the palms of your hands so that it forms a soft rope about ½ inch in diameter. Press this putty around the flange of your new strainer and press the strainer in place.

Then slide the rubber washer onto the spud from below. Next, slide the fiber (or paper) washer on, followed by the new locknut. Tighten the locknut until it no longer turns or until the strainer body also begins to turn. From above, clear the excess putty from the rim of the strainer and tighten the locknut again.

Loosen locknut with a spud wrench

Put putty on new basket flange

Installing a disposer in an existing sink

A disposer can be installed in any sink that has a full-size opening. A single-bowl sink is a little less work than a double-bowl sink. But neither is very difficult. All you will need is a disposer, a disposer waste kit, and access to electricity.

To install a disposer in an existing single-bowl sink just remove the waste line, trap, and sink-flange locknut from below and the sink strainer and flange from above. Clean any putty residue from the recessed sink flange. For a double-bowl sink, do the same thing but first remove the waste connector that joins the two drains to the P-trap.

With everything removed, you are ready to install the disposer drain flange. Press putty around the sink flange and press it into the recessed sink opening. Then slide the rubber gasket, fiber gasket, mounting ring, and mounting plate onto the flange from below. While holding everything in place, snap the retaining ring over the ridge on the sink flange. Tighten the screws on the mounting plate until nearly all putty is forced from between the sink and flange, then trim the putty.

With the flange mounted in the sink opening, attach the disposer. Just hold the disposer up to the mounting plate and turn it until the tabs on the top of the disposer seat in the ridges located on the mounting plate.

Some disposers fasten directly to the flange, without need of the mounting

ring-and-plate assembly, using a stainless-steel band instead. A rubber collar on the top of the disposer simply slides over the sink flange. Then the stainless-steel band is tightened in place with a nut driver or a screwdriver.

Once the disposer is installed, attach the waste lines and complete the electrical hookups as shown on the facing page.

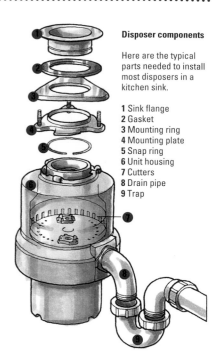

Disposer components

Here are the typical parts needed to install most disposers in a kitchen sink.

1 Sink flange
2 Gasket
3 Mounting ring
4 Mounting plate
5 Snap ring
6 Unit housing
7 Cutters
8 Drain pipe
9 Trap

Put putty on flange, then press into opening

Slide ring and gaskets over sink flange

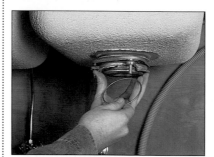
Slide plate onto flange and hold with ring

Lift disposer onto plate and turn until it seats

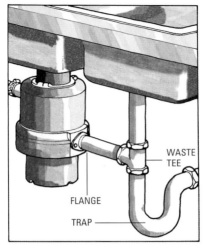

Typical disposer installation

WASTE TEE

FLANGE

TRAP

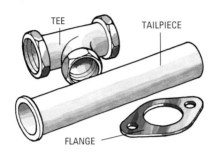

TEE

TAILPIECE

FLANGE

Components of a waste kit

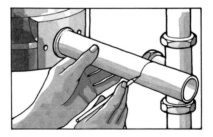

Mark and cut tailpiece

COMPRESSION NUT

COMPRESSION WASHER

Waste flange tailpiece

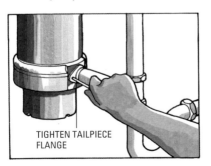

TIGHTEN TAILPIECE FLANGE

Fasten the flange screws

Most disposers on the market today come with a discharge tube that connects directly to the P-trap under your sink. These tubes work only if you are installing a disposer in a single-bowl sink or if you are replacing a disposer that was previously hooked up to its own trap. Otherwise, you'll need to install a waste kit.

Waste line connections

When connecting a disposer under a double-bowl sink, both compartments can be drained through a single trap. To make this connection, do not use the discharge tube that came with the disposer. Instead, buy a disposer waste kit. This kit consists of a tee, a tailpiece with a gasket, and a flange. Install the tee vertically between the P-trap and the tailpiece extension from the other sink. The center of the tee branch opening should be only slightly lower than the discharge opening on the disposer.

With the tee installed at the proper height, slip the rubber gasket onto the rim end of the tailpiece and hold it between the disposer opening and the tee opening. The tailpiece will be longer than needed, so you will have to cut to fit. Mark the proper length on the tailpiece. Remember to include the depth of the tee hub in your measurement.

Next, slide the metal flange onto the tailpiece followed by the compression nut and compression ring. Insert the compression end of the tailpiece into the hub on the tee. Push the other end of the tailpiece into the disposer opening. Bolt the flange to the disposer and tighten the compression nut to the tee.

To keep cooking grease from clinging to the sidewalls of the disposer and drain, always run cold water through your disposer when the motor is on. Cold water causes grease to coagulate and flow through the pipes. Hot water thins grease and allows it to build up in pipes.

If you are installing a disposer in a sink that has not had a disposer before, you will have to find some way to get electricity to the disposer and to a switch near the sink. If the basement ceiling beneath your sink is not finished, the easiest alternative is to run a separate cable from your service panel to a wall-mounted switch and then to your disposer. To meet code requirements, however, any cable that's inside the cabinet must be encased in flexible conduit.

If you don't like this option, consider converting an existing receptacle box above your counter into a switch box, if local code allow it. Just fish a short length of wire into the cabinet and over to the disposer.

Once inside the cabinet, the electrical hookup is simple. Remove the coverplate from the bottom of the disposer and pull out the white and black wires. Then, using plastic wire connectors, join the two insulated wires from the switch box to the insulated wires in the disposer. Connect black to black and white to white. Then fasten the uninsulated ground wire from the switch cable to the grounding screw located inside the disposer. Replace the coverplate and test the disposer.

If you are not comfortable making electrical repairs like this, consider hiring an electrician for the job.

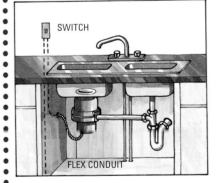

SWITCH

FLEX CONDUIT

Standard electrical hookup

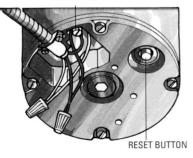

GROUND SCREW

RESET BUTTON

Bottom view of disposer

Servicing your disposer
Disposers work very well on most foods but have real problems with anything hard or stringy. Chicken bones, fruit seeds, eggshells, and celery can stop a disposer cold. When the motor pulls against too much resistance, a safety breaker built into the disposer will trip, cutting the power to the motor. To get a stopped disposer started again, first dislodge the motor blades from the blockage. To do this, use the wrench that came with the disposer to reverse the motor manually. The wrench should fit into a key slot on the bottom side of the disposer. Turn the motor back and forth until it spins easily in both directions. Next, find the reset button on the underside of the disposer and press it. Finally, run cold water through the disposer drain and turn on the disposer. This wrench and reset procedure will free most blockages. If the disposer stops again, repeat the procedure.

Installing a dishwasher

Like all things mechanical, dishwashers wear out. Hiring someone to replace yours can easily add $100 to the price of a new one. Dishwashers are not terribly difficult to install, but one precaution is in order. Because you must work with both electricity and water, make sure that you shut off the electricity at the main service panel before beginning.

Dishwasher components
Here's what you'll find when you remove the access panel on a typical dishwasher.
1 Water supply
2 Compression fitting
3 Dishwasher ell
4 Solenoid valve
5 Electrical box
6 Leveling leg

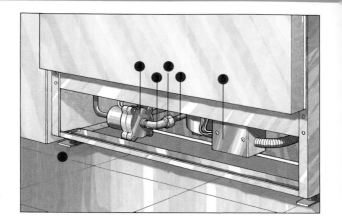

Removing your old dishwasher

After shutting off the electrical current to your old dishwasher, look under the sink for the valve that shuts off the water. If you find no valve isolating your dishwasher, you will have to shut off the supply at the meter.

With the water shut off, disconnect the discharge hose from the garbage disposer or the dishwasher tailpiece under the sink. Next, lift off the cover panel beneath the dishwasher door. This will give you access to the water and electrical connections. You may have to open the door to gain access to these screws.

Under the dishwasher, on the left-hand side near the front, you will find the water supply pipe and fitting attached to the solenoid valve. In most cases, the supply pipe will be ⅜-inch soft copper and the fitting will be a ½-inch threaded male pipe by ⅜-inch compression angle adapter. This fitting is used so universally on dishwashers that it is called a "dishwasher ell." Loosen the compression nut and pull the copper tubing out. Keep a shallow cake pan handy to catch the water trapped in the line. Leave the copper tubing in place under the dishwasher. In most cases it can be connected directly to the new dishwasher unit.

Near the solenoid valve you will see the metal box that contains the electrical connections. Undo the screws from the coverplate and pull the wires out of the box. Undo the wire connectors and save them for the new installation.

Most dishwashers are fitted with brackets that fasten to the underside of the countertop. Remove the screws from these brackets, then turn each of the leveling legs in so that the top of the dishwasher will clear the edge of the countertop. Tilt the dishwasher back and slide a large piece of cardboard under both front legs. This will keep you from damaging your floor covering. With everything disconnected and the cardboard in place, ease the old dishwasher out. Before hauling it away, however, tip it up and remove the dishwasher ell from the water supply inlet. You may need it for your new supply connection.

Testing for leaks
Before replacing the access panel, run the dishwasher through an entire cycle so that you can check your work. If the frame of the dishwasher vibrates too much, you may need to adjust one of the leveling legs. If a small amount of water appears beneath the water connection, a quick tightening of compression nut will usually correct the problem. (Be careful not to overtighten.) If the pump motor or electrical features fail to work, check the circuit fuse or breaker.

Remove access panel from bottom of unit

Remove screws that hold unit to countertop

Slowly pull out old unit to prevent floor damage

Installing your new unit

First, remove the access panel from the new dishwasher and thread the dishwasher ell into place. Be sure to use Teflon tape or pipe-joint compound on the male threads of the ell. Tighten the ell until nearly snug. Then tighten one more round until the compression nut points in the direction of the water supply pipe.

Slide the dishwasher up to the cabinet and start the drain hose through the existing opening at the back of the cabinet. Slowly push the dishwasher into place. As the dishwasher goes in, pull the discharge hose into the sink cabinet.

Align the sides of the dishwasher evenly in the cabinet. Then adjust the leveling legs. Open and shut the door to test it. If the door rubs against the cabinet, adjust the dishwasher and then fasten the brackets to the countertop with short screws.

Level new unit by adjusting threaded legs

Attach access panel with screws under door

Connecting the discharge hose

You can attach your dishwasher discharge hose directly to your sink waste line with a waste tee fitting. But usually it's more convenient to run the hose into your garbage disposer.

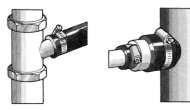

Washer tee fitting   **Hose adapter kit**

Disposers have fittings for just this purpose. If the hose from your dishwasher fits tightly on the disposer drain nipple then just attach the hose with a hose clamp. If the hose is too small, you'll have to install an adapter kit on the disposer. This is nothing more than a stepped rubber fitting that allows you to hook different size hoses to the disposer.

The most important thing to remember when hooking up a discharge hose is that the hose must arch high up in the cabinet before descending to the disposer or waste tee fitting. If your kitchen sink ever backs up, bacteria-laden sewage will flow into your dishwasher if no loop is there to stop it.

Some codes may require that a vacuum breaker be installed in the discharge hose. This provides an air gap to prevent siphoning, and because the hose connects to it just under the countertop, it creates its own loop. The most likely spot to install a vacuum breaker is in the fourth hole in your sink. If no extra sink hole exists, cut a hole in your countertop with a holesaw. The top half of the breaker will fit on top of the counter and the hose attachments will fit underneath.

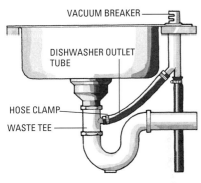

Some codes require a vacuum breaker

Making the water connection

If the previous water connection was made in ⅜-inch soft copper pipe, the new connection will be easy. With the dishwasher ell transferred from the old dishwasher to the new, all you will have to do is apply pipe-joint compound to the ferrule already on the pipe, insert the end of the copper into the ell, and tighten the compression nut.

If your old dishwasher was piped in rigid copper with soldered joints, the process becomes a little more complicated. Rigid copper supply pipes enter the dishwasher compartment in one of two ways.

Dishwasher ell

The most common approach is directly through the floor. In this case a union is located under the dishwasher, and a valve is located just below the floor in the basement. If the water supply does not come through the floor, then it will take off from the hot water supply line in the sink cabinet, enter the dishwasher compartment, and travel along the floor to the dishwasher water inlet. In either case, it is usually best to cut the supply line just after the valve and install a ⅜-by-⅜-inch compression adapter. You will then be able to run ⅜-inch soft copper pipe through the cabinet wall or kitchen floor to the compression end of the dishwasher ell. If manufacturer specifications insist on larger supply lines, use larger soft copper pipe.

Apply Teflon tape to threads on dishwasher ell

Tighten ell into solenoid with adjustable wrench

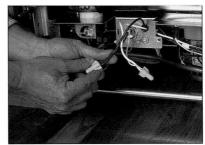

Attach supply line to ell with compression fitting

Making the electrical connection

Most codes require that any nonmetallic sheathed cable that extends into the dishwasher compartment be encased in flexible conduit. If your wire is not encased, now is a good time to do it. Just slide a length of conduit over the wire until it enters the drywall. Then cut the other end so that it can be fastened to the electrical box on the dishwasher.

With the conduit in place, use wire connectors to join the wires inside the box. Attach black to black, white to white, and fasten the ground wire to the green grounding screw inside the box.

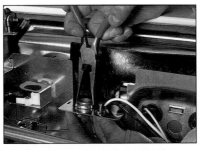

Install a cable connector in the electrical box

Join wires with wire connectors

Pour mineral oil into dishwasher to protect seals when machine won't be used for a couple of weeks.

Keep your dishwasher running smoothly
If you are installing your home's first dishwasher, you should have your kitchen drain line cleaned. Often a partially plugged drain line will accommodate the relatively low output of a kitchen sink, but when a dishwasher is added, the line will overflow. If you snake the line first, you will prevent the chance of water damage. Because a dishwasher forces a lot of water through a drain line and because that water is always very hot, a snaked kitchen line will remain clean almost indefinitely.

Dishwashers are designed to retain some water. Their pumps contain rubber O-rings and seals that must stay wet. Without this water, your dishwasher's seals will dry out, causing the pump to seize up or leak. If you are going to be away from your home for two weeks or longer, pour a cup or two of mineral oil into the base of your dishwasher. The oil will float on top of the water and seal it so that evaporation does not occur.

Contrary to popular belief, dishwashers do not sterilize dishes. The water temperature would have to be at least 180° F to sterilize, and water at that temperature is a safety hazard at your faucets. You should set your water heater between 135 and 140° F.

Toilet installation

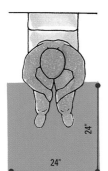

There are several reasons why you might remove a toilet. If you want to install a new one, of course, you'll first have to remove the old. You might need to repair part of the bathroom floor or replace a broken toilet flange. Or you might want to install new flooring in the whole room and therefore need to take out the toilet and reset it afterward. Installing a toilet is not a difficult job, but it is one that contains a number of pitfalls. Avoiding these pitfalls is at least half the job.

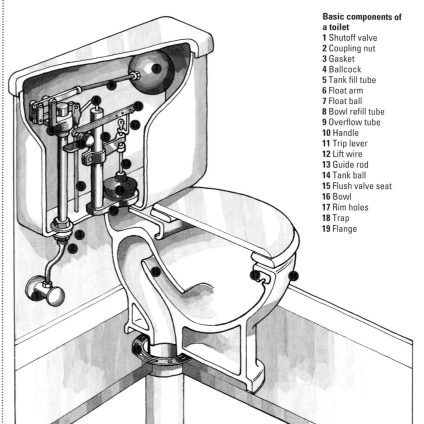

Basic components of a toilet
1 Shutoff valve
2 Coupling nut
3 Gasket
4 Ballcock
5 Tank fill tube
6 Float arm
7 Float ball
8 Bowl refill tube
9 Overflow tube
10 Handle
11 Trip lever
12 Lift wire
13 Guide rod
14 Tank ball
15 Flush valve seat
16 Bowl
17 Rim holes
18 Trap
19 Flange

Removing a toilet

While toilets are heavy and unwieldy, they are also fragile. To complicate the matter, old brass bolts and working parts become brittle with age and fall apart easily. If you wish only to remove a toilet in order to lay flooring, don't separate the tank from the bowl. While the unit will be heavier to move, you will avoid the possibility of damaging tank bolts and spud gasket seals.

Turn off the valve and remove riser pipe

Start by shutting off the water at the supply valve. Then flush the toilet and sponge the remaining water out of the tank. When the tank is dry, use a paper cup to dip the remaining water out of the bowl. Then undo the water supply at the valve.

Next, pry the bolt caps from the base of the toilet. Under these caps you will find the closet bolts. Older models may have four bolts instead of the two bolts found on more modern stools. The front two bolts will be lag-bolts with removable nuts and the back two will be standard closet bolts mounted through the toilet flange. Use a small adjustable wrench to remove the nuts.

Remove caps, then nuts, on closet bolts

When the closet nuts are loose and the supply pipe disconnected, rock the bowl slightly in each direction to break it free from the floor and bowl gasket. Then grab the toilet by the bowl rim just in front of the tank and lift up. Because the bowl gasket will be sticky and dirty, have a newspaper ready to set the toilet on. Then use a putty knife to scrape the remaining wax or putty from the toilet and the flange. Discard the old closet bolts.

Rock toilet from side to side, then lift

Resetting a toilet

Before resetting a toilet, you will need to buy a new bowl gasket (usually called a wax ring) and two new closet bolts. Begin by sliding the new closet bolts into the slots in the closet flange and center them so that each is the same distance away from the back wall. Then press the wax ring down on the flange.

Lift the toilet by the bowl rim near the tank and carry it over to the flange. Carefully align the holes in the bowl with the bolts and slowly set the stool down. Press down evenly with all your weight. Then slide the washers and nuts onto the bolts and tighten the nuts slowly, working from one bolt to another. When the base meets the floor and the nuts on the closet bolts seem snug, try rocking the bowl a little. If it moves, tighten the closet nuts another round. If the bowl does not move, stop. Both flanges and toilet bowls can break if you overtighten the bolts. Retighten after a few days if needed.

Remove old wax ring with putty knife

Slide bolts into flange, then add new wax ring

Lower toilet into place and install nuts on bolts

The water connection

Bringing water to the tank

If you are resetting a toilet that you've recently taken up, chances are you will be able to use the original supply riser. First, apply pipe-joint compound to the compression ferrule. Then insert the compression end of the riser into the shutoff valve and slide the other end into the ballcock fitting. If necessary, bend the riser slightly to gain the clearance you need. When both ends are in place, straighten the pipe and tighten the nuts.

If you added a new layer of flooring, you can't use the original supply riser. Installing a new one will probably be easier anyway, thanks to improved materials and designs.

While standard chrome-plated copper supply risers are bendable, they kink very easily and, once this happens, can't be used. To avoid this problem, choose chrome-plated supplies that are ribbed. These are very flexible and almost impossible to kink.

Also on the market are plastic supply tubes encased in stainless-steel mesh. The plastic makes this tubing flexible and the steel mesh makes it durable. These tubes cost more but in the long run are probably worth it. Sink risers are also available in stainless-steel-wrapped plastic.

No matter which type of supply riser you choose, you will find that the end that connects to the ballcock will be shaped to accept either a flat washer or a cone washer. The other end is designed to accept the compression nut and ferrule from the shutoff valve.

If your supply riser must be cut to length, hold it against the ballcock threads and estimate how much you will have to bend it to make it meet the stool valve. Then make the two bends as near to the ballcock end of the tube as possible. To avoid kinking the tube, apply steady, even pressure at several points along the length.

Hold the riser in place again and mark where the cut should be made. Be sure to add the depth of the valve socket to the length of the pipe. Use a tubing cutter to make the cut. Then slide the ballcock nut on the pipe from the bottom end, followed by the compression nut and ferrule. Fit the compression end into the shutoff valve socket and push the other end against the ballcock. Tighten the compression nut one full turn after you feel resistance. To tighten the ballcock nut, reach into the tank and hold the ballcock to keep it from spinning.

If you use flexible risers, you won't have to cut anything. Just measure the distance from the shutoff valve to the ballcock and buy a riser that's just a little longer than this measurement.

Next, turn on the water slowly at the shutoff valve and check for leaks. If you find water dripping at either joint just tighten the nut slightly until it stops.

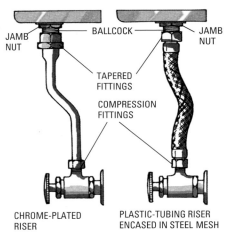

JAMB NUT — BALLCOCK — JAMB NUT
TAPERED FITTINGS
COMPRESSION FITTINGS
CHROME-PLATED RISER
PLASTIC-TUBING RISER ENCASED IN STEEL MESH

Bending pipe

A bending spring is the cheapest and easiest tool for making bends in small-diameter copper pipes. The spring is made of hardened steel and is designed to support the walls of the pipe while it's being bent. This prevents the pipe from kinking. Some bending springs are made to fit inside the pipe, others are meant to slide over the pipe.

To bend small copper pipes like supply risers, slide a spring over the outside of the pipe so it supports the area you want to bend. Hold the tube against your knee and bend it to the required angle. The bent tube might grip the spring, depending on how tight the bend is. If this happens just pull the spring off with a pair of pliers.

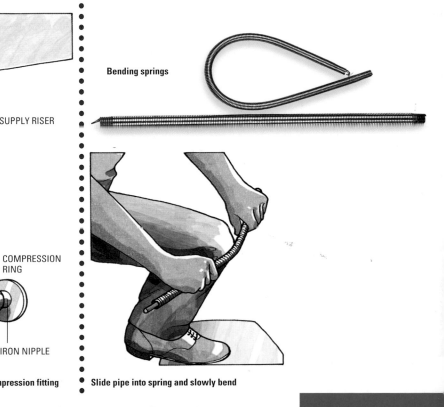

Bending springs

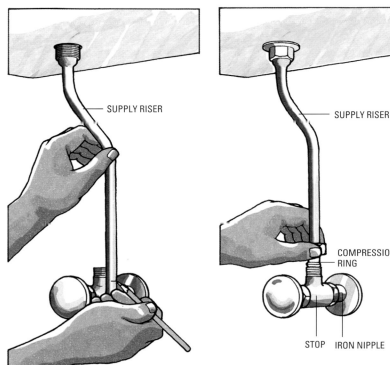

SUPPLY RISER

SUPPLY RISER

COMPRESSION RING

STOP   IRON NIPPLE

Hold riser in place, mark length, and cut

Connect riser to valve with compression fitting

Slide pipe into spring and slowly bend

Installing a new toilet

Your new toilet will come in two boxes. One will contain the bowl and the other the tank. You will have to install the bowl first, but open both boxes. Inside the tank box, you will find closet-bolt caps and retainers that are needed to install the bowl.

Fitting a new toilet

Begin by inserting new closet bolts in the slots of the toilet flange that's attached to the floor. Make sure both bolts are the same distance from the wall behind the toilet. Then center the new wax ring on the flange and press it down to make even contact. With the bolts and wax in place, lift the bowl over the flange and guide the closet bolts through the holes in the bowl base. If there is a slight angle in the position of the bowl, straighten it before you press down to fully seat the bowl. Then slide the closet-bolt cap retainer rings and washers over the bolts and thread the nuts on. Tighten the nuts until you feel steady resistance, then push down on the bowl again and tighten the nuts another turn. Do not overtighten these nuts. It is always better to tighten them more after the toilet has settled than to break the vitreous china bowl during installation.

BACK WALL   SIDE WALL

12"   15"

CLOSET FLANGE

Clearances for toilet flange

SHIM

Level bowl with shims

Tank assembly components

1 Tank bolt	**4** Tank cushion
2 Rubber washer	**5** Spud nut
3 Tank washer	**6** Spud washer

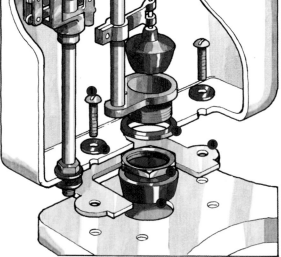

Setting the tank

The same package that contained the bowl caps will contain a large rubber spud washer and tank bolts and washers. Press the spud washer over the flush valve spud nut that protrudes from the tank. Then slide a rubber washer onto each tank bolt and push the bolts into the tank holes. If your toilet came with a tank cushion, place it on the bowl now. Set the tank on the bowl so the bolts go through the matching holes in the bowl. Install a washer and nut on each bolt and tighten them slowly, working from one bolt to the other to equalize pressure. Tighten them only until you feel firm resistance. With some models, the tank will not sit down on the bowl completely. It will remain somewhat suspended by the spud washer.

Slide tank bolts through bottom of tank

Carefully lower tank onto bowl

Making the water connection

Given the choices now available in toilet supply risers, you are likely to choose one of the flexible types and avoid cutting and shaping chrome-plate copper pipe altogether. Flexible supplies cost a little more, but are much easier to use. Just buy one that's the right length for the job.

The item most likely to wear out and often the most difficult to remove is your toilet seat. The nuts on metal seat bolts almost always rust or corrode to the bolts. When you attempt to loosen these nuts, the bolts, which are molded into the seat hinge, break loose inside the hinge and turn in place. The only alternative left is to saw the bolts off at bowl level with a small hacksaw.

To avoid chipping or scarring the porcelain surface, tape some cardboard on to the toilet rim in front of the seat hinge. By doing this you'll be able to lay the saw blade flat on the bowl and cut under the seat hinge. It's tedious work, but once done it should not need to be done again. Most seats manufactured today use plastic bolts and nuts.

Once you are rid of your old-fashioned seat with its brass bolts, your next replacement will be much easier. When shopping for a seat and lid, choose a painted wooden one. The plastic models on the market are not as sturdy.

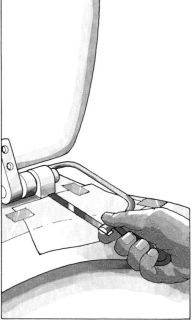

Protect bowl from saw with cardboard scrap

Riser made of plastic tubing encased in steel mesh

Repairing toilet flanges

When a toilet is allowed to leak for months at a time, the water almost always damages the floor around it. If you have dry rot around your toilet, you will have to take up the toilet and replace a section of the floor. This is an involved task, but not a difficult one.

Take up the toilet and cut out the rotted flooring with a circular saw. Then measure the area and cut a plywood replacement to fit the removed section. Measure and cut the opening for the toilet flange, keeping in mind that the flange rim must rest on top of the plywood.

Cut the plywood in two pieces so the center of the flange opening is the center of the cut. Slide each plywood half under the flange and nail down. Then screw the flange to the new floor.

Slide plywood under flange

Toilet flanges do occasionally break. The method of repair depends mostly upon the material of the flange and soil pipe connected to it. Cast-iron flanges break most easily because of the nature of the metal. Brass flanges can also become brittle with age and break, while copper flanges will tear out at the slots. Plastic flanges can also tear or break at the slots. And, of course, any flange connected to a lead riser is easily threatened. When a toilet is tightened down too much, either the stool or the flange will likely break.

Replacing a cast-iron flange

If your cast-iron flange breaks at one of its side slots, you may be able to effect a quick fix that is also permanent: You can buy a simple strap-metal repair item that works quite well in most situations. The strap is curved and shaped to slide under an existing flange. Just insert a closet bolt through the repair strap and slide the strap under the broken side of the flange. The strap is usually long enough to catch under the remaining edges of the existing flange. The pressure from the closet bolt keeps the repair piece tightly in place.

If your cast-iron flange is badly broken, you will need to replace it. To do so, first take up the toilet and clean the excess wax from the flange. If the flange is screwed to the floor, remove the screws. Then use an old screwdriver and hammer to pry the

lead out of the joint between the flange and soil pipe. Hammer the screwdriver into the lead about ½ inch deep and pry up as you go.

Once you have the old flange out, slide the new flange over the soil pipe and make sure that both-closet bolt slots are the same distance from the back wall. Then use heavy-duty nonferrous wood screws to fasten the flange to the floor. To make a leak-proof lead-and-oakum joint, push oakum into the joint and press it down so that it seats against the rim of the flange. Then use a hammer and packing iron to pack the oakum completely around the joint. Add more oakum until you have filled the joint two-thirds full. Finally, pack the remainder of the joint with lead wool until the hub is full.

Repair strap and broken flange

Removing a cast-iron flange and lead riser

Many older homes have cast-iron flanges connected to lead risers. Because lead is soft and becomes brittle with age, this combination should be replaced. Lead risers were used because lead is easier to work than cast iron. One end of the riser is bonded to a cast-iron insert that fits inside the nearest hub of cast-iron waste pipe. The other end comes through the bathroom floor and is flared out under a flat, cast-iron flange. The best solution is to take out the flange and most of the lead riser and convert to plastic.

First remove the flange from the floor. Then cut the lead where it meets the cast-iron insert. Install a 4-by-3-inch no-hub coupling over the insert and continue with a suitable length of plastic pipe topped off with a plastic flange. Remember to keep the closet bolt holes 12 inches from the wall.

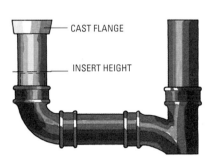

CAST FLANGE

INSERT HEIGHT

Flange connection with a lead riser

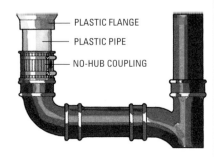

PLASTIC FLANGE

PLASTIC PIPE

NO-HUB COUPLING

Flange connection with a plastic pipe

Replacing a plastic flange

On plastic flanges, usually one of the slots breaks or tears loose. If the ceiling below your stool is open, such as in a basement, the easiest way to remove a plastic stool flange is to cut the waste pipe just below the flange. Then remove the flange screws and pull the damaged flange out.

Buy a new flange and a coupling. Then glue the new flange to a short stub of pipe and join the pipe to the waste line with a coupling. Make sure the bolt slots are the same distance from the back wall before the glue sets. Then screw the flange to the floor and reset the toilet.

If the waste pipe is 4-inch plastic, cut the lip of the flange from above using a reciprocating saw. Saw around the joint where the top of the soil pipe meets the flange, then glue the new flange inside the waste pipe and screw the flange to the floor.

Glue plastic flange to waste pipe

Toilet repairs

Toilets are a marvel of mechanical simplicity. With only a few moving parts, your toilet is responsible for nearly half the water used in your home every day. It is easy to take toilets for granted, until they start to malfunction. Then we wonder how so few parts can cause so much trouble.

When you come to understand how a toilet really works, repair will no longer be a mystery. Mechanically, the components of a two-piece toilet haven't changed much since the turn of the century. The changes that have been made are generally modest, mostly stemming from the need to conserve water. You can expect toilets in the future to flush with much less water than they use today. Even so, the age-old concept of gravity-flow flush valves and float-controlled ballcocks is likely to endure.

How toilets work

The typical toilet has only three mechanical components: trip lever, flush valve, and ballcock. The design of the toilet allows it to work so simply.

A two-piece toilet consists of a bowl, which rests on the floor, and a tank, which mounts on the bowl. The bowl contains a built-in trap that holds a consistent amount of water. The water trapped in the bowl keeps the bowl clean and keeps sewer gases from escaping from waste pipes.

The rim of the bowl is hollow. Water from the tank rushes into the rim and sprays through holes on its underside (and through a tube exiting opposite the drain opening). These holes are drilled at an angle, which causes the water to stream down the sides of the bowl at an angle. This angled spray serves two very important purposes. It cleans the sides of the bowl, and it starts the water in the bowl spiraling into the trap, which starts the siphoning action that pulls the water out of the bowl, over the trap, and into the waste pipe. Once the water in the bowl begins siphoning over the trap, the water draining out of the tank keeps the siphon going until all the waste is gone. When the tank is empty and the flow is stopped, the siphon breaks, which causes the water climbing the trap to fall back into the bowl.

The tank is less a matter of design than of mechanics. All the tank does is

hold water. Water is brought into the tank through a ballcock and is released through a flush valve. When you press down on the flush lever, a chain pulls a ball or flapper off the flush valve opening. Water then rushes into the bowl. The water level drops in the tank, which lowers the ballcock float, which opens the ballcock to incoming water. When most of the water passes through the flush valve, the ball or flapper settles back into place and the tank begins to fill again. When the water level reaches a certain point, the float shuts off the incoming flow of water through the ballcock.

This early toilet design features a separate elevated tank mounted high on the wall. The flush lever was activated by pulling on a chain.

This mid-twentieth-century design features a separate tank and bowl connected by chrome-plated piping. The flush handle is mounted on the tank.

SPIRALING WATER

HOLLOW RIM

This contemporary toilet has a much more compact design. It still has a separate tank but it rests directly on the bowl and it uses less water than its predecessors. No connective piping is needed. The flush lever is still mounted on the front of the tank.

Repairing a ballcock

When a ballcock assembly wears out, some external component may break or the diaphragm may become too porous or brittle to make the seal. If an external part breaks, you will have to replace the entire ballcock assembly. If the internal seals wear out, you can replace them without replacing the ballcock. The type of ballcock you have, its age, and the convenient availability of parts will have a lot to do with the repair choices you make.

Replacing a ballcock seal

If the ballcock in your toilet is made of brass and has been in service for many years, you should probably replace it. If your toilet is not that old, or if the ballcock is made of plastic, you can probably get by with changing only the diaphragm seals. Start by shutting off the water below the toilet, or at the meter, and flushing the water. Remove the screws on the diaphragm cover and lift off the float-arm assembly and cover. Place them aside. Remove all rubber washers

Remove diaphragm cover for access

and gaskets from the float-arm assembly and diaphragm and examine the rim of the diaphragm seat. If you can feel pits in the rim surface, you will have to replace the entire ballcock. If not, take the rubber washers and gaskets to your local plumbing outlet and buy replacement parts to match them.

Clean the entire mechanism to remove any sediment or rust flakes that may have entered through the supply piping. Then cover the new rubber washers and gaskets with heat-proof grease, press them in place, and reattach the cover.

Apply heat-proof grease to all parts.

Replacing a ballcock

To install a replacement ballcock, first shut off the water. Then flush the bowl and sponge all remaining water out of the tank. Remove the nut that attaches the ballcock to the supply line and the jamb nut that holds the ballcock to the tank. Pull the ballcock straight up and out of the tank. If putty was used, scrape the residue from the bottom of the tank and clean the area with a rag.

To insure a leak-proof connection, apply pipe-joint compound to the new ballcock gasket. Then insert the shank of the ballcock through the hole in the tank. From underneath the tank, thread the jamb nut onto the ballcock and tighten it with your fingers. Before tightening the nut completely, make sure that the float will not rub against the tank wall or catch on the flush valve overflow. Then tighten the jamb nut with a wrench until the gasket is flattened out and the nut feels tight. Fasten the refill tube to the inside of the overflow tube.

It's a good idea to replace the supply riser when you install a new ballcock. Be sure to coat the cone washer on the top of the riser with pipe-joint compound before you attach it to the ballcock.

Adjusting the performance of the new ballcock is done by bending the brass float arm. Bend it up for higher water, down for lower water. The water level should be about one inch below the overflow tube.

Remove supply line and jamb nut to free ballcock

Lift old ballcock out and lower new one in

When replacing a ballcock, you will find several designs on the market. Still widely used is the traditional brass ballcock with float-arm assembly. The term "ballcock" refers to this specific mechanism. The ball on the end of a float arm rises and falls with the water level, thus closing and opening a valve-cock mechanism. This design was used for so long that all mechanisms that fill a tank are often called ballcocks, even though their floats are not ball-shaped or their valves float-operated. Brass ballcocks will last a long time, but they are expensive.

The Fluidmaster design offers two advantages. First, it is available with antisiphon valves, and second, it can be easily twisted apart at valve level if you need to clean the diaphragm. This second feature is important if you live in an older home, where mineral deposits from aging pipes frequently lodge under the diaphragm.

A third design, called a Fillmaster, uses no float at all. Instead, a built-in regulator allows a measured amount of water into the tank and then shuts off automatically. This lets you easily adjust the water volume to meet the needs of the type of toilet you have.

Fillmaster valve

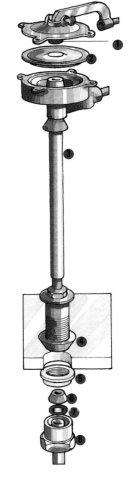

Fluidmaster valve

Brass ballcock components
1 Valve
2 Diaphragm
3 Refill tube
4 Rubber gasket
5 Jamb nut
6 Cone washer
7 Washer
8 Supply riser

Flush valves

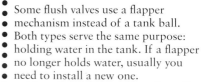

Flush valves can be very persistent sources of trouble. Luckily, most flush valve problems can be corrected with replacement tank balls.

Flush valve components
1 Plastic cup
2 Bowl refill tube
3 Trip lever
4 Overflow tube
5 Lift wires
6 Lift wire guide
7 Tank ball
8 Flush valve
9 Lever
10 Valve seat
11 Lift rod
12 Clip

Adjusting a tank ball

For a flush valve to work properly, the tank ball must drop smoothly and seat tightly. This motion is controlled by the lift wires, which can be adjusted in two ways. The trip lever has multiple holes for attaching the upper lift wire. Pick the one that yields the best results. The travel of the bottom wire is controlled by the lift wire guide that is clamped to the overflow pipe. Loosen this clamp to move the guide.

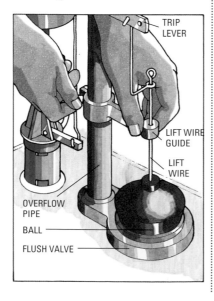

TRIP LEVER

LIFT WIRE GUIDE

LIFT WIRE

OVERFLOW PIPE

BALL

FLUSH VALVE

Replacing a tank ball and assembly

If your tank ball is damaged and needs to be replaced, start by shutting off the water to the toilet. Then reach into the tank, hold the ball still, and unthread the lift wire from the top of the ball. If the ball is very old and brittle, the threaded inset may tear out of the rubber. If this happens, hold the inset with pliers and back the lift wire out.

With the tank ball removed, check the valve seat for calcium buildup and sand the valve seat if necessary. Then slide the lower lift wire through the lift wire guide and thread it into the new tank ball. If either lift wire is bent, replace it.

The lift wire guide is mounted on the overflow tube and controls the travel of the lower lift wire. You adjust it by loosening its clamp screw and moving the guide's position. Sometimes this screw can be very stubborn. Work carefully with it to avoid breaking off the overflow tube in the flush valve. If this happens, you can replace the tube if you put in the effort. But in most cases it makes more sense to replace the whole flush valve.

Hold the upper lift wire next to the trip level and move the wire and ball up and down to determine where the upper wire should be fastened. Feed the upper wire through the best hole and bend it over on the other side.

Then fill the tank with water and flush the toilet several times. Make any necessary adjustments.

To remove ball, first lift it out of flush valve

Hold ball firmly and unthread the lift wire

Some flush valves use a flapper mechanism instead of a tank ball. Both types serve the same purpose: holding water in the tank. If a flapper no longer holds water, usually you need to install a new one.

To replace a flapper, first shut off the water to the tank. Then reach into the tank and carefully pull the rubber eyelets off the flush valve pegs. Disconnect the chain from the trip lever and discard the old flapper. It's a good idea to scour the seat rim with steel wool or emery cloth to remove any calcium buildup.

Some flush valves have no pegs to mount the flapper. In this case, slide the collar of the flapper over the overflow tube until it seats against the bottom of the flush valve. If your flush valve does have pegs, hook the flapper's eyelets over these pegs. Universal flappers, which work for both types of valves, are commonly available. They include instructions for both installations. After the flapper is in place, hook the chain to the trip lever so that there is not more than ½-inch slack in the chain.

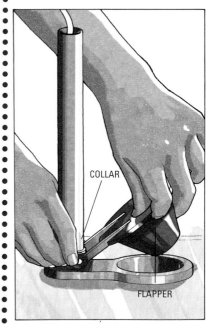

COLLAR

FLAPPER

To install flapper, slide collar to bottom of tube

Attach flapper chain to hole in trip lever

Faulty flush valves

If a flush valve seat is pitted or defective in any way, replacing the flapper or tank ball will do little good. The best solution is to separate the tank from the bowl and replace the entire flush valve. If this seems too intimidating, you can install a replacement seat over the defective seat.

Dealing with a faulty flush valve

Installing a replacement seat

A seat replacement kit consists of a stainless-steel seat rim, a flapper ball carriage, a flapper ball, and epoxy putty. To install a seat replacement kit, you must first remove the flapper or tank ball and dry the defective flush valve completely. Press the new seat over the old so the epoxy is flattened evenly against both surfaces. Then allow the epoxy to dry.

Replacing a flush valve

A more permanent and much preferred solution is to replace the entire flush valve. To do this, you must first remove the tank from the bowl. Because tank bolts are likely to break in the process, you should buy new tank bolts when you buy the replacement flush valve. And it's a good idea to replace the spud washer as long as the tank is being removed.

Flush the bowl and then sponge out all the water in the tank. Disconnect the water supply tube at the ballcock. Then remove the two or three tank bolts that hold the tank to the bowl. Lift the tank straight up and lay it on its side on the floor. Remove the large rubber spud washer from the flush valve spud. Then use a spud wrench or large adjustable pliers to undo the spud nut from the old flush valve assembly.

If any putty or pipe-joint compound is stuck to the bottom of the tank, scrape it clean with a putty knife and sand the area around the opening. Then apply pipe-joint compound to the new spud washer. Insert the flush valve through the tank opening and fasten it in place with the new spud nut. Make sure that the overflow tube

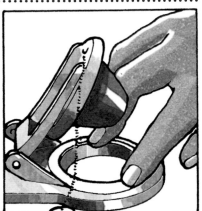
Press new replacement seat into flush valve

is not in the way of the float arm inside the tank. Then press the new rubber spud washer over the spud nut and set the tank back on the bowl.

Apply pipe-joint compound to the rubber washers on the tank bolts and slide the bolts through the tank holes and bowl holes. (Some tanks require that you fasten the tank bolts to the tank with a second set of nuts and washers before setting the tank in place. Other models require rubber spacers, or a cushion, between the tank and the bowl.) Then tighten the tank bolts a little at a time until the tank rests firmly on the bowl, and reconnect the water supply line.

Finally, attach the flapper or tank ball to the overflow tube and make any necessary adjustments so the flapper or ball seats properly on the flush valve. After the toilet has been flushed several times satisfactorily, check for tank leaks by running your hand under the tank and around the tank bolts. If you find a few drips, tighten the tank bolts.

REPLACING A FAULTY TRIP LEVER

Replacing a trip lever is not difficult, but the left-hand threads of the retaining nut have stumped many beginner plumbers. The threads are machined on the shank counterclockwise so that the downward motion of the flush lever will not loosen the nut.

Take the lid off the tank and use an adjustable wrench to loosen the retaining nut. When the nut is loose, slide it off of the trip lever. (Some models have set screws instead of retaining nuts.) Then pull the lever out through the tank opening.

To install a new trip lever, feed the lever into the opening until the handle seats. Then slide the nut over the lever until it makes a right-angle turn and rests against the threads of the shank. Tighten the nut and connect the flapper chain or tank-ball wire to the most convenient hole in the lever. Test and make any needed adjustments.

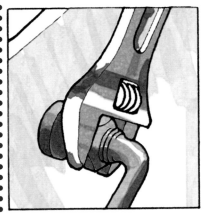
Loosen trip-lever nut by turning clockwise

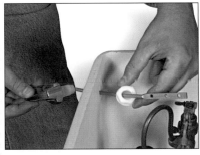
Slide the new trip lever through the tank hole

Coat the spud washer with pipe-joint compound

Attach the tank to the bowl with tank bolts

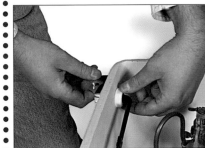
Tighten the nut on the handle threads

357

Maintaining toilets

Dealing with sweating tanks

Condensation appears on the outside of a toilet tank when cold water from the water system meets the warm humid air of a bathroom. The water that collects on the surface of the tank eventually falls to the floor, often causing water damage over time.

Air-conditioned homes do not tend to have tank-sweating problems because air conditioners dehumidify as they cool. If your home is not air-conditioned, your best alternative is to insulate the tank from the inside. There are polystyrene insulating liners on the market, but you can just as easily make your own, using ½-inch polystyrene or foam rubber.

Drain and dry the tank. Cut a piece for each wall and several pieces for the bottom of the tank. Then glue them in place with silicone cement

and be sure to allow the glue to dry for a full day.

You can also reduce the temperature extremes by mixing hot water with the cold before it enters the tank. This method wastes hot water, of course, and unless you install a check valve on the hot-water side of the connection, the other fixtures in your home can back-siphon some of the heated water through their cold-water lines.

A temperature valve is available for this purpose. In a typical installation, the temperature valve should be installed just below the ballcock. You attach the cold water supply to this valve. Then you tap into the hot water supply of your lavatory and run a ⅜-inch soft copper line to the temperature valve. If you have access from below, in an unfinished basement for example, you can tap into the hot-water line below the floor.

Glue foam rubber or polystyrene to the inside of the tank

Repairing wall-mounted toilet tanks

Repairing a leaking flush ell
Loosen the nuts and wrap the threads with sealant tape.

Many older toilets have wall-mounted tanks that are joined to their bowls by means of a 90-degree pipe, called a "flush ell." While the working parts of these toilets are the same as in newer models, dealing with flush ells requires special care. When a flush ell leaks, carefully undo the nuts with a pipe wrench and clean the threads and the ell thoroughly. Then wrap the threads with Teflon sealant tape and tighten the nuts in place again. When tightening the spud nut, be sure to

hold on to the ell firmly to avoid cracking it.

Because wall-mounted tank toilets waste so much water, and because their flush ells make them harder to repair, you should think about replacing them when they need extensive work. For minor repairs, choose methods that do not require taking off the tank. For example, instead of replacing a worn flush valve, install a stainless-steel flush valve seat replacement.

Every toilet bowl has a rim and most rims are filled with holes that allow the water from the tank to wash the sides of the bowl before going down the drain. If your toilet's flush seems sluggish and the bowl doesn't clean well, the rim holes are probably restricted or clogged. Often, this is the result of calcified mineral deposits left by hard water. To remove these calcified minerals, pour vinegar into the overflow tube inside the tank. Let it stand for about 30 minutes.

After the vinegar has had a chance to loosen the deposits, ream each hole with a wire. A 1-foot length of coiled 12-gauge electrical wire works well for this job. But if some holes are heavily clogged, use an Allen wrench as a reaming tool. Use a hand mirror to see under the rim because porcelain can chip easily, take your time and don't exert too much force.

It's also a good idea to use a wire to clean out the siphon jet hole at the bottom of the bowl. This hole can be clogged from mineral deposits too.

Clean toilet rim holes with an Allen wrench

Use a wire to clean siphon jet hole

Bathtub installation

For many years, bathtub designs consisted of various size free-standing tubs. Today, most tubs are of standard dimensions and are built into the bathroom walls with an apron covering the side of the tub left exposed. Except for whirlpools, basic designs have changed very little in the last forty years, but some important material changes have taken place. Tubs today can be made of enameled cast iron, porcelain-covered steel, or molded fiberglass. The installation of tubs, however, remains much the same as it has always been.

Installing a built-in tub

To install a tub, you will need a framed opening that is 60 1/16 inches long by at least 31 inches deep. On the drain opening side, cut a hole in the floor that is 8 inches wide by 12 inches long. Center this hole 15 inches from the back wall. Then nail blocking between the studs all around the tub, centering the blocking 14 inches above the floor.

Slide the tub into the opening slowly. Keep your feet and fingers out of the way. If your tub is made of fiberglass or steel, it should move pretty easily. But if your tub is a 375-pound cast-iron model, you may have to pry it into place with a 2x4.

To attach a steel or fiberglass tub, just screw through the lip of the tub and into the blocking you installed between the studs. Cast-iron tubs have no lip and are held in place by the subflooring and wall finish alone.

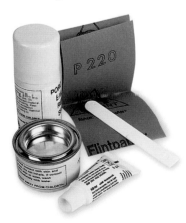

Minor tub-surface damage can be repaired with touchup kits. But major resurfacing should be done by professionals.

Installing a waste and overflow drain

The waste and overflow drain you buy will come in several pieces. Start by locating the drain shoe, drain gasket, and drain strainer. Wrap a small roll of plumber's putty around the flange of the strainer. Then reach below the tub and hold the drain shoe against the tub opening with its rubber gasket sandwiched between the drain shoe and the tub. Thread the strainer into the drain shoe.

Next, assemble the overflow tube, tripwaste tee, and tailpiece, and connect the tee to the drain shoe with the compression nuts provided. You can also attach the tailpiece to the drain trap at this time.

When the waste and overflow components are assembled, you will be ready to install and adjust the tripwaste mechanism. Feed the plunger into the overflow tube and fasten the coverplate screws.

Adjusting a tripwaste

There are two basic tripwaste designs. One has a plunger cylinder attached to the end of the lift linkage. In the down position, this cylinder slides into the tee and closes it. The other design features a pop-up lever and plug in the drain opening of the strainer. When the spring is in the down position, the pop-up lever pushes the plug up and drains the tub.

Pop-up tripwaste
Pull stopper from drain to adjust.

BRASS YOKE

THREADED ROD

LOCKNUT

Plunger tripwaste
Pull plunger from overflow hole to adjust. Turn locknut as needed.

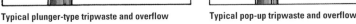

COVER PLATE

TRIP LEVER

OVERFLOW TUBE

LIFT LINKAGE

PLUNGER

SEAT

TRIP-WASTE TEE

DRAIN SHOE

STRAINER

TAILPIECE

Typical plunger-type tripwaste and overflow

LIFT LINKAGE

SPRING

STOPPER

ROCKER LINKAGE

Typical pop-up tripwaste and overflow

Valves and maintenance

Tub valves and showerheads

Most tub/shower valves on the market come with a diverter spout and showerhead. Start by installing the faucet body. Bring ½-inch copper water supply pipe up in the tub wall to a height of 28 inches. Then cut a 44-inch length of copper for the shower riser and a 4½-inch length for the tub spout nipple. Thread or solder the valve in place, close enough to the wall so that the coverplate screws will reach through the tile and drywall and into the faucet. Then solder a sweat/FIP fitting, called a "drop-eared ell," to the shower riser and to the spout leg. Temporarily install the showerhead and tub spout and turn on both the hot and cold sides of the valve to check for leaks.

After checking for leaks, remove the showerhead and tub spout and finish the walls with drywall and tile. Thread the showerhead into its fitting with Teflon sealant tape. To install the spout, measure from the surface of the tile to ⅛ inch inside the spout fitting and buy a ½-inch nipple that length. Wrap sealant tape around both ends of the nipple and thread the nipple into the spout fitting. Then turn the spout onto the nipple and caulk around the spout and faucet coverplate.

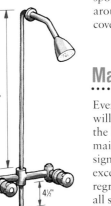

44"

4½"

Piping dimensions
Rough-in a tub valve 28 inches from the floor.

Push grout into joints

Maintaining tub tile walls

Eventually, every tiled tub/shower wall will need repair, but you can extend the life of your tile with a few simple maintenance procedures. The danger signs are loose or missing grout and excessive mildew in grout joints. To regrout a tiled wall, start by digging all soft or loose grout from between tiles with a grout removal tool. These are available from any tile outlet. All joints that need regrouting should be scraped to a depth of at least ¹⁄₁₆ inch. Then wipe away the loose grout.

With the tile prepared, select a small container of premixed, ready-to-use grout and force a liberal amount into each prepared joint with your finger. Use a damp sponge to smooth the grout. Wipe in large diagonal patterns until the grout is uniform. Then allow it to set for one-half hour and wipe the surface again to remove any residue. After the grout has cured for 24 hours, apply clear silicone sealer to the entire wall with a soft cloth.

Replacing ceramic tiles

When water is allowed to seep behind tiles, it can ruin both the tile mastic and the drywall. Eventually, tiles will loosen and fall out. To replace them, you may need to remove all tiles that have come in contact with moisture and replace a section of drywall.

Use a knife or screwdriver to pry under the tiles. If tiles come up easily, take them out. Then cut out the affected drywall and nail a new piece of moisture-resistant drywall in its place. If the edges fit together neatly, you will not have to tape the seams. Prime the new drywall with clear sealer or oil-base paint and allow the primer to dry completely.

To strip the paper and mastic from the removed tile, soak each tile in very hot water and scrape it clean with a putty knife. Lay the tiles out on the floor in the order in which they will go back on. Apply wall-grade tile mastic to the wall or tile with a notched trowel. A ⅛-inch notch will provide enough gap in the cement to hold the tile to the wall.

With the cement in place, press the old tiles back onto the wall. Clean away any tile cement from the tile surfaces and allow the cement to cure for 72 hours. (If you grout the joints too soon, the gases escaping from the cement will cause pinholes to appear in the grout.) When the cement has cured, grout the new tile joints and seal the entire wall with clear silicone sealer.

Apply cement with a notched trowel

Cleaning a tub drain

Often slow-draining tripwastes are partially clogged or need only minor adjustments. Start by undoing the screws that hold the coverplate to the overflow opening and taking the coverplate off. Then, pull the tripwaste linkage up and out of the overflow tube. Clean any hair buildup from the mechanism. On the tripwaste lift linkage you will see either adjustment slots or a threaded adjustment rod with a locknut. If you have a slot adjustment, pinch the two bottom wires together and move them up or down into the next slot level. If your tripwaste has a threaded adjustment, loosen the locknut and turn it up or down about ⅛ inch and retighten the locknut. Then slide the tripwaste back into the overflow and replace the coverplate.

If you do not find a clog at the tripwaste mechanism, you will have to snake the overflow pipe. Because tubs are snaked through the overflow and not through the drain, you will need to remove the coverplate and tripwaste components. Feed a hand snake into the overflow until you feel resistance at the trap bend. When you feel the trap, start cranking the snake in a clockwise direction while pushing the cable slightly. After you crank through the trap, pull the snake out and replace the tripwaste and coverplate.

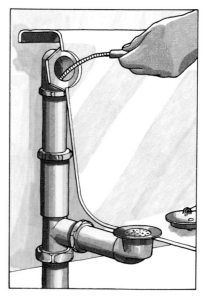

Snake drain through the overflow pipe

Installing showers

Shower stalls come in several varieties and, these days, in quite a few different colors. All-metal or plastic free-standing showers are considered the low end of the market. They can be installed anywhere near a floor drain and are popular in unfinished basements. They are often thought of as utility showers. One-piece fiberglass stalls come in different sizes and colors and are built into framed walls. They are popular in finished bathrooms, both upstairs and down. They always drain into dedicated traps and are plumbed conventionally. A more traditional shower consists of a separate pan built into a framed wall and plumbed into a dedicated trap. The framed walls are covered with moisture-resistant drywall or concrete board and finished with ceramic tile, molded plastic, or fiberglass shower walls.

Installing a free-standing shower

A free-standing shower consists of a raised pan, three wall panels, corner braces, a drain spud, a valve, and a showerhead. All of these parts will come in a box and must be assembled on site.

Start by setting up the pan and plumbing the drainpipe to the nearest floor drain. Then install the walls and corner braces and fasten the walls to the pan according to directions supplied with the shower.

Next, assemble the valve and shower riser and mount the valve and showerhead to the plumbing wall of

the shower. Some free-standing shower stalls will have predrilled valve holes, but other models will have to be drilled. The manufacturer usually supplies a template for this job.

Run surface piping to the nearest floor drain.

Plumbing the drain pipe

A free-standing shower stall

Installing a one-piece fiberglass shower

To install a one-piece fiberglass shower, start by framing the walls. The width of the opening should not be more than 1/16 inch wider than the width of the fiberglass stall. The depth of the opening should exceed the front drywall lip of the shower by more than 2 inches. With the framing completed, cut the drainhole in the floor. To do this, take the measurements from the bottom of the shower stall to find the center of the drain, and make the opening at least 5 inches in diameter so you will have room to work.

Next, install the drain assembly in the pan opening. Wrap the underside of the drain flange with plumber's putty and press it into the opening. Then slide the gasket in place from below and tighten the spud nut.

With the drain installed, you are ready to set the shower in its frame. Because fiberglass shower floors tend to flex, it is a good idea to support the floor with a little perlite plaster. Mix enough of this plaster to cover the

wooden floor 1 inch deep and about 1½ feet extending around the drainhole. Then set the shower in place on top of the plaster. Level the shower walls and step into the shower to settle the base into the plaster. Nail the lip of the shower walls to the studs with galvanized roofing nails and connect the drain trap below the floor.

With the stall in place, measure for the shower-valve cut. The valve should be 48 inches off the floor and the showerhead should be 6 feet or more above the floor. Use a holesaw to cut the shower-valve holes. Solder the shower valve, supply lines, and showerhead riser together and mount this assembly on the framed wall. Make sure the valve extends through the shower wall. With the valve in place, install the showerhead. Then connect the water supply lines to the water system and test the solder joints under full pressure to make sure there are no leaks. Install and finish drywall on the exposed framed walls and paint.

Framing the opening
Frame an opening to match the size of the shower.

Hardboard shield
Use a piece of hardboard to protect the shower when driving nails through the lip.

Installing showers

Installing a shower pan

Like a one-piece shower, a shower pan is installed in a framed opening. Simply frame the stall as you would with a one-piece shower and cut the drain opening in the floor. Install the drain flange in the pan, using putty under the flange, and set the pan in place.

Many shower pans are designed so the drainpipe from the trap extends up, through the drain flange, to just below the drain screen. To seal this joint, insert a rubber gasket around the pipe. Push it in with your hands or tap it with a hammer and packing tool.

With the pan installed and connected to the drain line, install the valve and showerhead piping in the framed wall. Test the piping and cover the walls with moisture-resistant drywall. Then cover the drywall with ceramic tile or a molded shower surround.

Trace the drain opening of shower pan on floor

Check height of drain riser to top of shower pan

Shower pan
This versatile fixture is a good way to start a stall-shower installation. Once you have the pan installed properly, you can add drywall and ceramic tile above to cover the walls. Or you can install one of the many different shower surround wall kits.

Install rubber gasket to seal drain riser to pan

Installing a tub or shower surround

Molded fiberglass or plastic tub and shower surrounds are easy to install and offer long-term durability. The appeal of these molded shower walls is that they have very few seams and therefore few opportunities to leak. The only situation that inhibits the use of surrounds is crooked walls. Even with out-of-plumb walls, a little bottom edge trimming will create an effective seal.

Most tub or shower surrounds come in three pieces. You will have to cut the valve and spout access holes, but beyond that, they are ready to go. Before installing any of the panels, put a level on all walls and on the top of the tub or shower pan to make sure they are reasonably plumb and level. If everything is straight and level, mark the exact center of the back wall in the room. Then mark the center of the back shower wall panel.

Apply several beads of panel adhesive to the back of the center panel. Then peel the paper from the adhesive strips around the edges, if present. Lift the panel up to the back tub or shower pan rim so that the bottom of the panel is an inch away from the wall. Rest the panel on several match sticks laid on the back rim. When the center of the panel is aligned with the center of the back wall, press the bottom of the panel against the wall. Work from bottom to top until the adhesive strip has sealed the entire panel. Then rub the panel firmly with the palm of your hand to flatten the panel to the wall.

Next, install the corner panel opposite the plumbing wall. Use the same method you used for the back panel, but press the corner in first. The corner panel will lap the back panel by several inches.

To cut the valve handles and tub spout in the plumbing wall panel, remove the spout and handles and measure from the tub rim and inside corner. Use a holesaw to cut the openings. Even a small cutting error will ruin the panel, so double-check all measurements before cutting. With the holes made, slide the panel over the valve stems and spout pipe to make sure that everything fits. Then apply panel adhesive, peel the paper from the adhesive strips and press the panel in place, once again starting at the corner.

When the adhesive dries, caulk the bottom seam and the valve flanges with white silicone sealant and both corners with latex tub and tile caulk.

Cut shower-pipe hole in panel with hole saw

Test-fit panel to check that holes are right

Apply adhesive to panel back and install panel

Water heaters

It is hard to imagine living an active life without instant access to hot water. When your water heater fails, don't panic. A little troubleshooting, adjustment, and repair may extend its life.

Water heaters are fairly simple appliances, but when problems arise, they can present an array of confusing symptoms. Because problems can occur in any part of your hot-water systems, don't limit your investigation to the heater alone. The diagnostic charts on the next page will help you locate the source of your hot-water troubles.

The piping system

In some cases, water-heater problems turn out to be piping problems instead. For example, high operating costs can often be traced to dripping faucets or leaking pipes. Several dripping faucets in your home can waste hundreds of gallons of water a year. A simple, inexpensive faucet repair can pay for itself quickly, in the energy it saves.

Long uninsulated piping runs also waste hot water. When you draw water from a faucet at the end of a run, hot water from the tank must first push the cooled water through the pipe. This not only wastes water but energy as well. Uninsulated pipes dissipate heat much as a radiator does. To keep the energy you buy from escaping through the walls of hot-water pipes, you should consider insulating all hot-water lines.

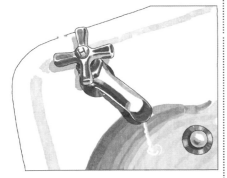
Dripping hot-water faucets are big energy wasters

Problems inside the tank

An aging water system can carry sediment into a tank, or sediment may collect in flakes of calcium and lime. In electric models, sediment-covered heating elements will burn out quickly. In gas water heaters, sediment accumulates in the bottom of the tank and forms a barrier between the heat source and the water. Not only does sediment make your heater very inefficient but air bubbles created by the heat percolate through the sediment and cause a continuous rumbling sound. So if your electric heater burns up lower elements frequently, or if your heater rumbles, sediment may be the culprit.

To remove sediment, drain as much water as possible from the tank. Then turn the water supply on and allow the new water to flush through the drain valve for a few minutes.

Dip tubes

A dip tube is a plastic pipe that delivers incoming cold water to the heat source near the tank bottom. Occasionally, a dip tube will slip through the cold-water inlet fitting and fall into the tank. When this happens, cold water entering the tank is drawn through the hot-water outlet without being heated. To replace a dip tube, disconnect the inlet pipe from the tank. Then slide a new dip tube into the fitting and reconnect the inlet pipe.

Anode rods

New water heaters are equipped with magnesium anode rods that prevent rust from developing in the porcelain tank lining. An anode rod acts as a sacrificial element to draw rust and corrosion to itself. These rods are usually troublefree, but problems can occur when water has an unusually high concentration of dissolved mineral salts. As a result, the water will have a gassy odor or taste. To correct this, replace the magnesium rod with an aluminum rod.

Relief valves

A relief valve keeps a heater from exploding in the event a thermostat becomes stuck. When pressure builds and the water gets too hot, the relief valve opens until the pressure is equalized. However, the spring mechanism in some valves weakens with age and the valves release water with any slight variation in pressure. To correct this, simply remove the old valve and thread in a new one.

To remove sediment, drain tank with garden hose

Remove cold inlet pipe and slide dip tube in place

To remove anode, unscrew from tank and pull out

Screw new valve into side of tank

GAS WATER-HEATER DIAGNOSTIC CHART

SYMPTOMS AND CONDITIONS

CAUSES	Burner will not light	Burner flame floats—Lifts off	Burner flame yellow—Lazy	Burner flame noisy	Burner flame too high	Burner pops when turned off or on	Flame burns at orifice	Pilot will not stay lit	High operating costs	Insufficient hot water	Slow hot-water recovery	Pounding and steaming at faucet	Dripping relief valve	Thermostat fails to close	Condensation	Combustion odors	Smoking—Carbon formation	Pilot flame too small	Pilot flame too large	SOLUTIONS
Insufficient secondary air			●		●										●	●				Provide ventilation
Dirt in main burner orifice	●		●		●	●			●	●	●					●	●	●		Clean—Install dirt trap
Dirt in pilot burner orifice								●										●		Clean—Install dirt trap
Flue clogged			●	●				●	●		●					●	●	●		Remove—Blow clean—Reinstall
Pilot line clogged	●							●										●		Clean—Install dirt trap
Burner line clogged	●			●																Clean—Check source and correct
Wrong pilot burner	●							●									●	●		Replace with correct pilot burner
Loose thermocouple								●												Finger-tight plus 1/4 turn
Defective thermocouple lead	●							●												Replace thermocouple
Defective thermostat	●					●					●		●		●					Replace thermostat—(Call plumber)
Improper calibration									●	●	●	●	●	●						Replace—(Call plumber)
Heater in confined area	●	●	●												●	●	●			Install vent in wall or door
Heater not connected to the flue		●	●		●										●	●	●			Provide and connect to proper flue
Sediment or lime in tank									●	●	●	●								Drain and flush—Repeat
Heater too small									●	●	●									Upgrade to larger heater
Gas leaks									●											Check with utility—Repair immediately
Excess draft		●		●					●		●									Check source, stop draft
Long runs of exposed piping									●	●										Insulate hot lines only
Surge from washer solenoid valve												●								Insulate air cushion pipe
Faulty relief valve												●								Install rated T&P valve—Soon
Dip tube broken										●	●	●								Replace dip tube

ELECTRIC WATER-HEATER DIAGNOSTIC CHART

SYMPTOMS AND CONDITIONS

CAUSES	No hot water	Insufficient hot water	Slow hot-water recovery	Steaming and pounding at faucet	High operating costs	Dripping relief valve	Excessive relief valve operation	Condensation	Element failure	Blown fuse, tripped circuit breaker	Service wires charred or hot	Continuous operation	Singing thermostat	Wet heater insulation	Gas odor or taste in water	Fluctuating temperatures	Rusty or discolored water	Rumbling, pounding in tank	SOLUTIONS
No power	●									●									Check fuses, breakers—Reset
Undersize heater		●		●								●				●			Install larger heater
Undersize elements		●	●									●							Replace with rated element
Wrong wiring connections	●	●		●					●	●	●								See manufacturer's instructions
No relief valve				●															Install relief valve—Soon
Leaking faucets		●		●										●					Locate and repair
Leaks around heating elements	●			●				●						●					Tighten tank flange
Sediment or lime in tank		●		●													●	●	Drain and flush—Water treatment?
Lime formation on elements		●	●														●	●	Replace elements
Thermostat not flush with tank		●	●	●								●	●			●			Reposition
Faulty wiring connection	●	●	●						●	●		●				●			Locate, reconnect
Faulty ground		●	●	●							●								See maker's grounding instructions
Short	●		●	●					●	●	●								Locate short circuit—Correct
Gas from mangnesium anode rod														●			●		Install aluminum anode rod
Damage from electrolysis																	●		Install dielectric unions
Excessive mineral deposits			●														●		Flush tank—Install water filter
Improper calibration	●		●	●	●	●	●	●				●							Replace thermostat—(Call plumber)
Eroded anode rod																●	●		Replace
Faulty thermostat	●	●	●	●	●		●	●								●	●		Replace—(Call plumber)
Faulty high limit (ECO)	●	●	●	●								●					●		Replace
Open high limit (ECO)	●																		Reset button or replace
Dip tube broken		●	●		●											●			Replace dip tube

Gas water-heater problems

A typical gas water heater consists of a steel tank, a layer of insulation, and a sheetmetal jacket. The bottom of the tank is heated by a fixed gas burner that is controlled by a thermocouple and a regulator valve. To vent excess heat and noxious fumes, a gas heater tank is equipped with a hollow tube, through its center, that connects to a house flue.

A supply of secondary air

For a gas heater to burn evenly and efficiently, it must have an ample supply of combustion air. If your water heater shares space with a furnace and clothes dryer, then a continuous air supply is especially important, because they compete with the heater for air. When a heater is starved for air, the flame will burn orange, jump, and pop. An orange flame means higher operating costs. Be sure that the heater has a sufficient supply of combustion air by opening doors in confined areas or by installing louvered vents in the doors.

A clogged flue

A clogged flue is caused by rust or debris that accumulates at tight bends in the flue piping. A clogged flue is a serious heath hazard. Deadly carbon gases, unable to vent through the flue, are forced into living quarters. An easy way to check that the flue is working properly is to place a burning match, or burning piece of cardboard, near the flue hat while the heater is on. The smoke should be drawn into the flue. To locate an obstruction, turn the heater to pilot and disassemble the vent pipes. Inspect and clean each piece of pipe, then reassemble the flue.

Dirt in gas lines

Dirt in gas lines often makes its way into the heater's control mechanism. A dirty pilot line or burner line will cause the heater to burn unevenly or to stop burning entirely. To clean these lines, disconnect them from the regulator and slide a thin wire through each line. Then blow air through the lines. If dirt is lodged in the gas control valve, call a plumber. Control valves are delicate mechanisms that can be dangerous if serviced improperly.

Thermocouple breakdown

A thermocouple is a thick copper wire that has a heat sensor on one end and a plug on the other. Heat from the pilot flame sends a tiny millivolt charge through the wire, which causes the plug to open the control valve. When a thermocouple's sensor burns out, the heater's magnetic safety valve remains closed and the pilot light won't burn. To replace a thermocouple, turn off the gas and disconnect the entire burner assembly from the control valve. Remove the thermocouple from its retainer clip near the pilot and snap a new one in its place. Be sure to position the sensor directly in line with the pilot flame. Finally, reconnect the burner assembly to the control valve.

Gas leaks

If you smell a strong gas odor, it's likely there is a dangerous gas leak. Leave the house immediately and call your gas or utility company. If you smell only a light trace of gas, it may be a leaky pipe joint. To find the leak, brush every joint with a mixture of dish detergent and warm water. Soap bubbles will appear around the leaky joint. Shut off the gas at the meter. Bleed the line at the union located above the heater and ventilate the area.

Take apart the leaking joint and clean the fitting and pipe thoroughly with a wire brush. Then reassemble the parts with pipe-joint compound. Tighten all the joints. Turn on the gas, bleed the air from the line, and retest all the new joints with soap and warm water.

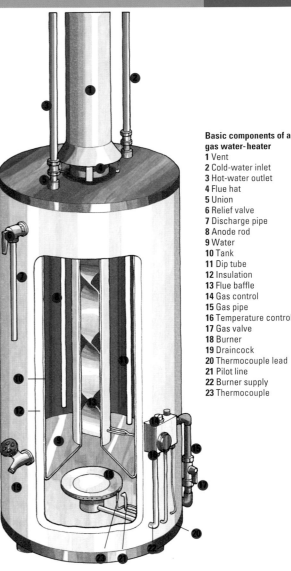

Basic components of a gas water-heater
1 Vent
2 Cold-water inlet
3 Hot-water outlet
4 Flue hat
5 Union
6 Relief valve
7 Discharge pipe
8 Anode rod
9 Water
10 Tank
11 Dip tube
12 Insulation
13 Flue baffle
14 Gas control
15 Gas pipe
16 Temperature control
17 Gas valve
18 Burner
19 Draincock
20 Thermocouple lead
21 Pilot line
22 Burner supply
23 Thermocouple

PILOT
THERMOCOUPLE
RETAINING CLIP SCREW
Loosen clip screw to remove thermocouple

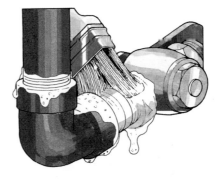

Test for gas leaks with soap and water mixture

Problems with electric water heaters

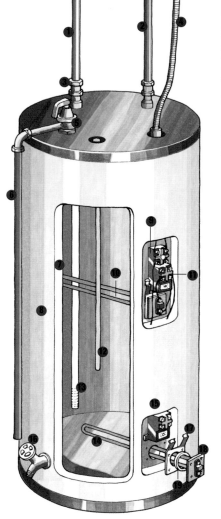

Basic components of an electric water heater
1 Cold-water inlet
2 Hot-water outlet
3 Union
4 Power cable
5 Relief valve
6 Discharge pipe
7 Insulation
8 Tank
9 High-limit switch
10 Upper element
11 Upper thermostat
12 Anode rod
13 Dip tube
14 Lower element
15 Lower thermostat
16 Draincock
17 Bracket
18 Element flange
19 Gasket

If your electric water heater fails, first check for burned-out fuses or tripped circuit breakers at the main service panel. If the problem is not in the service panel, go to the heater. Remove the access panels and press the reset button on each thermostat and listen for a ticking noise caused by expansion as the elements begin to heat up. If this procedure doesn't produce hot water, the problem may be in the wiring, thermostats, or elements.

Loose wires

Remove the access panels for both heating elements and check to see if any wire has come loose from its terminal. If a wire is loose or disconnected, turn off the power to the heater, then loosen the terminal screw, bend the end of the wire around it, and tighten the screw.

Defective thermostat element

To determine if the problem is in the element, thermostat, or high-limit protector, test each part with a volt-ohmmeter (VOM). If you do not have a VOM, try simple logic. If the heater produces plenty of warm water but no hot water, then the top element or thermostat is probably defective. If you get a few gallons of very hot water followed by cool water, then the bottom element or thermostat probably needs replacing. Since elements fail much more often than thermostats, assume a faulty element or test with a VOM.

terminals. (Some elements thread into a threaded tank opening, while others bolt to a gasket flange.) Before turning the power on, fill the tank with water and bleed all trapped air through the faucets. An element that is energized when dry will burn out in seconds.

Finally, replace the insulation, thermostat protection plates, and access panel. Then turn on the power. If after 45 minutes you still don't have sufficient hot water, a replacement thermostat is in order.

Replacing a thermostat

Shut off the power and disconnect the wires from the thermostat's terminals. Pry out the old thermostat and snap the new one into the clip. Then reconnect the wires, replace the insulation, and turn the power back on. Allow both elements to complete their heating cycles and then test the water temperature at the faucets using a meat thermometer. Adjust the thermostat until the water temperature is between 130° and 140° F.

Replacing an element

To replace a defective element, first shut off the power and water supply to the heater. Next, drain the tank to a level below the element to be replaced. Disconnect the wires from the terminals and unscrew the element. Pull the element straight out of the tank. Then clean the gasket surface, coat it lightly with pipe-joint compound and seat a new gasket. Attach the new element to the heater and reconnect the wires to the

New designs in electric water heaters

For years, electric water heaters have been made with metal storage tanks. All other components were replaceable, but when a tank developed a leak, the entire heater had to be replaced. The longevity of the tank, then, determined the longevity of the heater. While most manufacturers still prefer metal tanks, some offer plastic tanks. Because plastic cannot rust through, and because mineral salts will not adhere to it, this new design has real potential.

Another recent design rejects the principle of storing hot water entirely. The makers of this design maintain that heating and reheating stored water is too wasteful. They offer, instead, a system that heats cold water as it passes through a heating element. In this way, only the water used is heated. With careful use and planning, these units should offer real savings. If you regularly take showers while your clothes washer or dishwasher is operating, then this system may have trouble keeping up. In any case, consider your needs before investing.

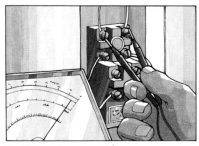

Troubleshoot thermostat with an ohmmeter

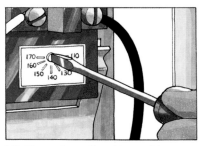

Adjust temperature setting with screwdriver

Water softeners

The water we pump into our homes varies greatly in quality from region to region, and even from well to well. The degree of mineral content in groundwater accounts for these differences and can also account for a few health and plumbing problems as well. Most municipal water systems provide water that falls within tolerable limits of hardness and dissolved mineral salts. Others, especially rural systems, do not. When mineral levels are too high, water must be treated or filtered to bring it within acceptable tolerances for domestic use.

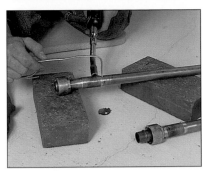

To install softener, join union stubs to risers

Water softeners

The purpose of a water softener is to substitute sodium for calcium, magnesium, or iron. These minerals, in sufficient concentrations, can cause clogged pipes and appliances and can give drinking water a foul smell. Water softeners neutralize these minerals, which makes conditioned water feel softer. It helps eliminate soap scum on fixtures and reduces the amount of mineral sediment in water heaters.

If soap does not dissolve easily in your water or if mineral buildup occurs on your fixtures, then you may need a softener. Have your water tested by a local lab to get a good reading of the mineral content.

If you do need a water softener, consider isolating your main cold-water drinking faucets and your outdoor hydrants. Softeners naturally raise the salt content of drinking water, which presents some health risks, especially for those on low-sodium diets. And, of course it doesn't make sense to pay for soft water that you use to wash the car or water the garden.

The easiest installation in a home with finished basement ceilings is to tie the intake of the softener to the inlet line of your water heater. With a hot-water-only installation, you get soft water where you need it most, in your clothes washer and dishwasher. You will also get some soft water in your tub/shower or wherever you mix hot and cold water.

But, for a more complete installation, you should tie the softener into the incoming water trunk line before it reaches any branch fittings. To isolate cold-water drinking faucets and outdoor sillcocks or hydrants, cut and cap the branch fittings that serve these lines and tie all hard-water lines in at a new location, somewhere between the meter and the soft-water inlet fitting.

All water softeners must be equipped with a three-way bypass valve. You can buy a three-way valve and splice it into the inlet and outlet lines of the softener. Or you can make one yourself, by first installing a separate globe valve in the inlet and outlet lines. Then install a tee in each pipe above these valves, joined by a third valve that acts as a bypass. When the softener is in service, the two line valves are open and the center valve is closed. When the softener is not in service, the two line valves are closed and the center valve is opened to allow water to pass through without going to the softener.

Attach purge line and overflow tube to unit head

Connect riser-pipe unions to bypass valve

Push softener into place against wall

Solder risers to water supply pipes

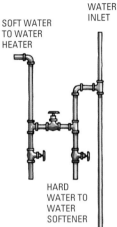

Water softener piping
You can make your own 3-way bypass valve for a water softener installation by following this diagram.

SOFT WATER TO WATER HEATER

HARD-WATER INLET

HARD WATER TO WATER SOFTENER

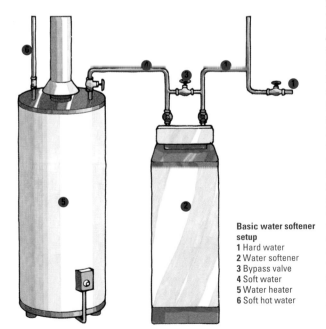

Basic water softener setup
1 Hard water
2 Water softener
3 Bypass valve
4 Soft water
5 Water heater
6 Soft hot water

Water filters

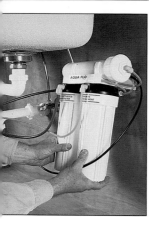

Installing in-line filters

In-line filters are good at removing sediment and organic and inorganic contaminants in gas, liquid, and particle form. Carbon filters are some of the most popular. In-line filters must be installed in a vertical position in the main water line of the house—before the line branches off to any fixtures or appliances.

Begin work by draining the water system. Then cut out a section of pipe (usually about 14 inches long) to accommodate the top of the filter body and two short piping stubs on both sides. Install a male adapter, with a pipe stub soldered in the end, on both sides of the filter. Then install a shutoff valve on both of the stubs so you can turn off the water flow at any time. If you use valves that have a compression fitting on one end, you won't have to solder the stubs to the valves. To maintain electrical grounding for your home, add a jumper cable over the top of the filter.

In-line filter
Removes common contaminants from home water systems.

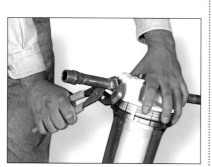
Install adapters with stubs in both sides of filter.

Install shutoff valve on both sides of the filter.

Add jumper wire to maintain electrical grounding.

The quality of the drinking water in this country is very high, from large cities to small rural towns. But that doesn't mean that every glass of tap water is entirely safe. Municipal treatment can vary from day to day, and countless private wells were tested only when they were drilled, not since. For these reasons and others, more people are starting to treat their own drinking water. The good news is that there's an equipment solution for just about every water problem. The bad news is that no single piece of equipment handles all the problems.

Installing reverse-osmosis filters

Reverse-osmosis (RO) filters are very good at removing nitrates and hazardous chemical pollutants. But they don't remove biological contaminants. If you have both problems, need have to install two filtering systems.

RO units work by forcing water through a permeable membrane that does the filtering. Because this membrane is so dense, the filter can't handle high water volumes. RO units are not designed for complete plumbing system filtration. They're usually installed under kitchen sinks to purify drinking and cooking water.

To install one, first assemble the filter according to the manufacturer's instructions. Then mount it on the inside wall of your kitchen-sink cabinet. Slide the water-storage tank into the cabinet and connect the tank to the filter with the tubing provided.

The unit comes with a countertop-mounted dispensing faucet. It can be installed in the sink, if you remove the spray hose, or on the countertop next to the sink. If you put it on the countertop, you'll have to bore a hole through the counter to mount it. Attach supply tubing from the storage tank to this faucet.

To tap into the household water, install a saddle tap on the cold water supply line that serves the kitchen sink. Then run tubing from the tap to the filter unit.

This filter requires a drain connection to the kitchen-sink waste line. Drill a hole in this pipe and install a drain saddle according to the instructions supplied with the filter. Connect a hose from this saddle to the drain port on the filter.

Turn on the water to the filter and flush at least two full tanks of water through the faucet before using the water for drinking or cooking. This should take a couple of days. Be patient. The kits come with a preservative solution inside that can cause flu-like symptoms unless it is flushed out completely.

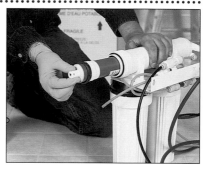
Install filter cartridge.

Mount dispenser in sink hole.

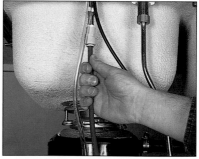
Attach supply tube to dispenser.

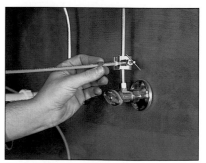
Attach supply tube to saddle valve.

Rural septic systems

The most common private waste-disposal system in this country is the septic system. It's composed of two major parts: a septic tank, which is a storage unit for house waste, and a leach field, which disperses the waste into the ground after it has been broken down in the septic tank. Both of these are buried underground as is the piping that connects them. Raw-sewage cesspools, for obvious reasons, are no longer permitted for residential use. When well maintained, a septic system can last the life of a house. When not maintained, a system can fail in five years. Once it fails, it can't be reclaimed. A new system is needed at a great cost.

Mound leach field

If a septic system fails it will usually be in the winter or early spring. The reasons are twofold. First, frozen soil releases no water through plant roots and little through evaporation. This means that leach fields in winter are relegated to simple storage troughs, nearly filled with water. Second, spring is often the wettest time of year. These two conditions make for wetter, oxygen-saturated soil around the leach fields, which, in turn, slows or reduces the nitrification of effluent. At some point the leach fields can hold no more water and the system backs up.

To circumvent this, researchers developed a leach field that was built above ground in the shape of a mound. With sufficient ground slope between the tank and the leach field, effluent flows directly into the mound. When the terrain is flat, a pump is used to lift the waste to mound level.

The mound is constructed of a layered aggregate containing a gridwork of perforated pipe. Because sewage is warm when leaving the tank, the mound does not freeze and evaporation occurs through the top as well as through the four sides, even in winter. Mound systems are still new in parts of the country, but most health departments will allow their use.

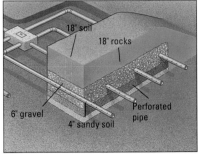

Mound system construction details

Septic tanks

To understand the need for routine maintenance, you must first understand how a septic system works. As raw sewage is drained into the septic tank, bacteria break the sewage down into gray water, bottom sludge, and surface scum. As more sewage enters the tank, gray water rises through a baffle and floats out into the leach field. Once in the field, around 60 percent of the gray water is consumed by plants. The remaining 40 percent is lost through surface evaporation. The nitrate residue left behind is then consumed by another kind of bacteria found only in the top 4 feet of soil.

Because of the scum and sludge left in the tank, your septic tank must be pumped out every two or three years. If you do not have your tank pumped, the sludge at the bottom will rise, thus reducing the capacity of the tank. The scum will continue to build up at the top of the tank until it is deep enough to make its way through the baffle and into the leach field. Once inside the leach field, it will coat the walls of the trench and clog

the gravel storage area. When the walls of the leach field are sealed, the leach field will fail.

To keep your septic tank and leach field in working order, have the tank pumped at least once every three to four years and avoid planting trees near the tank or on top of the leach field.

Basic components of a typical septic system
1 Septic tank
2 Access cover
3 House sewer pipe
4 Baffle
5 Distribution box
6 Gravel
7 Leach field
8 Perforated pipe

Repairing a collapsed culvert leach field

Some leach fields use concrete half-culverts (inverted on concrete blocks) instead of perforated pipe. Culverts can break when a vehicle is driven over them. If a section does collapse, you can dig it up and replace it. Though you can do this work by hand, it makes a lot of sense to hire an excavator with a backhoe to do it for you.

Because leach fields work best near the surface, you will find the top of the culvert only a foot or two down. Dig the dirt above the culvert away and keep it to one side of the ditch. When you hit gravel, dig it out of the trench

and store it on the other side.

Each culvert will be 3 to 4 feet long. When you've removed the gravel from around the broken one, pull it out. Clean most of the gravel out of the ditch and set a new length of half culvert on the blocks. Push the gravel back into the ditch until the dome of the culvert is covered. Then lay landscape fabric over the gravel and fill the remainder of the ditch with dirt. Because uncompacted dirt will settle in time, leave a 4-inch mound over the trench. Then soak the dirt and replace the sod or plant new grass.

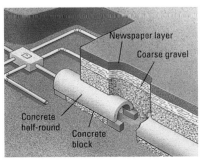

Typical culvert leach field installation

Sprinkler systems

With the introduction of plastic pipe and fittings to the plumbing market, simple do-it-yourself sprinkler systems are a lot easier to install, even in cold weather climates. Still, the most difficult aspect of any in-ground sprinkler job is digging all the pipe trenches. If you don't want to make this harder than it already is, plan your layout carefully before you set a spade to the ground.

Installing a system

You will have to make a scale drawing of your lawn and include features such as driveways and sidewalks, which may present piping barriers. You should be able to cover your lawn evenly by matching sprinkler heads to specific areas. Use single-direction pop-up heads for terraces and flower gardens, 45- and 90-degree heads for corners and along drives, and 360-degree heads for open spaces. No matter which combination you use, you will have some overlap. Overlapping patterns are not a real problem because coverage is lighter the farther away from the heads. By researching the products on the market, you can get a good idea of how each head works and in which situation each should be used. You can do the layout yourself or get help from your local dealer.

Another important factor in planning your system is the water pressure in your home. With high pressure, amd just a few good heads, you may be able to feed all heads from a single line and valve. But, with less pressure and a bigger system, you need to divide the system up into two or three separately controlled lines so that one section can be charged at a time. Most sprinkler dealers will lend you a pressure gauge designed to be used on outside faucets. When testing for water pressure, make sure that none of the indoor fixtures is running at the same time.

Joining plastic pipe
Plastic pipe is easily assembled. Use cleaning solvent and rag to prepare joints. Then join parts with solvent cement.

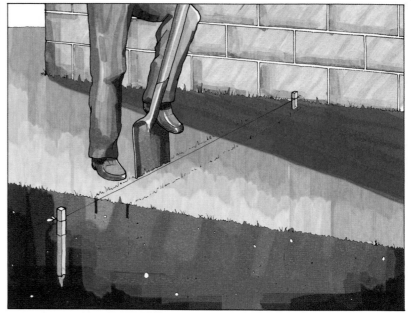
Lay out your trench lines with string, then cut through the sod with a flat-blade shovel or spade

Glue tees into pipe at head locations

Test fit heads to check proper height

Apply Teflon tape to fitting before final assembly

Insert drain fittings into drain tees

Place gravel under drains to prevent clogging

Glue piping lines to zone-control valves

Water wells

Making water connections

With all heads installed, replace the sod all the way up to the house connection. At the house, you will have to bore a hole into the basement to access your water supply. This is best done through a first-floor rim joist. But make the hole wherever it's convenient. You also need to install a vacuum breaker in the water line that goes into the house. (A vacuum breaker is necessary to keep your in-house plumbing from back-siphoning any contaminated water. It also allows your sprinkler heads to drain properly.) Run a copper pipe from the vacuum breaker down to the ground and attach it to the plastic sprinkler pipe with an adapter and an elbow. Use copper pipe on the other side of the breaker to enter the house.

Permanent indoor connections

Once the pipe is through the basement wall, you have to join it to a cold water supply line in the house. Choose the one nearest to the hole. Shut off and drain the house water. Then cut the pipe and install a tee in this line. Because the supply line will likely be ¾-inch diameter, you'll have to increase the pipe diameter to the 1-inch size used outdoors. Also install a full flow shutoff valve at this point.

Before you complete the joint between the outside and inside lines, install a boiler drain valve just below where the sprinkler line comes into the house. This valve will help you seasonally drain the system, before winter.

When all the assembly is complete, turn on the water, bleed the air out of the lines, and check for any leaks.

Install vacuum breaker on outside wall of house.

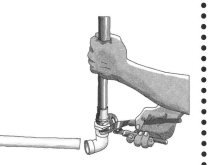

Join system pipes with adapter and elbow.

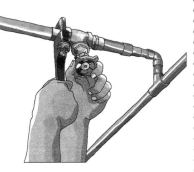

Install tee and shutoff valve in house water line.

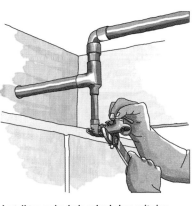

Install tee and a drain valve below exit pipe.

Submersible pumps

If you live in a city or a town, you probably don't think much about how water gets to your house. All you need to know is how to open the tap. But if you move a few miles outside of town, this picture could change. Most rural homes have their own wells and must maintain a fairly complicated system that gets water from the ground to the tap.

There are several different systems that accomplish this. One of the most common is the submersible pump system. This consists of a cylindrical pump that is lowered in the casing to the bottom of a deep well. It's connected to a storage tank in the house with plastic pipe. It's also connected to the electric system with waterproof cable. When the pressure switch senses reduced pressure in the storage tank it turns on the pump and more water is delivered.

To keep the system from freezing in northern climates, the pipe that joins the pump and the tank is installed below the local frost line.

The pumps are durable and last a long time. But when they wear out, the well cap is removed and the pump and all the piping is pulled up through the top of the well.

Water-well pressure switch

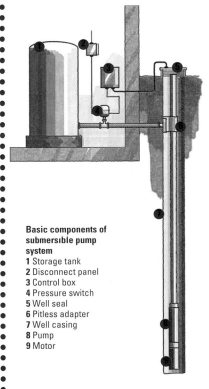

Basic components of submersible pump system
1 Storage tank
2 Disconnect panel
3 Control box
4 Pressure switch
5 Well seal
6 Pitless adapter
7 Well casing
8 Pump
9 Motor

Plumbing outdoors

Outdoor plumbing can be a welcome alternative to stringing garden hoses across your yard. A freezeless spigot, often called a hydrant, in your garden is a lot more convenient and less annoying than a bunch of hoses. A seepage pit to serve a drain in your garage workshop can also make life easier. Fortunately, outdoor plumbing is not much more difficult to install than indoor plumbing. The obvious difference is that, in some places, outdoor plumbing must be able to withstand subzero temperatures.

Freezeless yard hydrants

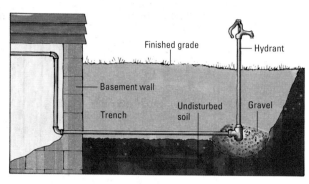

Typical yard hydrant installation. Supply piping is below frost line.

Yard hydrants have their shutoff locations buried below frost level. When you lift the handle at the top of the hydrant, you pull a long stem inside the casing upward. The stopper at the lower end of the stem is lifted out of its seat and water travels up through the pipe casing to the spout. When you push the handle down, the stem pushes the stopper back into its seat and interrupts the flow of water. The water left standing in the casing then drains back through an opening at the bottom of the hydrant, just below frost level.

Installing a hydrant

Whether you bring water from a basement wall or a buried rural line, you will have to rent a trenching machine. The depth of the trench you dig will be dictated by how deeply the ground freezes in your area. Hydrants can be purchased in several lengths for a variety of conditions. A 5-foot depth is common in colder climates.

If you intend to bring water from a house system through a basement wall, simply start the trencher a few inches away from the wall and trench to the hydrant location. At the hydrant location, force the trencher to dig a foot or so deeper. Then, trench a few feet past where the hydrant will be located to avoid having loose soil fall back into the trench.

With the trench ready, measure carefully and drill directly into the

open trench from inside the basement. Then slide one end of a coil of buriable plastic pipe through the wall from the outside and reel the coil out in the trench to the hydrant location. Leave the hydrant end of the coil out of the ditch so that you can attach the brass conversion fitting. Attach this fitting to the supply pipe with stainless-steel hose clamps. Before putting the hydrant in the trench, pour about 50 pounds of gravel into the deeper section of the ditch. This will provide a small reservoir for the drain water from the hydrant. Set the hydrant in place and pour a few more pounds of gravel around the hydrant. Then backfill the trench and make the connection to a convenient supply line inside the house.

Seepage pits are miniature leach fields designed to dispose of gray water discharged from remote floor drains. If your drainage system is served by a municipal sewer, seepage pits will not be needed, and, in most cases, not allowed. If, however, your home is in a rural area, a seepage pit can save you the trouble of tapping into your septic system when outbuildings are some distance from the house.

The size of the pit you build will depend upon anticipated volume. For a garage or workshop, a 3- or 4-foot inside diameter is often sufficient. Before starting the job, however, check with local code authorities for structural guidelines.

Begin by digging a more or less round pit roughly 5 feet deep and 5 feet in diameter. Then lay a starter course of concrete blocks side by side around the outside walls of the pit. Follow with a series of courses until you are within 1½ feet of the finished grade. At this point, you can trench the drainage pipe to the pit. If you slide the drainpipe through an opening in one of the top blocks, it will be held permanently in place. Finally, construct a cover from treated lumber.

In sandy soil, tape a few layers of newspaper around the outside perimeter of the block to keep the soil from sifting in when you backfill. The newspaper will decompose after the soil settles. Regrade the ground and plant some grass.

Remove hydrant head to service parts

Lift out valve stem to replace old stopper

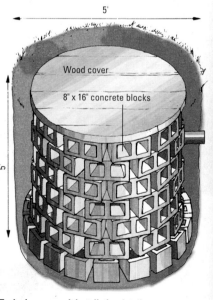

5'

5'

Wood cover

8" x 16" concrete blocks

Typical seepage pit installation details

Attach vacuum-breaker fitting to sillcocks to prevent back-siphoning of polluted water into house supply lines.

Open fires

For centuries open fires were our only domestic heating. Inefficient and wasteful, their only benefits were the radiant heat from the burning fuel and some milder warmth from heated chimneys. They are nowadays used mainly as attractive focal points in homes heated by more modern means.

How an open fire works

To burn well, any fire needs a good supply of oxygen **(1)** and a means for its smoke and gases to escape **(2)**. If either of these is cut off, the fire will be stifled and will eventually go out.

The domestic open fire is built on a barred grate **(3)** through which ash and debris fall and oxygen is sucked up into the base of the fire to maintain combustion.

As the fuel burns, it gives off heated gases which expand and become lighter than the surrounding air so that they rise **(4)**. To prevent the gases and smoke from drifting out and filling the room, a chimney above the fire gives them an escape route, taking them above the roof level of the house to be discharged in the outside air.

As the hot gases rise, they cause suction at the bottom of the fire that draws in a supply of oxygen to keep it burning. For this reason, a good fire needs not only an effective chimney but also good ventilation in the room where it is burning, so that the air consumed by the fire can be continually replenished.

In modern homes or older homes with new, tightly sealed doors and windows, a fire may not burn properly due to a lack of consistent air supply. In these cases, extra ventilation must be provided—either through a dedicated fireplace vent or by simply opening a window slightly to admit the necessary air.

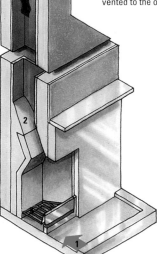

Oxygen in, smoke out
1 Air is sucked in as the smoke rises.
2 Smoke escapes up the narrow flue.
3 The grate lets air in and allows ash to collect underneath.
4 Smoke and gases are vented to the outside.

Sweeping chimneys

- **Vacuum sweeping**
You can have a chimney cleaned with a special vacuum cleaner. Its nozzle, inserted through a cover over the fire opening, sucks the soot out of the chimney. Although this is a relatively clean method, it may not remove heavy soot deposits or other obstructions.

- **Chemical cleaning**
There are chemicals that will remove light deposits and help prevent a buildup in the future. In liquid or powder form, they are sprinkled onto a hot fire, producing a nontoxic gas that causes soot to crumble away from inside the chimney. Keep in mind, though, that a thorough cleaning by brush is considered the best approach.

All solid fuels give off dust, ash, acids, and tarry substances as they burn, and this material is carried up through the chimney, where a part of it condenses and collects as a substance called creosote. If too much creosote collects in a chimney, it not only reduces the gas flow (and prevents the fire from burning properly) it can even cause a blockage. More importantly, the creosote can ignite, causing a potentially dangerous chimney fire.

To prevent creosote buildup, clean your chimney at least once a year before the heating season. It may be necessary to clean the chimney again during the heating season—especially if an efficient, airtight wood stove is in use or green wood has been burned. It's a good idea to have your chimney inspected by a professional chimney sweep, as well.

Though it's a dirty job, you can clean a chimney without making a great deal of mess to be cleaned up afterward, provided you take some care. You can rent the brushes, but be sure to get a size that matches your chimney. (It should fit tightly.) Modern ones have nylon bristles and fiberglass extension rods.

Remove all loose items from the fireplace surround and hearth, then roll back the carpet and cover it with a drop cloth or newspapers for protection. Drape a large old sheet or blanket over the surround, weighting it down along the top and leaning something heavy against each side to form a seal with the edges.

Actual cleaning may be done by pushing a brush up from a fireplace or by forcing it down from the chimney top. If the roof is dangerous or the chimney is covered by a chimney cap, sweep from inside the house. (You may have to remove the damper plate at the base of the flue to fit the brushes in.) If possible, sweep from the top down. To do this, first be sure the fireplace opening is tightly covered with drop cloths. From the roof, insert the brush into the chimney and push it down toward the fireplace opening. Thread on additional rods as required to reach the proper depth, and work the brushes up and down. When you reach the bottom, withdraw the brush. Wait 1 hour for the dust to settle, then vacuum the debris from the fireplace floor using a heavy-duty industrial vacuum cleaner available from rental centers.

Though using a brush is a time-honored and effective way of sweeping a chimney, in recent years other methods have been found to help with this dirty job (see left).

Cleaning from above
Insert brush and rods at chimney top. Brush up and down, threading on additional rods as required.

Sweeping a chimney
Seal off the fireplace with an old sheet and feed the brush rods up under it.

Curing a smoky fireplace

A well-functioning fireplace is the product of many design elements. When fireplace smoke drifts into the room, rather than escaping up the chimney, there may be several causes. If the fireplace has always been a smoky one, chances are that its construction includes one or more design flaws. If the condition is a recent development, solving the problem may require only a simple adjustment or cleaning.

Regulating draft
Regulate chimney draft by adjusting damper. Operate adjusting arm using poker when fire is burning.

Remedying simple problems

If the fireplace smokes only occasionally or has just begun to smoke, run through this checklist of minor adjustments. First, be certain that when the fire is burning, the damper is fully open.

Most dampers can be adjusted when hot by pushing the protruding end of the handle with a poker. Check, too, that the chimney is free of obstructions, especially if a normally clean-burning fireplace suddenly starts smoking. Along with this, make sure that the chimney is regularly cleaned. Accumulated soot and creosote can eventually cause smoking

and, worse, a chimney fire.

Check that the fire is built well back in the firebox so that no burning logs project beyond the fireplace opening. Try raising the height of the fire several inches by placing the logs on a grate elevated on firebricks. Inadequate intake of air—too little to support combustion or feed the chimney's draft—may also be the culprit, especially if you have altered the ventilation pattern in the room by adding insulation and weather stripping. To alleviate this cause of a smoky fireplace, open a door or window to admit more air.

Correcting chimney faults

To produce an updraft, air must flow steadily across the opening at the top of a chimney. This creates a partial vacuum within, which aids in drawing the heated air from the fireplace. In order for the air to be unobstructed as it flows, a chimney must be at least 3 feet higher than any object within a 10-foot radius, including roof peaks, trees, television antennas, or other chimneys. If you cannot increase the height of a too-short chimney by adding to it,

attaching a chimney cap or smoke puller (a fan mounted in the chimney opening) may help. Before undertaking such modifications, consult a professional chimney sweep or mason.

Uncapped chimneys should have a sloping cowl of mortar on all four sides to direct passing air up and over the opening. Otherwise, air striking the chimney will eddy and swirl erratically, which may cause an uneven flow of air from the fireplace.

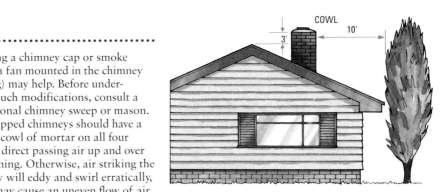

Correcting fireplace proportions

To draw smoke upward properly, the dimensions of the chimney flue must bear a certain proportional relationship to those of the brick-lined or steel-lined area where the fire is actually built (called the firebox). Also, the firebox itself must be built to a certain shape in order to both reflect heat outward and direct smoke upward. Often, either the firebox is built too large for the flue rising inside the chimney or the flue (usually a retrofit inserted into a chimney that was originally built without one) is too small.

One solution is to fit a metal fireplace hood, available from fireplace and woodstove supply stores and some home centers, across the top of the fireplace opening to decrease its overall size and also to smoke that might otherwise seep out. To install the

hood, first determine how large it must be by holding a piece of metal or dampened plywood across the top of the fireplace when a fire is burning. As the fireplace begins to smoke, gradually lower the sheet of material until the smoking is contained. Buy a hood this size. Most hoods attach to the fireplace surround by means of special masonry hangers.

Another solution is to fit glass doors across the entire front opening of the fireplace. These, too, are available in many sizes from fireplace and woodstove stores, as well as home centers. Although some heat may be lost to the room when the doors are closed, the fire is entirely enclosed and smoke is completely contained. There are also energy-efficient models that actually enhance the amount of heat produced by the fireplace.

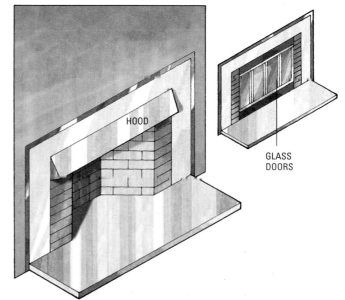

Remedies for smoky fireplaces
A hood or glass doors can prevent smoke from entering a room.

Removing a fireplace

To take out an antique fire surround and hearth is easy enough, but it can create a lot of dust and debris. Any hammering is likely to cause quantities of soot to fall down the chimney. Before you start, clean the chimney, move all furniture away from the fireplace, roll back the carpet, and cover everything with drop cloths. There is a good demand for Victorian fire surrounds, and some are valuable. If you remove yours undamaged, you may be able to sell it.

Removing the hearth

Most old-fashioned hearths were laid after the fire surround had been fitted, and so must come out first. But, check beforehand that your surround has not been installed on top of the hearth.

Wear safety goggles and heavy gloves against flying debris, and use a 2-pound sledgehammer and a bricklayer's chisel to break the mortar bond between the hearth and the subhearth below. Knocking in wood wedges will help. Lever the hearth free with a crowbar or the blade of a strong garden spade and lift it clear. It will be heavy, so get someone to help.

Some older hearths are laid level with the surrounding floorboards and have a layer of tiles on top of them. Here, all that's needed is to lift the tiles off carefully with a bricklayer's chisel.

Removing the surround

Most fire surrounds are held to the wall by screws that are driven through metal lugs set around their edges. They will be concealed by the plaster on the chimney. To find the lugs, chip away a 1-inch strip of plaster around the surround, then expose the lugs completely and take out the screws. If they are rusted and immovable, soak them in penetrating oil, leave for a few hours, and try again. If that fails, drill out their heads. The surround will be heavy, so have some help available when you lever it from the wall and lower it carefully onto the floor.

Brick and stone surrounds
A brick or stone surround can be removed a piece at a time, using a bricklayer's chisel to break the mortar joints. There may also be metal ties holding it to the wall.

Marble surrounds
Marble surrounds are made in sections, so remove the shelf first, then the frieze or lintel, and last, the side jambs.

Wooden surrounds
A wooden surround will probably be held by screws driven through its sides and top into strips that are fixed to the chimney inside the surround. The screwheads will be hidden by wooden plugs or filler. Chisel these out, remove the screws, and lift away the surround.

Cast-iron fireplace
Some old fireplace surrounds are in demand. Paint can be stripped from cast-iron surrounds, as shown above.

● **Saving a surround**
Fire surrounds can be very heavy, especially stone, slate, or marble ones. If you wish to keep yours intact for sale, lay an old mattress in front of it before you pull it from the wall so it will be less likely to break if it should fall.

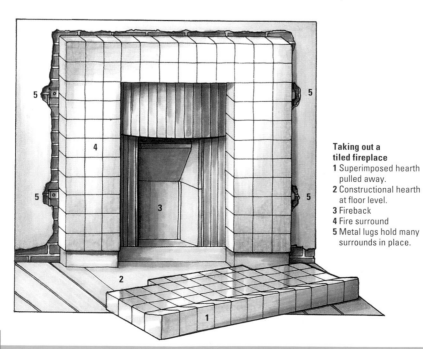

Taking out a tiled fireplace
1 Superimposed hearth pulled away.
2 Constructional hearth at floor level.
3 Fireback
4 Fire surround
5 Metal lugs hold many surrounds in place.

Cracked or broken tiles in a hearth or fire surround should be replaced with new ones, but you may not be able to match those in an old fireplace. One solution here is to buy some new tiles that pleasantly complement or contrast with the originals and replace more than just the damaged one or two, making a random or symmetrical pattern.

Break out the damaged tile with a hammer and cold chisel, working from the center of the tile outward. Wear thick gloves and safety goggles, and protect nearby surfaces with drop cloths. When the tile is out, remove all traces of old adhesive or mortar and vacuum up the dust.

If necessary, cut the new tile to shape. Spread heat-resistant tile adhesive thickly on its back and on the surface where it is to go. Don't get adhesive on its edges or on the edges of surrounding tiles. Set the tile in place, taking care that the clearance is equal all around, and wipe off any excess adhesive. Leave it to set and then apply grout.

If you are replacing only one tile, it's not worth buying a large quantity of adhesive. Instead, mix a paste from coarse sawdust and wood glue, which will work just as well. If the tile is very close to the fire, you can use some fire cement.

Chipping out a damaged tile
Start in the middle and work out to the edges. Clean out all old mortar or adhesive.

● Complete retiling
If a lot of the tiles are damaged or crazed, your best option may be to retile the entire surround and hearth. This is much less trouble than it sounds, as you can simply stick the new tiles directly on top of the old ones. First make sure that the old tiles are clean and remove any loose pieces, then apply your tile adhesive and stick the tiles on in the ordinary way.

Sealing a fireplace opening

If you have removed an old fireplace, you can close the opening by bricking it up or by covering it with drywall. The latter will make it easier to reinstall the fireplace at a later date. In either case, fit a ventilator in the opening just above the baseboard. The airflow through the chimney will prevent condensation from forming and seeping through the brickwork to damage wall decorations.

Restoring the floor

If the floor is solid, you need only bring the subhearth up level with it, using cement. You can also do this with a wood floor, if it is to be carpeted. If you want exposed floorboards, the subhearth will have to be broken away with a hammer and cold chisel to make room for new floor framing and floorboards.

Sealing the opening with bricks

If you wish to brick up the firebox opening, remove bricks from alternate courses at the edges of the opening so that the new brickwork can be "toothed in." Provide ventilation for the chimney by fitting a brick vent in the center of the brickwork and just above baseboard level. Plaster the brickwork and allow it to dry out thoroughly before you redecorate the wall. Finally, lever the old pieces of baseboard from the ends of the fireplace and replace them with a full-length piece from corner to corner.

Sealing the opening with drywall

Cut a panel from ½-inch drywall and nail it onto a wood frame mounted inside the fire opening. Use 2 x 4 lumber for the frame. Nail it into the opening with masonry nails, setting it in so that when the drywall is nailed on, it will lie flush with the surrounding wall if it is to be papered or painted to match the other walls in the room. Place the frame ⅛ inch deeper if you plan to add a plaster skim coat to the surface of the drywall. After decorating or plastering the panel, fit a ventilator in the center as shown below.

An inset frame to support plasterboard

An unused chimney must be ventilated

Closing the chimney top

When you close off a fireplace opening, you will have to cap the chimney in such a way as to keep rain out while allowing the air from the vent in the room to escape. Use a half-round ridge tile bedded in cement or a metal cowl, either of which will do the job.

Commercial cowl   **Half-round ridge tile**

In the past 30 years or so, traditional fireplaces have vanished from many older houses, swept away in the name of modernization. But now they are being appreciated again and even sought after. You can install an old-fashioned fireplace with simple tools and a few weekends of work.

Most period fire surrounds are held in place by lugs screwed to the wall, but some can be attached with mortar. A plaster surround can be held with dabs of bonding plaster.

First, remove a strip of plaster from around the fire opening, about 2 inches wider all around than the surround.

If the surround incorporates a cast-iron centerpiece, it must be fitted first. Most of them simply stand on the back hearth, but some have lugs for screwing to the wall. If yours has lugs, use metal wall plugs or expansion bolts. Fit lengths of fiberglass-rope packing where the grate or centerpiece touches the fireback.

Hold the surround in place, mark the wall for the screw holes, and drill them. Use a level to check that the surround is upright and the mantel horizontal, and make any needed corrections by fitting wooden wedges behind the surround or bending the lugs backward or forward.

An alternative method for plaster surrounds is to apply mortar or plaster to the wall and prop the surround against it with boards until the mortar or plaster sets.

Replace the hearth or build a new one. Set the hearth on dabs of mortar and point around the edges with the same material.

Replaster the wall and fit new baseboard molding between the hearth and the corners of the chimney masonry.

Hold the mantleshelf of a marble surround in place with a 2 x 4 prop until the adhesive sets.

Inserts and surrounds

Once discarded as outdated and worthless, antique fireplaces are now much sought after—both for the character they impart to a living space and for the improved resale value they bring to an older home. To reinstall a fireplace insert or surround that was once removed, you can either buy an original example from an architectural salvage company or choose from the range of good-quality reproductions and contemporary designs available today.

Before you rebuild your old fireplace, however, be sure to see that the fireplace opening, hearth, and chimney are all in good condition. It's best to get a professional inspection. And, bring your plans to your local building codes office or building inspector to make sure your project conforms to all the appropriate regulations.

Fireplace styles
When reinstating a fireplace, choose one that suits the period style of your home.

Insert and surround

Position the insert into the fireplace so it's centered in the opening. Check that it's plumb and square. If the opening is larger than the front plate of the insert, fill in the space at the sides with mortared bricks. If there's space above the insert, add a concrete lintel supported by brickwork at each side. If the opening is not in the center of the chimney, move the insert sideways to accommodate the chimney location.

Position the surround temporarily to see that it fits snugly against the wall and insert the grate. If necessary, pull the insert forward to butt up against the back of the surround. Now remove the surround, pack a fiberglass-rope gasket behind the rim of the insert, and seal the gap with an appropriate cement. If necessary, use heat-resistant anchors and threaded fasteners to secure the components to the masonry.

One-piece surround

The method for installing a surround will depend on its design. If you have an antique, modifications may be required and it's often best to get expert help. Wooden and cast-iron types are usually made in one piece and secured with threaded fasteners at each side.

Hold the surround against the wall and center it. Check that the surround is level and plumb, then mark the positions of any fasteners. Remove the surround, install anchors in the wall, and screw the surround in place. Use mortar to shape the channel, or throat, that connects the firebox with the flue.

Easy-to-install fireplace inserts, consisting of an energy-efficient tubular fireplace grate and blower unit, plus glass doors that fully cover the fireplace opening, are widely available and can significantly boost the amount of heat produced by an ordinary fireplace.

Although there are many different varieties, installation of most combination inserts involves first assembling the grate, usually by bolting the convection tubes to the grate supports that elevate the unit off the firebox floor. Then the unit is installed in the firebox and the doors are assembled and secured. Many grates are freestanding, and are simply slid in and out of the firebox for periodic cleaning.

The tops of the convection tubes generally sit against a vented portion along the top of the doorframe, so that the heated air rising through them as the fire burns is directed outward. A blower assembly is attached to the lower portion of the door to draw the air needed for combustion into the lower ends of the tubes and assist in forcing it upward and out again, into the room.

The doors themselves fit around the perimeter of the fireplace surround and are held in place with masonry bolts. Installation is usually a matter of drilling into the masonry, installing bolt anchors, then attaching the doorframe using the bolts supplied with the unit. In addition, most manufacturers recommend sealing the gap between the insert frame and the fireplace surround with fiberglass rope to prevent heat leaks.

Reduce size of the opening if necessary

Fill void behind insert with concrete

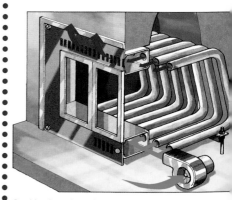

Combination tube and glass-door insert
This installs easily and increases fireplace efficiency.

Wood heaters and insets

A modern enclosed fireplace, or room heater, can be freestanding or inset (built in). Both are very efficient at heating individual rooms and can help offset the cost of conventional central heating. The toughened-glass doors of closed fireplaces and insets allow the glow of the fire to be seen, and they open in order for extra fuel to be added.

A freestanding heater on the hearth

Freestanding room heaters are designed to stand on the hearth, forward of the chimney masonry. They radiate extra warmth from their surfaces, but their size can make them obtrusive in small rooms. You may also have to extend the hearth as required by your local building code.

A heater of this type has a flue outlet at its rear which is connected to the chimney, and the easiest way of arranging this is to run the stovepipe into a metal backplate that closes off the fire opening. The projecting end of the outlet must be at least 4 inches from the back wall of the firebox.

The closure plate should be an appropriate fireproof panel—check with a woodstove supply store to find the latest type available. Use metal wall anchors to hold the screws, and seal the joint between the plate and the opening with fiberglass rope and heat-resistant cement.

Alternatively, stovepipes for freestanding heaters can be fitted into the fireplace damper opening after removing the damper plate.

1 A backplate closes off fire opening

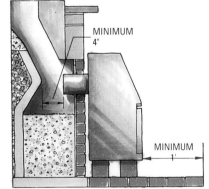

2 Important measurements for room heater

A freestanding heater in the fireplace

Some freestanding room heaters are designed to stand in the fire opening. This type of heater has a flue outlet in its top that must be connected to a closure plate set in the base of the chimney.

The plate can be metal or precast concrete. To make room enough to fit it, remove some bricks from the chimney masonry just above the opening but below the load-bearing lintel. If the plate is concrete, take out a course of bricks around the bottom of the chimney to support it properly. You can insert a metal plate into a cleared-out mortar joint or fasten it with expansion bolts. Bed the plate on heat-resistant cement, sealing the edges above and below. Check that the heater's outlet enters the chimney flue, and seal the plate joint with fiberglass rope and an appropriate cement.

A horizontal plate seals off chimney

An inset room heater

An inset room heater has its flue outlet mounted on top, to be connected to a chimney closure plate or stovepipe rising through the chimney.

This type of appliance is designed to fill and seal the fire opening completely, so to install one you may have to modify your present fireplace surround or even, if the opening is very large, build a new one. The sides of the surround must be exactly at right angles to the hearth, as the front portion of the heater's casing has to be sealed to both. If the surround and the hearth form an odd angle, a good seal with the heater casing will be impossible. The seal can be made with fiberglass-rope packing material.

More often, inset room heaters are screwed down to the firebox floor, and some may need a vermiculite-based infill around the back of the casing that must be in place before the chimney closure plate is fitted and the flue outlet connected.

Some come supplied with their own fire surrounds, complete with drop-in closure plates designed to make their installation easier.

Finish the job by restoring the fireplace brickwork, and replaster if necessary.

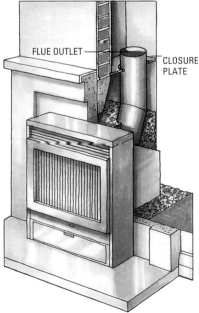

Inset room heater
The flue outlet connects to a horizontal closure plate in the base of the chimney. Some heaters require an infill behind the casing.

Installing a flue liner

If your house was built before World War II, there's a good chance that its chimney is unlined, and is simply a rectangular duct whose brickwork is either stuccoed with cement or exposed. Over the years, corrosive elements in the rising combustion gases eat into the chimney's mortar and brickwork and weaken it, allowing condensation to pass through and form damp patches on the outside and, in extreme cases, letting smoke seep through. This is particularly true where coal or woodburning appliances are in use.

Choosing a flue liner

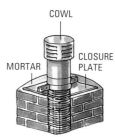

COWL
CLOSURE PLATE
MORTAR

An approved cowl for a gas heater

You can deal with these problems by installing a flue liner, which will prevent the corrosive elements from reaching the brick and mortar. It will also reduce the size of the flue, speeding up the flow of gases and preventing their cooling and condensing. The draft of air through the flue will improve, and the fire will burn more efficiently.

However, it is important to fit the type of liner that's appropriate to the kind of heating appliance being used and to be sure the size is large enough to keep the fireplace from smoking. Ask the stove dealer or building inspector. Linings are tubes, one-piece or in sections, of metal or other rigid, noncombustible material.

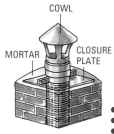

COWL
CLOSURE PLATE
MORTAR

An approved cowl for oil-fired heaters

Casting a flue liner
Professional installers can cast a flue liner in your unlined chimney. A deflated tube is lowered into the chimney. It is inflated, and a lightweight semiliquid mixture is poured into the gap between the tube and the flue. When the mixture has set, the tube is deflated and removed, leaving a smooth-bore flue liner.

SAFE ACCESS

You can rent easy-to-use, light-alloy roof scaffolding. Two units will make a half platform for a central or side chimney; four will provide an all-around platform.

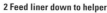
Scaffolding is essential for safe working

Installing a one-piece flue liner

A popular type of liner is a one-piece, flexible, corrugated tube of stainless steel that is easily fed into a chimney that has bends in it. Unfortunately, this type of liner is not suitable for use with coal or wood-burning appliances. To install it you must get onto the roof and erect scaffolding around the chimney (see below left).

First sweep the chimney, then chop away the mortar around the base of the chimney pot, if installed, with a hammer and cold chisel. Carefully remove the pot—it will be heavy—and lower it to the ground on a rope. Clean up the top of the chimney to expose the brickwork.

The liner is fed into the chimney from the top. Drop a strong weighted line down the chimney **(1)** and attach its other end to the conical end piece of the flue liner. Have an assistant pull gently on the line from below while you feed the liner down into the chimney **(2)**. When the conical end piece emerges below, remove it and connect the liner to a closure plate set across the base of the chimney, or to the flue outlet of the heating appliance. Seal the joint with fiberglass packing and some appropriate cement.

Return to the roof, fit the top closure plate, and bed it in mortar laid on the top of the chimney, adding extra mortar to match the original **(3)**. Finally, fit a cowl to the top of the liner—choose one appropriate to the heating appliance being used (see far left).

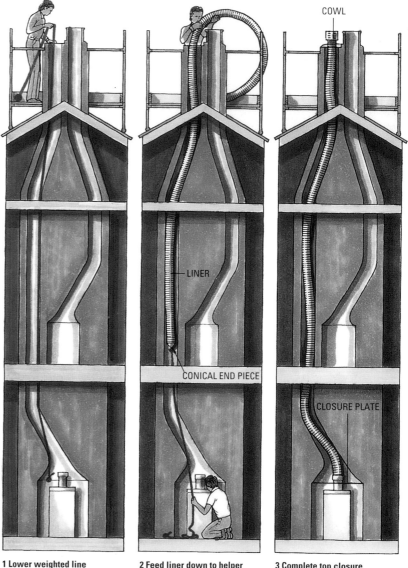

COWL
LINER
CONICAL END PIECE
CLOSURE PLATE

1 Lower weighted line   **2 Feed liner down to helper**   **3 Complete top closure**

Because a sectional flue liner has the space around it filled with a lightweight concrete that strengthens and insulates the chimney, it needs a good foundation for the added weight. Like the one-piece liner (see opposite), it is inserted from the top. First, cement a steel baseplate across the bottom of the chimney.

Tie the first flue section to a rope and lower it into the chimney. Connect the next section to it by one of the supplied steel collars and lower the two farther down. Continue adding sections and lowering the liner until it reaches the baseplate, then seal it in place.

If there are any bends in the chimney, you will have to break into it at those points to feed the sections in. This may be a job for a professional.

To fill in the chimney around the liner, use concrete made with a lightweight aggregate such as expanded clay or vermiculite. Pour this into the chimney around the liner and finish off the mortar cap at the top.

One of the most economical ways to keep a room warm is by means of a modern, slow-combustion wood-burning stove—if you have access to cheap wood. Like fireplace inserts or inset room heaters, they can be stood on the hearth with rear flue outlets or installed in the fireplace with top-mounted outlets. A good wood-burning stove can burn all day or night on one load of wood.

If a wood-burning stove is installed in place of a fireplace, it's best placed forward of the masonry so that you get the full benefit of the heat that radiates from its surfaces. You can stand it on an existing hearth, provided that the hearth projects the required minimum as indicated by your local building code or the literature that came with the stove. Otherwise, you will have to construct an appropriate fireproof base. Again, your building office will have guidelines and requirements. Common materials for this job are stone, brick, or tile.

A wood-burning stove can be connected to a stainless-steel, insulated flue and this can be passed through a vertical back closure plate that seals off an existing fireplace opening, or through a horizontal plate that closes

off the base of the chimney. More commonly, the stovepipe connects to a masonry chimney through a metal fitting called a thimble that's installed in the brickwork. Ventilated thimbles and fiberglass packing are used for passage through walls when there is no other option for installation.

If an insulated, stainless-steel flue is used, make sure the stovepipe connects through a T-fitting so the bottom extension of the fitting can be removed for cleaning.

It's important to follow local fire codes and building regulations when installing a woodstove. These generally include setting the unit at a safe distance from combustibles, making a positive connection between the stovepipe and flue, and being sure the flue extends at least 36 inches above the roof.

Wood-burning stoves
Available in a range of traditional designs, wood-burning stoves epitomize country living.

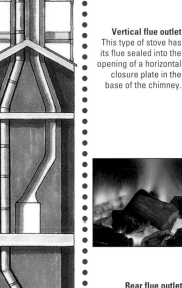

Remove chimney pot and mortar before you begin.

Sections are joined with steel collars or interlocking joints.

Where chimney bends, break a hole through the masonry to feed flue sections into the lower part of the chimney.

Use ready-made bends or cut straight sections with a masonry saw to make a miter joint.

A lightweight concrete fills the gap around the liner.

Cement baseplate to a concrete lintel, or attach it to angle-iron supports.

A sectional flue liner
Installing a sectional flue liner can be such a complicated procedure that it is worth getting a price from a professional before you decide to tackle the job yourself.

Vertical flue outlet
This type of stove has its flue sealed into the opening of a horizontal closure plate in the base of the chimney.

Rear flue outlet
A rear flue outlet allows the stove to stand clear of the fireplace.

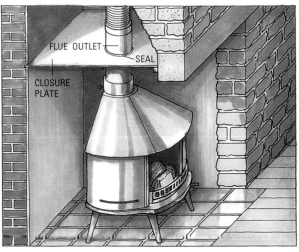

FLUE OUTLET
SEAL
CLOSURE PLATE

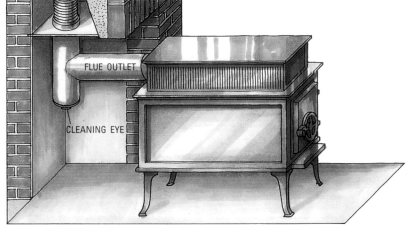

FLUE OUTLET
CLEANING EYE

Forced-air heating

Forced-air systems

Modern forced-air heating systems consist of a furnace that heats air, a large squirrel-cage blower that circulates that air, and a system of air ducts through which the heated air is directed throughout the house. A secondary system of ducts is also part of the system. Through it, cool air returns to the furnace.

Because of the size and unwieldy nature of the air ducts, forced hot-air heating systems are almost always installed during new construction. From the main duct that leads away from the blower chamber, the delivery ducts branch off, running between floor joists and wall studs to their openings at registers located in outside walls or in the floor near them. Cool air returns through larger, centrally located ducts in the floor. Since hot air rises and cold air falls, the warm air rising along the outside walls heats the rooms, then circulates and cools on the way to the return ducts. This creates a convection current that serves the entire enclosed area.

In large systems, the ductwork is configured to create heating zones—groups of rooms served by a single branch of the system that can be isolated from the rest. By the use of dampers, which physically close off key ducts (dampers are operated manually or by thermostats), the amount of heat directed throughout the house can be economically adjusted so that unused rooms receive less heat.

A central heating system supplies heat from a single source to selected rooms—or to all the rooms—in the house. It is a much more efficient arrangement than having an individual heater in each room, as there is only one appliance to be controlled, cleaned, and maintained.

Central heating systems are categorized by the medium used to deliver the heat from its source to the various outlets around the house. The three most common systems are forced-air, circulating hot water, and steam. Heat sources for these are normally a gas- or oil-fired furnace (though in some areas coal-fueled and even wood-fueled systems are used), which in turn heats either water in a boiler or air passing through a heat exchanger. Electric heating systems, which derive heat through simple resistance wiring, or which feed heated air through a blower, are less popular systems, due to expensive energy costs. Their advantages, however, are cleanliness and high efficiency.

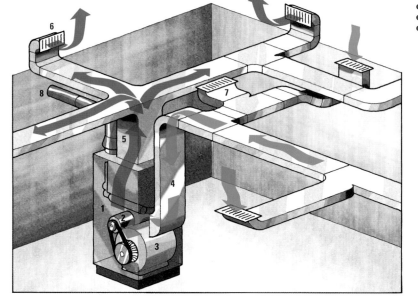

Typical gas-fired forced-air heating system
1 Furnace (gas)
2 Motor
3 Blower
4 Cold-air return
5 Warm-air delivery
6 Warm-air registers
7 Cold-air registers
8 Exhaust (to chimney)

Balancing a forced-air heating system

Adjusting the air flowing through a forced-air heating system—a process called balancing—assures that each room receives just the right amount of heat. While the individual registers at the ends of each duct can be manually adjusted or shut, a better system utilizes strategically located dampers mounted inside the ductwork.

Dampers are controlled by means of a handle on the outside of the duct. Turning the handle so it's parallel with the run of the duct allows maximum airflow. Turning it the other way reduces airflow. To balance the system, simply adjust the dampers until the appropriate settings are achieved. The process is simple, but, because each room requires 6 to 8 hours to become properly heated, takes time. Balance the system during a cold spell, when the furnace is running at its peak. Begin by closing down the damper to the most uncomfortably hot area nearest the furnace. This will send greater amounts of heat to more distant registers. After waiting the required heating-up time, move on to the next hot area and adjust the damper there. You can judge the temperature by how the room feels or by holding a thermometer a few feet above the floor.

After you've adjusted all the dampers once (a process that may have taken a week or more), go back and make minor adjustments to any areas that seem too warm or cool. When you're finished, mark the damper handle positions on the ductwork so that they are permanently recorded.

If, after balancing, areas at the far end of duct runs are still too cool, a common solution is to increase the speed of the squirrel-cage blower. This is done by adjusting or replacing one of the drive pulleys on the motor. However, since increasing blower speed places additional strain on the motor, consult a furnace service technician before you make the change.

Hot-water and steam heating

Circulating hot water

The most popular form of central heating is a circulating hot-water system. Water is heated to between 120° and 180°F in a furnace-fired boiler and then is forced by one or more circulator pumps through a system of pipes leading to and from radiators or convectors located throughout the house. Some layouts pump water through a single loop of pipe, off of which branch piping both feeds hot water and returns cooled water to each radiator in sequence. With these systems, careful balancing (as for forced-air systems) is necessary to assure that radiators at the far end of the pipe loop obtain sufficient heat. A better type of layout is one made up of two sets of pipe runs, one to carry only the hot water and one to return only the cooled. These systems require far less adjustment, since water flowing to the farthest radiator does not become mixed with cooled water returning from radiators along the way. Hot-water systems usually include an expansion tank, which contains air, located near the boiler. As water in the system becomes heated and expands, the air in the tank is compressed. This places the water in the system under pressure and prevents it from becoming steam.

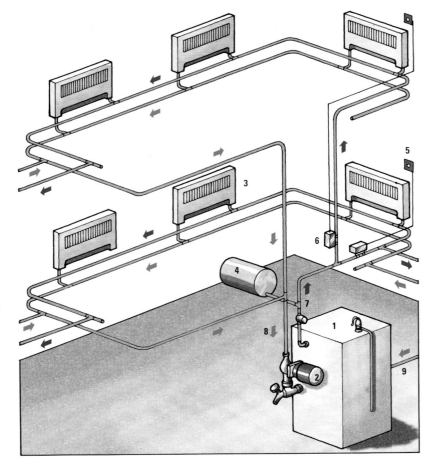

Hot-water system
The water heated by the boiler (1) is driven by a circulator pump (2) through a two-pipe system to radiators or convector heaters (3), which give off heat as the hot water flows through them, gradually warming the rooms to the required temperature. The water then returns to the boiler to be reheated. An expansion tank (4) handles the excess volume of water created by heating. Thermostats (5) regulate the heat delivered to specific zones in the house by triggering control valves (6) or multiple circulators. In the diagram, red indicates the flow of hot water from the boiler (7) and blue shows the return flow (8). Water is supplied by the household plumbing system (9).

Steam heat

Few contemporary homes are built with steam heating systems. However, they are still to be found in many older homes, especially those built prior to World War II. Steam systems operate much like a single-pipe, circulating hot-water system (see above). Water, heated in a boiler until it becomes steam travels under its own pressure through a single pipe a loop around the house. From this pipe, branch lines serve the radiators. As the steam cools by giving up its heat to the radiators, it changes back to water and returns to the boiler by gravity through the same pipe that delivered the steam. Steam systems require neither a circulator nor an expansion tank. Piping must, however, slope downward from all points toward the boiler, and balancing is necessary to properly distribute steam to each room. In addition, steam radiators must be frequently drained of both air and water to remain in working order.

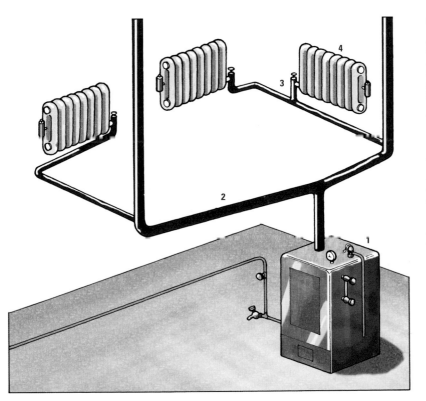

Steam systems
In a single-pipe steam system, steam moves from the boiler (1) around the perimeter of the house through a single pipe that forms a loop (2). Flow and return pipes (3) divert the steam to each radiator (4). From the radiator, the heat moves to the objects in the room and the steam condenses. The water then flows back through the pipes to the boiler. Larger radiators may be required at the end of the loop in order to compensate for heat loss.

Electric heat

Condensing furnaces

Standard furnaces extract heat from the burners by means of a heat exchanger—a series of cells through which the household air moves as it's warmed by the hot exhaust gases surrounding the outside of the cell walls. These traditional furnaces capture about 65 percent of the heat they generate at the burners. The rest goes up the chimney.

To capture more of the wasted heat, condensing furnaces have a second heat exchanger that increases efficiency up to about 94 percent. However, because so much heat has been removed from the exhaust, it no longer rises through the chimney on its own. Therefore, these modern furnaces have induced-draft blowers to move the cool gases outdoors through plastic pipes. At these low temperatures, corrosive elements condense from the exhaust and must be drained away. Secondary heat exchangers must be highly corrosion resistant to handle the condensate that occurs.

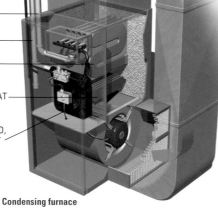

OUTDOOR COMBUSTION AIR

EXHAUST

PRIMARY HEAT EXCHANGER

SECONDARY HEAT EXCHANGER

VARIABLE-SPEED, INDUCED-DRAFT BLOWER

Condensing furnace

Combination boilers

Combination boilers provide both hot water for the heating system and a separate supply of instant hot water for taps and showers. Because there's no separate water heater, the system is easier to install, takes up less space, and is more economical to operate.

The main drawback is a fairly slow flow rate—so it takes longer to fill a bath, and it's sometimes not possible to use several hot taps at the same time. However, improved versions overcome these problems by incorporating a small built-in hot-water storage tank.

Electric central heating systems have long been popular in Europe, and have been available in the United States for many years. Their popularity reached its peak during the 1960s, prior to the worldwide increase in energy costs, which has subsequently caused large-scale electric heating systems to be expensive to operate. Still, electric heat offers distinct advantages. It provides quick, efficient, draft-free warmth—and since no fuel is actually burned, there's no need for a chimney or fuel tank.

Because most electric systems operate on the principle of radiant, rather than convective, heat, they provide the most uniform heat and achieve their greatest energy efficiency when installed over the greatest possible area. Many small, low-intensity units covering a broad area produce better results than only a few high-intensity units widely spaced.

Baseboard heaters

Electric baseboard heaters are the most popular form of electric heat in the United States. Each unit contains one or more horizontal heating elements, the entire unit being thermostatically controlled. Baseboard heaters are generally installed in groups that are controlled by a common thermostat. This makes it easy to independently adjust the heat in the various areas of the home.

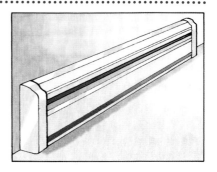

Wall heaters

Individual electric wall heaters are often installed in special-use areas such as bathrooms and laundry rooms to provide supplementary or occasional heat. Installed between the studs of wall framing, most of these units include a small fan which aids in quickly circulating heated air throughout the room. Like baseboard heaters, these small wall heaters are thermostatically controlled.

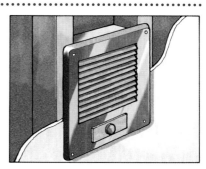

Electric furnace

Like oil- or gas-fired forced-air furnaces, electric furnaces heat air which is then delivered throughout the house via ductwork. Electric furnaces, though, are small and require no fuel tank, chimney, or vents. They usually consist of several cookstove-type heating elements plus a squirrel-cage blower. While generally expensive to operate, electric furnaces can make sense where electricity is inexpensive and easy maintenance desired.

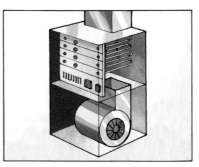

Radiant ceiling panels

Flexible and rigid panels containing electric heating grids are available for retrofitting or new construction. Some types fasten to standard framing prior to installation of the finished ceiling; others are embedded in gypsum and may be installed using drywall screws or nails.

Fuel-burning furnaces

The furnace is the heart of any heating system, whether forced-air, circulating hot water, or steam. Most household furnaces today are heated by gas or oil. To operate properly and efficiently, these furnaces require regular adjustment and periodic care. If carefully maintained, however, modern furnaces are economical heat producers and will provide years of dependable service, often equal to the life of the house. Here are the basics for understanding how typical systems work.

Oil burners

Oil burners spray fuel oil into a combustion chamber where the oil/air mixture is then ignited to produce heat. The most popular burner design is the pressure (gun) type. Another type, called a vaporizing or pot burner, is less common, but you may find it in older installations or where a smaller heat output is required.

In a high-pressure oil burner, a fine spray of oil is pumped under pressure through a nozzle. Here, it mixes with air and is ignited by a high-voltage electric spark derived from a transformer that's supplied with household current. Low-pressure burners are somewhat similar, the difference being that the oil and air are mixed before exiting the nozzle and pumped into the combustion chamber under far less pressure and through a

much larger opening.

Vaporizing burners do not operate under pressure. The combustion area consists of an enclosed shallow pan into which oil is admitted by regulating a manually operated valve. The oil in the pan is ignited by hand, or by a simple electric igniter. The heat from the burning oil causes more oil to vaporize and combine with air, to burn in the combustion chamber. Air is brought to the combustion chamber by either natural draft or a blower. Because vaporizing oil burners are compact and make very little noise, they are sometimes installed in kitchens or utility rooms. Pressure-type oil burners, on the other hand, are nearly always installed in basements. Vaporizing burners require a finer grade of oil to operate.

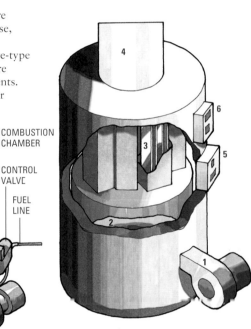

Pressure burner — BLOWER — FUEL LINE

COMBUSTION CHAMBER — AIR TUBE

Vaporizing burner — COMBUSTION CHAMBER — CONTROL VALVE — FUEL LINE — OIL POOL (POT)

Parts of an oil furnace
1 Motor/blower
2 Combustion chamber
3 Heat exchanger
4 Chimney vent
5 On/off switch
6 Combination gauge

Typical oil burner (shown equipped for circulating hot water)

Gas burners

Gas burners are far simpler than oil burners and, since gas itself burns much more cleanly than fuel oil, require less regular maintenance. Still, they should be cleaned and serviced at least every two or three years.

Whether supplied by natural gas or liquefied petroleum (LP gas), furnaces of this type consist merely of a burner assembly and a gas-regulating valve. The burners may be of a type that spread their flame over a large area, or they may merely have multiple openings

(or jets), as on a gas kitchen range.

For safety, gas burners incorporate a thermocouple device that shuts off the gas-supply valve when no heat is detected in the combustion area. Should the odor of gas ever be detected near a gas burner, immediately open windows, extinguish any open flames or cigarettes, then leave the house and telephone your gas or utility company. To avoid generating a small spark that may be enough to ignite escaping gas, do not touch electrical switches.

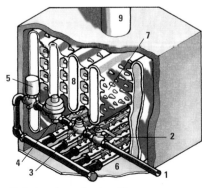

Parts of a gas furnace
1 Gas supply
2 Manual shutoff valve
3 Thermocouple
4 Pressure regulator
5 Automatic supply valve
6 Burners
7 Combustion chamber
8 Heat exchanger
9 Chimney vent

Typical gas burner (equipped for circulating hot water)

Radiators and convectors

STEAM UNITS

The hot water from a boiler is pumped through the house along narrow pipes that are connected either to radiators or to special convector heaters. These units extract heat from the water and transfer it out to the objects and air in the room.

You can feel radiant heat being emitted directly from the hot surface of an appliance, but convected heat warms the air that comes into contact with the hot surface. As the warmed air rises toward the ceiling, it allows cooler air to flow in around the appliance, and this air in turn is warmed and moves upward. Eventually, a steady but very gentle circulation of air takes place in the room, and the temperature gradually rises until it reaches the setting on the room thermostat.

Radiators

Ordinary radiators are made of heavy cast iron which absorbs heat and then radiates it for a long time. For hot-water use only, lightweight radiators made of pressed sheetmetal are sometimes available as imports. In either type, water flows in through a manually adjustable valve at one corner and then out through a return valve at the other (except in the case of most steam radiators—see sidebar at right). A bleed valve is placed near the top of the radiator on the end opposite the inflow valve to let air out and prevent air locks, which stop the radiator from heating up properly. Cast-iron radiators are normally freestanding. However, special brackets are available to hang them from sturdy

wall studs. Sheetmetal radiators are usually hung on the wall.

Despite their name, radiators deliver only about half their output as radiant heat—the rest is emitted through natural convection as the surrounding air comes into contact with the hot surfaces of the radiator.

Radiators come in a wide range of sizes, and the larger they are, the greater their heat output. Maximum efficiency dictates that radiators be fully exposed in a room, not recessed or covered by a vented housing. Nor should they be painted or hidden behind furniture or drapes. A better way to deal with unsightly radiators is to replace them with less obtrusive convectors.

Decorative radiators
As a rule, flat-panel radiators are designed to be unobtrusive. If you prefer something more conspicuous, choose from one of the more colorful styles. Some radiators are chromed.

Cast-iron radiator
1 The manual valve controls incoming water.
2 The return valve controls water leaving the radiator, and is adjusted to keep the radiator hot.
3 The bleed valve purges the radiator of air.

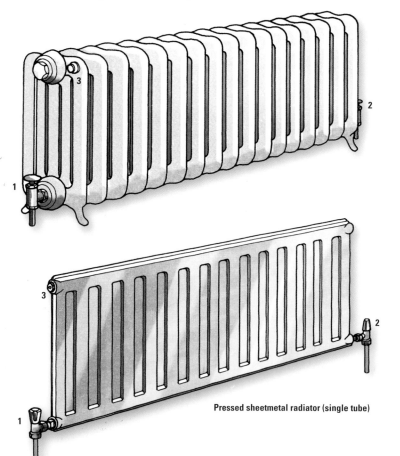

Heat emission
As it's heated by the radiator, convected air flows upward and is replaced by cooler air near the base of the radiator. In addition, heat radiates from the surface of the panel.

Pressed sheetmetal radiator (single tube)

Cast-iron radiators designed for steam heat look similar to those used for hot water and, with minor modifications, are interchangeable. In most cases, steam radiators have only one pipe connecting them with the main supply line. Water that has condensed as the steam gives up its heat makes its way back to the boiler the way it came. The other difference is that in place of a bleed valve, steam radiators have an automatic vent built into the end of the radiator opposite the inlet pipe. The vent permits air to bleed out automatically as the radiator fills with steam. However, the steam itself does not escape.

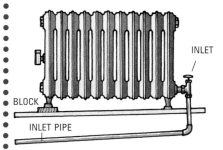

To cure a noisy radiator, block end so unit slopes toward inlet. Pipe should slope toward boiler.

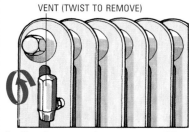

If radiator heats unevenly, remove vent and listen for escaping air. Replace with new vent.

Maintenance

Many steam radiators produce knocking and banging noises as they heat up. The sound is actually made by water that has become trapped striking the walls of the radiator or piping as the steam seeks to get past. To cure the condition, make sure that the radiator slopes slightly downward toward the inlet pipe and the pipe itself slopes downward toward the boiler.

If the radiator will not heat properly all the way across, suspect a blocked vent. Air that cannot escape prevents steam from diffusing throughout the radiator. Shortly after turning on the heat, unscrew the vent and remove it. As the steam rises, air should escape from the hole, followed by steam, indicating that the radiator itself is functioning properly. Buy a new vent and install it in place of the old one.

Placing your heaters

Most modern hot-water systems use relatively inexpensive convection heaters. You can also install convectors in your circulating hot-water heating system to replace conventional cast-iron radiators.

Unlike radiators, convection heaters emit none of their heat in the form of direct radiation. The hot water from the boiler passes through a finned pipe inside the heater. The fins absorb the heat and transfer it to the air around them. Once the air warms, it moves up and escapes through an opening at the top of the heater. At the same time, cool air is drawn in through the open bottom to replace the air that left.

Most convection heaters have a damper that can be set to control the airflow, and many are designed for inconspicuous mounting at baseboard level, similar to electric heating units. A variation on the basic convection heater is one with a fan that accelerates the airflow across the heated fins. This results in faster heating.

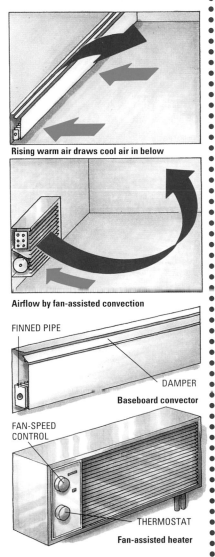

Rising warm air draws cool air in below

Airflow by fan-assisted convection

FINNED PIPE

DAMPER

Baseboard convector

FAN-SPEED
CONTROL

THERMOSTAT

Fan-assisted heater

At one time, central heating radiators or convectors were nearly always placed under windows to offset the cold glass surfaces and cut the drafts caused by warmed air cooling against them. However, with modern, thermally-effective double-glazed windows these problems are less severe and you can place radiators or convectors with an eye to maximum comfort.

Convenience and cost

Your radiators and convection heaters can be positioned anywhere that's convenient. However, it's best to keep in mind the shape of the room and the distance from the boiler, so costly pipe runs are kept to a reasonable minimum.

While double glazing means that the heaters don't necessarily need to be placed under the windows, there is a slight drawback to placing them against walls. The warm air rising from them will tend to discolor the paint or wallpaper above. You can guard against this by fitting radiator shelves immediately above them to direct the warm air away from the walls.

Never hang curtains or stand furniture in front of radiators or convectors. They will absorb radiated heat, and curtains will trap convected heat between themselves and the walls. While convectors radiate almost no heat, you should never prevent warm air from leaving the heater nor cool air from being drawn into it.

A room's shape should also affect your decisions regarding the positioning of heaters and how many you need. For example, you cannot heat a large L-shaped room from a single radiator in its short end. A heating contractor can determine the number and sizes of units required and the best placement of each.

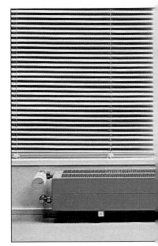

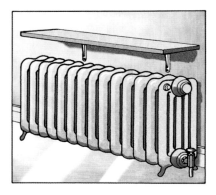

A shelf directs warm air clear of the wall

Selecting the size of heaters

A house loses heat whenever a door or window is opened because of cold drafts and by conduction through the actual materials that make up the doors, windows, walls, floors, ceilings, and roof of the structure. To work out the heating needs of the rooms in a house, the heating contractor has to take into account the rate at which they lose heat. This varies with the materials and construction. For example, heat is lost more quickly through a solid brick wall than through an insulated wood-frame wall. Also, the temperature on the other side of walls, floors, and ceilings comes into the equation.

The contractor also needs to know the temperature to which each room must be heated, and there are standard levels for particular rooms. A heat-loss analysis will be made to produce the heating requirement for each room, and radiators or convectors are selected with the appropriate outputs. Then all the heat output figures are totaled to give the output required from the boiler.

When you install your central heating, be sure to choose radiators and convection heaters that meet the standards approved by your local building inspector.

Ideal room temperatures
While most of us are happy to choose our room temperatures to suit our lifestyles and tastes, the professional who designs your heating system will make certain assumptions and may offer you suggestions. The following chart is an example of temperature settings for particular areas in the home. It may be used as a starting point for designing the system that suits you best.

ROOM TEMPERATURE	
Living room	**70°F (21°C)**
Dining room	**70°F (21°C)**
Kitchen	**60°F (16°C)**
Hall/landing	**65°F (18°C)**
Bedroom	**60°F (16°C)**
Bathroom	**72°F (23°C)**

Heating system controls

A range of automatic control systems and devices for circulating central heating can, if used sensibly, enable you to make real savings in operating costs. They can ensure that your system never "burns up money" by producing unwanted heat.

Three basic devices
While considerable sophistication is now available in automatic control, the systems can be divided into three main types: temperature controllers (thermostats), automatic on/off switches (timers and programmers), and heating circuit controllers (zone valves).

These devices can be used individually or in combination to provide a very high level of control.

It must be added that automatic controls are really effective only with gas- or oil-fired boilers, which can be switched on and off at will. Linked to coal or wood systems, which take time to react to controls, the systems will be less effective and can be dangerous.

Room thermostat

Programmer or timer

ZONE CONTROL VALVES

It is not often that all the rooms in a house are in use at once. During the day it is normal for the upstairs rooms to be unused for long periods, and to heat them continuously would be wasteful. A better idea is to divide your system into heating zones—the usual ones being upstairs and downstairs—and heat those areas only when it's necessary.

Control is provided by motorized valves linked to a timer that directs the flow of hot water through preselected pipes at specific times. Alternatively, zone valves can be used to provide zone temperature control by being linked to individual zone thermostats. In many cases, circulator pumps piped to specific zones and controlled by thermostats do the same job.

Heating controls
There are several ways to control the temperature:
1 Programmable type controls the boiler and pump.
2 A timer is used to control a zone valve. It can be used to regulate boiler and pump.
3 Room thermometer controls pump or a zone valve.
4 A nonelectric radiator valve controls an individual heater.

Thermostats

All steam and hot-water systems incorporate thermostats to prevent overheating. A gas- or oil-fired tank will have one that can be set to alter heat output by switching the unit on and off. Another, called an aquastat, can be set to monitor the temperature of the water circulating through the pipes.

Room thermostats are common forms of central heating control, often the only ones fitted. They are placed in rooms where temperatures usually remain fairly stable, and work on the assumption that any rise or drop in room temperature will be matched by similar ones throughout the house. Room thermostats control temperatures through simple on/off switching of the heating unit, or its pump if a boiler must run constantly to provide a constant supply of domestic hot water.

The room thermostat's drawback is that it can make no allowance for local temperature changes in other rooms caused, for example, by the sun shining through a window or a separate heater being switched on. Much more sophisticated temperature control is provided by thermostatic radiator valves, which can be fitted to radiators instead of the standard manually operated inlet valves. Temperature sensors open and close them, varying heat output to maintain the desired temperatures in individual rooms.

Thermostatic radiator valves need not be fitted in every room. You can use one to reduce the heat in a kitchen or reduce the temperature in a bathroom while using a room thermostat to regulate the temperature in the rest of the house or in separate zones.

Other available thermostatic controls include devices for regulating the temperature of domestic hot water and for giving frost protection to a unit switched off during winter vacations.

Timers and programmers

You can save a lot in running costs by ensuring that your heating system is not working when you don't need it—while you're out, for instance, or while you sleep. A timer can be set to switch the system on and off to suit the regular schedule of the family. It can switch on and warm the house just before you get up, then off again just before you leave for work, on again when you come home, and so on.

The simpler timers offer two "on" and two "off" settings which are repeated daily, though a manual override allows variations for weekends and such. More sophisticated programmable versions offer a number of on/off options—even a different one for each day of the week—as well as control of hot water.

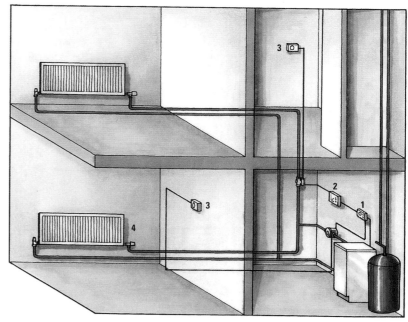

A motorized zone-control valve

Furnace maintenance

Routine cleaning, maintenance, and adjustment will give your central heating furnace a longer life and prolong its efficiency.

Both gas- and oil-fired furnaces should be serviced once a year by qualified service persons, but you can do a certain amount of cleaning and tuning up yourself.

Maintaining gas burners

Because gas furnaces involve less complicated equipment and technology than oil burners (combining gas and air for combustion is much easier than combining fuel oil and air), frequent maintenance of gas furnaces is less necessary than with oil-fired units. Inspection of the flame and pilot mechanisms should be carried out yearly by a professional service technician, of course. Cleaning—a task suitable for do-it-yourselfers—normally need take place only every two or three years. Before beginning any maintenance task, be certain to turn off the main gas supply line, pilot light, and burners.

Servicing oil burners

Here are several maintenance chores you can perform that do not involve making adjustments to the combustion components of the furnace. Unless you are skilled and have the proper testing instruments, leave that to a service professional. Before starting any maintenance task, turn the furnace completely off.

Cleaning a pressure-type oil burner

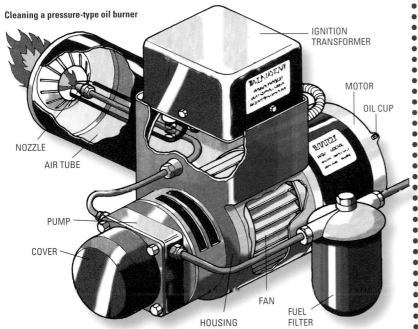

IGNITION TRANSFORMER

MOTOR

OIL CUP

NOZZLE

AIR TUBE

PUMP

COVER

FAN

HOUSING

FUEL FILTER

The very high efficiency of modern gas and oil furnaces largely depends on their being regularly checked and serviced. It should be done annually, and because the mechanisms involved are so complex, the work should be done by qualified service technicians. For either type of furnace, you can arrange a contract—with either the original installer or the fuel supplier—for regular maintenance.

Gas-fired installations

Many gas utilities offer a choice of service arrangements for gas furnaces. These cover their own installations, but they can often be arranged for systems put in by other installers on the condition that the utility inspects the installation before writing the contract.

The simplest maintenance plan provides for an annual check and adjustment of the furnace. If any repairs are found to be necessary, either at the time of the regular check or at other times during the year, the labor and the required parts will be charged separately. But, for an extra fee it is possible to have both free labor and free parts for furnace repairs at any time of the year. Most utilities will also extend the arrangement to include a check of the whole heating system at the same time that the furnace is checked.

It may be that your own installer can offer you a similar choice of service plans. The best course is to compare the charges and decide which gives the best value for your money.

Oil-fired installations

The installers of oil-fired systems and the suppliers of fuel oil offer service plans similar to those outlined above. The choice of plans ranges from the simple checkup each year to complete coverage for new parts and labor if and when any repairs should become necessary.

Change fuel filter
Place pan beneath filter area. Unscrew cup. Remove and replace cartridge and gasket.

Lubricate motor
Locate oil cups at each end of motor (if none are present, motor is maintenance free). Squirt 3 to 6 drops of 10W nondetergent electric motor oil in each cup. Do not over-lubricate.

Clean pump strainer
Remove pump cover and gasket. Soak strainer in solvent, then brush clean with toothbrush. Replace using new gasket. (Note: Some pumps do not have strainers.)

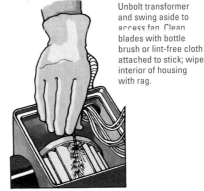

Clean fan
Unbolt transformer and swing aside to access fan. Clean blades with bottle brush or lint-free cloth attached to stick; wipe interior of housing with rag.

Draining a hot-water system : REFILLING THE SYSTEM

Circulating hot-water systems rarely need complete draining. However, if the water has become overly contaminated, or if a component fails and must be removed for replacement by following the procedures outlined here, the task of removing the water from the boiler and piping can be done fairly easily.

Steps in draining hot-water system
1 Extinguish furnace
2 Shut off water supply line.
3 Open draincock
4 Open radiator bleed valves.
5 Drain expansion tank

Draining the system

The most frequent reason for draining a hot-water system is excessive rust in the circulating water. Each year, a small amount of water should be drained from the boiler into a clear glass by way of the draincock (usually located near the base of the unit). If the water appears unusually cloudy, it's best to drain the system, then flush it clean and refill it.

Begin by turning off the furnace. Remember that with a gas furnace this means also turning off the pilot flame and main gas inlet. Next, turn off the water supply line to the boiler. Connect a garden hose to the draincock and lead the other end of the hose to a floor drain. If no drain is present, position a bucket beneath the draincock. After waiting until you are certain the water has cooled sufficiently, open the draincock and let the water drain out. While it is draining, open the bleed valves on the radiators in the house to avoid creating a partial vacuum (which prevents complete drainage). At the same time, drain the expansion tank (see below).

Flushing
To rid the boiler of accumulated rust and sediment, leave the draincock open after the water stops flowing, then reopen the water supply line to admit fresh water into the system. When the water runs clear, close the draincock and let the boiler fill.

When you are ready to refill the boiler, close the draincock used for flushing the system. If you wish to add a commercial rust inhibitor to reduce further corrosion in the pipes, close the water supply line, remove the pressure-relief valve from the boiler tank and pour the recommended amount of inhibitor (see manufacturer's instructions) into the hole. When you're done, replace the valve and reopen the water supply line. Wait until the boiler fills, then turn on the furnace. Close the radiator bleed valves when you hear water rising in the radiators. Wait several hours with the system running, then bleed all the radiators.

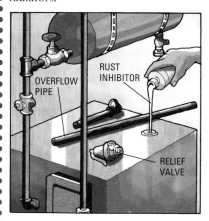

Draining the expansion tank

Conventional expansion tanks are merely cylinders partially filled with water. As the water in the circulating system heats and expands, air present in the tank is compressed, relieving the excess system pressure and also preventing the hot water from turning to steam. Over a period of time, however, most tanks gradually accumulate too much water, which forces the air out and thus prevents the tank from functioning properly. The solution is to drain the tank, an operation that must also be done if the entire system is to be drained.

To drain a conventional expansion tank, attach a garden hose to the draincock, usually located on the underside of the tank. Close off the inlet pipe leading to the tank, then open the draincock. If no inlet valve is present, you must drain the entire system in order to drain the tank.

Diaphragm expansion tanks
Some expansion tanks physically separate air and water by means of a rubber partition, or diaphragm, that divides the tank into two chambers. Instead of draining the water from such tanks, periodically recharge them with air. To do the job, first check the air pressure in the chamber using an ordinary tire-pressure gauge attached to the recharge valve, usually located on the underside of the tank. Then use a bicycle pump or compressor to add air until the gauge indicates that you've reached the tank's recommended pressure. If you find that your diaphragm tank requires even moderately frequent recharging, there's a good chance that it's leaking and should be replaced.

Diaphragm expansion tanks never need draining.
1 Diaphragm
2 Air
3 Water
To recharge air chamber, use a bicycle pump.

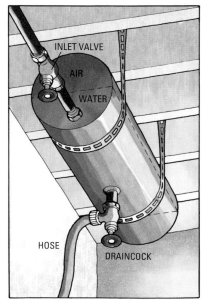

Conventional expansion tank

Bleeding the system

You can remove an individual radiator while the wall behind it is decorated without having to drain the whole system. You simply close the valves at the ends of the radiator, drain it, and then remove it.

Shut off both valves, turning the shank of the return valve clockwise with a key or an adjustable wrench (**1**). Note the number of turns needed to close it so you can reopen it by the same number of turns later.

Make sure that you have plenty of rags for mopping up spills, a jug, and a large bowl, as the water in the radiator will be very dirty. Also, roll back the floorcovering before you start, if possible.

Unscrew the capnut that holds one of the valves to the adapter in the end of the radiator (**2**). Hold the jug under the joint and open the bleed valve slowly to let the water drain out. Transfer the water from jug to bowl and keep going until no more can be drained.

Unscrew the capnut that holds the other valve on the radiator. If the radiator is not freestanding, lift it free from its wall brackets (**3**) and drain any remaining water into the bowl. Unscrew the wall brackets to decorate.

To replace the radiator after decorating, screw the brackets back in place, hang the radiator on them, and tighten the capnuts on both valves. Close the bleed valve and open both radiator valves. Adjust the return valve by the same number of turns you used to close it. Finally, use the bleed valve to release any trapped air.

Trapped air prevents radiators from fully heating through, and regular intake of air can cause corrosion. If a radiator feels cooler at the top than at the bottom, it's likely that a pocket of air has formed inside it and stopped circulation of the water. Getting the air out of a radiator, or bleeding it, is a simple procedure.

Opening a bleed valve

Bleed radiators with the circulator running. Each radiator has a bleed valve at one of its top corners, near the end opposite the water inlet. Usually the valve is slotted for a screwdriver, but on many new models the valve has a square-section shank in the center of the round plug. You should have been given a key to fit these shanks by the installer, but if you weren't, you can buy one at a plumbing supply store.

Use the key to turn the shank of the valve counterclockwise about a quarter of a turn. It shouldn't be necessary to turn it farther, but have a small container handy to catch any spurting water if you do open the valve too far.

You will hear a hissing sound as the air escapes. Keep the key on the shank of the valve, and when the hissing stops and the first dribble of water appears, close the valve tightly.

Under no circumstances should you open the valve any more than is needed to let the air out, or remove it completely, as this will produce a deluge of water.

Releasing trapped air in a radiator.
If your radiator requires a key, keep it in a handy place, where you can find it on short notice.

Fitting an automatic bleed valve

If you find yourself having to bleed one particular radiator regularly, it will save you trouble if you replace its bleed valve with an automatic one that will allow air to escape but not water.

To do the job, first drain the water from the system, then use your bleed-valve key to unscrew the old valve completely out of the drain plug (**1**). Wind some Teflon tape around the threads of the automatic valve (**2**) and screw it fingertight into the blanking plug (**3**).

Refill the system; if any water appears around the threads of the new valve, tighten it farther with an adjustable wrench (**4**).

If, when the system is going again, the radiator still feels cool on top, it may be that a larger amount of air has collected than the new bleed valve can cope with. In this case, unscrew the valve until you hear air hissing out. Tighten it again when the hissing stops and the first trickle of water appears.

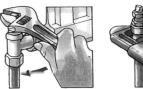

1 Close valve

2 Unscrew capnut

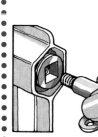

3 Final draining
Lift radiator from brackets and drain off any remaining water.

1 Unscrew old valve

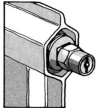

2 Tape new threads

3 Screw it fingertight

4 Stop any leak in use

Replacing radiator valves

Like faucets, radiator valves can develop leaks—which are usually relatively easy to cure. Occasionally, however, it's necessary to replace a faulty valve.

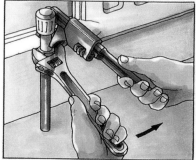

Curing a leaking radiator valve

If an inlet valve or return valve on a radiator seems to be leaking, it's most likely that one of the capnuts that secures it to the water pipe and to the radiator's valve adapter needs some tightening up.

Tighten the suspect capnut with an adjustable wrench while you hold the body of the valve with a pipe wrench to prevent it from moving. If this doesn't work, the valve will have to be replaced.

If the leak seems to be from the valve adapter in the radiator, the joint will have to be repaired in the same way as when a new valve is fitted (see below). If the leak seems to be from the valve spindle, tighten the gland nut (see left) or replace the valve.

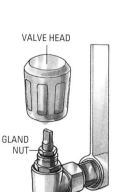

VALVE HEAD

GLAND NUT

Tightening gland nut
Tighten the gland nut with a wrench to stop a leak from a radiator valve spindle. If the leak persists, replace the valve.

Replacing a worn or damaged valve

Be sure that the new valve is exactly like the old one, or it may not align with the water pipe. Drain the heating system and lay rags under the valve to catch any remaining water that may come out.

Hold the body of the valve with a pipe wrench and use an adjustable wrench to unscrew the capnuts that hold the valve to the water pipe and to the adapter in the end of the radiator (**1**). Lift the valve from the end of the pipe (**2**). If the valve being replaced is a return valve, don't remove it before you have closed it, counting the number of turns needed so that you can open the new valve by the same number to balance the radiator. Unscrew the adapter from the radiator (**3**). You may be able to do this with an adjustable wrench, or you may need an Allen wrench, depending on the adapter.

Fitting the new valve

Ensure that the threads in the end of the radiator are clean and wind Teflon tape four or five times around the thread of the new valve's adapter, then screw it into the end of the radiator by hand and tighten it further one and one-half turns with an adjustable or Allen wrench.

Slide the valve capnut and a new ferrule over the end of the water pipe and fit the valve to the end of the pipe (**4**), but don't tighten the capnuts yet. First align the valve body with the adapter and tighten the capnut that holds them together (**5**). Hold the valve body firm with a wrench while you do this. Now tighten the capnut that holds the valve to the water pipe (**6**).

Finally, refill the system, check for leaks, and tighten the capnuts again if necessary.

DEALING WITH A JAMMED FERRULE

If the ferrule is jammed onto the pipe, cut the pipe off below floorboard level and make up a new section. Join it to the old pipe by means of either a soldered joint or a compression joint.

NEW SECTION OF PIPE

New section replaces pipe with jammed ferrule

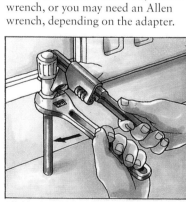

1 Hold valve firm and loosen both capnuts

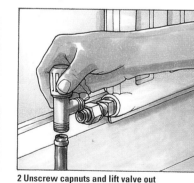

2 Unscrew capnuts and lift valve out

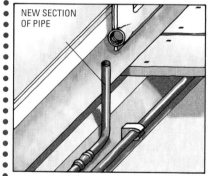

3 Remove valve adapter from radiator

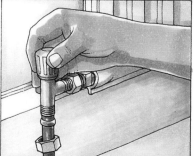

4 Fit new adapter, then fit new valve on pipe

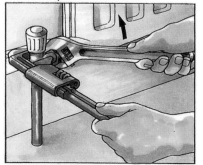

5 Connect valve to adapter and tighten capnut

6 Tighten capnut that holds valve to pipe

Replacing a radiator

Try to obtain a new radiator exactly the same size as the one you're planning to replace. This makes the job relatively easy.

Simple replacement

Drain and remove the old radiator. Once it's away from the wall, unscrew the valve adapters from the bottom with an adjustable wrench or, if necessary, an Allen wrench. Unscrew the bleed valve with its key, and then the two drain plugs from the top of the radiator, using a square or hexagonal Allen wrench (**1**).

With steel wool, clean up the threads of both adapters and both plugs (**2**), then wind four or five turns of Teflon tape around the threads (**3**). Screw them into the new radiator and install the bleed valve into the plug.

Position the new radiator and connect the valves to their adapters. Open the valves and fill and bleed the radiators.

1 Removing the plug
Use an Allen wrench to unscrew the drain plug at the end of the radiator.

2 Cleaning the threads
Use steel wool to clean any corrosion from the threads of both drain plugs and valve adapters.

3 Taping the threads
Make the threaded joints watertight by wrapping Teflon tape several times around each component before screwing them into the new radiator.

Installing a different radiator

The replacement job will require somewhat more work if you can't get a radiator of the same type as the old one. If the replacement is not freestanding, you'll have to fit new wall brackets. Possibly, you'll also have to alter the water pipes.

Drain the system. Then, for a wall-hung unit, take the old brackets off the wall. Lay the new radiator facedown on the floor and slide one of its brackets onto the hangers welded to the back of the radiator. Measure from the top of the bracket to the bottom of the radiator, add 4 or 5 inches for clearance under the radiator, then mark a horizontal line on the wall that distance from the floor. Now measure the distance between the centers of the radiator hangers and make two marks on the horizontal line that distance apart and at equal distances from the two water pipes (**1**).

Line up the brackets with the pencil marks, mark their mounting screw holes, drill and plug the holes, and install the brackets (**2**).

Lift up the floorboards below the radiator and cut off the vertical portions of the inlet and return pipes. Connect the valves to the radiator and hang it on its brackets. Slip a short length of pipe into each valve as a guide for any further trimming of the pipes. Solder these lengths to the original pipes (**3**), then connect the new pipes to the valves. Refill the system and check for leaks.

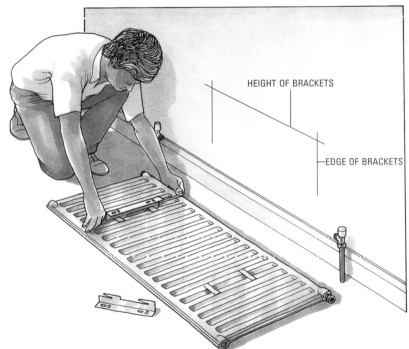

HEIGHT OF BRACKETS

EDGE OF BRACKETS

1 Transferring the measurements
Measure the positions of the radiator brackets and transfer these dimensions to the wall.

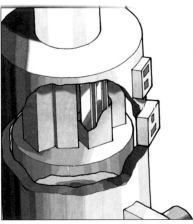

2 Securing the brackets
Screw the mounting brackets to the wall.

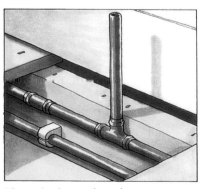

3 Connecting the new pipework
Make sure the vertical section of pipe aligns with the radiator valve.

Servicing a pump

Forced hot-water heating depends on a steady cycle of hot water, from boiler to radiators and back to the boiler, for reheating. This is the pump's job. A faulty pump means poor circulation. A failed pump means no circulation.

Bleeding the pump

If your radiators don't seem to be warming up, though you can hear or feel the pump running, it's likely that an air lock has formed in the pump and its impeller is spinning in air. The air must be bled from the pump, a job that's done in the same way as bleeding a radiator. You'll find a screw-in valve for the purpose in the pump's outer casing. The valve's position varies with different makes, but it is usually marked.

Switch off the pump, have a jar on hand to catch any water, and open the valve with a screwdriver or vent key. Open it just until you hear air hissing out. When the hissing stops and water appears, close the valve fully.

Open bleed valve with screwdriver

Adjusting the pump

There are two kinds of circulator pumps: fixed-head and variable-head. Fixed-head units run at a single speed, forcing the water to move through the system at a fixed rate. Variable-head pumps can be adjusted to run at different speeds, circulating the water at different rates.

When a variable-head pump is fitted as part of a hot-water system, the installer adjusts its speed after balancing all the radiators so that each room reaches its optimum temperature. If you find that your rooms are not as warm as you would like, though you have opened the radiator valves fully, you can adjust the pump speed. But first check that all radiators show the same temperature drop between their inlets and outlets. You can get clip-on thermometers for

the job from a plumber's supply store. You will need a pair of them.

Clip one thermometer to the feed pipe just below the radiator valve and the other to the return pipe below its valve (**1**). The difference between the temperatures registered by the two should be about 20°F. If it is not, uncover the return valve and close it further (to increase the difference) or open it more (to reduce the difference).

Having balanced the radiators, you can now adjust the pump. Switch it off and then turn the speed adjustment up (**2**), one step at a time, until you are getting the overall temperatures you want. You may be able to work the adjustment by hand, or you may need some special tool, such as an Allen wrench, depending on the make and model of your pump.

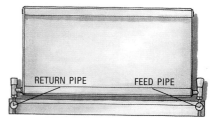

RETURN PIPE   FEED PIPE

1 Clip thermometers to radiator pipes

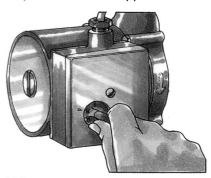
2 Adjust pump speed to alter temperature

Bridging the gap
Modern pumps are sometimes smaller than equivalent older models. If this is the case, buy a converter designed to bridge the gap between the existing pipes.

Replacing a worn pump

If you have to replace your circulator pump, be quite sure that the one you buy is of exactly the same make and model as the old one. If that's not possible, get advice from a service technician.

Turn off the boiler and close the isolating valves on each side of the pump. If there are no isolating valves, you will have to drain the whole system.

Find the electrical circuit that supplies the circulating pump and shut off the circuit breaker at the service panel. Then, take the coverplate off the pump and disconnect its wiring (**1**).

Have a bowl or bucket on hand to catch any water left in the pump, and use old rags for any mopping up that you may have to do. Undo the retaining nuts that hold the pump to the valves or the pipes with an adjustable wrench

(**2**) and catch the water as it flows out.

Remove the pump and fit the new one in its place, taking care to properly install any sealing washers that are provided with the new unit (**3**). Then tighten the retaining nuts.

Take the coverplate off the new pump, feed in the electrical cable, connect the wires to the pump's terminals (**4**), and replace the coverplate. If the pump is of the variable-head type (see above), set the speed control to the speed indicated on the old pump.

Open both isolating valves (or if the system has been drained, refill it). Check the pump connections for leaks and tighten them if necessary. Then open the pump's bleed valve to release any air that may have become trapped in it. Finally, switch the pump's circuit breaker on at the service panel and test the pump.

1 Remove coverplate

2 Undo connecting nuts

3 Attach new pump

4 Connect wires

Replacing a control valve

If a motorized valve won't open, its electric motor may have failed. Before replacing the motor, use a voltage tester to see whether it's receiving power. If it is, install a new motor.

There is no need to drain the system. Switch off the electrical supply to the heating system at the service panel—don't merely turn off the programmer, as motorized valves have a permanent live feed.

Once the power is off, remove the cover and undo the single screw that holds the motor in place **(1)**. Open the valve, using the manual lever, and lift out the motor **(2)**. Disconnect the two motor wires by cutting off the connectors.

Insert a new motor—available from a plumbing supply dealer—and let the lever spring back to the closed position. Install and tighten the retaining screw. Strip the ends and connect the wires, using the new connectors **(3)**.

Replace the valve cover and test the operation by turning on the power and running the system.

Control valves are a means by which timers and thermostats adjust the level of heating. Worn or faulty control valves can seriously impair the reliability of the system, and should therefore be repaired or replaced promptly.

Replacing a faulty valve

When you buy a new valve, make sure it is exactly the same as the one you are replacing.

Drain the system. Then turn off the power to the valve by removing the fuse or switching off the circuit breaker that protects the heating system's circuit.

The cable from the valve will be wired to an adjacent junction box, which is also connected to the heating system's other controls. Take the cover off the box and disconnect the wiring for the valve. Make a note of the terminals used, so it will be easy to connect the new unit.

To remove the old valve, cut through the pipe on each side **(1)**. When installing the new valve, bridge the gap with short sections of pipe and slip couplings **(2)**. After soldering the slip couplings, tighten the valve capnuts **(3)**. Connect the valve's cable to the junction box, then turn on the power to the circuit.

Two-port control valve
A two-port valve seals off a section of pipe when the water has reached the required temperature.

1 Releasing the motor retaining screw
Remove cover and then retaining screw

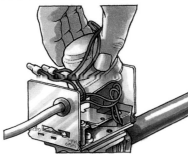

2 Removing the motor
Push lever to open valve, then lift out motor

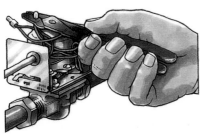

3 Fitting the new motor
Join wires, using two supplied connectors

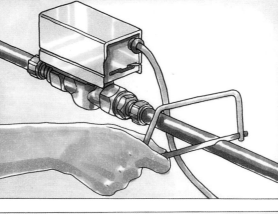

1 Removing the valve
If you're unable to disconnect the valve, use a hacksaw to cut through the pipe on each side.

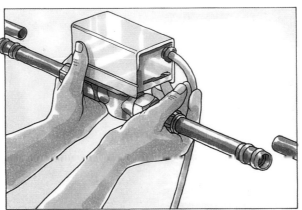

2 Fitting the new valve
With the new valve connected to short pipes, slide the slip couplings along the stubs and fit the assembly to the existing piping.

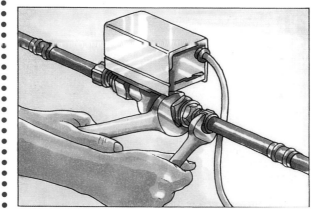

3 Tightening the nuts
After soldering the joints, tighten the valve capnuts on each side, using a pair of open-end wrenches. Refill the heating system and check that the valve is working properly.

Three-port control valve
This type of valve can isolate the central heating from the hot-water circuit.

Slip couplings
A slip coupling slides along the pipe, so it's easy to bridge gaps in fixed lengths of piping.

Hot-water radiant heat

With the availability of reliable plastic tubing, sophisticated controls, and efficient insulation, in-floor, hot-water radiant heat has become a viable and affordable form of central heating. Manufacturers have developed a range of systems to suit virtually any situation. The same companies generally offer a design service aimed at providing a heating system that satisfies the customer's specific requirements. In many cases, the technology can be applied to older homes, as well as to new construction.

BENEFITS OF RADIANT HEATING

● **Combining systems**
You can have radiators upstairs and in-floor heating downstairs. A mixing manifold will allow you to combine the two systems, using the same boiler.

● **Maintaining in-floor heating**
The heating elements are virtually maintenance free. If the flow through the pipework becomes restricted, the circuit can be flushed with water by attaching a hose to the manifold.

Although it's easier to install a radiant heating system while a house is being built, retrofitting it in an existing building is by no means impossible. And, there's no reason why in-floor radiant heat can't be made to work alongside a traditional hot-water system—it could provide the ideal solution for heating a new extension or updating a bathroom or kitchen.

Compared with a standard hot-water system, an in-floor heating system radiates heat more evenly and over a wider area. This has the effect of reducing hot and cold spots within the room and produces a more comfortable environment, where the air is warmest at floor level and cools as it rises toward the ceiling.

Radiant heating is also energy-efficient, because it operates at a lower temperature than other central heating systems. And, because there's more even temperature throughout a room, the thermostat can be set a degree or two lower, yet the house still feels warm and cozy. The net result is a saving on fuel costs with an increase in comfort.

Because there are no radiators or convectors permanently secured to the walls, you have greater freedom in decorating your rooms and arranging furniture. The floors can be finished with any conventional covering, but the thermal resistance of the flooring needs to be taken into account when the system is designed.

Underfloor heating systems

In-floor heating can be incorporated in any type of floor construction, including solid concrete floors and various types of wood flooring. The heat emanates from a continuous length of plastic tubing that snakes across the floor, forming parallel loops and covering an area of one or more rooms.

The entire system is divided into separate zones to provide custom temperature control in specific areas. Each zone is controlled by a thermostat, and is connected to a multivalve manifold that forms the heart of the system. The manifold controls the temperature of the water and the flow rate to the various zones. Once a room or zone reaches its required temperature, a valve automatically shuts off that part of the circuit. A flow meter for each of the zones allows the circuits to be balanced when setting up the system, and subsequently monitors system performance.

The manifold, which is installed in an accessible place above floor level, is connected to the boiler through a conventional circulation pump.

Methods for installing radiant heating

When radiant heating is installed in a new building, the plastic tubes are often set into a solid concrete floor (1). Flooring insulation is laid over the base concrete, and rows of special pipe clips are fixed to the insulation. (Sometimes a metal mesh is used instead of the clips.) The flexible heating tubes are then clipped into place at the required spacings, and a concrete slab is poured on top.

With a floating-wood floor (2), a layer of grooved insulation is laid over the concrete base, and the pipes are set in aluminum diffusion plates inserted in the grooves. The entire floor area is then covered with an edge-bonded chipboard or a similar underlayment.

The heating pipes can be fastened with spacer clips to the underside of a standard wooden floor (3). In this situation, clearance holes are drilled through the joists at strategic points to permit a continuous run of pipework. Reflective foil and thick blanket insulation are then installed below the pipes.

It is possible to lay the pipes on top of an existing floor, but this method raises the floor level by the thickness of the pipe assembly and the new flooring.

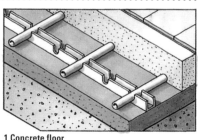

1 Concrete floor

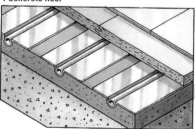

2 Floating-wood floor

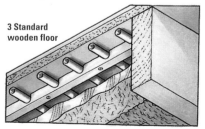

3 Standard wooden floor

Installing radiant heating

Added to an existing radiator system, in-floor hot-water heating makes a good choice for heating a new extension. The absence of radiators means you can decorate as you like, and make use of large windows. The concrete slab that might be used for such a project provides an ideal base for this form of heating.

WHERE TO START

To do the work yourself, first locate a supplier who can provide instructions and a plan for your project. The company will need a detailed description of your planned extension, and also a drawing of your house, including the specifications of your present hot-water system. From this information you'll receive a schematic of your new heating system and the price for all the components.

Your options

The simplest type of system is connected to the pipework of your existing radiator circuit. Heat for the extension will be available only when the existing hot-water system is running, although the temperature in the extension can be controlled independently by a thermostat connected to a motorized zone valve and the in-floor hot-water heating pump.

For full control, the flow and return pipes for the in-floor system must be connected directly to the boiler, and the thermostat must be wired to switch the boiler on and off and to control the temperature in the new space.

If it proves impossible to utilize the existing heating system, or if the boiler has insufficient capacity and cannot be upgraded, then you'll need to install an independent boiler and pump system to heat the extension.

The basic plumbing system

Your supplier will suggest the best point to connect your new plumbing to the existing hot-water circuit. It can be at any convenient point, provided that the performance of your radiators will not be affected.

The pipes connecting the manifold for the in-floor heating to the radiator circuit can be metal or plastic, and they can be the same size as (but not larger than) the existing pipes. Again, your supplier will advise what to use.

The flow and return pipes from the manifold to the house extension circuit (illustrated here, as an example) are connected to individual zone distributors, which in turn are connected to the flexible underfloor-heating tubes.

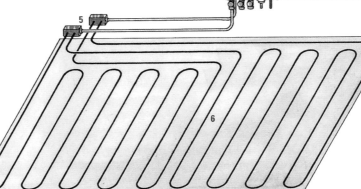

Basic system
1 Flow and return pipes from existing central heating circuit
2 Water-temperature mixing valve
3 Pump
4 Manifold with zone valves
5 Zone distributors
6 Radiant-heating tube

Floor construction
1 Gravel
2 Vapor barrier
3 Concrete base
4 Insulation
5 Edge insulation
6 Pipe clips and pipe
7 Floor slab
8 Floor tiles

Constructing the floor

To build an extension that will be served by radiant hot-water heat, you will need to excavate the site and pour a concrete slab that conforms to your local building codes. Check with your codes office for details. The slab should include a vapor barrier. Allow for a layer of floor insulation under the slab—a minimum of 2-inch, flooring-grade expanded polystyrene or 1¼-inch extruded polyurethane (check with your building inspector). The floor should be finished with a 2½-inch concrete slab, plus the preferred floor covering.

When laying the floor insulation slabs, install a strip of 1-inch-thick insulation around the edges. This is to prevent cold from penetrating the baseboard and the floor slab.

Cut a hole through the house wall to connect the new system to the old.

Installing the system

Mount the manifold in a convenient place and connect the two distributor blocks below it—one for the flow, the other for the return. Run the flow and return pipes back into the house, ready for connecting to the existing central heating circuit. Install your new pump and a mixing valve in the flow and return pipes.

Following the layout supplied by the system's manufacturer, press the spikes of the pipe clips into the insulation at the prescribed spacing **(1)**. Lay out the heating tubes for both coils, and clip them into place.

Push the end of one of the coils into the flow distributor, and the other end of the same coil into the return distributor **(2)**. Connect the other coil similarly.

Connect the flow and return pipes to the house's hot-water system—it pays to insert a pair of isolating valves at this point, so that you can shut off the new circuit for maintenance. Fill, flush out, and check the new system for leaks.

Pour concrete composed of 4 parts sand and 1 part cement, with a plasticizer additive. Allow it to set for at least three weeks before laying your floor covering—don't use heat to accelerate the drying.

Fit the thermostat at head height, out of direct sunlight. Make the electrical connections, then set the thermostat to control the circuit pump and zone valve, following the instructions supplied.

1 Press pipe clips into place

2 Push tubing into distributors

Heating system troubleshooting

When heating systems fail to work properly, they can exhibit all sorts of symptoms, some of which can be difficult to diagnose without specialized knowledge and experience. However, it pays to check out the more commons faults, summarized below, before calling for a repair technician.

Hissing or banging sounds from boiler or pipework

Overheating caused by:

- Blocked chimney (with coal furnace).
  Check flueway for substantial soot fall. Sweep chimney.

- Heavy mineral deposits in system due to hard water.
  Shut down boiler and pump. Treat system with a descaler, then drain, flush, and refill system.

- Faulty boiler thermostat.
  Shut down boiler. Leave pump working to circulate water, to cool system quickly. When it's cool, operate boiler thermostat control. If you don't hear a clicking sound, call in a repair person.

- Incorrectly sloping pipework (with steam systems).
  Check to see that radiators and pipe runs carrying steam slope downward at all points so that water can travel freely back to boiler. Insert wooden wedges under improperly sloping radiators. Rehang improperly pitched pipe. Check results using spirit level.

- Circulating pump not working (with coal furnace).
  Shut down boiler, then check that the pump is switched on. If pump won't work, turn off power and check wired connections to it. If pump seems to be running but outlet pipe is cool, check for air lock by using bleed screw. If pump is still not working, shut it down, drain system, remove pump, and check it for blockage. Clean pump or replace it if necessary.

Pressure-relief valve on circulating hot-water boiler opens, sending water through overflow pipe

- Excess pressure in piping caused by malfunctioning expansion tank.
  Drain conventional tank by first closing inlet valve leading to tank, then opening draincock on underside of tank. For tanks with diaphragm design, recharge air chamber using bicycle pump, or replace tank.

All radiators remain cool, though boiler is operating normally

- Pump not working.
  Check pump by listening or feeling for motor vibration. If pump is running, check for air lock by opening bleed valve. If this has no effect, the pump outlet may be blocked. Switch off boiler and pump, remove pump, and clean or replace as necessary.

- Pump thermostat or timer is set incorrectly or is faulty.
  Check thermostat or timer setting and reset if necessary. If this makes no difference, switch off power and check wiring connections. If connections are in good order, call in repair person.

Radiators in one part of house do not warm up

- Timer or thermostat that controls zone valve faulty or not set properly.
  Check timer or thermostat setting and reset if necessary. If this has no effect, switch off the power supply and check wired connections. If this makes no difference, call in repair person.

- Zone valve itself faulty.
  Drain system and replace valve.

Single radiator does not warm up

- Manual inlet valve closed.
  Check setting of valve and open it if it is necessary.

- Thermostatic radiator valve faulty or not set properly.
  Check setting of valve and reset it if necessary. If this has no effect, drain radiator and replace valve.

- Return valve not set properly.
  Remove return-valve cover and adjust valve setting until radiator seems as warm as those in adjacent rooms. Have valve properly balanced during next service visit.

- Inlet/outlet blocked by corrosion.
  Close inlet and return valves, remove radiator; flush out and refit or replace as necessary.

Area at top of radiator stays cool while the bottom is warm

- Air lock at top of radiator preventing water from circulating fully.
  Operate bleed valve to release the trapped air.

Cool patch in center of radiator while top and ends are warm

- Heavy deposits of corrosion at bottom of radiator are restricting circulation of water.
  Close inlet and return valves, remove radiator, flush out, then refit or replace as necessary.

Water leaking from system

- Loose pipe unions at joints, pump connections, boiler connections, etc.
  Switch off boiler and turn furnace off completely; switch off pump and tighten leaking joints. If this has no effect, drain the system and remake joints completely.

- Split or punctured pipes.
  Wrap damaged pipes in rags temporarily, switch off boiler and pump, and make a temporary repair with hose or commercial leak sealant. Drain system and fit new pipe.

Boiler not working

- Thermostat set too low.
  Check that room or boiler thermostat is set correctly.

- Timer or programmer not working.
  Check that unit is switched on and set correctly. Have it replaced if the fault persists.

- Pilot light goes out.
  Relight a gas-boiler pilot light following the manufacturer's instructions, which are usually found on the back of the boiler's front panel. If the pilot fails to ignite after second try, have the unit replaced.

Planning a garden

Consider the details
(above and bottom)
Period cast ornaments
that add character to a
garden need not cost a
fortune.

Juxtaposing textures
Create eye-catching
focal points, using
well-considered
combinations of
natural form and
texture.

Planning on a small scale *(right)*
Good garden design does not rely on having a large
plot of land. Here, curved shapes draw the eye
through a delightful array of foliage and flowers
planted around a beautifully manicured lawn and a
small but perfectly balanced fishpond.

Designing a garden is not an exact science. You may, for example, find that plants don't thrive in a particular spot, even though you have selected species that are recommended for your soil conditions and for the amount of sunlight your garden receives. And trees don't always conform to the size specified in a catalog. Nevertheless, forward planning can help avoid some of the more unfortunate mistakes, such as laying a patio where it will be in shade for most of the day, or digging a fishpond that's too small to create the conditions required for fish. Concentrate on planning the more permanent features first, taking into consideration how they will affect the planted areas of the garden that are to follow.

Deciding on the approach

Before you put pencil to paper, think about the type of garden you want, and ask yourself whether it will sit happily with your house and its immediate surroundings. Is it to be a formal garden, laid out in straight lines and geometric patterns—a style that often marries successfully with modern houses? Or do you prefer the more relaxed style of a rambling cottage garden? If you opt for the latter, remember that natural informality may not be as easy to achieve as you think, and your planting scheme will probably take several years to mature into the romantic garden you have in mind. Or maybe you're attracted to the idea of a Japanese-style garden—in effect a blend of both these styles, with every plant, stone, and pool of water carefully positioned, so that the garden bears all the hallmarks of a man-made landscape and yet conveys a sense of natural harmony.

Getting inspired

There's no shortage of material from which you can draw inspiration—there are countless books and magazines devoted to garden planning and design. Since no two gardens are completely alike, you probably won't find a plan that fits your plot exactly, but you may be able to adapt a design to suit your needs, or integrate some eye-catching details into your scheme.

Visiting real gardens is an even better way of getting inspired. Although large country estates and city parks are designed on a grand scale, you will be able to glean from them how mature shrubs should look or how plants, stone, and water can be used in a rock or water garden.

Don't forget that your friends may have had to tackle problems similar to your own—and if nothing else, you may learn from their mistakes!

SURVEYING THE PLOT

In order to make the best use of your plot of land, you need to take fairly accurate measurements and check the prevailing conditions.

Measuring up
Make a note of the overall dimensions of your plot. At the same time, check the diagonal measurements, because your garden may not be the perfect rectangle or square it appears to be. The diagonals are especially important when plotting irregular shapes.

Slopes and gradients
Check how the ground slopes. You don't need an accurate survey, but at least jot down the direction of the slope and plot the points where the gradient begins and ends. You can get some idea of the differences in level by using a long straightedge and a level. Place one end of the straightedge on the top of a bank, for example, and measure the vertical distance from the other end to the foot of the slope.

Keep any useful features
Plot the position of existing features, such as pathways, areas of lawn, and established trees.

How about the weather?
Check the passage of the sun and the direction of prevailing winds. Don't forget that the angle of the sun will be higher in summer, and that a screen of deciduous trees will be less effective as a windbreak when the leaves fall.

Soil conditions
The type of soil you have in your garden is bound to influence your choice of plants, but you can easily adjust soil content by adding peat or fertilizers. Clay soil is heavy when wet, and tends to crack when dry. A sandy soil feels gritty and loose in dry conditions. Acidic peat soil is dark brown and flaky. Pale-colored, chalky soil will not support acid-loving plants. Any soil that contains too many stones or gravel is unsuitable as topsoil.

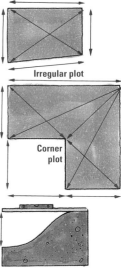

Measuring a plot
To draw an accurate plan, take down the overall dimensions, including the diagonals.

Irregular plot

Corner plot

Sloping site

Gauging a slope
Use a straightedge and a level to measure the height of a bank.

Theme gardens
Deciding on a style or theme for your garden will help you with the overall planning right from the start. The very different themes shown here include the seemingly random planting of a colorful cottage garden, the pleasing symmetry of a formal layout, and the "natural" informality of a Japanese-style garden that, in reality, is constructed with care from selected rocks, pebbles, and sculptural foliage.

Planning in greater detail

Armed with all the measurements you've taken, make a simple drawing to try out your ideas. Then, to make sure that your plan will work in reality, mark out the shapes and plot the important features in your garden.

Drawing a plan

Draw a plan of your garden on paper. It must be a properly scaled plan, or you are sure to make some errors, but it need not be professionally perfect. Use graph paper to plot the dimensions, but do the actual drawing on tracing paper laid over the grid, so you can try out several ideas and adapt your plan without having to redraw it each time.

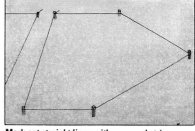
Draw a garden plan on tracing paper

Plotting your design on the ground

Planning on paper is only the first stage. Gardens are rarely seen from above, so it is essential to plot the design on the ground to check your dimensions and view the features from different angles.

A pond or patio that seems enormous on paper may look pathetically small in reality. Other shortcomings, such as the way a tree will block the view from your proposed patio, become obvious once you lay out the plan full size.

Plot individual features by driving pegs into the ground and stretching string lines between them.

Use a rope tied to a peg to scribe arcs on the ground, and mark the curved lines with stakes or a row of bricks. A garden hose provides the ideal aid for marking out less regular curves. If you can scrape areas clear of weeds, that will define the shapes still further.

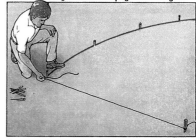
Mark out straight lines with pegs and string

Practical experiments

When you have marked out your design, carry out a few experiments to check that it is practicable.

Will it be possible, for instance, for two people to pass each other on the garden path without having to step into the flowerbeds? Can you set down a wheelbarrow on the path without one of its legs slipping into the pond?

Try placing some furniture on the area you have marked out for your patio to make sure there is enough room to relax comfortably and sit down to a meal with visitors. Most people build a patio alongside the house, but if you have to put it elsewhere to find a sunny spot, will it become a chore to walk back and forth with drinks and snacks?

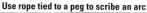
Use rope tied to a peg to scribe an arc

Siting a pond

Position a pond to avoid overhanging trees, and in an area where it will catch at least half a day's sunlight. Check that you can reach it with a hose and that you can run electrical cables to power a pump or lighting.

Common sense safety

Don't make your garden an obstacle course. A narrow path alongside a pond, for example, may be hazardous or intimidating for an elderly relative, and low walls or planters near the edge of a patio could cause someone to trip.

Try out irregular curves with a garden hose

Driveways and parking spaces

Allow a minimum width of 10 feet for a driveway, making sure there is enough room to open the doors of a car parked alongside a wall. And bear in mind that vehicles larger than your own might need to use the drive or parking space. If possible, allow room for the turning circle of your car; make sure you will have a clear view of the traffic when you pull out into the road.

Don't neglect your neighbors

There are legal restrictions regarding what you can erect in your garden. However, even if you have a free license, it's worth consulting your neighbors in case anything you're planning might inconvenience them. A wall or row of trees that throws shade across a neighbor's patio or blocks the light to their windows could be the source of a bitter dispute that lasts for years.

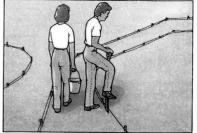
Make sure two people can pass on a path

Plotting curved features
Use rope tied to a peg to lay out circles and arcs on the ground.

Tree roots and foundations

There's a widely held belief that climbing plants, especially ivy, will damage any masonry wall.

If exterior stucco or the mortar between bricks or stonework is in poor condition, then a vigorous ivy plant will undoubtedly weaken the structure as its aerial roots attempt to extract moisture from the masonry. The roots will invade broken joints and, on finding a source of nourishment for the main plant, expand and burst the weakened material. This encourages damp to penetrate the wall.

However, when clinging to sound masonry, ivy can do no more than climb using its suckerlike roots for support.

This growth can be controlled with the aid of training wires. As long as the structure is sound and free from damp, there is even some benefit in allowing a plant to clothe a wall, since its close-growing mat of leaves, mostly with their drip tips pointing downward, acts as insulation and provides some protection against the elements.

Climbers must be pruned regularly, so they don't penetrate between the roofing or clog gutters and down-spouts. If a robust climber is allowed to grow unchecked, the weight of the mature plant may eventually topple a weakened wall.

When planning your garden, you will probably want to include one or two trees. Think carefully, however, about your choice of trees and their position—they could potentially be damaging to the structure of your house if planted too near to it.

Siting trees

Tree roots searching for moisture can do considerable harm to a house's drainage system. Large roots can fracture rigid pipes and penetrate joints, eventually blocking drainage.

Before planting a tree close to the house, find out how far its root system is likely to spread. One solution is to estimate its likely maximum height, and take this as a guide as to how far from the house you should plant the tree.

If you think an existing tree is likely to cause problems in the future, don't be tempted to chop it down without consulting your local planning depart-ment—some trees are protected by preservation orders, and you could be fined if you cut down a protected tree without permission. A better solution is to hire a professional tree surgeon, who may be able to solve the problem by pruning the branches and roots.

Cracks: subsidence and heave

Minor cracks in foundation walls are often the result of shrinkage as the structure dries out. Such cracks are not serious and can be repaired during normal maintenance. More serious structural cracks, on the other hand are due to movement of the foundations. Trees planted too close to a building can add to the problem by removing moisture from the site, causing subsidence of the foundations as the supporting earth collapses. Tree felling can be just as damaging; the surrounding soil, which has stabilized over the years, swells as it takes up the moisture that had previously been removed by the tree's root system. As a result, upward movement of the ground—known as heave—distorts the foundations, and cracks begin to appear.

Training wires
Growth can be controlled by fixing horizontal wires at the required height.

Subsidence
A mature tree growing close to a house can draw so much water from the ground that the earth subsides, causing damage to the foundations.

Don't allow climbers to get out of control

Heave
When a mature tree is felled, the earth can absorb more water, causing it to swell until it displaces the foundations of the building.

Choosing fences

Log fencing
Construct your own informal fencing, using split logs nailed to horizontal rails.

A fence is the most popular form of boundary marker or garden screen, primarily because it is relatively inexpensive and takes very little time to erect, compared with building a wall.

Value for money
In the short term a fence is cheaper than a masonry wall, although one can argue that the cost of maintenance and replacement over a very long period eventually cancels out the savings. Wood has a comparatively short life, because it is susceptible to insect infestation and rot when exposed to the elements. However, a fence can last for years if it is treated regularly with a preservative. And, if you're prepared to spend a little more money on plastic or concrete components, then your fence will be virtually maintenance free.

Selecting your fencing

You may be surprised by how much fencing you need to surround even a small garden. It's worth considering the available options carefully, to make sure you invest your money in a fence that will meet your needs. Unless your priority is to keep neighborhood children or animals out of your garden, privacy is most likely to be the prime consideration. There are a number of privacy options, but you may have to compromise to some extent if you plan to erect a fence on a site exposed to strong prevailing winds. In this situation, you will need a fence that will act as a windbreak without offering so much resistance that the posts work loose within a couple of seasons.

Planning and planning permission

As a general rule, you can build a fence up to 6 feet high without hav-ing to obtain planning permission. However, if your boundary adjoins a highway, you may not be allowed to erect any barrier higher than 3 feet. In addition, there could be restrictions on fencing if the land surrounding your house has been designed as an open-plan area. Even so, many authorities will permit you to erect low boundary markers such as post-and-chain fencing.

Discuss your plans with your neighbors, because you will need their permission if you want to work from both sides of the boundary when erecting the fence. Check the exact line of the boundary to make certain that you don't encroach upon your neighbor's land. The fenceposts should run along the boundary or on your side of the line; before you dismantle an old fence, make sure that it is indeed yours to demolish.

If a neighbor is unwilling to replace an unsightly fence and won't even allow you to replace it at your expense, there is nothing to stop you from erecting another fence alongside the original one, provided that it's on your property.

Although it is an unwritten law that a good neighbor erects a fence with the post and rails facing his or her own property, there are usually no legal restrictions that could force you to do so.

Types of fencing

Chain-link fencing

Chain-link fencing

Consisting of wire netting stretched between posts, chain-link fencing is purely functional. A true chain-link fence is made from strong galvanized or plastic-coated wire mesh that is suspended from a heavy-gauge cable, known as a straining wire, strung between the posts. You can make a cheap fence from soft wire netting or chicken wire, but it will not be durable and it will stretch if a large animal leans against it.

Decorative wire fencing, which is available at many garden centers, is designed primarily for marking boundaries or supporting lightweight climbing plants. Except in a remote rural location, any chain-link fence will benefit from a screen of climbers or hedging plants.

Trellis fencing

Trellis fencing

An open trellis, constructed from thin softwood or from cedar lath, is designed primarily to help plants climb a wall, but rigid panels made from softwood battens can be used in conjunction with fenceposts to erect a substantial freestanding screen. Most garden centers stock a wide range of these decorative panels. A similar fence made from split rustic poles nailed to heavy rails and posts forms a strong and attractive barrier.

Post-and-chain fencing

Post-and-chain fencing

A post-and-chain fence is no more than a decorative feature intended to prevent people from inadvertently wandering off a path or pavement onto a lawn or flowerbed. This type of fencing is constructed by stringing lengths of painted metal or plastic chain between short posts sunk into the ground.

Types of fencing

Closedboard fencing

A closedboard fence is made by nailing overlapping strips (sometimes called featherboards) to horizontal rails. Featherboards are sawn planks that taper across their width, from ⅜ inch at the thicker edge down to about ⅛ inch. The boards are usually 4 or 6 inches wide. The best quality featherboards are made from cedar, but softwood is the usual choice in view of the amount of lumber required to make a long closedboard fence. Although it is expensive, closedboard fencing forms a screen that is both strong and attractive. Because the boards are attached vertically, the fence is quite difficult to climb from the outside—which makes it ideal for keeping intruders out.

Closedboard fencing

Prefabricated panel fencing

Fences made from prefabricated panels nailed between posts are very popular, perhaps because they are so easy to erect. Standard fence panels are 6 feet wide and range in height from 2 to 6 feet. They are supplied in 1-foot gradations. Most fence panels are made from interwoven or overlapping strips of wood sandwiched between a frame of sawn lumber.

Overlapping-strip panels are usually designated as "lap" panels. When the strips have a natural wavy edge, they are sometimes called rustic lap.

Any panel fence tends to be a good value for the money and will provide reasonably durable screening, but if privacy is a consideration, choose the lapped type, as interwoven strips can shrink in the summer, leaving gaps in the fence.

Panel fencing

Interlap fencing

An interlap fence is made by nailing square-edged boards to horizontal rails, fixing the boards alternately on one side, then the other. Spacing is a matter of choice. You can overlap the edges of the boards for privacy, or space them apart to create a more decorative effect. This type of fencing is a sensible choice for a windy site. Although it's a sturdy screen, it permits a strong wind to pass through the gaps between the boards, reducing the amount of pressure exerted on the fence. Being equally attractive from either side, an interlap fence is perfect as boundary screening.

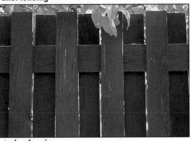
Interlap fencing

Picket fencing

The traditional low picket fence is still popular as a barrier at the front of the house, particularly where a high fence would look out of place. Narrow, vertical pickets with rounded or pointed tops are spaced at about 2 inches apart. Because they are time consuming to build by hand, some picket fences are sold as ready-made panels constructed from plastic or softwood to keep down the cost.

Picket fencing

Ranch-style fencing

Low-level fences—made from simple horizontal rails fixed to short posts—are the modern counterpart of picket fencing. Used extensively to divide up building plots in some housing developments, ranch-style fencing is often painted, although clear-finished or stained lumber is just as attractive and much more durable. Softwood and some hardwoods are commonly used for this kind of fencing, but plastic ranch-style fences are also popular for their clean, crisp appearance. And, because there's no need to repaint them, very little maintenance is necessary.

Ranch-style fencing

Concrete fencing

A cast-concrete fence is maintenance free, and it provides the security and permanence of a wall built from brick or stone. Interlocking horizontal sections are built one upon the other, up to the required height. Each vertical stack is supported by grooves cast into the sides of concrete fenceposts. This relatively heavy fencing would be dangerous if the posts were not firmly embedded in concrete.

Concrete fencing

Fenceposts

Whatever type of fence you decide to erect, its strength and durability will rely on good-quality posts set solidly in the ground. Erecting the posts carefully and accurately is crucial to the longevity of the fence, and may save you having to either rebuild or repair it in the future.

Types of post

In some cases, the nature of the fencing will determine the choice of post. Concrete fencing, for example, has to be supported by compatible concrete posts. Generally, though, you can choose the material and style of post that suits the appearance of the fence.

Timber posts

Most fences are supported by square-section wood posts. Standard fence-post sizes are 3 or 4 inches square, but gate posts are often 5, 6, or 8 inches square. Unless you ask specifically for hardwood, most lumberyards supply pretreated softwood posts.

Plastic posts

Extruded PVC (polyvinyl chloride) posts are supplied with plastic fencing, together with molded-plastic end caps and other plastic components.

Concrete posts

A variety of reinforced-concrete posts, usually 4 inches square, are produced to suit different styles of fence—drilled for chain-link fixings, mortised for rails, and recessed or grooved for panels. Special corner and end posts are notched to accommodate bracing struts for chain-link fencing.

Metal posts

Steel posts are made to support chain-link fences, and wrought-iron gates are often hung from plastic-coated steel posts. Steel posts are very sturdy, but are not usually considered the most attractive option for residential use.

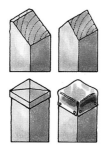

Capping fenceposts
If you simply cut the end of a wood post square, the top of the post will rot relatively quickly. The solution is to cut a single or double bevel to shed the rainwater, or nail a wooden or galvanized-metal cap over the end of the post.

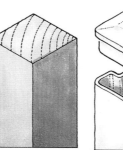

Square wood post   **Capped plastic post**

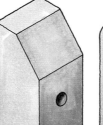

Drilled concrete post   **Mortised concrete post**

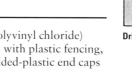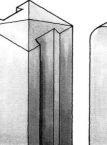

Grooved concrete post   **Notched end post**

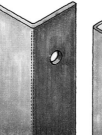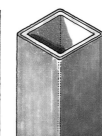

Angle-iron post   **Tubular-steel post**

Preserving fenceposts

Immersing fenceposts
Wood that is to be in contact with the ground benefits from prolonged immersion in a polyethelene-lined trough of chemical wood preserver.

Even when a wood fencepost is pretreated to prevent rot, you can make doubly sure by soaking the base of each post in a bucket of chemical preserver overnight. Untreated wood needs to be immersed for a similar period in a polyethelene-lined trough filled with the preserver.

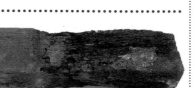

Untreated timber posts quickly succumb to rot.

REMOVING OLD FENCEPOSTS

If you are replacing a dilapidated fence, it may prove convenient to put the new posts in the same position as the old.

Begin by dismantling the boards and rails, or cut through the hardware so you can remove the fence panels. If any of the posts are bedded firmly, or sunk into concrete, you will have to pry them out.
   Start by removing the topsoil from around each post to loosen it. Drive large nails into two opposite faces of the post, about one foot from the ground. Bind a length of rope around the post, just below the nails, and tie the ends to the tip of a pry board. Build a pile of bricks or place a concrete building block close to the post, and use it as a fulcrum to lever the post out of the ground.

Removing a rotted fencepost
Use a pry board to lever a post out of the ground.

Fixing to a wall

If a fence runs up to the house, attach the first post to the wall, using three expanding masonry bolts. Place a washer under each bolt head to stop the wood from being crushed. Using a level, check that the post is vertical and, if need be, drive shims between the post and wall to make adjustments.

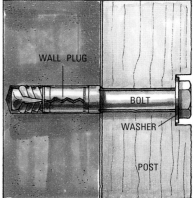

WALL PLUG
BOLT
WASHER
POST

Bolting a post to a wall
If you are attaching a prefabricated panel against a wall-fixed post, counterbore the bolts so that the heads lie flush with the surface of the wood.

Erecting fenceposts

The type of fence you choose dictates whether you need to erect all the posts first or put them up one at a time, along with the other components. If you are building a prefabricated panel fence, for example, fix the posts as you erect the fence; but if you are putting up chain-link fencing, complete the run of posts first.

Marking out a row of fenceposts

Drive a peg into the ground at each end of the fence run, and stretch a length of string between the pegs to align the row of posts. If possible, adjust the spacing to avoid obstructions such as large tree roots.

If one or more posts have to be inserted across a paved patio, either lift enough slabs to allow you to dig the required holes, or mark out the patio for bolt-down, metal post sockets (see right).

Erecting the posts

Digging the hole
Bury one quarter of each post to provide a firm foundation. You can rent posthole augers to remove the central core of earth. Twist the tool to drive it into the ground **(1)** and pull it out after every 6 inches to remove the soil. When you have reached a sufficient depth, taper the sides of the hole slightly so that you can backfill easily around the post.

Anchoring the post
Pack a layer of broken bricks or small stones into the bottom of the hole to support the base of the post and provide drainage. Get someone to hold the post upright while you brace it with boards nailed to the post and to stakes driven into the ground. Use guy ropes to support a concrete post. Check with a level that the post is vertical **(2)**.

Pack some more soil around the post, leaving a hole about 1 foot deep for filling with concrete. Fill up with a fast-setting dry concrete mix made specially for erecting fence posts, then pour in the recommended amount of water. Alternatively, mix up general-purpose concrete and tamp it into the hole with the end of a board **(3)**. Form the concrete just above the level of the soil, and smooth it to slope away from the post **(4)**. This will help shed rainwater and prevent rot.

Leave the concrete to harden before removing the braces. Support a panel fence temporarily, with braces wedged against the posts.

1 Dig the posthole

2 Brace the post

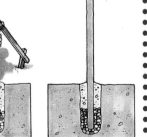
3 Fill with concrete

4 Slope the concrete

Supporting end posts

Chain-link fenceposts made of wood must resist the tension of the straining wires. Brace each end post (and some of the intermediate ones, over a long run) with a strut made from a length of fencepost. Shape the end of the strut to fit a notch cut into the post **(1)** and nail it in place. You can order special precast-concrete end posts and struts.

Anchor the post in the ground in the usual way, but dig a trench about 18 inches deep alongside for the strut. Wedge a brick under the end of the strut before packing the soil around the post and strut. Fill the trench up to ground level with concrete **(2)**. Support a corner post with two struts set at right angles.

1 Notch the post

2 Concrete the end post

Instead of digging holes for your fenceposts, you can place the base of each post into a square socket attached to a metal spike that is driven into firm ground. Similar sockets can be bolted to existing paving or set in fresh concrete.

Use 2-foot spikes for fences up to 4 feet high, and 30-inch spikes for a 6-foot fence. Place a scrap of hardwood post into the socket to protect the metal and then drive the spike partly into the ground with a sledgehammer.

Hold a level against the socket to make certain the spike is vertical **(1)**, then hammer the spike into the ground until only the socket is visible. Insert the post and, depending on the type of spike, secure it by screwing through the side of the socket or by tightening clamping bolts **(2)**. If you're putting up a panel fence, use the edge of a fixed panel to position the next spike **(3)**.

1 Use a level to check that spike is vertical

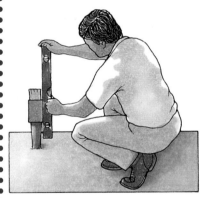

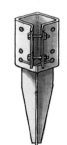
2 Fix the post

3 Position next spike

Fencepost spikes

Bolted sockets
Bolt this type of socket to existing patios and concrete drives.

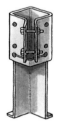
Embedded sockets
Embed these sockets in wet concrete.

Repair socket
Allows replacement of rotten or broken posts set in concrete. Cut off the old post flush with the concrete and then drive the spike into the center of the stump

Putting up chain-link fencing

To support chain-link fencing, set out a row of wood, concrete, or steel posts, spacing them no more than 10 feet apart. Brace the end posts with struts to resist the pull exerted by the straining wires. A long run needs a braced intermediate post every 200 feet or so.

Using wood posts

Support chain-link fencing on straining wires (see right). Since it's impossible to tension this heavy-gauge wire by hand, large straining bolts are used to stretch it between the posts: one to coincide with the top of the fencing, one about 6 inches from the ground, and a third, if required, midway between.

Drill ⅜-inch-diameter holes right through the posts, insert a bolt into each hole, and fit a washer and nut **(1)**, leaving enough thread to provide about 2 inches of movement once you begin to apply tension to the wire.

Pass the end of the wire through the eye of a bolt, then twist it around itself with pliers **(2)**. Stretch the wire along the run of fencing, stapling it to each post and strut **(3)**, but leave enough slack for the wire to move when tensioned.

Cut the wire to length and twist it through the bolt at the other end of the fence. Tension the wire from both ends by turning the nuts with a wrench **(4)**.

Standard straining bolts provide enough tension for the average garden fence, but over a long run of fencing—200 feet or more—use a turnbuckle for each wire, applying tension with a wrench (see left).

Using concrete posts

Fix straining wires to concrete posts, using a special bolt and cleat (see right). Bolt a stretcher bar to the cleats when erecting the wire netting.

Secure the straining wires to intermediate posts by using a length of galvanized wire passed through each of the predrilled holes.

Using steel posts

Stretcher bars with winding brackets for applying tension to straining wires are supplied with steel fenceposts (see right). As you pass a straining wire from end to end, pass it through the predrilled hole in every intermediate post.

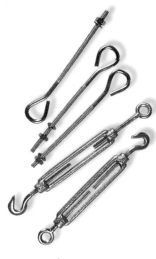

Using a turnbuckle
Apply tension by turning the turnbuckle with an open-end wrench.

KNUCKLE
SPIRAL

Joining wire mesh
Chain-link fencing is usually supplied in 80-foot lengths. To join one roll to another, unfold the knuckles at each end of the first wire spiral, then turn the spiral counter-clockwise to withdraw it from the mesh. Connect the two rolls by rethreading the loose spiral in a clockwise direction through each link of the mesh. Bend the knuckle over at the top and bottom.

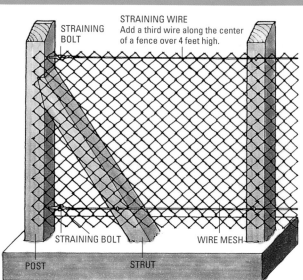

STRAINING BOLT
STRAINING WIRE
Add a third wire along the center of a fence over 4 feet high.

STRAINING BOLT
WIRE MESH
POST
STRUT

Chain-link fencing

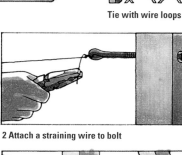

Attaching the mesh
Staple each end link to the post. Unroll the mesh and pull it taut. Tie it to straining wires every 1 foot with galvanized wire. Attach to post at far end.

Staple mesh to post

Tie with wire loops

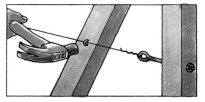

1 Insert a straining bolt in end post

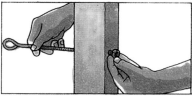

2 Attach a straining wire to bolt

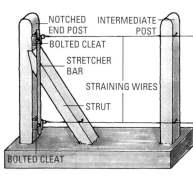

3 Staple the wire to each post and strut

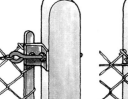

4 Tension the bolt at the far end of fence

NOTCHED
END POST
INTERMEDIATE
POST
BOLTED CLEAT
STRETCHER BAR
STRAINING WIRES
STRUT
BOLTED CLEAT

Concrete fence posts

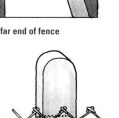

Cleat and stretcher bar

Tie wire to post

END POST
WINDING BRACKET
STRETCHER BAR
STRAINING WIRES
STRUT
WINDING BRACKET   INTERMEDIATE POST

Steel posts

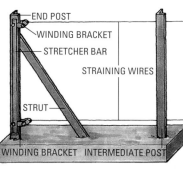

Winding bracket

Pass wire through post

The boards used to panel a closedboard fence are nailed to triangular-section rails mortised into the fenceposts. Concrete posts, and some wooden ones, are supplied ready-mortised, but if you buy standard wood posts, you'll either have to cut the mortises yourself or use end brackets (see right) instead. Space fenceposts no more than 10 feet apart.

The ends of the fence boards are liable to rot, especially if they are in contact with the ground, so install horizontal boards at the foot of the fence. Nail capping strips across the tops of the boards.

The rails take most of the strain when a closedboard fence is buffeted by high winds.

Not surprisingly, the rails often crack across the middle or break where the tenon enters the mortise. Galvanized-metal brackets are made for repairing broken rails.

You can use end brackets to construct a new fence, instead of cutting mortises for the rails. However, it will not be as strong as a fence built with mortise-and-tenon joints.

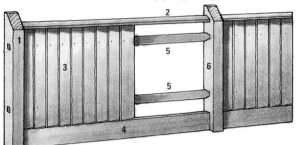

Closedboard fencing
1 End post
2 Capping strip
3 Fence boards
4 Baseboard
5 Rail
6 Intermediate post

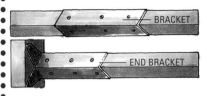
BRACKET

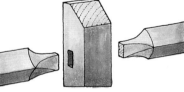
END BRACKET

Erecting the framework

When using plain wooden posts, mark and cut mortises for the rails about 6 inches above and below where the fence boards will be attached. For fencing over 4 feet high, cut mortises for a third rail midway between the others. Position the mortises 1 inch from the front face of each post.

As you erect the fence, cut the rails to length and shape a tenon on each end, using a coarse rasp or Surform file **(1)**. Paint preservative onto the shaped ends and into the mortises before you assemble the rails.

Erect the first fencepost and pack soil around its base. Get someone to hold the post steady while you fit the rails and erect the next post, tapping it

onto the ends of the rails with a mallet **(2)**. Check that the rails are horizontal and the posts vertical before packing soil around the second post. Construct the entire run of posts and rails in the same way. If you can't maneuver the last post onto the tenoned rails, cut the rails square and attach them to the post with metal end brackets.

Check the whole run once more to ensure that the rails are bedded firmly in their mortises and that the framework is true, then secure each rail by driving a nail through the post into the tenon **(3)** or by drilling a hole and inserting a wooden dowel. Pack concrete around each post and leave it to set.

1 Shape rails to fit the mortises

Closedboard fencing

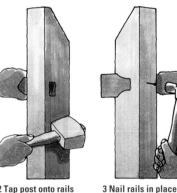

2 Tap post onto rails   **3 Nail rails in place**

Installing the boards

Baseboards
Some concrete posts are mortised to take baseboards; in this case, fit the boards at the same time as the rails. If concrete posts are not mortised, bed treated wooden cleats into the concrete filling at the base of each post, and screw the baseboard to the cleat when the concrete has set.

To fit baseboards to wooden posts, nail cleats to the foot of each post, then nail the boards to the cleats **(4)**. Some metal post sockets are made with brackets for attaching baseboards.

Fence boards
Cut the fence boards to length and treat the endgrain with preservative.

Stand the first fence board on the baseboard, butting its thicker edge against the post. Nail the board to the rails with galvanized nails about ¾ inch from the thick edge. Place the next board in position, overlapping the thin edge of the fixed board by ½ inch. Check that it's vertical, then nail it in the same way. Don't drive a nail through both boards, or they may split if the wood shrinks. To space the other boards equally, make a spacer block from a scrap of wood **(5)**. Plane the last board to fit against the next post and attach it, this time with two nails per rail **(6)**. Finally, nail capping strips across the tops of the fence boards, cut the posts to length, and cap them.

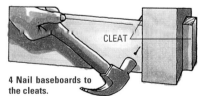
CLEAT

4 Nail baseboards to the cleats.

Capping the fence
Nail a wooden capping strip to the ends of the fence boards to shed rainwater.

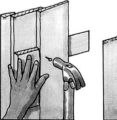

5 Use a spacer block to position fence boards   **6 Attach last board with two nails**

Erecting panel fences

To prevent a fencing panel from rotting, either install baseboards, as on a closed-board fence, or leave a gap at the bottom by supporting a panel temporarily on two bricks while you attach it to the fenceposts.

Using wood posts

Pack the first post into its hole with soil, then get someone to hold a panel against the post while you toenail through the frame into the post (**1**). If you can work from both sides, drive three nails from each side of the fence. If the wood used for the frame is likely to split, blunt the nails by tapping their points with a hammer.

You can also use galvanized-metal angle brackets to secure the panels (**2**). Construct the entire fence by erecting panels and posts alternately.

Install pressure-treated baseboards, and nail capping strips across the panels if they have not already been installed by the manufacturer. Finally, cut each post to length and cap it.

Wedge struts made from scrap lumber against each post to keep it vertical, then top up the holes with concrete. If you're unable to work from both sides, you will have to fill each hole as you build the fence.

Using concrete posts

Grooved concrete posts will support panels without the need for additional hardware (**3**). Recessed concrete posts are supplied with metal brackets for attaching the panels (**4**).

Building a panel fence
Posts and panels are erected alternately. Dig a hole for the post (**1**) and hold it upright with packed soil. Support a panel on bricks (**2**) and get a helper to push it against the post (**3**) while you nail it (**4**). Install baseboards (**5**) and capping strips (**6**), then cap the posts (**7**). Fill the holes with concrete (**8**) and allow it to set.

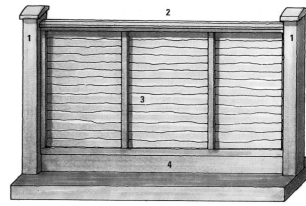

Panel fence
1 Fenceposts
2 Capping strip
3 Prefabricated panel
4 Baseboard

1 Nail the panel through its frame

2 Or use angle brackets to attach panels to posts

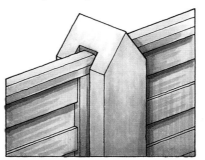
3 Concrete post grooved to take panels

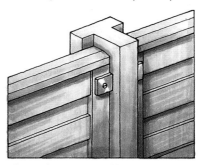
4 Recessed concrete post with hanging brackets

Post-and-rail fences

A simple ranch-style fence is no more than a series of horizontal rails attached to short posts concreted into the ground. A picket fence is similar, but with vertical pickets attached to the rails.

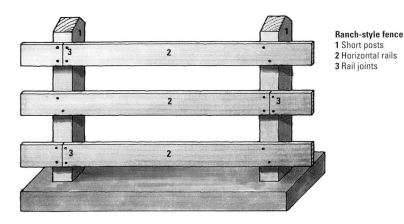

Ranch-style fence
1 Short posts
2 Horizontal rails
3 Rail joints

Fixing horizontal rails

You can screw the rails directly to the posts (**1**), but the fence is likely to last longer if you cut a shallow notch in the post to locate each rail before attaching it permanently in place (**2**).

Join two horizontal rails by butting them over a fencepost (**3**). Arrange to stagger such joints so that you don't end up with all the rails butted on the same posts (**4**).

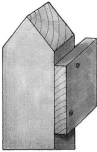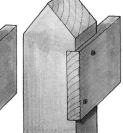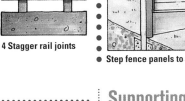

1 Screw rail to post   2 Or notch it first   3 Butt rails on posts   4 Stagger rail joints

Installing picket panels

When constructing a low picket fence from manufactured panels, which are designed to fit between the posts, it is best to buy or make steel saddle brackets for attaching a pair of panels to each post. Be sure to prime and paint homemade brackets to keep the steel from rusting.

Use a metal bracket to attach picket-fence panels

Crossways slope
If a slope runs across your property so that a neighbor's yard is higher than your own, either build brick retaining walls between the posts or set paving slabs in concrete to hold back the soil.

Downhill slope
The posts need to be set vertically, even when you are erecting a fence on a sloping site. Chain-link fencing or ranch-style rails can follow the slope of the land if you wish; but fence panels should be stepped, and the triangular gaps beneath them filled with base-boards or retaining walls.

Retaining wall for a crossways slope

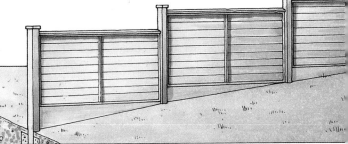

Step fence panels to allow for a downhill slope

Supporting a rotted post

Buried wood posts often rot below ground level, leaving a perfectly sound section above. To save an old post, you can make a passable repair by bracing the upper section with a short concrete post.

Erecting the post
First, dig the soil from around the rotted stump and remove it. Install a concrete post and pack soil around it (**1**), then fill the hole with concrete (**2**). Drill pilot holes in the wooden post for lagscrews (**3**). Insert the screws, using a wrench to draw the old post tightly against the new one.

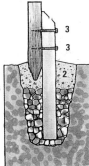

Building plastic ranch-style fencing
The basic construction of a plastic fence is similar to one built from wood, but follow the manufacturer's instructions concerning the method for joining the rails to the posts.

Choosing a gate

Browsing through lumberyards and home centers, you'll find that gates are grouped according to their intended location, because it's where a gate is hung that has the greatest influence on its design and style. When choosing a gate, give due consideration to the character of the house and its surroundings. Buy a gate that matches the style of fence or complements the wall from which it is hung. If in doubt, aim for simplicity.

Side gates

An unprotected side entrance is an open invitation for intruders to slip in unnoticed and gain access to the back of your house. Side gates are designed to deter burglars while affording easy access for visitors. These gates are usually between 6 and 7 feet high and are made from either wrought iron or wood. Wood gates are heavy and are therefore braced with strong diagonal members to keep them rigid. With security in mind, choose a closedboard or tongue-and-grooved gate because their vertical boards are difficult to climb. Attach strong hinges to the top and bottom.

Entrance gates

An entrance gate is designed as much for its appearance as its function, but it must be sturdy enough to withstand frequent use. For this reason, wood gates are often braced with a diagonal strut running from the top of the latch stile down to the bottom of the hinge stile. Don't hang a gate with the strut running the other way, or the bracing will not work as well.

Common fence styles are reflected in the type of entrance gates you can buy. Picket, closedboard, and ranch-style gates are all available, and there are simple frame-and-panel gates made with solid wood or exterior-grade plywood panels that serve to keep the frame rigid. If the tops of both the stiles are cut at an angle, they will tend to shed rainwater, reducing the likelihood of wet rot.

Decorative iron gates are often used for entrances, but make sure the style is appropriate for the building and its location. A large, ornate gate can look out of place in front of a simple modern house.

Driveway gates

First, decide whether hanging a gate across your driveway is a good idea. Stepping out of your car in order to open the gate can be a problem unless there's plenty of room to pull the car off the road.

Driveway gates invariably open into the property, so if the drive slopes up from the road, make sure there's adequate ground clearance for a wide gate. You can also hang two smaller gates that meet in the center.

Gateposts and piers

Gateposts and masonry piers need to be anchored securely to the ground in order to take the leverage exerted by a heavy gate.

Choose hardwood posts whenever possible, and select the size according to the weight of the gate. Posts that are 4 inches square are adequate for entrance gates, but use 5-inch posts for gates that are 6 feet high. For a gate across a drive, choose posts that are 6 or even 8 inches square.

If you opt for concrete gateposts, look for posts predrilled to accept hinges and a catch. Otherwise, you may have to screw these fittings to a strip of wood bolted to the post.

Square or cylindrical tubular-steel posts are available with hinge pins, gate-stops, and catches welded in place. Unless they have been coated with plastic at the factory, steel posts must be painted to protect them from rust.

A pair of masonry piers is another possibility. Each pier should be at least 16 inches square and built on a firm concrete footing. For heavy gates, the hinge pier should be reinforced with rebar buried in the footing and running up through the pier.

Gate styles

Side gates

Entrance gates

Driveway gates

Hardware for gates

A range of specialized hardware has been developed for hanging heavy garden gates, to cope with the strain involved.

Hinges

Strap hinges
Most side and entrance gates are hung on strap hinges. Screw the longer flap to the gate rail, and the vertical flap to the face of the post. Heavy gates require a hinge that's bolted through the top rail. Wide driveway gates are hung from double strap hinges, made with long flaps bolted on each side of the top rail.

Hinge pins
Collars, welded to metal gates, drop over hinge pins that are attached to the gateposts. To prevent a gate from being lifted off, drill a hole through the top pin and install a split pin and washer.

Latches and catches

Automatic latches
Simple wood gates are usually outfitted with a latch that operates automatically as the gate is closed.

Thumb latches
Pass the lifter bar of a thumb latch through a slot cut in the gate, then screw the handle to the front. Attach the latch beam to the inner face, so the lifter bar can raise the beam from the hooked keeper fixed to the gatepost.

Ring latches
A ring latch works in a similar way to a thumb latch but is usually operated from inside only, by twisting the ring handle to lift the latch beam.

Chelsea catches
Pivoting on a bolt that passes through the stile of a driveway gate, a Chelsea catch drops into a slot in the catch plate, which is screwed to the gatepost.

Loop-over catches
When hanging a pair of wide gates, one is fixed with a bolt that slides into a socket buried into the ground. A U-shaped metal catch on the other gate drops over the stile of the fixed gate.

Materials for gates

Many wood gates are made from relatively cheap softwood, but a wood such as cedar or oak will last longer. Many so-called wrought-iron gates are actually made from mild-steel bar, which must be primed and painted to prevent rust.

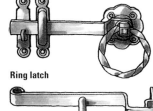
Strap hinge

Heavy-duty strap hinge

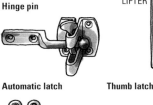
Double strap hinge

LATCH BEAM

KEEPER

LIFTER

Hinge pin

Automatic latch   **Thumb latch**

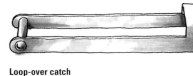
Ring latch

Chelsea catch

Loop-over catch

Erecting gateposts

Gateposts are set in concrete like ordinary fenceposts, but the postholes are linked by a concrete bridge that provides extra support.

Erecting gateposts
Lay the gate on the ground with a post on each side. Check that the posts are parallel and that they are the required distance apart to accommodate hinges and catch. Nail two boards from post to post and another diagonally to keep the posts in line while you erect them **(1)**.

Dig a trench 1 foot wide across the entrance, making it long enough to accommodate both posts. It need be no deeper than 1 foot in the center, but dig an adequate posthole at each end—about 18 inches deep for a low entrance gate, or 2 feet deep for a taller side gate.

Set the braced gateposts in the holes with soil and concrete, using temporary braces to hold them upright until the concrete has set **(2)**. Fill the trench with concrete, and either level it flush with the surrounding ground or allow for the thickness of some paving.

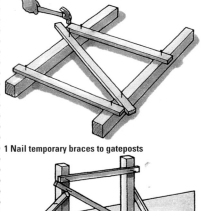
1 Nail temporary braces to gateposts

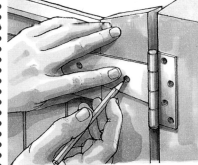
2 Support the posts until concrete sets

Mark positions of the hinges and catch

Driveway gateposts
Hang wide, farm-style gates on posts set in holes 3 feet deep. Erect the latch post in concrete, like any fencepost, but bolt a heavy piece of wood across the base of the hinge post before anchoring it in concrete.

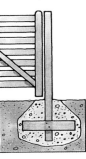
Supporting wide gates
Bolt a piece of wood to the hinge post to help support the weight of a wide gate.

Hanging a gate
Stand the gate between the posts and prop it up on a pair of bricks or wood blocks to hold it the required height off the ground. Tap in pairs of wedges on each side of the gate until it is held securely. Then mark the positions of the hinges and catch.

Masonry: building walls

Whatever kind of masonry structure you are building, the basic techniques are broadly similar. However, it's well worth hiring a professional builder or mason when the structure is complicated or extensive, especially if it will have to bear considerable loads or stress.

Amateur masons

It's difficult to suggest which aspects of bricklaying are likely to overstretch the capabilities of a do-it-yourselfer, as this differs from one individual to another and depends on the nature of the job. Clearly, it would be foolish for anyone to try to build a two-story house without having had a lot of experience or professional training. And even building a high boundary wall, which is simple in terms of technique, may be too difficult if the wall is very long or moves down, up, or across a sloping yard.

The simple answer is to practice with relatively low retaining walls, screens, and dividing walls until you have mastered the skills of laying bricks and blocks solidly one upon another and have developed the ability to build a wall that is straight and absolutely plumb.

Walls for different locations

Retaining walls

A retaining wall is designed to hold back a bank of earth when terracing a sloping site. Raised planting beds often serve a similar purpose.

Provided it's not excessively high, a retaining wall is quite easy to build, although, strictly speaking, it should slope back into the bank to resist the weight of the earth. You must also allow for drainage, in order to reduce water pressure behind the wall.

Retaining walls can be constructed with bricks, concrete blocks, or stone. Sometimes they are piled up, but in many cases traditional mortar is used for the joints.

Boundary walls

A brick or stone wall that surrounds your property provides security and privacy while creating an attractive background for trees and shrubs.

New bricks complement a formal garden or a modern setting, while secondhand materials or undressed stone blend well with an old, established garden. If you aren't able to match existing masonry exactly, disguise the difference in color by brushing liquid fertilizer onto the wall to encourage lichen to grow. You can also hide the junction with a climbing plant.

You usually need a building permit to build a wall higher than 3 feet if it's near a highway, or over 6 feet high elsewhere.

Dividing walls

Many people like to divide up a yard with walls in order to add interest to an otherwise featureless site. For example, you can build a wall to form a visual break between a patio and an area of grass, or perhaps to define the edge of a pathway. This type of dividing wall is often no more than 2 feet high.

Your material options are many, but concrete blocks with textured surfaces and standard bricks are very popular.

Screen walls

Screens are dividing walls that provide a degree of privacy without completely masking the property beyond. They are usually built with decorative pierced blocks, sometimes combined with brick or solid-block bases and piers.

Stone retaining wall

Decorative concrete-block screen

Boundary wall of yellow brick

Cast concrete blocks make attractive dividing walls

Choosing bricks

Thousands of different types of bricks are produced in this country and around the world. Generally, your choice will be limited to bricks manufactured in your local area, because long-distance hauling of these heavy materials is too expensive for most applications. When buying brick, it's important to understand the basic classifications as they relate to size, appearance, and weathering characteristics.

Varieties of brick

Face brick
Face bricks are suitable for any type of exposed brickwork. They are weather- and frost-resistant. Being visible, face bricks are made as much for their appearance as for their structural qualities, and, as such, are available in the widest range of colors and textures. Face bricks are graded carefully to meet standards of strength, water absorption, and uniformity of shape. A trip to your local lumberyard, home center, or masonry supply outlet will present you with more choices than you thought possible.

Building brick
Building bricks are cheap general-purpose bricks used primarily for interior brickwork that will be plastered or stuccoed over when finished. They are not color matched carefully, but the mottled effect of an exposed wall built with building bricks can be attractive.

Although they can be damaged or cracked by frost if used in structural applications in exposed exterior locations, building bricks can be used for freestanding garden walls.

Firebrick
Firebricks are pale yellow in color and are made from specially chosen clays that are carefully fired to provide a highly heat-resistant product. They are designed for lining fireplaces, kilns, and barbecues. They must be laid up with heat-resistant mortar.

Durability of bricks

Building brick is manufactured in three grades that have different weathering characteristics and indicate the conditions a particular kind of brick is best suited to. For any particular project, check which kind of brick is required by your local building department.

Type SW (severe weathering) bricks are best suited for outdoor projects in areas prone to prolonged periods of freezing. Always choose type SW brick for patios and driveways. While there is a separate classification for bricks known as paving bricks, these are meant for public, high-traffic areas and are not required for residential projects.

Type MW (moderate weathering) can be used outdoors in areas where there is little or no frost. In most cases type MW bricks can be used for constructing garden walls, even in cold regions.

Type NW (no weathering) bricks are meant only for indoor use, but they can be used occasionally for outdoor structures that will be protected by an overhang from the ravages of driven rain and snow.

Types of bricks

Ordering bricks
Bricks are normally sold by the thousand, but most retailers are usually willing to sell them in smaller quantities. It is cheaper to order them directly from the manufacturer, but only if you buy a load large enough to make the shipping economical.

Estimating quantities
The size of a standard brick is 2¼ x 3¾ x 8 inches. But because dimensions may vary by a fraction of an inch, even within the same batch of bricks, manufacturers normally specify a nominal size which includes an additional ¼ to ½ inch to each dimension to allow for the mortar joint. To calculate how many bricks you need, allow about 48 bricks for every square yard of a wall. Add 5 percent for cutting and breakage.

Solid bricks
The majority of bricks are solid throughout, either flat on all surfaces or with a depression known as a "frog" on one face. When filled with mortar, the frog keys the bricks.

Cored or perforated bricks
Cored bricks have holes through them, performing the same function as the frog. A wall made with cored bricks must be covered on top with a course of solid bricks.

Special shapes
Specially shaped bricks are made for decorative brickwork. Masons draw upon the full range when building structures such as arches and chamfered or rounded corners.

Seconds
Seconds are secondhand, rather than second-rate, bricks. They should be cheaper than new bricks, but demand can inflate prices. Using seconds might be the only way you can match the color of weathered brickwork.

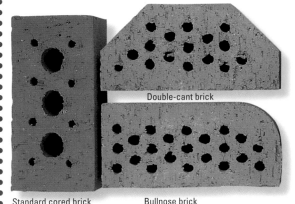

Standard cored brick · Double-cant brick · Bullnose brick

Standard brick with frog · Cut brick for shaped corner · Half-round brick

Brick dimensions

8 in. · 3-3/4 in. · 2-1/4 in.

• **Storing bricks**
When bricks are delivered, have them unloaded as near as possible to the building site and stack them carefully on a flat, dry base. Cover the stack with a tarp until you're ready to use the bricks, to prevent them from becoming saturated with rain.

Brick color and texture

The popularity of brick as a building material stems largely from its range of subtle colors and textures, which actually improve with weathering. Weathered brick can be difficult to match by using a manufacturer's catalog, so try to borrow samples from your supplier's stock—or, if you have spare bricks, take one to the supplier to compare it with new bricks.

Color

The color of bricks is largely determined by the type of clay used in their manufacture, although the color is modified by the addition of certain minerals and by the temperature of the firing. Large manufacturers supply a wide variety of colors, and you can also buy brindled (multicolored or mottled) bricks, which are useful for blending with existing masonry.

Texture

Texture is as important to the appearance of a brick wall as color. Simple rough or smooth textures are created by the choice of materials. Others are imposed upon the clay by scratching, rolling, brushing, and so on. A brick may be textured all over, or on the sides and ends only.

Brick colors and textures
A small selection from the wide range of colors and textures.
1 Smooth blended
2 Handmade
3 Sand-faced yellow
4 Smooth blue engineering
5 Sand-faced grey
6 Smooth red stock
7 Wire-cut brindle
8 Textured multibuff
9 London stock (second)
10 Wire cut blue
11 Red common
12 Coarse fletton
13 Molded fletton
14 Drag wire multired

Pattern formed by projecting headers

Decorative combination of colored bricks

Second-hand molded bricks

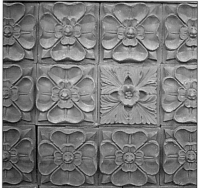

Sometimes whole panels are available

Weathered antique bricks are popular

Choosing concrete blocks

Cast concrete blocks were introduced as a cheap substitute for bricks that were to be covered with plaster or stucco, but they have long since overtaken brick for any number of applications—especially for foundation work. They come in a wide variety of sizes, shapes, colors, and textures and can be used just about anywhere.

Types of block

Lightweight concrete blocks
Made from aerated concrete, these blocks can be carried easily in one hand, which enables masons to build walls quickly and safely. Aerated blocks can be drilled and cut to shape easily, using common hand and power tools. They are used extensively for the construction of both internal and external walls.

Standard concrete blocks
Made from relatively heavy concrete, these are also known as dense concrete blocks. Most of these blocks are nearly hollow on the inside; they just have supporting ribs between the two outer faces. This makes the blocks lighter and provides a hollow space in which to install reinforcing bars (rebars) and concrete.

Varieties of block

Structural blocks
Simple rectangular blocks, cement gray or white in color, are most often used for foundation work. They cost less than bricks and are much faster to install. Another common use of these simple blocks is in the structural core of a wall that will be covered with stucco or plaster later. These blocks are often made with a zigzag keyed surface that allows the finish material to grip the surface better.

Facing blocks
These are blocks with one decorative face for walls that will be entirely exposed. They are often made to resemble natural stone by including some crushed stone aggregate in the mix or by creating a rough, textured surface. These blocks are used for covering the surface of a structural block wall or for freestanding landscape walls. A wide variety of shapes, sizes, colors, and surface textures is available.

Qualities of block

Loadbearing blocks
Structural blocks are used to construct the loadbearing walls of a building, typically the perimeter foundation walls and occasionally an interior loadbearing wall that supports a central beam. In some situations, lightweight aerated concrete blocks can be used. Generally, though, foundation work calls for standard dense concrete blocks.

Nonloadbearing blocks
These blocks are used to build internal dividing partitions. They are either lightweight aerated blocks or low-density foam concrete blocks. They are easy to handle and install, but are

rarely used in loadbearing applications.

Insulating blocks
Foamed concrete blocks are often used in commercial applications for the interior side of a standard concrete or concrete-block wall. They have good insulating properties and frequently meet the minimum building code requirements for wall R-values without the need to add secondary insulation.

Newer ultralight foam blocks offer even higher R-values, and some residential foundation systems use these blocks exclusively. They are laid up dry, their cores are filled with concrete, and the outside is parged.

When the blocks are delivered, have them unloaded as near as possible to the construction site to save time and reduce the possibility of damage in transit—they are quite brittle and chip easily. Stack them on a flat, dry base and protect them from rain and frost with a tarpaulin or a polyethelene sheet.

Available sizes
Standard blocks are nominally 16 inches long by 8 inches high by 8 inches thick. Many other sizes are available as well, including half and three-quarter units. Available shapes vary widely: Units with keyed ends are used in ordinary wall construction and square-end blocks are used for corners. Single and double bullnose units can be used for decorative designs, and other blocks are made for doorjambs and lintels.

Estimating quantities
To calculate the number required, you must divide a given area of wall by the dimensions of a specific type of block. Blocks are sometimes specified with the mortar joints on the ends, and on the top and bottom. This generally adds ⅜ inch to both dimensions. Because concrete blocks are almost always laid in single courses, the thickness of the block is always specified as the actual dimension.

Sizes of structural blocks
The nominal size of a block refers to the length and height only, including the mortar joints. But block thicknesses are always specified as the actual size.

Screen blocks

Pierced concrete blocks are used for building decorative screens. The blocks are not bonded like brickwork or structural blocks, and therefore require supporting piers made from matching pilaster blocks. These are made with channels that hold the sides of the pierced blocks. Solid blocks finish the tops of the screen blocks and piers.

Screen blocks should not be used to build loadbearing walls. However, they can support lightweight structures, like garden arbors.

Screen block

Pilaster block

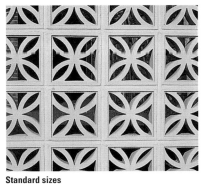

Standard sizes
Decorative screen blocks are usually 1 foot square and 3¾ inches thick.

Stone: natural and artificial

Artificial stone blocks, made from poured concrete, can look very convincing, especially after they've weathered. Depending on where you live, these blocks may be easier to obtain than natural building stone, and are usually cheaper. But, from the standpoint of pure appearance, nothing can surpass a quarried stone such as granite or sandstone.

Natural stone
Whether it's roughly hewn or finely dressed, natural stone is durable and weathers beautifully.

Natural stone

Limestone, sandstone, and granite are all suitable materials for building walls. Slate and other flat stones are commonly used for walkways and garden paths, but can also be used for walls.

Stone bought in its natural state (undressed) is classified as random rubble. It is perfect for building dry-stone walls in both formal and informal settings. For more regular appearance, ask for semidressed stone, which is cut into reasonably uniform blocks, but still has uneven surfaces. Fully dressed stone has flat surfaces cut by a machine. The cost of stone increases in proportion to the degree of preparation it has undergone.

In practical terms, the type of stone you can use for walls depends almost entirely on where you happen to live. The cost of shipping for large quantities of stone from far away is prohibitively high for most people. Besides, a structure built from indigenous stone is more likely to fit in well with the prevailing architecture in your area.

Where to obtain stone

If you live in or very near a city, obtaining natural stone can be a problem. You may be able to easily buy a few small boulders for a rock garden from a local garden center. But the cost of buying enough natural stone for even a short wall can be prohibitive. If you don't want to use artificial stone made from cast concrete, you can rent a truck, drive to the nearest quarry,and transport the stone yourself.

Another source of material is a demolition site. This is usually the cheapest approach, though prices for this material can vary greatly. And, you not only have to rent a truck, but must also be prepared for a lot of hard work loading and unloading the stone.

Estimating quantities

Most quarries sell stone by the ton. When you have worked out the dimensions of the wall, visit the nearest quarry and look at the different stone they have available. Get their advice on the quantity of stone you'll need for your job and quotes for the cost of the stone if they deliver it, or if you pick it up.

Artificial-stone wall
(below)
Cast concrete blocks that simulate real stonework are used to construct attractive walls and planters.

Slate-effect wall
(below right)
Good-quality concrete blockwork is difficult to distinguish from real stone once it has weathered. What looks like thin pieces of slate are actually cast as large interlocking blocks that can be laid quickly.

Semidressed, natural stone blocks

Dry-stone retaining wall

Flat stone wall

Undressed stone boundary wall

Artificial-stone blocks

The outside faces of concrete blocks made specifically for garden use are textured to resemble natural stone. These blocks can be laid dry on top of a simple mortar base, or bonded together with mortar like conventional stonework. Artificial stone is available in undressed, semidressed, and fully dressed units.

When you are building a wall, mortar is used to bind together the bricks, concrete blocks, or stones. The durability of the wall depends to a large extent upon the quality of the mortar used in its construction. If it's mixed correctly, mortar is strong yet flexible. But if the ingredients are in the wrong proportions, the mortar is likely to be weak, or so hard that it is prone to cracking. If too much water is added to the mix, the mortar will be squeezed out of the joints by the weight of the masonry. If the mortar is too dry, then adhesion will be poor.

BRICKLAYERS' TERMS

Bricklayers use a number of specialized words and phrases to describe their craft and materials. Terms used frequently are listed below; others are described as they occur.

- **BRICK FACES** *The surfaces of a brick.*
- **Stretcher faces**—the long sides of a brick.
- **Header faces**—the short ends of a brick.
- **Bedding faces**—the top and bottom surfaces.
- **Frog**—the depression in one bedding face.

- **COURSE** *A horizontal row of bricks.*
- **Stretcher course**—a single course with stretcher faces visible.
- **Header course**—a single course with header faces visible.
- **Coping**—the top course designed to protect the wall from rainwater.
- **Bond**—the pattern produced by staggering alternate courses so that vertical joints are not aligned one above the other.
- **Stretcher**—a single brick from a stretcher course.
- **Header**—a single brick from a header course.
- **Closure brick**—the last brick laid in a course.

- **CUT BRICKS** *Bricks cut to even up the bond.*
- **Bat**—a brick cut across its width (e.g. half-bat, three-quarter bat).
- **Queen closer**—a brick cut along its length.

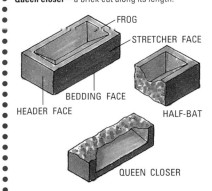

FROG
STRETCHER FACE
BEDDING FACE
HEADER FACE
HALF-BAT
QUEEN CLOSER

The ingredients of mortar

General-purpose mortar is usually mixed on site from bulk materials. It's made from portland cement, hydrated lime, and sand, mixed together with enough water to make a workable paste.

Cement is the hardening agent that binds the other ingredients together. The lime slows down the drying process and prevents the mortar from setting too quickly. It also makes the mix flow well, so that it fills gaps in the masonry and adheres to the texture of blocks or bricks. Sand acts as an aggregate, adding body to the mortar and reducing the possibility of shrinkage. For general-purpose mortar, fine builder's sand is ideal.

Plasticizers
If you're laying masonry in a period of cold weather, substitute a plasticizer for the lime. Plasticizer produces an aerated mortar in which the tiny air bubbles allow water to expand in freezing conditions, thus reducing the risk of cracking. Premixed masonry cement, which has an aerating agent, is ready for mixing with sand.

Ready-mixed mortar
This type of mortar contains all the essential ingredients mixed to the correct proportions—you simply add water. It is a more expensive way of buying mortar, but it's convenient to use and available in small quantities.

Mixing mortar

Mortar should be discarded if it isn't used within two hours of being mixed, so make only as much as you can use within that time. An average of about two minutes for laying each brick is a reasonable estimate.

Choose a flat site to mix the materials—a sheet of plywood will do—and dampen it slightly to prevent it from absorbing water from the mortar. Make a pile of half the amount of sand to be used, then add the other ingredients. Put the rest of the sand on top, and mix the dry materials thoroughly.

Scoop a depression in the pile and add clean tap water. Never use contaminated or salty water. Push the dry mix from around the edge of the pile into the water until it has absorbed enough for you to blend the mix with a shovel, using a chopping action. Add more water, little by little, until the mortar has a butterlike consistency slipping easily from the shovel, but firm enough to hold its shape if you make a hollow in the mix. If the sides of the hollow collapse, add more dry ingredients until the mortar firms up. Make sure the mortar is sufficiently moist; dry mortar won't form a strong bond with the masonry.

If the mortar stiffens up while you are working, add just enough water to restore the consistency.

Correct consistency
The mortar mix should be firm enough to hold its shape when you make a depression in the mix.

Proportions for masonry mixes

Mix the ingredients according to the prevailing conditions at the building site. Use a general-purpose mortar for moderate conditions where the wall is reasonably sheltered. A stronger mix is required for severe conditions where the wall will be exposed to wind and driving rain, or if the site is elevated or near the coast. If you are using plasticizer rather than lime, follow the manufacturer's instructions regarding the quantity you should add to the sand.

• **Estimating quantity**
As a rough guide to estimating how much mortar you will need when building a wall, allow approximately 1 cubic yard of sand (other ingredients in proportion) to lay about 1600 bricks.

• **Masonry cement**
A ready-mixed cement that is used without adding lime or plasticizer.

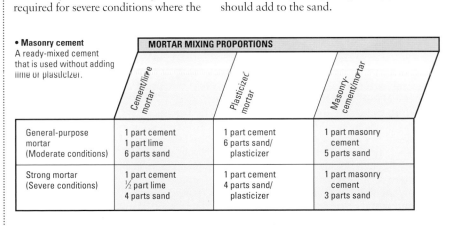

MORTAR MIXING PROPORTIONS	Cement/lime mortar	Plasticized mortar	Masonry-cement mortar
General-purpose mortar (Moderate conditions)	1 part cement 1 part lime 6 parts sand	1 part cement 6 parts sand/ plasticizer	1 part masonry cement 5 parts sand
Strong mortar (Severe conditions)	1 part cement ½ part lime 4 parts sand	1 part cement 4 parts sand/ plasticizer	1 part masonry cement 3 parts sand

Bonding brickwork

Stretcher bond

Flemish bond

Honeycomb bond

Although mortar is extremely strong under compression, its tensile strength is relatively weak. If bricks were stacked one upon the other, so that the vertical joints were continuous, any movement within the wall would pull the joints apart and the structure would be seriously weakened. Bonding the brickwork staggers the vertical joints, transmitting the load along the entire length of the wall. Try out the bond of your choice by dry-laying a few bricks before you embark upon building the wall.

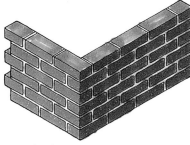

Stretcher bond

The stretcher bond is the simplest form of bonding. It is used for single-thickness walls in many different applications from facing walls on wood-framed houses to retaining walls and boundary walls in the yard. Half-bats are used to complete the bond at the end of a straight wall, while a corner is formed by alternating headers and stretchers.

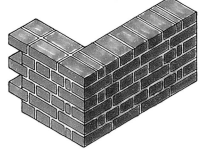

English bond

If you were to build a wall 8½ inches thick by laying courses in a stretcher bond side by side, there would be a weak vertical joint running centrally down the wall. An English bond strengthens the wall by using alternate courses of headers. Staggered joints are maintained at the end of the wall and at right-angle corners by inserting a queen closer before the last header.

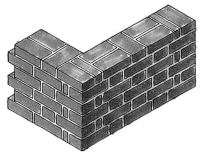

Flemish bond

The Flemish bond is another method used for building a solid wall 8½ inches thick. Every course is laid with alternate headers and stretchers. Stagger the joint at the end of a course and at corners by laying a queen closer before the header.

Decorative bonds

Stretcher, English, and Flemish bonds are designed to construct strong walls; decorative qualities are incidental. Other bonds, used primarily for their visual effect, are suitable for low, nonloadbearing walls only. They need to be supported by a conventionally bonded base and by piers.

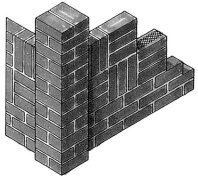

Stack bonding

Laying bricks in groups of three creates a basket-weave effect. Strengthen the continuous vertical joints with wall ties.

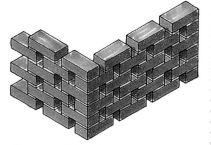

Honeycomb bond

Build an open decorative screen by using a stretcher-like bond with a quarter-bat-size space between each brick. This type of screen has to be built with care, in order to keep the bond regular. Cut quarter-bats to fill the gaps in the top course.

It is easy enough to appreciate the loads and stresses imposed upon the walls of a house or outbuilding, and hence the need for solid foundations with adequate methods of reinforcement and protection to prevent them from collapsing. But it is not so obvious that even a simple garden wall requires similar measures to ensure its stability. It's merely irritating if a low dividing wall or planter falls apart, but a serious injury could result from the collapse of a heavy boundary wall.

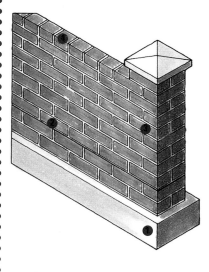

The basic structure of a wall

Unless you design and build a wall in the correct manner, it will not be strong and stable.

1 Footings
A wall must be built upon a solid concrete platform known as a footing. The dimensions of the footing vary according to the height and weight of the wall.

2 Bonding
The staggered pattern of the bricks is not merely decorative. It's designed primarily to spread the static load along the wall and to tie the individual bricks together.

3 Piers
Straight walls that exceed a certain height and length must be buttressed at regular intervals with thick columns of brickwork, known as piers. These resist the sideways pressure caused by high winds.

4 Coping
The coping prevents frost damage by shedding rainwater from the top of the wall, where it could seep into the upper brick joints.

Footings for garden walls

Your local building department establishes the size and reinforcement of the footings required to support masonry walls, especially loadbearing walls. Usually garden walls can be built on concrete footings laid in a simple trench with straight sides.

Size of footings

A footing needs to be substantial enough to support the weight of the wall. The surrounding soil must be firm and well drained, to avoid possible subsidence. It's not a good idea to set footings in ground that has been backfilled recently, such as a new building site. Take care to avoid tree roots and drainpipes.

Dig the trench deeper than the footing itself, so that the first one or two courses of brick are below ground level. This will allow for an adequate depth of soil for planting right up to the wall.

If the soil is not firmly packed when you reach the required depth, dig deeper until you reach a firm level. Then fill the bottom of the trench with compacted gravel up to the lowest level of the proposed footing.

RECOMMENDED DIMENSIONS FOR FOOTINGS			
Type of wall	Height of wall	Depth of footing	Width of footing
One brick thick	Up to 3 feet	4 to 6 inches	12 inches
Two bricks thick	Up to 3 feet	9 to 12 inches	18 inches
Two bricks thick	Between 3 and 6 feet	16 to 18 inches	18 to 24 inches
Retaining wall	Up to 3 feet	6 to 12 inches	16 to 18 inches

Setting out the footings

For a straight footing, set up two form boards (see below right), made from ¾-inch-thick lumber nailed to stakes that are driven into the ground at each end of the proposed trench. Position outside the work area.

Drive nails into the top edge of each board and stretch lines between them to mark the front and back edges of the wall. Then drive nails into the boards on each side of the wall lines to indicate the width of the footing, and stretch other lines between these nails (**1**).

When you're satisfied that the layout is accurate, remove the lines marking the wall. But leave their nails in place, so that you can replace the lines when you come to lay the bricks.

Place a level against the remaining lines to mark the edge of the footing on the ground (**2**). Mark the ends of the footing, which should extend beyond the end of the wall by half the wall's thickness. Before you remove the lines, mark out each edge of the trench on the ground, using a spade. Leave the form boards in place.

Turning corners
If your wall is going to have a right-angled corner, set up two sets of profile boards. Check carefully that the lines form a true right angle, using the 3-4-5 right-triangle method (**3**).

Digging the trench
Excavate the trench, keeping the sides vertical, and check that the bottom is level, using a long straight piece of wood and a level.

Drive a stake into the bottom of the trench near one end, until the top of the stake represents the depth of the footing. Drive in more stakes at about 3 foot intervals and check that the tops are level (**4**).

Filling the trench
Mix up the concrete, then pour it into the trench. Trowel the surface until it is exactly level with the top of the stakes. Leave the stakes in place, and allow the footing to harden thoroughly before laying up the wall.

If the ground slopes gently, simply ignore the gradient and make footings perfectly level. If the site slopes noticeably, make a stepped footing by placing plywood form stops across the trench at regular intervals. Calculate the height and length of the steps, using multiples of normal brick size.

Support plywood form stops with stakes.

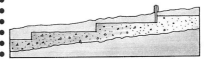

Section through a stepped footing
A typical stepped concrete footing, with one of the plywood form stops in place.

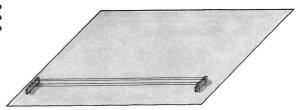

1 Stretched lines indicate width of wall and footing

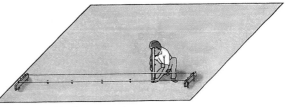

2 Mark width of footing on ground

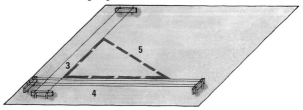

3 A triangle measuring 3, 4, and 5 units makes a right angle

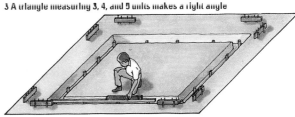

4 Check that tops of stakes are level

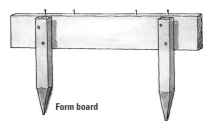

Form board

Laying bricks

Spreading a bed of mortar requires practice before you can do it at speed—so at first concentrate on laying bricks accurately. Using mortar of exactly the right consistency helps to keep the visible faces of the bricks clean. In hot, dry weather, dampen the footings and bricks before you begin, but let any surface water evaporate before you lay the bricks.

Basic bricklaying techniques

Hold the trowel with your thumb in line with the handle and pointing toward the tip of the blade (**1**).

Scoop some mortar out of the pile and shape it roughly to match the dimensions of the trowel blade. Pick up the mortar by sliding the blade under the pile, settling the mortar onto the trowel with a slight jerk of the wrist (**2**).

Spread the mortar along the top course by aligning the edge of the trowel with the centerline of the bricks. As you tip the blade to deposit the mortar, draw the trowel back toward you to stretch the bed over at least two to three bricks (**3**). Furrow the mortar by pressing the point of the trowel along the center of the bed (**4**).

Pick up a brick with your other hand (**5**), but don't extend your thumb too far onto the stretcher face or it will

disturb the mason's line (see opposite) as you place the brick in position. Press the brick into the bed, picking up excess mortar squeezed from the joint by sliding the edge of the trowel along the face of the wall (**6**).

Spread mortar onto the header of the next brick, making a neat ⅜-inch bed for the header joint (**7**). Press the brick against its neighbor, scooping off excess mortar with the trowel.

Having laid three bricks, use a level to check that they are flat and level. Make any adjustments by tapping them down with the trowel handle (**8**).

Hold the level along the outer edge of the bricks to check that they are in line. To move a brick sideways without knocking it off its mortar bed, tap the upper edge with the trowel at about 45 degrees (**9**).

Tools for basic bricklaying
While you can improvise some of the tools you need, you should buy the specialized mason's tools shown here to get the best results.

Hammer

Cold chisel

Pointing trowel

Level

Brick trowel

Cutting bricks
To cut brick, use a cold chisel to mark the line on all faces by tapping gently with a hammer. Realign the blade on the visible stretcher face and strike the chisel firmly.

• **Brick cleaner**
Wash mortar off your tools as soon as the job is finished.

1 The correct way to hold a brick trowel

2 Scoop some mortar onto trowel

3 Spread bed of mortar along course

4 Furrow mortar with point of trowel

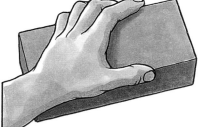

5 Pick up brick with your thumb on edge

6 Push brick down and remove excess mortar

7 Spread mortar onto head of next brick

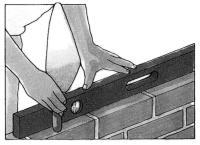

8 Level course of bricks with trowel handle

9 Tap bricks sideways to align them

Over a certain height, a single-width brick wall is structurally weak unless it either is supported with piers or changes direction by forming right-angle corners. The ability to construct accurate right-angle corners is a requirement for building most structures, even simple garden planters.

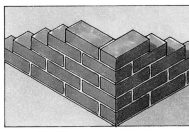

A stepped lead for a corner

Setting out the corners

Mark out the footings and the face of the wall by stretching string lines between form boards. When the footings have been filled and the concrete has set, either use a plumb line or hold a level lightly against the lines to mark the corners and the face of the wall on the footing **(1)**. Join up the marks on the concrete, using a pencil and a straight board, then check the accuracy of the corners with a builder's square. Finally, check that the alignment is straight by stretching a string line between the corner marks.

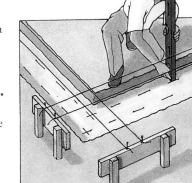

1 Mark face of wall on footing

Mason's line
Bricklayers use a nylon line as a guide for keeping bricks level. The line is stretched between two flat nails that are driven into vertical joints at each end of the wall.

Building corners

Construct the corners first, as a series of steps. Spread a bed of mortar on the footing, and then lay three bricks in both directions against the marked line. Using a level, make sure the bricks are level in all directions, including across the diagonal **(2)**.

Build the corners to a height of five stepped courses, using a marked gauge stick to measure the height of each course as you proceed **(3)**. Use alternate headers and stretchers to form the actual point of the corner.

Plumb the corner, and check the alignment of the stepped bricks by holding a level against the sides of the wall **(4)**.

2 Level first course of bricks

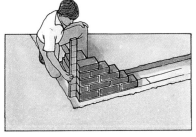

3 Check height with gauge stick

4 Check that steps are in line

Building the straight sections

Stretch a mason's line between the corners so that it aligns perfectly with the top of the first course **(5)**.

Lay the first straight course of bricks from both ends toward the middle. As you near the middle point, lay the last few bricks dry to make certain they will fit. If necessary, cut the central or closure brick to fit. Mortar the bricks in place, and finish by spreading mortar onto both ends of the closure brick and onto the header faces of the bricks on each side **(6)**. Scoop off excess mortar with the trowel. Lay subsequent courses between the leads in the same way, raising the mason's line each time.

To build the wall higher, raise the corners first to the required height, and then fill in between with bricks.

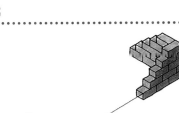

5 Stretch a mason's line along first course

6 Lay the last, or closure, brick carefully

Coping the wall
You could finish the wall by laying the last course frog side down. Or use a series of half-bats laid on end to get a more professional look.

• Protecting a wall
To protect the brick-work from rain or frost, cover newly built walls overnight with a tarp or sheets of polyethylene. Weight down the edges of the covers with bricks.

Pointing brickwork

Pointing the mortar between the bricks makes for packed, watertight joints and also enhances the appearance of the wall. Well-struck joints and clean bricks are essential for the wall to look professionally built. For best results, the mortar must be shaped when it has just the right consistency.

Consistency of the mortar

If the mortar is still too wet, the joint will not be crisp and you may drag mortar out from between the bricks. On the other hand, if it's left to harden too long, pointing will be difficult and you may leave dark marks on the joint.

Test the consistency of the mortar by pressing your thumb into a joint. If it holds a clear impression without sticking to your thumb, the mortar is just right for pointing. Because it's important to start shaping the joints at exactly the right moment, you may have to point the work in stages before you can complete the wall. Shape the joints to match existing brickwork, or choose a profile that is suitable for the prevailing weather conditions.

Shaping the mortar joints

Flush joint

Rubbed joint

V-joint

Raked joint

Weatherstruck joint

Flush joint
After using the edge of your trowel to scrape the mortar flush, stipple the joints with a stiff bristle brush to expose the sand aggregate.

Concave (rubbed) joint
Buy a shaped jointing tool to make a rubbed joint, or improvise with a length of bent tubing. Scrape the mortar flush first, then drag the tool along the joints. Finish the vertical joints, then shape the horizontal ones. This is a utilitarian joint, ideal for a wall built with secondhand bricks that are not good enough to take a crisp joint.

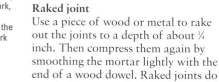

Shape mortar with jointing tool

V-joint
Produced in a similar way to the rubbed joint, the V-joint gives a very sharp finish to new brickwork and sheds rainwater well.

Raked joint
Use a piece of wood or metal to rake out the joints to a depth of about ¼ inch. Then compress them again by smoothing the mortar lightly with the end of a wood dowel. Raked joints do not shed water, so they are not suitable for an exposed site.

Weatherstruck joint
The angled weatherstruck joint will withstand harsh conditions. Use a small pointing trowel to shape the vertical joints (**1**). They can slope to the left or right, but be consistent.

Shape the horizontal joints, allowing the mortar to spill out slightly at the base of each joint. Finish the joint by cutting off excess mortar with a tool called a Frenchman, which is like a table knife with its tip bent at 90 degrees. You can improvise one by bending a strip of metal. Make a neat, straight edge to the mortar, using a board aligned with the bottom of each joint to guide the tool (**2**). Nail two scraps of wood to the board to hold it away from the wall.

1 Shape weatherstruck joint with trowel

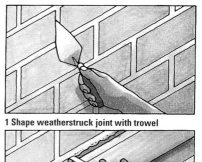

2 Remove excess mortar with Frenchman.

Cleaning the brickwork
Let the shaped joints harden a little before cleaning scraps of mortar from the face of the wall with a medium-soft brush. Sweep the brush lightly across the joints to avoid damaging the mortar.

The coping—which forms the top course of the wall—protects the brickwork from weathering and gives the wall a finished appearance.

Technically, a coping that is flush with both faces of the wall is called a capping. A true coping projects from the face, so that water drips clear and doesn't leave a stain on the brickwork.

Finish a wall with a coping of matching bricks, or create a pleasing contrast with differently colored or textured bricks. You can also buy special coping bricks that are designed to shed rainwater more efficiently than other bricks.

Stone or cast concrete slabs are popular for coping walls. Both are quick to lay and when installed on low walls, can form comfortable bench seating.

On an exposed site, consider installing a tile and brick coping. This design is eye-catching and protects the wall by shedding rainwater away from most of the bricks.

Brick coping
Specially shaped coping bricks are designed to shed rainwater.

Slab coping
Choose a stone or concrete slab that is wider than the wall itself.

Tile and brick coping
Lay flat roof tiles beneath a coping of bricks. The projecting tiles shed water clear of the wall.

• Colored mortar
You can change the appearance of mortar by adding colored powder to the mix. Make a trial batch to see how it looks when the mortar is dry.

When you are ready to point the brickwork, rake out the joints and refill them with the colored mortar. Work carefully to avoid staining the bricks.

Building intersecting walls

When building new walls that intersect at right angles, either join them by bonding the brickwork (see below) or take the easier option and link them with wall ties at every third course. If the intersecting wall is more than 6 feet long, make the junction a control joint by using straight metal strips as wall ties.

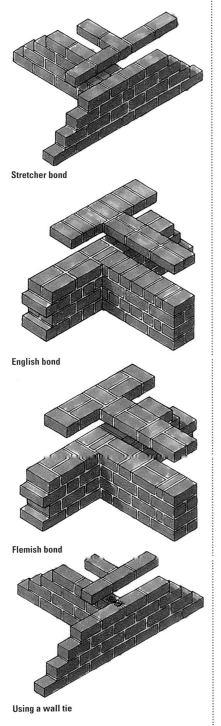

Stretcher bond

English bond

Flemish bond

Using a wall tie

Building up to a wall

Some brick house walls have what is called a damp-proof course (DPC). This consists of a layer of impervious material built into the mortar bed about 6 inches above ground level. When you build a new wall that intersects with a house wall that has a DPC, you should include a DPC in the new wall. Use a roll of bituminous roofing felt that matches the thickness of the new wall.

First, locate the house's DPC and build the first few courses of the new wall up to that level. Then spread a thin bed of mortar on the bricks and lay the DPC on it with the end of the roll turned up against the existing wall **(1)**. The next course of bricks will trap the DPC between the end brick and the house wall. Lay more mortar on top of the DPC to produce a standard ⅜-inch-thick joint, ready for laying the next course in the normal way. If you have to join rolls of felt, overlap the ends by at least 6 inches.

Tying in the new wall

The traditional method for linking a new wall with an existing structure involves chopping recesses in the brickwork at every fourth course. End bricks of the new wall are set into the recesses, bonding the two structures together **(2)**. However, a simpler method is to bolt to the wall a special stainless-metal connector, which is designed to anchor bricks or concrete blocks, using special wall ties. Standard connectors will accommodate walls from 4 to 10 inches thick.

Bolt a connector to the old wall, just above the DPC, if one exists **(3)**. Use anchor bolts recommended by the connector-plate manufacturer.

Mortar the end of a brick before laying it against the connector **(4)**. At every third course, hook a wall tie into one of the lugs in the connector and bed each tie in the mortar joint **(5)**.

Wall connector ties

1 Lap existing DPC with new roll

2 Interlock new wall with existing wall

3 But it is easier to use a special connector

4 Lay bricks against connector

5 Bed special wall tie in mortar joint

425

Brick piers

A pier is a freestanding column of masonry that is used for such things as a support for a porch or a pergola or to form an individual gatepost. When a column is built as part of a wall, it is more accurately termed a pilaster. In practice, however, the word column is often used to mean either structure. To avoid confusion, any supporting brick column will be described here as a pier.

Structural considerations

A freestanding wall over a certain length and height must be reinforced at regular intervals by piers. The straight sections of wall have to be tied to the piers, either by a brick bond or by inserting metal wall ties in every third course of bricks.

Whatever its height, any single-width brick wall would benefit from supporting piers at each end and at gateways,

where it is most vulnerable. Piers also serve to improve the appearance of this type of wall.

Piers that are more than 3 feet high, especially those supporting gates, should be built around steel reinforcing rods set in the concrete footings. Whether reinforcing is included or not, allow for the size of the piers when planning any footings.

Designing the piers

Piers should be placed no more than 10 feet apart in walls over a certain height (see chart below). The wall itself can be flush with one face of each pier, but the structure is stronger if the wall is centered on the piers.

Piers should be a minimum of twice the thickness of a wall that is 4 inches thick. But build piers 14 inches square to buttress a wall 8 inches thick or when reinforcement is required, such as for gates.

INCORPORATING PIERS IN A BRICK WALL		
Thickness of wall	Maximum height without piers	Maximum pier spacing
4 inches	18 inches	10 feet
8 inches	4 feet 6 inches	10 feet

If you prefer the appearance of bonded brick piers, construct them as shown below. It is easier, however, to use wall ties to reinforce continuous vertical joints in the brickwork, especially when building walls centered on piers.

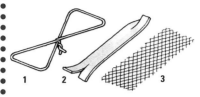

Wall ties
Various types of galvanized-metal wall ties are available: wire bent into a butterfly shape (**1**), stamped steel strips with forked ends, known as fish tails (**2**), and expanded-metal mesh strips (**3**).

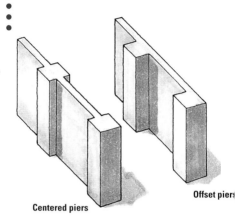

Centered piers   Offset piers

Bonding piers
While it's simpler to tie a wall to a pier with wall ties, it's relatively easy to bond a pier into a wall that is a single brick wide.

Color key
You will have to cut certain bricks to bond a pier into a straight wall. Whole bricks are colored with a light tone, three-quarter bats with a medium tone, and half-bats with a dark tone.

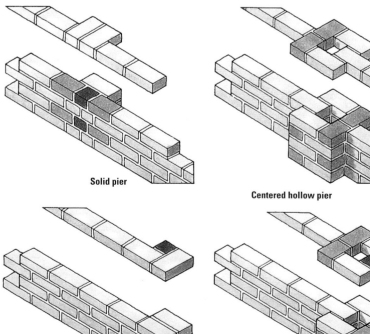

Solid pier

Centered hollow pier

Offset hollow pier

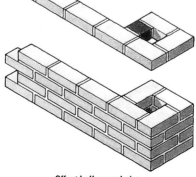

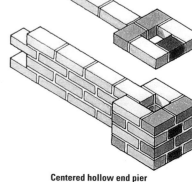

Solid end pier

Centered hollow end pier

Offset hollow end pier

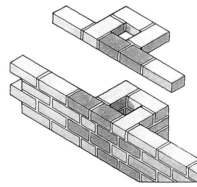

Building piers

On the concrete footing, accurately mark out the positions of the piers and the face of the wall. Lay the first course of bricks for the piers, using a mason's line stretched between two stakes to align them (1). Adjust the position of the line if necessary, and fill in between with the first straight course, working from both ends toward the middle (2). Build alternate pier and wall courses, checking that the bricks are laid level and the faces and corners of the piers are vertical. At every third course, push metal wall ties into the mortar bed to span the joints between the wall and the piers (3). Continue in the same way to the required height of the wall, then raise the piers by at least one extra course (4). Lay a coping along the wall and cap the piers with concrete or stone slabs (5).

1 Lay pier bases
Stretch a mason's line to position the bases of the piers.

2 Lay first wall course
Use the line to keep the first course of bricks straight.

3 Install pier ties
Join the piers to the wall by inserting wall ties into every third course. Put a tie into every second course for a gate pier.

4 Raise the piers
Build the piers higher than the wall to allow for a decorative coping along the top course.

5 Lay the coping
Lay coping on wall bricks and cap the piers.

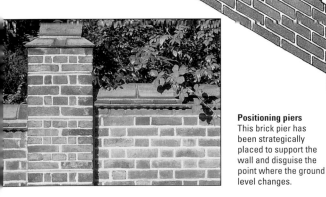

Positioning piers
This brick pier has been strategically placed to support the wall and disguise the point where the ground level changes.

Control joints

Although it's not noticeable, a brick wall moves from time to time as a result of ground settlement and expansion and contraction of the materials. Over short distances the movement is so slight that it has hardly any effect on the brickwork, but in a long wall it can crack the structure.

To compensate for this movement, build continuous mortar-free vertical joints into the wall at intervals of about 20 feet. Although these control joints can be placed in a straight section of wall, it is neater and more convenient to place them where the wall meets a pier. In this situation, build the pier and the wall as usual, but omit the mortar from the header joints of the wall. Instead of inserting standard wall ties, embed a flat galvanized strip in the mortar bed. Lightly grease one half of the strip with automotive grease or petroleum jelly, so that it can slide lengthwise to allow for movement and yet still key the wall and the pier together. When the wall is complete, fill the joint from both sides with caulk.

Adding reinforcement

Use ⅝-inch steel reinforcing bars to strengthen brick piers. If the pier is less than 3 feet high, use a single continuous length of bar (1). For taller piers, embed a bent starter bar in the footing, projecting a minimum of 20 inches above the level of the concrete. As the work proceeds, use galvanized wire to bind extension bars to the starter bars (2), up to 2 inches below the top of the pier. Fill in around the rebar with concrete as you build the pier. Pack the concrete very carefully so that you don't disturb the brickwork.

Control joint

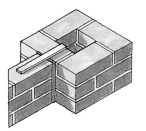

Making a control joint
When making a control joint, tie the pier to the wall with galvanized-metal strips, shown here before the bed of mortar is laid. Caulk is squeezed into the vertical joint between the wall and the pier.

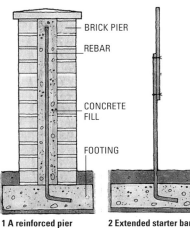

BRICK PIER

REBAR

CONCRETE FILL

FOOTING

1 A reinforced pier   **2 Extended starter bar**

Building with concrete blocks

Colorful block walls
High-quality blocks decorated with smooth masonry paint make a welcome change from the usual monotonous gray concrete.

Don't dampen concrete blocks before you lay them because wet blocks may shrink and crack the mortar joints as the wall dries out. Block walls need the same type of concrete footings and mortar mixes as brick walls.

Because concrete blocks are made in a greater variety of sizes, you can build a wall of many different thicknesses, using a simple stretcher bond.

Make the mortar joints flush with the surface of a wall that is going to be covered with stucco or plaster. For painted or exposed blocks, point the joints using a style that will enhance the appearance or performance of the wall.

Block types (from top)
Solid top block
Corner block
Basic block
Solid block

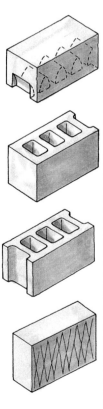

CONTROL JOINTS

Walls over 20 feet long should be built with a continuous vertical control joint to allow for expansion. Place an unmortared joint in a straight section of wall or against a pier, and bridge the gap with galvanized-metal strips, as for brick walls. Fill the vertical joint with flexible caulk.

If you need to insert a control joint in a partition wall, it's convenient to form the joint at a door opening. Install it around one end of the lintel and then vertically to the ceiling. Having filled the joint with mortar in the normal way, rake it out to a depth of ¾ inch on both sides of the wall, then fill the joint flush with caulk.

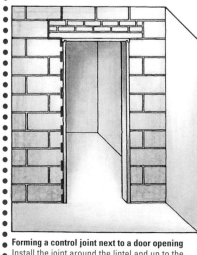

Forming a control joint next to a door opening
Install the joint around the lintel and up to the ceiling on both sides of the wall.

Building a partition wall

It is usual to divide up large interior spaces with nonloadbearing stud partitions. But if your house is built on a concrete slab, an alternative is to use concrete blocks.

If you're going to install a doorway in the partition, plan its position to avoid cutting too many blocks. You will need to allow for the wood doorframe, as well as a precast lintel to support the masonry above the opening. Fill the space above the lintel with concrete bricks.

Bolt metal connectors to the existing structure in order to support each end of the new partition wall. Plumb the connectors accurately to make sure the new wall is built perfectly plumb.

Lay the first course of blocks without mortar, across the room, to check their spacing and to determine the position of any doorways. Mark the positions of the blocks before building steps at each end, as explained earlier for brick walls. Check for accuracy with a level, and then fill in between the ends with blocks.

Lay another three courses, anchoring the end blocks to the connectors with wall ties in every joint. Leave the mortar to harden overnight before you continue with the wall.

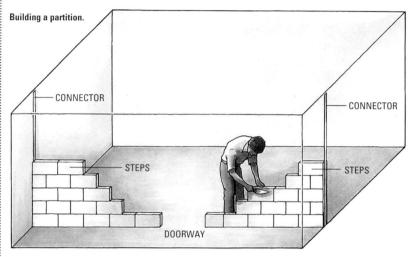

Building a partition.

CONNECTOR

CONNECTOR

STEPS

STEPS

DOORWAY

Building intersecting walls

Butt intersecting walls together with a continuous vertical joint between them, but anchor the structure with wire-mesh wall ties (**1**). If you build a wall with heavyweight hollow blocks, use heavy metal tie bars with a bend at each end. Fill the block voids with mortar to embed the ends of the bars (**2**). Install a tie in every course.

1 Wire-mesh wall ties for solid blocks
2 Metal tie bar for hollow blocks

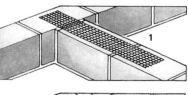

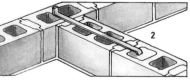

Cutting blocks

If you don't have a masonry-saw blade, cut a concrete block by scoring a line around it using a cold chisel. Deepen the line into a groove by striking the chisel sharply with hammer, working your way around the block until it eventually fractures along the chiseled groove.

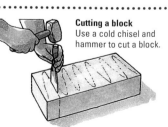

Cutting a block
Use a cold chisel and hammer to cut a block.

Building a block screen

Cavity walls are used in the construction of buildings to prevent moisture from seeping to the interior. This is achieved by building two independent masonry walls with a gap between them. The gap provides a degree of thermal insulation, but the insulation value increases significantly if you install insulation in the cavity.

The exterior wall of most cavity walls is constructed with bricks. The inner wall is sometimes built with bricks too, but more often with concrete blocks. Whatever type of masonry is used, both walls must be tied together with wall ties spanning the gap. Cavity walls are likely to be loadbearing, so they have to be built accurately. Hire a professional for this job, and make sure he or she avoids dropping mortar into the gap. If mortar collects at the base of the cavity, or even on one of the wall ties, moisture can bridge the gap and enter the interior of the room.

Basic bricklaying techniques and tools are used to build a pierced concrete screen, but the blocks are stack-bonded with continuous vertical joints.

If a screen wall is to be built higher than 2 feet, it must be reinforced vertically with ⅝-inch steel rebars and horizontally with galvanized mesh strips. Build a screen with supporting piers no more than 10 feet apart, using matching pilaster blocks. If you prefer the appearance of contrasting masonry, construct a base and piers from bricks (see below right).

Constructing a screen

Install concrete footings, making them twice the width of the pilaster blocks. Embed rebars in the concrete, and support them with ropes until the concrete sets.

Lower a pilaster block over the first bar, setting it onto a bed of mortar laid around the base of the bar. Check that the block is perfectly plumb and level, and that its side channel faces the next pier. Pack mortar or concrete into its core, then proceed with two more blocks so that the pier corresponds to the height of two mortared screen blocks (**1**). Construct each pier in the same way. Intermediate piers will have a channel on both sides.

Allow the mortar to harden overnight, then lay a mortar bed for two screen blocks next to the first pier. Cover the vertical edge of a screen block with mortar and press it into the pier channel (**2**). Tap the block into the mortar bed and check that it's level. Mortar the next

block and place it alongside the first. When covering screen blocks with mortar, take care to keep the faces clean by making a neat chamfered bed of mortar (**3**).

Lay two more blocks against the next pier. Stretch a mason's line to gauge the top edge of the first course, then lay the rest of the blocks toward the center, making sure that the vertical joints are aligned perfectly. Before building any higher, embed a wire reinforcing strip running from pier to pier in the next mortar bed (**4**). Continue to build the piers and screen up to a maximum height of 6 feet 6 inches, inserting a wire strip into alternate courses. Finally, lay coping units on top of each pier and along the top of the screen (**5**).

If you don't like the appearance of ordinary mortar joints, rake out some of the mortar and repoint with mortar made with silver sand. A concave rubbed joint suits decorative screening.

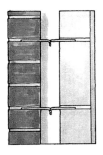

Cavity wall construction
A section through a typical cavity wall built with an exterior wall of bricks tied to an inner wall of plastered concrete blocks.

Building a brick base and piers
You can construct a garden wall using a combination of bricks and concrete screen blocks. Build a low base of bricks with reinforced piers spaced to accommodate the blocks. Build the piers and lay the blocks between them, reinforcing the joints with galvanized mesh strips, as described at left. Insert standard wall ties in alternate courses to provide additional support.

Reinforcing a high wall
Any screen built higher than 2 feet should be reinforced vertically with ⅝-inch steel rebars. Galvanized mesh strips should be embedded in the horizontal mortar joints.

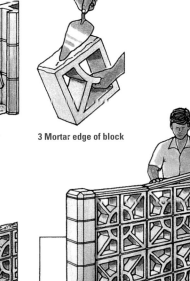

1 Build piers

2 Fit block to pier

3 Mortar edge of block

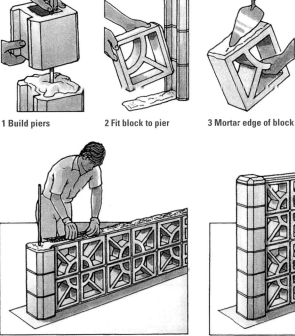

4 Lay wire reinforcing strip into mortar

5 Lay coping units along wall

Building with stone

Constructing walls with natural stone requires a different approach than building with bricks or concrete blocks. A stone wall has to be as stable as one built with any other masonry product, but its visual appeal relies on the courses being less regular. In fact, it's impossible to have regular courses when a wall is built with undressed stone.

Structural considerations

Not all stone walls are built with mortar, although it is often used with dressed or semidressed stone in order to provide additional stability.

Usually walls are tapered, with heavy, flat stones laid at the base of the wall, followed by proportionally smaller stones as the height increases.

This traditional form of construction was developed to prevent walls made with unmortared stones from toppling sideways when subjected to high winds or the weight of farm animals.

Far from detracting from its appearance, this informal construction suits a country style perfectly.

Dry-stone wall
Traditional dry-stone wall is stable without having to fill the joints with mortar.

Building a dry-stone wall

As described above, a true dry-stone wall relies on the careful selection and placement of stones to provide stability. However, there's no reason why you can't introduce mortar, particularly within the core of the wall, and still maintain the appearance of dry-stone structure. Another way to help stabilize a wall is to bed the stones in soil, packing it firmly into the crevices as you lay each course. This enables you to add suitable plants to the wall, even during its construction.

When you are selecting the stone,

watch for flat stones in a variety of sizes and make sure you have some that are large enough to run the full width of the wall, especially at the base of the structure. Placed at regular intervals, these bonding stones are important components because they tie the loose stones into a cohesive structure.

Even a low wall will inevitably include some heavy stones. When you lift them, keep your back straight and your feet together, using the muscles of your legs to take the strain.

Pointed stonework
Mortar is required for buildings and substantial freestanding walls constructed from dressed or semidressed stone.

Constructing the wall

Assuming you're using soil as your joint material, spread a 1-inch layer over the footing and then place a substantial bonding stone across the width to form the bed of the first course (**1**). Lay other stones, about the same height as the bonding stone, along each side of the wall, pressing them down into the soil to make a firm base. It's worth stretching a mason's line along each side of the

wall to help you make a reasonably straight base.

Lay smaller stones between to fill out the base of the wall (**2**), then pack more soil into all the crevices.

Spread another layer of soil on top of the base and lay a second course of stones, bridging the joints between the stones below (**3**). Press the stones down firmly, so they lean in toward the center of the wall. As you proceed, check by

A dry-stone wall must be tapered, beginning with a wide base, followed by stones that slope in toward the middle of the wall.

For a wall about 3½ feet high—it's risky to build a dry-stone wall any higher—the base should be no less than 18 inches wide. And you need to provide a minimum slope of 1 inch for every 2 feet of height.

Traditionally, the base of this type of wall rests on a bed of sand about 4 inches deep. This sand should lay on compacted soil at the bottom of a shallow trench.

For a more reliable foundation, lay a 4-inch concrete footing, making it about 4 inches wider than the wall on each side.

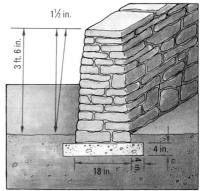

Proportions of stone wall

eye that the course is about level and remember to include bonding stones at regular intervals.

You can introduce plants into the larger crevices or hammer smaller stones into the cracks to lock large stones in place (**4**).

At the top of the wall, either fill the core with soil for plants or lay large, flat coping stones in place. Finally, brush any loose soil from the faces of the stones.

1 Lay wide bonding stone across end of wall

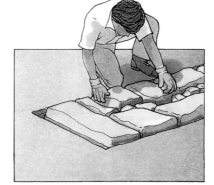

2 Fill out base with small stones

3 Lay second course of stones

4 Fill cracks

Retaining walls are designed to hold back a bank of soil. But don't try to cut into a steep bank and restrain it with a single high wall. Apart from the obvious dangers of the wall collapsing, terracing the slope with a series of low walls is a more sensible solution, which offers opportunities for creative landscaping.

Choosing your materials

Both bricks and concrete blocks make sturdy retaining walls, provided they are reinforced with metal bars buried in a sound concrete footing. Either run the bars through hollow concrete blocks **(1)** or build a double brick wall, like a miniature cavity wall, using wall ties to bind bothh sides together **(2)**.

The mass and weight of natural stone make it ideal for retaining walls.

A stone wall should be tapered to an angle of 2 inches for every 1 foot of height, so that the wall actually leans into the bank **(3)**. For safety, don't build higher than 3½ feet.

A skillful builder could construct a perfectly safe dry-stone retaining wall, but unless you have had some experience with this work, it's a better idea to use mortar for more rigidity.

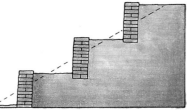

Terracing with retaining walls

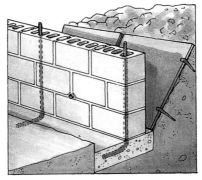

1 A retaining wall of hollow concrete blocks

2 Use two walls of brick tied together

3 Lean stone wall against bank of soil

Constructing the wall

Excavate the soil to provide enough room to dig the footing and construct the wall. If the bank is loosely packed, restrain it temporarily with sheets of scrap plywood or similar sheeting. Drive long steel pegs into the bank to hold the sheets in place **(1)**. Install the footing at the base of the bank, and allow it to set before you begin building the wall.

Use conventional techniques to build a block or brick wall. Lay uncut stones as if you were building a dry-stone wall, but set each course on mortar. If you use regular stone blocks, stagger the joints and select stones of different proportions to add variety to the wall. Set the stones in mortar.

You must allow for drainage behind the wall, or else the soil will become water-saturated. So when you lay the second course of stones, embed ¾-inch plastic pipes in the mortar, angling them very slightly toward the base of the wall. Lay the pipes 3 feet apart, making sure that they pass right through the wall and project a little from the face **(2)**.

FINISHING STONE WALLS

When the wall is complete, rake out the joints so that it looks like a traditional dry-stone wall.

An old paintbrush is a useful tool for smoothing the mortar in deep crevices to create firm, watertight joints. It is best to finish regular stone walls with concave rubbed joints.

Allow the mortar to set for a day or two before filling behind the wall. Lay gravel at the base to cover the drainage pipes, and firmly pack soil against the rest of the wall. Provide a generous layer of topsoil to finish the backfilling.

1 Hold back earth with scrap plywood

2 Set plastic pipes in wall for drainage

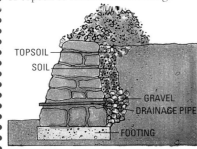

TOPSOIL
SOIL
GRAVEL
DRAINAGE PIPE
FOOTING

Filling behind a stone wall

Pathways, driveways, and patios

For some people, installing any type of hardscaping (pathways, walls, driveways, and patios) is considered almost antithetical to the whole idea of gardening. They must envision a complete yard devoid of plants, trees, and grass. But for the rest of us, introducing hard elements like stone, brick, or concrete for a variety of uses not only makes our landscaping work better, it also creates a textured counterpoint to all the plantings that surround the hardscaping.

Paved patio
A patio area that's surrounded by stone or brick walls makes a perfect retreat.

Sometimes, a hard and unyielding surface can be softened by the addition of foliage.

Hardscape design
The marriage of different materials offers numerous possibilities. It may be convenient to define areas for walks or patios, but these are only names to describe the function of those particular areas. There's no reason why you cannot blend one area into another by using the same material throughout, or by employing similar colors to link one type of paving with another.

Having so many choices at your disposal does have its drawbacks: There's a strong temptation to experiment with any and every combination. But a few well-chosen materials that complement the house and its surroundings produce an effect that's far more appealing.

Working with concrete

Concrete is more versatile than some people think. It may appear to be a rather drab, utilitarian material for garden use, but you can add texture and color to ordinary concrete, or use one of the many types of cast concrete slabs and bricks made for paving patios, paths, and driveways.

Ingredients of concrete

Concrete in its simplest form consists of cement and fine particles of stone (sand and pebbles), known as aggregate. The dry ingredients are mixed with water to create a chemical reaction with the cement, which binds the aggregate into a hard, dense material.

The initial hardening process takes place quite quickly. The mix becomes unworkable after a couple of hours, depending on the temperature and humidity. But the concrete has no real strength for three to seven days.

The hardening process continues for up to a month, or as long as there is moisture still present within the concrete. Moisture is essential to the reaction. Consequently, concrete must not be allowed to dry out too quickly during the first few days.

Cement

Standard portland cement, sold in 90-lb. bags, is used for on-site mixing of concrete. In its dry condition, it is a fine gray powder.

Sand

Sharp sand, a fairly coarse and gritty material, constitutes part of the aggregate of a concrete mix. Don't buy fine builder's sand that is used for mortar. And avoid unwashed or beach sand, both of which contain impurities that can affect the quality of the concrete.

Lumberyards and masonry supply outlets sell sharp sand loose by the cubic yard. For small jobs, it's also available in large plastic bags that are easy to transport in your car.

Coarse aggregate

Coarse aggregate is gravel or crushed stone composed of stones that range in size from about ¼ to ¾ inch for normal use. It's usually sold in bulk cubic yards, like sand. But it is sometimes available in bags.

Pigments

Special pigments can be added to a concrete mix in order to color it, but it's difficult to guarantee an even color from one batch to another.

Combined aggregate

In some areas, masonry supply outlets sell a combined aggregate (sometimes called ballast) that is a sand and gravel mix in the proper proportions for concrete use.

Dry-mix concrete

You can buy dry cement—sand and aggregate mixed to the required proportions—for making concrete. Choose the proportion that best suits the job you have in mind. The dry ingredients for erecting fenceposts make up one typical ready-mixed product.

Concrete mix is sold in various-size bags up to 100 pounds. Available from the usual outlets, this is a more expensive way of buying concrete ingredients, but it's a simple and convenient method of ordering exactly the amount you need. Before you add water, make sure the ingredients are mixed thoroughly.

Water

Use ordinary tap water. Impurities and salt contained in river or sea water are detrimental to concrete.

Admixtures

Various additives (called admixtures) are available for concrete work. Air-entrainment is one that's frequently used during cold weather to avoid the damage done by freeze-and-thaw cycles. This is not something you can add to your concrete mix. It has to be done at a concrete plant.

Ready-mix concrete

Ready-mix concrete is delivered by truck. You can stipulate the type of mix you want when ordering. There's usually a minimum order of at least a couple of cubic yards. But sometimes a truck will have a small amount left from a previous order and will drop it off at your job on the way back to the concrete plant.

Rent a small mixing machine if you have to prepare a large volume of concrete, but for most jobs it's more convenient to mix it by hand. It isn't necessary to weigh the ingredients—simply mix them by volume, choosing the proportions that suit the job at hand.

Mixing by hand

Use two large buckets to measure the ingredients, one for the cement and (in order to keep the cement perfectly dry) another identical bucket for the sand and coarse aggregate. Using two shovels is also a good idea.

Measure the materials accurately, leveling them with the rim of the bucket. Tap the side of the bucket with the shovel as you load it with sand or cement, so that the loose particles are shaken down.

Mix the sand and coarse aggregate first, on a hard, flat surface. Scoop a depression in the pile for the cement, and mix all the ingredients until the mixture is an even color.

Form another depression and add some water. Push the dry ingredients into the water from around the edge until the surface water has been absorbed, then mix the batch by chopping the concrete with the shovel **(1)**. Add more water, then turn the concrete from the bottom of the pile and chop it as before until the whole batch has an even consistency.

To test the workability of the mix, form a series of ridges by dragging the blade of the shovel across the pile **(2)**. The surface of the concrete should be flat and even in texture, and the ridges should hold their shape without slumping.

1 Mixing ingredients
Mix the ingredients by chopping the concrete mix with the shovel. Turn the mix over and chop again.

2 Testing the mix
Make ridges with the back of the shovel to test the workability of the mix.

Mixing by machine

Make sure you set the concrete mixer on a hard, level surface and that the drum is upright before you start the motor. Use a bucket to pour half the required coarse aggregate into the drum and add water. Add the sand and cement alternately in small batches, plus the rest of the aggregate. Keep on adding water little by little along with the other ingredients.

Let the batch mix for a few minutes. Then tilt the drum of the mixer while it is still rotating and turn out some of the concrete into a wheelbarrow, so you can test its consistency (see above). If necessary, return the concrete to the mixer to adjust it.

Machine safety
When you rent a concrete mixer, take the time to read the safety advice that's supplied with the machine.

• Make sure you understand the operating instructions before you turn the machine on.
• Shim the mixer with blocks of woods until it is level and stable.
• Never put your hands or shovel into the drum while the mixer is running.
• Don't lean over a rotating drum to inspect the contents.
• Wear goggles and gloves when mixing concrete.

Storing materials

If you buy sand and aggregate in sacks, use as much as you require for the job and keep the rest bagged up until you need it again. Loose ingredients should be piled separately on a hard surface or on thick polyethylene sheets. Cover the piles with weighted sheets of plastic.

Storing cement is more critical. It's usually sold in paper sacks, which will

absorb moisture from the ground, so pile them on a board. It's best to keep cement in a dry shed or garage. But if you have to store it outdoors, cover the bags with sheets of plastic weighted down with bricks.

Once a bag is opened, cement will absorb moisture from the air, so keep a partly used bag sealed in a plastic bag.

READY-MIXED CONCRETE

If you need a lot of concrete for a driveway or large patio, it may be worth ordering a delivery of ready-mixed concrete from a local supplier.

Always contact the supplier well in advance to discuss your particular requirements. Specify the proportions of the ingredients, and say whether you require a retarding agent to slow down the setting time. (Once a normal mix of concrete is delivered, you will have about 2 hours in which to finish the job. A retarding agent can add a couple of hours to the setting time.) Tell the supplier exactly what you need the concrete for, and accept his advice. For quantities of less than 8 cubic yards, you may have to shop around for a supplier who is willing to deliver without tacking on an additional charge.

In order to avoid moving the concrete too far by wheelbarrow, you will want it discharged as close to the site as possible, if not directly into place. However, the chute on a delivery truck can reach only so far, and if the vehicle is too large or heavy to drive onto your property, you will need several helpers to move the concrete while it is still workable. A single cubic yard of concrete will fill 25 to 30 wheelbarrows. If it takes longer than 30 to 40 minutes to discharge the load, you may have to pay extra.

Professional mixing

Some companies may deliver concrete ingredients and mix them to your specifications on the spot. You have to move the concrete in a wheelbarrow and pour it into place. This is a good option if you can't figure out exactly how much concrete you need.

Storing sand and aggregate
Piles of sand and aggregate with dividing board

Storing cement
Raise bags of cement off the ground and cover them with plastic sheeting.

Designing concrete paving

Designing simple concrete pads may not be very complicated, but there are important factors to consider if the concrete is to be durable. At the least, you will have to decide on the thickness of the concrete that is needed to support the weight of traffic, and the surface slope required to drain off water.

When the area of concrete is large, or a complicated shape, you need to incorporate control joints to allow the material to expand and contract. If a pad is for a habitable building, it must include a vapor barrier to exclude moisture rising from the ground. Even the proportions of sand, cement, and aggregate used in the mix have to be considered carefully.

• Sloping floors
Although you can build upon a perfectly flat base, it is a good idea to slope the floor toward the door of a garage or outbuilding that is to be scrubbed out from time to time. Alternatively, slope a floor in two directions toward the middle to form a shallow drain that runs to the door.

Deciding on the slope

A freestanding pad can be laid perfectly level, especially to support a small outbuilding. But a very slight slope or fall will prevent water from collecting in puddles if you have failed to get the concrete absolutely flat. If a pad is laid directly against a house, it must have a definite fall away from the building, and any parking area or driveway must shed water to provide adequate traction for vehicles and to minimize the formation of ice.

USE OF PAVING	ANGLE OF FALL
Pathways	Not required
Driveways	1 inch per yard
Patios Parking spaces	1 inch per yard
Pads for garages and outbuilding	½ inch per yard

Irregular shapes
Insert control joints at 90 degrees to edges.

Recommended thicknesses for concrete

The normal thicknesses recommended for concrete paving assume it will be laid on a firm subsoil. If the soil is clay or peat, increase the thickness by about 50 percent. The same applies to a new site, where the soil may not be compacted. Unless the concrete is for pedestrian traffic only, lay a subbase of compacted gravel below the paving. This will absorb ground movement without affecting the concrete itself. A subbase is not essential for a very lightweight structure, such as a small wood shed, or for a modest-size patio.

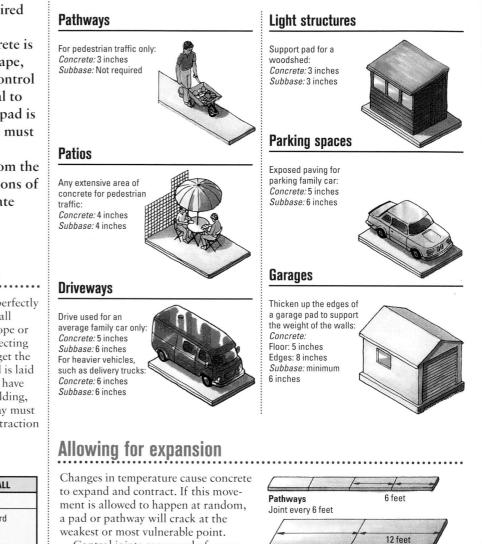

Pathways
For pedestrian traffic only:
Concrete: 3 inches
Subbase: Not required

Patios
Any extensive area of concrete for pedestrian traffic:
Concrete: 4 inches
Subbase: 4 inches

Driveways
Drive used for an average family car only:
Concrete: 5 inches
Subbase: 6 inches
For heavier vehicles, such as delivery trucks:
Concrete: 6 inches
Subbase: 6 inches

Light structures
Support pad for a woodshed:
Concrete: 3 inches
Subbase: 3 inches

Parking spaces
Exposed paving for parking family car:
Concrete: 5 inches
Subbase: 6 inches

Garages
Thicken up the edges of a garage pad to support the weight of the walls:
Concrete:
Floor: 5 inches
Edges: 8 inches
Subbase: minimum 6 inches

Allowing for expansion

Changes in temperature cause concrete to expand and contract. If this movement is allowed to happen at random, a pad or pathway will crack at the weakest or most vulnerable point.

Control joints composed of a compressible material will either absorb the movement or concentrate the force in predetermined areas where it will do little harm. The joints should meet the sides of a concrete area at more-or-less 90 degrees. Always place a control joint between concrete and a wall.

Positioning control joints
The exact position of the control joints will depend on the area and shape of the concrete.

Pathways
Joint every 6 feet
6 feet

Drives/parking spaces
Joint every 12 feet
12 feet

12 feet

Concrete pads
Joints no more than 12 feet apart and around any floor drains.

Divide a pad into equal bays if:
• The length is more than twice the width.
• The longest dimension is more than 40 times the thickness.
• The longest dimension exceeds 12 feet

Calculating quantities

To estimate the amount of materials that will be required, you need to calculate the volume of concrete in the finished pad, path, or drive. Measure the surface area of the site and multiply that figure by the thickness of the concrete.

Estimating quantities of concrete

Use the grid diagram to estimate the volume of concrete you will need, by reading off the area of the site in square yards and tracing it across horizontally to meet the angled line indicating the thickness of the concrete. Trace the line up to find the volume in cubic yards.

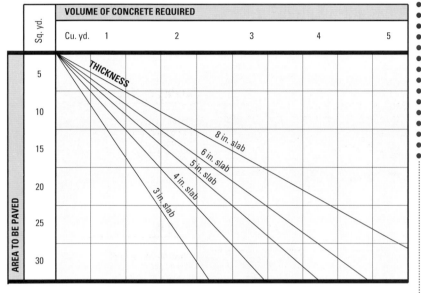

Estimating quantities of ingredients

Use the bar charts below to estimate the quantities of cement, sand, and aggregate you will require to mix up the volume of concrete arrived at by using the chart above.

The figures are based on the quantity of ingredients required to mix 1 cubic yard of concrete for a particular type of mix, plus about 10 percent to allow for waste.

CUBIC YARDS OF CONCRETE									
	1.00	1.50	2.00	2.50	3.00	3.50	4.00	4.50	5.00
GENERAL-PURPOSE MIX									
Cement (94-lb. bag)	7.00	10.50	14.00	17.50	21.00	24.50	28.00	31.50	35.00
plus Sand (cubic yard)	0.50	0.75	1.00	1.25	1.50	1.75	2.00	2.25	2.50
Aggregate (cubic yard)	0.75	1.15	1.50	1.90	2.25	2.65	3.00	3.40	3.75
or Ballast (cubic yard)	0.90	1.35	1.80	2.25	2.70	3.15	3.60	4.05	4.50
FOUNDATION MIX									
Cement (94-lb. bag)	6.00	9.00	12.00	15.00	18.00	21.00	24.00	27.00	30.00
plus Sand (cubic yard)	0.55	0.80	1.10	1.40	1.65	1.95	2.20	2.50	2.75
Aggregate (cubic yard)	0.75	1.15	1.50	1.90	2.25	2.65	3.00	3.40	3.75
or Ballast (cubic yard)	1.00	1.50	2.00	2.50	3.00	3.50	4.00	4.50	5.00
PAVING MIX									
Cement (94-lb. bag)	9.00	13.50	18.00	22.50	27.00	31.50	36.00	40.50	45.00
plus Sand (cubic yard)	0.45	0.70	0.90	1.15	1.35	1.60	1.80	2.00	2.25
Aggregate (cubic yard)	0.75	1.15	1.50	1.90	2.25	2.65	3.00	3.40	3.75
or Ballast (cubic yard)	1.00	1.50	2.00	2.50	3.00	3.50	4.00	4.50	5.00

Keep the shovel as clean as possible between mixing batches of concrete, and at the end of a working day wash all traces of concrete from your tools and wheelbarrow.

When you have finished using a concrete mixer, add a few shovels of coarse aggregate and a little water, then run the machine for a couple of minutes to scour the inside of the drum. Dump the aggregate, then hose out the drum with clean water.

Shovel unused concrete into sacks, ready for disposal at a refuse dump, and wash the mixing area with a stiff broom. Never hose concrete or any of the separate ingredients into a drain.

CALCULATING AREAS

Squares and rectangles
Calculate the area of rectangular paving by multiplying width by length.

Example:
2 ft. x 3 ft. = 6 sq. ft.
78 in. x 117 in. = 9126 sq. in. or 7 sq. yd.

Circles
Use the formula πr^2 to calculate the area of a circle ($\pi = 3.14$, r = radius of circle).

Example:
3.14×2 ft.^{2} = 3.14×4 = 12.56 sq. ft.
3.14×78 in.^{2} = 3.14×6084 = 19,104 sq. in. or 14.75 sq. yd.

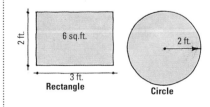

Rectangle   Circle

Irregular shapes

Square-up an irregular shape to calculate area.

Pouring a concrete pad

Installing a simple pad as a base for a small shed or similar structure involves all the basic principles of concrete work including building a retaining formwork, and pouring, leveling, and finishing the surface. Provided the base is less than 6 feet square, there's no need to include control joints.

Mixing concrete by volume
Whatever container you use to measure out the ingredients (shovel, bucket, or wheelbarrow), the proportions remain the same.

MIXING CONCRETE BY VOLUME			
Type of mix		Proportions	For 1 cu.yd. concrete
GENERAL PURPOSE			
Use in most situations including covered pads other than garage floors.	plus	1 part cement	7 bags (94 lb. each)
		2 parts sand	0.5 cu. yd.
	or	3 parts aggregate	0.7 cu. yd.
		4 parts ballast	0.9 cu. yd.
FOUNDATION			
Use for footings at the base of masonry walls.	plus	1 part cement	6 bags (94 lb. each)
		2½ parts sand	0.5 cu. yd.
	or	3½ parts aggregate	0.7 cu. yd.
		5 parts ballast	1.0 cu. yd.
PAVING			
Use for parking areas, drives, footpaths, and garage floors.	plus	1 part cement	9 bags (94 lb. each)
		1½ parts sand	0.4 cu. yd.
	or	2½ parts aggregate	0.7 cu. yd.
		3½ parts ballast	1.0 cu. yd.

Excavating the site

First, mark out the area of the pad with string lines attached to pegs driven into the ground outside the work area (**1**). Remove the lines to excavate the site, but replace them afterward to help position the forms that will hold the concrete in place.

Remove the topsoil and vegetation within the site down to a level that allows for the combined thickness of concrete and subbase. Extend the area of excavation about 6 inches outside the space allowed for the pad. Cut back any roots you encounter and, if there's any turf, put it aside to cover the backfill surrounding the completed pad. Finally, level the bottom of the excavation by dragging a board across it (**2**) and compact the soil with a lawn roller or plate compactor.

Erecting the formwork

Until the concrete sets hard, it must be supported all round by forms. For a straightforward rectangular slab, construct the forms from standard ¾-inch-thick lumber. The planks, which must be as wide as the finished depth of concrete, need to be held in place temporarily with 2 x 2-inch wood stakes. Scrap lumber, as long as it's straight, works well for forms. If you have to join boards, butt them end to end, nailing a cleat on the outside (**3**).

Using the string lines as a guide, erect one board at the high end of the slab and drive stakes behind it at about 3-foot intervals or less, with one for each corner. The tops of the stakes and board must be level and need to correspond exactly to the proposed surface of the slab. Nail the board to the stakes (**4**).

Set up another board opposite the first one, but before you nail it to the stakes, check it for level with the first board using a level and a straightedge. Work out the difference in level from one side of the pad to the other. For example, a pad that is about 8 feet wide should drop about 1 inch over that distance. Tape a shim of scrap wood to one end of the straightedge and, with the shim resting on the low stakes, place the other end on the opposite board (**5**). Drive down each low stake until the spirit level reads horizontal, and then nail the board flush with the tops of the stakes.

Erect the ends of the form. Allowing the boards to overshoot at the corners will make it easier to dismantle them when the concrete has set (**6**). Use the straightedge, this time without the shim, to level the boards from end to end.

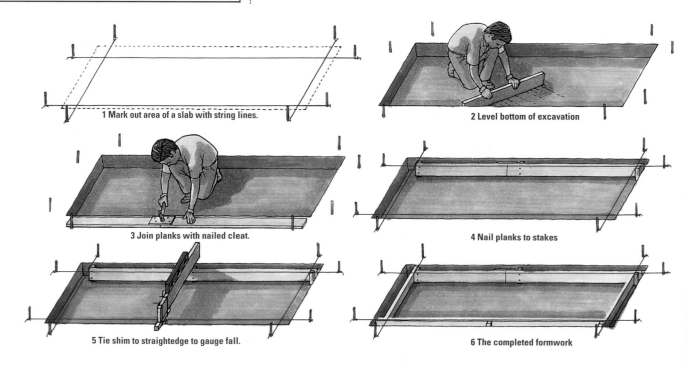

1 Mark out area of a slab with string lines.

2 Level bottom of excavation

3 Join planks with nailed cleat.

4 Nail planks to stakes

5 Tie shim to straightedge to gauge fall.

6 The completed formwork

Laying the subbase

Bank run gravel, a natural mixture of gravel and sand, is an ideal material for a subbase. But you can use crushed stone or screened gravel too. Be sure to remove any scrap building materials and vegetation from the subbase material. Then level its surface and compact it with a roller or a tamper made from a 4 x 4 with a wood pad nailed to the bottom (**7**). If there are any stubborn lumps, break them up with a heavy hammer. Fill in low spots with more subbase material until the subbase reaches the underside of the form boards.

Filling with concrete

Mix the concrete as near to the site as you can and transport the fresh mix to the form in a wheelbarrow. Set up a firm runway using scaffolding boards if the ground is soft, especially around the perimeter of the forms.

Dampen the subbase and formwork with a fine spray, and let surface water evaporate before tipping the concrete in place. Start filling from one end of the site and push the concrete firmly into the corners (**8**). Rake it level until the concrete stands about ¾ inch above the level of the boards.

Tamp down the concrete with the edge of a 2-inch-thick plank that is long enough to reach across the forms. Starting at one end of the site, compact the concrete with steady blows of the plank, moving it along by a couple of inches each time (**9**). Cover the whole area twice and then remove excess concrete, using the plank with a sawing action (**10**). Fill any low spots, then compact and level the concrete once more.

To retain the moisture, cover the pad with sheets of polyethylene, taped at the joints and held down with bricks around the edge (**11**). Try to avoid laying concrete in very cold weather. But if that's unavoidable, use ready-mix concrete treated to resist freezing for the job.

It's perfectly safe to walk on the concrete after three days, but leave it for about a week before removing the forms and erecting a shed or similar outbuilding.

Extending a slab
If you want to enlarge your patio, simply butt a new section of concrete against the existing pad. The butt joint will in itself serve as a control joint.

To add a narrow strip to a pad (so that you can erect a larger shed, for example), drill holes in the edge of the pad and use epoxy adhesive to glue in short lengths of rebar before pouring the fresh concrete.

Finishing the edges
If any of the edges are exposed, the sharp corners could cause a painful injury. Use an edging float to smooth and round the edges.

7 Level subbase with lawn roller or tamper tool

8 Pour concrete, starting in one corner

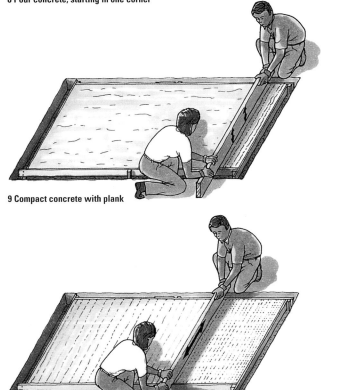

9 Compact concrete with plank

10 Use sawing action to remove excess concrete

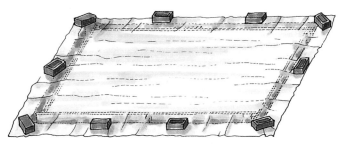

11 Cover pad with sheets of polyethylene

Walks and driveways

Walks and drives are laid and compacted in the same way as rectangular pads, using similar forms to contain the concrete. However, the shape of most walks and driveways makes the inclusion of control joints essential, to allow for expansion and contraction. You will have to install a subbase beneath a driveway, but a footpath can be laid on compacted soil leveled with sand. Establish a slight fall across the site to shed rainwater.

1 A water level made from garden hose

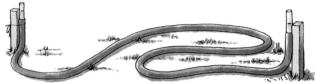

2 Level form using reference pegs

A sloping drive
If you build a driveway on a sloping site, make the transition from level ground as gentle as possible. If the drive runs toward a garage, make the last 6 feet slope up toward the garage door. Press a pole lengthwise into the wet concrete at the lowest point, and remove it. This will create a path for water to drain away.

5 Expansion strip with concrete and nails

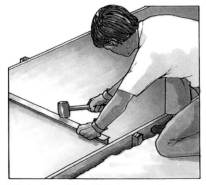

6 Make dummy joint with T-shaped steel

Laying out paths and drives

Excavate the site, allowing for the thickness of the subbase and concrete. Level the bottom of the excavation as accurately as you can, using a board to scrape the surface flat.

Drive accurately leveled pegs into the ground along the site to act as reference points for the form boards. Space them about 6 feet apart along the center of the walk. Drive in the first peg until its top corresponds exactly to the proposed surface of the concrete. Use either a long straightedge and a level or a water level to position every other peg.

To make a water level, push a short length of transparent plastic tubing into each end of an ordinary garden hose.

Holding both ends together, fill the hose with water until it appears in the tube at both ends. Then mark the level on both tubes. As long as the ends remain open, the water level at each end is constant, enabling you to establish a level over any distance, even around obstacles or corners. When you move the hose, plug both ends to retain the water.

Tie one end of the hose to the first reference peg, ensuring that the marked level aligns with the top of the peg. Use the other end to establish the level of every other peg along the pathway (1).

To set a fall with a water level, make a mark on one tube below the surface of the water and use that as a gauge for the top of the peg.

Erecting formwork

Construct forms from ¾-inch-thick boards and 2 x 2 stakes. To check for level, rest a straightedge on the nearest reference peg (2).

If the driveway or walk is very long, wood forms can be expensive. It may be cheaper to rent metal forms (3). Standard forms are made from rigid

units, but flexible sections are available to form curves.

If you want to bend wood forms, make a series of closely spaced parallel saw cuts across the width of the plank in the area of the curve (4). The board is less likely to break if you place the saw cuts on the inside of the bend.

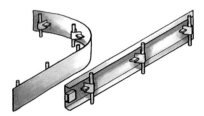

3 Curved and straight metal forms

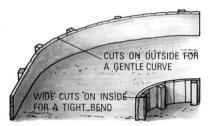

CUTS ON OUTSIDE FOR A GENTLE CURVE

WIDE CUTS ON INSIDE FOR A TIGHT BEND

4 Curved forms made with wood planks

Installing control joints

Install a permanent expansion joint every 6 to 8 feet for a walk, and every 13 or 14 feet along a driveway. For a patio, you can install similar joints or use alternate-bay construction (see facing page).

Expansion-joint material is available at masonry supply outlets. It's usually about ½ inch thick. Cut each expansion strip to fit exactly between the formwork and to match the depth of the concrete. Before pouring, hold the control joints in place with mounds of concrete and nails driven into the formwork on each side of the strip (5). As you fill the formwork, pack more concrete on both sides of each joint and tamp toward the strip from both

sides, so that it is not dislodged.

On a narrow path, to prevent the concrete from cracking between joints, cut ¾-inch-deep grooves across the concrete to form dummy joints alternating with the physical ones. The simplest method is to cut a length of T-section steel to fit between the form boards. Place the strip on the surface of the wet concrete and tap it down with a mallet (6). Carefully lift the strip out of the concrete to leave a neat impression. If the concrete moves after it's dry, a crack will develop unnoticed at the bottom of the groove. Install expansion material between the concrete and an adjoining wall, or other obstructions, to absorb expansion.

Surface finishes

It is not always possible to pour all the concrete in a single operation. In such cases, it's easier to divide the form in half with additional planks, to create two separate bays.

By filling alternate bays with concrete, you have plenty of time to finish each section and more room in which to maneuver. It is a convenient way to lay a large patio—which would be practically impossible to pour and finish in one go—and it is the only method you can use for driveways or walks that butt against a wall. Alternate-bay construction is also frequently used for building a driveway on a steep slope, to prevent the heavy, wet concrete from slumping downhill.

There is no need to install control joints when using bay construction, but you may want to form dummy joints for a neat appearance (see facing page).

Laying concrete next to a wall

Stand in the empty bays so you can pour and smooth the concrete against the wall. When the first bays have set hard, remove the intermediate form boards and fill the gaps. Trowel the surface level with the set concrete. Don't use a vehicle on a concrete driveway for 10 days after pouring.

Finishing concrete bays next to wall

The surface finish produced by striking off concrete with a plain screed board is adequate for a workmanlike foundation slab, walk, or driveway. But you can produce a range of other finishes using simple hand tools and basic skills.

Create smooth finish with wooden float

Float finishes

You can smooth the poured concrete by sweeping a wooden float across the surface, or make an even finer texture by finishing with a steel float. Let the concrete dry out a little before using a float, or you will bring water to the top and weaken it, which will eventually result in a dusty residue on the hardened concrete. Bridge the formwork with a thick plank so that you can reach the center, or rent a steel float with a long handle for large slabs.

Brush-finished concrete

Brush finishes

To produce a finely textured surface, draw a yard broom across the setting concrete. Finish the concrete initially with a wooden float and then make parallel passes with the broom, held at a low angle in order to avoid tearing the surface.

Texture surface with broom

Exposed aggregate finish

Embedding small stones or pebbles in the surface makes a very attractive and practical finish, although you will need a little practice in order to do it successfully.

Scatter dampened pebbles onto the freshly laid concrete and embed them firmly with a short board until they are flush with the surface **(1)**. Place a plank across the forms and apply your full weight to make sure the surface is even. Let the floor harden for a while until all the surface water has evaporated, then use a very fine spray and a brush to wash away the cement from around the pebbles until they protrude **(2)**. Cover the concrete for about 24 hours, then lightly wash the surface again to clean any sediment off the pebbles. Cover the concrete again, and let it harden thoroughly.

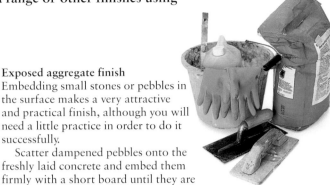

1 Tamp pebbles into fresh concrete

2 Wash cement from around the pebbles

Exposed aggregate finish

Paving slabs

If your only experience of paving slabs is the rather bland variety used for many public walkways and courtyards, then cast concrete paving may not seem like an attractive option for the landscaping around your house. But it pays to look around. There's a wide variety of residential pavers in many different shapes and colors.

Colors and textures

Paving slabs are made by hydraulic pressing or casting in molds to create the desired surface finish. Pigments and selected aggregates added to the concrete mix are used to create the illusion of a range of muted colors or natural stone. Combining two or more colors or textures within the same area of paving can be very striking.

Regular or informal paving
Constructing a simple grid from square slabs (left) is relatively easy. Though more difficult to lay, mixed paving (below) is richer in texture, color, and shape.

SHAPES AND SIZES

Although some manufacturers offer a wider choice than others, there's a fairly standard range of shapes and modular sizes. It is possible to carry the largest slabs without help, but it's a good idea to get an assistant to help maneuver them carefully into place.

Square and rectangular
A single size and shape can be employed to make gridlike patterns or, when staggered, to create a bonded brick effect. Use rectangular slabs to form a basket-weave or herringbone pattern. Or combine different sizes to create the impression of random paving, or mix slabs with a different type of paving to create a colorful contrast.

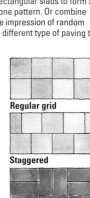

Regular grid

Staggered

Colorful combination

Basket-weave pattern

Herringbone pattern

Random paving

Hexagonal
Hexagonal slabs form honeycomb patterns. Use half-slabs to edge areas that are paved in straight lines.

Half-hexagonal slabs

Hexagonal slab

Honeycomb pattern

Tapered slabs
Use tapered slabs to edge ponds and for encircling trees or making curved steps. Progressively larger slabs can be used for laying circular areas of paving.

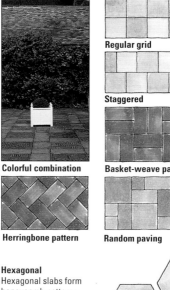

Circular slabs
Circular slabs make perfect individual stepping-stones across a lawn or flowerbed, but for a wide area, fill the spaces between with stones or gravel.

Butted circular slabs

Laying paving

Laying paving slabs involves a good deal of physical labor, but in terms of technique it's no more complicated than tiling a wall. Accurate planning and careful placement, especially during the early stages, will help you achieve top-notch results.

CUTTING PAVING SLABS

It is often necessary to trim concrete paving slabs to size in order to fit narrow margins or to fill in around obstructions such as walls and trees.

Mark a line across a slab with chalk or a soft pencil. Place the slab on a bed of sand and, using a cold chisel and hammer, chisel a groove about ⅛ inch deep along the line (1). When cutting a thick slab, continue the groove down both of the edges and across the underside.

Turn the slab facedown and, with the hammer, tap firmly along the groove until the slab splits (2). If need be, clean up the edge with the cold chisel. To obtain a perfect cut, use a masonry blade in a portable circular saw. Be prepared for a lot of dust. Wear goggles, a respirator, and gloves.

1 Cut a groove with cold chisel

2 Strike block over groove with a hammer

Protecting your eyes

When cutting slabs with a bolster chisel or an angle grinder, always protect your eyes by wearing plastic goggles. An angle grinder throws up a great deal of dust, so it is advisable to wear a simple gauze face mask, too.

Laying out the area of paving

Wherever practical, plan an area of paving so that it can be laid with whole slabs only. This eliminates the time-consuming task of cutting units to fit. Use pegs and string to mark out the perimeter of the paved area, and check the measurements before you excavate.

You can use a straight wall as a reference line and measure away from it. If possible, leave a 4- to-6-inch margin of gravel between the paving and wall. A gravel margin not only saves time and money by using fewer slabs, but also provides an area for planting climbers and for adequate drainage to keep the wall dry.

Establish a slope of ⅛ inch per yard across the paving, so that most of the surface water will drain into the surrounding yard. If the paving area is bounded by structures on all four sides, you should install a drain before laying the pavers.

Because paving slabs are made to fairly precise dimensions, marking out an area simply involves accurate measurement, allowing for a ¼- to ⅜-inch gap between the slabs. Some slabs have sloping edges to provide a tapered joint (1). These pavers should be butted edge to edge.

Preparing a base for paving

Paving slabs must be laid upon a firm, level base, but the depth and substance of that base depends on the type of soil and the proposed use of the paving.

For straightforward patios and walks, remove vegetation and topsoil to allow for the thickness of the slabs, plus a 1½-inch layer of sharp sand, and an extra ¾ inch so the paving will be below the level of surrounding turf, in order to prevent damage to your lawn mower. Compact the soil with a garden roller, and then spread the sand with a rake and level it by scraping and tamping with a length of 2 x 6 (2).

To support heavier loads, or if the soil is composed of clay or peat, lay a subbase of firmly compacted gravel or crushed stone to a depth of 3 or 4 inches before spreading the sand to level the surface. If you plan to park vehicles on the paving, increase the depth of the gravel or stone to about 6 inches.

Laying the paving slabs

Set up string lines again as a guide and lay the edging slabs on the sand, working in both directions from a corner. When you are satisfied with their positions, lift the slabs one at a time, so you can set them on a bed of firm mortar (1 part cement to 4 parts sand). Lay a fist-size spot under each corner, and one more to support the center of the slab (3). If you intend to drive vehicles across the slabs, lay a continuous bed of mortar about 2 inches thick.

Lay three slabs at a time, inserting wooden spacers between them. Level each slab by tapping with a hammer and a block of wood to protect the surface (4). Check the alignment.

Gauge the slope across the paving by setting up reference pegs along the high side. Drive them into the ground until the top of each corresponds to the finished surface of the paving, and then use a straightedge with a wood block tacked to one end to check the fall on the slabs (5). Lay the remainder of the slabs, each time working out from the corner in order to keep the joints square. Remove the spacers before the mortar sets.

Filling the joints

Don't walk on the paving for two to three days, until the mortar has set. If you have to cross the area, lay planks across the slabs to spread the load.

To fill the gaps between the paving slabs, brush a dry mortar mix of 1 part cement to 3 parts sand into the open joints (6). Remove any surplus material from the surface of the paving, then sprinkle the area with a very fine spray of water to consolidate the mortar. Avoid dry-mortaring if rain is in the forecast. It can wash out the mortar.

Cutting slabs

1 Tapered joint

2 Level sand base

3 Lay spots of mortar

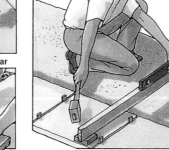

4 Level slabs   **5 Check fall with level**

6 Fill joints

Laying fieldstone paving

Informal walks and patios laid with irregular-shaped paving stones have always been popular. The random effect, which many people find more appealing than the geometry of neatly laid slabs, is also very easy to achieve. A good eye for proportion and shape is more important than a practiced technique.

Materials for crazing paving

You can use broken flat stones like slate or bluestone if you are able to find enough. These materials are quarried into flat sections and then are cut into pieces with square edges. Randomly-broken flat stones can be obtained at a very reasonable price if you can collect them yourself. Select stones about 1½ to 2 inches thick, in a pleasing variety of shapes, colors, and sizes.

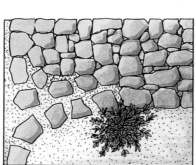

Walkway made of broken pieces of flat stone

LAYING A BASE

You can set out string lines to define straight edges for stone paving, although edges will never be as precise as those made with regular cast concrete slabs.

You can also allow the stones to form an irregular junction with grass, perhaps setting one or two stones out from the edge. Lay a bed of sharp sand for the stones, as described for laying paving slabs.

Create an irregular edge to stone paving.

Laying the stones

Arrange an area of fieldstones (sometimes called flagstones), selecting them for a close fit but avoiding too many straight, continuous joints. Use a cold chisel and hammer to trim those that don't quite fit. Reserve larger stones for the perimeter. Small stones tend to break away.

Use a mallet or a block of wood and a hammer to bed each stone into the sand **(1)** until they are all perfectly stable and reasonably level. Having bedded an area approximately 1 square yard, use a straightedge and level to check the stones **(2)**. If necessary, add or remove sand beneath individual stones until the area is level. When the main area is complete, fill in the larger gaps with small stones, tapping them into place with a mallet **(3)**.

Fill the joints by spreading more sand across the surface and sweeping it into the joints from all directions **(4)**. You can also mix up a stiff, almost dry, mortar and press it into the joints with a trowel, leaving no gaps. Use an old paintbrush to smooth the mortared joints, then wipe the stones clean.

1 Bed stones in sand base

2 Check level across several stones

3 Fill gaps with small stones

4 Sweep dry sand into joints

Laying stepping-stones

Place individual stones across a lawn to form a row of stepping-stones. Cut around the edge of each stone with a spade or trowel and remove the area of turf directly beneath. Scoop out the soil to allow for a 1-inch bed of sharp sand plus the stone, which must be about ¾ inch below the level of the surrounding turf. Tap the stone into the sand until it no longer rocks when you step on it.

Cut around stepping-stone with trowel

Stepping-stones form a garden walkway

Paving with bricks

Unlike brick walls, which must be bonded in a certain way for stability, brick paths, patios, and car-parking areas can be laid to any pattern that appeals to you. Try out your ideas on graph paper, using the examples shown below for inspiration.

Concrete bricks, which have one finished surface, are often chamfered all round to define their shape and emphasize whatever pattern you choose. Many bricks have spacers molded into the sides to help form accurate joints. House bricks can be laid on edge or facedown, showing the wide face normally unseen in a wall.

Bricks make charming paths and walkways. The wide variety of textures and colors offers nearly endless pattern possibilities. But choose the type of brick carefully, keeping in mind the sort of use your paving will have to serve.

Brick paving

Ordinary house bricks are often used for paths and small patios, even though there is the risk of spalling in freezing conditions—unless they happen to be engineering bricks. Slightly uneven texture and color are the two big reasons why secondhand bricks (from demolition sites) are in demand for paving projects.

House bricks are not really suitable if the paved area is a parking space or driveway, especially one used by heavy vehicles. For a surface that will be durable under these severe conditions, use concrete bricks instead. These are generally slightly smaller than standard house bricks. In fact, there are many variations in shape, size, and color, making possible a wide range of approaches.

Brick pavers
Pavers are available in a variety of colors, styles, and shapes. Textured units are ideal for non-slip garden walkways (top left). Mottled bricks make functional and eye-catching driveways and parking areas (top right).

Herringbone pattern with straight edging

Angled herringbone with straight edging

Whole bricks surrounding colored half-bats

Staggered basket-weave pattern

Stretcher bond pattern

Cane weave pattern

Providing a base for brick paving

Lay brick walkways and patios on a 3-inch-thick gravel base, covered with a 2-inch layer of compacted, slightly damp sharp sand. When laying concrete bricks for a drive, you need to increase the depth of the gravel to 6 inches. Fully compact the gravel, so that sand from the bedding course is not lost to the subbase.

Provide a slope (for water runoff) on patios and drives, as described earlier for concrete. In cold climates this slope is especially important. If the water pools, it can freeze into a sheet of ice.

Retaining edges

Unless the brick path is laid against a wall or some similar structure, the edges of the paving must be contained by a permanent restraint. Lumber treated with chemical preservative is one solution, constructed like the formwork for concrete. The edging boards should be flush with the surface of the path, but drive the stakes below ground so that they can be covered by soil or turf **(1)**.

Concrete paving, in particular, needs a more substantial edging of bricks set in concrete **(2)**. Dig a trench that is deep and wide enough to take a row of bricks on end plus a concrete foundation. Lay the bricks while the concrete is still wet. Hold them in place temporarily with a staked board while you pack more concrete behind the edging. Once the concrete has set, remove the board and lay gravel and sand in the excavation.

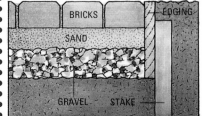

1 Wood retaining edge

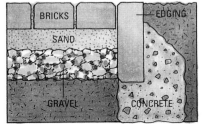

2 Brick retaining edge

Brick paving

Having chosen your bricks, prepared the ground, and set retaining edges, you can start laying your paving. Laying bricks over a wide area can be time consuming, so it helps if at least two people can work together, dividing up the various tasks between them. Also, it's well worth the extra expense of renting tools that will make the work faster and more efficient.

Special tool
Use a gas-powered, vibrating-plate compactor to prepare the subbase and to embed the pavers.

Mottled-brick garden path

Interlocking concrete pavers

Concrete-brick path edged with flush pavers

Paving with character
(left)
Many people think that modern concrete pavers are suitable only for driveways and parking spaces. Here, small plain units made in a variety of subtle colors are used to create a distinctive circular patio. Shaped paving slabs are made specifically for laying in circular patterns, but provided the units are relatively small, curved shapes can be accommodated simply by including slightly tapered joints between the pavers.

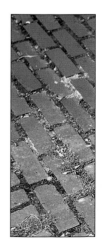

Laying concrete bricks

Compacting and leveling the sand

When the bricks are first laid on the sand they should project ⅜ inch above the edging restraints, to allow for bedding them into the base later (**1**).

Spread sand to about two-thirds of its finished thickness across the area to be paved and then compact it, using a rented plate compactor (facing page).

Spread more sand on top and level it with a notched board that spans the edging (**2**). If the area is too wide for a single board, lay leveling guides on the gravel base and scrape the sand to the required depth using a straightedge (**3**). Then remove the guides and fill the voids carefully with sand.

Bedding in the bricks

Lay the bricks on the sand in your chosen pattern. Start at one end of the site, kneeling on a board placed across the bricks (**4**). Never stand on the bed of sand. Lay whole bricks only, leaving any gaps at the edges to be filled with cut bricks after you have laid an area of approximately 2 square yards. Butt the bricks together tightly. Fill any of the remaining spaces with bricks cut with a cold chisel and hammer. If you have a lot of cuts to make, consider renting a hydraulic brick cutter. It cuts bricks quickly and cleanly.

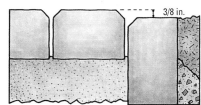
1 Start by laying bricks 3/8 inch above edging

2 Level sand with notched board

3 For wide areas use guide boards

4 Lay bricks in your chosen pattern

When the area of paving is complete, run the vibrating plate over the surface two or three times, until it has worked the bricks down into the sand flush with the outer edging (**5**).

Vibrating the bricks will work some sand up between them; complete the job by brushing more kiln-dried, joint-filling sand across the finished paving and vibrating it into the open joints.

5 A plate compactor levels and embeds bricks

A large patio or parking space may have to accommodate an existing drain cover, which often spoils the appearance of the job. The solution is to replace this cover with a special hollow version that is designed to be filled with pavers so the cover will merge into the surrounding paving.

Another common problem is draining rainwater from a large flat area of paving. One solution is to install a linear drainage channel that will carry water to the storm sewer.

Access cover
The metal frame of an access cover should be embedded in concrete, which is then covered with pavers that run up to the rim of the access hole. Make sure the rim is just below the finished surface of the paving.

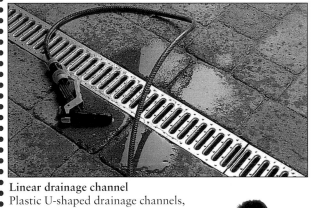

Linear drainage channel
Plastic U-shaped drainage channels, linked end to end, are embedded in a 4-inch-thick concrete base, which holds the channel in place. The first row of bricks on each side of the channel is embedded in the concrete, and should finish ⅛ to ¼ inch above the level of the plastic or metal grating used to cover the channel.

A special endcap is available for connecting to a main sewer, or you can drain the water into a dry well about 4 feet square and at least 4 feet deep. Fill the dry well with coarse gravel or crushed stone.

Hydraulic brick cutter

Access cover

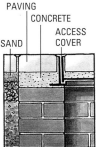
PAVING
CONCRETE
ACCESS
COVER
SAND
Frame embedded in concrete

Cutting the channel
Use a handsaw to cut a plastic drainage channel to length.

Cobblestones and gravel

Cobblestones and gravel are used more for their decorative qualities than as practical paving. Cobbles, in particular, are uncomfortable to walk on and, although a firmly consolidated area of gravel is fine for vehicles, walking on a gravel footpath can be annoying. Both materials come into their own, however, when used as a contrast for areas of flat paving slabs or bricks, and to set off plantings of any type.

• Compacting gravel
A lightweight garden roller is fine for compacting soil or sand, but use one weighing at least 200 pounds when you want to compact gravel. You can also rent a vibrating plate compactor to do the job.

Making a gravel garden
(below)
To lay an area of gravel for plantings, simply excavate the soil to accept a bed of fine gravel about 1 inch deep. Either set the gravel ¾ inch below the level of the lawn or edge the gravel garden with bricks or flat stones. Scrape away a small area of gravel to allow for planting, then sprinkle the gravel back again to cover the soil right up to the plant.

Laying decorative cobbles

Cobbles can be laid loose, usually with larger rocks and plants. However, they are often set in mortar or concrete to create more formal areas.

Compact a subbase of gravel and cover it with a leveled layer of dry concrete mix, about 2 inches deep. Press the cobbles into the dry mix, packing them tightly together and leaving them projecting well above the concrete mix. Use a heavy board to tamp the area level (**1**), then lightly sprinkle the whole area with water. This will begin the concrete-hardening process and also clean the surfaces of the cobbles.

Press cobbles into dry concrete mix

Laying gravel

If an area of gravel is going to be used as a pathway or for vehicles, construct retaining edges of brick, concrete pavers, or pressure-treated boards. This will stop the gravel from being spread outside the planned area.

To construct a gravel drive, the subbase and the gravel itself must be compacted and leveled to prevent cars from skidding and churning up the material. Lay a 6-inch bed of compacted bank-run gravel, topped with 2 inches of very coarse gravel mixed with sand. Roll it flat, then rake a 1-inch layer of fine pea gravel across the surface and roll it down.

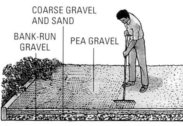

COARSE GRAVEL AND SAND
BANK-RUN GRAVEL
PEA GRAVEL

Rake pea gravel across surface of drive

If you live in a rural area where large logs are plentiful, or when a mature tree has been cut down on your property, you can use 6-inch lengths of sawn wood, set on end, to make a practical and attractive footpath. Lay the sections together in a pleasing pattern, or use large individual pieces as stepping-stones. Hold wood rot at bay by soaking the sawn sections in chemical preservative for at least 24 hours.

Laying a log pathway

Excavate the area of the pathway to a depth of 8 inches, then spread a 2-inch deep layer of gravel and sand mix across the bottom. Level the bed by using a straight board and compact it with a lawn roller or plate compactor.

Place the logs on end on the bed, arranging them to create a pleasing combination of shapes and sizes (**1**). Work the logs down into the sand until they stand firmly and evenly. Then fill the spaces by pouring more sand and gravel between them (**2**). Finally, brush the filler across the pathway in all directions until the gaps between the logs are flush with the surrounding surfaces (**3**). If any of the logs stand too high, so they could cause someone to trip, tap them down with a heavy hammer.

If you want to introduce a few low-growing plants between the logs, scrape out some sand and gravel and replace it with the appropriate soil.

1 Arrange logs on end

2 Shovel sand and gravel mix between logs

3 Brush filler mix into joints

Resurfacing with macadam

As an alternative to macadam, completely resurface a walk or driveway with natural stone chips embedded in a bitumen emulsion.

Stone chips, in a variety of colors, are available in 50-pound bags, one of which will cover about 3 square yards. Apply weed killer and fill any holes as explained for macadam (see right).

Bitumen emulsion sets by evaporation, but it won't be completely waterproof for approximately 12 hours after it has been laid. So check the weather forecast to avoid wet conditions. You can lay emulsion on a damp surface, but not when it's icy.

Applying the emulsion

Apply emulsion, available in 10-, 50-, and 400-pound drums. A 10-pound drum will cover about 8 square yards, provided the surface is dense macadam or concrete. However, an open-textured surface will absorb much more bitumen emulsion. Pour the emulsion into a bucket to make it easier to use. Brush it out over the surface with a stiff broom. Follow the directions on the container and don't spread it too thin.

Spreading the chips

Having brushed out one bucket of emulsion, spread the stone chips evenly with a garden spade. Hold the spade horizontally just above the surface and gently shake the chips off the edge of the blade. Don't pile them on too thickly, just make sure the emulsion is covered completely.

Cover an area of about 6 square yards and then roll the chips to press them in. When the entire area is covered, roll it once more. If traces of bitumen show between the chips, mask them with a little sharp sand and roll again.

You can walk or drive on the dressed surface immediately. One week later, gently sweep away surplus chips. You can patch any bare areas that may have appeared by retreating them with emulsion and chips.

Sprinkle layer of chips with spade

You can dress up an old macadam path or driveway, or any sound but unsightly paved area, by resurfacing with cold-cure macadam. It's a durable surface and is ready to use directly from the bag.

Choosing the materials

Cold-cure macadam is sold in 50-pound bags that cover about 10 square feet each at a thickness of about ½ inch. Both red and black versions are available. Some products are sold with a separate bag of decorative stone chips for embedding in the soft macadam as an alternative finish.

Macadam can be laid in almost any weather, but it is much easier to level and roll flat on a warm, dry day. If you have to work in cold weather, store the materials in a warm place the night before using them.

Although it's not essential, edging with either bricks or concrete pavers will improve the appearance of the finished surface.

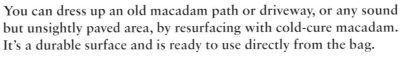

Dealing with weeds
Treat the surface with weed killer two days before applying cold-cure macadam.

Preparing the surface

Pull up all weeds and grass growing between the old paving, then apply a strong weed killer to the surface two days before you lay the tarmac.

Sweep the area clean, and level any potholes: Cut the sides vertical and remove dust and debris from the hole, then paint with bitumen emulsion supplied by the macadam manufacturer. Wait for the emulsion to turn black before filling the hole with ¾-inch layers of macadam, compacting each layer until the surface is level.

Mask any surrounding walls and other objects. Then apply a tack coat of bitumen emulsion to the entire surface to make a firm bond between the new macadam and the old paving. Stir the emulsion with a stick before pouring it from the container. Then spread it thinly, using a stiff-bristled broom.

Try not to splash, and avoid leaving puddles, especially at the foot of a slope. Let the tack coat set for about 20 minutes, and in the meantime wash the broom in hot, soapy water.

Apply tack coat of bitumen emulsion

Applying the macadam

Rake the macadam to make a layer about ¼ inch thick **(1)**, and use a straight board to scrape the surface flat. Press down any stubborn lumps with your foot. Before the initial rolling, spread the contents of no more than three sacks. Keep the roller wet **(2)** to avoid picking up specks of macadam. Don't run the roller onto grass or gravel, or you may roll particles into the macadam.

Spread and roll the macadam over the whole area, then compact it by rolling it thoroughly in several directions. Lightly scatter the stone chips, if you want **(3)**, before making your final pass with the roller.

You can walk on the finished surface immediately, but avoid wearing high-heeled shoes. Don't drive on it for a day or two. And if you have to erect a ladder on the new surface, spread the load by placing a board under the feet.

• **Laying a new path**
Although cold-cure macadam is primarily a resurfacing material, it can be applied to a new gravel base that has been compacted firmly, leveled, and sealed with a generous coat of bitumen emulsion.

• **Treating surfaces for heavy wear**
Vehicle tires often cause excessive wear at entrances to driveways and on any curves. Treat the worn areas with a ¾-inch rolled layer of cold-cure macadam. Apply a dressing of stone chips if you want.

• **Double dressing**
If the surface you are dressing is in a very poor condition or is very loose, apply a first coat of bitumen emulsion. Cover with stone chips and roll thoroughly. Two days later, sweep away any loose chips and apply a second coat of emulsion.

1 Level macadam

2 Keep roller wet

3 Scatter stone chips

Building garden steps

Designing landscaping for a sloping site offers plenty of possibilities for creating attractive outdoor features, such as multilevel patios, terraced planting beds, and undulating walkways. To be able to move from one level to another safely usually requires some steps.

Designing steps

If you have a large yard where the slope is very gradual, a series of steps with wide treads and low risers can make an impressive feature. If the slope is steep, you can avoid a staircase appearance by constructing a flight of steps composed of a few treads interposed with wide, flat landings, at which points the flight can change direction to add further interest and offer a different view of the yard. In fact, a shallow flight can be virtually a series of landings, perhaps circular in plan, sweeping up the slope in a curve.

For steps to be both comfortable and safe to use, the proportion of tread (the part you stand on) to riser (the vertical part of the step) is important. As a rough guide, construct steps so that the depth of the tread (from front to back) plus twice the height of the riser equals about 2 feet. For example, match 1-foot treads with 6-inch risers, 14-inch treads with 5-inch risers, and so on. Avoid making treads less than 1 foot deep, or risers higher than 7 inches.

• Dealing with slippery steps
Steps can become dangerously slippery if algae is allowed to build up on the treads. Brush affected steps with a solution of 1 part household bleach to 4 parts water. After 48 hours, wash them with clean water and repeat the treatment if the fungal growth is heavy. You can also treat the steps with a fungicidal solution, but follow the manufacturer's instructions carefully.

Using concrete slabs

Concrete paving slabs in their various forms are ideal for making firm, flat treads for landscape steps. Construct the risers from concrete blocks or bricks, allowing the treads to overhang by 1 to 2 inches in order to cast shadow lines to define the edge of the steps.

So you can gauge the number of steps required, measure the difference in height from the top of the slope to the bottom. Next, mark the position of the risers with pegs, and roughly shape the steps in the soil (**1**).

Either lay concrete slabs, embedded in sand, flush with the ground at the foot of the slope, or dig a trench for a gravel subbase and 4 to 6 inches of concrete to support the first riser (**2**). When the concrete has set, construct the riser from two courses of mortared bricks, checking the alignment with a level (**3**). Fill behind the riser with compacted gravel until it is level, then lay the tread on a bed of mortar (**4**). Using a level as a guide, tap down the tread until it slopes very slightly toward its front edge, in order to shed rainwater and prevent ice forming in cold weather.

Measure from the front edge of the tread to mark the position of the next riser on the slabs (**5**), then construct the next step in the same way. Set the final tread flush with the paved area or lawn at the top of the steps.

Landscaping each side

It is usually possible to landscape the slope at each side of a flight of steps with grass or plantings to prevent the soil from washing down onto the steps. Another solution is to retain the soil with large stones, perhaps extending into a rock garden on one or both sides. Eventually, spreading plants will soften the hard-edge appearance of the paving, but you should cut back overhanging growth that threatens to mask the front edges of the treads and cause someone to stumble.

1 Cut shape of steps in soil

2 Dig footing for first riser

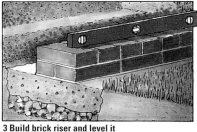
3 Build brick riser and level it

4 Lay tread on mortar

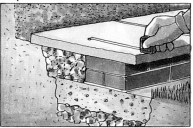
5 Mark position of next riser

Paved steps built with natural stone risers

Paving-slab steps
A section through a simple flight of garden steps built with brick risers and paving slabs.
1 Concrete footing
2 Brick riser
3 Gravel backfill
4 Paving slab tread

Building log steps

Pouring new steps in concrete requires such complicated formwork that the end result hardly justifies the effort involved, especially when it's much easier to build attractive steps from cast concrete pavers and blocks. But if you already have a flight of concrete steps, you should keep them in good condition.

Like other forms of masonry, concrete suffers from spalling, whereby frost breaks down the surface of the material and fragments flake off. Spalling frequently occurs along the front edges of steps where foot traffic adds to the problem. Repair broken edges as soon as you can. Not only do they look bad, but damaged steps are not as safe as they should be.

Building up broken edges

Wearing safety goggles and gloves, chip away concrete around the damaged area and provide a good grip for fresh concrete. Cut a board to the height of the riser and prop it against the step with bricks (**1**). Mix up a small batch of general-purpose concrete, adding a little PVA (polyvinyl acetate) bonding agent to help it adhere to the step. Dilute some bonding agent with water (3 parts water to 1 part bonding agent) and brush it onto the damaged area. When the surface becomes tacky, fill the hole with concrete mix flush with the edge of the board (**2**). Finish the edge with an edging trowel, running it against the board (**3**).

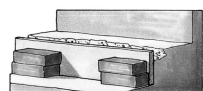

1 Prop board against riser

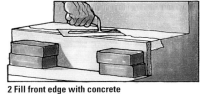

2 Fill front edge with concrete

3 Run edging trowel against board

You can use sawn lengths of timber to build attractive steps that suit an informal landscape design. It's best to construct risers that are more or less the same height, otherwise someone may stumble. Because it's not always possible to obtain uniform logs, you may have to make up the height of the riser with two or more thinner logs. You can buy pressure-treated logs, machined with a flat surface on two faces. If you use untreated lumber, soak it in chemical preservative overnight before using it.

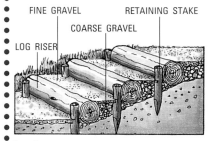

FINE GRAVEL   RETAINING STAKE
COARSE GRAVEL
LOG RISER

Log steps

Remove any turf and cut a regular slope in the bank, then compact the soil by treading it down. Sharpen stakes, cut from logs, that are about 3 inches in diameter and drive them into the ground, one at each end of a step (**1**).

Place a heavy log behind the stakes, bedding it down in the soil until it is level (**2**), and pack coarse gravel behind it to construct the tread of the step (**3**). To finish the step, shovel a layer of fine gravel on top of the coarse gravel. Rake the gravel level with the top of the riser.

If you're unable to obtain large logs, you can build a step from two or three smaller logs, holding them against the stakes with gravel as you construct the riser (**4**). Finish by laying a gravel path at the top and bottom of the flight of steps.

1 Drive stake at each end of step

2 Place log behind stakes

3 Fill behind log with coarse gravel

4 Make up riser with two smaller logs

Making curved steps

To build a series of curved steps, choose materials that will make construction as easy as possible. One option is to use tapered concrete slabs for the treads, designing the circumference of the steps to suit the proportions of the slabs.

Or use bricks laid flat or on edge to build the risers. Set the bricks to radiate from the center of the curve, and fill the slightly tapered joints with

mortar. Use a length of string attached to a peg driven into the ground as an improvised compass to mark out the curve of each step.

After roughly shaping the soil, lay a concrete foundation for the bottom riser. Build the risers and treads as you would for regular paving-slab steps (see facing page), using the improvised string compass as a guide.

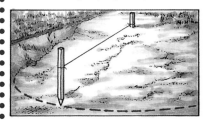

Mark edge with an improvised compass

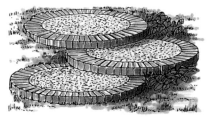

Concrete steps

Log steps

Curved steps

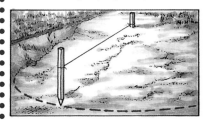

Paved circular landing

Building circular landings
To construct a circular landing (left), build the risers with bricks. When the mortar has set, fill the area of the landing with compacted gravel up to the top of the risers.

Creating water gardens

There is nothing like running water to enliven a garden. Waterfalls and fountains have an almost mesmerizing fascination, and the sound of trickling water has a delightfully soothing effect. Even a small area of still water will support all manner of interesting pond life and plants—with the additional bonus of trees, rocks, and sky being reflected in its placid surface.

Well worth it
A well-balanced, healthy pond requires careful construction and regular maintenance. This effort will be repaid many times over, especially if you include some form of running water to add sound and sparkling light to the scene.

Pond liners

It isn't a matter of simple chance that the number of garden ponds has greatly increased in recent years. Their popularity is in large part due to the availability of easily installed rigid and flexible pond liners, which make it possible to create a water garden by putting in just a few days' work.

In the past it was necessary to line a pond with concrete. While it is true that concrete is a very versatile material, there is always the possibility of a leak developing through cracks caused by ground movement or the force of expanding ice. There are no such worries with flexible liners or those made from rigid plastic. Building forms for a concrete pond involves both labor and expense, and when the pond is finished it has to be left to season for about a month, during which time it needs to be emptied and refilled a number of times to ensure that the water will be safe for fish and plant life. In contrast, you can introduce plants into a pool lined with plastic or rubber as soon as the water is warm, which takes no more than a few days.

Ordering a flexible liner

Use a simple formula to calculate the size liner you will need. Disregard any complicated shapes, planting shelves, and so on. Simply take the overall length and width of the pond and add twice the maximum depth to each dimension to arrive at the size of the liner. If possible, adapt your design to fall within the nearest stock liner size.

POND DIMENSIONS	
Length	9 ft. 9 in.
Width	6 ft. 6 in.
Depth	1 ft. 6 in.
SIZE OF LINER	
Length	9 ft. 9 in. + 3 ft. = 12 ft. 9 in.
Width	6 ft. 6 in. + 3 ft. = 9 ft. 6 in.

Choosing a pond liner

The advantages of manufactured pond liners over concrete are fairly obvious, but there are a number of options to choose from, depending on the size and shape of the pond you wish to create and how much you are planning to spend.

Pond under construction
This ambitious project utilizes a flexible liner in the construction of a water garden.

Rigid plastic liners

Regular visitors to garden centers will be familiar with the range of preformed plastic pond liners. A rigid liner is in effect a one-piece pond—including planting shelves and, in some cases, recessed troughs to accommodate marsh or bog gardens.

The best pond liners are those made from rigid fiberglass, which is very strong and is also resistant to damage from frost or ice. Almost as good, and more economical, are liners made from vacuum-formed plastic. Provided they are handled with care and installed correctly, rigid plastic pond liners are practically leakproof. A very substantial water garden can be created with a carefully selected series of pond liners linked together by watercourses.

Rigid pond liner
Rigid liners are molded from plastic.

Flexible liners

For complete freedom of design, choose a flexible sheet liner that will hug the contours of any shape and size pond. Flexible plastic pond liners range from inexpensive polyvinyl acetate and polyethylene sheets to better-quality low-density polyethylene and nylon-reinforced PVC. Plastic liners, especially those reinforced with nylon, are guaranteed for many years of normal use—but if you want your pond to last for 20 years or more, choose a thicker membrane made from synthetic butyl rubber. Black and stone-colored butyl liners are made in a wide range of stock sizes, up to 22 x 35 feet, and larger liners can be available as special orders.

Flexible liner
High-quality flexible pond liners are made from butyl rubber.

451

Constructing a pond

A pond must be sited correctly if it is to have any chance of maturing into an attractive, clear stretch of water. Don't place a pond under deciduous trees: Falling leaves will pollute the water as they decay, causing fish to become ill or die. Some trees are especially poisonous.

• Accommodating a sloping site
On a sloping site, build up the low side with soil, planting grass up to the paving surround. Either cut back the higher side and build a low retaining wall or embed stones in the soil to create a rock garden.

The need for sunlight
Although sunlight promotes the growth of algae, which cause ponds to turn a pea-green color, it is also necessary to encourage the growth of other water plants. An abundance of oxygenating plants will compete with the algae for mineral salts and, aided by the shade that is cast by floating and marginal plants, will help to keep the pond clear.

Volume of water
The pond's dimensions are important in creating harmony between plants and fish. It is difficult to maintain the right conditions for clear water in a pond that is less than 40 square feet in surface area. But the volume of water is even more vital. A pond up to about 100 square feet in area needs 18 inches depth. As the area increases, you will have to dig deeper, to 2 feet or more, although it's hardly ever necessary to dig deeper than 2½ feet.

Designing the shape of your pond
Although there's a huge variety of rigid plastic liners available, you are limited to the shapes selected by the manufacturers. There are no such limitations if you use a flexible pond liner, though curved shapes take up the slack better than straight-sided pools do.

The profile of the pond must be designed to fulfill certain requirements. To grow marginal plants, you will need a shelf 9 inches wide around the edge of the pond, 9 inches below the surface of the water. This will take a standard 6-inch planting crate, with ample water above, and you can always raise the crate on bricks if necessary. The sides of the pond should slope at about 20 degrees, to prevent the collapse of soil during construction and to allow the liner to stretch without creating too many creases. It will also allow a sheet of ice to float upward without damaging the liner. Judge the angle by measuring 3 inches in for every 9 inches of depth. If the soil is very sandy, increase the angle of slope slightly for extra stability.

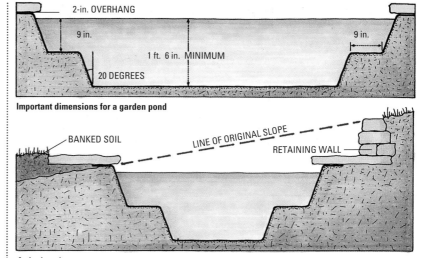

Important dimensions for a garden pond

A sloping site

Installing a rigid liner

Stand a rigid pond liner in position and prop it up with cardboard boxes to check its orientation and to mark its perimeter on the ground.

Use a level to plot key points on the ground **(1)** and mark them with small pegs. You will need to dig outside this line, so absolute accuracy is not required.

As you remove the topsoil, either take it away in a wheelbarrow or pile it close by, ready to incorporate into a rock garden later. Lay a straightedge across the top and measure the depth of the excavation **(2)**, including marginal shelves. Keep the excavation as close as possible to the shape of the liner, but extend it by 6 inches on all sides. Compact the base and cover it

with a layer of sand 1 inch deep.

Lower the liner and push it down firmly into the sand. Check that the pool is level **(3)** and wedge it temporarily with wooden boards until it is backfilled.

Start to fill the liner with water from a hose and, at the same time, pour soil or sand behind the liner **(4)**. There's no need to hurry because it will take some time to fill the pool. But try to keep pace with the level of the water. Reach into the excavation and pack soil under the marginal shelves with your hands.

When the liner is firmly bedded, finish the edge with stones as shown for a flexible liner (on the facing page) or plant grass to cover the rim of the liner.

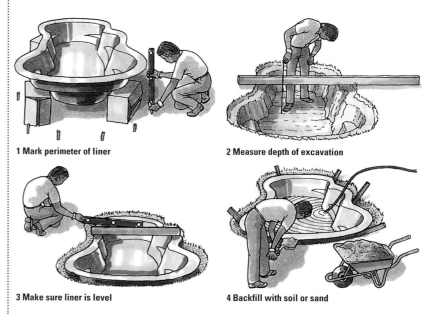

1 Mark perimeter of liner

2 Measure depth of excavation

3 Make sure liner is level

4 Backfill with soil or sand

Mark out the shape of the pond on the ground using a garden hose for the curved areas. Before you start excavating the soil, look down from an upstairs window (if possible) at the shape to make sure you are happy with the proportions of your pond.

Excavating the pond

Excavate the pond to the level of the planting shelf, then mark and dig out the deeper sections (1). Remove sharp stones and roots from the sides and bottom of the excavation.

The stones surrounding the pond need to be ¾ inch below the turf. Cut back the turf to allow for the stones and then, every 3 feet or so, drive wood pegs into the exposed surround. Level the tops of all the pegs, and use a straightedge (2) to check the level across the pond as well. Remove or pack soil around the pegs to bring the entire surround to a consistent level.

When the pond's surround is level, remove the pegs and, to cushion the liner, spread a ½- to 1-inch-thick layer of slightly damp sand over the base and sides of the excavation (3). Pack the sand carefully into the soil.

Installing the liner

Drape the liner across the excavation with an even overlap all around. Hold it in place with bricks while you fill it with water from a hose (4). Filling a large pond will take several hours, but check the liner regularly, moving the bricks as it stretches. A few creases are inevitable, but you can avoid most of them if you keep the liner taut and press it into shape as the water rises.

When the level reaches 2 inches below the edge, turn off the water. Cut off the extra liner with scissors, leaving a 6-inch overlap all around (5). Push long nails through the overlap into the soil, so the liner can't slip.

Laying the surround

Select flat stones that follow the shape of the pond, with a reasonably close fit between them. Let the stones project over the water by about 2 inches.

Wearing goggles, use a cold chisel and hammer to cut stones to fit any gaps. Lift the stones one or two at a time and bed them on two or three strategically placed mounds of mortar: 1 part cement to 3 parts soft sand (6).

Tap the stones level with a mallet and fill the joints with a trowel. Use an old paintbrush to smooth the joints flush. Don't drop mortar into the water, or you will have to empty and refill the pond before introducing fish or plants.

Every garden pond needs more water from time to time. And, as many gardeners know, it's all too easy to forget to turn off the water and flood the garden when the pond overflows. As a precaution, build a simple drain beneath the pond's edging stones to allow excess water to escape. This drain can also provide easy access for electrical cables servicing a pump or lights.

Cut corrugated-plastic sheet into two strips, about 6 inches wide and long enough to run under the edging stones. Pop-rivet the strips together to make a channel about 1 inch deep (1).

Scrape earth and sand from beneath the liner to accommodate the channel (2), then lay edging stones on top to hold it in place. Dig a small trench behind the channel and fill it with gravel, topped off with fine crushed stone up to the level of the edging.

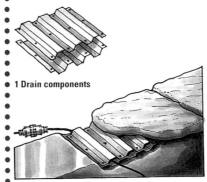

1 Drain components

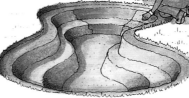

2 Place drain beneath edging stones

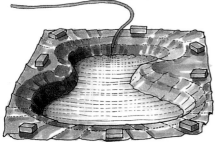

1 Dig excavation as accurately as possible

2 Level edge using wood pegs

3 Line excavation with damp sand

4 Stretch liner by filling pond

5 Cut flexible liner to fit

6 Lay edging stones to complete pond

453

Raised-edge ponds

If you want a more formal pond, you can build a raised edge using bricks or concrete blocks. A surround about 18 inches high serves as a deterrent for small children while also providing comfortable seating. If you prefer a lower wall, say 9 inches high, create planting shelves at ground level, digging the pond deeper in the center. Place planting crates on blocks around the edge of a deep raised pond.

Building the edging

Pour 4- to 6-inch-deep concrete footings to support walls. Below is shown a typical cavity wall built to match the width of flat coping stones. The coping stones overhang the water's edge by 2 inches and the outer wall side by ½ to ¾ inch. To save money, you may prefer to use common bricks or plain concrete blocks for the inner side, while reserving costlier decorative bricks or blocks for the outer side of the wall.

A raised pond can be lined with a standard flexible liner, or you can order a prefabricated fitted liner to reduce the amount of creasing at the corners.

Trap the edge of the liner underneath the coping stones.

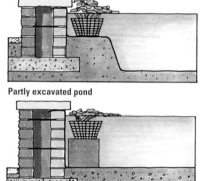

Partly excavated pond

Fully raised pond built with a cavity wall

Raised-edge pond
A beautifully designed water feature, built from artificial stone. The small cascade is powered by a submersible pump.

Alternative pond edging

Edging a pond with flat stones provides a safe and attractive footpath that is useful for tending water plants and fish, but often a more natural setting is desired, particularly for small pools in a rock garden. Incorporate a shelf around the pond for edging rocks. If you install them carefully, there is no need to mortar them in place. Add rocks behind the edging to cover the liner **(1)**.

In order to create a shallow, beach-like edging, slope the soil at a very shallow angle and lay large pebbles or flat rocks on the liner. You can merge them with a rock garden, or let them form a natural waterline **(2)**.

To discourage neighborhood cats from poaching fish from your pond, create an edging of trailing plants. Without a firm foothold, cats won't try to reach into the water. Embed a strip of soft wire netting in the mortar below flat edging stones, and cut the strip to overhang the water by about 6 inches as a support for the plants **(3)**. Once the plants are established, they will disguise the exposed edge of the pool liner.

1 Rock-edged pond

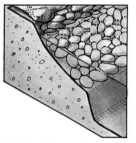

2 Pebble-strewn shelf

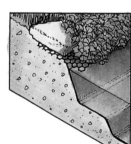

3 A wire edge supports plants

Submersible pumps for fountains and waterfalls are driven either by standard 120-volt power from the house service panel or by low voltage supplied through a transformer such as the ones used for low-voltage outdoor lighting. The combination of 120-volt electricity and water can be fatal. If you don't have experience working with electrical systems, hire a licensed electrician to install the necessary equipment.

A low-voltage pump is perfectly safe, and can be installed and wired simply. Place the pump in the water and run its cable under the edging stones to a transformer installed inside the house. Run the pump regularly, even in the winter, to keep it in good working order. Clean the pump and its filter according to the manufacturer's instructions.

Place a submersible waterfall pump close to the edge of the pond so that you can reach it to disconnect the supply hose when you need to service the pump. Stand a fountain unit on a flat stone or prop it up on bricks, so the jet of water is vertical. Plant water lilies some distance away from a fountain, because falling water will cause the flowers to close up.

Extra-low-voltage cascade pump and transformer

Combination fountain and cascade pump

Solar-powered pumps and lights

Solar-powered fountain pumps and lights can be bought as complete kits, including a panel of solar cells.

The lighting units contain a battery that stores the electricity produced by the solar cells during the day, and releases it to the lamps during the night. The pumps are designed to operate continuously. Solar-powered devices are not sufficiently powerful to supply cascades or spotlights.

A waterfall running through a tastefully planted rock garden adds another dimension to a water garden. The technique for building a series of waterways is not as complicated as you might expect. While working on them, you can do much of the groundwork needed to create the rock garden. Providing running water is also an ideal way of filtering your pond.

You will be surprised at the amount of soil produced by excavating a pond. To avoid waste and the trouble of transporting it elsewhere, use it to create a pool-side rock garden. If you include a filter and a small reservoir on the higher ground, you can pump water from the main pond through the filter into the reservoir and have it return via a waterfall.

If you order them from a garden center, buying a large number of natural stones to give the impression of a real rocky outcrop can be extremely expensive. A cheaper way is to use hollow-cast reproduction rocks that after some weathering can look very realistic. Or you can order natural stones direct from a quarry and have them delivered or pick them up yourself, and buy or rent a heavy-duty wheelbarrow to make the work easier.

A rock garden and waterfall are best built as one project, but for the sake of clarity they are described separately here.

Creating a waterfall

Rigid liner manufacturers make molded waterfall kits for embedding in rock gardens—you simply cover the edges with stones, soil, and trailing plants. You may prefer to create your own custom-made waterway, using pieces of flexible liner.

Installing the liner
So that the waterfall can discharge directly into the main pond, form a small inlet at the side of the pond by extending a large flap of flexible liner **(1)**. Build shallow banks at each side of the inlet and line it with stones. Create a stepped waterway ascending in stages to the reservoir. Line the waterway with flexible liner, overlapping the ends on the face of each waterfall. Tuck the edge of each lower piece of liner under the edge of the piece above, and hold the pieces in place with stones.

To retain water in small pools along the waterway, cut each step with a slope toward the rear **(2)** and place stones along the lip for the desired effect **(3)**. A flat stone will produce a sheet of water; a layer of pebbles will create rippling water.

As the construction work progresses, test the waterway by running water from a garden hose. It's difficult to adjust the angle of the stones once the waterway is done.

Bury the flexible hose from the pump in the rock garden—making sure there are no sharp bends, which would restrict the flow of water. Attach the hose to the filter tank at the top of the waterway **(4)**. Conceal the tank behind rocks where it can discharge filtered water into the reservoir.

A rigid plastic reservoir will have a lip molded in one edge, which allows water to escape down the waterway. If you use flexible liner to construct a reservoir **(5)**, you will need to shape the edge to form a low point **(6)** and support a flat stone over the opening in order to hide the liner.

Filter tanks
Pumps usually have built-in foam filters, but these are not sufficient to keep the water in a sizable pond clear and healthy enough for fish. It is preferable to install a plastic tank containing a combination of foam filters that will remove debris, plus a layer of biological filter medium to take out pollutants created by rotting vegetation.

Custom-made watercourse
This cross section shows a series of small waterfalls running from a reservoir to a pond.

1 Inlet   **4** Hose run to filter tank
2 Sloped step   **5** Reservoir
3 Edging stone   **6** Reservoir outlet

AVOIDING BACK STRAIN

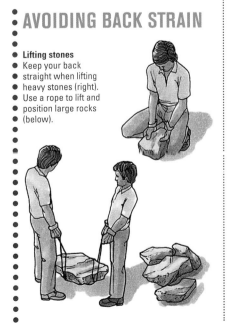

Lifting stones
● Keep your back straight when lifting heavy stones (right).
● Use a rope to lift and position large rocks (below).

Constructing a rock garden

To create an illusion of layers of rock, select and place each stone in a rock garden carefully. Stones placed haphazardly at odd angles tend to resemble a heap rather than a natural outcrop. Take care not to strain yourself when lifting rocks. Keep your feet together and use your leg muscles to do the work, keeping your back as straight as possible. To move a particularly heavy rock, slip a rope around it (see left).

Lay large, flat rocks to form the front edge of the rock garden, placing soil behind and between them to form a flat, level platform. Compact the soil to make sure there are no air pockets, which can damage the roots of plants.

Lay subsequent layers of rock behind the first ones, but not in a regular pattern. Place some to create steep embankments, others to form a gradual slope of wide steps. Brush soil off the rocks as the work progresses.

Pockets of soil for plantings will be formed naturally as you are laying the stones, but plan larger areas of soil for specimen shrubs or dwarf trees.

Building a rock garden
A rock garden should have irregular steps along its front edge.

Creating a pebble pool

One of the pleasures of a secluded garden is to be able to appreciate the natural sounds of rustling trees, singing birds, and, if you're particularly fortunate, the rippling of running water. As a rule, nature will provide the wind and the birds, but most of us have to supply the sound of running water ourselves. Given sufficient space, most people choose a fountain or a small waterfall trickling into a garden pond. But what if you have only a small garden or patio? A space-saving water feature offers an ideal solution. This doesn't have to involve anything more than a submersible recirculating pump installed in a small plastic pool set in the ground and covered with decorative pebbles. This type of water feature can be located next to the house, within earshot of the windows and doors.

Small-scale water feature
One pot rests on the rim of the other.

PEBBLES DISGUISE HOSE

HOSE FROM PUMP

TRAY

BACKFILL

PUMP

SUMP

Installing a molded pool

Molded plastic pools take the form of shallow round or square trays with a deep bucket for the center section or sump. A perforated or molded lid is provided to cover the sump, and to support the pebbles that are used to hide the feature once it's been installed.

Excavating the pool
Start by digging a hole slightly larger than the size of the tray. Make the hole deep enough to set the edge of the tray level with or just below the surface of the patio. You also need to allow for a layer of sand to be placed at the base of the hole. Set the sump in place and partially fill it with water to help keep it steady. Carefully backfill the sides with soil or sand. Then build up the backfill until the sump and tray are well supported and level.

Installing the pump
Following the manufacturer's instructions, connect the pump's cable to your power supply. If you are in any doubt about the installation, hire a licensed electrician.

Drill a discreet hole in a convenient place just above the house foundation for the pump's cable, and seal the gap around the cable with silicone caulk.

Connect a length of hose to the pump's water outlet and then place the pump in the sump, which you can now fill with water. Test that the pump is working. Lead the hose to one side and put the lid in place. It may be necessary to trim the edge of the lid in order to accommodate the hose.

Making the waterfall
Two ceramic plant pots can make an attractive waterfall. Balance one of the pots at an angle on the rim of the other one, and stand them on the tray. Feed the end of the hose into the drain hole in the bottom of the angled pot, and then seal the hole with silicone caulk. You may find this is easier to do if you disconnect the hose from the pump once the hose has been cut to length.

With the pots in position, place some attractive random-size pebbles around them to cover the pond tray. Put a few pebbles inside the angled pot, to weight it down and to conceal the end of the hose. Arrange potted plants to help disguise the hose at the rear. Run the pump, and try various arrangements of pebbles in and around the pots to create an attractive cascade of falling water.

ROUTINE MAINTENANCE

Add water to the buried pond occasionally to make up for natural evaporation. At the end of the season, remove the pump and clean the filter. This will mean rearranging the pebbles, which provides an opportunity to remove leaf litter and other debris.

Water pump
For a patio water feature, choose a small waterfall pump. If you're in doubt about the performance of a particular unit, talk to your supplier and read the manufacturer's literature.

Ever since well-to-do people used them to raise exotic plants and as places for relaxation, conservatories have been desirable additions to our homes. Today, with double glazing and efficient heating, they are used to extend the house, not only to provide an indoor garden but as living and dining rooms, workrooms, studios, and sometimes kitchens.

Conservatories are made in a range of standard sizes and styles. They are available in kit form for building yourself, but are usually professionally installed.

The materials used for constructing conservatories may include wood framing combined with low masonry walls, or they may be built primarily from aluminum or PVC components in either a traditional or modern style.

The transparent sections of the roof may be constructed with glass panes or consist of double-wall or triple-wall polycarbonate sheets.

For security reasons and to conserve energy, double-glazed sealed units are now the most commonly used glazing for the windows and doors.

It is worth studying the range of available designs in order to choose a conservatory that suits the style of your house. For example, a decorative Victorian-style conservatory might be acceptable for an ornate or period house, but it would probably look out of place alongside a modern building. On the other hand, a simple modern conservatory can sometimes look perfectly at home with an older house. The overall proportions of the conservatory and the quality of the construction and the building materials are important factors to consider, too.

From the practical point of view, bear in mind that wood frames and panels need painting from time to time, and even stained frames benefit from an occasional touchup with wood stain. Like PVC frames, factory-finished aluminum frames should require little, if any, maintenance.

Heating and ventilation

Conservatories need efficient temperature controls if they are not to be too hot in summer or too cold in winter. The large expanse of glass is designed to absorb natural heat from the sun quickly, but it can just as quickly lose heat during cold weather.

Double glazing is essential to retain the heat gained from sunlight, particularly if a conservatory is to be used all year round. Ideally, low-emissivity glass should be installed, as it reflects the absorbed heat back into the room. However, during the winter months, when the sun's rays are weak and outside temperatures are low, it's necessary to provide internal heating. This is usually supplied by an extension to the house's central heating system or by individual space heaters.

During the summer, the heat can rise to uncomfortable levels. One way to overcome this is to install blinds for both the windows and the roof. Special heat-reflective blinds provide shade in the summer and reduce heat loss in the winter. Conservatory suppliers usually can provide blinds to meet your requirements. Another option is to stick special self-adhesive vinyl sheeting to the glazing. This reusable material can be applied to the inside or the outside, and is held in place by static electricity only.

However effective your blinds may be, good ventilation is essential, not only to deflect heat in summer but also to reduce condensation in winter. Most conservatories have operable windows or vents to provide cross-ventilation. Roof ventilators are normally manually operated, but temperature-controlled automatic systems are also available.

The period style of this conservatory complements the character of the house and garden.

Choosing the site

Some areas of the country may not require a building permit for a small conservatory or greenhouse addition, but most certainly will. A quick trip to your local building department should answer any questions you may have about structure size, location, and style.

Before committing to your preferred design, check the manufacturer's specification in order to establish the size of the conservatory in relation to your site. Make sure there are no problems with drainage and with the proximity of trees or other features.

Apart from such practical concerns, which may include ensuring a means of access from the house, your choice of location should take into consideration the direction of the sun. A conservatory built on a south-facing wall will benefit from sunlight all the year round and, as a result, would provide a cozy environment in the winter. However, in high summer the same conservatory is likely to become unpleasantly hot unless you provide efficient ventilation and shade.

A west-facing conservatory receives less direct sunlight, but could allow you to enjoy the setting sun during the late afternoon and evening. East-facing conservatories are ideal for an informal breakfast, with the possibility of early-morning sunshine. A north-facing site will receive little direct sunlight, and to be comfortable will usually require heating for most of the winter. A corner site may provide you with a wide range of benefits for much of the day.

Building conservatories

Although a conservatory is a relatively lightweight structure, it nevertheless requires a strong base. Your existing patio, for example, will probably not be suitable. A concrete base is the usual solution. But a special metal-frame platform, which requires less site preparation, is a possible alternative.

Conservatory suppliers will specify a typical base for their products. But because sites vary, you'll have to consult with your local building department to establish its requirements for foundations, perimeter drainage, and proper ventilation.

Extended living space
A well-constructed and insulated conservatory will add space and value to your home.

Types of concrete base

A typical base for a conservatory is a slab of concrete 4 to 6 inches thick, laid over well-compacted gravel that is a minimum of 4 inches thick. It should also have footings around the perimeter that conform with local building codes and suit the ground conditions. The base may be constructed as a monolithic concrete slab, which combines the footings (1). Or it can be built like a conventional foundation with concrete footings that support masonry walls, which surround the concrete slab (2).

The floor must incorporate a continuous vapor barrier underneath the slab to prevent water vapor and moisture from rising through the slab.

Constructing a base

A standard conventional foundation is described here. Start by marking out the finished floor level with a chalkline on the house wall. Using form boards, lay out the area of the foundation, following closely the dimensions supplied by the conservatory manufacturer. Use a plumb line to check whether the house wall is vertical. If it leans out, set the base dimensions from the plumb line, not the wall.

The footings should be 1 foot wide for a wall of single-brick construction, or 18 inches wide for a cavity wall with a 2-inch cavity. For most sites, the footings will need to be at least 16 inches thick, starting at a depth required by your local building department. Dig the necessary trenches and pour in concrete to the required level.

Once the concrete has set, excavate the area within the footings, allowing for the thickness of the floorcovering, concrete slab, insulation board (if required), and the compacted gravel base. Lay the perimeter wall up to at least 6 inches above ground level.

When the mortar has set, lay a bed of well-compacted gravel in the excavation and cover it with 2 inches of sand. Screed the sand until it is level. Then lay a polyethylene vapor barrier over the sand, with the edges of the sheet overlapping the inside surface of the walls.

Insulation board is an excellent product and you should seriously consider installing it before you pour the slab. It will keep the floor warmer in the winter and cooler in the summer. Not all building codes require underslab insulation, but it's well worth the money.

Complete the base (usually after you erect the frame) by pouring a concrete slab, followed, when fully dry, by the floorcovering.

Erecting the frame
The frame sills must be installed level, and the modular frames mounted squarely. Following the manufacturer's instructions, erect the frame units. Any gaps at the junctions with the wall of the house should be filled with silicone caulk.

The roof-wall rafter should also be sealed and covered with a traditional aluminum flashing. If the house wall is brick, the step flashing should be tucked into mortar joints. If the house has wood siding, the flashing should be installed underneath the siding shingles or clapboards. The manufacturer's directions should explain how the flashing is joined to the conservatory roof framing.

INSULATING

- Some building codes require under-floor insulation only in rooms that are permanently open to the rest of the house. However, it makes sense to include insulation in any case, because it will help conserve energy.

- Foam insulation board, up to 2 inches thick, is installed as the floor is being laid. Insulation is normally placed under the concrete slab (1), but it can be placed just below the floorcovering (2). If the flooring is thin, like sheet vinyl, the insulation must go below the slab. If the flooring is solid wood, the insulation can go between furring strips nailed to the concrete slab.

FLOOR FINISH
VAPOR BARRIER
CONCRETE BASE
GRAVEL
SOIL

1 Monolithic slab foundation

KNEE WALL
VAPOR BARRIER   FLOOR
CONCRETE SLAB
GRAVEL
SOIL
CONCRETE FOOTING

2 Conventional foundation

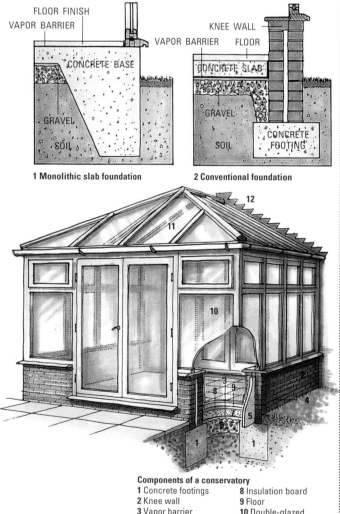

Components of a conservatory
1 Concrete footings
2 Knee wall
3 Vapor barrier
4 Damp-proof course
5 Cavity insulation
6 Gravel
7 Concrete slab
8 Insulation board
9 Floor
10 Double-glazed wall units
11 Double-glazed roof units
12 Flashing

CONCRETE SLAB
INSULATION
FLOORING
VAPOR BARRIER

1 Insulation under concrete slab

FLOORING
INSULATION
VAPOR BA
CONCRETE SLAB

2 Insulation under flooring

Woodworking tools

If you talk to people who make a living using tools, you will find that they guard them jealously: they are loath to lend their tools and even less likely to borrow them. The way a person uses or sharpens a tool – even his or her working stance – will shape and modify it until it works better for its owner than in other hands. This is particularly noticeable with old wooden tools. If you examine the sole of a well-used wooden jack plane, for example, you will see that it has worn unevenly to suit the style of one person. Even the handle of a new plane feels unfamiliar after the feel of a plane you have used for years.

When it comes to building up a kit, the choice of tools is equally personal. No two professionals' tool kits are identical, and each might select different tools to do the same job. The tools shown and described on these pages will enable you to tackle all but the most specialized tasks involved in repairing, maintaining, extending, and decorating your home and garden, although the final choice is yours.

Very few people buy a complete set of tools all at once. Apart from the considerable cost, it makes more sense to buy tools as you need them. You may prefer to do your own decorating yet hire a professional for electrical work, in which case you are better off spending your money on good-quality brushes, rollers, or scrapers than spreading it thinly on a wider range of cheaper tools. We have therefore listed the essential tools for each "trade" under specific headings – plumber's tools, decorator's tools, and so on. But a great many tools are common to all trades, and you will find that you will gradually add to your collection as you tackle a growing range of activities.

Tools can cost a lot of money, but it's worth buying the best you can afford, for top-quality tools are always a wise investment. Not only will they perform well but they will last longer, provided that they are used, stored, and maintained properly. Power tools are especially expensive, so unless you plan to use them regularly it may be more economical to rent them. Make sure that rented tools are in good condition and ask for a set of written instructions or a demonstration before you leave the rental store.

It's impossible to produce first-class work with cutting tools that are blunt; they are also more dangerous than sharp ones. Keep the blades in good condition and discard disposable blades when they no longer cut smoothly and easily. You can sharpen and maintain hand tools yourself, but it's advisable to have power tools serviced professionally.

WOODWORKER'S TOOLS

A full woodworking tool set is enormous, but for general home maintenance you can make do with a fairly limited selection. The most essential tools are listed in the page margins as a guide to building up a basic kit.

TOOLS FOR MEASURING AND MARKING

* * * * * * * * * *

Take care of your measuring and marking tools. If they are thrown carelessly into a tool box, try squares can be knocked out of true, and gauges will become blunt and inaccurate.

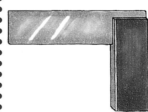

Tape measure and folding rule
A folding boxwood rule is the traditional cabinet-maker's tool, but a modern tape measure is more versatile.

Choose a tape that is about 25 feet long, and which can be locked open at any point so that even a large workpiece can be measured single-handedly.

Don't let the spring-loaded tape snap back into its case, or the hook riveted to the end of the tape will eventually work loose.

Try square
A try square is used for checking the accuracy of jointed corners and planed lumber and also for marking out workpieces that are to be cut "squared."

Choose a try square that has the blade and handle cut from a single L-shaped piece of metal – one with a straight blade riveted to the handle may lose its accuracy.

Some try squares are made with the top of the stock cut at 45 degrees for marking miter joints.

It's worth buying the largest square you can afford: they are available with blades up to 1 foot long.

Checking an internal angle

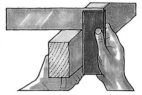

Checking planed lumber
View the work against the light to check you are planing square.

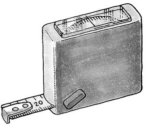

Combination square
A combination square is a very versatile tool. Essentially, it is a try square, but instead of a fixed blade it has a calibrated rule that slides in the stock to make a blade of any length up to 12 inches. This serves as a useful depth gauge. The head has an angled face for marking miters and incorporates a small spirit level for checking vertical and horizontal surfaces.

Checking for level
To use the tool as a spirit level, remove the blade and place the stock on the horizontal surface.

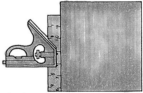

Checking verticals
Place the blade against a vertical face and read the spirit level to check it is perpendicular.

Sliding bevel
A sliding bevel is similar to a standard try square, but its blade can be adjusted to check or mark any angle.

Marking knife

Before sawing lumber, mark the cutting line with a knife – this is more accurate than using a pencil and helps to keep the wood fibers from tearing out when you saw across the grain. The blade of a marking knife is ground on one side only; run the flat face against the square or bevel.

Marking gauge

With a marking gauge, you can score a line parallel to an edge. Slide the fence along the beam until it is the required distance from the pin. Press the face of the fence against the edge of the workpiece and, with the pin touching the wood's surface, push the tool away from you to scribe the line.

Cutting gauge

If you try to score a line across the grain with a marking gauge, the pin will tear the surface; whereas a cutting gauge – which has a small sharp blade – is ideal for the purpose. The blade is held in place by a removable wedge.

Mortise gauge

This type of gauge has two pins, one fixed and the other movable, for marking the parallel sides of mortise-and-tenon joints. First set the points to match the width of the mortise chisel, then adjust the stock to place the mortise the required distance from the edge of the wood. Carefully mark the ends of the mortise, using a try square (**1**), then score the two lines with the gauge (**2**). With the same setting, mark the tenon on the rail.

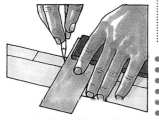

1 Mark the limits of the mortise

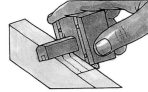

2 Score the lines

HANDSAWS

Handsaws, with their flexible unsupported blades, are used to cut solid lumber and manufactured panels such as plywood and hardboard. All handsaws are similar in appearance but each type is made with different-shaped teeth that are designed for a specific purpose.

Ripsaw

The ripsaw is designed for a ripping cut – sawing solid lumber along its length. Each of its teeth is like a tiny chisel that slices the wood along the grain. Alternate teeth are "set" (bent outward in opposite directions) so that the "kerf" (the groove that's cut) is slightly wider than the thickness of the blade. If saws were not set, they would jam in the kerf.

Crosscut saw

Unlike ripsaw teeth, which are filed square with the face of the blade, crosscutting teeth are filed at an angle to form points that score lines along both sides of the kerf before the wood in between is removed. This allows the saw to cut across the grain of solid lumber without tearing the fibers. The teeth on crosscut saws are also set to provide clearance and keep the tool from binding in the kerf.

Panel saw

The teeth of a panel saw are set and shaped like those of a crosscut saw but, being smaller and closer together, they cut a finer kerf. The saw is used for cutting man-made boards such as plywood and hardboard.

STORING SAWS

Glue dowel pegs into a stout board and screw it to the wall. Hang your saws from the pegs, protecting their teeth with removable plastic strips.

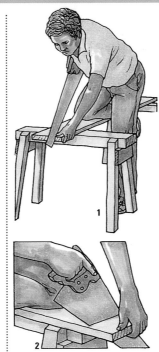

1

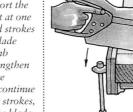

2

Using handsaws

Hold the saw with your forefinger extended towards the tip of the blade. This keeps the blade in line with your forearm and helps you to make a straight cut.

When ripsawing, support the board on sawhorses. Start at one end using short backward strokes only, steadying the saw blade with the tip of your thumb against its flat face (1). Lengthen your stroke once you have established the kerf, and continue cutting with slow regular strokes, using the full length of the blade. When necessary, move the sawhorses to provide a clear path for the blade. As you approach the end of the board, turn it round and start a fresh cut from that end, sawing back to meet the original kerf.

When crosscutting, support the waste with your free hand (2) and finish the cut with slow gentle strokes to avoid breaking off the last few wood fibers.

BACKSAWS

The blade of a backsaw is stiffened with a heavy metal strip folded over its top edge. The relatively fine teeth make it ideal for cutting joints.

Tenon saw

A tenon saw has small teeth shaped and set like those of a crosscut saw. It is the perfect saw for general-purpose woodworking and joinery.

Dovetail saw

Because the tails and pins of a dovetail joint run with the grain, the teeth of a dovetail saw are like miniature ripsaw teeth. Use this saw for fine cabinet-making.

Gent's saw

This cheap alternative to a dovetail saw has a straight handle.

Using backsaws

Support the work in a vice or on a bench hook and hold the saw at a shallow angle to establish the kerf. As the cut progresses, gradually level the blade until you are sawing parallel to the face of the wood.

Using a bench hook

A bench hook is a simple jig, used when crosscutting narrow pieces of wood with a backsaw. Steady the "hook" against the front edge of the bench, then clamp the work firmly against the top block with one hand.

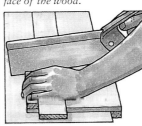

Using a miter box

A miter box has slots set at 45 degrees to guide the saw blade when you are cutting miter joints. There are also slots set at 90 degrees to guide the blade when cutting square butt joints.

● **Essential tools**
Tape measure
Combination square
Marking knife
Marking gauge
Crosscut saw
Tenon saw

461

Woodworking tools

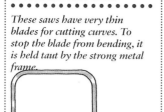

COPING AND FRET SAWS

These saws have very thin blades for cutting curves. To stop the blade from bending, it is held taut by the strong metal frame.

Coping saw
A coping saw has teeth that are coarse enough to cut fairly thick wood as well as relatively thin man-made boards.

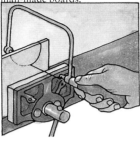

Using a coping saw
The blade is held between pins that swivel so you can turn it in the direction of the cut, swinging the frame out of the way.

Fitting a coping-saw blade
A coping-saw's blade has to be replaced if it breaks or when it gets dull. Loosen the handle with a few counterclockwise turns. Hook the new blade into the pin farthest from the handle, then press the frame down on your workbench and locate the other end of the blade. Tension the blade by turning the handle clockwise. Make sure the teeth point toward the handle and that the two pins are aligned so the blade isn't twisted.

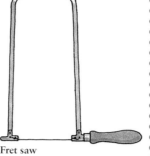

Fret saw
A fret-saw blade is so fine that the spring of the frame is able to keep it under tension. The blade is held at each end by a thumb-screw and plate, with the teeth pointing toward the handle.

Using a fret saw
Hold the wood over the edge of the workbench so you can saw with the blade upright, pulling on it from below.

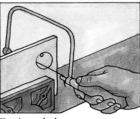

Cutting a hole
Use a coping saw to cut a large hole in a piece of wood. Lay out the cut line and drill a small hole inside the area. Pass the blade through the small hole, then connect it to the saw frame. Cut out the hole, adjusting the angle of the blade to the frame as required, then dismantle the saw in order to free the blade.

KEYHOLE SAW

A keyhole saw is designed for cutting holes in panels. Having a blade that is wider than a coping saw's, it's easier to use on straight cuts. As there's no frame to restrict its movement, this saw can be used for jobs such as cutting the slot for a letter box.

SHARPENING SAWS

To cut properly, saws must be sharpened carefully with special tools, so you may prefer to have them sharpened professionally, especially any that are finer than a tenon saw. If you want to keep them in tip-top condition yourself, you will need to buy a saw file for sharpening the teeth and a saw set for bending the teeth to the required angle.

Saw-sharpening tools
A saw file is tapered and triangular in cross section. In theory, its length should relate precisely to the spacing of the saw's teeth, but in practice you can use one file about 6in long for handsaws and another, about 4in long, for a tenon saw. Some people use a file guide, which is placed over the saw's teeth and keeps the file at a constant angle while in use.

Closing the handles of a saw set squeezes the saw tooth between a plunger and an angled anvil, which you set first to correspond with the number of tooth points per 1in on the saw blade (**1**). To set the anvil, close the handles and release the locking screw at the end of the tool. Turn the anvil until the required setting number on its edge aligns with the plunger, then tighten the locking screw.

Jointing a saw
*Jointing restores all of a saw's teeth to the same height. It is not absolutely essential every time a saw is sharpened, but a light jointing will produce a spot of bright metal on each point that will help you to sharpen the teeth evenly. Near the top edge of a block of hardwood, cut a groove that will grip a smooth flat file (**2**). Clamp the saw, teeth pointing up, between two battens held in a vice and, with the wood block held against the flat of the blade, pass the file two or three times along the tops of the teeth (**3**) so that each one shows a tiny spot of bright metal.*

Setting the teeth
*Adjust the saw set to the right number of points (see above) and, starting at one end of the saw, place the set over the first tooth facing away from you. Align the plunger with the center of the tooth. Hold the set steady and squeeze the handles together (**4**). Set every other tooth – those facing away from you – then turn the saw round and set those in between.*

(Continued opposite)

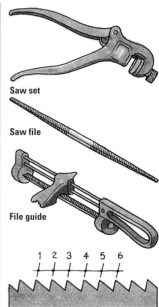

Saw set

Saw file

File guide

1 2 3 4 5 6

1 Count the number of points per 1in

2 Mount a file in a hardwood block

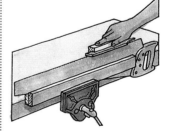

3 Top the saw with the file

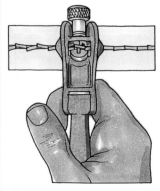

4 Set the saw teeth

SHARPENING SAWS

Sharpening a ripsaw

Clamp the blade between two battens with its teeth projecting just above the edges of the wood. Starting near the toe of the saw, place the saw file on the first tooth bent away from you, and against the leading edge of the tooth next to it. Holding the file square to the blade (5), make two or three strokes until the edge of the tooth is shiny right up to its point and half of the bright jointing spot has disappeared. Working towards the handle, file alternate teeth in this way, then turn the saw round and sharpen those in between until the bright spots are completely removed.

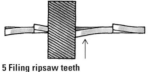

5 Filing ripsaw teeth

Sharpening a crosscut saw

Use a similar method, but hold the file at an angle of 65 degrees to the blade (6), with the tip of the file pointing in the direction of the saw handle.

6 Filing the teeth of a crosscut saw

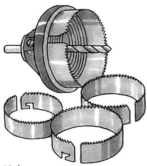

Hole saw

You can buy a set of hole saws for cutting perfectly round holes of different diameters. These are attached to an arbor and drill bit that's then secured in the chuck of a power drill. Place the tip of the twist drill at the center of the required hole, set the power tool to a slow speed, and push the revolving saw against the wood. Always place a piece of scrap stock behind the work to keep the saw from breaking out the back of the workpiece.

POWER SAWS

Power saws are invaluable for cutting heavy lumber and large manufactured panels such as plywood. Cordless saws are convenient, but their batteries provide sufficient power only for relatively short periods.

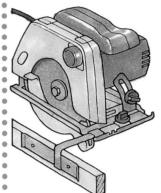

Portable circular saw

When you buy or rent a circular saw for general use, choose one with a blade no smaller than 7¼ inch in diameter. Its motor will be powerful enough to cut thick lumber and man-made materials without straining the saw or scorching the work. You can buy blades designed specifically for ripping or crosscutting, but a sharp combination blade can perform both functions reasonably well. The best-quality blades have carbide-tipped teeth. There are also special blades and abrasive discs for cutting metal, stone, and masonry. On most circular saws, you can adjust the angle of the blade for cutting bevels.

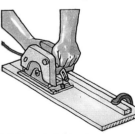

Making straight cuts

Circular saws have removable fences to guide the blade parallel to the edge of the work. When necessary, you can extend the fence by screwing a batten to it. Alternatively, clamp a strip of wood onto the work to guide the edge of the saw's sole plate.

Clamping the strip at different angles across the wood allows you to make miters and other beveled cuts.

Sawing freehand

When accuracy of cut is not too important you can use a circular saw freehand, employing the notch in the base plate as a sight to guide the blade along a marked line. Place the tip of the baseplate on the work and align the notch with the line. Turn the saw on and advance the saw steadily.

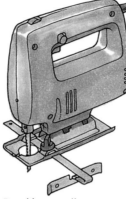

Reciprocating saws

With blades up to 6in long, these saws are especially useful for such jobs as cutting openings in stud partitions.

Portable power jigsaw

Corded and cordless jigsaws are primarily for making curved cuts in lumber and man-made materials. Although they invariably have guide fences for straight cutting, the fences are rarely sturdy enough to stop the blade from wandering. Discard jigsaw blades when they become dull. As jigsaw blades are fairly cheap, it's worth buying some of the special blades for cutting plastics, metal, drywall, and ceramics.

Using a jigsaw

Rest the front of the base plate on the edge of the work, squeeze the trigger, and then advance the blade into the work. Don't force or twist the blade, or it will break. When you turn the saw off, wait until the blade stops moving before you put the saw down.

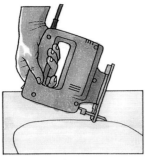

1 Preparing to plunge-cut

Cutting holes with a jigsaw

The simplest way to cut a large hole in a panel is first to drill a starter hole into which you can insert the jigsaw blade, but you can start by "plunge cutting." Tilt the jigsaw onto the front edge of its baseplate, with the tip of the blade just above the surface of the work (1); then turn on the saw and gradually lower the blade into the wood until it is upright and the base plate is flat on the surface.

CIRCULAR-SAW SAFETY

A circular saw is perfectly safe to use provided that you follow the manufacturer's handling and fitting instructions carefully, and observe the following rules:

- Always unplug a circular saw before you adjust or change the blade.
- Don't use a dull blade. Have it sharpened professionally.
- Install new blades according to supplied instructions. Check that the teeth at the bottom of the blade are facing in the direction of the cut.
- Circular saws must have a fixed blade guard and a lower guard that swings back as the cut proceeds. Never use the saw without these guards in place, and always make sure that the lower guard closes automatically when the blade clears the work.
- The work must be securely held, either on sawhorses or a workbench.
- Never have the power cord in front of the saw blade.
- Don't force the blade into the wood. If it jams in the kerf, back off a little until it returns to full speed.
- Make sure the blade has stopped spinning before you put down a circular saw.
- Don't wear loose clothing, or a necktie or necklace, as any of these could become entangled in the machine.

Saw bench

For heavy-duty work, it might be worth buying a bench top table saw. These are essentially circular saws mounted upside down in a table. They come with a miter gauge and rip fence for making accurate crosscuts and ripping cuts.

● **Essential tools**
Power jigsaw

Woodworking tools

BENCH PLANES

Bench planes are general-purpose tools for smoothing wood to make joints between boards or to level the surface of several boards glued together. Bench planes are all similar in design, differing only in the length of the sole.

Jointer plane
This is the longest bench plane, with a sole as much as 2ft long. The jointer is designed for truing up the long edges of boards that are to be butted and glued together. It is also useful for leveling large flat panels, since the long sole bridges minor irregularities so the blade can shave them down – whereas a plane with a shorter sole would simply follow the uneven surface.

Jack plane
A 14 to 15in-long jack plane is a good all-purpose tool. If you can afford only one bench plane, choose a jack plane.

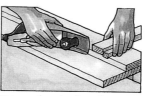

Smoothing plane
A finely set smoothing plane is used for putting the final surface on a piece of wood after it has been reduced to size with a jack plane or jointer plane.

STORING PLANES

It is good practice never to place a plane sole-down on the bench while you are working – always lay it on its side.

Similarly, a plane should be stored on its side and with the blade withdrawn to protect its cutting edge.

For long-term storage, dismantle and clean the plane, then wipe all bare metal parts with an oily rag to prevent rusting. Dispose of oil-soaked rags safely – they are a fire risk if kept in a workshop.

● **Essential tools**
Jack plane
Block plane

1 Checking the blade angle

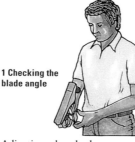

Adjusting a bench plane
*Before you use a bench plane, adjust the angle and depth of the blade. Check the angle by "sighting" down the sole of the plane from the toe **(1)**, and use the lateral-adjustment lever behind the blade to set the cutting edge so that it projects an equal amount across the width of the sole. Use the knurled adjusting nut in front of the handle to set the depth to take off a fine shaving.*

Planing a square edge
Keep the plane flat on the edge of the work by holding the toe down with the thumb of your free hand and press the fingers of the same hand against the side of the wood to guide the tool on a straight path.

Planing a wide flat surface
To plane a wide surface as flat as possible, first work across it diagonally in two directions, following the general direction of the grain. Check that the work is flat by holding a steel straight-edge against the surface, then finish by planing parallel with the grain, taking very fine shavings.

Block plane
The blade of a block plane is mounted at a shallow angle so that its edge can slice smoothly through the end grain of the wood. Since it is small and light-weight (you can hold the tool in the palm of one hand), a block plane is also ideal for all kinds of fine trimming and shaping.

Trimming end grain
Cut a line all round the work with a marking knife, then set the workpiece vertically in a vice. To prevent the wood splitting, form a chamfer down to the line on one edge by planing toward the center. Plane the end square, working from the other edge down to the marked line until you have removed the chamfer.

Using a shooting board
You can also trim end grain, using a bench plane on its side, running on a jig known as a shooting board. The blade must be sharp and finely set. Holding the work against the jig's stop prevents the wood splitting.

Shoulder plane
A shoulder plane is not a tool you need every day, but, because its blade spans the width of its squarely machined body, it is ideal for trimming the square shoulders of large joints and rabbets. With the front of the body removed, the exposed blade can trim a rabbet right up to a stopped end.

Power planers
A power planer is particularly useful for smoothing and shaping large pieces of wood, and it is perfect for trimming the bottom edge of a door in order to accommodate a new carpet. When the tool is fitted with a fence, its revolving cutter can be used for planing rabbets. Some power planes can be fixed upside down in a bench-mounted frame so that you can pass timber across the cutters, using both hands.

SPOKESHAVES

A spokeshave is a miniature plane for shaping curved edges.

Use one that has a flat base to shape convex curves, and one with a convex base when shaping concave curves. When using either tool, shape the curve from two directions so as to work with the grain at all times. Sharpen a spokeshave cutter as you would the blade of a plane.

Adjusting the cutter
Use the two adjusting screws to produce a fine setting, then tighten the locking screw to secure the spokeshave's cutter.

Using a spokeshave
With your thumbs on the back edges of the handles, push the spokeshave away from you. Rock the tool backward or forward as you work to produce a continuous shaving.

Woodworking tools

MOLDING PLANES

Woodworkers often need to cut grooves in wood, both with and across the grain, and to plane rabbets or moldings along the edges of workpieces.

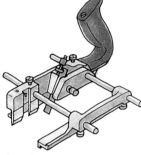

Plow plane
A plow plane takes narrow blades for cutting grooves. You can only use it in the direction of the grain.

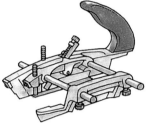

Combination plane
A combination plane can be used, with a variety of shaped blades, to cut grooves or rabbets and a number of molding profiles. It has a pair of vertically adjusting blades – called "spurs" – that cut parallel lines ahead of the main blade in order to prevent tearing the wood fibers when a dado is planed across the grain. You can also use a combination plane to cut tongue-and-groove joints along the edges of boards.

Rabbet plane
A rabbet plane is similar to a bench plane, but its blade spans the whole width of the sole. With its depth gauge and guide fence set to the required dimensions, the plane will cut any number of identical rabbets.

1 Starting a molding

Using molding planes
Whether you are using a plow, combination or rabbet plane, follow the maker's instructions for setting the depth gauge and fence, which together control the position of the blade relative to the surface and edge of the wood.

Hold the fence against the edge of the workpiece at the far end and make short strokes to begin the molding (1) – and then move backward, making longer and longer strokes until the depth gauge rests on the surface of the wood. Finish with one continuous pass along the length of the workpiece.

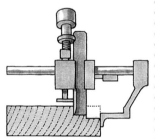

Cutting an extra-wide rabbet
If you need to cut a rabbet wider than the standard blade, first plane a rabbet on the outer edge, then adjust the fence to make a second cut that will make up the required width.

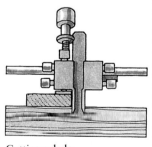

Cutting a dado
When using a combination plane to cut a dado (a groove across the grain), remove the fence and clamp a batten across the workpiece in order to guide the body of the plane.

SHARPENING PLANES

To keep its sharp cutting edge, a plane blade must be honed on a flat oilstone. Choose one with a medium grit on one side to remove metal quickly and fine grit on the other side for the final honing of the edge.

LEVER CAP   CAP IRON   BLADE
LATERAL-ADJUSTMENT LEVER
BOLT
ADJUSTMENT NUT

Removing and replacing a blade
The blade of a bench or block plane is clamped in place by a metal lever cap. Slacken the lever to remove the cap and lift the blade out of the plane. The blade of a bench plane has a cap iron bolted to it to break and curl the shavings as they are trimmed from the wood. Undo the bolt with a screwdriver and remove the cap iron before you sharpen the blade.

When you replace the cap iron, place it across the blade (1), then swivel it until the two are aligned (2), making sure you don't drag the cap iron across the cutting edge in the process. Now slide the iron to about ¹⁄₃₂ to ¹⁄₁₆in of the edge (3).

Honing a blade
The cutting edge of a plane blade will have been ground to an angle of about 25 degrees. The object of sharpening it on an oilstone is to hone the leading edge only to about 30 degrees.

Hold the blade against the stone at the correct angle and rub it back and forth to produce a sharp edge. A wide blade must be held at an angle across the stone so that the whole edge is in contact with the surface (1). Keep the stone lubricated with a little oil while you work.

Honing creates a burr along the cutting edge. Remove it by laying the back face of the blade flat on the stone (2) and making several passes along the surface.

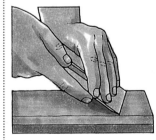

1 Hone the cutting edge

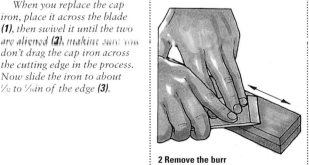

2 Remove the burr

Using a honing guide
To be certain that you are honing a blade to the correct angle, clamp it in a honing guide and roll the guide back and forth on the surface of the oilstone to sharpen the blade.

Repairing a chipped cutting edge
If you chip the cutting edge of a plane blade (against a nail, for example), regrind it on a bench grinder. Hold the blade against the tool rest and move the cutting edge from side to side against the revolving wheel until it is straight and clean. Use only light pressure and dip the blade into water regularly to cool it. Finally, sharpen the ground edge by honing it on an oilstone.

● **Essential tools**
Combination oilstone

Woodworking tools

ROUTERS

A router plane is used to finish the bottom of a dado after most of the waste has been cut out with a chisel. An electric router is a sophisticated tool that replicates the various tasks performed by a combination plane. A router bit revolves so fast that it produces as clean a cut across the grain as with it.

Router plane

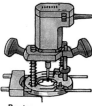

Router

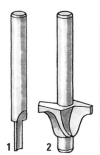

Router bits
1 Straight bit
2 Ogee bit

● Essentials tools
Firmer chisels
  ⅛ to 1in
Bevel-edge chisels
  ½ to 1in
Gouges
  Select sizes as required
Mortise chisels
  Select sizes as required

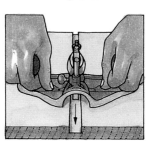

Using a router plane
To pare the bottom of a dado, hold one handle of the router in each hand and push it away from you, as you would a plane.

Using a router
Always let the bit reach full speed before you allow it to come into contact with the work, and lift it clear of the workpiece before you switch off. For safety and good control, feed the router against the bit rotation when cutting the edges of lumber.

Router cutters and bits
Router plane cutters have square shafts that clamp into the tool and are adjusted vertically to set the chisel-like cutting edges at the required depth.

Bits for electric routers are secured in a collet at the base of the tool and are locked in place by tightening a nut. Some router bits have a fixed or ball-bearing pilot that's held against the stock edge to guide the cut and prevent it from cutting too deeply. Bits without a pilot must be used with a fence, guide bushing, or shop-made guide strip.

High-speed steel bits are relatively inexpensive but dull quickly – especially in hard wood. Carbide-tipped bits stay sharp far longer.

Follow the manufacturer's instructions when fitting and adjusting router bits and cutters.

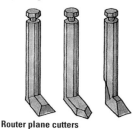

Router plane cutters

Sharpening a router plane cutter
Hone dull router plane cutters on an oilstone. Position the stone so the cutter's shaft will clear the bench, then rub the cutter from side to side on the stone.

Cutting grooves and dadoes
*To cut a groove parallel to an edge, set the adjustable guide fence (**1**) or run the edge of the base against a guide strip clamped to the work (**2**). To cut a wide groove, use two parallel strips to guide the bit along the outer edges (**3**), then remove the waste from the center.*

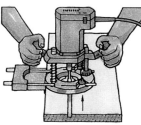

1 Using a fence

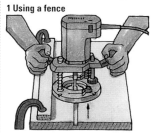

2 Using a guide strip

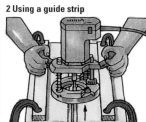

3 Cutting a wide groove

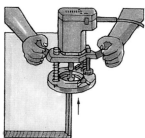

Cutting edge moldings
Rest the base of the router on the surface of the work and when the cutter has reached full speed, feed it against and along the edge of the workpiece.

If you need to shape all four edges of a rectangular piece of wood, rout the end grain first and then run the bit along each side of the work.

SHARPENING ROUTER BITS

Although it is possible to touch up high-speed steel router bits with a stone or grinder, it is generally better to replace them when they get dull. Sharpening carbide bits requires special tooling and the job should be done by a professional.

CHISELS AND GOUGES

Chisels are general-purpose woodcutting tools but are used mostly to remove the waste from joints or to pare and trim them to size. The size of a chisel refers to the width of its cutting edge. Although chisels range in width from ⅛ to 2in, a selection of sizes up to 1in should be sufficient for most woodworking purposes.

Gouges are similar to wood chisels but their blades are curved in cross section for work such as cutting the shoulders of a joint to fit against a turned leg or scooping out the waste from a "finger pull" on a drawer front or sliding cupboard door.

Wood chisels and gouges have handles made of wood or impact-resistant plastic.

Firmer chisel
A firmer chisel has a strong, flat rectangular-section blade for chopping out waste wood. It is strong enough to be driven with a mallet or hammer – though you should never use a hammer on a wooden handle.

Bevel-edge chisel
A bevel-edge chisel is used for paring – especially for trimming undercuts such as dovetail joints or dadoes. The bevels enable you to work the blade in spaces that would be inaccessible to a firmer chisel. However, a bevel-edge chisel is not as strong as a firmer chisel and may break if it is used for heavy work. If a little extra force is needed to drive the chisel forward, use the ball of your hand or tap gently with a wooden mallet.

Mortise chisel
A mortise chisel has a thick blade, rectangular in section, for chopping and levering the waste out of mortise joints. Because this type of chisel is often driven with a mallet, a shock-absorbent leather washer is fitted between the blade and the ferrule.

Chopping out waste wood
Don't chop out too much waste at one time – the wood will split or the chisel will be driven over the line of the joint, resulting in a poor fit. Remove the waste a little at a time, working back to the marked line. Use a mallet at first but finish off by hand.

Paring with a chisel
Finish a joint by paring away very thin shavings, using a bevel-edge chisel. Control the blade with finger and thumb, steadying your hand against the work, while applying pressure to the tip of the handle with your other hand.

Woodworking tools

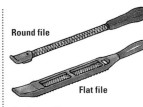

In-cannel gouge

Out-cannel gouge

Gouges

The cutting edge of an in-cannel gouge is formed by grinding the inside of the curved blade. This type of gouge is used for trimming rounded shoulders.

An out-cannel gouge is ground on the outside so that the blade will not be driven into the wood when it is being used to scoop out shallow recesses.

STORING CHISELS

You can make a rack for chisels and gouges by gluing spacer blocks between two strips of plywood, leaving a slot for the blades. Screw the rack to the wall behind your workbench so the tools are within easy reach.

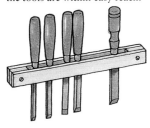

RASPS AND SURFORMS

Rasps are coarse files used for shaping free curves by wearing away the wood. Traditional rasps have teeth formed in the solid metal. Surform files have thin perforated blades made by punching out regularly spaced teeth with their cutting edges facing forward, leaving holes in the metal through which the wood shavings fall. As a result, Surform files cut faster than rasps and without clogging.

Cabinet rasp

Flat rasp

Round rasp

Rasps

Traditional rasps are available in various degrees of coarseness, designated bastard, second-cut and smooth. Their names refer to their shapes: a cabinet rasp is half-round, with one flat and one curved face; a flat rasp has two flat faces and one cutting edge; a round rasp is circular in section, tapering towards the tip.

Round file

Flat file

Surform files

A round Surform file has a detachable handle and thumb-grip at the tip. A flat Surform has a disposable blade that fits into a hollow metal frame.

Using a rasp

Steady the point of a rasp with your fingertips, applying forward pressure with your other hand. Don't use a rasp or file without fitting a handle – holding the bare pointed tang is dangerous.

Cleaning a rasp
When a rasp becomes clogged with wood fibers, clear the teeth with a fine wire brush or file card made for the purpose.

SANDPAPER

Sandpaper is used for putting a final smooth finish on wood. Always sand in the direction of the grain. Tiny scratches made by cross-grain sanding may not appear obvious until a stain or varnish is applied. Though flat surfaces are often sanded smooth, you can get a better finish with a cabinet scraper.

Sanding by hand

Abrasive papers – still widely referred to as "sandpapers" – are graded by the size and spacing of the grit. There are coarse, medium, and fine grits, but they are also designated by number (the higher the number, the finer the grit). On "open-coat" papers the particles are spaced wide apart to reduce clogging. The more tightly packed "closed-coat" papers produce a finer finish.

TYPES OF ABRASIVE

Flint paper is inexpensive and relatively soft. Use it for the first stages of sanding, especially on softwoods.

Garnet paper is much harder than flint paper and produces a better finish. Reddish in color, it is used for sanding softwoods and hardwoods.

Silicon-carbide paper (usually known as wet-and-dry paper) is most widely used for smoothing paintwork – but you can also use it dry to produce an extra-smooth finish on hardwoods.

Using abrasive papers

*Fold the sheet of paper over the edge of a bench and tear it into convenient strips. To smooth flat surfaces or square edges, wrap a strip of paper round a sanding block **(1)**; on curves, use your fingertips to apply the paper. To sand moldings, wrap a strip of abrasive paper round a dowel **(2)** or shaped block.*

As the work proceeds, use progressively finer grades of paper. Before the final sanding, dampen the wood with water to raise the grain. When the wood is dry, sand it with a very fine abrasive for a perfect finish.

To sand end grain, first rub the grain with your fingers: the wood feels rougher in one direction than the other. Sand the grain in the smoother direction only, back and forth.

When the grit gets clogged with wood dust, clear it by tapping the paper against the bench, or use a fine wire brush.

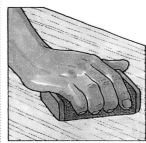

1 Sanding a flat surface

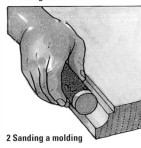

2 Sanding a molding

Sharpen a chisel as you would a plane blade – but hone it across the whole surface of the oilstone in a figure eight pattern to avoid uneven wear on the stone.

Honing an out-cannel gouge

*Stand to the side of the oilstone and rub the bevel of the gouge along the stone from end to end in a figure eight pattern **(1)**. At the same time, rock the blade from side to side to hone the curved edge evenly. Remove the burr from the inside of the cutting edge with a slipstone **(2)** – a small oilstone shaped to fit a variety of gouge sizes.*

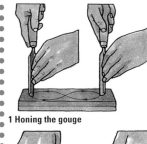

1 Honing the gouge

2 Removing the burr

Honing an in-cannel gouge

*Sharpen the bevel on the inside of an in-cannel gouge by honing with a slipstone **(1)**, then remove the burr by holding the back of the blade flat on an oilstone and rocking it from side to side while sliding it up and down the surface of the stone **(2)**.*

1 Sharpening the edge

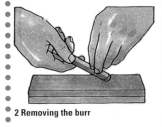

2 Removing the burr

● **Essential tools**
Combination oilstone
Slipstone
Range of sandpaper
Sanding block
Surform files

Woodworking tools

POWER SANDERS

Power sanders ease the chore of sanding large surfaces but rarely produce a surface good enough for a clear finish – so a final sanding by hand is required.

Belt sander

A belt sander has a continuous loop of abrasive paper passing around a revolving drum at each end. A flat plate between the two drums presses the moving abrasive against the wood.

Using a belt sander

Turn on the machine and lower it gently onto the work, then make forward and backward passes with the sander, holding it parallel to the grain. The weight of the machine provides enough pressure to do the work, especially when the abrasive belt is fresh. Cover the surface with overlapping passes but don't let the sander ride over the edges of the work or it will round them over. Lift the sander from the surface before you turn it off, and don't put the tool down until the belt comes to a stop.

Following the manufacturer's instructions, change to a finer-grade belt to remove the marks left by the previous sanding.

Finishing sanders

A finishing sander produces a surface that needs only a light sanding by hand before you apply a clear finish. On this type of sander, a strip of sandpaper is stretched across a flat rubber pad that is moved by the motor in a tight, rapid orbital pattern.

Specialized orbital sanders with small triangular plates are designed for sanding in tight corners. Use only light pressure – otherwise the paper will leave tiny swirl marks on the wood.

A cordless finishing sander is convenient for working outdoors.

● **Essential tools**
Flat cabinet scraper
Finishing sander or orbital disc sander

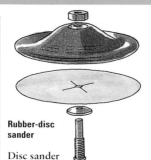

Rubber-disc sander

Disc sander

The simplest disc sander is a flexible rubber pad with a central shaft that is gripped in the chuck of an electric drill. An abrasive-paper disc is bolted to the face of the pad. This type of sander is not suitable for fine woodwork, since it inevitably leaves swirling scratch marks that have to be removed with a finishing sander or cabinet scraper before a clear finish can be applied. However, it is a handy tool for rough work in areas a belt sander can't reach.

Using a rubber-disc sander

With the drill running, flex the edge of the rubber disc against the wood. Keep the sander moving along the work to avoid deep scratching.

Foam drum sander

This flexible plastic-foam drum covered by an abrasive-paper band is driven by a central shaft that fits into the chuck of a power drill. The drum deforms against irregularly curved workpieces.

Random-orbit sander

A random-orbit sander has a sanding disc that moves eccentrically as it rotates. This leaves the surface of the wood virtually free of the typical swirl marks left by orbital sanders. The flexible backing pad copes with curved surfaces.

WOOD SCRAPERS

Scrapers produce an extremely smooth surface finish on wood. Whereas sandpaper leaves minute scratches on the surface, scrapers remove fine shavings.

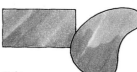

Cabinet scraper

This is a simple rectangle of thin steel used for scraping flat surfaces. Curved-edge versions are used for working moldings and carved wood.

Using a cabinet scraper

Hold the scraper in both hands and press it into a slightly curved shape with your thumbs. Tilt the scraper away from you and work diagonally across the surface in two directions to scrape the wood flat. Finally, scrape lightly in the direction of the grain.

SHARPENING A CABINET SCRAPER

A cabinet scraper is sharpened by raising a burr along its edge. Straight and curved scrapers are both sharpened in a similar way, although it's harder to turn an even burr along a curved edge.

*First, draw-file the edge of the scraper and hone it perfectly square on a whetstone (**1**). To raise the burr, hold the scraper flat on a workbench then stroke the edge firmly several times with the curved back of a gouge (**2**). This stretches the metal along the edge of the scraper, which produces the burr. Turn the burr to project from the face of the scraper by holding the scraper upright on the bench and stroking the burred corner with the gouge held at an angle to the face (**3**).*

Standard hook scraper

DISPOSABLE BLADE

Long-handled hook scraper

Hook scraper

A hook scraper's disposable blade slides into a clip at the end of a wooden handle. Simply pull the scraper toward you along the grain of the wood, applying light pressure.

1 Hone the edge square

2 Raise the burr

3 Turn the burr over

Woodworking tools

DRILLS AND BRACES

The electric drill is so versatile, it has more or less replaced the brace and hand drill in many household tool kits.

Brace
A brace is designed for boring holes that have a relatively large diameter. The bit is driven into the wood by the turning force on the handle, plus pressure on the head of the tool.

A good-quality brace has a ratchet so you can turn the bit in one direction only when working in a confined space where a full turn of the handle isn't possible.

1 Tightening the chuck

Brace bits
Brace bits have a square-section tang that fits into the jaws of the tool's chuck.

To install a bit, grip the chuck in one hand and turn the handle of the brace clockwise to open the jaws. Drop the bit into the chuck, then tighten the chuck on the bit by turning the handle in the counterclockwise direction.

Auger bit
An auger bit has helical twists along its shank that remove the waste as the bit bores into the wood. Being the same diameter as the cutting tip, the twisted shank keeps the bit straight when you are boring deep holes. A tapered lead screw helps to draw the bit into the wood, and knife-edge spurs cut the perimeter of the hole before the bit enters the wood.

Expansive bit
This bit has an adjustable spurred cutter for boring holes of up to 3in in diameter.

Center bit
This type of bit is fast-cutting because it has no helical twists to create friction, but it tends to wander off line.

It's best for drilling plywood and similar panel stock because the holes are never very deep. Its relatively short shank makes it useful in confined spaces.

Using a brace
When using a brace, don't let the bit break through the back of the work and split the wood. As soon as the lead screw emerges, turn the work over and complete the hole from the other side.

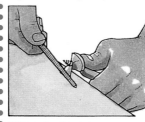

Hand drill
For small-diameter holes use a hand drill. Some models have a cast body enclosing the drive mechanism to keep gear wheels and pinions free from dust.

Using a hand drill
Center the drill bit on the work. This is easier if the center for the hole has been marked with an awl. Give the bit a start by moving the handle back and forth until the bit bites into the wood, then crank the handle to drive the bit clockwise.

Twist drills
Use standard twist drills with a hand drill. To fit a twist drill, open the tool's chuck by turning it counterclockwise. Insert the bit and then turn the chuck clockwise to tighten it. Check that a very small twist drill is centered accurately between the chuck's three jaws.

SHARPENING TWIST DRILLS

It is possible to sharpen a dull twist drill on a bench grinder, but it takes practice to center the point. An electric sharpener centers the point automatically. Insert the tip of the drill in the appropriate hole in the top of the machine and switch on for a few seconds to grind one cutting edge; then rotate the drill one half turn to position the other edge and repeat the process.

SHARPENING BRACE BITS

Brace bits are sharpened with flat and triangular files.

Put an edge on a spur by stroking its inside face with a flat file (1), then rest the point of the bit on a bench and sharpen the cutting edge with a triangular file (2).

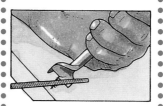

1 Sharpening the spur

2 Sharpening the edge

Power drill
Modern drills sold for the DIY market are now as sophisticated as those that were once made for the professional trade only. It is worth buying a drill with a powerful motor that can cope with a wide range of jobs.

Cordless power drill
Drills powered by rechargeable batteries do away with the need for an extension cord in order to reach a remote work site or work at the top of a ladder. Choose a cordless drill that has variable speed for driving woodscrews, and a hammer action for drilling into masonry. It is convenient to have a spare battery so that you are able to continue working while recharging a dead battery.

SELECTING USEFUL FEATURES

Before you buy an electric drill, make sure it has all the features you are likely to require.

- **Variable speed**
With a variable-speed drill, you are able to select the ideal speed for drilling different materials. A slow speed uses the drill's power to produce more torque (turning force) for drilling into masonry or metal; a high speed produces a clean cut when drilling wood. Some tools have a dial for selecting maximum speed. On most drills, however, speed is varied by the pressure on the trigger.

Variable speed is essential if you want to use a power drill for driving screws.

- **Trigger lock**
A trigger-lock button sets the drill for continuous running when it is used to drive accessories.

- **Chuck size**
The chuck's size refers to the maximum diameter of drill shank it can accommodate. A ⅜ or ½in chuck is adequate for most purposes, though there are drills with a chuck size of ⅝in. You can drill holes of a diameter greater than the chuck size by using special bits with reduced shanks.

- **Percussion or hammer action**
Moving a switch converts some electric drills from smooth rotation to a hammer action that delivers several hundred blows per minute to the revolving chuck. This action is used only when drilling into brick, stone, or concrete; the hammer vibration helps to break up hard particles ahead of specially toughened masonry bits. Helical flutes along the shank of the bit clear the debris from the hole.

- **Reverse rotation**
If you want to use a screwdriver bit with your power drill, make sure its rotation can be reversed – so you can take screws out as well as to insert them.

- **Grips**
A power drill often has both a pistol-grip handle and a second handgrip for steadying the drill. Some manufacturers provide an extra handle that bolts onto the rear of the drill to enable you to exert maximum pressure behind the bit.

● **Essential tools**
Set of twist drills
Power drill

Woodworking tools

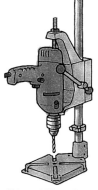

Using a drill stand
To bore holes that are absolutely square to the face of the work, mount your power drill in a vertical drill stand.

● **Essential tools**
Set of spade or power-bore bits
Countersink bit
Claw hammer
Cross-peen hammer
Pin hammer
Carpenter's mallet
Pincers
Nail set

POWER-DRILL BITS

A variety of bits can be used in a power drill, depending on the kind of hole you want to bore.

Twist drills
You can use standard twist drills of any size up to the maximum opening of the chuck. To bore larger holes, use reduced-shank twist drills.

Power-bore bit

Spade bit

Power-bore and spade bits
With power-bore and spade bits you can drill holes up to 1½in in diameter. Both produce minimal friction. Place the sharp lead point of the bit on the center of the hole before squeezing the trigger of the drill.

Countersink
To sink the head of a flathead screw flush with the surface of the work, make a tapered recess in the top of the clearance hole with a countersink. These bits can be used with a hand drill or a brace, but a high-speed power drill forms a neater recess.

Unless you use a drill stand (see left), the countersink may "chatter" if the hole has already been drilled, producing a rough recess. When using a power drill without a stand, it's sometimes better to make the countersink recess first, then drill the hole itself in the center.

Screwdriver bits
With slot- or Phillips head screwdriver bits, you can use your electric drill as a power screwdriver. The drill must be reversible for withdrawing screws, and have variable speed.

Plug cutter
This special bit cuts cylindrical plugs of wood for concealing the heads of screws sunk below the surface of the work.

Brad point bit
This is a twist drill with a sharp lead point and cutting spurs that help keep it on line when you are boring holes for dowel joints.

Drill and countersink bit
This bit makes the pilot hole, clearance hole, and countersink recess for a woodscrew in a single operation. As it is matched to one specific screw size, it is only worth buying when you are planning to use a fair number of identical screws.

Fitting a power-drill bit
In a standard chuck, three self-centering jaws are closed onto the bit using a toothed key called a chuck key. Turn the chuck counterclockwise to open its jaws, and remove the bit.

Installing a drill bit into a fast-action keyless chuck couldn't be simpler. Turn the chuck ring counterclockwise by hand to open it. To tighten the chuck, turn the chuck ring in the opposite direction while your other hand keeps the shaft from rotating.

USING A POWER DRILL SAFELY

● Choose a drill with a double-insulated, plastic body.
● Always unplug a drill before installing bits, accessories or attachments.
● Remove a chuck key before switching on the drill.
● Don't wear loose clothing, or a necktie or necklace, while using a drill.
● Use a heavy-duty extension cord that's designed for power tool use.
● Never lift a drill by its cord.

Doweling jig
A doweling jig clamped to the work ensures alignment of dowel holes and also keeps the drill bit perpendicular to the work.

HAMMERS AND MALLETS

Driving a nail is so simple that one hammer would seem to be as effective as another, but using one that is the right shape and weight for the job makes for easier, trouble-free work.

A mallet has its own specific uses and should not be used for hammering nails.

Wood-handle hammer

Steel-shaft hammer

Claw hammer
This is a heavy general-purpose hammer and probably the most useful one to have in a basic tool kit. The claw at the back of the head is for prying out nails. In order to cope with the leverage, the hammer head has to be fixed firmly to a strong shaft.

The traditional wood-handle hammer head has a deep, square socket into which the handle is driven and wedged. An all-metal claw hammer won't bend or break and the head can't work loose. Fiberglass-shaft hammers are also available, and rubber grips are both comfortable and shock-absorbing.

Cross-peen hammer
For tasks that are too delicate for a heavy claw hammer, use a medium-weight cross-peen hammer. Its wedge-shaped peen is for starting a small nail held between finger and thumb.

Pin hammer
A small lightweight pin hammer is the perfect tool for tapping in tiny nails, brads, and tacks.

Using a hammer
Set a nail in wood with one or two taps of the hammer until it stands upright without support, then drive it home with firm steady blows, keeping your wrist straight and the hammer face square to the nailhead.

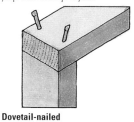

Hammering small nails
If the nail is very small, either set it with the hammer peen or push it through a piece of thin cardboard to steady it. Just before you tap the nail flush with the wood, tear the card away.

Using a nail set
A nail set is a punch with a hollow-ground tip used for sinking nails below the surface of the wood. Nail sets are made in several sizes for use with large and small nails. Having driven the nail almost flush, hold the set upright between thumb and fingertips and place its tip on the protruding nailhead, then tap the tool with your hammer. With a heavy hammer very little force is needed to sink the nail.

Blind nailing
To hide a nail fixing, lift a flap of wood with a gouge, sink the nail with a nail set, then glue the flap and clamp it flat.

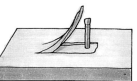

Dovetail-nailed

Toe-nailed

Making a strong nailed joint
The grip between the nails and the wood is usually enough to hold the joint together, but for stronger joints drive the nails in at an angle. When angled nails fasten wood onto the end grain of another member, the technique is called dovetail-nailing; when they pass through the side of a section it's called toe-nailing.

Woodworking tools

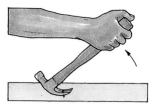

Removing a bent nail
If you bend a nail while driving it in with a claw hammer, pry it out by sliding the claw under the nailhead and pulling back on the end of the handle. The hammer's curved head will roll on the wood without doing too much damage, but you can protect the work by placing thick cardboard or hardboard under the hammer head.

A thick shim of this kind will also give you extra leverage for removing a long nail.

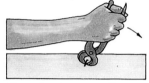

If a nailhead is too small to catch in a claw hammer, lever it out with carpenter's pincers. Grip the nail with the jaws resting on the wood, squeeze the handles together, and roll the pincers away from you. As with a claw hammer, cardboard, or hardboard shims will protect the wood.

Sanding a hammer head
You are more likely to bend nails if your hammer head is slick. Rub the hammer's face on fine sandpaper for a better grip.

Carpenter's mallet
A carpenter's mallet is for driving a chisel or gouge into wood. Its striking faces are angled so as to deliver square blows to the end of the chisel. Tighten a loose mallet head by tapping the top of the tapered handle on a bench.

Soft-faced mallet
Though you can use a hardwood carpenter's mallet to knock joints together or apart, a soft-faced rubber, plastic, or leather mallet is less likely to mark the wood.

SCREWDRIVERS

A woodworker's tool kit needs to include a number of screwdrivers because it is important to match the size of the driver to the screw. If you use a screwdriver with a tip that is slightly too big or too small, it is likely to slip out of the slot as you turn it, damaging both the screw and the surrounding wood.

Cabinet screwdriver
A cabinet screwdriver has a shaft that is ground on two sides to produce a flat, square tip. It may have a hardwood handle, strengthened with a metal ferrule, or a plastic one molded onto the shaft.

Phillips-head screwdriver
Use a matching Phillips-head screwdriver to drive screws that have cross slots. Using a flat-tip driver to turn a Phillips-head screw invariably damages the screw's head.

Ratchet screwdriver
Using a ratchet screwdriver, you can insert and remove screws without having to adjust your grip on the handle of the driver.

You can select clockwise or counterclockwise rotation or lock the ratchet and use the tool like an ordinary screwdriver.

Pump-action screwdriver
A straight thrust of the tool causes the tip of a pump-action screwdriver to rotate. The spring-loaded shaft moves in and out of a hollow handle, which contains a ratchet mechanism that controls the direction of rotation. Interchangeable Phillips-head and flat-tipped bits fit into a chuck at the end of the shaft.

Power screwdriver
A cordless electric screwdriver, which takes interchangeable bits, is especially convenient for working in confined spaces.

HONING A FLAT TIP

When worn, a screwdriver tip no longer grips screws properly. To reshape the tip, hone it on an whetstone, then file the end square.

Driving a woodscrew
You may split the wood if you drive in a screw without boring a hole for it first. To make a starter hole for a small screw, place the flat tip of a bradawl **(1)** *across the grain of the wood, then press it in and twist. To guide a large screw, drill a pilot hole, followed by a clearance hole for the shank* **(2)**. *For the pilot hole, use a drill bit slightly narrower than the thread of the screw, but drill the clearance hole slightly larger than the screw's shank.*

Use a countersink to make recesses to accommodate the heads of flathead screws.

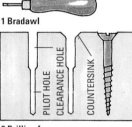

1 Bradawl

2 Drilling for screws

Lubricating a screw
If a screw is a tight fit in the hole you have drilled for it, withdraw it slightly and put a little wax or snap on its shank.

Extracting old screws
Before attempting to extract a painted-over screw, scrape the paint from the slot with the end of a hacksaw blade – or, for the best results, place a corner of the screwdriver tip in the slot and tap it sideways until it fits snugly, then extract the screw.

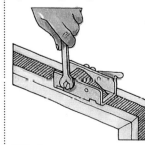

Clearing a screw slot

When a screw's slot has been completely stripped, remove the head with a power drill. Mark the center of the head with a metal punch, then use progressively larger drill bits to remove the metal in stages.

CLAMPS

Clamps are for holding joints together while the glue sets. They are also used to assemble structures temporarily to see if they work or fit, and for holding small workpieces on a bench while you are working on them.

Bar clamp
A bar clamp is a long metal bar with a screw-adjustable jaw at one end. and another jaw that can be fixed at any point by inserting a metal peg in one of a series of holes along the bar. Bar clamps are for clamping large frames or panels. When you need a deeper reach, fast-action bar clamps are the answer. These have a fixed jaw at the top and a threaded sliding jaw to apply the necessary pressure.

Clamp heads
If you need an extra long bar clamp, use a pair of clamp heads that can be installed on a piece of lumber that serves as a bar. Alternatively, pipe clamps are commonly available. These are used with ½ or ¾in black-iron pipe of whatever length is required for the job.

C-clamp
A screw-adjusted C-clamp grips the work between the adjustable foot and the cast-metal frame. You're likely to need at least one 6in and one 12in C-clamp.

Frame and miter clamps
The four plastic corner blocks of a simple frame clamp hold the glued corners of a mitered frame while a cord is pulled tight around the blocks to apply equal pressure on all four joints.

A miter clamp holds one joint at a time. Made of cast metal, it clamps the two mitered members against a right-angle fence.

Web clamp
A web clamp acts like a frame clamp. Use one to form a tourniquet around a large frame. The nylon webbing is tensioned by adjusting a ratchet mechanism with a wrench or screwdriver.

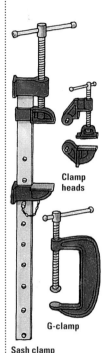

Clamp heads

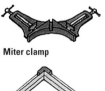

G-clamp

Sash clamp

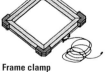

Miter clamp

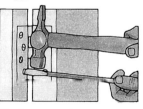

Frame clamp

● **Essential tools**
Flat-tip screwdriver
Phillips-head screwdriver
Bradawl
C-clamps

Woodworking tools

Clamping a frame

Prepare and adjust your bar clamps before you glue and assemble a frame. If you waste time adjusting them after the glue has been applied, the glue may begin to set before you can close the joints properly. Set the sliding jaws to accommodate the frame and make sure that the adjustable jaws will have enough movement to tighten the joints. Place the clamps in line with the joints, using softwood shims to protect the work from the metal jaws. Apply pressure gradually, first with one clamp, then the other, until the joints are tightly closed (1).

Check that the frame is square by measuring both diagonals. If they aren't equal, set the clamps at a slight angle to the frame to pull it square by squeezing the long diagonal (2).

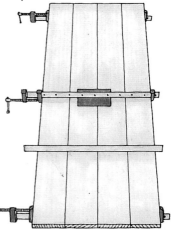

1 Bar clamps square to a frame

2 Sash clamps set at an angle to the frame

Clamping boards together

To clamp several glued boards edge to edge, use at least three bar clamps. Place one of the clamps on top of the assembly to keep the boards from bowing under the pressure of the other two. A long bar clamp will bend as you tighten it, so protect the wood by inserting strips of hardboard between the bars and the work.

Lay a straightedge across the clamped boards to check that the panel is flat. If it isn't, correct the distortion by slackening or tightening the clamps.

If a board is misaligned, tap it into position by placing a softwood block across the joint and striking the block firmly with a heavy hammer.

● **Essentials tools**
Portable bench

Use at least three clamps to the glue boards together.

BENCHES AND VICES

A woodworking bench must be strong and rigid. Working with heavy lumber and manufactured panels puts a considerable strain on a bench, and the stress imposed by sawing and hammering will eventually weaken a poorly constructed one.

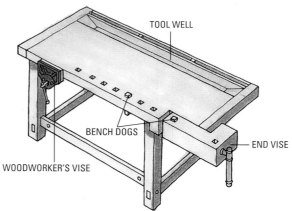

TOOL WELL

BENCH DOGS

WOODWORKER'S VISE

END VISE

Woodworker's bench

The hardwood underframe of a traditional woodworker's bench is constructed with large double-wedged mortise-and-tenon joints.

The longer rails are usually bolted to the rigid end frames so that the bench can be dismantled to facilitate removal. The thick hardwood top is normally made of beech. A storage recess or tool well keeps the top free from tools, so you can lay large boards on it.

Better-quality benches have an end vise, built onto one end of the top, for clamping long sections of wood between metal pegs called bench dogs.

BENCH-TOP VISE

ADJUSTING HANDLE

PLASTIC PEGS HOLD WORKPIECES

ADJUSTING HANDLE

Portable bench

A portable workbench can be folded away between jobs. The two halves of the thick plywood top are, in effect, vise jaws, operated by adjusting handles at the ends of the bench. Because the handles work independently, the jaws can hold tapered work-pieces. Plastic pegs fit into holes in the top to hold work laid flat on it; they can be arranged to hold irregular shapes.

Clamp-on vice

A lightweight vise can be clamped temporarily to the edge of any top. Although not as good as a proper woodworker's vise, it is a lot cheaper.

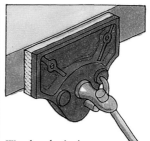

Woodworker's vice

A feature of most benches is a large woodworker's vise. This is normally screwed to the underside of the top, close to one leg, so that the top will not flex when you are working on wood held in the vise. Wooden pads fastened inside the jaws protect the work from the metal edges.

A quick-release lever on the front of the vise allows you to open and shut the jaws quickly, turning the handle only for final adjustments.

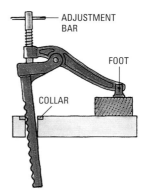

ADJUSTMENT BAR

FOOT

COLLAR

Holdfast

A holdfast is a bench-mounted clamp for holding a workpiece firmly against the top. The notched shaft of the clamp is slipped into a metal collar that is let into the bench.

When pressure is applied with the clamp's adjustment bar, the shaft rocks over to lock in the collar, and the foot at the end of the pivoting arm bears down on the workpiece. A pair of holdfasts, one at each end of the bench, is ideal for clamping long boards.

Woodworking joints

BASIC WOODWORKING JOINTS

Craftsmen have invented countless ingenious ways of joining
pieces of wood together. Some
are as decorative as they are
practical, but for general joinery
and home maintenance only a
few basic woodworking joints
are needed.

BUTT JOINTS

When you cut a piece of wood
square and butt it against its
neighbor you need some kind of
mechanical fastener to hold the
joint together, as the end grain
doesn't glue strongly enough for
adhesive alone to be used.

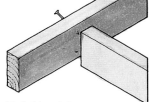

Nailed butt joints
When you nail-fix a butt joint,
drive the nails in at an angle to
clamp the two pieces together.

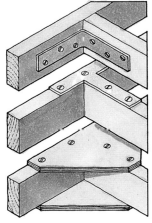

Bracket and gusset joint
A screwed-on metal right-angle
bracket or T-bracket makes a
strong, though not very attractive, butt joint. Similarly, you can
reinforce a butt joint by nailing
or screwing a plywood gusset
across it.

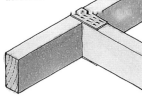

Plate connectors
The sharp pointed teeth of
metal plate connectors
hammered onto a butt joint grip
the wood like a bed of nails.

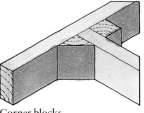

Corner blocks
Either nail and glue or screw a
square or triangular block of
wood in the corner between two
components.

LAP JOINT

You can make a simple lap joint
by laying one square-cut board
across another and fixing them
with nails or screws.

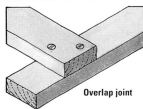

Overlap joint

Making an lap joint
*Clamp the components together
accurately with a C-clamp, and
drill pilot and clearance holes for
the screws. Remove the clamp,
apply glue, and then screw the
components together.*

HALF-LAP JOINTS

Half-lap joints can be adapted to
join lengths of wood at a corner
or T-joint, or where components
cross one another.

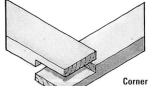

**Corner
half-lap joint**

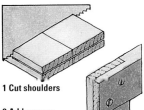

1 Cut shoulders

2 Add screws

Cutting a corner half-lap joint
*To join two pieces of wood at a
corner, cut down half the
thicknesses at each end. Then
clamp the components side by
side and cut their shoulders
simultaneously (1).*
  *Reinforce the glued joint with
screws (2).*

Cutting a T half-lap joint
*Lay the cross rail on the side rail
(1) and mark the width of the
dado on it with a marking knife,
extending the lines halfway down
each edge of the rail.*
  *With a marking gauge set to
exactly half the thickness of the
rails, score the center lines on
both rails (2). Mark the shoulder
of the tongue on the cross rail
(3), allowing for a tongue
slightly longer than the width of
the side rail. Hold the cross rail
at an angle in a vise (4) and saw
down to the shoulder on one
edge, keeping to the waste side
of the line. Then turn the rail
around and saw down to the
shoulder on the opposite edge.
Finally, saw down square to the
shoulder line (5) and remove the
waste by sawing across the
shoulder line (6).*
  *To cut the dado in the side rail,
saw down both the shoulder lines
to the halfway mark, then make
several saw cuts across the waste
(7). Pare out the waste with a
chisel down to the marked lines,
working from both sides (8).*
  *Glue and assemble the joint.
When it has set, plane the end
of the tongue flush.*

1 Mark the dado

2 Score the center lines

3 Mark the shoulder

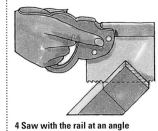

4 Saw with the rail at an angle

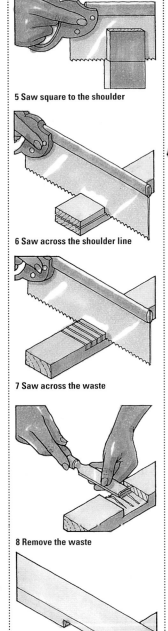

5 Saw square to the shoulder

6 Saw across the shoulder line

7 Saw across the waste

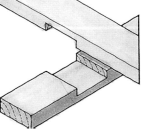

8 Remove the waste

Cutting a cross half-lap joint
*To make a cross half-lap joint,
hold the two components
together, side by side, and mark
both joints simultaneously.
Then separate the components
and saw across the shoulder
lines and remove the waste with
a chisel as described above.*

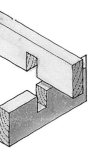

**Edge-to-edge half-lap
joint**
Clamp the two parts
together, then mark
and saw both halves
of the joint. Remove
the clamps and chisel out
the waste.

Woodworking joints

RABBETED CORNER JOINT

This is a simple joint for joining two wide boards at a corner.

Rabbet joint

Cutting a rabbet joint
Cut the square-ended board first and use it to mark out the width of the rabbet on the other board (**1**). *Set a marking gauge to about half the stock thickness and mark out the rabbet depth* (**2**). *Cut the rabbet with a tenon saw, then glue and nail the joint.*

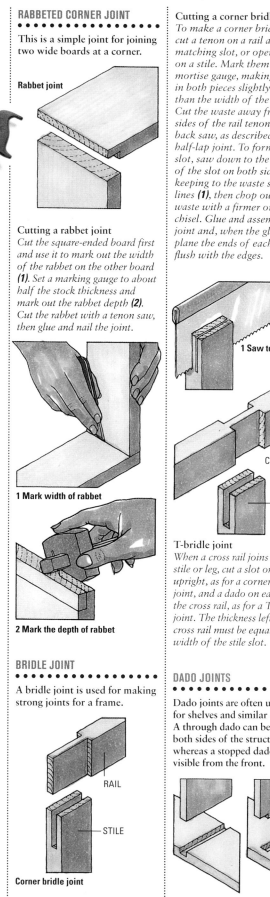

1 Mark width of rabbet

2 Mark the depth of rabbet

BRIDLE JOINT

A bridle joint is used for making strong joints for a frame.

RAIL

STILE

Corner bridle joint

Cutting a corner bridle joint
To make a corner bridle joint, cut a tenon on a rail and a matching slot, or open mortise, on a stile. Mark them with a mortise gauge, making the cuts in both pieces slightly longer than the width of the pieces. Cut the waste away from both sides of the rail tenon with a back saw, as described for a T half-lap joint. To form the stile slot, saw down to the bottom of the slot on both sides, keeping to the waste side of the lines (**1**), *then chop out the waste with a firmer or mortise chisel. Glue and assemble the joint and, when the glue has set, plane the ends of each piece flush with the edges.*

1 Saw to slot bottom

CROSS RAIL

STILE

T-bridle joint
When a cross rail joins an upright stile or leg, cut a slot on the upright, as for a corner bridle joint, and a dado on each side of the cross rail, as for a T-half-lap joint. The thickness left in the cross rail must be equal to the width of the stile slot.

DADO JOINTS

Dado joints are often used for shelves and similar structures. A through dado can be seen from both sides of the structure, whereas a stopped dado is not visible from the front.

Through dado   **Stopped dado**

Cutting a through dado
Square the end of one board and use it to mark out the width of the dado on the other board (**1**), *then with a marking gauge set to about a third of the board's thickness, mark the depth of the dado on both edges* (**2**). *Saw along both sides of the dado* (**3**), *keeping just on the waste side of the two lines, then chisel out the waste, working from both edges of the board* (**4**). *A hand router is the ideal tool for levelling the bottom of the dado; otherwise, pare it flat with the chisel.*

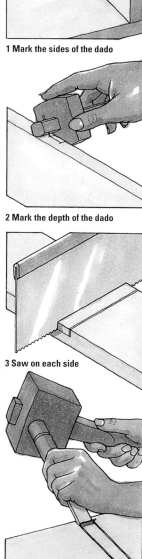

1 Mark the sides of the dado

2 Mark the depth of the dado

3 Saw on each side

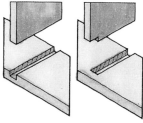

4 Chisel out the waste

Cutting a stopped dado
First, mark out the dado as described left – but stop about ¼in short of the front edge. To give the saw clearance, remove about 1½in of the dado at the stopped end, first with a drill and then with a chisel (**1**). *Saw down both sides of the dado and pare out the waste to leave a level bottom. In the front corner of the other board, cut a notch* (**2**) *to fit the stopped dado so the two edges lie flush when assembled.*

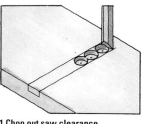

1 Chop out saw clearance

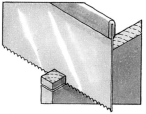

2 Cut a notch

DOWEL JOINTS

Dowel joints are strong and versatile. They can secure butt-jointed rails, mitered frames and long boards butted edge to edge. Use dowels that are about one-third the thickness of the wood.

Doweled butt joint

Doweled miter joint

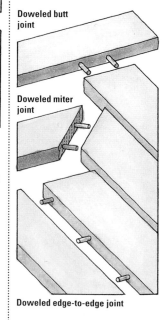

Doweled edge-to-edge joint

Cutting a dowel joint

When joining boards end to edge, cut dowels about 1½ in long; otherwise, saw the dowels to a length equal to two-thirds the width of the rails. File chamfers on both ends of each dowel and saw a groove along each one (1) so air and surplus glue can escape when the joint is assembled. To save time, buy ready-cut and chamfered dowels that are grooved all around.

If you are using a doweling jig, then you won't need to mark the centers of the dowel holes. Otherwise, use a marking gauge to lay out the centerline on both pieces (2), drive finishing nails into the edge of the side rail to mark the dowel-hole centers, then cut them to short sharp points with pliers (3). Line up the rails, push them together so the metal points mark the end grain of the adjoining piece (4), and then pull out the nails.

Using a power drill with the appropriate bit, bore the holes to a depth just over half the length of the dowels; then glue and clamp the joint. Drilling accurate dowel holes is much easier if the drill is mounted in a vertical drill stand.

1 Saw slot for glue to escape

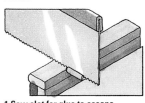
2 Score centerlines

3 Cut pins to sharp points

4 Mark centers on adjoining piece

MORTISE-AND-TENON JOINTS

A mortise and tenon is a strong joint for narrow components – and essential for chair and table frames. A through tenon can be wedged for extra strength, but a stopped tenon is neater.

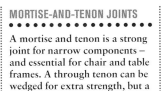
Stopped mortise and tenon
STILE
RAIL

Cutting a mortise and tenon

Mark the width of the mortise, using the rail as a guide (1), and mark the shoulder of the tenon all around the rail (2) so that the tenon's length is two-thirds the width of the stile. Set a mortise gauge to one-third of the rail's thickness and mark both mortise and tenon (3).

Cut the tenon as described for a bridle joint. Remove the waste from the mortise with an electric drill (preferably mounted in a drill stand), then square up its ends and sides with a chisel (4).

Glue and clamp the joint.

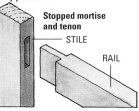
1 Mark width of mortise

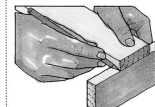
2 Mark tenon shoulder

3 Mark thickness of joint

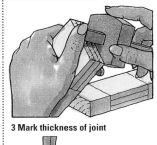
4 Chop out remaining waste

WEDGES   SAW CUTS
Through mortise and tenon

Cutting a through tenon

When a tenon is to pass right through a side rail, cut it slightly longer than the width of the rail and saw two slots through it. Glue and assemble the joint, then drive glued hardwood wedges into the saw cuts to expand the tenon in the mortise. When the glue has set, plane the wedges and the tenon flush with the rail.

MITER JOINT

Miter joints are used for joining corners of frames. They are also especially useful for decorative moldings and skirting boards.

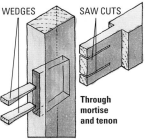
Miter joint

Cutting a miter joint

A right-angle miter joint is made by sawing the ends of two rails to 45 degrees in a miter box, then butting them together. Trim the miters with a finely set plane on a shooting board and assemble the glued joint in a miter clamp. If the meeting faces of the rails are fairly large, glue alone will hold them together; but you can reinforce a miter joint by sawing two slots across the corner and gluing strips of veneer into them (1). Plane the veneers flush with the rails after the glue has set.

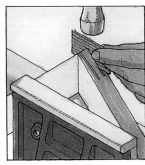
1 Inserting veneer strips

SCARF JOINT

A scarf joint is used for joining two lengths of wood end to end.

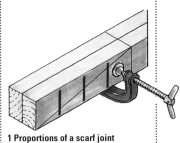
Scarf joint

Making a scarf joint

Clamp the two lengths side by side, with their ends and edges flush, and mark out the angled cut. The length of a scarf joint should be at least four times the width of the stock (1). Saw and plane both lengths down to the marked line simultaneously, then unclamp them. Glue the two angled faces together, securing them with battens and clamps while the glue sets (2).

If the scarf joint is likely to be subjected to a great deal of stress, you can reinforce it with plywood plates screwed to both sides of the rails (3).

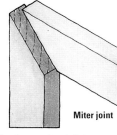
1 Proportions of a scarf joint

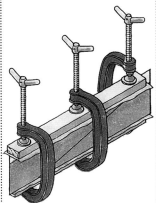
2 Clamp joint with G-clamps

3 Reinforced scarf joint

Building tools

Using a mortar hawk
A mortar hawk makes tuckpointing mortar joints very easy. Place the lip of the hawk just under a horizontal joint and scrape the mortar into place with a jointer or pointing trowel.

● **Essential tools**
Brick trowel
Pointing trowel
Plasterer's trowel
Mortarboard
Hawk
Spirit level
Try square
Plumb line

BUILDER'S TOOLS

A specialist builder—such as a plasterer, finish carpenter, or bricklayer—needs only a limited set of tools, whereas the amateur is more like a one-man general builder who has to be able to tackle all kinds of construction and repair work, and therefore requires a much wider range of tools than the specialist.

The selection suggested here is for renovating and improving the structure of your home and for such tasks as building or restoring garden structures and laying paving. Electrical work, decorating, and plumbing call for other sets of tools.

FLOATS AND TROWELS

For a professional builder, floats and trowels have their specific uses, but in home maintenance a repointing trowel may often be the ideal tool for patching small areas of plaster, or a plasterer's trowel for smoothing concrete.

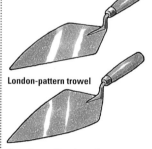

London-pattern trowel

Canadian-pattern trowel

Brick and block trowels
A brick or block trowel is for handling and placing mortar when laying bricks or concrete blocks. A professional might use one with a blade as long as 1 foot, but such a trowel is too heavy and unwieldy for the amateur.

The blade of a **London-pattern trowel** has one curved edge for cutting bricks, a skill that takes practice to perfect; the blade's other edge is straight, for picking up mortar. You can buy left-handed versions of this trowel or opt for a similar trowel with two straight edges.

A *Canadian-pattern trowel* (sometimes called a Philadelphia brick trowel) is also symmetrical, having a wide blade with two curved edges.

Pointing trowel
A pointing trowel is designed for repairing and shaping mortar joints between bricks. The blade is only 3 to 4 inches long.

Jointer
Use a jointer to shape the mortar joints between bricks. Its narrow blade is dragged along the mortar joint, and the curved front end is used for shaping the verticals.

Wooden float
A wooden float is for applying and smoothing concrete to a fine, attractive texture. The more expensive ones have detachable handles, so their wooden blades can be replaced when they wear out. Similar floats made from plastic are also available.

Plasterer's trowel
A plasterer's trowel is a steel float for applying plaster and cement renderings to walls. It is also dampened and used for "polishing"—smoothing the surface of the material when it has firmed up. Some builders prefer to apply stucco with a heavy trowel and finish it with a more flexible blade, but you need to be quite skilled to exploit such subtle differences.

BOARDS FOR CARRYING MORTAR OR PLASTER

Any conveniently sized sheet of ½- or ¼-inch exterior-grade plywood can be used as a mixing board for plaster or mortar. A panel about 3 feet square makes an ideal mixing board, while a smaller board, about 2 feet square, is convenient for carrying the material to the work site. Screwing battens to the underside of either board makes it easier to lift and carry.

You will also need a small lightweight hawk for carrying pointing mortar or plaster. Make one by nailing a block of wood underneath a plywood board so that you can plug a handle into it.

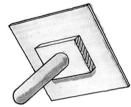

A home-made hawk

LEVELING AND MEASURING TOOLS

You can make some leveling and measuring tools yourself—but don't skimp on essentials, such as a good spirit level and a robust tape measure.

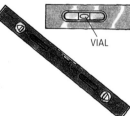

VIAL

Spirit level
A spirit level is a machine-made straightedge incorporating special glass tubes or vials that contain a liquid. In each vial an air bubble floats. When a bubble rests exactly between two lines marked on the glass, that indicates that the structure on which the level is held is precisely horizontal or vertical, depending on the orientation of the vial.

Buy a wooden or lightweight aluminum level, 2 to 3 feet long. A well-made one is very strong, but treat it with care and always clean mortar or plaster from it before it sets.

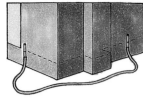

Water level
You can make a water level by plugging short lengths of transparent plastic tubing into the two ends of a garden hose; fill the hose with water until it appears in both tubes. Since water level remains constant, the levels in the tubes are always identical and so can be used for marking identical heights, even over long distances and round obstacles and bends.

Builder's square
A large square is useful when setting out brick or concrete-block corners. The best squares are stamped out of sheetmetal, but you can make a serviceable one by cutting out a right-angle triangle from thick plywood with a hypotenuse of about 2 feet 6 inches. Cut out the center of the triangle to reduce the weight.

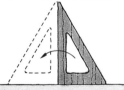

Checking a square
Accuracy is important, so check the square by placing it against a perfectly straight board on the floor. Draw a line against the square to make a right angle with the board, then flop the square to see if it forms the same angle from the other side.

Try square
Use a try square for marking out square cuts or joints on lumber.

Making a plumb line
Any small, heavy weight hung on a length of fine string can act as a plumb line for judging whether a structure or surface is vertical.

Building tools

Bricklayer's line
This is a nylon line used as a guide for laying bricks or blocks level. It is stretched between two flat-bladed pins, which are driven into vertical joints at the ends of a wall or between line blocks that hook over the bricks at the ends of a course. As a substitute, you can stretch string between two stakes driven into the ground outside the line of the wall.

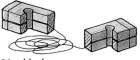

Steel pins and line
You can buy special flat-bladed pins to hold a line that guides in laying a straight course of bricks.

Line blocks
The blocks grip the corners of the bricks or blocks at the end of a course; the line passes through their slots.

Straightedge
Any length of straight rigid lumber can be used to check whether a surface is flat or, in conjunction with a spirit level, to see whether two points are at the same height.

Story pole
For gauging the height of brick courses, calibrate a softwood batten by making saw cuts across it at intervals equal to the thickness of a brick plus one mortar joint. Blocks of wood at each end enable a story pole to span irregularities.

Tape measure
An ordinary retractable steel tape measure is adequate for most purposes, but if you need to measure a large plot, buy a wind-up tape, 50 to 100 feet in length.

Marking gauge
A marking gauge has a sharp steel point for scoring a line on lumber parallel to the edge. It has an adjustable fence that keeps the point a constant distance from the edge.

HAMMERS

Several types of hammer are useful on a building site.

Claw hammer
Choose a strong claw hammer for building stud walls, nailing floorboards, making doorframes and window frames, and putting up garden fencing.

Hand sledge
A heavy hand sledge is used for driving cold chisels and for a variety of demolition jobs. It is also useful for driving large masonry nails into walls.

Sledgehammer
Buy a sledgehammer if you have to break up concrete or masonry. It's also the best tool for driving stakes or fence posts into the ground, though you can make do with a hand sledge if the ground is not too hard.

Mallet
A wooden carpenter's mallet is the proper tool for driving a wood chisel. But you can use a metal hammer instead if the chisel has an impact-resistant plastic handle.

SAWS

Every builder needs a range of handsaws, but consider buying a circular saw when you have to cut a lot of heavy structural lumber—especially if you have a lot of ripping to do, which is a very tiring job when done by hand.

Special saws are available for cutting metal and even for sawing through masonry.

Panel saw
All kinds of manufactured panels are used in house construction, so it is worth investing in a good panel saw.

It can also be used for cutting large structural lumber to the required lengths.

General-purpose saw
A single handsaw that can be used equally well for ripping solid planks lengthwise and crosscutting them to size is a useful tool to have on a building site. A saw with hardened teeth is also an asset.

Backsaw
This is a good saw for accurately cutting small pieces of trim, paneling, and joints. The metal stiffening along the top of the blade keeps it rigid and prevents the saw from wandering off line.

Keyhole saw
This small saw has a narrow tapered blade for cutting holes in lumber and panel stock.

Coping saw
A coping saw has a frame that holds a fairly coarse but very narrow blade under tension for cutting curves in wood.

Floorboard saw
If you pry a floorboard above its neighbors, you can cut across it with an ordinary tenon saw, but the curved cutting edge of a floorboard saw makes it easier to avoid damaging the boards on either side.

Hacksaw
The hardened-steel blades of a hacksaw have fine teeth for cutting metal. Use one to cut steel concrete-reinforcing rods or small pieces of sheetmetal.

All-purpose saw
An all-purpose saw is able to cut wood, metal, plastics, and building boards. The short frameless blade has a low-friction coating.

This type of saw is especially useful for cutting scrap lumber, which may contain nails or screws that would dull the blade of an ordinary saw.

Power jigsaw
Use a jigsaw to cut curves in wood or metal. It is also handy for cutting holes in fixed wall panels and for sawing through floorboards. A cordless saw is useful for small jobs.

Circular saw
A circular saw will quickly and accurately rip lumber or manufactured panels down to size. As well as saving you the effort of handsawing large stock, a sharp power saw produces such a clean cut that there is often no need for planing afterwards. If your preference is for a cordless circular saw, buy a spare battery and keep it charged.

Reciprocating saw
A reciprocating saw is a two-handed power saw that has a long pointed blade. It is powerful enough to saw sections of heavy lumber, and can even cut through a complete stud wall. With a change of blade, you can use a reciprocating saw to cut metal pipes. Both cordless and corded versions are available.

Gas-engine masonry saw
A gas-engine masonry saw is strictly a rental item. Still, there is no substitute for one when it comes to masonry demolition.

DRILLS

A powerful electric drill is invaluable to a builder. A cordless version is useful when you have to bore holes outdoors or in attics and cellars that lack convenient electrical outlets.

Power drill
Buy a good-quality power drill, plus a range of twist drills and spade or power-bore bits for drilling wood. Make sure the drill has a percussion or hammer action for drilling masonry walls. For masonry you need special drill bits tipped with tungsten carbide. The smaller ones are matched to the size of standard wall plugs; there are also much larger ones that have reduced shanks, so they can be used in a standard drill chuck.

Brace
A brace is the ideal hand tool for drilling large holes in lumber. In addition, when fitted with a screwdriver bit, it provides the necessary power for driving or removing large woodscrews.

Drilling masonry for wall plugs
Set the drill to hammer action and low speed. Wrap tape around the bit to mark the depth to be drilled, allowing for slightly more depth than the length of the plug, as dust will pack down into the hole as the plug is inserted. Drill the hole in stages, partly withdrawing the bit at times to clear the debris.

To protect paintwork and floor coverings from falling dust, tape a paper bag just below the position of the hole before drilling.

● **Essential tools**
Straightedge
Tape measure
Claw hammer
Hand sledge
Panel saw
Tenon saw
Hacksaw
Keyhole saw
Power jigsaw
Power drill
Masonry bits
Brace and bits

Building tools

Crowbar

A crowbar, or wrecking bar, is used for demolishing lumber framework. Force the flat tip between the components and use the leverage of the long shaft to pry them apart. Choose a crowbar that has a claw at one end for removing large nails.

Slater's ripper

To replace individual slates or wooden shingles you must cut their fixing nails without disturbing the pieces overlapping them, and for this you need a slater's ripper. Pass the long hooked blade up between the shingles, locate one of the hooks over the fixing nail, and pull down sharply to cut it.

● Essential tools
Glass cutter
Putty knife
Cold chisel
Brick chisel
Spade
Shovel
Rake
Wheelbarrow
Cabinet screwdriver
Phillips-head
  screwdriver
Jack plane

GLAZIER'S TOOLS

Glass is such a hard and brittle material that it can only be worked with specialized tools.

Glass cutter

A glass cutter does not actually cut glass but merely scores a line in it. This is done by a tiny hardened-steel wheel or a chip of industrial diamond mounted in a penlike holder. The glass breaks along the scored line when pressure is applied to it.

Beam-compass cutter

A beam-compass cutter is for scoring circles on glass that enable you to either cut a round hole or create a circular pane. The cutting wheel is mounted at the end of an adjustable beam that turns on a central pivot that's attached to the glass by a suction cup.

Spear-point glass drill

A glass drill has a flat tungsten-steel tip shaped like a spearhead. The shape of the tip is designed to reduce friction that would otherwise crack the glass, but it does need lubricating with oil or water during drilling.

Hacking knife

A hacking knife is often a shop-made tool with a heavy steel blade for chipping old putty out of window rabbets in order to remove the glass. To use it, place the point between the putty and the frame, then tap the back of the blade with a hammer.

Putty knife

The blade of a putty knife is used for shaping and smoothing fresh putty when reglazing a window. You can choose between a chisel type with a thick, stiff blade, or a standard putty knife with a thin, flexible blade. Putty knives are also useful for removing paint and other light-duty scraping jobs.

CHISELS

As well as chisels for cutting and paring wood joints, you'll need some special ones when you are working on masonry.

Cold chisel

Cold chisels are made from solid-steel-hexagonal-section rod. They are primarily for cutting metal bars and chopping the heads off rivets, but a builder will use one for cutting a notch in brickwork or for chopping hardware embedded in brick.

Slip a plastic safety sleeve over the chisel to protect your hand from a misplaced blow with a hammer.

Plugging chisel

A plugging chisel has a narrow, flat tip for cutting out old or eroded pointing. It's worth having when you have a large area of brickwork to repoint.

Brick chisel

The wide blade of a brick chisel is designed for cutting bricks and concrete blocks. It is also useful for other heavy chopping and prying jobs.

WORK GLOVES

Wear strong work gloves whenever you are carrying paving rubble, concrete blocks, or rough lumber. Ordinary gardening gloves are better than none, but they won't last very long on a building site. The best work gloves have leather palms and fingers, although you may prefer a pair with ventilated backs for comfort in hot weather.

DIGGING TOOLS

Much building work requires some kind of digging—for making footing trenches and holes for concrete pads, sinking rows of postholes, and so on. You probably have the basic tools in your garden shed; the others you can rent.

Pickax

Use a medium-weight pickax to break up heavily compacted soil—especially if it contains a lot of buried rubble.

Mattock

The wide blade of a mattock is ideal for breaking up heavy clay soil, and it's better than an ordinary pickax for ground that's riddled with tree roots.

Spade

Buy a good-quality spade for excavating soil and mixing concrete. One with a stainless-steel blade is best, but alloy steel lasts reasonably well. Choose a strong hardwood or reinforced fiberglass shaft with a D-shaped handle that's riveted with metal plates on its crosspiece. Make sure the hollow shaft socket and blade are forged in one piece.

Although square spade blades seem to be more popular, many builders prefer a round-mouth spade with a long pole handle for digging deep holes and trenches.

Shovel

You can use a spade for mixing and placing concrete or mortar, but the raised edges of a shovel retain it better.

Garden rake

Use an ordinary garden rake for spreading gravel or leveling wet concrete. Be sure to wash your rake before concrete sets on it.

Posthole auger

Rent a posthole auger to dig narrow holes for fence- and gateposts. You drive it into the ground like a corkscrew, then pull out the plugs of earth.

Wheelbarrow

Most garden wheelbarrows are not strong enough for construction, which generally involves carting heavy loads of rubble and wet concrete. Unless the tubular underframe of the wheelbarrow is rigidly braced, the wheelbarrow's thin metal body will distort and may well spill its load as you are crossing rough ground.

Check, too, that the axle is fastened securely—a cheap wheelbarrow can lose its wheel as you are tipping a load into place.

SCREWDRIVERS

Most people gradually acquire an assortment of screwdrivers over a period of time, as and when the need arises. Alternatively, buy a power screwdriver with a range of bits or buy screwdriver bits for your power drill.

Cabinet screwdriver

Buy at least one large flat-tip screwdriver. The fixed variety is quite adequate, but a pump-action one, which drives large screws very quickly, is useful when assembling large projects.

Phillips-head screwdriver

Choose the size and type of Phillips-head screwdriver to suit the work at hand. There is no "most-useful size," as each driver must fit a screw slot exactly.

PLANES

Furniture building may call for molding or grooving planes, but most household joinery needs only a light pass to remove saw marks and leave a fairly smooth finish.

Jack plane

A jack plane, which is a medium-size bench plane, is the most versatile general-purpose tool.

Decorating tools

DECORATOR'S TOOL KIT

Most do-it-yourselfers collect a fairly extensive set of tools for decorating their houses or apartments. Although traditionalists will want to stick to time-tested tools and to materials of proven reliability, others may prefer to try recent innovations aimed at making the work easier and faster for the home decorator.

TOOLS FOR PREPARATION

Whether you're tiling, painting, or papering, make sure the surface to which the materials will be applied is sound and clean.

Straight scraper

Serrated scraper

Wallpaper and paint scrapers

The wide, stiff blade of a scraper is for removing softened paint or soaked wallpaper. The best scrapers have high-quality steel blades and riveted handles.

One with a blade 4 to 5 inches wide is best for stripping wallpaper, while a narrow one, no more than 1 inch wide, is better for removing paint from window frames and doorframes.

A serrated scraper will score impervious wallcoverings so that water or stripping solution can penetrate faster, but take care not to damage the wall itself.

Vinyl gloves

Most people wear ordinary household "rubber" gloves as protection for their hands when washing down or preparing paintwork—but tough PVC work gloves are more durable and will protect your skin against many harmful chemicals.

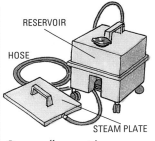

RESERVOIR

HOSE

STEAM PLATE

Steam wallpaper stripper

To remove wallpaper quickly (especially thick wallcoverings), either buy or rent an electric steam-generating stripper.

All steam strippers work on similar principles—but follow any specific safety instructions that come with the machine.

Using a steam stripper

Fill the stripper's reservoir with water and plug the tool into an outlet. Hold the steaming plate against the wallpaper until it is soft enough to be removed with a scraper. You will find that some wallcoverings take longer to soften than others.

Wallpaper scorer

Running a scorer across a wall punches minute perforations through the paper so that water or steam can penetrate faster. Some wallpaper scorers can be mounted on an extension handle.

Straight-sided shavehook

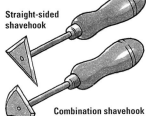

Combination shavehook

Shavehook

This is a special scraper for removing old paint and varnish. A straight-sided triangular shavehook is fine for scraping flat surfaces, but one with a combination blade can be used on concave and convex moldings too. Pull the shavehook towards you to remove the softened paint.

Heat gun

The gas blowtorch was once the professional's tool for softening old paint that required stripping, but the modern electric heat gun is much easier to use. It is as efficient as a blowtorch, but there's less risk of scorching woodwork. With most heat guns, you can adjust the temperature. Interchangeable nozzles are designed to concentrate the heated air or direct it away from windowpanes.

Drywall knife

A filling knife looks like a paint scraper but has a flexible blade for forcing filler into cracks in wood or plaster. Areas of damaged wall can be patched with large versions of this tool.

Wire brush

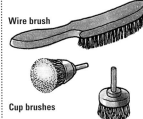

Cup brushes

Wire brushes

You can use a wire brush with steel-wire bristles to remove flaking paint and particles of rust from metalwork before repainting it. However, the job becomes easier if you use a rotary wire cup brush fitted into the chuck of an electric drill. Whatever method you use, wear goggles or safety glasses to protect your eyes.

Caulking guns

Caulk is used to seal joints between materials with different rates of expansion, which would eventually crack a rigid filler. You can buy caulk that you squeeze direct from a plastic tube, but it's more easily applied from a cartridge installed in a caulking gun.

Tack rag

A resin-impregnted cloth called a tack rag is ideal for picking up particles of dust and hard paint from a surface that's been prepared for painting. If you can't get a tack rag, use a lint-free cloth dampened with mineral spirits.

Dusting brush

A dusting brush has long soft bristles for clearing dust out of moldings and crevices just before painting. You can use an ordinary paintbrush, provided you keep it clean and dry.

SANDPAPER

Waterproof sandpaper is used for smoothing new paintwork or varnish before applying the final coat. It consists of silicon-carbide particles glued to a waterproof backing paper. Dip a piece in water and rub the paintwork until a slurry of paint and water forms. Wipe it off with a cloth before it dries; then rinse the paper clean and continue.

Alternatively, use a hard-foam block that's coated with silicon-carbide particles. These are somewhat easier to handle than a folded sheet of paper, which can tear or distort after a comparatively short period.

Masking tape

Low-tack self-adhesive tape is used to mask off wood trim or glass in order to keep an area free of paint when you are decorating adjacent surfaces.

Wide tape, up to 6 inches in width, is used to protect fitted carpets while you are painting baseboards.

Woodworking tools

As well as the decorating tools described here, you will need a basic woodworking tool kit for repairing damaged floorboards or window frames and for such jobs as installing wall paneling or building shelves.

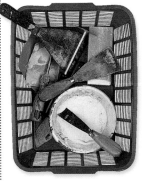

● **Essential tools**
Wallpaper scraper
Combination
  shavehook
Drywall knife
Heat gun
Wire brush

Decorating tools

PAINTBRUSHES

Quality natural-bristle paintbrushes are made from black bristle or white ox hair.

Synthetic-bristle brushes are generally less expensive than natural bristle and are quite adequate for the home decorator.

Bristle types

Natural bristle is ideal for paintbrushes, since each hair tapers naturally and splits at the tip into even finer filaments that hold paint well. Bristle is also tough and resilient and meant for use with oil-based paint only.

Synthetic "bristle" (usually made of nylon or polyester) resembles real bristle, and a good-quality nylon or polyester brush will serve most painters as well as a bristle one.

Paint bucket
To carry paint to a work site, pour a little into a cheap, lightweight plastic paint bucket.

Choosing a brush

The bristles, or filaments, of a good brush are densely packed. When you fan them with your fingers they should spring back into shape immediately. Flex the tip of the brush against your hand to see if any bristles work loose. Even a good brush will shed a few bristles at first, but never clumps of them. The ferrule should be fixed firmly to the handle.

½-inch   **1-inch**   **2-inch**

Straight paintbrushes

The bristles or filaments are set in plastic and bound to the wooden or plastic handle with a pressed-metal ferrule. You will need several sizes, up to 3 inches, for painting, varnishing, and staining, woodwork.

● **Essential tools**
Flat brushes
(½-inch, 1-inch, and 2-inch)
Wall brush (6-inch)

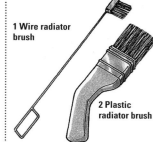

Cutting-in brush

The bristles of a cutting-in brush are cut at an angle so that you can paint windows right up into the corners and against the glass. Most painters keep a few sizes on hand.

Paint shield

Glass scraper

Paint shield and scraper

There are various plastic and metal shields for protecting glass when you are painting windows. If the glass does get spattered, it can be cleaned with a razor scraper.

SPECIAL-EFFECT BRUSHES AND TOOLS

You will need to invest in a few specialized brushes and tools in order to paint your walls, ceilings, and woodwork with colorful textures. Most can be bought inexpensively from paint stores and home centers.

Dragging brush

This brush has extra-long flexible bristles that leave linear striations in wet glaze.

Stippling brush

This is a wide flat brush with short bristles that are dabbed against a glazed surface to apply or remove color.

Stencil brush

A stencil brush has short stiff bristles. The paint is stippled through a cut-ut template that defines the shape to be painted.

Wood grainers

Special brushes and paint applicators are used to create wood-grain effects with paints and glazes. The delicate bristles of a softener, for example, blur the outlines of graining, while steel, rubber, or plastic combs can be dragged through glaze to copy straight-grained wood. A heart grainer is used to create bold heartwood graining, and other effects are achieved using rolled-up or folded scraps of cloth.

1 Wire radiator brush

2 Plastic radiator brush

Radiator brush

Unless you take a radiator off the wall for decorating, you will need a special brush to paint the back of it and the wall behind. There are two types of radiator brush. The one has a standard flat paintbrush head at right angles to a long wire handle (**1**); the other is like an ordinary paintbrush but has an angled plastic handle (**2**).

Wall brush

When applying latex paint by brush, use a straight 6-inch wall brush designed for the purpose.

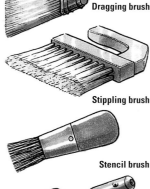

Dragging brush

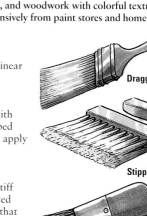

Stippling brush

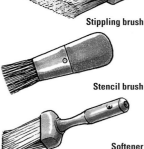

Stencil brush

Softener

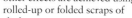

Graining combs

Heart grainer

CLEANING PAINTBRUSHES

● **Water-based paints**
As soon as you finish working, wash the filaments with warm soapy water, flexing them between your fingers to work the paint out of the roots. Then rinse the brush in clean water and shake out the excess. Smooth the bristles and slip an elastic band around their tips to hold the shape of the filling while it is drying.

Holding the shape of a brush

● **Solvent-based paints**
If you're using solvent-based paints, you can suspend the brush overnight in solvent. Squeeze out the solvent before you resume painting on the next day.

When you have finished painting, brush the excess paint onto newspaper, then soak the brush in a bowl of thinner overnight. Rinse the brush with clean thinner before storing it to remove all traces of paint.

Soaking a brush

● **Hardened paint**
If paint has hardened on a brush, soften it by soaking the bristles in brush cleaner. It will then become soft enough to wash out with hot water. If the old paint is very stubborn, dip the bristles in some paint stripper.

STORING PAINTBRUSHES

Before storing a clean paint-brush, fold paper over it and secure the paper to the ferrule with an elastic band.

Decorating tools

PAINT PADS

Paint pads help inexperienced painters apply paints and stains quickly and evenly. Although they aren't universally popular, no one would dispute their usefulness for painting large flat areas. Paint pads are unlikely to drip paint provided they are loaded properly.

Standard pads

There is a range of rectangular paint pads for decorating walls, ceilings, and flat woodwork. These standard pads have short synthetic pile on their painting surfaces and are generally made with D-shaped handles.

Corner pad

A synthetic pad wrapped around a triangular applicator spreads paint simultaneously onto both sides of an internal corner. Paint into the corner first, then pick up the wet edges and continue with a standard pad.

Sash pad

A sash pad has a small sole for painting windows. Most sash pads incorporate plastic guides to stop them from straying onto the glass.

HYDRAULIC PAINT APPLICATOR

Using a hydraulic applicator saves you having to reload your paint pad when cutting in around windows and doorframes. Changing to a corner pad allows you to paint around the edges of a room before finishing the job with a roller.

With the tool in contact with the wall or ceiling, squeeze the applicator's trigger to deliver the paint to the pad. When the paint starts to run dry, remove the pad and refill the applicator from the paint can.

CLEANING PAINT PADS

Before dipping a new pad into paint for the first time, brush it with a clothes brush to remove any loose fibers.

- When you have finished painting, blot the pad on old newspaper, then wash it in the appropriate solvent—water, mineral spirits, or brush cleaner, or any special thinners recommended by the paint manufacturer. Squeeze the foam and rub the pile with gloved fingertips, then wash the pad in hot soapy water and rinse it.

- A new paint pad that has just been used for the first time may appear to be stained by paint even after it has been washed. However, the color will not contaminate the next batch of fresh paint.

Pad tray

Pads and trays are sometimes sold as sets. If you buy a separate pad tray, look for one with a loading roller that distributes paint evenly onto the sole of a pad drawn across it.

Extension handles

Relatively wide flat pads are made with hollow handles that thread onto extension poles to help you to reach up to the ceiling.

Filling the applicator
Insert the tip into the paint and slowly draw back the handle.

PAINT ROLLERS

A paint roller is the ideal tool for painting a large area of wall or ceiling quickly. The cylindrical covers that apply the paint are interchangeable, and slide onto a revolving sprung-wire frame attached to the roller handle. The covers are very easy to swap or to remove for washing.

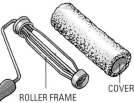

ROLLER FRAME   COVER

Sizes of roller covers

Sleeves for standard paint rollers are 7 and 9 inches long, but it is also possible to buy even larger sizes for specialized jobs.

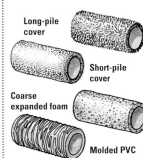

Long-pile cover

Short-pile cover

Coarse expanded foam

Molded PVC

Types of roller sleeves

You can buy roller covers of various materials to suit different surface textures and kinds of paint. Most covers are made of **sheepskin** or **synthetic fiber**, cropped to different lengths. A sheepskin cover can hold more paint than one that is made from synthetic fiber but costs about 25 percent more.

Choose a **long-pile cover** for applying paint to rough or textured surfaces such as masonry walls. A **medium-pile cover** is best for painting medium rough surfaces such as rough wood. For gloss paints, use a **short-pile cover**.

Inexpensive **plastic-foam covers** are unsatisfactory for applying paint on any surface where the quality of finish is important. They leave air bubbles in the painted surface, and the foam often distorts as it dries after washing. But they are cheap enough to be thrown away after use with finishes, such as asphalt-based paint, that would be difficult to remove even from a short-pile sleeve.

Use a **coarse expanded-foam** *cover* for applying textured paints and coatings. There are also **molded PVC rollers** with embossed surfaces to create patterns.

Extending a roller

If your roller has a hollow handle, you can thread it onto an extension pole to enable you to reach a ceiling from the floor. A hydraulic extension sucks paint into its hollow handle, then feeds it back to the roller as you work.

CLEANING A ROLLER

Remove most of the excess paint by running the roller back and forth across some old newspaper. If you are planning to use the roller next day, apply a few drops of the appropriate thinners to the cover and then wrap it in plastic. Otherwise, clean, wash, and rinse the sleeve before the paint has time to dry.

- **Water-based paints**
  If you've been using latex or acrylic paint, flush most of it out under running water, then massage a little liquid detergent into the pile of the sleeve and flush it again.

- **Solvent-based paints**
  To remove solvent-based paints, pour some thinner into the roller tray and slowly roll the sleeve back and forth in it. Squeeze the roller and agitate the pile with gloved hands. When the paint has dissolved, wash the sleeve in hot soapy water.

Roller tray

A paint roller is loaded from a sloping plastic or metal tray, the deep end of which acts as a paint reservoir. Load the roller by rolling paint from the deep end up and down the tray's ribbed slope once or twice to get an even distribution on the cover.

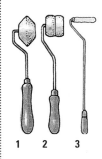

1   2   3

1 Corner roller

You can't paint into a corner with a standard roller. So unless there are to be different adjacent colors, paint the corner first with a shaped corner roller.

2 Pipe roller

A pipe roller has two narrow sleeves mounted side by side. These locate over the cylindrical pipework, enabling you to paint it.

3 Radiator roller

This is a thin roller on a long wire handle for painting behind radiators and pipes.

- **Essential tools**
2-inch and 8-inch standard pads
Sash pad
Large roller and selection of covers
Roller tray

Decorating tools

PAINT-SPRAYING EQUIPMENT

Spraying is so fast and efficient that it's worth considering when you are planning to paint the outside walls of a building. Spraying equipment is readily available, even from large DIY stores, and you can rent it. It's possible to spray most exterior paints and finishes if they are thinned properly, but tell the rental store which paint you intend to use so they can supply the right spray gun with the correct nozzle. Get goggles and a respirator at the same time.

Preparation

As far as possible, plan to work on a dry and windless day. Also, allow time to mask off windows, doors and pipework.

Follow the setting-up and handling instructions supplied with the equipment, and if you are new to the work, practice beforehand on an inconspicuous section of wall.

Compressor-operated spray

With this equipment, the paint is mixed with compressed air to emerge as a fine spray. It is generally not used for applying paint on large areas, but for painting and finishing smaller projects and furniture.

The trigger opens a valve to admit air, and at the same time opens the paint outlet at the nozzle. The paint is drawn from a container, usually mounted below the gun, and mixes with air at the tip. Most guns have air-delivery horns at the sides of the nozzle in order to produce a fan-shaped spray.

Spraying reinforced paints
Rent a special gravity-fed spray gun to apply heavily textured finishes. The material is loaded into a hopper on top of the gun.

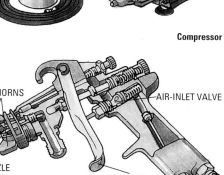

Compressor

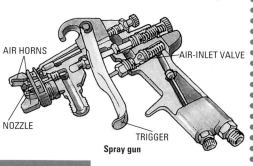

AIR HORNS

AIR-INLET VALVE

NOZZLE

TRIGGER

Spray gun

Airless sprayer

In an airless sprayer, an electric pump delivers the paint itself at high pressure to the spray gun. The paint is picked up through a plastic tube inserted in the paint container, and the pump forces it through a high-pressure hose to

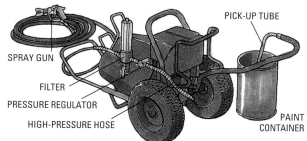

PICK-UP TUBE

SPRAY GUN

FILTER

PRESSURE REGULATOR

HIGH-PRESSURE HOSE

PAINT CONTAINER

a filter and pressure regulator, which you adjust to produce the required spray pattern.

The paint leaves the nozzle at such high pressure that it can penetrate skin. Most spray guns of this kind have safety shields on their nozzles.

USING SPRAYERS SAFELY

Follow safety recommendations supplied with the sprayer, and take the following precautions:

● Wear goggles and a respirator when spraying.
● Don't spray indoors without proper ventilation.
● Atomized oil paint is highly flammable, so turn off all lights and never smoke when you are spraying.
● Don't leave the equipment unattended, especially where there are children or pets.
● If the gun has a safety lock, engage it whenever you are not actually spraying.
● Unplug the equipment and release the pressure in the hose before trying to clear a blocked nozzle.
● Never aim the gun at yourself or anyone else. If you should accidentally spray your skin with an airless gun, seek medical advice immediately.

CLEANING A SPRAY GUN

Empty out any paint that is left in the container and add some thinner. Spray the thinner until it emerges clear, then release the pressure and dismantle the spray nozzle. Clean the parts with a solvent-dampened rag and wipe out the container.

COMMON SPRAYING FAULTS

Streaked paintwork

An uneven, streaked finish will result if you do not overlap the passes of the gun.

Patchy paintwork

Coverage won't be consistent if you move the gun in an arc. Keep it pointing directly at the wall and moving parallel to it.

Orange-peel texture

A wrinkled paint film resembling the texture of orange peel is usually caused by spraying paint that is too thick. Alternatively, if the paint seems to be the right consistency, you may be moving the gun too slowly.

Paint runs

Runs will occur if you apply too much paint—probably through holding the gun too close to the surface you are spraying.

Powdery finish

This is caused by paint drying before it reaches the wall. The remedy is to hold the gun a little closer to the wall's surface.

Spattering

If the pressure is too high, the finish will look speckled. To avoid spattering, lower the pressure until the finish is satisfactory.

Spitting

A partly clogged nozzle will make the gun splutter. Clear the nozzle with a stiff bristle from a brush (never use wire) and then wipe it with a rag dampened in paint thinner.

PAPERHANGER'S TOOLS

You can improvise some of the tools needed for paperhanging. However, the right equipment is inexpensive, so it's worth having a decent kit.

Tape measure

A steel tape measure is best for measuring walls and ceilings in order to estimate the amount of wallcovering you will need.

Plumb bob and line

Chalkline

Plumb line

A plumb line has a pointed metal weight called a plumb bob. It is used to mark the position of one edge of a strip of wallpaper. Hold the end of the line close to the ceiling, allow the weight to come to rest, and then mark the wall at points down the length of the line.

A chalkline has a string that retracts into a hollow case that contains colored chalk, so the string is coated with chalk every time it is withdrawn. With the string stretched taut, snap it like a bowstring to leave a line on the wall or ceiling. A chalkline can be used like a plumb line, or stretched at any angle between two points.

Paste brush

Use either a wide wall brush or a short-pile roller to apply paste to the back of wallcoverings.

Clean either tool by washing it in warm water.

Decorating tools

PAPERHANGER'S TABLE

You can paste wallcoverings on any flat surface, but a dedicated pasting table provides a much more convenient working surface. It stands higher than the average dining table, but is only 1 inch wider than a standard roll of wallpaper, which makes it easier to spread paste without getting it onto the worktop. The table's frame folds flat and the top is hinged, so the table be carried from room to room and stored in a small space.

Paperhanger's brush
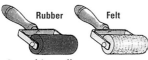

This is used for smoothing wallcoverings onto a wall or ceiling. Its bristles should be soft so as not to damage delicate paper but springy enough to provide the pressure to squeeze out air bubbles and excess paste. Wash the brush in warm water when you finish work to prevent paste hardening on the bristles.

Seam roller
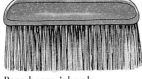

Use a hardwood or plastic seam roller to press down the seams between strips of wallpaper, but don't use one on embossed or delicate wallcoverings.

Smoothing roller

Rubber **Felt**
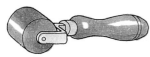

There are rubber rollers for squeezing trapped air from under wallcoverings, but use a felt one on delicate or flocked papers.

Paperhanger's scissors

Any fairly large scissors can be used for trimming wallpaper to length, but special paperhanger's scissors have extra-long blades to achieve a straight cut.

Utility knife

Use a knife to trim paper around light fittings and switches and to achieve perfect butt joints by cutting through overlapping edges of paper. The knife must be sharp to avoid tearing, so use one with disposable blades that you can change as soon as one gets dull. Some knives have double-ended blades clamped in the handle. Others have retractable blades that are snapped off in short sections to leave a new sharp edge.

TILING TOOLS

Most of the tools in a tiler's kit are for applying ceramic wall and floor tiles. Different tools are required for laying soft tiles and vinyl sheeting.

Level

You will need a level to ensure that horizontal and vertical runs of tile will be level and plumb.

Profile gauge

A profile gauge is used for copying the shape of door moldings or pipework. It provides a pattern so you can fit soft floor coverings. As you press the steel pins of the profile gauge against the object you wish to copy, they slide back, replicating the shape.

Notched trowel

Make a ridged bed of adhesive or mortar for tiles by drawing the toothed edge of a plastic spreader or steel tiler's trowel through the material.

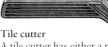

Tile cutter

A tile cutter has either a pointed tungsten-carbide tip or a steel wheel (similar to a glass cutter's) for scoring the glazed surface of ceramic tiles. The tile snaps cleanly along the scored line.

Tile saw

A tile saw has a bent-metal frame that holds a thin wire rod under tension. The rod is coated with particles of tungsten-carbide, which are hard enough to cut through ceramic tiles. As the rod is circular in section, it will cut in any direction, making it possible to saw along curved lines.

Grout spreader or rubber float

The spreader has a hard-rubber blade mounted in a plastic handle. The float looks similar to a wooden float but has a rubber sole. Both tools are used for spreading grout into the gaps between ceramic tiles.

Nibblers

It is impossible to snap a very narrow strip off a ceramic tile. Instead, score the line with a tile cutter, then break off the waste little by little with tile nibblers. These resemble pincers but have sharper jaws, made of tungsten-carbide, that open automatically when you relax your grip on the spring-loaded handles.

Tile sander

To smooth a rough, cut tile edge, use specially made abrasive-coated mesh.

TILE-CUTTING JIGS

A jig makes it much easier to cut and fit tiles at the edges of walls, floors, and ceilings. You can use a marking-and-cutting jig to measure the gap and cut the tiles for these narrow strips.

Using a marking-and-cutting jig

To measure the size of the tile, slide the jig open until one pointer is against the adjacent wall and the other is against the edge of the last whole tile (1). The jig automatically makes an allowance for grouting.

Fit the jig over the tile to be cut and use a tile cutter to score the glaze through the slot in the jig (2). The cutter comes with a pair of pliers with angled jaws for snapping the tile in two (3).

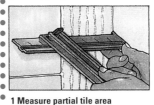

1 Measure partial tile area

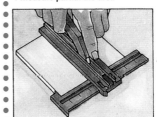

2 Score glazed surface

3 Snap tile with special pliers

Score-and-snap tile cutter

If you need to cut a lot of tiles, especially thick floor tiles, buy a sturdy score-and-snap cutter. After pushing the cutting wheel across the tile's glazed surface, press down on the lever to snap the tile.

Powered wet saw

If you need to cut thick unglazed tiles, rent a powered wet saw with a diamond-coated blade. The same tool is ideal for cutting corners out of ceramic tiles that have to be fitted around an electrical outlet or switch.

● **Essential tools**
Tape measure
Plumb line
Paste brush
Paperhanger's brush
Seam roller
Scissors
Utility knife
Paperhanger's table
Level
Notched trowel
Tile cutter
Nibblers
Tile saw
Float

Plumbing tools

PLUMBER'S AND METALWORKER'S TOOLS

While easy-to-work plastic pipe is used extensively in residential plumbing, particularly for drain and vent systems, it only comprises part of the plumbing picture. Brass fittings and pipe made from copper dominate typical water supply systems, and cast-iron waste and vent pipe is still found in many older homes. Therefore, a good part of a plumber's tool kit includes tools for working with metal.

EQUIPMENT FOR REMOVING BLOCKAGES

You don't have to get a plumber to clear blocked fixtures, pipes, or even large drains. All the necessary equipment can be bought or rented.

Plunger
This is a simple but effective tool for clearing a blockage from a sink, toilet, or bath. A pumping action on the rubber cup forces air and water along the pipe to disperse the blockage. When you buy a plunger, make sure the cup is large enough to cover the drain. If you have more than one bathroom, buy one for each room.

Drain auger
A flexible coiled-wire drain auger will pass through small-diameter waste pipes to clear blockages. Pass the corkscrew-like head into the waste pipe until it reaches the blockage, clamp the cranked handle onto the other end, and then turn it to rotate the head and engage the blockage. Push and pull the auger till the pipe is clear.

Also available are rotary drain augers that are powered by an electric drill. These may have a reach of 20 feet and are capable of navigating the tight turns in drain traps.

● **Essential tools**
Plunger
Scriber
Center punch
Steel rule
Try square
General-purpose hacksaw

Small-wire auger
The short, coiled-wire drainpipe auger is designed for clearing toilets and drain traps. To operate it, the handle is rotated in a rigid, hollow shaft while the auger end is pushed into the drain. The auger has a vinyl guard to keep the fixture from getting scratched.

SET OF RODS

PLUNGER   CORKSCREW   SCRAPER

Drain rods
You may be able to rent a complete set of rods and fittings for clearing main drains. The rods come in 3-foot, 3-inch lengths of polypropylene with threaded brass connectors.

The clearing heads comprise a double-worm corkscrew fitting, a 4-inch rubber plunger, and a hinged scraper for clearing the clogged section of drain piping.

MEASURING AND MARKING TOOLS

Tools for measuring and marking metal are very similar to those used for wood, but they are made and calibrated for greater accuracy because metal parts must fit with precision.

Scriber
For precise work, use a pointed hardened-steel scriber to mark lines on sheetmetal or a piece of steel or cast-iron pipe.

Spring dividers
Spring dividers are similar to a pencil compass, but both legs have steel points. These are adjusted to the required spacing by a knurled nut on a threaded rod that links the legs.

Using spring dividers
Use dividers to step off divisions along a line (1) or to scribe circles (2). By running one point against the edge of a workpiece, you can scribe a line parallel with the edge (3).

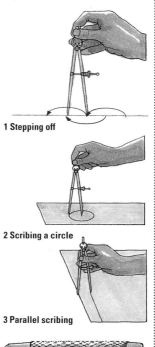

1 Stepping off

2 Scribing a circle

3 Parallel scribing

Center punch
A center punch is an inexpensive tool for marking the centers of holes to be drilled.

Using a center punch
With its point on dead center, strike the punch with a hammer. If the mark is not accurate, angle the punch toward the true center, tap it to extend the mark in that direction, and then mark the center again.

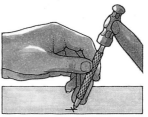

Correcting a misplaced center mark

Steel rule
You will need a long tape measure for estimating pipe runs and positioning appliances, but use a 1- or 2-foot steel rule for marking out components when accuracy is required.

Try square
You can use a woodworker's try square to mark or check right angles; however, an all-metal engineer's try square is precision-made for metalwork. The small notch between blade and stock allows the tool to fit properly against a right-angled workpiece even when the corner is burred by filing. For general-purpose work, choose a 6-inch try square.

METAL-CUTTING TOOLS

You can cut solid bar, sheet, and tubular metal with an ordinary hacksaw, but there are tools specifically designed for cutting sheetmetal and pipes.

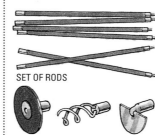

General-purpose hacksaw
A modern hacksaw has a tubular-steel frame with a light cast-metal handle. The frame is adjustable to accommodate replaceable blades of different lengths, which are tensioned by tightening a wingnut.

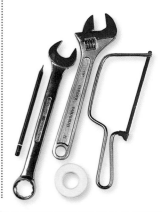

Plumbing tools

CHOOSING HACKSAW BLADES

You can buy 8-, 10-, and 12-inch hacksaw blades. Try the different lengths till you find the one that suits you best. Choose the hardness and size of teeth according to the type of metal you are planning to cut.

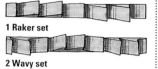

1 Raker set

2 Wavy set

Size and set of teeth
A coarse hacksaw blade has 14 to 18 teeth per 1 in; a fine blade has 24 to 32. The teeth are set (bent sideways) to make a cut wider than the blade's thickness, to prevent it jamming in the work. Coarse teeth are "raker set" **(1)**, with pairs of teeth bent to opposite sides and separated by a tooth left in line with the blade to clear metal waste from the kerf (cut). Fine teeth are too small to be raker set, and the whole row is "wavy set" **(2)**. Use a coarse blade for cutting soft metals like brass and aluminum, which would clog fine teeth; and a fine blade for thin sheet and the harder metals.

Hardness
A hacksaw blade must be harder than the metal it is cutting or its teeth will quickly dull. A carbon-steel blade will cut most metals, but there are high-speed steel blades that stay sharp longer and are less prone to losing teeth. However, being rigid and brittle, they break easily. Blades of high-speed steel combined with a flexible metal backing, called bimetal blades, are nearly unbreakable.

Installing a hacksaw blade
With its teeth pointing away from the handle, slip a new blade onto the pins at each end of the hacksaw frame. Apply tension with the wingnut. If the new blade tends to wander off-line as you cut, tighten the wingnut.

Turning a blade
Sometimes it's easier to work with the blade at right angles to the frame. To do so, rotate the blade-mounting pins a quarter turn before fitting the blade.

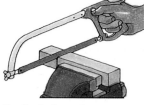

Turn first kerf away from you

Sawing metal bar
Hold the work in a vise, with the marked cutting line as close to the jaws as possible. Start the cut on the waste side of the line with short strokes until the kerf is about 1/16-inch deep; then turn the bar 90 degrees in the vise so that the kerf faces away from you and cut a similar kerf in the new face. Continue in this way until the kerf runs right around the bar, then cut through the bar with long steady strokes. Steady the end of the saw with your free hand and put a little light oil on the blade if necessary.

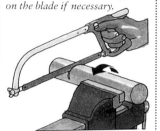

Sawing rod or pipe
As you cut a cylindrical rod or pipe, rotate it away from you until the kerf runs right around the work before you sever it.

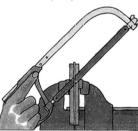

Sawing sheetmetal
To saw a small piece of sheet-metal, sandwich it between two strips of wood clamped in a vise. Adjust the metal to place the cutting line close to the strips, then saw down the waste side with steady strokes and the blade angled to the work. To cut a thin sheet of metal, clamp it between two pieces of plywood and cut through all three layers simultaneously.

Sawing a groove
To cut a slot or groove wider than a standard hacksaw blade, fit two or more identical blades in the frame at the same time.

Junior hacksaw
Use a junior hacksaw for cutting small-bore tubing and thin metal rod. The simplest ones have a solid spring-steel frame that holds the blade under tension.

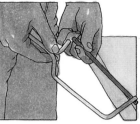

Fitting a new blade
To fit a blade, locate it in the slot at the front of the frame and bow the frame against a workbench until the blade fits in the rear slot.

Metalworker's vise
A large metalworker's vise has to be bolted to the workbench, but smaller ones can be clamped on. Slip plastic or brass liners over the jaws of a vise to protect workpieces held in it.

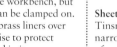

Cold chisel
Plumbers use cold chisels for hacking old pipes out of masonry. They are also useful for chopping the heads off rivets and cutting metal rod. Sharpen the tip of the chisel on a bench grinder.

Straight snips

Universal snips

Tinsnips
Tinsnips are used for cutting sheet metal. *Straight snips* have wide blades for cutting straight edges. If you try to cut curves with them, the waste usually gets caught against the blades; but it is possible to cut a convex curve by progressively removing small straight pieces of waste down to the marked line. *Universal snips* have thick narrow blades that cut a curve in one pass and will also make straight cuts.

Using tinsnips
As you cut along the marked line, let the waste curl away below the sheet. To cut thick sheet metal, clamp one handle of the snips in a vise, so you can apply your full weight to the other one.
Try not to close the jaws completely every time, as that can cause a jagged edge on the metal. Wear thick gloves when cutting sheetmetal.

SHARPENING SNIPS

Clamp one handle in a vise and sharpen the cutting edge with a smooth file. File the other edge and finish by removing the burrs from the backs of the blades with a slipstone.

Sheetmetal cutter
Tinsnips tend to distort a narrow strip cut from the edge of a metal sheet. However, the strip remains perfectly flat when removed with a sheet-metal cutter. The same tool is also suited to cutting rigid plastic sheet, which cracks if it is distorted by tinsnips.

Tube cutter
A tube cutter slices tubing exactly 90 degrees to its length. The pipe is clamped between the cutting wheel and an adjustable slide with two rollers and is cut as the tool is moved around it. The adjusting screw is tightened between each revolution.
Pipe and tubing can also be cut with a hacksaw or reciprocating saw.

Chain-link cutter
Cut large-diameter cast-iron pipe with a chain-link cutter. Wrap the chain round the pipe, locate the end link in the clamp, and tighten the adjuster until the cutter on each link bites into the metal. Work the handle back and forth to score the pipe and continue tightening the adjuster intermittently until the pipe is severed.

● **Essential tools**
Hacksaw
Cold chisel
Tinsnips
Tube cutter

Sheetmetal cutter

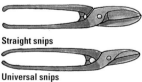

Tube cutter

Chain-link cutter

Plumbing tools

DRILLS AND PUNCHES

Special-quality steel bits are made for drilling holes in metal.

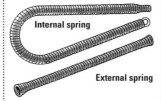

Twist drills

Metal-cutting twist drills are similar to the ones used for wood but they are made from high-speed steel and their tips are ground to a shallower angle. Use them in a power drill or drill press at a slow speed.

Mark the metal with a center punch to locate the drill point, and clamp the work in a vise, to the bed of a drill press or to a work surface. Drill slowly and steadily, and keep the bit oiled.

When drilling sheetmetal, the bit can jam and produce a ragged hole as it exits on the opposite side of the workpiece. As a precaution, clamp the work between pieces of plywood and drill through all three layers.

For ease in starting a hole in metal, especially when the hole center hasn't been marked with a punch, choose a drill bit with a split-point design, or similar feature. These bits are less likely to skate across the surface when starting the hole.

Metal hole-punch kit

Another option for making holes is to use a metal hole-punch kit. This features a lever-activated hand tool, and dies and punches for creating holes in aluminum, brass, copper, plastic, and mild steel.

To use the hole-punch kit, first mark the hole location on the workpiece. Then, position the punch over the mark and firmly squeeze the handles together to drive the cutting die through the metal.

● **Essential tools**
High-speed twist drills
Power drill
Bending springs
Soft mallet
Soldering iron
Gas torch

METAL BENDERS

Thick or hard metal must be heated before it can be bent successfully, but soft copper piping and sheetmetal can be bent while cold.

Internal spring

External spring

Bending springs

You can bend small-diameter pipes over your knee, but their walls must be supported with a coiled spring to prevent them from buckling.

Push an internal spring inside the pipe, or slide an external one over it. Either type of spring must fit the pipe exactly.

CURVED FORMERS

STRAIGHT FORMERS

Tube bender

With a tube bender, a pipe is bent over one of two fixed curved formers that are designed to give the optimum radii for plumbing and to support the walls of the pipe during bending. Each has a matching straight former, which is placed between the pipe and a steel roller on a movable lever. Operating this lever bends the pipe over the curved former.

Soft mallet

Soft mallets have a head made of coiled rawhide, hard rubber or plastic. They are used in bending strip or sheetmetal, which would be damaged by a metal hammer.

To bend sheetmetal at a right angle, clamp it between straight boards along the bending line. Start at one end and bend the metal over one of the boards by tapping it with the mallet. Don't attempt the full bend at once, but work along the sheet, increasing the angle gradually and keeping it constant along the length until the metal lies flat on the batten. Tap out any kinks.

TOOLS FOR JOINING METAL

You can make permanent watertight joints with solder, a molten alloy that acts like a glue when it cools and solidifies.

Mechanical fasteners such as compression joints, rivets, and nuts and bolts are also used for joining metal.

SOLDERS

Solders are special alloys for joining metals and are designed to melt at temperatures lower than the melting points of the metals to be joined. Soft solder melts at 365°F to 482°F. Brazing, a method of hard soldering involving a copper and zinc alloy, requires the even higher temperature of 1562°F to 1832°F.

Solder is available as a coiled wire or a thick rod. Use soft solder for copper and brass plumbing fittings and pipe.

FLUX

To be soldered successfully, a joint must be perfectly clean and free of oxides. Even after the metal has been cleaned with steel wool or emery cloth, oxides form immediately, making a positive bond between the solder and metal impossible. Flux is used to form a chemical barrier against oxidation.

Corrosive or "active" flux, applied with a brush, dissolves oxides but must be washed from the surface with water as soon as the solder solidifies, or it will go on corroding the metal.

A "passive" flux, in paste form, is used where it is impossible to wash the joint thoroughly. Although it does not dissolve oxides, it excludes them adequately for soldering copper plumbing joints and electrical connections.

Another alternative is to use wire solder containing flux in a hollow core. The flux flows just before the solder melts.

Soldering irons

For successful soldering, the work has to become hot enough for the solder to melt and flow—otherwise it solidifies before it can completely penetrate the joint. A soldering iron is used to apply the necessary heat.

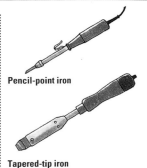
Pencil-point iron

Tapered-tip iron

At one time, soldering irons were simply heated in a fire, but today's electric versions are far handier to use because the temperature is both controllable and constant.

Use a low-powered pencil-point iron for soldering electrical connections. To bring sheetmetal up to working temperature, use a larger iron with a tapered tip.

For more control and versatility, choose a trigger-activated soldering gun. These often have two wattage ranges, the lower for fine work and the higher for heavier jobs.

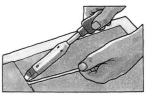

Tinning a soldering iron

The tip of a soldering iron must be coated with solder to keep it oxide-free and maintain its performance. Clean the cool tip with a file; then heat it to working temperature, dip it in flux, and apply an even coat of solder.

Using a soldering iron

Clean the mating surfaces of the joint to a bright finish and coat them with flux, then clamp the joint tightly between two wooden strips so it does not move out of position. Apply the hot iron along the joint to heat the metal thoroughly, and then run its tip along the edge of the joint, following closely with the solder. The solder flows immediately into a properly heated joint.

Plumbing tools

Gas torch

Even a large soldering iron can't heat thick metal fast enough to compensate for heat loss from the joint, and this is very much the situation when you solder copper pipe. Although the copper unions have very thin walls, the pipe on each side dissipates so much heat that a soldering iron cannot get the joint itself hot enough to form a watertight soldered seal. Instead, use a gas torch with an intensely hot flame to heat the work quickly. The torch runs on propane or MAPP gas contained under pressure in a disposable metal canister that screws onto the gas inlet. Open the control valve and light the gas released from the nozzle, then adjust the valve until the flame roars and is bright blue. Use the hottest part of the flame—about the middle of its length—to heat the joint.

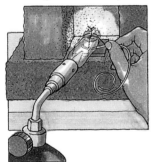

Hard soldering and brazing

Use a gas torch for brazing and hard soldering. Clean and flux the work—if possible with an active flux—then wire or clamp the parts together. Place the assembly on a fireproof mat or surround it with firebricks. Bring the joint to red heat with the torch, then dip a stick of the appropriate alloy in flux and apply it to the joint.

When the joint is cool, chip off hardened flux, wash the metal thoroughly in hot water, and finish the joint with a file.

Fireproof mat

It's a good idea to buy a special fireproof mat from a plumbing supply outlet to protect flammable surfaces from the heat of a gas torch.

Heat gun

Some heat guns designed for stripping paint can also be used for thawing frozen pipe. You can vary the temperature of an electronic gun from about 200°F to over 1000°F. A heat shield on the nozzle reflects the heat back onto the work.

RIVET

Blind riveter

Join thin sheetmetal with a blind riveter, a hand-operated tool with plierlike handles. It uses special rivets with long shanks that break off, leaving slightly raised heads on both sides of the work.

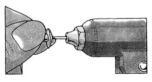

1 Insert the rivet

2 Squeeze the handles

Using a riveter

Clamp the two sheets together and drill holes right through the metal, matching the diameter of the rivets and spaced regularly along the joint. Open the handles of the riveter and insert the rivet shank in the head (1). Push the rivet through a hole in the workpiece and, while pressing the tool hard against the metal, squeeze the handles to compress the rivet head on the far side (2). When the rivet is fully expanded, the shank will snap off in the tool.

A professional plumber uses a great variety of wrenches on a wide range of fittings and fasteners. However, there is no need to buy them all, since you can rent ones that you need only occasionally.

Open-end wrench

A set of open-end wrenches is essential for a plumber or metalworker. In many cases, pipes run into a fitting or accessory, and the only tool you can use is a wrench with open jaws.

The wrenches are usually double-ended and combine two sizes. In some sets, the sizes are duplicated so you can turn two identical nuts simultaneously, as when tightening or loosening a compression joint, for example.

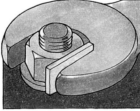

Achieving a tight fit
A wrench must be a good fit or it will round the corners of the nut. In an emergency, pack out the jaws with a thin shim of metal if you don't have the right wrench for the job.

Box-end wrench

The closed head of a box-end wrench is stronger and fits better than an open-ended tool.

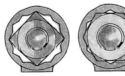

Square nut   **Hexagonal nut**

Choosing a box-end wrench

Choose a twelve-point wrench for speed and the ability to handle both square and hexagonal nuts. A six-point wrench, however, grips a hexhead fastener more securely. You can buy combination wrenches that have one closed end and one open end.

Socket tube

A socket tube is a steel tube with hexagonal ends. The turning force is applied with a bar slipped through holes drilled in the tube. Don't use a very long bar. Too much leverage may strip the thread of the fitting or distort the walls of the tube.

Adjustable wrench

An adjustable wrench, with its movable jaw, is not as strong as an open-end or box-end wrench, but it is often the only tool that will fit a large or painted nut. It's also ideal when an odd-size fastener is encountered. Make sure the spanner fits the nut snugly by rocking it slightly as you tighten the jaws; grip the nut with the back of the jaws. If you use just the tips, they can spring apart slightly under force and the wrench will slip.

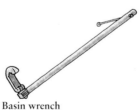

Basin wrench

A basin wrench provides under-the-sink access to the nut that holds a sink faucet to the counter. It has a pivoting jaw that can be set for either tightening or loosening.

Radiator wrench

Use this simple wrench, made from hexagonal-section steel rod, to remove radiator drain plugs. One end is ground to fit plugs that have square sockets.

● **Essential tools**
Blind riveter
Open-end wrenches
Adjustable wrench

Plumbing tools

Pipe wrench
The adjustable toothed jaws of a pipe wrench are for gripping pipe and fittings. As force is applied, the jaws tighten.

Chain wrench
A chain wrench does the same job as a pipe wrench but can be used on pipe and fittings with a very large diameter. Wrap the chain tightly around the work and engage it with the hook at the end of the wrench, then lever the handle toward the toothed jaw to apply turning force.

Smooth-jaw adjustable wrench
This older-style wrench is ideal for gripping and manipulating chromed fittings because its large smooth jaws will not damage the surface of the metal.

Strap wrench
With a strap wrench you can disconnect a tub spout or other chromed fitting without damaging its surface. Wrap the strap around the pipe, pass its end through the slot in the head of the tool, and pull it tight. Levering on the handle rotates the pipe.

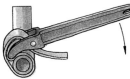

Locking pliers
Locking pliers clamp onto the work. They grip round stock or damaged nuts and are often used as a small clamp.

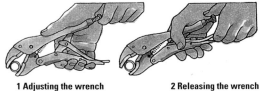

1 Adjusting the wrench   **2 Releasing the wrench**

Using locking pliers
To close the jaws, squeeze the handles while slowly turning the adjusting screw clockwise (1). Eventually the jaws will snap together, gripping the work securely. To release the tool's grip on the work, pull the release lever (2).

● **Essential tools**
Locking pliers
Second-cut and smooth flat files
Second-cut and smooth half-round files

FILES
Files are used for shaping and smoothing metal components and removing sharp edges.

CLASSIFYING FILES
The working faces of a file are composed of parallel ridges, or teeth, set at about 70 degrees to its edges. A file is classified according to the size and spacing of its teeth and whether it has one or two sets of teeth.

Single-cut file

Double-cut file

A **single-cut file** has one set of teeth virtually covering each of its faces. A **double-cut file** has a second set of identical teeth crossing the first at a 45-degree angle. Some files are single-cut on one side and double-cut on the other.

The spacing of teeth relates directly to their size: the finer the teeth, the more closely packed they are. Degrees of coarseness are expressed as number of teeth per 1 inch. Use progressively finer files to remove marks left by coarser ones.

File classification:

Bastard file–*c*oarse grade (26 teeth per 1 inch), used for initial shaping.
Second-cut file–medium grade (36 teeth per 1 inch), used for preliminary smoothing.
Smooth file–fine grade (47 teeth per 1 inch), used for final smoothing.

CLEANING A FILE
Soft metal tends to clog file teeth. When a file stops cutting efficiently, brush along the teeth with a fine wire brush called a file card, then rub chalk on the file to help reduce clogging in future.

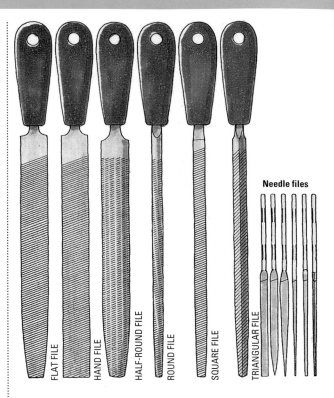

FLAT FILE   HAND FILE   HALF-ROUND FILE   ROUND FILE   SQUARE FILE   TRIANGULAR FILE

Needle files

Flat file
A flat file tapers from its pointed tang to its tip, in both width and thickness. Both faces and both edges are toothed.

Hand file
Hand files are parallel-sided but tapered in their thickness. Most of them have one smooth edge for filing up to a corner without damaging it.

Half-round file
This tool has one rounded face for shaping inside curves.

Round file
A round file is for shaping tight curves and enlarging holes.

Square file
Square files are used for cutting narrow slots and smoothing the edges of small rectangular holes.

Triangular file
Triangular files are designed for accurately shaping and smoothing undercut apertures of less than 90 degrees.

Needle files
These are miniature versions of standard files and are made in extra-fine grades. Needle files are used for precise work and to sharpen brace bits.

FILE SAFETY
Always install a wooden or plastic handle on the tang of a file before you use it.

1 Installing a file handle

2 Knock a handle from tang

If an unprotected file catches on the work, then the tang could be driven into the palm of your hand. Having installed a handle, tap its end on a bench to tighten its grip **(1)**.

To remove a handle, hold the blade of the file in one hand and strike the ferrule away from you with a block of wood **(2)**.

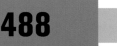

Plumbing tools

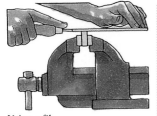

Using a file
When using any file, keep it flat on the work and avoid rocking it during forward strokes. Hold it steady, with the fingers of one hand resting on its tip, and make slow firm strokes with the full length of the file. Bear down only on the forward, cutting stroke and hold the work low in the vise to avoid vibration.

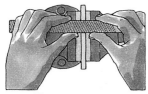

Draw-filing
You can give metal a smooth finish by draw-filing. With both hands, hold a smooth file at right angles to the work and slide the tool backwards and forwards along the surface. Finally, polish the workpiece with emery cloth wrapped around the file.

PLIERS

Pliers are for improving your grip on small components and for bending and shaping metal rod and wire.

Slip-joint pliers
For general-purpose work, buy a sturdy pair of slip-joint pliers. The toothed jaws have a curved section for gripping round stock, and most models have a shear for cutting wire.

Tongue-and-groove or waterpump pliers
The special feature of tongue-and-groove pliers is a movable pivot for enlarging the jaw spacing. The extra-long handles give a good grip on pipes and other fittings.

FINISHING METAL

Before painting or soldering metal, always make sure it is clean and rust-free.

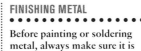

Wire brush
Use a steel-wire hand brush to clean rusty or corroded metal.

Steel wool
Steel wool is a mass of very thin steel filaments. It is used to remove file marks and to clean corrosion and dirt from metal.

Emery cloth and paper
Emery is a natural black grit which, when backed with paper or cloth, is ideal for polishing metals. There is a range of grades from coarse to fine. For the best finish, use progressively finer abrasives as the work proceeds.

1 Glue paper to a board

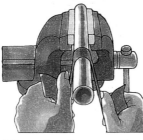

2 Clean a pipe with an emery strip

Using emery cloth and paper
To avoid rounding the crisp edges of a flat component, glue a sheet of emery paper to a board and rub the metal on the abrasive (1).

To finish round stock or pipes, loop a strip of emery cloth over the work and pull alternately on each end (2).

Buffing wheel
Metals can be brought to a shine by hand, using a liquid metal polish and a soft cloth; but for a really high gloss, use a buffing wheel in a bench-mounted power drill or grinder.

Using a buffing wheel
After applying a stick of buffing compound (a fine abrasive with wax) to the revolving wheel, move the work from side to side against the lower half, keeping any edges facing downwards.

Reseating tool
If the seat of a tap has become so worn that even fitting a new washer won't produce a perfect seal, use a reseating tool to grind the seat flat.

Remove the tap's faucet handle, stem, and stem nut, then screw the cone of the reseating tool into the faucet valve cavity. Turn the knurled adjuster to lower the cutter onto the worn seat, and then turn the bar to grind the seat.

WOODWORKING TOOLS

A plumber needs a set of basic woodworking tools in order to lift floorboards, notch joists for pipe runs, and other odd jobs.

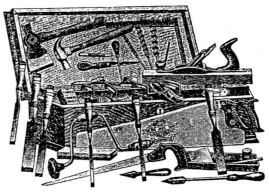

● **Essential tools and materials**
Pliers
Wire brush
Steel wool
Emery cloth
Emery paper

Electrical tools

Flashlight
Keep a flashlight handy for checking your service panel when a fuse blows or breaker trips. You may also need extra light when working on connections in the basement or attic (a flashlight that stands on its own is particularly helpful).

● **Essential tools**
Screwdrivers
Wire cutters
Wire strippers
Power drill and bits
Flashlight
Voltage tester
Continuity tester
General-purpose tools

ELECTRICIAN'S TOOLS

You need only a fairly limited range of tools to make electrical connections, but an extensive general-purpose tool kit is required for making cable runs and for installing electrical accessories and appliances.

SCREWDRIVERS

Buy good screwdrivers in a range of sizes for tightening electrical terminals. Fixed-blade screwdrivers and multibit versions with interchangeable tips stored in the handle are both handy to have.

Insulated and noninsulated screwdrivers
An electric circuit should be turned off before working on it. But it's still a good idea to use a fully insulated screwdriver. An insulated screwdriver has a plastic handle and a plastic insulating sleeve on its shaft.

Use an ordinary noninsulated screwdriver with a bare shaft for general work such as fastening mounting boxes to walls.

KNEEPADS

Protect your knees when working on outlet receptacles and other devices or appliances near the floor.

WIRE CUTTERS

Use wire cutters for cropping cable and flex to length.

Electrician's side-cutting pliers
These are heavy-duty pliers that have large jaws and shears and padded handles. You can use them to cut wire and cable.

Diagonal cutters
Diagonal cutters will cut thick conductors more effectively than will electrician's pliers, but you'll need a hacksaw to cut heavy cable, flexible conduit, and other metal components.

WIRE STRIPPERS

There are various tools for cutting or stripping the plastic insulation that covers cables and flexible cords.

Multi-tool

Wire strippers
To remove the insulation from cable, use a pair of wire strippers with jaws shaped to cut through the covering without damaging the conductor. There is a multipurpose version that can cut screws and conductors and strip insulation.

Utility knife
A knife with sharp disposable blades is best for slitting and peeling the sheathing around electrical cable.

DRILLS

When you run circuit wiring, you need a drill with several special-purpose bits for boring through wood and masonry.

Auger
Some electricians employ a long wood-boring auger to drill through the wall plate and framing when they're running a switch cable from an attic down to its mounting box.

Power drill
A cordless power drill is ideal for boring cable holes through framing and for securing junction, receptacle, and switch boxes in place. As well as twist bits and screwdriving bits, you'll need auger bits and perhaps carbide-tipped bits for boring through brick walls.

If you shorten the shaft of a wide-tipped spade bit, you can use it in a power drill between floor joists.

TESTERS

Even when you have turned off the power at the service panel, use a tester to check that the circuit is safe to work on.

Voltage tester
Be sure to buy a twin-probe tester that's intended for use on a household electrical system.

Always check that the tester is functioning properly before and after you use it by testing it on a circuit you know to be live.

Following the manufacturer's instructions, place one probe on the neutral terminal and the other one on the live terminal that is to be tested. If the bulb illuminates, the circuit is live; if it doesn't illuminate, try again between the ground terminal and each of the live and neutral terminals. If the bulb still doesn't light up, you can assume the circuit is not live, provided you have checked the tester.

Continuity tester
A continuity tester will indicate whether current will pass from one terminal to another, so it's ideal for diagnosing short circuits, broken wires, or improper grounding. Alternatively, buy a multitester that combines the functions of continuity testing and voltage testing.

Using a continuity tester
The following is an example of how a continuity tester can be used. Be sure to switch off the power at the service panel before making any tests.

To determine whether two accessible cable ends are part of the same cable, twist two of the conductors together at one end. Then apply the tester's probes to the same conductors at the other end (1) and depress the circuit-testing button on the tester. The bulb should light up and, with some testers, there may also be an audible signal. Untwist the conductors. Then make the test again. If the bulb doesn't illuminate, the two ends don't belong to the same cable.

To check whether a plug-in appliance is safely grounded, apply one probe to the ground pin of the plug and touch an unpainted part of the metal casing of the appliance with the other probe (2). Depress the test button. If the ground

connection is good, the bulb will illuminate.
    Don't use the appliance if the bulb illuminates when you apply the probe to either of the plug's other pins (3). If the appliance is defective, have it repaired by a service technician or simply replace it with a new one.

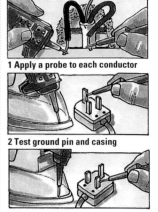

1 Apply a probe to each conductor

2 Test ground pin and casing

3 Test one other pin and casing

GENERAL-PURPOSE TOOLS

Every electrician needs tools for dealing with the house structure as it affects running cable and securing electrical components.

Claw hammer
For nailing cable straps to walls and framing.

Hand sledge
For use with a cold chisel.

Cold chisel
For cutting through old electrical components, plaster, and brickwork.

Wood chisels
For notching and trimming house framing.

Power jigsaw or reciprocating saw
For cutting through walls and floors and making other miscellaneous cuts.

Floorboard saw
This is the best tool for cutting across a pried-up board.

Level
For checking that mounting boxes are secured plumb.

Drywall knife
For making wall repairs after installing boxes and cable.

Adjustable wrench
A single adjustable wrench is easy to carry and handles the wide range of hexhead fasteners that might be encountered.

Softwoods and hardwoods

LUMBER AND MAN-MADE BOARDS

Lumber is classified into two main groups, softwood and hardwood, according to the type of tree it comes from. Softwoods are from coniferous trees such as firs and pines, hardwoods are from deciduous broad-leaved trees. Most softwoods are in fact softer than most hardwoods, but that is not invariably the case.

Some hardwoods, particularly from tropical rain forests, are now endangered species—so look at the product labeling or check with the supplier to make sure that the lumber has come from a sustainable source.

SOFTWOODS

Most of the wood you see in a lumberyard is softwood, as it is much cheaper than hardwoods and is more widely used for structural house framing, floor-boards, stairs, and the simpler kinds of domestic furniture. Common softwoods are pine, spruce, fir, cedar, and redwood.

Buying softwood

Most softwood is available in rough and smooth versions called, respectively, rough and surfaced lumber. Unplaned lumber is often used in coarse utility construction, such as barns or small bridges, or on jobs where it will be out of sight.

Wherever appearance is important, you need planed wood—lumber that has been run through a surface planer after having been saw roughly to size. Planed lumber, or S4S (surfaced four sides)—is always slightly thinner and narrower than its nominal dimensions. Machine planing takes about ½ to ⅜in. off the width and about ¼ to ⅛in from the thickness of the sawn wood. For example, you can expect 1in.-thick softwood lumber to be ⅜in thick, and 2 by 4 construction stock to be 1½in thick by 3½in wide. Surfaced 1in hardwood lumber is generally 13/16in thick. Because the actual planed size varies with the type of wood and it is saw size, it's necessary to check with your lumber dealer before buying wood for a critical project.

Traditionally, lumber was measured in board feet, where a board foot is a volume quantity equaling a 1 by 12 by 12 in piece of wood. While mills still deal in this system, home centers designate quantity by nominal size and actual length.

Choosing softwood

A number of defects that can be found in softwood should be avoided, especially when appearance is important. For this reason, it is best to pick out the wood yourself. If that's not possible, be sure to order extra and examine each piece so that you can use the stock in the most effective manner.

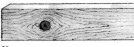

Knots

Knots can look attractive in pine boards, but they must be "live" knots—the glossy brown ones. The black "dead" knots will shrink and may drop out.

Warping

Distorted timber is another common problem. Look along the edges of each board to check that it is straight. A typical defect is warp, or curve across the end. A bowed board is curved along its length and a twisted board has ends that are not parallel.

End shakes

These are splits at the ends of boards caused by rapid drying. Take these into account when you buy lumber.

Heart shakes

These are splits that occur along radial lines in the log. When they are combined at the center of the tree, they are known as star shakes.

Cup shakes

These occur parallel to the tree's annual rings—the layers of new wood that grow each year. Typically, a board cut from the center of the tree may have the central ring split away from the other ones along its length.

Surface checking

This is fine cracking on the surface of timber. Very fine cracks may be removed by planing, or filled if the work is to be painted. Wood with wider cracks should be rejected.

Other defects

Watch out for irregularities such as remaining bark, damage from rough handling in the yard, and water staining.

Standard sizes and sections

Planed softwood comes in a variety of standard thicknesses and widths—from nominal 1-to 6 in thicknesses and nominal 2 to 12in widths. Standard lengths are from 4 to 16 feet in 2 foot intervals.

Planed softwood can also be bought milled as tongue-and-groove stock for flooring or paneling, and machined into a variety of sectional shapes known as moldings designed for use as baseboards, door and window trim, and picture frames.

Cutting to size

Lumberyards will generally cut a board to the approximate length you want—unless that would leave a piece too small to be sold. However, don't expect a finished cut—to be sure of obtaining the exact size you need, buy the wood slightly longer and carefully cut it to size yourself. At one time, dealers had the machinery to plane stock to the specific thickness that you required. If your dealer can't do this, try a local woodworking shop or cabinetmaker.

Seasoning wood

When a log is sawn into boards, it contains a high level of moisture. As the wood dries, the board shrinks and warps. To make the wood stable, it's dried, or seasoned, to an acceptable level before you buy it. Most lumber is seasoned by kiln drying, but as it is often exposed to humidity in an open lumberyard, the moisture level can rise again. It's best to let the wood dry out and stabilize indoors for at least a week—preferably in the room where it will be used. Stack the lumber with dry spacers in between so the air can circulate.

HARDWOODS

Hardwoods are generally more expensive than softwoods, and usually have to be bought from specialty lumber suppliers. Some dealers, though, may carry oak or other domestic hardwoods for interior trim.

Ordering hardwoods

Like softwoods, commonly stocked hardwoods are listed in nominal sizes. However, you'll also find hardwood thickness indicated in multiples of ¼in. For example, 4/4 stock is nominally 1in thick, while 8/4 material is 2in thick. Hardwood is available through mail-order distributors, local mills, and some lumberyards. It can be bought rough, surfaced on two faces, or planed on all four surfaces.

Most hardwoods are sold in relatively knot-free grades, but pieces can suffer from warping, shakes, and checks. The figure and color of the wood may vary from tree to tree of the same species, will be affected by the way it is cut from the log. This makes buying rough lumber, where the color and grain are obscured, a risky process—especially if you're trying to match wood in your home. Also, remember that finished furniture and woodwork is often stained, and even clear varnishes and natural aging can change the color of the wood. When matching wood, or looking for a specific appearance, it always pays to ask your dealer if you're unsure.

Working with hardwoods

Because hardwoods are generally tougher than softwoods, tools need to be sharpened more frequently and honed to a fine cutting edge. Carbide-tipped, circular saw blades and router bits are better choices than high-speed steel.

Screws require drilled pilot holes, not only to ease driving, but to prevent splitting the hardwood. Pilot holes must be carefully sized to match the screws that will be used.

The dust that's created when working hardwoods can be unpleasant. It is therefore best to wear a dust mask or respirator—especially when sanding.

Hardwood veneers

Veneers are thin slices of wood cut from a log. The way they're sliced, around or through the log, for example, affects the grain pattern. Hardwood veneers are used in fine custom furniture and also as face layers for plywood and other manufactured panels. Most lumber dealers stock a small range of common veneer plywoods. More exotic veneers and veneered panels are available through mail-order.

Manufactured panels

These days, much of the furniture and cabinetwork in your home—indeed, your home itself—is probably not made with solid lumber, but with manufactured wood products. In most cases, these are made in a convenient sheet form that's easy to cut and allows for simple joinery.

Panel stock has other advantages, as well. Typically these products are more stable than solid wood, so warping and shrinkage are less of a concern—and, in some cases, nonexistent. The uniform, flat surfaces are also easy to finish.

Many panels are offered with attractive hardwood-veneer surfaces, or durable, easy-to-clean melamine surfaces.

On the down side, panel edges generally need to be covered with either a veneer or solid-wood edge banding. And thin veneer faces are not only somewhat delicate, but they can be easily sanded through if you're not careful.

Plywood

Plywood is probably the most familiar manufactured panel. It's available in many grades and for a range of uses—from home construction to furniture making. It's made by gluing thin veneers together under high pressure. These may be of the same thickness throughout, or the core veneers may be thicker than the face veneers. To maintain stability, the veneers are laid in an odd number with the grain direction alternating from one layer to the next. This also means that the grain of the face veneers will be parallel.

Softwood plywood is made from softwood veneer and is graded by the quality of the face veneers. For example, A/C fir plywood has one blemish-free face while the opposite face has defects. This grade would be suitable for painted cabinetwork. C/D plywood, on the other hand, would be used in construction where its appearance is hidden by siding or flooring.

Hardwood plywood has an alternating veneer core like softwood plywood, but its face veneers are hardwood. Most lumberyards will carry common species such as oak, birch, and lauan (a mahogany-like wood), but a wider selection is available through specialty dealers.

Typical lumberyard-grade plywood will have voids in the core created by gaps and defects in the thicker interior plies. Quality, uniform veneer plywood is available, usually with birch veneers, at a higher cost. Marine-grade plywood is another option where core quality is a concern. Medium-density overlay (MDO) is a softwood plywood that has faces of resin-impregnated paper. It has very smooth, easily painted faces, and it's a good choice for outdoor projects and signage.

Plywood sizes

Typical thicknesses range from ¼ to ¾ inch, while some specialty plywood, such as bending plywood, can be found as thin as ⅛ inch. Most plywood is sold in 4 x 8-foot sheets, but home centers often sell hardwood veneer-plywoods in partial sheets.

Particleboard

Particleboard is a relatively cheap material commonly used to make modern cabinet furniture. The board is manufactured by gluing small softwood particles together under pressure. There are several grades, including standard and moisture-resistant types for flooring and roofing.

Standard particleboard, which is sanded smooth on both sides, can be filled and primed for painting. It also makes a good substrate for veneer and is often the choice for kitchen countertops that are to receive a plastic laminate surface. You'll also find particleboard sold with hardwood veneer or melamine faces. The melamine-faced particleboard is a good choice for kitchen cabinets and bookcases.

Particleboard sizes

Standard particleboard sheets range in thickness between ¼ and 1⅛ inches. The panels are 4 x 8 feet in size.

You'll find melamine faced particleboard sold in oversize 49 x 97-inch sheets so they can be cut in foot increments with little waste. Melamine-faced panels range in thickness between ¼ and ¾ inch.

Lumber-core panels

A lumber-core panel consists of a core of rectangular-section wood strips sandwiched between layers of pressure-bonded veneer. It is used where structural strength and stability are needed, for an unsupported span of worktable, for example, or for shelving that has to bear a heavy load. Lumber core is an excellent material for veneering—but like plywood and particleboard, exposed edges need to be covered with edge banding. Lumber core is less popular than other panels.

Lumber-core panel sizes

These panels come in 4 x 8-foot sheets, ½ and ¾ inch thick.

Hardboard

Hardboard is a dense, thin sheet material made from compressed softwood pulp and resins. It is not as strong as other panels, but it is inexpensive and very stable.

There are several varieties of hardboard including S1S (smooth one side), S2S (smooth two sides), and it's offered in standard grade, service grade, and tempered. Tempered hardboard is tougher and more moisture resistant than the standard and service grades.

In addition to flat, solid panels, perforated hardboard is available and is often used with metal hangers for tool storage. Textured hardboard has a decorative molded surface and is commonly used for house siding.

Uses and sizes

Standard hardboard is relatively light, easy to cut, and ideal for small sliding doors, cabinet backs and drawer bottoms, and as an underlay for floor coverings.

Standard hardboard sheets measure 4 x 8 feet. Thicknesses are ⅛ and ¼ inch.

Fiberboards

Like hardboard, these are made from compressed wood fiber and synthetic resin in various densities.

Medium-density fiberboard (MDF) is a dense material with fine, smooth surfaces on both sides. The edges machine well, making them easy to finish with paint. MDF is an ideal substrate for veneer and plastic laminate because it is stable and flat. However, it's very heavy and does not hold screws that well. MDF is made in a range of thicknesses from ½ to ⅞ inch. You'll find it in 4 x 8 sheets.

Man-made boards
1 Plywood
2 Particleboard
3 Lumber core
4 Standard hardboard
5 Perforated hardboard
6 Textured hardboard
7 Medium-density fiberboard (MDF)

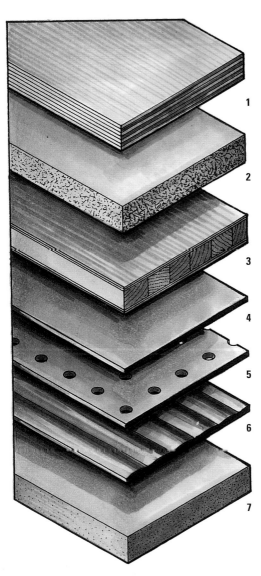

Moldings and adhesives

MOLDINGS

Both softwoods and hardwoods are used for making moldings. The cheaper softwoods are generally used for the larger moldings such as baseboard and casing, although some are made in hardwood. Smaller profiles, for picture framing and decorative cover moldings, are often made from hardwoods. Period-style moldings are generally more ornate than modern profiles. If you need to replace a wooden molding but can't find the right shape, it is possible to have the molding made by a custom millwork shop. Simply supply them with a pattern or sample piece.

Molding sections
1 Astragal
2 Double astragal
3 Glass bead
4 Chair rail
5 Straight corner
6 Round corner
7 Ogee
8 Quarter-round
9 Half-round
10 Beaded lip
11 Screen mold
12 Parting bead
13 Beaded stop
14 Triangle
15 Cove
16 Casing
17 Apron
18 Picture rail
19 Baseboard

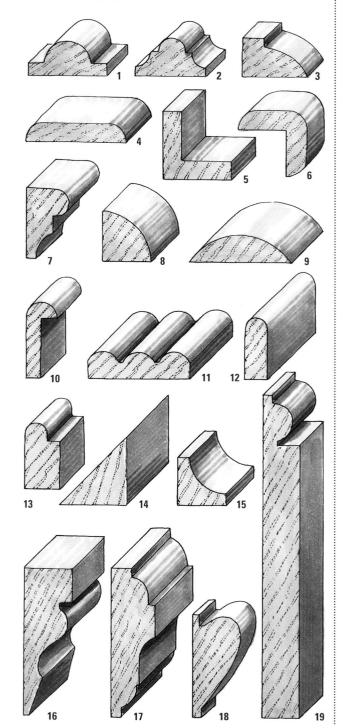

ADHESIVES

Modern adhesives are greatly superior to the old glues they have supplanted. Although there is no true universal glue that will stick anything to anything, you can bond most materials if you use the appropriate adhesive. There are a great many general-purpose and specific-purpose glues; those discussed here relate to the procedures dealt with in this book.

Woodworking
To glue wood for use indoors, apply a polyvinyl acetate (PVA) woodworking glue to the mating surfaces. Clamp or weight the work while the glue cures. To clean away excess, wait until the glue skins over, then slice off the excess with a sharp chisel. The joint can be handled within 30 minutes, and the bond will be complete in 24 hours.

Outdoors, use water-resistant, exterior PVA glue for garden furniture and similar projects. For maximum water resistance, however, use a powdered, plastic-resin glue that you mix with water or a two-part resorcinol adhesive. The two parts are first mixed together in the correct proportions, then applied to the mating surfaces. Epoxy adhesives are also two-part products. For small projects, syringe-like applicators are available to mix just the right amount of resin and hardener for the job. Large projects can be assembled with marine epoxy available from dealers that sell boat-building supplies. All of these adhesives require the work to be held together with clamps, screws, nails, or other fasteners while the glue sets.

Gluing plastic laminates
Contact adhesive is the standard material for gluing plastic laminate to wood and other surfaces. This type of adhesive is applied to both surfaces with a short-nap roller or brush. After it has dried to the touch, the pieces are brought into contact, at which point they instantly adhere. To avoid misalignment, keep large pieces of laminate separated from the substrate with dowels. Then, remove the dowels in order while pressing the laminate in place. Some new contact cements retain a degree of adjustability after assembly. New water-based contact cements are safer to use and require only water for cleanup.

Fixing floor coverings
Flooring adhesives need to be versatile enough to bond a wide range of coverings—cork, vinyl, linoleum, and many others—to a range of substrates such as plywood underlayment or concrete. They must also be able to withstand regular floor-washing and the spillage of various liquids. Such multipurpose flooring adhesives are made from synthetic resin or latex. They will stick almost any covering to any floor surface. They are semiflexible and will not crack or fail due to slight movement of the covering.

Attaching ceiling tiles
Expanded polystyrene ceiling tiles can be glued to plaster and drywall surfaces, using a synthetic latex-based adhesive. These adhesives have gap-filling properties that allow the material to be fixed effectively to rough or uneven surfaces. They also allow some degree of movement so that the tiles can be adjusted after they have been stuck in place.

Attaching ceramic tiles
Ceramic wall tiles are bonded in place with adhesive that is available ready-mixed or in powder form. Some are dual-purpose, for use as an adhesive and grout. Ordinary "thin-bed" adhesives are for tiling on fairly flat surfaces, and there are "thick-bed" ones for use on rough and uneven surfaces.

Use a water-resistant version for kitchens and bathrooms. Epoxy-based grouts resist mold growth and help keep kitchens and bathrooms germ-free.

Ceramic floor tiles are usually laid with a cement-based tile adhesive. Thick quarry tiles are sometimes laid on a sand-and-cement mortar—to which a special builder's adhesive, PVA bonding agent, can be added to improve adhesion (a method also used for repairing sand-and-cement stucco and concrete).

Gluing metals
Metals can be glued with epoxy-resin adhesives, which produce a powerful bond. The adhesives come in two parts, a resin and a hardener, supplied in separate tubes or a special double syringe-like dispenser.

(Continued opposite)

Adhesives

Epoxy-resin adhesives are also generally suitable for joining glass, ceramics, fiberglass, and plastic. However, some products will not join all of these materials, so make sure you get the right adhesive for the job.

Cyanoacrylates

The cyanoacrylates, or "super glues," come close to being universal adhesives that will glue anything. They rapidly bond a great many materials, including human skin—so take great care when handling them (see "Adhesive Solvents," right).

Usually supplied in tubes with fine nozzles, superglues must be used sparingly. Most are thin liquids, but a gel type is also available. They are commonly used for joining small objects made of metal, glass, ceramic, fiberglass, or rigid plastic.

Urethane adhesive

Urethane glue is a highly versatile adhesive that not only works on wood, but bonds stone, metal, ceramics, and a wide range of synthetic materials. It's also completely waterproof and has good gap-filling characteristics. It's popular among woodworkers as it has a relatively long open time (the time it takes the glue to begin setting). Unlike other glues, it requires some moisture to cure.

Glue guns

An electric "hot-melt" glue gun is loaded with a rod of solid glue that melts under heat; the glue is discharged as a liquid onto the work when the gun is activated. The components are pressed or clamped together and the glue bonds as it cools. Glue guns are useful for accurate spot-gluing, and there is a choice of glue rods for use with various materials. The glues cool and set within 20 to 90 seconds.

Cold gun-applied adhesive for fixing wallboards and ceiling tiles is supplied in cartridges fitted with nozzles. When you squeeze the gun's trigger, a ram pushes on the base of the cartridge and forces out the glue.

ADHESIVE SOLVENTS

When using an adhesive, you will inevitably put some where you don't want it. So have the right solvent handy for the glue in question and use it promptly. The more the glue has set, the harder it is to remove, and once the glue has set, it may be impossible to dissolve it. With epoxy, for example, sanding it off may be the only practical way to remove it once it has cured. No matter what adhesive you use, always check the label to find out what the manufacturer recommends for cleaning up

ADHESIVE	SOLVENT
PVA woodworking glue	Water
Plastic-resin	Water
Standard contact cement	Acetone
Water-based contact cement	Water
Synthetic-latex	Water
Epoxy-resin	Acetone or lacquer thinner (check manufacturer's instructions)
Cyanoacrylates (superglues)	Special manufacturer's solvent
Urethane	Alcohol or thinner

Use this chart as a guide for gluing the materials on the left to those across the top.	WOOD AND MAN-MADE BOARDS	MASONRY	PLASTER	METAL	STONE	GLASS	CERAMIC	RIGID PLASTIC/ FIBERGLASS
WOOD/MAN-MADE BOARDS	1,2,4,9	4	5,9	4,9	4,9	4,8,9	4,9	4,9
METAL	4,9			4,7,8	4,7,8	4,7,8	4,7,8	4,7,8
PLASTIC LAMINATES	3	3	3		3			3
FLOOR COVERINGS	5,6	5,6			5,6		5,6	
CEILING TILES/PANELS	6,8,9	6,8,9	6,8,9		6,8,9			
CERAMIC	4,9	8	8	4,7,8	8	4,7	4,7	4
STONE	4,9	4		4,7,8	4	4	8	8,9
GLASS	4,8,9	4	4	4,7,8	4	4,7,8	4,7	4,8
RIGID PLASTICS/FIBERGLASS	4,9			4,7,8	8,9	4,8	4	4,7,8

KEY TO TYPES OF ADHESIVES
1 PVA woodworking
2 Plastic-resin/ resorcinol and urea
3 Rubber-based contact
4 Epoxy-resin
5 Rubber-resin
6 Synthetic-latex
7 Cyanoacrylates
8 PVA tile adhesive
9 Urethane

Nails

FASTENERS

A crucial aspect of any assembly is choosing the right fastening. As well as the time-honored variety of nails and screws for wood, and nuts, bolts, and rivets for metal, there are a number of special devices that speed and simplify many jobs.

NAILS
● ● ● ● ● ● ● ● ● ● ● ● ●

Nails, used with or without glue, provide an inexpensive, quick, and simple fastening method for woodworkers. And there are also many special types of nails for other purposes. Here are a few that you may find.

● **Preventing split wood**
To avoid splitting, blunt the point of a nail with a light hammer blow. A blunt nail punches its way through wood instead of forcing the fibers apart.

● **Removing a dent from wood**
If you dent wood with a hammer blow, put a few drops of hot water on the dent and let the wood swell. When it is dry, smooth the wood with abrasive paper.

COMMON NAIL SIZES

Penny size	Length (in.)	Approx. No. per lb.
2d	1"	847
3d	1¼"	543
4d	1½"	296
5d	1¾"	254
6d	2"	167
7d	2¼"	150
8d	2½"	101
9d	2¾"	92
10d	3"	66
12d	3¼"	66
16d	3½"	47
20d	4"	30
30d	4½"	23
40d	5	17
50d	5½"	13
60d	6"	11

Common nail
Rough general carpentry. Bright steel or galvanized finish, 1 to 6 inches long (2d to 60d).

Finishing nail
Joinery. Head can be set below the surface and covered with wood filler. Bright steel finish, 1 to 4 inches (2d to 20d).

Cement-coated common nail
General carpentry. Thinner and lighter than common nails, with greater holding power. Are ⅛ to ¼ inch shorter than common nails with the same penny designation. Size: ⅞ to 5¼ inches.

Annular-ring nail
For securing manufactured panels such as plywood. Bright or blued steel, ¾ to 4 inches long (2d to 20d).

Spiral-shank nail
General-purpose. Twisted shank gives extra grip. Bright or blued steel, ¾ to 4 inches long (2d to 20d).

Cut nails
Rectangular cross-section nail for carpentry and securing to masonry. Steel, 1 to 6 inches long.

Cut flooring nail
For nailing floorboards to joists. Steel, 1½ to 4 inches long.

Powder-set nail
Joining wood to concrete. Nails are set by a special tool that uses a gunpowder charge. Hardened steel, 1½ to 3⁷⁄₁₆ inches long.

Panel nail
Attaching hardboard or light plywood paneling. Blued or enameled steel, ½ to 3½ inches.

Veneer nail (molding nail)
For applying veneers and small moldings. Bright steel, ⅝ to 2 inches.

Roofing nail
Applying shingles to sloped roofs. Galvanized steel, ¾ to 4 inches long.

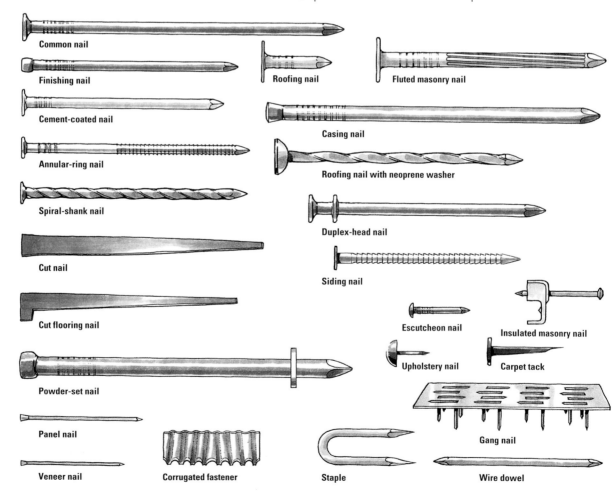

Common nail

Finishing nail

Cement-coated nail

Annular-ring nail

Spiral-shank nail

Cut nail

Cut flooring nail

Powder-set nail

Panel nail

Veneer nail

Roofing nail

Fluted masonry nail

Casing nail

Roofing nail with neoprene washer

Duplex-head nail

Siding nail

Corrugated fastener

Escutcheon nail

Upholstery nail

Insulated masonry nail

Carpet tack

Gang nail

Staple

Wire dowel

Screws

Fluted masonry nail
For fastening wood to concrete or brick masonry. Hardened steel, ½ to 4 inches long.

Casing nail
General carpentry. Conical head rather than the round head of a finishing nail. Often has a depression in the head to accept a nail set. Steel, 1 to 5 inches long.

Roofing nail with neoprene washer
For use in flat roofing, skylights, or solar panels where potential for leaks is high. Galvanized steel, 1½ to 2½ inches long.

Duplex-head nail
For temporary construction and bracing where the nails must be removed. Bright or galvanized steel, 1¾ to 4½ inches long.

Siding nail
For securing exterior siding and wall shingles. Galvanized steel, 1¼ to 2 inches long.

Escutcheon nail
For fixing keyhole plates etc. Brass, ⅝ or ¾ inch long.

Insulated masonry nail
For securing electric cable to masonry. The nail is driven through a plastic cable clip. Available in various shapes and sizes.

Upholstery nail
For upholstering furniture. Domed decorative head. Brass, bronze, chromed, or antique, ⅛ to ½ inch long.

Carpet tack
For carpeting and attaching fabric to wood. Blued, coppered, or galvanized, ¼ to 1¼ inches long.

Gang nail
For making rough butted or mitered wood joints, used in the construction of wooden roof trusses.

Staple
Rough carpentry, and for fastening fencing wire. Bright steel or galvanized, ⅜ to 1½ inch long.

Wire dowel
Often a shop-made fastener for wood. One point enters each component for hidden nailing. Steel, 1½ to 2 inches long.

SCREWS

Screws are manufactured with a range of head shapes suited to various purposes, and in a choice of materials and finishes. They are usually made of mild steel, but hardened steel is also used.

Solid-brass and stainless-steel screws do not rust. Steel screws are sometimes plated with zinc, chromium, or brass to make them corrosion resistant. There are also bronzed and japanned screws.

Screw fastening
While nails are fine for framing and finish carpentry, screws are a better choice for joining wooden parts that must fit precisely, or for attaching other materials to wood. Screws provide a strong clamping force, and they can be removed to allow disassembly or adjustment without damage to the parts. When combined with glue, they can be used to hold joints tight without the need for clamps.

Screw threads
Traditional woodscrews have a plain "full" shank below the head. The shank is about one-third the length of the screw.

More modern screws have a modified thread that may be single or double. They have a sharp point that makes starting easier, and a shank that's smaller in diameter than the thread. Drywall screws are of this type, and they can be driven into softwood with a drill/driver and without the need for a pilot hole. However, when fastening near the end of a workpiece, or in a piece that's relatively thin, it's always best to bore a pilot hole to prevent splitting.

Screwheads
There are four basic screwheads.

- **Flathead,** *for work where the screw must be recessed, either flush with the surface or below it. It usually requires a hole that's recessed with a countersink. Drywall and decking screws have a flat head but are often driven without a pilot hole or countersink.*
- **Roundhead,** *often used when the screw is expected to be removed, or with sheet material that is too thin for countersinking.*
- **Oval-head,** *a roundhead screw that requires a countersunk hole, often used for attaching hardware to wood.*
- **Panhead,** *similar to roundhead but mainly found on self-tapping screws used for joining sheetmetal.*

A further subdivision of screws covers the shape of the recess in the head and the type of tool required to drive the screw. Both Phillips-head and square-drive screws are better suited to power driving with a drill/driver.

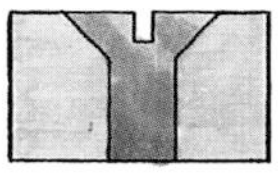
Flathead

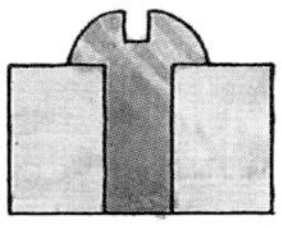
Roundhead

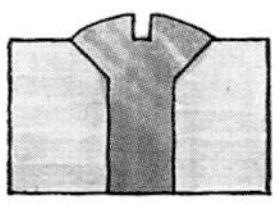
Oval-head

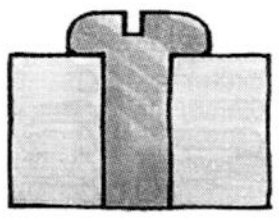
Pan-head

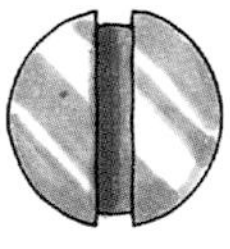
Slot-head

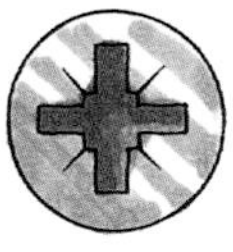
Phillips-head

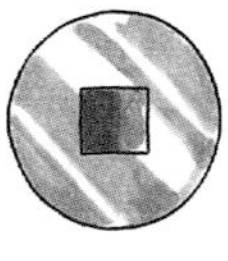
Square-drive

Sizes and gauges
In addition to head type, all screws are described in terms of their length and gauge, which is expressed as a number from 1 to 20. For example, a designation such as a 1½ No. 8 fh (flathead) woodscrew describes the length, gauge, and type of head. The thicker the screw, the higher its gauge number. The gauges in most general use are 4, 6, 8, and 10.

The length of a screw is the distance between its pointed tip and the part of the head that lies flush with the work surface. Woodscrews are made in lengths ranging from ½ to 6 inches—but not every combination of length, head shape, and material is available, let alone stocked in every gauge. The widest choice is generally to be found within gauges 6 to 12.

Cups, sockets, and caps
Countersunk and oval-head screws may be used with metal screw cups, which improve their clamping force and also make for a neat appearance. Plastic sockets with snap-on caps are also available to conceal the heads of screws. Also, there are simple semidomed plastic caps that plug into flush-mounted Phillips heads.

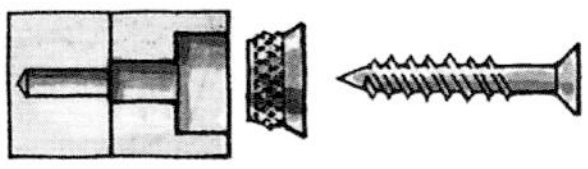
Flush screw cup

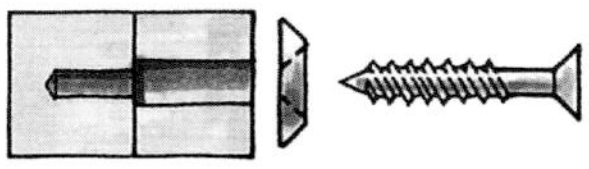
Surface screw cup

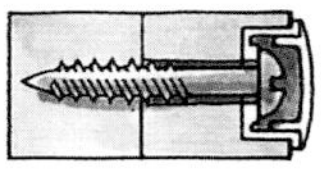
Plastic socket and cap

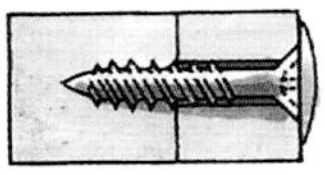
Plastic cap

Types and uses
The traditional woodscrew has changed little since it was developed in the last century. However, since the introduction of man-made boards and drill/drivers, manufacturers have produced new thread and head forms.

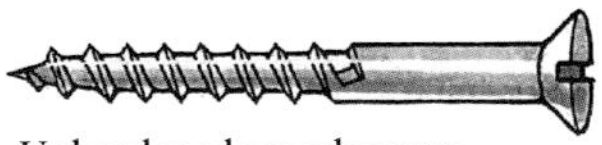

Unhardened woodscrews
The standard woodscrew, with its single-helix thread, is made in the widest range of sizes, head types, and materials. It is suitable for most woods and is particularly suited for fixing hardware such as hinges, locks, and catches. This type of screw requires a pilot hole and shank-clearance hole to be drilled prior to fitting.

Length: ⅜ to 6 inches. Gauge: 2 to 18.

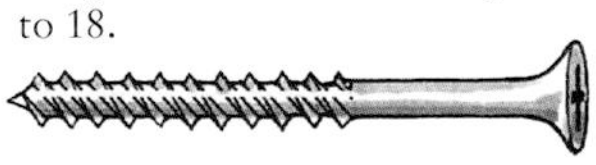

Hardened-steel woodscrews
Flathead or roundhead screws, often with twin steep-pitch threads, are best for fast driving. They can be used with all types of solid wood and man-made boards. The hardened metal makes it possible to drive into a range of relatively soft materials without the need for pilot holes.

Length: ½ to 4 inches. Gauge: 3 to 12.

(Continued overleaf)

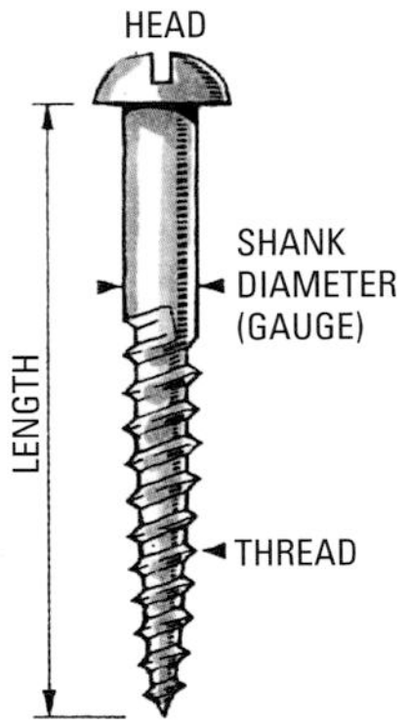

Parts of a screw
The basic terminology for describing a woodscrew.

Screws and mounting hardware

General-purpose screws
These hardened-steel screws are designed for manufactured panels but work well in solid wood, too. They're made with countersunk heads only, and they have a single-helix thread.

Although pilot holes are required for most materials, you can drive small-diameter screws directly into softwoods or low-density man-made boards.

Length: 1/2 to 4 inches.

Decking screws
These hardened-steel screws are designed to be driven into treated wood used for deck construction with the use of a pilot hole. You'll find them galvanized or coated to resist corrosion.

Length: 1 to 4 inches. Gauge: 8 to 10.

Drywall screws
A special range of hardened, easily driven screws are made for attaching drywall to wooden framing or studs. Each screw has a sharp point for drilling its own hole and a bugle-shaped, flat head that enables it to bed down into the panel material. These screws are often used as general-purpose screws.

Length: 1 to 3 inches.

Security screws
The heads of these flathead screws have special slots that permit the screw to be driven into the work but reject the tip of the screwdriver when the action is reversed in an attempt to remove the screw. The latest type has twin threads and is for use with slot-head screwdrivers.

Length: ¼ to 2 inches. Gauge: 6 to 12.

Lag screws
Lag screws are made from unhardened steel, and are used for heavy-duty applications such as building a workbench. They have a hexagonal or square head and are driven into the work with a wrench. Use washers to keep the heads from cutting into the wood.

Length: 1 to 6 inches. Diameter: ¼ to ½ inch.

Self-tapping screws
Self-tapping screws are designed to cut their own thread in materials such as plastics, thin sheetmetal, and ductwork. They are made from case-hardened steel and are normally available in four head forms, flathead, oval-head, panhead and flange head. Hexhead screws are available for driving by hand with a nut driver or with a drill/driver and socket.

Length: ¼ to 2½ inches. Gauge: 4 to 14.

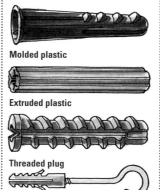

Masonry screws
These extra-hard screws with a special dual thread can be driven directly into all types of masonry without the need for anchors.

Length: 2¼ to 4 inches. Diameter/gauge: ³⁄₁₆ and ¼ inch.

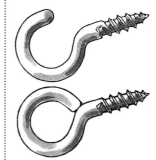

Screw hooks and eyes
Made of steel, screw hooks and eyes have a conventional woodscrew thread for fastening to a wall or panel. Plain or shouldered screw hooks are made in various sizes and with round or square-shaped hooks, either bright-plated or plastic-coated. The hooks provide securing points for cords, chains, and so on.

WALL MOUNTINGS

To fasten to anything other than solid wood or thick wooden panels, special hardware is available. These products range from simple plugs, or anchors, that hold a woodscrew in a hole drilled in brick or masonry, to elaborate heavy-duty devices complete with bolts. There are also special devices for mounting to hollow walls.

Molded plastic

Extruded plastic

Threaded plug

Clothesline fixing

Anchors
These relatively simple mounting devices anchor a variety of screws.

There are light to medium-weight molded-plastic anchors that take a range of standard-gauge woodscrews, generally from No. 4 to No. 14. Some are color-coded for easy recognition.

An anchor is pushed into a drilled hole, and then the screw is driven into the plug, which expands to grip the sides of the hole.

Extruded-plastic anchors are straight fluted tubes that accommodate only the thread of the screw, so have to be cut shorter than the depth of the hole. They are cheaper than molded plugs, but less convenient.

Threaded anchors are for use in walls of crumbly material like aerated concrete. These plugs have a coarse thread on the outside and are screwed into the soft material to provide a socket for screws. A hole in masonry or brick that's too irregular to take an anchor can be filled with mortar. When the mortar sets, bore a hole with a hammer drill and insert the appropriate anchor.

Lead shields are available for fastening to masonry. There's also a type of anchor with a coarse thread and a sharp point that cuts its own hole in a plasterboard wall.

Heavy-duty nylon anchors *come complete with coach screws or with screw hooks (for use as clothesline attachments, for example).*

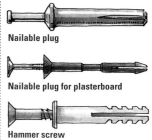

Expansion bolts
These are for making very rugged mountings. There are various designs, but all work on the same basic principle: a bolt is screwed into a segmented metal or plastic shell and engages the thread of an expander. As the bolt is tightened, the expander forces the segments apart to grip the sides of the hole. Hooks and eyes that employ a similar principle are also available.

Nailable plug

Nailable plug for plasterboard

Hammer screw

Nailable plugs
These can be used in place of anchors and screws. There are two types: One has a flanged expansion sleeve with a masonry nail; the other has an anchor and "hammer screw." Both types are hammered into a drilled hole, but only the hammer screw can be removed, using a screwdriver. These plugs are often used for securing furring strips and other woodwork to a masonry substrate.

Plastic frame fastener

Metal-sleeved frame fastener

Frame fasteners
These are designed to speed up screw fastening in wood, plastic or metal door and window frames by eliminating the need to mark out and predrill holes.

Supplied with a plated screw or bolt, these long fittings are available with plastic plugs or split, metal expanding sleeves.

The item to be secured is first set in position and a clearance hole drilled through it into the wall. The frame fastener is then inserted and the screw tightened.

Hollow-wall fasteners

There are many different devices for fastening to the hollow walls of drywall on studs, lath and plaster, and so on. They typically feature an expansion mechanism that grips the inside of the wall.

Plastic toggles and *collapsible anchors all have segments that open out or fold up against the inside face of the drywall or panel.*

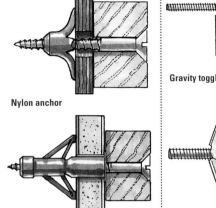

Nylon anchor

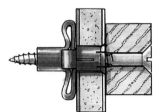

Toggle cavity anchor

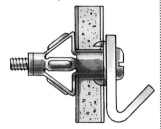

Plastic collapsible anchor

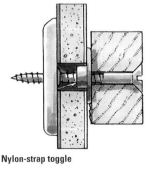

Metal collapsible anchor

A rubber anchor has a steel bolt which, when tightened, draws up an internal nut that makes the rubber sleeve bulge out behind the panel.

Rubber-sleeve anchor

Metal gravity toggles and spring *toggles have arms that open out inside the cavity. A gravity toggle has a single arm, pivoted near one end so that its own weight causes it to drop. A spring toggle has two spring-loaded arms that fly open when they are clear of the hole and a bolt that draws them tight up against the panel.*

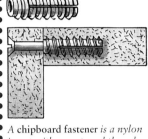

Gravity toggle

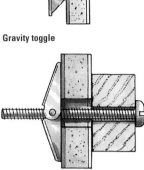

Spring toggle

A nylon-strap toggle has an arm that is held firmly behind the panel by a thin plastic strap while the screw is driven into its pilot hole. The strap is cut off after installation.

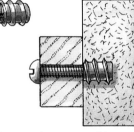

Nylon-strap toggle

Some anchors remain in the hole if the screw has to be removed. Others, such as nylon anchors and spring toggles, will be lost in the cavity. A rubber anchor can be removed and then used again.

None of these devices should be used for a heavy load. Instead, locate the wall studs and fasten directly to them. On lath-and-plaster walls, even for moderate loads use the larger spring and gravity toggles, rather than plug-type fasteners.

KNOCK-DOWN FITTINGS

Woodscrews in their various forms serve as simple and effective fasteners for most jobs. However, there are times when the project may require reinforcement or an alternative mechanical fitting in order to hold the parts together. Knock-down fittings allow components to be easily put together and easily taken apart.

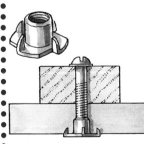

A chipboard fastener is a nylon insert with an external thread that is driven into a hole in the face or edge of chipboard to provide a secure fixing for woodscrews.

Screw sockets *are metal inserts that are threaded internally to receive a bolt. These sockets make neat concealed fixings.*

Teenuts *are used to make strong bolt fastenings in wood. When the metal nut is pressed into the back of a hole drilled in the component, the projecting prongs bite into the wood.*

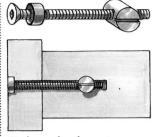

Steel cross dowels are strong fasteners for joining the ends of rails to side panels or stiles. The dowel is housed in a stopped hole drilled in one side or face of the rail. A threaded hole through the side of the dowel receives a bolt. A clearance hole for the bolt is drilled in the end of the rail.

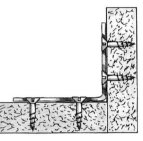

Angle brackets are used to join panels or boards at right angles. They're a good solution when speed of construction and reasonable strength is a priority. Various other types of metal reinforcing plates and brackets are also available.

A

ABS pipe
Acrylonitrile butadiene styrene pipe, a plastic pipe used in plumbing systems.

Admixture
Any of various additives made for concrete and mortar mixes which provide or improve specific qualities such as appearance or weather resistance.

Adze
An axelike tool with an arched blade set in the handle at a 90-degree angle.

Aggregate
Particles of sand or stone mixed with cement and water to make concrete, or mortar, or added to paint for a textured finish.

Air lock
A blockage caused by trapped air, as in a pipe.

Air-entrainment
An admixture that traps air in concrete to improve its weathering capabilities.

Angle iron
A metal fixture made to join pieces at an angle.

Anthropometrics
The study and measurement of the proportions of the human body.

Aquastat
A device for regulating the temperature of water.

Axminster
A manufacturing process for producing pile-tufted carpet with a woven backing.

B

Back-siphon
The flowing back of used or polluted water from a plumbing fixture into the pipe which feeds it; due to reduced pressure in the pipe.

Backfill
To refill, also, the material used for refilling.

Ballast
A sand and gravel mix used as aggregate for making concrete.

Baluster
One of a set of vertical posts supporting a stair handrail.

Balustrade
A handrail along the top of the balusters (posts) on a staircase or landing.

Banister
A balustrade, a handrail along a staircase.

Batt
A flat, insulating filler, as of fiberglass or mineral fiber.

Batten
A narrow strip of wood.

Blind nailing
A nailing technique that leaves no visible nailhead on the surface of the workpiece. Nails are driven at an angle.

Blocking
A short piece of wood between studs or joists, providing extra strength to a framework.

Bore
The hollow part of a pipe or tube, also, to drill a hole.

Brown coat
The middle layer of stucco, applied after the first, or scratch, coat and before the finish coat.

BTU
British Thermal Units. The amount of energy required to raise the temperature of one pound of water by 1 degree Fahrenheit. Used as an energy-rating guide to air conditioners and other appliances.

Builder's sand
A fine, filtered sand used in cement or mortar mixes.

Burr
The rough, raised edge left on a workpiece after cutting or filing.

C

Came, cames
The grooved lead rod or rods that hold the glass in a stained-glass window.

Carnauba
A wax used in polishes, derived from a South American palm species.

Casing
The wooden molding around a door or window opening.

Caulk
A paste material used to seal seams and joints for weather or moisture protection. Also, to seal such joints by applying caulk.

Cavity wall
A wall of two separate masonry skins with an air space between them.

Chamfer
A narrow, flat surface on the edge of a workpiece, normally at a 45-degree angle to adjacent surfaces. Also, to plane the angled surface.

Chlordane
A liquid insecticide.

Circuit
A path through which electricity flows.

Clerestory
An outer, windowed wall which rises above the surrounding roof.

Conductor
A component, usually a length of wire, along which an electrical current will pass.

Coping
Cutting a curved shape in wood. Also, a decorative molding covering a wall.

Cornice
The decorative molding course between walls and ceiling.

Counterbore
To cut a hole which allows the head of a bolt or screw to lie below a surface, also, the hole itself.

Countersink
To cut a tapered recess which allows the head of a screw to lie flush with a surface, also, the tapered recess itself.

Course
A continuous layer of bricks, masonry, tiles, or other wallcovering.

Cove molding
A decorative molding with a concave section or with a trough for hidden lighting.

Cowl
A chimney covering which helps to control airflow.

CPVC
Chlorinated polyvinyl chloride, a plastic pipe used in water supply lines.

Crazing
A crackled glaze coating for ceramic tiles.

Creosote
A flammable, tarry substance, exuded from burning wood, that forms on the inside walls of chimneys.

Cup
The bending that occurs in wood, especially across the width of a plank.

D

Dado
A groove cut into a piece of wood to make a joint, running across the grain.

Damp-proof course
A layer of impervious material that prevents moisture from rising through the ground into the walls of a masonry building.

Deadmen
A T-shaped brace used to support workpieces, such as drywall, on a ceiling during installation.

Dormer
A vertical window projecting from a sloping roof.

DPC
Damp-proof course.

Draftproof
To make a structure impervious to drafts through insulation and construction.

Drip groove
A groove cut or molded in the underside of a door or windowsill to prevent rainwater from running back to the wall.

E

Eaves
The lower edge of a sloping roof that project beyond the walls.

Efflorescence
A white, powdery deposit caused by soluble salts migrating to the surface of masonry.

Endgrain
The surface of wood exposed after cutting across the fibers.

EPA
The Environmental Protection Agency.

Escutcheon
A flat ring of protective material surrounding an object, such as a flange around a keyhole.

Expanded clay
A cement aggregate.

Extension
A length of electrical cable for temporarily connecting an appliance to a wall socket. Also, a structural addition to an existing building.

F

Face edge
In woodworking, the surface planed square to the face side.

Face side
In woodworking, the face of lumber to be exposed to view in the finished product.

Fall
A downward slope.

Glossary

Fascia board
Strip of wood which covers the ends of rafters and to which gutters are attached.

Feather
To wear away or smooth an edge until it is undetectable.

Featherboards
Overlapping planks that taper across their width, from a wide edge to a thin edge.

Fence
An adjustable guide to keep the cutting edge of a tool a set distance from the edge of a workpiece.

Ferrule
A supportive sleeve or ring encircling a pipe, or joint.

Fire surround
A nonflammable metal or ceramic structure, often decorative, surrounding a fireplace.

Fish tails
A metal wall tie with forked ends used to reinforce vertical joints in brickwork.

Flashing
A weatherproof junction between a roof and a wall or chimney, or between one roof and another.

Float glass
A glass made through a molten-metal/flotation process, used in double glazing.

Flue
The chimney pipe or other passageway which carries smoke to the outer air.

Flux
A paste used in soldering that assists in the fusion of one metal to another.

Footing
A narrow concrete foundation for a wall.

Formwork
A frame which provides a mold for setting wet concrete, for floors, paths, and stairs.

Frog
The angled depression in one face of a type of brick.

Frost line
The boundary below which soil will not freeze.

Furring strips
Parallel strips of wood fixed to a wall or ceiling to provide a framework for attaching panels.

Fuse box
The service box where the main electrical service is connected to the house ciruitry.

G

Gable roof
Two sloping roofs joined at a center ridge, forming a triangular shape.

Gambrel roof
A roof with the slope broken into two different pitches, generally one at a sharper and one at a shallower angle.

Galvanized
Covered with a protective coating of zinc.

Gel
A substance with a thick, jellylike consistency.

GFCI
Ground fault circuit interrupter.

Glazier
A glassworker.

Glazing
Architectural glasswork, glass windows, or doors.

Grain
The general direction of wood fibers. Also, the patterns produced on the surface of lumber by cutting through the fibers.

Grommet
A ring of rubber or plastic lining a hole to protect material from degrading.

Ground
A connection, as a wire, or rod, that provides a path of least resistance connecting electricity with the earth, providing a safety feature.

Gypsum
A mineral material used in drywall.

H

Hardscaping
The paths, brickwork, patios, walls, and other built portions of a landscape design.

Hardwood
Timber cut from deciduous trees.

Header
The top horizontal member of a wooden frame.

Heave
An upward swelling of the ground caused by freezing.

Helical
Spiral in form.

Hip roof
A roof with four sides, all sloping up to the center.

Housing
A long, narrow channel cut across the general direction of wood grain to form part of a joint. Also, a casing for an object.

House wraps
Modern semipermeable vapor barriers used to exterior walls before siding is installed.

Humidistat
An device that measures and regulates the degree of humidity.

I

I-beam
An I-shaped steel supporting beam.

Insulation
Materials used to reduce the transmission of heat or sound. Also, nonconductive material surrounding electrical wires or connections to prevent the passage of electricity.

J

Jack studs
Shorter studs that support headers.

Jalousie
A window with horizontal glass louvers that adjust to allow airflow.

Jamb
A vertical upright that forms the side of an opening, or the framework of the opening as a whole.

Joist
A horizontal wooden beam used to support a floor or ceiling.

K

Kerf
The groove cut by a saw.

K-value
A measurement of heat-conducting properties, used in the construction industry to rate the insulation capability of building materials.

Key, keyed, keying
To prepare a surface by abrading it so that it coatings such as glue or plaster will adhere.

Knee kicker
A device used in carpet installation to tighten the carpet along the surface.

Knurled
Impressed with a series of fine grooves designed to improve the grip.

L

Lath
Narrow strips of material nailed to walls, joists, etc., to provide support for plaster.

LB box
An electrical housing which allows you to connect electrical conduit at right angles.

Lead
A stepped section of brickwork built at each end of a wall to act as a guide to the intermediate coursing.

Level
To make perfectly horizontal or vertical. Also, an instrument, with a visible bubble of liquid, which measures the level quality of a structure.

Lintel
A loadbearing horizontal member above an opening, such as a door.

Low-E glass
Low-emissivity glass.

Low-emissivity
A treated glass that blocks heat radiation.

LP gas
Liquid petroleum gas.

M

Marine plywood
Plywood meeting specific requirements governing continuing immersion in water.

Mastic
A construction adhesive.

Mattock
An axelike digging tool.

MDF
Medium-density fiberboard, a manufactured board used in construction.

MDO
Medium-density overlay.

Mineral wool
A fibrous, insulating fabric.

Miter
A joint formed between two workpieces by cutting bevels of equal angles at the ends of each piece. Also, to cut such a joint.

Mortise
A slot cut in lumber or other material to receive a matching tongue or tenon.

Mullion
A thin, vertical divider between panes of a window or door.

Muntin
A central vertical member of a panel door.

N

NEC
National Electrical Code.

Neutral
The part of an electrical circuit that carries the flow of current back to source. Also, a terminal to which the neutral connection is made. Alternatively, a muted color.

Newel
A decorative vertical post supporting the handrail on a staircase or landing.

Nosing
The front edge of a stair tread.

O

OSB
Oriented strand board.

Oxidize
To form a layer of metal oxide, as in rusting.

P

P.E.
Professional engineer's degree.

Parge
To coat with plaster.

PB pipe
Polybutylene pipe, formerly used in plumbing systems, now outdated but still found in some older homes.

Penetrating oil
A thin lubricant which will seep between corroded components.

Pentachlorophenol
A substance used as a fungicide and preserver for wood.

Pergola
A decorative landscaping structure with vertical supports and an open roof.

PEX
Cross-linked polyethylene, a pipe used in plumbing, mainly for in-floor radiant heat systems.

Pier
A supporting column built at intervals into brick or block walls.

Pilaster
A columnar pier supporting and projecting slightly out from the surrounding wall.

Pile
Raised fibers which stand out from a backing material, as in carpet.

Pilot hole
A small-diameter hole drilled when setting a woodscrew to act as a guide for the screw's thread.

Plaster of paris
A powder mixed with water to make a paste for molded plasterwork and repairs.

Plinth
A decorative block forming a base.

Plumb
To check the vertical aspect of a workpiece or structure for level. Also, a weighted line used to check the vertical.

Pointing
To form the mortar joints binding bricks together.

Polyethylene
A moisture-resistant, lightweight plastic.

Polyurethane
A polymer used in rigid foams and in various protective coatings.

Portland cement
A fine-grained aggregate of clay and limestone or similar substances.

Positive
The part of an electrical circuit which carries the flow of current, also called live.

Primer
The first coat of a paint system, serving to protect the workpiece and reduce absorption of subsequent coats.

Purlin
A horizontal beam that provides intermediate support for rafters or sheet roofing.

PVA
Polyvinyl acetate, a vinyl compound used in some woodworking glues.

PVC
Polyvinyl chloride, a plastic pipe in plumbing systems.

R

Rabbet
A stepped recess along the edge of a workpiece, usually as part of a joint. Also, to cut such a recess.

Raceway
A channel for holding electrical cable.

Radius
The measurement of a circle by a line from the center to the circumference of the circle.

Rafter
One of a set of parallel sloping beams that form the main structural element of a roof.

Ratchet
A device that permits movement in one direction only by restricting the reversal of a toothed wheel or rack.

Rebar
Steel reinforcing rod, used in concrete to add strength.

Retrofit
To refit a mechanism or structure so that it will have added qualities or capabilities.

Riser
The vertical part of a step. Also, a pipe which supplies water, by pressure, to upward locations.

RO
Reverse osmosis filter.

Rock wool
A mineral fiber material used for insulation.

Run
The horizontal measurement between the top and bottom risers of a stair or the depth of one tread.

R-value
A measurement of a substance's ability to impede thermal passage, and so, its heat insulating quality.

S

Sash
The framework holding the panes of the window, also, the whole operable part of the window.

Scratch coat
The bottom, or first, layer of stucco.

Screed
A thin layer of mortar applied to give a smooth surface to concrete or other mortar. Also, to smooth a concrete surface until it is flat.

Scribe
To mark or score a guiding line on a surface.

Sheathing
The outer layer of insulation surrounding electrical cable. Also, the outer covering of a stud-framed wall that is applied beneath the wall siding.

Shiplap
Rabbeted boards that overlap the edges of adjacent boards, allowing them to make a flush joint.

Short circuit
The accidental rerouting of electricity to ground which increases the flow of current and blows a fuse.

Short grain
When the general direction of wood fibers lies across a narrow section of lumber.

Sill
The lowest horizontal member of a stud partition. Also, the lowest horizontal member of a door or window frame.

Slake
To treat with or soak in water.

Sleeper wall
A low masonry wall used as an intermediate support for first-floor joists.

Soffits
The underside of a part of a building such as the eaves, or archway.

Softwood
Timber cut from coniferous trees.

Solder
The process of heating metal to a fluid state and fusing metal pieces together.

Sole plate
The sill of a stud partition, also called bottom plate.

Spalling
Flaking of the outer face of masonry caused by expanding moisture in icy conditions.

Squint corner
A pinched corner on bricks or blocks.

STC
Sound transmission rating.

Stile
A vertical side member of a door or window sash.

Stringer
A board, which runs from one floor level to another, into which staircase treads and risers are jointed.

Stucco
A thin layer of cement-based mortar applied to walls to provide a protective or decorative finish. Also, to apply the mortar.

Stud partition
An interior stud-framed dividing wall.

Studs
The vertical members of a stud-framed wall.

Subsidence
A sinking of the ground caused by the shrinkage of excessively dry soil.

T

Tamp
To pack down firmly with repeated blows.

T&P relief valve
A regulating valve in a water heater which opens to release pressure.

TBTO
Tributyltin oxide, a fungicide used in liquid wood preservative to protect wood from weather and infestation.

Tempered glass
Glass treated to strengthen it and to cause it to break into pellets rather than shards.

Template
A cutout pattern to help shape something accurately.

Tenon
A projecting tongue on the end of a workpiece which fits in a corresponding mortise.

Terminal
A connection for an electrical conductor.

Thermostat
A temperature-regulating mechanism.

Thimble
A lining for an opening in a roof for a chimney.

Thinner
A solvent used to dilute paint or varnish.

Thixotropic
Paints having a gel consistency until they are stirred and applied, at which point they become liquified.

Toenail
To fasten by driving nails in at an angle.

Topcoat
The outer layer of a paint system.

Torque
A rotational force.

Trap
A bent section of pipe in a plumbing system, below a bath, sink, etc., which holds standing water to prevent the passage of gases.

Tread
The horizontal part of a step.

Trisodium phosphate
A chemical compound used in cleaning solutions.

Truss
A rigid framework, and the members thereof, forming a support structure.

Turnbuckle
A tightening device.

U

Undercoat
A layer or layers of paint used to obliterate the color of a primer and build a protective layer of paint before applying a topcoat.

U-value
A measurement of insulating properties.

V

Valance
A decorative banding for curtains and window openings.

Vanes
The vertical panels or slats on vertical window and door blinds.

Vapor barrier
A layer of impervious material which prevents the passage of moisture-laden air.

Vermiculite
A light, water-absorbent mineral material, used as a soil additive.

VOC
Volatile organic compound.

VOM
Volt-ohmmeter, a device which measures electrical resistance in ohms.

W

Wall angle
A metal angled piece, as an angle iron, used to fasten two surfaces at a joint, as for fixing a suspended ceiling system to walls.

Wall plate
A horizontal member placed along the top of a wall to support the ends of joists and spread their load.

Wall tie
A usually metal piece used to reinforce joints in brickwork and masonry.

Waney edge
A natural wavy edge on a plank, sometimes still covered by bark.

Weather strip
Thin strips of various materials set around structural openings to keep out the weather.

Wilton
A weaving method used in floorcoverings in which a pile is woven into a backing.

Winders
Tapered treads on a circular or curving staircase, in which one end of the tread is wider than the other.

Workpiece
An object in the process of being shaped, produced, or otherwise worked on.

Wye
A Y-shaped piece.

Index

Index

Shop Guide

CUSTOMARY TO METRIC (CONVERSION)

LINEAR MEASURE

inches	millimeters
1/16	1.5875
1/8	3.2
3/16	4.8
1/4	6.35
5/16	7.9
3/8	9.5
7/16	11.1
1/2	12.7
9/16	14.3
5/8	15.9
11/16	17.5
3/4	19.05
12/16	20.6
7/8	22.2
15/16	23.8
1	25.4

inches	centimeters
1	2.54
2	5.1
3	7.6
4	10.2
5	12.7
6	15.2
7	17.8
8	20.3
9	22.9
10	25.4
11	27.9
12	30.5

feet	centimeters	meters
1	30.48	.3048
2	61	.61
3	91	.91
4	122	1.22
5	152	1.52
6	183	1.83
7	213	2.13
8	244	2.44
9	274	2.74
10	305	3.05
50	1524	15.24
100	3048	30.48

1 yard = .9144 meters
1 rod = 5.0292 meters
1 mile = 1.6 kilometers
1 nautical mile = 1.852 kilometers

WEIGHTS

ounces	grams
1	28.3
2	56.7
3	85
4	113
5	142
6	170
7	198
8	227
9	255
10	283
11	312
12	340
13	369
14	397
15	425
16	454

Formula: ounces x 28.3495 = grams

pounds	kilograms
1	.45
2	.9
3	1.4
4	1.8
5	2.3
6	2.7
7	3.2
8	3.6
9	4.1
10	4.5

1 short ton (2000 lbs) =
907 kilograms (kg)

Formula: pounds x .4536 = kilograms

MISCELLANEOUS

1 British thermal unit (Btu) (mean)
= 1055.9 joules

1 horsepower = 745.7 watts
= .75 kilowatts

caliber (diameter of a firearm's bore in
hundredths of an inch) = .254
millimeters (mm)

1 atmosphere pressure = 101,325
pascals (newtons per sq meter)

1 pound per square inch (psi) = 6895
pascals

1 pound per square foot = 47.9 pascals

1 knot = 1.85 kilometers per hour

1 mile per hour = 1.6093 kilometers
per hour

FLUID MEASURE

(Milliliters [ml] and cubic centimeters
[cc] are equivalent, but it is customary
to use milliliters for liquids.)

1 cu in	=	16.39 ml
1 fl oz	=	29.6 ml
1 cup	=	237 ml
1 pint	=	473 ml
1 quart	=	946 ml
	=	.946 liters
1 gallon	=	3785 ml
	=	3.785 liters

Formula:
fluid ounces x 29.5735 = milliliters

VOLUME

1 cu in	=	16.39 cubic centimeters (cc)
1 cu ft	=	28,316.7 cc
1 bushel	=	35,239.1 cc
1 peck	=	8809.8 cc

AREA

1 sq in	=	6.45 sq cm
1 sq ft	=	929 sq cm
	=	.093 sq meters
1 sq yd	=	.84 sq meters
1 acre	=	4047 sq meters
	=	.4047 hectares
1 sq mile	=	2,589,988 sq meters
	=	259 hectares
	=	2.59 sq kilometers